THE CHRONOLOGICAL TRACKING
OF THE
AMERICAN CIVIL WAR
PER THE OFFICIAL RECORDS
OF THE
WAR OF THE REBELLION

by Ronald A. Mosocco
Foreward by Arthur W. Bergeron, Jr.

SECOND EDITION

Published by
James River Publications
102 Maple Lane
Williamsburg, Virginia 23185-8106
(804) 220-4912

1st Edition - 1994

2nd Edition - Revised - 1995

FOREWORD

"The Civil War is probably the most significant single experience in our national existence," said historian Bruce Catton. He continued, "It was certainly the biggest tragedy in American history and, at the same time, probably did more to shape our future than any other event." The incredible enthusiasm generated by the spectacular PBS series "The Civil War" and the movies "Gettysburg" and "Glory" certainly evidences the enduring deep popular interest in this watershed of our national history.

During the Civil War Centennial, it seemed as if the number of books published on the conflict had reached an unsurpassable peak. That has proven a false assumption. As interest in the war has grown steadily not waned, so has the number of new books on the war. For example, a bibliography of the battle of Gettysburg contains more than 250 pages. This book was published in 1982, so it is more than a decade out-of-date. Some skeptics have argued that there are too many Civil War books in print. Reference books like Ronald Mosocco's will always have a market because the new people who become captivated with the Civil War will rely on books like his to feed their increasing appetites for information.

Battles and leaders continue to fascinate Civil War enthusiasts. The indispensable source for those subjects is the massive set of books entitled <u>War of the Rebellion: Official Records of Union and Confederate Armies</u>. Based upon the chronologies printed at the beginning of each volume of the <u>Official Records</u>, Mosocco's book covers events from the secession of South Carolina on December 20, 1860, until the death on December 21, 1865, of a Confederate general who had become ill while still on active duty. By scanning a page, a reader can discover what was going on all over the country. For example, on the same day that the Pickett-Pettigrew-Trimble Charge rolled across the fields at Gettysburg, Pennsylvania, other engagements and events were happening: John Hunt Morgan's Confederate cavalry raiders fought a skirmish at Columbia, Kentucky; Union troops evacuated Suffolk, Virginia; and Federal scouts skirmished with Confederates near Memphis, Tennessee. The book is more than just a chronology of campaigns and battles, however. It includes appointments and promotions of Union and Confederate generals, assignments of officers to various army and departmental commands, and the deaths of generals.

Ronald Mosocco has obviously worked long and hard putting together <u>The Chronological Tracking of the American Civil War Per the Official Records of the War of the Rebellion.</u> His effort is a worthy addition to the literature of that conflict.

Arthur W. Bergeron, Jr.
Baton Rouge, Louisiana

Dedicated to those valiant men
who freely gave the ultimate in sacrifice
for their Beliefs, for their God,
and for their Country.

<u>The American Civil War.</u> There is no war more written about, debated, discussed, analyzed and relived through re-enactments than the American War between the States. There are volumes upon volumes of works done on the reasons causing this war; on individual military battles, campaigns and the generals who led the men of the Blue and of the Grey headfirst into the history books, as well as the Presidents, Abraham Lincoln of the National Government and Jefferson Davis, leader of the Confederate States of America. Every minute troop movement and strategy has been analyzed, pro and con, and debated by enthusiasts as to the "what if," or "what could have been" done differently that could have changed or altered the final outcome.

It is this same fascination so many hold for this period in American History, when the people and the nation as a whole, were still innocent, that drew me to this era of time in our nation. A time when most of our natural resources were still waiting to be explored and tapped; of the wide open spaces yet to be conquered. When over half the country was still wild, untamed, and for the most part, uncharted. New states were being added. Congress was carving up additional large sections of land into territories. There were stories of wild savages and vast herds of buffalo roaming the plains. Where the majority of hard working men and women, with their simple way of life, could still be found down on the farm. It was also an exciting period of American life for the adventurous as the expanding railroads opened up new areas; at the same time where men felt comfortable in their small well knit communities, attending Church services on Sunday and feeling overall content with their lives, hoping the same for their offspring. However, dark storm clouds were on the horizon. The very fabric of our society was threatened to be torn apart due to some major issues that, over time, were moving to centerstage. Of all the causes credited with the development of this war, the one most prevalent is the issue of slavery. However, this book was not written and compiled to concentrate on these issues, but are presented here only as a backdrop to the content of this book.

My personal interest in the Civil War, like so many others, led me to read and enjoy all the numerous books available on any particular interest I had for this epic struggle. I thoroughly engross myself in studying and analyzing over and over again the dynamic pictures of Matthew Brady, Alexander Gardner, and Timothy O'Sullivan, to name a few of the famous photographers of the Civil War. For me, I can remember the black and white pictures taken when I was a child, and at times, for those fleeting moments I can mentally feel myself a part of Brady's camera view; not just someone casually looking at his pictures, but being present when the negative was exposed, observing first hand the images frozen for all time.

This undying interest led me to purchase a complete set of the Official Records of the War of the Rebellion in 1985-86. Thanks goes out to my understanding wife, Doris, on our limited budget. The hours I spent reading them induced me to work compiling notes for future reference. As time went by and my notes took more of a serious nature, Doris suggested a book that could be shared with other Civil War buffs, historians and students.

Therefore, this book was prepared to present to the reader every event reported in the 128 volume set of the Official Records. The **"Official Records of the War of the Rebellion"** is the "Bible" for the serious researchers of the American Civil War. The Official Records are comprised of all essential military communications generated during the war that were not lost or destroyed. After every military encounter, movement, or activity, military commanders were required to file a report as to their command's involvement. In many instances this would entail reports filed by the General commanding the army down to the Colonel of an individual regiment. As can be expected, there are

far more Union reports than Confederate; many being destroyed, such as when the fleeing Rebels burned the South's capital of Richmond, VA. Nevertheless, there are thousands of reports which are incorporated in the Official Records; from the large battles and campaigns that have literally hundreds of reports by the various generals and colonels on both sides, down to the obscure skirmish where there may be only one report filed by a Union colonel. With single reports, the author can only reflect how the one side saw it and reported it. With events of multiple reports from both sides I have tried to balance the different opinions the two opposing sides had on the outcome of their encounter. In addition, there are numerous events in the O/R that reflect sections of a particular volume. This book reflects those events, such as operations in a military district for a certain time period.

After the Civil War, Congress of the United States approved an act on June 23, 1874, and appropriated funds "to enable the Secretary of War" to compile "all reports, letters, telegrams, and general orders not heretofore copied or printed, and properly arranged in chronological order." Work had originally begun by a resolution of Congress of May 19, 1864, and continued with books being released as they were completed starting in the early fall of 1880 and continuing until the year 1900. Today, hardly a book is, or could be, written on the Civil War without the author citing the Official Records or **"O/R"** as they are commonly known, as source reference material.

After years of working at it, I hope you will thoroughly enjoy the final product. The approach to my book was to present every event reflected in the O/R, all in chronological and alphabetical order. Additional events deemed by the author to be of importance have been added that are not in the O/R due to their being outside the immediate realm of the military scope that the O/R are comprised.

One of the main goals of the author was to walk the reader through the Civil War in its entirety without becoming too voluminous by echoing the vast pages of the O/R itself. To avoid "not being able to see the forest because of the trees." To this end, I have moved through the war years in ever increasing detail; starting out with basic abbreviated information on December, 1860, and 1861, the year both the North and South must learn to fight a war; moving into 1862 where the two immature sides send many a brave man to their grave in intense fighting as they size each other's military might up. Many a good man will sacrifice the ultimate for their country in the early battles. As 1863 moves into the meat of the war, so does this book as it begins to pick up and describe to the reader a little more detail information on events taking place; to 1864 where by now all hell has broken loose and everything appears to be totally out of control, concluding with 1865 when the South finally ran out of steam, both militarily and economically; the South's will to continue the struggle being shattered. My book follows this pattern providing more indepth detail presentation of the events occurring as time progresses. This will allow the reader to observe numerous events from a macro overview, down to more detailed reporting by war's end.

In addition to all military events reflected in the O/R, I believe it was important to reflect all 1,008 Confederate and Union generals who reached official military rank during the American Civil War; their promotion dates and the date that many gave their lives for their country. For these were the elite group of men who directed the war, leading their armies and commands in a struggle for ultimate victory. With over 600,000 men sacrificing their lives during the Civil War, only a scant minority would not be under the command of one of the men on this distinguished list. The reader, through careful study, can track the generals in chronological order of promotion. Some names will be very familiar to the reader; others will become so, as you move through this book. This book does not report any of those awarded the "brevet" level as this rank was largely used by the Federal government to award those for political rather than military reason. Nor can this book omit those

generals not worthy of being mentioned in the same breath as the others. Some will drop off into obscurity, while others will never get the true recognition they deserve, while still others will not live long enough to "see this thing through to the end." In addition, many a brave Colonel will be mortally wounded or permanently disabled thereby thinning the ranks of qualified men eligible for advancement to General.

The ranks used by the Federal and Confederate Governments were very similar, except for the rank of Full general which the Federals did not use. In addition, only one Union general, Ulysses S. Grant, achieved the status of Lieut. General, besides the retired Federal General, Winfield Scott. However, Scott's rank of Lieut. Gen. was earned by means of "brevet." The Confederacy, on the other hand, liberally used the two top general ranks.

Confederate	Federal
General (full)	not used
Lieutenant General	Lieutenant General
Major General	Major General
Brigadier General	Brigadier General
Colonel	Colonel
Lieutenant Colonel	Lieutenant Colonel
Major	Major
Captain	Captain
Lieutenant	Lieutenant
Sergeant	Sergeant
Corporal	Corporal
Private	Private

(Some of the lower ranks had various grades, such as 1st and 2nd Lieutenant, and Sergeant Major, Quartermaster Sergeant, Ordnance Sergeant and 1st (or Orderly) Sergeant, in addition to ranks such as Surgeon and Adjutant-General (a Colonel) etc.)

Typical arrangement for the armies by 1863 through 1865:
- Army - usually commanded by General, Lieut. General or Maj. General
- Corps - usually commanded by General, Lieut. General or Maj. General
- Division - usually commanded by Lieut. General or Maj. General
- Brigade - usually commanded by a Brig. General or Colonel
- Regiment - usually commanded by a Colonel or Lieut. Colonel

How this book is arranged:

Each date is arranged in chronological as well as alphabetical order as follows:

1) the death of generals in order of descending rank (alphabetically, Confederate [CSA] before Union [USA]), unless the death occurred during that day's battle, which that general will then immediately follow.

2) the promotion of generals in order of descending rank, C.S.A. before U.S.A.

3) events occurring in alphabetical order by state, territory or area, etc.; example, all events in

Alabama precede Georgia, which precede North Carolina, which precede Virginia. The exception to this are campaigns, expeditions, reconnaissances, etc. that are a major topic; then the individual events will normally follow that event. Example is on July 5, 1863, the Jackson, Mississippi Campaign begins that runs from July 5th through July 25th, 1863. The skirmish at Birdsong, MS, is part of this campaign, therefore it follows the above, although out of alphabetical order.

4) In order to avoid duplication of the same information time and time again, the author has, in many instances, not listed as to what campaign certain military events belong. For example, the Gettysburg Campaign which the O/R reflects beginning June 3, 1863 and ending August 1, 1863 has many skirmishes and encounters during this period in Virginia, Maryland and Pennsylvania. In lieu of pointing this out at each event, the astute reader will grasp that these encounters are part of the Gettysburg Campaign.

Commonly used terms in the Official Records - as you work your way through the pages, you will be aware of the frequent use of certain key words, the most frequent being the term "skirmish." Although the author has yet to find an exact definition, I believe it to mean all the encounters of hostile forces engaged in a fire fight on a small scale; small scale usually consisting of a thousand men or less.

The reader will also note the repeated use of the following military terms: action, advance, affair, attack, battle, bombardment, campaign, capture, destruction, engagement, evacuation, expedition, occupation, operations, reconnaissance, retreat, scout, siege, surrender, withdraw, and so on.

The Cautious Use of Numbers and Statistics. As the reader moves through this book, you will notice not much information and space dedicated to the "big" battles. There are plenty of well written books on these engagements and unfortunately there is not enough room to expand on them here. Reporting is done in capsule form. Losses of the two sides in the major engagements are normally listed in total. With the format used, it was deemed unimportant in many instances to get across to the reader how many men the blue bellies lost versus the johnny rebs; this has sometimes become the determining factor of who's winning and who's losing; the body count factor that the author normally finds irrelevant and wishes to avoid. During this period, it was exceedingly difficult to keep exact numbers of casualties. Many men were listed as missing; their bodies were never found as they hobbled off the battlefield, mortally wounded, to die in the bushes; while still others called it quits and deserted to go home. Others were wounded and sent to hospitals where they later died of infections or diseases. Were they a mortality of the battlefield or the surgeon's knife? Besides, can the modern day student on the Civil War fully comprehend the staggering casualties amassed at Antietam, Gettysburg, Chickamauga or Shiloh, to name a few battles? I assume the reader is more wary of that notion. However, I do begin to reflect individual casualties to show how many men were losing their lives in those small skirmishes that never hit the front pages of the history books. Of how on October 13, 1863, near Indiantown, NC, Rebel guerrillas ambush the Federal Cavalry command as they leave the area after having captured a local guerrilla; traveling down a dirt road, and surrounded by thick woods on both sides, the Yankees lose some good boys that night. Or, of how on September 4, 1863, 3 or 4 boys of the 18th Iowa were captured by guerrillas at Quincy, MO, taken out of town into the countryside and executed. Bear in mind, the Yankees had no monopoly of losing lives; the Rebs fought just as hard for this distinction.

The reader must never forget that as you move through the pages of this book that, except in few instances, every time the Union soldier ran up against the Rebels, somebody usually got killed. This

is true in every skirmish, battle and encounter. You must not lose sight of the fact that boys were spilling their blood every day for their cause; so if numbers of casualties are not mentioned on any particular day, they were still happening, none-the-less. Saddles were being emptied; boys were going out on expeditions and scouts, only to run into the enemy, see death first hand; carrying their friends back in excruciating pain from their battlewounds received during these confrontations. We hope the reader is observant to the fact that while I have tried to cram as much information into this book it would be impossible to write in detail about every event taking place, and keep this book within a reasonable size. By presenting many events on a brief but revealing outline, the reader must be able to visualize the unwritten that is taking place.

Personally, I can visualize the rounded shape of the earth far below the clouds. Looking down from the heavens as night is fast approaching, the countryside is barely recognizable. The dim of the approaching night reflects the instantaneous lights flickering from the barrels of mens' muskets as they send more valiant lads to their deaths. The numerous flashes, like a vast yard full of fireflies. Their souls being carried upward towards the heavens, appearing as gray hearts with wings.. there to the left are tens of hearts. over to the right, are more.. This procession continued for four years, as the heavens opened up to accept the good men who left the ongoing battles below, having given all they could; leaving the rest to be played out by others..

You will be able to follow all the events of the Civil War, either on a day by day basis, or by tracking the events in a military district, or by following the events incurred by a specific army, region, campaign, etc. For example, you may want to follow the Army of Northern Virginia and/or the Army of the Potomac to observe the ongoing events on the eastern front in Virginia. Or, you may have an interest in the bushwacking and guerrilla warfare played out in the Missouri, Arkansas region. Some will thoroughly enjoy following the chain of events taken by Ulysses S. Grant in his brilliant siege and capture of Vicksburg, then on to the east to effectively end the rebellion of the South, culminating with Lee's surrender at Appomattox Court-House. Still others may be very interested in reading the events between the Native American Indians and the whiteman. It is curious to see who really has the right to call what color of the skin as "savages."

I would also like to point out that, wherever possible, the book highlights the names of Union and Confederate steamers, rams, schooners, transports, ironclads, gunboats, mortar boats, as well as other sailing vessels, such as Rebel blockade runners, that are reflected throughout the O/R. The reader should be aware of the importance of the overwhelming military naval strength the Union exerted over the South, which contributed to the ultimate downfall of the Confederacy. The Federal North Atlantic Blockading Squadron off the Eastern Seaboard as well as those operating in the Gulf, eventually and effectively cutting off the life blood of imports the Confederacy came so heavily to depend on. The Union ironclads, mortar boats, and transports contributed to the Union domination of the Mississippi River and surrounding waterways, the National Government able to move troops rapidly along these controlled river systems.

While recognizing the importance of controlling the waterways, we must not neglect to point out the importance of the railroads as a modern means of transportation and the telegraph lines as a very important communication system of this time period. The North had a substantial advantage in these areas. The reader will note the numerous campaigns against the railroad lines; Maj. Gen. William T. Sherman, USA, for example, dealing a destructive blow on the Southern railway lines on his way from Atlanta, during his famous march to the sea.

As this is an all inclusive book for listing all military events, bear in mind that as the author reports the daily occurrences as reflected by the officers' reports in the O/R, that it is by no means a complete delivery systems of everything that happened during the Civil War. In addition, it would be impossible to give a synopsis of every event in the O/R and keep the size of this book manageable. For that, the reader must use the Official Records to do further research, as it would be impossible to lay to pen every event the men experienced; of how during a skirmish with Indians, a Yankee soldier is on the receiving end of a arrow that enters his back going through the body and traveling along the arm and wedging in his elbow. Yes, the book reflects the attack by Indians and the reporting of casualties, but not the injury this particular soldier experienced. That is why I urge the reader to slowly absorb the events taking place; do not rush through this book; rather use this book and your imagination as a tool to sit and ponder what is actually taking place. Follow the elusive John Singleton Mosby as he dominates his superior opponent in his part of the Confederacy; of the brilliance of Nathan Bedford Forrest; of the destructive effect of Philip Henry Sheridan along with William Tecumseh Sherman and Ulysses Simpson Grant. Of the southern stars of Robert Edward Lee, Stonewall Jackson, and James Longstreet, to name a few. Of how as the war progressed, the Federal expeditions were chewing up and destroying vital Confederate provisions the South could ill afford to lose.

In the back of this book are reprinted maps from the Atlas of the Official Records of the United States for the periods 1861-1865 showing the location of towns, cities and rivers, as well as the designated military divisions that are reflected so often in this book. I urge the reader to frequently use these maps as they track the ongoing events, noting how the military departments and divisions were reallocated as the war developed.

I have also enclosed a spreadsheet example specimen that can be used by those interested in tracking individual army corps through commanders and military assignments. The reader will find the vast number of command changes, as well as the movement of the various army corps, divisions, and other troop commands. Feel free to copy this spreadsheet and use this format as the reader wishes.

For those readers who show a further interest into the details of the war, I have presented the Organization of the Military commands during some of the largest better known military engagements experienced in the Civil War. This will give the individual an analysis of an entire command on one page; this has never before been available in this format.

I urge you to use this book frequently as one reads articles and books on the Civil War. Refer to it, and observe the dates leading up to and following the material you are studying. For if it adds to your appreciation of the Civil War, then I can say I have accomplished what I have set out to do.

I hope you enjoy this book enough to where you may suggest to others with similar interests they purchase a copy.

I would like to give credit and appreciation to the various authors who came before me and who helped to instill my passion for the Civil War. I highly recommend the books that are listed in the back of this book.

I would like to thank my lovely wife, Doris, and my daughters, Melinda, Michelle, and Darcy, who patiently watched their husband and father dedicate a couple of years to complete this project. Hopefully now, life can get back to normal. A big thanks to all the folks I have met during my first attempt into the realm of publishing; I appreciate their friendly and supportive attitude. And finally, a sincere thank you to Frank, Bill, and Clif Hannah, as well as Kay Moore, at Multi-Print of Hampton, VA, who made me feel like one of the family. A special thanks to Frank Hannah, who showed the same enthusiasm for the production of this book as I have. With his knowledge and similar fascination for the Civil War, made this a most enjoyable experience.

TABLE OF CONTENTS

12	20	1860	The following are the Four General Officers in the Union Regular Army at the outbreak of the Civil War: **<u>Brevet Lieutenant General Winfield Scott, U.S.A.</u>** **Brevet Major General David E. Twiggs,** **U.S.A.** **Brevet Major General John Ellis Wool,** **U.S.A.** **Brigadier General William Selby Harney,** USA
12	20	1860	The ordinance of secession is adopted by the South Carolina Convention, by the unanimous vote of 169 to 0 in the Institute Hall, Charleston, SC.
12	26	1860	The United States troops, under the command of Maj. Robert Robert Anderson, US Army, (hereafter abbreviated USA), are transferred from Fort Moultrie to Fort Sumter, Charleston Harbor, Charleston, SC.
12	26	1860	The United States Revenue Cutter, the **William Aiken,** surrenders to the South Carolina state forces, Charleston Harbor, Charleston, SC.
12	27	1860	Castle Pickney and Fort Moultrie are seized by the South Carolina state troops, Charleston Harbor, Charleston, SC.
12	30	1860	The United States Arsenal at Charleston, SC, is seized by the South Carolina state troops.

1861.

	Sunday.	Monday.	Tuesday.	Wednesday.	Thursday.	Friday.	Saturday.
Jan			1	2	3	4	5
	6	7	8	9	10	11	12
	13	14	15	16	17	18	19
	20	21	22	23	24	25	26
	27	28	29	30	31		
Feb						1	2
	3	4	5	6	7	8	9
	10	11	12	13	14	15	16
	17	18	19	20	21	22	23
	24	25	26	27	28		
March						1	2
	3	4	5	6	7	8	9
	10	11	12	13	14	15	16
	17	18	19	20	21	22	23
	24	25	26	27	28	29	30
	31						
April		1	2	3	4	5	6
	7	8	9	10	11	12	13
	14	15	16	17	18	19	20
	21	22	23	24	25	26	27
	28	29	30				
May				1	2	3	4
	5	6	7	8	9	10	11
	12	13	14	15	16	17	18
	19	20	21	22	23	24	25
	26	27	28	29	30	31	
June							1
	2	3	4	5	6	7	8
	9	10	11	12	13	14	15
	16	17	18	19	20	21	22
	23	24	25	26	27	28	29
	30						
July		1	2	3	4	5	6
	7	8	9	10	11	12	13
	14	15	16	17	18	19	20
	21	22	23	24	25	26	27
	28	29	30	31			
August					1	2	3
	4	5	6	7	8	9	10
	11	12	13	14	15	16	17
	18	19	20	21	22	23	24
	25	26	27	28	29	30	31
Sept	1	2	3	4	5	6	7
	8	9	10	11	12	13	14
	15	16	17	18	19	20	21
	22	23	24	25	26	27	28
	29	30					
October			1	2	3	4	5
	6	7	8	9	10	11	12
	13	14	15	16	17	18	19
	20	21	22	23	24	25	26
	27	28	29	30	31		
Nov						1	2
	3	4	5	6	7	8	9
	10	11	12	13	14	15	16
	17	18	19	20	21	22	23
	24	25	26	27	28	29	30
Dec	1	2	3	4	5	6	7
	8	9	10	11	12	13	14
	15	16	17	18	19	20	21
	22	23	24	25	26	27	28
	29	30	31				

VIII

MONTH	DAY	YEAR	ACT
01	2	1861	President James Buchanan refuses to receive a letter from the South Carolina Commissioners, who, wanting to reach an agreeable solution, inform the President of the situation of Major Robert Anderson's USA, men at Fort Sumter, SC, and of their unprotected position. This letter prompts the United States Government to order reinforcements for Fort Sumter, SC.
01	2	1861	**Fort Johnson, Charleston Harbor, SC,** which has been **evacuated by** the US troops and stands empty, is seized by the South Carolina state troops.
01	2	1861	The US Government orders that the naval vessel, the **USS Brooklyn,** stationed at Norfolk, VA, be readied for the possible aid of Fort Sumter, Charleston Harbor, SC.
01	2	1861	Col. Charles Pomeroy Stone, Inspector General, USA, is placed in charge of securing the safety of the nation's capital, Washington, DC.
01	3	1861	The War Department overturns the former Secretary of War, John Buchanan Floyd's orders to remove weapons from many US Arsenals, which could fall into the hands of the Southern States Governments.
01	3	1861	Fort Pulaski, Savannah River, GA, is seized by the Georgia state troops, by order of Governor Joseph E. Brown.
01	4	1861	The US Arsenal at Mount Vernon, AL, under Capt. Jesse L. Reno, is seized by the Alabama state troops by order of Governor A. B. Moore.
01	5	1861	Forts Morgan and Gaines, AL, are seized by the Alabama state troops in an attempt to protect Mobile, AL.
01	5	1861	The 1st expedition for the relief of Fort Sumter, Charleston, SC, sails from New York Harbor, New York, by order of Gen. Winfield Scott, USA, consisting of 250 men on the merchant ship, **Star of the West,** who summarily overrides the decision to use the **USS Brooklyn,** stationed at Norfolk, VA.
01	5	1861	The US Senators from the southern states of Alabama, Arkansas, Florida, Georgia, Louisiana, Mississippi, and Texas meet in Washington, DC, to discuss the options of seceding from the United States.
01	6	1861	The US Arsenal at Apalachicola, FL, is seized by the Florida state troops.
01	7	1861	Fort Marion, Saint Augustine, FL, is seized by the Florida state troops. The US government is unable or unwilling to provoke a confrontation with the various state troops at this point, not trying to prevent the seizure of the Fort.
01	8	1861	The US troops at Fort Barrancas, FL, fire on a party of Rebel men who attempt to move on the fort, unlike the peaceful seizure of Fort Marion the day before.
01	9	1861	The ordinance of secession is adopted at Jackson, MS, by the state of Mississippi, by the overwhelming vote of 84-15, becoming the 2nd state to secede.
01	9	1861	Fort Johnston, NC, is seized by the rebellious citizens of Smithville, North Carolina. (2nd seizure 4/16/1861)
01	9	1861	The steamship, **Star of the West,** is fired upon by the South Carolina state troops, Charleston Harbor, SC, while attempting to bring food as well as reinforcements to the beleaguered fort. With shots fired, but no damage done, the **Star of the West** retreats, heading back to New York City.
01	10	1861	The ordinance of secession is adopted at Tallahassee, FL, by Florida, by the convincing vote of 62-7, becoming the 3rd state to secede from the Union.
01	10	1861	The US troops are transferred from Barrancas Barracks to Fort Pickens, Santa Rosa Island, Pensacola Harbor, FL, by the order of Lieut. Adam Jacoby Slemmer, US 1st Artillery.
01	10	1861	The US Arsenal/Barracks at Baton Rouge, LA, is seized by the Louisiana state troops led by Braxton Bragg, by order of Louisiana Governor Thomas O. Moore.
01	10	1861	Fort Caswell is seized by the citizens of Smithville and Wilmington, North Carolina. (2nd seizure 4/16/1861).
01	11	1861	The ordinance of secession is adopted at Montgomery, AL, by Alabama, becoming the 4th state to secede, by a smaller margin but vast majority, 61-39.
01	11	1861	Forts Jackson and Saint Phillip, LA, at the mouth of the Mississippi River, below New Orleans, are seized by the Louisiana state troops, by order of Governor Thomas O. Moore.
01	11	1861	The surrender of Fort Sumter, Charleston Harbor SC, is demanded of Major Robert Anderson, USA, by South Carolina Governor, Francis W. Pickens, and is refused.
01	12	1861	The Mississippi House of Representatives get up and leave the United States Congress.
01	12	1861	Barrancas Barracks, Fort Barrancas and Fort McRee, and the Navy-yard at Pensacola, FL, are seized by the Florida state troops.

MONTH	DAY	YEAR	ACT
01	12	1861	The surrender of Fort Pickens, FL, is demanded by the Florida state troops after capturing the above facilities, but is refused.
01	13	1861	President James Buchanan, receives the envoys from Major Robert Anderson, USA, (Lieut. J. Norman Hall) and from the South Carolina Governor, Francis W. Pickens, (J. W. Hayne), regarding the status of Fort Sumter, SC. President Buchanan, while not trying to provoke a hostile reaction, emphasizes that Fort Sumter, SC, will not be turned over to the South Carolina state authorities.
01	14	1861	Fort Taylor, Key West, FL, is garrisoned by the US troops under Capt. John M. Brannan, 1st US Artillery. This fort will prove invaluable in the US effort to blockade Southern Ports, by providing coal to the US ships' boilers.
01	14	1861	Fort Pike, near New Orleans, LA, is seized by the Louisiana state troops.
01	15	1861	The 2nd demand is made for the surrender of Fort Pickens, FL.
01	15	1861	The Depts. of California and Oregon are merged into the Dept. of the Pacific.
01	15	1861	Col. Albert Sidney Johnston, 2nd US Cavalry, Brvt. Brig. Gen. USA, assumes the command of the Dept. of the Pacific.
01	16	1861	**Operations in the vicinity of Humboldt, CA.** 1/16-5/18/1861.
01	18	1861	The 3rd demand is made for the surrender of Fort Pickens, Pensacola Harbor, FL, and refused by Lieut. Adam Slemmer, USA.
01	18	1861	Fort Jefferson, Dry Tortugas, off Key West, FL, is garrisoned by the US troops, under Bvt. Maj. Lewis G. Arnold, to be used to hold political prisoners.
01	19	1861	The ordinance of secession is adopted at Milledgeville, by Georgia by the overwhelming vote of 208-89, the 5th state to secede.
01	20	1861	Fort Massachusetts, Ship Island, at the mouth of the Mississippi River, Gulf of Mexico, is seized by the Mississippi state troops, a key refueling point for Union vessels and key in the defense of New Orleans, LA.
01	21	1861	Mississippi Senator, and former US Secretary of War, Jefferson Davis, bids farewell in his speech from the US Congress chambers, in addition to the following senators: a) Clement C. Clay, Jr. - from Alabama b) Benjamin Fitzpatrick - from Alabama c) Stephen R. Mallory - from Florida d) David L. Yulee - from Florida
01	24	1861	US Arsenal at Augusta, GA, is seized by the Georgia state troops, Col. A. R. Lawton, commanding.
01	24	1861	Union re-inforcements for Fort Pickens, FL, sail from Fortress Monroe, VA.
01	26	1861	The Oglethorpe Barracks and Fort Jackson, Savannah, GA, are seized by the State troops by order of Governor Joseph Brown.
01	26	1861	The ordinance of secession is overwhelming adopted by the Louisiana State Convention at Baton Rouge, by a vote of 113-17. the 6th state to secede.
01	28	1861	The US property in the hands of the US Army Officers is seized at New Orleans, LA.
01	28	1861	Fort Macomb, near New Orleans, LA, is seized by the Louisiana state troops, 1st Regiment, Louisiana Infantry.
01	29	1861	Kansas receives the votes in Congress to enter the Union as the thirty-fourth state and as a "free" state, under the Wyandotte Constitution.
01	29	1861	The US revenue cutter, **Robert McClelland,** is seized by the Louisiana state troops, near New Orleans, LA.
01	30	1861	The US revenue schooner, **Lewis Cass,** is seized by the Alabama state troops in Mobile Bay, AL.
01	30	1861	President-elect Abraham Lincoln leaves Springfield, IL, and travels to Coles County, IL, to visit his step-mother, Sarah Bush Lincoln.
01	31	1861	The US Branch Mint and the Customs House are seized by the state troops in New Orleans, LA, in addition to the seizure of the U.S. schooner, **Washington.**
02	1	1861	At Austin TX, the ordinance of secession is adopted by the Texas Convention, as the 7th state which votes to leave the Union. The vote is almost unanimous, with the final vote being 166-7.
02	3	1861	Former law partners, Judah Benjamin and John Slidell, from Louisiana, leave Washington, DC, and their Senate positions, for Baton Rouge, LA.

| --- | --- | --- | --- |

02	4	1861	The Peace Convention, headed by former President John Tyler, convenes in Washington, DC, in their attempt to head off hostilities. 20 Northern states are represented; the Southern states are do not attend.
02	5	1861	Plans are being made in Montgomery, AL, for the inauguration of the Government of the Confederate States of America.
02	5	1861	Civil authorities of Texas appoint a commission to confer with the US officer commanding that military department there.
02	5	1861	The Peace Convention convening in Washington, DC, attempts to devise a means of settling this dispute between the states in a non-violent solution.
02	5	1861	Federal scouts from Fort Walla Walla, Washington Territory and Fort Dallas, Oregon Territory, to the Umatilla River and to Willow and Butter Creeks, Oregon, with skirmishes with Indians **(8th and 10th)** on the Columbus River. 2/5-17/1861.
02	6	1861	The US steamer, **Brooklyn,** arrives off Pensacola, FL, with Federal re-inforcements for Fort Pickens.
02	7	1861	The **Choctaw Indian Nation** declares its adherence to the Southern States.
02	8	1861	The Constitution of the Confederate States of America is adopted by the convention held in Montgomery, AL, which is similar to the U.S. Constitution, except for certain provisions which allows for slavery and for states' rights.
02	8	1861	The US Arsenal at Little Rock, AR, under Capt. James Totten, is seized by the Arkansas state troops, by order of Gov. Henry M. Rector.
02	9	1861	The Confederate Convention in Montgomery, AL, votes unanimously to elect the 1st President and the Vice-President of the Confederate States of America, (CSA), as follows: a) **Jefferson Davis** - President, from Mississippi b) **Alexander Stephens** - Vice-President, from Georgia
02	9	1861	Fort Pickens, FL, refuses to receive the Federal troops that arrived on the US steamer, **Brooklyn,** in order to keep the status quo.
02	9	1861	The state of Tennessee decides against holding a State Convention to address the issue of secession.
02	9	1861	Bvt. Maj. Gen. David E. Twiggs, USA, appoints a military commission to meet the commissioners of Texas.
02	10	1861	Jefferson Davis is surprised to receive word at his plantation home in Mississippi, of his election as the 1st (and only) President of the Confederate States of America.
02	11	1861	President-elect, Abraham Lincoln, leaves Springfield, IL, for his inauguration at Washington, DC, never to return alive.
02	11	1861	President-elect Jefferson Davis, leaves Brierfield Plantation, MS, for his inauguration at Montgomery, AL.
02	12	1861	The US Ordnance at Napoleon, AR, is seized by the Arkansas state troops there.
02	12	1861	Both Lincoln and Davis speak out on secession, Davis in Mississippi, and Lincoln, at Cincinnati, OH.
02	13	1861	President-elect Abraham Lincoln addresses the Ohio State Legislature, at Columbus, OH.
02	15	1861	President-elect Abraham Lincoln delivers his speech at Pittsburgh, PA, then traveling on to Cleveland, OH.
02	15	1861	The Peace Convention, meeting in Washington, DC, continues to debate and drag on, not reaching any conclusions.
02	15	1861	Raphael Semmes, who will later command the **CSS Sumter** and the **CSS Alabama,** resigns his US Naval Commission, Washington, DC.
02	16	1861	The US Arsenal and Barracks at San Antonio, TX, is seized by the Texas state troops.
02	16	1861	The Texas commissioners demand the surrender of all the US military posts and public property in Texas.
02	18	1861	CSA President Jefferson Davis is sworn in at Montgomery, AL, ahead of USA President Abraham Lincoln.
02	18	1861	Bvt. Maj. Gen. David E. Twiggs, USA, commanding the Dept. of Texas, surrenders all US military posts\public property to the Texas authorities, agree US troops are to retain their arms and to retire unmolested. However this is considered by many an act of treason on Twiggs' part.
02	18	1861	President-elect Abraham Lincoln delivers his speech at Buffalo and Albany, NY, on his way to Washington, DC, still attempting to reconcile any differences between the Northern and Southern States.
02	19	1861	The following Confederate Cabinet Members are chosen at Montgomery, AL: a) **Judah P. Benjamin** - Attorney General, from LA b) **Stephen R. Mallory** - Secretary of Navy, from FL c) **Christopher G. Memminger** - Secretary of Treasury, from SC

			d) **John H. Reagan** - Postmaster General, from TX
			e) **Robert Toombs** - Secretary of State, from GA
			f) **Leroy Pope Walker** - Secretary of War, from AL
02	19	1861	The US Paymaster officer is seized at New Orleans, LA.
02	19	1861	President-elect Abraham Lincoln delivers his speech at New York City, NY.
02	19	1861	Bvt. Maj. Gen. David E. Twiggs, USA, is superseded by Col. Carlos A. Waite, USA, in the Dept. of Texas, at Camp Verde, TX.
02	20	1861	The Confederate Government in Montgomery, AL, establishes the Confederate Dept. of the Navy.
02	21	1861	The US Property at Brazos Santiago, TX, is seized by the Texas state troops.
02	21	1861	Camp Cooper, TX, is abandoned by the Union forces.
02	22	1861	President-elect Abraham Lincoln delivers his speech at Philadelphia, and Harrisburg, PA, and due to death threats, leaves for Washington, DC, incognito, under the protection of the well known detective, **Allen Pinkerton.**
02	23	1861	In a referendum, the voters of Texas vote 3 to 1 to secede.
02	23	1861	President-elect Abraham Lincoln arrives in the nation's capital, Washington, DC.
02	26	1861	Camp Colorado, TX, is abandoned by the Union forces, led by Capt. E. Kirby Smith, 2nd US Cavalry.
02	27	1861	The Peace Conference assembled in Washington, DC, continues to work towards a peaceful solution.
02	28	1861	The US Congress votes to create the **Colorado Territory.**
02	28	1861	Pro-Unionists in North Carolina win in their bid to suppress a state convention to be held for the issue of secession.
03	1	1861	**Pierre Gustave Toutant Beauregard,** CSA, is appointed Brig. Gen.
03	1	1861	**Edwin Vose Sumner,** USA, is appointed Brig. Gen.
03	1	1861	The Government of the Confederate States of America, (CSA) assumes control of the military affairs at Charleston, South Carolina.
03	1	1861	Bvt. Maj. Gen. David E. Twiggs, USA, in Texas, is dismissed from the US Military service by order of President Buchanan.
03	2	1861	The US Congress votes to create the **Dakota Territory,** consisting of North and South Dakota, Montana and Wyoming.
03	2	1861	The Peace Convention sponsors a Constitutional amendment in Congress by Senator John J. Crittenden, of KY, which is defeated, and climaxes the end of the Peace Convention, as it now becomes clear there will be no compromise.
03	2	1861	The US Congress votes to create the **Nevada Territory.**
03	2	1861	The US revenue cutter, **Henry Dodge,** is seized at Galveston, TX, by the Texas state troops.
03	3	1861	Brig. Gen. Pierre Gustave Toutant Beauregard, CSA, assumes the Confederate command at Charleston Harbor, SC.
03	3	1861	Bvt. Lieut. Gen. Winfield Scott, USA, determines that the relief of Fort Sumter, SC, is not practical.
03	4	1861	**Abraham Lincoln is sworn in as the 16th President of the United States of America,** at Washington, DC, in front of a crowd, with troops and sharpshooters positioned in case of a rumored assassination attempt.
03	4	1861	President Abraham Lincoln's initial cabinet consisted of:
			a) **Edward Bates** - Attorney General, from MO
			b) **Montgomery Blair** - Postmaster General, from MD
			c) **Simon Cameron** - Secretary of War, from PA
			d) **Salmon P. Chase** - Secretary of Treasury, from OH
			e) **William H. Seward** - Secretary of State, from NY
			f) **Caleb Blood Smith** - Secretary of Interior, from IN
			g) **Gideon Welles** - Secretary of Navy, from CT
03	5	1861	All US troops in the Dept. of Texas are ordered to the coast for transportation to the state of New York.
03	6	1861	Envoys, Martin J. Crawford, John Forsyth and A. B. Brown, from the Confederate Government continue to try to establish meetings with the new Federal government, even though Abraham Lincoln refuses to meet with them.

03	7	1861	**Braxton Bragg,** CSA, is appointed Brig. Gen.
03	7	1861	**Samuel Cooper,** CSA, is appointed Brig. Gen.
03	7	1861	Camp Verde, TX, is abandoned by the Union forces.
03	7	1861	Ringgold Barracks, TX, is abandoned by the Union forces.
03	11	1861	Brig. Gen. Braxton Bragg, CSA, from North Carolina, assumes the command of all the Confederate forces in Florida.
03	12	1861	Fort McIntosh, TX, is abandoned by the Union forces, led by Maj. C. C. Sibley, 3rd US Infantry.
03	13	1861	Capt. Nathaniel Lyon, 2d US Infantry, is assigned to the command of the Saint Louis, MO, Arsenal, with subsequent orders to arm the loyal citizens and execute the laws of the United States of America.
03	13	1861	President Abraham Lincoln continues to refuse to meet with any Confederate envoys so as to not imply the acceptance of the Government of the Confederacy.
03	15	1861	Camp Wood, TX, is abandoned by the Union forces.
03	16	1861	The Arizona (Territory) State Convention held at Mesilla, votes to leave the Union.
03	17	1861	Camp Hudson, TX, is abandoned by the Union forces.
03	18	1861	The Arkansas State Convention held at Little Rock, AR, votes against seceding, 39-35, but agrees to another vote later in the year.
03	18	1861	Lieut. Adam Jacoby Slemmer, USA, who is commanding at Fort Pickens, FL, returns 4 fugitive slaves to their masters.
03	18	1861	The Governor of Texas, **Sam Houston,** quietly leaves office rather than swear allegiance to the Confederacy.
03	18	1861	The affair with Indians on the Columbia River, near the Kootenay River, the Washington Territory.
03	19	1861	Fort Clark, TX, is abandoned by the Union forces.
03	19	1861	Fort Inge, TX, is abandoned by the Union forces.
03	19	1861	Fort Lancaster, TX, is abandoned by the Union forces.
03	20	1861	Fort Brown, TX, is abandoned by the Union forces, led by Lieut. Col. Electus Backus, 3rd US Infantry.
03	20	1861	Fort Duncan, TX, is abandoned by the Union forces, led by Bvt. Maj. O. L. Shepherd, 3rd US Infantry.
03	21	1861	The Confederate seizure of the US supply ship sloop, the **USS Isabella,** at Mobile, AL, on its way to Pensacola, FL.
03	22	1861	Col. William W. Loring, USA, assumes the command of the Dept. of New Mexico (Territory).
03	23	1861	Brig. Gen. Edwin Vose Sumner, USA, is assigned to the command of the Dept. of the Pacific.
03	23	1861	Fort Chadbourne, TX, is abandoned by the Union forces.
03	26	1861	Col. Earl Van Dorn, CSA, reports of his arrival in Texas for the purpose of securing the adhesion of the US troops to the Confederate cause.
03	29	1861	Fort Mason, TX, is abandoned by the Union forces.
03	29	1861	President Abraham Lincoln, decides to send a force to supply the troops at Fort Sumter, SC, in lieu of an evacuation.
03	31	1861	Fort Bliss, TX, is abandoned by the Union forces.
04	1	1861	President Abraham Lincoln secretly orders the **USS Powhatan** to the aid of Fort Pickens, Pensacola, FL, from Fort Sumter, SC.
04	3	1861	The schooner, **Rhoda H. Shannon,** is fired upon by the Confederate batteries on Morris Island, Charleston Harbor, SC.
04	4	1861	President Abraham Lincoln writes a letter to Maj. Robert Anderson, USA, to hold Fort Sumter, Charleston Harbor, SC.
04	4	1861	The Virginia State Convention votes against holding a referendum on secession by the vote of 89-45.
04	5	1861	Fort Quitman, TX, is abandoned by the Union forces.
04	8	1861	Federal re-inforcements for Fort Pickens, FL, sail from New York Harbor, NY, aboard the Federal cutter, **Harriet Lane.**
04	9	1861	Two more vessels leave New York Harbor, NY, for Fort Sumter, SC, including the US steamer, the **USS Baltic.**

04	10	1861	The 2nd expedition for the relief of Fort Sumter, SC, sails from New York Harbor, while the **USS Pawnee** sails from Hampton Roads, VA.
04	11	1861	Col. Earl Van Dorn, CSA, is ordered to assume the command in Texas and make prisoners of all the US troops remaining in the State who refuse to espouse the Confederate cause.
04	11	1861	The evacuation of Fort Sumter, SC, is demanded by Brig. Gen. Pierre Gustave Toutant Beauregard, CSA.
04	12	1861	**The Bombardment, Evacuation, and Surrender of Fort Sumter, SC,** by Maj. Robert Anderson, after meeting with Confederate Commissioners, Col. James Chestnut, Lt. Col. A. R Chisolm, and Capt. Stephen D. Lee, refusing to surrender. 4/12-14/1861.
04	12	1861	**The Civil War is (un)Officially begun.**
04	12	1861	The re-inforcements from Fortress Monroe, VA, and a detachment of marines, land on Santa Rosa Island, at Fort Pickens, Pensacola, FL.
04	13	1861	**Alexander Robert Lawton,** CSA, is appointed Brig. Gen.
04	13	1861	Bvt. Col. Harvey Brown, 2nd US Artillery, assumes the command of the Dept. of Florida.
04	13	1861	**Maj. Robert Anderson, USA, surrenders Fort Sumter, SC,** to the Confederate authorities at Charleston, SC, after enduring continuous shelling by Confederate batteries.
04	13	1861	Fort Davis, TX is abandoned by the Union forces.
04	14	1861	Skirmishes with Indians on Van Dusen's Creek, near the Mad River, CA. 4/14-15/1861.
04	14	1861	President Abraham Lincoln, Washington, DC, issues a call for volunteer men of 75,000 to support the Union.
04	15	1861	Fort Macon, NC, is seized by the North Carolina state troops.
04	15	1861	The Governors of Kentucky and North Carolina refuse to furnish any militia to the United States.
04	15	1861	**Fort Sumter, SC, is evacuated** by the Federal forces, under Maj. Robert Anderson, USA. In the firing of a final salute to the US flag, an explosion of gunpowder occurs, resulting in 2 Federal dead and 2 wounded.
04	16	1861	Fort Washita, Indian Territory, **Chickasaw Indian Nation,** is abandoned by the Union forces.
04	16	1861	Fort Caswell, at the mouth of the Cape Fear River, NC, and Fort Johnston, at Smithville, NC, are seized by the North Carolina state troops.
04	17	1861	Federal re-inforcements from New York, aboard the **USS Powhatan,** arrive at Fort Pickens, FL.
04	17	1861	Secessionists from Maryland meet in Baltimore.
04	17	1861	The Governor of Missouri and the States of Tennessee and Kentucky refuse to furnish the quota of militia to the United States as requested by President Abraham Lincoln.
04	17	1861	The US steamer, **Star of the West,** is captured by the troops under Col. Earl Van Dorn, CSA, near Indianola, TX.
04	17	1861	The ordnance of secession, by secret ballot, is adopted by the Virginia Convention by a somewhat close vote of 88-55.
04	18	1861	The US Army subsistence stores are seized at Pine Bluff, AR.
04	18	1861	Maj. Gen. William B. Taliaferro is assigned to the command of the Virginia forces at Norfolk, VA.
04	18	1861	The US Armory at Harper's Ferry, WV, is abandoned and burned by its garrison.
04	18	1861	Lieut. Col. Robert Edward Lee USA, alledgingly turns down an offer by President Abraham Lincoln to command the Union forces.
04	19	1861	The conflict between the US troops, the 6th MA, and the 26th PA, en route to Washington DC, and the angry mob in Baltimore, MD, resulting in over 40 casualties.
04	19	1861	Maj. Gen. Robert Patterson, PA Militia, is assigned to the command over the States of Delaware, Pennsylvania, Maryland and the District of Columbia.
04	20	1861	The burning of the railroad bridges is ordered by the mayor, to prevent the passage of Union troops through Baltimore, MD. 4/20-26/1861.
04	20	1861	Brig. Gen. Benjamin F. Butler, USA, with the 4th MA, arrives at Annapolis, MD, to support Fortress Monroe, VA.
04	20	1861	The US Arsenal at Liberty, MO, is seized by state forces.
04	20	1861	The Federal expedition to destroy the Gosport Naval Yard dry-dock at Norfolk, VA, is ordered by Commandant Charles S. McCauley, where several ships, including the **USS Merrimac,** and supplies are burned.

04	20	1861	**Lieut. Col. Robert E. Lee USA, resigns his federal position,** deciding to side with his state of Virginia.
04	21	1861	Rioting continues in Baltimore, MD.
04	21	1861	Anti-secessionists meet in Monongahela County, VA, to show their support for the Union and not the Confederacy.
04	21	1861	Col. Earl Van Dorn, CSA, assumes the command of the Confederate forces in Texas.
04	22	1861	The Governor of Arkansas, Henry M. Rector, refuses to furnish the quota of militia requested by President Abraham Lincoln.
04	22	1861	Illinois state militia troops **occupy Cairo, IL,** at the junction of the Ohio and Mississippi Rivers.
04	22	1861	The US Arsenal at Fayetteville, NC, is seized by the North Carolina state troops.
04	23	1861	**Milledge Luke Bonham,** CSA, is appointed Brig. Gen.
04	23	1861	**George Brinton McClellan,** **U.S.A.,** is appointed Maj. Gen.
04	23	1861	Fort Smith, AR, is seized by the Arkansas state troops.
04	23	1861	Brig. Gen. Benjamin F. Butler, USA, offers to use US troops in co-operation with the Governor of Maryland to repress an apprehended slave insurrection there.
04	23	1861	Col. Carlos A. Waite, USA, commanding the Dept. of Texas, and his staff officers, are made prisoners of war at San Antonio, along with a company of the 8th US Infantry.
04	23	1861	Maj. Gen. Robert E. Lee, VA Volunteers is assigned to the command of the military and naval forces in the Confederate State of Virginia.
04	23	1861	Maj. Gen. Walter Gwynn, VA Volunteers, is assigned to the command of the Virginia state forces in and about Norfolk, VA.
04	23	1861	Maj. Gen. Joseph E. Johnston, VA Volunteers, is assigned to the command of the Virginia state forces in and about Richmond, VA.
04	25	1861	Capt. James H. Stokes removes 12,500 muskets from the Federal arsenal in St. Louis, MO, transporting them to the Pro-union militia troops in Illinois.
04	25	1861	Brig. Gen. Edwin Vose Sumner, USA, assumes the command of the Dept. of the Pacific, relieving Col. Albert Sidney Johnston, 2nd US Cavalry, Brevet Brig. Gen., USA, who recently resigned to join the Confederacy.
04	25	1861	Fort Stockton, TX, is abandoned by the Union forces.
04	25	1861	The US troops under Maj. Caleb C. Sibley, USA, surrender near Indianola, TX, as prisoners of war to Col. Earl Van Dorn, CSA, and sign a parole not to take up arms against the Confederate states until exchanged.
04	25	1861	The capture of US troops at Saluria, TX.
04	25	1861	The 7th NY Infantry arrives in Washington, DC, for its defense.
04	27	1861	**John Henry Winder,** CSA, is appointed Brig. Gen.
04	27	1861	Lieut. Gen. Winfield Scott, USA, announces the suspension of the **writ of habeas corpus,** between Philadelphia and Washington, DC, by the direction of President Lincoln.
04	27	1861	Maj. Gen. Robert Patterson, PA Militia, is assigned to the command of the Dept. of Pennsylvania.
04	27	1861	Brig. Gen. Benjamin F. Butler, MA Militia, is assigned to the command of the Dept. of Annapolis, MD.
04	27	1861	Col. Thomas J. Jackson, VA Volunteers, is assigned to the command of the Virginia state troops at and about Harper's Ferry, WV.
04	27	1861	The Virginia State Convention offers Richmond to the Confederacy as its capitol, in lieu of Montgomery, AL, which is strategically too far away from the events of the day.
04	27	1861	Col. Joseph K. F. Mansfield, USA, is assigned to the command of the Dept. of Washington, DC.
04	29	1861	The State of Maryland Convention, at Annapolis, votes down secession by the vote of 53-13.
04	30	1861	**Robert Selden Garnett,** CSA, is appointed Brig. Gen.
04	30	1861	President Lincoln orders the Federal troops to evacuate the forts in the Indian Territory, leaving the following Indian Nations under the jurisdiction of the Confederate States: a) **Cherokee** Indian Nation b) **Chickasaw** Indian Nation c) **Choctaw** Indian Nation d) **Creek** Indian Nation e) **Seminole** Indian Nation
04	30	1861	Fort Washita, the Indian Territory, is abandoned by Lieut. Col. William H. Emory, 1st US Cavalry, as he marches his troops north toward Fort Leavenworth, KS.

| 04 | 30 | 1861 | Maj. Caleb C. Sibley's, USA, detachment of paroled US troops sail for New York, from Texas. |

05	1	1861	**Joseph Eggleston Johnston,** CSA, is appointed Brig. Gen.
05	1	1861	Fort Washita, the Indian Territory, and near Texas, is occupied by the Texas militia.
05	1	1861	Funeral services are held in Boston, MA, for the Union soldiers killed in the Baltimore, MD, riots.
05	1	1861	Volunteer forces to support the Union are called out in the Nebraska Territory, by Governor Samuel W. Black.
05	1	1861	Brig. Gen. Robert E. Lee, CSA, sends Confederate troops to Harper's Ferry, VA, under the command of Col. Thomas J. Jackson, VA Militia, to remove all military equipment.
05	1	1861	The mouth of the James River, and Hampton Roads, VA, is blockaded by an assortment of US Navy vessels.

05	3	1861	President Lincoln creates the Dept. of the Ohio, consisting of Illinois, Indiana and Ohio, and assigns George Brinton McClellan, Maj. Gen. of Ohio Militia, to its command.
05	3	1861	Governor John Letcher of Virginia issues a call for additional volunteer forces.
05	3	1861	In Washington, DC, Bvt. Lieut. Gen. Winfield Scott develops the **Anaconda Plan,** whereby the Union envelopes the Southern states by use of a Naval blockade of all major ports, a plan that can be credited with aiding in the eventual downfall of the Confederacy.

| 05 | 4 | 1861 | The US Ordnance Stores are seized at Kansas City, MO. |
| 05 | 4 | 1861 | Col. G. A. Porterfield, CSA, is assigned to command of the States forces in Northwestern Virginia (WV). |

| 05 | 5 | 1861 | Fort Arbuckle and Fort Cobb, of the Indian Territory, the **Chickasaw Indian Nation,** are abandoned, by Lieut. Col. William H. Emory, 1st US Cavalry, on his march to Fort Leavenworth, KS. |
| 05 | 5 | 1861 | Alexandria, VA, is abandoned by the Virginia state troops. (Subsequently Reoccupied). |

05	6	1861	The ordnance of secession is adopted by the Arkansas Convention, at Little Rock, by the overwhelming vote of 69-1 in favor of secession.
05	6	1861	Brig. Gen. Daniel M. Frost, Missouri State Militia, establishes a camp of instructions near Saint Louis, by the direction of the Governor of Missouri.
05	6	1861	The State Legislature of Tennessee, votes 66-25 in favor of secession, to set the tone for the upcoming general election which will determine the issue of secession.

| 05 | 7 | 1861 | With the general population of Tennessee split over secession, a riot breaks out in Knoxville, which results in many injuries and one fatality. |
| 05 | 7 | 1861 | The routes between Philadelphia, Harrisburg and Washington, DC, via Baltimore, are re-established. |

| 05 | 8 | 1861 | The US steamer **Baltic,** and the **USS Constitution,** prepare to move the US Naval Academy from Baltimore, MD, to Newport, RI, due to the unrest in Maryland. |

| 05 | 9 | 1861 | The detachment of US troops under the command of Bvt. Lieut. Col. Isaac V.D. Reeve, USA, surrender at San Lucas Spring, TX, to the command under Col. Earn Van Dorn, CSA. |
| 05 | 9 | 1861 | The exchange of shots between the US steamer, **USS Yankee,** and the Confederate shore batteries at Gloucester Point, across from Yorktown, VA, on the York River. |

05	10	1861	Capt. Nathaniel Lyon, 2nd US Infantry, with a force of US volunteers, comprised of the 1st, 3rd, and 4th Missouri Reserves, makes prisoners of General Daniel Marsh Frost, and his entire command of over 625 men of the Missouri Militia.
05	10	1861	Capt. Nathaniel Lyon, 2nd US Infantry, along with 5th Missouri Reserves, capture Camp Jackson, which is near Saint Louis, MO. A Pro-secession crowd congregates which starts a riot that breaks out resulting in over 30 killed.
05	10	1861	The first blockade patrol of Charleston Harbor, SC, is begun with the **USS Niagara.**
05	10	1861	Col. Earn Van Dorn, CSA, reports to his Confederate Govt. of the capture of the last columns of US troops in Texas.

05	11	1861	**Ben McCulloch,** CSA, is appointed Brig. Gen.
05	11	1861	Pro-Union demonstrations are held in San Francisco, CA.
05	11	1861	Riot in Saint Louis, MO, continues from the previous day which results in several additional deaths. The 5th Missouri Reserve Regiment eventually squelches the secessionists uproar.
05	11	1861	Brig. Gen. William S. Harney, USA, resumes the command of the Dept. of the West.
05	11	1861	Pro-Union demonstrations are held in Wheeling, VA.

| 05 | 13 | 1861 | Brig. Gen. Ben. McCulloch, CSA, is assigned to the command in the Indian Territory. **(later to become the state of Oklahoma).** |

05	13	1861	Moving from the Relay Station, **Baltimore, MD, is occupied** without the official authorization of Bvt. Lieut. Gen. Winfield Scott, USA, by the troops, including the 6th and 8th MA troops led by Massachusetts Militia Brig. Gen. Benjamin Franklin Butler, a political military appointee.
05	13	1861	Maj. Gen. George B. McClellan, USA, assumes the command of the Dept. of Ohio, now embracing a portion of Western Virginia.
05	14	1861	**Robert Edward Lee,** CSA, is appointed Brig. Gen.
05	14	1861	**John Charles Fremont, U.S.A,** is appointed Maj. Gen.
05	14	1861	The following are appointed Union Brigadier Generals:

Irvin McDowell, USA
Joseph King Fenno Mansfield, USA
Montgomery Cunningham Meigs, USA
Erastus Barnard Tyler, USA

05	14	1861	The seizure of a train of railroad cars and locomotives at Harper's Ferry, WV, and on the **Baltimore and Ohio Railroad,** by direction of Col. Thomas Jonathan Jackson, VA Militia.
05	14	1861	President Abraham Lincoln orders Major Robert Anderson, USA, to provide aid to the Kentucky Unionists even though the state has claimed neutrality.
05	15	1861	**Robert Anderson,** USA, is appointed Brig. Gen.
05	15	1861	**George Archibald McCall,** USA, is appointed Brig. Gen.
05	15	1861	Bvt. Maj. Gen. George Cadwalader, PA Militia, supersedes Brig. Gen. Benjamin F. Butler, USA, in the Dept. of Annapolis, MD. Brig. Gen. Butler will be ordered to the command at Fortress Monroe, Hampton Roads, VA.
05	15	1861	The Federal expedition from Saint Louis to Potosi, MO, by order of Brig. Gen. Nathaniel Lyon, USA, to assist Pro-Union citizens .
05	15	1861	Brig. Gen. Joseph Eggleston Johnston, CSA, is assigned to the command of troops near Harper's Ferry, VA.
05	16	1861	**Samuel Cooper, C.S.A., is appointed full Confederate General.**
05	16	1861	**Benjamin Franklin Butler, U.S.A.,** is appointed Maj. Gen. **John Adams Dix, U.S.A.,** is appointed Maj. Gen.
05	16	1861	**William Starke Rosecrans,** USA, is appointed Brig. Gen.
05	16	1861	President Abraham Lincoln empowers Bvt. Maj. Gen. George Cadwalader, USA, to arrest any persons under certain circumstances, MD, etal.
05	16	1861	President Abraham Lincoln orders US Navy Commander, John Rodgers, to take charge of the naval operations in the rivers in the West, most importantly the Mississippi River.
05	16	1861	Capt. Nelson Cole, 5th MO Infantry, enters Potosi and arrests a number of anti-Union citizens.
05	16	1861	Tennessee is officially admitted to the Confederacy with the transparent manipulation by Governor Isham Harris.
05	17	1861	The following are appointed Union Brigadier Generals:

Don Carlos Buell, USA
James Cooper, USA
Darius Nash Couch, USA
Jacob Dolson Cox, USA
Samuel Ryan Curtis, USA
William Buel Franklin, USA
Ulysses Simpson Grant, USA
Charles Smith Hamilton, USA
Samuel Peter Heintzelman, USA
Joseph Hooker, USA
Philip Kearny, USA
Benjamin Franklin Kelley, USA
Erasmus Darwin Keyes, USA
Rufus Ring, USA
Frederick West Lander USA
Nathaniel Lyon, USA
John Alexander McClernand, USA
William Reading Montgomery, USA
John Walcott Phelps, USA
John Pope, USA
Andrew Porter, USA

Fitz John Porter,	USA
Benjamin Mayberry Prentiss,	USA
Joseph Jones Reynolds,	USA
Robert Cumming Schenck,	USA
Thomas West Sherman,	USA
William Tecumseh Sherman,	USA
Franz Sigel,	USA
Charles Pomeroy Stone,	USA
Alpheus Starkey Williams,	USA

05	18	1861	Arkansas is admitted to the Confederacy.
05	18	1861	Engagement between the US steamer, **Monticello,** and the battery at Sewell's Point, VA. 5/18-19/1861.
05	18	1861	The US Navy essentially seals off Northern Virginia with the naval blockade of the Rappahannock River.
05	19	1861	The Union blockade continues its attack on the Confederate shore batteries at Sewell's Point, near Hampton Roads, VA.
05	20	1861	**William Wing Loring,** CSA, is appointed Brig. Gen.
05	20	1861	The Capital of the Confederacy is to be moved to the City of Richmond, VA, by the vote of the Confederate Provisional Congress, Montgomery, AL.
05	20	1861	The ordinance of secession is adopted by the North Carolina Convention, held at Raleigh, NC, the 11th state to secede.
05	21	1861	Col. John B. Magruder, Provisional Army of VA, is assigned to the command at Yorktown, VA.
05	21	1861	Brig. Gen. M. L. Bonham, CSA, is assigned to the command on the **"Alexandria Line,"** VA.
05	21	1861	The convention and proclamation between Brig. Gen. Harney, USA, and Maj. Gen. Sterling Price, the Missouri State Guard, whereby Harney agreed not to bring any Federal troops into the state if Price can maintain law and order, effectively giving control to the Pro-southern force.
05	22	1861	**Charles Clark,** CSA, is appointed Brig. Gen.
05	22	1861	**David Emanuel Twiggs,** CSA, is appointed Brig. Gen.
05	22	1861	Maj. Gen. Benjamin F. Butler, MA Militia, is assigned to the command at Fort Monroe, Hampton, VA.
05	23	1861	**John Buchanan Floyd,** CSA, is appointed Brig. Gen.
05	23	1861	**Operations against Indians on the Mad and Eel Rivers, California,** with skirmishes as follows: a) near Larrabee's Ranch, (May 23rd) b) on the Eel River, **(May 26th)** c) on the South Fork of the Eel River **(May 28th)** d) the Keatuck Creek **(May 30th)** e) opposite Bell Spring on the Eel River **(June 4th),** f) near Larrabee's House **(June 2nd and 8th)** g) South Fork of the Eel River, **(June 14th and 16th)** h) near Kettenshaw, **(June 17th)** 5/23-6/17/1861.
05	23	1861	Demonstration on Hampton, VA, by Maj. Gen. Benjamin Butler.
05	23	1861	Brig. Gen. Benjamin Huger, VA Volunteers, is assigned to the command at Norfolk, VA.
05	23	1861	The State of Virginia votes to secede from the Union by the margin of 3 to 1. However, the Western part of the state prepares to break away from the rest of Virginia, remaining loyal to the Federal Government.
05	24	1861	The Union Army advances into Virginia and **occupies Arlington Heights and Alexandria, VA.** In the process of removing a Confederate flag from a hotel, **Col. Elmer Ephraim Ellsworth,** of the 11th NY Regiment, is shot dead by the inns keeper, **Mr. James Jackson,** who in turn, is subsequently killed by **Pvt. Francis E. Brownell,** some of the very first casualties of the Civil War.
05	24	1861	Maj. Gen. Benjamin F. Butler, USA, from Fortress Monroe, Hampton, VA, announces to President Lincoln of his determination to employ in the Federal cause fugitive slaves of disloyal owners, causing a political stir as Butler looks upon slaves as contraband, refusing to release 3 Negro slaves.
05	25	1861	The publication of the Honorable William G. Brownlow's editorial, in the Knoxville, TN, Whig, "Murder will out," upon which his subsequent arrest is based by CSA officials.
05	25	1861	President Abraham Lincoln attends the funeral for **Col. Elmer Ellsworth,** after laying in rest at the White House.
05	26	1861	Federal Naval blockade is established on New Orleans, LA, by the **USS Brooklyn.**

MONTH	DAY	YEAR	ACT
05	26	1861	**Chief Justice Roger B. Taney,** of the US Supreme Court, issues a **writ of habeas corpus.** His opinion is in the matter of Prisoner John Merryman, MD, who was arrested by Maj. Gen. George Cadwalder, while trying to recruit Confederate soldiers. Taney orders that Mr. Merryman be set free.
05	26	1861	The advance upon and the **occupation of Grafton, WV,** by the Union troops. 5/26-30/1861.
05	26	1861	Lincoln's 1st Postmaster, Francis Preston Blair, Jr, announces postal services will be cut with the Confederate States on May 31, 1861, Washington, DC.
05	27	1861	The **occupation of Newport News, VA,** by the Union troops led by Maj. Gen. Benjamin Franklin Butler, USA, from Fortress Monroe, near Hampton, VA. 5/27-29/1861.
05	28	1861	Federal Naval blockade is established on Savannah, GA, by the **USS Union.**
05	28	1861	Brig. Gen. Irvin McDowell, USA, assumes the command of the Dept. of Northeastern Virginia.
05	29	1861	Union Secretary of War, Simon Cameron, accepts Miss Dorothea Dix's offer to establish Federal Military hospitals.
05	30	1861	**Albert Sidney Johnston, CSA. is appointed full Confederate General.**
05	30	1861	The **occupation of Grafton, WV,** by the Union troops, led by Col. Benjamin F. Kelley, USA, under Maj. Gen. George B. McClellan, USA, to protect the **Baltimore and Ohio Railroad,** Washington's leading link to the western states and territories. 5/26-30/1861.
05	30	1861	Honorable Simon Cameron, Secretary of War, directs Maj. Gen. Benjamin F. Butler, USA, not to surrender any fugitive slaves to disloyal owners; Maj. Gen Butler is stationed at Fortress Monroe, VA.
05	30	1861	Across Hampton Roads from Newport News, VA, the Confederates raise the scuttled **USS Merrimack,** after it was burned to the water level, by the evacuating Federals, April 20, 1861, at the Gosport Naval Yard Dry-dock, Norfolk, VA.
05	31	1861	Union troops, which were ordered by President Lincoln to evacuate their forts in the Indian Territory, arrive at Fort Leavenworth, KS. The route they followed is named after one of their guides, the honorable Mr. Jesse Chisholm, afterwards to always be remembered as **"The Chisholm Trail."**
05	31	1861	Brig. Gen. Nathaniel Lyon, USA, supersedes Brig. Gen. William Selby Harney in Missouri.
05	31	1861	The **"Alexandria Line,"** VA, command is given to Brig. Gen. Pierre Gustave Toutant Beauregard, CSA.
05	31	1861	Federal attack on the Aquia Creek Batteries, VA. 5/31-6/1/1861
06	1	1861	Skirmishes at Arlington Mills and Fairfax Court-House, VA. **Capt. John Q. Marr,** CSA, is killed and is one of the early Confederate casualties of the war.
06	2	1861	Brig. Gen. Pierre Gustave Toutant Beauregard, CSA, supersedes Brig. Gen. Milledge Luke Bonham, CSA, in the command of the **"Alexandria Line,"** (also referred to as the **"Department of Alexandria,"** also known as the **"Potomac Department,"** afterwards known as the **"Army of the Potomac."**
06	3	1861	**Stephen Arnold Douglas,** 'The Little Giant,' the Democratic candidate for the US Presidency against Republican, Abraham Lincoln, dies at the age of fortyeight, at Springfield, IL.
06	3	1861	Action at Philippi, WV, where Col. G. A. Porterfield, CSA, is routed. Maj. Gen. George B. McClellan, USA, receives credit for the victory, although not involved. The Pro-Union men use the lack of Confederate forces forces in the area to launch a spearhead against secession.
06	5	1861	The following are appointed Confederate Brigadier Generals: **Earl Van Dorn,** CSA **Theophilus Hunter Holmes,** CSA **Henry Alexander Wise,** CSA
06	5	1861	The **USS Niagara** captures the Confederate schooner, **Aid,** off the coast of Mobile, AL.
06	5	1861	Attack upon Pig Point Batteries, near Hampton, VA, on the James River, by the Federal Steamer, the **Harriet Lane.**
06	6	1861	The State of Missouri is transferred to the Dept. of the Ohio, commanded by Maj. Gen. George B. McClellan, USA.
06	6	1861	Brig. Gen. Henry Alexander Wise, CSA, ex-governor of Virginia, is ordered to command the CSA troops in the Kanawha Valley, WV.
06	7	1861	Confederate reconnaissance from Yorktown to Newport News, VA, by the Chatham Grays, VA Cavalry.
06	8	1861	The State of Tennessee reports that the general election favors secession from the Union by a 2 to 1 vote. This serves only to confirm the course of action already taken by the State Legislature, led by Governor Isham Harris, although eastern Tennessee will remain staunch Pro-Union.

06	8	1861	Brig. Gen. Robert S. Garnett, CSA, is assigned to the command of troops in Northwestern VA, (WV) after the June 3rd, incident at Philippi, WV.
06	8	1861	The Virginia state troops are transferred to the Confederate States of America by Virginia Governor, John Letcher.
06	10	1861	The engagement at Big Bethel, or Bethel Church, VA, 8 miles from Newport News, VA. Maj. Gen. Benjamin F. Butler, USA, is defeated by Col. John Bankhead Magruder, CSA, and retreats back to Fortress Monroe, Hampton, VA.
06	10	1861	Brig. Gen. Pierre Gustave Toutant Beauregard, CSA, is placed in the command of all the Confederate forces in the Virginia counties of Prince William, Fairfax, and Loudoun.
06	10	1861	**The Rockville MD, Expedition,** Col. Charles Stone, 14th US Infantry, commanding an early Federal expedition from Washington, D.C., to Edwards' Ferry, Potomac River, MD. 6/10-7/7/1861.
06	11	1861	Col. Edward Richard Sprigg Canby, USA, reports that Col. Loring, USA, has abandoned his command of the Union Dept. of New Mexico Territory; Loring having given his allegiance to the Confederacy.
06	11	1861	Col. Edward Richard Sprigg Canby, 19th US Infantry, is placed in general charge of affairs in the Federal Dept. of the New Mexico Territory.
06	11	1861	Skirmish at Romney, WV, with Col. Lew Wallace, USA, 11th IN.
06	12	1861	Missouri Governor Claiborne Jackson puts out a call for 50,000 volunteer men to enlist in the Confederacy to repel the ongoing Federal attempts to conquer the state.
06	13	1861	Descent of the Union troops on, and **occupation of, Romney, WV,** led by Col. Lew. Wallace, USA, 11th IN Infantry, commanding, who then returns back to Cumberland, MD.
06	14	1861	**<u>Robert Edward Lee, C.S.A., is appointed Full Confederate General.</u>**
06	14	1861	**Stephen Augustus Hurlbut,** USA, is appointed Brig. Gen.
06	14	1861	Federal expedition near Seneca Mills, MD, under Brig. Gen. Charles P. Stone, USA, with skirmish.
06	14	1861	**Harper's Ferry, WV, is evacuated** by Brig. Gen. Joseph E. Johnston, CSA, after receiving word of the potential arrival of Federal troops from the west under Maj. Gen. George Brinton McClellan, and from the north under Gen. Robert Patterson; Johnston withdrawing to the vicinity of Winchester, VA.
06	15	1861	The Federal **occupation of Edwards' and Conrads' ferries, Potomac River,** MD, by Brig. Gen. Charles P. Stone, USA.
06	17	1861	The following are appointed Confederate Brigadier Generals: **Barnard Elliott Bee,** CSA **Richard Stoddert Ewell,** CSA **William Joseph Hardee,** CSA **Benjamin Huger,** CSA **Thomas Jonathan "Stonewall" Jackson,** CSA **David Rumph Jones,** CSA **James "Old Pete" Longstreet,** CSA **John Bankhead Magruder,** CSA **John Clifford Pemberton,** CSA **Henry Hopkins Sibley,** CSA **Edmund Kirby Smith,** CSA
06	17	1861	**Frederick West Lander,** USA, is appointed Brig. Gen.
06	17	1861	Engagement at Boonville, MO, sees Brig. Gen. Nathaniel Lyon, USA, inflicting a Confederate defeat under Pro-South Governor Claiborne Jackson. This further opens up the Missouri River to the Union.
06	17	1861	Jefferson City, MO, is controlled by Union forces under Brig. Gen. Nathaniel Lyon, USA.
06	17	1861	Affair at Conrad's Ferry, MD, with Brig. Gen. Charles P. Stone, USA.
06	17	1861	President Abraham Lincoln intently watches the new hot air balloon invention of **Professor Thaddeus S. C. Lowe,** as a potential military observation weapon.
06	17	1861	Skirmish near Vienna, VA, with Col. Maxcy Gregg, CSA, 1st S.C.
06	18	1861	Skirmish at Edward's Ferry, MD, with Brig. Gen. Charles P. Stone, USA.
06	18	1861	Skirmish at Camp Cole, MO, with Pro-Union Home Guards.
06	19	1861	Skirmish at New Creek, WV.
06	19	1861	Pro-Unionists of Virginia meet in Wheeling, WV, to elect Francis Henry Pierpont as the provisional governor of the potential new state of **West Virginia.**

MONTH	DAY	YEAR	ACT
06	22	1861	Col. Harvey Brown, USA, commanding at Fort Pickens, FL, reports to the War Dept. that he will not return any fugitive slaves to their masters unless he is ordered so.
06	22	1861	Pro-union men meet in Greeneville, TN, to pledge allegiance to the United States.
06	23	1861	The Federal blockade ship, the **USS Massachusetts,** captures 4 blockade runners in the Gulf of Mexico.
06	23	1861	Skirmish at Righter, WV.
06	24	1861	Maj. Gen. Nathaniel P. Banks, USA, is directed to "quietly seize" the Baltimore, MD, Police Commissioners.
06	24	1861	Skirmish at Jackson, MO.
06	24	1861	Affair on the Rappahannock River, 12 miles below Urbanna, VA.
06	25	1861	**Leonidas Polk, C.S.A.,** is appointed Maj. Gen.
06	25	1861	Mathias Point, VA, Potomac River, is attacked by Federal gunboats.
06	26	1861	Skirmishes at Frankfort and on Patterson Creek, or Kelley's Island, WV, with Col. Lew. Wallace, 11 IN.
06	27	1861	The attack on Mathias Point, VA, York River, by the Federal gunboats, **Pawnee** and **Freeborn,** are repelled as they attempt to land Union forces.
06	27	1861	Mr. George P. Kane, Marshal of the Police of Baltimore, MD, is arrested.
06	27	1861	The Confederate capture of the side-wheeler, **St. Nicholas,** near Baltimore, MD, led by George N. Holllins.
06	30	1861	Pursued by the **USS Brooklyn,** the Confederate warship, the **CSS Sumter,** slips past the Union blockade at the mouth of the Mississippi River, near New Orleans, LA, and heads for the open seas.
07	1	1861	The US War Dept. issues orders for raising troops in Kentucky and Tennessee even though Tennessee voted on May 6, 1861, to secede from the Union, while Kentucky has voted to remain neutral in this disagreement over states' rights.
07	1	1861	Maj. Gen. Nathaniel P. Banks, USA, reports the arrest of the Baltimore Police Commissioners. Subsequently he has a proclamation which he pitches to the good citizens of Baltimore, MD.
07	2	1861	**Operations in the Shenandoah Valley, VA.** 07/02-25/1861.
07	2	1861	Brig. Gen. Robert Patterson's, USA, command crosses the Potomac River at Williamsport, MD, in an attempt to prevent Brig. Gen. Joseph E. Johnston's, CSA, forces in the Shenandoah Valley from moving to reinforce the Confederate forces at Manassas, VA, led by Brig. Gen. P. G. T. Beauregard, CSA.
07	2	1861	Engagement at Falling Waters, or Hoke's Run, WV, or Haynesville, or Martinsburg, MD, in the area of Western Virginia, which results in a Federal victory by Patterson, USA.
07	2	1861	The new Legislature of Western Virginia convenes at Wheeling, WV, under the auspices of the Federal Government.
07	3	1861	Fort McLane, the New Mexico Territory, is abandoned.
07	3	1861	The Western Dept. is constituted. (of the states of Missouri, Arkansas, Kansas and the Indian Territory).
07	3	1861	The New Mexico Territory is embraced into the Western Dept.
07	3	1861	**Martinsburg, WV, is occupied** by the Union forces of Brig. Gen. Robert Patterson, USA, causing the Confederate forces of Brig. Gen. Joseph Eggleston Johnston's, CSA, men to retreat.
07	4	1861	**Joseph Eggleston Johnston, C.S.A., is appointed full Confederate General.**
07	4	1861	Skirmish at Farmington, below St. Louis, MO.
07	4	1861	Skirmish at Harper's Ferry, WV, with Brig. Gen. Robert Patterson's USA forces and Brig. Gen. Joseph E. Johnston's, CSA, men.
07	4	1861	President Abraham Lincoln uses the Fourth of July to issue a request for an additional 400,000 men to volunteer.
07	5	1861	The Engagement near Carthage, MO, which embraces the actions at Dry Fork Creek and Brier Fork, in southwest MO, has the Confederate forces under Missouri Governor Claiborne Jackson forcing a Union retreat toward Carthage, MO, led by Brig. Gen. Franz Sigel, USA. Sigel to have a lackluster military career.
07	5	1861	Brig. Gen. Ben. McCulloch, CSA, at Neosho, MO, captures and paroles 80 Union soldiers belonging to the command of Brig. Gen. Franz Sigel, USA.
07	5	1861	Skirmish near Newport News, near Curtis' Farm, VA, with Brig. Gen. John B. Magruder's, CSA, forces, and Maj. Gen. Benjamin F. Butler, USA.

07	6	1861	The **CSS Sumter** arrives at Cienfuegos, Cuba with the following captured Union vessels: **Albert Adams, Cuba, Ben Dunning, Lewis Kilham, Machia, Niad,** and the **West Wind.**
07	6	1861	The Confederate Privateer, the **Jefferson Davis,** captures the Union vessels, **Enchantress** and the **John Welsh,** off Cape Hatteras, NC.
07	6	1861	The **Campaign in West Virginia.** 07/6-17/1861
07	6	1861	Skirmishes at Middle (Creek) Fork Ridge, or Buckhannon, WV. 7/6-7/1861.
07	7	1861	The Confederate Privateer, the **Jefferson Davis,** captures the Union vessel, **S. J. Waring,** in the Atlantic, off New Jersey.
07	7	1861	Skirmish at Great Falls, VA.
07	7	1861	Skirmishes at Belington and Laurel Hill, WV. 7/7-12/1861.
07	7	1861	Skirmish at Glenville, WV.
07	8	1861	**Richard Caswell Gatlin,** CSA, is appointed Brig. Gen.
07	8	1861	The Confederate camp at Florida, MO, is attacked and dispersed by loyal Union State troops.
07	8	1861	Brig. Gen. Henry Hopkins Sibley, CSA, is ordered to Texas to expel the Union forces from the New Mexico Territory.
07	9	1861	The following are appointed Confederate Brigadier Generals: **Benjamin Franklin Cheatham,** CSA **Daniel Smith Donelson,** CSA **Gideon Johnson Pillow,** CSA **Felix Kirk Zollicoffer,** CSA
07	9	1861	Skirmishes at and near Monroe Station, MO, with Col. Robert F. Smith, USA, 16th IL Infantry. 7/9-11/861.
07	9	1861	Maj. Gen. Leonidas Polk, CSA, telegraphs to the Richmond, VA, authorities that "no time is to be lost in East Tennessee."
07	9	1861	Skirmish at Vienna, VA.
07	9	1861	The US House of Representatives resolves that it is not the duty of Union soldiers to capture and return fugitive slaves.
07	10	1861	**Daniel Harvey Hill,** CSA, is appointed Brig. Gen.
07	10	1861	**Jones Mitchell Withers,** CSA, is appointed Brig. Gen.
07	10	1861	The Confederacy signs a peace treaty with the **Creek Indian Nation** tribe, the Indian Territory.
07	10	1861	Fort Breckinridge, the New Mexico Territory, is abandoned.
07	10	1861	Skirmish at Rich Mountain, WV, between Brig. Gen. Robert S. Garnett, CSA, and Brig. Gen. William S. Rosecrans, USA, under Maj. Gen. George B. McClellan, USA.
07	11	1861	Maj. Gen. Nathaniel Prentiss Banks, USA, supersedes Bvt. Maj. Gen. George Cadwalader, PA Troops, in command of the Dept. of Annapolis, MD.
07	11	1861	**Engagement at Rich Mountain, and Laurel Hill, WV,** where overall commanding general, Maj. Gen. George B. McClellan, USA, claims victory over Brig. Gen. Robert S. Garnett, CSA, as Garnett withdraws into the Cheat River Valley, WV.
07	12	1861	The Confederacy signs peace treaties with the **Chickasaw** and the **Choctaw** Indian nation tribes, in the Indian Territory.
07	12	1861	Lieut. Col. John Pegram's, CSA, forces surrender to Brig. Gen. William Starke Rosecrans, USA, after the engagement at Rich Mountain, WV, at Beverly, WV.
07	12	1861	**Beverly, WV is occupied** by Maj. Gen. George B. McClellan, USA, as the Confederates retreat from Laurel Hill, WV.
07	12	1861	Brig. Gen. Jacob Dolson Cox's, USA, forces move to confront Brig. Gen. Henry Alexander Wise's, CSA forces in the area surrounding the Valley of the Great Kanawha, WV.
07	12	1861	Skirmish near Newport News, VA, with Maj. Gen. Benjamin F. Butler, USA.
07	13	1861	Maj. Gen. Leonidas Polk, CSA, assumes the command of the Confederate Dept. No. 2, KY, etal.
07	13	1861	Skirmish at the Red House, near Barboursville, WV.
07	13	1861	**Action at Carrick's (or Corrick's), Ford, Cheat River, WV**, with Maj. Gen. George B. McClellan, USA soundly defeating the Confederates, and giving the Federals virtual control over WV.
07	13	1861	**Brig. Gen. Robert Selden Garnett, CSA,** is the first Civil War General to die, mortally wounded while setting up a skirmish line and fighting a rear guard action, during the action at Carrick's Ford.

| 07 | 13 | 1861 | The descent of the Union troops upon Romney, WV, by Maj. Gen. George B. McClellan, USA. |

07	14	1861	The **USS Daylight** begins the initial blockade of the Confederate port of Wilmington, N.C.
07	14	1861	Brig. Gen. Henry Rootes Jackson, CSA, is ordered to the command of the Confederate forces in West Virginia, following the death of Brig. Gen. Robert Selden Garnett, CSA.
07	14	1861	Federal reconnaissance from Alexandria, VA, towards Fairfax Court-House, VA, by Col. Thomas A Davies, 16th NY.

07	15	1861	The military forces, stores, and etc. of Arkansas, are transferred to the Confederate States.
07	15	1861	Skirmish at Mexico, MO.
07	15	1861	Skirmish at Wentzville, or Millsville, MO. 7/15-17/1861.
07	15	1861	Action near Vienna, VA.
07	15	1861	Skirmish at Bowman's Place, on the Cheat River, WV.
07	15	1861	Skirmish near Bunker Hill, WV, north of Winchester, VA.
07	15	1861	The Confederate forces **evacuate Harper's Ferry, WV.**

| 07 | 16 | 1861 | **Forward to Richmond! The Bull Run, or the Manassas Campaign, VA.** 07/16-22/1861. The advance of the Union army under Brig. Gen. Irvin McDowell, USA, toward Manassas, and Centreville, VA. |
| 07 | 16 | 1861 | Skirmish at Barboursville, WV, between Brig. Gen. Jacob D. Cox, USA, and Brig. Gen. Henry A. Wise, CSA. |

07	17	1861	Skirmish at Fulton, MO.
07	17	1861	Skirmish at Parkersville, MO. 7/17-19/1861.
07	17	1861	The Confederate Army retires to the line of Bull Run, VA.
07	17	1861	Skirmish at Fairfax Court-House, VA.
07	17	1861	Skirmish at Vienna, or Bunker Hill, VA.
07	17	1861	Action at Scarey Creek, or Scarrytown, WV, between Brig. Gen. Jacob D. Cox's, USA, advance and Brig. Gen. Henry A. Wise, CSA.

07	18	1861	**Richard Heron Anderson,** CSA, is appointed Brig. Gen.
07	18	1861	Action near Harrisonville, and Parkersville, MO, as reported by Maj. R. T. Van Horn, Missouri Reserve Corps.
07	18	1861	Skirmish at Martinsburg, MO.
07	18	1861	**Action at Blackburn's Ford, VA,** where Brig. Gen. James Longstreet's, CSA, forces withstand Maj. Gen. Irvin McDowell's, USA, Federal probe, under Brig. Gen. Daniel Tyler, USA.
07	18	1861	Skirmish at Mitchell's Ford, VA, with Brig. Gen. James Longstreet.
07	18	1861	The main body of Confederate Forces under Brig. Gen. Joseph E. Johnston, CSA, in the Shenandoah Valley, VA, are withdrawn to re-inforce the troops under Brig. Gen. P.G.T. Beauregard, CSA, in the Bull Run, or Manassas Campaign, VA.

07	19	1861	**Robert Augustus Toombs,** CSA, is appointed Brig. Gen.
07	19	1861	Affair on the Back River Road, VA.
07	19	1861	Affair near New Market Bridge, VA.

| 07 | 20 | 1861 | Federal expedition from Springfield to Forsyth, MO. 7/20-25/1861. |
| 07 | 20 | 1861 | Brig. Gen. William W. Loring, CSA, is assigned to the command of the "Northwestern Army" (WV). |

07	21	1861	**Pierre Gustave Toutant Beauregard, CSA, is appointed full Confederate General.**
07	21	1861	The following are appointed Confederate Brigadier Generals: **Jubal Anderson Early,** CSA **Samuel Jones,** CSA **William Henry Chase Whiting,** CSA
07	21	1861	**James Brewerton Ricketts,** USA, is appointed Brig. Gen.
07	21	1861	Skirmish with Indians on the South Fork of the Eel River, CA.
07	21	1861	**The Battle of Bull Run, or Manassas, VA,** with activity around Sudley Springs Ford, Matthews Hill, Henry House, Stone House, Robinson House, Stone Bridge, Cub Run Bridge, etc, which results in a resounding Federal defeat for Brig. Gen. Irvin McDowell, USA, and a jubilant victory for the joint command of Gens. Joseph E. Johnston, and P.G.T. Beauregard, CSA.
07	21	1861	**Brig. Gen. Barnard Elliott Bee, CSA,** is mortally wounded while leading is men during the Battle of Bull Run, or Manassas, VA, dying the next day. Bee is best remembered for giving **Thomas Jonathan Jackson** his nickname of **"Stonewall."**
07	21	1861	The Retreat of the Union Army from Bull Run, or Manassas, VA
07	21	1861	Maj. Gen. Nathaniel P. Banks, USA, is ordered to relieve Maj. Gen. Patterson, USA, in the command of

the Dept. of the Shenandoah, VA, for allowing Gen. Joseph E. Johnston, CSA, to transfer his troops unopposed to Manassas, VA, from the Shenandoah Valley.

| 07 | 21 | 1861 | Skirmish at Charlestown, WV, between Brig. Gens. Jacob D. Cox, USA, and Henry A. Wise, CSA. |

07	22	1861	**Brig. Gen. Barnard Elliott Bee, CSA,** dies in his cabin headquarters from wounds received yesterday at the Battle of Bull Run, or Manassas, VA.
07	22	1861	Brig. Gen. William J. Hardee, CSA, assumes the command of the Confederate forces in Northwestern Arkansas.
07	22	1861	Skirmish at Etna, MO.
07	22	1861	Skirmish at, and **occupation of, Forsyth, MO,** by Brig. Gen. Thomas Sweeny, USA.
07	22	1861	The Pro-South Governor of Missouri, Claiborne Jackson, continues to declare his administration is the only legal ruling body of Missouri, even though the Missouri State Convention votes to abstain from leaving the Union.
07	22	1861	Maj. Gen. George Brinton McClellan, USA, is ordered to Washington, DC.

07	23	1861	Brig. Gen. William Starke Rosecrans, USA, assumes the command of the Dept. of the Ohio, embracing a portion of Western Virginia, and replacing Maj. Gen. George B. McClellan, USA.
07	23	1861	Maj. Gen. John A. Dix, USA, assumes the command of the Dept. of Maryland.
07	23	1861	Fort Buchanan, the New Mexico Territory, is abandoned by the Union forces.

07	24	1861	Action at Blue Mills, MO.
07	24	1861	Operations at Back River, VA, with a general troop skirmish.
07	24	1861	Brig. Gen. Henry Wise, CSA retreats up the Kanawha Valley, WV, evacuating the area around Charleston, WV, and retreating to Gauley Bridge, after the action at Tyler Mountain with Brig. Gen. Jacob Cox, USA, who **occupies Charleston.**

07	25	1861	Maj. Gen. John C. Fremont, USA, assumes the command of the Western Dept., at St. Louis, MO, who will soon generate much controversy over his policies and administration of events in this military district.
07	25	1861	Skirmish at Dug Springs, MO.
07	25	1861	Skirmishes at Harrisonville, MO. 7/25-27/1861.
07	25	1861	Skirmish at Mesilla, the New Mexico Territory, with Federal troops from Fort Fillmore, under Maj. Isaac Lynde, USA, who stave off the Confederates.
07	25	1861	Maj. Gen. John Adams Dix, USA, assumes the command of the Dept. of Pennsylvania.
07	25	1861	Maj. Gen. Nathaniel Prentiss Banks, USA, assumes command of the Dept. of the Shenandoah Valley, VA, superseding Maj. Gen. Robert Patterson, USA.
07	25	1861	**Robert Mercer Taliaferro Hunter** replaces **Robert Toombs** as the Confederate Secretary of State, Toombs resigning for a military appointment.

07	26	1861	Skirmish at McCulla's Store, MO.
07	26	1861	Fort Fillmore, the New Mexico Territory, is abandoned, by Maj. Isaac Lynde, even though having a 2 to 1 numerical advantage over Capt. John Baylor, CSA.
07	26	1861	Brig. Gen. Felix Kirk Zollicoffer, CSA, is assigned to the command in East Tennessee.

| 07 | 27 | 1861 | The Union forces under Maj. Isaac Lynde, USA, 7th US Infantry, from Fort Fillmore, surrender at San Augustine Springs, the New Mexico Territory, to Capt. John R. Baylor, CSA. |
| 07 | 27 | 1861 | Maj. Gen. George Brinton McClellan, USA, assumes the command of the **Division (later Army) of the Potomac,** VA, appointed by President Abraham Lincoln, to replace Maj. Gen. Irwin McDowell, USA, after his disastrous defeat at Bull Run, or Manassas, VA. |

| 07 | 28 | 1861 | **New Madrid,** in southeastern MO, on the Mississippi River, **is occupied** by the Confederates. |

07	29	1861	The Baltimore MD Police Commissioners, from their prison, memorialize Congress for redress.
07	29	1861	Skirmish at Edwards Ferry, MD.
07	29	1861	Brig. Gen. John Pope, USA, assumes the command in North Missouri, with the instructions to protect the railroads and and to suppress all local disorders.

| 07 | 30 | 1861 | The Missouri State Convention votes 56-25 to elect a new governor (Pro-Union). |

| 07 | 31 | 1861 | The Pro-Union Missouri State Convention elects Hamilton R. Gramble as the new governor of Missouri, replacing Claiborne Jackson. |
| 07 | 31 | 1861 | Brig. Gen. John Pope, USA, issues General Order Number 3, and formulates a plan for the suppression of the lawless elements and permanent pacification of North Missouri. |

07	31	1861	The Army of the State of Tennessee is transferred to the Confederate States of America.
08	1	1861	**Arnold Elzey,** CSA, is appointed Brig. Gen.
08	1	1861	**Lawrence Pike Graham,** USA, is appointed Brig. Gen.
08	1	1861	Police Commissioner Charles Howard addresses US Secretary, Simon Cameron, and Bvt. Lieut. General Winfield Scott, protesting against the alleged harsh treatment of the political prisoners at Fort Lafayette, MD.
08	1	1861	Skirmish at Edina, MO.
08	1	1861	After his capture of Fort Fillmore, New Mexico Territory, on July 26, 1861, Capt. John Baylor, CSA, declares that all the territory in New Mexico and Arizona south of the 34th parallel, belongs to the Confederacy.
08	1	1861	**Gen. Robert Edward Lee,** CSA, is ordered to take command of the Confederate forces in West Virginia, by order of President Jefferson Davis, following the debacle on July 13, 1861 at Carrick's Ford, WV; Lee replaces Brig. Gen. William W. Loring.
08	2	1861	Federal reconnaissance from Ironton to Centreville, MO, with Col. B. Gratz Brown, 4th MO Infantry.
08	2	1861	Skirmish at Dug Springs, MO, near Springfield, Brig. Gen. Ben McCulloch, CSA, pitted against Brig. Gen. Nathaniel Lyon, USA.
08	2	1861	Fort Stanton, New Mexico Territory, near Messilla, is abandoned due to the efforts of Capt. John Baylor, CSA.
08	3	1861	**Lorenzo Thomas,** USA, is appointed Brig. Gen.
08	3	1861	**James Wolfe Ripley,** USA, is appointed Brig. Gen.
08	3	1861	Federal scout from Fort Crook to Round Valley, CA, with skirmish **(August 5th)** with Indians in the Upper Pitt River Valley, CA. 8/3-12/1861.
08	3	1861	Skirmish at McCulla's Store, MO.
08	3	1861	Governor Isham G. Harris, of Tennessee, proposes to visit Richmond, VA, to confer with the Confederate authorities upon the threatening aspect of affairs in East Tennessee.
08	3	1861	**John LaMountain** makes the first reported balloon ascent from a ship, the **Fanny,** off Hampton Roads, Hampton, VA.
08	4	1861	The Honorable Thomas A. R. Nelson is arrested on his way to the Union lines by the Confederate soldiers, TN.
08	5	1861	The blockade runner, the **CSS Alvarado,** is captured and burned off the Florida coast near Fernandina, FL, by the US steamer, the **USS Vincennes.**
08	5	1861	Skirmish at Athens, MO.
08	5	1861	Brig. Gen. Nathaniel Lyon, USA, retreats from Dug Springs, MO, towards Springfield, due to reports of advancing Confederates
08	5	1861	Skirmish in Virginia, opposite Point of Rocks, MD.
08	6	1861	**Ambrose Everett Burnside,** USA, is appointed Brig. Gen.
08	6	1861	Federal camp "Dick Robinson" is established near Lexington, KY, to bolster the standing of Pro-Union men there.
08	7	1861	Federal expedition to Price's Landing, Commerce, Benton, and Hamburg, MO, with Union troops ferried on the US steamer, **Luella,** under Maj. John McDonald, 8th MO Infantry. 8/7-10/1861
08	7	1861	The US War Dept. signs a contract with **Mr. James B. Eads,** of St. Louis, MO, to construct the following seven iron clad gunboats which will become the main military force of the Union's western river operations: a) **USS Cairo** b) **USS Carondolet** c) **USS Cincinnati** d) **USS Louisville** e) **USS Mound City** f) **USS Pittsburg** g) **USS St. Louis**
08	7	1861	**Hampton, VA, is burned** by Brig. Gen. John B. Magruder, CSA, in part for Maj. Gen. Benjamin Butler's, USA, position of not returning slaves to their owners, while using Hampton to house them.
08	8	1861	**Henry Hayes Lockwood,** USA, is appointed Brig. Gen.
08	8	1861	Brig. Gen. Ulysses S. Grant, USA, assumes the command of the District of Ironton, MO.

08	8	1861	The Indian attack on an emigrant train, near the Great Salt Lake, the Utah Territory. 8/8-9/1861.
08	8	1861	Skirmish at Lovettsville, VA.
08	9	1861	**Daniel Ruggles,** CSA, is appointed Brig. Gen.
08	9	1861	**Isaac Ridgeway Trimble,** CSA, is appointed Brig. Gen.
08	9	1861	The following are appointed Union Brigadier Generals:

Louis Ludwig Blenker, USA
John Henry Martindale, USA
George Webb Morrell, USA
Israel Bush Richardson, USA
Henry Warner Slocum, USA
James Samuel Wadsworth, USA

08	10	1861	**Samuel Davis Sturgis,** USA, is appointed Brig. Gen.
08	10	1861	**The Battle of Oak Hills, Springfield, or Wilson's Creek, MO,** results in another Confederate victory following Bull Run, or Manassas, VA. Brig. Gen. Nathaniel Lyon, USA, is mortally wounded, Brig. Gen. Samuel Sturgis, USA, assumes command and retreats to Rolla, MO, conceding a large portion of Missouri to the Confederates. Brig. Gen. Ben McCulloch, CSA, combines forces with the State Militia of Missouri under Sterling Price to defeat the Union troops.
08	10	1861	**Brig. Gen. Nathaniel Lyon, USA,** is mortally wounded, shot dead from atop his horse while waving his hat and directing the position of the Union troops.
08	10	1861	Skirmish at Potosi, MO, with Brig. Gen. Ulysses S. Grant, USA.
08	11	1861	Affair at Hamburg, MO, with Brig Gen. M. Jeff Thompson, MO State Guard.
08	11	1861	Brig. Gen. John Buchanan Floyd, CSA, assumes the command of the Confederate forces in the Valley of the Kanawha, WV.
08	12	1861	The following wooden Union gunboats, which were converted riverboats, arrive at Cario, IL, which will support all Federal river operations until the ironclads can be built:

a) **USS Conestoga**
b) **USS Lexington**
c) **USS Tyler**

08	12	1861	**Apache Indians** led by Chief Nicholas attack and kill about 15 Confederate soldiers south of Fort Davis, in the Big Bend country, Texas. The Confederates, in their effort to control the entire southwest, want to appease all the Indian tribes, and do nothing in return.
08	13	1861	**William Farrar Smith,** USA, is appointed Brig. Gen.
08	13	1861	**George Stoneman,** USA, is appointed Brig. Gen.
08	13	1861	President Jefferson Davis, CSA, orders that the Honorable Thomas A. R. Nelson, of Tennessee, for opposing his state's action regarding secession, be discharged.
08	13	1861	Skirmish near Grafton, WV.
08	14	1861	**James William Denver,** USA, is appointed Brig. Gen.
08	14	1861	Martial law is declared in Saint Louis, MO, by Maj. Gen. John Charles Fremont, USA.
08	14	1861	Brig. Gen. Earl Van Dorn, CSA, is relieved from, and Brig. Gen. Paul O. Hebert, CSA, is assigned to, the command of the Confederate forces in Texas.
08	14	1861	The 79th NY Regiment mutinies in the Army of the Potomac, due to lack of furloughs.
08	15	1861	The following are appointed Confederate Brigadier Generals:

George Bibb Crittenden, CSA
John Breckinridge Grayson, CSA
Albert Pike, CSA
Roswell Sabine Ripley, CSA

08	15	1861	Federal expedition from Fort Crook to the Pitt River, CA, with skirmish **(19th)** with Indians near Kellogg's Lake. 8/15-22/1861.
08	15	1861	The states of Kentucky and Tennessee are constituted the Dept. of the Cumberland, under the command of Brig. Gen. Robert Anderson, USA, recently of Fort Sumter, Charleston, SC, fame.
08	15	1861	Federal expedition to Saint Genevieve, MO, aboard the US steamer, **Hannibal City,** led by Maj. John McDonald, 8th MO Infantry. 8/15-16/1861.
08	15	1861	The 2nd ME Regiment, like the 79th NY, threatens mutiny in the Army of the Potomac, which results in the transfer of some 60 men to duty on Dry Tortugas, off Key West, FL.

08	16	1861	Federal expedition to Fredericktown, MO.
08	16	1861	Federal operations around Kirksville, MO. 08/16-21/1861
08	16	1861	Mauraders fire into a passenger train upon the Hannibal and Saint Joseph Railroad, MO.
08	16	1861	Many New York City, NY, newspapers are charged by the Federal Government with publishing Pro-Southern articles.
08	17	1861	**Paul Octave Hebert,** CSA, is appointed Brig. Gen.
08	17	1861	**George Henry Thomas,** USA, is appointed Brig. Gen.
08	17	1861	**Egbert Ludovicus Viele,** USA, is appointed Brig. Gen.
08	17	1861	Skirmish at Brunswick, MO.
08	17	1861	Affairs at Hunnewell and Palmyra, MO, where Confederates are reported to have fired into a train that was carrying Union troops.
08	17	1861	Bvt. Maj. John Ellis Wool, USA, supersedes Maj. Gen. Benjamin F. Butler, USA, in the command of the Dept. of Virginia.
08	17	1861	The Depts. of Northeastern Virginia, of Washington, and of the Shenandoah are merged into the Dept. (Army) of the Potomac.
08	18	1861	The Confederate privateer, **Jefferson Davis,** runs aground and sinks off St. Augustine, FL, ending a most destructive career.
08	18	1861	Skirmish at Sandy Hook, MD.
08	18	1861	Federal scout to Accotink, and the subsequent skirmish at the Pohick Church, VA, about 12 miles south of Alexandria, VA, with the 1st NY Cavalry, sent by Brig. Gen. William B. Franklin, USA.
08	19	1861	**Henry Wager Halleck, U.S.A.,** is appointed Maj. Gen.
08	19	1861	**John James Peck,** USA, is appointed Brig. Gen.
08	19	1861	**James Shields,** USA, is appointed Brig. Gen.
08	19	1861	Skirmish at Charleston, or Bird's Point, MO, across the river from Cairo, IL, with a Union victory over the Missouri State Guard.
08	19	1861	Skirmish at Klapsford, MO.
08	19	1861	Newspaper offices in Easton and West Chester, PA, are raided by Pro-unionist men, while the editor of the Haverhill, MA, newspaper is tarred and feathered by an anti-South mob.
08	20	1861	**William Farquhar Barry,** USA, is appointed Brig. Gen.
08	20	1861	**John Fulton Reynolds,** USA, is appointed Brig. Gen.
08	20	1861	Confederate attack on the railroad train near Lookout Station, MO.
08	20	1861	Skirmish at Fish Lake, MO.
08	20	1861	Brig. Gen. Richard Caswell Gatlin, CSA, assumes the command of the defenses of North Carolina.
08	20	1861	Maj. Gen. George B. McClellan, USA, assumes the command of the Dept., or Army of the Potomac, VA.
08	20	1861	Skirmish at the Hawk's Nest, WV.
08	20	1861	Skirmish at Laurel Fork Creek, WV.
08	21	1861	Brig. Gen. John Breckinridge Grayson, CSA, is assigned to the command of the Confederate Dept. of Middle and East Florida.
08	21	1861	Skirmishes at Jonesborough, MO. 8/21-22/1861.
08	21	1861	Brig. Gen. Roswell Sabine Ripley, CSA, is assigned to the command of the Confederate Dept. of South Carolina.
08	22	1861	The Federal capture of the steamers, the **CSS W.B. Terry,** and the mail steamboat, **Samuel Orr,** by the **USS Lexington,** at Paducah, KY.
08	23	1861	Skirmish at Medoe, MO.
08	23	1861	Skirmish near Fort Craig, the New Mexico Territory.
08	23	1861	The engagement of the US steamers, **Yankee,** and the **Release,** (ice-boat) with the batteries at the mouth of the Potomac Creek, VA, that are commanded by Col. R. M. Cary, 30th VA Infantry.
08	23	1861	Skirmish at Springfield, WV.
08	24	1861	The Dept. of Pennsylvania is absorbed into the Dept. of the Potomac, also known as **"The Army of the Potomac."**
08	24	1861	Jefferson Davis, Richmond, VA, appoints the following commissioners to represent the Confederacy in Europe: a) John Slidell - France

                    b) James M. Mason - Great Britain
                    c) Pierre A. Rost   -   Spain

08	25	1861	**Operations against Indians about Fort Stanton, the New Mexico Territory,** by Lieut. John R. Pulliam, CSA. 8/25-9/8/1861.
08	25	1861	Federal scout into Virginia from Great Falls, MD.
08	25	1861	Skirmish with the **Apache Indians** near Fort Bliss, TX, by Lieut. Col. John R. Baylor, CSA.
08	25	1861	Skirmish near Piggot's Mill (Big Run), WV, with Brig. Gen. Henry A. Wise, CSA; meanwhile his camp is currently severely disabled by measles.
08	26	1861	Col. Benjamin L. Beall, 1st US Dragoons, is assigned to the command the District of Oregon.
08	26	1861	Skirmish at Blue's House WV.
08	26	1861	Action at Cross-Lanes, near Summerville, WV, which results in an overwhelming Confederate victory by Brig. Gen John B. Floyd, CSA, surprising Col. Tyler, 27th Ohio Infantry as his men ate breakfast.
08	26	1861	Skirmishes at Wayne Court-House, WV. 8/26-27/1861.
08	26	1861	The US ships, **Cumberland, Fanny, Harriet Lane, Minnesota, Monticello, Pawnee, Susquehanna,** and the **Wabash,** under the command of Commodore Silas Stringham, USN, in conjunction with Maj. Gen. Benjamin F. Butler, USA, sail from Hampton Roads, VA, for the North Carolina Coast at Cape Hatteras with 900 Union soldiers to attack Forts Clark and Hatteras.
08	27	1861	Skirmish at Antietam Iron Works, MD, north of the Potomac.
08	27	1861	The US expeditionary force lands Federal troops at Cape Hatteras, Hatteras Inlet, NC.
08	27	1861	The Confederates abandon Fort Clark, NC, near Cape Hatteras.
08	27	1861	Skirmishes at Ball's Cross-Roads, VA. 8/27-28/1861.
08	28	1861	**Operations in Southeastern Missouri.** 8/25-9/5/1861.
08	28	1861	Skirmish at Ball's Mills, MO.
08	28	1861	The Federal Capture of the Confederate batteries at Hatteras Inlet, NC, including Fort Hatteras and Fort Clark, NC. 8/28-29/1861.
08	28	1861	Skirmishes near Bailey's Corners, (or Cross-Roads), VA, below Washington, DC, with the 2nd and 3rd MI Infantry. 8/28-30/1861.
08	28	1861	The War Dept., at Washington DC, directs that certain paroled prisoners are to be discharged from the military service of the United States.
08	29	1861	Skirmish at Morse's Mills, near Lexington, MO.
08	30	1861	The Honorable Montgomery Blair recommends that certain Baltimore, MD, newspapers be suppressed.
08	30	1861	**Operations in Northeastern Missouri.** 8/30-9/7/1861.
08	30	1861	In an action that President Abraham Lincoln later calls "dictatorial," and totally without any authorization, Maj. Gen. John Charles Fremont, USA, declares all of the following: 1) The "Emancipation Proclamation," 2) proclaims martial law in Missouri and his purpose is to confiscate the property and liberate the slaves of disloyal owners. 3) orders the arrest of all disloyal persons found within the Union lines to be armed. 4) directs the extreme penalty of the law be inflicted on the destroyers of railroad and telegraph lines, bridges, etc.
08	31	1861	The following are appointed Union Brigadier Generals: **John Joseph Abercrombie,** USA **Silas Casey,** USA **Abram Duryee,** USA **George Gordon Meade,** USA **John Sedgwick,** USA **Charles Ferguson Smith,** USA
08	31	1861	Skirmish at Munson's Hill, or the Little River Turnpike, VA, with Col. George W. Taylor, 3rd NJ Infantry.
09	1	1861	**Thomas Leonidas Crittenden,** USA, is appointed Brig. Gen.
09	1	1861	Skirmish near Fort Scott, KS.
09	1	1861	Brig. Gen. Ulysses S. Grant, USA, based at Cape Girardeau, MO, assumes the command of the Federal forces in Southeastern Missouri.

09	1	1861	Skirmish at Bennett's Mills, MO.
09	1	1861	Federal expeditions through Jefferson County, MO. 9/1-3/1861.
09	1	1861	Skirmish at Blue Creek, WV.
09	1	1861	Skirmish at Boone Court-House, WV.
09	1	1861	Skirmish at Burlington, WV.

09 2 1861 **James McKinstry,** USA, is appointed Brig. Gen.

09 2 1861 Destruction of the US dry-dock at Pensacola, FL.

09 2 1861 Brig. Gen. M. Jeff. Thompson, CSA, issues a proclamation threatening retaliation, in Missouri, because of Maj. Gen. Charles Fremont's, USA, proclamation.

09 2 1861 Expeditions toward Columbia, Boone County, and Iberia, MO.

09 2 1861 Skirmish at Dallas, MO.

09 2 1861 Action at Dry Wood Creek, or Fort Scott, MO.

09 2 1861 Arkansas and all the military operations in Missouri is placed under the command of Maj. Gen. Leonidas Polk, CSA, commanding the Confederate Dept. Number Two, which already includes Confederate operations along the Mississippi River and in Tennessee.

09 2 1861 Skirmish at Beller's Mill, near Harper's Ferry, WV.

09 2 1861 Skirmish near the Hawk's Nest, WV, with Brig. Gen. Henry A. Wise, CSA.

09 2 1861 Skirmish at Worthington, WV.

09 3 1861 **Joseph Anderson,** CSA, is appointed Brig. Gen.

09 3 1861 The following are appointed Union Brigadier Generals:

Ebenezer Dumont,	USA
Oliver otis Howard,	USA
Charles Davis Jameson,	USA
Alexander McDowell McCook,	USA
Robert Huston Milroy,	USA
Elezear Arthus Paine,	USA
Daniel Edgar Sickles,	USA
Lewis Wallace,	USA

09 3 1861 **The advance of the Confederate forces,** led by Maj. Gen. Gideon Pillow, CSA, into Kentucky, which up until now, had declared its neutrality, including the **occupation of Columbus, and Hickman, KY.**

09 3 1861 Brig. Gen. Gideon Johnson Pillow, CSA, and Col. William Henry L. Wallace, the 11th IL Infantry, negotiate an exchange of prisoners of war in Missouri.

09 3 1861 Maj. Gen. Joseph Reid Anderson, CSA, is ordered to North Carolina.

09 4 1861 The **USS Jamestown** captures and burns the blockade runner, the **Col. Long,** off the coast of Georgia.

09 4 1861 Engagement at Hickman and Columbus, KY, with the Union gunboats, **USS Lexington** and the **USS Tyler,** and the Confederate shore batteries along with the **CSS Jackson.**

09 4 1861 Skirmish at Great Falls, MD, with Brig. Gen. George A. McCall, USA, with his 6th Regiment suffering terribly with typhoid fever.

09 4 1861 Action at Shelbina, MO, with Brig. Gen. Stephen A. Hurlbut, USA, **evacuating Shelbina.**

09 4 1861 Brig. Gen. Earl Van Dorn CSA, transfers the command of the Dept. of Texas to Col. Henry Eustace McCulloch, 1st TX Rifles.

09 5 1861 Skirmish at Papinsville, MO.

09 5 1861 President Lincoln meets with Bvt. Lieut. Gen. Winfield Scott to discuss the future of Maj. Gen. John C. Fremont, USA, at his St. Louis, MO, post.

09 6 1861 Brig. Gen. Charles Ferguson Smith, USA, is assigned to the command in Western Kentucky.

09 6 1861 **Paducah, KY,** near the the Cumberland River, and at the mouth of the Ohio and Tennessee Rivers is **occupied by** the Union forces, led by Brig. Gen. Ulysses S. Grant, USA, as an obstacle to the Confederates entrance in Kentucky on 9/3/1861.

09 6 1861 Skirmish at Monticello Bridge, MO.

09 6 1861 Skirmish at Rowell's Run, WV.

09 7 1861 The following are appointed Union Brigadier Generals:

Daniel Butterfield,	USA
Willis Arnold Gorman,	USA
Charles Mynn Thruston,	USA

09	7	1861	Skirmish with Indians near the Santa Ana Canyon, CA.
09	7	1861	Federal expedition to Big Springs, MO, by Col. Alvin P. Hovey, USA, 24th IN Infantry.
09	8	1861	Federal operations against **Green's Confederate guerrillas** in Missouri, by Brig. Gen. John Pope, USA. 9/8-9/1861
09	8	1861	Federal reconnaissance from Cairo, IL, and the engagement at Lucas Bend, MO, Brig. Gen. Ulysses S. Grant, USA, supported by the Union gunboats, **Conestoga** and **Lexington.** 9/8-10/1861.
09	9	1861	**Ormsby MacKnight Mitchel,** USA, is appointed Brig. Gen.
09	9	1861	President Lincoln orders Maj. Gen. David Hunter, USA, to St. Louis, MO, to "assist" Maj. Gen. John Charles Fremont, USA, who is becoming a nuisance to Lincoln.
09	9	1861	Skirmish at Shepherdstown, WV.
09	10	1861	Brig. Gen. George Henry Thomas, USA, is assigned to the command at the training Camp Dick Robinson, Eastern Kentucky.
09	10	1861	Federal reconnaissance toward Norfolk, MO, by Brig. Gen. John McClernand, USA.
09	10	1861	Skirmish at Lewinsville, VA, with men from the 79th NY and the 5th WI.
09	10	1861	**Engagement at Carnifex Ferry, WV**, with Union troops led by Brig. Gen. William Starke Rosecrans, USA, forcing a general Confederate retreat, led by Brig. Gen. John B. Floyd, CSA, and Brig. Gen. Henry A. Wise, CSA, toward Dogwood Gap and Sewell Mountain.
09	11	1861	President Abraham Lincoln issues an order modifying the proclamation of Maj. Gen. John C. Fremont, USA, in Missouri, to conform to the act of Congress.
09	11	1861	Federal reconnaissance from the Chain Bridge to Lewinsville, VA, and action at Lewinsville, with Col. JEB Stuart's 1st VA Cavalry, and Brig. Gen. William F. Smith's, USA, men, including the 79th NY; Maj. Gen. George B. McClellan, USA, restoring the colors of the 79th NY, which had mutinied.
09	11	1861	Operations in Cheat Mountain, WV, including actions and skirmishes at the following places: a) Cheat Mountain Pass b) Cheat Summit c) Point Mountain Turnpike d) and Elk Water. Brig. Gen. John Fulton Reynolds', USA, troops defeat the Confederates led by Gen. Robert E. Lee, CSA, which cuts off Western Virginia from the rest of the state. Gen. Lee considers his assault a complete failure, as do many other Confederates.
09	12	1861	**Braxton Bragg, C.S.A.,** is appointed Maj. Gen.
09	12	1861	Maj. Gen. George Brinton McClellan, USA, after various conferences with the President and with the Secretary of War, orders the arrest of the disloyal members of the Maryland Legislature as well as other citizens of the state, which occurs. 09/12-17/1861.
09	12	1861	Maj. Gen. John Charles Fremont, USA, issues the deeds of manumission to two slaves of a disloyal owner in Missouri.
09	12	1861	Skirmish at Black River, near Ironton, MO, with Maj. Gavitt, 1st IN Infantry.
09	12	1861	Skirmish at Petersburg, WV.
09	12	1861	Skirmish near Peytona, WV.
09	13	1861	**The Siege of Lexington, MO,** by Brig. Gen. Sterling Price, CSA. 9/13-20/1861.
09	13	1861	Action at Boonville, MO, with Col. Jefferson C. Davis, 22 IN.
09	13	1861	Col. Benjamin L. Beall, 1st US Dragoons, assumes the command of the District of Oregon.
09	14	1861	**Simon Bolivar Buckner,** CSA, is appointed Brig. Gen.
09	14	1861	**Edward Otho Cresap Ord,** USA, is appointed Brig. Gen.
09	14	1861	Col. George Wright, 9th US Infantry, is assigned to the command of all the Federal troops serving in Southern CA.
09	14	1861	Federal descent on the Pensacola, FL, navy-yard with the destruction of the Confederate Privateer, **Judah,** by the men from the **USS Colorado,** under Col. Harvey Brown, 5th US Art.
09	14	1861	Skirmish at Old Randolph, MO.
09	14	1861	The **USS Albatross** captures the Confederate blockade runner, the **Alabama,** near the mouth of the Potomac River, VA.
09	15	1861	Skirmish at Pritchard's Mill, or Darnestown, VA, near the Antietam Ford, MD, with Col. John W. Geary 28th PA Vol.
09	15	1861	Gen. Albert Sidney Johnston, CSA, supersedes Maj. Gen. Leonidas Polk, CSA, in the command of the

Confederate Dept. Number 2 in Missouri, etal.

09	16	1861	**William Nelson,** USA, is appointed Brig. Gen.
09	16	1861	**Horatio Gouverneur Wright,** USA, is appointed Brig. Gen.
09	16	1861	The **USS Conestoga** captures a couple Confederate vessels in the Cumberland River, KY.
09	16	1861	Skirmish opposite Seneca Creek, near Poolesville, MD, with a party from the 34th NY, Col. La Dew.
09	16	1861	The Confederate forces **evacuate Ship Island, MS,** which will be used in the future by the Union forces as a base of operations for refueling the blockading squadron along the Gulf Coast. Men from the **USS Massachusetts** take possession.
09	16	1861	Skirmish at Magruder's Ferry, VA.
09	16	1861	Action at Princeton, WV.

09	17	1861	**Leroy Pope Walker,** CSA, is appointed Brig. Gen.
09	17	1861	Brig. Gen. Benjamin Mayberry Prentiss, USA, is assigned to the command along and north of the **Hannibal and St. Joseph Railroad, MO.**
09	17	1861	Action at Blue Mills Landing, MO.
09	17	1861	Skirmish at Morristown, MO.

09	18	1861	**William Thomas Ward,** USA, is appointed Brig. Gen.
09	18	1861	Capt. Samuel Francis DuPont, USN, assumes command of the **South Atlantic Blockading Squadron.**
09	18	1861	Brig. Gen. Simon Bolivar Buckner, CSA, assumes the command of the Confederate Central Division of Kentucky.
09	18	1861	Bowling Green, KY, **is occupied** by the Confederates.
09	18	1861	Federal agents seize employees of a Louisville, KY, newspaper, accused of writing Pro-Southern newspaper articles..
09	18	1861	Skirmish near Berlin, MD.
09	18	1861	Brig. Gen. Paul Octave Hebert, CSA, assumes the command of the Confederate Dept. of Texas.

09	19	1861	**Gustavus Woodson Smith, C.S.A.,** is appointed Maj. Gen.
09	19	1861	**Earl Van Dorn,** **C.S.A.,** is appointed Maj. Gen.
09	19	1861	**John Blair Smith Todd,** USA, is appointed Brig. Gen.
09	19	1861	The Dept. of the Ohio is reorganized, KY, etal.
09	19	1861	Action at Barboursville, KY, where Brig. Gen. Felix Kirk Zollicoffer, CSA, causes a general retreat of Federal troops from the area.
09	19	1861	The Dept. of Western Virginia is constituted.

09	20	1861	**Mayfield, KY, is evacuated** by the Confederate forces.
09	20	1861	The Maryland political prisoners are sent to Fort Lafayette, NY, while Maryland Governor Thomas H. Hicks, indorses the act of arrest.
09	20	1861	Skirmish opposite Seneca Creek, MD.
09	20	1861	Maj. Gen. Sterling Price, the Missouri State Guard, **captures Lexington, MO,** and the US forces under the command of Col. James A. Mulligan, of the 23d IL Infantry, after a week long siege. Maj. Gen. John Charles Fremont, USA, is further criticized for not sending relief to Col. Mulligan.

09	21	1861	**Albert Gallatin Blanchard,** CSA, is appointed Brig. Gen.
09	21	1861	**Edward Dickinson Baker, U.S.A.,** is appointed Maj. Gen.
09	21	1861	Federal reconnaissance toward Columbus, and skirmish at Mayfield Creek, KY, by Brig. Gen. Ulysses S. Grant, USA. 9/21-22/1861.
09	21	1861	Brig. Gen. Ormsby MacKnight Mitchel, USA, assumes the command of the Dept. of the Ohio, KY. which will soon be absorbed into the Army of the Cumberland.
09	21	1861	Gen. Joseph E. Johnston, CSA, calls upon the state of Tennessee for 30,000 men.
09	21	1861	Maj. Gen. Leonidas Polk is assigned to the command of the 1st (or Western) Division, the Confederate Dept. No. 2, TN.
09	21	1861	Gen. Robert E. Lee, CSA, is in immediate command of the Confederate forces in the Valley of the Kanawha, WV.

09	22	1861	Skirmish at Eliott's Mills or Camp Crittenden MO.
09	22	1861	The destruction by **burning of Osceola, or Papinsville,** MO, by the Federal Kansas Jayhawkers, led by Mr. James H. Lane.
09	22	1861	Gen. Joseph E. Johnston, CSA, calls upon the states of Arkansas and Mississippi for 10,000 men each,

for service in Confederate Dept. Number 2, TN, etal.

| 09 | 23 | 1861 | **Gabriel James Rains,** CSA, is appointed Brig. Gen. |
| 09 | 23 | 1861 | The following are appointed Union Brigadier Generals: |

			John Gross Barnard,	USA
			Winfield Scott Hancock,	USA
			John Newton,	USA
			Innis Newton Palmer,	USA
			Stewart Van Vliet,	USA
			Seth Williams,	USA

09	23	1861	Affair at Albany, KY, with Brig. Gen. Felix Zollicoffer, CSA.
09	23	1861	Maj. Gen. Charles Fremont, USA, closes a St. Louis, MO, newspaper, the **Evening News,** for criticizing his (in)actions regarding Lexington.
09	23	1861	Skirmish at Cassville, WV.
09	23	1861	The Confederate descent upon Romney, WV, including the affairs at Mechanicsburg Gap and Hanging Rock Pass, with the advancing Rebels.

| 09 | 24 | 1861 | **James Ewell Brown (JEB) Stuart,** CSA, is appointed Brig. Gen. |
| 09 | 24 | 1861 | Skirmish at Point of Rocks, MD, with Col. John Geary, 28th PA Vols. |

09	25	1861	**Thomas Fenwick Drayton,** CSA, is appointed Brig. Gen.
09	25	1861	**Lafayette McLaws,** CSA, is appointed Brig. Gen.
09	25	1861	The District of Southern California is created, Col. George, 9th US Infantry, is assigned to its command, consisting of the following counties:

a) Buena Vista   d) San Bernardino
b) Los Angeles   e) San Diego
c) Santa Barbara   f) San Luis Obispo
                     g) Tulare

09	25	1861	Federal expedition from San Bernardino to the Temecula Ranch and Oak Grove, CA. 9/25-10/5/1861.
09	25	1861	Skirmish at Canada Alamosa, the New Mexico Territory.
09	25	1861	Brig. Gen. Henry Alexander Wise, CSA, is relieved from command in West(ern) Virginia.
09	25	1861	Maj. Gen. Gustavus Woodson Smith, CSA, is assigned to the command of the 2nd Army Corps, the Army of Northern Virginia.
09	25	1861	Engagement at Freestone Point, VA, with the Union fleet and the Confederate shore batteries, under Col. Louis T. Wigfall, 1st TX Infantry,
09	25	1861	Federal reconnaissance to, and skirmish near, Lewinsville, VA, with Brig. Gen. William F. Smith's, USA men.
09	25	1861	Action at Kanawha Gap, near Chapmanville, WV, between Gen. Robert. E. Lee, CSA, and Brig. Gen. William S. Rosecrans, USA.

09	26	1861	Federal expedition from Cumberland Ford, KY, including skirmish at Laurel Bridge, Laurel County, and the capture of Salt Works in Clay County, KY, by Brig. Gen. Felix K. Zollicoffer, CSA. 9/26-30/1861.
09	26	1861	The destruction of the locks at the mouth of the Muddy River, near Lucas Bend, KY, by Brig. Gen. Simon B. Buckner, CSA.
09	26	1861	Skirmish at Hunter's farm, near Belmont, MO.
09	26	1861	Skirmish near Fort Thorn, the New Mexico Territory.

| 09 | 27 | 1861 | Skirmish near Norfolk, MO, with Col. R. J. Oglesby, 8 IL. |

09	28	1861	**Thomas Carmichael Hindman,** CSA, is appointed Brig. Gen.
09	28	1861	**Edward Denison Morgan,** U.S.A., is appointed Maj. Gen.
09	28	1861	The following are appointed Union Brigadier Generals:

			John Milton Brannan,	USA
			William Thomas Harbaugh Brooks,	USA
			William Wallace Burns,	USA
			William Henry French,	USA
			John Porter Hatch,	USA
			Randolph Barnes Narcy,	USA
			Isaac Ingalls Stevens,	USA
			David Sloane Stanley,	USA

			William Kerley Strong, USA
			George Sykes, USA
			Thomas Williams, USA
			George Wright, USA
09	28	1861	Affair near Vanderburgh's house, Munson's Hill, near Bailey's Cross-Roads, VA, with a Confederate retreat, Col. Edward D. Baker, 71st PA Infantry commanding.
09	29	1861	Affairs at Albany KY, and Travisville, TN, with Col. William A. Hoskins, USA, 12th KY Infantry.
09	29	1861	Skirmish at Hopkinsville, KY, with Brig. Gen. Simon B. Buckner, CSA.
09	29	1861	Skirmish at Berlin, MD.
09	29	1861	Brig. Gen. Daniel Henry Hill, CSA, is ordered to North Carolina.
09	29	1861	Accidental mishap at Munson's Hill, or Camp Advance, VA, with the 69th PA Infantry firing a volley into their sister regiment, the 71st PA, with fatalities.
09	30	1861	**Adley Hogan Gladden,** CSA, is appointed Brig. Gen.
09	30	1861	**Albin Francisco Schoepf,** USA, is appointed Brig. Gen.
09	30	1861	Confederate operations against the Indians from Camp Robledo, the New Mexico Territory, by Capt. R. Hardeman, CSA Scout.
09	30	1861	Ex-Marshal George P. Kane, from Fort Lafayette, MD, writes to President Lincoln, calling the President's attention to his (mis)treatment there.
09	30	1861	The Rev. William Blount Carter lays before Brig. Gen. George Henry Thomas, USA, of a scheme to burn the railway bridges in East Tennessee.
10	1	1861	The following are appointed Union Brigadier Generals:
			John Gray Foster, USA
			James Scott Negley, USA
			Lovell Harrison Rousseau, USA
			Nelancthon Smith Wade, USA
10	1	1861	The Dept. of New England is constituted, under the command of Maj. Gen. Benjamin F. Butler, USA. (This department is created in connection with the organization of the **Gulf Expedition to New Orleans,** LA, and was thereafter discontinued on February 20, 1862).
10	1	1861	The capture of the US transport, the **Fanny,** by the Confederate vessels, **Curlew, Junaluska,** and **Raleigh,** near Chicamacomico, or Loggerhead Inlet, Pamlico Sound, NC.
10	1	1861	The Confederate Council of War, which is attended by among others, President Jefferson Davis, Gen. Joseph Eggleston Johnson, Gen. Pierre Gustave Toutant Beauregard, and Maj. Gen. Gustavus Woodson Smith, CSA, meets at Centreville, VA, to discuss Southern strategy of an offensive war in VA, which is decided against at this time due to lack of proper readiness of men and material.
10	2	1861	The Confederacy sign a peace treaty with the **Great Osage Indian Nation** tribe, the Indian Territory.
10	2	1861	Federal expedition from Bird's Point, near Cario, IL, to Charleston, MO, and attack on the rebel camp there.
10	2	1861	Skirmish at Chapmansville, VA, ends in a Confederate defeat.
10	2	1861	Skirmish at Springfield Station, VA, about 12 miles south of Washington, DC.
10	3	1861	Governor Thomas O. Moore, of Louisiana, bans the shipment of cotton from his state to Europe in order to place pressure on the European nations to officially recognize the Confederacy as a nation.
10	3	1861	Federal expedition to, and the capture of the Pohick Church, 12 miles from Alexandria, VA, by the Federal troops under Col. Christian, 26th NY, sent by Brig. Gen. Henry W. Slocum, USA.
10	3	1861	Skirmish of cavalry at Springfield Station, VA, under Col. Pratt, 31st NY Infantry, sent by Brig. Gen. William Franklin, USA.
10	3	1861	**The Engagement at Greenbrier, WV,** that results in the total rout of the Confederates. The Federal troops capture valuable livestock, Brig. Gen. Joseph J. Reynolds, USA, defeating Brig. Gen. William W. Loring, CSA.
10	4	1861	The Confederacy signs treaties with the following Indian nation tribes:
			a) **Cherokee (Oct 7th)**
			b) **Seneca**
			c) **Shawnee**
10	4	1861	Col. George Wright, 9th US Infantry, assumes the command of the District of Southern California.
10	4	1861	Skirmish at Buffalo Hill, KY.

MONTH	DAY	YEAR	ACT
10	4	1861	Skirmish near Edwards Ferry, MD, with Brig. Gen. Charles P. Stone, USA.
10	4	1861	The **USS South Carolina** captures two blockade runners, the **Ezilda** and **Joseph H. Toone,** off the Southwest Pass of the Mississippi River, near New Orleans, LA.
10	4	1861	Skirmish at Alamoosa, near Fort Craig, the New Mexico Territory.
10	4	1861	Affair at Chicamacomico, NC, with the Confederates unable to retake key bases now under Union control commanded by Maj. Gen. John E. Wool, USA.
10	4	1861	**Professor Thaddeus Lowe** demonstrates a balloon ascent to President Abraham Lincoln, in Washington, DC.
10	5	1861	Federal expedition to Oak Grove and the Temecula Ranch, CA, to determine the reported location of Rebel men.
10	5	1861	Brig. Gen. Joseph King Fenno Mansfield, USA, is assigned to the command at Hatteras Inlet, NC.
10	6	1861	The **Pony Express,** after only 18 months, is discontinued.
10	6	1861	The capture of the Confederate blockade runner, **Alert,** off Charleston, SC.
10	7	1861	The following are appointed Confederate Major Generals:

William Joseph Hardee,	C.S.A.
Theophilus Hunter Holmes,	C.S.A.
Benjamin Huger,	C.S.A.
Thomas Jonathan "Stonewall" Jackson,	C.S.A.
James "Pete" Longstreet,	C.S.A.
Mansfield Lovell,	C.S.A.
John Bankhead Magruder,	C.S.A.

MONTH	DAY	YEAR	ACT
10	7	1861	Maj. Gen. Braxton Bragg's, CSA, command is extended over the coast and state of Alabama.
10	7	1861	Federal reconnaissance from Cairo, IL, to Lucas Bend, MO, by Brig. Gen. Ulysses S. Grant, USA aboard the **USS Lexington** and the **USS Tyler.**
10	7	1861	President Abraham Lincoln sends Secretary of War, Simon Cameron to deliver a letter to Brig. Gen. Samuel R. Curtis, USA, which asks Curtis if he believed Maj. Gen. John C. Fremont, USA, should be relieved of command.
10	8	1861	**Alexander Peter Stewart,** CSA, is appointed Brig. Gen.
10	8	1861	**Lovell Harrison Rousseau, U.S.A.,** appointed Maj. Gen.
10	8	1861	Brig. Gen. William T. Sherman, USA, supersedes Brig. Gen. Robert Anderson, USA, the hero of Fort Sumter, SC, in the command of the Dept. of the Cumberland, Kentucky and Tennessee, with his headquarters at Lousiville, KY. Anderson is relieved due to his failing health, and apparent nervous breakdown, never to command again, eventually retiring from the US Army in 1863.
10	8	1861	Action at Hillsborough, KY.
10	9	1861	Action on Santa Rosa Island, Pensacola Bay FL, with the Confederate assault on the Federal batteries, led by Brig. Gen. Richard Heron Anderson, CSA, but is repulsed by the Federal troops stationed on the island at Fort Pickens.
10	10	1861	Brig. Gen. E. Kirby Smith, CSA, is assigned to the command of the Dept. of Middle and East Florida. (subsequently this order is revoked).
10	10	1861	Brig. Gen. Ormsby McKnight Mitchel, USA, is ordered to organize an expedition into East Tennessee.
10	11	1861	**Edmund Kirby Smith, C.S.A.,** is appointed Maj. Gen.
10	11	1861	**Richard Johnson,** USA, is appointed Brig. Gen.
10	11	1861	**Thomas John Wood,** USA, is appointed Brig. Gen.
10	11	1861	Lieut. Col. Albemarle Cady, 7th US Infantry, is assigned to the command of the District of Oregon.
10	11	1861	**Operations against Indians (Lipans) from Fort Inge, TX,** by Serg. W. Barrett, CSA Cavalry. 10/11-16/1861
10	11	1861	Brig. Gen. William S. Rosecrans, USA, assumes the command of the Dept. of Western Virginia.
10	11	1861	Skirmish at Harper's Ferry, WV.
10	12	1861	**John Porter McCown,** CSA, is appointed Brig. Gen.
10	12	1861	Skirmish near Upton's Hill, KY.
10	12	1861	Naval encounter near New Orleans, LA, between the **USS Richmond, USS Vincennes** and the **CSS Manassas,** with the two Union vessels retreating, and subsequent action at Bayles' Cross Roads, LA.
10	12	1861	The **Union's 1st ironclad,** the **St. Louis,** is launched at Carondelet, MO.

10	12	1861	Skirmishes near Clintonville and on the Pomme de Terro, or Cameron, MO, after Maj. Gen. John C. Fremont, USA, advances from St. Louis, MO, to avoid further criticism for his inactivity while the Confederates operate in the area. 10/12-13/1861.
10	12	1861	Operations about Ironton and Fredericktown, MO, with the advance of Merriwether Jeff Thompson's, Confederate Partisan forces from Stoddard County, MO; Thompson being the ex-mayor of St. Louis, and commanding his own independent command.
10	12	1861	Confederate Commissioners to France and Great Britain, Msrs. John Slidell and James Mason, slip through the Union blockade of Charleston, SC, aboard the **Theodora,** which is bound for Cuba en route for Europe.
10	13	1861	Action at Wet Glaze, or Shanghai, or Dutch or Monday's Hollow, near Henrytown, MO.
10	13	1861	Brig. Gen. Thomas Williams, USA, supersedes Brig. Gen. Joseph K. F. Mansfield, USA, in command at Hatteras Inlet, NC.
10	13	1861	Skirmish at Cotton Hill, WV.
10	14	1861	The Confederate Dept. of Alabama and West Florida is constituted, under the command of Maj. Gen. Braxton Bragg, CSA.
10	14	1861	Col. George Wright, 9th US Infantry, transfers the command of the District of Southern California to Col. James H. Carleton, 1st California Infantry.
10	14	1861	Skirmish at Beckwith's farm, 12 miles from Bird's Point, and the subsequent fight at Underwood's farm, near Bird's Point, MO.
10	14	1861	Affair at Linn Creek, MO, with the 29th IL Infantry.
10	14	1861	The Honorable Simon Cameron, US Secretary of War, authorizes Brig. Gen. Thomas West Sherman, USA, commanding at Port Royal, SC, to organize and arm, if necessary, squads of fugitive, captured slaves.
10	15	1861	Skirmishes near and at Blackwell Station and the destruction of the Big River Bridge, near Potosi, MO, with M. Jeff Thompson's Confederates capturing 33 men from the 38th IL Regiment.
10	15	1861	Operations about Ironton and Fredericktown, MO.
10	15	1861	Skirmish on the Little River Turnpike, VA, with Lieut. Col. Isaac M. Tucker, 2nd NJ Infantry.
10	16	1861	The Federal troops descend upon, and **occupy Lexington, MO.**
10	16	1861	Skirmish near Linn Creek, MO, with Maj. Clark Wright, Fremont Battalion, MO Cavalry.
10	16	1861	Skirmish at Warsaw, MO.
10	16	1861	Skirmish at Bolivar Heights, near Harper's Ferry, WV, with **Lieut. Col. Turner Ashby, CSA, Cavalry.**
10	17	1861	Skirmishes at Fredericktown, MO. 10/17-18/1861.
10	18	1861	**Lloyd Tilghman,** CSA, is appointed Brig. Gen.
10	18	1861	Skirmish near Rockcastle Hills, KY.
10	18	1861	Maj. Gen. Mansfield Lovell, CSA, supersedes Maj. Gen. David Twiggs, CSA, in the command of Dept. Number 1, consisting of Louisiana and Texas.
10	18	1861	Union forces under Col. Joseph Bennett Plummer, 11th Missouri Infantry, advance from Cape Girardeau, MO, toward M. Jeff Thompson's Confederate Partisans which results in the following skirmish at Warrensburg, MO.
10	18	1861	Federal gunboat reconnaissance down the Mississippi River, MO.
10	18	1861	Skirmish at Warrensburg, MO.
10	18	1861	Federal reconnaissance towards the Occoquan River, VA, by Brig. Gen. Israel B. Richardson, USA.
10	19	1861	Action at the Big Hurricane Creek, MO.
10	19	1861	**Operations in the Kanawha and the New River Region, WV,** with Brig. Gen. William S. Rosecrans, USA, and Brig. Gen. John B. Floyd, CSA. 10/19-11/16/1861.
10	19	1861	Skirmishes on the New River, WV. 10/19-21/1861.
10	20	1861	Union forces under Col. William Passmore Carlin, 38th Illinois Infantry, advance from Pilot Knob, MO.
10	20	1861	Brig. Gen. Edwin Vose Sumner, USA, relinquishes the command of the Dept. of the Pacific to Col. George Wright, 9th US Infantry.
10	20	1861	Federal reconnaissance to Hunter's Mill and Thorton Station, VA, near Leesburg, VA, by Brig. Gen. Charles P. Stone, USA.
10	21	1861	The following are appointed Confederate Brigadier Generals: **Philip St. George Cocke CSA**

			Nathan George Evans, CSA
			Robert Emmett Rodes, CSA
			Richard Taylor, CSA
			James Heyward Trapier, CSA
			Louis Trezevant Wigfall, CSA
			Cadmus Marcellus Wilcox, CSA

10   21   1861   **Brig. Gen. John Breckinridge Grayson, CSA,** dies at Tallahassee, FL, from lung disease, three days after his 55th birthday.

10   21   1861   Action at Rockcastle Hills, or Camp Wildcat, KY, with Brig. Gen. Felix Zollicoffer, CSA, attacking Brig. Gen. A. Schoepf, USA.

10   21   1861   The Federal expedition under the command of Brig. Gen. Thomas W. Sherman, USA, sails from Annapolis, MD, for the South Carolina coast.

10   21   1861   Engagement at Fredericktown, MO, with Col. J. B. Plummer, USA.

10   21   1861   Operations on the Potomac, near Leesburg, VA, including:

     a) **Engagement (or Battle of) Ball's Bluff, or of Leesburg, VA,** and the resulting skirmish on the Leesburg road (Oct. 21st). The Union troops are ferried across the Potomac here and downstream at Edwards Ferry, and march up the steep banks; they are pressed back, with many killed as they leap down the steep banks while many others drown as they attempt to recross the Potomac. The Confederates under Brig. Gen. Nathan George "Shanks" Evans, CSA, rout the Federals, under Brig. Gen. Charles Pomeroy Stone, USA. Although taking direct orders from Maj. Gen. George B. McClellan, Gen. Stone's military career is destroyed with the untimely death of **Maj. Gen. Edward Dickinson Baker, USA,** who is also a Senator from Oregon, and a close personal friend of President Lincoln. His death will eventually cause the Congress to create the **"Committee of the Conduct of the War,"** which will politically be used to attack various Union officers. This committee will have the political power to derail or sidetrack any Federal officer's career who was not careful.

     b) Action near Edwards Ferry **(Oct. 22nd).**

10   21   1861   Skirmish at Young's Mill, near Newport News, VA, with Brig. Gen. John B. Magruder, CSA.

10   22   1861   **Joseph Bennett Plummer,** USA, is appointed Brig. Gen.

10   22   1861   Affairs around Budd's Ferry, MD, against Confederate shore batteries located near Shipping Point between the Chopawamsic and Quantico Creeks, MD.

10   22   1861   Skirmish at Buffalo Springs, MO.

10   22   1861   Brig. Gen. James Heyward Trapier, CSA, is assigned to the command of the Confederate Dept. of Middle and East Florida.

10   22   1861   The **Confederate Department (Army) of Northern Virginia** is constituted, with the following command appointments:

     a) Gen. Joseph E. Johnston,   overall command.

     b) Gen. Pierre G. T. Beauregard,   Potomac District.

     c) Maj. Gen. Theophilus Hunter Holmes,   Aquia District.

     d) Maj. Gen. Thomas Jonathan Jackson,   Valley District.

10   22   1861   Brig. Gen. Benjamin Franklin Kelley, USA, is assigned to the command of the Federal Dept. of Harper's Ferry, WV, and Cumberland, MD.

10   22   1861   After his visit to Washington, DC, William Blount Carter enters East Tennessee to organize parties to destroy the railway bridges there.

10   23   1861   **Samuel Gibbs French,** CSA, is appointed Brig. Gen.

10   23   1861   Skirmish near Hodgensville, KY.

10   23   1861   Skirmish at West Liberty, KY, with Brig. Gen. William Nelson, USA.

10   23   1861   Lieut. Col. Albemarle Cady, 7th US Infantry, relieves Col. Benjamin L. Beall, 1st US Cavalry, in the command of the District of Oregon.

10   23   1861   Federal reconnaissance in the Kanawha Valley, WV. 10/23-27/1861.

10   23   1861   Skirmish at Gauley, WV.

10   24   1861   Attack on Camp Joe Underwood, KY, by Col. R. D. Allison, CSA, 14th TN Infantry.

10   24   1861   Maj. Gen. David Hunter, USA, is ordered to supersede Maj. Gen. John Charles Fremont, USA, in the command of the Western Dept., MO, etal.

10   24   1861   President Lincoln attends the funeral for **Maj. Gen. Edward D. Baker,** killed October 21, 1861, at the Battle of Ball's Bluff, or Leesburg, VA.

10   25   1861   Action at Springfield, or Wilson's Creek, MO, consisting of Maj. Gen. John Fremont's, USA, Cavalry

			charge into Springfield, MO, that routs the small Confederate force there.
10	25	1861	Construction continues on the **USS Monitor,** at Greenpoint, NY, with the laying of its keel.
10	26	1861	**William Henry Carroll,** CSA, is appointed Brig. Gen.
10	26	1861	Brig. Gen. Alexander Robert Lawton, CSA, is assigned to the command of the Confederate Dept. of Georgia.
10	26	1861	Federal expedition to Eddyville and skirmish at Saratoga, KY, by Brig. Gen. C. F. Smith, USA, transported aboard the **USS Conestgoga.**
10	26	1861	Maj. Gen. John Charles Fremont, USA, commanding the Western Dept., and Maj. Gen. Sterling Price, Missouri State Guard, commanding the Confederate forces in Missouri, conclude an agreement for the exchange of POW's.
10	26	1861	Col. George Wright, 9th US Infantry, assumes the command of the Dept. of the Pacific.
10	26	1861	Action at Romney, or Mill Creek Mills, WV, where Brig. Gen. Benjamin F. Kelley, USA, forces a Confederate withdrawal.
10	26	1861	Skirmish at the South Branch Bridge, WV.
10	26	1861	Skirmish near Springfield, WV.
10	27	1861	The **CSS Sumter** captures and burns the US schooner, **Trowbridge,** in the Atlantic Ocean.
10	27	1861	Skirmish at Plattsburg, MO.
10	27	1861	Skirmish near Spring Hill, MO, as Maj. Gen. John Fremont, USA, contends he will pursue and defend Springfield, MO, from the advancing Brig. Gen. Sterling Price, CSA, who in actuality, is retreating. Fremont hopes any orders on their way from Lincoln will now not be delivered.
10	27	1861	The **USS Lexington** captures and burns three Confederate ships at Chincoteaque Inlet, VA.
10	28	1861	Gen. Albert Sidney Johnston, CSA, assumes the immediate command of the Confederate Army Corps of Central Kentucky, at Bowling Green, KY, relieving Brig. Gen. Simon Bolivar Buckner, CSA.
10	28	1861	Skirmish at Laurel Bridge, Laurel County, KY.
10	28	1861	Skirmish near Budd's Ferry, MD, with new Confederate shore batteries, and Brig. Gen. Joseph Hooker, USA.
10	28	1861	Federal expedition to Fulton, MO, by **Brig. Gen. Chester Harding, Jr,** USA.
10	29	1861	**Hugh Weedon Mercer,** CSA, is appointed Brig. Gen.
10	29	1861	Skirmishes at and near Woodbury, and Morgantown, KY, with Kentucky Volunteers against Mississippi Cavalry.
10	29	1861	Brig. Gen. Thomas West Sherman's and Flag Officer Samuel Francis DuPont's expedition to capture Port Royal, SC, sails from Hampton Roads, VA, with a total of 77 ships. They run into severe weather at sea, and if successful in their attempt to capture the town, would use it as a refueling depot for the Atlantic blockading fleet.
10	30	1861	**Humphrey Marshall,** CSA, is appointed Brig. Gen.
10	31	1861	Skirmish near Morgantown, KY, with a Confederate attack on a Federal camp repulsed.
10	31	1861	Skirmish at Greenbrier, WV.
11	1	1861	**George Washington Cullum,** USA, is appointed Brig. Gen.
11	1	1861	Maj. Gen. George B. McClellan, US Army, 34 yrs of age, supersedes 75 year old Bvt. Lieut. Gen. Winfield Scott in the **Command of the Armies of the United States.**
11	1	1861	Brig. Gen. Humphrey Marshall, CSA, is ordered to Eastern Kentucky.
11	1	1861	Maj. Gen. John Adam Dix, USA, issues his proclamation of his determination to protect the ballot box in MD, etal.
11	1	1861	Federal expedition from Rolla, MO, against Freeman's forces. 11/1-9/1861.
11	1	1861	Skirmish at Renick, Randolph County, MO.
11	1	1861	A convoy ship sinks off Cape Hatteras, NC, a part of the Port Royal, SC, expedition.
11	1	1861	The beginning of negotiations for the release and exchange of the US officers and men surrendered in Texas.
11	1	1861	Skirmish with Indians on the Peosi River, TX, by Col. H. E. McCulloch, CSA.
11	1	1861	Skirmishes near Gauley Bridge, or Cotton Hill, WV, with Confederate attacks under Brig. Gen. John Buchanan Floyd, CSA, failing to dislodge the Union forces under Brig. Gen. William Starke Rosecrans, USA. 11/1-3/1861.
11	2	1861	**John Cabell Breckenridge,** CSA, is appointed Brig. Gen.
11	2	1861	Gen. John Charles Fremont, USA, is relieved by Maj. Gen. David Hunter, USA, in Missouri, etal.
11	2	1861	Federal operations from Bird's Point, Cape Girardeau, and Ironton, MO, against M. Jeff Thompson's

Partisan Confederate forces. 11/2-12/1861.

11	3	1861	Federal expedition into Lower Maryland, by Brig. Gens. Oliver O. Howard and George Sykes, USA. 11/3-11/1861.
11	4	1861	Maj. Gen. John Adams Dix, USA, directs that Negroes not be allowed to come within certain military lines in Maryland.
11	4	1861	**Operations in the Valley District, VA.** 11/4/1861-2/21/1862
11	4	1861	**Maj. Gen. Thomas Jonathan "Stonewall" Jackson,** CSA, assumes the command of the Shenandoah Valley District, at Winchester, VA.
11	5	1861	The coasts of South Carolina, Georgia, and East Florida are constituted a Confederate Dept., under the command of **Gen. Robert Edward Lee,** CSA.
11	5	1861	The Federal **occupation of Prestonburg, KY,** by Brig. Gen. William Nelson, USA.
11	6	1861	Action at Little Santa Fe, MO.
11	6	1861	Confederate President Jefferson Davis and Vice-Pres. Alexander Stephens are re-elected to office in the elections held in the South, Richmond, VA, for 6 yrs.
11	6	1861	Operations at Townsend's Ferry, New River, WV. 11/6-15/1861.
11	7	1861	Maj. Gen. George B. McClellan, USA, in a letter counsels Brig. Gen. Don Carlos Buell, appointed to command in Kentucky, to respect the constitutional rights of Kentuckians in their slave property.
11	7	1861	**Engagement at Belmont, MO,** and demonstration from Paducah, upon Columbus, KY. Brig. Gen. Ulysses S. Grant's, USA, expedition is driven back to their transports on the Mississippi River by Maj. Gen. Leonidas Polk, CSA, who sent troops across the river.
11	7	1861	**The Bombardment and subsequent capture of Forts Beauregard (at Bay Point) and Walker (at Hilton Head), Port Royal Bay, SC,** by the US Navy led by Flag Officer Samuel F. DuPont, and Brig. Gen. Thomas W. Sherman, USA which are strategically located between Charleston, SC, and Savannah, GA.
11	7	1861	Maj. Gen. David Hunter, USA, the successor of Gen. John C. Fremont, USA, repudiates the Fremont-Price convention in Missouri of October 26, 1861.
11	8	1861	Capt. Charles Wilkes, of the **USS San Jacinto,** stops the British mail ship, **Trent,** off the coast of Cuba, and captures the two Confederate Commissioners to France and England, James Mason and John Slidell.
11	8	1861	Brig. Gen. William Tecumseh Sherman, USA, commanding the Dept. of the Cumberland, expresses his opinion that fugitive slaves must be delivered by upon an application of their masters, in conformity to the laws of the state of Kentucky.
11	8	1861	Engagement at Ivy Mountain and skirmish at Piketon, or Fry Mountain, KY, Brig. Gen. William Nelson, USA, fighting Col. John Williams, CSA. 11/8-9/1861.
11	8	1861	Federal reconnaissance on Hilton Head, SC, toward Beaufort, by the recently landed Union troops, under Brig. Gen. Thomas W. Sherman, USA.
11	8	1861	Gen. Robert E. Lee, CSA, assumes the command of the Dept. of South Carolina, Georgia and East Florida.
11	8	1861	Revolt of the Unionists (mountaineers) East Tennessee, with the destruction of railroad bridges and uprising against the Confederate troops there under by Brig. Gen. Felix Zollicoffer, CSA. 11/8-9/1861.
11	8	1861	The capture and burning of the schooner, **CSS Royal Yacht,** in the Bolivar Channel, off Galveston Harbor, TX, by the frigate, the **USS Santee.**
11	9	1861	**George Bibb Crittenden, C.S.A.,** is appointed Maj. Gen.
11	9	1861	**Jeremiah Tilford Boyle,** USA, is appointed Brig. Gen.
11	9	1861	The Dept. of Kansas is constituted, under the command of Maj. Gen. David Hunter, USA.
11	9	1861	The Dept. of the Ohio is reorganized so as to embrace the states of Kentucky, east of the Cumberland River, Ohio, Indiana, Michigan, and Tennessee, under the command of Brig. Gen. Don Carlos Buell, USA, who supersedes Brig. Gen. William T. Sherman, USA.
11	9	1861	The Dept. of Missouri is constituted, which included Arkansas, Illinois, Kentucky west of the Cumberland River and Missouri, under the command of Maj. Gen. Henry Wager Halleck, USA.
11	9	1861	The Dept. of New Mexico is re-established under the command of Col. Edward Richard S. Canby, USA.
11	9	1861	The Federal **occupation of Beaufort, SC,** by Brig. Gen. Thomas W. Sherman's, USA, recently landed expeditionary forces.
11	9	1861	Federal expedition to Mathias Point, VA , on the York River, by Brig. Gens. Joseph Hooker and Daniel E. Sickles, USA.

11	10	1861	Federal expedition from Hilton Head to Braddock's Point, SC, as Brig. Gen. Thomas W. Sherman, USA, continues to press on. 11/10-11/1861.
11	10	1861	Skirmish near Bristol, TN, with the uprising Unionists.
11	10	1861	Skirmishes at Blake's Farm, Cotton Hill, or Gauley Bridge, WV, with Brig. Gen. Jacob D. Cox, USA. 11/10-11/1861.
11	10	1861	Affair at Guyandotte, WV.
11	11	1861	Maj. Gen. George B. McClellan, USA, escorts Bvt. Lieut. Gen. Winfield Scott, USA, retired, to the railroad depot for his retirement at West Point. McClellan feels confident now with Scott out of the way.
11	11	1861	Action at Little Blue, MO, between Federal **Kansas Jayhawkers,** and Pro-southern men.
11	11	1861	The energetic efforts of Governor Harris and the Richmond, VA, Confederate government to suppress the insurrection in East Tennessee. 11/11-20/1861.
11	11	1861	The failure of the Federal efforts to succor the East Tennessee unionists. 11/11-12/1861.
11	11	1861	Maj. Gen. George B. Crittenden, CSA, is assigned to the command of the District of Cumberland Gap, TN.
11	11	1861	Skirmish near New Market Bridge, which is close to Fortress Monroe, Hampton, VA.
11	12	1861	**Richard Griffith,** CSA, is appointed Brig. Gen.
11	12	1861	The following are appointed Union Brigadier Generals:

Christopher Columbus Augur, USA
Schuyler Hamilton, USA
George Washington Morgan, USA
Jesse Lee Reno, USA
Julius Stahel, USA

11	12	1861	Governor Hicks protests against the release of the obnoxious members of the Maryland Legislature.
11	12	1861	Federal reconnaissance to Pohick Church and the Occoquan Creek, VA, by Brig. Gen. Samuel P. Heintzelman, USA.
11	12	1861	Skirmish on Laurel Creek, Cotton, Hill, WV.
11	13	1861	Federal expedition from Greenville to Doniphan, MO. 11/13-15/1861.
11	13	1861	Federal scout through Texas and Wright Counties, MO. 11/13-18/1861.
11	13	1861	Skirmish near Romney, WV.
11	13	1861	Maj. Gen. George B. McClellan, USA, snubs President Abraham Lincoln by retiring to bed, rudely refusing to meet with Lincoln, as Lincoln patiently waits in his parlor. This will be the last time Lincoln calls on McClellan; from now on, McClellan will be summoned to the White House.
11	14	1861	**William Montgomery Gardner,** CSA, is appointed Brig. Gen.
11	14	1861	**Richard Brooke Garnett,** CSA, is appointed Brig. Gen.
11	14	1861	Affair at the mouth of the Mattawoman Creek, MD, by Brig. Gen. Joseph Hooker, USA.
11	14	1861	The Federal expedition through the Virginia Counties of Accomac and Northampton. 11/14-22/1861.
11	14	1861	Skirmish on the road from Fayetteville to Raleigh, WV.
11	14	1861	Skirmishes at and near McCoy's Mill, WV.
11	15	1861	Brig. Gen. Don Carlos Buell, USA, assumes the command of the Dept. of the Ohio, KY, etal, replacing Brig. Gen. William T. Sherman, USA.
11	15	1861	The Unionists' camp near Chattanooga, TN, is dispersed by the Confederates.
11	15	1861	The **USS San Jacinto** arrives at Fortress Monroe, VA, and transfers Confederate Commissioners, Mason and Slidell, as prisoners of war, to Fort Warren, Boston Harbor, MA, arriving November 24, 1861. This creates an **international incident** with England, which is undesired by President Lincoln.
11	15	1861	The **US Christian Commission** is organized, to help furnish supplies, nurses, and friendship to the Union men, by the **Young Men's Christian Association (YMCA).**
11	16	1861	**Lawrence O'Bryan Branch,** CSA, is appointed Brig. Gen.
11	16	1861	**William Mahone,** CSA, is appointed Brig. Gen.
11	16	1861	Capt. D. N. Ingraham, CSN, is assigned to duty in Charleston Harbor, SC.
11	16	1861	William Blount Carter escapes to the Union lines and reports to Brig. Gen. George Henry Thomas, USA, of the success of his enterprise in East Tennessee, of burning bridges, etc.
11	16	1861	The capture of a Union foraging party at Doolan's Farm, VA, in the vicinity of Taylor's Corner and Falls Church, VA.
11	17	1861	Skirmish at Cypress Bridge, near Rumsey, McClean County, KY.
11	18	1861	Col. James H. Carleton, 1st California Infantry, is relieved from command of the District of Southern CA.

11	18	1861	Confederate soldiers convene at Russellville, KY, and elect to secede from the Union, creating two state governments, similar to Missouri, North Carolina, and later, Virginia (West).
11	18	1861	Skirmish at Palmyra, MO.
11	18	1861	Confederate attack on the steamer, **Platte Valley,** Price's Landing, MO.
11	18	1861	Confederate capture of a wagon train near Warrensburg, MO.
11	18	1861	Pro-unionists meet at Hatteras, denounce session, and elect **Marble Nash Taylor,** as Provisional Governor of North Carolina.
11	18	1861	The capture of Unionists charged with burning bridges at Doe River, East TN.
11	18	1861	Skirmish on the road from Falls Church to Fairfax Court-House, VA, with Lieut. Col. Fitzhugh Lee, 1st VA Cavalry.
11	19	1861	**Operations in the Indian Territory.** 11/19-1/4/1862.
11	19	1861	Engagement at Round Mountain, Indian Territory, with Capt. M. J. Brinson, CSA, 9th Texas Infantry, and Pro-South **Cherokee Indians** engaging **Creek Indians.**
11	19	1861	Maj. Gen. Henry Wager Halleck, USA, assumes the command of the Dept. of Missouri.
11	19	1861	Brig. Gen. George Wright, USA, is formally assigned to the command of the Dept. of the Pacific.
11	19	1861	Gen. Albert Sidney Johnston, CSA, calls upon Tennessee for all the militia and volunteer force than can be armed.
11	19	1861	Skirmish at Wirt Court-House, WV.
11	20	1861	The pursuit and the capture of the Showalter Party at Warner's Ranch, in the San Jose Valley, CA, southeast of Los Angeles, 18 Confederates, including their leader, Mr. Daniel Showalter, are captured on 11/29/1861.
11	20	1861	Maj. Gen. David Hunter, USA, assumes the command of the Dept. of Kansas.
11	20	1861	Skirmish at Brownsville, KY, with Brig. Gen. Thomas C. Hindman, CSA.
11	20	1861	Maj. Gen. Henry Wager Halleck, USA, issues General Orders No. 3, excluding fugitive slaves from the military camps in the Dept. of the Missouri.
11	20	1861	Skirmish at Butler, MO.
11	20	1861	Skirmish at Little Santa Fe, MO.
11	20	1861	Col. William B. Wood, CSA, announces to the Honorable Judah P. Benjamin, Confederate Secretary of War, the suppression of the East Tennessee rebellion.
11	20	1861	Brig. Gen. John Buchanan Floyd, CSA, withdraws his troops from the vicinity of the Gauley River, WV.
11	21	1861	The following are appointed Union Brigadier Generals: **Philip St. George Cooke,** USA **Thomas Jefferson McKean,** USA **John McAllister Schofield,** USA
11	21	1861	10,000 Confederate volunteers are called out in Mississippi for the defense of Columbus, KY, etc, by Gen. Albert Sidney Johnston, CSA.
11	21	1861	The Confederate destruction of the US stores at Warsaw, MO.
11	21	1861	Brig. Gen. Lloyd Tilghman, CSA, is assigned to the command of Forts Henry and Donelson, on the Tennessee and Cumberland Rivers, TN, south of the Kentucky-Tennessee state line.
11	21	1861	**Judah Benjamin replaces Leroy Pope Walker** as the Confederate **Secretary of War;** Maj. Gen. Braxton Bragg's brother, **Thomas Bragg,** ascends to Mr. Benjamin's position of **Attorney General,** Richmond, VA.
11	22	1861	The Confederate Dept. of the Indian Territory is established, under the command of Brig. Gen. Albert Pike, CSA.
11	22	1861	The Bombardment of the Confederate lines, under Maj. Gen. Braxton Bragg, CSA, commanding the Army of Pensacola, about Pensacola, FL, including Forts Barrancas and McRee, by Union forces, including the vessels, **USS Richmond,** and the **USS Niagara.** 1/22-23/1861.
11	23	1861	**John Grubb Parke,** USA, is appointed Brig. Gen.
11	23	1861	**Zealous Bates Tower,** USA, is appointed Brig. Gen.
11	24	1861	The Union forces, with the assistance of the **USS August, Flo, Pocahontas, Savannah,** and **Seneca, occupy Tybee Island,** on the Savannah River near Savannah, GA, and inproximity to Fort Pulaski, near Savannah, GA.
11	24	1861	**Col. Nathan Bedford Forrest's Confederate expedition to Caseyville, Eddyville, etc., KY, the beginning of an illustrious military career.** 11/24-12/5/1861.

11	24	1861	The **USS Jacinto** delivers Confederate Commissioners, Mason and Slidell, to Fort Warren, Boston Harbor, MA.
11	24	1861	Skirmish at Johnstown, MO.
11	24	1861	Skirmish at Lancaster, MO.
11	25	1861	The Honorable Judah P. Benjamin, the new Confederate Secretary of War, from Richmond, VA, orders the captured bridge-burners in East Tennessee to be tried by **drum-head court-martial, and hanged,** if found guilty.
11	25	1861	The Confederate Naval Dept. is in the process of converting the **USS Merrimack,** into the Confederate iron-clad renamed, the **CSS Virginia.**
11	26	1861	Skirmish at Independence, or Little Blue, MO.
11	26	1861	Federal expedition to Dranesville, VA, and skirmish, with Brig. Gen. George A. McCall, USA. 11/26-27/1861
11	26	1861	Skirmish near Vienna, VA, with a Confederate victory.
11	26	1861	The Pro-Union convention held in Wheeling, WV, adopts a resolution to secede from Virginia and form a new state comprised of the western part of Virginia.
11	27	1861	Maj. Gen. George B. McClellan, USA, earnestly urges upon Brig. Gen. Don Carlos Buell, USA, for an advance into East Tennessee.
11	27	1861	Skirmish near Fairfax Court-House, VA.
11	27	1861	The **Ship Island, Mississippi, Expedition** sails from Hampton Roads, VA, with the mission to establish a base of operations against New Orleans, LA and vicinity.
11	28	1861	Brig. Gen. Benjamin Mayberry Prentiss, USA, assumes the command of the District of North Missouri.
11	28	1861	Missouri is admitted as a member of the Confederate States of America. (CSA), Richmond, VA.
11	29	1861	**John Franklin Farnsworth,** USA, is appointed Brig. Gen.
11	29	1861	The capture of the Confederate Showalter Party at Warner's Ranch, southeast of Los Angeles, CA.
11	29	1861	Brig. Gen. John McAllister Schofield, USA, assumes the command of the Missouri Militia.
11	29	1861	Judge Humphreys issues a **writ of habeas corpus** in the cases of certain bridge-burners. The writ, however, is not obeyed by the military, East Tennessee, etal.
11	30	1861	Skirmish at Grand River, or Black Walnut Creek, near Sedalia, MO.
11	30	1861	Skirmish near the mouth of Little Cacapon River, WV, where bushwackers capture some of Brig. Gen. Benjamin F. Kelly's, USA, horses.
12	1	1861	Skirmishes near Camp Goggin, KY. 12/1-2/1861.
12	1	1861	Federal gunboat demonstrations (3) on Fort Holt, KY.
12	1	1861	**Operations about Mills Springs and Somerset, KY,** with Brig. Gen. Albin Schoeph, USA battling Brig. Gen. Felix K. Zollicoffer, CSA. 12/1-13/1861.
12	1	1861	Skirmish at Whippoorwill Creek, KY.
12	1	1861	Skirmish at Shanghai, MO.
12	1	1861	**The hanging of the Pro-Union bridge-burners in East Tennessee.** 11-12/1861.
12	2	1861	Brig. Gen. James William Denver, USA, is assigned to the command of all troops in the state of Kansas.
12	2	1861	Skirmish at Annandale, VA, with Brig. Gen. Louis Blenker, USA.
12	3	1861	Skirmish at Salem, MO, with Col. John B. Wyman, USA, 13th IL.
12	3	1861	Federal scout through Saline County, MO, by Maj. George C. Marshall, 2nd MO Cavalry. 12/3-12/1861.
12	3	1861	Brig. Gen. John Pope, USA, assumes the command of all the forces between the Missouri and Osage Rivers.
12	3	1861	**Ship Island, Mississippi, is occupied** by the Union forces under Maj. Gen. Benjamin F. Butler, USA with the assistance of the steamship, **USS Constitution.**
12	3	1861	Skirmish at Vienna, VA, with the capture of the entire Federal detachment of the 3rd PA Cavalry.
12	4	1861	The Confederate expedition to, and the destruction of, the Bacon Creek Bridge, near Munfordville, KY, by **Col. John Hunt Morgan,** CSA. 12/4-7/1861.
12	4	1861	The Confederate raiding party is repulsed by the Union citizens of Dunksburg, MO.
12	4	1861	Skirmish at Burke's Station, VA, south of Washington, DC.
12	5	1861	Maj. Gen. William Joseph Hardee, CSA, assumes the command of the Confederate Central Army of Kentucky.

12	5	1861	Confederate scout in the vicinity of Russellville, KY, by Capt. I. F. Harrison, CSA, Brig. Gen. Wirt Adams' MS Cavalry. 12/5-8/1861.
12	5	1861	Federal expedition through the Current Hills, MO, by Col. John B. Wyman, USA, 13th IL Infantry. 12/5-9/1861.
12	6	1861	Federal expedition to Port Royal Ferry and Beaufort, SC. 12/6-7/1861.
12	6	1861	The Honorable William G. Brownlow is arrested at Knoxville, TN, on a civil warrant for treason.
12	6	1861	Federal expedition to Gunnell's Farm, near Dranesville, VA, by a foraging raid by Brig. Gen. George Gordon Meade, USA.
12	7	1861	The **USS Santiago de Cuba** stops the English vessel, the **Eugenia Smith,** capturing Confederate agent, **Mr. James W. Zacharie,** off New Orleans, LA, which is similar to the **Trent** incident and the Slidell and Mason captures.
12	8	1861	The **CSS Sumter** captures the whaler vessel, the **Eben Dodge,** in the Atlantic Ocean.
12	8	1861	Skirmish at Fishing Creek, near Somerset, KY.
12	8	1861	Skirmish at Dam No. 5, Chesapeake and Ohio Canal, on the Potomac River, VA.
12	8	1861	Skirmish near Romney, WV.
12	9	1861	The engagement at Chusto-Talasah, or Bird Creek or High Shoal, Indian Territory, later known as Tulsa, OK, between Pro-Confederate Indians, **Cherokee, Chickasaw** and **Choctaw,** and Pro-Union **Creek** Indians.
12	9	1861	Skirmish at Union Mills, MO.
12	9	1861	The US Senate Committee overwhelming votes to establish the **Joint Committee on the Conduct of the War,** due, in part, to the fiasco at Ball's Bluff, VA.
12	10	1861	Kentucky is admitted as the 13th State of the Confederacy.
12	10	1861	The House Judiciary Committee reports back the Baltimore MD Police Commissioners' memorial, and asks to be discharged from its further consideration, MD, etal.
12	11	1861	Skirmish near Bertrand, MO.
12	11	1861	Tragedy strikes Charleston, SC, as an uncontrollable fire sweeps through the city, destroying half of the city, including the business district.
12	11	1861	Skirmish at Dam No. 4, Chesapeake and Ohio Canal, VA.
12	12	1861	The Dept. of Alabama and West Florida, is extended to embrace Pasagoula Bay and that portion of Mississippi east of the Pasagoula River.
12	12	1861	The District of Humboldt is created, to consist of the following Northern California Counties: a) Del Norte d) Mendocino b) Humboldt e) Napa c) Klamath f) Sonoma g) Trinity Col. Francis J. Lippitt, 2nd California Infantry, is assigned to its command.
12	12	1861	Skirmish at Gradyville, KY.
12	12	1861	Skirmish at Charleston, MO.
12	12	1861	Skirmish at Greenbrier River, WV.
12	13	1861	**Edward Johnson,** CSA, is appointed Brig. Gen.
12	13	1861	**Engagement at Camp Alleghany, Buffalo Mountain, WV.** Brig. Gen. Robert Huston Milroy's, USA, troops force the Confederates to retreat to Stauton, VA, while the Union soldiers remove to Cheat Mountain, WV.
12	14	1861	**Maxcy Gregg,** CSA, is appointed Brig. Gen.
12	14	1861	Brig. Gen. Henry Hopkins Sibley, CSA, assumes the command of the Confederate forces on the Upper Rio Grande River and in New Mexico and Arizona.
12	15	1861	**Jefferson Columbus Davis,** USA, is appointed Brig. Gen.
12	15	1861	Operations on the Lower Potomac, MD, by Brig. Gen. Samuel Gibbs French, CSA. 12/15-17/1861.
12	15	1861	The capture of the Confederate sloop, **Victory,** on the Lower Potomac, MD.
12	15	1861	Federal expedition to Meadow Bluff, WV. 12/15-21/1861.
12	15	1861	Affair in Roane County, WV.
12	16	1861	**Henry Constantine Wayne,** CSA, is appointed Brig. Gen.

12	17	1861	Action at Rowlett's Station, or Munfordville, or Woodsonville, Green River, KY, with men from Brig. Gen. Alexander McD. McCook, USA, pitted against Brig. Gen. Thomas C. Hindman, CSA.
12	17	1861	Skirmish on Chisolm's Island, SC, with Brig. Gen. Isaac I. Stevens, USA.
12	17	1861	Skirmish at, followed by the **evacuation of, Rockville, SC, near Hilton Head,** by the Confederate forces.
12	17	1861	The trial, condemnation and **pardon of Harrison Self,** a bridge-burner in East Tennessee. 12/17-27/1861.
12	17	1861	Maj. Gen. Thomas Jonathan "Stonewall" Jackson's, CSA, operations against Dam No. 5, Chesapeake and Ohio Canal, Potomac River, VA. 12/17-21/1861.
12	18	1861	Federal reconnaissance from Somerset to Mill Springs, KY.
12	18	1861	Skirmish at Blackwater Creek, or Milford, or also called Shawnee Mound, MO, with Brig. Gen. John Pope, USA.
12	18	1861	Federal scout from Rolla towards Houston, MO, by Maj. Gen. Henry W. Halleck, USA.
12	18	1861	Federal reconnaissance to Pohick Church, VA, 12 miles south of Alexandria, VA.
12	19	1861	Skirmish at Point of Rocks, MD, along the Potomac River.
12	20	1861	**William High Keim,** USA, is appointed Brig. Gen.
12	20	1861	**John McCauley Palmer,** USA, is appointed Brig. Gen.
12	20	1861	**Two warships of the English Royal Navy convoy troops to Canada** in case a satisfactory solution to the "Trent" affair is not achieved.
12	20	1861	A stone fleet, consisting of old whaling vessels, are sunk by the Federal Navy to prevent (unsuccessfully) Confederate blockade runners from entering Charleston Harbor, SC.
12	20	1861	Engagement at Dranesville, VA, between Brig. Gen. George A. McCall, USA, and Brig. Gen. JEB Stuart, CSA, Cavalry.
12	21	1861	Brig. Gen. Henry Alexander Wise, CSA, is assigned to duty in North Carolina, being removed from Western Virginia for his lackluster performance.
12	21	1861	Skirmish at Hudson, MO.
12	21	1861	The British Minister, **Lord Lyons,** continue to meet with the Secretary of State William H. Seward regarding the **"Trent" Affair.**
12	22	1861	Skirmish at New Market Bridge, near Newport News, VA.
12	23	1861	**Cols. James Abram Garfield and Marshall's, USA, Operations in Eastern Kentucky.** 12/23-1/30/1862.
12	23	1861	Union forces advance from Louisa, KY.
12	23	1861	Skirmish at Dayton, MO.
12	23	1861	Federal Expedition to Lexington, MO, by Brig. Gen. John Pope, USA, and his Cavalry.
12	24	1861	**Raleigh Edward Colston,** CSA, is appointed Brig. Gen.
12	24	1861	Skirmish at Wadesburg, MO.
12	24	1861	Federal scout towards Fairfax Court-House, VA. 12/24-25/1861.
12	25	1861	Skirmish at Grider's Ferry, Cumberland River, KY.
12	25	1861	Skirmish at Fort Frederick, MD.
12	25	1861	Brig. Gen. Ulysses S. Grant, USA, commanding the District of Southeast Missouri, orders all fugitive slaves to be expelled from Fort Holt, KY.
12	25	1861	Brig. Gen. Samuel Ryan Curtis, USA, is assigned to the command of the Southwestern District of Missouri.
12	25	1861	Federal expedition to Danville, MO, by Col. George G. Todd, 10th MO Infantry.
12	25	1861	The Confederate blockade runner schooner, **William H. Northrup,** is captured off Cape Fear, NC, by the **USS Fernandina.**
12	25	1861	Skirmish at Cherry Run, WV.
12	26	1861	**Brig. Gen. Philip St. George Cocke, CSA,** commits suicide at his home, "Belmead," Powhatan County, VA, after having his health deteriorate for 8 months in the field.
12	26	1861	Engagement at Chustenahlah, Indian Territory, Cherokee Nation, between Confederates and some Pro-Union **Creek** Indians led by **Hopoeithleyohola.**
12	26	1861	Martial law is proclaimed in Saint Louis, MO, and in and about all railroads in the State of Missouri, is

			issued by Maj. Gen. Henry Wager Halleck, USA.
12	26	1861	The US Government **orders the release of James Mason and John Slidell** from Fort Warren, Boston Harbor, MA.
12	27	1861	Nolle prosequi entered in Brownlow's case, and he is discharged from civil into military custody, East TN.
12	27	1861	Skirmish near Hallsville, MO, with Brig. Gen. Benjamin M. Prentiss, USA.
12	27	1861	Confederate skirmish with **Creeks** and **Seminoles** in Indian Territory, by **Col. Stand Watie, CSA,** 2nd Cherokee Mounted Rifles, Cherokee Nation.
12	28	1861	Federal expedition to Camp Beauregard and Viola, KY, by Brig. Gen. Lewis Wallace, USA 12/28-31/1861
12	28	1861	Action at Sacramento, KY, with Brig. Gen. Thomas L. Crittenden, USA, fighting Col. Nathan Bedford Forrest's, CSA, Cavalry.
12	28	1861	Action at Mount Zion Church, MO, with Brig. Gen. Benjamin Mayberry Prentiss, USA.
12	28	1861	**Beckley (or Raleigh Court-House), WV, is occupied** by the Union forces.
12	29	1861	Confederate scout after Hopoeithleyohola in the Indian Territory, with skirmishing continuing with the Pro-Union **Creek** Indians, who were leaving the Indian Territory, headed for Kansas, and being pursued by the Pro-southern Indian Nation tribes of **Cherokee, Chickasaw, Choctaw,** and **Seminole.** 12/29-1/4/1862.
12	29	1861	Confederate descent upon Commerce, MO, and the unsuccessful attack on the steamer **City of Alton,** by Brig. Gen. M. Jeff Thompson's Partisan Confederates.
12	29	1861	The Federal **capture of Suttonville (Braxton Court-House),** and skirmishes in the following WV counties: a) Braxton b) Clay c) Webster
12	30	1861	Confederate Commissioners James Mason and John Slidell are released to Lord Lyons, British Minister, **which virtually ends this international incident.**
12	31	1861	Both contending governments prepare to usher in a New Year.

1862.

	Sunday.	Monday.	Tuesday.	Wednesday.	Thursday.	Friday.	Saturday.
Jan	.....	.....	.....	1	2	3	4
	5	6	7	8	9	10	11
	12	13	14	15	16	17	18
	19	20	21	22	23	24	25
	26	27	28	29	30	31	.....
Feb	.....	.....	.....	.....	.....	.....	1
	2	3	4	5	6	7	8
	9	10	11	12	13	14	15
	16	17	18	19	20	21	22
	23	24	25	26	27	28	
March ..	.....	.....	.....	.....	.....	.....	1
	2	3	4	5	6	7	8
	9	10	11	12	13	14	15
	16	17	18	19	20	21	22
	28	24	25	26	27	28	29
	30	31	.....	.....	.....	.....	.....
April	.....	.....	1	2	3	4	5
	6	7	8	9	10	11	12
	13	14	15	16	17	18	19
	20	21	22	23	24	25	26
	27	28	29	30	.....	.....	.....
May	.....	.....	.....	.....	1	2	3
	4	5	6	7	8	9	10
	11	12	13	14	15	16	17
	18	19	20	21	22	23	24
	25	26	27	28	29	30	31
June	1	2	3	4	5	6	7
	8	9	10	11	12	13	14
	15	16	17	18	19	20	21
	22	23	24	25	26	27	28
	29	30	.....	.....	.....	.....	.....
July	.....	.....	1	2	3	4	5
	6	7	8	9	10	11	12
	13	14	15	16	17	18	19
	20	21	22	23	24	25	26
	27	28	29	30	31	.....	.....
August	.....	.....	.....	.....	.....	1	2
	3	4	5	6	7	8	9
	10	11	12	13	14	15	16
	17	18	19	20	21	22	23
	24	25	26	27	28	29	30
	31	.....	.....	.....	.....	.....	.....
Sept	.....	1	2	3	4	5	6
	7	8	9	10	11	12	13
	14	15	16	17	18	19	20
	21	22	23	24	25	26	27
	28	29	30	.....	.....	.....	.....
October	.....	.....	.....	1	2	3	4
	5	6	7	8	9	10	11
	12	13	14	15	16	17	18
	19	20	21	22	23	24	25
	26	27	28	29	30	31	.....
Nov	.....	.....	.....	.....	.....	.....	1
	2	3	4	5	6	7	8
	9	10	11	12	13	14	15
	16	17	18	19	20	21	22
	23	24	25	26	27	28	29
	30	.....	.....	.....	.....	.....	.....
Dec	.....	1	2	3	4	5	6
	7	8	9	10	11	12	13
	14	15	16	17	18	19	20
	21	22	23	24	25	26	27
	28	29	30	31	.....	.....	.....

01	1	1862	**The Federal Bombardment of Forts McRee and Barranacas, Pensacola Harbor, FL,** against Maj. Gen. Braxton Bragg, CSA, commanding the Confederate Army of Pensacola, FL.
01	1	1862	The Federal expedition from Morristown to Dayton and Rose Hill, MO, skirmish en route, and the **destruction of Dayton,** MO, by Lieut. Col. D. R. Anthony, 1st KS Cavalry. 1/1-3/1862.
01	1	1862	Engagement at Port Royal Ferry, Coosaw River, SC, with the Confederates removing their batteries.
01	2	1862	The Honorable William G. Brownlow states his case to President Jefferson Davis, and asks leave to withdraw from the Confederacy, East Tennessee.
01	3	1862	Skirmish at Hunnewell, MO.
01	3	1862	Federal reconnaissance from Camp Hamilton to **Big Bethel, VA,** and the **occupation** of the town by the Federal troops.
01	3	1862	Skirmishes at Bath, (Berkeley Springs) WV, with Maj. Gen. "Stonewall" Jackson, CSA, arriving from Winchester, VA, in an attempt to destroy dams along the Chesapeake and Ohio Canal, as well as the **Baltimore and Ohio Railroad,** on his way to Romney, WV. (referred to as the **Romney Campaign**). 1/3-4/1862.
01	3	1862	The descent upon and skirmish at Huntersville, WV, with Brig. Gen. Edward Johnson, CSA.
01	4	1862	The **occupation of Bath, WV,** by Maj. Gen. Thomas J. Jackson, CSA.
01	4	1862	Skirmishes at Slane's Cross-Roads, Great Cacapon Bridge, Sir John's Run, and Alpine Depot, WV, with Maj. Gen. Thomas J. Jackson, CSA.
01	5	1862	The bombardment of Hancock, MD, by Maj. Gen. Thomas J. Jackson's Confederate artillery batteries firing across the Potomac River. 1/5-6/1862.
01	5	1862	Operations in Johnson and La Fayette Counties, MO, and skirmish at Columbus, MO, with Lieut. Col. D. R. Anthony, 1st KS Cav. 1/5-12/1862.
01	6	1862	**Henry Heth,** CSA, is appointed Brig. Gen.
01	6	1862	Brig. Gen. Schuyler Hamilton, USA, assumes the command of the Saint Louis District, MO.
01	7	1862	**Johnson Kelly Duncan**, CSA, is appointed Brig. Gen.
01	7	1862	Skirmish at Jennie's Creek or Paintsville, KY.
01	7	1862	The Dept. of North Carolina is constituted, to be commanded by Brig. Gen. Ambrose Everett Burnside, USA.
01	7	1862	Skirmish at Hanging Rock Pass (Blue's Gap), near Romney WV, with a Confederate defeat by Col. Dunning's Union troops, as Maj. Gen. Thomas J. Jackson, CSA, continues to press his men forward in the blinding snow and freezing weather, withdrawing from the Hancock, MD, area to Romney, WV.
01	8	1862	Skirmish at Fishing Creek, near Somerset, KY.
01	8	1862	Skirmish at Charleston, MO, or Silver Creek, or Sugar Creek, and Roan's Tan-yard, with the rout of the Confederate camp there.
01	8	1862	Action at Roan's Tan-yard, Silver Creek, MO.
01	8	1862	Skirmish on the Dry Fork of the Cheat River, WV.
01	9	1862	**John George Walker,** CSA, is appointed Brig. Gen.
01	9	1862	Col. Francis J. Lippitt, 2nd California Infantry, assumes command of the Humboldt Military District, CA.
01	9	1862	Skirmish at Columbus, MO.
01	9	1862	Skirmish near Pohick Run, VA.
01	10	1862	Federal expedition into Kentucky from Cairo, IL, led by Brig. Gen. Ulysses S. Grant, USA, and Brig. Gen. John McClernand, USA. 1/10-21/1862.
01	10	1862	Engagement at Middle Creek, near Prestonburg, KY, with Col. James Abram Garfield, USA, receiving the promotion to Brig. Gen. the following day due to his perceived victory over Brig. Gen. Humphrey Marshall, CSA.
01	10	1862	The Confederate Trans-Mississippi District of Dept. No. 2, is organized, under the command of Maj. Gen. Earl Van Dorn, CSA.
01	10	1862	**Romney, WV, is evacuated** by the Union force, and subsequently **occupied** by Maj. Gen. Stonewall Jackson, CSA.
01	11	1862	**James Abram Garfield,** USA, is appointed Brig. Gen.
01	11	1862	The Dept. of Key West, FL, is constituted, under the command of Brig. Gen. John Milton Brannan, USA.
01	11	1862	**Writ of habeas corpus** is issued in the case of Daniel Smith and six other bridge-burners in East TN.
01	11	1862	**The Burnside Expedition,** with about 100 ships, sails from Fort Monroe, VA, the VA Peninsula, for the North Carolina Coast, including Roanoke Island, NC.

01	11	1862	Due to rumors of corruption in the War Dept., **Mr. Simon Cameron resigns as the Secretary of War,** Washington, DC.
01	12	1862	Maj. Gen. Sterling Price, Missouri State Guard, writes Maj. Gen. Henry Wager Halleck, USA, commanding the Dept. of the Missouri, to protest against the capital punishment of his men for burning bridges.
01	12	1862	Federal expedition to Logan Court-House and the Guyandotte Valley, WV, as reported by Col. Edward Siber, 37th IL. 1/12-23/1862.
01	13	1862	The Burnside Expedition arrives off Hatteras Inlet, NC, and begins crossing into Pamlico Sound.
01	13	1862	Brig. Gen. Ambrose Everett Burnside, USA, assumes the command of the Dept. of North Carolina.
01	13	1862	President Lincoln appoints **Edwin Stanton** as the new Federal Secretary of War, Washington, DC.
01	14	1862	**John Clifford Pemberton, C.S.A.,** is appointed Maj. Gen.
01	14	1862	**John Ring Jackson,** CSA, is appointed Brig. Gen.
01	14	1862	**George Edward Pickett,** CSA, is appointed Brig. Gen.
01	14	1862	The US Gunboat reconnaissance to Columbus, KY, bombarding Confederate positions along the way.
01	15	1862	Federal expeditions to Benton, Bloomfield, and Dallas, MO. 1/15-17/1862.
01	15	1862	Federal reconnaissance from Paducah, KY, to Fort Henry, TN, a combined joint effort of Brig. Gen. Ulysses S. Grant, USA, along with Brig. Gen. John McClernand, USA, and Federal gunboats, against Brig. Gen. Lloyd Tilghman, CSA. 1/15-25/1862.
01	16	1862	The Union Naval descent upon Cedar Keys, FL, with the destruction of seven small Confederate blockade runners, by men from the **USS Hatteras.**
01	17	1862	**Federal Gunboat demonstrations on Fort Henry, on the Tennessee River, TN,** led by Brig. Gen. Charles Ferguson Smith, USA, in conjunction with the 1/15/1862 advance under Brig. Gen. John McClernand, USA, as heavy ice blocked the Mississippi River some twenty miles below St. Louis, MO. 1/17-22/1862.
01	18	1862	The Confederate Territory of Arizona is formed, comprised of the southern portion of the Federal Territory of New Mexico.
01	18	1862	Former President of the United States of America, John Tyler, is buried today along the James River, in the **Hollywood Cemetery, Richmond, VA.** He will be joined here the next 4 years by numerous Confederate generals as well as many other brave men.
01	19	1862	**The Engagement at Logan's Cross-Roads, or Beech Grove, (Battle) on Fishing Creek, near Mill Springs, KY,** sees Brig. Gen. George H. Thomas, USA, whipping Brig. Gens. Felix Zollicoffer and George B. Crittenden, CSA, forcing a CSA retreat across the Cumberland River, the Confederate defensive line in Kentucky suffers irreparable damage.
01	19	1862	**Brig. Gen. Felix Kirk Zollicoffer, CSA,** is mortally wounded, dying instantly from a Federal Regiment Volley that he was not aware of, at the engagement near Mill Springs, KY.
01	20	1862	Contest over the British schooner **Andracita,** formerly the **J.W. Wilder,** off the coast of Alabama, with the Federals capturing this blockade runner.
01	20	1862	Operations in and about Atchison, KS, with Capt. Irving W. Fuller, 1st MO Cavalry. 1/20-24/1862.
01	20	1862	A second stone fleet is sunk at the entrance to Charleston Harbor, SC, by the Federals in an attempt to prevent Confederate blockade runners for using the harbor.
01	21	1862	Brig. Gen. John Alexander McClernand, USA, returns to his base of operations at Columbus, KY.
01	22	1862	Skirmish at Knobnoster, MO.
01	22	1862	Federal **occupation of Lebanon, MO.**
01	22	1862	Brig. Gen. Henry Alexander Wise, CSA, is assigned to the Confederate command at Roanoke Island, NC.
01	22	1862	Federal expedition to Edisto Island, SC, by the Port Royal Federal force under Brig Gen. Ambrose Everett Burnside, USA. 1/22-25/1862.
01	22	1862	Maj. Gen. Thomas J. Jackson, CSA, returns to Winchester, VA, from his stay in Romney, WV.
01	23	1862	The blockade runner, **Calhoun,** is captured by Federal vessels, near New Orleans, LA.
01	23	1862	A third stone fleet is sunk at the entrance to Charleston Harbor, SC, by the Federals in an attempt prevent Confederate blockade runners for using the harbor.
01	24	1862	**Richard Stoddert Ewell,** C.S.A., is appointed Maj. Gen.
01	24	1862	**Bushrod Rust Johnson,** CSA, is appointed Brig. Gen.
01	24	1862	**James McQueen McIntosh,** CSA, is appointed Brig. Gen.

01	24	1862	**Lewis Golding Arnold,** USA, is appointed Brig. Gen.
01	24	1862	Federal expedition to the Little Sandy and Piketon, KY. 1/24-30/1862
01	25	1862	The Federal expedition at Hatteras Inlet continues to struggle to cross the sand bar at Pamlico Sound, NC.
01	26	1862	Federal reconnaissance to Wilmington Narrows, or Freeborn's Cut, GA, with naval engagement. 1/26-28/1862.
01	26	1862	Gen. Pierre Gustave Toutant Beauregard, CSA, is ordered from the Potomac District, VA, to Columbus, KY, to assist Gen. Albert Sidney Johnston, CSA.
01	27	1862	Brig. Gen. Jones Mitchell Withers, CSA, is assigned to the command of the Army of Mobile, AL.
01	27	1862	Brig. Gen. Samuel Jones, CSA, is assigned to the command of the Army of Pensacola, FL.
01	27	1862	Frustrated with Maj. Gen. George B. McClellan's continued delay, President Lincoln issues **General War Order Number 1,** ordering a general movement of the US land and naval forces against the Rebels.
01	28	1862	Operations near Greensburg and Lebanon, KY, by Col. John Hunt Morgan, CSA, against Lieut. Col. T. C. H. Smith, USA, 1st OH Cavalry. 1/28-2/2/1862.
01	29	1862	**Frederick Steele,** USA, is appointed Brig. Gen.
01	29	1862	Federal expedition to Blue Springs, MO, by Capt. William S. Oliver, 7th MO Infantry, in search of the notorious guerrilla, **William Clarke Quantrill.** 1/29-2/3/1862.
01	29	1862	Maj. Gen. Earl Van Dorn, CSA, assumes the command of the Confederate Trans-Mississippi District, MO.
01	29	1862	Affair at Lee's House, near the Occoquan Bridge, on the Occoquan River, VA, south of Washington, DC, as a Federal excursion breaks up a Confederate dance.
01	30	1862	The Federal's first ironclad, the **USS Monitor,** is launched at Greenpoint, Long Island, NY, with its designer, Swedish born John Ericsson, on hand.
01	30	1862	Confederate Commissioners, James Mason and John Slidell, finally arrive at Southampton, England, after being captured and released by the Federal authorities.
01	31	1862	President Abraham Lincoln issues **Special War Order Number 1,** which is specifically directed at Maj. Gen. George B. McLellan, USA, and orders a Federal advance on Manassas before February 22, 1862.
02	1	1862	**Ethan Allen Hitchcock, U.S.A.,** is appointed Maj. Gen.
02	1	1862	Skirmish at Bowling Green, KY.
02	1	1862	The Confederate forces enter the New Mexico Territory.
02	2	1862	Skirmish in Morgan County, TN, with Lieut. Col. J. W. White, CSA, 1st TN Cavalry.
02	3	1862	The following are appointed Union Brigadier Generals: **John Wynn Davidson,** USA **William Scott Ketcham,** USA **Thomas Francis Meagher,** USA
02	3	1862	The call goes out for 71,000 volunteers from the State of Missouri for Confederate service.
02	3	1862	Federal reconnaissance to Occoquan Village, VA, by Col. Stephen G. Champlin, 3rd MI Infantry.
02	4	1862	Federal gunboat reconnaissance to Fort Henry, TN, on the Tennessee River, while transport ships leave Cairo, IL, for Paducah, KY, under Brig. Gen. Ulysses S. Grant, USA, who is aboard the **USS Cincinnati.**
02	5	1862	Col. James H. Carleton, 1st California Infantry, resumes the command of the District of Southern CA.
02	5	1862	Brig. Gen. Charles Ferguson Smith, USA, **captures Fort Heiman,** on the bluffs above Fort Henry, TN, from Brig. Gen. Lloyd Tilghman, CSA.
02	6	1862	Federal naval expedition to Florence, AL, by the gunboats, **USS Conestoga, USS Lexington,** and the **USS Tyler,** led by Lieut. Commander S.L. Phelps, USN. 2/6-10/1862.
02	6	1862	Reconnaissance to Wright River, SC.
02	6	1862	**The Capture of Fort Henry, TN,** by the Union naval forces under Flag Officer Andrew Foote. Brig. Gen. Lloyd Tilghman, CSA surrenders the fort of about 90 men, sending the majority of his forces to Fort Donelson, TN, ten miles away on the Cumberland River, prior to surrendering, with the following Federal gunboats participating in the attack: a) **USS Carondelet** b) **USS Cincinnati** c) **USS Conestoga** d) **USS Essex**

e) **USS Lexington**
f) **USS Saint Louis**
g) **USS Tyler.**

02	7	1862	Brig. Gen. Bushrod Rust Johnson, CSA, assumes the command at Fort Donelson, TN.
02	7	1862	Federal expedition to Flint Hill and Hunter's Mill, VA, near Fairfax Court-House, by Maj. Joseph L. Moss, 5th PA Cavalry.
02	7	1862	In honor of Flag Officer Foote, Brig. Gen. John A. McClernand, USA, **renames Fort Henry to Fort Foote, TN.**
02	7	1862	To avoid capture by the **USS Conestoga,** the Confederates burn the vessels, **Appleton Belle, Lynn Boyd,** and the **Samuel Orr,** on the Tennessee River.
02	7	1862	Union forces **reoccupy Romney, WV,** as Maj. Gen. Thomas J. Jackson, CSA, withdraws to Winchester, VA.
02	8	1862	Martial law is declared throughout the State of Kansas.
02	8	1862	Affair at Bolivar, MO.
02	8	1862	The Confederate steamers, **Sallie Wood** and **Muscle,** are captured at Chickasaw, AL, by the **USS Conestoga.**
02	8	1862	**The Battle of Roanoke Island, NC,** Albemarle Sound, with Col. Shaw, CSA, filling in for a sick Brig. Gen. Henry Alexander Wise, CSA, surrenders their position to the Union forces under Brig. Gen. Ambrose E. Burnside, USA, and with the participation of the following Union gunboats: **Brinker, Ceres, Chasseur, Commodore, Barney, Commodore Perry, Delaware, Granite, Hetzel, Hunchback, Hussar, Lockwood, Louisiana, Morse, Pickett, Pioneer, Putnam, J. N. Seymour, Shawseen, Southfield, Stars and Stripes, Underwriter, Valley City, Vidette,** and the **Whitehead.**
02	8	1862	Union gunboats move from Roanoke Island, NC, up the Pasquotank River toward Elizabeth City, NC.
02	8	1862	Skirmish at Linn Creek, VA.
02	8	1862	Skirmish at the mouth of the Blue Stone, Mercer County, WV, by Lieut. Col. William E. Peters, CSA, 45th VA Infantry.
02	9	1862	Skirmish at Marshfield, MO, with Brig. Gen. Samuel Curtis, USA.
02	9	1862	Brig. Gen. Gideon Johnson Pillow, CSA, assumes the command at Fort Donelson, TN.
02	10	1862	**James Patton Anderson, CSA,** is promoted to Brig. Gen.
02	10	1862	Action at Elizabeth City, or Cobb's Point, NC, between Union gunboats and Confederate forces with the loss of all remaining Confederate ships, including the **CSS Ellis, Fanny, Forrest, Seabird,** and the **Black Warrior.** The following Union gunboats participated: **Brinker, Ceres, Commodore Perry, Delaware, Hetzel, Louisiana, Morse, Putnam, J. N. Seymour, Shawseen, Underwriter, Valley City,** and the **Whitehead.**
02	10	1862	Skirmish on Barnwell's Island, SC.
02	11	1862	**Bowling Green, KY, is evacuated** by the Confederates, as Brig. Gen. John McClernand, USA, under Brig. Gen. Ulysses S. Grant, USA, move from Fort Henry (Foote), TN, while Union gunboats move toward Fort Donelson, TN.
02	11	1862	Operations at Arkansas Pass, TX, by Maj. Daniel D. Shea, CSA. 2/11-13/1862.
02	12	1862	**Howell Cobb,** CSA, is appointed Brig. Gen.
02	12	1862	**George Wythe Randolph,** CSA, is appointed Brig. Gen.
02	12	1862	**Henry Morris Naglee,** USA, is appointed Brig. Gen.
02	12	1862	Skirmish at Springfield, MO, with Brig. Gen. Samuel Curtis, USA.
02	12	1862	Brig. Gen. Ambrose E. Burnside's Federal forces **occupy Edenton, NC,** as the Confederates **evacuate.**
02	12	1862	**The Siege and Capture of Fort Donelson, TN,** with Brig. Gen. Ulysses S. Grant, USA, surrounding the fort, as well as Dover, TN, while Federal gunboats prepare to attack from the Cumberland River. 2/12-16/1862.
02	12	1862	Skirmish at Moorefield, WV.
02	13	1862	**James Ronald Chalmers,** CSA, is appointed Brig. Gen.
02	13	1862	**Joseph Brevard Kershaw,** CSA, is appointed Brig. Gen.
02	13	1862	Skirmish at Fort Heiman, KY, due to the Fort Donelson, TN, siege, with Lieut. Col. J. H. Miller, CSA, 1st Battalion Mississippi Cavalry, defending.
02	13	1862	Federal **occupation of Springfield, MO.**
02	13	1862	Brig. Gen. John Buchanan Floyd, CSA, assumes the command at Fort Donelson, TN, while Federal

MONTH	DAY	YEAR	ACT
			troops under Brig. Gens. John Alexander McClernand, and Charles Ferguson Smith begin their attack, along with the **USS Carondelet.**
02	13	1862	Skirmish at Blooming Gap, VA.
02	14	1862	**Joseph Lewis Hogg,** CSA, is appointed Brig. Gen.
02	14	1862	Brig. Gen. William Tecumseh Sherman, USA, is assigned to the command of the District of Cairo, IL.
02	14	1862	**Bowling Green, KY,** is **evacuated** by the Confederates and **occupied by** the Union forces under Brig. Gen. Ormsby M. Mitchel, USA. 2/14-15/1862.
02	14	1862	Skirmish at Flat Lick Ford, KY.
02	14	1862	Skirmish at Crane Creek, MO, with Brig. Gen. Samuel Curtis,, USA.
02	14	1862	Skirmish near Cumberland Gap, TN, with the Confederate post defended by Col. James E. Rains, CSA, against Lieut. Col. Munday, USA, 1st Kentucky Cavalry.
02	14	1862	The Federal ironclads, **St. Louis** and **Louisville,** are severely damaged during the siege of Fort Donelson, TN.
02	14	1862	Brig. Gen. Ulysses Simpson Grant, USA, is assigned to the command of the District of West Tennessee.
02	14	1862	Affair at Bloomery Gap, WV.
02	15	1862	**William Wing Loring, C.S.A.,** is appointed Maj. Gen.
02	15	1862	Action at Venus Point, GA.
02	15	1862	Brig. Gen. John McAllister Schofield, USA, assumes the command of the District of Saint Louis, MO.
02	15	1862	Skirmish near Flat Creek, MO.
02	15	1862	Federal expedition from Cairo, IL, to Eastport, MS, by the US gunboats, Lieut. William Gwin USA, aboard the **USS Tyler,** commanding. 02/15-22/1862.
02	15	1862	Brig. Gen. John Buchanan Floyd, CSA, passes the Confederate command of Fort Donelson, TN, to Brig. Gen. Gideon Johnson Pillow, CSA, who in turn, passes the command to Brig. Gen. Simon Bolivar Buckner, CSA, which allows the former two to escape through the Union lines with a portion of their commands towards Nashville. Lieut. Col. Nathan Bedford Forrest, CSA, leads his cavalry command to safety prior to Buckner's surrender of the Fort, opting not to surrender.
02	16	1862	Action at Potts' Hill, Sugar Creek, AR.
02	16	1862	Brig. Gen. Simon Bolivar Bucker, CSA, **surrenders Fort Donelson, TN,** to Brig. Gen. Ulysses Simpson Grant, USA, under Grant's **"unconditional terms of surrender."** The Cumberland and Tennessee Rivers are now under Federal control.
02	17	1862	**Ulysses Simpson Grant, U.S.A.,** is appointed Maj. Gen.
02	17	1862	**David Bell Birney,** USA, is appointed Brig. Gen.
02	17	1862	Action at Sugar Creek, or Pea Ridge, AR, with Brig. Gen. Samuel R. Curtis, USA.
02	18	1862	Action at Bentonville, AR, with Brig. Gen. Samuel R. Curtis, USA.
02	18	1862	Skirmish at Independence, MO.
02	18	1862	Federal expedition to Mount Vernon, MO, by Capt. Mudgett, 3rd IA Cavalry. 2/18-19/1862.
02	18	1862	Federal expedition to Winton, NC and skirmish on February 19th. 2/18-20/1862.
02	19	1862	Skirmish at West Plains, MO.
02	19	1862	Federal expedition into Currituck Sound, NC. 2/19-20/1862.
02	19	1862	**Clarksville, TN, and Fort Defiance are occupied** by the Union forces under Brig. Gen. Charles Ferguson Smith, USA.
02	20	1862	Gov. Isham Harris of Tennessee moves the state capital from Nashville to Memphis, away from the Union advance, while Gen. Albert S. Johnston, CSA, moves his men toward Murfreesboro, TN.
02	20	1862	President and Mrs. Abraham Lincoln mourn the loss of their 12 year old son, **William Wallace "Willie" Lincoln,** to one of the scourges of their time, typhoid fever. Mrs. Lincoln will experience many more painful episodes in her life, eventually causing her mental imbalance that will be with her for the rest of her life.
02	21	1862	The Engagement at Valverde, the New Mexico Territory, near Fort Craig, with Brig. Gen. Henry Hopkins Sibley, CSA, routing Col. Edward Richard Sprigg Canby, USA.
02	21	1862	Convicted slave trader, **Nathaniel Gordon, is hung** in New York City, New York.
02	22	1862	Brig. Gen. Lewis Golding Arnold, USA, supersedes Col. Harvey Brown, US Artillery, in the command of the Dept. of Florida.
02	22	1862	Skirmish at Independence, MO.
02	22	1862	Engagement in Arkansas Bay, TX, with Capt. Benjamin F. Neal, CSA.
02	22	1862	Federal expedition to Vienna and Flint Hill, VA, by Col. Max Friedman, 5th PA Cavalry.

02	22	1862	President Jefferson Davis is inaugurated in Richmond, VA.

02   22   1862   President Jefferson Davis is inaugurated in Richmond, VA.

02   23   1862   **Fayetteville, AR,** is occupied by the Union forces, under Brig. Gen. Samuel R. Curtis, USA, and Brig. Gen. A. Asboth, USA.

02   23   1862   The Dept. of the Gulf is constituted, under the command of Maj. Gen. Benjamin Franklin Butler, USA, FL, AL, etal.

02   23   1862   Brig. Gen. John Pope, USA, assumes the command of the Army of Mississippi, assembling at Commerce, MO.

02   23   1862   Federal reconnaissance from Greenville, MO, and skirmish. 2/23-25/1862.

02   23   1862   Federal reconnaissance to Pea Ridge Prairie, MO, and skirmish. 2/23-24/1862.

02   23   1862   Federal reconnaissance on the Bull River and Schooner Channel, SC.

02   23   1862   Gen. Albert Sidney Johnston, CSA, assumes the immediate command of the Central Army, TN, etal.

02   23   1862   **Nashville, TN, is evacuated** by the Confederates under Brig. Gen. Nathan Bedford Forrest, CSA, and **occupied** by the Federal forces under Brig. Gen. Don Carlos Buell, USA. 2/23-25/1862.

02   24   1862   Skirmish at Mingo Creek, near Saint Francisville, MO.

02   24   1862   Skirmish at New Madrid, MO.

02   24   1862   Affair at Lewis' Chapel, near Pohick Church, VA, 12 miles south of Alexandria, VA, with Brig. Gen. Samuel P. Heinztelman, USA.

02   24   1862   Skirmish at Mason's Neck, Occoquan, VA.

02   24   1862   Federal **occupation of Harper's Ferry, WV,** by Maj. Gen. Nathaniel Prentiss Banks, USA.

02   25   1862   Skirmish at Keetsville, Barry County, MO, with Brig. Gen. Samuel R. Curtis, USA, and the Texas Rangers.

02   25   1862   Maj. Gen. Edmund Kirby Smith, CSA, is assigned to the command in East Tennessee.

02   25   1862   **Operations in Loudoun County, VA.** 2/25-5/6/1862.

02   26   1862   **Ambrose Powell Hill,**   CSA, is appointed Brig. Gen.

02   26   1862   **James Johnston Pettigrew,** CSA, is appointed Brig. Gen.

02   26   1862   Skirmish at Keytesville, MO.

02   26   1862   Maj. Gen. John Porter McCown, CSA, assumes the command at Madrid Bend, MO.

02   26   1862   Confederate scout to Nashville, TN, by Col. John Hunt Morgan, CSA.

02   27   1862   The following are appointed Confederate Brigadier Generals:
Danville Leadbetter,   CSA.
William Whann Mackall,   CSA.
Carter Littlepage Stevenson, CSA.

02   27   1862   President Jefferson Davis is given the authority by the Confederate Congress to suspend **habeas corpus,** similar to actions taken by President Abraham Lincoln.

02   28   1862   Affair at Osage Springs, near Fayetteville, AR.

02   28   1862   Brig. Gen. Samuel Jones, CSA, supersedes Maj. Gen. Braxton Bragg, CSA, in the command of the Dept. of Alabama and West Florida.

02   28   1862   The Florida Federal expedition sails from Warsaw Sound, GA.

02   28   1862   **Operations at New Madris, MO, and Island No. 10,** and the descent upon Union City, TN. 2/28-4/8/1862.

02   28   1862   Union forces, under Brig. Gen. John Pope, USA, advance from Commerce upon New Madrid, and Island No. 10, MO.

02   28   1862   **Charleston, VA, is occupied** by the Federal forces.

03   1   1862   **Robert Ransom, Jr.,**   CSA, is appointed Brig. Gen.

03   1   1862   **Charles Sidney Winder,**   CSA, is appointed Brig. Gen.

03   1   1862   **David Hunter,**   U.S.A., is appointed Maj. Gen.

03   1   1862   **Irvin McDowell,**   U.S.A., is appointed Maj. Gen.

03   1   1862   **John McArthur,**   USA, is appointed Brig. Gen.

03   1   1862   Skirmish near Sikeston, MO.

03   1   1862   Engagement at Pittsburg Landing, TN, between Brig. Gen. George W. Cullum, USA, and Union gunboats, **USS Lexington** and **USS Tyler,** and Confederate batteries.

03   2   1862   **Brig. Gen. Frederick West Lander, USA,** dies at Camp Chase, Paw Paw, WV, from camp fever (dysentery) contracted the previous weeks while moving his command in the Shenandoah Valley, VA.

03	2	1862	**Columbus, KY, is evacuated** by Maj. Gen. Leonidas Polk, CSA, and **occupied** by Brig. Gen. George W. Cullum, USA. 3/2-3/1862.
03	2	1862	Skirmish near New Madrid, MO.
03	2	1862	Albuquerque, New Mexico Territory, is abandoned by the Union forces under Capt. Herbert M. Enos, USA.
03	2	1862	Naval engagement at Pittsburg Landing, TN, with the US gunboats, **Lexington,** and **Tyler.**
03	3	1862	**Daniel Marsh Frost,** CSA, is appointed Brig. Gen.
03	3	1862	**John Bell Hood,** CSA, is appointed Brig. Gen.
03	3	1862	Federal reconnaissance to Berryville, AR. 3/3-7/1862.
03	3	1862	**Amelia Island, FL, is evacuated** by the Confederate forces.
03	3	1862	**The siege and capture of New Madrid, MO.** 3/3-14/1862.
03	3	1862	The Confederate **capture of Cubero,** the New Mexico Territory.
03	3	1862	Gen. Robert Edward Lee, CSA, is called to Richmond, VA, by President Jefferson Davis, to act as military advisor.
03	3	1862	Skirmish at, and **occupation of, Martinsburg, WV,** by the Federals troops.
03	4	1862	The following are appointed Confederate Brigadier Generals:

			Hamilton Prioleau Bee, CSA
			Thomas James Churchill, CSA
			Patrick Ronayne Cleburne, CSA
			Winfield Scott Featherston, CSA
			Samuel Bell Maxey, CSA
			Albert Rust, CSA
			William Booth Taliaferro, CSA

03	4	1862	**Andrew Johnson,** USA, is appointed Brig. Gen.
03	4	1862	Maj. Gen. Braxton Bragg, CSA, announces his resumption of the command of the Dept. of Alabama and West Florida.
03	4	1862	**Amelia Island, FL, is occupied** by the Union forces.
03	4	1862	**Santa Fe, New Mexico Territory, is abandoned** by the Union forces, under Capt. Herbert M. Enos, USA, and subsequently **occupied** by Brig. Gen. Henry Hopkins Sibley, CSA.
03	4	1862	Federal scout through Laclede, Wright, and Douglas Counties, MO, including skirmishes at Fox Creek **(March 7th)** and Mountain Grove **(March 9th),** by Col. George E. Waring, Jr, 4th MO Cavalry. 3/4-11/1862.
03	4	1862	Maj. Gen. John Clifford Pemberton, CSA, assumes the command of Dept. of South Carolina, Georgia, and East Florida, replacing Gen. Robert E. Lee, CSA, who was ordered to Richmond, VA, the day before.
03	5	1862	**James Morrison Hawes,** CSA, is appointed Brig. Gen.
03	5	1862	**James Gallant Spears,** USA, is appointed Brig. Gen.
03	5	1862	Gen. Pierre Gustave Toutant Beauregard, CSA, assumes command of the Army of the Mississippi, based at Jackson, TN.
03	5	1862	Skirmish near Pohick Church, or Occoquan, VA, with Col. Alexander Hays, 63rd PA Infantry.
03	5	1862	Skirmish at Bunker Hill, north of Winchester, VA, with Brig. Gen. Alpheus S. Williams, USA.
03	6	1862	**Sterling Price,** C.S.A., is appointed Maj. Gen.
03	6	1862	**George Hume Steuart,** CSA, is appointed Brig. Gen.
03	6	1862	**The Battle of Pea Ridge, or Elkhorn Tavern, AR,** north of Fayetteville, which results in a Union victory under Brig. Gen. Samuel Ryan Curtis, USA, opposing Brig. Gens. Earl Van Dorn, Ben McCulloch, and Albert Pike, CSA. 3/6-8/1862.
03	6	1862	The **USS Monitor,** under tow by the tugboat **Seth Law,** leaves New York Harbor, NY, accompanied by the Federal vessels, **USS Currituck,** and the **USS Sachem.**
03	7	1862	**William Duncan Smith,** CSA, is appointed Brig. Gen.
03	7	1862	**Thomas Alfred Davies,** USA, is appointed Brig. Gen.
03	7	1862	**Brig. Gen. Ben McCulloch, CSA,** the second highest ranking brigadier of the Confederacy, is mortally wounded, shot in the chest by a Federal Sharpshooter at the Battle of Pea Ridge, or Elkhorn Tavern, AR.
03	7	1862	**Brig. Gen. James McQueen McIntosh, CSA,** dies within minutes of Brig. Gen. McCulloch, after being shot through the heart during his cavalry charge into the Federal lines, Battle of Pea Ridge, or Elkhorn Tavern.
03	7	1862	**Brig. Gen. William Yarnel Slack, CSA,** is mortally wounded by a musket ball in the hip, only inches from a similar wound received at the earlier Battle at Springfield, dying on March 21, 1862.
03	7	1862	Federal reconnaissance up the Savannah River and to Elba Island, GA. 3/7-11/1862.

03	7	1862	Skirmish at Bob's Creek, MO, by Lieut. Col. Arnold Krekel, 1st Battalion MO Cavalry Militia.
03	7	1862	Skirmish at Fox Creek, MO.
03	7	1862	Engagement at Point Pleasant, MO.
03	7	1862	Operations in Saline County, MO. 3/7-10/1862.
03	7	1862	The advance of the Army of the Potomac to Centreville and Manassas, VA, under Maj. Gen. George B. McClellan, USA. 3/7-11/1862.
03	7	1862	**Withdrawal** of the Confederate forces from **Evansport, Dumfries, Manassas, and Occoquan, VA,** under Gen. Joseph Eggleston Johnston, CSA. 3/7-9/1862.
03	7	1862	Skirmish near Winchester, VA, with Brig. Gen. Alpheus S. Williams, USA, and Lieut. Col. Turner Ashby, CSA Cavalry.
03	8	1862	**James Edwin Slaughter,** CSA, is appointed Brig. Gen.
03	8	1862	Col. Thomas M. Jones, 27th Miss. Infantry, is assigned to the command at Pensacola, FL.
03	8	1862	Brig. Gen. William T. Sherman's, USA, division embarks at Paducah, KY, for the Tennessee River.
03	8	1862	Operations about Rolla, MO, with MO Cavalry and Infantry. 3/8-9/1862.
03	8	1862	**Chattanooga, TN, is occupied** by the Confederates, under Brig. Gen. John B. Floyd, CSA.
03	8	1862	Skirmish near Nashville, TN, with Capt. John Hunt Morgan, CSA.
03	8	1862	By the direction of Confederate Secretary Judah Benjamin, the Honorable William G. Brownlow is escorted to the Union lines, East Tennessee.
03	8	1862	Col. James Dada Morgan's, USA, operations near Nashville, TN.
03	8	1862	Naval engagement in Hampton Roads, VA, and the destruction of the US frigate **Congress** and the sloop of war **Cumberland,** with severe damage to the warship, **USS Minnesota,** by the Confederate iron-clad **Virginia,** (formerly the **Merrimac**) 3/8-9/1862.
03	8	1862	The **occupation of Leesburg, VA,** by the Union forces.
03	9	1862	**Charles William Field,** CSA, is appointed Brig. Gen.
03	9	1862	Skirmish on Big Creek, MO, where Lieut. Col. Arnold Krekel, 1st Battalion MO Cavalry, killed the notorious **Ted Sharp,** who killed Dr. Cleveland, another notoriously bad character, at the Virginia Hotel, a few days before.
03	9	1862	Skirmish at Mountain Grove, MO, with the MO Infantry.
03	9	1862	Skirmish on Granny White's Pike, near Nashville, TN, with Col. John S. Scott, CSA, 1st LA Cavalry.
03	9	1862	Federal expedition towards Purdy and operations about Crump's Landing, TN, by Brig. Gen. Charles F. Smith, USA. 3/9-14/1862.
03	9	1862	Maj. Gen. Edmund Kirby Smith, CSA, assumes the command in East Tennessee.
03	9	1862	**Naval engagement at Hampton Roads, VA,** between the 1st ironclads, the **USS Monitor,** and the **CSS Merrimac,** which fight to a draw, after the following US vessels are attacked by the **CSS Merrimac: Congress, Cumberland,** and the **Minnesota.**
03	9	1862	Skirmish at Sangster's Station, VA.
03	10	1862	The following are appointed Confederate Major Generals: **Benjamin Franklin Cheatham, C.S.A.** **David Rumph Jones,** **C.S.A.** **John Porter McCown,** **C.S.A.**
03	10	1862	**William Henry Forney,** CSA, is appointed Brig. Gen.
03	10	1862	Skirmish in La Fayette County, MO.
03	10	1862	Skirmish at Jacksborough, Big Creek Gap, TN.
03	10	1862	Skirmish at Burke's Station, VA.
03	11	1862	The following are appointed Confederate Brigadier Generals: **Seth Maxwell Barton,** CSA. **Paul Jones Semmes,** CSA. **Lucius Marshall Walker,** CSA.
03	11	1862	The Depts. of Kansas, of the Missouri, and part of the Ohio, are merged into the Dept. of the Mississippi, under Maj. Gen. Henry Wager Halleck, USA.
03	11	1862	Brig. Gens. John Buchanan Floyd, CSA, and Gideon Johnson Pillow, CSA, are relieved from command by Jefferson Davis for their role at Fort Donelson, TN.
03	11	1862	Skirmish near Paris, TN, with Maj. Gen. Ulysses S. Grant, USA.
03	11	1862	Maj. Gen. George B. McClellan, USA, is relieved from the command of the Armies of the United States- retaining command of the Army of the Potomac, VA, etal.

03	11	1862	Skirmish at Stephenson's Station, near Winchester, VA.
03	11	1862	**Winchester, VA, is abandoned** by the Confederate forces under Maj. Gen. Thomas Jonathan "Stonewall" Jackson, CSA, and subsequently **occupied** by the Union forces. 3/11-12/1862.
03	11	1862	The Dept. of Western Virginia is merged into the Mountain Dept.
03	12	1862	**Jacksonville, FL, is occupied** by Union forces from the **USS Ottawa,** under Lieut. T. H. Stevens, USN.
03	12	1862	Skirmish near Aubrey, KS, with Col. Robert H. Graham, 8 KS Infantry.
03	12	1862	Skirmish near Lebanon, MO.
03	12	1862	Skirmish at Lexington, MO.
03	13	1862	**John Bordenave Villepigue,** CSA, is appointed Brig. Gen.
03	13	1862	**Daniel Tyler,** USA, is appointed Brig. Gen.
03	13	1862	Action at Spring River, AR.
03	13	1862	Maj. Gen. Henry Wager Halleck, USA, assumes the command of the Dept. of the Mississippi.
03	13	1862	The destruction of the Beach Creek Bridge, on the **Mobile and Ohio Railroad,** TN.
03	13	1862	The US Army Corps are organized in the **Army of the Potomac,** VA, under the following Army Corp Commanders:

a) Maj. Gen. Irvin McDowell, I Army Corps
b) Brig. Gen. Edwin Vose Sumner, II Army Corps
c) Brig. Gen. Samuel Peter Heintzelman, III Army Corps
d) Brig. Gen. Erasmus Darwin Keyes, IV Army Corps
e) Maj. Gen. Nathaniel Prentiss Banks, V Army Corps

03	13	1862	Gen. Robert E. Lee, CSA, is charged with the conduct of military operations in the Armies of the Confederacy.
03	13	1862	Additional Article of War is approved forbidding all officers and soldiers of the US Army from aiding in the capture and return of fugitive slaves to their disloyal owners, VA, etal.
03	14	1862	The following are appointed Confederate Brigadier Generals:

John Stevens Bowen, CSA
Benjamin Hardin Helm, CSA
Henry Eustace McCulloch, CSA

03	14	1862	**Andrew Jackson Smith,** USA, is appointed Brig. Gen.
03	14	1862	Brig. Gen. James Heyward Trapier, CSA, is assigned command of the Confederate Dept. of Middle and East Florida.
03	14	1862	The **capture of New Madrid, MO,** by Brig. Gen. John Pope, USA, as Maj. Gen. John P. McCown, CSA, retreats to Island No. 10.
03	14	1862	**The Battle of New Berne, NC.** Brig. Gen. Ambrose E. Burnside, USA, **captures** the town, while Brig. Gen. Lawrence O'Bryan, CSA, retreats.
03	14	1862	Maj. Gen. John Clifford Pemberton, CSA, is assigned command of Confederate Dept. of South Carolina and Georgia.
03	14	1862	Federal expedition from Savannah, TN, to Yellow Creek, MS, and the **occupation of Pittsburg Landing,** TN, with Brig. Gen. William T. Sherman, USA, commanding. 3/14-17/1862.
03	14	1862	Skirmishes at Big Creek Gap and Jacksborough, TN, with Maj. Gen. E. Kirby Smith, CSA.
03	14	1862	Federal reconnaissance to Cedar Run, VA, by Brig. Gen. George Stoneman, USA.
03	14	1862	Brig. Gen. William Starke Rosecrans, USA, assumes the command of the Mountain Dept., VA, etal.
03	15	1862	The Dept. of Florida is merged into the Dept. of the South, Maj. Gen. David Hunter, USA, commanding, which will include the states South Carolina, Georgia, and Florida, headquartered at Hilton Head, SC.
03	15	1862	Skirmish near Marshall, MO.
03	15	1862	**The Siege and Capture of Island No. 10, MO,** by Maj. Gen. Ulysses S. Grant, USA, and the union gunboats under Flag Officer Foote, USN. 3/15-4/7/1862.
03	15	1862	Capt. John Hunt Morgan's, CSA, operations about Gallatin, TN. 3/15-18/1862.
03	16	1862	Action at Pound Gap, KY, with Brig. Gen. James A. Garfield, USA, and Brig. Gen. Humphrey Marshall, CSA.
03	16	1862	Skirmish near Marshall, MO.
03	16	1862	Skirmish near Pittsburg Landing, or Black Jack Forest, TN.
03	17	1862	The following are appointed Union Brigadier Generals:

William Hemsley Emory, USA
Orris Sanford Ferry, USA

Isaac Ferdinand Quinby, USA

03	17	1862	Action at Riddle's Point, MO.
03	17	1862	The Army of the Potomac, Maj. Gen. George B. McClellan, USA, commanding, begins to embark on navy transports for the Virginia Peninsula at Alexandria, VA, headed for Fortress Monroe, near Hampton, VA.

03	18	1862	**Dabney Herndon Maury,** CSA, is appointed Brig. Gen.
03	18	1862	**Ambrose Everett Burnside, U.S.A.,** is appointed Maj. Gen.
03	18	1862	Skirmish at Spring River, or Salem, AR.
03	18	1862	Confederate troops under Gen. Albert Sidney Johnson, CSA, begin arriving at Corinth, MS, from Murfreesboro, TN.
03	18	1862	Federal operations in Johnson, Saint Clair, and Henry Counties, MO, including skirmish near Leesville, MO, by Brig. Gen. James Totten, USA. **(March 19th).** 3/18-30/1862
03	18	1862	Engagement at Point Pleasant, MO.
03	18	1862	Skirmish at Middletown, VA.
03	18	1862	President Jefferson Davis appoints **Judah Benjamin as Secretary of State.** Benjamin is currently acting as the Confederate **Secretary of War,** who will be replaced by **George W. Randolph,** Richmond, VA.

03	19	1862	**Samuel Jones,** C.S.A., is appointed Maj. Gen.
03	19	1862	**Daniel Phineas Woodbury,** USA, is appointed Brig. Gen.
03	19	1862	Federal expedition from Camp Latham to Owen's River, CA, with skirmish with Indians **(April 9th)** near Bishop's Creek, in the Owen's River Valley, California. 3/19-4/28/1862.
03	19	1862	Col. W.S. Dilworth, CSA, is assigned to the command of the Dept. of Florida, vice Trapier, is ordered to Alabama.
03	19	1862	Federal expedition to Carthage, MO, by Lieut. Col. Powell Clayton, 5th KS Cavalry. 3/19-20/1862.
03	19	1862	Federal operations in Johnson County, MO, by Brig. Gen. James Totten, USA. 3/19-23/1862.
03	19	1862	Brig. Gen. Joseph R. Anderson, CSA, supersedes Brig. Gen. Richard C. Gatlin, CSA, in the command of the Confederate Dept. of North Carolina.
03	19	1862	Federal reconnaissance on May River, SC. 3/19-24/1862.
03	19	1862	Skirmish at Strasburg, VA; Maj. Gen. Thomas J. Jackson, CSA, causes a Federal retreat, by Brig. Gen. James Shields, USA.
03	19	1862	Skirmish at Elk Mountain, WV.

03	20	1862	**States Rights Gist,** CSA, is appointed Brig. Gen.
03	20	1862	**John Seldon Roane,** CSA, is appointed Brig. Gen.
03	20	1862	**Marsena Rudolph Patrick,** USA, is appointed Brig. Gen.
03	20	1862	Maj. Gen. Benjamin Franklin Butler, USA, assumes the command of the Dept. of the Gulf, at Ship Island, MS, in preparation of a Federal attack on New Orleans, LA.
03	20	1862	Federal expedition to Washington, NC, from New Berne, by Maj. Gen. Ambrose E. Burnside, USA. 3/20-21/1862.
03	20	1862	Federal operations near Bluffton, SC, including affairs at Buckingham and Hunting Island, SC.
03	20	1862	Federal reconnaissance to Dumfries, VA. 3/20-21/1862.
03	20	1862	Maj. Gen. Nathaniel P. Banks, USA, assumes the command of the 5th Army Corps, as Banks is ordered to remove the majority of his command to the defense of Washington, DC, the remaining portion in the Shenandoah Valley is withdrawing towards Winchester from Strasburg, and is pursued by Maj. Gen. Thomas Jonathan "Stonewall" Jackson, VA.
03	20	1862	Federal reconnaissance to Gainesville, about 9 miles from Manassas Junction, VA, by Brig. Gen. Oliver O. Howard, USA.
03	20	1862	Skirmish at Philippi, WV.

03	21	1862	**Brig. Gen. William Yarnel Slack, CSA,** dies from wounds he received on March 7, 1862, at the Battle of Pea Ridge, or Elkhorn Tavern, AR.
03	21	1862	The following are appointed Union Major Generals:

Samuel Ryan Curtis, U.S.A.
John Alexander McClernand, U.S.A.
William Starke Rosecrans, U.S.A.
Lewis Wallace, U.S.A.

03	21	1862	The following are appointed Union Brigadier Generals:

Alexander Sandor Asboth, USA
Henry Beebee Carrington, USA
John Cook, USA

James Craig,	USA
Speed Smith Fry,	USA
Henry Moses Judah,	USA
Jacob Gartner Lauman,	USA
John Alexander Logan,	USA
Robert Latimer McCook,	USA
Horatio Phillips Van Cleve,	USA
William Harvey Lamb Wallace,	USA

03 21 1862 Naval engagement at Mosquito Inlet, FL, with the Union gunboats: **Henry Andrew, Penguin,** and the **Union.**

03 21 1862 The Federal **occupation of Washington, NC,** by Maj. Gen. Ambrose E. Burnside, USA.

03 21 1862 Affair at McKay's Farm, between Humansville and Warsaw, MO.

03 21 1862 Federal reconnaissance to and skirmish at Cumberland Gap, TN, against Maj. Gen. E. Kirby Smith, CSA. 3/21-23/1862.

03 22 1862 The following are appointed Union Major Generals:

Don Carlos Buell,	**U.S.A.**
John Pope,	**U.S.A.**
Franz Sigel,	**U.S.A.**

Richard James Oglesby, USA, is appointed Brig. Gen.

03 22 1862 **Operations in the Humboldt Military Division, CA.** 3/22-8/31/1862.

03 22 1862 Skirmish at Little Santa Fe, or Independence, MO, as the 2nd KS Cavalry, under Col. Robert B. Mitchell, USA, search for the notorious guerrilla, William Clarke Quantrill.

03 22 1862 The British vessel, the **Oreto,** embarks from Liverpool, England, for Nassau, the Bahamas Islands, which was sold to the Confederacy and will be renamed the **CSS Florida.**

03 22 1862 Skirmish on the Post Oak, MO.

03 22 1862 Skirmish at Kearnstown, VA, as Brig. Gen. James Shields, USA, encounters Maj. Gen. Thomas Jonathan "Stonewall" Jackson, CSA.

03 22 1862 The Middle Military Dept. is constituted, under the command of Maj. Gen. John A. Dix, USA, headquartered at Baltimore, MD.

03 23 1862 Affair at Smyrna, FL.

03 23 1862 Skirmish at Carthage, MO.

03 23 1862 Federal expedition from Point Pleasant, near New Madrid, to Little River, MO, by Maj. Jonas Rowalt, 7th IL Cavalry.

03 23 1862 **The Federal Siege of Fort Macon,** near Beaufort, NC, by Brig. Gen. John Grubb Parke's, USA, Union soldiers under Maj. Gen. Ambrose Everett Burnside, USA. 3/23-4/26/1862.

03 23 1862 **The Battle of Kernstown, VA,** about 3 miles south of Winchester, VA, officially begins Stonewall Jackson's **Valley Campaign,** which results in a Confederate withdrawal from the vicinity of Brig. Gen. James Shields, USA, men. This obscure battle has the effect of freezing Maj. Gen. Irvin McDowell, USA, in Washington, and Maj. Gen. Nathaniel P. Banks, USA, at Harper's Ferry, WV, not permitting them to reinforce Maj. Gen. George B. McClellan's **Peninsula Campaign.**

03 24 1862 **Mahlon Dickerson Manson,** USA, is appointed Brig. Gen.

03 24 1862 Federal scout in Saint Clair and Henry Counties, MO.

03 24 1862 Maj. Gen. Theophilus Hunter Holmes, CSA, supersedes Brig. Gen. Joseph Reid Anderson, CSA, in command of the Dept. of North Carolina.

03 24 1862 Skirmish at Camp Jackson, TN.

03 24 1862 The last of Gen. Albert S. Johnston's, CSA, Army arrives at Corinth, MS, from Murfreesboro, TN, in preparation of their defense against Maj. Gen. Ulysses S. Grant, USA, who is currently at Pittsburg Landing.

03 25 1862 Federal expedition in Moniteau County, MO, and skirmish en route, by Brig. Gen. James Totten, USA. 3/25-28/1862.

03 25 1862 Federal reconnaissance to Agnew's Ferry, TN, with Lieut. Mortimer Neely, 5th IA Cavalry.

03 25 1862 Federal reconnaissance from Murfreesborough to Shelbyville, Tullahoma, Manchester, and McMinnville, TN. 3/25-28/1862.

03 25 1862 Skirmish at Mount Jackson, VA.

03 26 1862 **Daniel Harvey Hill,**   **C.S.A.,** is appointed Maj. Gen.

03 26 1862 **William Nelson Pendleton,** CSA, is appointed Brig. Gen.

03	26	1862	**Gordon Granger,** USA, is appointed Brig. Gen.
03	26	1862	Skirmish near Denver City, Colorado Territory, results in the capture of 50 Confederate cavalrymen.
03	26	1862	Skirmish near Gouge's Mill, 15 miles east of Boonville, MO.
03	26	1862	Action at Humansville, MO, where State militia repel the Confederates.
03	26	1862	Skirmish at Warrensburg, or near Briar, MO.
03	26	1862	Action on the Post Oak, at mouth of the Brier, MO, with Brig. Gen. James Totten, USA.
03	26	1862	Skirmish at Apache Canon, near Johnson's Ranch, the New Mexico Territory results in a Union victory as they withdraw to Pigeon's Ranch, near Glorieta, under Maj. John M. Chivington, 1st Colorado Infantry.
03	26	1862	The Confederate Dept. of Henrico, under the command of Brig. Gen. John Henry Winder, CSA, is extended to embrace the city of Petersburg and vicinity, VA.
03	27	1862	Federal reconnaissance on Santa Rosa Island, FL, by Brig. Gen. Lewis G. Arnold, USA. 3/27-31/1862.
03	27	1862	Gen. Joseph Eggleston Johnston, CSA, is ordered to re-enforce the Army of the Peninsula, CSA, under Maj. Gen. John Bankhead Magruder, CSA, VA.
03	27	1862	Operations in the vicinity of Middleburg and White Plains, VA, as Col. Jonathan W. Geary, USA, 28th PA, discovers burnt bridges, cut telegraph wires, etc. 3/27-31/1862.
03	28	1862	Federal reconnaissance near the mouth of Saint Augustine Creek, GA.
03	28	1862	Engagement at Glorieta, La Glorieta Pass, or Pigeon's Ranch, near Sante Fe, New Mexico Territory, with Col. William Read Scurry, CSA, besting Col. John Potts Slough, USA.
03	28	1862	Skirmish near Johnson's Ranch, or Apache Canon, or Glorieta, New Mexico Territory; Confederate supply wagons are attacked by Maj. John Chivington, USA, forcing a Confederates retreat to Sante Fe, New Mexico Territory.
03	28	1862	**The Cumberland Gap Campaign, TN.** 3/28-6/18/1862.
03	28	1862	Brig. Gen. George Washington Morgan, USA, is assigned to the command of 7th Division, Army of the Ohio, and is ordered to operate against Cumberland Gap, TN, the important mountain pass connecting Kentucky, Tennessee, and Virginia.
03	28	1862	Confederate expedition into Scott and Morgan Counties, TN, by Maj. Gen. E. Kirby Smith, CSA.
03	28	1862	Operations on the **Orange and Alexandria Railroad,** VA, with affairs at the Bealeton and the Rappahannock Stations, VA, and the Union **occupation of Shipping Point, VA,** by Brig. Gen. Oliver O. Howard, USA. 3/28-31/1862.
03	29	1862	The Confederate Armies of Kentucky and Mississippi are consolidated under the **Army of the Mississippi** with the following Army Corps Commands, currently based at Corinth, MS: a) Gen. Albert Sidney Johnston, Commanding b) Gen. Pierre Gustave Toutant Beauregard, 2nd in Command c) Maj. Gen. Leonidas Polk, I Corps d) Maj. Gen. Braxton Bragg, II Corps e) Maj. Gen. William Joseph Hardee, III Corps f) Maj. Gen. George Bibb Crittenden, Reserve Corps
03	29	1862	Skirmish on the Blackwater, near Warrensburg, MO.
03	29	1862	Affair on Edisto Island, SC.
03	29	1862	Maj. Gen. John Charles Fremont, USA, supersedes Brig. Gen. William S. Rosecrans, USA, in command of the Mountain Dept., VA, as Rosecrans will be transferred to the West.
03	30	1862	Affairs on Wilmington and Whitemarsh Islands, GA. 3/30-31/1862.
03	30	1862	Skirmish near Clinton, MO, with detachment from the 1st IA Cavalry.
03	30	1862	Federal descent upon Union City, TN. 3/30-31/1862.
03	31	1862	**Granville Mellen Dodge,** USA, is appointed Brig. Gen.
03	31	1862	Brig. Gen. William Whann Mackall, CSA, supersedes Maj. Gen. John Porter McCown, CSA, in the command at New Madrid Bend, and at Island No. 10, Mississippi River, MO.
03	31	1862	Skirmish at Pink Hill, MO, with the 1st MO Cavalry.
03	31	1862	Skirmish at Deep Gully, NC.
03	31	1862	Maj. Gen. David Hunter, USA, assumes the command of the Dept. of the South, i.e., South Carolina, Georgia, and Florida.
03	31	1862	Federal expedition to Paris, TN, by Capt. William A. Haw, 5th IA Cavalry. 3/31-4/2/1862.
03	31	1862	Skirmish on the Purdy Road near Adamsville, TN, with Brig. Gen. Lewis Wallace, USA.
03	31	1862	The Federal **capture of Union City, TN.**
03	31	1862	Brig. Gen. Louis (Ludwig) Blenker's, USA, Division is ordered to the Mountain (a.k.a. Fremont's) Dept., VA.

04	1	1862	**Lewis Addison Armistead,** CSA, is appointed Brig. Gen.
04	1	1862	**Andrew Atkinson Humphreys,** USA, is appointed Brig. Gen.
04	1	1862	**Adolph Wilhelm August Friedrich von Seinwehr,** USA, is appointed Brig. Gen.
04	1	1862	Skirmish at Doniphan, MO, with Brig. Gen. Frederick Steele, USA.
04	1	1862	Skirmish on the Little Sni, MO, with Brig. Gen. James Totten, USA.
04	1	1862	Federal gunboat expedition on the Tennessee River, from Pittsburg Landing, TN, to Eastport, MS, and Chickasaw, AL.
04	1	1862	The Headquarters, Army of the Potomac, **is transferred** to the vicinity of Fortress Monroe, near Hampton, VA, consisting of 12 Federal Divisions, under Maj. Gen. George B. McClellan, USA.
04	1	1862	Skirmish at Salem, VA, as Maj. Gen. Thomas J. Jackson, CSA, retreats up the Shenandoah Valley, protected by his cavalry, under Col. Turner Ashby, CSA.
04	1	1862	Advance of the Union forces from Strasburg to Woodstock and Edenburg, VA, under Maj. Gen. Nathaniel Banks, USA. 4/1-2/1862.
04	2	1862	Brig. Gen. James William Denver, USA, assumes the command of the District of Kansas.
04	2	1862	Federal reconnaissance from Cape Girardeau to Jackson, Whitewater, and Dallas, MO. 4/2-4/1862.
04	2	1862	Skirmish near Doniphan, at Putnam's Ferry, MO.
04	2	1862	Skirmish near Walkersville, MO.
04	2	1862	Skirmish at Stony Creek, near Edenburg, VA.
04	2	1862	Federal reconnaissance to the Rappahannock River, VA, as Maj. Gen. George B. McClellan, USA, arrives at Fortress Monroe, near Hampton, VA, aboard the US steamer, **Commodore.**
04	3	1862	Federal troops **occupy Apalachicola, FL.**
04	3	1862	Gen. Albert S. Johnston, CSA, enroute from Corinth, MS, to clash with Maj. Gen. Ulysses S. Grant, USA, at Pittsburg Landing and Shiloh Church, TN, is hampered by bad weather.
04	3	1862	Skirmish near Monterey, TN, with Brig. Gen. James R. Chalmers, CSA.
04	3	1862	Federal expedition from Ship Island, to Biloxi and Pass Christian, MS, against Maj. Gen. Mansfield Lovell's, CSA forces. 04/3-4/1862.
04	3	1862	Skirmish at Moorefield, WV.
04	3	1862	The US Senate votes 29 to 14 to abolish slavery in the District of Columbia.
04	4	1862	Affair at Table Bluff, CA.
04	4	1862	Under the cover of darkness and a severe thunderstorm, the **USS Carondelet,** runs the Confederate batteries at Island No. 10, passing below the fort through a canal cut by the Union forces.
04	4	1862	Skirmish at Lawrenceburg, TN, with Brig. Gen. Milo S. Hascall, USA.
04	4	1862	Skirmish near Pittsburg Landing, at Crump's Landing, or Adamsville, TN, as Gen. Albert S. Johnston, CSA, advances toward Maj. Gen. Ulysses S. Grant, USA.
04	4	1862	Skirmish at Howard's Mills near Cockletown, VA.
04	4	1862	**The Advance of the Army of the Potomac,** from the vicinity of Fortress Monroe, toward Yorktown, VA.
04	4	1862	Skirmish at Great Bethel, VA.
04	4	1862	The Depts. of the Rappahannock (under Maj. Gen. Irvin McDowell) and the Shenandoah (under Maj. Gen. Nathaniel P. Banks) are constituted, VA.
04	4	1862	The 1st US Army Corps (McDowell's) is detached from the Army of the Potomac and is merged into the Dept. of the Rappahannock, VA, which places McDowell in a position to protect Washington, DC.
04	4	1862	The 5th US Army Corps (Bank's) is merged into the Dept. of the Shenandoah, VA.
04	5	1862	**Joseph Finegan,** CSA, is appointed Brig. Gen.
04	5	1862	The **occupation of Edisto Island, SC,** by Federal troops.
04	5	1862	Affair at San Luis Pass, TX, including the destruction of the Confederate steamer, **Columbia.** 4/5-6/1862.
04	5	1862	**The Federal Siege of Yorktown, VA,** by Maj. Gen. George B. McClellan's Army of the Potomac, against Gen. Joseph E. Johnston, and Maj. Gen. John B. Magruder, CSA. 4/5-5/4/1862.
04	5	1862	Skirmish near Lee's Mill, VA.
04	5	1862	Skirmish near the junction of the Warwick and the Yorktown Roads, VA.
04	6	1862	**Braxton Bragg, C.S.A., is appointed Full General.**
04	6	1862	**Jones Mitchell Withers, C.S.A.,** is appointed Maj. Gen.
04	6	1862	Skirmish near Fort Anderson, CA.
04	6	1862	Confederate expedition from Greeneville, TN, into Laurel Valley, NC, by Maj. Gen. E. Kirby Smith, CSA. 4/6-11/1862.
04	6	1862	**The Battle of Pittsburg Landing, or Shiloh, TN,** with fighting around Shiloh Church, the Sunken Road,

the Hornet's Nest, at the Blood Pond, and the Peach Orchard, as the battle swayed back and forth with Maj. Gen. Ulysses S. Grant, USA, retreating to the protection of the Union gunboats, **USS Lexington,** and the **USS Tyler,** and with Maj. Gen. Don Carlos Buell, USA, arriving with reinforcements, force a general Confederate retreat, now under Gen. P. G. T. Beauregard, CSA, as Gen. Albert S. Johnston, CSA, is mortally wounded, one of about 23,500 casualties. 4/6-7/1862.

04	6	1862	**Full General Albert Sidney Johnston, CSA,** has his femoral artery in his leg severed by a musketball, and bleeds to death after refusing to send for his Confederate doctors who are busy caring for the Federal wounded, at the Battle of Shiloh, TN.
04	6	1862	**Brig. Gen. Adley Hogan Gladden, CSA,** is mortally wounded at the Battle of Shiloh, TN, requiring his arm to be amputated from a shell fragment, and dying six days later near Corinth, MS, on April 12, 1862.
04	6	1862	**Brig. Gen. William Harvey Lamb Wallace, USA,** is mortally wounded at the Battle of Pittsburg Landing, or Shiloh, TN, while leading his men in a retreat, after assisting Brig. Gen. Benjamin Mayberry Prentiss, in defending the "Hornet's Nest," Shiloh, TN, dying at Savannah, TN, April 10, 1862.
04	6	1862	**Col. Daniel Weisiger Adams, CSA,** 1st LA, loses his right eye at the Battle of Shiloh, to become a Brig. Gen.
04	7	1862	Affair at Saint Andrew's Bay, FL. with Capt. R. S. Smith, CSA, Marianna Dragoons.
04	7	1862	Maj. Gen. John Clifford Pemberton's, CSA, command is extended over Middle and Eastern Florida.
04	7	1862	The Union ironclads, **USS Mississippi** and the **USS Pensacola,** enter the lower Mississippi River in preparation of an assault on New Orleans, LA.
04	7	1862	The Federal gunboat, **USS Pittsburg,** runs the CSA batteries at Island No. 10, New Madrid, MO, and joins the **USS Carondelet,** through the channel that Maj. Gen. John Pope's men cut in the Mississippi River around Island No. 10.
04	7	1862	Federal expedition to Elizabeth City, NC, by Lieut. Col. Griffin, 6th NH Infantry, aboard the steamers **Ceres, Eagle, Putnam** and the **Virginia.** 4/7-8/1862.
04	7	1862	Skirmish at Foy's Plantation, NC.
04	7	1862	Skirmish near Newport, NC, as Capt. John Boothe, CSA, attacks Lieut. Col. James Wilson's, USA, pickets on the Cedar Point Road.
04	7	1862	Federal raid on the Confederate line of communications between Chattanooga, TN, and Marietta, GA. 4/7-12/1862.
04	7	1862	Skirmish at Columbia Furnace, VA.
04	7	1862	Federal reconnaissance to the Rappahannock River, VA, by Lieut. Col. Thomas J. Lucas, 16th IN Infantry, to obtain positions of the Confederate Army of Northern Virginia.
04	8	1862	**James Gillpatrick Blunt,** USA, is appointed Brig. Gen.
04	8	1862	**Robert Byington Mitchell,** USA, is appointed Brig. Gen.
04	8	1862	Skirmish near Arcata, CA.
04	8	1862	Brig. Gen. Joseph Finegan, CSA, is assigned to the command of the Dept. of Middle and Eastern Florida.
04	8	1862	Skirmish near Corinth, MS.
04	8	1862	Skirmish at Medicine Creek, MO, Brig Gen Ben Loan, MO Militia.
04	8	1862	Federal scout through Gadfly, Newtonia, Granby, Neosho, and Valley of the Indian Creek, MO, and skirmishes.
04	8	1862	Skirmish near Warrensburg, MO.
04	8	1862	Skirmish near Warsaw, MO.
04	8	1862	Skirmish at Albuquerque, the New Mexico Territory, as Col. Edward R. S. Canby, 19th US Infantry, commanding the Dept. of New Mexico, forces Brig. Gen. Henry H. Sibley, CSA, to retreat southward along the Rio Grande River.
04	8	1862	Martial law is declared in East Tennessee.
04	8	1862	**The Confederate Garrison at Island No. 10, is surrendered at Tiptonville, TN,** to Maj. Gen. John Pope, USA.
04	8	1862	Federal reconnaissance from the Shiloh, or Pittsburg Landing, TN, battlefield, by Maj. Gen. Ulysses S. Grant, USA, as Gen. Pierre G. T. Beaurgeard, CSA, retreats toward Corinth, MS.
04	9	1862	Action at Owen's River, California.
04	9	1862	**Jacksonville, FL, is evacuated** by the Union forces.
04	9	1862	Brig. Gen. Mosby Monroe Parsons, MO, State Guard, assumes the command of the Confederate Missouri State Guard.
04	9	1862	Federal scout to Shiloh Camp, on Hoyle's Run, near Quincy, MO, and skirmishes; scout to Little Niangua, Hickory County, MO; and scout from Humansville to Montevallo, Vernon County, MO.

| 04 | 9 | 1862 | Skirmish at Jackson, MO, with the MO Cavalry Militia. |
| 04 | 9 | 1862 | Federal reconnaissances in front of Yorktown, VA. 4/9-11/1862. |

04	10	1862	**Brig. Gen. William Harvey Lamb Wallace, USA,** dies at Maj. Gen. Ulysses S. Grant's, USA, headquarters at Savannah, TN, from wounds received April 6, 1862, at the Battle of Shiloh, TN.
04	10	1862	Col. Ferris Forman, 4th California Infantry, assumes the command of the District of Southern California.
04	10	1862	Skirmish near Fernandina, FL.
04	10	1862	**The bombardment and capture of Fort Pulaski, GA,** near Savannah, GA; Brig. Gen. Quincy A. Gillmore, USA, attacking from nearby Tybee Island, and using men from the **USS Wabash.** 4/10-11/1862.
04	10	1862	Brig. Gen. Samuel Davis Sturgis, USA, assumes the command of the District of Kansas.
04	10	1862	Brig. Gen. John McAllister Schofield, USA, is placed in the immediate command in Missouri.
04	11	1862	The following are appointed Confederate Brigadier Generals:
			William Nelson Rector Beall, CSA
			Franklin Gardner, CSA
			Martin Luther Smith, CSA
04	11	1862	The following are appointed Union Major Generals:
			Cassius Marcellus Clay, U.S.A.
			Ormsby MacKnight Mitchel, U.S.A.
04	11	1862	**Francis Engle Patterson,** USA, is appointed Brig. Gen.
04	11	1862	**Huntsville, AL,** near Chattanooga, TN, and on the **Memphis and Charleston Railroad, is occupied** by the Union forces by Brig. Gen. Ormsby Mitchel, USA, Maj. Gen. E. Kirby Smith, CSA, defending.
04	11	1862	Skirmish near Shiloh, MO, about 15 miles southeast of Osceola, with a raid on a Rebel camp by Brig. Gen. James Totten, USA.
04	11	1862	The US House of Representatives votes 93-39 to gradually abolish slavery in the District of Columbia.
04	11	1862	Skirmish at Wartrace, TN, with Maj. Gen. E. Kirby Smith, CSA.
04	11	1862	Confederate Naval Operations in Hampton Roads VA, as the **CSS Virginia (Merrimac)** captures three Union merchant ships.
04	12	1862	**Brig. Gen. Adley Hogan Gladden, CSA,** dies near Corinth, MS, from complications of his wound received at the Battle of Shiloh, TN, on April 6, 1862.
04	12	1862	**William Yarnel Slack,** CSA, is appointed Brig. Gen.
04	12	1862	Federal expedition to Bear Creek, AL, by Brig. Gen. William T. Sherman, USA. 4/12-13/1862.
04	12	1862	The **Great Locomotive Chase** begins at Marietta, GA, as Mr. James J. Andrews commandeers the Confederate locomotive, **General,** is pursued and finally caught by the locomotive, **Texas,** north of Ringgold, GA. 8 were eventually executed, Andrews included; 8 escaped from prison, and 6 were paroled.
04	12	1862	Skirmish at the Little Blue River, MO.
04	12	1862	Skirmish at Monterey, VA, with Brig. Gen. Robert Milroy, USA.
04	12	1862	The command of Gen. Joseph E. Johnston, CSA, is extended over the Depts. of Norfolk and the Peninsula, VA.
04	12	1862	Maj. Gen. Nathaniel Prentiss Banks, USA, assumes the command of the Dept. of the Shenandoah, VA.
04	12	1862	Federal raid from Fairmont to Valley River and Boothsville, Marion County, WV, sent by Brig. Gen. Benjamin F. Kelley, USA, to capture or kill certain individuals in the area trying to raise companies of volunteers for the Confederate cause; the raid being successful with most of the men killed.
04	13	1862	**Decatur, AL,** on the Tennessee River, **is occupied** by the Union forces, commanded by Brig. Gen. Ormsby Mitchel, USA.
04	13	1862	Federal expedition from Southern California, under Brig. Gen. James H. Carleton, USA, through Arizona to Northwestern Texas and New Mexico Territory, gradually forcing the Confederates to **evacuate** the **New Mexico Territory.** 4/13-9/20/1862.
04	13	1862	Maj. Gen. David Hunter, USA, orders the emancipation of slaves at Fort Pulaski and on Cockspur Island, GA.
04	13	1862	Federal reconnaissance on Corinth, MS and Purdy, TN, roads.
04	13	1862	Pursuit of the Confederate forces, including skirmish at Peralta, the New Mexico Territory, by Col. Edward R.S. Canby, USA. 4/13-22/1862.
04	13	1862	Skirmish at Gillett's Farm, Pebbly Run, NC, with the 2nd NC Volunteers.
04	14	1862	The following are appointed Confederate Major Generals:
			John Cabell Breckenridge, C.S.A.
			Thomas Carmichael Hindman, C.S.A.
04	14	1862	The following are appointed Confederate Brigadier Generals:

			Thomas Jordan, CSA
			William Preston, CSA
04	14	1862	**Cuvier Grover,** USA, is appointed Brig. Gen.
04	14	1862	**Amiel Weeks Whipple,** USA, is appointed Brig. Gen.
04	14	1862	Skirmish at Diamond Grove, MO.
04	14	1862	Skirmish near Montevallo, MO, with Rebel jayhawkers.
04	14	1862	Skirmish near the Sante Fe Road, MO, with a Union attack on William Clarke Quantrill's guerrillas.
04	14	1862	Skirmish Walkersville, MO.
04	14	1862	Skirmish at Pollocksville, NC.
04	14	1862	Federal reconnaissance on Seabrook Island, SC, to 1 mile from Rockville, SC, under cover of the Federal gunboat, **Pocahontas.**
04	14	1862	Fort Pillow, TN, on the Mississippi River, is bombarded by Union mortar and gunboats.
04	15	1862	**Julius Adolph de Lagnel,** CSA, is appointed Brig. Gen.
04	15	1862	The following are appointed Union Brigadier Generals:
			Benjamin Alvord, USA
			Napoleon Bonaparte Buford, USA
			Charles Devens, Jr., USA
			George Lucas Hartsuff, USA
			Rufus Saxton, USA
			Carl Schurz, USA
			William Sooy Smith, USA
			James Henry Van Alen, USA
04	15	1862	Skirmish at Picacho Pass, near Tucson, the Arizona Territory.
04	15	1862	Skirmish at Lost Creek, MO.
04	15	1862	Skirmish at Peralta, the New Mexico Territory.
04	15	1862	Maj. Gen. Earl Van Dorn's, CSA, Confederate forces are ordered to Memphis, TN.
04	15	1862	Skirmish at Pea Ridge, TN.
04	15	1862	Federal reconnaissance to the Rappahannock River, VA, led by Capt. Robert F. Dyer, USA, 1st ME Cavalry, is repulsed near Bealeton, VA.
04	16	1862	The following are appointed Confederate Brigadier Generals:
			John Echols, CSA
			Lewis Henry Little, CSA
			George Earl Maney, CSA
			Jean Jacques Alfred Alexander Mouton, CSA
			Roger Atkinson Pryor, CSA
			John Stuart Williams, CSA
04	16	1862	**Nathan Kimball,** USA, is appointed Brig. Gen.
04	16	1862	**Tuscumbia, AL, is occupied** by the Union forces.
04	16	1862	Skirmish on Whitemarsh Island, or Wilmington Island, GA, due to an advance ordered by Brig. Gen. Quincy A. Gillmore, USA.
04	16	1862	Flag Officer Daniel Glasgow Farragut, USN, moves his naval fleet to below Forts Jackson and St. Philip, Mississippi River, near New Orleans, LA, the mortar fleet of Commander (later Admiral) David Dixon Porter, USN, as well as Union transports carrying Maj. Gen. Benjamin F. Butler's, USA, men, joining Farragut.
04	16	1862	Skirmish near Blackwater Creek, MO, with mounted bushwackers.
04	16	1862	Skirmish at Savannah, TN.
04	16	1862	Skirmish at Columbia Furnace, VA, with Maj. Gen. Banks, USA.
04	16	1862	Engagement at Lee's Mill, Burnt Chimneys, or Dam No. 1, VA.
04	16	1862	Federal reconnaissance to Liberty Church, VA, as Lieut. Col. Willard Sayles, 1st RI Cavalry, arrests the blacksmith Willis.
04	16	1862	Federal reconnaissance to the Rappahannock River, VA, as Maj. Robert C. Anthony, 1st RI Cavalry is forced to retreat, near the blacksmith Willis' home.
04	16	1862	The Confederate government prepares to enact the law of conscription of all able bodied men, age 18 to 35 years old, Richmond, VA.
04	17	1862	Skirmish at Warsaw, MO.
04	17	1862	Skirmish at Monterey, TN, near Corinth, MS.

04	17	1862	The Confederate capture of about 475 Union refugees at Woodson's Gap, TN, by Maj. Gen. E. Kirby Smith, CSA.
04	17	1862	Skirmishes near Falmouth and the **occupation (18th) of Fredericksburg, VA,** by the Union forces, under Maj. Gen. Irvin McDowell, USA. 4/17-19/1862.
04	17	1862	Federal **occupation of Mount Jackson,** skirmish at Rude's Hill, and the **occupation of New Market, VA,** by Maj. Gen. Nathaniel P. Banks, USA.
04	17	1862	Skirmish at Piedmont, VA.
04	17	1862	Skirmish at Holly River, WV.
04	17	1862	Federal expedition from Summerville (Nicholas Court-House) to Addison, WV, as Maj. Ebenezer B. Andrews, 36th OH Infantry skirmishes with bushwackers. 4/17-21/1862.
04	18	1862	Brig. Gen. Joseph Finegan, CSA, assumes the command of the Confederate Dept. of Middle and East Florida.
04	18	1862	**The Federal Bombardment and Capture of Forts Jackson and Saint Philip, LA,** by Flag Officer David Farragut's gunboats and Commander David Porter's mortar fleet. **4/18-28/1862.**
04	18	1862	Col. Justus Steinberger, 1st Washington Territory Infantry, is assigned to command of the District of the Oregon Territory.
04	18	1862	Skirmish at, and the **occupation of, Falmouth, VA,** across from Fredericksburg, VA, by Maj. Gen. Irvin McDowell, USA.
04	18	1862	Federal reconnaissance to the Rappahannock River, VA, under Brig. Gen. John J. Abercrombie, USA.
04	18	1862	Skirmish at Chapmanville, WV.
04	19	1862	Skirmish at Talbot's Ferry, near Yellville, AR, with the Federal destruction of Confederate saltworks.
04	19	1862	Engagement at South Mills, or Camden, Camden County, NC, with Brig. Gen. Jesse L. Reno, USA, under Maj. Gen. Ambrose E. Burnside, USA, and Maj. Gen. Benjamin Huger, CSA.
04	19	1862	Skirmish on the Trent Road, NC.
04	19	1862	Brig. Gen. Rufus Saxton, USA, is assigned to special duty in the Dept. of the South, SC, etal.
04	19	1862	Skirmish on Edisto Island, SC.
04	19	1862	Skirmish on the South Fork of the Shenandoah River, near Luray, VA.
04	19	1862	Federal **occupation of Sparta, VA,** by Maj. Gen. Nathaniel P. Banks, USA.
04	20	1862	**Henry Prince,** USA, is appointed Brig. Gen.
04	20	1862	Men from the **USS Itasca** and the **USS Pinola** employ a night raid to remove some of the Confederate river obstructions below Forts Jackson and St. Philip, Mississippi River, near New Orleans, LA.
04	20	1862	Maj. Gen. Irvin McDowell, USA, meets Abraham Lincoln near Fredericksburg, VA, on the Aquia Creek, and travels with the President to Washington, DC.
04	20	1862	The Federal blockade on the Rappahannock River report capturing the following Confederate vessels: **Eureka, Falcon, Lookout, Monterey, Reindeer, Roundout, Sarah Ann, Sea Flower,** and the **Sydney Jones.**
04	21	1862	Skirmish at Pocahontas, AR.
04	21	1862	The families of Messrs. Brownlow, Johnson, Maynard, and other Union men are ordered to leave the Confederacy, East Tennessee.
04	21	1862	Skirmish at Monterey, VA.
04	22	1862	The Confederate capture of Union launches belonging to the **USS Arthur,** in Arkansas Pass, TX.
04	22	1862	**Harrisonburg, VA, is occupied** by Union forces.
04	22	1862	The Federal **occupation of,** and skirmish near, **Luray, VA,** by Maj. Gen. Nathaniel P. Banks, USA.
04	22	1862	Maj. Gen. William Buel Franklin's, USA, Division arrives at Yorktown, VA.
04	23	1862	Skirmish at Bridgeport, AL.
04	23	1862	Federal forces successfully blockade the Chesapeake and Albemarle Canal, NC.
04	23	1862	Skirmish at Grass Lick, between Lost River and Cacapon, WV, with guerrillas.
04	24	1862	Skirmish at Tuscumbia, AL.
04	24	1862	The batteries of Forts Jackson and St. Philip are successfully passed by Flag Officer Daniel Farragut's naval fleet, and after confronting the Confederate ram, **CSS Manassas,** moves unabated on New Orleans, LA.
04	24	1862	Skirmish on the Corinth, MS, road.
04	24	1862	Skirmish at Lick Creek, TN.
04	24	1862	Skirmish on the Shelbyville Road, TN.
04	24	1862	Skirmish 9 miles from Harrisonburg, VA.
04	25	1862	**Maj. Gen. Charles Ferguson Smith, USA,** dies from a combination of an infection to his leg and camp fever (dysentery) at Union Headquarters, Savannah, TN. Unable to lead the Federal command at Shiloh, TN,

			one of his former subordinates, Maj. Gen. Ulysses Simpson Grant, USA, commands the Federal operations.
04	25	1862	The following are appointed Union Major Generals:

George Cadwalader,   **U.S.A.**
George Henry Thomas,   **U.S.A.**

04	25	1862	The following are appointed Union Brigadier Generals:

Samuel Wylie Crawford,   USA
John White Geary,   USA
William Alexander Hammond,   USA
Milo Smith Hascall,   USA
Henry Walton Wessells,   USA

04	25	1862	Skirmish at Tuscumbia, AL.
04	25	1862	**New Orleans, LA, is captured by the US Navy,** under Flag Officer Daniel Farragut, USN, as Maj. Gen. Mansfield Lovell, CSA, **evacuates** New Orleans, officially surrendered by civilians April 29, 1862.
04	25	1862	Skirmish on the Corinth, MS, Road.
04	25	1862	Skirmish on the Osage, near Monagan Springs, MO, with a small band of **jayhawkers,** while in the morning 30,000 Federal rations were delivered by the steamer **Silver Lake.**
04	25	1862	Affair at Socorro, the New Mexico Territory.
04	25	1862	Col. Moses White, CSA, **surrenders Fort Macon, NC,** to Brig. Gen. John Grubb Parke, USA, with the assistance of the Union gunboats, **Chippewa, Daylight, Gemsbok,** and the **Georgia.** 4/25-26/1862.
04	26	1862	**Leonard Fulton Ross,** USA, is appointed Brig. Gen.
04	26	1862	**Alfred Howe Terry,** USA, is appointed Brig. Gen.
04	26	1862	Skirmishes on the Eel River and near Fort Baker, CA.
04	26	1862	Skirmish at Neosho, MO, with Confederate aligned **Choctaw, Chickasaw** and **Cherokee** Indians.
04	26	1862	Skirmish at Turnback Creek, MO.
04	26	1862	Skirmish at Arkins' Mill, TN.
04	26	1862	Confederate scout on the Forked Deer River, TN. 4/26-26/1862.
04	26	1862	Skirmish at the Gordonsville and Keezletown Cross-Roads, VA, in front of Yorktown, VA.
04	27	1862	Skirmish at Bridgeport, AL.
04	27	1862	**Forts Livingston, Pike and Wood, are captured** by the Union forces, near New Orleans, LA.
04	27	1862	**Fort Quitman, is abandoned** by the Confederates, near New Orleans, LA, and a blockade runner is also captured.
04	27	1862	Skirmish near Haughton's Mill, Horton's Mills, or Pollocksville Road, NC, with Col. Baron Egloffstein, 103 NY Infantry.
04	27	1862	Skirmish at Pea Ridge, TN, with Maj. Gen. John McClernand, USA.
04	27	1862	Skirmish at McGaheysville, VA, and Swift Run Bridge, in the vicinity of Harrisonburg, VA, with Union cavalry.
04	28	1862	The following are appointed Union Brigadier Generals:

Absalom Baird,   USA
George Dashiell Bayard,   USA
William Plummer Benton,   USA
Henry Bohlen,   USA
John Curtis Caldwell,   USA
James Henry Carleton,   USA
Thomas Turpin Crittenden,   USA
Neal Dow,   USA
Quincy Adams Gillmore,   USA
George Sears Greene,   USA
Pleasant Adam Hackleman,   USA
John Cleveland Robinson,   USA
Isaac Peace Rodman,   USA
Truman Seymour,   USA
James Clifford Veatch,   USA
Max Weber,   USA

04	28	1862	Skirmish at Bolivar, AL.
04	28	1862	Skirmish at Paint Rock Bridge, AL.

04	28	1862	The British **Oreto** (soon to be **CSS Florida**) arrives at Nassau, the Bahamas Islands.
04	28	1862	Brig. Gen. John Horace Forney, CSA, is assigned to the command of the Dept. of Alabama and West Florida.
04	28	1862	**The surrender of Fort Jackson and Fort Saint Philip,** outside New Orleans, LA, by the Confederate forces there, after Flag Officer Daniel Farragut **captured New Orleans, LA,** rendering these forts useless.
04	28	1862	Federal scouts on the Marias-des-Cygnes and the Elk Fork Rivers, MO.
04	28	1862	Skirmish at Warsaw, MO.
04	28	1862	Skirmish at Cumberland Mountain, TN.
04	28	1862	Skirmish near Monterey, TN, by Maj. Gen. John Pope, USA.
04	28	1862	Federal expedition to Purdy, TN. 4/28-29/1862.
04	29	1862	Action at West Bridge, near Bridgeport, AL, by Brig. Gen. Ormsby Mitchel, USA.
04	29	1862	The Federal advance from Pittsburg Landing, under Maj. Gen. Henry W. Halleck, USA, upon, and the siege of Corinth, MS, and the pursuit of the Confederate forces to Guntown, MS, under Gen. Pierre Gustave Toutant Beauregard, CSA.
04	29	1862	Skirmish near Batchelder's Creek, NC, with Maj. Andrew Elwell, the 23 MA Infantry.
04	29	1862	Engagements at Pineberry Battery, Williston, White Point, SC, with the destruction of the Confederate battery at Pineberry.
04	29	1862	Skirmish near Cumberland Gap, TN.
04	29	1862	Federal raid on the **Mobile and Ohio Railroad,** near Bethel Station, TN.
04	29	1862	Skirmish near Monterey, TN.
04	29	1862	The Federal **occupation of Purdy, TN.**
04	30	1862	**Abram Sanders Piatt,** USA, is appointed Brig. Gen.
04	30	1862	The Reorganization of the Union **Armies of the Mississippi,** with the following command assignments: Maj. Gen. George Henry Thomas, Right Wing Maj. Gen. John Pope, Left Wing Maj. Gen. John Alexander McClernand, Reserve Wing Maj. Gen. Don Carlos Buell, commands Army of the Ohio Maj. Gen. Ulysses S. Grant, overall 2nd in command
04	30	1862	Maj. Gen. Thomas J. **Stonewall** Jackson, CSA, moves toward Stauton from Elk Run, near Swift Run Gap, Shenandoah Valley, VA.
05	1	1862	**William Tecumseh Sherman, U.S.A.,** is appointed Maj. Gen.
05	1	1862	**Samuel Powhatan Carter,** USA, is appointed Brig. Gen.
05	1	1862	Federal operations in vicinity of Athens, Mooresville, Limestone Bridge, and Elk River, AL, with Maj. Gen. Ormsby M. Mitchel, USA. 5/1-2/1862.
05	1	1862	**New Orleans, LA, is occupied by the Union forces,** under Maj. Gen. Benjamin F. Butler, USA.
05	1	1862	Skirmish near Pulaski, TN, with Col. John Hunt Morgan, CSA.
05	1	1862	Skirmish at Rapidan Station, VA.
05	1	1862	Skirmish on Camp Creek, in the Stone River Valley, WV, and on the Lewisburg road, with Brig. Gen. Jacob D. Cox, USA.
05	1	1862	Skirmish at Clark's Hollow, WV.
05	2	1862	**John Gibbon,** USA, is appointed Brig. Gen.
05	2	1862	Skirmish at Litchfield, AR.
05	2	1862	The Federal Dept. of Kansas is re-established, under the command of Brig. Gen. James G. Blunt, USA.
05	2	1862	Skirmish near Deep Gully, Trenton Road, NC, with Lieut. Charles H. Pope, 1st RI Lt Art, Corporal Martindale is killed instantly.
05	2	1862	Federal expedition from Trenton to Paris and Dresden, and skirmish near Lockridge's Mill, TN. 5/2-9/1862.
05	2	1862	Skirmishes at Trevillan's Depot and Louisa Court-House, VA.
05	3	1862	**Edward Otho Cresap Ord, U.S.A.** is appointed Maj. Gen.
05	3	1862	Skirmish at Batesville, AR, with Brig. Gen. Samuel Curtis, USA.
05	3	1862	The destruction of bridges on Lookout Creek, near Lookout Mountain, GA.
05	3	1862	Skirmish at Watkins' Ferry, GA.
05	3	1862	Federal reconnaissance to and skirmish at Farmington, MS, between Maj. Gen. Henry W. Halleck, USA, and Gen. P.G.T. Beauregard, CSA.
05	3	1862	Federal reconnaissances to the **Memphis and Charleston Railroad,** MS.

05	3	1862	**Yorktown, VA, is evacuated** by the Confederates, under Gen. Joseph E. Johnston, CSA, and Maj. Gen John Magruder, CSA, before Maj. Gen. George B. McClellan, USA, could use his heavy artillery siege guns.
05	3	1862	Martial law is proclaimed in Southwest Virginia.
05	4	1862	**Tucson, the New Mexico Territory, is evacuated** by the Confederate forces there.
05	4	1862	Skirmish at Farmington Heights, near Corinth, MS, by Maj. Gen. Henry W. Halleck, USA.
05	4	1862	Skirmish at Licking, MO.
05	4	1862	Federal raid on the **Mobile and Ohio Railroad** near Bethel and skirmish near Purdy, TN.
05	4	1862	Skirmish at Pulaski, TN.
05	4	1862	Skirmish at Columbia Bridge, VA.
05	4	1862	Federal reconnaissance to Culpeper Court-House, VA. 5/4-5/1862.
05	4	1862	**Yorktown, VA is occupied** by the Union forces, moving on toward Williamsburg, VA.
05	4	1862	Skirmishes near Williamsburg, VA, with Brig. Gen. George B. Stoneman, USA, Chief of Cavalry, and Brig. Gen. JEB Stuart, CSA, and his Confederate Cavalry.
05	4	1862	Skirmish at Franklin, WV.
05	4	1862	Skirmish at Princeton, WV.
05	5	1862	**Samuel Peter Heintzelman, U.S.A.,** is appointed Maj. Gen.
05	5	1862	Brig. Gen. James G. Blunt, USA, assumes the command of the Dept. of Kansas.
05	5	1862	Skirmish at Lockridge Mills, or Dresden, KY.
05	5	1862	Action at Lebanon, TN, with Brig. Gen. Ebenezer Dumont, USA.
05	5	1862	Col. Justus Steinberger, 1st Washington Territory Infantry, relieves Col. Albemarle Cady, 7th US Infantry, in command of the District of Oregon.
05	5	1862	**The Battle of Williamsburg, VA,** between Maj. Gens. James Longstreet and Daniel H. Hill, CSA, fighting a rear guard delaying action with the advancing Federals led by Joseph Hooker and Philip Kearney, under Maj. Gen. George B. McClellan, USA, the Peninsula Campaign.
05	5	1862	President Abraham Lincoln sails to Fortress Monroe, VA, to observe first hand the advance of the Army of the Potomac.
05	6	1862	Skirmish on White River, AR.
05	6	1862	**Williamsburg, VA, is occupied** by the Union forces, as the **Chocura, Sebago,** and the **USS Wachusett** sail up the York River, mostly unopposed, toward West Point, VA.
05	6	1862	Skirmish near Harrisonburg, VA, as Maj. Gen. Stonewall Jackson, CSA, moving from Conrad's Store, VA, forces Maj. Gen. Nathaniel P. Banks, USA, to withdraw toward Strasburg, VA, as Jackson turns his attention to the Union forces at McDowell, WV.
05	6	1862	Skirmish at Camp McDonald and Arnoldsburg, WV.
05	7	1862	Skirmish at Croghan's Ranch, CA.
05	7	1862	Maj. Gen. Braxton Bragg, CSA, assumes the command of the Confederate Army of the Mississippi.
05	7	1862	Skirmish at Horse Creek, MO.
05	7	1862	Federal expedition from Roanoke Island toward Gatesville, NC, by Col. Rush C. Hawkins, USA. 5/7-8/1862.
05	7	1862	Skirmish at Purdy, TN.
05	7	1862	Federal reconnaissance to Mulberry Point, James River, VA, by Maj. Robert Morris, USA, 6th PA Cav. 5/7-8/1862.
05	7	1862	Action at Somerville Heights, VA, on the south fork of the Shenandoah River, with Maj. Gen. Stonewall Jackson, CSA.
05	7	1862	**Engagement at West Point, Barhamsville, or Eltham's Landing, VA.** Maj. Gen. Gustavus Woodson Smith, CSA, retreating from **Williamsburg, VA,** and Brig. Gen. William Buel Franklin, USA, attacking the Confederate supply train.
05	7	1862	Skirmish at and near Wardensville, WV, Maj. Gen. John C. Fremont, USA, searching for guerrillas who murdered a party of officers, zouaves, and convalescent soldiers on their way from Winchester to Moorefield.
05	8	1862	Skirmish at Elkton Station, near Athens, AL.
05	8	1862	Confederate arsenal at **Baton Rouge, LA, is captured** by a landing party from the **USS Iroquois.**
05	8	1862	Federal reconnaissance toward Corinth, MS, by Maj. Gen. Henry W. Halleck, USA.
05	8	1862	Skirmish at Glendale, near Corinth, MS.
05	8	1862	**Engagement near McDowell (Bull Pasture Mountain), VA,** as Maj. Gen. Thomas Jonathan "Stonewall" Jackson, CSA, repulses and pursues Brig. Gen. Robert Cumming Schenck, USA, toward Franklin, WV.

05	8	1862	Maj. Gen. William W. Loring, CSA, is assigned to the command of the Army of Southwest Virginia.
05	8	1862	US Naval demonstration upon Sewell's Point, off Hampton, VA.
05	9	1862	**George William Tyler,** USA, is appointed Brig. Gen.
05	9	1862	**The Evacuation of Pensacola, FL, by the Confederates, and its occupation by the Union forces,** under Brig. Gen. Lewis G. Arnold, USA.
05	9	1862	Maj. Gen. David Hunter, USA, **orders the emancipation of all slaves** in Florida, Georgia, and South Carolina, and also authorizes the arming of all able-bodied negroes in those states, without the approval of President Abraham Lincoln.
05	9	1862	Skirmish near Corinth, MS, with Maj. Gen. Henry W. Halleck, USA, advancing against Gen. P. G. T. Beauregard, CSA.
05	9	1862	Engagement at Farmington, MS.
05	9	1862	Skirmish on the Elk River, near Bethel, TN.
05	9	1862	Skirmish near McDowell, WV, as Maj. Gen. Stonewall Jackson, CSA, pursues the retreating Federals toward Franklin, WV.
05	9	1862	**Norfolk, VA, is evacuated by the Confederate forces,** as the Confederates cede an important naval base to the Federals.
05	9	1862	Skirmish at Slatersville, or New Kent Court-House, VA.
05	10	1862	Skirmish at Lamb's Ferry, AL.
05	10	1862	Federal reconnaissance on the Alabama Road toward Sharp's Mill, MS.
05	10	1862	Skirmish near Farmington, MS.
05	10	1862	Skirmish near Bloomfield, MO, with the Union capture of Confederate supplies.
05	10	1862	Naval engagement at Plum Point, near Fort Pillow, TN, with the Confederate sinking of the Union ironclads, **USS Cincinnati,** and the **USS Mound City.**
05	10	1862	**Norfolk and Portsmouth, VA, are occupied** by the Union forces under Maj. Gen. John E. Wool, USA, as President Abraham Lincoln is on hand to personally observe the undertaking.
05	10	1862	Skirmishes near Franklin, WV, as Brig. Gen. Robert C. Schenck, USA, sends a party to kill bushwackers who beat one of his men to death. 5/10-12/1862.
05	10	1862	Action at Giles Court-House, WV, with Brig. Gen. Henry Heth, CSA.
05	11	1862	Brig. Gen. John Selden Roane, CSA, is assigned to the command in Arkansas.
05	11	1862	Affair at Cave City, KY, where Col. John Hunt Morgan, CSA, captured a passenger train on the **Louisville and Nashville Railroad,** KY.
05	11	1862	Skirmish at Pulaski, TN.
05	11	1862	With the loss of Norfolk, VA, the Confederates destroy their ironclad, the **CSS Merrimac, James River, VA,** as she no longer has a port to call home, and was forced to move up the James River into water too shallow; a Confederate frustration.
05	11	1862	Skirmish on Bowling Green Road, near Fredericksburg VA.
05	11	1862	Skirmish at Princeton, WV.
05	12	1862	Skirmish near Farmington, MS, between Gen. P.G.T. Beauregard, CSA, and Maj. Gen. Henry Wager Halleck, USA.
05	12	1862	**The Surrender of Natchez, MS,** is demanded, and subsequently **occupied** by the naval forces of the **USS Iroquois,** and the **USS Oneida,** under Flag Officer Daniel Farragut, USN. 5/12-13/1862.
05	12	1862	Skirmish at Monterey, TN.
05	12	1862	Skirmish at Lewisburg, WV.
05	13	1862	Federal **occupation of Rogersville** and skirmish at Lamb's Ferry, AL, with Brig. Gen. Ormsby Mitchel, USA. 5/13-14/1862.
05	13	1862	Federal raid on the **Memphis and Charleston Railroad** near Corinth, MS.
05	13	1862	The abduction of the Confederate steamer, **Planter,** from the Southern Wharf, Charleston Harbor, SC, by its' all black crew of 8.
05	13	1862	Skirmish at Baltimore Cross-Roads, near the New Kent Court-House, VA.
05	13	1862	Affair on Rappahannock River, VA, with Brig. Gen. Bayard, USA.
05	14	1862	Skirmish at Cotton Plant, AR.
05	14	1862	Skirmish with Indians at Angel's Ranch on the Mad River, CA.
05	14	1862	Skirmish on the **Memphis and Charleston Railroad,** near Corinth, MS, with Maj. Gen. Henry W. Halleck. USA.

05	14	1862	Skirmish at Fayetteville, TN.
05	14	1862	Federal raid on the **Mobile and Ohio Railroad,** TN.
05	14	1862	Skirmish at Gaines' Cross-Roads, VA, with Maj. Gen. George B. McClellan's, USA, advancing Federal army on Richmond, VA.
05	15	1862	**James Green Martin,** CSA, is appointed Brig. Gen.
05	15	1862	Skirmish at Chalk Bluff, AR, with the ferry there seized by the Federals.
05	15	1862	Col. James H. Carleton, 1st CA Infantry, relinquishes command of the District of Southern California.
05	15	1862	Federal expedition from California to the Arizona and New Mexico Territories, is organized as the Column from California, Col. James H. Carleton, 1st California Infantry, commanding.
05	15	1862	The infamous ironclad, **CSS Alabama,** is launched from its' berth at Liverpool, England.
05	15	1862	Maj. Gen. Benjamin F. Butler, USA, solidifies his notoriety in the south by issuing Order No. 28, which accuses any woman of pandering her profession who verbally insults any Federal soldier stationed at New Orleans, LA.
05	15	1862	Skirmish near Butler, Bates County, MO.
05	15	1862	Federal scout to Little Blue and skirmish near Independence, MO, with a Confederate ambush. 5/15-17/1862.
05	15	1862	Skirmishes near Trenton Bridge, at Young's Cross-Roads, and Pollocksville, NC, with Col. Thomas J. C. Amory, 17th MA Infantry, commanding 1st Brigade, 1st Division. 5/15-16/1862.
05	15	1862	Federal naval demonstration upon Galveston, TX.
05	15	1862	Federal reconnaissance toward the **Memphis and Charleston Railroad** and skirmish, TN.
05	15	1862	The engagement at **Fort Darling,** James River, VA, near Drewry's Bluffs, about 8 miles south of Richmond, VA, with Confederate defenses repulsing the following Union ironclads: **Aroostook, Galena, Maratanza, Monitor,** and the **Port Royal,** under Commander William Smith, USN, who is aboard the steamer **USS Wachusett.**
05	15	1862	Skirmish at Gaines' Cross-Roads, Rappahannock County, VA, as Gen. Joseph E. Johnston, CSA, withdraws his forces to within 3 miles of his nation's capitol, **Richmond, VA.**
05	15	1862	**Operations in the Shenandoah Valley, VA.** 5/15-6/17/1862.
05	15	1862	Maj. Gen. Thomas Jonathan "Stonewall" Jackson's, CSA, Confederate command returns from McDowell to the Shenandoah Valley, VA.
05	15	1862	Skirmish at Linden, VA, as Confederate guerrillas attack Brig. Gen. Jonathan Geary, USA.
05	15	1862	Actions at and in the vicinity of Princeton, and Ravenswood, WV, with Maj. Gen. John C. Fremont, USA. 05/15-17/1862.
05	15	1862	Skirmish at Ravenswood, WV.
05	15	1862	Action at Wolf Creek, WV, as Brig. Gen. Humphrey Marshall, CSA, under Brig. Gen. Henry Heth, CSA, is routed; Heth falls back to Jackson's River Depot.
05	16	1862	**Brig. Gen. Joseph Lewis Hogg, CSA,** dies from dysentery, near Shiloh, TN, shortly after joining Gen. Pierre Gustave Toutant Beauregard's, CSA, Confederate Army.
05	16	1862	**John Ellis Wool, U.S.A.,** is appointed Maj. Gen.
05	16	1862	Maj. Gen. Benjamin F. Butler, USA, continues his insult to the citizens of New Orleans by closing down two newspapers, the **Bee,** and the **Delta,** New Orleans, LA.
05	16	1862	Federal operations in Dunklin County, MO, and the capture of the Rebel steamer, **Daniel E. Miller,** at Hornersville, MO. 5/16-20/1862.
05	17	1862	**Thomas Lanier Clingman,** CSA, is appointed Brig. Gen.
05	17	1862	**Alvin Peterson Hovey,** USA, is appointed Brig. Gen.
05	17	1862	Skirmish on the Little Red River, AR, with the Confederate capture of a Union foraging party and wagons.
05	17	1862	Col. George W. Bowie, 5th California Infantry, assumes the command of the District of Southern California.
05	17	1862	Action at Russell's House, near Corinth, MS, with Maj. Gen. Henry Wager Halleck, USA, continuing to advance on Corinth.
05	17	1862	Federal expedition up the Pamunkey River, VA, aboard the tug boat, **Seth Lowe.**
05	17	1862	Maj. Gen. Irvin McDowell, USA, at Fredericksburg, VA, is ordered to form a junction with the Army of the Potomac and move upon Richmond, VA, in co-operation with Maj. Gen. George Brinton McClellan, USA.
05	18	1862	**Brig. Gen. William High Keim, USA,** dies at Harrisburg, PA, from camp fever (dysentery) developed during the Peninsula Campaign, VA.
05	18	1862	**Operations about Vicksburg, MS, and Baton Rouge, LA.** 5/18-8/6/1862 .
05	18	1862	The surrender of Vicksburg, MS, is demanded by Maj. Gen. Benjamin F. Butler, USA, and by Flag

Officer Daniel Farragut and refused by Brig. Gen. Martin Luther Smith, CSA.

05	18	1862	Federal reconnaissance toward Old Church and Cold Harbor, VA. 5/18-19/1862.
05	18	1862	Maj. Gen. William Buel Franklin, USA, assumes the command of the 6th US Army Corps, the Army of the Potomac, the Peninsula Campaign, VA.
05	18	1862	Brig. Gen. Fitz John Porter, USA, assumes the command of the 5th US Army Corps (which has been reorganized), the Peninsula Campaign, VA.
05	18	1862	Skirmish at Woodstock, VA, with Maj. Gen. Stonewall Jackson, CSA, and Maj. Gen. Nathaniel Prentiss Banks, USA.
05	19	1862	Skirmish at Searcy Landing, AR, a very bloody skirmish.
05	19	1862	President Abraham Lincoln modifies Maj. Gen. David Hunter's proclamation freeing slaves in his military Dept. of Georgia, South Carolina and Florida.
05	19	1862	Skirmish near Farmington, MS.
05	19	1862	Skirmish at Clinton, NC.
05	19	1862	Federal expedition down the Mississippi to Fort Pillow, TN, by Brig. Gen. Isaac F. Quinby, USA. 5/19-23/1862.
05	19	1862	Skirmish at City Point, James River, VA, with Capt. William H. Willis, CSA, 4th GA Infantry, attacking a Union landing party.
05	19	1862	Skirmish at Gaines' Mill, VA.
05	20	1862	**Tucson, the Arizona Territory, is occupied** by Union forces.
05	20	1862	President Abraham Lincoln, signs the **Homestead Act,** which opens up the Western Frontier, giving up to 160 acres to those willing to develop the land for a five year period, for a small fee.
05	20	1862	Affair on Crooked River, FL, where a Confederate ambush kills or captures most of Union landing party.
05	20	1862	Federal Gunboat (2) bombardment of Cole's Island, SC.
05	20	1862	Skirmish on Elk River, TN.
05	20	1862	Operations about Bottom's Bridge, Chickahominy River, VA, under Brig. Gen. Erasmus D. Keyes, USA, commanding the 4th US Army Corps, the Army of the Potomac. 5/20-23/1862.
05	20	1862	Federal raid on the **Virginia Central Railroad** at Jackson's River Depot, 10 miles from Covington, VA, to destroy bridges.
05	21	1862	Skirmish at Village Creek, AR.
05	21	1862	Skirmish at Widow Serratt's, near Corinth, MS, with Maj. Gen. Henry Wager Halleck, USA.
05	21	1862	Affair at Paraje, the New Mexico Territory.
05	21	1862	Affair near Battery Island, SC.
05	21	1862	The Union Army advances across Bottom's Bridge, on the Chickahominy River, VA.
05	21	1862	Confederate reconnaissance from Front Royal to Browntown, VA, as Maj. Gen. Richard S. Ewell, CSA, combines his forces under Maj. Gen. Thomas J. Jackson, CSA.
05	22	1862	Federal reconnaissance to Burnsville and Iuka, MS. 5/22-23/1862
05	22	1862	Skirmish near Farmington, MS, between Maj. Gen. Henry W. Halleck, USA, and Gen. P. G. T. Beauregard, CSA.
05	22	1862	Skirmish at Florida, MO.
05	22	1862	Skirmish at the Trenton and Pollocksville Cross-Roads, NC, near New Berne, NC.
05	22	1862	Confederate expedition to John's Island, SC, in search of Union landing parties to drive off.
05	22	1862	Skirmish at Winchester, TN.
05	22	1862	President Lincoln meets with Maj. Gen. Irvin McDowell, USA, at Fredericksburg, VA, to discuss strategy.
05	22	1862	Maj. Gen. Thomas J. Jackson, CSA, crosses Luray Gap, of the Massanutten Mountain, toward Front Royal, Shenandoah Valley, VA.
05	22	1862	Federal reconnaissance to New Castle and Hanovertown Ferries, VA, by Col. Richard H. Rush, 6th PA Cavalry. (Lancers).
05	23	1862	**Lafayette McLaws, C.S.A.,** is appointed Maj. Gen.
05	23	1862	The following are appointed Confederate Brigadier Generals:

Daniel Weisiger Adams,   CSA
Turner Ashby,   CSA
Samuel Garland, Jr.,   CSA
Wade Hampton,   CSA
Robert Hopkins Hatton,   CSA

05	23	1862	Affair near Fort Craig, the New Mexico Territory.

MONTH	DAY	YEAR	ACT
05	23	1862	Federal reconnaissance from Bottom's Bridge toward Richmond VA.
05	23	1862	Skirmish at Buckton Station, VA.
05	23	1862	Skirmish at Ellison's Mill near Mechanicsville, VA.
05	23	1862	**Action at Front Royal, VA,** as Maj. Gen. Stonewall Jackson, CSA, defeats Maj. Gen. Nathaniel Prentiss Banks, USA.
05	23	1862	Skirmish at Hogan's, near New Bridge, VA.
05	23	1862	Action at Lewisburg, WV, where Brig. Gen. Jacob D. Cox, USA, routs Brig. Gen. Henry Heth, CSA.
05	24	1862	Maj. Gen. Nathaniel Prentiss Banks', USA, command retreats to Williamsport, MD. 5/24-26/1862.
05	24	1862	Skirmish near Corinth, MS.
05	24	1862	Federal expedition to Spring Hill, MO, against Rebel jayhawkers.
05	24	1862	Skirmish at Winchester, TN.
05	24	1862	Skirmish at Berryville, VA, with Maj. Gen. Thomas J. Jackson, CSA.
05	24	1862	Federal reconnaissance toward Hanover Court-House, VA, by Col. Richard H. Rush, 6th PA Cavalry (Lancers).
05	24	1862	Skirmish at Linden, VA.
05	24	1862	Skirmish at Mechanicsville, VA.
05	24	1862	Action at Middletown, VA, with Maj. Gen. Thomas J. Jackson, CSA.
05	24	1862	Skirmish at New Bridge, VA, with Maj. Gen. George B. McClellan, USA.
05	24	1862	Action at Newtown, VA.
05	24	1862	Skirmish at Seven Pines, VA, with Maj. Gen. George B. McClellan, USA.
05	24	1862	Skirmish at Strasburg, VA, with Maj. Gen. Thomas Jackson, CSA.
05	24	1862	Maj. Gen. Irvin McDowell's, USA, orders to move upon Richmond, VA, in co-operation with the **Army of Potomac,** Maj. Gen. George B. McClellan, USA, commanding, are suspended. Maj. Gen. Irvin McDowell is ordered to put 20,000 men in motion for the Shenandoah Valley, VA, and to capture Maj. Gen. Thomas J. **"Stonewall"** Jackson, CSA.
05	24	1862	Maj. Gen. John Charles Fremont, USA, is ordered to move from Franklin, WV, against and to cut off Maj. Gen. Thomas Jonathan **"Stonewall"** Jackson, CSA, who is operating in the Shenandoah Valley, VA.
05	24	1862	**Operations about Harper's Ferry, WV.** 5/24-30/1862.
05	25	1862	Call is made by the US Secretary of War, **Edwin Stanton,** for all Volunteers and Militia in Illinois, Indiana, Iowa, Maine, Massachusetts, Michigan, New Hampshire, New York, Ohio, Pennsylvania, Rhode Island, Vermont and Wisconsin.
05	25	1862	Operations about Miami and Waverly, MO, and skirmish, with marauding rebels. 5/25-28/1862.
05	25	1862	Affair between James and Dixon's Islands, SC, with damage to the steamer, **Chesterfield.**
05	25	1862	Federal expedition from Bottom's Bridge to the James River, VA, by Lieut. Frank C. Davis, 3rd PA Cavalry. 5/25-26/1862.
05	25	1862	**Engagement at Winchester, VA,** as Maj. Gen. Nathaniel P. Banks', USA, men are routed by Maj. Gen. Thomas J. Jackson, CSA, and retreat toward Harper's Ferry, WV.
05	26	1862	**Ambrose Powell Hill, C.S.A.,** is appointed Maj. Gen.
05	26	1862	**Louis Hebert,** CSA, is appointed Brig. Gen.
05	26	1862	**John Creed Moore,** CSA, is appointed Brig. Gen.
05	26	1862	The Confederate Trans-Mississippi Dept. is extended to include Arkansas, the Indian Territory, Missouri, West Louisiana, and Texas.
05	26	1862	Skirmish at Calico Rock, AR.
05	26	1862	Federal reconnaissance from Jacksonport toward Augusta and Des Arc, AR, and skirmish at the Cache River Bridge, AR. **(May 28th).**
05	26	1862	Affair at Grand Gulf, MS.
05	26	1862	The Confederate Dept. No. 2 is extended to embrace Mississippi south of the 33d parallel and west of the Pascagoula and the Chickasawha Rivers, and Louisiana east of the Mississippi.
05	26	1862	Skirmish at Crow's Station, near Licking, MO, with a Rebel attack and partial destruction of the Union wagon train.
05	26	1862	Federal reconnaissance toward Hanover Court-House, VA.
05	26	1862	**Winchester, VA, is occupied** by Maj. Gen. Thomas J. "Stonewall" Jackson, CSA.
05	26	1862	Skirmish near Franklin, WV.
05	27	1862	Skirmish at Big Indian Creek, near Searcy Landing, White County, AR, with the Union forage train.
05	27	1862	Federal expeditions from Searcy Landing to West Point, Searcy, and Bayou Des Arc, AR, and skirmishes.

05	27	1862	Skirmish on Bridge Creek, near Corinth, MS.
05	27	1862	Skirmish at Monagan Springs, near Osceola, MO.
05	27	1862	Engagement at Hanover Court-House, VA, (27th) and operations **(28th-29th)** in that vicinity. 5/27-29/1862.
05	27	1862	Skirmish at Loudoun Heights, VA, by Maj. Gen. Thomas J. Jackson, CSA, advancing upon Harper's Ferry, WV, and as Maj. Gen. Nathaniel P. Banks, USA, retreats across the Potomac River, at Williamsport, MD.
05	27	1862	Skirmish at Slash Church, VA.
05	27	1862	Skirmish at White Oaks, VA.
05	28	1862	The Confederate District of West Louisiana is constituted, under the command of Brig. Gen. Paul O. Hebert.
05	28	1862	Skirmishes in front of Corinth, MS, Maj. Gen. Henry W. Halleck, USA, advancing against Gen. P. G. T. Beauregard, CSA.
05	28	1862	The destruction of the Confederate supplies at Ashland, VA.
05	28	1862	The **Virginia Central Railroad** Bridge, on the South Anna River, VA, is destroyed by Union forces.
05	28	1862	Skirmish at Charlestown, WV, with Maj. Gen. Thomas **"Stonewall"** Jackson, CSA.
05	29	1862	Skirmish at Whitesburg, AL.
05	29	1862	Skirmish at the Kickapoo Bottom, near Sylamore, and west of Searcy, AR.
05	29	1862	Skirmish near Booneville, MS.
05	29	1862	Skirmishes in front of Corinth, MS.
05	29	1862	Skirmish at Pocotaligo, SC.
05	29	1862	The **Richmond and Fredericksburg Railroad** Bridge, on the South Anna River, VA, is destroyed.
05	29	1862	Skirmish near Seven Pines, on the Chickahominy River, VA.
05	29	1862	Skirmish near Wardensville, WV.
05	30	1862	**The Capture of Booneville, MS.**
05	30	1862	**Corinth, MS, is evacuated** by the Confederates and **occupied** by Maj. Gen. Henry W. Halleck, USA, as Gen. P.G.T. Beauregard, CSA, retreats toward Tupelo, MS.
05	30	1862	The Federal destruction of the Cypress Creek and Tuscumbia Bridges, near Booneville, MS.
05	30	1862	Skirmish at Tranter's Creek, near Washington, NC, with Capt. George F. Jocknick, 3rd NY Cavalry.
05	30	1862	Martial law is declared in Texas.
05	30	1862	Skirmish near Fair Oaks, VA.
05	30	1862	**Action at Front Royal, VA,** as Brig. Gen. James Shields, USA, **occupies** the town.
05	30	1862	Skirmish near Zuni, VA.
05	30	1862	Skirmish at Lewisburg, WV.
05	30	1862	Federal raid to Shaver's River, WV, against guerrillas.
05	31	1862	**Silas Casey,** **U.S.A.** is appointed Maj. Gen.
05	31	1862	**Edwin Vose Sumner,** **U.S.A.,** is appointed Maj. Gen.
05	31	1862	**Edward Richard Sprigg Canby,** USA, is appointed Brig. Gen.
05	31	1862	Skirmish with Indians on the Eel River, near Van Dusen's Creek, CA.
05	31	1862	Skirmish at Tuscumbia Creek, MS.
05	31	1862	Maj. Gen. Thomas Carmichael Hindman, CSA, assumes the command of the Trans-Mississippi District.
05	31	1862	Skirmish on Salt River, near Florida, MO.
05	31	1862	Skirmish near Neosho, MO, with Rebel guerrillas, and Confederate aligned **Cherokees** under Stand Watie.
05	31	1862	Skirmish near Waynesville, MO.
05	31	1862	**The Battle of Fair Oaks, or Seven Pines, VA,** as Gen. Joseph Johnston, CSA, attacks the two isolated advanced Union corps across the rising Chickahominy River under Maj. Gens. Samuel P. Heintzelman and Erasmus Keyes, USA. Maj. Gen. Edwin V. Sumner, USA, moving across the Chickahominy River to deflect any further Confederate attacks, with Gen. Joseph E. Johnston, CSA, seriously wounded in the action taking place, being replaced the next day by Robert E. Lee, CSA, who breaks off the attack. 5/31-6/1/1862.
05	31	1862	**Brig. Gen. Robert Hopkins Hatton, C.S.A.,** is instantly killed during the intense fighting at the Battle of Fair Oaks, VA, in thick underbrush, only 8 days after receiving his commission as brigadier general.
05	31	1862	Skirmish near Front Royal, VA.
05	31	1862	Maj. Gen. Thomas J. **"Stonewall"** Jackson's CSA, retires from Winchester, VA.
06	1	1862	**Joseph Hooker, U.S.A.,** is appointed Maj. Gen.
06	1	1862	Operations in Oregon County, MO, and skirmish at Eleven Points, MO, with Union forages and guerrillas. 6/1-5/1862.
06	1	1862	**Gen. Robert Edward Lee, CSA, assumes the command of the Confederate Army of Northern**

<u>Virginia.</u>

06	1	1862	The Dept. of Virginia is extended and embraced in Maj. Gen. George Brinton McClellan's command, Maj. Gen. John Ellis Wool, USA, being assigned to the Middle Dept. and Maj. Gen. John Adams Dix, USA, to the command at Fortress Monroe, VA.
06	1	1862	Federal reconnaissance beyond Seven Pines, VA. 6/1-2/1862.
06	1	1862	Skirmish at Mount Carmel, on the Strasburg and Stauton Road, near Strasburg, VA; Maj. Gen. Thomas Jonathan "Stonewall" Jackson, CSA, vs. Maj. Gen. Irvin McDowell, USA.
06	2	1862	Affair at Galloway's Farm near Jacksonport, AR, with the advance guard of Maj. Gen. Earl Van Dorn, CSA.
06	2	1862	Skirmish on the Little Blue, Jackson County, MO.
06	2	1862	Skirmish at Tranter's Creek, NC.
06	2	1862	Federal expedition to Wormley's Ferry, Pamunkey River, VA.
06	2	1862	Skirmishes at Strasburg and Woodstock, VA, with Maj. Gen. Thomas J. Jackson, CSA.

06 3 1862   The following are appointed Confederate Brigadier Generals:

      James Jay Archer,   CSA
      James Lawson Kemper,   CSA
      William Dorsey Pender,   CSA
      Ambrose Ransom Wright,   CSA

06	3	1862	Col. George F. Shepley, 12th Maine Infantry, is appointed the Military Governor of Louisiana.
06	3	1862	Affair near Rienzi, MS, with Maj. Gen. John Pope, USA.
06	3	1862	Federal reconnaissance toward Baldwyn and Carrollsville, MS.
06	3	1862	Skirmish on James Island, SC, at Legare's Point, near Charleston, SC.
06	3	1862	**Fort Pillow, TN, near Memphis, TN, is evacuated** by the Confederates and **occupied** by the Union forces as the Federals continue their attempt to capture Memphis, TN. 6/3-5/1862.
06	3	1862	North Carolina, west of the Blue Ridge, is added to the Dept. of East Tennessee.
06	3	1862	Action near Harrisonburg, VA.
06	3	1862	Maj. Gen. George McClellan, USA, orders a reconnaissance to the James River, VA, to communicate with the Union fleet. 6/3-7/1862 .
06	3	1862	Skirmish at Mount Jackson, VA, with Maj. Gen. Thomas J. "Stonewall" Jackson, CSA.
06	3	1862	Skirmish at Tom's Brook, VA, with Maj. Gen. Thomas J. "Stonewall" Jackson, CSA.
06	4	1862	Skirmishes at Huntsville, AL, with Maj. Gen. Ormsby M. Mitchel, USA. 6/4-5/1862.
06	4	1862	Skirmish at Woodville, AL.
06	4	1862	Skirmishes at Osborn's and Wolf's Creeks, Blackland, MS.
06	4	1862	Federal scouts to Miami, Cambridge, Frankfort, Waverly, Pink Hill, etc. MO. 6/4-10/1862.
06	4	1862	Skirmish at Sweeden's Cove, near Jasper, TN, with Maj. Gen. Orsby M. Mitchel, USA.
06	4	1862	Skirmish at Big Bend, WV, with Maj. Gen. Thomas J. Jackson, CSA, as he continued to pull back up the Shenandoah Valley, VA.
06	5	1862	Skirmish at Little Red River, AR.
06	5	1862	Skirmish at Round Grove, the Indian Territory.
06	5	1862	Skirmish near Sedalia, MO.
06	5	1862	Action at Tranter's Creek, NC, with Lieut. Col. Francis A. Osborn, 24th MA Infantry.
06	5	1862	Skirmish at New Bridge, VA.
06	6	1862	Skirmishes with Indians at Daley's Ferry and on the Mad River, near Arcata, CA. 6/6-7/1862.
06	6	1862	Skirmish at Grand River, Indian Territory.
06	6	1862	Skirmish near Tompkinsville, KY, with Col. Edward C. Williams, 9th PA Cavalry.
06	6	1862	Federal reconnaissance from Booneville toward Baldwyn, MS, and skirmish.
06	6	1862	Action near Harrisonburg, VA, with Maj. Gen. T. Jackson, CSA.
06	6	1862	**Brig. Gen. Turner Ashby, C.S.A.,** is mortally wounded while fighting a rear guard action, while defending Maj. Gen. Stonewall Jackson's CSA, withdrawal up the Shenandoah Valley toward Port Republic, a few miles south of the town of Harrisonburg, VA.
06	6	1862	Affair at Port Royal Ferry, SC, where a Rebel landing party burns the ferry-house and crossing flats used by the Federals.
06	6	1862	Naval engagement off Memphis, TN, and the **occupation of Memphis** by the Union forces, which effectively opens up the Mississippi River in this area. Union gunboats involved included: **USS Benton, Carondelet, Cairo, Louisville,** and the **St. Louis,** in addition to the **US Rams, Monarch** and the **Queen of the West.**

06	7	1862	Skirmishes at Fairview and Little Red River, AR.
06	7	1862	Skirmish in the Mattole Valley, CA.
06	7	1862	Federal expedition from Baton Rouge, LA. 6/7-9/1862.
06	7	1862	Maj. Gen. Benjamin Franklin Butler, USA, orders the **hanging of** a **William B. Mumford** for the removal of the US flag flying over the US Mint, New Orleans, LA.
06	7	1862	Skirmish on John's Island, SC.
06	7	1862	Federal attack on Chattanooga, TN, by Maj. Gen. Ormsby M. Mitchel, USA; Maj. Gen. E. Kirby Smith, CSA, defending. 6/7-8/1862.
06	7	1862	The Federal **capture of Jackson, TN.**
06	7	1862	Skirmish at Readyville, TN.
06	7	1862	Federal cavalry reconnaissance on the east bank of the Chickahominy River, near the outskirts of Richmond, VA.
06	7	1862	Skirmish near Harrisonburg, VA, with Maj. Gen. Thomas J. **"Stonewall"** Jackson, CSA.
06	7	1862	Skirmish at Big Bend, WV.
06	8	1862	Martial law is declared in Arizona.
06	8	1862	Skirmish at Fawn Prairie, near Liscombe's Hill, CA.
06	8	1862	The Dept. of the Mississippi is extended (in orders) to embrace all of Kentucky and Tennessee.
06	8	1862	Affairs on John's Island, near Secessionville, SC, with the Federals withdrawing to Legareville, SC. 6/8-9/1862.
06	8	1862	**The Battle of Cross Keys, VA,** as Maj. Gen. Charles Fremont's, USA, attack is repulsed by Maj. Gen. Richard S. Ewell, CSA, a part of Maj. Gen. Thomas J. Jackson's, CSA, command.
06	8	1862	**Engagement at Port Republic, VA,** as Maj. Gen. Thomas J. Jackson, CSA, defeats Maj. Gen. James Shields, USA, column under Brig. Gen. Erastus B. Tyler, as the **Federal plan** to destroy Jackson from two directions in a pincher movement **is a total failure.** 6/8-9/1862.
06	8	1862	The rearrangement of the Mountain Dept. and the Dept. of the Shenandoah, VA.
06	8	1862	Maj. Gen. Irvin McDowell USA, is ordered, under the conditions stated, to operate in the direction of Richmond, VA, to aid Maj. Gen. George B. McClellan, USA, and break off his combined pursuit with Maj. Gens. Charles Fremont, and James Shields, USA, of Maj. Gen. Thomas J. Jackson, CSA, in the Shenandoah Valley, VA.
06	8	1862	Skirmish near Fair Oaks, VA, with Maj. Gen. McClellan, USA.
06	8	1862	Federal reconnaissance on the New Market Road, VA.
06	8	1862	Skirmish at Big Bend, WV.
06	8	1862	Skirmish at Muddy Creek, about 1 mile from Palestine, WV.
06	9	1862	**George Burgwyn Anderson,** CSA, is appointed Brig. Gen.
06	9	1862	**Beverly Holcombe Robertson,** CSA, is appointed Brig. Gen.
06	9	1862	The following are appointed Union Brigadier Generals:
			Stephen Gano Burbridge, USA
			George Henry Gordon, USA
			Charles Griffin, USA
			Julius White, USA
06	9	1862	Federal reconnaissance to Baldwyn and Guntown, MS, south of Corinth, MS, and skirmish. 6/9-10/1862.
06	9	1862	Engagement at Grand Gulf, MS, with Confederate shore batteries and the **USS Itasca** and the **USS Wissahickon.**
06	9	1862	Maj. Gen. John Ellis Wool, USA, assumes the command of the Middle Military Dept., VA.
06	9	1862	Maj. Gen. Shield's US division is ordered back to Luray, en route for Fredericksburg, VA.
06	9	1862	Maj. Gen. Thomas Jonathan **"Stonewall"** Jackson, CSA's **Valley Campaign** is effectively and successfully ended.
06	10	1862	Operations on the White River, AR, 8 miles below Saint Charles, with the disabling of the gunboat, **USS Mound City.** 6/10-7/14/1862.
06	10	1862	Skirmish on James Island, SC, near Charleston, SC, with Union pickets.
06	10	1862	Skirmish at Rogers' Gap, TN.
06	10	1862	Skirmish at Wilson's Gap, TN.
06	10	1862	Skirmish at Winchester, TN.
06	10	1862	Maj. Gens. Ulysses Simpson Grant, Don Carlos Buell, and John Pope, USA, are ordered to resume the command of their separate Union Army Corps, TN, etal.

| 06 | 10 | 1862 | Skirmish at the mouth of West Fork, WV. |
| 06 | 11 | 1862 | The following are appointed Union Brigadier Generals: |

Washington Lafayette Elliott, USA
Albion Parris Howe, USA
Green Clay Smith, USA

06	11	1862	Federal expedition from Camp Latham to Owen's River, CA, with skirmish **(June 24)** at Owen's Lake. 6/11-10/8/1862.
06	11	1862	Skirmish with hostile Indians on the Mad River, CA.
06	11	1862	Skirmishes in Big Creek Gap, KY. 6/11-13/1862.
06	11	1862	Skirmish near Monterey, Owen County, KY.
06	11	1862	Skirmish near Booneville, MS.
06	11	1862	Skirmish near Cassville, MO, with Rebel guerrillas.
06	11	1862	Skirmish at Deep Water, MO, with Rebels who crossed the Osage at Taberville.
06	11	1862	Skirmish at Pink Hill, MO, with **William Clake Quantrill's** guerrillas attacking the Federal mail escort between Independence and Harrisonville.
06	11	1862	Skirmishes in Big Creek Gap, TN 6/11-12/1862.
06	11	1862	Maj. Gen. John Charles Fremont's, US Army, is withdrawn to Mount Jackson, VA. 6/11-12/1862.
06	11	1862	Confederate re-enforcements are sent from the Army of Northern Virginia to the Valley District, VA.
06	12	1862	Skirmish near Jacksonport, AR.
06	12	1862	Skirmish at Waddell's Farm, near Village Creek, AR, as the Federals load up their 36 wagons with confiscated corn and bacon, compliments of Mr. Waddell.
06	12	1862	Federal reconnaissance on Hutchinson's Island, SC.
06	12	1862	Brig. Gen. George Archibald McCall's, USA, division re-enforces the Army of the Potomac, VA. 6/12-13/1862.
06	12	1862	Maj. Gen. Thomas Jonathan "Stonewall" Jackson's CSA, command encamps near Weyer's Cave, VA.
06	13	1862	Affair at White House, near Hilton Head, SC.
06	13	1862	**Maj. Gen. James Ewell Brown Stuart's, CSA, Cavalry Raid** around Maj. Gen. George Brinton McClellan, USA, and the Army of the Potomac, threatens the US supply lines, and lowers Federal morale, with the following skirmishes: a) at Hawes' Shop, b) Old Church, and c) at Garlick's Landing, VA. 6/13-15/1862.
06	13	1862	Skirmish near Mount Jackson, VA.
06	13	1862	Skirmish at New Market, VA.
06	14	1862	Federal expedition from Pensacola to Milton, FL. 6/14-15/1862.
06	14	1862	Skirmish at Clear Creek, near Baldwyn, MS, with Col. John F. Lay, CSA.
06	14	1862	Confederate bushwackers fire into a railroad train near Turnstall Station, VA, killing 4 and wounding 8.
06	15	1862	The US Naval descent upon and bombardment of Saint Mark's, FL.
06	15	1862	The Federal expedition to Holly Springs and skirmish at the Tallahatchie Bridge, MS, with Brig. Gen. William T. Sherman, USA. 6/15-18/1862.
06	15	1862	Action at Big Creek Gap, TN.
06	15	1862	Parley between Brig. Gen. Howell Cobb, CSA, and Col. Thomas M. Key, USA, under flag of truce, with discussions for the exchange of prisoners, VA.
06	15	1862	Federal reconnaissance to the vicinity of New Market, VA.
06	15	1862	Skirmish near Seven Pines, VA, with Brig. Gen. Daniel E. Sickles, USA, commanding the 2nd Brigade, as Maj. Gen. George B. McClellan, USA, continues on his campaign for Richmond, VA.
06	16	1862	Federal scout from Batesville to Fairview, Denmark, Hilcher's Ferry, and Bush's Ford, AR. 6-17/1862.
06	16	1862	The **Emigrant Road expedition** from Omaha, Nebraska Territory, to Portland, Oregon Territory. 6/16-10/30/1862.
06	16	1862	The engagement at Secessionville, James Island, SC, results in Brig. Gen. Nathan G. Evans, CSA, repulsing Brig. Gen. Henry W. Benham, USA, who disobeyed orders and attacked.
06	16	1862	Skirmish at Winchester, TN.
06	17	1862	Engagement at Saint Charles, White River, AR, with the US Gunboats: **Conestoga, Lexington, Mound City,** and **St. Louis,** the **Mound City's** boiler explodes, killing/wounding 100 men.
06	17	1862	Skirmish near Smithville, AR, killing a few bushwackers.

06	17	1862	Skirmish at Pass Manchac, LA, where Union forces with the help of the Union gunboat, **New London,** attack the Confederate positions.
06	17	1862	Gen. Braxton Bragg, CSA, temporarily supersedes the ailing Gen. P.G.T. Beauregard, CSA, in the command of Dept. No. 2, or the Western Dept., around Tupelo, MS, etal.
06	17	1862	Skirmish at Eminence, MO.
06	17	1862	Skirmish near Warrensburg, MO, with Rebel bushwackers.
06	17	1862	Maj. Gen. Thomas Jackson's CSA forces move from Weyer's Cave for the Virginia Peninsula, to assist **Gen. Robert E. Lee,** CSA, and the **Army of Northern Virginia's** attempt to repulse the **Army of the Potomac's** advance on Richmond, VA, under Maj. Gen. George McClellan, USA.
06	17	1862	Maj. Gen. Charles Fremont, USA, resigns his position after refusing to serve under Maj. Gen. John Pope, USA, who Lincoln is bringing east to command the **newly created Army of Virginia.** Fremont is replaced by Maj. Gen. Franz Sigel, USA.
06	18	1862	Skirmish at Wilson's Gap, KY, and TN, and the **occupation of Cumberland Gap** by Brig. Gen. George W. Morgan, USA.
06	18	1862	Skirmish at Hambright's Station, MO.
06	18	1862	Brig. Gen. Paul O. Hebert, CSA, assumes command of the District of Texas.
06	18	1862	**The Reserve Army Corps,** under the command of Brig. Gen. Samuel D. Sturgis, USA, is constituted, VA.
06	18	1862	Skirmish near Fair Oaks, VA with Brig. Gen. Joseph Hooker,USA.
06	18	1862	Skirmish on the Nine Mile or the Williamsburg Road, near Richmond, VA, with Brig. Gen. J. B. Kershaw, CSA.
06	18	1862	Skirmish near Winchester, VA.
06	19	1862	Federal expedition to the Blue Mountains and skirmish near Knight's Cove, AR, with Rebel guerrillas.
06	19	1862	Skirmish on the Charles City Road, near Richmond, VA, as Col. William L. Brown, USA, 20th IN Infantry withdraws.
06	19	1862	Skirmish near Winchester, VA.
06	19	1862	President Abraham Lincoln signed into law legislation prohibiting slavery in all US territories.
06	20	1862	Affairs in Owen County, KY, and skirmish near Lusby's Mill, with Confederate guerrillas. 6/20-23/1862.
06	20	1862	Skirmish at Bayou des Allemands, LA.
06	20	1862	**Federal expedition from Baton Rouge, LA, to Vicksburg, MS,** with joint operations under Admiral Daniel Farragut and Brig. Gen. Thomas Williams, USA. 6/20-7/24/1862.
06	20	1862	Maj. Gen. John P. McCown, CSA, assumes the command of the Army of the West, MS, etal.
06	20	1862	Gen. Braxton Bragg, CSA, is assigned to the command of Dept. No. 2, Maj. Gen. Earl Van Dorn, CSA, is transferred to the command of the Dept. of Southern Mississippi and East Louisiana, which includes the defenses of Vicksburg, MS.
06	20	1862	Affair at Gill's Bluff, James River, VA.
06	20	1862	Artillery affair near New Bridge, VA.
06	21	1862	Federal expedition to Hernando, MS, with skirmish at Coldwater Station, MS, as the Union attempt to ambush M. Jeff Thompson's Confederate guerrillas, meets with limited success.
06	21	1862	Engagement at Simmons' Bluff, SC, with Federal gunboats.
06	21	1862	Skirmish at Rankin's Ferry, near Jasper, TN.
06	21	1862	Skirmish at Battle Creek, TN.
06	21	1862	The Confederate Dept. of North Carolina is extended to the south bank of the James River, VA.
06	21	1862	Skirmish near Fair Oaks Station, VA.
06	22	1862	Skirmish at Bayou des Allemands or Raceland, near Algiers, LA.
06	22	1862	Federal expedition from Ship Island, aboard the steamer, **Creole,** to Pass Christian, MS, to capture any Rebel vessels in the vicinity. None around.
06	22	1862	Federal scout from Strasburg to Moorefield and New Creek, WV, and Winchester, VA. 6/22-30/1862.
06	22	1862	Federal reconnaissance to the left of White Oak Swamp, VA, about 16 miles south of Richmond, VA, with Brig. Gen. Erasmus D. Keyes, USA, under Maj. Gen. George B. McClellan, USA. 6/22-23/1862.
06	23	1862	**John Robert Jones,** CSA, is appointed Brig. Gen.
06	23	1862	Federal reconnaissance toward Augusta, AR.
06	23	1862	Skirmish at Pineville, MO, with a rout of the Confederates.
06	23	1862	Skirmish near Raytown, MO, results in a Union retreat.
06	23	1862	Operations about Sibley and Pink Hill, MO, including the capture of certain Confederates implicated in capturing and plundering the steamer, **Little Blue.** 6/23-7/1/1862.

06	23	1862	Brig. Gen. Benjamin Alvord, USA, is assigned to the command of the District of Oregon.
06	23	1862	Operations around New Kent Court-House, VA, as Capt. Robert B. Ward, 11th PA Cavalry, moves to capture a Pro-south Mr. Toler.
06	23	1862	President Lincoln leaves Washington, DC, for New York and West Point, to confer with retired Bvt. Lieut. Gen. Winfield Scott, USA, on the current state of military affairs.
06	24	1862	Skirmish at Hamilton's Plantation, near Grand Gulf MS.
06	24	1862	Federal reconnaissance from Washington to Tranter's Creek, NC, by Capt. George F. Jocknick, 3rd NY Cavalry Company I.
06	24	1862	Skirmish near Mechanicsville, VA, just north of Richmond, VA.
06	24	1862	Skirmish at Milford, VA, with Maj. Charles H. Town, 1st MI Cavalry.
06	24	1862	The **Confederate troops evacuate White House Landing, VA,** as Maj. Gen. George McClellan, USA, continues his approach on Richmond.
06	25	1862	Skirmish at Yellville, on the Little Red River, AR.
06	25	1862	Skirmish near Pensacola, FL.
06	25	1862	The Confederate Dept. No. 1 is merged into Dept. No. 2, under the command of General Braxton Bragg, CSA, MS, etal.
06	25	1862	Affair near La Fayette Station, about a mile from Germantown, TN, as Confederate Cavalry derail and burn a train.
06	25	1862	The **Army of Virginia,** under the command of Maj. Gen. John Pope, USA, and the **1st, 2nd and 3rd US Army Corps of Virginia** are constituted.
06	25	1862	**The Seven Days Battles, VA.** 6/25-7/1/1862.
06	25	1862	Engagement at Oak Grove, King's School-House, French's Field, or the Orchard, VA, between Maj. Gen. Benjamin Huger, CSA, and Maj. Gen. Samuel P. Heintzelman, USA. (7 Days Battle)
06	25	1862	Skirmish near Ashland, VA.
06	25	1862	Skirmish at Mungo Flats, WV.
06	25	1862	President Lincoln returns to Washington, DC, from West Point, after visiting with retired Bvt. Lieut. Gen. Winfield Scott, USA.
06	26	1862	Skirmish at Cherry Grove, Schuyler County, MO.
06	26	1862	Engagement at Point of Rocks, Appomattox River, VA.
06	26	1862	**The Battle of Mechanicsville, Beaver Dam Creek, or Ellison's Mill, VA,** as Maj. Gen. A. P. Hill crosses the Chickahominy River at Meadow Bridge, and pushes Brig. Gen. Fitz John Porter, USA, out of Mechanicsville back to Beaver Dan Creek and Ellison's Mill, VA.
06	26	1862	Skirmish at Meadow Bridge, near Mechanicsville, VA.
06	26	1862	Gen. George Stoneman's USA operations, including the destruction of stores at White House Landing, VA, as Maj. Gen. George B. McClellan, USA, decides to move his base of operations from the Pamunkey to Harrison's Landing, on the James River, VA. 6/26-7/2/1862.
06	26	1862	Skirmish at Atlee's Station, VA, on the **Virginia Central Railroad.**
06	26	1862	Skirmish near Hanover Court-House, VA.
06	26	1862	Skirmishes at Hundley's Corner, VA. 6/26-27/1862.
06	26	1862	The Mountain Dept. and the Dept. of the Rappahannock and of the Shenandoah are merged into the Army of Virginia.
06	26	1862	Maj. Gens. Nathaniel P. Banks and Irvin McDowell, USA, assume command of the 2nd and 3rd US Army Corps, the newly created Army of VA.
06	27	1862	Skirmish at Stewart's Plantation, AR, with a Rebel ambush of a Union forage train, about 8 miles from Village Creek.
06	27	1862	Federal reconnaissance to the Williams' Bridge, Amite River, LA, and skirmish. 6/27-29/1862.
06	27	1862	Gen. Braxton Bragg assumes permanent command of Confederate Dept. No. 2, MS, as Federal mortars continued to bombard Vicksburg, MS.
06	27	1862	**The Battle of Gaines' Mill, Cold Harbor, or the Chickahominy River, VA,** as Brig. Gens. John Bell Hood, and George Pickett, CSA, finally break through Brig. Gen. Fitz John Porter's, USA, lines; Maj. Gen. Thomas J. Jackson, CSA, again failing to attack in a timely matter.
06	27	1862	Skirmish at Fair Oaks, VA, with Maj. Gen. John Magruder, CSA.
06	27	1862	Action at Garnett's Farm, VA, with the Federals retreating toward Harrison Landing, VA, and the protection of US Gunboats.
06	28	1862	Skirmishes at and near Blackland, MS, as Confederate Cavalry attack Brig. Gen. William S. Rosecrans',

			USA, cavalry pickets here.
06	28	1862	The Federal naval bombardment of Vicksburg, MS, and the passage of the batteries by the Union fleet under Admiral Daniel Farragut, USN.
06	28	1862	Operations in Johnson County, MO, with Federal orders to shoot every armed bushwacker on the spot, which occurs. 6/28-29/1862.
06	28	1862	The Federal **evacuation of James Island, SC,** and the current halt to the Union's attempt to capture Charleston, SC. 6/28-7/7/1862.
06	28	1862	Skirmish at Sparta, TN.
06	28	1862	Confederate Department No. 2 is extended, TN, etal.
06	28	1862	Skirmish at Dispatch Station, on the **Richmond and York Railroad,** VA, with Maj. Gen. George McClellan, USA.
06	28	1862	Federal naval expedition from Fort Monroe, VA, to open up communications with the retreating Army of the Potomac, from Richmond, towards Harrison Landing, VA. 6/28-7/4/1862.
06	28	1862	Action at Garnett's and Golding's Farms, VA, as Maj. Gen. George B. McClellan, USA, continues his retreat to the James River, at **Harrison Landing,** or also known as **Berkeley Plantation, VA.**
06	29	1862	The capture of the British steamer, **Ann,** a blockade runner, under the guns of Fort Morgan, AL.
06	29	1862	The Confederate Dept. of Alabama, and West Florida is discontinued.
06	29	1862	Federal reconnaissance from Front Royal to Luray, VA, and skirmish. 6/29-30/1862.
06	29	1862	Skirmish on the James River Road, near Willis' Church, VA.
06	29	1862	Skirmish at Jordan's Ford, VA.
06	29	1862	**The Battle of Savage Station,** on the **Richmond and York River Railroad, VA.**
06	29	1862	**Brig. Gen. Richard Griffith, C.S.A.,** is mortally wounded at the Battle of Savage Station, and is transported to, but dies the same day in Richmond, VA.
06	29	1862	**The Engagement at Peach Orchard, or Allen's Farm, near Fair Oaks Station, VA,** as Gen. Robert E. Lee, CSA, continues to press on against the retreating Army of the Potomac.
06	29	1862	Skirmish on the Williamsburg Road, near Fair Oaks Station, VA.
06	29	1862	Maj. Gen. Franz Sigel, US Army, assumes the command of the 1st US Army Corp, the Army of Virginia.
06	29	1862	Affair at Moorefield, WV.
06	30	1862	**William Bowen Campbell,** USA, is appointed Brig. Gen.
06	30	1862	Skirmish at Adams' Bluff, AR.
06	30	1862	The Federal naval bombardment of Tampa, FL. 6/30-7/1/1862.
06	30	1862	Skirmish at Henderson, KY.
06	30	1862	Affair at Powell River, TN.
06	30	1862	Skirmish at Rising (or Morning) Sun, TN, as Confederate Cavalry harass Maj. Gen. Ulysses S. Grant's, USA, supply train.
06	30	1862	**The Battle of Glendale, Nelson's Farm, Charles City Cross-Roads, New Market Cross Roads, Frazier's Farm, White Oak Swamp, Turkey Bend, or Willis' Church, VA,** as Maj. Gen. George B. McClellan, USA, repulses Maj. Gen. James Longstreet, CSA, with McClellan retreating to Malvern Hill.
06	30	1862	Skirmish at Jones' Bridge, VA.
06	30	1862	Skirmish near New Kent Court-House, VA.
06	30	1862	Engagement at Turkey Bridge, or Malvern Cliff, VA.
06	30	1862	Engagement at White Oak Swamp Bridge, VA.
07	1	1862	**Philip Henry Sheridan,** USA, is appointed Brig. Gen.
07	1	1862	**James Madison Tuttle,** USA, is appointed Brig. Gen.
07	1	1862	Action near Booneville, MS, where Brig. Gen. Philip H. Sheridan, USA, defeats Confederate forces there.
07	1	1862	Skirmish near Holly Springs, MS.
07	1	1862	The naval fleets under Flag Officers Daniel Farragut and Charles Davis, USN, combine forces north of Vicksburg, MS, on the Mississippi River.
07	1	1862	Skirmish at Cherry Grove, Schuyler County, MO, 6 miles from the Iowa border, with Rebel marauders.
07	1	1862	**The Battle of Malvern Hill, or Crew's or Poindexter's Farm, VA,** (day 7 of the Seven Days' Battle), with Maj. Gen. George B. McClellan, USA, inflicting severe casualties on Gen. Robert E. Lee's charging Confederates, and Gen. Lee retreating. Lee will repeat the same mistake a year later, at Gettysburg, PA. Lee does end the immediate Federal threat on Richmond, VA, as the 7 Days' Battle produced approximately 36,000 total Confederate and Union casualties.
07	1	1862	Skirmish near Fort Furnace, Powell's Big Fort Valley, VA, with Brig. Gen. John W. Geary, USA.

MONTH	DAY	YEAR	ACT
07	1	1862	The US Government approves the building of a trans-continental railroad across the west, which will become the **Union Pacific and the Central Pacific Railroad.**
07	1	1862	The US Government enacts the first Federal Income Tax Law.
07	2	1862	Skirmish at Huntsville, AL.
07	2	1862	Attack on Cutterback's House on Van Dusen's Creek, CA.
07	2	1862	The **Confederate Districts of the Mississippi and of the Gulf** are constituted, under the command of Maj. Gen. Van Dorn and Brig. Gen. John H. Forney, CSA.
07	2	1862	Confederate Dept. No. 2, is extended, and Maj. Gen. Leonidas Polk, CSA, is announced as 2nd in command TN, etal.
07	2	1862	Affair near Haxall's Landing or Elvington Heights, VA.
07	2	1862	Skirmish at Malvern Hill, VA.
07	2	1862	Skirmish near New Kent Court-House, VA.
07	2	1862	Federal reconnaissance up Powell's Big Fort Valley, VA.
07	2	1862	President Lincoln signs into law the **Morrill Act,** which gives each state 30,000 acres for each senator and representative for proposed future agricultural and mechanical schools, which was the beginning of the land grant universities.
07	3	1862	Skirmish near Russellville, AL, between Cavalry soldiers.
07	3	1862	Skirmish at Locust Grove, the Indian Territory, with Pro-Union Indians.
07	3	1862	Union mortar boats continue to bombard Vicksburg, MS.
07	3	1862	Maj. Gen. Sterling Price, CSA, assumes the command of the Confederate **Army of the West,** TN, etal.
07	3	1862	Skirmishes near Herring Creek, or Harrison's Landing, VA. 7/3-4/1862.
07	3	1862	Federal reconnaissance from Harrison's Landing, on the Charles City Road, VA.
07	4	1862	The following are appointed Union Major Generals: **Darius Nash Couch,** U.S.A. **Philip Kearny,** U.S.A. **Alexander McDowell McCook,** U.S.A. **George Webb Morrell,** U.S.A. **John James Peck,** U.S.A. **Fitz John Porter,** U.S.A. **Israel Bush Richardson,** U.S.A. **John Sedgwick,** U.S.A. **Henry Warner Slocum,** U.S.A. **William Farrar Smith,** U.S.A.
07	4	1862	**Confederate Col. John Hunt Morgan's 1st Kentucky Raid.** 7/4-28/1862, begins with Morgan's command setting out from Knoxville, TN.
07	4	1862	Affair at Port Royal Ferry, SC.
07	4	1862	Confederate attack on the US vessels near Velasco, TX.
07	4	1862	Federal reconnaissance from Harrison's Landing, VA.
07	4	1862	The capture of the Confederate gunboat, **CSS Teaser,** on the James River, as it attempted to launch an observation ballon made of old silk frocks.
07	4	1862	Skirmish at Westover, VA.
07	5	1862	Federal expedition from Ponchatoula, LA, to catch the individuals responsible for the murder of two Union soldiers. 7/5-8/1862.
07	5	1862	Skirmish on the Hatchie River, MS.
07	5	1862	Maj. Gen. William J. Hardee, CSA, is temporarily commanding the **Army of the Mississippi.**
07	5	1862	Skirmish at Battle Creek, TN.
07	5	1862	Affair at Walden's Ridge, TN.
07	5	1862	Confederate operations against the Union shipping on the James River, VA. 7/5-6/1862.
07	6	1862	Skirmish at Bayou Cache, AR, between Augusta and Clarendon with the advance of the Federal **Army of the Southwest.**
07	6	1862	Skirmish at Grand Prairie, near Aberdeen, AR.
07	6	1862	Federal expedition toward Blackwater and Chapel Hill, MO, with the Federals acting like bushwackers. 7/6-9/1862.
07	6	1862	Federal scout from Waynesville to the Big Piney, MO. 7/6-8/1862.
07	6	1862	Skirmish at Salem, MO.

MONTH	DAY	YEAR	ACT
07	6	1862	Maj. Gen. Ambrose Burnside, USA, sails from Cape Hatteras, NC, with re-enforcements for the **Army of the Potomac,** at Harrison's Landing, VA, leaving Brig. Gen. John G. Foster, USA, in command of the Dept. of North Carolina.
07	7	1862	Action at Bayou Cache, or Cotton Plant, Cache River, and skirmishes at Round Hill, Hill's Plantation, and at Bayou de View, AR.
07	7	1862	Skirmish near Devall's Bluff, AR.
07	7	1862	Skirmish at Inman Hollow, MO.
07	7	1862	Skirmish near Newark, MO.
07	7	1862	Operations in the District of Oregon. 7/7/1862-10/6/1863.
07	7	1862	Brig. Gen. Benjamin Alvord, USA, assumes the command of the District of Oregon.
07	7	1862	Operations about Cumberland Gap, TN. 7/7-11/1862.
07	7	1862	Operations in Arkansas Pass, TX. 7/7-17/1862.
07	7	1862	Federal reconnaissance from Yorktown, VA. 7/7-9/1862.
07	8	1862	Skirmish at Black Run, on the Black River, MO.
07	8	1862	Skirmish at Pleasant Hill, MO, with a Federal attack on the guerrilla, William Clarke Quantrill's camp.
07	8	1862	President Lincoln travels aboard the **USS Ariel** up the James River to meet with Maj. Gen. George B. McClellan at Harrison's Landing, VA.
07	9	1862	Skirmish near Aberdeen, AR.
07	9	1862	Affair at the Weaverville Crossing of the Mad River, CA.
07	9	1862	Col. John Hunt Morgan's Rebel troops **capture Tompkinsville, KY.**
07	9	1862	Skirmish at Lotspeich Farm, near Wadesburg, MO.
07	9	1862	Union troops **capture Hamilton, NC,** Roanoke River, with the aid of the Federal gunboats, **USS Ceres, USS Perry,** and the **USS Shawseen.**
07	9	1862	Confederate expedition to Fenwick's Island, SC.
07	9	1862	Federal demonstration against Pocotaligo, SC. 7/9-10/1862.
07	9	1862	Federal reconnaissance on the Long Bridge Road, VA.
07	10	1862	Federal expedition to Guntown, MS, where under flag of truce, the opposing forces exchanged newspapers, discussed topics of the day, etc. 7/10-11/1862.
07	10	1862	Federal reconnaissance from Harrison's Landing toward White Oak Swamp, VA, and skirmish.
07	11	1862	Maj. Gen. Henry Wager **"Old Brains"** Halleck, USA, is assigned to command as **General-in Chief** of all the US land forces.
07	11	1862	Skirmishes at Sears' House and Big Creek Bluff, near Pleasant Hill, MO.
07	11	1862	Federal reconnaissance from Harrison's Landing, beyond Charles City Court-House, VA, toward Williamsburg, VA.
07	12	1862	Federal expedition from Decatur, AL, and skirmish near Davis' Gap. 7/12-16/1862.
07	12	1862	The skirmish near and **capture of Lebanon, KY,** which is part of Col. John Hunt Morgan's Confederate Raid. This causes alarm for the citizens of Cincinnati, OH, Evansville, IL, and of Frankfort, Lexington, and Louisville, KY.
07	12	1862	Federal reconnaissance to Culpeper, Orange, and Madison Court-Houses, by Maj. Gen. John Pope, USA. 7/12-17/1862.
07	13	1862	The Confederate Missouri State Guard is relieved from duty east of the Mississippi River and ordered to join Maj. Gen. Thomas Carmichael Hindman, CSA.
07	13	1862	The action at, and the **Union surrender of Murfreesborough, TN,** by Brig. Gen. Thomas Crittenden's troops to **Col. Nathan Bedford Forrest's Confederate Cavalry troops.**
07	13	1862	Skirmish near Wolf River, TN, as Confederate Cavalry attack and burn part of Maj. Gen. William T. Sherman's, USA, 5th Division, Army of the Tennessee, supply train.
07	13	1862	Maj. Gen. Thomas Jackson's Confederate forces advance from Hanover Court-House upon Gordonsville, VA.
07	13	1862	Skirmish at Rapidan Station, VA, with the Union destruction of a Confederate bridge.
07	14	1862	**Richard Heron Anderson, C.S.A.,** is appointed Maj. Gen.
07	14	1862	Skirmish at Batesville, AR.
07	14	1862	Skirmish near Helena, AR.
07	14	1862	Federal reconnaissances from Grand River to Fort Gibson, Tahlequah, and Park Hill, Indian Territory and skirmishes with Pro-South **Cherokees.** 7/14-17/1862
07	14	1862	Skirmish near Mackville, KY, with Col. John Hunt Morgan, CSA.

| 07 | 15 | 1862 | **Maj. Gen. David Emanuel Twiggs, C.S.A.,** dies of old age near Augusta, GA. |

07 15 1862 **Maj. Gen. David Emanuel Twiggs, C.S.A.,** dies of old age near Augusta, GA.

07 15 1862 Action near Fayetteville, AR, with a Federal Cavalry victory.

07 15 1862 Skirmish at Apache Pass, the New Mexico Territory with **Apache** Indians, and Federal troops from California.

07 15 1862 Engagement between the **CSS Arkansas,** and the Union gunboats, **USS Carondelet, Essex, Tyler,** and the **Queen of the West,** on the Yazoo River, about Vicksburg, MS. The damaged **CSS Arkansas** retired to under the protection of Confederate batteries of Vicksburg, MS.

07 15 1862 Skirmish at Wallace's Cross-Roads, near Decatur, TN.

07 15 1862 Skirmish near Middletown, VA.

07 15 1862 Skirmish at Orange Court-House, VA.

07 16 1862 The following are appointed Union Brigadier Generals:

Jacob Ammen,	USA
Catharinus Putnam Buckingham,	USA
Charles Cruft,	USA
Francis Jay Herron,	USA
Alfred Pleasonton,	USA
Benjamin Stone Roberts,	USA
Frederick Salomon,	USA
Joshua Woodrow Sill,	USA
Morgan Lewis Smith,	USA
Fitz-Henry Warren,	USA
Cadwallader Colden Washburn,	USA

07 16 1862 Maj. Gen. Henry Halleck, USA, relinquishes immediate command of the troops in the Dept. of the Mississippi, to assume his new role as General-in-chief of all US land forces.

07 16 1862 The District of West Tennessee, Maj. Gen. Ulysses S. Grant, USA, commanding, is extended to embrace the Army of the Mississippi.

07 16 1862 Maj. Gen. Theophilus H. Holmes, CSA, is assigned to the command of the Confederate Trans-Mississippi Dept.

07 16 1862 Federal reconnaissance from Westover, on the Richmond Road, VA.

07 17 1862 **St. John Richardson Liddell,**   CSA, is appointed Brig. Gen.

07 17 1862 **Thomas Leonidas Crittenden,** U.S.A., is appointed Maj. Gen.

07 17 1862 **William Nelson,**   U.S.A., is appointed Maj. Gen.

07 17 1862 The following are appointed Union Brigadier Generals:

Henry Shaw Briggs,	USA
John Cochrane,	USA
Conrad Feger Jackson,	USA
James Dada Morgan,	USA
James Blair Steedman,	USA
Henry Dwight Terry,	USA
John Basil Turchin,	USA
August von Willich,	USA

07 17 1862 Col. John Hunt Morgan's, CSA, Cavalry Raiding party **captures Cynthiana, KY.**

07 17 1862 Maj. Gen. Ulysses S. Grant, USA, assumes the command of all Federal troops in the Armies of the Tennessee and of the Mississippi and in the Districts of Cairo and of the Mississippi.

07 17 1862 Maj. Gen. Daniel Henry Hill, CSA, is assigned to command of the Dept. of North Carolina.

07 17 1862 Skirmish between Mount Pleasant and Columbia, TN.

07 17 1862 Skirmish near, and the **capture of, Gordonsville, VA,** by Maj. Gen. John Pope, USA.

07 17 1862 Due to a shortage of metal coins, President Lincoln signed into law a bill authorizing the use of postage stamps as money.

07 18 1862 The following are appointed Union Major Generals:

John Gray Foster,	U.S.A.
John Grubb Parke,	U.S.A.
Joseph King Fenno Mansfield,	U.S.A.
Jesse Lee Reno,	U.S.A.
Isaac Ingalls Stevens,	U.S.A. (posthumously)

07 18 1862 **George Foster Shepley,** USA, is appointed Brig. Gen.

07	18	1862	**The Confederate raid and capture of Henderson, KY, below Evansville, IN, and Newburg, IN,** by Col. John Hunt Morgan's, CSA, Cavalry.
07	18	1862	The Confederate Dept. No. 2, is extended to embrace all of Mississippi, East Louisiana, and West Florida.
07	18	1862	Skirmish near Memphis, MO, with severe Union losses due to a Confederate ambush.
07	18	1862	The Confederate Dept. of East Tennessee is extended.
07	19	1862	**James Streshly Jackson,** USA, is appointed Brig. Gen.
07	19	1862	**John Smith Phelps,** USA, is appointed Brig. Gen.
07	19	1862	Skirmish near Paris, or Owensville, KY, with the Federals surprising Col. John Hunt Morgan's CSA Cavalry raiding party.
07	19	1862	Federal scout in Polk and Dallas Counties, MO. 7/19-23/1862.
07	19	1862	Confederate Guerrilla raid on Brownsville, TN.
07	19	1862	Federal expedition from Fredericksburg to Beaver Dam Station, VA, with the destruction of Confederate supplies. 7/19-20/1862.
07	20	1862	Skirmish at Gaines' Landing, AR, with Brig. Gen. Samuel Curtis, USA.
07	20	1862	Affair at Hatchie Bottom, MS, where a Union Cavalry company is surrounded and captured.
07	20	1862	Skirmish at Greenville, MO, where the Confederates overrun the Federal camp there in a surprise attack.
07	20	1862	Skirmish at Taberville, MO.
07	21	1862	The following are appointed Confederate Brigadier Generals: **Nathan Bedford Forrest,** CSA **Martin Edwin Green,** CSA **Johnson Hagood,** CSA
07	21	1862	**The Confederate Army of the Mississippi is ordered to Chattanooga, TN.**
07	21	1862	Maj. Gen. Sterling Price, CSA, assumes the command of the Confederate District of the Tennessee.
07	21	1862	Skirmishes around Nashville, TN, with the burning of bridges and capture of Union pickets by the Confederates.
07	21	1862	The **occupation of Luray, VA,** by the Federal troops.
07	22	1862	**Micah Jenkins,** CSA, is appointed Brig. Gen.
07	22	1862	Engagement with the **CSS Arkansas,** about Vicksburg, MS, by the **USS Essex,** and the Union ram, **Queen of the West,** with both Union vessels retreating with damages.
07	22	1862	Skirmish at Florida, MO.
07	22	1862	Col. John Hunt Morgan, CSA, arrives at Livingston, TN, after his foray into Kentucky.
07	22	1862	The following Union Major Generals assume command in the Dept. of Virginia: Maj. Gen. John A. Dix, USA, 7th US Army Corps. Maj. Gen. Ambrose E. Burnside, USA, 9th US Army Corps.
07	22	1862	Federal reconnaissance to James City and Madison Court-House, VA, with Brig. Gen. George D. Bayard, USA. 7/22-24/1862.
07	22	1862	Federal scout in King William, King and Queen, and Gloucester Counties, VA. 7/22-30/1862.
07	22	1862	Federal reconnaissances from Luray to Columbia Bridge White House Ford, VA.
07	22	1862	Affair at Verdon, VA, with Maj. Gen. JEB Stuart's, CSA, Cavalry.
07	22	1862	Affair near Westover, VA.
07	23	1862	Maj. Gen. Henry W. Halleck assumes the command of the **Federal Armies of the United States.**
07	23	1862	Federal expedition from Helena, AR, aboard the steamboat, **Catahoula,** to Coldwater, and skirmish at White Oak Bayou, MS. 7/23-25/1862.
07	23	1862	Extra Union mortar boats on the Mississippi River are transferred to the James River to support Maj. Gen. George B. McClellan's, USA, the **Army of the Potomac.**
07	23	1862	Skirmish on the Blackwater, near Columbus, MO, with guerrillas.
07	23	1862	Skirmish at Boles' Farm, near Florida, MO.
07	23	1862	Gen. Braxton Bragg's, CSA, army is moving from Tupelo, MS, en route to Chattanooga, TN, via railroad, which will take his forces to Mobile, then Montgomery, AL, and Atlanta, GA.
07	23	1862	Skirmishes near Carmel Church, VA, with Federal Cavalry under Brig. Gen. Rufus King and Col. Judson Kilpartick, USA, destroying Confederate supplies, and finally driven off by Maj. Gen. JEB Stuart's, CSA, Cavalry.
07	24	1862	**Fitzhugh Lee,** CSA, is appointed Brig. Gen.

07	24	1862	Federal Cavalry expedition from Helena to Marianna, AR. 7/24-26/1862.
07	24	1862	Skirmish on the Amite River, near Benton's Ferry, LA, where a Union surprise attack overwhelms the Confederates.
07	24	1862	Skirmish at White Oak Bayou, MS.
07	24	1862	Skirmish at Moore's Mill, near Fulton, MO.
07	24	1862	Skirmishes near Sante Fe, MO. 7/24-25/1862.
07	24	1862	Former President **Martin Van Buren,** dies at Lindenwald, NY, at the age of 79.
07	24	1862	Federal expeditions from New Berne to Trenton and Pollocksville, and etc., NC, under Brig. Gen. John G. Foster, USA. 7/24-28/1862.
07	24	1862	Federal reconnaissance from Fredericksburg toward Orange Court-House, VA, by Brig. Gen. John Gibbon, USA. 7/24-26/1862.
07	24	1862	Federal scout in Wyoming County, WV, to Flat Top, Barke's, Peak's, and Milam's Ridges, etc, near the Guyandotte River.
07	25	1862	**James Ewell Brown, "JEB," Stuart, C.S.A.,** is appointed a Major General of the Confederacy.
07	25	1862	**Harry Thompson Hays,** CSA, is appointed Brig. Gen.
07	25	1862	Skirmish at Courtland, or Courtland Bridge, AL, with a Confederate rout. Maj. Gen. Don Carlos Buell, USA, upset over the surprise, issues a stern embarrassing letter to the army pointing out the names of the Union soldiers who were surprised.
07	25	1862	Skirmish at and near Trinity, AL.
07	25	1862	Federal expedition to Lake Pontchartrain, Pass Manchac, and up the Tehefuncta and Pearl Rivers, LA, with skirmishes. 7/25-8/2/1862.
07	25	1862	Confederate expedition from Holly Springs, MS, to Bolivar and Jackson, TN, as **Col. Joseph Wheeler's,** CSA, Cavalry penetrates 70 miles behind Union lines burning bridges, etc. 7/25-8/1/1862.
07	25	1862	Skirmishes near Mountain Store, and the Big Piney, MO. 7/25-26/1862.
07	25	1862	Skirmish at Clinton Ferry, TN, with a Confederate retreat away from the Union foraging party.
07	25	1862	Affair at Summerville, WV, as Confederate Cavalry surprise the Union post there in the middle of the night.
07	26	1862	Action near Spangler's Mill, near Jonesborough, AL, as Gen. Braxton Bragg, CSA, forces Maj. Gen. Ulysses S. Grant's, USA, men to retreat.
07	26	1862	Federal scout in Southeastern Missouri, and skirmishes, **(July 28th),** at Bollinger's Mill, MO. 7/26-29/1862.
07	26	1862	Skirmish at Mill Creek, near Pollocksville, NC.
07	26	1862	Federal reconnaissance from Newport to Young's Cross-Roads, NC, and skirmish **(July 27th).** 7/26-29/1862.
07	26	1862	Skirmish at Tazewell, TN.
07	26	1862	Federal reconnaissance toward Orange Court-House, VA, by order of Brig. Gen. Samuel W. Crawford, USA.
07	27	1862	**John Buford,** USA, is appointed Brig. Gen.
07	27	1862	Federal expedition from Woodville to Guntersville, AL, and skirmishes: **(July 28th)** at Guntersville **(July 29th)** at Law's Landing, and **(July 29th)** at Old Deposit Ferry, AL. 7/27-30/1862.
07	27	1862	Skirmish at Bayou Bernard, near Fort Gibson, the Indian Territory.
07	27	1862	Skirmish at Covington, LA.
07	27	1862	Skirmish at Madisonville, LA.
07	27	1862	Federal expedition from Rienzi to Ripley, MS. 7/27-29/1862.
07	27	1862	Operations in Carroll, Ray, and Livingston Counties, MO. 7/27-8/4/1862.
07	27	1862	Skirmish at Brown's Spring, MO.
07	27	1862	Affair near Toone's Station, or Lower Post Ferry, TN.
07	27	1862	Skirmish at Flat Top Mountain, WV.
07	28	1862	**Richard Taylor, C.S.A.,** is appointed Maj. Gen.
07	28	1862	Skirmish at Stevenson, AL.
07	28	1862	Federal expedition from Helena To Old Town and Trenton, AR. 7/28-31/1862.
07	28	1862	Indian attack on Whitney's Ranch, near Fort Anderson, CA.
07	28	1862	Skirmish at Cross Timbers, MO.

Month	Day	Year	Act
07	28	1862	Action at Moore's Mill, near Fulton, MO.
07	28	1862	Federal scout in Pettis County, MO, from near Sedalia. 7/28-31/1862.
07	28	1862	Federal expedition from Batchelder's Creek, on the Neuse River Road, NC, with Capt. Charles D. Sanford, 12th MA Cavalry.
07	28	1862	Skirmish near Humboldt, TN.
07	28	1862	Col. John Hunt Morgan's Confederate Cavalry command arrives at Livingston, TN.
07	28	1862	Federal reconnaissance from Culpeper to Raccoon Ford, VA.
07	29	1862	Skirmish near Albee's Ranch, CA.
07	29	1862	Skirmish at Russellville, KY, with Confederate guerrillas.
07	29	1862	Skirmish at Arrow Rock, MO.
07	29	1862	Skirmish at Bloomfield, MO.
07	29	1862	Federal operations in Saline County, MO, with guerrillas. 7/9-8/2/1862 .
07	29	1862	Affair at Hatchie Bottom, near Denmark, TN, as Brig. Gen. John Logan's, USA, cavalry is routed by Confederate cavalry.
07	29	1862	Federal reconnaissance from Harrison's Landing to Saint Mary's Church, VA.
07	29	1862	Operations about Orange Court-House, VA.
07	29	1862	The infamous lady, **"Belle Boyd"** is arrested by Union troops near Warrenton, VA, and charged with spying for the Confederacy. Sent to the Old Capitol Prison, Washington, DC, she was released August 8, 1862, due to lack of evidence.
07	30	1862	Affair with Indians at Miller's Ranch, near Elk Camp, CA.
07	30	1862	Maj. Gen. Theopilus Holmes, CSA, assumes the command of the Confederate Trans-Mississippi Department.
07	30	1862	Skirmish at Paris, KY.
07	30	1862	Skirmish at Clark's Mill, Chariton County, MO.
07	30	1862	Maj. Gen. George B. McClellan, USA, is ordered to remove his sick, from Harrison's Landing, VA, as this is the initial effort of plans to remove the **Army of the Potomac** back towards Washington, DC.
07	30	1862	Federal reconnaissance from Harrison's Landing to Jones' Ford, or Coggin's Point, Chickahominy River, VA.
07	31	1862	Confederate attack on the Union camps and shipping between Shirley and Harrison's Landing, VA. 7/31-8/1/1862.
08	1	1862	The following are appointed Union Brigadier Generals: **Michael Corcoran,** USA **George Crook,** USA **James Irvin Gregg,** USA
08	1	1862	Skirmish near Carrollton, MO.
08	1	1862	Skirmish at Forsyth, or Ozark, MO, with guerrillas.
08	1	1862	Skirmish at Grand River, MO.
08	1	1862	Skirmish at Barnett's Ford, near Harrison's Landing, VA.
08	2	1862	Skirmish at Jonesborough, AR, as the Texas Rangers rout the Federals.
08	2	1862	Skirmish near Totten's Plantation, Coahoma County, MS.
08	2	1862	Skirmish at Austin, Tunica County, MS.
08	2	1862	Skirmish on Clear Creek, near Taberville, MO.
08	2	1862	Operations at Cumberland Gap and skirmish **(August 6th)** near Tazewell, TN. 8/2-6/1862.
08	2	1862	Federal reconnaissance from Harrison's Landing and the Union **reoccupation of Malvern Hill, VA.** 8/2-8/1862.
08	2	1862	Skirmish at **Orange Court-House, VA,** with Maj. Gen. John Pope, USA, forces occupying the place, and forcing out Confederate Cavalry troops.
08	2	1862	Operations about Wyoming Court-House, WV, with a Rebel Cavalry raid from Jeffersonville. 8/2-8/1862.
08	2	1862	Federal scout from Meadow Bluff to the Greenbrier River, WV. 8/2-5/1862.
08	3	1862	Skirmishes at L'Anguille Ferry, Jackson, and Scatterville, AR.
08	3	1862	The capture of the British blockade runner, **Columbia,** by the Federal steamer, **Santiago de Cuba,** off the Bahamas.
08	3	1862	Skirmish near Morganfield, KY.
08	3	1862	Skirmish at Chariton Bridge, MO.
08	3	1862	Skirmish on Nonconah Creek, near Sparta, TN.

08	3	1862	Maj. Gen. George McClellan, USA, is ordered to remove his forces to Aquia Creek, VA, near Fredericksburg, and to Alexandria, VA, and to assist Maj. Gen. John Pope, USA, in the defense of Washington, DC. McClellan strongly disagrees with Maj. Gen. Henry W. Halleck, USA, as he believes his army should continue operations on the Virginia Peninsula.
08	3	1862	Federal reconnaissance on the south side of the James River and skirmish at Sycamore Church, near Petersburg, VA.
08	3	1862	Skirmish on Greenbrier River, WV.
08	4	1862	Confederate attack on Union pickets near Woodville, AL, (August 4th) and a Federal reconnaissance from Woodville to Guntersville, AL. **(August 5th-7th).**
08	4	1862	Federal expedition from Helena to Clarendon, AR. 8/4-17/1862.
08	4	1862	President Lincoln declines the offer of two black Indiana regiments, suggesting they be used as laborers instead.
08	4	1862	Federal reconnaissance from Jacinto to Bay Springs, MS, and skirmish. 8/4-7/1862.
08	4	1862	Skirmish at Gayoso, MO.
08	4	1862	Federal scout on Sinking Creek, MO, about 25 miles southeast of Salem, MO, with the Federals surprising the Rebels. 8/4-11/1862.
08	4	1862	Skirmish on White River, near Forsyth, MO.
08	4	1862	Federal reconnaissance from Coggins Point beyond Sycamore Church, and White Oak Swamp Bridge, VA. 8/4-5/1862.
08	4	1862	Maj. Gen. James Ewell Brown Stuart's CSA, Cavalry expedition from Hanover Court-House to the vicinity of Fredericksburg, VA. 8/4-8/1862.
08	4	1862	Maj. Gen. Ambrose E. Burnside, USA, arrives with his forces from North Carolina at Aquia Creek, north of Fredericksburg, VA, to assist Maj. Gen. John Pope, USA, in the defense of the anticipated advance of the Confederates under Gen. Robert E. Lee, CSA.
08	5	1862	**Albert Gallatin Jenkins,** CSA, is appointed Brig. Gen.
08	5	1862	Skirmish near New Market, AL, where Brig. Gen. Robert Latimer McCook, USA, is mortally wounded.
08	5	1862	**Brig. Gen. Robert Latimer McCook, USA,** is mortally wounded, murdered by Capt. Frank Gurley, CSA, shot in the abdomen, dying the following day near Decherd, TN. Scouting the area for a campsite for his troops, between Athens, GA, and Decherd, TN, he was riding in a carriage because of camp fever he developed, was overcome by Confederate partisans and shot by one Capt. Frank Gurley.
08	5	1862	Federal expedition from Helena to the mouth of the White River, AR, with the Union gunboat, **Benton,** the steamers, **Iatan, Louisville,** and the **Mound City,** and the rams, **Bragg, Monarch,** and **Switzerland.** 8/5-8/1862.
08	5	1862	**Engagement at Baton Rouge, LA,** including the CSS gunboat, **CSS Arkansas,** with the Confederates, under Maj. Gen. John C. Breckinridge, CSA, repulsed by Brig. Gen. Thomas Williams, USA.
08	5	1862	**Brig. Gen. Thomas Williams, USA,** is instantly killed at Baton Rouge, LA, while leading his men against the Confederate forces under Maj. Gen. John Cabell Breckinridge, CSA, receiving his death wound in the chest by a Confederate musketball, at the beginning of the Union countercharge.
08	5	1862	Skirmish near Cravensville, Daviess County, MO.
08	5	1862	Skirmish at **Montevallo, MO,** with the Union **occupation** of the town.
08	5	1862	Skirmish at Sparta, TN.
08	5	1862	Federal expedition from Fredericksburg to Frederick's Hall Station, VA, with skirmishes, as Brig. Gen. Gibbon, USA, is engaged. 8/5-8/1862.
08	5	1862	Engagement at Malvern Hill, VA.
08	5	1862	Skirmish at Thornburg, or Massaponax Church, VA.
08	5	1862	Skirmish at White Oak Swamp Bridge, VA.
08	5	1862	Skirmish at Wyoming Court-House, WV.
08	6	1862	**Brig. Gen. Robert Latimer McCook, USA,** of the famous **"fighting McCooks"** from Ohio, dies from the excruciating stomach wound received the day before near Decherd, TN.
08	6	1862	**William Edwin Starke,** CSA, is appointed Brig. Gen.
08	6	1862	Skirmish near Fort Gaston, CA.
08	6	1862	Destruction of the **CSS Arkansas,** about Vicksburg, MS, after attacked by the Union gunboats, the **USS Cayuga, Essex, Ratahdin, Kineo,** and **Sumter.**
08	6	1862	Action at Kirksville, MO.
08	6	1862	Col. P. Edward Connor, 3d California Infantry, assumes the command of the District of Utah.
08	6	1862	Skirmish at Malvern Hill, VA, with a general Federal retreat.

08	6	1862	Action at Thornburg, Mattapony or Massaponax Church, VA.
08	6	1862	Skirmish at Beech Creek, WV.
08	6	1862	Skirmish at Pack's Ferry, New River, WV, with Brig. Gen. Jacob D. Cox, USA, pitted against Maj. Gen. William W. Loring, CSA.
08	7	1862	**Francis Preston Blair, Jr.,** USA, is appointed Brig. Gen.
08	7	1862	**Richard Busteed,** USA, is appointed Brig. Gen.
08	7	1862	Confederate attack on, and capture of, the convalescent train near Moseley's Plantation, about 2.5 miles from Decatur, AL.
08	7	1862	Federal reconnaissances from Pensacola to Bagdad and Milton, FL, where the Federals remove much needed cut lumber from the local burnt sawmills. 8/7-10/1862.
08	7	1862	Skirmish near Montevallo, MO.
08	7	1862	Federal scout from Ozark to Forysth, MO, and skirmishes. 8/7-9/1862.
08	7	1862	Skirmish at Rocky Bluff, Platte County, MO.
08	7	1862	Skirmish near Fort Fillmore, the New Mexico Territory.
08	7	1862	Skirmish at Wood Springs, 5 miles east of Dyersburg, TN, where Union Cavalry surprise and totally rout Jackson's Cavalry.
08	7	1862	Skirmish at Wolftown, VA, 4 miles south of Thoroughfare Mountain.
08	8	1862	Due to continued guerrilla firing into railroad cars, local ministers are arrested by the Union troops and placed aboard each train, at Huntsville, AL. The firing ceases.
08	8	1862	West Florida is transferred from the Dept. of the South to the Dept. of the Gulf.
08	8	1862	Skirmish near Newtonia, MO.
08	8	1862	Skirmish on Panther Creek, MO.
08	8	1862	Skirmish near Stockton, Macon County, MO.
08	8	1862	Action near Madison Court-House, VA.
08	8	1862	Skirmish near Slaughter's House, VA.
08	9	1862	**Brig. Gen. Joseph Bennett Plummer, USA,** dies near Corinth, MS, while in camp, from camp fever.
08	9	1862	**Christopher Columbus Auger, U.S.A.,** is appointed Maj. Gen.
08	9	1862	**The Battle of Cedar Run, or Cedar (or Slaughter) Mountain, VA,** sees Maj. Gen. Stonewall Jackson's forces defeating Maj. Gen. John Pope, USA, and Maj. Gen. A. P. Hill, CSA, beating back a Federal offensive under Maj. Gen. Nathaniel Banks, USA. Total casualties approximate 3,700.
08	9	1862	**Brig. Gen. Charles Sidney Winder, CSA,** is horribly wounded and mangled by a Federal artillery shell at the Battle of Cedar Run, VA, and dies within hours.
08	9	1862	US Naval bombardment of Donaldsonville, LA.
08	9	1862	Skirmish at Salem, MO.
08	9	1862	Skirmishes at Walnut Creek, and at Sears' Ford, Chariton River, MO.
08	9	1862	Federal expedition from Fort Walla Walla to the Grande Ronde Prairie, the Washington Territory, with affair with Indians **(August 14th)** at the Grande Ronde Prairie. 8/9-22/1862.
08	10	1862	The capture of the Confederate steamer, **General Lee,** in the Savannah River, near Fort Pulaski, GA.
08	10	1862	Affair at Bayou Sara, LA, where the Union ironclad, **Essex,** protected a Union transport that followed and removed a large quantity of sugar from the area.
08	10	1862	Skirmish at Linn Creek, MO.
08	10	1862	Skirmish at Switzer's Mill, MO.
08	10	1862	Federal reconnaissance from Brownsville, TN, toward the mouth of the Hatchie River. 8/10-11/1862.
08	10	1862	Affair on the Neuces River near Fort Clark, TX.
08	10	1862	Skirmish at Cedar Run, near Culpeper, VA.
08	11	1862	Skirmish near Helena, AR.
08	11	1862	Skirmish at Brown's Plantation, MS.
08	11	1862	Skirmish at Compton's Ferry, or Little Compton, Grand River, MO, including a 250 miles pursuit of Rebel irregulars.
08	11	1862	Action at and the **surrender of Independence, MO,** to Confederate irregular guerrillas, including **William Clarke Quantrill.**
08	11	1862	Skirmish at Taberville, MO.
08	11	1862	Affair near Kinderhook, TN, with Rebel guerrillas.
08	11	1862	Skirmish at Saulsbury, TN, with the rout of guerrilla cavalry.
08	11	1862	Skirmish near Williamsport, TN.

08	11	1862	Affair at Velasco, TX.
08	11	1862	Maj. Gen. Thomas J. "Stonewall" Jackson's Confederate corps retires to the vicinity of Gordonsville, VA, south of the Rapidan River.
08	12	1862	**William Barksdale,** CSA, is promoted Brig. Gen.
08	12	1862	Federal expedition from Fort Leavenworth, KS, to Independence, MO, as the Confederates threaten Kansas City, MO. 8/12-14/1862.
08	12	1862	Federal expedition from Camp Gamble, MO, in search of guerrillas. 8/12-18/1862.
08	12	1862	Skirmish between Stockton, Cedar County, and Humansville, MO.
08	12	1862	Skirmish at Van Buren, Carter County, MO.
08	12	1862	Col. John Hunt Morgan's CSA, Cavalry **captures Gallatin, TN,** and destroys bridges in that vicinity (August 12th) and skirmish **(August 13th).** 8/12-13/1862.
08	12	1862	The Federal capture of the **Breaker** and the destruction of the **Elma** and the **Hannah,** by the **USS Arthur,** in Corpus Christi Bay, TX.
08	13	1862	Skirmish on Yellow Creek, or Muscle Fork, Chariton River, MO, results in a Confederate defeat.
08	13	1862	Engagement on the Black River, SC, some 20 miles above Georgetown, SC.
08	13	1862	Skirmish at Huntsville, Scott County, TN.
08	13	1862	Skirmish near Medon, TN, and 15 miles south of Jackson, TN.
08	13	1862	Orders are issued for the movement of the Confederate **Army of Northern Virginia** from the Peninsula to Gordonsville, VA.
08	13	1862	Federal reconnaissance toward Orange Court-House, VA, and skirmish.
08	13	1862	Over 70 men are lost as the Federal steamers, **George Peabody** and the **West Point,** collide in the Potomac River, VA.
08	13	1862	Skirmishes at Blue Stone, WV. 8/13-14/1862.
08	14	1862	Skirmish near Barry, MO, with the Union burning of certain suspected guerrillas' homes.
08	14	1862	Federal expedition from Ozark to Forsyth, MO. 8/14-17/1862.
08	14	1862	Federal reconnaissance from Newport to Swansborough, NC, with Col. Charles A. Heckman, 9th NJ Infantry. 8/14-15/1862.
08	14	1862	Skirmish near Mount Pleasant, TN, with guerrillas.
08	14	1862	The 3d and 5th US Army Corps move from Harrison's Landing for Aquia Creek, VA, aboard US transports. 8/14-15/1862.
08	14	1862	Operations of the Federal Cavalry covering the rear of the Army of of the Potomac from Harrison's Landing to Williamsburg, VA. 8/14-19/1862.
08	15	1862	Skirmish at Clarendon, AR.
08	15	1862	Gen. Braxton Bragg, CSA, resumes command of the Confederate **Army of the Mississippi.**
08	15	1862	Federal expedition from Fredericksburg to Port Royal, VA. 8/15-16/1862.
08	16	1862	**Edward Dorr Tracy,** CSA, is appointed Brig. Gen.
08	16	1862	**Federal Naval expedition from Helena, AR,** down the Mississippi and up the Yazoo River. 8/16-27/1862.
08	16	1862	The Confederate **Army of Kentucky** under Maj. Gen. E. Kirby Smith, CSA, crosses the Cumberland Mountains into Kentucky.
08	16	1862	Skirmish at Horn Lake Creek, MS, with guerrillas.
08	16	1862	Action at Lone Jack, MO, with an initial Confederate victory.
08	16	1862	Operations about Cumberland Gap, TN, including action at London, Kentucky, and skirmishes at Flat Lick, Kentucky, and Pine Mountain, TN. **(August 17th)** 8/16-22/1862.
08	16	1862	Skirmish at Meriwether's Ferry, Obion River, TN.
08	16	1862	The Federal naval bombardment of Corpus Christi, TX. 8/16-18/1862.
08	16	1862	**The Campaign in Northern Virginia.** 8/16-9/2/1862.
08	16	1862	The Confederate **Army of Northern Virginia** moves from Gordonsville, VA, as Gen. Robert E. Lee, CSA, advances towards Maj. Gen. John Pope, USA, the **Army of Virginia,** and Maj. Gen. George B. McClellan, USA, the **Army of the Potomac.**
08	16	1862	Federal reconnaissance toward Louisa Court-House, VA. 8/16-17/1862.
08	16	1862	Skirmish at Wire Bridge, WV.
08	17	1862	Federal expedition from Fort Leavenworth, KS, to Hickory Grove, 8/17-27/1862.
08	17	1862	Skirmish near Mammoth Cave, KY, with the capture of guerrillas.

08	17	1862	**The uprising of the Sioux Indians,** who, after facing starvation, attack settlers near Acton, MN. 8/17-9/23/1862.
08	17	1862	Federal reconnaissance toward Forge Bridge, VA.
08	17	1862	Maj. Gen. James Ewell Brown Stuart, CSA, is assigned to the command of all the cavalry of the **Army of Northern Virginia.**
08	18	1862	Affair at Milliken's Bend, LA, and the capture of the Confederate steamer **Fair Play,** near Bolivar, MS.
08	18	1862	The **Sioux Indian** ambush of Union troops at Redwood Ferry, MN.
08	18	1862	Skirmish at White Oak Ridge, MO.
08	18	1862	Col. R. Mason, 71st OH, **surrenders Clarksville, TN,** to the Confederate forces, without a fight, and is subsequently relieved of command.
08	18	1862	Skirmish near Dyersburg, TN, with the rout of small band of rebels.
08	18	1862	The capture of 2 Rebel steamboats, on the Tennessee River, near Waggoner's and Walker's Landing.
08	18	1862	The Union **Army of Virginia** retires to the north bank of the Rappahannock River, VA, and awaits reinforcements from the **Army of the Potomac.** 8/18-19/1862.
08	18	1862	Skirmishes near Rapidan Station and on Clark's Mountain, VA.
08	18	1862	Skirmish at Huttonsville, WV.
08	19	1862	**James Birdseye McPherson,** USA, is appointed Brig. Gen.
08	19	1862	**Orlando Bolivar Willcox,** USA, is appointed Brig. Gen.
08	19	1862	Skirmish on Clear Creek, AR.
08	19	1862	Federal scout from Woodville to Guntersville, AL, and vicinity. 8/19-20/1862.
08	19	1862	**Federal Expedition against the Snake Indians in Idaho.** 19-10/11/1862.
08	19	1862	Skirmish at Tallulah, LA.
08	19	1862	**Sioux Indians** move on New Ulm, MN, past Fort Ridgely.
08	19	1862	Federal expedition from Rienzi to Marietta and Bay Springs, MS, and skirmishes. 8/19-21/1862.
08	19	1862	The **US Dept. of the Ohio** is re-established, comprising of Illinois, Indiana, Michigan, Ohio, Wisconsin, and Kentucky east of the Tennessee River; Maj. Gen. Horatio G. Wright, USA, commanding.
08	19	1862	**Col. John Hunt Morgan's, CSA, raid on the Louisville and Nashville Railroad,** with skirmishes: a) at Pilot Knob, b) Drakes' Creek, and c) Manscoe Creek, near Edgefield Junction **(Aug. 20th),** and d) action **(Aug. 21st)** on the Hartsville Road, near Gallatin, TN. 8/19-21/1862.
08	20	1862	Skirmish at Baton Rouge, LA.
08	20	1862	Maj. Gen. Richard Taylor, CSA, is assigned to the command of the District of West Louisiana.
08	20	1862	The **Sioux Indians** unsuccessfully attack Fort Ridgely, MN.
08	20	1862	Federal scout in Wayne, Stoddard, and Dunklin Counties, MO, including Bloomfield, Four Mile, Union Mills, MO. 8/20-27/1862.
08	20	1862	Skirmish at Pilot Knob, or Edgefield Junction, TN.
08	20	1862	The Districts of Arkansas, Louisiana, and Texas are constituted into the **Confederate Trans-Mississippi Dept.**
08	20	1862	The **Army of the Potomac** embarks for Aquia Creek and for Alexandria, VA, with the 5th US Army Corps embarking at Newport News, VA. 8/20-9/10/1862.
08	20	1862	Skirmishes at Raccoon Ford, Stevensburg, Brandy Station, Rappahannock Station, and near Kelly's Ford, VA. Maj. Gen. John Pope, USA vs. Maj. Gen. Stonewall Jackson.
08	21	1862	Skirmish at Light Prairie, near Arcata, CA.
08	21	1862	**Baton Rouge, LA, is evacuated** by the Union forces, and after the Union ironclads **Essex and No. 7,** laying offshore, threaten to shell the city if occupied by Confederates, a local citizen committee meet with the commander of **No. 7,** and he promises not to bombard the city.
08	21	1862	Skirmish at Neosho, MO, with Rebel guerrillas.
08	21	1862	Affair on Pinckney Island, SC, with a Confederate surprise attack on a Federal company posted there, with prisoners.
08	21	1862	The Union forces **surrender Gallatin, TN.**
08	21	1862	Skirmishes along the Rappahannock River, at Kelly's, Beverly (or Cunningham's), and Freeman's Fords, etc., VA.
08	21	1862	The 3rd US Army Corps sails from Yorktown, VA, for Alexandria, and Aquia Creek, VA.
08	22	1862	**Brig. Gen. Henry Bohlen, USA,** is mortally wounded while retreating with his command across the

			river at Freeman's Ford, Rappahannock River, VA from Maj. Gen. Stonewall Jackson's Confederate forces.
08	22	1862	**John Reese Kenly,** USA, is appointed Brig. Gen.
08	22	1862	**Alexander Schimmelfennig,** USA, is appointed Brig. Gen.
08	22	1862	Skirmish at Trinity, near Decatur, AL.
08	22	1862	Action with the **Sioux Indians** at Fort Ridgely, MN, with the Federals repelling repeated Indian attacks.
08	22	1862	Confederate raid on Catlett's Station, VA, as Maj. Gen. JEB Stuart, CSA, captures Maj. Gen. John Pope's personal belongings. A major embarrassment for Pope.
08	22	1862	Actions at Freeman's Fords and Hazel River and skirmishes along the Rappahannock River, VA.
08	22	1862	**Brig. Gen. Albert Gallatin Jenkins' Confederate Cavalry Expedition into WV and Ohio.** 8/22-9/19/1862.
08	23	1862	**Matthew Duncan Ector,** CSA, is appointed Brig. Gen.
08	23	1862	Affair 1 mile from Trinity, AL, as the Rebels derail and burn a train, while under fire from Brig. Gen. William S. Rosecrans, USA.
08	23	1862	Affair on Little River, CA.
08	23	1862	Action at Big Hill, KY, with a Federal rout.
08	23	1862	Affair at Bayou Sara, LA, as the Union gunboat, **Essex,** accompanied by a troop transport, begins shelling the place.
08	23	1862	Skirmish at Greenville, MS.
08	23	1862	Skirmish at Four Mile, MO.
08	23	1862	Skirmish at Hickory Grove, MO, as Rebels threaten Kansas City.
08	23	1862	Skirmish near Wayman's Mill, or Spring Creek, MO.
08	23	1862	Maj. Gen. Horatio G. Wright, USA, assumes the command of the Dept. of the Ohio, TN, etal.
08	23	1862	Skirmish near Fort Donelson, TN.
08	23	1862	Action at Beverly Ford, VA.
08	23	1862	Skirmish at Fant's Ford, VA.
08	23	1862	The 6th US Army Corps embarks at Fort Monroe, VA, for the Washington, DC, area and the Aquia Creek.
08	23	1862	Actions at Sulphur (or Warrenton) Springs, VA. 8/23-24/1862.
08	23	1862	The capture of a Union train between Harper's Ferry, WV, and Winchester, VA.
08	23	1862	Affair at Smithfield, or Smithfield Springs, VA.
08	23	1862	Engagement at Rappahannock Station, VA.
08	23	1862	Skirmish at Moorefield, WV.
08	24	1862	The **CSS Alabama** is officially commissioned off the island of Terceira, Azores, to begin a two year career of plundering US merchant vessels.
08	24	1862	Affair near Bloomfield, MO.
08	24	1862	Skirmish on Coon Creek, near Lamar, MO.
08	24	1862	Skirmish on Crooked Creek, near Dallas, MO.
08	24	1862	Federal scout from Salem to Current River, MO. 8/24-28/1862.
08	24	1862	Maj. Gen. John Porter McCown, CSA, is assigned temporarily to command of the Dept. of East Tennessee.
08	24	1862	Actions at Waterloo Bridge, VA, **Second Bull Run,** as Gen Robert E. Lee, CSA, puts his army in motion northward. 8/24-25/1862.
08	25	1862	**John Potts Slough,** USA, is appointed Brig. Gen.
08	25	1862	Skirmish at Madisonville, KY.
08	25	1862	Skirmish at Red Bird Creek, KY.
08	25	1862	Skirmish at Bolivar, MS.
08	25	1862	Fearing further **Sioux Indian** attacks, **New Ulm, MN, is evacuated** by the citizens and the Federal garrison there.
08	25	1862	Skirmish at Fort Donelson, TN.
08	25	1862	Skirmish at Sulphur Springs, VA.
08	26	1862	The capture of the Confederate steamer, **Fair Play,** by Maj. Gen. Samuel R. Curtis, USA.
08	26	1862	Col. James H. Carleton, 1st CA Infantry is assigned to the command of the Department of New Mexico.
08	26	1862	Skirmish near Rienzi, MS, with **Col. Philip H. Sheridan, USA.**
08	26	1862	Skirmish at Fort Donelson, and at Cumberland Iron Works, Cumberland Gap, TN.

08	26	1862	The 2nd US Army Corps embarks at Fort Monroe, VA, for Northern Virginia.
08	26	1862	The **capture of Manassas Station, VA,** by Maj. Gen. Stonewall Jackson's troops, under Brig. Gen. Fitzhugh Lee, CSA's cavalry.
08	26	1862	Skirmishes at Bristoe Station, Bull Run Bridge, Gainesville, Hay Market, Manassas Junction, and Sulphur Springs, VA, as Maj. Gen. Thomas J. "Stonewall" Jackson, CSA, pushes his Confederate Army Corps of the **Army of Northern Virginia** through Thoroughfare Gap in the Bull Mountains.
08	27	1862	Skirmish at Bridgeport, AL, and the attack on Fort McCook, Battle Creek, TN, as the Federals burn the fort and retreat.
08	27	1862	Skirmish near Kossuth, MS.
08	27	1862	Skirmish near Cumberland Gap, TN.
08	27	1862	Skirmish near Murfreesborough, TN.
08	27	1862	Skirmish near Reynolds' Station, on the **Nashville and the Decatur Railroad,** TN.
08	27	1862	Skirmish on Richland Creek, near Pulaski, TN.
08	27	1862	Skirmish at Round Mountain, 2.5 miles from Woodbury, TN, as Brig. Gen. Nathan Bedford Forrest's, CSA, Cavalry is repulsed.
08	27	1862	**Operations of Brig. Gen. Joseph Wheeler's Cavalry in Tennessee and Kentucky.** 8/7-10/22/1862
08	27	1862	Brig. Gen. Joseph Wheeler's CSA command crosses the Tennessee River at Chattanooga.
08	27	1862	The Confederate **Army of the Mississippi,** under Gen. Braxton Bragg, CSA, crosses the Tennessee River. 8/27-28/1862.
08	27	1862	Skirmish at Buckland Bridge (Broad Run), VA.
08	27	1862	Action at Bull Run Bridge, VA, between Maj. Gen. John Pope, USA, and Maj. Gen. Thomas J. Jackson, CSA.
08	27	1862	Engagement at Kettle Run, near Bristoe Station, VA, results in a Union victory by Maj. Gen. Joseph Hooker, USA.
08	27	1862	Skirmish near Salem, VA.
08	27	1862	Skirmish at Waterford, VA.
08	28	1862	**Edward Aylesworth Perry,** CSA, is appointed Brig. Gen.
08	28	1862	Federal expedition from Helena to Eunice, AR, with the gunboat, **USS Pittsburg,** and the steamers, **Iatan** and **White Cloud.** 8/28-9/3/1862.
08	28	1862	Skirmish near Corinth, MS.
08	28	1862	Skirmish at Ashley, MO.
08	28	1862	Skirmish in Howard County, MO.
08	28	1862	Skirmishes at Centreville, Lewis' Ford, and Hay Market, VA.
08	28	1862	Engagement near Gainesville, VA.
08	28	1862	**The Engagement at Thoroughfare Gap, VA,** as Gen. Robert E. Lee, CSA, along with Maj. Gen. James Longstreet, CSA, force their way through toward Manassas, VA, and Maj. Gen. Stonewall Jackson, CSA.
08	29	1862	**John Gregg,** CSA, is appointed Brig. Gen.
08	29	1862	**Godfrey Weitzel,** USA, is appointed Brig. Gen.
08	29	1862	Skirmish between Big Hill and Richmond, KY.
08	29	1862	Engagement between the **USS Anglo-American** and the Port Hudson, LA, Confederate batteries.
08	29	1862	Skirmish near Saint Charles Court-House, LA.
08	29	1862	Skirmish at Bloomfield, MO.
08	29	1862	Skirmish near Iberia, MO.
08	29	1862	Federal expeditions from Waynesville, MO, with skirmish at the California House, etc. 8/29-9/?/1862.
08	29	1862	Brig. Gen. Frederick Steele, USA, assumes the command of the **Army of the Southwest,** MO, etal.
08	29	1862	Gen. Pierre G. T. Beauregard, CSA, assumes the command of the Confederate Dept. of South Carolina and Georgia, relieving Maj. Gen. John C. Pemberton, CSA.
08	29	1862	Skirmishes at Short Mountain Cross-Roads (Aug. 29th), and Little Ford **(Aug. 30th),** near McMinnville, TN. 8/29-30/1862.
08	29	1862	**The Battle of Groveton, or Manassas Plains, VA,** as Maj. Gen. Thomas J. Jackson, CSA, encounters Maj. Gens. John Pope, Fitz John Porter, and Irvin McDowell, USA.
08	30	1862	**John Calvin Brown,** CSA, is promoted Brig. Gen.
08	30	1862	**Robert Cumming Schenck, U.S.A.,** is appointed Maj. Gen.
08	30	1862	Skirmish near Larkinsville, AL.
08	30	1862	The **District of Arizona** is constituted to comprise of all the territory from Fort Thorn, the New Mexico Territory, along the north bank of the Rio Grande River to Fort Quitman, TX.

08	30	1862	**The Battle of Richmond, KY, or the Engagements at the Mount Zion Church, White's Farm, and at Richmond, KY,** as the advancing Maj. Gen. E. Kirby Smith, CSA, forces a Union retreat toward Louisville, KY.
08	30	1862	Skirmish near Plymouth, NC.
08	30	1862	Skirmish at Altamont, TN.
08	30	1862	Operations on the **Mississippi Central Railroad.** 8/30-9/1/1862.
08	30	1862	Skirmish near Bolivar, TN, on the **Mississippi Central Railroad.**
08	30	1862	**The Battle of Bull Run, Groveton Heights, or the Battle of Second Manassas, VA,** results in an overwhelming Confederate victory by Gen. Robert E. Lee, CSA, as the Federals retreat toward Centreville, VA, being pushed back by Maj. Gens. Jackson and Longstreet, CSA; Maj. Gen. George B. McClellan, USA, failing to reinforce Maj. Gen. John Pope, USA; Richmond, VA, is relieved from any Union advance at a total cost of about 25,000 casualties on both sides.
08	30	1862	**Brig. Gen. George William Taylor, USA,** is mortally wounded at the Second Battle of Bull Run, VA, by a Confederate artillery canister shot, while leading his men against the entrenched position of Brig. Gen. Isaac Ridgeway Trimble, CSA's Confederate troops, dying September 1, 1862.
08	30	1862	Skirmishes at Lewis' Ford and Waterloo Bridge, VA.
08	30	1862	Maj. Gen. Gustavus W. Smith, CSA, assumes the command of the defenses of Richmond, VA.
08	30	1862	Skirmish at Buckhannon, WV.
08	31	1862	**Samuel Gibbs French, C.S.A.,** is appointed Maj. Gen.
08	31	1862	Skirmish at Stevenson, AL.
08	31	1862	Skirmish at Yates' Ford, KY, on the Kentucky River.
08	31	1862	Skirmish near Marietta, MS.
08	31	1862	Skirmish at Little River Bridge, MO.
08	31	1862	Skirmish at Rogers' Gap, TN, as the Confederates there are dispersed by Brig. Gen. George W. Morgan, USA.
08	31	1862	Skirmishes at Medon Station, TN, on the **Mississippi Central Railroad.**
08	31	1862	Skirmish near Toone's Station, TN, the **Mississippi Central Railroad.**
08	31	1862	The capture of the US transport **W.B. Terry** on the Tennessee River, after running aground.
08	31	1862	Operations about Centreville and Chantilly, VA, with Maj. Gen. John Pope, USA attempting to consolidate his forces, while Gen. Robert E. Lee, CSA, sent Maj. Gen. Thomas J. Jackson, CSA, to flank Pope's position.
08	31	1862	Skirmish at Franklin, VA.
08	31	1862	Union troops **evacuate Fredericksburg, VA,** leaving behind vast supplies.
08	31	1862	Skirmish at Germantown, VA.
08	31	1862	The Confederate **capture of Weston, WV.**
09	1	1862	**Brig. Gen. George William Taylor, USA,** dies from wounds received two days before at the Second Battle of Manassas, or Bull Run, VA.
09	1	1862	**Alfred Holt Colquitt,** CSA, is appointed Brig. Gen.
09	1	1862	**Junius Daniel,** CSA, is appointed Brig. Gen.
09	1	1862	Skirmish at Huntsville, AL.
09	1	1862	Skirmish at Morganfield, KY.
09	1	1862	Skirmish at Tait's Ferry, Kentucky River, KY.
09	1	1862	Skirmish at Uniontown, KY.
09	1	1862	Skirmish at Putnam, MO.
09	1	1862	Skirmishes at Neosho and Spring River, MO.
09	1	1862	Maj. Gen. Ormsby M. Mitchel, USA, is assigned to the command of the Dept. of the South, SC, etal.
09	1	1862	Maj. Gen. John Porter McCown, CSA, assumes the command of the Dept. of East Tennessee.
09	1	1862	Skirmish at Britton's Lane, near Denmark, TN, on the **Mississippi Central Railroad.**
09	1	1862	The Proclamation declaring martial law in Texas is annulled.
09	1	1862	**The Battle of Chantilly, or Ox Hill, VA,** concludes the 2nd Battle of Bull Run; Maj. Gen. Pope, USA, retreats towards Washington, DC.
09	1	1862	**Maj. Gen. Philip Kearny, USA,** is instantly killed at the Battle of Chantilly, VA, receiving multiple gunshot wounds after unknowingly riding directly into the Confederate battle line, refusing to be captured, he spurred his horse to flee.
09	1	1862	**Maj. Gen. Isaac Ingalls Stevens, USA,** is instantly killed at the Battle of Chantilly, VA, shot through the head by a Confederate soldier.
09	1	1862	Skirmish at Glenville, WV.

09	2	1862	**Abraham Buford,** CSA, is promoted Brig. Gen.
09	2	1862	**Lexington, KY, is occupied** by Maj. Gen. E. Kirby Smith, CSA, as Gen. Braxton Bragg, CSA, marches north from Chattanooga, TN.
09	2	1862	Action with the **Sioux Indians** at Acton, MN.
09	2	1862	Action with the **Sioux Indians** at Birch Cooley, MN.
09	2	1862	Raid into Ohio, by Jenkins' Confederate Cavalry command.
09	2	1862	Skirmish near Memphis, TN.
09	2	1862	Skirmish near Nashville, TN.
09	2	1862	The **Army of Virginia** is merged into the **Army of the Potomac,** under the command of Maj. Gen. George B. McClellan, USA, leaving Maj. Gen. John Pope, USA, without a command.
09	2	1862	Skirmishes near Fairfax Court-House, Falls Church, and Vienna, VA, as Maj. Gen. Pope, USA, retreats to Washington, DC.
09	2	1862	Affair at Flint Hill, VA.
09	2	1862	Skirmish near Leesburg, VA, results in a rout of the Federals.
09	2	1862	Federal expedition from Suffolk, VA, to cut off some Rebel recruits on their way to Richmond, VA. 9/2-3/1862.
09	2	1862	**Winchester, VA, is evacuated** by Brig. Gen. Julius White, USA.
09	2	1862	Surrender of Union forces at Spencer Court-House, WV, to Brig. Gen. Albert G. Jenkins', CSA, Cavalry Raid.
09	3	1862	Action with Indians at Fort Abercrombie, the Dakota Territory.
09	3	1862	Maj. Gen. E. Kirby Smith's CSA troops **occupy Frankfort,** the state capital of Kentucky.
09	3	1862	Skirmish at Geiger's Lake, or Slaughterville, KY.
09	3	1862	**The Maryland (Antietam) Campaign.** 9/3-20/1862.
09	3	1862	Skirmish at Edwards Ferry, MD. 9/3-4/1862.
09	3	1862	Skirmish at Monocacy Aqueduct, MD. 9/3-4/1862.
09	3	1862	Skirmish at Neosho, MO.
09	3	1862	Brig. Gen. Alpheus S. Williams, USA, assumes the command of the 2nd US Army Corps, the **Army of Virginia.**
09	3	1862	Maj. Gen. Jesse L. Reno, USA, assumes the command of the 9th US Army Corps, the **Army of Virginia.**
09	3	1862	The 10th US Army Corps is constituted under the command of Maj. Gen. Ormsby M. Mitchel, USA, SC, etal.
09	3	1862	Skirmishes at Falls Church, VA. 9/3-4/1862.
09	3	1862	The **Confederate Army of Northern Virginia** marches toward Leesburg, VA.
09	3	1862	The **occupation of Winchester, VA,** by the Confederate forces.
09	3	1862	Skirmish at Bunker Hill, WV. 9/3-4/1862.
09	3	1862	Reconnaissance from Harper's Ferry to Lovettsville and Charlestown, WV. 9/3-4/1862.
09	3	1862	Skirmish near Martinsburg, WV.
09	3	1862	Skirmish at Ravenswood, WV.
09	3	1862	Skirmish at Weston, WV.
09	4	1862	**Charles Champion Gilbert,** USA, is appointed Brig. Gen.
09	4	1862	The CSA Steamer, **Oreto** eludes the Union vessel, **Oneida,** and arrives safely through the Union blockade at Mobile Bay, AL.
09	4	1862	Skirmish at Shelbyville, KY.
09	4	1862	Affairs at Boutte Station and Bayou des Allemands, LA, after the Texas Rangers ambush some Federals, are pursued into the local swamps, with many captured, by Maj. Gen. Benjamin F. Butler, USA. 9/4-5/1862.
09	4	1862	Skirmishes at Point of Rocks and Berlin, MD. 9/4-5/1862.
09	4	1862	Skirmishes at Poolesville, MD. 9/4-5/1862.
09	4	1862	Skirmish with the **Sioux Indians** at Hutchinson, MN.
09	4	1862	Federal scouts in Callaway County, MO.
09	4	1862	Skirmish at Prairie Chapel, MO.
09	4	1862	Brig. Gen. Albert Gallatin Jenkin's, CSA, Cavalry raid into Ohio and West Virginia continues.
09	4	1862	The **Army of Northern Virginia** crosses the Potomac by the fords near Leesburg, VA, into Maryland, as the Federals **evacuate Frederick, MD.** 9/4-7/1862.
09	5	1862	The following are appointed Union Brigadier Generals: **Herman Haupt,** USA **Charles Edward Hovey,** USA **Gabriel Rene Paul,** USA

09	5	1862	The **CSS Alabama** captures and burns her first Union target, the **Ocmulgee,** eastern Atlantic, near the Azores.
09	5	1862	The command of the District of Western Arizona is shuffled as follows: Maj. David Ferguson, 1st CA Cavalry, is relieved of command; Col. Joseph R. West, 1st CA Infantry, assumes command; Maj. Theodore A. Coult, 5th CA Infantry, is assigned to command.
09	5	1862	Skirmish near Madisonville, KY.
09	5	1862	Brig. Gen. Daniel Ruggles, CSA, is assigned to the command of the District of the Mississippi.
09	5	1862	Federal scout toward Holly Springs and skirmish at Olive Branch, MS, by Brig. Gen. Benjamin H. Grierson, USA. 9/5-6/1862 .
09	5	1862	Skirmish at Neoso, MO.
09	5	1862	Brig. Gen. John M. Brannan, USA, is temporarily in command of the Dept. of the South, SC.
09	5	1862	Skirmish at Burnt Bridge, near Humboldt, TN.
09	5	1862	Federal expedition from Fort Donelson to Clarksville, TN, and skirmishes **(Sept. 6th)** at New Providence and **(Sept. 7th)** at Riggin's Hill, TN. 9/5-10/1862.
09	5	1862	The **armies of the Potomac and Virginia** being consolidated, Maj. Gen. John Pope, USA, is relieved and ordered to report to the Secretary of War, VA, etal.
09	6	1862	Skirmish at La Grange, AR.
09	6	1862	Skirmish with **Sioux Indians** at Fort Abercrombie, the Dakota Territory.
09	6	1862	The **Dept. of the Northwest** is created to embrace Wisconsin, Iowa, Minnesota, and the Territories of Nebraska and Dakota.
09	6	1862	Maj. Gen. John Pope, USA, is assigned to the command of the Dept. of the Northwest, MN, to deal with the Indian uprisings, a new diminished future role for John Pope.
09	6	1862	**Frederick, MD, is occupied** by Maj. Gen. Stonewall Jackson, CSA.
09	6	1862	Skirmish south of Roanoke, MO, with a Union attack on the guerrilla camp there.
09	6	1862	Confederate attack on Washington, NC.
09	6	1862	Affair on the Gallatin Road, TN.
09	6	1862	The Union **evacuation of Aquia Creek, VA,** near Fredericksburg, and the destruction of property there.
09	6	1862	**Campaign in the Kanawha Valley, WV,** by Maj. Gen. William W. Loring, CSA. 9/6-16/1862.
09	6	1862	Maj. Gen. Loring's Confederate command moves from the Narrows, WV .
09	7	1862	The following are appointed Union Brigadier Generals: **Joseph Bradford Carr,** USA **Thomas Leiper Kane,** USA **Gershom Mott,** USA **Nelson Taylor,** USA
09	7	1862	Union forces **occupy Bowling Green, KY.**
09	7	1862	Federal **surrender** of the outpost at **Shepherdsville, KY.**
09	7	1862	Federal expedition from Carrollton and vicinity of Saint Charles Court-House, LA, and skirmish. 9/7-8/1862.
09	7	1862	Engagement between the **USS Essex** and the Port Hudson, LA, batteries.
09	7	1862	Skirmish at Point of Rocks, or Poolesville, MD.
09	7	1862	Skirmish at Lancaster, MO, with Rebel guerrillas.
09	7	1862	Skirmish near Murfreesborough, TN, with Gen. Braxton Bragg, CSA.
09	7	1862	Skirmish at Pine Mountain Gap, TN.
09	7	1862	Skirmish at Riggin's Hill, near Clarksville, TN.
09	7	1862	Maj. Gen. Joseph Hooker, USA, assumes the command of the 3rd US Army Corps, the Army of Virginia, relieving Maj. Gen. Irvin McDowell, USA.
09	7	1862	Skirmish at Darkesville, WV.
09	8	1862	Skirmish at Redwood Creek, CA.
09	8	1862	Affair at the Kentucky Line, with Brig. Gen. Joseph Wheeler's Cavalry, CSA.
09	8	1862	Skirmish at Barboursville, KY.
09	8	1862	Skirmish at Poolesville, MD.
09	8	1862	Federal expedition to the Coldwater and Hernando, MS. 9/8-13/1862.
09	8	1862	Federal expedition from Fort Leavenworth, KS, through Jackson, Cass, Johnson, and La Fayette Counties, MO, in pursuit of Quantrill's band of guerrillas. 9/8-23/1862.
09	8	1862	Maj. Gen. Nathaniel P. Banks, USA, assumes the command of the Defenses of Washington, DC.
09	9	1862	**William Rufus Terrill,** USA, is appointed Brig. Gen.

MONTH	DAY	YEAR	ACT
09	9	1862	The **CSS Alabama** continues its hunt for Union vessels, burning the **Alert, Ocean Rover, Starlight,** and the **Weather Gauge,** during the last 3 days, near the Azores, eastern Atlantic Ocean.
09	9	1862	Skirmishes on the Franklin and Scottsville Roads, KY.
09	9	1862	Skirmishes at Monocacy Church and Barnesville, MD, as Gen. Robert E. Lee, CSA, presses on into Maryland.
09	9	1862	Skirmish at Big Creek, MO.
09	9	1862	Skirmish at Cockrum Cross-Roads, MS.
09	9	1862	Skirmish at Rienzi, MS.
09	9	1862	Skirmish at Columbia, TN.
09	9	1862	Skirmish at Williamsburg, VA, with Federals under Maj. Gen. John A Dix, USA, Dept. of VA, being routed by Rebels; Maj. Jacob P. Wilson, 5th PA Cavalry, after being brought in front of a Court of Court-Martial for cowardice, is found not guilty, and restored to previous rank.
09	9	1862	Maj. Gen. Samuel P. Heintzelman, USA is placed in command of the Defenses of Washington, DC, south of the Potomac River.
09	10	1862	**Edward Ferraro,** USA, is appointed Brig. Gen.
09	10	1862	**James Nagle,** USA, is appointed Brig. Gen.
09	10	1862	Skirmish at Fort Mitchel, near Covington, KY.
09	10	1862	Skirmish at Log Church, KY.
09	10	1862	Skirmish at Woodburn, KY.
09	10	1862	Skirmish near Boonsborough, MD.
09	10	1862	Skirmish near Frederick, MD.
09	10	1862	Skirmishes at Sugar Loaf Mountain, MD. 9/10-11/1862.
09	10	1862	Skirmish with the **Sioux Indians** at Sauk Centre, MN.
09	10	1862	Cincinnati, OH, prepares for a Confederate invasion, from the likes of Brig. Gen. John Hunt Morgan, Maj. Gen. E. Kirby Smith and/or Gen. Braxton Bragg, CSA.
09	10	1862	Skirmish on the Kilkenny River, SC.
09	10	1862	Skirmish at Columbia, TN.
09	10	1862	Operations at Rogers' and Big Creek Gaps, TN.
09	10	1862	Action at Fayetteville, WV.
09	11	1862	Federal expedition from Clarendon to Lawrenceville and Saint Charles, AR. 9/11-13/1862.
09	11	1862	Engagement at Saint John's Bluff, FL., with the Confederate shore batteries there.
09	11	1862	Skirmish at Smith's, KY, as Maj. Gen. E. Kirby Smith, CSA, **captures Maysville, KY,** and is within striking distance of Cincinnati, OH.
09	11	1862	Action at Bloomfield, MO.
09	11	1862	Skirmish between Williamsport, MD, and Martinsburg, WV.
09	11	1862	Skirmishes at Cotton Hill, Gauley (or Miller's) Ferry, Armstrong's Creek, and near Cannelton, WV.
09	12	1862	The following are appointed Confederate Brigadier Generals: **James Fleming Fagan,** CSA **Allison Nelson,** CSA **William Read Scurry,** CSA **Francis Ashbury Shoup,** CSA **William Steele,** CSA
09	12	1862	Skirmish at Brandenburg, KY.
09	12	1862	**Glasgow, KY, is occupied** by Maj. Gen. E. Kirby Smith, CSA.
09	12	1862	Skirmish near Woodburn, KY.
09	12	1862	Skirmishes at Frederick, MD, Maj. Gen. McClellan, USA commanding.
09	12	1862	Skirmish at the Coldwater Railroad Bridge, MS.
09	12	1862	Federal scout in Loudoun County, VA, and skirmish **(Sept. 14th)** near Leesburg, VA. 9/12-17/1862.
09	12	1862	The **1st, 2nd and 3rd US Army Corps,** the **Army of Virginia,** are designated respectively as the **11th, 12th and the 1st US Army Corps,** the **Army of the Potomac,** VA.
09	12	1862	**The Confederate Siege and Capture of Harper's Ferry, WV** including action on Maryland and Bolivar Heights. 9/12-15/1862.
09	12	1862	Skirmish at Hurricane Bridge, WV.
09	13	1862	**Calvin Edward Pratt,** USA, is appointed Brig. Gen.
09	13	1862	Federal expedition to Pass Manchac and Ponchatoula, LA, and skirmish, as the Federals burn telegraph and post offices there, etc. 9/13-15/1862.

09	13	1862	Skirmishes at Catoctin Mountain, Middletown, Jefferson, and South Mountain, MD.
09	13	1862	Skirmish near Bragg's Farm, near Whaley's Mill, MO.
09	13	1862	Skirmish at Newtonia, MO.
09	13	1862	Skirmish on Strother Fork of the Black River, Iron County, MO.
09	13	1862	Skirmish near Iuka, MS, with Confederate Cavalry.
09	13	1862	Operations at Flour Bluffs, TX. 9/13-14/1862.
09	13	1862	**Gen. Robert E. Lee's Special Order No. 191,** which details Lee's offensive strategy, is found by Union soldiers, VA, which gives Maj. Gen. George B. McClellan a decisive edge in the upcoming campaign at Antietam, MD.
09	13	1862	Maj. Gen. John Sedgwick, USA, is assigned to command of the 12th Corps, Army of the Potomac.
09	13	1862	Action at, and **evacuation of, Charleston, WV,** by Union forces, due to the forces under Maj. Gen. William W. Loring, CSA.
09	14	1862	Skirmish at Henderson, KY.
09	14	1862	Confederate siege of Munfordville and Woodsonville, KY, as Gen. Braxton Bragg, CSA, and Maj. Gen. Don Carlos Buell, USA, clash. 9/14-17/1862.
09	14	1862	Skirmish at Burnsville, MS.
09	14	1862	Skirmish near Petersville, MD.
09	14	1862	**The Battle of South Mountain, (Boonsborough, Boonsborough Gap,** or **Turner's Pass),** and **Crampton's Pass, MD,** as Maj. Gen. William B. Franklin, USA, attempts to force a crossing to aid the Union forces at Harpers Ferry, WV, which results in approximately 5,000 total casualties.
09	14	1862	**Brig. Gen. Samuel Garland, Jr., CSA,** is mortally wounded defending Fox's Gap, at South Mountain, VA.
09	14	1862	**Maj. Gen. Jesse Lee Reno, USA,** is mortally wounded at the head of his command, while attacking the Confederate forces defending Fox's Gap, South Mountain, VA.
09	14	1862	Brig. Gen. Jacob D. Cox, USA, assumes the command of the 9th US Army Corps, Army of the Potomac.
09	15	1862	**Joseph Robert Davis,** CSA, is appointed Brig. Gen.
09	15	1862	**William Henry Fitzhugh Lee,** CSA, is appointed Brig. Gen.
09	15	1862	**Henry Jackson Hunt,** USA, is appointed Brig. Gen.
09	15	1862	Skirmish at Boonsborough, MD.
09	15	1862	Skirmish on the Antietam Creek, near Keedysville, MD.
09	15	1862	Federal scout in Ralls County, MO. 9/15-20/1862.
09	15	1862	Maj. Gen. Stonewall Jackson, CSA, **captures Harper's Ferry, WV.**
09	15	1862	Maj. Gen. Joseph King Fenno Mansfield, USA, assumes the command of the 12th US Army Corps, Army of the Potomac, just 2 days before being mortally wounded.
09	16	1862	Skirmish near Oakland Station, near Munfordville, KY.
09	16	1862	**The Battle of Antietam, or Sharpsburg, MD,** 9/16-17/1862.
09	16	1862	Skirmish in Monroe County, MO.
09	16	1862	Federal reconnaissance from Burnsville toward Iuka, MS and skirmish.
09	16	1862	Federal reconnaissance toward Thoroughfare Gap and Aldie, VA.
09	16	1862	Federal reconnaissance from Upton's Hill to Leesburg, VA, and skirmish. 9/16-19/1862.
09	16	1862	Union forces reach the Ohio River from the Kanawha Valley, WV.
09	17	1862	The following are appointed Union Major Generals: **Gordon Granger,** U.S.A. **Schuyler Hamilton,** U.S.A. **Stephen Augustus Hurlbut,** U.S.A.
09	17	1862	**The Battle of Antietam, or Sharpsburg, MD,** with Maj. Gen. George B. McClellan, USA, and Gen. Robert E. Lee, CSA, fighting the deadliest one day battle on Sept. 17, 1862, with over 23,000 casualties, at sites including the East Woods, West Woods, the Cornfield, the Bloody Lane, the Dunkard Church, Burnside's Bridge, Mumma's farm, near the Piper Farmhouse, etc. Lee withdraws across the Potomac, and McClellan failing to push the issue. The battle essentially ends in a draw. 9/16-17/1862.
09	17	1862	**Brig. Gen. George Burgwyn Anderson, CSA,** is mortally wounded at the Battle of Antietam, MD, after being shot in the foot which required amputation at Raleigh, NC. Failing to recover, he died October 16, 1862.
09	17	1862	**Brig. Gen. Lawrence O'Bryan Branch, CSA,** is instantly killed by a Federal sharpshooter, at the Battle of Antietam, MD, while his commanding officer, Maj. Gen. A.P. Hill, meets with his brigade commanders of Archer, Gregg, and Branch, shortly after Hill arrives from Harper's Ferry, and saves the day for the Confederates.

09	17	1862	**Brig. Gen. William Edwin Starke, CSA,** is mortally wounded at the Battle of Antietam, MD, after being shot three times, and surviving for only a few hours.
09	17	1862	**Maj. Gen. Joseph Ring Fenno Mansfield, USA,** is mortally wounded at the Battle of Antietam, MD, receiving his death wound to his stomach while leading his men out of the East Woods towards the Confederate position in the West Woods, dying the next day.
09	17	1862	**Maj. Gen. Israel Bush Richardson, USA,** is mortally wounded at the Battle of Antientam MD, while valiantly encouraging his men on near the Sunken Lane, finally succumbing to his wounds two months later on November 3, 1862.
09	17	1862	**Brig. Gen. Isaac Peace Rodman, USA,** is mortally wounded at the Battle of Antietam, MD, receiving his death wound to his chest by a Confederate musketball, while leading his men against Maj. Gen. Ambrose Powell Hill's Confederate forces, who just arrived from Harper's Ferry, WV, after Rodman's men forded the Antietam Creek above the infamous **"Burnside's Bridge,"** dying two weeks later on September 30, 1862.
09	17	1862	Engagement at Saint John's Bluff, FL, with the Confederate shore battery there and 5 Union gunboats.
09	17	1862	**The Federal Evacuation of Cumberland Gap, TN,** by Brig. Gen. George W. Morgan, USA, and the march of its garrison to Greensburg, KY. 9/17-10/3/1862.
09	17	1862	Union troops **surrender Munfordville, KY,** to Gen. Braxton Bragg, CSA.
09	17	1862	Skirmishes on the Bowling Green Road and at Merry Oaks, KY.
09	17	1862	Skirmish near Falmouth, KY.
09	17	1862	Operations at and about Shiloh, NC. 9/17-20/1862.
09	17	1862	Maj. Gen. Ormsby M. Mitchel, USA, assumes the command of the Dept. of the South, SC. etal.
09	17	1862	Skirmish near Durhamville, TN.
09	17	1862	Maj. Gen. George G. Meade, USA, assumes the command of the 1st US Army Corps, Army of the Potomac.
09	17	1862	Brig. Gen. Alpheus S. Williams, USA, assumes the command of the 12th US Army Corps, Army of the Potomac.
09	18	1862	**Maj. Gen. Joseph Ring Fenno Mansfield, USA,** dies near Sharpsburg, MD, from his battle wound received the previous day.
09	18	1862	The **CSS Alabama** continues to destroy Federal whaling vessels, near the Azores, Atlantic Ocean, including the **Altahama, Courser, Elisha Dunbar, Benjamin Tucker,** and the **Virginia.**
09	18	1862	Skirmish near Cave City, KY.
09	18	1862	Skirmish near Florence, KY.
09	18	1862	Affair at Glasgow, KY, with the capture of many Confederates.
09	18	1862	Skirmish at Owensborough, KY.
09	18	1862	Skirmish at Rienzi, MS.
09	18	1862	Brig. Gen. James H. Carleton, USA, relieves Brig. Gen. Edward R. S. Canby in command of the Dept. of New Mexico.
09	18	1862	Operations about Forts Henry and Donelson, TN, and skirmish. 9/18-23/1862.
09	18	1862	The Confederate Army of Northern Virginia recrosses the Potomac River near Shepherdstown, WV after losing thousands of valiant brave men at Antietam, MD. 9/18-19/1862.
09	19	1862	**William Edwin Baldwin,** CSA, is promoted Brig. Gen.
09	19	1862	**William Edmondson Jones,** CSA, is appointed Brig. Gen.
09	19	1862	**Charles Smith Hamilton,** U.S.A., is appointed Maj. Gen.
09	19	1862	The following are appointed Union Brigadier Generals: **Francis Channing Barlow,** USA **Gustavus Adolphus Smith,** USA **Francis Laurens Vinton,** USA
09	19	1862	Skirmish near Helena, AR, with Federal pickets and Texas Rangers.
09	19	1862	Operations in the Indian Territory. 9/19-24/1862.
09	19	1862	Skirmishes at Horse Cave and Bear Wallow, KY.
09	19	1862	Skirmish at Southerland's Farm, KY.
09	19	1862	Skirmishes at Sharpsburg, Shepherdstown (Blackford's, or Boteler's) Ford, and near Williamsport, MD, as Maj. Gen. George B. McClellan, USA, begins to move after the retreating Confederate Army of the Northern Virginia.
09	19	1862	Skirmish at Barnett's Corners, MS.
09	19	1862	Confederate small arms attack on the **Queen of the West,** near Bolivar, MS.
09	19	1862	**The Engagement at Iuka, MS.** Maj. Gen. William S. Rosecrans, USA, defeats Maj. Gen. Sterling Price,

			CSA. Total casualties approximate 2,350.
09	19	1862	**Brig. Gen. Lewis Henry Little, C.S.A.,** is instantly killed by a musketball to the forehead, while he sat on his horse talking with Maj. Gen. Sterling Price, and Brig. Generals Louis Hebert, and John Wilkins Whitfield, at the engagement at Iuka, MS; the Minie Ball passing under Gen. Price's arm and striking **Lewis Henry Little** in the forehead.
09	19	1862	Skirmish at Peyton's Mill, MS, between Cavalry forces.
09	19	1862	Skirmish at Prentiss, MS.
09	19	1862	**The Dept. of Missouri is re-established** and also embraces the **Dept. of Kansas, which is discontinued.**
09	19	1862	Skirmish at Hickory Grove, MO.
09	19	1862	Affair at Mount Vernon, MO.
09	19	1862	The **Confederate Dept. of North Carolina and Southern Virginia. (Dept. of Virginia and of North Carolina)** is constituted, under the command of Maj. Gen. Gustavus W. Smith, CSA.
09	19	1862	Skirmishes at Brentwood, TN. 9/19-20/1862.
09	19	1862	West Virginia is transferred to the Federal Dept. of the Ohio.
09	20	1862	Skirmish near Helena, AR.
09	20	1862	Actions near **Munfordville, KY,** with Maj. Gen. Don Carlos Buell, USA, **reoccupying** the town, as Gen. Braxton Bragg, CSA, moves to Bardstown to effect a hookup with Maj. Gen. E. Kirby Smith, CSA. 9/20-21/1862.
09	20	1862	Skirmish near Hagerstown, MD.
09	20	1862	Skirmish near Williamsport, MD.
09	20	1862	Skirmish on the Fulton Road, south of Iuka, MS.
09	20	1862	Skirmish at Shirley's Ford, Spring River, MO.
09	20	1862	Affair near Shiloh, NC, with the Union landing party from the ironclad, **USS Lancer.**
09	20	1862	Federal expedition from Bolivar to Grand Junction and La Grange, TN, and skirmish. 9/20-22/1862.
09	20	1862	Skirmish at Ashby's Gap, VA.
09	20	1862	Skirmish at Point Pleasant, WV.
09	20	1862	Action near Shepherdstown, WV.
09	21	1862	Affair at the San Pedro Crossing, the Arizona Territory.
09	21	1862	Affair on the Yreka Road, near Fort Crook, CA.
09	21	1862	Federal expedition from Carrollton to Donaldsonville, LA, and skirmish, as the Federal landing party after sugar, etc, was forced to retreat, in a hurry. 9/21-25/1862.
09	21	1862	Skirmish at Cassville, MO.
09	21	1862	Skirmish near Van Buren, TN.
09	22	1862	**John Crawford Vaughn,** CSA, is appointed Brig. Gen.
09	22	1862	Skirmish at Vinegar Hill, KY.
09	22	1862	Skirmish at Ashby's Gap, VA, as the Federals advance on the retreating Confederate supply wagon train.
09	22	1862	Union forces **reoccupy Harper's Ferry, WV.**
09	23	1862	Skirmish at McGuire's Ferry, AR.
09	23	1862	Action with **Sioux Indians** at Fort Abercrombie, the Dakota Territory.
09	23	1862	Action with **Sioux Indians** at Wood Lake, near Yellow Medicine, MN, with Col. Henry Hastings Sibley, USA, capturing over 1,000 Indians.
09	23	1862	Federal expedition to Eureka, Boone County, MO. 9/23-24/1862.
09	23	1862	The **Dept. of the Tennessee** is constituted, under the command of Maj. Gen. George H. Thomas, USA. (but, it is inoperative).
09	23	1862	Skirmish at Wolf Creek Bridge, near Memphis, TN.
09	24	1862	**Mason Brayman,** USA, is appointed Brig. Gen.
09	24	1862	**Nathaniel James Jackson,** USA, is appointed Brig. Gen.
09	24	1862	Maj. Gen. Samuel R. Curtis, USA, assumes the command of the Dept. of Missouri.
09	24	1862	Skirmish at Granby, MO.
09	24	1862	Gen. P.G.T. Beauregard, CSA, relieves Maj. Gen. John C. Pemberton in the command of the Dept. of South Carolina and Georgia.
09	24	1862	Affair on Skull Creek, SC.
09	24	1862	Engagement at Sabine Pass, TX. 9/24-25/1862.
09	24	1862	The District of West Tennessee is reorganized. Maj. Gens. Sherman, Ord, and Rosecrans, and Brig. Gen. Quinby, USA, are assigned to divisions.

09	25	1862	**George Washington Getty,** USA, is appointed Brig. Gen.
09	25	1862	Skirmish at Ashbysburg, KY.
09	25	1862	Skirmish near Snow's Pond, KY, as Maj. Gen. Don Carlos Buell, USA, arrives at Louisville, KY, ahead of Gen. Braxton Bragg, CSA.
09	25	1862	Skirmish at Davis' Bridge, Hatchie River, TN, with guerrillas.
09	25	1862	The **burning of Randolph, TN,** by Maj. Gen. William T. Sherman, USA.
09	25	1862	Federal Cavalry reconnaissance from Shepherdstown, WV, found the Confederates camped 2 miles out from Sherpherdstown.
09	25	1862	Federal expedition from Centreville to Bristoe Station and Warrenton Junction, VA. 9/25-28/1862.
09	26	1862	The following are appointed Union Brigadier Generals: **William Woods Averell,** USA **Alfred Sully,** USA **Gouverneur Kemble Warren,** USA
09	26	1862	Federal expedition from Helena to Jeffersonville and Marianna, AR.
09	26	1862	Federal expedition from Helena to La Grange, AR.
09	26	1862	Skirmish with **Sioux Indians** at Fort Abercrombie, the Dakota Territory.
09	26	1862	Action at West Liberty, KY.
09	26	1862	Skirmish near Cambridge, MO, as the Federals walk into an ambush.
09	26	1862	Skirmish at Pocahontas, TN.
09	26	1862	Skirmish near Catlett's Station, VA.
09	26	1862	Federal expedition from Point Pleasant, up the Kanawha River, to Buffalo, WV, and skirmish with Brig. Gen. Albert G. Jenkins, CSA. 9/26-27/1862.
09	27	1862	Skirmishes at Augusta and Brookville, KY. 9/27-28/1862.
09	27	1862	Skirmish near Iuka, MS.
09	27	1862	The following Confederate command assignments took place: a) Maj. Gen. John P. McCown, CSA - Dept. of East Tennessee b) Maj. Gen. Samuel Jones, CSA - District of Middle TN.
09	27	1862	Affair on Taylor's Bayou, near Beaumont, TX, as the Federals are unsuccessful in burning the **Eastern Texas Railroad** bridge. Confederates stationed there are suffering from measles and yellow fever.
09	27	1862	Federal reconnaissance from Harper's Ferry toward Charlestown, WV.
09	28	1862	Maj. Gen. Hindman, CSA, is assigned to the command of the 1st Corps, Army of the West, Arkansas, Missouri, etc.
09	28	1862	Skirmish near Lebanon Junction, KY.
09	28	1862	Federal expedition from Columbus, KY, to Covington, Durhamville, and Fort Randolph, TN. 9/28-10/5/1862.
09	28	1862	Skirmish near Friar's Point, MS.
09	28	1862	Skirmish at Standing Stone, WV.
09	29	1862	**Maj. Gen. William Nelson, USA,** is shot dead in the lobby of the Gault House, Louisville, KY, after being confronted by **Brig. Gen. Jefferson Columbus Davis, USA,** who Nelson argued with on prior occasions and provoked Davis by slapping him only moments before the shooting. Although it appears to have been cold blooded murder, Davis was never formally charged with anything.
09	29	1862	**Henry Hastings Sibley,** USA, is appointed Brig. Gen.
09	29	1862	Brig. Gen. Douglas H. Cooper, CSA, is appointed Superintendent of Indian Affairs, MO, the Indian Territory, etal.
09	29	1862	Skirmish on the Elizabethtown Road, KY.
09	29	1862	The capture of the 3rd Georgia Cavalry, near New Haven, KY. Col. Martin J. Crawford, CSA, has his rank and pay suspended for 3 months by the Confederate Court-Martial Board, for allowing such capture to take place.
09	29	1862	Maj. Joseph John F. Reynolds, USA, assumes the command of the 1st US Army Corps, Army of the Potomac, VA.
09	29	1862	Federal Cavalry expedition from Centreville to Warrenton and Buckland Mills, VA, where many sick and wounded Confederates are captured and paroled.
09	30	1862	**Brig. Gen. Isaac Peace Rodman, USA,** dies from chest wounds received at the Battle of Antietam, MD.
09	30	1862	Federal reconnaissance on May and Savannah Rivers, GA, aboard the transports, **Planter and Starlight** to destroy Confederate saltworks. 9/30-10/3/1862.

09	30	1862	Skirmish near Louisville, KY.
09	30	1862	Skirmishes at Russellville and Glasgow, KY.
09	30	1862	Federal reconnaissance from Rienzi, MS, to the Hatchie River.
09	30	1862	Skirmish on Clear Fork, near Warrensburg, MO.
09	30	1862	Engagement at Newtonia, MO, between Brig. Gen. Frederick Salomon, USA, and Col. Douglas H. Cooper, CSA.
09	30	1862	Skirmishes in Scotland and Boone Counties, MO.
09	30	1862	Federal expedition from Fort Ruby, the Nevada Territory, to Camp Douglas, the Utah Territory, with affairs **(Oct. 11th and 15th)** on the Humboldt River, the Nevada Territory. 9/30-10/29/1862.
09	30	1862	Federal expedition from Hilton Head, SC, to Saint John's Bluff, FL. 9/30-10/13/1862.
09	30	1862	Skirmish at Goodlettsville, TN.
09	30	1862	Skirmish near Glenville, WV, with Union cavalrymen.
10	1	1862	**Robert Seaman Granger,** USA, is appointed Brig. Gen.
10	1	1862	Engagement at Saint John's Bluff, FL.
10	1	1862	Skirmish on the Bardstown Pike, near Mount Washington, KY.
10	1	1862	Skirmish on the Fern Creek, Louisville, and Frankfort Road, KY.
10	1	1862	Skirmish on the Louisville Pike, KY.
10	1	1862	The **Confederate Dept. of Mississippi, and East Louisiana,** is constituted, under the command of Maj. Gen. John C. Pemberton, CSA, which included Vicksburg, MS, and who will replace Maj. Gen. Earl Van Dorn, CSA, after being defeated at Corinth, MS.
10	1	1862	Skirmish at Davis' Bridge, MS.
10	1	1862	Skirmish at Ruckersville, MS.
10	1	1862	Skirmish at Davis' Bridge, TN.
10	1	1862	Skirmish near Nashville, TN.
10	1	1862	Federal reconnaissance from Sharpsburg, MD, to Shepherdstown and Martinsburg, WV, and skirmishes en route.
10	1	1862	President Lincoln travels to Harper's Ferry, WV, to meet with Maj. Gen. George B. McClellan, USA.
10	1	1862	Federal reconnaissance from Harper's Ferry, WV, to Leesburg, VA. 10/1-2/1862.
10	2	1862	**Evander McIvor Law,** CSA, is appointed Brig. Gen.
10	2	1862	**Francis Barretto Spinola,** USA, is appointed Brig. Gen.
10	2	1862	Skirmishes between Mayport Mills and Saint John's Bluff, FL.
10	2	1862	Skirmish on the Shepherdsville Road, KY.
10	2	1862	Skirmish at Baldwyn, MS.
10	2	1862	Skirmish near Ramer's Crossing, the **Mobile and Ohio Railroad,** MS.
10	2	1862	Skirmish near Columbia, MO, as the Federals routs guerrillas.
10	2	1862	Federal destruction of the railroad depot near Beaumont, TX, and the Eastern Texas Bridge. Confederates still greatly suffering from the measles and yellow fever.
10	2	1862	Operations at Blue's Gap (or Hanging Rock), Little Cacapon Bridge, and Paw Paw Tunnel, WV, including Maj. Gen. JEB Stuart's capture of a Union company. **(Oct. 4th).** 10/2-4/1862.
10	2	1862	President Lincoln visits with Maj. Gen. George B. McClellan, USA, in the field in the vicinity of Antietam, MD to see first hand the status of the Army of the Potomac and to prod McClellan to move quickly after the damaged Army of Northern Virginia.
10	3	1862	**William Brimage Bate,** CSA, is promoted Brig. Gen.
10	3	1862	The Federal **capture of Saint John's Bluff, FL.**
10	3	1862	Skirmish at Cedar Church, near Shepherdsville, KY.
10	3	1862	Skirmish at Jollification, MO.
10	3	1862	**The Battle of Corinth, MS,** sees Maj. Gens. Earl Van Dorn and Sterling Price pushing Maj. Gen. William S. Rosecrans, USA, back towards the defenses of Corinth, but failing to take this important rail center, they retreat toward Chewalla, 10 miles north west of Corinth on 10/4/1862. Total casualties approximate 6,750. 10/3-4/1862.
10	3	1862	The Battle of Corinth, MS, concludes with the pursuit of the Confederate forces. 10/3-12/1862.
10	3	1862	**Brig. Gen. Pleasant Adam Hackleman, USA,** is mortally wounded at the Battle of Corinth, MS, while attempting to rally his men against the Confederate onslaught. He died later that night at the Tishomingo Hotel, Corinth, MS.
10	3	1862	Affair near La Fayette Landing, TN, with a Union scouting party.
10	3	1862	Skirmish on the Blackwater, near Franklin, VA, with Maj. Gen. John Dix, USA, Dept. of VA, attempting

			to attack the movable bridge thrown up by the Confederates.
10	3	1862	Affair on the Blackwater, near Zuni, VA.
10	4	1862	**Brig. Gen. William Duncan Smith, CSA,** dies from the yellow fever at Charleston, SC.
10	4	1862	**Dabney Herndon Maury, C.S.A.,** is appointed Maj. Gen.
10	4	1862	The following are appointed Union Brigadier Generals:

Joseph Jackson Barlett,   USA
John Milton Thayer,   USA
John Henry Hobart Ward, USA

10	4	1862	Skirmish near Bardstown, on the Bardstown Pike, KY.
10	4	1862	Skirmish near Clay Village, KY.
10	4	1862	Engagement near Donaldsonville, LA.
10	4	1862	Affair at Granby, MO.
10	4	1862	Skirmish in Monroe County, MO.
10	4	1862	Skirmish at Newtonia, MO, with Brig. Gen. John M. Schofield, USA.
10	4	1862	Skirmish near Middleton, TN.
10	4	1862	Federal reconnaissance from Conrad's Ferry, Potomac River, into Virginia.
10	4	1862	Federal reconnaissance from Loudoun Heights to Neersville and Hillsborough, VA. 10/4-6/1862.
10	4	1862	President Lincoln returns to Washington, DC, after visiting with Maj. Gen. George B. McClellan, USA, in the field.
10	5	1862	**Federal recapture of Jacksonville, FL.**
10	5	1862	Attack on the camp of the "Union Brigade" at Corinth, MS.
10	5	1862	Engagement at Hatchie (or Davis') Bridge, Big Hatchie, or Metamora, MS, ends the Battle of Corinth, as Maj. Gen. Van Dorn, CSA, moves toward Holly Springs, and Maj. Gen. Edward Otho Ord's, USA, troops regroup.
10	5	1862	Skirmish at Cole Camp, MO.
10	5	1862	Skirmish at Sims' Cove, on Cedar Creek, MO.
10	5	1862	Skirmishes near Chewalla and Big Hill, TN.
10	5	1862	Skirmish at Fort Riley, near Nashville, TN.
10	5	1862	Skirmish at Neely's Bend, Cumberland River, TN.
10	5	1862	**Galveston, TX, is captured** by the Union Naval fleet.
10	6	1862	**Jacob Dolson Cox, U.S.A.,** is appointed Maj. Gen.
10	6	1862	**Solomon Meredith,** USA, is appointed Brig. Gen.
10	6	1862	Federal expedition from Jacksonville to Lake Beresford, FL. 10/6-9/1862.
10	6	1862	Brig. Gen. Joseph Finegan, CSA, is assigned to the command of East Florida. Brig. Gen. John H. Forney, CSA, is assigned to the command of West Florida.
10	6	1862	Skirmishes at Fair Grounds, Springfield, Burnt Cross-Roads, Beach Fork, and Grassy Mound, KY, as Gen. Braxton Bragg, CSA, withdraws towards Harrodsburg.
10	6	1862	Maj. Gen. Don Carlos Buell, USA, **occupies Bardstown, KY,** while in pursuit of Gen. Braxton Bragg, CSA.
10	6	1862	Skirmish at Liberty, MO.
10	6	1862	Skirmish at Sibley, MO.
10	6	1862	Skirmish at Big Birch, WV.
10	6	1862	Federal reconnaissance from Bolivar Heights toward Charlestown, WV.
10	7	1862	**Brig. Gen. Allison Nelson, CSA,** dies of camp fever in camp, near Austin, AR, after getting sick on 9/27/62.
10	7	1862	Middle and East Florida is embraced in General Pierre G.T. Beauregard's Confederate command of Florida's southeast coast.
10	7	1862	The Federals capture Governor Milton of Florida.
10	7	1862	Skirmishes at Brown Hill and Perryville, KY, as Maj. Gen. Don Carlos Buell, USA, continues to pursue Gen. Braxton Bragg, CSA.
10	7	1862	Maj. Gen. Gordon Granger, CSA, is assigned to the command of the Army of Kentucky.
10	7	1862	Skirmish near Box Ford, Hatchie River, MS.
10	7	1862	Skirmish near Ripley, MS.
10	7	1862	Skirmish near Ruckersville, MS.
10	7	1862	Brig. Gen. Eugene Asa Carr, USA, assumes the command of the Army of the Southwest, MO, AR, etal.

10	7	1862	Skirmish near New Franklin, Howard County, MO.
10	7	1862	Skirmish at Newtonia, MO.
10	7	1862	Skirmish near La Vergne, TN, results in a Union victory.
10	7	1862	Maj. Gen. Darius N. Couch, USA, supersedes Maj. Gen. Edwin V. Sumner in the command of the 2nd US Army Corps, the Army of the Potomac.
10	8	1862	**Elkanah Brackin Greer,** CSA, is appointed Brig. Gen.
10	8	1862	**James Birdseye McPherson, U.S.A.,** is appointed Maj. Gen.
10	8	1862	Skirmish at Lawrenceburg, KY.
10	8	1862	**The Battle of Perryville, or Chaplin Hills, KY,** the only major battle fought in Kentucky, with Maj. Gen. Don Carlos Buell, USA, forcing Gen. Braxton Bragg, CSA, to retreat to the southeast, effectively ending the last major Confederate threat on Kentucky. Total casualties approximate 7,600.
10	8	1862	**Brig. Gen. James Streshly Jackson, USA,** is mortally wounded at the Battle of Perryville, KY, while leading his command.
10	8	1862	**Brig. Gen. William Rufus Terrill, USA,** is mortally wounded at the Battle of Perryville, KY, receiving his death wound from a Confederate artillery shell fragment and dying the same day in a field hospital.
10	8	1862	Brig. Gen. Orlando B. Wilcox, USA, supersedes Brig. Gen. Jacob D. Cox in the command of the 9th US Army Corps, Army of the Potomac.
10	8	1862	Federal reconnaissance from Conrad's Ferry to Leesburg, VA.
10	8	1862	Federal reconnaissance from Fairfax Court-House to Aldie, VA, and skirmish, by Maj. Gen. Franz Sigel, USA. 10/8-9/1862.
10	9	1862	**James "Pete" Longstreet, C.S.A., is appointed Lieut. Gen.**
10	9	1862	**Edmund Kirby Smith, C.S.A., is appointed Lieut. Gen.**
10	9	1862	Action at Dry Ridge, Dog Walk, or Chesser's Store, near Salt River, KY, with Confederate Cavalry.
10	9	1862	Skirmishes on the Mackville Pike and Bardstown Road, KY.
10	9	1862	Skirmish at Four Locks, MD.
10	9	1862	Federal expedition from Fort Union to the Canadian River and Utah Creek, the New Mexico Territory, mainly a foraging expedition, but includes capturing some Mexicans trading with Indians; some dying from smallpox; being stopped and negotiating with Indians for mens' lives in exchange for some of the Federals' food, etc. 10/9-11/25/1862.
10	9	1862	Affair near Humboldt, TN.
10	9	1862	**Maj. Gen. James Ewell Brown Stuart's CSA, begins his expedition** into Maryland and Pennsylvania, with his 2nd ride around Maj. Gen. George B. McClellan's USA, troops of the Army of the Potomac. 10/9-12/1862.
10	10	1862	**The following Major Generals of the Confederacy are appointed Lieut. Generals:**
			William Joseph Hardee, C.S.A.
			Theophilus Hunter Holmes, C.S.A.
			Thomas Jonathan "Stonewall, Old Blue Light," Jackson, C.S.A.
			John Clifford Pemberton, C.S.A.
			Leonidas Polk, C.S.A.
10	10	1862	The following are appointed Confederate Major Generals:
			John Bell Hood, C.S.A.
			George Edward Pickett, C.S.A.
			Carter Littlepage Stevenson, C.S.A.
10	10	1862	**George Leonard Andrews,** USA, is appointed Brig. Gen.
10	10	1862	Skirmish at the Danville Cross-Roads, near Harrodsburg, KY.
10	10	1862	**Pursuit of the Confederate forces from Perryville to London, KY.** 10/10-22/1862.
10	10	1862	The Confederate capture of the Signal Station on Fairview Heights, MD, by Maj. Gen. JEB Stuart, CSA.
10	10	1862	Skirmishes at McCoy's, or Kinsell's, Ferry, and near Green Spring Furnance, MD.
10	10	1862	The **capture of Chambersburg, PA,** by Maj. Gen. J.E.B. Stuart, CSA.
10	10	1862	Skirmish at Medon Station, TN.
10	10	1862	Maj. Gen. John B. Magruder, CSA, is assigned to the command of the District of Texas.
10	11	1862	**James Bowen,** USA, is appointed Brig. Gen.
10	11	1862	Skirmish near Helena, AR.
10	11	1862	Skirmish at Danville, KY.
10	11	1862	**Harrodsburg, KY, is reoccupied** by the Union forces.

10	11	1862	Skirmish at Lawrenceburg, KY.
10	11	1862	The territories of Colorado and Nebraska are added to the Dept. of Missouri.
10	11	1862	Operations in Lewis, Clarke, Scotland, and Schuyler Counties, MO, including the capture of guerrillas.
10	11	1862	The **CSS Alabama** captures and burns the **Manchester,** off the coast of Nova Scotia, Canada.
10	11	1862	Skirmish near Gettysburg, PA, with JEB Stuart's CSA, Cavalry.
10	11	1862	The Confederate Congress in Richmond, VA, votes to exempt from conscription, all men owning 20 or more slaves, causing some to remark that it's a poor man's war.
10	12	1862	Federal expedition from Ozark, MO, toward Yellville, AR. 10/12-19/1862.
10	12	1862	Skirmish at Dick's Ford, KY.
10	12	1862	Skirmish near the mouth of the Monocacy, MD, as Maj. Gen. JEB Stuart, CSA, crosses the Potomac near Poolesville, and returning to Virginia.
10	12	1862	Skirmish at White's Ford, MD, with Maj. Gen. JEB Stuart, CSA.
10	12	1862	Skirmish near Arrow Rock, MO, with a guerrilla ambush on the Federal troops there.
10	12	1862	Maj. Gen. Earl Van Dorn, CSA, assumes the command of all the troops in the State of Mississippi.
10	13	1862	Skirmish at Harrodsburg, KY.
10	13	1862	Skirmish on the Lancaster Road, KY.
10	13	1862	Skirmish at New Franklin, MO.
10	13	1862	Skirmish on the Lebanon Road, near Nashville, TN.
10	13	1862	Col. Joseph Wheeler, CSA, is placed in command of all the cavalry of Gen. Braxton Bragg's Confederate Army, TN, etal.
10	13	1862	Operations about Paris, Snickersville, and Middlesburg, VA.
10	13	1862	Maj. Gen. Ambrose E. Burnside, USA, is assigned to the command of the Defenses of Harper's Ferry, WV.
10	13	1862	Maj. Gen. Jacob D. Cox, USA, assumes the command of the District of West Virginia.
10	14	1862	**Francis Redding Tilloou Nicholls,** CSA, is appointed Brig. Gen.
10	14	1862	**Gustave Paul Cluseret,** USA, is appointed Brig. Gen.
10	14	1862	Skirmish at Trenton, AR.
10	14	1862	Skirmishes at Lancaster and on the Crab Orchard Road, KY.
10	14	1862	Skirmish at Manchester, KY.
10	14	1862	Skirmishes near Mountan Gap, KY. 10/14-16/1862.
10	14	1862	Skirmish at Stanford, KY.
10	14	1862	Lieut. Gen. John C. Pemberton, CSA, assumes the command of the Confederate Dept. of the Mississippi and East Louisiana, including the forces intending to operate in Southwestern Tennessee.
10	14	1862	Skirmish at Hazel Bottom, MO.
10	15	1862	**Eliakim Parker Scammon,** USA, is appointed Brig. Gen.
10	15	1862	Skirmish at Fort Gibson, the Indian Territory.
10	15	1862	Skirmishes at Crab Orchard and Barren Mound, KY.
10	15	1862	Operations against guerrillas in the counties of Henry, Owen, and Gallatin, KY. 10/15-20/1862.
10	15	1862	Skirmish at Neely's Bend, Cumberland River, TN.
10	15	1862	Skirmish near Carrsville, VA.
10	16	1862	**Brig. Gen. George Burgwyn Anderson, CSA,** dies at Raleigh, NC, from complications of wounds received on September 17, 1862, at the Battle of Antietam, MD.
10	16	1862	Skirmishes at Shell's Mill, MO, and Elkhorn Tavern, AR.
10	16	1862	Operations in Bath, Powell, Estill, Clark, Montgomery, and Bourbon Counties, KY. 10/16-25/1862.
10	16	1862	Skirmishes at Mountain Gap and Mount Vernon, KY.
10	16	1862	Skirmishes near Mount Vernon, at Wild Cat Mountain, and Big Rockcastle Creek, KY.
10	16	1862	Federal reconnaissance of portion of Maj. Gen. George B. McClellan's Army of the Potomac from Sharpsburg, MD, to Smithfield, WV, including skirmishes near Kearneysville and Shepherdstown. 10/16-17/1862.
10	16	1862	Skirmish at Auxvasse Creek, Callaway County, MO, with the Federal attack on a guerrilla camp.
10	16	1862	Affair at Portland, MO.
10	16	1862	The **Dept. of the Tennessee** is constituted, under the command of Maj. Gen. Ulysses S. Grant, USA.
10	16	1862	Brig. Gen. John Echols, CSA, supersedes Maj. Gen. William W. Loring, CSA, in the command of the Dept. of Western Virginia.
10	16	1862	Federal reconnaissance of portion of Maj. Gen. George B. McClellan's army from Harper's Ferry to

Charlestown, WV, and skirmish en route.

10	17	1862	Skirmish at Mountain Home, AR.
10	17	1862	Skirmish at Sugar Creek, AR.
10	17	1862	Skirmishes about Camp Wild Cat, KY.
10	17	1862	Skirmishes at Valley Woods and Rocky Hill, KY.
10	17	1862	Skirmish at Lexington, MO.
10	17	1862	Civilian resistance to the Union draft in Carbon, Luzerne and Schuylkill Counties, PA, breaks out. 10/17-25/1862.
10	17	1862	Skirmish at Island No. 10, Mississippi River, with a Confederate attack.
10	17	1862	Federal expedition to Thoroughfare Gap, VA, and skirmish. 10/17-18/1862.

10	18	1862	Skirmish at Cross Hollow, AR.
10	18	1862	Skirmish near Helena, AR.
10	18	1862	Skirmish at Bloomfield, KY.
10	18	1862	Skirmishes at Cross-Roads, Big Hill, Little Rockcastle River, and Mountain Side, KY.
10	18	1862	Action at **Lexington, KY,** with Col. John Hunt Morgan's CSA troops routing the Federals, and Hunt entering the city.
10	18	1862	Skirmish at Nelson's Cross-Roads, KY.
10	18	1862	Skirmish at Rockcastle River, KY.
10	18	1862	Skirmish at California House, MO, with Rebel guerrillas.
10	18	1862	Skirmish near Uniontown, MO.
10	18	1862	Affair at Kirk's Bluff, SC.

10	19	1862	Skirmish at Bardstown, KY.
10	19	1862	The Confederate Army of Tennessee, under Gen. Braxton Bragg, CSA, retire through Cumberland Gap, KY, taking with it large amounts of confiscated supplies from Kentucky. 10/19-24/1862.
10	19	1862	Reconnaissance on Madison Road, KY.
10	19	1862	Skirmish at Pitman's Cross-Roads, KY.
10	19	1862	Skirmish at Wild Cat, KY.
10	19	1862	Skirmish at Bonnet Carre, Saint John Baptist Parrish, LA.
10	19	1862	Skirmish between Catlett's Station and Warrenton Junction VA.

10	20	1862	**Robert Hall Chilton,** CSA, is appointed Brig. Gen.
10	20	1862	Skirmish near Helena, AR.
10	20	1862	President Lincoln orders Maj. Gen. John McClernand, USA, to organize troops from Indiana, Illinois and Iowa for an independent expedition against Vicksburg, MS, which will in turn upset Maj. Gen. Ulysses S. Grant, USA's area command.
10	20	1862	Skirmish at Pitman's Cross-Roads, near Bardstown, KY.
10	20	1862	Skirmish near Wild Cat, KY.
10	20	1862	Skirmish near Marshfield, MO.
10	20	1862	Skirmish at Hermitage Ford, TN.
10	20	1862	Skirmish on the Gallatin Pike, near Nashville, TN, with Brig. Gen. Nathan Bedford Forrest, CSA, repelled.
10	20	1862	Maj. Gen. Henry W. Slocum, USA, assumes the command of the 12th US Army Corps, the Army of the Potomac.
10	20	1862	Skirmish at Hedgesville, WV.

10	21	1862	Skirmish near Simmons' Ranch, near Hydesville, CA.
10	21	1862	Federal expedition from Crab Orchard to Big Hill and Richmond, KY.
10	21	1862	Col. Joseph Wheeler's, CSA, command arrives at, and **seizes London, KY.**
10	21	1862	Skirmish at Pitman's Cross-Roads, KY.
10	21	1862	Federal scout to Collierville, Shelby Depot, Hickory, and Galloway Switch, TN, and skirmishes. 10/21-24/1862.
10	21	1862	Skirmish at Woodville, TN, with Rebel Partisan Rangers.
10	21	1862	Federal reconnaissance from Loudoun Heights to Lovettsville, VA, and skirmishes en route with the capture of Rebel foragers.

10	22	1862	Skirmish near Helena, AR.
10	22	1862	Skirmish at Huntsville, AR.
10	22	1862	Action at Old Fort Wayne, or Beattie's Prairie, near Maysville, Indian Territory, with fighting by the Pro-South **Cherokee** and **Creek Indians.**
10	22	1862	The pursuit of the Confederate forces from Perryville to London, KY, is discontinued.

10	22	1862	Skirmish near Van Buren, MO.
10	22	1862	Skirmish at Coosawhatchie, SC, and engagements at the Caston and Frampton Plantations, near Pocotaligo, or Yemassee, SC. 10/22-23/1862.
10	22	1862	Federal expedition from Fort Donelson to Waverly, TN, with skirmishes. 10/22-25/1862.
10	22	1862	Skirmish near Snickersville, VA.
10	23	1862	Federal destruction of the Confederate Goose Creek Salt-Works, near Manchester, KY. 10/23-24/1862.
10	23	1862	Skirmish at Clarkston, MO.
10	23	1862	Skirmishes near Waverly and Richland Creek, TN.
10	24	1862	Skirmish near Fayetteville, AR.
10	24	1862	Operations in the La Fourche District, LA. 10/24-11/6/1862.
10	24	1862	Federal expedition from Independence to Greenton, Chapel Hill, Hopewell, etc., MO. 10/24-26/1862.
10	24	1862	The **CSS Alabama** continues to prowl the Atlantic, this time burning the whaling vessel, **Lafayette,** off Halifax, Nova Scotia.
10	24	1862	Affair on Saint Helena Island, SC.
10	24	1862	The **Dept. of the Cumberland,** TN, is re-established, and Maj. Gen. William S. Rosecrans, USA, is assigned to command, Maj. Gen. Don Carlos Buell, USA, is relieved of command after failing to prevent Gen. Braxton Bragg from leaving Kentucky.
10	24	1862	The 13th US Army Corps is constituted, TN, etal.
10	24	1862	Maj. Gen. Leonidas Polk, CSA, is temporarily in command of Confederate Dept. No. 2, TN, etal.
10	24	1862	Skirmish near White Oak Springs, TN.
10	24	1862	Skirmishes at Manassas Junction and near Bristoe Station, VA.
10	25	1862	**Joseph Warren Revere,** USA, is appointed Brig. Gen.
10	25	1862	**Joseph Rodman West,** USA, is appointed Brig. Gen.
10	25	1862	Skirmish near Helena, AR.
10	25	1862	Skirmish at Lawrenceburg, KY.
10	25	1862	Federal **capture of Donaldsonville, LA,** by Brig. Gen. Godfrey Weitzel, USA, under Maj. Gen. Benjamin F. Butler, USA.
10	25	1862	Skirmish near Pike Creek and Eleven Points, MO.
10	25	1862	Maj. Gen. Ulysses S. Grant, USA, assumes the command of the 13th US Army Corps and the Dept. of the Tennessee.
10	25	1862	Skirmish near Zuni, VA, with Maj. Gen. John A. Dix, USA.
10	25	1862	President Lincoln continues to be frustrated with Maj. Gen. George B. McClellan's slowness and lack of initiative in advancing into Virginia and against the Confederate Army of Northern Virginia.
10	26	1862	The Union **Army of the Mississippi is discontinued.**
10	26	1862	Operations in Loudoun, Faquier, and Rappahannock Counties, VA, as Maj. Gen. George B. McClellan, USA, crosses the Potomac River with the Army of the Potomac. 10/26-11/10/1862.
10	27	1862	**William Henry Forney, C.S.A.,** is appointed Maj. Gen.
10	27	1862	**Preston Smith,** CSA, is appointed Brig. Gen.
10	27	1862	Skirmish at Fayetteville, AR. CSA troops retreat to around Boston Mountain, AR, as the Federals pursue.
10	27	1862	Skirmish at Pitman's Ferry, AR.
10	27	1862	Action at Georgia Landing or Bayou Lafourche, near Labadieville, LA, with the Confederates routed.
10	27	1862	The British steamer **Anglia,** is seized by the Federal naval blockade squadron, Bulls Bay, SC.
10	27	1862	Brig. Gen. John M. Brannan, USA, temporarily assumes the command of the Dept. of the South, vice Mitchel, deceased, SC, etal.
10	27	1862	Maj. Gen. William S. Rosecrans, USA, assumes the command of the 14th US Army Corps, TN.
10	27	1862	Union forces **occupy Halltown, VA,** as Maj. Gen. George B. McClellan, USA, advances into Virginia.
10	27	1862	Skirmish at Snicker's Gap, VA, as Gen. Robert E. Lee, CSA, begins to move his Army of Northern Virginia from the Shenandoah Valley to meet the Army of the Potomac.
10	27	1862	Maj. Gen. Samuel P. Heintzelman, USA, supersedes Maj. Gen. Nathaniel P. Banks, USA, in the command of the Defenses of Washington, DC.
10	28	1862	Action at McGuire's, AR.
10	28	1862	Action at Oxford Bend, White River, near Fayetteville, AR, forcing a Confederate retreat, by Brig. Gen. Samuel R. Curtis, USA, the **Army of the Frontier.**
10	28	1862	Skirmish near Waverly, TN.

| 10 | 28 | 1862 | Maj. Gen. John C. Breckinridge, CSA, assumes the command of the Army of Middle Tennessee. |

10	29	1862	**Alfred Cumming,** CSA, is appointed Brig. Gen.
10	29	1862	The capture of Confederate pickets opposite Williamsport, MD.
10	29	1862	Skirmish at Island Mound, MO.
10	29	1862	Affair at Sabine Pass, TX.
10	29	1862	Skirmish on the Blackwater, VA.
10	29	1862	Skirmish near Upperville, VA.
10	29	1862	Skirmish near Petersburg, WV, as the Federals overtake and recapture 200 head of cattle taken by JEB Stuart's Cavalry.

10	30	1862	**Maj. Gen. Ormsby MacKnight Mitchel, USA,** dies at Beaufort, SC, from yellow fever contracted while commanding the Federal Dept. of the South, based out of Hilton Head, SC.
10	30	1862	**William Stephen Walker,** CSA, is appointed Brig. Gen.
10	30	1862	**Joseph Wheeler,** CSA, is appointed Brig. Gen.
10	30	1862	Maj. Gen. William S. Rosecrans, USA, assumes the command of the Dept. of the Cumberland, superseding Maj. Gen. Don Carlos Buell, USA, TN, etal.
10	30	1862	Brig. Gen. George Stoneman, USA, supersedes Maj. Gen. Samuel Heintzelman in the command of the 3rd US Army Corps, the Army of the Potomac.

10	31	1862	Union forces advance from Bolivar and Corinth, MS, upon Grand Junction, TN. 10/31-11/1/1862.
10	31	1862	**Operations on the Mississippi Central Railroad from Bolivar, TN, to Coffeeville, MS.** 10/31-1/10/1863.
10	31	1862	Federal scout in Monroe County, MO.
10	31	1862	The Federal bombardment of Lavaca, TX.
10	31	1862	Skirmish at Aldie, VA.
10	31	1862	Skirmish at Franklin, VA.
10	31	1862	Skirmish near Mountville, VA.
10	31	1862	Skirmish at Snickersville, VA.
10	31	1862	Skirmish near the Falls of the Kanawha, WV.

| 11 | 1 | 1862 | The following are appointed Confederate Brigadier Generals: |

			George Thomas Anderson,	CSA
			Thomas Reade Rootes Cobb,	CSA
			John Rogers Cooke,	CSA
			Montgomery Dent Corse,	CSA
			George Pierce Doles,	CSA
			John Brown Gordon,	CSA
			Alfred Iverson Jr.,	CSA
			James Henry Lane,	CSA
			Elisha Franklin Paxton,	CSA
			Carnot Posey,	CSA
			Stephen Dodson Ramseur,	CSA
			Jerome Bonaparte Robertson,	CSA
			Edward Lloyd Thomas,	CSA

| 11 | 1 | 1862 | The following are appointed Union Brigadier Generals: |

			Richard Arnold,	USA
			William Passmore Carlin,	USA
			Alfred Washington Ellet,	USA

11	1	1862	Skirmish at La Grange, AR.
11	1	1862	Skirmish in Henderson County, KY.
11	1	1862	Federal naval operations on Berwick Bay, LA, including the capture of the Rebel steamer, **A.B. Seger.** 11/1-6/1862.
11	1	1862	Operations in Boone County, MO. 11/1-10/1862.
11	1	1862	Operations in Jackson County, MO, with the pursuit of Quantrill's guerrillas. 11/1-5/1862.
11	1	1862	Federal expedition from New Berne, NC, including skirmishes **(2nd)** at Little Creek and Rawle's Mill. 11/1-12/1862.
11	1	1862	The command of Gen. Braxton Bragg, CSA, is extended over the troops in the Dept. of East Tennessee.
11	1	1862	Skirmish at Berry's Ford Gap, VA.

11	1	1862	Skirmish at Philomont, VA, with Brig. Gen. Alfred Pleasanton, USA, Cavalry.
11	2	1862	Skirmish at Castleman's Ferry, near Snicker's Gap, VA, as Maj. Gen. George B. McClellan, USA, marches onward into Virginia.
11	2	1862	Skirmishes at Union and Upperville, VA. 11/2-3/1862.
11	3	1862	**Maj. Gen. Israel Bush Richardson, U.S.A.,** dies at the Pry House, Sharpsburg, MD, from wounds received on September 17, 1862, at the Battle of Antietam, MD.
11	3	1862	Federal scouts from Fort Crook, CA, and Fort Churchill, the Nevada Territory, to Honey Lake Valley, CA. 11/3-29/1862.
11	3	1862	Federal expedition along the coasts of Georgia and East Florida, aboard the steamer, **Darlington,** between Saint Simon's Island and Fernandina, to destroy Confederate saltworks and the rebel coastline picket stations. 11/3-10/1862.
11	3	1862	Skirmish near Harrisonville, Cass County, MO, as Quantrill's guerrillas attack and capture a Federal wagon train.
11	3	1862	Skirmish at Ashby's Gap, VA, as Maj. Gen. James Longstreet's Army Corps and Gen. Robert E. Lee arrive at Culpeper Court-House to front McClellan's advance, currently at Warrenton, VA, while Maj. Gen. Thomas J. Jackson's Army Corps remained in the Shenandoah Valley.
11	3	1862	Federal Cavalry reconnaissance to, and skirmish at, Snicker's Gap, VA.
11	3	1862	Gen. Braxton Bragg, CSA, resumes the command of the Confederate Dept. No. 2, TN, etal. (On Oct. 24, 1862, the command had been temporarily transferred to Lieut. Gen. Leonidas Polk, CSA).
11	4	1862	**Martin Luther Smith, C.S.A.,** is appointed Maj. Gen.
11	4	1862	The following are appointed Confederate Brigadier Generals: **William Robertson Boggs,** CSA **William George Mackey Davis,** CSA **Archibald Gracie, Jr.,** CSA **Evander McNair,** CSA **James Edward Rains,** CSA
11	4	1862	The Confederate saltworks at Kingsbury, GA, are destroyed by the Federal troops.
11	4	1862	Gen. P. G. T. Beauregard's Confederate command is extended to the Choctawhatchee River, SC.
11	4	1862	**La Grange and Grand Junction, TN, are occupied** by Maj. Gen. Ulysses S. Grant, USA, in preparation of an assault on Vicksburg, MS.
11	4	1862	Skirmish at Manassas Gap, VA.
11	4	1862	Skirmish at Markham's Station, VA.
11	4	1862	Skirmish at Salem, VA.
11	5	1862	The following are appointed Confederate Brigadier Generals: **Dandridge McRae,** CSA **Mosby Monroe Parsons,** CSA **James Camp Tappan,** CSA
11	5	1862	**Edwin Henry Stoughton,** USA, is appointed Brig. Gen.
11	5	1862	Federal expedition from Helena to Moro, AR. 11/5-8/1862.
11	5	1862	Affair near Piketon, KY.
11	5	1862	Skirmish at Jumpertown, MS, with Maj. Gen. Ulysses S. Grant, USA.
11	5	1862	Action at **Lamar, MO,** as a stubborn Confederate attack burns about one third of the town.
11	5	1862	Federal reconnaissance from La Grange toward Somerville, TN, by Maj. Gen. Ulysses S. Grant, USA.
11	5	1862	Action at Nashville, TN, with Brig. Gen. Nathan Bedford Forrest's, CSA, Cavalry attack on Brig. Gen. James S. Negley, USA.
11	5	1862	Action at Barbee's Cross-Roads, VA.
11	5	1862	Operations in Augusta, Bath, and Highland Counties, VA, and Pendleton and Pocahontas Counties, WV, as Brig. Gen. John H. Milroy, USA, sweeps the countryside, capturing 75 head of cattle. 11/5-14/1862.
11	5	1862	Federal reconnaissance to Manassas Gap, VA, and skirmish. 11/5-6/1862.
11	5	1862	Skirmish near Warrenton, VA.
11	6	1862	**Brig. Gen. Charles Davis Jameson, USA,** dies aboard a steamboat near Boston, MA, finally dying from typhoid fever contracted during the June, 1862, Battle of Seven Pines, VA.
11	6	1862	**Stephen Dill Lee,** CSA, is appointed Brig. Gen.
11	6	1862	Federal expeditions from Fort Scott, KS, and skirmishes with Quantrill's guerrillas. 11/6-11/1862.
11	6	1862	Skirmish at Garrettsburg, KY, as Brig. Gen. Thomas Ransom, USA, thwarts the Rebels in the area.

MONTH	DAY	YEAR	ACT
11	6	1862	Skirmish at Old Lamar, MS.
11	6	1862	Federal reconnaissance from La Grange, TN, toward Lamar, MS, and skirmish at Worsham's Creek, by Maj. Gen. Ulysses S. Grant.
11	6	1862	The following are officially assigned Corp Commands in the Confederate Army of Northern Virginia: 1st Army Corps: Lieut. Gen. James Longstreet, CSA. 2nd Army Corps: Lieut. Gen. Thomas J. Jackson, CSA.
11	6	1862	Skirmish at Warrenton, VA.
11	6	1862	Skirmish at Martinsburg, WV.
11	7	1862	**John Pegram,** CSA, is appointed Brig. Gen.
11	7	1862	Skirmish at Boonesborough, AR.
11	7	1862	Skirmish at Rhea's Mill, near Marianna, AR.
11	7	1862	Skirmish at Spaulding's, on the Sapello River, GA.
11	7	1862	The Confederate Army of the Mississippi receives new commanders as follows: Immediate command: Gen. Braxton Bragg, CSA 1st Army Corps: Lieut. Gen. Leonidas Polk, CSA 2nd Army Corps: Lieut. Gen. William J. Hardee, CSA
11	7	1862	Action at Clark's Mill, Big Beaver Creek, Douglas County, MO, near Vera Cruz, as the Confederates capture and parole about 100 Union troops of the Federal Army of the Frontier.
11	7	1862	Skirmish at Gallatin, TN, as Maj. Gen. William S. Rosecrans, USA, transfers the Army of the Cumberland from Kentucky to Nashville, TN.
11	7	1862	Skirmish at Tyree Springs, TN.
11	7	1862	Skirmish at White Range, TN.
11	7	1862	**Maj. Gen. George Brinton McClellan, USA,** is surprised to be informed that President Lincoln **has replaced him** with **Maj. Gen. Ambrose Everett Burnside, USA,** in command of the Army of the Potomac, VA, effectively ending McClellan's military career.
11	7	1862	Skirmish at Jefferson, VA.
11	7	1862	Skirmish at Rappahannock Station, VA.
11	7	1862	Skirmish at Waterloo Bridge, VA.
11	8	1862	**John George Walker, C.S.A.** is appointed Maj. Gen.
11	8	1862	Skirmish at Cove Creek, AR.
11	8	1862	Skirmishes at Marianna and La Grange, AR.
11	8	1862	The **CSS Alabama** continues plundering Union shipping by burning the **T.B. Wales,** in the Atlantic, near Bermuda.
11	8	1862	Skirmish near Cato, KS.
11	8	1862	Skirmish at Burkesville, KY.
11	8	1862	Maj. Gen. Nathaniel P. Banks, USA, is assigned to the command of the Dept. of the Gulf, LA, replacing Maj. Gen. Benjamin F. Butler, USA, who had earned a despicable reputation for his (mis)treatment of the citizens of New Orleans, LA, as President Lincoln continues to reshuffle his high command of officers.
11	8	1862	Federal expedition into the southern part of Missouri and the northern part of Arkansas. 11/8-13/1862.
11	8	1862	Brig. Gen. William Henry Chase Whiting, CSA, is assigned to the command of the defenses of the Cape Fear River, NC.
11	8	1862	Skirmish on the Cumberland River, near Gallatin, TN.
11	8	1862	Federal reconnaissance from La Grange, TN, and skirmishes at Old Lamar and Hudsonville, MS, by Maj. Gen. Ulysses S. Grant, USA. 11/8-9/1862.
11	8	1862	Skirmish at Hazel River, VA.
11	8	1862	Skirmish at Little Washington, VA.
11	8	1862	Skirmish at Rappahannock Station, VA.
11	8	1862	Affair near Snickersville, VA.
11	8	1862	Skirmish near Warrenton, VA.
11	8	1862	Col. John Daniel Imboden's, CSA, expedition from his camp on South Fort, Hardy County, into Tucker County, WV, and the **capture of Saint George.** 11/8-14/1862.
11	9	1862	**Brig. Gen. John Bordenave Villepigue, CSA,** dies at Port Hudson, LA, from camp fever sickness.
11	9	1862	Skirmishes at Boston Mountains, AR, and Dry Wood, MO.
11	9	1862	Skirmish between Fayetteville and Cane Hill, AR.
11	9	1862	Skirmish at Huntsville, MO.
11	9	1862	Skirmish at Lebanon, TN.

| 11 | 9 | 1862 | Skirmish at Silver Springs, TN. |

11 9 1862 Skirmish at Fredericksburg, VA, with a Union cavalry charge under Col. Ulric Dahlgren, USA, through the city. Gen. Robert E. Lee, CSA, holds a Court of Inquiry, into possible negligence on the part of his pickets. The outcome is that no charges are lodged by Lee.

11 9 1862 Skirmish at Newby's Cross-Roads, VA.

11 9 1862 Skirmish at **Philomont, VA,** where Rebel Cavalry **capture** the town and the tail end of a long Federal supply train.

11 9 1862 Skirmishes near Rappahannock Station, VA.

11 9 1862 Federal reconnaissance from Bolivar Heights to Rippon, WV.

11 9 1862 Federal expedition into Greenbrier County, WV. 11/9-11/1862.

11 9 1862 Skirmish on the South Fork of the Potomac, WV, between Brig. Gen. Benjamin F. Kelley, USA, and Col. John Daniel Imboden, CSA, Partisan Rangers.

11 10 1862 Action at Corbin's Cross-Roads, near Amissville, VA, as Gen. Robert E. Lee, CSA, orders Maj. Gen. JEB Stuart, CSA, to advance his calvary to detect if any Federals had crossed the Rappahannock River, VA.

11 10 1862 Skirmish at Gaines' Cross-Roads, VA.

11 10 1862 Skirmish at Markham's Station, VA.

11 10 1862 Operations along the **Orange and Alexandria Railroad,** VA. 11/10-12/1862.

11 10 1862 Maj. Gen. **"Little Mac"** George B. McClellan bades farewell to the US Army of the Potomac, near Warrenton, VA.

11 10 1862 Maj. Gen. Joseph Hooker, USA, supersedes **Maj. Gen. Fitz John Porter,** USA, in the command of the 5th US Army Corps, the Army of the Potomac, which effectively ends Porter's military career, as he will be cashiered from the army in 1863 for the blame he received for the Union failure at the 2nd Battle of Manassas or Bull Run, August 29th-30th, 1862.

11 10 1862 Brig. Gen. John S. Williams, CSA, is assigned to the command of the Dept. of Western Virginia.

11 10 1862 Skirmish at Charlestown, Jefferson County, WV.

11 11 1862 Confederate demonstration on New Berne, NC.

11 11 1862 Skirmish at Jefferson, VA.

11 12 1862 The capture of the Union courier station on Stone's River, TN.

11 12 1862 Operations about Suffolk, VA, including skirmishes at:
a) Providence Church (12th) and at
b) Blackwater Bridge, and **(Nov. 14th)** at Zuni, VA. 11/12-14/1862.

11 13 1862 Federal expedition from Beaufort to Doboy River, GA, with the capture of around 250,000 board feet of Confederate lumber, etc. 11/13-18/1862.

11 13 1862 Lieut. Gen. William J. Hardee, CSA, assumes the command of the 2nd Army Corps, the Confederate Army of the Mississippi.

11 13 1862 Skirmish at Holly Springs, MS, with the Union forces capturing the important railroad depot there.

11 13 1862 Skirmish near Nashville, TN.

11 13 1862 Gen. Braxton Bragg, CSA, Army of Tennessee, moves his troops from Chattanooga, toward Murfreesboro, TN, to unite his forces with Maj. Gen. John Cabell Breckinridge, CSA.

11 13 1862 Skirmishes at Sulphur Springs, VA. 11/13-14/1862.

11 14 1862 **Andrew Jackson Hamilton,** USA, is appointed Brig. Gen.

11 14 1862 Brig. Gen. Andrew Jackson Hamilton, USA, is appointed the military governor of Texas.

11 14 1862 General Braxton Bragg, CSA, arrives with his forces at Tullahoma, southeast of, and near, Nashville, TN.

11 14 1862 Skirmish at Jefferson, VA.

11 14 1862 Skirmish at Waterloo, VA.

11 14 1862 Maj. Gen. Ambrose Everett Burnside, USA, as the new commander, reorganizes the the Army of the Potomac, into three grand divisions with the following commanders:
a) **Right Grand Division**   - Maj. Gen. Edwin V. Sumner, USA
b) **Center Grand Division** - Maj. Gen. Joseph Hooker, USA
c) **Left Grand Division**   - Maj. Gen. William B. Franklin, USA

11 15 1862 **John Sappington Marmaduke,** CSA, is appointed Brig. Gen.

11 15 1862 Skirmish at Yocum Creek, MO.

11 15 1862 Federal reconnaissance from Edgefield Junction toward Clarksville, TN. 11/15-20/1862.

11	15	1862	Action at Warrenton, or Sulphur Springs, VA.
11	15	1862	The Confederate Secretary of War, **George W. Randolph,** unexpectantly resigns his cabinet post, Richmond, VA.
11	15	1862	Skirmish on the Guyandotte, WV.
11	16	1862	Operations about Cassville and Keetsvile, MO. 11/17-18/1862.
11	16	1862	Federal expedition from Helena against Arkansas Post, AR. 11/16-21/1862.
11	16	1862	Skirmish at Gloucester Point, VA.
11	16	1862	The Army of the Potomac sees the following commanders assume their respective commands:

a) Center Grand Division - Maj. Gen. Joseph Hooker, USA
b) Left Grand Division   - Maj. Gen. William B. Franklin, USA
c) 5th US Army Corps   - Brig Gen. Daniel Butterfield, USA
d) 6th US Army Corps   - Maj. Gen. William F. Smith, USA

11	16	1862	Affair at United States Ford, VA, as Maj. Gen. Ambrose E. Burnside, USA, moves the Army of the Potomac from Warrenton, VA, towards Fredericksburg, VA.
11	16	1862	Skirmish at Chester Gap, VA.
11	17	1862	The **USS San Jacinto** lies in wait off the Caribbean island of Martinique for the Confederate steamer, **CSS Alabama,** but fails to prevent her from leaving port.
11	17	1862	Operations about Cassville and Keetsville, MO.
11	17	1862	Federal expedition from Sparta, TN, into KY. 11/17-29/1862.
11	17	1862	Affair near Carrsville, VA, with Confederate Cavalry.
11	17	1862	Skirmish at Falmouth, on the Rappahannock River and across from Fredericksburg, VA, with the freshly arrived Army of the Potomac.
11	17	1862	President Jefferson Davis appoints **Maj. Gen. Gustavus Woodson Smith, CSA,** as acting Confederate Secretary of War, Richmond, VA.
11	18	1862	**John Austin Wharton,** CSA, is appointed Brig. Gen.
11	18	1862	Skirmish on Doboy River, GA. 11/18/1862.
11	18	1862	Skirmish at Core Creek, NC.
11	18	1862	Skirmish at Double Bridge, TN.
11	18	1862	Skirmish at Rural Hills, TN.
11	18	1862	Skirmish at Franklin, VA, where it looks like rain.
11	19	1862	**George Lucas Hartsuff, U.S.A.,** is appointed Maj. Gen.
11	19	1862	Federal expedition from Grand Junction, TN, to Ripley, MS, to determine Confederate troop strength at Vicksburg, MS. 11/19-20/1862.
11	19	1862	Skirmish near Tompkinsville, KY, with Confederate Cavalry.
11	19	1862	Skirmish at Tunnel Hill, KY.
11	19	1862	Skirmish at Pineville, MO.
11	19	1862	Federal reconnaissance toward La Vergne, TN.
11	19	1862	Skirmish at Philomont, VA.
11	20	1862	Federal reconnaissance toward Van Buren and Fort Smith, AR. 11/20-23/1862.
11	20	1862	Affair near Matagorda, TX, where a party from the US mortar vessel, **Henry James,** are captured after they went ashore to purchase food for the crew.
11	20	1862	The **Confederate Army of Tennessee is constituted,** to consist of the following Army Corps Commanders:

a) Lieut. Gen. Edmund Kirby Smith,   CSA
b) Lieut. Gen. Leonidas Polk,   CSA
c) Lieut. Gen. William Joseph Hardee, CSA

11	20	1862	Federal expedition from Camp Douglas to the Cache Valley, the Utah Territory, with skirmish **(23rd)** in the Cache Valley. 11/20-27/1862.
11	20	1862	Brig. Gen. John H. Martindale, USA, assumes the command as Military Governor of the District of Columbia.
11	21	1862	Affairs at Petite Anse Island, LA. 11/21-22/1862.
11	21	1862	Skirmish at Bayou Bonfouca, LA, as the local Partisan Rangers attack (and kill) men aboard the Federal steamer, **G. Brown.**
11	21	1862	The surrender of Fredericksburg, VA, is demanded by Maj. Gen. Ambrose E. Burnside, USA, and refused by the mayor, as Lieut. Gen. Thomas Stonewall Jackson moves his army corps from the

			Shenandoah Valley to join up with Gen. Robert E. Lee, and Lieut. Gen. James Longstreet, CSA, who are already at Fredericksburg, behind entrenched positions.
11	21	1862	President Jefferson Davis appoints **James A. Seddon** as the new Secretary of War, replacing acting secretary Maj. Gen. Gustavus Woodson Smith, CSA.
11	22	1862	**Brig. Gen. Francis Engle Patterson, USA,** dies near Fairfax Court-House, VA, in his tent, from a self inflicted gunshot wound to his head. Under investigation by his superiors for a possible act of cowardice by ordering (presumably) an unauthorized retreat, it was never determined whether the wound was accidental or intentional.
11	22	1862	The destruction of Confederate Salt-Works, Matthews County, VA.
11	22	1862	Federal reconnaissance from Williamsburg, VA, toward the Chickahominy River, by Maj. Gen. John A. Dix. USA.
11	22	1862	Skirmish near Halltown, WV.
11	22	1862	Skirmish near Winchester, VA.
11	22	1862	Federal expedition from Fort Ruby, the Nevada Territory, to the Sierra Nevada Mountains. 11/22-27/1862.
11	24	1862	**Clinton Bowen Fisk,** USA, is appointed Brig. Gen.
11	24	1862	Gen. Joseph E. Johnston, CSA, is assigned to the command embracing Western North Carolina, Tennessee, Northern Georgia, Alabama, Mississippi, and Eastern Louisiana, which places Gen. Braxton Bragg, CSA, in Tennessee, and Lieut. Gen. John C. Pemberton, CSA, at Vicksburg, MS, under his overall command.
11	24	1862	Skirmish near Tompkinsville, KY, with Confederate Cavalry.
11	24	1862	Federal expedition from Sharpsburg, MD, to Shepherdstown, WV, and skirmishes. 11/24-25/1862.
11	24	1862	Skirmish at Beaver Creek, MO.
11	24	1862	Federal expeditions from Greenfield into Jasper and Barton Counties, MO, with the southwestern counties swarming with Rebel guerrilla bands, including William Clarke Quantrill. 11/24-26/1862.
11	24	1862	Skirmish at Newtown, WV.
11	24	1862	Federal expedition from Summerville to Cold Knob Mountain, WV, and skirmish **(26th)** at Lewis' Mill, on Sinking Creek. 11/24-30/1862.
11	25	1862	Skirmish near Cane Hill, AR, as Brig. Gen. James G. Blunt, USA, attacks Brig. Gen. John S. Marmaduke, CSA, who is attempting to join up with Maj. Gen. Thomas Hindman, CSA, in their attempt to get north into Missouri.
11	25	1862	Federal expedition to Yellville, AR, with the destruction of Confederate saltworks. 11/25-29/1862.
11	25	1862	Skirmish at Calhoun, KY.
11	25	1862	Confederate raid on Poolesville, MD.
11	25	1862	The capture of the US steamer, **Ellis,** on the New River, NC.
11	25	1862	Skirmish at Clarksville, TN.
11	25	1862	The capture of Henderson's Station on the **Mobile and Ohio Railroad,** TN.
11	25	1862	Maj. Gen. Samuel Jones, CSA, is assigned to the command of the Trans-Allegheny, or Western, Dept. of Virginia.
11	26	1862	Affairs in Jackson and La Fayette counties, MO.
11	26	1862	Lieut. Gen. Leonidas Polk, CSA, assumes the command of **"Polk's Corps,"** the Army of Tennessee.
11	26	1862	Federal expedition from Edgefield to Harpeth Shoals, Clarksville, etc, TN. 11/26-12/1/1862.
11	26	1862	Federal reconnaissance to La Vergne, TN, and skirmish. 11/26-27/1862.
11	26	1862	Skirmish near Somerville, TN.
11	26	1862	Operations about Springfield, TN, including Union soldiers, while collecting food supplies, were attacked by bushwackers. 11/26-30/1862.
11	26	1862	President Lincoln travels to Aquia Creek, VA, to meet with Maj. Gen. Ambrose E. Burnside, USA, Army of the Potomac.
11	26	1862	Federal reconnaissance from Bolivar Heights to Charlestown, WV, and skirmish at Cockrall's Mill, WV.
11	27	1862	Federal expedition from Helena, AR, to the vicinity of Grenada, MS. 11/27-12/6/1862.
11	27	1862	The Confederate capture of the steamboat, **New River,** near New River Landing, LA.
11	27	1862	Skirmish at Carthage, MO.
11	27	1862	Skirmish at Mill Creek, TN, with the Texas Rangers.
11	27	1862	Maj. Gen. Ambrose E. Burnside, USA, meeting with President Lincoln, declines to use Lincoln's suggested strategy of using a three-pronged attack south of the Rappahannock River, choosing instead to make a direct assault on Gen. Robert E. Lee's Army of Northern Virginia lines.
11	28	1862	Action at Cane Hill, Boston Mountain and Boonsboro, AR, with Brig. Gen. James Gillpatrick Blunt, USA,

routing Brig. Gen. John Sappington Marmaduke, CSA, with Marmaduke retreating into the Boston Mountains.

| 11 | 28 | 1862 | Skirmish at the junction of the Coldwater and the Tallahatchie, MS. |

11   28   1862   Skirmishes at Holly Springs, MS, as the Federals build up supplies for their anticipated advance on Vicksburg, MS, under Maj. Gen. Ulysses S. Grant, USA. 11/28-29/1862.

11   28   1862   Skirmishes on the Carthage road, near Hartsville and Rome, TN, as the Federals recapture some of their supply wagons taken yesterday.

11   28   1862   Affair near Hartwood Church, VA.

11   28   1862   Federal reconnaissance from Chantilly to Snicker's Ferry and Berryville, VA, and skirmishes. 11/28-30/1862.

11   29   1862   In what will become by far the largest day for Union General appointments, other than April 15, 1865 when officer after officer were given the rank of Brevet General, which is not covered in this manual, due to the fact the brevets were handed out more in celebration of the Final Union victory over the Confederacy and right before most were mustered out of the service of the Federal Volunteer Army than those deserving such promotion, the following are appointed Union Major Generals:

Hiram Gregory Berry,	U.S.A.
Francis Preston Blair, Jr.,	U.S.A.
James Gillpatrick Blunt,	U.S.A.
Daniel Butterfield,	U.S.A.
Napoleon Jackson Tecumseh Dana,	U.S.A.
William Henry French,	U.S.A.
Winfield Scott Hancock,	U.S.A.
Francis Jay Herron,	U.S.A.
John Alexander Logan,	U.S.A.
George Gordon Meade,	U.S.A.
Robert Huston Milroy,	U.S.A.
Richard James Oglesby,	U.S.A.
John McCauley Palmer,	U.S.A.
Benjamin Mayberry Prentiss,	U.S.A.
John Fulton Reynolds,	U.S.A.
Joseph Jones Reynolds,	U.S.A.
John McAllister Schofield,	U.S.A.
Daniel Edgar Sickles,	U.S.A.
David Sloane Stanley,	U.S.A.
Frederick Steele,	U.S.A.
George Stoneman,	U.S.A.
George Sykes,	U.S.A.
Cadwallader Colden Washburn,	U.S.A.

11   29   1862   The following are appointed Union Brigadier Generals:

James Barnes,	USA
John Beatty,	USA
Samuel Beatty,	USA
Egbert Benson Brown,	USA
Robert Christie Buchanan,	USA
Ralph Pomeroy Buckland,	USA
Charles Thomas Campbell,	USA
Stephen Gardner Champlin,	USA
Joseph Tarr Copeland,	USA
Marcellus Monroe Crocker,	USA
Lysander Cutler,	USA
George Washington Deitzler,	USA
Elias Smith Dennis,	USA
Charles Cleveland Dodge,	USA
William Dwight,	USA
Hugh Boyle Ewing,	USA
Theophilus Toulmin Garrard,	USA
Charles Kinnaird Graham,	USA
David McMurtrie Gregg,	USA

James Allen Hardie,	USA
Edward Harland,	USA
William Harrow,	USA
Isham Nicholas Haynie,	USA
Alexander Hays,	USA
Charles Adam Heckman,	USA
Edward Winslow Hincks,	USA
Edward Henry Hobson,	USA
Lewis Cass Hunt,	USA
John Haskell King,	USA
Edward Needles Kirk,	USA
Joseph Farmer Knipe,	USA
Vladimir Kryzanowski,	USA
Michael Kelly Lawler,	USA
Albert Lindley Lee,	USA
Mortimer Dormer Leggett,	USA
William Haines Lytle,	USA
George Francis McGinnis,	USA
Nathaniel Collins McLean,	USA
James Winning McMillan,	USA
John McNeil,	USA
Gilman Marston,	USA
John Sanford Mason,	USA
Charles Leopold Matthies,	USA
Sullivan Amory Meredith,	USA
William Hopkins Morris,	USA
James St. Clair Morton,	USA
Thomas Hewson Neill,	USA
Franklin Stillman Nickerson	USA
William Ward Orme,	USA
Joshua Thomas Owen,	USA
Thomas Gamble Pitcher,	USA
Orlando Metcalfe Poe,	USA
Edward Elmer Potter,	USA
Thomas Edward Greenfield Ransom	USA
Thomas Algeo Rowley,	USA
Thomas Howard Ruger,	USA
David Allen Russell,	USA
Adam Jacoby Slemmer,	USA
John Eugene Smith,	USA
John Dunlap Stevenson,	USA
George Crockett Strong,	USA
David Stuart,	USA
Frederick Shearer Stumbaugh	USA
Thomas William Sweeny,	USA
Davis Tillson,	USA
Alfred Thomas Archimedes Torbert	USA
Robert Ogden Tyler,	USA
William Vandever,	USA
Israel Vogdes,	USA
George Day Wagner,	USA
Joseph Dana Webster,	USA
Thomas Welsh,	USA
Frank Wheaton,	USA
David Henry Williams,	USA
Nelson Grosvenor Williams,	USA

			Isaac Jones Wistar, USA
			Samuel Kosciuszko Zook, USA
11	29	1862	Ex-Marshal George B. Kane, of Baltimore, MD, after 17 months' imprisonment, arrives in Baltimore and denounces **Secretary of State William H. Seward** in a newspaper card.
11	29	1862	Skirmish at Lumpkin's Mill, MS.
11	29	1862	Skirmishes at Waterford, MS. 11/29-30/1862.
11	29	1862	Federal reconnaissance from Stewart's Ferry, Stone's River, to Baird's Mills, TN, and skirmishes en route. 11/29-12/1/1862.
11	29	1862	Maj. Gen. John B. Magruder, CSA, assumes the command of the District of Texas, New Mexico and Arizona.
11	30	1862	The federal warship, **Vanderbilt,** fails to capture the **CSS Alabama,** but instead the **CSS Alabama** captures and burns the vessel, **Parker Cook,** near the Leeward Islands, Atlantic Ocean.
11	30	1862	Skirmish at Chulahoma, MS.
11	30	1862	Skirmish on the Tallahatchie River, MS, with the destruction of the steamer, **New Moon.**
11	30	1862	Federal expedition from Rolla to the Ozark Mountains, MO, and skirmishes. 11/30-12/6/1862.
12	1	1862	Skirmish at Hudsonville, MS.
12	1	1862	Skirmishes about Oxford, MS. 12/1-3/1862.
12	1	1862	Skirmish on the Yocknapatalfa, near Mitchell's Cross-Roads, MS.
12	1	1862	Skirmish near Nolensville, TN.
12	1	1862	Skirmish at Beaver Dam Church, VA.
12	1	1862	Federal reconnaissance to Grove Church, near Hartwood, VA.
12	1	1862	Federal expedition to Westmoreland County, VA. 12/1-4/1862.
12	1	1862	Federal expedition toward Logan Court-House, WV. 12/1-10/1862.
12	1	1862	Skirmish at Romney, WV.
12	2	1862	**William Thompson Martin,** CSA, is appointed Brig. Gen.
12	2	1862	Skirmish on the Blackwater, near Franklin, VA.
12	2	1862	Federal reconnaissance from Bolivar Heights to Winchester, VA, and and skirmishes at Charlestown, WV, and Berryville, VA, etc. 12/2-6/1862.
12	2	1862	The capture of Union pickets near Dumfries, VA.
12	2	1862	Skirmish at Leeds' Ferry, Rappahannock River, VA, as the **Army of Northern Virginia** and the **Army of the Potomac** prepare to square off.
12	3	1862	Federal troops under Brig. Gen. Charles Edward Hovey, USA, **occupy Grenada, MS.**
12	3	1862	Skirmish at Oakland, MS.
12	3	1862	Skirmishes on the Yocknapatalfa, at Prophet, Spring Dale, and Free Bridges, MS, with Maj. Gen. Ulysses S. Grant, USA.
12	3	1862	Attack on the Union forage train on the Hardin Pike, near Nashville, TN.
12	3	1862	Skirmish at Moorefield, WV.
12	4	1862	**Arnold Jones Elsey, C.S.A.,** is appointed Maj. Gen.
12	4	1862	Federal operations about Cane Hill and Reed's Mountain, AR.
12	4	1862	Federal operations in Cherokee County, the Indian Territory, including skirmishes with the **Pin Indians.**
12	4	1862	Skirmish in Floyd County, KY.
12	4	1862	The capture of Union transports, and skirmishes near Prestonburg, KY. 12/4-5/1862.
12	4	1862	Affair near Oxford, MS.
12	4	1862	Skirmish at Water Valley, MS.
12	4	1862	Skirmish on the Franklin Pike, near Holly Tree Gap, TN.
12	4	1862	Gen. Joseph E. Johnston, CSA, assumes the command to which he was assigned Nov. 24, 1862, TN, etal.
12	4	1862	The capture of the Union outpost near Stewart's Ferry (or Ford's), Stone's River, TN.
12	4	1862	Engagement on the Rappahannock River, near Port Royal, and east of Fredericksburg, VA.
12	4	1862	Union forces **occupy Winchester, VA.**
12	5	1862	Engagement at Coffeeville, MS, where Maj. Gen. Ulysses S. Grant's, USA, cavalry is repulsed.
12	6	1862	Skirmish at Parkersville, MO.
12	6	1862	Skirmish near Kimbrough's Mill, Mill Creek, TN, as Brig. Gen. Joseph Wheeler, CSA, attacks and captures a portion of the Federal forage train.
12	7	1862	**The Battle of Prairie Grove, AR,** about 12 miles southwest of **Fayetteville, AR,** on the Illinois Creek, where Maj. Gen. Thomas C. Hindman, CSA, battled Maj. Gen. James Gillpatrick Blunt and Francis Jay

12	7	1862	Herron, USA, to a draw. Total casualties approximate 2,500.

12 7 1862 Affair at Padre Island, TX, where Confederates, testing the depth of the channel, is pursued by Federal ships, go ashore; they fire on and deal death upon the Federals, who retreat; later the same Confederates capture some Federal launches; all in one day!

12 7 1862 Action at Hartsville, TN, with Col. John Hunt Morgan, CSA, inflicting over 2,000 Union casualties under Col. A.B. Moore, USA.

12 7 1862 The Confederate Dept. of Mississippi and East Louisiana is reorganized as follows:
a) 1st Confederate Army Corp - Maj. Gen. Earl Van Dorn, CSA
b) 2nd Confederate Army Corp - Maj. Gen. Sterling Price, CSA

12 8 1862 Federal reconnaissance from Suffolk to the Blackwater and skirmishes at and about Zuni, VA. 12/8-12/1862.

12 9 1862 Skirmish at Mudtown, AR.

12 9 1862 Federal reconnaissance from Corinth, MS, toward Tuscumbia, AL, including skirmishes **(12th)** at Cherokee Station and Little Bear Creek, AL. 12/9-14/1862.

12 9 1862 Maj. Gen. Earl Van Dorn, CSA, is temporarily in command of the Confederate Army of the Mississippi.

12 9 1862 Federal expedition from Ozark, MO, into Marion County, AR, with the destruction of Confederate saltworks. 12/9-15/1862.

12 9 1862 Skirmish at Dobbins' Ferry, near La Vergne, TN, as Brig. Gen. Joseph Wheeler, CSA, attacks a Union forage train.

12 9 1862 Federal reconnaissance toward Franklin, and skirmish near Brentwood, TN.

12 9 1862 Brig. Gen. Julius Stahel, USA, is temporarily in command of the 11th US Army Corps, the Army of the Potomac, VA.

12 10 1862 Skirmish at Desert Station, LA.

12 10 1862 Confederate attack on and **partial burning of, Plymouth, NC,** with the US ironclad, **Southfield,** disabled in the attack.

12 10 1862 Port Royal, near and west of Fredericksburg, VA, is attacked by Union gunboats.

12 10 1862 Maj. Gen. Samuel Jones, CSA, assumes the command of the Confederate Western Dept. of Virginia.

12 11 1862 **John Hunt Morgan, CSA,** is appointed Brig. Gen.

12 11 1862 Federal expedition from New Berne to Goldsborough, NC. 12/11-20/1862.

12 11 1862 Skirmish on the Kinston Road, NC. 12/11-12/1862.

12 11 1862 Skirmish at La Vergne, TN, as Brig. Gen. Nathan Bedford Forrest, CSA, prepares a Cavalry raid on Maj. Gen. Ulysses S. Grant's, USA, line of communication.

12 11 1862 Skirmish near Nashville, TN.

12 11 1862 Federal reconnaissance from Nashville to Franklin, TN, and skirmishes on the Wilson Creek Pike and at Franklin. **(12th).** 12/11-12/1862.

12 11 1862 **The Battle of Fredericksburg, VA.** 12/11-15/1862.

12 11 1862 Maj. Gen. Ambrose E. Burnside's forces, under Maj. Gens. Edwin V. Sumner and William B. Franklin, USA, **occupy Fredericksburg, VA,** after driving back Brig. Gen. William Barksdale's, CSA, sharp-shooters who were contesting the laying of Union pontoon bridges across the Rappahannock River.

12 11 1862 Federal reconnaissance from Yorktown to Gloucester, Matthews, King and Queen, and Middlesex Counties, VA. 12/11-15/1862.

12 11 1862 Skirmish at Darkesville, WV.

12 12 1862 **Brig. Gen. Maxcy Gregg, CSA,** is mortally wounded at the Battle of Fredericksburg, VA, after his men had stacked their rifles, fearing no attack from the Federals, who thereupon charged, firing into the unprepared Confederates; Gregg dying three days later.

12 12 1862 Skirmishes at Cherokee Station and Little Bear Creek, AL.

12 12 1862 The Federal expedition up the Yazoo River, MS, witness the **first Union vessel to be sunk by a torpedo, the USS Cairo,** north of Vicksburg, MS.

12 12 1862 Union naval operations on the Neuse River, NC. 12/12-15/1862.

12 12 1862 Skirmish at Dumfries, VA.

12 12 1862 Skirmish between Harper's Ferry and Leesburg, VA.

12 12 1862 White's operations in Loudoun County, VA, and raid **(Dec. 14th)** on Poolesville, MD. 12/12-20/1862.

12 12 1862 Maj. Gen. Arnold Elsey, CSA, is assigned to the command of the Richmond, VA, defenses.

12 12 1862 Federal reconnaissance from North Mountain to Bunker Hill, WV.

12 13 1862 The following are appointed Confederate Major Generals:
Patrick Ronayne Cleburne,   C.S.A.

			Franklin Gardner, C.S.A.
			Ambrose Ransom Wright, C.S.A.
12	13	1862	The following are appointed Confederate Brigadier Generals:
			Zachariah Cantey Deas, CSA
			Roger Weightman Hanson, CSA
			Lucius Eugene Polk, CSA
			Edward Cary Walthall, CSA
			Marcus Joseph Wright, CSA

12 13 1862 Federal raid on the **Mobile and Ohio Railroad** from Corinth to Tupelo, MS. 12/13-19/1862.

12 13 1862 Skirmishes at Southwest Creek, NC. 12/13-14/1862.

12 13 1862 President Jefferson Davis is on hand at Murfreesboro, TN, to review Gen. Braxton Bragg's Confederate Army.

12 13 1862 **At Fredericksburg, VA,** Gen. Robert E. Lee's Confederates, under Lieut. Gens. James Longstreet and Thomas Stonewall Jackson, CSA, repel Burnsides' onslaught on the Stone Wall and Mayre's Heights, etc., under Maj. Gens. Edwin Sumner, William B. Franklin and Joseph Hooker, USA, with great slaughter to the charging Union men, and with total casualties nearing 18,000.

12 13 1862 **Brig. Gen. Thomas Reade Rootes Cobb, CSA,** is mortally wounded defending the **"Sunken Road,"** at the Battle of Fredericksburg, VA, bleeding to death after having his thigh shattered by a rifle shot.

12 13 1862 **Brig. Gen. George Dashiell Bayard, USA,** is mortally wounded by a shell fragment while at Brig. Gen. William Buel Franklin's Headquarters during the Battle of Fredericksburg, VA, dying the next day.

12 13 1862 **Brig. Gen. Conrad Feger Jackson, USA,** is mortally wounded at the Battle of Fredericksburg, VA, dying instantly after being shot in the head with a minie ball, while leading his troops.

12 13 1862 Skirmish at Leesburg, VA.

12 14 1862 **Brig. Gen. George Dashiell Bayard, USA,** dies from wounds he received the day before at the Battle of Fredericksburg, VA.

12 14 1862 Affair near Helena, AR, as the Texas Rangers execute a surprise attack on the Federals, capturing 23 outpost pickets.

12 14 1862 The Confederate District of the Gulf has Maj. Gen. John H. Forney, CSA, superseded in command by Brig. Gen. William W. Mackall, CSA, followed by Maj. Gen. Simon B. Buckner, CSA, assigned to command, LA, etal.

12 14 1862 The Confederate raid on Poolesville, MD.

12 14 1862 Federal expedition against the **Mobile and Ohio Railroad,** MS. 12/14-19/1862.

12 14 1862 Engagement at **Kinston, NC,** where Maj. Gen. John G. Foster, USA, moving from New Berne, NC, **captures** the town.

12 14 1862 Confederate attack on the Union forage train and skirmish on the Franklin Pike, near Nashville, TN.

12 14 1862 Maj. Gen. Ambrose E. Burnside, USA, withdraws the Army of the Potomac across the Rappahannock River to Stafford Heights.

12 14 1862 Skirmish at the Quaker village of Waterford, VA.

12 15 1862 **Brig. Gen. Maxcy Gregg, CSA,** dies from wounds received on December 12, 1862, at the Battle of Fredericksburg, VA.

12 15 1862 Skirmish at Neosho, MO.

12 15 1862 Affair at White Hall Bridge, NC, as Maj. Gen. John G. Foster, USA, advances on Goldsborough, NC.

12 15 1862 **Maj. Gen. Nathan Bedford Forrest's Confederate Expedition into West Tennessee,** to affect Grant's Union movement on Vicksburg, MS. 12/15-1/3/1863.

12 15 1862 Maj. Gen. Nathan Bedford Forrest's Confederate command crosses the Tennessee River at Clifton, TN.

12 15 1862 A violation of a flag of truce, TN, whereby under the flag, Confederate Cavalry charge and capture Union men, is claimed by Maj. Gen. William S. Rosecrans, USA, to Gen. Braxton Bragg, CSA. Bragg responds to Rosecrans by claiming his flag carrier was detained by the Federals, and therefore he refuses to return the POW's. 12/15-16/1862.

12 16 1862 Maj. Gen. Nathaniel P. Banks, USA, assumes the command of the 19th Army Corps, as Maj. Gen. Benjamin F. Butler, bades farewell to his troops at New Orleans, LA.

12 16 1862 Affairs at Mount Olive Station and Goshen Swamp, NC.

12 16 1862 Engagement at White Hall, NC, with Maj. Gen. John Foster, USA.

12 16 1862 Skirmish at Wardensville, WV.

12 17 1862 Maj. Gen. Nathaniel P. Banks, USA, supersedes Maj. Gen. Benjamin F. Butler, USA, in the command of the Dept. of the Gulf, at New Orleans, LA.

12	17	1862	**Baton Rouge, LA, is reoccupied** by Union forces.
12	17	1862	Maj. Gen. Ulysses S. Grant, USA, damages his reputation by issuing an order singling out Jews for continuing to deal in the illegal merchandising and speculation trade, which proves unfounded, but will haunt Grant into his years as President of the United States of America, even though Maj. Gen. Henry Halleck and President Lincoln rescind the order on January 4, 1863.
12	17	1862	Federal expedition from New Madrid to Clarkton, MO.
12	17	1862	Federal raid on Dudley Station, NC.
12	17	1862	Engagement at Goldsborough Bridge, NC, with Maj. Gen. John G. Foster, USA.
12	17	1862	Skirmish at Thompson's Bridge, NC.
12	17	1862	Federal reconnaissance to Diascund Bridge and Burnt Ordinary, near Richmond, VA.
12	18	1862	**Brig. Gen. Johnson Kelly Duncan, CSA,** dies at Knoxville, TN, from camp fever sickness.
12	18	1862	Skirmish near Water Valley, MS.
12	18	1862	The **US Army of the Tennessee** has the following assignments: a) Maj. Gen. John A. McClernand, USA, - 13th US Army Corps, b) Maj. Gen. William T. Sherman, USA, - 15th US Army Corps, c) Maj. Gen. Stephen A. Hurlbut, USA, - 16th US Army Corps, d) Maj. Gen. James B. McPherson, USA, - 17th US Army Corps, **(the 15th, 16th, and 17th US Army Corps are newly created)**
12	18	1862	Skirmish at Lexington, TN, where Brig. Gen. Nathan Beford Forrest, CSA, defeats the Union cavalry.
12	19	1862	Engagement near Jackson, TN, with Brig. Gen. Nathan Bedford Forrest, CSA, attacking the railroad and supply lines of Maj. Gens. Ulysses S. Grant and William S. Rosecrans, USA.
12	19	1862	Affairs at Carroll Station and Spring Creek, TN, with Brig. Gen. Nathan Bedford Forrest, CSA.
12	19	1862	Skirmish on the Occoquan, VA.
12	19	1862	Due to constant bickering between Secretary of State and Treasury, Seward and Chase, Seward offers to resign but Lincoln refuses to accept his resignation.
12	20	1862	Skirmish at Cane Hill, AR.
12	20	1862	Skirmish at Cold Water, MS.
12	20	1862	**Operations against Vicksburg, MS.** 12/20-1/3/1863.
12	20	1862	**The Federal Expedition under the command of Maj. Gen. William Tecumseh Sherman, USA,** embarks at Memphis, TN, for Vicksburg, MS.
12	20	1862	Federal operations against the Maj. Gen. Earl Van Dorn Confederate raid, MS. 12/20-28/1862.
12	20	1862	The Confederate **capture of Holly Springs, MS,** by Maj. Gen. Earl Van Dorn's CSA, troops moving from Grenada, MS, and capturing 1,500 of Maj. Gen. Ulysses S. Grant's men and over $1,500,000 of military supplies. Grant is now forced to withdraw to LaGrange, TN, and forgo his advance on Vicksburg, MS.
12	20	1862	**Brig. Gen. Samuel P. Carter's, USA, Raid into East Tennessee and Southwest Virginia.** 12/20/1862-1/5/1863.
12	20	1862	The Confederate **capture of Humboldt, TN,** by Maj. Gen. Nathan Bedford Forrest, CSA.
12	20	1862	Skirmish at Railroad Crossing, Forked Deer River, TN, with Maj. Gen. Nathan Bedford Forrest, CSA.
12	20	1862	The Confederate **capture of Trenton, TN,** by Maj. Gen. Nathan Bedford Forrest, CSA.
12	20	1862	Skirmishes at Kelly's Ford, VA. 12/20-22/1862.
12	20	1862	Skirmish near Occoquan, VA.
12	20	1862	Skirmish near Halltown, WV.
12	20	1862	Secretary of the Treasury, **Salmon P. Chase** also tenders his resignation, which President Lincoln refuses to accept.
12	21	1862	Federal expedition from Fayetteville to Huntsville, AR, including the capture of Confederate stragglers from the Battle of Prairie Grove.
12	21	1862	Skirmish at Van Buren, AR.
12	21	1862	Skirmish at Davis' Mill, MS.
12	21	1862	President Jefferson Davis visits Vicksburg, MS.
12	21	1862	Affair at Rutherford's Station, TN.
12	21	1862	The Confederate **capture of Union City, TN,** by Brig. Gen. Nathan Bedford Forrest, CSA.
12	21	1862	Skirmish on the Wilson Creek Pike, TN.
12	21	1862	Federal scout to Catlett's Station and Brentsville, VA. 12/21-23/1862.
12	21	1862	Federal reconnaissance from Potomac Creek Bridge toward Warrenton, VA. 12/21-22/1862.

12	21	1862	Federal reconnaissance from Stafford Court-House to Kellysville, VA. 12/21-23/1862.
12	21	1862	Skirmish at Strasburg, VA.
12	22	1862	**Brig. Gen. John Hunt Morgan's 2nd Confederate Kentucky Raid.** 12/22/1862-1/2/1863.
12	22	1862	Brig. Gen. John Hunt Morgan's, CSA, command sets out from Alexandria, near Carthage, TN, and crosses the Cumberland River, into Kentucky.
12	22	1862	Maj. Gen. Robert C. Schenck, USA, supersedes Gen. John E. Wool, USA, in the command of the Middle Military Dept, VA.
12	22	1862	Skirmishes near Windsor and at Joyner's Ferry, on the Blackwater, VA.
12	22	1862	Skirmish at Wardensville, WV.
12	22	1862	President Abraham Lincoln meets with Maj. Gen. Ambrose E. Burnside, USA, to discuss the recent battle, chain of events, and actions taken by various officers, at Fredericksburg, VA.
12	23	1862	Skirmish on the St. Francis Road, near Helena, AR, with the Texas Rangers surprising the Union outpost pickets, killing and capturing 18.
12	23	1862	Maj. Gen. Simon Buckner, CSA, assumes the command of the District of the Gulf, LA, etal.
12	23	1862	Skirmish at Ripley, MS.
12	23	1862	Federal operations in the Sugar Creek Hills, MO, in pursuit of various Rebel guerrilla bands. 12/23-31/1862.
12	23	1862	Lieut. Gen. Edmund Kirby Smith, CSA, resumes the command of the Dept. of East Tennessee.
12	23	1862	Skirmish near Nashville, TN, as the Confederates continue to harass the Union foraging parties, this time by the Texas Rangers, who capture the advance vedette of Maj. Gen. Philip H. Sheridan's, USA.
12	23	1862	Because of his treatment of New Orleans, LA, citizens while the Union Military Governor there, President Jefferson Davis declares Maj. Gen. Benjamin F. Butler, USA, a felon, punishable by death, if captured by the Confederates.
12	24	1862	**James Hewett Ledlie,** USA, is appointed Brig. Gen., arguably one of the worst generals of the war, and was in command and responsible for the disaster at the "Crater" outside Petersburg, VA, on July 30, 1864.
12	24	1862	Federal expedition from Helena, AR, to the Tallahatchie, MS.
12	24	1862	Skirmish at, and **occupation of Glasgow, KY**, by Brig. Gen. John Hunt Morgan, CSA, and his Confederate Cavalry Raiders.
12	24	1862	Skirmishes at Bolivar and Middleburg, TN.
12	24	1862	Skirmish near Nashville, TN.
12	24	1862	Federal expedition into East Tennessee, and skirmish at Perkins' Mill, on Elk Fort, December 28, 1862. 12/24/1862-1/1/1863.
12	24	1862	**Galveston, TX, is occupied** by Union forces.
12	24	1862	**The 18th US Army Corps is constituted,** under the command of Maj. Gen. John Gray Foster, USA, the Dept. of North Carolina.
12	25	1862	Maj. Gen. William T. Sherman's Federal expedition from Milliken's Bend, LA, to Dallas Station and Delhi, LA, in their operations against Vicksburg, MS. 12/25-26/1862.
12	25	1862	Skirmish at Bear Wallow, KY, with Brig. Gen John H. Morgan, CSA
12	25	1862	The **capture of Glasgow, KY,** by Brig. Gen. John H. Morgan, CSA.
12	25	1862	Skirmish on the Burkesville road, near Green's Chapel, KY, with Brig. Gen. John Hunt Morgan's Confederate Cavalry.
12	25	1862	Skirmish at Ripley, MS.
12	25	1862	Skirmish at Prim's blacksmith shop, Edmondson Pike, TN, with the Union party out foraging for corn.
12	25	1862	Skirmish on the Wilson Creek Pike, between Brentwood and Petersburg, TN, as Brig. Gen. John A. Wharton, CSA, Cavalry attacks the Union foraging party.
12	25	1862	Maj. Gen. George G. Meade, USA, assumes the command of the 5th US Army Corps, the Army of the Potomac, VA.
12	25	1862	Skirmish near Warrenton, VA.
12	25	1862	Federal reconnaissance from Martinsburg to Charlestown, WV.
12	25	1862	President Abraham and Mrs. Mary Todd Lincoln spends part of their Christmas day visiting wounded soldiers in various Washington, DC, hospitals.
12	26	1862	Skirmish at Bacon Creek, near Munfordville, KY, with Brig. Gen. John Hunt Morgan, CSA.
12	26	1862	The **capture** of the Union stockade at **Nolin, KY,** by Brig. Gen. John Hunt Morgan, CSA.

12	26	1862	The Federal capture of a guerrilla camp in the eastern part of Powell County, KY.
12	26	1862	President Abraham Lincoln decides not to stay the execution of 38 **Sioux Indians** for the Minnesota uprising and are hanged at Mankato, MN.
12	26	1862	**The Stone's River, or Murfreesborough Tennessee, Campaign.** 12/26/1862-1/5/1863.
12	26	1862	Skirmish at Franklin, TN, and the following Tennessee locations as Maj. Gen. William S. Rosecrans, USA, advances towards Gen. Braxton Bragg, CSA, who is at Murfreesboro, TN. This is the beginning of the Stone's River, Campaign.
12	26	1862	Skirmish at Knob Gap, TN.
12	26	1862	Skirmish at La Vergne, TN. 12/26-27/1862.
12	26	1862	Mutiny of the Anderson Cavalry, around Nashville, TN, of men from Pennsylvania.
12	26	1862	Skirmish at Nolensville, TN.
12	26	1862	Maj. Gen. John Sedgwick, USA, supersedes Gen. Darius N. Couch in the command of the 2nd US Army Corps, the Army of the Potomac, VA.
12	27	1862	**William Hays,** USA, is appointed Brig. Gen.
12	27	1862	The **capture** of the Union forces at **Elizabethtown, KY,** by Brig. Gen. John Hunt Morgan, CSA.
12	27	1862	Skirmishes at Chickasaw Bayou, MS, as Maj. Gen. William T. Sherman, USA, continues to advance on Vicksburg. 12/27-28/1862.
12	27	1862	Affair at Snyder's Mill, Yazoo River, MS, as Lieut. Gen. John Pemberton, CSA, contests Maj. Gen. William Sherman's advance.
12	27	1862	Skirmish at Elizabeth City, NC.
12	27	1862	Skirmish at Franklin, TN.
12	27	1862	Skirmish near Huntingdon, TN, with Maj. Gen. Nathan Bedford Forrest, CSA.
12	27	1862	Skirmish on the Jefferson Pike, at Stewart's Creek Bridge, TN.
12	27	1862	Skirmish on the Murfreesborough Pike, at Stewart's Creek Bridge, TN, as Maj. Gen. William S. Rosecrans marches on.
12	27	1862	Skirmish at Triune, TN.
12	27	1862	Federal Raid on Dumfries and Fairfax Station, VA, including action at Dumfries and skirmishes at and near Occoquan, at Fairfax Court-House, Chantilly, Frying Pan, etc. 12/27-29/1862.
12	28	1862	Skirmish at Dripping Springs, and the **capture of Van Buren, AR,** where Maj. Gen. James G. Blunt, USA, soundly defeats Maj. Gen. Thomas C. Hindman, CSA, including the destruction of the Rebel steamboats, **Notre, Key West** and **Rose Douglass.** Hindman also burns the steamers, **Eva** and **Arkansas.**
12	28	1862	Skirmish at Muldraugh's Hill, KY, (near Fort Knox) with Brig. Gen. John Hunt Morgan's Confederates blowing up a bridge, near President Abraham Lincoln's birthplace.
12	28	1862	Maj. Gen. Franklin Gardner, CSA, assumes the command at Port Hudson, LA.
12	28	1862	Union forces **evacuate New Madrid, MO.**
12	28	1862	Skirmishes near Suffolk and at Providence Church, VA.
12	29	1862	**John Adams,** CSA, is appointed to Brig. Gen.
12	29	1862	**William Hicks Jackson,** CSA, is appointed Brig. Gen.
12	29	1862	The **capture** of the Union stockade at **Boston, KY,** by Brig. Gen. John Hunt Morgan, CSA.
12	29	1862	Skirmish near Johnson's Ferry (or Hamilton's Ford), Rolling Fork, KY, with Brig. Gen. John Hunt Morgan, CSA.
12	29	1862	Affair near Plaquemine, LA, with Union cavalry.
12	29	1862	Maj. Gen. William T. Sherman's Federal assault on Chickasaw Bluffs, MS, in the vicinity of Vicksburg, is repulsed by the Confederates with massive Federal casualties.
12	29	1862	Skirmish at Huntingdon, TN, with Maj. Gen. Nathan Bedford Forrest, CSA.
12	29	1862	Skirmish at Lizzard's, between Triune and Murfreesborough, TN.
12	29	1862	The passage of Moccasin Gap, and the capture of Confederates on the Blountsville road, TN, by Brig. Gen. Samuel Carter's, USA, raid.
12	29	1862	Skirmishes near Murfreesborough, TN. 12/29-30/1862.
12	29	1862	Skirmish at Wilkinson's Cross-Roads (or Wilkerson's Cross-Roads), TN.
12	30	1862	Skirmish at New Haven, KY, with Brig. Gen. John Hunt Morgan, CSA.
12	30	1862	Affair at Springfield, KY, with Brig. Gen. John Hunt Morgan, CSA.
12	30	1862	The capture of Confederates at Blountsville, TN, by Brig. Gen. Samuel P. Carter's, USA, raid.
12	30	1862	The **capture of Carter's Depot,** and the destruction of the Watauga Railroad Bridge, TN, by Brig. Gen. Samuel Carter, USA.

12	30	1862	Skirmish at Clarksburg, TN, with Maj. Gen. Nathan Bedford Forrest, CSA.
12	30	1862	Skirmish at Huntingdon, TN, with Nathan Bedford Forrest, CSA.
12	30	1862	Skirmish at Jefferson, TN.
12	30	1862	Skirmish at La Vergne, TN.
12	30	1862	Skirmish at Nolensville, TN.
12	30	1862	Skirmish at Rock Spring, TN.
12	30	1862	The **capture of Union, TN,** and the destruction of the railroad bridge across the Holston River, by Brig. Gen. Samuel Powhatan Carter, USA.
12	30	1862	Federal expedition from Falmouth to Warrenton, VA. 12/30-31/1862.
12	30	1862	Federal expedition from Potomac Creek to Richards' and Ellis' Fords, VA. 12/30-31/1862.
12	31	1862	**Brig. Gen. John B. Marmaduke's, CSA, Confederate expedition into Missouri.** 12/31/1862-1/25/1863.
12	31	1862	Brig. Gen. John S. Marmaduke, CSA, moves from Lewisburg, AR, into Missouri.
12	31	1862	Affairs at Plaquemine, LA. 12/31-1/3/1863.
12	31	1862	Affair at Muldraugh's Hill, near New Market, KY, with Brig. Gen. John Hunt Morgan, CSA.
12	31	1862	The **USS Monitor** foundered in heavy seas off the coast of Cape Hatteras, NC, and sinks shortly after midnight.
12	31	1862	Skirmish at Overall's Creek, TN.
12	31	1862	Engagement at Red Mound, or Parker's Cross-Roads, TN, with Maj. Gen. Nathan Bedford Forrest's, CSA, Cavalry.
12	31	1862	**The Battle of Stone's River, or Murfreesboro, TN,** where Lieut. Gen. William J. Hardee's troops, under Gen. Braxton Bragg, CSA, attack Maj. Gen. William Starke Rosecrans, USA. 12/31/1862-1/3/1863.
12	31	1862	**Brig. Gen. James Edward Rains, CSA,** is mortally wounded while leading his men in a charge against a Federal battery, dying instantly from a rifle shot at the Battle of Murfreesboro, TN.
12	31	1862	**Brig. Gen. Edward Needles Kirk, USA,** is mortally wounded while leading his command at the Battle of Stone's River, TN, dying some months later at home on July 29, 1863.
12	31	1862	**Brig. Gen. Joshua Woodrow Sill, USA,** is instantly killed while leading his men at the Battle of Stone's River, TN. Rumors indicate he was wearing Brig. Gen. Philip Henry Sheridan's overcoat while he was shot.

1863.

	Sunday.	Monday.	Tuesday.	Wednesday.	Thursday.	Friday.	Saturday.		Sunday.	Monday.	Tuesday.	Wednesday.	Thursday.	Friday.	Saturday.
Jan	....	....	....	....	1	2	3	**July**	....	....	....	1	2	3	4
	4	5	6	7	8	9	10		5	6	7	8	9	10	11
	11	12	13	14	15	16	17		12	13	14	15	16	17	18
	18	19	20	21	22	23	24		19	20	21	22	23	24	25
	25	26	27	28	29	30	31		26	27	28	29	30	31	....
	....	....	....	....	....	....	....	**Aug**	....	....	....	....	....	....	1
Feb	1	2	3	4	5	6	7		2	3	4	5	6	7	8
	8	9	10	11	12	13	14		9	10	11	12	13	14	15
	15	16	17	18	19	20	21		16	17	18	19	20	21	22
	22	23	24	25	26	27	28		23	24	25	26	27	28	29
	....	....	....	....	....	....	....		30	31	....	....	....	....	....
Mar	1	2	3	4	5	6	7	**Sept**	....	....	1	2	3	4	5
	8	9	10	11	12	13	14		6	7	8	9	10	11	12
	15	16	17	18	19	20	21		13	14	15	16	17	18	19
	22	23	24	25	26	27	28		20	21	22	23	24	25	26
	29	30	31	....	....	....	....		27	28	29	30	....	....	....
Apr	....	....	....	1	2	3	4	**Oct**	....	....	....	1	2	3
	5	6	7	8	9	10	11		4	5	6	7	8	9	10
	12	13	14	15	16	17	18		11	12	13	14	15	16	17
	19	20	21	22	23	24	25		18	19	20	21	22	23	24
	26	27	28	29	30	....	....		25	26	27	28	29	30	31
May	....	....	....	....	....	1	2		....	....	....	....	....	....	....
	3	4	5	6	7	8	9	**Nov**	1	2	3	4	5	6	7
	10	11	12	13	14	15	16		8	9	10	11	12	13	14
	17	18	19	20	21	22	23		15	16	17	18	19	20	21
	24	25	26	27	28	29	30		22	23	24	25	26	27	28
	31	....	....	....	....	....	....		29	30	....	....	....	....	....
June	....	1	2	3	4	5	6	**Dec**	....	....	1	2	3	4	5
	7	8	9	10	11	12	13		6	7	8	9	10	11	12
	14	15	16	17	18	19	20		13	14	15	16	17	18	19
	21	22	23	24	25	26	27		20	21	22	23	24	25	26
	28	29	30	....	....	....	....		27	28	29	30	31	....	....

XI

MONTH	DAY	YEAR	ACT
01	1	1863	Affair at Helena, AR, as the Texas Rangers surprise and capture 30 Union pickets without firing a shot. Brig. Gen. Willis A. Gorman, USA, commanding, is furious.
01	1	1863	Skirmish at Bath Springs, MS.
01	1	1863	Skirmish near Clifton, TN, with Maj. Gen. Nathan Bedford Forrest, CSA.
01	1	1863	Skirmishes at Stewart's Creek and La Vergne, TN.
01	1	1863	All is relatively quiet around Stone's River, Murfreesboro, TN.
01	1	1863	The attack on the Federal Blockade fleet and the **recapture of Galveston, TX,** by Brig. Gen. John S. Marmaduke, CSA, with the capture of the US Gunboat, **Harriet Lane,** the destruction of the **Westfield,** while the **Clifton, Coryphaeus, Owasco,** and the **Sachem** flee.
01	1	1863	President Lincoln signs the Emancipation Proclamation, Washington, DC.
01	2	1863	**James Murrell Schackelford,** USA, is appointed Brig. Gen.
01	2	1863	Skirmish at White Spring, Boston Mountains, AR, with Brig. Gen. John S. Marmaduke, CSA.
01	2	1863	Union forces, under Maj. Gen. William T. Sherman, USA, re-embark and proceed to Milliken's Bend, LA, giving up in their attempt on Vicksburg, MS. 1/2-3/1863.
01	2	1863	**New Madrid, MO, is reoccupied** by the Union forces.
01	2	1863	Maj. Gen. Nathan Bedford Forrest's, CSA, Cavalry recrosses the Tennessee River at Clifton, TN.
01	2	1863	Brig. Gen. John Hunt Morgan's, CSA, Cavalry recrosses the Cumberland River, TN.
01	2	1863	Skirmish between Fort Donelson and Fort Henry, TN, with an attack by Spaulding's Confederate guerrillas with Spaulding being killed.
01	2	1863	The 2nd day of fighting at **Murfreesboro, or Stone's River, TN,** sees Maj. Gen. John C. Breckinridge, CSA, repulsed by Maj. Gen. William S. Rosecran, USA, with total combined casualties of about 24,500.
01	2	1863	**Brig. Gen. Roger Weightman Hanson, CSA,** is mortally wounded at the Battle of Murfreesboro, TN, while leading his men in a charge, dying two days later.
01	2	1863	Skirmish at Jonesville, Lee County, VA.
01	2	1863	Brig. Gen. James S. Wadsworth, USA, is temporarily in command of the 1st US Army Corps, the Army of the Potomac, VA.
01	2	1863	Skirmish at Bath Springs, WV.
01	2	1863	Federal expedition to Moorefield and Petersburg, WV. 1/2-5/1863.
01	3	1863	Affairs at Plaquemine, LA. 12/31/1862-1/3/1863.
01	3	1863	Skirmish at Burnsville, MS, as Gen. Braxton Bragg, CSA, retreats from Murfreesboro, toward Manchester and Tullahoma, leaving Maj. Gen. William S. Rosecrans, USA, in command of the battlefield, at Murfreesboro, TN.
01	3	1863	Skirmish near Clifton, TN, with Maj. Gen. Nathan Bedford Forrest, CSA.
01	3	1863	Skirmish at the Insane Asylum, or Cox's Hill, or Blood's, TN.
01	3	1863	Action at Somerville, TN.
01	3	1863	The Federal **Dept. of the East** is re-established, VA.
01	3	1863	Skirmish at Moorefield, WV, with the Confederate attack repulsed.
01	4	1863	**Brig. Gen. Roger Weightman Hanson, CSA,** dies from wounds he received at the Battle of Murfreesboro, TN on January 2, 1863.
01	4	1863	**The unauthorized Federal expedition by Maj. Gen. John A. McClernand, USA, against, and the successful capture of Arkansas Post or Fort Hindman, AR.** 1/4-17/1863.
01	4	1863	Maj. Gen. John A. McClernand, USA, assumes command of the Army of the Mississippi.
01	4	1863	The **unauthorized transfer of the Army of the Mississippi** from Milliken's Bend, LA, to the mouth of the White River, AR, by Maj. Gen. John A. McClernand, USA. 1/4-8/1863.
01	4	1863	Federal scout from Ozark, MO, to Dubuque, AR. 1/4-6/1863.
01	4	1863	Federal operations against Indians in the New Mexico Territory. 1/4-5/8/1863.
01	4	1863	The **USS Quaker City** captures a Confederate blockade runner off the coast of Charleston, SC.
01	4	1863	Skirmish on the Manchester Pike, TN, as Gen. Braxton Bragg, CSA, withdraws to Manchester, TN.
01	4	1863	Skirmish at Monterey, TN.
01	4	1863	Skirmish at Murfreesborough, TN.
01	4	1863	Maj. Gen. John F. Reynolds, USA, resumes the command of the 1st US Army Corps, the Army of the Potomac, VA.
01	5	1863	Maj. Gen. William T. Sherman, USA, assumes the command of the 2nd US Army Corps, the Army of the Mississippi, while en route with Maj. Gen. John McClernand towards Fort Hindman, AR.
01	5	1863	Skirmish at Lytle's Creek, on the Manchester Pike, TN.

01	5	1863	**Murfreesborough, TN, is occupied** by the Union forces.
01	5	1863	Skirmish on the Shelbyville Pike, TN.
01	5	1863	Skirmish at Cub Run, VA.
01	5	1863	Skirmish near Moorefield, WV.

01   6   1863   Skirmish at Fort Lawrence, Beaver Station, MO, where Brig. Gen. John Sappington Marmaduke, CSA, **burns Fort Lawrence.**

01   7   1863   Federal scout from Big Spring Creek to Rocky Ford, MS.

01   7   1863   **Ozark, MO, is captured** by Maj. Gen. Sterling Price, CSA, and Brig. Gen. John Sappington Marmaduke, CSA.

01   7   1863   Federal army and naval expedition from Yorktown to West Point and White House, VA, and destruction of Confederate supplies, under Maj. Gen. Erasmus D. Keyes, USA. 1/7-9/1863.

01   8   1863   **James Cantey,** CSA, is appointed Brig. Gen.

01   8   1863   Federal scout from Elkhorn to Berryville, AR, where they surprise and kill 10 Rebel bushwackers. 1/8-10/1863.

01   8   1863   Engagement at **Springfield, MO,** with Brig. Gen. John Marmaduke, CSA, being repulsed by the Union garrison there, **burns part of the town** and withdraws towards Rolla, MO.

01   8   1863   Skirmish at Knob Creek, near Ripley, TN.

01   8   1863   Brig. Gen. Joseph Wheeler's, CSA, Cavalry Raid, including affairs at Mill Creek, Harpeth Shoals, and Ashland, TN. 1/8-14/1863.

01   8   1863   Federal reconnaissance to Catlett's and Rappahannock Stations, VA, with skirmishes at Brentsville, Elk Run, etc. 1/8-10/1863.

01   8   1863   Federal Cavalry expedition from Suffolk toward the Blackwater, VA. 1/8-10/1863.

01   9   1863   Federal expedition from Huntsville, AR, to Buffalo River, near Kingston, AR.

01   9   1863   The loss of the US transport **Sparkling Sea,** near Key West, FL, after striking the coral reef there. The US gunboat, **Sagamore,** safely rescues the men aboard.

01   9   1863   The destruction of Confederate salt-works near St. Joseph's, FL, by the **USS Ethan Allen.**

01   9   1863   **Holly Springs, MS, is evacuated** by the Union forces. 1/9-10/1863.

01   9   1863   The **surrender** of the Union garrison at **Hartville, MO,** to Brig. Gen. John S. Marmaduke, CSA.

01   9   1863   The **US Army of the Cumberland, TN,** is divided into three army corps with the following corps commanders:
a) 14th US Army Corps - Maj. Gen. George H. Thomas, USA
b) 20th US Army Corps - Maj. Gen. Alexander McD. McCook, USA
c) 21st US Army Corps - Maj. Gen. Thomas L. Crittenden, USA

01   9   1863   Skirmish at Fairfax Court-House, VA.

01   9   1863   Skirmish near Providence Church, Suffolk, VA, where Maj. James N. Wheelan, USA, defeats Brig. Gen. Roger Atkinson Pryor, CSA.

01   10   1863   **Camille Armand Jules Marie Prince de Polignac,** CSA, is appointed Brig. Gen.

01   10   1863   **The Engagement at Arkansas Post, or Fort Hindman, on the Arkansas River, AR,** with the Confederate shore batteries and the Union gunboats, the **USS Baron de Kalb, Black Hawk, Cincinnati, Lexington, Louisville,** and the **Rattler.** 1/10-11/1863.

01   10   1863   Federal reconnaissance near Arkansas Post, or Fort Hindman, AR, where Maj. Gen. John McClernand, USA, surrounds Brig. Gen. Thomas James Churchill, CSA.

01   10   1863   Skirmish at Carrollton, AR.

01   10   1863   Brig. Gen. Thomas West Sherman, USA, assumes the command of the Defenses of New Orleans, LA.

01   10   1863   Skirmish at Clifton, TN.

01   10   1863   Maj. Gen. Franz Sigel, USA, assumes the command of the Reserve Grand Division, the Army of the Potomac, VA.

01   10   1863   **Maj. Gen. Fitz John Porter, USA, is court marshalled and cashiered** out of the Union army following the Military Court's decision he failed to follow orders at the Battle of 2nd Manassas, or Bull Run, VA, on August 29, 1862. Porter's guilt is questionable.

01   11   1863   **The Federal capture of Fort Hindman, AR,** commanded by Brig. Gen. Thomas J. Churchill, CSA, by the joint efforts of Maj. Gen. John McClernand, USA, and Admiral David Dixon Porter, USN.

01   11   1863   Engagement at Hartville, or Wood's Fork, MO, where Brig. Gen. John S. Marmaduke, CSA, is defeated by Col. Merrill, USA.

01	11	1863	Skirmish at Lowry's Ferry, TN.
01	11	1863	The **USS Gramphus Number Two** is destroyed and sunk by the Confederate forces near Memphis, TN, on the Mississippi River.
01	11	1863	Maj. Gen. James B. McPherson, USA, assumes the command of the 17th US Army Corps, TN, etal.
01	11	1863	The capture and sinking of the **USS Hatteras** off the coast of Galveston, TX, by the Confederate Raider, **CSS Alabama.**
01	12	1863	Skirmish at Lick Creek, about 12 miles from Helena, AR.
01	12	1863	Maj. Gen. William Tecumseh Sherman, USA, assumes command of the 15th US Army Corps, Army of the Tennessee, TN, etal.
01	12	1863	Maj. Gen. John E. Wool, USA, assumes the command of the Dept. of the East, VA, etal.
01	12	1863	President Jefferson Davis, in a speech to the 1st Confederate Congress, is still hoping for foreign recognition.
01	13	1863	**Daniel Ullmann,** USA, is appointed Brig. Gen.
01	13	1863	Federal expedition under Maj. Gen. John A. McClernand, USA from Helena up the White River, AR, and the **capture of Saint Charles, Clarendon, Devall's Bluff, and Des Arc,** and along with 6,000 Confederate soldiers.
01	13	1863	The **USS Columbia** runs aground off the coast of North Carolina and is burned by the Confederates a few days later.
01	13	1863	Skirmish at Chambers Creek, near Hamburg, TN.
01	13	1863	Federal reconnaissance from Murfreesborough to Nolensville and Versailles, TN. 1/13-15/1863.
01	13	1863	Federal reconnaissance from Nashville to Harpeth River and Cumberland River Shoals, TN. 1/13-19/1863.
01	13	1863	Federal expedition from Yorktown to West Point, VA.
01	14	1863	Western Arizona is transferred to the Dept. of New Mexico.
01	14	1863	Federal expedition to South Bend, Arkansas River, AR, under Maj. Gen. John A. McClernand, USA. 1/14-15/1863.
01	14	1863	Engagement at Bayou Teche, LA, where Brig. Gen. Godfrey Weitzel, USA, captures and destroys the Confederate gunboat, **Cotton.** The US gunboats **Calhoun, Diana, Estrella,** and the **Kinsman,** are also engaged.
01	14	1863	Lieut. Gen. Edmund Kirby Smith, CSA, is assigned to the command of the Army of the Southwest.
01	15	1863	**Maj. Gen. David Rumph Jones, CSA,** dies in Richmond, VA, from heart disease.
01	15	1863	**Mound City, AR, is burned** by the Union expeditionary forces.
01	16	1863	The Confederate privateer Raider, **Florida,** evades the Union blockade around Mobile, AL.
01	16	1863	A landing party from the Union gunboat, **USS Baron De Kalb,** captures Confederate supplies at Devall's Bluff, AR.
01	16	1863	Federal expedition from Fort Henry to Waverly, TN.
01	16	1863	Maj. Gen. John Sedgwick, USA, supersedes Brig. Gen. Orlando Bolivar Wilcox, USA, in the command of the 9th US Army Corps, the Army of the Potomac, VA.
01	17	1863	The following are appointed Confederate Major Generals: **Daniel Smith Donelson,** C.S.A. **Jubal Anderson Early,** C.S.A. **Isaac Ridgeway Trimble,** C.S.A.
01	17	1863	The following are appointed Confederate Brigadier Generals: **Henry Lewis Benning,** CSA **Robert Frederick Hoke,** CSA **Samuel McGowan,** CSA **William Tatum Wofford,** CSA
01	17	1863	The Army of the Mississippi, under Maj. Gen. John McClernand, USA, is ordered by Maj. Gen. Ulysses S. Grant, USA, to re-embark for Milliken's Bend, LA, near Vicksburg, MS, after moving against Arkansas Post, AR without authorization.
01	17	1863	Federal reconnaissance from New Berne to Pollocksville, Trenton, Young's Cross-Roads, and Onslow, NC, and skirmishes: **(19th)** at White Oak Creek and **(20th)** near Jacksonville, NC. 1/17-21/1863.
01	17	1863	Brig. Gen. Daniel Smith Donelson, CSA, is assigned to the command of the Dept. of East Tennessee, vice Brig. Gen. Henry Heth, CSA, is ordered to Virginia.
01	17	1863	Skirmish near Newtown, WV.
01	18	1863	Skirmish in the Cherokee Country, the Indian Territory.

| 01 | 19 | 1863 | Skirmish near Woodbury, TN. |

01 19 1863 Skirmish near Woodbury, TN.

01 19 1863 Federal scout from Williamsburg and skirmish at Burnt Ordinary, VA, with a small party of Confederate pickets.

01 19 1863 Maj. Gen Ambrose E. Burnside, USA, prepares to move two **Grand Divisions** of the **Army of the Potomac** under Maj. Gens. Joseph Hooker and William B. Franklin, USA, across the Rappahannock River at U.S. Ford, about 10 miles above Fredericksburg, VA.

01 19 1863 Maj. Gen. Carl Schurz, USA, is assigned to the command of the 11th US Army Corps, the Army of the Potomac.

01 20 1863 **Joseph Wheeler, C.S.A.,** is appointed Maj. Gen.

01 20 1863 The following are appointed Confederate Brigadier Generals:
Frank Crawford Armstrong, CSA
William Lewis Cabell, CSA
George Blake Cosby, CSA
Marcellus Augustus Stovall, CSA

01 20 1863 **Patterson, MO, is captured** by Brig. Gen. John Marmaduke, CSA.

01 20 1863 Maj. Gen. David Hunter, USA, resumes the command of the Dept. of the South, SC, etal.

01 20 1863 **The "Mud March," about Fredericksburg, VA,** by Maj. Gen. Ambrose E. Burnside's Union forces, damages the morale of these troops, in gruelling inclimate weather of a mixture of rain and snow, the Yankees return to their original positions after continuous marching in knee deep mud. 1/20-24/1863.

01 21 1863 Skirmish near Columbia, MO.

01 21 1863 President Jefferson Davis orders Gen. Joseph E. Johnston, CSA, to travel to Manchester, TN, to discuss with Gen. Braxton Bragg, CSA, his unexplained reasons for retreating from Murfreesboro, or Stone's River, TN.

01 21 1863 Federal reconnaissance from Murfreesborough to Auburn, Liberty, and Cainsville, TN. 1/21-22/1863.

01 21 1863 The capture of Union forage trains near Murfreesborough, TN.

01 21 1863 Skirmish on the Shelbyville Pike, TN.

01 21 1863 Confederate attack on the blockading squadron at Sabine Pass, TX, with two Union blockade vessels captured.

01 21 1863 **Maj. Gen. Fitz John Porter, USA, is officially cashiered** from the Union Army by order of President Lincoln. This order will be revoked in 1879 after a military review and Porter will be reinstated as a Colonel in the Regular Army in 1886 without any back pay.

01 22 1863 The **CSS Florida** captures and burns the vessels **Corris** and the **Windward,** off the coast of Cuba.

01 22 1863 Maj. Gen. Ulysses S. Grant, USA, assumes the command of all the troops in Arkansas within reach of his orders, relegating Maj. Gen. John McClernand, USA, to the role of a Corps commander.

01 22 1863 Maj. Gen. Joseph Wheeler, CSA, is assigned to the command of all the cavalry in Middle Tennessee.

01 22 1863 Skirmish in Pocahontas County, WV.

01 23 1863 Federal scout from Fayetteville to Van Buren, AR, with the capture of the Rebel steamer, **Julia Roan,** along with 200 Confederate men. 1/23-27/1863.

01 23 1863 Federal expedition from Beaufort, SC, up the Saint Mary's River, in Georgia and Florida, aboard the steamers, **John Adams, Planter, and Ben De Ford.** 1/23-2/1/1863.

01 23 1863 Skirmish on the Bradyville Pike, near Murfreesborough, TN.

01 23 1863 Skirmish at Carthage, TN.

01 23 1863 Partly due to frustration with the weather, Maj. Gen. Ambrose E. Burnside, USA, issues orders to remove his subordinate commanders, which is never approved by President Lincoln, and included: Maj. Gen. Joseph Hooker, Maj. Gen. William B. Franklin, Brig. Gen. John Newton, and Brig. Gen. William T. Brooks, USA. In addition to ruining his own military career, Burnside's accusations have a negative impact on any future advancement of Maj. Gen. William B. Franklin. The remaining generals see Hooker advancing to lead the Army of the Potomac with the others eventually being promoted to Major Generals.

01 24 1863 Skirmish at Woodbury, TN.

01 24 1863 Federal scouts in Fauquier County, VA. 1/24-26/1863.

01 25 1863 Brig. Gen. John S. Marmaduke, CSA, reaches Batesville, AR, which effectively ends his expedition into Missouri, that began 12/31/62.

01 25 1863 Federal scout between Bolivar, TN, and Ripley, MS, against guerrilla bands operating in the vicinity.

01 25 1863 Skirmish near Mill Creek, TN.

01 25 1863 Federal reconnaissance from Murfreesborough to Auburn, TN.

01 25 1863 President Abraham Lincoln meets in Washington, DC, with Maj. Gen. Ambrose E. Burnside, USA, and after refusing to dismiss many of Burnside's subordinate officers, Burnside in frustration offers to resign

and in so doing, President Lincoln orders Maj. Gen. Joseph Hooker, USA, to relieve Maj. Gen. Ambrose E. Burnside, in command of the Army of the Potomac; Maj. Gens. Edwin Vose Sumner and William Buer Franklin are also relieved from duty in the Army of the Potomac, VA.

01	26	1863	Skirmish at Mulberry Springs, AR.
01	26	1863	Skirmish at Township, FL.
01	26	1863	The **CSS Alabama** captures and burns the vessel **Golden Rule** off the coast off Santo Domingo.
01	26	1863	Skirmish at Grove Church, near Morrisville, VA.
01	26	1863	Skirmishes near Fairfax Court-House and at Middleburg, VA, with Union pickets and Capt. John S. **Mosby's Confederate Virginia Partisan Rangers.** 1/26-27/1863.

01 26 1863 In a shake-up in the command of the Army of the Potomac, President Lincoln orders the following removals/promotions:

    a) Maj. Gen. Joseph Hooker, USA, supersedes Maj. Gen. Ambrose Everett Burnside, USA, in command of the Army of the Potomac.

    b) Maj. Gen. Darius Nash Couch, USA, supersedes Maj. Gen. Edwin Vose Sumner, USA, in command of the Right Grand Division

    c) Maj. Gen. George Gordon Meade, USA, assumes command of the Center Grand Division

    d) Maj. Gen. Oliver Otis Howard, USA, supersedes Maj. Gen. John Sedgwick, USA, in command of the 2d US Army Corps

    e) Brig. Gen. Charles Griffin, USA, is temporarily in command of the 5th US Army Corps.

01	27	1863	Union naval attack on Fort McAllister, Genesis Point, on the Ogeechee River, south of Savannah, GA, by 5 Union vessels.
01	27	1863	Affair at Bloomfield, MO, with a Union Cavalry dash into town.
01	27	1863	Federal reconnaissance on the Neuse, Dover, and Trent Roads, NC, to ascertain the Rebels positions 1/27-28/1863.
01	27	1863	Affair near Germantown, TN, as Confederate Cavalry stage a surprise attack on a Union forage train.
01	27	1863	Skirmish at Deserted House, near Suffolk, VA.
01	28	1863	**John Daniel Imboden,** CSA, is appointed Brig. Gen.
01	28	1863	Skirmish at Indian Village, LA, force a Confederate retreat.
01	28	1863	Skirmish near Collierville, TN, with Rebel guerrillas.
01	28	1863	Federal scout from La Grange, TN, toward Ripley, MS. 1/28-30/1863.
01	28	1863	Skirmish near Nashville, TN.
01	28	1863	Skirmish near Yorkville, TN, with Union foraging parties who bring in 6 wagon loads of corn and 2,000 pounds of salted meats.
01	29	1863	Skirmish near Richmond, LA.
01	29	1863	Skirmish at Pinos Altos Mines, the New Mexico Territory, with Indians, as the Indians attack two Federal hunting parties.
01	29	1863	Confederate expedition to Daufuskie Island, SC.
01	29	1863	Federal engagement on the Bear River, or Battle Creek, the Utah Territory, 140 miles from Camp Douglas, with hostile Indians who had been murdering emigrants on the Overland Mail Route for the last 15 yrs. Over 220 Indians are reported killed.
01	30	1863	Maj. Gen. Ulysses S. Grant, USA, assumes the immediate command of the expedition against Vicksburg, MS.
01	30	1863	Skirmish at Dyersburg, TN.
01	30	1863	The Confederate capture of the US Steamer, **Isaac Smith,** in the Stono River, near Charleston, SC, after running aground.
01	30	1863	Engagement at the Deserted House, or Kelley's Store, near Suffolk, VA, where Brig. Gen. Roger A. Pryor, CSA, inflicts numerous casualties on Brig. Gen. Michael Corcoran, USA.
01	30	1863	Skirmish at Turner's Mills, VA.
01	31	1863	**William Smith,** CSA, is appointed Brig. Gen.
01	31	1863	Affair on Bull Island, SC, with Confederates arriving from nearby Sullivan's Island.
01	31	1863	Attack on the US naval blockading squadron off Charleston, SC, by the Confederate steam-ram, **CSS Chicora,** and the ironclad, **CSS Palmetto State,** which do extensive damage to the blockading vessels, **USS Keystone State,** and the **USS Mercedita.**
01	31	1863	Federal expedition from Murfreesborough to Franklin, TN, etc., including skirmishes: (Jan. 31st) at Unionville and Middleton, and

			(Jan. 31st and **Feb. 13th**) at Rover, TN. 1/31-2/13/1863.
01	31	1863	Maj. Gen. John A. McClernand, USA, assumes the command of the 13th US Army Corps, TN, etal.
01	31	1863	The 9th Army Corps is ordered to the Dept. of Virginia.
02	1	1863	The 2nd Union Naval attack on Fort McAllister, Genesis Point, south of Savannah, GA, with the Union gunboats, **USS Dawn, Seneca,** and the **Wissahickon,** and the mortar boat, **C. P. Williams.**
02	1	1863	Federal expedition from New Berne to Plymouth, NC, aboard the steamer, **Northerner.** 2/1-10/1863.
02	1	1863	Federal reconnaissance to Franklin and Brentwood, TN. 2/1-2/1863.
02	1	1863	The Union forces **occupy Franklin, TN.**
02	1	1863	Maj. Gen. George Sykes, USA, is placed in temporary command of the 5th US Army Corps, the Army of the Potomac, VA.
02	2	1863	Skirmish at the mouth of the Mulberry River, AR.
02	2	1863	Skirmish at Vine Prairie, White Oak River, AR.
02	2	1863	The passage of the Vicksburg and Warrenton, MS, batteries, by the Union ram, **Queen of the West;** the **Queen of the West** unable to capture the Confederate vessel, **City of Vicksburg,** and sustaining only minor damage by the Confederate shore batteries. 2/2-3/1863.
02	2	1863	Federal scouts and skirmishes in and about Mingo Swamp, MO. 2/2-13/1863.
02	2	1863	The (repeated) destruction of the Confederate Salt-Works at Wale's Head, Currituck Beach, NC, by the Federals transported by the US Steamer, **Halifax.**
02	2	1863	Federal reconnaissance in the vicinity of Saulsbury, TN, with nothing of worthy transpiring. 2/2-5/1863.
02	2	1863	Federal reconnaissance of the Rappahannock fords, and skirmish at Rappahannock Station, VA, with Maj. Gen. Joseph Hooker, USA.
02	2	1863	The **Dept. of Washington, DC,** is re-created, with the troops constituting the 22nd US Army Corps, VA, etal.
02	3	1863	Maj. Gen. Ulysses S. Grant's, USA, forces cut a path through the levee on the Yazoo River, near Yazoo Pass, MS, for transporting troops north of Vicksburg, MS.
02	3	1863	The capture of the Confederate steamers **Baker, Berwick Bay,** and the **Moro** by the Union Ram **Queen of the West,** near Vicksburg, MS.
02	3	1863	Skirmish at Mingo Swamp, MO.
02	3	1863	Attack on Fort Donelson, TN, by Confederate Cavalry under Brig. Gen. Nathan Bedford Forrest, CSA, and Maj. Gen. Joseph Wheeler, CSA, is repulsed with skirmishing at Cumberland Iron-Works, TN.
02	3	1863	Federal expedition from Murfreesborough to Auburn, Liberty, and Alexandria, TN. 2/3-5/1863.
02	4	1863	Skirmish at Batesville, AR, forces a retreat by Brig. Gen. John S. Marmaduke, CSA.
02	4	1863	Union troops are routed at Lake Providence, LA.
02	4	1863	Skirmish near Murfreesborough, TN, as the Rebel cavalry attack a Union foraging party.
02	4	1863	Maj. Gen. John Sedgwick, USA, supersedes Maj. Gen. William Farrar Smith, USA, in the command of the 6th US Army Corps, the Army of the Potomac, VA.
02	5	1863	Federal scout from Fayetteville to the Arkansas River, with skirmishes at Threlkeld's Ferry and near Van Buren, AR. 2/5-12/1863.
02	5	1863	Skirmish in Pope County, AR.
02	5	1863	Skirmish on Bear Creek, Johnson County, MO.
02	5	1863	Skirmish near Olive Branch Church, north of Williamsburg, VA.
02	5	1863	Federal operations at the Rappahannock Bridge and at Grove Church, VA, with the purpose of destroying the railroad bridge is called off due to a snow storm. 2/5-7/1863.
02	5	1863	The **Grand Divisions, Army of the Potomac, are abolished,** and the commanders are assigned to the command of US Army corps as follows: Maj. Gen. John F. Reynolds, USA - 1st US Army Corps Maj. Gen. Darius N. Couch, USA - 2d US Army Corps Maj. Gen. Daniel E. Sickles, USA - 3d US Army Corps Maj. Gen. George G. Meade, USA - 5th US Army Corps Maj. Gen. John Sedgwick, USA - 6th US Army Corps Maj. Gen. William F. Smith, USA - 9th US Army Corps Maj. Gen. Franz Sigel, USA - 11th US Army Corps Maj. Gen. Henry W. Slocum, USA - 12th US Army Corps Maj. Gen. George Stoneman, USA - US Cavalry Corps
02	5	1863	Union scout in a blinding snowstorm from Camp Piatt, across the Big Coal River at Thompson's farm, to

Wyoming County, and about 12 miles above Boone Court-House, WV; some men having their feet frozen. 2/5-8/1863.

02	6	1863	Federal scout in the vicinity of Fort Pillow, TN.
02	6	1863	Skirmish at Dranesville, VA.
02	6	1863	Skirmish at and near Millwood, VA, after the stage coach running between Martinsburg and Winchester was captured by guerrillas, who in turn were captured by the Yankees.
02	6	1863	Skirmish at Wiggenton's Mills, Aquia Creek, VA.
02	6	1863	The 9th US Army Corps, encamped around Falmouth and Aquia Creek, VA, Maj. Gen. William Farrar Smith, USA, commanding, is transferred aboard railroad cars and water transports, from the Army of the Potomac to Newport News, VA. 2/6-21/1863.
02	6	1863	The Federal Government officially turns down the offer by France's **Napoleon III** to mediate between the North & South.
02	7	1863	Lieut. Col. Harvey Lee, 4th California Infantry, assumes the command of the District of Southern California.
02	7	1863	Skirmish near Edenton, NC.
02	7	1863	Three blockade runners arrive safely at Charleston, SC.
02	7	1863	Skirmish near Murfreesborough, TN, with a Union foraging party.
02	7	1863	Confederates reopen Sabine Pass, near Galveston, TX, from the Union naval blockade.
02	7	1863	Skirmish at Olive Branch Church, near Williamsburg, VA, with Brig. Gen. Henry A. Wise, CSA, who blames the Union Cavalry for the burning of the library, etc, at **William & Mary College,** Williamsburg, VA. (5th PA Cavalry).
02	7	1863	Maj. Gen. Samuel P. Heintzelman, USA, assumes the command of the renewed Dept. of Washington, DC.
02	8	1863	Skirmish near Independence, MO, with guerrillas.
02	8	1863	Affair near Camp Sheldon, MS.
02	9	1863	**Alfred Eugene Jackson,** CSA, is appointed Brig. Gen.
02	9	1863	**William Henry Talbot Walker,** CSA, is appointed Brig. Gen.
02	9	1863	**Joseph Pannell Taylor,** USA, is appointed Brig. Gen.
02	9	1863	The **Confederate Southwestern Army** is extended to embrace the entire Trans-Mississippi Dept., AR.
02	9	1863	Affair near Moscow, TN, with guerrillas.
02	9	1863	Skirmish near Somerville, VA.
02	10	1863	Skirmish at Old River, LA, where Capt. Tucker, USA, repels the Confederates.
02	10	1863	Federal operations on the Red, Atchafalaya, and Black Rivers, LA, and the capture (**14th**) of the Union ram **Queen of the West.** 2/10-14/1863.
02	10	1863	Affair near Camp Sheldon, MS, with the capture of 6 Federal guns.
02	10	1863	Skirmish at Sarcoxie Prairie, MO.
02	10	1863	Skirmish at Batchelder's Creek, NC.
02	10	1863	Skirmish at Chantilly, VA.
02	10	1863	Federal operations in Westmoreland and Richmond Counties, VA, including the Union capture of 50 barrels of villainous whiskey. 2/10-16/1863.
02	10	1863	Federal expedition from Beverly into Pocahontas County, WV, to capture rebel recruiting parties and supplies. 2/10-12/1863.
02	12	1863	The **USS Conestoga** captures two Confederate steamers on the White River, AR.
02	12	1863	Federal operations on Bayou Plaquemine and Atchafalaya River, LA. 2/12-28/1863.
02	12	1863	The **Queen of the West** destroys a Confederate supply train along the Red River, LA.
02	12	1863	Federal expedition from Batchelder's Creek and skirmish (**13th**) at Sandy Ridge, NC, to ascertain the strength of the Rebels, with the capture of some Confederate smallarms. 2/12-13/1863.
02	12	1863	Union forces are defeated at Bolivar, TN, in a skirmish.
02	12	1863	Federal expedition from Belle Plain, aboard the steamer, **Edwin Lewis,** to Mattox Creek, Currioman and Nomini Bays, VA. 2/12-14/1863.
02	12	1863	Federal expedition from Pratt's Landing, aboard the steamer, **Alice Price,** down the Potomac to the Coan River and Heathsville, VA, and the destruction of 5 small rebel vessels.
02	12	1863	Skirmishes near Smithfield and Charlestown, WV.
02	12	1863	The capture and later destruction of the Yankee clipper **Jacob Bell,** with cargo valued at over $2 million by the **CSS Florida,** in the Caribbean Sea, West Indies.

02	13	1863	Skirmish near Washington, NC, as Union cavalry surprise and capture the Confederate's outpost picket headquarters and men.
02	13	1863	The **USS Indianola** successfully sails past the Vicksburg, MS, shore batteries as so many other Union vessels have done.
02	13	1863	Federal expedition from La Grange, TN, to Mount Pleasant and Lamar, MS. 2/13-14/1863.
02	13	1863	Skirmish at Dranesville, VA.
02	14	1863	Federal expedition to Greenville, MS, and Cypress Bend, AR, with skirmishes: a) at Cypress Bend, AR, **(19th)** and b) at Deer Creek and Fish Lake Bridge, near Greenville, MS. **(23rd)**. 2/14-26/1863.
02	14	1863	The **Queen of the West** captures the Confederate vessel, the **New Era Number Five,** and is subsequently captured by the Confederates after running aground. The **USS DeSoto** rescues the crew of the **Queen of the West** from capture on the Mississippi River, near Vicksburg.
02	14	1863	Affair about 3 miles from Union Mills, VA, as the Rebel cavalry lay an ambush on the Federal Cavalry.
02	14	1863	Affair on the Hillsborough Road, and Federal scout to Leesburg, VA.
02	15	1863	Skirmish at Arkadelphia, AR, with the guerrillas routed.
02	15	1863	Skirmishes near Auburn, TN, as the Federals attack a Rebel party attempting to burn a bridge; they are counterattacked by the Confederates.
02	15	1863	Skirmish near Cainsville, TN, where Brig. Gen. John Hunt Morgan, CSA, is repulsed by Col. Monroe, USA.
02	15	1863	Skirmish near Nolensville, TN, where Sgt. Holmes, USA, fends off the Confederates.
02	16	1863	Skirmish at Yazoo Pass, MS, as the Confederates contest the advance of Maj. Gen. Ulysses S. Grant, USA, on Vicksburg, MS.
02	16	1863	Maj. Gen. Stephen A. Hurlbut, USA, assumes the command of the 16th US Army Corps, MS, etal.
02	16	1863	Skirmish at Bradyville, TN.
02	16	1863	Maj. Gen. George Sykes, USA, is placed in temporary command of the 5th US Army Corps, the Army of the Potomac, VA.
02	16	1863	Affair near Romney, WV, as Rebel Cavalry capture a Union forage train and guards.
02	17	1863	Union forces burn **Hopefield, AR,** in retaliation after the Confederates from that town attack the **USS Hercules.**
02	17	1863	Maj. Gen. Samuel G. French, CSA, is placed in temporary command of the Dept. of North Carolina and Southern Virginia.
02	17	1863	The Union ironclad, **USS Indianola,** positions itself at the mouth of the Red River on the Mississippi River to disturb Confederate riverboats operating in the area.
02	17	1863	Union expedition from Lexington to Clifton, TN. 2/17-21/1863.
02	17	1863	Federal expedition from Memphis, TN, against Confederate guerrillas harassing the Federals rear.
02	17	1863	Federal expedition from Murfreesborough to Liberty, TN. 2/17-20/1863.
02	18	1863	Operations in Central Kentucky, including skirmishes at: **(Feb. 22nd)** at Coombs' Ferry, **(Feb. 24th)** at Stoner Bridge, and **(March 2nd)** at Slate Creek, near Mount Sterling, KY. 2/18-3/5/1863.
02	18	1863	The South Carolina Militia is called into service.
02	18	1863	Affair near Moscow, TN, with the Confederate attack on a Union forage train. The Federals lose 42 mules, 2 horses and 18 men.
02	18	1863	Maj. Gen. Thomas J. Wood, USA, is placed in temporary command of the 21st US Army Corps, TN, etal.
02	18	1863	Two divisions of Longstreet's Confederate Corps is ordered from the **Army of Northern Virginia,** near Fredericksburg, VA, to the defense of Richmond, VA.
02	19	1863	Federal expedition from Indian Village to Rosedale, LA.
02	19	1863	Skirmish near Coldwater River, MS, results in a Union victory, over Col. Wood, CSA.
02	19	1863	Skirmish near Yazoo Pass, MS, with Brig. Gen. Nathan Bedford Forrest, CSA, Cavalry and Maj. Gen. John A McClernand, USA.
02	19	1863	Federal scout into Barton and Jasper Counties, MO. 2/19-23/1863.
02	19	1863	Skirmish near Rover, TN.
02	19	1863	Skirmish at Leesburg, VA.
02	20	1863	Skirmish near Fort Halleck, the Dakota Territory with the **Ute Indians.**
02	20	1863	Skirmish on the Shelbyville Pike, TN.

02	21	1863	Skirmish at Prairie Station, MS.
02	21	1863	Federal reconnaissance from Franklin, on the Lewisburg, Columbia, and Carter Creek Roads, TN.
02	21	1863	Attack on the US gunboats **Freeborn** and **Dragon,** at Ware's Point, the Rappahannock River, VA.
02	22	1863	Federal Cavalry attack on Tuscumbia, AL, and the rear of Maj. Gen. Earl Van Dorn's Confederate column, capturing supplies.
02	22	1863	Skirmish on the Manchester Pike, TN, between pickets of Gen. Braxton Bragg, CSA, and Maj. Gen. William S. Rosecrans, USA.
02	23	1863	Affair at Athens, KY.
02	23	1863	Engagement of the US Steamers, **Dacotah** and the **Monticello,** at Fort Caswell, NC.
02	23	1863	Brig. Gens. Andrew A. Humphreys and Adolph von Steinwehr, USA, are temporarily and respectively commanding the 5th and the 11th US Army Corps, the Army of the Potomac, VA.
02	23	1863	Former US Secretary of War and Governor of Pennsylvania, **Simon Cameron,** resigns his post as Minister to Russia.
02	24	1863	The US Congress organizes the **Arizona Territory,** officially separating it from the **New Mexico Territory.**
02	24	1863	**The Yazoo Pass Expedition** (by Moon Lake, Yazoo Pass, and the Coldwater and Tallahatchee Rivers), including engagements **(March 11th, 13th, 16th, and April 2nd and the 4th)** at Fort Pemberton, near Greenwood, MS. 2/24-4/8.
02	24	1863	The Confederates capture and sink the Union gunboat, the **Indianola,** near Mr. Joe Davis' Plantation, below Vicksburg, on the Mississippi River, with the captured **Queen of the West.**
02	24	1863	Skirmish near Strasburg, VA.
02	25	1863	Maj. Gen. Daniel Harvey Hill, CSA, assumes the command of the Confederate troops in North Carolina.
02	25	1863	Skirmish at Chantilly, VA.
02	25	1863	Skirmish at Hartwood Church, VA, with Brig. Gen. Fitzhugh Lee's, CSA, Cavalry.
02	25	1863	Cavalry skirmishes near Winchester, Strasburg, and Woodstock, VA. 2/25-26/1863.
02	25	1863	The **USS Vanderbilt** captures the British blockade runner, **Peterhoff,** off St. Thomas, Virgin Islands, which almost causes an international incident, eventually the Peterhoff is released.
02	26	1863	The **Cherokee Indian Nation** cancels its treaty with the Confederacy, and realigns with the Federal Government.
02	26	1863	Confederate guerrillas capture a Union freight train laden with supplies near Woodbury, TN.
02	26	1863	Lieut. Gen. James Longstreet, CSA, assumes the command of the Dept. of Virginia and North Carolina.
02	26	1863	Affair 2 miles from Germantown, VA, as Capt. John S. Mosby's Cavalry routs the Federals there.
02	27	1863	Maj. Gen. Sterling Price, CSA, is ordered to the Confederate Trans-Mississippi Dept., AR, etal.
02	27	1863	Federal expedition from Fort Pillow, TN.
02	27	1863	Skirmish near Bloomington, on the Hatchie River, TN.
02	27	1863	Brig. Gen. James S. Wadsworth, USA, is temporarily in command of the 1st US Army Corps, the Army of the Potomac, VA.
02	27	1863	Federal scout from Centreville to Falmouth, VA. 2/27-28/1863.
02	28	1863	**Edward Johnson, C.S.A.,** is appointed Maj. Gen.
02	28	1863	The destruction of the Confederate steamer **Nashville (Rattlesnake),** by the **USS Montauk,** on the Ogeechee River, south of Savannah, GA; the **USS Seneca, Wissahickon,** and **Dawn** assisting.
02	28	1863	Federal naval attack on Fort McAllister, GA, following the above.
02	28	1863	Skirmish near Fort Gibson, the Indian Territory.
02	29	1863	**Daniel Chevilette Govan,** CSA, is appointed Brig. Gen.
03	1	1863	The Federal **capture of,** and skirmish near, **Bloomfield, MO.**
03	1	1863	Federal expedition from New Berne aboard the US steamer, **Escort,** to Swan Quarter, NC, and skirmishes **(3rd and 4th)** near Fairfield and Swan Quarter; the Union taking casualties; they receive the protection of the US gunboat, **North State.** 3/1-6/1863.
03	1	1863	Skirmish at Bradyville, TN, with Brig Gen. Nathan Bedford Forrest, CSA.
03	1	1863	Skirmish at Woodbury, TN.
03	2	1863	Federal expedition from New Orleans, LA, to the mouth of the Rio Grande River, TX. 3/2-30/1863.
03	2	1863	Skirmish near Neosho, MO.
03	2	1863	Skirmish near Eagleville, TN.

03	2	1863	Federal scout from La Grange, TN, to Hudsonville and Salem, MS, and Saulsbury, TN. 3/2-3/1863.
03	2	1863	Skirmish near Petersburg, TN.
03	2	1863	Skirmish near Aldie, VA, as Union cavalry are surprised while feeding their horses and with many captured by Rebel cavalry.
03	2	1863	The US Congress approves the massive officer promotions to November 29, 1862.
03	3	1863	Another unsuccessful Union naval attack on Fort McAlister, below Savannah, GA, by the gunboats, **USS Nahant, Passaic,** and the **Patapsco.**
03	3	1863	Confederate raid on Granby, MO, with a quick Rebel exit.
03	3	1863	Skirmish near Bear Creek, TN.
03	3	1863	Federal expedition from Concord Church to Chapel Hill, TN. 3/3-6/1863.
03	3	1863	Federal expedition from Murfreesborough to Woodbury, TN. 3/3-8/1863.
03	3	1863	Federal expedition from Belle Plain to Coan River and Machodee Creek, VA. 3/3-8/1863.
03	3	1863	The US Government creates the **Idaho Territory** from an area previously part of the **Washington Territory.**
03	4	1863	**Robert Brank Vance,** CSA, is appointed Brig. Gen.
03	4	1863	Skirmish (4th) near Franklin, TN, and engagement **(5th)** at Thompson's Station, or Spring Hill, TN, where Maj. Gen. Earl Van Dorn, CSA, captures several Union regiments under the command of Maj. Gen. William S. Rosecrans, USA. 3/4-5/1863.
03	4	1863	Federal expedition from Murfreesborough toward Columbia, TN, with skirmishes: (4th) at Rover and Unionville, **(5th)** at Chapel Hill **(9th)** at Thompson's Station and **(10th-11th)** at Rutherford Creek, TN. 3/4-14/1863.
03	4	1863	Skirmish at Independent Hill, Prince William County, which is 8 miles from Dumfries, VA.
03	5	1863	Skirmish near Fort Smith, AR.
03	5	1863	Federal expedition from Helena, AR, up the St. Francis and Little Rivers, with skirmish at Madison, AR. 3/5-12/1863.
03	5	1863	Federal operations in Newton and Jasper Counties, MO. 3/5-13/1863.
03	5	1863	Action near **Franklin, TN,** with the defeat of Col. Coburn, USA, and the **occupation** of the town by the Confederates.
03	6	1863	Federal expedition from Helena to Big and Lick Creeks, AR, and skirmishes. 3/6-10/1863.
03	6	1863	Skirmish on the White River, AR.
03	6	1863	Federal expedition from New Berne to Trenton, Pollocksville, Young's Cross-Roads, and Swansborough, NC. 3/6-10/1863.
03	6	1863	Federal demonstration on Kinston, NC, including skirmishes **(7th)** at Core Creek and near Dover, NC. 3/6-8/1863.
06	6	1863	Federal reconnaissance from Murfreesboro, including skirmishes near Christiana and at Middleton, TN. 3/6-6/1863.
03	7	1863	Lieut. Gen. E. Kirby Smith, CSA, assumes command of all the Confederate forces west of the Mississippi River, AR, etal.
03	7	1863	Maj. Gen. Nathaniel P. Banks, USA, moves to Baton Rouge, LA, from New Orleans, to join forces with Maj. Gen. Ulysses S. Grant, USA, with the joint effort against Vicksburg, MS.
03	7	1863	**Union operations against and about Port Hudson, LA,** by Maj. Gen. Ulysses S. Grant, USA. 3/7-27/1863.
03	7	1863	Federal expedition from New Berne, aboard the steamers, **Escort** and **Northerner,** and accompanied by the US gunboats, **North State** and **Allison,** to Mattamuskeet Lake, NC, with Col. Charles C. Dodge, USA, commanding the expedition, accusing the 103rd PA Volunteer Infantry of lack of discipline in the unauthorized burning and plundering of civilian farms and homes, as well as the insulting of local women. 3/7-14/1863.
03	7	1863	Federal expedition from Newport Barracks to Cedar Point, NC. 3/7-10/1863.
03	7	1863	Federal reconnaissance from Isle of Wight Court-House, VA, to Smithfield, Benn's Church and Chuckatuck, and skirmish **(9th)** near Windsor, VA, as Confederate cavalry move to block their advance. 3/7-9/1863.
03	7	1863	Skirmish at Green Spring Run, WV.

MONTH	DAY	YEAR	ACT
03	8	1863	Confederate expedition against New Berne, NC, with skirmishes **(13th-14th)** at Deep Gully, and **(14th)**, Confederate attack on Fort Anderson, led by Maj. Gen. Daniel Henry (DH) Hill, CSA. 3/8-16/1863.
03	8	1863	The capture of Brig. Gen. George Crook's, USA, forage train near Carthage, TN.
03	8	1863	Federal expedition from Collierville, TN. 3/8-12/1863.
03	8	1863	Federal expedition from Franklin to Columbia, TN, including skirmishes at Thompson's Station **(9th)** and at Rutherford Creek **(10th and 11th)**. 3/8-12/1863.
03	8	1863	Federal expedition from La Grange, and skirmishes **(9th** and **10th)** near Covington, TN, with Col. Benjamin H. Grierson, USA, Cavalry. 3/8-12/1863.
03	8	1863	Skirmish on the Harpeth River, near Triune, TN.
03	9	1863	Skirmish near Saint Augustine, FL, with a Union attack on the Confederate camp, Fort Peyton, 7 miles southwest of Saint Augustine.
03	9	1863	Affair at Fort McAllister, GA.
03	9	1863	Skirmish at Hazle Green, KY.
03	9	1863	Skirmishes on the Comite River, at Montesano Bridge, etc. LA. 3/9-10/1863.
03	9	1863	Federal expedition from Bloomfield, MO, to Chalk Bluff, AR, and to Gum Slough, Kennett, and Hornersville, MO, and skirmishes. 3/9-15/1863.
03	9	1863	Federal reconnaissance from Salem to Versailles, TN. 3/9-14/1863.
03	9	1863	Affair at Fairfax Court-House, VA, where **Capt. John Mosby's** Confederates **capture Brig. Gen. Edwin Henry Stoughton, USA, in his bed,** effectively ruining and ending his military career.
03	10	1863	**Operations in the Humboldt Military District, CA,** against hostile Indians. 3/10-7/10/1863.
03	10	1863	Union forces, mostly black, and led by Col. Higginson, USA, **reoccupy Jacksonville, FL.**
03	10	1863	President Jefferson Davis meets with Lieut. Gen. John C. Pemberton, CSA, at Vicksburg, MS.
03	10	1863	The Confederate demonstration on Plymouth, NC, is driven off by the nearby Union gunboats. 3/10-13/1863.
03	10	1863	Federal scout to La Fayette and Moscow, TN, and skirmish. 3/11-16/1863.
03	10	1863	Skirmish near Murfreesborough, TN.
03	10	1863	President Lincoln issues amnesty to all soldiers absent without leave if they report before April 1, 1863.
03	11	1863	**George Jerrison Stannard,** USA, is appointed Brig. Gen.
03	11	1863	Affair near Paris, KY.
03	11	1863	Confederates construct Fort Pemberton, near Greenwood, MS, under Maj. Gen. William W. Loring, CSA, to effectively deflect the Federal advance under Maj. Gen. Ulysses S. Grant against Vicksburg, MS.
03	12	1863	**Henry Baxter,** USA, is appointed Brig. Gen.
03	12	1863	Federal expedition from Columbia, KY, to Perryville, TN. 3/12-20/1863.
03	12	1863	Skirmish at Louisa, KY.
03	12	1863	Brig. Gen. William W. Morris, USA, is temporarily in command of the Middle Military Dept, VA.
03	12	1863	Federal scout from Camp Piatt through Boone, Wyoming, and Logan Counties, WV, finding many locals sympathetic to the southern cause, and suspected of being bushwackers. 3/12-16/1863.
03	13	1863	The following are appointed Union Brigadier Generals: **Thomas Ewing, Jr.,** USA **Abner Clark Harding,** USA **Robert Brown Potter,** USA **Hugh Thompson Reid,** USA
03	13	1863	The capture of Confederate conscripts near Charlotte, TN. 3/13-14/1863.
03	13	1863	Skirmish at Rover, TN, with Union cavalry and Brig Gen. John Austin Wharton, CSA.
03	13	1863	The 3rd Army Division, 9th US Army Corps, Maj. Gen. Smith, USA Commanding, is transferred from Newport News to Suffolk, VA. 3/13-16/1863.
03	13	1863	The Confederate Ordnance Laboratory, Brown's Island, near Richmond, VA, explodes, killing nearly 70, mostly women who are working in the munitions factory.
03	14	1863	**Thomas Greely Stevenson,** USA, is appointed Brig. Gen.
03	14	1863	Engagement between the Union fleet and the Port Hudson, LA, batteries, with the loss of the Federal gunboat, the **USS Mississippi,** while other gunboats safely pass. 3/14-15/1863.
03	14	1863	The **Steele's Bayou Expedition** (to Rolling Fork, MS, by Muddy Steele's, Black Bayou and Deer Creek), by Maj. Gen. Ulysses S. Grant, USA, on Vicksburg, MS, with skirmishes

a) on Deer Creek (**21st** and **22nd**) and
b) on Black Bayou (**24th** and **25th**). 3/14-27/1863.

| 03 | 14 | 1863 | Skirmish at Davis' Mill, TN. |

03	15	1863	The seizure of the Confederate schooner, **J.M. Chapman,** by the **USS Cyane,** San Francisco Harbor, CA.
03	15	1863	The English vessel, the **Britannia,** successfully evades the Union blockade and arrives in port at Wilmington, NC.
03	15	1863	Skirmishes near Hernando, MS, and on the Coldwater, 8 miles north of Holly Springs. 3/15-16/1863.
03	15	1863	Skirmish at Rover, TN.
03	15	1863	Affair near Dumfries, VA, with the capture of a Union patrol.
03	15	1863	Federal scout from Harper's Ferry to Leesburg, VA, who are ambushed by bushwackers.

03	16	1863	**Philip Henry Sheridan, U.S.A.,** is appointed Maj. Gen.
03	16	1863	The following are appointed Union Brigadier Generals: **Joseph Andrew Jackson Lightburn,** USA **Joseph Anthony Mower,** USA **Thomas Church Haskell Smith,** USA
03	16	1863	Federal expedition from Jackson to Trenton, TN. 3/16-18/1863.
03	16	1863	The Confederate Cavalry commands of Maj. Gen. Earl Van Dorn and Brig. Gen. Joseph Wheeler, CSA, are designated as the Confederate Army Corps, of the Army of Tennessee.

03	17	1863	The following are appointed Union Major Generals: **Carl Schurz, U.S.A.** **Julius Stahel, U.S.A.**
03	17	1863	Operations on the west bank of the Mississippi River, from Port Hudson, LA.
03	17	1863	Federal expedition from Montesano Bayou toward Port Hudson, LA.
03	17	1863	Skirmish at Bealeton Station, VA, with guerrillas.
03	17	1863	Skirmish about 5 miles from Franklin, VA.
03	17	1863	Affair at Herndon Station, VA, as Capt. John Mosby, CSA, and his Virginia Partisan Cavalry surprises and captures the 25 man Union reserve picket post there.
03	17	1863	Engagement at Kelly's Ford (Kellysville), VA, with the Cavalry of Brig. Gen. William Woods Averell, USA, and Brig. Gen. Fitzhugh Lee, CSA. The up and coming young **John Pelham,** CSA, is sadly killed as he watched the battle without participating, but merely observing as a spectator.
03	17	1863	Maj. Gen. Ambrose E. Burnside, USA, assumes the command of the 9th US Army Corps, currently at Suffolk, VA.

| 03 | 18 | 1863 | **One of the few days of rest and peace.** |
| 03 | 18 | 1863 | Lieut. Gen. Theophilus H. Holmes, CSA, assumes command of the Confederate District of Arkansas. |

03	19	1863	Skirmish on Frog Bayou, AR, with a small Union reconnoitering party besting the Rebel forces.
03	19	1863	Skirmish at Hazle Green, KY.
03	19	1863	Skirmish at Mount Sterling, KY.
03	19	1863	Reconnaissance to False River, LA.
03	19	1863	The passage of the Grand Gulf, MS, batteries by the Union gunboats, **USS Hartford** and the **USS Monongahela.**
03	19	1863	Federal scout toward Doniphan, MO. 3/19-23/1863.
03	19	1863	Skirmish near College Grove, TN.
03	19	1863	Skirmish at Liberty, TN, with attack on a Union forage train.
03	19	1863	Skirmish at Richland Station, TN.
03	19	1863	Skirmish at Spring Hill, TN, with Brig. Gen. Earl Van Dorn, CSA.
03	19	1863	Skirmish near Winchester, VA.
03	19	1863	Maj. Gen. John G. Parke, USA, assumes the command of the 9th US Army Corps, at Newport News, VA, with Maj. Gen. Ambrose E. Burnside, USA, as his superior.
03	19	1863	The 1st and 2nd Divisions, 9th US Army Corps, embark at Newport News, VA, for the **Dept. of the Ohio,** arriving at Bardstown and Lexington, KY via railroad cars through Pennsylvania and Ohio. The 3rd Division left Newport News, VA, for Suffolk, VA. 3/19-26/1863.

| 03 | 20 | 1863 | Affair in Saint Andrew's Bay, FL, where Confederates kill and capture most of a Union landing party that is up to mischief. |
| 03 | 20 | 1863 | Action at Vaught's Hill, near Milton, TN, with Col. Hall, USA, defeating the Confederates. |

03	21	1863	**Maj. Gen. Edwin Vose "Bull" Sumner, USA,** dies in Syracuse, NY, from natural causes, while he was travelling to his new assignment as the commander of the Dept. of Missouri. "So long, Sir."
03	21	1863	Skirmish on the Eel River, CA, with over 45 Indians killed and 37 squaws and children brought in as prisoners.
03	21	1863	Federal expedition from Bonnet Carre to the **Jackson Railroad** and the Amite River, LA. 3/21-29/1863.
03	21	1863	Federal expedition from New Orleans to Ponchatoula, LA, and skirmishes. 3/21-30/1863.
03	21	1863	Affair near Doniphan, MO.
03	21	1863	Confederate guerrilla attack on the Union railway train between Bolivar and Grand Junction, TN, which they are able to derail and burn.
03	21	1863	Federal scout from La Grange to Saulsbury, TN. 3/21-22/1863.
03	21	1863	Cavalry skirmish at Salem, TN.
03	21	1863	Skirmish at Triune, TN.
03	22	1863	Skirmish near the head of the White River, AR, as the Confederates attack a party of Union men assisting a beef contractor with his cattle.
03	22	1863	**Brig. Gen. John Pegram's Confederate expedition into Kentucky.** 3/22-4/1/1863.
03	22	1863	The **capture of Mount Sterling, KY,** by Col. R. S. Cluke, CSA, of Brig. Gen. John Hunt Morgan's Confederate Cavalry command.
03	22	1863	Skirmish at Blue Springs, near Independence, MO, with guerrillas.
03	22	1863	The destruction of the Confederate steamer, **Georgiana,** off the coast of Charleston, SC.
03	22	1863	Skirmish near Murfreesborough, TN.
03	22	1863	Affairs at Selecman's Ford, and at Mrs. Violett's, near Occoquan, VA, as the Confederates probably by men under Capt. John Mosby, CSA, capture yet another group of Union reserve pickets.
03	23	1863	Federal operations near Jacksonville, FL. 3/23-31/1863
03	23	1863	Attack on the Warrenton, MS, batteries, by the **Albatross** and the **Hartford,** below Vicksburg, MS.
03	23	1863	Skirmish at Winfield, NC, with the Confederate attack repulsed.
03	23	1863	Skirmish near Thompson's Station, TN, with Union cavalry.
03	23	1863	Skirmish on the Little River Turnpike, near Chantilly, VA, as Capt. John Mosby, CSA, routs the Federals, but is later caught off guard by charging Union cavalry while feeding their unbridled horses. Mosby orders a foot charge and scares off the Federals.
03	23	1863	The Confederate attack on **Williamsburg, VA,** is repulsed.
03	24	1863	Federal scout from Fayetteville, AR. 3/24-31/1863.
03	24	1863	Skirmish with Indians on the Eel River, CA.
03	24	1863	Affair in Ocklockonnee Bay, FL.
03	24	1863	Skirmishes at Danville, KY, with Brig. Gen. John Pegram, CSA. 3/24-26/1863.
03	24	1863	Federal expedition to Hermitage Landing, or Ponchatoula, LA.
03	24	1863	Federal scout from Bloomfield to Scatterville, MO. 3/24-4/1-1863.
03	24	1863	Skirmish at Rocky Hock Creek, NC.
03	24	1863	Skirmish on Davis' Mill road, near La Grange, TN, with Col. Benjamin H. Grierson, USA, Cavalry.
03	25	1863	Affair with Union wooden gunboats near Florence, AL, as Brig. Gen. Nathan Bedford Forrest's, CSA, Cavalry successfully moves to protect the several manufacturing establishments in the area.
03	25	1863	Skirmish at Jacksonville, FL.
03	25	1863	Skirmishes near Louisa, KY. 3/25-26/1863.
03	25	1863	Federal expedition to Booneville, MS. 3/25-4/1/1863.
03	25	1863	The passage of the Vicksburg, MS, batteries by the ironclad, **Switzerland,** and the destruction of the **Lancaster.**
03	25	1863	Actions at Brentwood, and at Franklin, on the Little Harpeth River, TN, including the capture of the Union command at Brentwood, by Brig. Gen. Nathan Bedford Forrest, CSA.
03	25	1863	Maj. Gen. Ambrose E. Burnside, USA, supersedes Maj. Gen. Horatio G. Wright, USA, in the command of the Dept. of the Ohio, TN, as Maj. Gen. Horatio G. Wright is relegated to a division commander in the Army of the Potomac, VA.
03	25	1863	Federal expedition from Belle Plain aboard the steamer, **W.W. Fraiser,** into Westmoreland County, VA, with large quantities of foodstuff seized. 3/25-29/1863.
03	25	1863	Affair at Norfolk, VA.
03	26	1863	Federal reconnaissance from Murfreesborough to Bradyville, TN.
03	26	1863	Federal expedition from Camp Douglas to the Cedar Mountains, the Utah Territory, and skirmish with Indians **(Goshutes)** believed to be spending the winter in the Mormon settlements of Tooele Valley and

who have been attacking the Overland Mail route **(April 1st)** at Cedar Fort, as the Federals charge the Mormons of encouraging the Indians, instead of aiding in punishing the Indians. 3/26-4/3/1863.

03	27	1863	Skirmish at Palatka, FL.
03	27	1863	Skirmish at Madisonville, KY.
03	27	1863	Skirmish on the Rio Bonito, the New Mexico Territory, with Indians. Arrows found indicate they were **Apaches.**
03	27	1863	Skirmish on the Woodbury Pike, TN, with Union cavalry.
03	28	1863	**Brig. Gen. James Cooper, USA,** dies while the commandant of the Federal prison, Camp Chase, near Columbus, OH, from camp fever sickness.
03	28	1863	Col. Ferris Forman, 4th California Infantry, is assigned to the command of the District of Southern California.
03	28	1863	Skirmishes at Danville and Hickman's Bridge, KY, with Brig. Gen. John Pegram, CSA.
03	28	1863	The capture of the steamer, **USS Diana,** near Pattersonville, LA, by Maj. Gen. Richard Taylor, CSA.
03	28	1863	The Confederate attack on and capture of the US steamer, **Sam. Gaty**, MO.
03	28	1863	Federal expedition from La Grange to Moscow and Macon, and action near Belmont, TN, under Col. Benjamin H. Grierson, USA. 3/28-4/3/1863.
03	28	1863	Skirmish at Hurricane Bridge, WV.
03	29	1863	Federal scouts from Fayetteville, AR, to Cassville, and Springfield, MO, to bring back wagon trains of weapons. 3/29-4/5/1863.
03	29	1863	Skirmish at Jacksonville, FL.
03	29	1863	Affair at Moscow, TN, as 12 Rebels capture the passenger train which held about 30 Union soldiers. Maj. Gen. Stephen A. Hurlbut, USA, is furious and refuses to receive these 30 soldiers if they are exchanged.
03	29	1863	Affair 5 miles from Dumfries, VA, on the Telegraph road.
03	29	1863	Skirmish at Kelly's Ford, VA.
03	29	1863	Skirmish at **Williamsburg, VA,** with the Confederates failing in their surprise attack to capture **Fort Magruder.** The Federals are enraged at the help given the Rebels by the local citizens.
03	29	1863	Maj. Gen. Carl Schurz, USA, assumes the command of the 11th US Army Corps, VA. etal.
03	30	1863	**John Newton,** U.S.A., is appointed Major General.
03	30	1863	**Patrick Edward Connor,** USA, is appointed Brig. Gen.
03	30	1863	Skirmish at Cross Hollow, AR.
03	30	1863	Skirmish at Tahlequah, the Indian Territory.
03	30	1863	Action at Dutton's Hill, near Somerset, KY, with a Union victory over Brig. Gen. John Pegram, CSA.
03	30	1863	Skirmish in Vernon County, MO, at "the Island."
03	30	1863	Skirmish near Deep Gully, NC, between the picket lines.
03	30	1863	The **Confederate siege of Washington, NC,** by Maj. Gen. Daniel Henry Hill, CSA, and the subsequent pursuit of the Confederate forces. 3/30-4/20/1863.
03	30	1863	Skirmish at Rodman's Point, on the Pamlico River, NC, as **Washington, NC, is invested** by the Confederate forces under Maj. Gen. D. H. Hill, CSA.
03	30	1863	Skirmish at Zoar Church, VA.
03	30	1863	Skirmish at Point Pleasant, WV.
03	31	1863	**Oliver Otis Howard,** U.S.A., is appointed Maj. Gen.
03	31	1863	Skirmishes at Clapper's Saw Mill, on Crooked Creek and at Cross Hollow, AR.
03	31	1863	**Jacksonville, FL, is evacuated** by the Union forces.
03	31	1863	The Union ironclads sink the **CSS Nashville,** in the Savannah River, GA.
03	31	1863	**Federal Operations from Milliken's Bend to New Carthage, LA.** 3/31-4/17/1863.
03	31	1863	Skirmish at Richmond, LA.
03	31	1863	Engagement at Grand Gulf, MS, with the passing of the shore batteries by the **Albatross, Hartford,** and the **Switzerland,** led by Admiral Daniel Farragut, USN.
03	31	1863	Skirmishes near Eagleville, TN, with Rebel cavalry. 3/31-4/1/1863.
03	31	1863	Skirmish near Franklin, TN.
03	31	1863	Federal scout from Lexington to the mouth of Duck River, TN. 3/31-4/3/1863.
04	1	1863	**William Babcock Hazen,** USA, is appointed Brig. Gen.
04	1	1863	**John Baillie McIntosh,** USA, is appointed Brig. Gen.
04	1	1863	Skirmish at Chalk Bluff and Clarendon, AR.

04	1	1863	Maj. Gen. Francis J. Herron, USA, supersedes Brig. Gen. John Schofield, USA, in the command of the Federal **Army of the Frontier.**
04	1	1863	Federal scout from Linden to White River, MO. 4/1-5/1863.
04	1	1863	Skirmish on the White River and at Carroll County, MO.
04	1	1863	Engagement at Rodman's Point, NC between Union gunboats and Confederate batteries, during Maj. Gen. D. H. Hill's, CSA, siege of Washington, NC.
04	1	1863	Skirmish on the Columbia Pike, TN.
04	1	1863	Federal expedition from Jackson, TN, to the Hatchie River, and skirmishes. 4/1-16/1863.
04	1	1863	Federal expedition from Murfreesborough to Lebanon, Carthage, and Liberty, TN, with the destruction of large quantities of Confederate wheat and bacon, etc. 4/1-8/1863.
04	1	1863	Lieut. Gen. James Longstreet's Confederate command is reorganized to consist of the following: **Dept. of North Carolina** - Maj. Gen. Daniel H. Hill, CSA **Dept. of Richmond, VA** - Maj. Gen. Arnold Elzey, CSA **Dept. of Southern Virginia** - Maj. Gen. Samuel G. French, CSA
04	1	1863	Skirmish near the mouth of Broad Run, Londoun County, VA, as Capt. John Mosby's 65 men are surprised by 200 Union cavalry; Mosby counterattacks, inflicting 107 Federal casualties.
04	1	1863	Federal expedition from Yorktown to Smith's and Byrd's Plantation, Ware River, VA, by the **USS Commodore Morris,** which proceeded to gather grain for the ship.
04	2	1863	Skirmish on the Little Rock Road, AR.
04	2	1863	Federal expedition to Greenville, Black Bayou, and Deer Creek, MS, with skirmishes, (**April 7th, 8th, and 10th**). 4/2-14/1863.
04	2	1863	Affair in Jackson County, MO.
04	2	1863	Engagement at Hill's Point, Pamlico River, NC, between Union gunboats and the Confederate batteries, under Maj. Gen. Hill.
04	2	1863	Federal scout in Beaver Creek Swamp, TN. 4/2-6/1863.
04	2	1863	Skirmish on the Carter Creek Pike, TN, with Union cavalry.
04	2	1863	Federal reconnaissance from Murfreesborough to Auburn, Liberty, Snow Hill, Cherry Valley, Statesville, Gainesville, and Lebanon, and skirmishes (**April 3rd**) at Snow Hill, or Smith's Ford, and at Liberty, TN. 4/2-6/1863.
04	2	1863	Federal expedition from Readyville to Woodbury, TN.
04	2	1863	Federal expedition from Camp Douglas to the Spanish Fork, the Utah Territory, and action (**4th**) with hostile Indians at the Spanish Fork Canon, with many Indian casualties and fatalities. 4/2-6/1863.
04	2	1863	Maj. Gen. Oliver O. Howard, USA, supersedes Maj. Gen. Carl Schurz, USA, in the command of the 11th US Army Corps, VA.
04	2	1863	**Bread riots** by hungry citizens occur in Richmond, VA. Jefferson Davis makes a speech in the streets to squelch the uprising of mostly poor women.
04	3	1863	Federal expedition from Camp Piatt through Logan and Cabell Counties, WV, and skirmish (**5th**) at Mud River. 4/3-6/1863.
04	3	1863	Federal scout from Fairfax Court-House to Middleburg, VA, with the capture of Rebels, horses, wagons, foodstuff, etc. 4/3-6/1863.
04	4	1863	Skirmish at Richmond, LA.
04	4	1863	Engagement at Rodman's Point, near Washington, NC, between Union gunboats and the Confederate batteries. 4/4-5/1863.
04	4	1863	Skirmish on the Lewisburg Pike, TN.
04	4	1863	Skirmish on Nonconnah Creek, near Memphis, TN.
04	4	1863	Skirmish at Woodbury, TN.
04	4	1863	Brig. Gen. Orlando B. Wilcox, USA, is temporarily in command of the 9th US Army Corps, the Dept. of the Ohio, TN, etal.
04	4	1863	President Lincoln travels to Fredericksburg, VA, to meet with Maj. Gen. Joseph Hooker, USA, to discuss military strategy.
04	5	1863	Skirmish near New Carthage, LA.
04	5	1863	Skirmish at Davis' Mill, TN.
04	5	1863	Federal scout from Grand Junction to Saulsbury, TN. 4/5-6/1863.
04	5	1863	Federal scout from La Grange, TN, to Early Grove and Mount Pleasant, MS. 4/5-7/1863.
04	6	1863	Skirmish at Town Creek, AL.

04	6	1863	Skirmish at James' Plantation, near New Carthage, LA.
04	6	1863	Skirmish at Nixonton, NC, with Union men on patrol.
04	6	1863	Skirmish at Davis' Mill, TN, with the capture of Union pickets.
04	6	1863	Skirmish near Green Hill, TN, with the capture of Rebel liquor.
04	6	1863	Maj. Gen. Erasmus Darwin Keyes, USA, is temporarily in the command of the Dept. of Virginia.
04	6	1863	Skirmishes near Burlington, and at Purgitsville and Goings' Ford, WV. 4/6-7/1863.
04	7	1863	Federal expedition from Fort Wright to Williams' Valley, CA, with skirmish **(9th)** in Williams' Valley, as the Union party hunted down in a blinding snowstorm a band of Indians thought to have killed a citizen. Refusing to surrender and detached from the main Indian party, the Federals shot and killed the party of six "bucks," capturing two old squaws who were sent to a reservation. 4/7-11/1863.
04	7	1863	The Confederate attack on the Union steamer **Barataria,** Amite River, LA, which after running aground, the Confederates burn the ship and retreat under the cover of darkness.
04	7	1863	Skirmish near Dunbar's Plantation, Bayou Vidal, LA.
04	7	1863	Engagement in Charleston Harbor, SC, pitting the US South Atlantic blockade squadron against the Confederate Shore batteries, with the following US ironclads: **Catskill, Keokuk, Montauk, Nahant, Nantucket, New Ironsides, Passaic, Patapsco,** and the **Weehawken.**
04	7	1863	Skirmish at Liberty, TN.
04	7	1863	Brig. Gen. Joseph Wheeler's Confederate Cavalry raid on the **Louisville and Nashville** and the **Nashville and Chattanooga Railroads,** including affair **(April 10th)** at Antioch Station, TN. 4/7-11/1863.
04	7	1863	Federal expedition from Gloucester Point to Gloucester Court-House, VA.
04	8	1863	Skirmish at St. Francis County, AR.
04	8	1863	Skirmish at James' Plantation, near New Carthage, LA, with Confederate forces deflecting Maj. Gen. John McClernand, USA.
04	8	1863	Skirmish on the Millwood Road, near Winchester, VA.
04	8	1863	President Lincoln reviews Maj. Gen. Joseph Hooker's army across the Rappahannock River from Fredericksburg, VA.
04	9	1863	**Halbert Eleazer Paine,** USA, is appointed Brig. Gen.
04	9	1863	**Hector Tyndale,** USA, is appointed Brig. Gen.
04	9	1863	Skirmish on the White River, AR.
04	9	1863	**Operations in West Louisiana.** 4/9-5/14/1863.
04	9	1863	Union forces cross Berwick Bay, LA. 4/9-11/1863
04	9	1863	Skirmish at Sedalia, MO.
04	9	1863	Action at Blount's Creek, NC, during Maj. Gen. Daniel Henry Hill's, CSA, siege of Washington, NC.
04	9	1863	The Confederate destruction of the Union steamer **George Washington,** near Beaufort, SC, after her ironclad escort, **Hale,** runs aground.
04	9	1863	Skirmish at Franklin, TN.
04	9	1863	Skirmish near the Obion River, at Antioch Station, TN.
04	9	1863	Confederate operations against Gloucester Point, VA, are repelled. 4/9-14/1863.
04	10	1863	Col. Ferris Forman, 4th California Infantry, assumes the command of the District of Southern California.
04	10	1863	Federal expedition from Humboldt to Cottonwood, KS.
04	10	1863	Skirmish on Folly Island, SC, with a Rebel attack on pickets.
04	10	1863	**Engagement at Franklin and the Harpeth River TN,** where Maj. Gen. Earl Van Dorn, CSA, and Maj. Gen. Gordon Granger, USA, fight to a draw.
04	10	1863	Federal scout from La Grange, TN, to Hudsonville, Lockhart's Mills, Mount Pleasant, and Early Grove, MS. 4/10-11/1863.
04	10	1863	President Lincoln returns to Washington, DC, after reviewing the Federal troops at Falmouth, VA, via Aquia Creek, VA.
04	11	1863	Skirmish near Squirrel Creek Crossing, the Colorado Territory, near Colorado City, with the capture of a couple guerrillas.
04	11	1863	Skirmish at Webber's Falls, the Indian Territory.
04	11	1863	Skirmish near Pattersonville, LA.
04	11	1863	Skirmish at Courtney's Plantation, MS.
04	11	1863	Federal scout from La Grange to Saulsbury, TN.
04	11	1863	Col. A. D. Streight, USA, leaves Nashville, TN, for a cavalry raid into Georgia.

04	11	1863	**The Confederate Siege of Suffolk, VA.** 4/11-5/4/1863.
04	11	1863	The Confederate Corps of the Army of Northern Virginia, under Lieut. Gen. James Longstreet, CSA, advance upon Suffolk, VA, with the following skirmish.
04	11	1863	Skirmish on the South Quay Road, near the Blackwater, VA.
04	11	1863	Skirmish at **Williamsburg, VA,** where the Confederates, under Brig. Gen. Henry Wise, CSA, again fail to capture **Fort Magruder.**
04	11	1863	Federal expedition from Camp Douglas to the Spanish Fork Canon, the Utah Territory, with skirmish with hostile Indians **(12th)** at Pleasant Grove, where the Federals desired to set up a base of operations against a band of hostile Indians who are attacking the **overland stage coaches** between Salt Lake City and Ruby Valley, and with action **(15th)** at Spanish Fork Canon. 4/11-20/1863.
04	11	1863	Federal scout from Beverly to Franklin, WV. 4/11-18/1863.
04	12	1863	Federal expedition from Camp Babbitt to Keysville, CA, against Indians, thought to be **Tehachapie** and **Owen's River Indians,** were surrounded; the old men and boys were released while the other "bucks" who no one could vouch for (about 35) **were either shot or sabered to death.** 4/12-24/1863.
04	12	1863	Affair on the Amite River, LA, where the Confederates attempt to recover guns, etc. from the scuttled Union gunboat there.
04	12	1863	Engagement at Fort Bisland (Bethel Place or Bayou Teche), near Centreville, LA, including the destruction of the **Queen of the West, (14th)** which was captured and in Confederate use. 4/12-13/1863.
04	12	1863	Destruction of the Confederate steamer, the **Stonewall Jackson,** just from Nassau, by her own crew who feared capture, near Long Island, SC. Foolishly they were not in immediate danger.
04	12	1863	Skirmish at Stewartsborough, TN, with a Confederate rout.
04	12	1863	Skirmishes on the Edenton, Providence Church, and Somerton Roads, VA, as Lieut. Gen. James Longstreet, CSA, moves on Suffolk, VA. 4/12-13/1863.
04	12	1863	Federal reconnaissance from Gloucester Point to the vicinity of Hickory Forks, VA, and the burning of a civilian grain mill.
04	12	1863	Federal reconnaissance from Winchester up Cedar Creek Valley, VA. 4/12-13/1863.
04	12	1863	President Lincoln receives a letter from Maj. Gen. Joseph Hooker, USA, who suggests a movement around Gen. Robert E. Lee's flank to Richmond, VA, which is contrary to their discussions just held where Lincoln reminded Hooker that Lee's Army must be Hooker's main goal.
04	13	1863	Skirmish at Porter's and McWilliams' Plantations, at Indian Bend, LA.
04	13	1863	Federal expeditions from New Berne to Swift Creek Village, NC, during Maj. Gen. D. H. Hill's, CSA, siege of Washington, NC. 4/13-21/1863.
04	13	1863	Maj. Gen. Ambrose E. Burnside, USA, commanding the Dept. of the Ohio, issues a proclamation to invoke the death penalty for anybody aiding the Southern cause.
04	13	1863	Skirmish about 3 miles from Chapel Hill, TN, with the destruction of a Confederate forage train.
04	13	1863	Skirmish at Elk Run, VA.
04	13	1863	Skirmish at Snicker's Ferry, VA.
04	14	1863	Engagement at Irish Bend, near Centreville, LA.
04	14	1863	The former Union gunboat, **Queen of the West,** now a Confederate ram, is sunk by Federal fire in Grand Lake, LA.
04	14	1863	Skirmish at Jeanerette, LA.
04	14	1863	Maj. Gen. Joseph Hooker's, USA, Federal Cavalry operations at Rappahannock Bridge, and at Kelly's, Welford's, and Beverly Ford, VA. 4/14-15/1863.
04	14	1863	Engagement at the mouth of West Branch and near the Norfleet House, Nansemond River, near Suffolk, VA, with Lieut. Gen. James Longstreet's, CSA advance on Suffolk, VA.
04	15	1863	The **CSS Alabama** captures two Federal whaling ships off the coast of the Brazilian island of Fernando de Noronha.
04	15	1863	Federal expeditions **(April 15th-May 2nd)** to Courtland, AL, and **(May 2nd-8th)** Tupelo, MS. 4/15-5/8/1863.
04	15	1863	Brig. Gen. Grenville M. Dodge's USA expedition from Corinth, MS, to Courtland, AL. 4/15-5/2/1863.
04	15	1863	Skirmish at Piketon, Pike County, KY.
04	15	1863	Skirmish near Dunbar's Plantation, Bayou Vidal, LA, as Maj. Gen. Ulysses S. Grant, USA, continues his latest advance on Vicksburg.
04	15	1863	**Franklin, LA, is occupied** by Maj. Gen. Nathaniel P. Banks, USA.
04	15	1863	The Confederate siege of Washington, NC, is raised.

04	15	1863	Federal expedition from La Grange to Saulsbury, TN.
04	15	1863	Skirmish on the Edenton Road, near Suffolk, VA, with Lieut. Gen. James Longstreet, CSA.
04	15	1863	Engagement near the Norfleet House, near Suffolk, VA.
04	16	1863	Skirmish at Paris, KY.
04	16	1863	Skirmish at Newtown, LA.
04	16	1863	The passage of the Vicksburg, MS, batteries by Union gunboats and transports, under Admiral David Porter, USN, including the following: **Benton, Carondolet, La Fayette, Louisville, Mound City, Pittsburg, Price,** and the **Tuscumbia,** and the chartered steamer transports, **Forest Queen, Henry Clay,** and the **Silver Wave,** which were protected with hay and cotton bales.
04	16	1863	Federal expedition from New Berne toward Kinston, NC, in pursuit of the retreating Maj. Gen. D. H. Hill, CSA. 4/16-21/1863.
04	16	1863	Affairs at Hill's and Rodman's Points, NC, after Maj. Gen. Daniel Henry Hill, CSA, ends his siege of Washington, NC.
04	16	1863	Skirmish near Eagleville, TN.
04	16	1863	Affair on the Pamunkey River, near West Point, VA, including the Confederate cannonading of two Union vessels, inflicting casualties; the vessels retreat down the York River.
04	17	1863	**Maj. Gen. Daniel Smith Donelson, CSA,** dies at Montevale Springs, TN, from natural causes.
04	17	1863	Actions and skirmishes at Lundy's Lane, Cherokee Station, Great Bear Creek, and Barton Station, AL.
04	17	1863	The **CSS Florida** destroys the **Commonwealth** off the coast of Brazil.
04	17	1863	Federal expedition from Saint Martinsville to Breaux Bridge and Opelousas, LA. 04/17-21/1863.
04	17	1863	Skirmish on the Amite River, LA.
04	17	1863	Action at Bayou Vermillion, LA.
04	17	1863	**Brig. Gen. John S. Marmaduke's, CSA, Expedition into Missouri.** 4/17-5/2/1863 .
04	17	1863	Skirmish on the White River, MO, near Relleford's Mill.
04	17	1863	Federal expedition from New Berne to Washington, NC. 4/17-19/1863.
04	17	1863	Skirmishes at Core Creek, NC, with Maj. Gen. D. H. Hill, CSA. 4/17-18/1863.
04	17	1863	**Col. Benjamin H. Grierson's USA Cavalry Raid** from La Grange, TN, to Baton Rouge, LA, to be made into a Hollywood movie starring John Wayne, named the **Horse Soldiers.** 4/17-5/2/1863.
04	17	1863	Skirmishing takes place generally along the lines during the siege of Suffolk, VA, by Lieut. Gen. James Longstreet, VA.
04	17	1863	Federal expedition from Winchester to Stump's Tannery, VA. 4/17-18/1863.
04	18	1863	Skirmish at Fayetteville, AR, with Brig. Gen. John S. Marmaduke's, CSA, raiding party being repulsed.
04	18	1863	The destruction of the CSA salt-works near New Iberia, LA.
04	18	1863	Skirmish at New Albany, MS, with Col. Benjamin H. Grierson, USA. 4/18-19/1863.
04	18	1863	Federal scout through Shannon County, MO.
04	18	1863	Federal scout from Salem to Sinking Creek, the Current River, and the Big Creek, MO. 4/18-22/1863.
04	18	1863	Skirmish at Hartsville, TN, as the Rebels capture much needed beef cattle.
04	18	1863	Federal expedition from Memphis, TN, to the Coldwater, MS, including action: (18th) at Hernando, and skirmish **(19th)** at Perry's Ferry. 4/18-24/1863.
04	18	1863	Affair at Sabine Pass, TX, as the Confederates rout the Union landing party.
04	18	1863	Affair near Johnstown, Harrison County, WV, with the Federals.
04	19	1863	Skirmish at Dickson Station, AL.
04	19	1863	Skirmish at Celina, KY, with the rout of the Confederates, destruction of their camp and capture of 100,000 lbs. of bacon, as well as other provisions.
04	19	1863	Skirmish at Creelsborough, KY.
04	19	1863	Skirmish at Pontotoc, MS, with Col. Benjamin H. Grierson, USA.
04	19	1863	Federal scout near Neosho, MO, and skirmish with bushwackers. 4/19-20/1863.
04	19	1863	Skirmish at Big Swift Creek, NC, with Maj. Gen. D.H. Hill, CSA.
04	19	1863	Skirmish at Trenton, TN.
04	19	1863	The Federal **capture of Battery Huger,** Hill's Point, on the Nansemond River, near Suffolk, VA.
04	19	1863	President Abraham Lincoln travels with Maj. Gen. Henry W. Halleck, USA, and Secretary of War, Edwin Stanton to Aquia Creek on a military fact finding mission.
04	20	1863	**Butte-a-la-Rose, LA, is captured** by the Union fleet.
04	20	1863	**Opelousas and Washington, LA, are occupied** by the Union army, under Maj. Gen. Nathaniel P. Banks, USA.

04	20	1863	Skirmish at Bloomfield, MO.
04	20	1863	Skirmish at Patterson, MO, with Brig. Gen. John S. Marmaduke, CSA.
04	20	1863	Skirmish at Sandy Ridge, NC, with Maj. Gen. D. H. Hill, CSA.

04 20 1863 Federal expedition from Murfreesborough to McMinnville, TN, including the destruction of the **McMinnville to Manchester Railroad,** etc. 4/20-30/1863.

04 20 1863 Federal expedition from Belle Plain to Port Conway and Port Royal, VA. 4/20-23/1863.

04 20 1863 Federal reconnaissance from Winchester toward Wardenville and Strasburg, VA, and skirmish, with loss of life.

04 20 1863 **Brig. Gen. John Imboden's, CSA, Confederate expedition** into West Virginia, including skirmishes:
a) at Beverly,   **(April 24th)**
b) at Janelew, and   **(May 5th)**
c) near Summerville, WV.   **(May 12th)**. 4/20-5/14/1863.

04 21 1863 Federal expedition from Opelousas, LA, to Barre's Landing and the capture of the Confederate steamer, **Ellen.**

04 21 1863 Skirmish at Palo Alto, MS, with Col. Benjamin H. Grierson, USA.

04 21 1863 **Brig. Gen. William E. "Grumble" Jones' Confederate Raid** on the **Northwestern (Baltimore and Ohio) Railroad,** VA, etal. 4/21-5/21/1863.

04 22 1863 **William Henry Chase Whiting, CSA,** is appointed Maj. Gen.

04 22 1863 **Henry DeLamar Clayton,**   CSA, is appointed Brig. Gen.

04 22 1863 Action at Rock Cut, near Tuscumbia, AL, with Brig. Gen. Grenville Dodge, USA, being defeated by Confederate forces.

04 22 1863 Skirmish on the Bayou Boeuf Road, near Washington, LA.

04 22 1863 **The passage of the Vicksburg and Warrenton, MS, batteries** by Union transports, after which President Jefferson Davis, CSA, suggests that Lieut. Gen. John Clifford Pemberton, CSA, send fire rafts down the Mississippi River, from Vicksburg, to obstruct the Union advance.

04 22 1863 Skirmish at Fredericktown, MO, with Brig. Gen. John S. Marmaduke, CSA.

04 22 1863 Skirmish at Hartsville, TN.

04 22 1863 **Operations in the Shenandoah Valley, VA.** 4/22-5/16/1863.

04 22 1863 Skirmish at Fisher's Hill, near Strasburg, VA, with a Confederate defeat by Union Majors McGee and White, USA.

04 22 1863 Federal expedition from Belle Plain to Port Conway and Port Royal, VA, with the capture of a wagon train and some mail. 4/22-24/1863.

04 22 1863 Skirmish at Point Pleasant, WV.

04 23 1863 Skirmishes at Dickson Station, Tuscumbia, Florence, and Leighton, AL.

04 23 1863 Skirmish near Creek Head, KY.

04 23 1863 Skirmish at Independence, MO.

04 23 1863 Skirmish on the Shelbyville Pike, TN.

04 23 1863 Affair at Chuckatuck, near Suffolk, VA.

04 24 1863 **Edward Augustus Wild,** USA, is appointed Brig. Gen.

04 24 1863 Federal operations against Indians in the Owen's River and adjacent valleys, CA, with captures, etc; one Indian tribe comes into Federal camp which had suffered severely from hunger and thirst amidst the severe winter cold, many of the women and children having died for want of water. 4/24-5/26/1863.

04 24 1863 Federal expedition to Lake Saint Joseph, LA.

04 24 1863 Skirmishes at Garlandville and Birmingham, MS, with Col. Benjamin H. Grierson's, USA, Cavalry raid.

04 24 1863 Skirmish at Mill, or Middle, Creek Bridges, MO, **Iron Mountain Railroad,** near St. Louis, MO, with Brig. Gen. John S. Marmaduke, CSA.

04 24 1863 Skirmish on the Edenton Road, near Suffolk, VA.

04 24 1863 Skirmish in Gilmer County, WV.

04 25 1863 Skirmish with **Apache Indians** near Fort Bowie, the Arizona Territory, who attacked the Federals and soon retreated thereafter.

04 25 1863 Skirmish at Webber's Falls, the Indian Territory, with the Pro-South **Cherokee Indians,** under Col. Stand Watie, CSA.

04 25 1863 Maj. Gen. Ulysses S. Grant's, USA, expedition to Hard Times Landing, LA, and skirmishes:
(26th) at Phelps' and Clark's Bayou, and,
(28th) at Choctaw Bayou, or Lake Bruin. 4/25-29/1863.

04	25	1863	Skirmish at Apache Pass, the New Mexico Territory, with **Apache Indians,** several of them having guns.
04	25	1863	Maj. Gen. Dabney H. Maury, CSA, assumes the command of the Dept. of East Tennessee.
04	25	1863	Federal expedition to Hard Times Landing, LA, with skirmishes **(26th)** at Phelps' and Clark's Bayous, and **(28th)** at Choctaw Bayou, or Lake Bruin. 4/25-29/1863.
04	25	1863	Skirmish at Greenland Gap, WV, with Brig. Gen. William E. "Grumble" Jones, CSA.
04	26	1863	**Arthur Middleton Manigault,** CSA, is appointed Brig. Gen.
04	26	1863	Col. Abel D. Streight's, USA, Cavalry raid from Tuscumbia, AL, toward Rome, GA. 4/26-5/3/1863.
04	26	1863	Federal expedition to Celina, KY. 4/26-29/1863.
04	26	1863	Federal expedition to Monticello, KY, and operations in Southeastern Kentucky. 4/26-5/12/1863.
04	26	1863	Federal expedition from Opelousas toward Niblett's Bluff, LA. 4/26-29/1863.
04	26	1863	Affair at Altamont, MD, with Brig. Gen. William E. "Grumble" Jones, CSA.
04	26	1863	Affair at Cranberry Summit, MD, with Brig. Gen. William E. "Grumble" Jones, CSA.
04	26	1863	Skirmish at Oakland, MD, with Brig. Gen. William E. "Grumble" Jones, CSA.
04	26	1863	Action at Cape Girardeau, MO, where Brig. Gen. John McNeil, USA repels Brig. Gen. John S. Marmaduke's, CSA, forces.
04	26	1863	Skirmish at Independence, MO.
04	26	1863	Skirmish near Jackson, MO, with Brig. Gen. John S. Marmaduke, CSA.
04	26	1863	Affair near College Grove, TN, with Rebel cavalry.
04	26	1863	Engagement at Duck River Island, or Little Rock Landing, TN, where the Texas Rangers are repelled.
04	26	1863	Skirmish at Oak Grove, VA.
04	26	1863	Skirmish at Burlington, WV.
04	26	1863	Skirmish at Portland, WV.
04	26	1863	Skirmish at Rowlesburg, WV, with Brig. Gen. William E. "Grumble" Jones, CSA.
04	27	1863	Skirmish at Town Creek, AL.
04	27	1863	Skirmish at Barboursville, KY.
04	27	1863	Skirmish at Negro Head Cut, near Woodburn, KY.
04	27	1863	Skirmishes at Jackson and near White Water Bridge, MO, with Brig. Gen. John Sappington Marmaduke, CSA.
04	27	1863	Federal expedition from New Berne toward Kinston, NC, and skirmish **(28th)** at Wise's Cross-Roads. 4/27-5/1/1863.
04	27	1863	Affair at Murray's Inlet, SC, with a Union landing party.
04	27	1863	Maj. Gen. Dabney H. Manry, CSA, is relieved by Maj. Gen. Simon B. Buckner, CSA, in the command of the Dept. of East Tennessee; Manry is then ordered to assume the command of the District of the Gulf, LA, etal.
04	27	1863	Skirmish on Carter Creek Pike, TN, with the surprise Federal attack on and capture of the Texas Legion, under Maj. Gen. Earl Van Dorn, CSA.
04	27	1863	**The Chancellorsville Campaign, VA,** as Maj. Gen. Joseph Hooker, USA, begins to move the Army of the Potomac from Falmouth, toward Chancellorsville, VA. 4/27-5/6/1863.
04	27	1863	Federal expedition from Yorktown beyond Hickory Forks, VA, and the destruction of large Confederate stores of food.
04	27	1863	Affair at Independence, WV, with Brig. Gen. William E. Jones, CSA.
04	27	1863	Affair at Morgantown, WV, with Brig. Gen. William E. Jones, CSA.
04	28	1863	Action at Town Creek, AL.
04	28	1863	Skirmish at Sand Mountain, GA.
04	28	1863	Skirmishes near Monticello, KY. 4/28-5/2/1863.
04	28	1863	Skirmish at Union Church, MS, with Col. Benjamin H. Grierson, USA.
04	28	1863	Maj. Gen. Joseph Hooker, USA, crosses the Rappahannock River, above Fredericksburg, leaving Maj. Gen. John Sedgwick, USA, to face Gen. Robert. E. Lee, CSA, the Chancellorsville Campaign.
04	29	1863	Federal expeditions from Opelousas to Chicotville and Bayou Boeuf, LA. 4/29-30/1863.
04	29	1863	Skirmish at Brookhaven, MS, with Col. Benjamin H. Grierson, USA.
04	29	1863	Federal demonstration against Haynes' and Drumgould's Bluffs, or engagement at Snyder's Mill, MS, by Maj. Gen. William T. Sherman, USA. 4/29-5/1/1863.
04	29	1863	The US Naval **bombardment of Grand Gulf, MS,** and the passage of the Confederate shore batteries, by the US gunboats, **USS Benton, Carondelet, Louisville, Mound City,** and the **Pittsburg.**
04	29	1863	Skirmish at Castor River, MO, with Brig. Gen. John S. Marmaduke, CSA.
04	29	1863	Federal reconnaissance on the Chapel Hill Pike, TN.
04	29	1863	Federal scout from La Grange, TN, into Northern Mississippi. 4/29-5/5/1~63.

MONTH	DAY	YEAR	ACT
04	29	1863	Federal reconnaissance from Murfreesborough, on Manchester Pike, TN. 4/29-5/2/1863.
04	29	1863	Skirmishes at Crook's Run and Germanna Ford, near Fredericksburg, VA, the Chancellorsville Campaign.
04	29	1863	Federal operations at Franklin's Crossing, or Deep Run, near Fredericksburg, VA. 4/29-5/2/1863.
04	29	1863	Federal operations at Pollock's Mill Creek (White Oak Run), or Fitzhugh's Crossing, near Fredericksburg, VA. 4/29-5/2/1863.
04	29	1863	Skirmish at Fairmont, WV, about 15 miles south of Morgantown, WV, with Brig. Gen. William E. Jones, CSA.
04	29	1863	Maj. Gen. John Stoneman, USA, Cavalry Raid, VA, beginning with the following: 4/29-5/7/1863.
04	29	1863	Skirmishes near Kellysville, Brandy Station, and Stevensburg, VA.
04	30	1863	Actions at Day's Gap, or Sand Mountain, Crooked Creek, and Hog Mountain, AL, with Col. Abel D. Streight's, USA, raid.
04	30	1863	Attack near Oak Camp, CA, as Indians ambush and capture a US Government pack train about 13 miles from Fort Gaston.
04	30	1863	Skirmish at Fort Gibson, the Indian Territory.
04	30	1863	Union troops under Maj. Gen. John McClernand, USA, cross the Mississippi River near Bruinsburg, MS, toward Vicksburg, MS.
04	30	1863	Skirmish at Bloomfield, MO, with Brig. Gen. John S. Marmaduke, CSA.
04	30	1863	Skirmishes at and near Chancellorsville, VA, as Maj. Gen. Joseph Hooker, USA, and the Army of the Potomac, make camp.
04	30	1863	Skirmish at Raccoon Ford, VA, with Maj. Gen. George Stoneman, USA.
04	30	1863	Skirmish near Spotsylvania Court-House, VA.
04	30	1863	Skirmish at Bridgeport, WV, with Brig. Gen. William E. "Grumble" Jones, CSA.
05	1	1863	Skirmishes at Blountsville and on the East Branch of the Big Warrior River, AL, with Col. Abel D. Streight's, USA, raid.
05	1	1863	Skirmishes at Chalk Bluff, Saint Francis River, near La Grange, AR, with Brig. Gen. John S. Marmaduke, CSA, which effectively ends his latest expedition into Missouri. 5/1-2/1863.
05	1	1863	Skirmish near La Grange, AR.
05	1	1863	Skirmishes near Greensburg and at Williams' Bridge, LA, with Col. Benjamin H. Grierson's, USA, Cavalry raid.
05	1	1863	Skirmish at Walls Post-Office, on the Amite River and north of Baton Rouge, LA, with Col. Benjamin H. Grierson, USA.
05	1	1863	Skirmish near Washington, LA.
05	1	1863	**The Battle of Port Gibson, or Thompson's Hill, MS,** with Brig. Gen. John S. Bowen, CSA, being defeated by Maj. Gen. John McClernand, USA. Total casualties approximate 1,700.
05	1	1863	**Brig. Gen. Edward Dorr Tracy, CSA,** is mortally wounded at the Battle of Port Gibson, MS, dying instantly from a chest wound.
05	1	1863	Skirmish at Chalk Bluff on the St. Francis River, MO, with Brig. Gen. John S. Marmaduke, CSA, effectively ending his Confederate raid into Missouri.
05	1	1863	Federal reconnaissance from Murfreesborough to Lizzard, TN.
05	1	1863	**The Battle of Chancellorsville, VA,** as Gen. Robert E. Lee, CSA, plans the offensive over a cracker barrel with Lieut. Gen. Thomas Stonewall Jackson, CSA, after Maj. Gen. Joseph Hooker, USA, unexpectedly goes on the defense once the opening shots are fired around the Chancellor House, VA. Jackson, on a long march, rolls up the Union flank. Action takes place around Catherine Furnace, Wilderness Church, Dowdall's Tavern, Hazel Grove, the Orange Plank Road, etc. 5/1-3/1863.
05	1	1863	Skirmish at Rapidan Station, VA, with Maj. Gen. George Stoneman, USA, and his Union Cavalry.
05	1	1863	Skirmish at South Quay Bridge, VA, near Suffolk, VA.
05	2	1863	**Lieut. Gen. Thomas Jonathan "Stonewall" Jackson, CSA,** is mortally wounded at the Battle of Chancellorsville, VA, by a volley from his own men who had mistaken his envoy as Federal cavalry during Jackson's evening reconnaissance, requiring amputation of his left arm, and dying eight days later on May 10, 1863.
05	2	1863	**Douglas Hancock Cooper,** CSA, is appointed Brig. Gen.
05	2	1863	Skirmish at Black Creek, near Gadsden, AL, with Col. Streight, USA.
05	2	1863	Action at Blount's Plantation, AL, with Col. Streight, USA.
05	2	1863	Skirmish near Centre, AL, with Col. Streight's, USA, raid.
05	2	1863	Federal expedition from Bowling Green, KY, to the Tennessee line. 5/2-6/1863.
05	2	1863	Skirmish at Roberts' Ford, Comite River, LA, as Col. Benjamin H. Grierson's, USA, Cavalry raid draws to an end.

MONTH	DAY	YEAR	ACT
05	2	1863	Skirmish on the South Fork of Bayou Pierre, MS, as Maj. Gen. Ulysses S. Grant continues his advance on Vicksburg, MS.
05	2	1863	Skirmish near Thompson's Station, TN.
05	2	1863	Skirmish at Ely's Ford, near Fredericksburg, VA.
05	2	1863	Maj. Gen. James Ewell Brown Stuart, CSA, is temporarily assigned to the command of the 2nd Army Corps, the Army of Northern Virginia, replacing Maj. Gen. A. P. Hill, CSA, who was wounded after taking over for the seriously wounded Lieut. Gen. Stonewall Jackson, CSA.
05	2	1863	Skirmish near Louisa Court-House, VA, with Union Cavalry under Maj. Gen. George Stoneman, USA.
05	2	1863	The Confederate forces under Lieut. Gen. James Longstreet, CSA, retire from the Suffolk, VA, vicinity, unable to assist Gen. Robert E. Lee, CSA during the Chancellorsville campaign. 5/2-4/1863.
05	2	1863	Skirmish near Lewisburg, WV, with a Union Cavalry attack.
05	3	1863	**Brig. Gen. Elisha Franklin Paxton, CSA,** is mortally wounded on the 2nd day of the Chancellorsville, VA, Battle, dying instantly from a rifle shot while leading an attack on the Federal lines.
05	3	1863	**Maj. Gen. Hiram Gregory Berry, USA,** is mortally wounded while attempting to regroup his command after Stonewall Jackson's surprise flank attack at the Battle of Chancellorsville, VA.
05	3	1863	**Brig. Gen. Edmund Kirby, USA,** is mortally wounded near the Chancellor House, while commanding an artillery battery, receiving a dangerous leg wound from cannon fire; failing to recover, he died on May 28, 1863. (Not to be confused with Edmund Kirby Smith, CSA)
05	3	1863	**Gouverneur Kemble Warren, U.S.A.,** is appointed Maj. Gen.
05	3	1863	Skirmish and surrender of Col. Streight, USA, to Brig. Gen. Nathan Bedford Forrest, CSA, near Cedar Bluff, AL, ending his Union raid. Col. Streight and his subordinate officers are sent to Libby Prison, Richmond, VA, later to be exchanged.
05	3	1863	The **evacuation of Grand Gulf, MS,** by the Confederates.
05	3	1863	Skirmishes on the North Fork of Bayou Pierre, at Willow Springs, Ingraham's Heights, Jones' Cross-Roads, Forty Hills, and Hankinson's Ferry, the Big Black River, MS.
05	3	1863	Federal scout in Cass and Bates Counties, MO, searching for guerrillas. 5/3-11/1863.
05	3	1863	Federal expedition on the Sante Fe Road, MO.
05	3	1863	Federal scout from Triune to Eagleville, TN.
05	3	1863	Affair at Saint Joseph's Island, TX, as the Confederates kill, capture, and rout the Federal landing party there.
05	3	1863	Skirmishes at Ashland and Hanover Station, VA.
05	3	1863	Skirmish at Chuckatuck, VA, near Suffolk, VA.
05	3	1863	**The Battle of Fredericksburg (or Mayre's Heights) and Salem Church (or Salem Heights), and near Banks' Ford, and Chancellorsville, VA, with skirmishes,** generally along the lines, as Maj. Gen. Joseph Hooker, USA, orders Maj. Gen. John Sedgwick, USA, to overrun the remaining Confederate lines holding Mayre's Heights.
05	3	1863	Skirmishes near Hill's Point and Reed's Ferry, on the Nansemond River, near Suffolk, VA, with Lieut. Gen. James Longstreet, CSA.
05	3	1863	Federal reconnaissance on the Providence Church Road, VA, near Suffolk, VA.
05	3	1863	Skirmish at South Anna Bridge, Ashland, VA, with Maj. Gen. George Stoneman's, USA, Cavalry.
05	3	1863	Skirmish at Warrenton Junction, VA, where Capt. John S. Mosby, CSA, surprises and captures Union cavalry; is then surprised himself by the 1st WV Cavalry and loses most of his prisoners.
05	4	1863	**Maj. Gen. Amiel Weeks Whipple, USA,** is mortally wounded during the ensuing fighting around Chancellorsville, VA, receiving his death wound from a Confederate sharpshooter in the stomach, and dying on May 7, 1863.
05	4	1863	Federal expedition to the Snake Indian Country, the Idaho Territory, against the **Snake Indians.** 5/4-10/26/1863.
05	4	1863	Engagement at Fort De Russy, the Red River, LA, with the US gunboat, **Albatross,** suffering severe damage, against the Rebel gunboat, **CSS Cotton.**
05	4	1863	Skirmish at Hankinson's Ferry, MS.
05	4	1863	The unsuccessful attempt of the Federal tugboat, **George Sturgess,** to pass the Vicksburg, MS, batteries, as she was sunk.
05	4	1863	Operations about Lexington, MO.
05	4	1863	Affair at Murray's Inlet, SC.
05	4	1863	Affair near Nashville, TN.
05	4	1863	Skirmishes at Flemmings' (Shannon's) Cross-Roads, Tunstall's Station, and Ashland Church, VA, with

MONTH	DAY	YEAR	ACT
			Maj. Gen. Stoneman, USA.
05	4	1863	Skirmishes at Hungary Station, Tunstall's Station, Hanovertown Ferry, and at Aylett's, VA. 5/4-5/1863.
05	4	1863	Skirmish at Leesville, VA, effectively ending the Confederate Suffolk, VA, Campaign, under Lieut. Gen. James Longstreet, CSA.
05	4	1863	Action at Salem Church, VA, as Maj. Gen. Joseph Hooker withdraws the Army of the Potomac across the Rappahannock River, effectively ending the Chancellorsville, VA, Campaign. Total casualties surpass 30,000.
05	4	1863	Federal scout from Winchester, VA, into Hampshire County, WV. 5/4-9/1863.
05	5	1863	Federal scout from Fort Scott, KS, to Sherwood, MO, and skirmishes with the Confederates encamped near Sherwood, on Centre Creek, MO, scattering the Rebels. 5/5-9/1863.
05	5	1863	Skirmish at Big Sandy Creek, MS.
05	5	1863	Action at King's Creek, near Tupelo, MS, with a Confederate defeat under Brig. Gen. Daniel Ruggles, CSA, by Col. Corwyn.
05	5	1863	Skirmish at Peletier's Mill, NC.
05	5	1863	The leading **Copperhead,** or **Peace Democrat, Clement Vallandigham,** is arrested at his home and taken to Maj. Gen. Ambrose E. Burnside's, Dept. of the Ohio headquarters in Cincinnati, OH.
05	5	1863	Affair at Obion Plank Road Crossing, TN.
05	5	1863	Skirmish at Rover, TN, with Rebel cavalry.
05	5	1863	Union expedition from Camp Douglas, the Utah Territory, to Soda Springs, on the Bear River, the Idaho Territory, for the purpose of establishing a new post in that region for the protection of the overland emigration to Oregon, California and the Bannock City Mines, in addition to searching for the **Sagwich Indians,** etal. 5/5-30/1863.
05	5	1863	Skirmish at Thompson's Cross-Roads, VA, with Maj. Gen. George Stoneman's, USA, Cavalry.
05	6	1863	Federal scout between the White and St. Francis Rivers, AR. 5/6-15/1863.
05	6	1863	Confederate scout from Creek Agency, the Indian Territory, to Jasper County, MO, with skirmishes at Martin's House, Centre Creek, and Sherman, MO, killing about 30 Federal white and black soldiers. The Federals returned the next day and **burned the town of Sherwood, MO.** 5/6-19/1863.
05	6	1863	Federal expedition from Bowling Green, KY, to the Tennessee State Line.
05	6	1863	The US Navy, under Admiral Porter, takes **possession of Alexandria, LA.**
05	6	1863	Maj. Gen. Ambrose P. Hill, CSA, is assigned to the command of the 2nd Army Corps, the Army of Northern Virginia, replacing the mortally wounded Lieut. Gen. Stonewall Jackson, now at Guiney's Station, VA.
05	6	1863	Skirmish at Warrenton, VA.
05	6	1863	Skirmish at West Union, WV, with Brig. Gen. William E. "Grumble" Jones, CSA.
05	7	1863	**Maj. Gen. Earl Van Dorn, CSA, is murdered** in his headquarters tent at Spring Hill, TN, by one Dr. Peters for alledgingly committing adultery with Dr. Peters' wife.
05	7	1863	**Maj. Gen. Amiel Weeks Whipple, USA,** dies from his stomach wound received at Chancellorsville, VA, on May 4, 1863, dying in a Washington, DC, hospital.
05	7	1863	Skirmish at Cajoude Arivaypo, in the San Andres Mountains, the New Mexico Territory, with **Apache Indians.**
05	7	1863	Maj. Gen. John Stoneman's command recrosses Raccoon Ford, VA, effectively ending his Cavalry raid in Virginia.
05	7	1863	**West Point, VA, is occupied** by the Union forces.
05	7	1863	Affair at Cairo Station, WV, with Brig. Gen. William E. "Grumble" Jones, CSA.
05	7	1863	Affair at Harrisville (Ritchie Court-House), WV, with Brig. Gen. William E. Jones, CSA.
05	7	1863	President Abraham Lincoln and Maj. Gen. Henry W. Halleck, USA, return to Washington, DC, after conferring with Maj. Gen. Joseph Hooker, USA.
05	8	1863	Skirmish near Grove Church, VA.
05	9	1863	**John Wilkins Whitfield,** CSA, is appointed Brig. Gen.
05	9	1863	Skirmish at Shelter Cove, CA, with Indians, and the capture and transfer of some squaws and children to the Mendocino Reservation.
05	9	1863	Skirmish at Alcorn's Distillery, near Monticello, KY.
05	9	1863	Federal operations on the Amite River and **Jackson Railroad,** and skirmishes at Ponchatoula, Independence Station, and Tickfaw Bridge, LA, under Brig. Gen. Thomas W. Sherman, USA, whose men capture lumber, cotton, etc, as well as Confederate soldiers, deserters, and furloughed men, etc. 5/9-18/1863.
05	9	1863	Skirmish at Bayou Tensas, near Lake Providence, LA.

MONTH	DAY	YEAR	ACT
05	9	1863	Skirmish near Big Sandy Creek, MS.
05	9	1863	Skirmishes at and near Utica, MS, with Maj. Gen. Ulysses S. Grant, USA. 5/9-10/1863.
05	9	1863	**Gen. Joseph E. Johnston, CSA, is ordered to Mississippi,** to assume the command of the Confederate forces there.
05	9	1863	Skirmish in Stone County, MO, with bushwackers.
05	9	1863	Affair near Caney Fork, TN, with Brig. Gen. Nathan Bedford Forrest's Confederate Cavalry.
05	9	1863	The destruction of the Federal oil-works at Oiltown, WV, by Brig. Gen. William E. "Grumble" Jones, CSA.
05	10	1863	**Lieut. Gen. Thomas "Stonewall" Jonathan Jackson, CSA,** dies in a small house near Guiney's Station, VA, from pneumonia developed after being wounded on May 2, 1863, at the Battle of Chancellorsville, VA.
05	10	1863	Action at Horseshoe Bottom, (or Bend), Cumberland River, KY.
05	10	1863	Skirmish at Phillips Fork, Red Bird Creek, KY.
05	10	1863	Skirmishes at Caledonia and Pin Hook, or Bayou Macon, LA.
05	10	1863	Union naval attack on Fort Beauregard, Ouachita River, LA, by 4 Union gunboats, with little damage.
05	11	1863	Skirmishes at Mount Vernon and Taylor's Creek, or Crowley's Ridge, AR, with Union Cavalry and Brig. Gen. John S. Marmaduke, CSA.
05	11	1863	Federal Cavalry raid on the **New Orleans and Jackson Railroad,** near Crystal Springs, MS, with destruction of railroad lines.
05	11	1863	Federal Cavalry expedition from La Grange, TN, to Panola, MS, and skirmishes: (11th) at Coldwater and **(14th)** at Walnut Hill, MS. 5/11-15/1863.
05	11	1863	Skirmish at La Fayette, TN.
05	11	1863	Skirmish at Warrenton, VA.
05	12	1863	Skirmish at Fourteen-Mile Creek, MS, with Maj. Gen. Sherman, USA.
05	12	1863	Skirmish at Greenville, MS.
05	12	1863	Engagement at Raymond, MS, with Maj. Gen. John A. Logan, USA, repelling Brig. Gen. John Gregg, CSA.
05	12	1863	Skirmish at Bloomfield, MO.
05	12	1863	Maj. Gen. Simon B. Buckner, CSA, assumes the command of the Dept. of East Tennessee.
05	12	1863	Federal reconnaissance from La Vergne, TN.
05	12	1863	Skirmish at Linden, TN.
05	12	1863	Federal reconnaissance from Murfreesborough toward Liberty and Lebanon, TN. 5/12-16/1863.
05	12	1863	Federal operations about Buck's and Front Royal Fords, the Shenandoah Valley, VA. 5/12-14/1863.
05	12	1863	Federal operations on the **Seaboard and Roanoke Railroad** and skirmishes **(15th-16th)** near Carrsville, VA, as Federal cannons drive off the attacking Confederates. 5/12-26/1863.
05	12	1863	Federal scout from Snicker's Ferry, and skirmish **(13th)** at Upperville, VA, with Capt. John S. Mosby, CSA and his Virginia Partisan Rangers. 5/12-14/1863.
05	13	1863	Skirmishes near Woodbury and South Union, KY, with the unsuccessful Rebel attack on the railroad train near South Union.
05	13	1863	Federal reconnaissance from Baton Rouge, LA.
05	13	1863	Skirmishes at Mississippi Springs and at Baldwin's and Hall's Ferries, MS, as Maj. Gen. Ulysses S. Grant, sent forward Maj. Gens. James McPherson and William T. Sherman toward Jackson, MS, and Maj. Gen. John McClernand, USA, north toward Clinton, MS.
05	13	1863	Federal scout from Newtonia to French Point and Centre Creek, MO, and skirmishes.
05	13	1863	Skirmishes near Woodburn and South Union, TN.
05	14	1863	Skirmish at Fort Gibson, the Indian Territory.
05	14	1863	Skirmish at Boyce's Bridge, Cotile Bayou, LA, with dismounted Confederate cavalry and Brig. Gen. Godfrey Weitzel, USA.
05	14	1863	Federal reconnaissance to Judge Boyce's Plantation, LA, and skirmish.
05	14	1863	Federal scouts from Merritt's Plantation, on the Clinton Road, LA, by Col. Benjamin H. Grierson, USA.
05	14	1863	Engagement at and **capture of Jackson, MS,** by Maj. Gen. Ulysses S. Grant's troops.
05	14	1863	Skirmish at Marsteller's Place, near Warrenton Junction, VA.
05	14	1863	The army of Maj. Gen. Nathaniel P. Banks, USA, is en route from Alexandria, LA, for operations against Port Hudson, LA, above Baton Rouge, LA.
05	15	1863	**John Marshall Jones,** CSA, is appointed Brig. Gen.
05	15	1863	**James Alexander Walker,** CSA, is appointed Brig. Gen.

MONTH	DAY	YEAR	ACT
05	15	1863	Skirmish at Fort Smith, AR.
05	15	1863	Skirmish at Big Creek, near Pleasant Hill, MO, with the guerrillas, under William Clarke Quantrill.
05	15	1863	The Confederate capture of the steamers, **Emily** and **Arrow** at Currituck Canal, near Elizabeth City, NC.
05	15	1863	Federal operations on the **Norfolk and Petersburg Railroad,** and skirmishes: (17th) near Providence Church, and (23rd) at Antioch Church and Barber's Cross-Roads, VA. 5/15-28/1863.
05	15	1863	Federal expedition from West Point, aboard the US gunboat, **Morse,** to Robinson's Plantation, King and Queen County, VA, where the Union burn his barn full of grain suspected of being used by the Confederates.
05	15	1863	Federal scout from Parkersburg into Calhoun County, WV. /15-22/1863.
05	16	1863	Skirmish at Tickfaw Bridge, LA.
05	16	1863	**The Battle of Champion's Hill, or Baker's Creek, MS,** force a Confederate retreat toward Vicksburg, and the Big Black River, MS, under Lieut. Gen. John C. Pemberton, CSA, by Maj. Gens. John A. McClernand and James B. McPherson, USA, with about 6,300 total casualties.
05	16	1863	**Brig. Gen. Lloyd Tilghman, CSA,** is mortally wounded at the Battle of Champion's Hill, MS, while directing the fire of his artillery battery, having a shell fragment pass through his chest.
05	16	1863	Skirmish at Carthage, MO.
05	16	1863	Skirmish at Berry's Ferry, VA, with Maj. Gen. John Milroy, USA.
05	16	1863	Skirmish at Piedmont Station, VA, with Maj. Gen. John Milroy, USA.
05	16	1863	Skirmish at Charlestown, WV, with Maj. Gen. John Milroy, USA.
05	16	1863	Skirmish at Elizabeth Court-House, WV.
05	16	1863	Skirmish at Ravenswood, WV.
05	17	1863	Operations on the west side of the Mississippi River, near Port Hudson, LA, by Maj. Gen. Nathaniel P. Banks, USA, as Confederate Cavalry capture pickets and cattle.
05	17	1863	Engagement at Big Black River Bridge, MS.
05	17	1863	Skirmish about 3 miles from Bridgeport, MS, with the 6th Missouri Cavalry capturing 2 wagons and about 160 prisoners.
05	17	1863	Skirmish on the Bradyville Pike, TN.
05	17	1863	Federal scout from La Grange, TN.
05	17	1863	Cavalry skirmish near Dumfries, VA.
05	18	1863	Affair near Cheneyville, LA, with Confederate Cavalry.
05	18	1863	Operations about Merritt's Plantation, and on the Bayou Sara Road, LA, with Confederate Cavalry. 5/18-19/1863.
05	18	1863	The Federal **capture of Haynes' Bluff, MS.**
05	18	1863	Skirmish near Island No. 82, about 15 miles from Greenville, MS, including the Federal vessel, **Crescent City.**
05	18	1863	Affair at Hog Island, Bates County, MO, with the destruction of Confederate food supplies, and the rebels fleeing to Henry County.
05	18	1863	Torpedo operations in Skull Creek and skirmish on Pope's Island, SC. 5/18-21/1863.
05	18	1863	Skirmish on Horn Lake Creek, TN, about 4 miles from Nonconnah.
05	18	1863	Skirmishes at and about Fayetteville, WV. 5/18-20/1863.
05	19	1863	**John Wesley Frazer,** CSA, is appointed Brig. Gen.
05	19	1863	**The Siege of Vicksburg, MS,** as Maj. Gen. Ulysses S. Grant, USA, surrounds Lieut. Gen. John C. Pemberton, CSA and the city, itself. 5/19-7/4/1863.
05	19	1863	Skirmish near Richfield, Clay County, MO, in an ambush setup by bushwackers.
05	19	1863	Federal scouts from La Grange, TN, and skirmish with Confederate cavalry 10 miles south of La Grange.
05	19	1863	Federal expedition, with the US gunboat, **Winnisimmet,** from Gloucester Point, into Matthews County, VA, with the Union requisitioning grain and cattle, etc, from the area. 5/19-22/1863
05	20	1863	**Thomas Green,** CSA, is appointed Brig. Gen.
05	20	1863	**David Bell Birney, U.S.A.,** is appointed Maj. Gen.
05	20	1863	**Adelbert Ames,** USA, is appointed Brig. Gen.
05	20	1863	Skirmish near Fort Gibson, the Indian Territory.
05	20	1863	Skirmish 1.5 miles from Cheneyville, LA, with Confederate Cavalry.
05	20	1863	Federal expedition to Yazoo City, MS, and skirmish (23rd) at Liverpool Landing, with no major happenings. 5/20-23/1863.
05	20	1863	Two blockade runners arrive safely at Charleston, SC, from Nassau, Bahamas, with two others are captured.

05	20	1863	Federal demonstration on Kinston and skirmishes **(22nd)** at Gum Swamp and **(23rd)** at Batchelder's Creek, NC, as Maj. Gen. John G. Foster, USA, attempts to put pressure on the Confederate army which is being depleted by men being deployed to other more urgent areas of the Confederacy. 5/20-23/1863.
05	20	1863	Federal scout from Clarksville, TN. 5/20-22/1863.
05	20	1863	Skirmish at Collierville, TN, with the Confederate Cavalry attack on the Union picket post #'s 4 and 5, with 1 killed and 9 missing. Another quick fire fight with loss of life.
05	20	1863	Skirmish at Salem, TN, with the 2nd Iowa Cavalry. It is quite active around here as of late.
05	20	1863	Federal operations, including the transports, **Manhattan** and **Tallaca,** in the Northern Neck (King George, Lancaster, Northumberland, Richmond, and Westmoreland Counties) and in Middlesex County, VA, with destruction of over 50 Rebel ships and an estimated $1,000,000 of Confederate supplies, etc. 5/20-26/1863.
05	21	1863	Federal scout from Cassville, MO, into Jasper and Newton Counties, MO, including skirmishes **(22nd)** at Bentonville, and **(26th)** near Carthage. 5/21-30/1863.
05	21	1863	**The Siege of Port Hudson, LA,** as Maj. Gen. Nathaniel P. Banks advances from Baton Rouge on the Clinton Road. 5/21-7/8/1863.
05	21	1863	Action at Plains Store, LA.
05	21	1863	Federal operations on the Teche Road, between Barre's Landing and Berwick, LA, as the Federals search for the plantation owner who shot and killed a Union private searching for sugar. The Federals run into a band of guerrillas with casualties. 5/21-26/1863.
05	21	1863	Federal guerrilla operations on the Sante Fe Road, near Kansas City, MO.
05	21	1863	Federal expedition from La Grange, TN, to Senatobia (Swamp), MS, and skirmish **(23rd)**. 5/21-26/1863.
05	21	1863	Federal expedition from Murfreesborough to Middleton, TN, and skirmish. 5/21-22/1863.
05	22	1863	**William Birney,** USA, is appointed Brig. Gen.
05	22	1863	Skirmish at Fort Gibson, the Indian Territory.
05	22	1863	The Federal steamer, **Louisiana Belle,** is unsuccessfully attacked near Barre's Landing, Bayou Teche, LA, by a band of guerrillas.
05	22	1863	Skirmish at Bayou Courtableau, LA.
05	22	1863	The assault on the Confederate lines in front of Vicksburg, MS, by Maj. Gen. Ulysses S. Grant, USA, ends in failure.
05	22	1863	Skirmish at Yellow Creek, TN.
05	22	1863	Maj. Gen. Winfield S. Hancock, USA, assumes the command of the 2nd US Army Corps, the Army of the Potomac, VA.
05	22	1863	Brig. Gen. Alfred Pleasonton, USA, assumes the command of the Cavalry Corps, Army of the Potomac, VA.
05	23	1863	**Richard Stoddert Ewell,** CSA, is appointed Lieut. Gen.
05	23	1863	**William Henry Talbot Walker,** CSA, is appointed Maj. Gen.
05	23	1863	**Gustavus Adolphus De Russy,** USA, is appointed Brig. Gen.
05	23	1863	**Rufus Ingalls,** USA, is appointed Brig. Gen.
05	23	1863	Federal expedition on the US steamboat, **Pike,** from Helena to Napoleon, AR, to obtain recruits of African descent, with skirmish near Island No. 65, on the Mississippi River. 5/23-26/1863 .
05	23	1863	Skirmishes on the Springfield and Plains Store Roads, LA.
05	23	1863	Skirmish at Haynes' Bluff, MS.
05	23	1863	Federal expedition from Memphis, TN, to Hernando, MS, with actions from the 2nd WI Cavalry, 5th OH, and 1st MO. 5/23-24/1863.
05	23	1863	Skirmish at Hartville, MO.
05	23	1863	Skirmish at Warrenton, VA.
05	23	1863	Skirmish at West Creek, WV.
05	24	1863	**Ambrose Powell Hill, C.S.A., is appointed Lieut. Gen.**
05	24	1863	**Henry Heth,** C.S.A., is appointed Maj. Gen.
05	24	1863	Skirmish at Mill Springs, KY.
05	24	1863	Skirmish at Mound Plantation, near Lake Providence, LA.
05	24	1863	Skirmish at **Austin, MS,** with the Federals **burning the town.**
05	24	1863	Skirmish at Mechanicsburg, MS.
05	24	1863	Federal expedition up the Yazoo and Big Sunflower Rivers, MS. 5/24-31/1863.
05	24	1863	Maj. Gen. John A. Schofield, USA, supersedes Maj. Gen. Samuel R. Curtis, USA, in command of the Dept. of Missouri.

05	24	1863	Skirmish at Woodbury, TN.
05	25	1863	**John Stevens Bowen, C.S.A.,** is appointed Maj. Gen.
05	25	1863	Skirmish at Polk's Plantation, near Helena, AR.
05	25	1863	The capture of two Union vessels off the coast of Bahia, Brazil, by the Confederate warship, the **CSS Alabama.**
05	25	1863	The capture of the Confederate steamers, the **Red Chief** and the **Starlight,** on the Mississippi River, LA.
05	25	1863	Skirmish at Centreville, LA.
05	25	1863	Skirmish at Thompson's Creek, LA.
05	25	1863	Skirmish near Woodbury, TN.
05	26	1863	**Robert Ransom, Jr., C.S.A.,** is appointed Maj. Gen.
05	26	1863	**Alexander Shaler,** USA, is appointed Brig. Gen.
05	26	1863	Federal scout from Fort Heiman, KY, into Tennessee. 5/26-6/1/1863.
05	26	1863	Federal expedition from Corinth, MS, to Florence, AL, and skirmishes: a) at Florence, **(28th)** and b) at Hamburg Landing, TN. **(29th** and **30th).** 5/26-31/1863.
05	26	1863	Federal expedition from Haynes' Bluff to Mechanicsburg, MS, and skirmishes, as Maj. Gen. Frank Blair, USA, believes he burned over 500,000 bushels of corn, plus bacon, etc. 5/26-6/4/1863.
05	26	1863	Skirmish at Mountain Store and Bush Creek, MO.
05	26	1863	Federal expedition from Bolivar to Wesley Camp, Somerville, and Antioch Church, TN, and skirmishes with Rebel guerrillas. 5/26-29/1863.
05	26	1863	Federal expedition from Memphis, TN, toward Hernando, MS, with the Federal capture of a couple horses, mules, and some arms.
05	26	1863	Former Ohio Congressman, **Clement L. Vallandigham** is banished from the Union and turned over to the Confederates near Murfreesboro, TN.
05	27	1863	**William Dorsey Pender, C.S.A.,** is appointed Maj. Gen.
05	27	1863	**Edward Payson Chapin, USA,** is appointed Brig. Gen.
05	27	1863	The **CSS Chattahoochie** accidently explodes and sinks on the Chattahoochie River, GA.
05	27	1863	Skirmish near Lake Providence, LA.
05	27	1863	The first Federal assault on Port Hudson, LA.
05	27	1863	**Brig. Gen. Edward Payson Chapin, USA,** is mortally wounded during the assault on Port Hudson, LA, while leading his men.
05	27	1863	The Confederate attack (and failure) on the Union gunboats near Greenwood, MS.
05	27	1863	Engagement between the **USS Cincinnati** and the Vicksburg, MS, batteries, with the destruction of the **USS Cincinnati.**
05	27	1863	Federal scout from Memphis, TN, toward Hernando, MS, as this scouting party captures a few horses, Negro contraband, take a long standing afternoon lunch, and find no Rebels. Effectively a safe scout, on **a nice spring day** with no loss of life. A rare occasion. But etched in their minds as the wind softly blew. an experience only they could have.
05	27	1863	Federal reconnaissance from Murfreesborough, on Manchester Pike, TN. 5/27-28/1863.
05	27	1863	Federal scout from Snicker's Ferry to Aldie, Fairfax Court-House, and Leesburg, VA. 5/27-29/1863.
05	28	1863	**Brig. Gen. Edmund Kirby, USA,** dies at the age of 23, in a Washington, DC, hospital from wounds received on the second day of the Battle of Chancellorsville, VA, on May 3, 1863.
05	28	1863	**Isham Warren Garrott,** CSA, is appointed Brig. Gen.
05	28	1863	**Edmund Kirby,** USA, is appointed Brig. Gen.
05	28	1863	Skirmish near Fort Gibson, the Indian Territory.
05	28	1863	The **54th Massachusetts Volunteers,** the first Union regiment comprised of black soldiers, embark from Boston, for Hilton Head, SC, under **Col. Robert Shaw, USA.**
05	28	1863	Skirmish near Austin, MS.
05	28	1863	The Confederate Dept. of North Carolina is extended to embrace Petersburg, VA, and the Appomattox River.
05	28	1863	Federal scout from Memphis, TN, toward Hernando, MS, with no encounters with the enemy, and more importantly, no loss of life, a rare event.
05	28	1863	Maj. Gen. George L. Hartsuff, USA, assumes the command of the 23rd US Army Corps, TN.
05	29	1863	Skirmish near Mill Springs, KY.
05	29	1863	President Lincoln refuses to accept Maj. Gen. Ambrose E. Burnside's resignation, after Lincoln rescinds

Burnside's imprisonment of Ohio Congressman, **Clement Vallandigham,** who was turned over to Confederate officials in Tennessee, on May 26, 1863, for attacking President Lincoln's administration regarding the ongoing American Civil War.

05	30	1863	Cavalry skirmish at Jordan's Store, TN.
05	30	1863	Affair at Point Isabel, TX, where the Union frigate, **Brooklyn,** transports troops against Confederates who, in fleeing, burn the schooner, **Eager.**
05	30	1863	Skirmish near Greenwich, VA, as Capt. John Singleton Mosby, CSA, attacks and burn the railroad train for Bealeton.
05	30	1863	The Confederate Army of Northern Virginia is reorganized into three army corps, under the command of the following:

    1st Army Corps - Lieut. Gen. James Longstreet, CSA
    2nd Army Corps - Lieut. Gen. Richard S. Ewell, CSA
    3rd Army Corps - Lieut. Gen. Ambrose P. Hill, CSA
    Cavalry Corps - Maj. Gen. James Ewell Brown Stuart, CSA

Ewell and Hill commanding the forces previously commanded by the late Lieut. Gen. "Stonewall" Jackson, CSA.

05	31	1863	Affair on James Island, SC.
05	31	1863	Skirmish at Warrenton, VA.
05	31	1863	**West Point, VA, is evacuated** by the Union forces, removing to Federal positions at Yorktown, VA.
06	1	1863	Maj. Gen. Ambrose E. Burnside, USA, commanding the Dept. of the Ohio, orders the seizure of the **Chicago Times** for its supposedly Pro-south views, which causes an uproar in Chicago, IL.
06	1	1863	Skirmish at Berwick, LA, as the Confederates' attack on the Union guards there is repulsed.
06	1	1863	Skirmish at Doniphan, MO.
06	1	1863	Skirmish near Rocheport, MO, with Confederate marauders.
06	1	1863	Affair at Waverly, MO, with Confederate guerrillas ambushing the Federals from the thick brush.
06	1	1863	Skirmish at Snicker's Gap, VA.
06	2	1863	**Alexander Peter Stewart, CSA,** is appointed Maj. Gen.
06	2	1863	Skirmish at Jamestown, KY.
06	2	1863	Federal expedition from Haynes' Bluff to Satartia and Mechanicsburg, MS. 6/2-8/1863.
06	2	1863	President Jefferson Davis orders **Clement L. Vallandigham** sent to Wilmington, NC, to be held under guard as an alien enemy.
06	2	1863	Union raid on the Combahee River, SC, around Field's Point.
06	2	1863	Skirmish at Strasburg, VA.
06	2	1863	Skirmish at Upperville, VA.
06	3	1863	**Benjamin Henry Grierson,** USA, is appointed Brig. Gen.
06	3	1863	**Operations in Northern Louisiana,** as Maj. Gen. Richard Taylor, CSA, and Brig. Gen. Elias S. Dennis, USA, square off, including Black troops from the 8th LA Infantry. 6/3-7/10/1863.
06	3	1863	Federal expedition to Clinton, LA, Port Hudson Campaign.
06	3	1863	Engagement with the Federal gunboats, **USS Switzerland** and the **USS Pittsburg,** and Confederate shore batteries, near Simsport, LA. With the Yankee vessels injured, they retreat.
06	3	1863	The transfer of the 9th US Army Corps from Kentucky to the vicinity of Vicksburg, MS. 6/3-17/1863.
06	3	1863	**The Gettysburg, PA, Campaign.** 6/3-8/1/1863.
06	3	1863	Gen. Robert E. Lee, CSA. begins to move his forces out of Fredericksburg, VA.
06	3	1863	Brig. Gen. Quincy A. Gillmore, USA, is assigned temporarily to the command of the Dept. of the South, SC, etal.
06	3	1863	**Col. Robert Gould Shaw, USA,** arrives at Port Royal, SC, with the Negro Regiment, the 54th MA.
06	3	1863	Skirmish near Murfreesborough, TN.
06	3	1863	Skirmish near Fayetteville, WV.
06	4	1863	Skirmish at Fayetteville, AR.
06	4	1863	Federal expedition from Fort Pulaski, GA, to Bluffton, SC.
06	4	1863	Skirmish at the Atchafalaya, LA.
06	4	1863	Affair at Lake Saint Joseph, LA.
06	4	1863	Engagement at Franklin, TN, with a failed Rebel attack.
06	4	1863	Operations on the Shelbyville Pike, near Murfreesborough, TN.

06	4	1863	Federal scout to Smithville, TN. 6/4-5/1863.
06	4	1863	Skirmish at Snow Hill, TN, with Maj. Gen. William S. Rosecrans, USA, and Gen. Braxton Bragg, CSA.
06	4	1863	Gen. Robert E. Lee, CSA, moves the 1st and 2nd Corp (Lieut. Gens. Longstreet and Ewell) to Culpeper, VA, keeping the 3rd Army Corps of the Army of Northern Virginia, under Lieut. Gen. A. P. Hill, CSA at Fredericksburg, VA. The Cavalry Corps under Maj. Gen. JEB Stuart, CSA, is sent on a protective covering of the army's advance.
06	4	1863	Skirmish at Frying Pan, VA.
06	4	1863	Skirmish on the Lawyers' road, near Fairfax Court-House, VA, as the Federals are ambushed by the Confederates after passing Frying Pan; the Federals regrouped and chased the Rebels to Aldie, the Yankee returning via Dranesville.
06	4	1863	Federal expedition from Yorktown to Walkerton and Aylett's, VA, aboard the US transport **Winnisimet,** accompanied by the US gunboats, **Commodore Morris, Commodore Jones,** and **Smith Briggs** up the Pamunkey River where at Aylett they destroy a Rebel iron foundry making rifle and cannon shot, burn a grist mill, capture horses, etc. Maj. Gen. George E. Pickett, CSA, is reported 10 miles away at Newtown with 10,000 Rebels. 6/4-5/1863.
06	4	1863	President Lincoln has Maj. Gen. Ambrose E. Burnside's order revoked regarding the seizure of a Chicago newspaper..
06	5	1863	Maj. Gen. John G. Parke, USA, resumes the command of the 9th Army Corps, around Vicksburg, MS.
06	5	1863	Federal reconnaissance through Gates County, NC, and down the Chowan River, into Gatesville, then towards Mintonsville and on toward Sandy Cross, capturing prisoners along the way. 6/5-7/1863.
06	5	1863	Skirmishes at Franklin's Crossing (or Deep Run), on the Rappahannock River, VA, with Maj. Gen. John Sedgwick's 6th Army Corps, attacking Lieut. Gen. A.P. Hill, CSA. 6/5-13/1863.
06	6	1863	**Edward Asbury O'Neal,** CSA, is appointed Brig. Gen.
06	6	1863	**Stephen Hinsdale Weed,** USA, is appointed Brig. Gen.
06	6	1863	Skirmish at Oak Camp, CA, about 15 miles from Fort Gaston, as Indians ambush a citizen pack train; the lucky survivors fleeing back to Fawn Prairie.
06	6	1863	Federal operations about Fort Gibson, the Indian Territory, including skirmishes **(June 16th)** on Greenleaf Prairie, mostly between Union and Confederate Indian Regiments. 6/6-20/1863.
06	6	1863	Skirmish at Shawneetown, KS.
06	6	1863	Skirmish at Waitsborough, KY.
06	6	1863	Skirmish near Richmond, LA.
06	6	1863	Skirmish on the Shelbyville Pike, TN.
06	6	1863	Skirmish near Berryville, VA, with Lieut. Gen. James "Old Pete" Longstreet, CSA.
06	7	1863	Skirmish near Edmonton, KY, as Rebel Cavalry capture part of a Yankee scouting party.
06	7	1863	**The Attacks on Young's Point and Milliken's Bend, LA,** with Brig. Gen. Henry E. McCulloch, CSA, attacking Brig. Gen. Thomas, USA, including the two Union gunboats, the **Choctaw** and the **Lexington,** McCulloch withdraws, as the **Black soldiers rebel and kill unarmed Confederate prisoners** after learning the Rebel's had done the same. **The Black Northern soldiers' hands are becoming dirty like so many others.**
06	7	1863	Operations in Louisiana, west of the Mississippi River. 6/7-7/13/1863 .
06	7	1863	President Jefferson Davis' plantation, **Brierfield, is burned** by the advancing Federal troops, below Vicksburg, MS.
06	7	1863	Federal expedition from Jackson, TN, across the Tennessee River.
06	7	1863	Federal expedition from Gainesville, VA, and skirmishes with Capt. John Mosby's and Maj. Gen. JEB Stuart's Confederate Cavalry at Waterloo, Barbee's, Front Royal, and near Strasburg, VA. 6/7-8/1863 .
06	8	1863	Affair near Brunswick, GA.
06	8	1863	Skirmish at Fort Scott, KS.
06	8	1863	Federal expedition from Glasgow, KY, to Burkesville and the Tennessee State Line, and skirmish **(June 9th)** at Kettle Creek, KY. 6/8-10/1863.
06	8	1863	Skirmish at Camp Cole, MO.
06	8	1863	Federal expedition from Pocahontas, TN, to Ripley, MS, with the Union capture of forage, a couple mules, horses, 97 sheep and 38 head of cattle. 6/8-9/1863.
06	8	1863	Skirmish at Triune, TN.
06	8	1863	Maj. Gen. JEB Stuart's Confederate Cavalry Corps is reviewed at Culpeper Court House by Gen. Robert E. Lee's Army of Northern Virginia of Lieut. Gens. James Longstreet and Richard S. Ewell's corps.

06	8	1863	Federal scout from Suffolk, VA, to South Mills, NC and a skirmish with a Rebel party and the capture of a small amount of Rebel supplies.
06	9	1863	Affairs at Monticello and Rocky Gap, KY.
06	9	1863	Action near Lake Providence, LA.
06	9	1863	Skirmish at Macon Ford, Big Black River, MS.
06	9	1863	The Federal **Depts. of the Monongahela and of the Susquehanna,** Pennsylvania, are constituted.
06	9	1863	Skirmish near Triune, TN.
06	9	1863	**The Engagements at Brandy Station (or Fleetwood Hill) and Beverly Ford, VA, results in the largest Cavalry battle** (about 20,000) during the Civil War; Maj. Gen. JEB Stuart, CSA, holds off Brig. Gen. Alfred Pleasonton, USA.
06	9	1863	Skirmish at Stevensburg, VA.
06	10	1863	**William Thomas Harbaugh Brooks, U.S.A., is** appointed Maj. Gen.
06	10	1863	Skirmish at Seneca Mills, MD, as Maj. John S. Mosby and his **Virginia Partisan Rangers** surprise and burn the Federal camp there before retiring back across the Potomac.
06	10	1863	Skirmish at Edwards Station, MS, as Admiral Daniel Farragut continues his almost nonstop mortar bombardment of Vicksburg, MS.
06	10	1863	Maj. Gen. William Thomas Harbaugh Brooks, USA, assumes the command of the Dept. of the Monongahela, PA.
06	10	1863	Maj. Gen. Darius Nash Couch, USA, assumes the command of the Dept. of the Susquehanna, PA.
06	10	1863	Federal scout on Middleton and Eagleville Pikes, TN.
06	10	1863	The capture of the Union steamer, **Maple Leaf,** off the coast of Cape Henry, VA, after leaving Fort Delaware with 97 Rebel prisoners who overpowered the Federals aboard ship.
06	10	1863	Lieut. Gen. Richard S. Ewell's, CSA, Corps of the Army of Northern Virginia leaves Culpeper, VA, and heads northwest towards Maryland.
06	11	1863	Skirmish at Burnsville, AL.
06	11	1863	Skirmish at Jacksonport, AR.
06	11	1863	The Federal attack and **burning of Darien, GA,** with the Negro Regiment of the 54th MA.
06	11	1863	Affair at Scottsville, KY.
06	11	1863	The capture of Confederate outposts, near Port Hudson, LA.
06	11	1863	Skirmish at Smith's Bridge, near Corinth, MS.
06	11	1863	As a protest, **Clement Vallandigham** is nominated for Governor of Ohio.
06	11	1863	Operations on Little Folly Island, SC, by the Union to destroy the already wrecked steamer, **Ruby,** near Charleston, SC.
06	11	1863	Action at Triune, TN, with Brig. Gen. Nathan Bedford Forrest, CSA.
06	11	1863	Skirmish at Diascund Bridge, VA.
06	11	1863	Skirmish near Suffolk, VA, as the Federals surprise a party of Rebels moving to attack the Union pickets, driving them off, and as usual, with loss of life.
06	11	1863	Federal expedition from Brightwood, DC, via Seneca Mills and Poolesville, MD, to Leesburg, Aldie, and Chantilly, VA. 6/11-13/1863.
06	12	1863	**Robert Sanford Foster,** USA, is appointed Brig. Gen.
06	12	1863	Pennsylvania Governor **Andrew Curtin** calls out the state militia.
06	12	1863	Brig. Gen. Quincy A. Gilmore, USA, supersedes Maj. Gen. David Hunter, USA, in the command of the Dept. of the South, SC.
06	12	1863	Federal scouts on the Salem Pike, TN.
06	12	1863	Federal expedition from Pocahontas, TN, to New Albany and Ripley, MS, with the destruction of several blacksmith shops, wagon shops, etc, and skirmishes. 6/12-14/1863.
06	12	1863	Federal expedition from Suffolk to the Blackwater, VA, against Maj. Gen. Daniel H. Hill, CSA; the Federals retire. 6/12-18/1863.
06	12	1863	Skirmishes at Newtown, Cedarville, and Middletown, VA, as Gen. Robert E. Lee's troops move for the Shenandoah Valley.
06	13	1863	**Matt Whitaker Ransom,** CSA, is appointed Brig. Gen.
06	13	1863	**Alfred Moore Scales,** CSA, is appointed Brig. Gen.
06	13	1863	**Capt. P. M. Everett's, USA, Raid** into Eastern Kentucky. 6/13-23/1863.
06	13	1863	Skirmish at Howard's Mills, KY, with Capt. Everett, USA.

06	13	1863	Skirmish near Mud Lick Springs, Bath County, KY, with Capt. Everett.
06	13	1863	Operations in Northeastern Mississippi, including skirmishes **(19th)** at New Albany and **(20th)** at Mud Creek. 6/13-22/1863.
06	13	1863	Federal scout on the Manchester Pike, TN.
06	13	1863	Skirmish at **Berryville, VA,** and **occupation** by Lieut. Gen. Richard Stoddert Ewell, CSA.
06	13	1863	Skirmish at Opequon Creek, near Winchester, VA.
06	13	1863	Skirmish at White Post, near Winchester, VA.
06	13	1863	**The Engagement (2nd) at Winchester, VA,** as Maj. Gen. Robert Huston Milroy's, USA, command is nearly totally captured by Lieut. Gen. Richard S. Ewell; Milroy personally escaping with a few hundred cavalry to Harper's Ferry, WV. 6/13-15/1863.
06	13	1863	Skirmish at Bunker Hill, WV.
06	14	1863	**Hugh Judson Kilpatrick,** USA, is appointed Brig. Gen.
06	14	1863	The **burning of Eunice, AR,** by the Federals after the Confederate attack on the Union ironclad, **USS Marmora.**
06	14	1863	**The second Union assault on Port Hudson, LA,** by Maj. Gen. Nathaniel P. Banks, USA.
06	14	1863	**Col. William P. Sanders' Raid** in East Tennessee. 6/14-24/1863.
06	14	1863	Col. William Sanders' command sets out from Mount Vernon, KY.
06	14	1863	Skirmish near Green Hill, TN.
06	14	1863	Skirmish at Berryville, VA.
06	14	1863	Skirmish at Nine-Mile Ordinary, VA.
06	14	1863	Skirmish at Martinsburg, WV.
06	15	1863	Action near Richmond, LA.
06	15	1863	Skirmish near Williamsport, MD.
06	15	1863	Federal operations in Northwestern Mississippi, as Maj. Gen. Stephen A. Hurlbut, USA, 16th US Army Corps, orders 1,900 Union cavalry at La Grange, to attack the railroad line at Panola, MS, and to sweep the country of forage, wheat, animals, etc. 6/15-25/1863.
06	15	1863	Maj. Gen. JEB Stuart's CSA raid on Chambersburg, PA, as Lieut. Gen. James Longstreet, CSA, begins to move his corps from Culpeper, VA, northwest through Asby's and Snicker's Gaps, VA.
06	15	1863	Federal expedition to and skirmish near, Lebanon, TN. 6/15-17/1863.
06	15	1863	Affair near Trenton, TN.
06	15	1863	The **CSS Tacony** continues to evade Union warships and attack Federal vessels off the Atlantic Coast, VA, causing great concern by the United States Government, Washington, DC.
06	16	1863	Federal expedition against the **Sioux Indians,** the Dakota Territory. 6/16-9/13/1863.
06	16	1863	Skirmishes at Maysville, Mount Carmel, and Fox Springs, KY, with Capt. P. M. Everett, USA.
06	16	1863	Action at Triplett's Bridge, Rowan County, KY, with Capt. P. M. Everett, USA.
06	16	1863	Confederate raid on the Union Lines, during the siege of Port Hudson, LA.
06	16	1863	Federal demonstration on Waterloo, LA.
06	16	1863	Skirmish at Quinn's Mills, on the Coldwater, MS.
06	16	1863	Skirmishes near Holly Springs, MS. 6/16-17/1863.
06	16	1863	Skirmish on the Jornada del Muerto desert, the New Mexico Territory.
06	16	1863	Affairs in Holmes County, OH, including the US forces putting down an insurrection of bushwackers. 6/16-20/1863.
06	16	1863	Federal expedition from La Grange, TN, to Panola, MS. 6/16-24/1863.
06	16	1863	Federal scout from Memphis to the Hatchie River, TN.
06	16	1863	The Confederates cross the Potomac River, VA, as Maj. Gens. Joseph Hooker and Henry W. Halleck, USA, argue over the telegraph lines as to Hooker's next move.
06	17	1863	**Brig. Gen. Isham Warren Garrott, CSA,** is mortally wounded on the Vicksburg, MS, skirmish line while firing a rifle at the Federal troops.
06	17	1863	The capture of the Confederate Steamer, **CSS Atlanta,** by the US ironclads, **Nahant,** and the **Weehawken,** on the Wilmington River, Warsaw Sound, GA.
06	17	1863	Col. Hines' Confederate Cavalry raid into Indiana, crossing the Ohio River at Rome, IN, moving to Paoli, and retreating.
06	17	1863	Skirmishes at Catoctin Creek and Point of Rocks, MD, as Gen. Robert E. Lee, CSA, moves into Maryland.

06	17	1863	The Confederate attack on Union transports on the Mississippi River, near Commerce, MS.
06	17	1863	Skirmish near Westport, MO.
06	17	1863	Affair near Wellington, MO, with bushwackers.
06	17	1863	Federal scout from Rocky Run to Dover and Core Creek, NC, with no confrontation with the Confederates. 6/17-18/1863.
06	17	1863	Confederate operations on the Mississippi River, near Memphis, TN, and attack on transports there, with damage to the steamers, **Golden Era and the Platte Valley.** 6/17-18/1863.
06	17	1863	Federal expedition from Pocahontas, TN, toward Pontotoc, MS. 6/17-22/1863.
06	17	1863	Affair at Wartburg, near Montgomery, TN, with Col. Sanders, USA.
06	17	1863	Action at Aldie, VA with Brig. Gen. Hugh Judson Kilpatrick, USA.
06	17	1863	Skirmishes at and near Middleburg, VA. 6/17-18/1863.
06	17	1863	Skirmish at Thoroughfare Gap, VA, with Lieut. Gen. James Longstreet, CSCA.
06	18	1863	Skirmish at Plaquemine, LA.
06	18	1863	Skirmish at Belmont, MS.
06	18	1863	Affair at Birdsong Ferry, Big Black River, MS, with Confederate Cavalry.
06	18	1863	Skirmish at the Coldwater Bridge, MS.
06	18	1863	Skirmish near Rocheport, MO.
06	18	1863	Skirmish on Edisto Island, SC, with a rebel attack on the Union pickets there.
06	18	1863	Skirmish near Aldie, VA.
06	18	1863	Federal scout on the Peninsula, VA, near the York River, and towards Barhamsville, above Williamsburg, VA, to locate the position of any Confederate forces.
06	18	1863	Federal scout from Camp Piatt, on the Big and Little Coal Rivers, WV, including 10 miles up the Pond Fork with no contact with enemy forces. 6/18-19/1863.
06	19	1863	Lieut. Col. James F. Curtis, of the 4th California Infantry, is assigned to the command the District of Southern CA, relieving Col. Ferris Forman, of the 4th CA Infantry.
06	19	1863	Confederate raid on Bayou Goula, LA.
06	19	1863	Maj. Gen. Edward O. Ord, USA, supersedes Maj. Gen. John A. McClernand, USA, in the command of the 13th US Army Corps, due to his continued insubordination to Maj. Gen. Grant, USA, the Vicksburg, MS, Campaign.
06	19	1863	Action on the Coldwater, near Hernando, MS.
06	19	1863	Skirmishes near Panola, MS. 6/19-20/1863.
06	19	1863	Skirmishes at Knoxville, TN, with Col. William Sanders, USA. 6/19/20/1863.
06	19	1863	Affair at Lenoir's Station, TN, with Col. William Sanders, USA.
06	19	1863	Skirmish at Triune, TN.
06	19	1863	Action at Middleburg, VA, as the Army of Northern Virginia moves north toward Pennsylvania.
06	20	1863	Engagement at La Fourche Crossing, LA. 6/20/21/1863.
06	20	1863	The Confederate **capture of Thibodeaux, LA.**
06	20	1863	Skirmish at Middletown, MD.
06	20	1863	Federal reconnaissance from Young's Point to Richmond, LA, during the operations against Vicksburg, MS, as the Union batteries continue to shell the city of Vicksburg, MS.
06	20	1863	Skirmish at Matthew's Ferry, on the Coldwater, MS.
06	20	1863	Skirmish near Senatobia, MS.
06	20	1863	Federal scout from Waynesville, MO, to Robideaux and Gasconade and near the Laclede County line. 6/20-23/1863.
06	20	1863	Skirmish at Dixon Springs, TN.
06	20	1863	Skirmish at Rogers' Gap, TN, with Col. William Sanders, USA.
06	20	1863	Skirmish at Strawberry Plains, TN, with Col. William Sanders, USA.
06	20	1863	Skirmish near Government Springs, the Utah Territory, with the **Ute Indians** who are threatening destruction to soldiers and the overland mail.
06	20	1863	Skirmish at Diascund Bridge, VA.
06	20	1863	**West Virginia is admitted as the 35th state to the Union.**
06	21	1863	Skirmish at Brashear City, LA.
06	21	1863	Skirmish at Frederick, MD, with Gen. Robert E. Lee's Confederate advance.
06	21	1863	Skirmish on the Helena Road, MS.
06	21	1863	Skirmish at Hudsonville, MS.

06	21	1863	Affair on Dixon's Island, SC, with a Confederate movement on the Union cavalry pickets, who retire when fired upon.
06	21	1863	Skirmish at Powder Springs Gap, TN, with Col. William Sanders, USA.
06	21	1863	Skirmish near Gainesville, VA.
06	21	1863	Skirmishes at and about Thoroughfare Gap and Hay Market, VA. with Gen. Robert E. Lee's Confederate advance. 7/21-25/1863.
06	21	1863	Engagement at Upperville, VA, with Robert E. Lee's, CSA advance, and Brig. Gen. H. Judson Kilpatrick, USA, Cavalry.
06	22	1863	**Alfred Pleasonton, U.S.A.,** is appointed Maj. Gen.
06	22	1863	Skirmish on the Big Black River, MS.
06	22	1863	Action at Hills' Plantation, near Bear Creek, MS.
06	22	1863	Skirmish at Jones' Plantation, near Birdsong Ferry, MS.
06	22	1863	The **CSS Tacony** captures 5 Union fishing boats off the coast of New England.
06	22	1863	Skirmish at Powell Valley, TN, with Col. William P. Sanders, USA.
06	22	1863	Skirmish at Greencastle, PA, with the Confederate advance.
06	22	1863	Skirmish near Aldie, VA, with the Confederate advance.
06	22	1863	Skirmish near Dover, VA, with the Confederate advance.
06	23	1863	**Alfred Napoleon Alexander Duffie,** USA, is appointed Brig. Gen.
06	23	1863	**Alexander Stewart Webb,** USA, is appointed Brig. Gen.
06	23	1863	The Confederates attack and **capture** the Union garrison at **Brashear City, LA.**
06	23	1863	Union raid on Brookhaven, and skirmish at Rocky Creek, near Ellisville, MS, and the destruction of several railroad cars. 6/23-26/1863.
06	23	1863	Skirmish at Papinsville, MO.
06	23	1863	Skirmishes at, and the Federal **destruction of, Sibley, MO,** after being fired on from within the town by bushwackers.
06	23	1863	Affair at Canon Station, the Nevada Territory, as a couple of Union privates leave the station without authorization to go hunting. They are captured by hostile Indians and mutilated.
06	23	1863	**The Middle Tennessee, or Tullahoma Campaign,** begins with the advance of the Federals under Maj. Gen. William S. Rosecrans, USA, against Gen. Braxton Bragg, CSA. 6/23-7/7/1863.
06	23	1863	Skirmishes at Rover and Unionville, TN.
06	23	1863	Federal expedition from Yorktown to the South Anna Bridge, VA, and subsequent skirmish, by order of Maj. Gen. John A. Dix, USA, commanding the US Dept. of Virginia. 6/23-28/1863.
06	24	1863	Col. William P. Sanders' command arrives at Boston, KY, effectively ending his raid into East Tennessee.
06	24	1863	The **capture** of Union forces at **Bayou Boeuf Crossing, LA.**
06	24	1863	Skirmish at Chacahoula Station, LA.
06	24	1863	Skirmishes at Mound Plantation and near Lake Providence, LA, during the operations against Vicksburg.
06	24	1863	Skirmish at Sharpsburg, MD, with Gen. Robert E. Lee, CSA.
06	24	1863	Skirmish at Big Spring Branch, TN, as Maj. Gen. William S. Rosecrans, USA, advances on Middle Tennessee and is confronted by Gen. Braxton Bragg, CSA.
06	24	1863	Skirmish near Bradyville, TN.
06	24	1863	Skirmish at Christiana, TN.
06	24	1863	Skirmishes at Hoover's Gap, TN. 6/24-26/1863.
06	24	1863	Skirmishes at Liberty Gap, TN. 6/24-27/1863.
06	24	1863	Skirmish at Middleton, TN.
06	24	1863	The **Dept. of West Virginia is constituted,** under the command of Brig. Gen. Benjamin Franklin Kelley, USA.
06	25	1863	**George Washington Custis Lee,** CSA, is appointed Brig. Gen.
06	25	1863	**Walter Chiles Witaker,** USA, is appointed Brig. Gen.
06	25	1863	Skirmish at Milliken's Bend, LA.
06	25	1863	Federal expedition from Snyder's Bluff to Greenville, MS, aboard Union transports. 6/25-7/1/1863.
06	25	1863	Skirmish near McConnellsburg, PA.
06	25	1863	The capture of the Federal main supply train by Maj. Gen. JEB Stuart's CSA Cavalry Corps, Gettysburg, PA, Campaign, as Stuart, in a costly move, becomes separated from the main body of the Confederate Army of Northern Virginia, unable to provide Gen. Robert E. Lee with much needed information as to the Federals' whereabouts.

| 06 | 25 | 1863 | Skirmish at Fosterville, TN. |
| 06 | 25 | 1863 | Skirmish at Guy's Gap, TN. |

06 26 1863 **Rear Admiral Andrew Hull Foote, USN,** dies in New York City from wounds sustained during the siege of Fort Donelson, TN, Feb. 13-16, 1862.

06 26 1863 The Confederate capture of some Union outposts during the siege of Port Hudson, LA.

06 26 1863 The Confederate descent on **Portland Harbor, Maine,** by the schooner, **Archer,** which had recently been captured by the Confederate vessel, **Taconey,** where after capturing 21 Union vessels in less than 3 weeks, fails to seize the Federal cutter, **Caleb Cushing,** and being destroyed in the process. 6/26-27/1863.

06 26 1863 Skirmish near Gettysburg, PA, as Maj. Gen. Jubal A. Early, CSA, passes through Gettysburg, on his way toward York, PA.

06 26 1863 Skirmish at Beech Grove, TN.

06 26 1863 Skirmish on Loup Creek, WV, as the Confederates stage a surprise attack on a Union party, capturing some prisoners.

06 27 1863 **Brig. Gen. Martin Edwin Green, CSA,** is mortally wounded by a Federal sharpshooter while scanning the enemy's position at Vicksburg, MS, shot through the head, and dying instantly.

06 27 1863 Action at Carthage, MO.

06 27 1863 The Army Corps of Lieut. Gens. James Longstreet and A. P. Hill, CSA, arrive at Chambersburg, PA.

06 27 1863 The **capture of York, PA,** by Maj. Gen. Jubal A. Early, CSA.

06 27 1863 Skirmish at Fairfield, TN.

06 27 1863 Skirmishes at Fosterville and Guy's Gap, TN.

06 27 1863 **Manchester, TN, is occupied** by the Union forces.

06 27 1863 Action at Shelbyville, TN.

06 27 1863 Skirmish near Fairfax Court-House, VA, with Maj. Gen. JEB Stuart's CSA Cavalry capturing some of the Union forces.

06 28 1863 Skirmish at Russellville, KY, with Rebel guerrillas.

06 28 1863 Confederate attack on Donaldsville, LA, by Brig. Gen. Thomas Hart Taylor, CSA.

06 28 1863 Skirmish between Offutt's Cross-Roads and Seneca, MD.

06 28 1863 Skirmish near Rockville, MD.

06 28 1863 Federal reconnaissance from Plymouth to Nichol's Mills, NC, who meet up with some Confederates in the dark; shots are fired with no loss of life.

06 28 1863 Skirmish at Fountain Dale, PA.

06 28 1863 Skirmish near Oyster Point, PA. 6/28-29/1863.

06 28 1863 Skirmish at Wrightsville, PA.

06 28 1863 Skirmish at Rover, TN.

06 28 1863 Affair on the Little River Turnpike, VA. 6/28-29/1863.

06 28 1863 <u>**Maj. Gen. George G. Meade, USA. relieves Maj. Gen. Joseph Hooker, USA. in the command of the Army of the Potomac. VA.**</u>

06 28 1863 Brig. Gen. Benjamin F. Kelley, USA, assumes the command of the Dept. of West Virginia.

06 29 1863 The following are appointed Union Brigadier Generals:
George Armstrong Custer, USA
Elon John Farnsworth, USA
Wesley Merritt, USA

06 29 1863 Skirmishes at Columbia and Creelsborough, KY.

06 29 1863 Skirmish at Mound Plantation, LA.

06 29 1863 Affairs at Lisbon and Poplar Springs, MD.

06 29 1863 Skirmish at Muddy Branch, MD.

06 29 1863 Skirmish at Westminster, MD, with Maj. Gen. JEB Stuart, CSA.

06 29 1863 Skirmishes at Messinger's Ferry, Big Black River, MS. 6/29-30/1863.

06 29 1863 Skirmish at McConnellsburg, PA, as the Northern and Southern armies continue to concentrate toward Cashtown and Gettysburg, PA.

06 29 1863 Skirmish at Decherd, TN, as Maj. Gen. William S. Rosecrans, USA, advances.

06 29 1863 Skirmish near Hillsborough, TN.

06 29 1863 Skirmish near Lexington, TN.

06 29 1863 Skirmishes near Tullahoma, TN. 6/29-30/1863.

| 06 | 29 | 1863 | Confederate expedition, under Col. William L. Jackson, CSA, to Beverly, WV. 6/29-7/4/1863. |

06	30	1863	Attack on Goodrich's Landing, LA.
06	30	1863	The Federal **evacuation of Maryland Heights, MD.**
06	30	1863	Skirmish at Westminster, MD.
06	30	1863	Skirmish near Hudson's River, Neosho River, MO.
06	30	1863	Skirmish at Fairfield, PA, as Lieut. Gen. Richard S. Ewell, CSA, heads towards Gettysburg, PA.
06	30	1863	Action at Hanover, PA, with Maj. Gen. JEB Stuart, CSA, who barely escape capture himself.
06	30	1863	Skirmish at Sporting Hill, near Harrisburg, PA.
06	30	1863	The Confederate forces under Gen. Braxton Bragg, CSA, **evacuate Tullahoma, TN,** and head for Chattanooga, TN.
06	30	1863	President Abraham Lincoln resists political pressure to reinstate Maj. Gen. George B. McClellan, USA, as commander of the Army of the Potomac.

07	1	1863	**Henry Harrison Walker,** CSA, is appointed Brig. Gen.
07	1	1863	**Erasmus Darwin Keyes, U.S.A.,** is appointed Maj. Gen.
07	1	1863	**John Parker Hawkins,** USA, is appointed Brig. Gen.
07	1	1863	**Joseph Gilbert Totten,** USA, is appointed Brig. Gen.
07	1	1863	Engagement at Cabin Creek, the Indian Territory, with Col. Stand Watie, CSA.
07	1	1863	Affair at Christianburg, KY, where Rebel forces capture and burn the passenger train on the **Louisville and Lexington Railroad.**
07	1	1863	Skirmish at Baltimore Cross-Roads, MD, Maj. Gen. D.H. Hill, CSA, defending against a Union advance.
07	1	1863	Skirmish at Edwards Station, MS, as Lieut. Gen. John C. Pemberton, CSA, is close to surrendering Vicksburg, MS.
07	1	1863	Skirmish at Carlisle, PA.
07	1	1863	**The Battle of Gettysburg, PA,** as Lieut. Gen. A. P. Hill, CSA, pushed back Brig. Gen. John Buford's USA cavalry and then infantry of the 1st US Army Corps under Maj. Gen. Abner Doubleday and the 11th US Army Corps under Maj. Gen. Oliver O. Howard; the Confederates **occupy Gettysburg,** as Lieut. Gen. Richard S. Ewell approaches from the north and fails to take the all important Cemetery Hill, as places such as the Chambersburg Pike, Cemetery Hill, Cemetery Ridge, Culp's Hill, Herr Ridge, McPherson's Ridge, Oak Ridge, the Railroad Cut, Spangler's Spring, Seminary Ridge, and Willoughby Run will forever lose their obscurity. 7/1-3/1863.
07	1	1863	**Maj. Gen. John Fulton Reynolds, USA,** commanding the 1st US Army Corps, is mortally wounded at Gettysburg, PA, along the Chambersburg Road near the edge of McPherson's Woods, while directing the leading Union troops who arrived to aid Brig. Gen. John Buford's cavalry command, being killed instantly by a Confederate sharpshooter, as he sat upon his horse.
07	1	1863	Skirmish near Bethpage Bridge, Elk River, TN.
07	1	1863	Skirmish near Bobo's Cross-Roads, TN.
07	1	1863	**Tullahoma, TN, is occupied** by Maj. Gen. William S. Rosecrans, USA, as his highly successful Tullahoma Campaign is drawing to a conclusion with Gen. Braxton Bragg, CSA, continuing to retreat toward Chattanooga, TN.
07	1	1863	Maj. Gen. Daniel Henry Hill, CSA, is temporarily assigned to the command of the troops in the Dept. of Richmond, VA.
07	1	1863	Federal expeditions from White House to South Anna River under Brig. Gen. George W. Getty, USA, commanding 2nd Division, 7th US Army Corps and to Bottom's Bridge, VA, under Maj. Gen. Erasmus D. Keyes, commanding 4th US Army Corps, meeting up with Maj. Gen. Daniel H. Hill, CSA. 7/1-7/1863.

07	2	1863	**The Second Day of the Battle of Gettysburg, PA,** sees Lieut. Gen. James Longstreet, CSA, pushing Maj. Gen. Daniel Sickles 3rd US Army Corps back from his unapproved forward position at the Peach Orchard, the Wheatfield, Devil's Den, and along the Emmitsburg Road. Maj. Gen. John Bell Hood's Texans are pushed back from their attack on the Big and Little Round Tops, as Maj. Gen. Gouverneur Kemble Warren, USA, saves the day; Maj. Gen. Jubal A. Early, CSA, under Lieut. Gen. Richard S. Ewell's, CSA, attack on Culp's Hill is too late in the day and uncoordinated with Longstreet's attack and fails.
07	2	1863	**Maj. Gen. William Dorsey Pender, CSA,** is mortally wounded on the 2nd day of the Battle of Gettysburg, PA, from a shell fragment that required the amputation of his leg, dying on July 18, 1863.
07	2	1863	**Brig. Gen. William Barksdale, CSA,** is mortally wounded during the Confederate assault on the Round

Tops, is captured by the Federals and died the following day.

| 07 | 2 | 1863 | **Brig. Gen. Paul Jones Semmes, CSA,** is mortally wounded during the Confederate assault on the Round Tops, dying eight days later on July 10, 1863. |

| 07 | 2 | 1863 | **Brig. Gen. Strong Vincent, USA,** is mortally wounded, receiving his death wound as he charged down Little Round Top to rally his men after Col. Joshua Lawrence Chamberlin's men, who raced down the mountain after the Confederates in a bayonet charge, dying at the age of 26, on July 7, 1863. |

| 07 | 2 | 1863 | **Brig. Gen. Stephen Hinsdale Weed, USA,** is mortally wounded, receiving a fatal chest wound as he led his men in assistance of Col. Joshua Lawrence Chamberlin's command as they used bayonets to charge down the Round Tops into the Confederate advancing battle line. |

| 07 | 2 | 1863 | **Brig. Gen. Samuel Kosciuszko Zook, USA,** is mortally wounded as he lead his command in a counterattack against Lieut. Gen. James Longstreet's, CSA, men, receiving his death wound in his stomach, being so severe he died shortly after midnight. |

| 07 | 2 | 1863 | **Brig. Gen. John Hunt Morgan's CSA raid into Kentucky, Indiana, and Ohio.** 7/2-26/1863. |

| 07 | 2 | 1863 | Brig. Gen. John Hunt Morgan's CSA command crosses the Cumberland River at and near Burkesville, TN. |

| 07 | 2 | 1863 | Skirmish at mouth of Coal Run, Pike County, KY. |

| 07 | 2 | 1863 | Skirmish at Marrowbone, KY, with Brig. Gen. John Hunt Morgan, CSA. |

| 07 | 2 | 1863 | Affair at Springfield Landing, during the siege of Port Hudson, LA. |

| 07 | 2 | 1863 | Skirmish near Chambersburg, PA. |

| 07 | 2 | 1863 | Skirmish at Hunterstown, PA. |

| 07 | 2 | 1863 | Skirmish at Estill Springs, TN, as Gen. Braxton Bragg, CSA, and Maj. Gen. William S. Rosecrans, USA, continue to spar. |

| 07 | 2 | 1863 | Skirmish at Morris' Ford, Elk River, TN. |

| 07 | 2 | 1863 | Skirmishes at Pelham and Elk River Bridge, TN. |

| 07 | 2 | 1863 | Skirmish at Rock Creek Ford, Elk River, TN. |

| 07 | 2 | 1863 | Skirmishes at Baltimore, or Crump's, Cross-Roads, and the Baltimore Store, VA, against Maj. Gen. D. H. Hill, CSA. |

| 07 | 2 | 1863 | Engagement at Beverly, WV, as Col. William L. Jackson, CSA, attacks Brig. Gen. William W. Averell, USA, and his cavalry. |

| 07 | 3 | 1863 | **The Third Day of the Battle of Gettysburg, PA,** sees Gen. Robert E. Lee, CSA, ordering Lieut. Gen. James Longstreet, CSA, to attack the center of Maj. Gen. George Gordon Meade's, USA, line. Longstreet and Lee disagree over the attack as well as the entire 3 day battle, Longstreet preferring to have moved to another location better suited to fight a defensive battle. The attack will become known as **Pickett's Charge,** although it consisted of the following Confederate divisions: |

a) **Maj. Gen. Henry Heth's Division,** commanded by **Brig. Gen. James Johnston Pettigrew,** Heth seriously wounded July 1st.

b) **Maj. Gen. Dorsey Pender's Division,** commanded by **Maj. Gen. Isaac Ridgeway Trimble,** Pender mortally wounded yesterday; Trimble will lose a leg and be captured today, not being exchanged until February, 1865.

c) **Maj. Gen. George Edward Pickett's Division.** Pickett's Charge is a total Confederate disaster, forcing Gen. Robert E. Lee, CSA, to limp back to Virginia, leaving behind in graves a solid core of fighting men his Army of Northern Virginia could not afford to lose; total casualties for the 3 days battle for both sides approximate 43,500.

| 07 | 3 | 1863 | **Brig. Gen. Lewis Addison Armistead, CSA,** is mortally wounded during Pickett's Charge, the Battle of Gettysburg, PA, with his hand on a Federal cannon at the apex of the copse of trees the Confederates were attempting to reach, captured by the Federals and dying two days later. |

| 07 | 3 | 1863 | **Brig. Gen. William Barksdale, CSA,** dies from wounds suffered the day before at Gettysburg, PA. |

| 07 | 3 | 1863 | **Brig. Gen. Richard Brooke Garnett, CSA,** is mortally wounded during Pickett's Charge, the bloody climax of the Battle of Gettysburg, PA, his body never located. |

| 07 | 3 | 1863 | **Brig. Gen. Elon John Farnsworth, USA,** is mortally wounded as his cavalry command counterattacks Lieut. Gen. James Longstreet's, CSA, flank following the repulse of Pickett's Charge, during the Battle of Gettysburg, PA. |

| 07 | 3 | 1863 | **Brig. Gen. Samuel Kosciuszko Zook, USA,** dies after being mortally wounded the day before at the Battle of Gettysburg. |

| 07 | 3 | 1863 | **Strong Vincent,** USA, is appointed Brig. Gen. after being mortally wounded. |

| 07 | 3 | 1863 | Confederate expedition to Ossabaw Island and McDonald's place, GA, where the Rebels surprise and |

			capture 2 pickets and 8 negroes, releasing 5 who couldn't fit in their small boat.
07	3	1863	Federal expedition from Beaver Creek, KY, into Southwestern Virginia, with skirmishes: a) at Pond Creek, KY, (**6th**) and b) at Gladesville, VA. (**7th**). 7/3-11/1863.
07	3	1863	Skirmish at Columbia, KY, with Brig. Gen. John Hunt Morgan, CSA.
07	3	1863	Federal scout from Salem, MO, with skirmish.
07	3	1863	Federal raid on the **Wilmington and Weldon Railroad, NC,** with the destruction of some railroad cars and equipment. 7/3-7/1863.
07	3	1863	Action at Fairfield, PA.
07	3	1863	Skirmish at Boiling Fork, near Winchester, TN.
07	3	1863	Federal scouts from Memphis, TN, on the Hernando and Horn Lake roads, with skirmishes just a few miles outside Memphis.
07	3	1863	**Suffolk, VA, is evacuated** by the Union forces.
07	4	1863	Engagement at Helena, AR, including the US ironclad, **Tyler,** as Maj. Gen. Benjamin M. Prentiss, USA, repels the Confederate attack under Lieut. Gen. Theophilus H. Holmes, CSA, and Maj. Gen. Sterling Price, CSA. Total casualties approximate 1,800, mostly Confederate.
07	4	1863	Engagement at Green River Bridge, or Tebb's Bend, KY, as Brig. Gen. John Hunt Morgan, CSA, is repulsed by the Union defenders.
07	4	1863	Skirmish near Emmitsburg, MD.
07	4	1863	Skirmish at Messinger's Ferry, Big Black River, MS.
07	4	1863	Lieut. Gen. John C. Pemberton, CSA, **surrenders Vicksburg, MS,** and about 29,000 Confederate soldiers to Maj. Gen. US (**Unconditional Surrender**) Grant, USA, which, except for Port Hudson, the entire Mississippi River is opened up.
07	4	1863	Skirmish at Cassville, MO.
07	4	1863	Affair in the Black Fork Hills, MO.
07	4	1863	Skirmish with Indians near Fort Craig, the New Mexico Territory.
07	4	1863	Skirmish at Fairfield Gap, PA.
07	4	1863	Action at Monterey Gap, PA.
07	4	1863	Skirmish at University Depot, TN.
07	4	1863	Skirmish at the South Anna Bridge, on the **Richmond and Fredericksburg Railroad,** north of Richmond, VA, with Maj. Gen. D. H. Hill, CSA, defending.
07	4	1863	Skirmish at Fayetteville, WV.
07	4	1863	Skirmish at Huttonsville, WV, with Col. William L. Jackson, CSA, and his Cavalry expedition.
07	5	1863	Skirmish at Bardstown, KY, with Brig. Gen. John H. Morgan, CSA.
07	5	1863	Skirmish at Franklin, KY.
07	5	1863	Skirmish at Lebanon, KY, with Brig. Gen. John H. Morgan, CSA.
07	5	1863	Skirmish at Woodburn, KY, where Rebel forces burn the depot.
07	5	1863	Skirmish at Smithsburg, MD, with Union Cavalry troops.
07	5	1863	**The Jackson, MS, Campaign.** 7/5-25/1863.
07	5	1863	Skirmish near Birdsong Ferry, MS.
07	5	1863	Skirmish at Cunningham's Cross-Roads, PA, as Gen. Robert E. Lee, CSA, retreated south toward Hagerstown, MD.
07	5	1863	Skirmish near Fairfield, PA.
07	5	1863	Skirmish near Greencastle, PA.
07	5	1863	Skirmish near Green Oak, PA.
07	5	1863	Skirmish near Mercersburg, PA.
07	5	1863	Skirmish at Steven's Furnace (also known as the Caledonia Iron-Works), PA.
07	5	1863	Federal expedition from Plymouth to Gardner's Bridge and Williamston, NC, under Brig. Gen. Henry W. Wessels, USA commanding the US District of Albemarle. 7/5-7/1863.
07	5	1863	Skirmish at Kenansville, NC, along the **Wilmington and Weldon Railroad.**
07	5	1863	Skirmish at **Warsaw, NC,** and **occupation** by the Federals, along the **Wilmington and Weldon Railroad.**
07	5	1863	Skirmish at Yellow Creek, TN.
07	6	1863	Action at Hagerstown, MD.
07	6	1863	Action at Williamsport, MD, where Maj. Gen. John Buford's, USA, Cavalry, is repulsed.

07	6	1863	Skirmishes at Jones' and Messinger's Ferries, or Bolton and Birdsong Ferries, MS, as Maj. Gen. William T. Sherman, USA, marches his Union forces on Jackson, MS.
07	6	1863	Skirmish at Free Bridge, or Quaker Bridge, near Trenton, NC, along the **Wilmington and Weldon Railroad.**
07	7	1863	**Brig. Gen. Strong Vincent, USA,** dies in a field hospital outside Gettysburg, PA, from his battle wound received on July 2, 1863.
07	7	1863	Skirmish with Indians at Grand Pass, the Idaho Territory, about 100 miles southwest of Fort Halleck.
07	7	1863	Skirmish near Cummings' Ferry, KY.
07	7	1863	Skirmish at Shepherdsville, KY, with Brig. Gen. John Hunt Morgan, CSA.
07	7	1863	Confederate attacks on Union gunboats and transports on the Mississippi River, LA, etal. 7/7-10/1863.
07	7	1863	Skirmish at Funkstown, MD.
07	7	1863	Skirmish at Downsville, MD.
07	7	1863	Federal **reoccupation of Maryland Heights, MD,** as President Abraham Lincoln is upset that Maj. Gen. George G. Meade, USA, will not strike a blow against the retreating Army of Northern Virginia.
07	7	1863	Skirmish near Baker's Creek, MS.
07	7	1863	Action at Iuka, MS, with Union Cavalry.
07	7	1863	Skirmish at Queen's Hill, MS.
07	7	1863	Skirmish at Ripley, MS.
07	7	1863	Skirmish near Dry Wood, MO, with Confederate guerrillas.
07	7	1863	**Operations against the Navajo Indians in the New Mexico Territory,** under Col. Kit Carson, USA. Carson finds the **Ute Indians** attacking and killing the hostile **Navajoes** on their own. Carson will use some **Zuni Indians** as guides. 7/7-8/19/1863.
07	7	1863	The Confederate Army of Tennessee, under Gen. Braxton Bragg, CSA, camps near Chattanooga, TN.
07	7	1863	Skirmish at Harper's Ferry, WV.
07	8	1863	**Gabriel Colvin Wharton,** CSA, is appointed Brig. Gen.
07	8	1863	Brig. Gen. John Hunt Morgan, CSA, crosses the Ohio River, at Cumming's Ferry and at Bradenburg, KY, near Louisville, into Indiana. 7/8-9/1863.
07	8	1863	Skirmish near Cumming's Ferry, Kentucky River, KY, with Brig. Gen. John Hunt Morgan, CSA.
07	8	1863	Action at Boonsborough, MD.
07	8	1863	Skirmish near Williamsport, MD.
07	8	1863	Skirmish near Bolton Depot, MS, near Vicksburg, MS.
07	8	1863	Skirmish near Clinton, MS.
07	8	1863	Federal scout from Germantown, TN, to within 8 miles of Hernando.
07	8	1863	**Maj. Gen. Andrew A. Humphreys,** USA, is announced as the **Chief of Staff,** the Army of the Potomac, VA, etal.
07	9	1863	Indian attack on a private train transporting Government stores to Fort Gaston, at Redwood Creek, CA, with 10 casualties out of 18 Union men with the wagon train.
07	9	1863	Skirmish at Corydon, Indiana, with Brig. Gen. John Morgan, CSA.
07	9	1863	Skirmish at Bradenburg, KY, with Brig. Gen. John Morgan, CSA.
07	9	1863	After learning of the surrender of Vicksburg, MS, Maj. Gen. Franklin Gardner, CSA, formally **surrenders Port Hudson, LA,** and about 6,500 men to Maj. Gen. Nathaniel P. Banks, USA, the last Confederate stronghold on the Mississippi River.
07	9	1863	Skirmish at Benevola (or Beaver Creek), MD, as Gen. Robert E. Lee, CSA, continued to move the Army of Northern Virginia back to Virginia soil.
07	9	1863	Skirmishes near Clinton and Jackson, MS, as Maj. Gen. William T. Sherman, USA, marches on Jackson.
07	9	1863	Explosion of artillery ammunition at Fort Lyon, VA, as Union soldiers inspect the shells, with the loss of 20 deaths and 14 wounded.
07	9	1863	Confederate expedition from Richmond to Mathias Point, VA.
07	10	1863	**Quincy Adams Gillmore, U.S.A.,** is appointed Maj. Gen.
07	10	1863	**Brig. Gen. Paul Jones Semmes, CSA,** dies at Martinsburg, WV, from wounds received on July 2nd, 1863, at the Battle of Gettysburg, PA.
07	10	1863	Skirmish at Salem, Indiana, with Brig. Gen. John H. Morgan, CSA.
07	10	1863	Skirmish on Martin Creek, KY.
07	10	1863	Skirmish near Clear Spring, MD.

07	10	1863	Skirmishes at and near Funkstown, MD. 7/10-13/1863.
07	10	1863	Skirmishes at and near Hagerstown, MD. 7/10-13/1863.
07	10	1863	Skirmishes at Jones' Cross-Roads, near Williamsport, MD. 7/10-13/1863.
07	10	1863	Skirmish at Old Antietam Forge, near Leitersburg, MD.
07	10	1863	Skirmish at Florence, MO.
07	10	1863	Skirmish with the **Navaho Indians** at Cook's Canon, the New Mexico Territory.
07	10	1863	**The Union Investment and Capture of Jackson, MS,** as Maj. Gen. William T. Sherman, USA, attempts to surround the city and the Confederate Dept. of the West, under Gen. Joseph E. Johnston, CSA. 7/10-17/1863.
07	10	1863	**Operations on Morris Island, SC,** including the Union assaults on Battery Wagner, etc. 7/10-9/7/1863.
07	10	1863	Union forces **occupy the south end of Morris Island, SC,** and prepare to assault CSA Battery Wagner, Charleston Harbor.
07	10	1863	Engagement at Willstown Bluff, Pon Pon River, SC, with the US steamer, **John Adams,** the transport, **Enoch Dean,** the small tug, **Governor Milton,** and the Confederate shore batteries. The Yankees retreat after burning large sums of rice, rice-fields, buildings, etc., around Williston, SC.
07	10	1863	Skirmish at Bolivar, TN, with Union cavalry. Maj. Gen. Nathan Bedford Forrest, CSA, is rumored to be in the vicinity.
07	10	1863	The **capture** of the Union outpost, including 100 men, at **Union City, TN,** by Confederate cavalry, under Col. J. B. Biffle, CSA.
07	11	1863	**Daniel Harvey Hill, C.S.A., is appointed Lieut. Gen.,** which because of his criticism of Gen. Braxton Bragg at Chickamauga, in the Chattanooga Campaign, President Jefferson Davis refused to nominate Hill to the Confederate Senate he had earlier appointed him to. This is one Confederate general who was never appreciated.
07	11	1863	Skirmish at Pekin, Indiana, with Brig. Gen. John Hunt Morgan, CSA.
07	11	1863	Skirmish at Stockton, MO, with bushwackers.
07	11	1863	The first Union assault on Battery Wagner, Morris Island, SC, led by Brig. Gen. Quincy A. Gillmore, USA, is repulsed.
07	11	1863	Federal reconnaissance from Cowan to Anderson, TN. 7/11-14/1863.
07	11	1863	Federal reconnaissance to, and skirmish (**12th**) at, Ashby's Gap, VA. 7/11-14/1863.
07	12	1863	Brig. Gen. John Hunt Morgan, CSA, arrives at Vernon, Indiana.
07	12	1863	Engagement on the La Fourche (Cox's Plantation, etc.), near Donaldsonville, LA. 7/12-13/1863.
07	12	1863	Skirmish near Canton, MS, between Maj. Gen. William T. Sherman, USA, and Gen. Joseph E. Johnston, CSA.
07	12	1863	Federal expedition from Vicksburg to Yazoo City, MS, aboard the **USS Baron De Kalb, Kenwood, New National and Signal;** the **Baron De Kalb** striking a torpedo and sinking. 7/12-21/1863.
07	12	1863	Skirmish near Switzler's Mill, Chariton County, MO.
07	13	1863	**Maj. Gen. John Stevens Bowen, CSA,** dies near Raymond, MS, from camp fever sickness developed during the siege of Vicksburg, MS.
07	13	1863	Federal expedition to Huntsville, AL, where they seize 300 contrabands, 500 cattle, and 500 horses and mules. 7/13-22/1863.
07	13	1863	Lieut. Col. Stephen G. Whipple, 1st Battalion of Mountaineers, California Volunteers, relieves Col. Francis J. Lippitt, 2nd California Infantry, in command of the Humboldt Military District.
07	13	1863	Draft riots take place at New York City and Troy, NY, Boston, MA, Portsmouth, NH, Wooster, OH, and Rutland, VT, with 50 to 60 rioters reported killed in New York City alone. 7/13-16/1863.
07	13	1863	**Natchez, MS, is occupied** by the Union expeditionary troops.
07	13	1863	**Yazoo City, MS, is occupied** by the Union expeditionary troops.
07	13	1863	Federal reconnaissance from Newport Barracks to Cedar Point and White Oak River, NC, with the assistance of the Union gunboat, **Wilson,** with little activity. 7/13-16/1863.
07	13	1863	Brig. Gen. John Hunt Morgan's, CSA, Confederate command enters the state of Ohio, and heads toward Cincinnati and Hamilton.
07	13	1863	Martial law is declared in Cincinnati, Covington, and Newport Ohio, due to Brig. Gen. John Hunt Morgan's CSA raid.
07	13	1863	Skirmishes on Forked Deer River, and at Jackson, TN, with the Federals finding over 30 barrels of whiskey. It was with great effort the commanding Union officer exerted to keep the town from being burned and totally looted by the inebriated Federals.

07	13	1863	Federal expedition from Fayetteville, WV, to Wytheville, VA, with skirmish with Confederates, the capturing of Rebel prisoners and the burning of part of the town before withdrawing, etc. 7/13-25/1863.
07	14	1863	The Action at Falling Waters, MD.
07	14	1863	**Brig. Gen. James Johnston Pettigrew, CSA,** is mortally wounded fighting a rear guard action with the Federal Cavalry at Falling Waters, MD, following the Confederate retreat after the Battle of Gettysburg, PA, and dying three days later.
07	14	1863	Skirmish near Williamsport, MD.
07	14	1863	Skirmish near Iuka, MS.
07	14	1863	Maj. Gen. William H. C. Whiting, CSA, is assigned to the command of the Dept. of North Carolina.
07	14	1863	Skirmish at Camp Dennison, near Cincinnati, OH, with Brig. Gen. John Hunt Morgan's, CSA, Cavalry raid.
07	14	1863	Confederate sortie from Battery Wagner, Morris Island, near Charleston, SC. 7/14-15/1863.
07	14	1863	The **capture of Fort Powhatan, James River, VA,** by Union naval forces, which opens the James River to Drewry's Bluff.
07	14	1863	Skirmish near Harper's Ferry, WV.
07	15	1863	The Confederate Cavalry **occupation of Hickman, KY.** 7/15-16/1863.
07	15	1863	The US **Depts. of North Carolina and Virginia** are consolidated.
07	15	1863	Skirmish on Forked Deer River, near Jackson, MS.
07	15	1863	Brig. Gen. John Hunt Morgan, CSA, is pursued from Cincinnati, OH, eastward towards the Ohio River.
07	15	1863	Federal expedition to Columbia and Centreville, TN.
07	15	1863	Skirmish on the Forked Deer Creek, TN, with Rebel Cavalry.
07	15	1863	Skirmish near Jackson, TN.
07	15	1863	Skirmish at Pulaski, TN.
07	15	1863	Skirmish at Halltown, WV, as Gen. Robert E. Lee, CSA, retreated into the Shenandoah Valley.
07	15	1863	Skirmish at Shepherdstown, WV.
07	15	1863	**By the middle of the month, it was becoming apparent that the noose around the Confederacy was beginning to tighten.**
07	16	1863	Skirmish at Bolton Depot, MS, with Maj. Gen. William T. Sherman, USA.
07	16	1863	Skirmish at Clinton, MS, with Maj. Gen. William Sherman, USA.
07	16	1863	Skirmish at Grant's Ferry, Pearl River, MS, with Maj. Gen. William Sherman.
07	16	1863	**Jackson, MS, is evacuated** by Gen. Joseph E. Johnston, CSA, and subsequently **occupied** by Maj. Gen. William T. Sherman, USA.
07	16	1863	Engagement near Grimball's Landing, James Island, SC, with the Confederate attack being repulsed, with the help of the US steam sloop, **Pawnee.**
07	16	1863	Federal scout from Germantown, to Collierville, Concordia, etc., TN. 7/16-20/1863.
07	16	1863	Skirmish at Shanghai, WV.
07	16	1863	Action at Shepherdstown, WV.
07	17	1863	**Brig. Gen. James Johnston Pettigrew, CSA,** dies near Bunker Hill, VA, from the wounds he received on July 14, 1863.
07	17	1863	**John Converse Starkweather,** USA, is appointed Brig. Gen.
07	17	1863	**William Denison Whipple,** USA, is appointed Brig. Gen.
07	17	1863	Skirmish with Indians at Elk Creek, near Honey Springs, the Indian Territory, with Maj. Gen. James G. Blunt, USA, routing the rebel force.
07	17	1863	Skirmish at Berlin, OH, with Brig. Gen. John H. Morgan, CSA.
07	17	1863	Skirmish near Hamden, OH, with Brig. Gen. John H. Morgan, CSA.
07	17	1863	Skirmish at Bear Creek, near Canton, MS.
07	17	1863	Federal expedition from New Berne to Swift Creek Village, NC, and subsequent skirmish. 7/17-20/1863.
07	17	1863	Skirmish on Stone's River, TN.
07	17	1863	Skirmish at Snicker's Gap, VA.
07	17	1863	Skirmish near North Mountain Station, or Wytheville, VA.
07	18	1863	**Maj. Gen. William Dorsey Pender, CSA,** dies near Stauton, VA, from the infection that set in after the amputation of his leg at the Battle of Gettysburg, PA, on July 2nd, 1863.
07	18	1863	**Francis Marion Cockrell,** CSA, is appointed Brig. Gen.
07	18	1863	**George Crockett Strong,** U.S.A., is appointed Maj. Gen.

07	18	1863	Skirmish at Des Allemands, LA.
07	18	1863	Skirmish at Brookhaven, MS.
07	18	1863	Federal scout from Cassville, MO, to Huntsville AR.
07	18	1863	Federal expedition from New Berne to Tarborough and Rocky Mount, NC, under Brig. Gen. Edward E. Potter, USA. 7/18-24/1863.
07	18	1863	Skirmish with Indians on the Rio Hondo, the New Mexico Territory.
07	18	1863	Skirmish at Pomeroy, OH, as the Federals were closing in on the worn out men of Brig. Gen. John Hunt Morgan, CSA.
07	18	1863	The capture of Union pickets near Germantown, TN, by a squad of Rebel Cavalry, who also tore up the railroad tracks 2 miles from Germantown.
07	18	1863	Skirmish near Memphis, TN.
07	18	1863	**The Union siege of Battery (Fort) Wagner, Morris Island, SC.** 7/14-9/7/1863.
07	18	1863	The 2nd Union assault on Battery (Fort) Wagner, Morris Island, SC, is repulsed with fearful casualties, which included the death of **Col. Robert G. Shaw, USA,** of the 54th Massachusetts Colored Infantry, which was made into a Hollywood movie "Glory." 7/14-15/1863.
07	18	1863	**Maj. Gen. George Crockett Strong, USA,** is mortally wounded while leading the assault on Battery (Fort) Wagner, Morris Island, SC, receiving a minie ball wound to his thigh, which led to his death in a New York City hospital on July 30, 1863.
07	18	1863	Maj. Gen. John G. Foster, USA, assumes the command of the Dept. of Virginia and North Carolina.
07	18	1863	Maj. Gen. John A. Dix, USA, assumes the command of the Dept. of the East, VA, etal.
07	18	1863	Skirmishes at and near Hedgesville and Martinsburg, WV. 7/18-19/1863.
07	19	1863	Action at Brandon, MS, with Maj. Gen. William T. Sherman, USA.
07	19	1863	Federal scouts from Danville, MS, surprise 2 Confederate camps and capture prisoners.
07	19	1863	Skirmish with Indians on the Rio de las Animas, the New Mexico Territory.
07	19	1863	**The Engagement near Buffington Island,** Ohio River, OH, where Brig. Gen. John Hunt Morgan's Confederate raiders are overwhelmed with the majority killed, wounded or captured by the joint US forces under Brig. Gen. Edward H. Hobson, USA, and Brig. Gen. James M. Shackelford, USA; Morgan escaping along the Ohio River towards Pennsylvania.
07	19	1863	Operations in the vicinity of Trenton, TN. 7/19-29/1863.
07	19	1863	Lieut. Gen. Daniel H. Hill, CSA, is assigned to the command of the 2nd Confederate Army Corps, relieving Lieut. Gen. William J. Hardee, Army of the Tennessee, under Gen. Braxton Bragg, CSA, TN, etal.
07	20	1863	Operations against Indians in Round Valley, CA, as the Federals track and kill a party of **Ukie Indians,** and capture and hang 5 Indian leaders in front of all the Indians in the Valley, and so on. 7/20-26/1863.
07	20	1863	Skirmish at Cabin Creek, the Indian Territory.
07	20	1863	Skirmish at Coal Hill, near Cheshire, OH, with Brig. Gen. John Hunt Morgan, CSA.
07	20	1863	Skirmish near Hockingport, OH, with Brig. Gen. John Hunt Morgan.
07	20	1863	Skirmishes at Tarborough and Sparta, NC, with Brig. Gen. Edward E. Potter, USA.
07	20	1863	Federal navel bombardment of Legare's Point, James Island, SC.
07	20	1863	Federal scouts from Memphis, TN to within 3 miles of Hernando, another within 24 miles from Memphis, burning some cotton. 7/20-21/1863.
07	20	1863	Skirmish at Ashby's Gap, VA, between Gen. Robert E. Lee's Confederate and Maj. Gen. George Meade's Federal forces.
07	20	1863	Skirmish near Berry's Ferry, VA, as Maj. Gen. George Meade, USA, begins to pursue Gen. Robert E. Lee, CSA, into Virginia.
07	20	1863	Brig. Gen. George W. Getty, USA, assumes the command of the 7th US Army Corps, Dept. of Virginia and North Carolina.
07	21	1863	**James Patrick Major,** CSA, is appointed Brig. Gen.
07	21	1863	Skirmish at Street's Ferry, NC, with Brig. Gen. Edward E. Potter, USA.
07	21	1863	Skirmishes at Chester Gap, VA, with Maj. Gen. JEB Stuart's, CSA, cavalry. 7/21-22/1863.
07	21	1863	Skirmishes at Manassas Gap, VA, the Blue Ridge Mountains, with Maj. Gen. JEB Stuart, CSA. 7/21-22/1863.
07	21	1863	Brig. Gen. John D. Imdoben, CSA, is assigned to the command of the Valley District, VA.
07	22	1863	Federal expedition from Clinton, KY, in the pursuit of Biffle's, Forrest's, and Newsom's Confederate cavalry. 7/22-27/1863.

07	22	1863	**Brashear City, LA, is reoccupied** by the Union forces.
07	22	1863	Skirmish at Scupperton, NC, with Brig. Gen. Edward E. Potter, USA.
07	22	1863	Skirmish at Eagleport, OH, with Brig. Gen. John Morgan, CSA.
07	22	1863	Federal scout in Sequatchie Valley, TN.
07	23	1863	The following are appointed Confederate Brigadier Generals: **Laurence Simmons Baker,** CSA **Samuel Wragg Ferguson,** CSA **Lundsford Lindsay Lomas,** CSA
07	23	1863	**Kenner Garrard,** USA, is appointed Brig. Gen.
07	23	1863	Skirmish at Rockville, OH, with the tired Brig. Gen. John Hunt Morgan.
07	23	1863	Federal expedition from Memphis to Raleigh, TN.
07	23	1863	Skirmish near Chester Gap, VA, Blue Ridge Mountains.
07	23	1863	Skirmish near Gaines' Cross-Roads, VA.
07	23	1863	Skirmish near Snicker's Gap, VA.
07	23	1863	Action at Wapping Heights, Manassas Gap, VA, as Maj. Gen. William H. French, USA, and the 3rd US Army Corps are repulsed by Lieut. Gen. Richard S. Ewell, CSA.
07	24	1863	Action with the **Sioux Indians,** at the Big Mound, the Dakota Territory.
07	24	1863	Skirmish in Dade County, MO, with guerrillas.
07	24	1863	Skirmish with Indians at Cook's Canon, the New Mexico Territory.
07	24	1863	Skirmish at Athens, OH, with Brig. Gen. John H. Morgan, CSA.
07	24	1863	Skirmish at Washington, OH, again reduces the manpower of Brig. Gen. John Hunt Morgan, CSA.
07	24	1863	Skirmish at Battle Mountain, near Newby's Cross-Roads, VA, as Lieut. Gen. James Longstreet arrives at Culpeper Court-House.
07	25	1863	Skirmish at Brownsville, AR.
07	25	1863	Skirmish near New Hope Station, KY, dispersing the Rebels.
07	25	1863	**Col. John S. Scott's Confederate Raid into Eastern Kentucky.** 7/25-8/6/1863.
07	25	1863	Skirmish at Williamsburg, KY, with Col. John S. Scott, CSA.
07	25	1863	Federal expedition from New Berne to Winton, aboard the steamers, **Colonel Rucker** and **Utica,** and skirmish at Potecasi Creek, NC, with destruction of Confederate cotton, supplies, and capture of prisoners. 7/25-31/1863.
07	25	1863	Skirmishes near Steubenville and Springfield, OH, with Brig. Gen. John Hunt Morgan, CSA.
07	25	1863	The Confederate Dept. of East Tennessee is merged into the Dept. of Tennessee, under the command of Gen. Braxton Bragg.
07	25	1863	Skirmish at Barbee's Cross-Roads, VA.
07	25	1863	Federal scout to Goose Creek, VA, who were sent to recapture horses and cattle stolen by the Rebels and being hidden on Lowe's Island, on the Upper Potomac. Federals run into parties of Maj. John S. Mosby's Cavalry twice. Besides, the river was swollen. The Federals call it off. 7/25-27/1863.
07	25	1863	Federal expedition to Gloucester Court-House, VA, and capture of supplies including the Rebel mail carrier with his mail just from Richmond.
07	25	1863	Federal expedition from Portsmouth, VA, to Jackson, NC, and skirmish with loss of life; Brig. Gen. Matt Whitaker, CSA, defending. 7/25-8/3/1863.
07	26	1863	Action at Dead Buffalo Lake with the **Sioux Indians,** the Dakota Territory.
07	26	1863	Skirmish at London, KY, with Scott's Confederate Raiders.
07	26	1863	Federal expedition from Natchez, MS, to Kingston, Liberty, and Woodville, burning a large cotton factory at the latter. 7/26-30/1863.
07	26	1863	Federal expedition from Plymouth to Foster's Mills, NC. 7/26-29/1863.
07	26	1863	Skirmish at Salineville, OH, where the remnants of Brig. Gen. John Hunt Morgan's CSA command surrenders near New Lisbon, or Salineville, OH, near the Pennsylvania border, where they are ordered to the Ohio State Penitentiary at Columbus, OH.
07	27	1863	Confederate attack on the steamer, **Paint Rock,** near Bridgeport, AL.
07	27	1863	Skirmish near Rogersville, KY, with Col. John S. Scott, CSA.
07	27	1863	Skirmish at the mouth of Bayou Teche, LA.
07	27	1863	Affair near Cassville, MO.
07	28	1863	**James Deshler,** CSA, is appointed Brig. Gen.

07	28	1863	**Otho French Strahl,** CSA, is appointed Brig. Gen.
07	28	1863	Action at Stony Lake, with the **Sioux Indians,** the Dakota Territory.
07	28	1863	Action at Richmond, KY, with Scott's Confederate Raiders.
07	28	1863	Skirmish at Marshall and High Grove, MO.
07	28	1863	Federal scout from Newtonia to Oliver's Prairie. 7/28-29/863.
07	28	1863	Maj. John S. Mosby's Confederate operations about Fairfax Court-House, as he captures a number of sutlers and their teams, and skirmish near Aldie, VA, as the Federals follow and are able to recapture all the wagons except 3, which Mosby burned. Mosby keeps his prisoners, though. 7/28-8/3/1863.
07	28	1863	Skirmish at Fayetteville, WV.
07	29	1863	**Brig. Gen. Edward Needles Kirk, USA,** dies at Sterling, IL, from his battle wounds received December 31, 1862, at the Battle of Murfreesboro, TN, lingering on until today.
07	29	1863	Skirmish near, and the Federal **occupation of, Bridgeport, AL.**
07	29	1863	Skirmishes at the Missouri River, with the **Sioux Indians,** the Dakota Territory. 7/29-30/1863.
07	29	1863	Skirmish at Paris, KY, with Scott's Confederate Raiders.
07	29	1863	Skirmish near Winchester, KY, with Scott's Confederate Raiders.
07	29	1863	Skirmish with Indians at Conchas Springs, the New Mexico Territory.
07	29	1863	Skirmish near Fort Donelson, TN.
07	29	1863	Brig. Gen. Innis N. Palmer, USA, assumes the command of the 18th US Army Corps, the Dept. of Virginia and North Carolina.
07	30	1863	**Maj. Gen. George Crockett Strong, USA,** dies in New York City, NY, from lockjaw, which developed from his battle wound received July 18, 1863, while leading the Union assault on Battery (Fort) Wagner, SC.
07	30	1863	Skirmish near Elm Springs, AR.
07	30	1863	A peace treaty is signed with bands of the **Shoshone Indians** at Fort Boise, in the Snake River Country, the Idaho Territory.
07	30	1863	Skirmish at Irvine, KY, as Col. John S. Scott's Confederate Raid into Eastern Kentucky continues.
07	30	1863	Skirmish near Lexington, MO.
07	30	1863	Skirmish at Marshall, MO.
07	30	1863	Confederate expedition to Barnwell's Island, SC, where they capture 31 Negroes, of whom 3 are men; the rest are women and children.
07	30	1863	Skirmish at Grand Junction, TN.
07	31	1863	Skirmish at Lancaster, KY, with Col. John S. Scott's Confederate Raiders.
07	31	1863	Skirmish at Paint Lick Bridge, KY, with Col. John S. Scott, CSA.
07	31	1863	Skirmish at Stanford, KY, with Col. John S. Scott, CSA.
07	31	1863	Skirmish at Saint Catharine's Creek, near Natchez, MS, with 1,500 Union mounted men of Maj. Gen. John A. Logan's command.
07	31	1863	Skirmishes at Kelly's Ford, VA. 7/31-8/1/1863.
07	31	1863	Skirmish at Morris' Mills, WV.
08	1	1863	**James Lawlor Kiernan,** USA, is appointed Brig. Gen.
08	1	1863	**The advance of the Union forces upon Little Rock, AR, and etc.** 8/1-9/14/1863.
08	1	1863	Brig. Gen. John Wynn Davidson's, USA, Cavalry Division moves from Wittsburg to Clarendon, AR. 8/1-8/1863.
08	1	1863	Federal expedition from Columbus to Hickman, KY.
08	1	1863	Skirmish at Smith's Shoals, Cumberland River, KY, as Col. John S. Scott, CSA, crosses back into Tennessee after capturing weapons, supplies, and destroying bridges. This ends his raid into Eastern Kentucky.
08	1	1863	Skirmish at Taylor's Farm, on the Little Blue River, MO.
08	1	1863	Affair at Round Ponds, near the Castor River, MO, with Union men killed in their sleep and their wagon train burned; and horses stolen by guerrillas. The men slept too close to the swamp with cover so dense that there was no time for the alarm to be made.
08	1	1863	Action at Brandy Station, VA, between Cavalry outfits.
08	1	1863	Federal expedition from Warrenton Junction toward the Blue Ridge Mountains, VA, with the capture of some of Maj. John S. Mosby's, CSA, men. 8/1-8/1863.
08	1	1863	**The 4th and 7th US Army Corps are discontinued.**
08	2	1863	Confederate scout from Pocahontas, AR, to Patterson, MO.

08	2	1863	Skirmish at Stumptown, MO, with bushwackers.
08	2	1863	The Federal attack on the CSA steamer, **Chesterfield,** at Cummings' Point, SC, during the operations on Morris Island.
08	2	1863	Skirmish at Newtown, VA.

| 08 | 3 | 1863 | The following are appointed Confederate Major Generals: |

Wade Hampton, C.S.A.
Fitzhugh Lee, C.S.A.
Stephen Dill Lee, C.S.A.
Cadmus Marcellus Wilcox, C.S.A.

08	3	1863	**Philip Dale Roddey,** CSA, is appointed Brig. Gen.
08	3	1863	Skirmish at Jackson, LA, as Union parties out collecting Negroes for the Black Union infantry are attacked, with casualties.
08	3	1863	The 9th US Army Corps re-embarks at Haynes' Bluff, near Vicksburg, MS, for service in Kentucky, etc., with the 1st Division arriving at Cincinnati, OH, on August 12, and the 2nd on August 20th. 8/3-8/1863.
08	3	1863	Skirmish at Ripley, MS.
08	3	1863	Federal scout from Fort Pillow, and Union City, TN, and skirmish near Denmark, TN, with a party of guerrillas.

| 08 | 4 | 1863 | The following are appointed Union Brigadier Generals: |

Jasper Adalmorn Maltby, USA
Samuel Allen Rice, USA
John Benjamin Sanborn, USA
Giles Alexander Smith, USA
Charles Robert Woods, USA

08	4	1863	Affair at the mouth of Vincent's Creek, SC, as Confederates are transported to skirmish with the Federals, capturing several and killing others.
08	4	1863	Federal reconnaissance to Rock Island Ferry, TN. 8/4-5/1863.
08	4	1863	Skirmish at Amissville, VA.
08	4	1863	Skirmish at Brandy Station, VA, with Brig. Gen. John Buford, USA, commanding the 1st Cavalry Division, the 1st US Army Corps.
08	4	1863	Federal expedition to Fairfax Court-House, VA.
08	4	1863	Federal army and naval reconnaissance on the James River, VA, to about 14 miles below Fort Darling, when the gunboat **Barney** strikes a torpedo and is forced to retire. The ironclad, **Sangamon,** and the tug, **Chassett** also assisted. **(6th)** 8/4-7/1863.
08	4	1863	Skirmish at Burlington, WV.

08	5	1863	Maj. Gen. Frederick Steele, USA, assumes command of the Federal forces at Helena, AR.
08	5	1863	Skirmish at Mount Pleasant, MS.
08	5	1863	Federal expedition from Kempsville, VA, into Currituck and Camden Counties, NC, with some Rebel prisoners. 8/5-12/1863.
08	5	1863	Engagement at Dutch Gap, James River, VA, with the US ironclads, **USS Cohassett,** and with the **USS Commodore Barney,** sustaining damages from the explosion of a Confederate electronic torpedo.
08	5	1863	Skirmish at Little Washington, VA.
08	5	1863	Skirmish near Rixeyville Ford, near Culpeper, VA.
08	5	1863	Skirmish at Muddy Run, VA, toward Culpeper, as the Union Cavalry under Brig. Gen. David McM. Gregg, USA, find a considerable force of the enemy.
08	5	1863	**Brig. Gen. William Wood Averell's, USA, raid into West Virginia.** 8/5-31/1863.
08	5	1863	Brig. Gen. William Averell's, USA, expedition sets out from Winchester, VA, into West Virginia.
08	5	1863	Skirmish at Cold Spring Gap, WV, with Brig. Gen. William W. Averell, USA.

08	6	1863	The Union vessel, the **Sea Bride,** is captured in the Atlantic Ocean, near Cape of Good Hope, by the Confederate raider, the **CSS Alabama.**
08	6	1863	Federal scout from Greenfield to Golden Grove and Carthage, MO. 8/6-9/1863.
08	6	1863	Federal scout from Spring River Mills, MO, and skirmishes. 8/6-11/1863.
08	6	1863	Federal scout from Lexington to the vicinity of Hopewell, MO. 8/6-9/1863 .
08	6	1863	Skirmish at Cacapon Mountain, WV, with Brig. Gen. William W. Averell, USA.
08	6	1863	Skirmish at Moorefield, WV.

08	6	1863	The capture and recapture of sutlers' wagons near Fairfax Court-House, VA, by Col. John Mosby, CSA.
08	7	1863	The 13th US Army Corps is assigned (from the Dept. of the Tennessee) to the Dept. of the Gulf, LA, with Maj. Gen. Cadwallader C. Washburn, USA, temporarily in command of the 13th US Army Corps, LA, etal.
08	7	1863	Skirmish near New Madrid, MO.
08	7	1863	Affair at Burke's Station, VA, as the Confederates attack the Union wood cutters along the railroad. The Rebels are beaten off.
08	8	1863	Skirmish at Rienzi, MS.
08	8	1863	Affair on Clear Creek, near Ball Town, MO.
08	8	1863	Skirmish at Waterford, VA, as the Rebels attack the Federal Cavalry not far from Harper's Ferry, WV.
08	8	1863	Gen. Robert E. Lee, CSA, depressed over the results at Gettysburg, PA, offers his resignation to President Jefferson Davis, who flatly rejects such notion.
08	9	1863	**Eppa Hunton,** CSA, is appointed Brig. Gen.
08	9	1863	Skirmish at Garden Hollow, near Pineville, MO.
08	9	1863	Federal scout from Cape Girardeau to the Ash Hills and Poplar Bluff, MO, and skirmish (**13th**) at the Ash Hills.
08	9	1863	Skirmish at Sparta, TN.
08	9	1863	Skirmish at Brandy Station, VA.
08	9	1863	Skirmish near Welford's Ford, VA, opposite Beverly Ford, where a Union party crosses and is almost immediately sent fleeing back across the river.
08	10	1863	**Thomas Pleasant Dockery,** CSA, is appointed Brig. Gen.
08	10	1863	Maj. Gen. Frederick Steele's, USA, column advances from Helena, AR, toward Little Rock.
08	10	1863	Skirmish at Bayou Tensas, LA.
08	10	1863	Federal expeditions from Big Black River, MS, and La Grange, TN, to Grenada, MS. 8/10-23/1863.
08	10	1863	Skirmish at Dayton, MO, with Rebel bushwackers.
08	10	1863	Mutiny at Galveston, TX, by Confederates over lack of adequate food supplies. 8/10-13/1863.
08	10	1863	The 13th US Army Corps, under Maj. Gen. Edward O. C. Ord, USA, is transferred from Vicksburg and Natchez, MS, to Carrollton, LA. 8/10-26/1863.
08	10	1863	Skirmish at Bayou Tensas, LA.
08	10	1863	Bvt. Brig. Gen. William W. Morris, USA, is temporarily in command of the Middle Dept. and the 8th US Army Corps, VA.
08	10	1863	Federal raid on the **Mississippi Central Railroad** from Big Black River, MS, to Memphis, TN, with skirmishes at: a) Payne's Plantation, near Grenada, MS. (**18th**); b) at Panola, MS. (**20th**), and c) at the Coldwater, MS. (**21st**).
08	11	1863	The following are appointed Union Brigadier Generals: **Robert Alexander Cameron,** USA **Alexander Chambers,** USA **John Murray Corse,** USA **Manning Ferguson Force,** USA **Walter Quintin Gresham,** USA **John Aaron Rawlins,** USA **Thomas Kilby Smith,** USA
08	11	1863	Confederate batteries at Battery Wagner, Fort Sumter, and on James Island, near Charleston, SC, open fire on the Union trenches on Morris Island, SC.
08	11	1863	The capture of a 19 wagon Union wagon train near Annandale, Fairfax County, VA, by Maj. John S. Mosby, CSA. Mosby continues to help supply Gen. Robert E. Lee's army.
08	11	1863	Federal expedition from Portsmouth, VA, to Edenton, NC, and skirmishes with loss of life. 8/11-19/1863.
08	12	1863	**William Smith,** C.S.A., is appointed Maj. Gen.
08	12	1863	**Benjamin Grubb Humphreys,** CSA, is appointed Brig. Gen.
08	12	1863	The 1st Division, 9th US Army Corps, arrives from Vicksburg, MS, at Covington, KY, en route to Tennessee.
08	12	1863	Skirmish at Big Black River Bridge, MS.

| 08 | 12 | 1863 | Union heavy Parrott batteries on Morris Island, SC, return fire against Fort Sumter and Battery Wagner, Charleston Harbor, SC. |

08   12   1863   Federal expedition from Memphis, TN, to Grenada, MS, with skirmishes at:
a) Craven's Plantation, MS, (**14th**), and at
b) Grenada, MS. (**17th**).

08   13   1863   Federal expedition up the White and Little Red Rivers, AR, including:
a) engagement at West Point (**14th**) and
b) skirmish at Harrison's Landing, AR, (**16th**) with the aid of the US gunboats, **USS Cricket, USS Lexington,** and the **USS Mariner,** as the Federals advance on Little Rock. 8/13-16/1863.

08   13   1863   Federal expedition against Indians, the Dakota Territory. 8/13-9/11/1863.

08   13   1863   Skirmish at Jacinto, MS.

08   13   1863   Skirmish at Pineville, MO.

08   14   1863   **Brig. Gen. Thomas Welsh, USA,** dies in Cincinnati, OH, from camp fever, (malaria) contracted during the Vicksburg, MS campaign, June, 1863.

08   14   1863   Skirmish at West Point, AR.

08   14   1863   Skirmish near Jack's Fork, MO.

08   14   1863   Skirmish near Wellington, MO, with bushwackers.

08   14   1863   Federal siege of Washington, NC.

08   14   1863   Federal scout in the Bull Run Mountains near Aldie and the village of Landmark, VA, returning by way of Hopewell Gap.

08   14   1863   The Confederate Cavalry capture of the Vine-Tree Signal Station, VA, with all the Union men and horses except for the officer in charge.

08   14   1863   Federal scout to Winchester, VA, to ascertain the movements of the Rebels and retrieve large quantities of supplies and telegraph wire collected by Gen. Robert E. Lee's Army, but who left it behind in their hurried exit from Winchester.

08   14   1863   Maj. Gen. John J. Peck, USA, assumes the command of the 11th US Army Corps, the Army of the Potomac, VA.

08   15   1863   Skirmish at Bentonville, AR.

08   15   1863   Skirmish at Beverly Ford, VA.

08   15   1863   Federal scout from Centreville to Aldie, VA, looking for Gen. John Mosby, CSA, and his partisan rangers, and returning with some Confederate prisoners. 8/15-19/1863.

08   15   1863   Skirmish at Hartwood Church, VA.

08   16   1863   Skirmish near Corinth, MS.

08   16   1863   **The Chickamauga, GA, Campaign.** 8/16-9/22/1863.

08   16   1863   The general advance of the Army of the Cumberland, Maj. Gen. William S. Rosecrans, USA, commanding, from Tullahoma toward the Tennessee River and Chattanooga, TN, in search of Gen. Braxton Bragg's Confederate Army of Tennessee, the Chickamauga, GA, Campaign. 8/16-17/1863.

08   16   1863   **The East Tennessee Campaign.** 8/16-10/19/1863.

08   16   1863   The general advance of the Dept. of the Ohio, Maj. Gen. Ambrose E. Burnside, USA, commanding, from Camp Nelson, near Lexington, KY, toward the Tennessee River and east Tennessee.

08   16   1863   Federal expedition from Memphis, TN to Hernando, MS, with skirmish (**17th**) near Panola, MS. 8/16-20/1863.

08   16   1863   Skirmish at Falls Church, VA.

08   16   1863   Maj. Gen. Gouverneur K. Warren, USA, supersedes Brig. Gen. William Hays, USA, in the command of the 2nd US Army Corps, the Army of the Potomac, VA.

08   17   1863   **Alvan Cullem Gillem,**   USA, is appointed Brig. Gen.

08   17   1863   **James Clay Rice,**   USA, is appointed Brig. Gen.

08   17   1863   Skirmish at Grand Prairie, AR.

08   17   1863   Federal expedition from Cape Girardeau and Pilot Knob, MO, to Pocahontas, AR. 8/17-26/1863.

08   17   1863   **The Bombardment of Fort Sumter, SC.** 8/17-12/31/1863.

08   17   1863   Fire is opened upon Fort Sumter and Battery Wagner from Federal batteries on Morris Island, and from Union gunboats, Charleston Harbor, SC.

08   17   1863   Skirmish at Calfkiller Creek, near Sparta, TN, with the advance of the Union Army, the Chickamauga Campaign.

08	18	1863	**Henry Brevard Davidson,** CSA, is appointed Brig. Gen.
08	18	1863	Skirmish near Albany, KY.
08	18	1863	Skirmish near Crab Orchard, KY.
08	18	1863	Skirmish with Indians at Pueblo Colorado, the New Mexico Territory.
08	18	1863	Skirmish near Pasquotank, NC.
08	18	1863	Skirmish at Bristoe Station, VA.
08	18	1863	President Abraham Lincoln test fires the new Spencer Repeating Carbine in the park, Washington, DC.
08	19	1863	**Henry Watkins Allen,** CSA, is appointed Brig. Gen.
08	19	1863	The capture of the Confederate signal station at Saint John's Mill, near Jacksonville, FL, by crew members of the **USS Hale** and the **USS Norwich.**
08	19	1863	Skirmish at Weems' Springs, TN.
08	19	1863	The destruction of Confederate saltpeter-works near Franklin, WV, by Brig. Gen. William Woods Averell, USA.
08	20	1863	**Cullen Andrews Battle,** CSA, is appointed Brig. Gen.
08	20	1863	**William Clarke Quantrill's Raid into Kansas, and the pursuit by the Union forces.** 8/20-28/1863.
08	20	1863	Maj. Gen. William B. Franklin, USA, assumes the command of the 29th US Army Corps, LA.
08	20	1863	The 2nd Division, 9th US Army Corps, arrives from Vicksburg, MS, at Covington, KY, en route for East Tennessee.
08	20	1863	Federal expedition aboard transports, from Vicksburg, MS, to Monroe, LA, including skirmishes **(24th)** at Bayou Macon and at Floyd. 8/20-9/2/1863.
08	20	1863	Operations against the **Navajo Indians** in the New Mexico Territory by Col. Kit Carson, USA, as Carson burns wheat fields, the **Ute Indians** kill some **Navajoes,** the **Zuni Indians** capture **Navajo** horses, etc, Carson's men shoot some **Navajoes** who are fighting with bows and arrows; **Mescalero Apache Indians** from the reservation at Fort Sumner assist the Federals, etc. 8/20-12/16/1863.
08	20	1863	The Confederates' unsuccessful attempt to destroy the US Steamer, the **USS New Ironsides,** off Charleston Harbor, SC, with a torpedo ship, as the Federals continue to bombard Fort Sumter for the 4th straight day. 8/20-21/1863.
08	20	1863	The District of Utah is declared to include the Territory of Utah, Camp Ruby, the Nevada Territory, and the new post at Soda Springs, the Idaho Territory.
08	21	1863	Skirmish at Maysville, AL, the Chickamauga Campaign.
08	21	1863	**The senseless massacre at Lawrence, KS,** by the Confederate irregular guerrilla raiders under William Clarke Quantrill, **murdering over 150 citizens;** this action is disavowed by the regular Confederate command.
08	21	1863	Skirmish near Brooklyn, KS, with Quantrill's guerrillas.
08	21	1863	Skirmish near Paola, KS, with Quantrill's guerrillas.
08	21	1863	Brig. Gen. Robert B. Potter, USA, assumes the command of the 9th US Army Corps, KY, etal.
08	21	1863	Skirmish at Coldwater, MS.
08	21	1863	**The Bombardment of Charleston, SC,** begins tonight by Brig. Gen. Quincy Adams Gillmore, USA, because Fort Sumter refuses to surrender. Gillmore is firing the **Swamp Angel,** a huge battery that fires 200 lb shells. 8/21-12/31/1863.
08	21	1863	The bombardment of Chattanooga, TN, by Maj. Gen. Williams S. Rosecrans, USA, the Chickamauga Campaign.
08	21	1863	Action at Shellmound, TN, the Chickamauga Campaign.
08	21	1863	Maj. Gen. John G. Foster, USA, resumes the command of the 18th US Army Corps, TN.
08	21	1863	Skirmish near Glenville, WV, with Confederate guerrillas.
08	22	1863	Affair at San Pedro Crossing, the Arizona Territory, with Indians armed with bows and arrows who dash through the station on horses and steal a couple Federal horses and a mule.
08	22	1863	Federal expedition from Fort Lapwai, the Idaho Territory, to the Meadows, in search of hostile **Snake Indians,** only to find some peaceful **Nez Perce Indians,** and the remains of a settler supposedly killed by Indians a month or two earlier. 8/22-9/20/1863.
08	22	1863	Skirmish on Big Creek, near Pleasant Hill, MO, with the retreating William Clarke Quantrill.
08	22	1863	The Federal battery, **Swamp Angel,** blows up while firing off rounds, during the bombardment of Fort Sumter, Charleston, SC.
08	22	1863	Federal expedition from Tracy City, TN, to the Tennessee River, by Maj. Gen. William S. Rosecrans, USA, the Chickamauga Campaign. 8/22-24/1863.

| 08 | 22 | 1863 | Skirmish at Stafford Court-House, VA. |
| 08 | 22 | 1863 | Skirmish at Huntersville, WV, with Brig. Gen. William W. Averell, USA, and his Union Cavalry. |

08 23 1863 Skirmish at Fayetteville, AR.

08 23 1863 Federal scout on Bennett's Bayou, MO, and skirmish.

08 23 1863 The Confederate capture of the US gunboats, **Satellite,** and the **Reliance,** on the Rappahannock River, VA, by Lieut. John Taylor Wood, CSN, who retreats with his prizes to Urbanna, VA.

08 23 1863 The capture and destruction of the English blockade-runner, **Hebe,** off Wilmington, NC, by the US Naval Blockade fleet.

08 24 1863 Skirmish at Gunter's Landing, near Port Deposit, AI, the Chickamauga Campaign.

08 24 1863 Federal scout to Barbee's Cross-Roads, VA, who learn that a company of the 6th VA Confederate Cavalry was recruited around Salem, and had a habit of coming down to the farms and assisting the farmers in the gathering of their crops. Judging from the scarcity of men on the farms and the amount of hay that is cut, indicates this must be the case.

08 24 1863 Skirmish at Coyle's Tavern, near Fairfax Court-House, VA.

08 24 1863 Skirmish near King George Court-House, VA, and Port Conway, with Union Cavalry under Brig. Gen. Judson Kilpatrick, USA.

08 24 1863 **Maj. John Mosby's Confederate Operations in Virginia,** including the attacking of the Union outpost near Waterloo, the burning of bridges, capturing prisoners, horses, mules, and sutler's goods near Warrenton Junction, Alexandria, etc. 8/24-9/30/1863.

08 24 1863 Skirmish near Warm Springs, VA, with Brig. Gen. William W. Averell, USA.

08 25 1863 **Jeremy Francis Gilmer,**   CSA, is appointed Brig. Gen.

08 25 1863 **William Andrew Quarles,**   CSA, is appointed Brig. Gen.

08 25 1863 Skirmish at Brownsville, AR.

08 25 1863 Because of the William C. Quantrill massacre at Lawrence, KS, Brig. Gen. Thomas Ewing, USA, at Kansas City, KS, orders all residents of Bates, Cass and Jackson counties, KS, to leave, allowing citizens loyal to the Union to remain at military posts. Great resentment that will last for years is generated by the estimated 20,000 people forced to evacuate their homes.

08 25 1863 Skirmishes near Hopewell, MO, with William C. Quantrill. 8/25-26/1863.

08 25 1863 Skirmish near Independence, MO.

08 25 1863 Federal scout from Sedalia, and skirmish (**26th**) at Clear Fork, MO. 8/25-28/1863.

08 25 1863 Skirmish near Waynesville, MO.

08 25 1863 The Union assault and failure on the Confederate rifle-pits, Battery Wagner on Morris Island, SC.

08 25 1863 Skirmish at Hartwood Church, Rappahannock River, VA.

08 25 1863 Skirmish near Lamb's Ferry, Chickahominy River, VA, as the landing party from a Union gunboat is driven back, by Brig. Gen. Henry A. Wise, CSA, commanding.

08 25 1863 Federal reconnaissance to Covington and the destruction of the saltpeter-works on Jackson's River, WV, by Brig. Gen. William W. Averell, USA.

08 26 1863 **Brig. Gen. John Buchanan Floyd, CSA,** dies near Abingdon, VA, due to his declining health.

08 26 1863 Skirmish near Bayou Meto, AR.

08 26 1863 Skirmish at Perryville, the Indian Territory, as Maj. Gen. James G. Blunt, USA, moves against Brig. Gen. William Steele, CSA, and Col. Stand Watie, CSA.

08 26 1863 The 2nd assault and successful capture of the Confederate rifle-pits, outside Battery Wagner on Morris Island, SC.

08 26 1863 Skirmishes at Harrison's Landing, TN, the Chickamauga Campaign. 8/26-27/1863.

08 26 1863 Federal expedition from **Williamsburg** to Bottom's Bridge, VA, and skirmishes with loss of life. 8/26-29/1863.

08 26 1863 Engagement at Rocky Gap, near White Sulphur Springs, WV, with Brig. Gen. William W. Averell, USA, Cavalry. 8/26-27/1863.

08 26 1863 Skirmishes during Brig. Gen. William Woods Averell's, USA, Cavalry raid into West Virginia and skirmishes:
a) near Moorefield (26th)
b) near Sutton (26th),
c) on Elk Run (**27th**), and
d) near Glenville (**27th**), WV. 8/26-28/1863.

08	27	1863	Affair at Fort Bowie, the Arizona Territory, as Indians on horseback on the road from Tucson, surround and run off with the entire stock of Union horses.
08	27	1863	Action at Bayou Meto, or Reed's Bridge, AR.
08	27	1863	Skirmish in Carter County, KY.
08	27	1863	Skirmish at Clark's Neck, Lawrence County, KY.
08	27	1863	Skirmish at Mount Pleasant, MS.
08	27	1863	Skirmish near Vicksburg, MS.
08	27	1863	Skirmish at the Narrows, near Shellmound, TN, the Chickamauga Campaign. 8/27-28/1863.
08	27	1863	Cavalry operations in Virginia, with Maj. Gen. JEB Stuart, CSA. 8/27-9/2/1863.
08	27	1863	Skirmish at Edwards Ferry, MD, with Maj. Gen. JEB Stuart, CSA.
08	27	1863	Skirmish at Little Washington, VA.
08	27	1863	Skirmish at Weaverville, VA.
08	27	1863	Skirmish at Ball's Mill, WV.
08	27	1863	Brig. Gen. William W. Averell's US Cavalry command retreats to Beverly, WV, effectively ending his raid in West Virginia. 8/27-31/1863.
08	28	1863	Federal reconnaissance from Stevenson, AL, to Trenton, GA, the Chickamauga Campaign. 8/28-31/1863.
08	28	1863	Federal expedition from Lexington, MO, into La Fayette, Johnson, Cass, and Henry Counties, MO.
08	28	1863	Skirmish at Jacksborough, TN.
08	28	1863	Skirmish at Hartwood Church, VA, with Maj. Gen. JEB Stuart, CSA.
08	29	1863	**Goode Bryan,** CSA, is appointed Brig. Gen.
08	29	1863	**William Whedbee Kirkland,** CSA, is appointed Brig. Gen.
08	29	1863	Skirmish at Caperton's Ferry, Tennessee River, AL, the Chickamauga Campaign.
08	29	1863	Union mutiny at Camp Hubbard, Thibodeaux, LA, where the two Union Private ringleaders are court martialed and shot to death in front of the entire command there. 8/29-30/1863.
08	29	1863	Skirmish at Texas Prairie, MO, with a gang of bushwackers.
08	29	1863	Five Confederate seamen drown during the initial trial run of the experimental submarine, **H.L. Hunley,** Charleston Harbor, Charleston, SC.
08	30	1863	Skirmish at Shallow Ford, Bayou Meto, AR.
08	30	1863	Due to the constant Union bombardment of Fort Sumter, the Confederates dig batteries out from under the rubble and start transferring them to Charleston, SC.
08	30	1863	Federal reconnaissance from Shellmound toward Chattanooga, TN, the Chickamauga Campaign. 8/30-31/1863.
08	30	1863	Federal expeditions to Leesburg, VA, as they root out a few Confederate stragglers from local farmhouses. 8/30-9/2/1863.
08	31	1863	Skirmish in Will's Valley, AL, the Chickamauga Campaign.
08	31	1863	Action on the Marais des Cygnes, KS.
08	31	1863	The Confederate transport, **Sumter,** is sunk by the Union batteries on Sullivan's Island, SC.
08	31	1863	Skirmish at Winter's Gap, TN.
08	31	1863	Maj. Gen. Robert C. Schenck, USA, resumes the command of the Middle Dept. and the 8th US Army Corps, VA.
08	31	1863	Brig. Gen. Alpheus S. Williams, USA, is temporarily in command of the 12th US Army Corps, the Army of the Potomac.
09	1	1863	The following are appointed Confederate Brigadier Generals: **Matthew Calbraith Butler,** CSA **Robert Daniel Johnston,** CSA **William Carter Wickham,** CSA,
09	1	1863	Skirmishes at Will's Creek and at Davis', Tap's, and Neal's Gaps, or Devil's Backbone, AL, the Chickamauga Campaign.
09	1	1863	Skirmishes at Devil's Backbone or Backbone Mountain, and at Jenny Lind, AR, as Maj. Gen. James G. Blunt's, USA, advance guard is ambushed on his return from pursuing Brig. Gen. William Steele, CSA, with loss of life.
09	1	1863	**Fort Smith, AR,** since **evacuated** by Brig. Gen. William L. Cabell, CSA, is now **occupied** by Maj. Gen. Frederick Steele, USA, and his Federal forces.
09	1	1863	Federal expeditions from Paducah, KY, and Union City, TN, to Conyersville, TN, and skirmish, **(5th)**. 9/1-10/1863.

MONTH	DAY	YEAR	ACT
09	1	1863	Federal expedition from Natchez, MS, to Harrisonburg, LA, including skirmishes: a) at Trinity (**2nd**) and b) near Harrisonburg, (**4th**) and the **capture of Fort Beauregard.** 9/1-7/1863.
09	1	1863	Maj. Gen. William S. Rosecrans, USA, and the Army of the Cumberland, crosses the Tennessee River, heading for Chattanooga, TN, and Gen. Braxton Bragg, CSA, and the Confederate Army of Tennessee.
09	1	1863	Skirmish at Barbee's Cross-Roads, VA, with Maj. Gen. JEB Stuart, CSA.
09	1	1863	Skirmish at Corbin's Cross-Roads, VA.
09	1	1863	Skirmish at Lamb's Creek Church, near Port Conway, VA.
09	1	1863	Skirmish at Leesburg, VA.
09	2	1863	Skirmish near Shallow Ford, Bayou Meto, AR.
09	2	1863	Confederate affair with, and the rout of, **Zapata's banditti,** near Mier, Mexico.
09	2	1863	**Knoxville, TN, is occupied** by the Maj. Gen. Ambrose E. Burnside, USA, effectively cutting the direct Confederate railway between Chattanooga and Virginia.
09	2	1863	Skirmish near Oak Shade, VA, near to Utz's Ford, Stark's Ford, Rixeyville Ford, and Corbin's Cross-Roads.
09	2	1863	The federal expedition against and the destruction of the captured Union gunboats, **Satellite,** and the **Reliance** at Port Conway, VA, by Brig. Gen. Judson Kilpatrick's, USA, cavalry.
09	2	1863	Affair near Rixey's Ford, VA, with Maj. Gen. JEB Stuart, CSA.
09	2	1863	Federal Cavalry expeditions from Martinsburg, WV, including affairs (**15th and l9th**) at Smithfield, WV, and at Strasburg, VA, with the capture of Confederate supplies, stragglers, etc. 9/2-23/1863.
09	3	1863	**Operations in the Humboldt Military District, CA,** against Indians. 9/3-12/31/1863.
09	3	1863	Skirmish with Indians in the Hoopa Valley, CA, as the mail carrier and escort, including some Chinamen, are captured, killed and mutilated by Indians.
09	3	1863	Action with Indians near White Stone Hill, the Dakota Territory.
09	3	1863	Skirmish near Alpine, GA, with Maj. Gen. William Rosecrans, the Chickamauga Campaign.
09	4	1863	Federal scout from Fort Lyon, the Colorado Territory, toward Fort Larned, KS.
09	4	1863	Affair at Quincy, MO, as a band of guerrillas dash into town firing their weapons which wounds and kill a few men. They also took 3 or 4 men of the 18th Iowa. The next morning reveals the guerillas killed the Iowa boys.
09	4	1863	Federal scout from Cold Water Grove, to Pleaseant Hill and Big Creek, MO, and skirmishes, where the Federals ambush and kill some 6 bushwackers.
09	4	1863	Federal boat expeditions against Battery Gregg, Morris, Island, SC. 9/4-6/1863.
09	4	1863	**The Sabine Pass (Texas) Expedition,** sets out from New Orleans, LA, under Maj. Gen. Nathaniel P. Banks, USA, with the assistance of the US gunboats, **USS Arizona, Clifton, Granite City,** and the **Sachem.** 9/4-11/1863.
09	4	1863	The Confederate's unsuccessful attempt by men under Maj. Gen. JEB Stuart, CSA, to capture Brig. Gen. Joseph J. Bartlett, USA, near New Baltimore, VA.
09	4	1863	Skirmish at Moorefield, WV.
09	4	1863	Skirmish at Petersburg Gap, WV, with Federals marching from Petersburg, WV.
09	5	1863	Skirmish at Lebanon, AL, as Maj. Gen. William S. Rosecrans, USA, and the Army of the Cumberland moves toward Braxton Bragg, CSA, and the Confederate Army of the Tennessee, the Chickamauga Campaign.
09	5	1863	The destruction of Confederate salt-works at Rawlingsville, AL, the Chickamauga Campaign.
09	5	1863	Federal reconnaissance from Winston's Gap into Broomtown Valley, AL, the Chickamauga Campaign.
09	5	1863	Skirmish near Maysville, AR, when a third of the Union escort are reported being drunk and loud mouthed, and run into some of William Quantrill's guerrillas. Big mistake on their part.
09	5	1863	Skirmish with Indians near White Stone Hill, the Dakota Territory, as the Union party looking for missing men from the action at White Stone Hill the other day, are attacked by 300 Indians.
09	5	1863	The English Government seizes the two newly built ironclads ordered by the Confederacy in the Liverpool shipyards which halts the growth of the Confederate navy, and leaves the **CSS Alabama** as the lone Confederate raider on the high seas.
09	5	1863	Skirmish near Alpine, GA, the Chickamauga Campaign.
09	5	1863	Skirmish at Tazewell, TN, as Maj. Gen. Ambrose E. Burnside, USA, moves from Knoxville, to assist Maj. Gen. William S. Rosecrans, USA, against Braxton Bragg, CSA.
09	6	1863	**Brig. Gen. Lucius Marshall Walker, CSA,** is mortally wounded in a pistol duel with Maj. Gen. John

			Sappingon Marmaduke, CSA, in a general disagreement over military affairs, dying the next day.
09	6	1863	Skirmish at Stevens' Gap, GA, with Maj. Gen. William S. Rosecrans, USA, the Chickamauga Campaign.
09	6	1863	Skirmishes at Summerville, GA, the Chickamauga Campaign. 9/6-7/1863.
09	6	1863	Guerrilla attack on the supply wagon train between Fort Scott, KS, and Carthage, MO, with the Federals recapturing wagons that initially were taken by the raiders.
09	6	1863	Skirmish in the Hutton Valley, MO.
09	6	1863	**Batteries Gregg and Wagner, Morris Island, SC, are evacuated** by the Confederates, under the command of Gen. Pierre G.T. Beauregard, and **occupied** by the Union forces under Brig. Gen. Quincy A. Gilmore, USA. 9/6-7/1863.
09	6	1863	Skirmishes near Sweet Water, TN, with Maj. Gen. Ambrose E. Burnside, USA.
09	6	1863	Skirmish at Carter's Run, VA, on the Aestham River, with Brig. Gen. David McM. Gregg, USA.
09	6	1863	Skirmish at Petersburg, WV.
09	7	1863	**Brig. Gen. Lucius Marshall Walker, CSA,** dies at Little Rock, AR, from wounds received in a pistol duel the day before with Maj. Gen. John S. Markaduke.
09	7	1863	**John Wesley Turner,** USA, is appointed Brig. Gen.
09	7	1863	Skirmish at Stevenson, AL, with Maj. Gen. William S. Rosecrans, USA, and Gen. Braxton Bragg, CSA, the Chickamauga Campaign.
09	7	1863	Skirmish at Ashley's Mills, or Ferry Landing, AR.
09	7	1863	Federal expedition to Big Lake, Mississippi County, AR, against guerrillas. 9/7-30/1863.
09	7	1863	Skirmish at Morgan's Ferry, on the Atchafalaya, LA.
09	7	1863	Skirmish at Holly Springs, MS.
09	7	1863	Skirmish near Jacinto (or Glendale), MS.
09	7	1863	Federal expedition from Springfield, MO, into Arkansas and the Indian Territory, and skirmish **(15th)** near Enterprise, MO.
09	7	1863	Affair on Battery Island, SC, as Brig. Gen. William B. Taliaferro, CSA, attacks the Union pickets under Brig. Gen. Quincy A. Gillmore, USA, destroying the bridge and landing to Horse Island in the process.
09	7	1863	Engagement in Charleston Harbor, SC, as the **USS Ironsides** and 5 monitors attack the Confederate batteries at Moultie and Sullivan's Islands, with damage to both sides. 9/7-8/1863.
09	7	1863	Federal reconnaissance toward Chattanooga and skirmish in Lookout Valley, TN, the Chickamauga Campaign.
09	7	1863	Federal operations about, and the **capture of, Cumberland Gap, TN.** 9/7-10/1863.
09	7	1863	Skirmish at Bath, WV.
09	8	1863	Skirmish at Winston's Gap, AL, the Chickamauga Campaign.
09	8	1863	Skirmishes in the Chiricahua Mountains, the Arizona Territory, where the Federals capture and burn an Indian camp, along with 1,000 pounds of their precious food. 9/8-9/1863.
09	8	1863	Skirmish at Alpine, GA, the Chickamauga Campaign.
09	8	1863	Skirmishes on the Atchafalaya, LA. 9/8-9/1863.
09	8	1863	Union boat attack, under Admiral Dahlgren, USN, on Fort Sumter, SC, as the Fort is being reduced to rubble, but this assault is repulsed with about 125 Union men killed, wounded or captured. 9/8-9/1863.
09	8	1863	The actions at Limestone Station and also at Telford's Sation, East TN.
09	8	1863	Engagement between Union gunboats and Maj. Gen. William B. Franklin, USA, (of Bank's command) and Maj. Gen. John B. Magruder, CSA, results in a Federal defeat.
09	8	1863	Skirmish at Brandy Station, VA.
09	8	1863	Skirmish at Beech Fork, Calhoun County, WV.
09	8	1863	Skirmish at Sutton, WV.
09	9	1863	**Howell Cobb, C.S.A.,** is appointed Maj. Gen.
09	9	1863	Skirmish at Lookout Mountain, GA, the Chickamauga Campaign.
09	9	1863	**Chattanooga, TN, is occupied** by Maj. Gen. William S. Rosecrans, USA, as Gen. Braxton Bragg, CSA, retreats toward Lafayette, GA.
09	9	1863	Skirmish at Webber's Falls, the Indian Territory.
09	9	1863	Skirmish at Friar's Island, TN, the Chickamauga Campaign.
09	9	1863	The **1st Confederate Army Corps under Lieut. Gen. James Longstreet** is detached from the Army of Northern Virginia, and **ordered to Tennessee,** to assist Gen. Braxton Bragg, arriving Sept. 18-19, 1863, having to travel by rail, through North Carolina and to Atlanta, GA, to reach Bragg's army, revealing the South's inferior railroad system.

09	10	1863	**Abner Monroe Perrin,** CSA, is appointed Brig. Gen.
09	10	1863	The engagement at Bayou Fourche, as the Confederate Trans-Mississippi, under Lieut. Gen. E. Kirby Smith is in serious jeopardy, as **Little Rock AR, is evacuated** by Maj. Gen. Sterling Price, CSA, and occupied by Maj. Gen. Frederick Steele, USA; Price retreats to Rockport and Arkadelphia, AR. 9/10-14/1863.
09	10	1863	Federal reconnaissance from Alpine toward Rome, La Fayette, and Summerville, GA, and skirmish at Summerville, the Chickamauga Campaign.
09	10	1863	Skirmishes at Pea Vine Creek and near Graysville, GA, the Chickamauga Campaign.
09	10	1863	Skirmish at Brimstone Creek, KY, with Maj. Gen. Ambrose E. Burnside, USA.
09	10	1863	Skirmish at Athens, East TN.
09	10	1863	Federal scout to Middleburg, VA. 9/10-11/1863.
09	11	1863	Skirmish at Waldron, AR.
09	11	1863	The mutiny in Terrell's Texas Confederate Cavalry is put down.
09	11	1863	Federal reconnaissance toward Rome, GA, the Chickamauga Campaign.
09	11	1863	Skirmish near Blue Bird Gap, GA, the Chickamauga Campaign.
09	11	1863	Skirmish near Rossville, GA, the Chickamauga Campaign.
09	11	1863	Skirmishes near Lee and Gordon's Mills, GA, the Chickamauga Campaign. 9/11-13/1863.
09	11	1863	Skirmish at Davis' Cross-Roads (or Davis' House), near Dug Gap, GA, the Chickamauga Campaign.
09	11	1863	Skirmish near Ringgold, GA, the Chickamauga Campaign.
09	11	1863	Skirmish near Greenville, KY.
09	11	1863	Federal expedition from La Grange to Toone's Station, TN, with skirmish (**16th**) at Montezuma. 9/11-16/1863.
09	11	1863	Skirmish at Baldwin's Ferry, Big Black River, MS.
09	11	1863	Skirmish near Greenville, KY.
09	11	1863	Federal expedition from Corinth, MS, to Henderson, TN, with skirmishes: a) at Clark's Creek Church (**13th**) and b) near Henderson, TN. (**14th**). 9/11-16/1863.
09	11	1863	Affair at Moorefield, 9 miles from Petersburg, WV.
09	11	1863	Federal scout from Camp Piatt (Fayetteville), WV, to the Marsh Fork of the Coal River. 9/11-13/1863.
09	11	1863	Maj. Gen. Ambrose E. Burnside, USA, currently commanding the Dept. of the Ohio, and closing in on Gen. Braxton Bragg, tenders his resignation, but it is refused by President Abraham Lincoln.
09	12	1863	**Henry Lawrence Eustis,** USA, is appointed Brig. Gen.
09	12	1863	Skirmish near Brownsville, AR.
09	12	1863	Skirmish at Alpine, GA, as the battle for Chattanooga heats up.
09	12	1863	Skirmish at Dirt Town, GA, the Chickamauga Campaign.
09	12	1863	Skirmish on the La Fayette road, near Chattooga River, GA, the Chickamauga Campaign.
09	12	1863	Skirmish near Leet's Tan-yard, or Rock Spring, GA, the Chickamauga Campaign.
09	12	1863	Skirmish at Sterling's Plantation, near Morganza, LA.
09	12	1863	Affair near Houston, Texas County, MO.
09	12	1863	Skirmish at South Mills, NC.
09	12	1863	Skirmish at Rheatown, East TN.
09	12	1863	Skirmish near Bristoe Station, VA.
09	12	1863	Skirmish at White Plains, VA.
09	12	1863	Skirmish in Roane County, WV.
09	12	1863	Federal scout from Harper's Ferry, WV, into Loudoun County, and skirmish (**14th**) near Leesburg, VA. 9/12-16/1863.
09	13	1863	Federal reconnaissance from Henderson's Gap, AL, to La Fayette, GA, and skirmish, the Chickamauga Campaign.
09	13	1863	Federal reconnaissance from Lee and Gordon's Mills toward La Fayette, GA, and skirmish, the Chickamauga Campaign.
09	13	1863	Skirmish near Summerville, GA, the Chickamauga Campaign.
09	13	1863	Federal expedition from Fort Larned, KS, to Booth's Ranch, on the Arkansas River, KS.
09	13	1863	Federal scouting near Lake Ponchartrain, LA. 9/13-10/2/1863.
09	13	1863	Maj. Gen. Ulysses S. Grant, USA, commanding the Army of the Tennessee, is ordered to send all of his available forces to Corinth and Tuscumbia, MS, to support Maj. Gen. Rosecrans, USA, on the Tennessee River.

09	13	1863	Guerrilla attack on, and skirmish near, Salem, MO.
09	13	1863	The capture of the Union telegraph party near Lowndes' Mill, Combahee River, SC, as the Confederates use Negro dogs to track and capture some of the Union soldiers and Negroes who aided them. 9/13-14/1863.
09	13	1863	Skirmish at Paris, TN.
09	13	1863	The advance of the Union forces from the Rappahannock to the Rapidan River, VA, as Gen. Robert E. Lee, CSA, withdraws across the Rapidan River, from Culpeper to Orange, VA, due to the weakening of his command with the transfer of Lieut. Gen. James Longstreet's command to Tennessee, to bolster Gen. Braxton Bragg, CSA, with the following skirmishes: 9/13-17/1863.
09	13	1863	Skirmishes at Brandy Station, Muddy Run, Culpeper Court-House, Pony Mountain, and Stevensburg, VA.
09	13	1863	Maj. Gen. Henry W. Slocum, USA, resumes the command of the 12th US Army Corps, the Army of the Potomac, VA, etal.
09	13	1863	Confederates scout in West Virginia.
09	14	1863	**Alexander Welch Reynolds,** CSA, is appointed Brig. Gen.
09	14	1863	Skirmish near La Fayette, GA, the Chickamauga Campaign.
09	14	1863	The Confederate attack on Vidalia, LA, is repulsed.
09	14	1863	Federal reconnaissance to the Blackwater River, VA, with skirmishes. 9/14-17/1863.
09	14	1863	Skirmish in Smyth County, VA.
09	14	1863	Skirmishes at Somerville, Raccoon and Robertson's Fords, and Rapidan Station, VA, as the Army of the Potomac (Meade) moves against the Army of Northern Virginia. (Lee). 9/14-16/1863.
09	14	1863	Skirmish at Cheat Mountain Pass, WV.
09	15	1863	**George Douglas Ramsay,** USA, is appointed Brig. Gen.
09	15	1863	Skirmishes at Catlett's Gap, Pigeon Mountain, GA, as Maj. Gen. William S. Rosecrans, USA, and Gen. Braxton Bragg, CSA, concentrate their forces, the Chickamauga Campaign. 9/15-18/1863.
09	15	1863	Skirmish at Summerville, GA, the Chickamauga Campaign.
09	15	1863	Skirmish at Trion Factory, GA, the Chickamauga Campaign.
09	15	1863	Maj. Gen. Edward O. C. Ord, USA, resumes the command of the 13th US Army Corps, the Dept. of the Gulf, LA, etal.
09	15	1863	Federal scout from Greenfield, MO, where a Union private is caught and murdered. The Federals retaliate and burn everything from a pigpen to a mansion on Cedar and Horse Creeks.
09	15	1863	Skirmish at Enterprise, Jackson County, MO, at William C. Quantrill's camp.
09	15	1863	Federal scout from Fort Wingate to Ojo Redondo (Jacob's Well), the New Mexico Territory, where the Federals capture some **Navajoes,** destroy some vegetable and wheat fields, and the **Zuni Indians** show off some of their scalps taken in a war party against the **Navajoes,** etc. 9/15-10/5/1863.
09	15	1863	The explosion of a magazine, believed to be due to faulty ammunition, at Battery Cheves, James Island, near Charleston, SC, kills 6 Confederate soldiers.
09	15	1863	Federal expedition from Great Bridge, VA, to Indiantown, NC, where the Federals are ambushed, with loss of life. 9/15-19/1863.
09	15	1863	Affair near Kempsville, VA.
09	16	1863	Skirmish at Brownsville, AR.
09	16	1863	Skirmishes near Lee and Gordon's Mills, on Chickamauga Creek, GA, 12 miles south of Chattanooga, as Maj. Gen. William S. Rosecrans concentrates around here, and Alpine, GA, the Chickamauga Campaign. 9/16-18/1863.
09	16	1863	Skirmish at Smithfield, WV.
09	17	1863	Skirmish at Neal's Gap, AL, the Chickamauga Campaign.
09	17	1863	Skirmish at Owen's Ford, West Chickamauga Creek, GA, as Gen. Braxton Bragg, CSA, loses the opportunity to attack the separated corps of Maj. Gen. William S. Rosecrans', USA, Army, blaming his subordinates for failing to attack as instructed, while Rosecrans concentrated his forces, the Chickamauga Campaign.
09	17	1863	Federal reconnaissance from Rossville and skirmish at Ringgold, GA, the Chickamauga Campaign.
09	17	1863	Skirmish on Horse Creek, MO.
09	17	1863	The major ingredients for the bloodiest battle of the war in the Western Department (Chickamauga) are beginning to gel.

09	17	1863	Skirmish at Raccoon Ford, on the Rapidan River, VA, as the Union forces move from the Rappahannock to the Rapidan River.
09	18	1863	**Edmund Winston Pettus,** CSA, is appointed Brig. Gen.
09	18	1863	**Thomas Neville Waul,** CSA, is appointed Brig. Gen.
09	18	1863	Skirmishes at Pea Vine Bridge, Alexander's and Reed's Bridges, Dryer's Ford, Spring Creek, and near Stevens' Gap, GA, as Gen. Braxton Bragg, CSA, moves most of his forces from Ringgold across West Chickamuaga Creek as he is being reinforced by Lieut. Gen. James Longstreet's, CSA Army Corps, fresh from the Army of Northern Virginia. So as to not be outflanked, Maj. Gen. William S. Rosecrans, USA, moves Maj. Gen. George H. Thomas' USA Army Corps toward Chattanooga, TN, the Chickamauga Campaign.
09	18	1863	Skirmish at Calhoun, East TN, with Maj. Gen. Ambrose E. Burnside, USA.
09	18	1863	Skirmish at Cleveland, TN.
09	18	1863	Affair near Fort Donelson, TN.
09	18	1863	Skirmish at Kingsport, TN.
09	18	1863	Skirmish at Crooked Run, VA, near Bristol, TN.
09	18	1863	The Confederate capture of schooners **Alliance** (later burned), **J.J. Houseman, Samuel Pearsall** and the **Alexandria,** on the Chesapeake Bay, near Eastville, VA, by one Capt. John Y. Beall. 9/18-23/1863.
09	19	1863	**Henry Warner Birge,** USA, is appointed Brig. Gen.
09	19	1863	**Charles Garrison Harker,** USA, is appointed Brig. Gen.
09	19	1863	Skirmish on the Greenwell Springs Road, near Baton Rouge, LA.
09	19	1863	Skirmish at Bristol, TN.
09	19	1863	**The Battle of Chickamauga, GA,** begins with Brig. Gen. Nathan Bedford Forrest's, CSA, unmounted Cavalry pitted against Maj. Gen. George H. Thomas, USA, with the following generals joining in: Alexander McDowell McCook, USA, and James Longstreet and Leonidas Polk, CSA. 9/19-20/1863.
09	19	1863	**Brig. Gen. Preston Smith, CSA,** is mortally wounded during the Battle of Chickamauga, GA, while directing a night attack, receiving a volley from the Federal detachment of soldiers he accidently rode into.
09	19	1863	Skirmish at Como, TN.
09	19	1863	Federal expedition from Fort Pillow to Jackson, TN. 9/19-25/1863.
09	19	1863	Skirmish at Raccoon Ford, VA.
09	20	1863	**John Bell Hood, C.S.A., is appointed Lieut. Gen.**
09	20	1863	Federal expedition from Paducah, KY, to McLemoresville, TN. 9/20-30/1863.
09	20	1863	Skirmish at Morgan's Ferry, on the Atchafalaya, LA.
09	20	1863	Skirmish at Hornersville, MO.
09	20	1863	**The Battle of Chickamauga, GA,** rages on as the Confederates under Lieut. Gen. James Longstreet, CSA, eventually force a Union retreat toward Chattannooga, TN, by Maj. Gens. Rosecrans, McCook and Crittenden, while Maj. Gen. George H. Thomas, USA, earns his nickname, **"The Rock of Chickamauga,"** as he stubbornly refuses to retreat from his defensive position at Snodgrass Hill, finally withdrawing toward Rossville. Total casualties approximates 34,500.
09	20	1863	**Brig. Gen. James Deshler, CSA,** is mortally wounded at the Battle of Chickamauga, GA, dying instantly from a federal artillery shell while inspecting his troops prior to an assault on the Federal line.
09	20	1863	**Brig. Gen. Benjamin Hardin Helm, CSA,** is mortally wounded at the Battle of Chickamauga, GA, while leading his men on an assault on the Federal lines, dying the next day.
09	20	1863	**Brig. Gen. William Haines Lytle, USA,** is mortally wounded at the Battle of Chickamauga, GA, while leading his men in a charge against the Confederate battle line, to give the retreating Union troops time to escape.
09	20	1863	Skirmishes at Carter's Depot, East TN. 9/20-21/1863.
09	20	1863	Action at Zollicoffer, East TN, with Maj. Gen. Ambrose E. Burnside. USA. 9/20-21/1863.
09	20	1863	Affair on Shaver Mountain, WV, in the vicinity of Buckhannon and Huttonsville, WV, with casualties.
09	21	1863	**Brig. Gen. Benjamin Hardin Helm, CSA,** dies from battle wounds received the day before at the Battle of Chickamauga, GA, whose death is mourned by his brother-in-law, President Abraham Lincoln, and his sister, Mary Todd Lincoln.
09	21	1863	**Armistead Lindsay Long,** CSA, is appointed Brig. Gen.
09	21	1863	Skirmishes at Rossville, Lookout Church, and Dry Valley, GA, the Chickamauga Campaign.
09	21	1863	The Army of the Cumberland retreats to Chattanooga, TN, as Gen. Braxton Bragg, CSA, fails to order a

thrust against the defeated Federals, thus missing a major opportunity to inflict further damages on the defeated Union army, the Chickamauga Campaign. 9/21-22/1863.

09	21	1863	Action at Jonesborough, TN.
09	21	1863	Skirmish at Fisher's Hill, VA.
09	21	1863	Skirmish at Madison Court-House, VA, with the Federal reconnaissance party.
09	21	1863	Federal operations about Princess Anne Court-House, VA, near Fog Island, Back Bay and to Knott's Island, in the Great Dismal Swamp where guerrillas were supposed to be camping. 9/21-25/1863.
09	21	1863	Federal reconnaissance across the Rapidan River, VA, including to Madison Court-House, Wolftown, Burtonsville, Standardsville, Orange Court-House, and Liberty Mills with the capture of Confederate supply wagons and beef-cattle near Gordonsville, by Brig. Gens. John Buford and Judson Kilpatrick's US Cavalry. 9/21-23/1863.
09	21	1863	Skirmishes at White's Ford, VA, with the Federal reconnaissance party that crossed the Rapidan River. 9/21-22/1863.
09	21	1863	Federal scout from Harper's Ferry, WV, into Loudoun County Valley, VA, and skirmish (**25th**) near Upperville, VA, with men under Maj. John S. Mosby, CSA. 9/21-26/1863.
09	21	1863	Affair at Moorefield, WV.
09	22	1863	**Col. Joseph O. Shelby's Confederate Raid in Arkansas and Missouri.** 9/22-10/26/1863.
09	22	1863	Col. Joseph Orville Shelby, CSA, sets out from Arkadelphia, AR, for a raid through Arkansas and Missouri.
09	22	1863	Federal destruction of the Hudson Place Salt-Works, near Darien, GA.
09	22	1863	Skirmish at Marrow Bone Creek, KY.
09	22	1863	Skirmish at Rockville, MD.
09	22	1863	Federal scout in La Fayette County, MO, and skirmishes. 9/22-25/1863 .
09	22	1863	**The 1st, 2d,** and **4th Divisions** of the **15th US Army Corps,** under Maj. Gen. Ulysses S. Grant, USA, **Army of the Tennessee,** start en route from Vicksburg, MS, to Chattanooga, TN, to assist the desperate and hemmed in Maj. Gen. William S. Rosecrans, USA. 9/22-30/1863.
09	22	1863	Engagement at Blountsville, TN.
09	22	1863	Skirmish at Carter's Depot, TN.
09	22	1863	Skirmishes at Missionary Ridge and Shallow Ford Gap, near Chattanooga, TN, bring the Chickamuaga Campaign to a close as Gen. Braxton Bragg occupies the high ground of Missionary Ridge and Lookout Mountain surrounding Chattanooga and the Union Army of the Cumberland, the Chickamauga Campaign.
09	22	1863	Skirmish between Centreville and Warrenton, VA.
09	22	1863	Skirmish at Orange Court-House, VA.
09	22	1863	Skirmish at Raccoon Ford, VA.
09	23	1863	**Henry Rootes Jackson,** CSA, is appointed Brig. Gen.
09	23	1863	Skirmish near the Bayou Meto Bridge, AR.
09	23	1863	Affair opposite Donaldsonville, LA, with Confederate Cavalry.
09	23	1863	Maj. Gen. George E. Pickett, CSA, is assigned to the command of the Confederate Dept. of North Carolina.
09	23	1863	Skirmishes in front of Chattanooga, TN. 9/23-26/1863.
09	23	1863	Skirmish at Cumberland Gap, TN, with Maj. Gen. Ambrose E. Burnside, USA.
09	23	1863	Skirmishes at Summertown and Lookout Mountain, TN.
09	23	1863	Skirmishes near Liberty Mills and at Robertson's Ford, on the Rapidan River, VA.
09	24	1863	Federal expeditions from Carrollton and Baton Rouge to the New River and to the Amite River, LA. 9/24-29/1863.
09	24	1863	Skirmish at Zollicoffer, TN.
09	24	1863	Skirmish at Bristoe Station, VA.
09	24	1863	The **transfer** of the **11th** and **12th US Army Corps** from the **Army of the Potomac** to the **Army of the Cumberland,** to support Maj. Gen. William S. Rosecrans in Alabama, is ordered by President Lincoln and accomplished in lightning speed. 9/24-10/3/1863.
09	24	1863	Maj. Gen. Joseph Hooker, USA, is assigned to the command of the 11th and 12th US Army Corps.
09	24	1863	Skirmish at Greenbrier Bridge, about 21 miles from Huttonsville, WV.
09	25	1863	**William Wirt Adams,** CSA, is appointed Brig Gen.
09	25	1863	Federal operations in the vicinity of Baton Rouge, LA.

09	25	1863	Skirmish at Athens, TN.
09	25	1863	Skirmishes at Calhoun and Charleston, TN.
09	25	1863	Brig. Gen. Mahlon D. Manson, USA, assumes the command of the 23d US Army Corps, TN, etal.
09	25	1863	The capture of a (unnamed) Confederate steamer near White House, VA, about 12 miles above West Point on the Pamunkey River.
09	25	1863	Skirmish at Seneca Trace Crossing, Cheat River, WV, with an attack by Brig. Gen. John D. Imboden, CSA, with loss of life.
09	25	1863	President Abraham Lincoln is upset with Maj. Gen. Ambrose E. Burnside's inability to assist Maj. Gen. William S. Rosecrans, USA, at Chattanooga, TN; however, Burnside is having his own problems.
09	26	1863	Skirmish at Hunt's Mill, near Larkinsville, AL.
09	26	1863	Skirmish at Cassville, MO.
09	26	1863	Maj. Gen. William Henry Chase Whiting, CSA, is assigned to the separate command of the District of Cape Fear and the Defenses of Wilmington, NC.
09	26	1863	Skirmish at Calhoun, TN.
09	26	1863	Skirmish near Winchester, TN.
09	26	1863	Skirmish at Richards' Ford, VA, as a Rebel force coming from Stafford Court-House capture's the Union picket post there.
09	27	1863	Federal expedition from Goodrich's Landing to Bayou Macon, LA. 9/27-29/1863.
09	27	1863	Skirmish at Moffat's Station, Franklin County, AR, with Col. Joseph O. Shelby's Raiding Confederates.
09	27	1863	Federal scout in Bates County, MO, south of Butler.
09	27	1863	Skirmish at Newtonia, MO.
09	27	1863	Federal expedition from Corinth, MS, into West Tennessee, with skirmish at Swallow Bluffs, TN. (**Sept. 30th**). 9/27-10/1/1863.
09	27	1863	Federal expedition from Messinger's Ford, Big Black River, to Yazoo City, MS, with skirmishes at: a) Brownsville, (**Sept. 28th**) and b) Moore's Ford, near Benton (**Sept. 29th**). 9/27-10/1/1863.
09	27	1863	Skirmish at Athens, East TN, with Maj. Gen. Ambrose E. Burnside, USA.
09	27	1863	Skirmish at Locke's Mill, near Moscow, TN.
09	27	1863	Skirmish near Philadelphia, TN, with Maj. Gen. Ambrose E. Burnside, USA.
09	27	1863	Federal scout for guerrillas on Hazel Run, VA. 9/27-28/1863.
09	28	1863	The following are appointed Confederate Brigadier Generals: **James Byron Gordon,** CSA **Thomas Lafayette Rosser,** CSA **Pierce Manning Butler Young,** CSA
09	28	1863	As Maj. Gen. William S. Rosecrans, USA, blames his subordinates for the Union defeat at Chickamauga, GA, Maj. Gens. Alexander McDowell McCook and Thomas L. Crittenden are relieved of command of their respective US Army Corps and ordered to Indianapolis, IN, where a **Court of Inquiry** will look into their conduct at Chickamauga.
09	28	1863	Skirmish at Buell's Ford, TN.
09	28	1863	Skirmish at Jonesborough, TN.
09	29	1863	Federal action at Stirling's Plantation, on the Fordoche, near Morganza, LA, with Maj. Gen. Nathaniel P. Banks, USA.
09	29	1863	Federal expedition from Pilot Knob to Oregon County, MO, and to Pochontas, AR. 9/29-10/26/1863.
09	29	1863	Skirmish at Friendship Church, TN.
09	29	1863	Skirmish at Leesburg, TN.
09	30	1863	**Joseph Horace Lewis,** CSA, is appointed Brig. Gen.
09	30	1863	**James Argyle Smith,** CSA, is appointed Brig. Gen.
09	30	1863	Skirmish at Cotton Port Ford, Tennessee River, TN, because of the following Confederate Cavalry raid:
09	30	1863	Maj. Gen. Joseph Wheeler and Brig. Gen. Philip D. Roddey's Confederate raid on Maj. Gen. William S. Rosecrans' US Army of the Cumberland's communications, TN. 9/30-10/17/1863.
09	30	1863	The destruction of Confederate Salt-works on the Back Bay, Princess Anne County, near Norfolk, VA. Salt being valued at $5 per bushel. The Rebels lose the production capacity of 6 bushels per day.
09	30	1863	Skirmish at Neersville, VA.
09	30	1863	Skirmish at Woodville, VA.

10	1	1863	**James Abram Garfield, U.S.A.,** is appointed Maj. Gen.
10	1	1863	Skirmish at Elizabethtown, AR.
10	1	1863	Skirmish at Mountain Gap, or Anderson's Gap, near Smith's Cross-Roads, TN, with Maj. Gen. Joseph Wheeler's, CSA, Cavalry.
10	1	1863	The 11th and 12th US Army Corps, arrive at Nashville, enroute to the aid of Maj. Gen. William S. Rosecrans, USA.
10	1	1863	Skirmish near Auburn, VA, with the Army of Northern Virginia.
10	1	1863	Skirmish near Culpeper Court-House, VA.
10	1	1863	Skirmish at Lewinsville, VA, with a surprise Confederate attack and capture of Federal prisoners, horses and loss of Federal life.
10	1	1863	The capture of Union pickets on the north side of Robertson's River, VA, by Maj. Gen. JEB Stuart's, CSA, Cavalry.
10	1	1863	Skirmish near Harper's Ferry, WV.
10	2	1863	Skirmish at Vance's Store, AR.
10	2	1863	Skirmish at Carthage, MO.
10	2	1863	Skirmish at Anderson's Cross-Roads, TN.
10	2	1863	Skirmish near Chattanooga, TN, with Maj. Gen. Joseph Wheeler's CSA Cavalry, contesting the roads into Chattanooga.
10	2	1863	Skirmish near Dunlap, TN.
10	2	1863	Skirmish at Greeneville, TN.
10	2	1863	Skirmish on the Valley road, near Jasper, TN.
10	2	1863	Skirmish at Pitt's Cross-Roads, Sequatchie Valley, TN, on the only open road available for the 11th and 12th US Army Corps, currently at Bridgeport, AL, to reach Chattanooga, in through the Sequatchie Valley.
10	3	1863	**Operations in the Bayou Teche Country, LA.** 10/3-11/30/1863.
10	3	1863	The Union forces, under the command of Maj. Gen. William B. Franklin, USA, are ordered to advance by Maj. Gen. Nathaniel P. Banks, USA, westward from Berwick Bay and New Iberia, LA, in another attempt on the Sabine, TX, area.
10	3	1863	Skirmish at Forked Deer Creek, MS.
10	3	1863	Operations in Bates and Vernon Counties, MO. 10/3-7/1863.
10	3	1863	Skirmish at Bear Creek, TN.
10	3	1863	Skirmish at Hill's Gap, near Beersheba, TN, with Maj. Gen. Joseph Wheeler's, USA, Cavalry.
10	3	1863	Affair at, and **capture of, McMinnville, TN,** by Maj. Gen. Joseph Wheeler's, USA, Cavalry.
10	3	1863	Skirmish at Lewinsville, VA.
10	4	1863	**Mark Perrin Lowrey,** CSA, is appointed Brig. Gen.
10	4	1863	Affair at Nelson's Bridge, near New Iberia, LA, as Maj. Gen. William B. Franklin, USA, pressed on toward the Sabine, TX.
10	4	1863	Skirmish near the Widow Wheeler's, 15 miles southwest of Neosho, MO, with guerrillas.
10	4	1863	Action at Neosho, MO, with Col. James O. Shelby's, CSA, Raid.
10	4	1863	Skirmish at Oregon, or Bowers' Mill, MO, with Col. James O. Shelby.
10	4	1863	**Brig. Gen. James Ronald Chalmer's Confederate raid in West Tennessee and North Mississippi.** 10/4-17/1863.
10	4	1863	Skirmishes near McMinnville, TN.
10	4	1863	Federal expedition from Yorktown to Matthews County, VA, with the assistance of Union gunboats, **Commodore Jones, Putnam, and Stepping Stones,** and the Army gunboats, **Flora Temple, C.P. Smith, Smith Briggs, General Jesup, West End, Sam. Ruatan, Young Rover,** and the transport **Maple Leaf,** with the destruction of over 150 small boats and sloops, and the capture of beef cattle enroute to Richmond. The Federals state the countryside is full of forage, corn, fodder, and oats, while sheep, poultry, and cattle abound. 10/4-9/1863.
10	5	1863	Skirmish on the Greenwell Springs Road, LA.
10	5	1863	Skirmish at New Albany, MS, with Brig. Gen. James Ronald Chalmers', CSA, Confederate raid.
10	5	1863	Skirmish at Greenfield, MO, with Col. Joseph O. Shelby, CSA.
10	5	1863	Skirmish at Stockton, MO, with Col. Joseph O. Shelby, CSA.
10	5	1863	Skirmish at Syracuse, MO, with guerrillas who were on their way to join up with Col. Joseph O. Shelby's, CSA, raiding party.

10	5	1863	The Confederates attempt and fail to blow up the US Steamer, the **New Ironsides,** off Charleston Harbor, SC, by the cigar shaped, semi-submarine vessel, the **David.**
10	5	1863	Skirmish at Blue Springs, TN.
10	5	1863	The **2nd Division, 7th US Army Corps,** in addition to Maj. Gen. Joseph Hooker's **11th and 12th US Army Corps** from Virginia and portions of Maj. Gen. Ulysses S. Grant's **15th US Army Corps** from the Vicksburg, MS, area, starts en route from Memphis to Chattanooga, TN.
10	5	1863	Skirmish near Readyville, TN, with Maj. Gen. Joseph Wheeler, CSA.
10	5	1863	Skirmish and the destruction of the important Stone's River Railroad Bridge, near Murfreesborough, TN, by Maj. Gen. Joseph Wheeler, CSA, increasing the lack of food flowing into the beleaguered **Army of the Cumberland** at Chattanooga, TN.
10	6	1863	Col. William Clarke Quantrill's Confederate attack on Maj. Gen. James Gillpatrick Blunt's, USA, escort at Baxter Springs, KS.
10	6	1863	Skirmish at Baxter Springs, KS, as Quantrill's guerrillas ambush the Federals, killing men and burning Union wagons.
10	6	1863	Skirmish at Glasgow, KY, with Maj. Gen. Ambrose E. Burnside, USA.
10	6	1863	Skirmish in Morgan County, KY.
10	6	1863	Skirmish at Lockhart's Mill, on Coldwater River, MS, with Brig. Gen. James Ronald Chalmer's CSA Confederate Cavalry Raid.
10	6	1863	Skirmish at Humansville, MO, with Col. Joseph O. Shelby, CSA.
10	6	1863	Affair at Christiana, TN, with Maj. Gen. Joseph Wheeler, CSA.
10	6	1863	Skirmish at Garrison's Creek, near Fosterville, TN, with Maj. Gen. Wheeler, CSA.
10	6	1863	Skirmish at Readyville, TN, with Maj. Gen. Wheeler, CSA.
10	6	1863	Skirmish at Wartrace, TN, with Maj. Gen. Joseph Wheeler, CSA.
10	6	1863	Affair near Catlett's Station, VA, where the Rebels capture a couple of Union Cavalrymen on patrol.
10	6	1863	President Jefferson Davis travels to Charleston, SC, and to visit with Gen. Braxton Bragg, CSA, who is laying siege to Chattanooga, TN, and the Federal Army of the Cumberland.
10	7	1863	Skirmish at Evening Shade and Ferry's Ford, AR.
10	7	1863	Federal scout in the Spring River country of AR. 10/7-10/1863.
10	7	1863	Skirmish with Indians in the **Choctaw Nation,** the Indian Territory.
10	7	1863	Federal expedition from Sedalia to Marshall, MO. 10/7-17/1863.
10	7	1863	Skirmish near Warsaw, MO, with Col. Joseph O. Shelby, CSA.
10	7	1863	Action at Farmington, TN, with Maj. Gen. Joseph Wheeler, CSA.
10	7	1863	Skirmish at Blue Springs, TN, with Maj. Gen. Joseph Wheeler, CSA.
10	7	1863	Skirmish at Sims' farm, near Shelbyville, TN, with Maj. Gen. Joseph Wheeler, CSA.
10	7	1863	Skirmish at Hazel River, VA.
10	7	1863	Skirmish at Mitchell's Ford, Rapidan River, VA.
10	7	1863	Affair at Utz's Ford, Rapidan River, VA, where Maj. Gen. JEB Stuart, CSA, attacks, kills and captures Union pickets, taking horses and military equipment with him.
10	7	1863	Skirmishes at Charlestown and Summit Point, WV, with Confederate cavalry.
10	8	1863	**Leroy Augustus Stafford,** CSA, is appointed Brig. Gen.
10	8	1863	Federal reconnaissance to Olympian Springs, KY, the East Tennessee Campaign. 10/8-11/1863.
10	8	1863	Action at Salem, MS.
10	8	1863	Skirmish near Chattanooga, TN.
10	8	1863	Skirmish near James City, VA.
10	8	1863	Skirmishes along Robertson's River, VA.
10	9	1863	Maj. Gen. Joseph Wheeler's Confederate column recross the Tennessee River at Muscle Shoals, AL, returning to their base of operations at Chattanoga, TN.
10	9	1863	Skirmishes at Vermillion Bayou, LA, with Maj. Gen. William B. Franklin, USA. 10/9-10/1863.
10	9	1863	Skirmish near Cole Camp, MO, with Col. Joseph O. Shelby, CSA.
10	9	1863	Skirmish at Cleveland, TN, with Maj. Gen. Ambrose E. Burnside, USA.
10	9	1863	Affair at the Railroad Tunnel, near Cowan, TN.
10	9	1863	Skirmish on Elk River, TN.
10	9	1863	Skirmish at Sugar Creek, TN.
10	9	1863	**The Bristoe, Virginia Campaign,** as Gen. Robert E. Lee, CSA, crosses the Rapidan and tries to outflank Maj. Gen. George G. Meade, USA, to get to Washington, DC, since the Army of the Potomac has been

weakened by sending troops to Chattanooga, TN. 10/9-22/1863.

| 10 | 9 | 1863 | Skirmish near James City, VA, is the start of the Bristoe Campaign. |

10 9 1863 — Federal expedition to Chesnessex Creek, VA, and vicinity around Chincoteague Light-House where the Federals burn the Confederate schooner **Columbia,** near the head of Pocomoke Sound, VA. 10/9-13/1863.

10 10 1863 — Action at Tulip, AR.

10 10 1863 — Skirmish at Salyersville, KY, the East TN Campaign.

10 10 1863 — Skirmish at Ingraham's Plantation, near Port Gibson, MS.

10 10 1863 — Affair at La Mine Bridge, MO, with Col. Joseph O. Shelby, CSA.

10 10 1863 — Skirmish at Syracuse, MO, with Col. Joseph O. Shelby, CSA.

10 10 1863 — Affair at Tipton, MO, with Col. Joseph O. Shelby, CSA.

10 10 1863 — Federal expedition from New Berne to Elizabeth City and Edenton, NC, as the Pro-Union feeling is rapidly spreading in this region. Nearly 1,000 Confederate troops are needed to enforce the conscription. Many Pro-Northern friends can be found in Elizabeth City, NC, as per Maj. Gen. John J. Peck, USA, Commanding the Dept. of Virginia and North Carolina. However, guerrillas still abound. 10/10-17/1863.

10 10 1863 — Action at Blue Springs, East TN Campaign.

10 10 1863 — President Jefferson Davis arrives in Chattanooga, TN, to discuss strategy with Gen. Braxton Bragg, and quiet the underlying unrest with Bragg's subordinates.

10 10 1863 — Federal expedition from Gallatin to Carthage, TN, with skirmish (10th) near Hartsville. 10/10-14/1863.

10 10 1863 — Federal expedition from Memphis, TN, to Hernando, MS, with skirmish (**11th**) near Hernando. 10/10-11/1863.

10 10 1863 — Skirmishes at Sweet Water, East TN Campaign. 10/10-11/1863.

10 10 1863 — Maj. Gen. Gordon Granger, USA, assumes the command of the **4th US Army Corps,** formed by the consolidation of the **20th** and the **21st US Army Corps,** TN, etal.

10 10 1863 — Skirmishes at Raccoon, Germanna, and Morton's Fords, VA, between Gen. Robert E. Lee's and Maj. Gen. George Meade's troops, maneuvering for position.

10 10 1863 — Skirmishes at Russell's Ford, on Robertson's River, Bethsaida Church, and James City, VA, the Bristoe Campaign.

10 11 1863 — Confederate demonstration against Fayetteville, AR.

10 11 1863 — Skirmish at Brazil Creek, **Choctaw Nation,** the Indian Territory.

10 11 1863 — Skirmishes at, and the **capture of, Boonville, MO,** on the Missouri River, by Col. Joseph O. Shelby's, CSA, Cavalry. 10/11-12/1863.

10 11 1863 — Action at Collierville, TN, with Brig. Gen James Ronald Chalmers, CSA.

10 11 1863 — Skirmishes at Henderson's Mill and Rheatown, East TN.

10 11 1863 — Skirmish near Culpeper Court-House, VA, with Gen. Robert E. Lee, CSA.

10 11 1863 — Skirmishes at Griffinsburg, Culpeper, and Brandy Station, VA.

10 11 1863 — Skirmishes at Morton's Ford, Stevensburg, and near Kelly's Ford, VA, with Gen. Robert E. Lee, CSA.

10 11 1863 — Skirmish near Warrenton, or Sulphur Springs, VA, with Gen. Robert E. Lee, CSA.

10 11 1863 — Skirmish at Salt Lick Bridge, WV.

10 12 1863 — Skirmish at Buckhorn Tavern, near New Market, AL, with Maj. Gen. Joseph Wheeler's, CSA, Confederate Cavalry.

10 12 1863 — The attack on the Confederate blockade runner under the walls of Fort Morgan, AL. (The US gunboat, **Kanawha,** Lieut. Commander W. K. Mayo, and the US tender, **Eugenie,** Lieut. H. W. Miller are engaged).

10 12 1863 — Skirmish at Tulip, AR.

10 12 1863 — Federal scout from Fort Garland, the Colorado Territory, and the killing of the **outlaw Espanoza.** The heads of two rebels were severed from their bodies and delivered to the commandant at Fort Garland.

10 12 1863 — Skirmish at Webber's Falls, the Indian Territory.

10 12 1863 — Skirmish at West Liberty, KY, the East TN Campaign.

10 12 1863 — Skirmish at Ingram's Mill, and Wyatt's, near Byhalia, MS.

10 12 1863 — Skirmish at Quinn and Jackson's Mill, MS, with Brig. Gen. J. Ronald Chalmers, CSA.

10 12 1863 — Skirmishes at Merrill's Crossing to Lamine Crossing, and Dug Ford, near Jonesborough, MO, with Col. Joseph O. Shelby, CSA.

10 12 1863 — Federal scout from Vienna through Thornton, Hendrick's (Herndon) Station, Frying Pan, to Gum

Springs, VA, in search of Maj. John S. Mosby, CSA, who had gone toward Fairfax Court- House. 10/12-13/1863.

10	12	1863	Skirmish at Brandy Station, or Fleetwood, VA, and all the following with Gen. Robert E. Lee, CSA, the Bristoe Campaign.
10	12	1863	Skirmish at Hartwood Church, VA.
10	12	1863	Skirmishes at Jeffersonton and Gaines' Cross-Roads, VA.
10	12	1863	Action at Warrenton, or Sulphur Springs, VA.
10	13	1863	Skirmish at Maysville, AL, with Maj. Gen. Joseph Wheeler, CSA.
10	13	1863	Action at Wyatt, MS, with Brig. Gen. James R. Chalmers, CSA.
10	13	1863	Action at Marshall, MO, with Col. Joseph O. Shelby, CSA.
10	13	1863	**Clement L. Vallandigham,** exiled in Canada, is soundly defeated in his race for Governor of Ohio.
10	13	1863	Skirmishes at Fayetteville, TN.
10	13	1863	Action at Auburn, VA, with Gen. Robert E. Lee, CSA, and Maj. Gen. George G. Meade, USA.
10	13	1863	Federal scout from Great Bridge, VA, to Indiantown, NC, including the capture of a notorious guerrilla **Silas F. Gregory,** engaged in arming and feeding the local guerrillas. However, after having gone less than a mile, the Federals are fired upon from the woods by guerrillas, killing and injuring Union soldiers, which allows time for Mr. Silas Gregory to escape.
10	13	1863	Skirmishes near Warrenton and at Fox's Ford, VA, between Maj. Gen. George G. Meade, USA, and Gen. Robert E. Lee, CSA.
10	13	1863	Skirmish at Bulltown, WV, as Confederate forces surround the town and demand a surrender which the Federals refuse to do. After fighting and casualties on both sides, the Confederates withdraw towards Sutton.
10	13	1863	Skirmish at Burlington, WV.
10	14	1863	Skirmish at **Creek Agency,** the Indian Territory.
10	14	1863	Skirmishes at Carrion Crow Bayou, LA, with Maj. Gen. William B. Franklin, USA. 10/14-15/1863.
10	14	1863	Federal expedition from Messinger's Ferry, on the Big Black River, toward Canton, MS. 10/14-20/1863.
10	14	1863	Federal expeditions from Natchez and Fort Adams, MS, to Red River, LA, with skirmish at Red River. (14th). 10/14-20/1863.
10	14	1863	Skirmish near Man's Creek, Shannon County, MO.
10	14	1863	Skirmish at Scott's Ford, MO, with Col. Joseph O. Shelby, CSA.
10	14	1863	Skirmish at Blountsville, TN.
10	14	1863	Skirmish near Loudoun, TN.
10	14	1863	**The Engagement at Bristoe Station, VA,** where Maj. Gen. A.P. Hill, CSA, attacks the retreating rearguard forces of Maj. Gen. George Meade, USA, but is repulsed.
10	14	1863	**Brig. Gen. Carnot Posey, CSA,** is slightly wounded at the engagement at Bristoe Station, VA; however, infection sets in on the wound, and unable to recover, he dies on November 13, 1863.
10	14	1863	Skirmishes at Saint Stephen's Church, Catlett's Station, Gainesville, and Grove Church, and near Centreville and Brentsville, VA, the Bristoe Campaign.
10	14	1863	Skirmish at Salt Lick Bridge, WV, with Brig. Gen. William W. Averell's, USA, Cavalry which chase the Confederates toward Addison, in Webster County.
10	14	1863	Maj. Gen. Christopher C. Augur, USA, supersedes Maj. Gen. Samuel P. Heintzelman, USA, in the command of the Dept. of Washington, DC, and the 22nd US Army Corps.
10	15	1863	Skirmish at **Creek Agency,** the Indian Territory.
10	15	1863	Skirmish at Brownsville, MS.
10	15	1863	Skirmishes on the Canton Road, near Brownsville, MS.
10	15	1863	Skirmish at Cross Timbers, MO, with Col. Joseph O. Shelby, CSA.
10	15	1863	The Confederate experimental submarine, **H.L. Hunley,** sinks along with 8 crewmembers, including its inventor, Huntley, Charleston Harbor, Charleston, SC.
10	15	1863	Skirmish at Bristol, TN.
10	15	1863	Skirmish near Philadelphia, TN.
10	15	1863	Skirmishes at McLean's, or Liberty Mills, Blackburn's, and Mitchell's Fords, on Bull Run, and Manassas and Oak Hill, VA, the Bristoe Campaign.
10	15	1863	Affair near Hedgesville, WV, as the Federals capture the entire party of 37 Confederates attempting to burn the Back Creek Bridge.

10	16	1863	Engagement at Fort Brooke, Tampa Bay, FL, with the destruction of two Confederate blockade runners by the US ironclads, the **Tahoma,** and the **Adele.**
10	16	1863	Skirmish at Grand Coteau, LA, with Maj. Gen. William B. Franklin, USA.
10	16	1863	Federal expedition from Natchez, MS, to Red River, LA. 10/16-20/1863.
10	16	1863	Skirmish at Treadwell's, near Clinton, and Vernon Cross-Roads, MS.
10	16	1863	The **Military Division of the Mississippi** (consisting of the: a) **Dept. of the Cumberland,** b) **Dept. of the Ohio,** and of the c) **Dept. of the Tennessee,** is created, and Maj. Gen. Ulysses S. Grant, USA, is assigned to assigned to the command. Maj. Gen. George H. Thomas, USA, is ordered to command the Dept. of the Cumberland, vice Maj. Gen. William S. Rosecrans, USA, is relieved of command, partly due to the Union loss at Chickamauga, GA.. Rosecrans' military career is effectively over.
10	16	1863	Skirmish on Deer Creek, MO, with Col. Joseph O. Shelby, CSA.
10	16	1863	Skirmishes near and at Humansville, MO, with Col. Joseph O. Shelby, CSA.
10	16	1863	Skirmish at Johnstown, MO, with Col. Joseph O. Shelby, CSA.
10	16	1863	Affairs at Pungo Landing, NC, as the Federals leave Great Bridge, VA, aboard the steamer, **Fawn,** are fired upon from shore, sustaining casualties. The Federals land and burn the houses from where the shots came from and also find the tugboat, **White,** and other small craft destroyed by the Confederates. 10/16-17/1863.
10	16	1863	Skirmish near Island No. 10, TN.
10	17	1863	Action at Bogue Chitto Creek, MS.
10	17	1863	Skirmish at Robinson's Mills, near Livingston, MS.
10	17	1863	Skirmish near Satartia, MS.
10	17	1863	Skirmish in Cedar County, MO, with Col. Joseph O. Shelby, CSA.
10	17	1863	Skirmish near Camden Court-House, NC, where the rear of a Union Cavalry detachment is fired upon by guerrillas concealed in the swamps. The Union men in the rear were not so lucky.
10	17	1863	Affair at Accotink, VA.
10	17	1863	Skirmish at Berryville, VA.
10	17	1863	Skirmishes at Groveton, VA, Bristoe Campaign. 10/17-18/1863.
10	17	1863	Skirmishes at Manassas Junction and Frying Pan Church, near Pohick Church, VA, as Gen. Robert E. Lee, CSA, withdraws from Bull Run toward the Rappahannock River, VA, the Bristoe Campaign.
10	17	1863	Affair at Stuart's, near Chantilly, VA.
10	18	1863	**William Price Sanders,** USA, is appointed Brig. Gen.
10	18	1863	Skirmish at Carrion Crow Bayou, LA, with Maj. Gen. William B. Franklin, USA.
10	18	1863	Skirmish on the Livingston road, near Clinton, MS.
10	18	1863	Maj. Gen. Ulysses S. Grant, USA, assumes the command of the Military Division of the Mississippi, which consists of all Union troops between the Mississippi River and the Cumberland Mountains.
10	18	1863	Skirmish at Carthage, MO, with Col. Joseph O. Shelby, CSA.
10	18	1863	Affair near Annandale, VA, where Maj. John Singleton Mosby, CSA, and his **Virginia Partisan Rangers** capture over 100 horses and mules, several wagons loaded with valuable stores, and between 75 and 100 prisoners, arms, equipment, etc, without sustaining any losses.
10	18	1863	Skirmish at Bristoe Station, VA, as Gen. Robert E. Lee, CSA, withdraws to around Orange Coury-House.
10	18	1863	The Confederate Army of Northern Virginia is established on the line of the Rappahannock River, VA, under the command of Gen. Robert E. Lee, CSA.
10	18	1863	The Confederate attack, under Brig. Gen. John D. Imboden, CSA, commanding the Valley District, on **Charleston, WV,** and skirmishes on the road to Berryville, VA, as Imboden surrounds Charlestown and **captures** the entire Union force there of 250 men, mostly the 9th Maryland.
10	19	1863	**Lucius Fairchild,** USA, is appointed Brig. Gen.
10	19	1863	Skirmish at Grand Coteau, LA, with Maj. Gen. William B. Franklin, USA.
10	19	1863	Skirmish at Smith's Bridge, MS.
10	19	1863	Skirmish at Honey Creek, MO, with bushwackers.
10	19	1863	Affair at Murrell's Inlet, (Myrtle Beach), SC, as the Confederates capture 11 Federals of a landing party arriving on barges who set out to recover the cargo aboard the blockade runner, **the Rover,** which ran aground here. The Confederates got the cargo as well as some prisoners.
10	19	1863	Skirmish at Spurgeon's Mill, TN.

10	19	1863	Skirmish at Zollicoffer, TN.
10	19	1863	The action at Buckland Mills, VA, or the **Buckland Races,** where Maj. Gen. JEB Stuart, CSA, routed Brig. Gen. H. Judson Kilpatrick's, USA, Cavalry forces, during the Bristoe Campaign.
10	19	1863	Skirmishes at Gainesville, New Baltimore, Catlett's Station, and Hay Market, VA, the Bristoe Campaign.
10	20	1863	Federal reconnaissance from Bridgeport toward Trenton, AL, with skirmish and capture of a few Confederates and their horses.
10	20	1863	Maj. Gen. Cadwallader C. Washburn, USA, assumes the command of the 13th US Army Corps, MS, etal.
10	20	1863	Skirmish at Treadwell's Plantation, MS.
10	20	1863	Skirmish at Warm Springs, NC, as a Rebel attack on the pickets here is repulsed; similar to last night although a picket of 10 Rebel men were captured then.
10	20	1863	**Operations on the Memphis and Charleston Railroad, TN,** etal. 10/20-29/1863.
10	20	1863	Skirmishes at Barton's and Dickson's Stations and Cane Creek, AL, on the **Memphis and Charleston Railroad.**
10	20	1863	Action at Philadelphia, TN, as Confederate Cavalry forces under Col. George G. Dibrell attack a wagon train belonging to Maj. Gen. Ambrose E. Burnsides, USA, commanding the Dept. of the Ohio, inflicting 479 casualties on the Federals in the process.
10	20	1863	**Maj. Gen. George H. Thomas, USA, supersedes Maj. Gen. William S. Rosecrans, USA, in the command of the Army of the Cumberland, TN,** etal.
10	20	1863	The Confederate cavalry, under Maj. Gen. JEB Stuart, CSA, retires across the Rappahannock River, VA, the Bristoe Campaign.
10	21	1863	Action at Cherokee Station, AL, on the **Memphis and Charleston Railroad.**
10	21	1863	Skirmishes at Opelousas and Barre's Landing, LA, with the **occupation of Opelousas, LA,** by Maj. Gen. William Buel Franklin, USA.
10	21	1863	Affair in Greenton Valley, near Hopewell, MO, with bushwackers.
10	21	1863	Skirmish at Sulphur Springs, TN.
10	21	1863	Federal scout from Charleston to Boone County Court-House, WV, and around Turtle Creek, Six-Mile Creek, and the Spruce Fork of Coal River, finding no enemy except a few stragglers who are made prisoners. 10/21-22/1863.
10	22	1863	Skirmish near Volney, Logan County, KY, with a complete rout of the Confederates. Unfortunately, a local citizen was shot dead when he refused to allow the Federals to confiscate his horse.
10	22	1863	Destruction of the steamer, **Mist,** near Ship Island, on the Mississippi River, by a band of Confederates.
10	22	1863	Skirmish at Brownsville, MS.
10	22	1863	Mutiny at Bloomfield, MO, by the subordinate officers of the 6th Missouri Cavalry, against their Colonel. A Court of Inquiry is held and all 5 subordinate officers are dismissed from the Union Army.
10	22	1863	Federal scout from Germantown, TN, to Chulahoma, MS, with little activity. It's a good thing as the men's clothing and most of their ammunition was thoroughly soaked with the heavy rain downpour. 10/22-24/1863.
10	22	1863	Skirmish at New Madrid Bend, TN.
10	22	1863	Affair near Annandale, some 3 miles from Fairfax Court-House and near the Little River turnpike, VA, as the Federals run into a squad of Maj. John S. **Mosby's Virginia Partisan Rangers** who were looking for government horses and sutlers' wagons. Mosby loses some good men today.
10	22	1863	Skirmishes at the Rappahannock Bridge, and near Bealeton, or Beverly Ford, VA, effectively ending the Bristoe, VA Campaign.
10	23	1863	Skirmish at Warm Springs, NC.
10	23	1863	Skirmish at Sweet Water, TN.
10	23	1863	**Lieut. Gen. Leonidas Polk, CSA, is transferred from the Army of Tennessee to the Army of the Mississippi,** partially due to the inability of Polk to get along with Gen. Braxton Bragg, a long time friend and supporter of President Jefferson Davis, while vice Lieut. Gen. William J. Hardee, CSA, is reassigned to the Army of the Tennessee, as President Davis continues his tour of the deep South.
10	23	1863	Skirmish at Fayetteville, VA.
10	23	1863	Skirmish near Rappahannock Station, VA.
10	24	1863	Skirmishes at Tuscumbia, AL. 10/24-25/1863.
10	24	1863	Skirmish at the Buffalo Mountains, AR, with Col. Shelby, CSA.
10	24	1863	Federal expedition from Goodrich's Landing, LA, to Griffin's Landing, Washington County, and Catfish

Point, MS, aboard the steamers, **Adams, Baltic, Fairchild, and Horner,** capturing a Rebel agent with $12,000 in Confederate money who was purchasing livestock to feed the Confederates soldiers. Many fine fat hogs, etc, were sent to the ram **Monarch,** lying off Greenville. The Federals also captured the rebel mail-carrier, cotton, etc. The Confederates burn the steamer, **Allen Collier,** that had landed opposite Laconia, AR. The Federals burn the plantation and home of a local well-known guerrilla, setting the family out in the lawn, as many similar instances take place.10/24-11/24/1863.

10	24	1863	Skirmish at Washington, LA, with Maj. Gen. William B. Franklin, USA.
10	24	1863	Skirmish near Harrisonville, MO, with Col. Joseph Shelby, CSA.
10	24	1863	**Maj. Gen. William T. Sherman, USA, assumes the command of the Army of the Tennessee,** with vice Maj. Gen. Ulysses S. Grant, USA, commanding the Military Division of the Mississippi, and arriving at Chattanooga, TN, to take charge and orders a supply line, **"the cracker line,"** to be established for the beleaguered Union troops there.
10	24	1863	Skirmish at Bealeton, VA.
10	24	1863	Skirmish at Liberty, VA.
10	25	1863	Action at Pine Bluff, AR.
10	25	1863	Skirmishes at Philadelphia, TN. 10/25-26/1863.
10	25	1863	Skirmishes at and near Bealeton, VA. 10/25-26/1863.
10	26	1863	**Stephen Miller,** USA, is appointed Brig. Gen.
10	26	1863	Skirmishes near Cane Creek and at Barton's Station, AL, on the **Memphis and Charleston Railroad.**
10	26	1863	Skirmish in Johnson County, AR, with Col. Joseph Shelby, CSA.
10	26	1863	Maj. Gen. Napoleon J. T. Dana, USA, assumes the command of the 13th US Army Corps, LA, etal.
10	26	1863	Skirmish at Vincent's Cross-Roads, near Bay Springs, MS, as the Federals move to intercept a raiding party reported to be on their return from Walker County, AL; many men are killed in the dense woods, many more are missing, but never found.
10	26	1863	Federal scout from Cape Girardeau to Doniphan, MO, and Pocahontas, AR. 10/26-11/12/1863.
10	26	1863	Skirmish at King's House, near Waynesville, MO.
10	26	1863	Skirmish at Warm Springs, NC.
10	26	1863	**2nd massive Federal bombardment of Fort Sumter, Charleston Harbor, SC, gets under way.**
10	26	1863	**The Reopening of the Tennessee River, (the "cracker line")** by Maj. Gen. Joseph Hooker, USA, from Virginia, crosses the river at Bridgeport, AL, moving eastward toward Chattanooga, TN, including skirmish at: a) Brown's Ferry, **(27th)** and engagement at b) Wauhatchie, TN. **(28th** and **29th)** 10/26-29/1863.
10	26	1863	Skirmish at Jones' Hill, TN.
10	26	1863	Skirmishes at and near Sweet Water, TN. 10/26-27/1863.
10	26	1863	Confederate attack led by Maj. John S. Mosby, CSA, and 50 Partisan Rangers, on a 50 wagon train 2 miles from New Baltimore, and Warrenton where there are large Union camps. Union cavalry arrives in time to prevent Mosby from burning many wagons, although he does make off with 145 horses and mules and upwards of 30 Negroes and Yankees before losing many of his horses in the dark. Tomorrow, he'll try to recover them.
10	26	1863	Skirmish at Ravenswood, WV.
10	27	1863	**Isaac Fitzgerald Shepard,** USA, is appointed Brig. Gen.
10	27	1863	Skirmish at Little Bear Creek, AL, on the **Memphis and Charleston Railroad.**
10	27	1863	Skirmish at Tulip, AR.
10	27	1863	Federal expedition from Cape Girardeau to Clarkton, MO. 10/27-11/15/1863.
10	27	1863	Skirmish in Cherokee County, NC, when Brig. Gen. Alfred J. Vaughn, Jr, CSA, along with Pro-Southern Indians, overtook **Goldman Bryson** and his mounted robbers, killing two and capturing 17 along with 30 horses. The following day, Vaughn catches up with and kills **Mr. Bryson** and another carrying orders from Maj. Gen. Ambrose Burnside, USA.
10	27	1863	Skirmish at Clinch Mountain, TN.
10	27	1863	Federal scout from Columbia toward Pulaski, TN, and skirmish.
10	27	1863	**The Rio Grande Expedition,** under Maj. Gen. Nathaniel P. Banks, USA, and operations on the coast of Texas, as Banks will attempt to establish a base of operations in Texas despite past failures at Sabine Pass and on the Teche. 10/27-12/2/1863.
10	27	1863	Federal expedition under the command of Maj. Gen. Nathaniel Banks, USA, sails from the mouth of the

			Mississippi River.
10	27	1863	Skirmishes near Bealeton and Rappahannock Station, VA.
10	27	1863	Skirmish on Sandy River, near Elizabeth, WV.
10	28	1863	The Federal Cavalry **occupation of Arkadelphia, AR.**
10	28	1863	Skirmish at Clarksville, TN.
10	28	1863	Skirmish at Leiper's Ferry, TN.
10	28	1863	Brig. Gen. John W. Geary, USA, of Maj. Gen. Joseph Hooker's command, repels Lieut. Gen. James Longstreet's night attack at Wauhatchie, in Lookout Valley, TN, as Longstreet fails in his attempt to break the Union's newly established **"cracker line."**
10	28	1863	Maj. Gen. John M. Palmer, USA, assumes the command of the 14th US Army Corps, TN, etal.
10	28	1863	The mutiny of Capt. Adrian I. Vidal, CSA, and followers who attack, kill, and wound some Confederate soldiers, many eventually being caught themselves and dealt with accordingly, at Fort Brown, TX.
10	29	1863	**Edward Higgins,** CSA, is appointed Brig. Gen.
10	29	1863	President Jefferson Davis continues with his trip through the deep south, visiting Atlanta, GA.
10	29	1863	Skirmish at Cherokee Station, AL, on the **Memphis and Charleston Railroad.**
10	29	1863	Skirmish at Ozark, MO.
10	29	1863	Federal scout from Pilot Knob to Alton and Doniphan, MO, with the killing and capture of guerrillas. 10/29-11/5/1863.
10	29	1863	Affair near Warsaw, MO.
10	29	1863	Skirmish at Centreville, TN, as Maj. Gen. George H. Thomas' USA, Cavalry attack and rout of the Confederates, killing, wounding and capturing close to 90 Rebels.
10	29	1863	Federal scout from Winchester to Fayetteville, TN, by way of Lynchburg, with skirmish. The Union men bring back beef cattle, horses and mules.10/29-11/2/1863.
10	29	1863	Maj. Gen. Frank P. Blair, Jr., USA, assumes the command of the 15th US Army Corps, TN, etal.
10	30	1863	**James Harrison Wilson,** USA, is appointed Brig. Gen.
10	30	1863	Skirmish at Fourteen Mile Creek, the Indian Territory.
10	30	1863	Skirmish at Salyersville, KY.
10	30	1863	Affair near Opelousas, LA, with Maj. Gen. William B. Franklin, USA.
10	30	1863	Affair at Ford's Mill, near New Berne, NC, with casualties.
10	30	1863	The federal steamer, **Chattanooga,** delivers supplies to the famished Union defenders at Chattanooga, TN.
10	30	1863	Skirmish at Leiper's Ferry, Holston River, TN.
10	30	1863	Skirmish near Catlett's Station, VA.
10	31	1863	**Brig. Gen. (Retired) Louis Ludwig Blenker, USA,** dies on his farm, in Rockland County, NY, having resigned from the Union Army Ranks on March 31, 1863.
10	31	1863	Skirmish at Barton's Station, AL.
10	31	1863	Skirmish at Washington, LA, with Maj. Gen. William B. Franklin, USA.
10	31	1863	Skirmish at Yazoo City, MS.
10	31	1863	The Federal bombardment of Fort Sumter, Charleston Harbor, SC, continues to reduce the fort to rubble.
10	31	1863	Affair near Weaverville, VA, as the Confederates surround and capture 3 Union tents with sleeping men inside who were supposed to be guarding the cattle within a mile or two of Federal Army headquarters. This causes a Union officer to write that rebel marauders are numerous along the Warrenton pike and between that and the railroad, and daily shoot and capture men almost in sight of headquarters.
11	1	1863	<u>**Ulysses Simpson Grant is appointed the sole Lieut. General in the Union Army.**</u>
11	1	1863	The Union forces under Maj. Gen. William B. Franklin, USA, retire from Opelousas to New Iberia, LA. 11/1-17/1863.
11	1	1863	Federal scout from Bovina to Baldwin's Ferry, MS, with no encounters with the enemy. One of the few days a force traverses the back country roads passing many small farms and houses with no loss of life. A fine day to be alive.
11	1	1863	Skirmish at Quinn and Jackson's Mill, MS.
11	1	1863	Skirmish at Eastport, TN.
11	1	1863	Skirmish at Fayetteville, TN.
11	1	1863	Skirmish with Indians on the Gila, the New Mexico Territory.
11	1	1863	Skirmish at Catlett's Station, VA.

MONTH	DAY	YEAR	ACT
11	1	1863	Federal expeditions from Beverly and Charleston against Lewisburg, WV. 11/1-17/1863.
11	1	1863	Brig. Gen. William W. Averell's US Cavalry command sets out from Beverly, WV, against Lewisburg.
11	2	1863	Skirmish at Bayou Bourbeau, LA, as Maj. Gen. William B. Franklin, USA, retires from Opelousas.
11	2	1863	Skirmish at Corinth, MS.
11	2	1863	President Jefferson Davis arrives at Charleston, SC, and observes first hand the continued Federal bombardment of Fort Sumter.
11	2	1863	Skirmish at Centreville, TN.
11	2	1863	Skirmish at Piney Factory, TN.
11	2	1863	**Brazos Island, TX, is occupied** by the expeditionary Union forces under Maj. Gen. Nathaniel P. Banks, USA, arriving from New Orleans, LA, aboard the **USS Monongahela, Owasco,** and the **Virginia.**
11	2	1863	Brig. Gen. John McNeil, USA, assumes command of the District of the Frontier.
11	3	1863	Engagement at Bayou Bourbeau, near Grand Coteau, LA, with Maj. Gen. William B. Franklin, USA.
11	3	1863	Skirmish at Carrion Crow Bayou, LA, with Maj. Gen. William B. Franklin, USA.
11	3	1863	Skirmish at Quinn and Jackson's Mill, Coldwater River, MS, on the **Memphis and Charleston Railroad.**
11	3	1863	Action at Collierville, TN, on the **Memphis and Charleston Railroad,** as Brig. Gen. John Ronald Chalmers, CSA, attacks the Federals with no success, losing 95 men in the process.
11	3	1863	Skirmish at Lawrenceburg, TN, as the Federals move against Col. Albert Cooper's Confederate camp there, with decent success.
11	3	1863	Confederate operations on the **Memphis and Charleston Railroad,** TN. 11/3-5/1863.
11	3	1863	Confederate scout about Catlett's Station, VA, by Maj. John S. Mosby, CSA, who surprises, kills, and captures Union soldiers of Brig. Gen. Judson Kilpatrick's, USA, Cavalry.
11	3	1863	Brig. Gen. Alfred N. A. Duffie's USA Cavalry command sets out from Charleston, WV, to join up with Brig. Gen. William W. Averell's USA, Cavalry expedition.
11	4	1863	Skirmish at Maysville, AL.
11	4	1863	Skirmish in the Pinal Mountains on the Gila River, the Arizona Territory.
11	4	1863	Federal expedition from Houston to Jack's Fork, and in Reynolds, Shannon, and Oregon counties, MO.
11	4	1863	Skirmish near Lexington, MO, with bushwackers.
11	4	1863	Skirmish at and near Neosho, MO. 11/4-6/1863.
11	4	1863	Federal expedition aboard transports and supported by the Union gunboats, **Delaware, Miami** and **Whitehead,** up the Chowan River, NC, to within 2 miles of the mouth of the Blackwater. 11/4-9/1863.
11	4	1863	Skirmish near Rocky Run, NC, with bushwackers.
11	4	1863	**The Knoxville (Tennessee) Campaign.** 11/4-12/23/1863.
11	4	1863	**Lieut. Gen. James Longstreet's Confederate Corps is detached from the Army of Tennessee,** in part due to his inability to get along with Gen. Braxton Bragg, CSA, and his operations against Maj. Gen. Ambrose E. Burnside's, USA, Union forces in East Tennessee, around Knoxville, TN.
11	4	1863	Skirmish at Motley's Ford, Little Tennessee River, TN, as the Federals got near the river just as a Confederate regiment was crossing the river. They charged them and drove them into the river, where at least 50 were killed or drowned in crossing.
11	4	1863	Skirmish at Falmouth, VA.
11	4	1863	Skirmish near Cackleytown, WV, during the Union Cavalry expedition to Lewisburg, WV
11	5	1863	Skirmish at Vermillionville, LA, with Maj. Gen. William B. Franklin, USA.
11	5	1863	Skirmish at Holly Springs, MS.
11	5	1863	Skirmish at Neosho, MO.
11	5	1863	Skirmish at La Fayette, TN, on the **Memphis and Charleston Railroad.**
11	5	1863	Skirmish in Loudon County, TN, with loss of life, similar to all other skirmishes.
11	5	1863	Skirmish at Moscow, TN, as Lieut. Gen. Ulysses S. Grant impatiently hopes that Maj. Gen. William T. Sherman, USA, arrives at Chattanooga before Lieut. Gen. James Longstreet, CSA, arrives against Maj. Gen. Ambrose E. Burnside, USA, at Knoxville, TN, on the **Memphis and Charleston Railroad.**
11	5	1863	**Confederate Maj. John Mosby's Operations in Virginia,** as Mosby reports capturing 75 Union Cavalrymen, over 100 mules and horses, plus wagons, arms, and equipment, and earning the reputation of the area he operated in as **"Mosby's Confederacy."** 11/5-22/1863.
11	5	1863	Skirmish at Hartwood Church, VA.
11	5	1863	Skirmish at Mill Point, WV, as the Union cavalry expedition presses on towards Lewisburg, WV.

11	6	1863	**Adin Ballou Underwood,** USA, is appointed Brig. Gen.
11	6	1863	Action at Rogersville, TN, as Brig. Gen. William E. "Grumble" Jones, CSA, Cavalry **captures Rogersville,** along with 775 prisoners, 32 wagons, ambulances, 1,000 horses, etc. However, by the time the horses got to headquarters, only 300 remained. Maj. Gen. Robert Ransom, Jr., CSA, commanding the District of Southwestern Virginia and East Tennessee believes the "missing" horses were appropriated by the men and may have been sent off and sold. Free enterprise at work? OR insubordination?
11	6	1863	**Brownsville and Point Isabel, TX, is occupied** by Maj. Gen. Nathaniel P. Banks' USA, expeditionary forces.
11	6	1863	Skirmish near Falmouth, VA.
11	6	1863	Engagement at Droop Mountain, WV, as Brig. Gen. William W. Averell's, USA, cavalry command continues to advance, defeating Brig. Gen. John Echols, CSA.
11	6	1863	Skirmish at Little Sewell Mountain, WV, with Brig. Gen. William W. Averell, USA.
11	7	1863	Federal expedition from Fayetteville, AR, to Frog Bayou, AR, and skirmishes (**9th**) near Huntsville and (**10th**) near Kingston. 11/7-13/1863.
11	7	1863	The advance of the Army of the Potomac to the line of the Rappahannock, VA. 11/7-8/1863.
11	7	1863	Engagement at Rappahannock Station, VA.
11	7	1863	Action at Kelly's Ford, VA, where Maj. Gen. George G. Meade, USA, forces Gen. Robert E. Lee to retreat to the Rapidan River.
11	7	1863	The capture of Union pickets near Warrenton, VA, who are paroled and released. Their Colonel is furious, charging them with cowardice, and upset as they were sitting down apart from their arms, making coffee when they were captured.
11	7	1863	The **capture of Lewisburg, WV,** by Brig. Gens. William W. Averell, and Alfred N. A. Duffie, USA, cavalry.
11	7	1863	Skirmish near Muddy Creek, WV, with Brig. Gen. William W. Averell, USA.
11	8	1863	Skirmish at Clarksville, AR.
11	8	1863	Skirmish at Bayou Tunica, or Tunica Bend, LA.
11	8	1863	Skirmish at Vermillionville, LA, with Maj. Gen. William B. Franklin, USA.
11	8	1863	**Maj. Gen. John C. Breckinridge, CSA, supersedes Lieut. Gen. Daniel H. Hill, CSA,** in the command of the 2nd Confederate Army Corps, the Army of Tennessee, in part due to Hill's inability to get along with Gen. Braxton Bragg, CSA.
11	8	1863	Skirmish at Warrenton, or Sulphur, Springs, VA, as Maj. Gen. George G. Meade, USA, moves the Army of the Potomac forward, including the following 5 skirmishes:
11	8	1863	Skirmish at Brandy Station, VA.
11	8	1863	Skirmish at Jeffersonton, VA.
11	8	1863	Skirmish at Muddy Run, near Culpeper Court-House, VA.
11	8	1863	Skirmish at Rixeyville, VA.
11	8	1863	Skirmish at Stevensburg, VA.
11	8	1863	Skirmish at Second Creek, on the road to Union, WV, with Brig. Gen. William W. Averell, USA.
11	9	1863	Skirmish in the **Choctaw Nation,** the Indian Territory.
11	9	1863	Skirmish near Bayou Sara, LA, as Confederate cavalry chase the Federals back to their ironclads, capturing prisoners and a wagon train.
11	9	1863	Skirmish near Indian Bayou, LA.
11	9	1863	Federal operations near Weldon, NC.
11	9	1863	Skirmish near Covington, VA, with the Union Cavalry expedition forces under Brig. Gen. William W. Averell, USA.
11	9	1863	Federal expedition from **Williamsburg** toward New Kent Court House, VA, where the Federals returned to **Williamsburg** with 30 wagons filled with corn gathered from the fields of 3 locals farmers. The Confederates on hand were not strong enough to prevent such action. 11/9-10/1863.
11	9	1863	President Jefferson Davis returns to Richmond, VA, from his trip into the deep south amid a snowstorm.
11	9	1863	President Abraham Lincoln spends the evening at the theater watching John Wilkes Booth star in "The Marble Heart."
11	10	1863	**William Thompson Martin, CSA,** is appointed Maj. Gen.
11	10	1863	**John Austin Wharton, C.S.A.,** is appointed Maj. Gen.
11	10	1863	Federal expedition from Benton to Mount Ida, AR, and skirmish (**11th**) at Caddo Gap. 11/10-16/1863.
11	10	1863	Federal expedition from Skipwith's Landing to Tallulah Court-House, MS, the Federals marching

			through a "deserted and abandoned country," with no enemy encounters. 11/10-13/1863.
11	10	1863	Federal expedition from Springfield, MO, to Huntsville, Carrollton, and Berryville, AR, in an attempt to mop up Confederate guerrilla operations, as well as above expeditions.
11	10	1863	Skirmish on Elk Mountain, near Hillsborough, WV, with Brig. Gen. William W. Averell, USA.
11	11	1863	Skirmish in the Fouche-le-Faix Mountains, AR.
11	11	1863	Skirmish at Greenleaf Prairie, the Indian Territory.
11	11	1863	Skirmishes at Carrion Crow and Vermillion Bayous, Bayou Teche country, LA, with Maj. Gen. William B. Franklin, USA.
11	11	1863	Skirmish near Natchez, MS.
11	11	1863	**Maj. Gen. Benjamin F. Butler, USA, supersedes Maj. Gen. John G. Foster, USA, in the command of the Dept. of Virginia and North Carolina.**
11	11	1863	Confederate raid on Suffolk, VA, where a company of cavalry dash through into the town, capturing 1 wagon, 8 fine horses and 7 prisoners.
11	12	1863	Skirmish at Roseville, AR.
11	12	1863	Skirmish at Greenlcaf Prairic, the Indian Territory.
11	12	1863	Operations about Saint Martinsville, Bayou Teche country, LA, with Maj. Gen. William B. Franklin, USA.
11	12	1863	Skirmish at Corinth, MS.
11	12	1863	Skirmish near Cumberland Gap, TN, as the Federal Cavalry arrives just in time to recapture the 21 wagon forage train sent out that was in the process of being captured by the Confederates. After loss of life, the Rebels high tail it out of there.
11	12	1863	Lieut. Gen. James Longstreet's Confederate Corps along with Maj. Gen. Joseph Wheeler's Cavalry Command arrives at Loudon, TN, for a combined assault on Maj. Gen. Ambrose E. Burnside, USA, at Knoxville, TN.
11	13	1863	**Brig. Gen. Carnot Posey, CSA,** dies at Charlottesville, VA, from infection that set in from the wound received October 14, 1863 at the engagement at Bristoe Station, VA.
11	13	1863	Skirmish at Mount Ida, AR, with a Union attack on the Confederate camp there.
11	13	1863	Skirmishes with Indians near the Big Bar on the South Fork of the Trinity River, CA, with various encounters and Indian deaths, including the 2 Indians and 3 squaws that were dressing a beef they had killed for food; the squaws escaped. The Indians were buried. 11/13-14/1863.
11	13	1863	Federal reconnaissance to the entrance of the Cape Fear River, NC. 11/13-14/1863.
11	13	1863	Skirmish at Blythe's Ferry, Tennessee River, TN.
11	13	1863	Skirmish at Palmyra, TN.
11	13	1863	Skirmish near Winchester, VA.
11	13	1863	Brig. Gen. Alfred N. A. Duffie's, USA, Cavalry command reaches Charleston, WV, part of the Cavalry expedition to Lewisburg.
11	14	1863	Federal expedition from Maysville to Whitesburg and Decatur, AL, sent to thoroughly scout the country situated between the **Memphis and Charleston Railroad** and the Tennessee River, and drive out or capture the marauding rebel bands known to be roving over that country, pressing horses, mules, cattle, sheep, hogs, wheat, etc. and running them across the river for Confederate use. The plantations in this area are very large, generally 2,000 to 4,000 acres each. Corn, horses, etc. are in abundant supply. 11/14-17/1863.
11	14	1863	Federal expedition from Helena, AR, aboard the steamer, **Hamilton Belle.**
11	14	1863	Skirmishes at Danville, MS. 11/14-15/1863.
11	14	1863	Skirmish at Huff's Ferry, TN, the Knoxville, TN, Campaign.
11	14	1863	Skirmish at Little River, TN, the Knoxville, TN, Campaign.
11	14	1863	Skirmish at Maryville, TN, the Knoxville, TN, Campaign.
11	14	1863	Skirmish at Rockford, TN.
11	14	1863	Affairs on the Eastern Shore of Virginia, where John Y. Beall, master in the Rebel navy, and his crew of 14 men land on the Chesapeake shore whose object was the capture of a steamer. Unfortunately for Beall and his men, they are the ones captured. Beall admits being responsible for the capture of other Union vessels in the past. 11/14-15/1863.
11	14	1863	Brig. Gen. Nathan Bedford Forrest, CSA, is assigned to the Confederate command of West Tennessee.
11	14	1863	Skirmish at Tyson's Cross-Roads, VA.
11	14	1863	Federal scout from Martinsburg, to Pughtown, up to the head of Cedar Creek, at Van Buren Furnace, WV,

where a few Confederate Cavalrymen and horses are captured. 11/14-18/1863.

11	15	1863	Skirmish in Newton County, AR.
11	15	1863	Maj. Gen. William T. Sherman, USA, arrives with his Union troops at Bridgeport, AL, enroute to the relief of Chattanooga, TN, under Lieut. Gen. Ulysses S. Grant, USA.
11	15	1863	Federal expedition from Vidalia to Trinity, LA. 11/15-16/1863.
11	15	1863	Confederate demonstration on John's Island, SC, as the Rebels unsuccessfully attempt to destroy the bridge connecting Seabrook and Kiawah Islands. The Federals are well equipped with vessels, having 11 schooners, 3 steamers, 3 brigs and 2 gunboats in the harbor, a definite advantage in this area.
11	15	1863	Skirmish at Lenoir's Station, TN, the Knoxville, TN, Campaign.
11	15	1863	Skirmish at Loudon, TN, the Knoxville, TN, Campaign.
11	15	1863	Skirmish at Pillowville, TN, as the Federals attack and rout a Confederate conscripting party, killing some in the process.
11	15	1863	Skirmish at Stock Creek, TN, the Knoxville, TN, Campaign.
11	15	1863	Federal expedition from Charlestown, WV, to near New Market, VA, and skirmishes (**16th**) at:

a) Woodstock, where the Federals capture the Rebel mail carrier and a wagon with four barrels of apple brandy intended for Brig. Gen. John D. Imboden's, CSA, camp.

b) Edenburg, and skirmish with Confederate pickets there, and

c) Mount Jackson, VA, with Confederate Cavalry and later on with bushwackers. 11/15-18/1863.

11	16	1863	The following are appointed Confederate Brigadier Generals:

James Holt Clanton,	CSA
Jesse Johnson Finley,	CSA
William Young Conn Humes,	CSA
John Hebert Kelly,	CSA
John Tyler Morgan,	CSA
Claudius Charles Wilson,	CSA

11	16	1863	Federal expedition from Vidalia to Trinity, LA.
11	16	1863	Engagement between the US Monitors and the Confederate batteries on Sullivan's Island, SC, with some severe nasty wounds causing death to some brave young men.
11	16	1863	Engagement at Campbell's Station, TN, where Lieut. Gen. James Longstreet, CSA, is unsuccessful in his attempt to cut off Maj. Gen. Ambrose E. Burnside's retreat to Knoxville, TN, the Knoxville, TN, Campaign.
11	16	1863	Skirmishes at and about Kingston, East TN, the Knoxville, TN, Campaign. 11/16-23/1863.
11	16	1863	Skirmish near Knoxville, TN, the Knoxville, TN, Campaign.
11	16	1863	Maj. Gen. Nathaniel P. Banks, USA, **occupies Corpus Christi, TX.**
11	16	1863	Affair at Germantown, VA, with Confederate Cavalry, probably some of Maj. John S. Mosby's Virginia Partisan Rangers.
11	16	1863	Federal expedition from Yorktown into Matthews County, VA, with the destruction of over 30 small boats, and the capture of some Confederate seamen, and with Union refugees coming in with the troops to avoid the Confederate conscription. 11/16-19/1863.
11	16	1863	Skirmish near Burlington, WV, where in addition to the events taking place with the Federal expedition on 11/15/1863 from Charlestown, Brig. Gen. John D. Imboden's, CSA, men attack a train of 80 wagons near Burlington, Hampshire County, WV, fleeing before setting fire to them, but removing with them 25 prisoners as well as 245 good horses.
11	17	1863	Skirmish near Willow Creek on the Trinity River, CA, with Indians.
11	17	1863	Skirmish at Bay Saint Louis, MS.
11	17	1863	Federal scout around Houston, MO. 11/17-11/26/1863.
11	17	1863	The massive Union bombardment of Fort Sumter, SC, continues.
11	17	1863	**The Siege of Knoxville, TN,** begins by Lieut. Gen. James Longstreet, CSA, the Knoxville, TN, Campaign. 11/17-12/4/1863.
11	17	1863	The capture of the Confederate battery at Arkansas Pass, TX, by Maj. Gen. Nathaniel P. Banks' USA, expeditionary forces.
11	17	1863	Brig. Gen. William W. Averell's US Cavalry command reaches New Creek, WV, effectively ending his successful cavalry expedition to Lewisburg, WV.
11	18	1863	**Brig. Gen. William Price Sanders, USA,** is mortally wounded by Lieut. Gen. James Longstreet's, CSA,

men as Sanders led his command to check the advance of the Confederates near Knoxville, TN, expiring the next day in a hotel room in Knoxville, TN.

11	18	1863	**Alfred Jefferson Vaughan, Jr,** CSA, is appointed Brig. Gen.
11	18	1863	Skirmish at Trenton, GA.
11	18	1863	Skirmish at Carrion Crow Bayou, LA, with Maj. Gen. William B. Franklin, USA.
11	18	1863	Federal expedition from Skipwith's Landing to Roebuck Lake, MS. 11/18-22/1863.
11	18	1863	Confederate operations against the United States gunboats, **USS Carondelet, USS Choctaw,** and the **USS Franklin** and transports near Hog Point, Mississippi River. 11/18-21/1863.
11	18	1863	Skirmish on Shoal and Turkey Creek, Jasper County, MO.
11	18	1863	Cavalry skirmish near Germanna Ford, VA, with Brig. Gen. George A. Custer, USA, pitted against Maj. Gen. Wade Hampton, CSA.
11	18	1863	Federal reconnaissance from Vienna toward the Blue Ridge Mountains, VA, in an effort to capture guerrillas, with the successful capture of a few of Maj. John S. Mosby's Virginian Partisan Rangers. 11/18-23/1863.
11	19	1863	**Brig. Gen. William Price Sanders, USA,** dies in the Knoxville, TN, hotel, the **Lamar,** from wounds received the day before.
11	19	1863	Skirmish near Lawrenceville, AR, at Dr. Green's farm.
11	19	1863	Federal gunboat demonstration upon Fort Sumter, SC. The Fort holds on. 11/19-20/1863.
11	19	1863	Skirmish at Colwell's Ford, TN.
11	19	1863	Federal scout from Memphis, TN, to Hernando, MS.
11	19	1863	President Abraham Lincoln, following the main speaker of the day, Edward Everett, delivers his famous, **"Gettysburg Address,"** in dedication of the fallen at the battle, and of the Federal Cemetery, at Gettysburg, PA.
11	19	1863	Skirmish at Meriwether's Ferry, near Union City, TN, as the Federals whip the Confederates. Capt. Franklin Moore, 2nd IL Cavalry states, "We came, we saw, we conquered," Well, at least at this encounter. Many, many more to follow.
11	19	1863	Skirmish at Mulberry Gap, TN, as the mounted Federals charge though a Rebel camp, killing and capturing some Confederates.
11	19	1863	Skirmish near Grove Church, VA.
11	20	1863	Skirmish at Camp Pratt, LA, with Maj. Gen. William B. Franklin, USA.
11	20	1863	Skirmish at Vermillion Bayou, LA.
11	20	1863	Fort Sumter, SC, continues to hold on against the heavy continuous Union bombardment.
11	20	1863	Skirmish at Sparta, TN.
11	21	1863	Affair at Jacksonport, AR, with a guerrilla ambush.
11	21	1863	Federal scout from Fort Pillow, TN, about 125 strong, capturing some Rebels pickets on duty, as they are overwhelmed. 11/21-22/1863.
11	21	1863	Federal expedition from Island No. 10, aboard the steamer, **O'Brien,** to Tiptonville, TN, destroying two Rebel boats, capturing 5 barrels of salt, contraband, etc., and removing the seized property to the **O'Brien.**
11	21	1863	Federal expedition from Bealeton toward Thoroughfare Gap, VA, as the Federals are successful in capturing a couple of Maj. John S. Mosby's Partisan Rangers.
11	21	1863	Affair at Liberty, VA, where some of Maj. John S. Mosby's Partisan Rangers attack and capture the horses from 3 wagons and 2 ambulances.
11	21	1863	President Abraham Lincoln is confined to bed with a mild case of smallpox, and believing his recent speech at Gettysburg, PA, was a failure.
11	22	1863	**Brig. Gen. Michael Corcoran, USA,** dies near Fairfax Court-House, VA, when the horse he was riding falls, killing him.
11	22	1863	Affair on Lake Borgne, LA.
11	22	1863	Skirmish at Camp Davies, MS, as the Federals drive the attacking Confederates away from their camp towards Rienzi, MS.
11	22	1863	Skirmish at Fayette, MS.
11	22	1863	Skirmish near Houston, MO.
11	22	1863	Skirmish at Winchester, TN.
11	22	1863	The expedition against and the **capture of Fort Esperanza, Matagorda Island, TX,** by Maj. Gen. Nathaniel P. Banks, USA. 11/22-30/1863.

11	23	1863	Affair at Bayou Portage, Grand Lake, LA, with Maj. Gen. William B. Franklin, USA.
11	23	1863	Federal scout from Houston, MO. 11/23-29/1863.
11	23	1863	Federal expedition from Springfield to Howell, Morgan and Wright counties, MO.
11	23	1863	Assault on the Confederate lines about Knoxville, TN, the Knoxville, TN, Campaign.
11	23	1863	Assault on the Union lines about Knoxville, TN, the Knoxville, TN, Campaign.
11	23	1863	**The Chattanooga-Ringgold, TN, Campaign.** 11/23-27/1863.
11	23	1863	Skirmishes at Orchard Knob, or Indian Hill, and Bushy Knob, TN, with the Federal troops under Maj. Gen. William T. Sherman, USA, occupying Orchard Knob, and establishing an entrenched position for Lieut. Gen. Ulysses S. Grant, USA.
11	23	1863	Skirmish at Cedar Bayou, TX, with Maj. Gen. Nathaniel P Banks, USA.
11	23	1863	Federal expedition to Rio Grande City, TX, by Maj. Gen. William P. Banks, USA.
11	24	1863	Skirmish at Clarksville, AR.
11	24	1863	Federal scout from Salem to Bushy and Pigeon Creeks, Gladen Valley, and Dry Fork, MO. 11/24-27/1863.
11	24	1863	Skirmish near Cunningham's Bluff, SC, as the Federals are successful in liberating 27 slaves on the Heyward plantation. The Rebels attack sending a pack of bloodhounds on the Yankees who bayonet the dogs. Men also died today.
11	24	1863	Raid on the **East Tennessee and Georgia Railroad,** with skirmishes at: a) Charleston, TN. (**26th**), and b) Cleveland, TN. (**27th**). 11/24-27/1863.
11	24	1863	**The Battle of Lookout Mountain, TN, or the Battle Above the Clouds,** as Maj. Gen. Joseph Hooker, USA, forces the Confederates to retreat from Craven's Farm on Lookout Mountain to Missionary Ridge.
11	24	1863	Skirmish at the foot of Missionary Ridge, TN, as Maj. Gen. William T. Sherman, prepares to take the ridge. 11/24-27/1863.
11	24	1863	Action at Kingston, TN, with Lieut. Gen. James Longstreet, CSA. the Knoxville, TN, Campaign.
11	24	1863	Skirmishes at and near Sparta, TN, as the Federals capture horses, arms, ammunition, etc.
11	24	1863	Skirmish near Little Boston, VA, as the Union infantry pickets are captured. The Union party sent to find the vedettes are also attacked and some of these Union men are also captured. Brig. Gen. Wesley Merritt, USA, Cavalry, comments that because the Rebels launch effective attacks with only 50 to 100 men the entire region has to be carefully watched.
11	24	1863	Skirmish near Woodville, VA.
11	25	1863	Skirmish in Crawford County, AR.
11	25	1863	Affair at Camp Pratt, LA, with Maj. Gen. William B. Franklin, USA.
11	25	1863	Skirmish near Vermillion Bayou, LA, with Maj. Gen. William B. Franklin, USA.
11	25	1863	Skirmish on the Big Piney, MO.
11	25	1863	Skirmish at Farmington, MO.
11	25	1863	Skirmish near Waynesville, MO.
11	25	1863	Skirmish near Greenville, NC, where the Federals attack the Rebel camp there, capturing over 50 prisoners and 100 stand of arms, etc.
11	25	1863	**The Battle of Missionary Ridge, TN,** with Maj. Gen. Patrick R. Cleburne, CSA, repelling Maj. Gen. William T. Sherman at Tunnel Hill and the north end of Missionary Ridge; Maj. Gen. Joseph Hooker, USA, not making much progress; Maj. Gen. George H. Thomas, USA, assaulting and breaking the center of the Confederate lines, forcing Gen. Braxton Bragg, CSA, to retreat across the Chickamauga Creek, Lieut. Gen. William J. Hardee, CSA, protecting the rear flank from the pursuing Maj. Gen. Philip H. Sheridan, USA. Total casualties approximate 12,500.
11	25	1863	Skirmish near Yankeetown, TN.
11	25	1863	Affair between Sangster's and Devereux Stations, VA, where Confederate guerrillas capture 23 teamsters and woodcutters along with 50 mules.
11	26	1863	Skirmish near Graysville, GA, with Maj. Gen. Patrick Cleburne, CSA.
11	26	1863	Federal scout from Columbia, KY, to the south side of the Cumberland River.
11	26	1863	Skirmish near Woodson, MO.
11	26	1863	Skirmish at Plymouth, NC.
11	26	1863	Skirmish at Warm Springs, NC.
11	26	1863	Brig. Gen. Washington L. Elliott, USA, is ordered, with all available cavalry from the Army of the Cumberland, into East Tennessee, the Knoxville, TN, Campaign.

11	26	1863	Skirmish at Chickamauga Station, TN, and the following as Maj. Gens. George H. Thomas, and William T. Sherman, USA, confront the rear guard of Gen. Braxton Bragg's CSA army, led by Maj. Gen. Patrick R. Cleburne, CSA, which is retreating toward Ringgold, GA.
11	26	1863	Skirmish in Pea Vine Valley, TN, with Maj. Gen. Patrick Cleburne, CSA.
11	26	1863	Skirmish at Pigeon Hills, TN.
11	26	1863	Skirmishes at and near Sparta, TN.
11	26	1863	Skirmish at Brentsville, VA.
11	26	1863	**The Mine Run Campaign, VA.** 11/26-12/2/1863.
11	26	1863	The Army of the Potomac crosses the Rapidan, VA, under Maj. Gen. George Gordon Meade, USA, with the following skirmishes.
11	26	1863	Skirmish at Morton's Ford, VA, as Maj. Gen. George Gordon Meade presses on.
11	26	1863	Skirmishes at and near Raccoon Ford, VA, with Maj. Gen. George Gordon Meade, USA. 11/26-27/1863.
11	27	1863	**Brig. Gen. Claudius Charles Wilson, CSA,** dies of camp fever sickness at Ringgold, Ga.
11	27	1863	Engagement at Ringgold Gap, Taylor's Ridge, GA.
11	27	1863	Skirmish at La Fayette, KY, where the attacking Rebel force steals all the Union horses they could find, crossing the Cumberland River and to safety aboard the steam-boat, **Duke.**
11	27	1863	Skirmish at **Monticello, KY,** as the Confederates **capture** the town and the Federal garrison there consisting of 153 Federals.
11	27	1863	**Brig. Gen. John Hunt Morgan, CSA, escapes from the Ohio State Penitentiary, Columbus, OH,** along with some of his subordinate officers, making it safely back to Confederate lines.
11	27	1863	**Maj. Gen. Gordon Granger, USA, is ordered, with 2nd and 3rd US Army Divisions, of the 4th Army US Army Corps, (Army of the Cumberland),** to the relief of Maj. Gen. Ambrose E. Burnside, USA, under siege by Lieut. Gen. James Longstreet, CSA, at Knoxville, TN.
11	27	1863	Skirmish at Catlett's Station, VA.
11	27	1863	Action near New Hope Church, VA, with Gen. Robert E. Lee, CSA.
11	27	1863	The engagement at Payne's Farm, VA, and following as Gen. Robert E. Lee, CSA, contests the advance of the Army of the Potomac, and Maj. Gen. George G. Meade, USA.
11	27	1863	Skirmishes at Robertson's Tavern, or Locust Grove, VA, with Gen. Robert E. Lee, USA.
11	27	1863	The capture of a Union wagon train near the Wilderness Church, VA, by Gen. Robert E. Lee's, CSA, Confederates.
11	28	1863	Skirmish near Molino, MS, on the **Memphis and Charleston Railroad.**
11	28	1863	Brig. Gen. (soon to be Maj. Gen.) Nathan Bedford Forrest's operations against the **Memphis and Charleston Railroad,** in West Tennessee. 11/28-12/10/1863.
11	28	1863	Maj. Gen. William T. Sherman's, USA, march to the relief of Knoxville, TN, with the **2nd Brigade, 2nd Division, Cavalry Corps,** and with Maj. Gen. Gordon Granger's command, the **11th US Army Corps,** the **2nd Division, 14th US Army Corps** and part of the **15th US Army Corps,** the Army of the Cumberland, the Knoxville, TN, Campaign. 11/28-12/6/1863.
11	28	1863	Skirmishes along Mine Run, VA, by Maj. Gen. George Meade, USA.
11	29	1863	Skirmishes on the Cumberland River, KY, where the pursuing Federals capture 15 Rebels and kill the notorious thief and rebel, Capt. Belbo.
11	29	1863	Attack on Bloomfield, MO, and the pursuit of the Confederates to Brown's Ferry, AR. 11/29-30/1863.
11	29	1863	**The Assault on Fort Sanders, (or Fort Loudon) Knoxville, TN,** by Lieut. Gen. James Longstreet, CSA, is repulsed and the last attempt by the Confederates to eradicate the Federals from Knoxville, TN, is effectively ended, as Longstreet will retreat toward Virginia, fully aware that reinforcements under Maj. Gen. William T. Sherman, USA, are on their way.
11	29	1863	Confederate **evacuation of Fort Esperanza,** Matagorda Bay, TX.
11	29	1863	Skirmish at Brentsville, VA.
11	29	1863	Skirmish near Jonesville, VA.
11	29	1863	Skirmish at New Hope Church, VA, the Mine Run Campaign.
11	29	1863	Action at Parker's Store, VA, the Mine Run Campaign.
11	29	1863	President Abraham Lincoln begins his recovery from smallpox.
11	30	1863	Skirmish at Salyersville, KY.
11	30	1863	Skirmish near Port Hudson, LA.
11	30	1863	Skirmish at Vermillion Bayou, LA, with Maj. Gen. William B. Franklin, USA.

11	30	1863	Affair at Charleston, TN, the Knoxville, TN, Campaign.
11	30	1863	Federal scouts to New Madrid Bend, TN, to conscript all able-bodied men subject to military duty. During the night, the Confederates conscripted quite a few men from the same area. Both sides seizing horses, saddles, corn, etc. 11/30-12/3/1863.
11	30	1863	Skirmish at Yankeetown, TN, where the Federals drive the Confederates across the river, the commanding Federal claiming he would take no prisoners.
11	30	1863	Federal **occupation of Fort Esperanza,** Matagorda Bay, TX.
11	30	1863	Skirmish at Licking Run Bridge, VA, as Maj. Gen. George G. Meade, USA, begins to realize his futility in attacking Gen. Robert E. Lee's position, and will give up the Mine Run Campaign, VA, within the next couple of days.
11	30	1863	Skirmishes along Mine Run, VA.
11	30	1863	Skirmish near Raccoon Ford, VA, the Mine Run Campaign.
12	1	1863	Skirmish near Benton, AR.
12	1	1863	Skirmish at Devall's Bluff, AR, with guerrillas.
12	1	1863	Affairs at Mount Sterling and Jackson, KY, where Maj. Gen. Samuel Jones, CSA, reports the Confederates attacked and burned $700,000 worth of stores at Mount Sterling and Jackson, capturing 250 horses, inflicting 100 Union casualties, all this without losing a man. 12/1-10/1863.
12	1	1863	Skirmish at Salyersville, KY, as the Confederates attack the Union outpost there.
12	1	1863	Federal operations about Natchez, MS, and skirmish **(7th)**, as Maj. Gen. James B. McPherson, USA, commanding the 17 US Army Corps, attacks Brig. Gen. Wirt Adams, CSA, at Camp Cotton, forcing a Confederate retreat. 12/1-10/1863.
12	1	1863	Skirmish at Ripley, MS, on the **Memphis and Charleston Railroad** with Brig. Gen. Nathan Bedford Forrest, CSA.
12	1	1863	Affair with the **Ponca Indians,** near Niobrara, the Nebraska Territory.
12	1	1863	Skirmish at Cedar Point, NC.
12	1	1863	Skirmish near Maynardville, TN, with Maj. Gen. Ambrose E. Burnside, USA, the Knoxville, TN, Campaign.
12	1	1863	Federal scouts from Pulaski, TN, and skirmishes, with Confederate cavalry near Florence and at Rawhide with Rebels prisoners.
12	1	1863	Skirmish at Jennings' Farm, near Ely's Ford, VA.
12	1	1863	Skirmish near Jonesville, VA, as the attacking Federal cavalry arriving from Cumberland Gap, force some of Maj. Gen. Joseph Wheeler's, CSA, Cavalry to retreat in confusion, losing men, lives, horses, etc. to the Yankees.
12	1	1863	The Army of the Potomac, under Maj. Gen. George G. Meade, USA, retires across the Rapidan River, after the Federal repulse at Mine Run, VA, and goes into winter quarters, effectively ending the Mine Run Campaign that began on 11/26/1863.
12	1	1863	Reputed Confederate spy, **Belle Boyd,** is released from prison at Washington, DC, and sent to Richmond, VA, due to her suffering from typhoid fever, and warned never to return to the Union lines.
12	2	1863	Federal scout from Waldron, AR, to Mount Ida, Caddo Gap, and Dallas, MO. 12/2-7/1863.
12	2	1863	**Lieut. Gen. William J. Hardee, CSA, supersedes Gen. Braxton Bragg, CSA,** in the command of the Army of Tennessee, at Dalton, GA, after Gen. Bragg asks President Jefferson Davis to be relieved of command following the Confederate setbacks in the Tennessee arena of warfare.
12	2	1863	Skirmish at Philadelphia, TN.
12	2	1863	The Federal descent on Saulsbury, TN, on the **Memphis and Charleston Railroad.**
12	2	1863	Action at Walker's Ford, Clinch River, TN, the Knoxville, TN, Campaign.
12	3	1863	**Robert Vinkler Richardson,** CSA, is appointed Brig. Gen.
12	3	1863	Skirmish at Greenville, KY.
12	3	1863	Affair at Saint Martinsville, LA, where Union cavalry charge and capture a Confederate party of 18 soldiers.
12	3	1863	Lieut. Gen. James Longstreet, CSA, moves his Confederate forces toward Russellville, TN, for winter quarters, which effectively ends the Knoxville, TN, campaign; the Confederates receiving one disaster after another in Tennessee.
12	3	1863	Skirmish at Log Mountain, in East TN, the Knoxville, TN, Campaign.
12	3	1863	Action at Wolf River Bridge, near Moscow, TN, on the **Memphis and Charleston Railroad.** 12/3-4/1863.

12	3	1863	Skirmish at Ellis' Ford, VA.

12	4	1863	**Nathan Bedford Forrest, C.S.A.,** is appointed Maj. Gen.
12	4	1863	Affair at Ripley, MS, on the **Memphis and Charleston Railroad.**
12	4	1863	Skirmish with Indians at Niobrara, the Nebraska Territory.
12	4	1863	The Federals bombard Fort Sumter, SC, with over 1,300 rounds the last several days.
12	4	1863	Skirmish near Kingston, TN, the Knoxville, TN, Campaign.
12	4	1863	Skirmish at La Fayette, TN, on the **Memphis and Charleston Railroad.**
12	4	1863	Skirmishes at and near Loudon, TN, the Knoxville, TN, Campaign. 12/4-5/1863.
12	4	1863	Skirmish at Meadow Bluff, WV.

12	5	1863	Federal reconnaissance from Little Rock and skirmish (**8th**) at Princeton, AR. 12/5-13/1863.
12	5	1863	Federal reconnaissance from Rossville to Ringgold, GA.
12	5	1863	Federal scouts from Columbia, KY, into Clinton and other counties, with 4 skirmishes, and with the capture of horses and some of Brig. Gen. Samuel W. Ferguson's meanest Confederate "guerrillas." Brig. Gen. Edward H. Hobson, USA, writes to his commander wondering if the best thing to do would be to shoot the prisoners. 12/5-10/1863.
12	5	1863	Federal scout from New Berne toward Kinston, NC, where the Union guide gets the troops lost in the swamp, and they finally return with little else happening.
12	5	1863	Affair at Murrell's or Murray's Inlet, (Myrtle Beach), SC, ends with the Union boat expedition being repelled near Magnolia Beach.
12	5	1863	Skirmish at Crab Gap, TN.
12	5	1863	Skirmish at Walker's Ford, Clinch River, TN, the Knoxville, TN, Campaign.
12	5	1863	Brig. Gen. Henry H. Lockwood, USA, supersedes Maj. Gen. Robert C. Schenck, USA, in the command of the Middle Dept. and the 8th US Army Corps, VA, etal.
12	5	1863	Federal expedition from Norfolk, VA, aboard steamers and aided by the Union gunboats **Flora Temple** and the **Coleman,** to South Mills, Camden Court House, etc. NC, with many different events occurring including the hanging of a guerrilla with a placard stating "this guerrilla hanged by order of Brig. Gen. Edward A. Wild, USA." 12/5-24/1863.
12	5	1863	Skirmish at Raccoon Ford, VA.

12	6	1863	A strong wave swamps and sinks the blockading Union ironclad, the **Weehawken,** off Charleston Harbor, Charleston, SC.
12	6	1863	Skirmish at Clinch Mountain, TN, the Knoxville, TN, Campaign.
12	6	1863	Affair near Fayetteville, TN.
12	6	1863	Skirmish at Cheat River, WV.

12	7	1863	Skirmish at Independence, MS.
12	7	1863	Skirmish at Rutledge, TN, the Knoxville, TN, Campaign.
12	7	1863	Skirmish at Eagleville, TN.
12	7	1863	Federal scout in Hampshire, Hardy, Frederick, and Shenandoah Counties, and the destruction of the Columbian Iron Works, WV, which are 15 miles west of Woodstock and an equal distance from Mount Jackson, VA. 12/7-11/1863.
12	7	1863	President Jefferson Davis addresses the 4th session of the 1st Confederate Congress, Richmond, VA.
12	7	1863	The 38th US Congress convenes in Washington, DC.

12	8	1863	Skirmish near **Scottsville, KY,** as the attacking Confederates **capture** the town, along with the Union garrison there, with commissary stores, etc.
12	8	1863	The Federal merchant vessel, **Chesapeake,** is seized by a group of Northern Copperheads, off the coast of Cape Cod, MA.
12	8	1863	**The Federal Raid on the Virginia and Tennessee Railroad,** and demonstrations up the Shenandoah Valley from the Kanawha Valley, WV. 12/8-25/1863.
12	8	1863	Brig. Gen. Eliakim P. Scammon's, USA, command advances from the Kanawha Valley, WV.
12	8	1863	Brig. Gen. William W. Averell's, USA, command advances from New Creek, WV.

12	9	1863	Federal scout from Waldron down Dutch Creek, AR.
12	9	1863	**Maj. Gen. John G. Foster, USA, supersedes Maj. Gen. Ambrose E. Burnside, USA,** in the command of the **Dept. of the Ohio,** KY, etal, at Burnside's request, following the criticism of his various actions, including his failure to support Maj. Gen. William. S. Rosecrans, USA, at Chickamauga, GA.

12	9	1863	The mutiny of black troops at Fort Jackson, LA, after two black soldiers are punished by whipping. The insurrection is put down by the white officers.
12	9	1863	Skirmish at Okolona, MS.
12	9	1863	Federal scout from Houston, MO, in pursuit of Rebel marauders.
12	9	1863	Blockade runners are being captured all along the Union blockade; today the **Minna,** is captured off Charleston, SC.
12	9	1863	Skirmishes at and near Bean's Station, TN, the Knoxville, TN, Campaign. 12/9-13/1863.
12	9	1863	Affair at Cumberland Mountain, on the road to Crossville, TN.
12	9	1863	Affairs at and near Lewinsville, VA, with an attack on the Union men by Maj. John S. Mosby, CSA.
12	10	1863	The Federal descent upon the Confederate Salt-Works in Choctawhatchie Bay, FL. 12/10-19/1863.
12	10	1863	Skirmish at Hertford, NC.
12	10	1863	Skirmish at Gatlinsburg, TN, as Lieut. Gen. James Longstreet, CSA, concentrates his forces around Greeneville, TN, the Knoxville, TN, Campaign.
12	10	1863	Skirmish at Long Ford, TN, the Knoxville, TN, Campaign.
12	10	1863	Federal scout from Memphis, TN, to 1.5 miles east of Buntyn Station, where they happen upon a couple Rebels cutting the telegraph wires, who manage to escape.
12	10	1863	Skirmish at Morristown, TN, the Knoxville, TN, Campaign.
12	10	1863	Affair at Russellville, TN, the Knoxville, TN, Campaign.
12	10	1863	Brig. Gen. William Wells', USA, command advances from Harper's Ferry, WV, in conjunction with Brig. Gen. William W. Averell, USA.
12	11	1863	Federal scout from Waldron to Dallas, AR. 12/11-13/1863.
12	11	1863	Maj. Gen. John G. Foster, USA, supersedes Maj. Gen. Ambrose E. Burnside, USA, in command of the Dept. of the Ohio, the Knoxville, TN, Campaign.
12	11	1863	Maj. Gen. John A. Logan, USA, supersedes Maj. Gen. Frank P. Blair, Jr, USA, in the command of the 15th US Army Corps, Knoxville, TN.
12	11	1863	Federal scout from Pulaski, TN, to Florence, AL, and skirmish (**12th**) on Shoal Creek, near Wayland Springs, TN, which the Yankees arrive back in camp with 35 prisoners and the 2 Rebels accused of the murder of two Yankee soldiers. 12/11-17/1863.
12	11	1863	Skirmishes at Big Sewell and Meadow Bluff, WV, with the Federal expedition party.
12	11	1863	Skirmish at Marling's Bottom Bridge, WV, with a Federal expedition party.
12	12	1863	Skirmish at La Fayette, GA, where the Federal Cavalry captures Rebel prisoners there, camps for the night at Pigeon Ridge, 5 miles from La Fayette, crosses the Chickamauga at a bridge 3 miles above Crawfish Springs, and scouts through McLemore's Cove, without encountering the enemy before returning to camp.
12	12	1863	Skirmish at Cheek's Cross-Roads, near Knoxville, TN, the Knoxville, TN, Campaign.
12	12	1863	Skirmishes at Russellville, TN, the Knoxville, TN, Campaign. 12/12-13/1863.
12	12	1863	Brig. Gen. Samuel D. Sturgis, USA, is assigned to the command of all the cavalry serving in the Dept. of the Ohio, TN, , the Knoxville, TN, Campaign.
12	12	1863	Skirmishes at and near Strasburg, VA. 12/12-13/1863.
12	12	1863	Federal expedition from **Williamsburg** to Charles City Court-House, VA, and skirmish, as the Federals capture a sizeable amount of supplies, horses, etc, in addition to 90 prisoners. 12/12-14/1863.
12	12	1863	Skirmish at Gatewood's, WV, with Brig. Gen. William W. Averell, USA.
12	12	1863	Skirmishes at Lewisburg and Greenbrier River, WV, with an Union Cavalry expedition.
12	13	1863	Skirmish at Meriwether's Ferry, Bayou Boeuf, AR.
12	13	1863	Skirmish at Ringgold, GA.
12	13	1863	Skirmish near Dandridge's Mill, East TN, the Knoxville, TN, Campaign.
12	13	1863	Skirmish at Farley's Mill, Holston River, East TN, the Knoxville, TN, Campaign.
12	13	1863	Skirmish at La Grange, TN.
12	13	1863	Affair at Germantown, VA, as Maj. John S. Mosby's Partisan Rangers crawl up and shoot (without warning), mortally wounding 2 Federals and capturing 5 horses and their equipments.
12	13	1863	Skirmish at Powell's River, near Stickleyville, VA, where the Confederates retire towards Abingdon after loss of life and prisoners.
12	13	1863	Skirmishes near Strasburg, VA, with Brig. Gen. William W. Averell, USA.
12	13	1863	Affair at Hurricane Bridge, WV, with Brig. Gen. William W. Averery, USA.

MONTH	DAY	YEAR	ACT
12	14	1863	Skirmish at Caddo Mill, AR.
12	14	1863	Federal reconnaissance from Rossville to La Fayette, GA.
12	14	1863	The engagement at Bean's Station, TN, as Lieut. Gen. James Longstreet, CSA, pushes Brig. Gen. James M. Shackelford, USA, out of his path on his way to Greeneville, TN, the Knoxville, TN, Campaign.
12	14	1863	Skirmish at Clinch Gap, TN, the Knoxville, TN, Campaign.
12	14	1863	The Confederate capture of a Union wagon train, near Clinch Mountain Gap, TN, as the Federals unsuccessfully counterattack.
12	14	1863	Skirmish at Granger's Mill, TN, the Knoxville, TN, Campaign.
12	14	1863	Skirmish near Morristown, TN, the Knoxville, TN, Campaign.
12	14	1863	Miscellaneous Cavalry affairs in Virginia, including various Rebels attacks on the Union forces with the capture of men and supplies by Maj. Gen. JEB Stuart's Confederate Cavalrymen. 12/14-24/1863.
12	14	1863	Affair 1.5 miles from Catlett's Station, VA, as Rebel guerrillas dressed in Union overcoats ride up and shoot 2 Union colonels, among others.
12	14	1863	Skirmish on the Blue Sulphur road, near Meadow Bluff, WV, with Brig. Gen. William W. Averell, USA, and his expeditionary force.
12	14	1863	Mrs. Mary Todd Lincoln's half-sister, who was married to Brig. Gen. Benjamin H. Helm, CSA, and who had died September 21, 1863, is granted Federal amnesty by President Abraham Lincoln, Washington, DC, after taking the loyalty oath to the Union.
12	15	1863	**Joseph Orville Shelby,** CSA, is appointed Brig. Gen.
12	15	1863	Maj. Gen. Thomas C. Hindman, CSA, supersedes Maj. Gen. John C. Breckinridge, CSA, in the command of the 2nd Confederate Army Corps, the Army of Tennessee.
12	15	1863	Skirmish at Bean's Station, TN, the Knoxville, TN, Campaign.
12	15	1863	Skirmish near Livingston, TN.
12	15	1863	Affair near Pulaski, TN.
12	15	1863	Skirmish at Sangster's Station, VA.
12	15	1863	Maj. Gen. Jubal A. Early, CSA, is assigned to the command of the Valley District, VA.
12	16	1863	**John Buford, U.S.A.,** is appointed Maj. Gen.
12	16	1863	**Maj. Gen. John Buford, USA,** dies in Washington, DC, from camp fever (typhoid) developed while in the Union Cavalry during the Rappahannock Campaign, October of 1863, and was best known for his role at Gettysburg, PA, initially holding off the Confederates under the command of Lieut. Gen. Ambrose Powell Hill, CSA, and portrayed by Sam Elliott in the movie, "Gettysburg.".
12	16	1863	Federal scout from Fayetteville, AR, including skirmishes (**23rd**) at Stroud's Store and (**25th**) on Buffalo River. 12/16-31/1863.
12	16	1863	Confederate demonstration on Fort Gibson, the Indian Territory.
12	16	1863	Skirmish near Springfield, MO.
12	16	1863	Skirmish near Free Bridge, NC, as Yankees and Rebels clash after the Yankees moved to bring in the Union lines the families of some Rebel deserters.
12	16	1863	Skirmishes at and near Blain's Cross-Roads, TN, the Knoxville, TN, Campaign. 12/16-19/1863.
12	16	1863	Skirmish at Rutledge, TN, the Knoxville, TN, Campaign.
12	16	1863	Federal descent upon Salem, VA, led by Brig. Gen. William W. Averell, USA.
12	16	1863	Skirmish at Upperville, VA.
12	16	1863	Maj. Gen. John C. Caldwell, USA, is temporarily in command of the 2nd US Army Corps, the Army of the Potomac, VA.
12	16	1863	**Gen. Joseph E. Johnston, CSA, is assigned to the command of the Confederate Dept of Tennessee, superseding Lieut. Gen. William H. Hardee, CSA,** and leaving Lieut. Gen. Leonidas Polk, CSA, in command of the Army of Mississippi.
12	17	1863	The federal recapture of the Union merchant ship, **Chesapeake,** from Northern Copperheads, at Sambro Harbor, Nova Scotia, Canada, by the **USS Ella** and **Annie.**
12	17	1863	Skirmish at Rodney, and at Port Gibson, MS.
12	17	1863	Federal expedition from Washington to Chicoa Creek, 13 miles from Washington, NC, with skirmish.
12	17	1863	Skirmish at Sangster's Station, VA, as the Federals were caught off guard when the telegraph operator was too intoxicated to notice the attack. Besides, the Federal cavalry present could not understand English and its officer couldn't speak German to give commands. A fiasco.
12	18	1863	**Augustus Louis Chetlain,** USA, is appointed Brig. Gen.
12	18	1863	Skirmish near Sheldon's Place, Barren Fork, the Indian Territory, with Col. Stand Watie's Confederates.

12	18	1863	Operations in Northern Mississippi and West Tennessee. 12/18-31/1863.
12	18	1863	Skirmish at Indiantown or Sandy Swamp, NC.
12	18	1863	Skirmish at Bean's Station, TN, the Knoxville, TN, Campaign.
12	18	1863	Skirmish at Rutledge, TN, the Knoxville, TN, Campaign.
12	18	1863	Affair near Culpeper, VA, with a quick Confederate cavalry dash on the Union pickets on the Sperryville road, capturing one Yankee.
12	18	1863	Federal scout from Vienna to Middleburg, VA, against Confederate guerrillas, and the capture of a few of Maj. John S. Mosby's Virginia Partisans. 12/18-20/1863.
12	19	1863	**John Randolph Chambliss, Jr,** CSA, is appointed Brig. Gen.
12	19	1863	Skirmish with Indians at Barren Fork, the Indian Territory.
12	19	1863	Skirmish at Stone's Mill, TN, the Knoxville, TN, Campaign.
12	19	1863	Skirmishes on Jackson's River, near Covington, VA, with Brig. Gen. William W. Averell, USA.
12	19	1863	Skirmish at Scott's, on Barber's Creek, VA, with Brig. Gen. William W. Averell, USA.
12	20	1863	Federal scout from Lexington, MO.
12	21	1863	**Lawrence Sullivan Ross,** CSA, is appointed Brig. Gen.
12	21	1863	Federal scout from Rossville to La Fayette, GA, with the capture of Rebel prisoners, citizens, forage, etc. 12/21-23/1863.
12	21	1863	Federal scout from Rocky Run toward Trenton, NC, in an effort to capture Rebel guerrillas. 12/21-24/1863.
12	21	1863	Skirmish at Clinch River, TN, the Knoxville, TN, Campaign.
12	21	1863	Skirmish at McMinnville, TN.
12	21	1863	Brig. Gen. Jacob D. Cox, USA, supersedes Brig. Gen. Mahlon D. Manson, USA, in the command of the 23rd US Army Corps, TN, the Knoxville, TN, Campaign.
12	21	1863	Federal expedition from Bealeton to Luray, VA, and skirmishes, including the burning of a large 3 story tannery at Luray, etc. 12/21-23/1863.
12	21	1863	Affair near Hunter's Mill, VA, as guerrillas fire on and seriously wound a couple of Yankees on the road to Fairfax Court-House.
12	22	1863	Skirmish at Fayette, MS.
12	22	1863	Lieut. Gen. Leonidas Polk, CSA, is assigned to the command of the Dept. of Mississippi and East Louisiana. (temporarily in command of the Dept. of Tennessee).
12	22	1863	Skirmish at Cleveland, TN, where the attacking Rebels force a Union retreat. Lieut. Jacob Bedtelyon, 4th MI Cavalry is very fortunate as his chest is only bruised from a spent Confederate minie ball.
12	22	1863	Federal scouts near Dandridge, TN, and skirmish, the Knoxville, TN, Campaign. 12/22-23/1863.
12	22	1863	Confederate winter quarters are established at and about Russellville, TN, by Lieut. Gen. James Longstreet, CSA, effectively ending the Knoxville, TN, Campaign.
12	23	1863	Skirmish at Jacksonport, AR.
12	23	1863	Skirmish near Corinth, MS, where the Confederates ambush the 3rd IL Cavalry, who suffer casualties.
12	23	1863	**Lieut. Gen. Leonidas Polk, CSA, assumes the command of the "Dept. of the Southwest"** (Mississippi, and East Louisiana).
12	23	1863	Confederate attack on Centreville, MO, and the pursuit of the Confederates, including a skirmish **(25th)** at Pulliam's, whereby the Federals recaptured the men taken by the Rebels. 12/23-25/1863.
12	23	1863	Federal reconnaissance from Blain's Cross-Roads to Powder Spring Gap, TN.
12	23	1863	Skirmish at Mulberry Village, TN, where a Confederate party captures a Union forage train and 6 Federals, tie their hands behind their backs and shoot them execution style. One Federal Lieutenant escapes by diving into the river but suffers critically from exposure to the cold. The Federals pick the remaining men out of the river; only one other survived. One young lad had an aged destitute mother depending upon him for support.
12	23	1863	Skirmish near Culpeper Court House, VA.
12	24	1863	Skirmish at Rodney, MS.
12	24	1863	Federal scout from Cassville, MO, to ascertain the movements of Col. Stand Watie, CSA, and his Indians. 12/24-29/1863.
12	24	1863	Skirmish at Estenaula, TN, between Brig. Gen. Benjamin H. Grierson's, USA, Cavalry and Maj. Gen. Nathan Bedford Forrest's, CSA, Cavalry.
12	24	1863	Action at Hay's Ferry, near Dandridge, TN.

12	24	1863	Skirmish at Jack's Creek, TN, between Brig. Gen. Benjamin H. Grierson's, USA, Cavalry and Maj. Gen. Nathan Bedford Forrest's, CSA, Cavalry.
12	24	1863	Operations near Mossy Creek and Dandridge, TN. 12/24-28/1863.
12	24	1863	Skirmishes at Peck's House, near New Market, and at Mossy Creek Station, TN.
12	24	1863	Affair near Germantown, VA, as mounted Confederate irregulars again swoop in and capture the 4 vedettes stationed on the road near Germantown, in the Fairfax, VA, area.
12	24	1863	Skirmish in Lee County, VA.
12	25	1863	Skirmish with Indians near Fort Gaston, CA.
12	25	1863	Engagement at Fort Brooke, FL, with the Federal attack on the fort by the gunboat, **Tahoma** and an unnamed schooner.
12	25	1863	The destruction of the Confederate Salt-works on Bear Inlet, NC, and another 2 miles up towards Swansborough, as the Federals travel aboard the gunboats **Howquah** and **Daylight.** The Union men suffered intensely from the cold, having to wade from the boats to shore.
12	25	1863	A Confederate attack inflict severe damages on the **USS Marblehead,** in Stono River, off Legareville and near John's Island, SC. The **USS Pawnee** tries to render assistance.
12	25	1863	Federal scout from Vienna to Leesburg, VA, and skirmish, as the Federals go house to house looking for any of Mosby's Partisans, and capturing 8 men in the process. 12/25-27/1863.
12	25	1863	Brig. Gen. William W. Averell's, USA, Cavalry command reaches Beverly, WV, effectively ending his raid on the **Virginia and Tennessee Railroad,** started 12/8/1863.
12	26	1863	**William Anderson Pile,** USA, is appointed Brig. Gen.
12	26	1863	Skirmish at Sand Mountain, AL.
12	26	1863	Skirmish with Indians near Fort Gaston, CA.
12	26	1863	Skirmish near Fort Gibson, the Indian Territory.
12	26	1863	The **CSS Alabama,** captures and burns two large vessels, the **Highlander,** and the **Sonora,** near the Straits of Malacca.
12	26	1863	Skirmish at Port Gibson, MS.
12	26	1863	Federal scout from Forsyth, MO, to Batesville, AR. 12/26-1/2/1864.
12	26	1863	Federal scout from Salem, MO, against guerrillas. 12/26-28/1863.
12	26	1863	Skirmish at Mossy Creek, TN.
12	26	1863	Skirmish near New Castle, TN, between Brig. Gen. Benjamin H. Grierson's, USA, Cavalry and Maj. Gen. Nathan Bedford Forrest's, CSA, Cavalry.
12	26	1863	Skirmish at Somerville, TN, between Brig. Gen. Benjamin H. Grierson's, USA, Cavalry and Maj. Gen. Nathan Bedford Forrest's, CSA, Cavalry.
12	27	1863	**Gen. Joseph E. Johnston, CSA, assumes the command of the Confederate Dept. of Tennessee, at Dalton, GA.**
12	27	1863	President Lincoln spends the day visiting Confederate P.O.W.'s at Point Lookout, MD.
12	27	1863	Federal expedition from Newport Barracks to Young's Cross-Roads, Swansborough, and Jackson, NC. 12/27-29/1863.
12	27	1863	Skirmish at Huntingdon, TN.
12	27	1863	Skirmish at Talbott's Station, TN.
12	27	1863	Skirmish between Brig. Gen. Benjamin H. Grierson's, USA, Cavalry and Maj. Gen. Nathan Bedford Forrest's, CSA, Cavalry, at the following places: a) at Collierville, TN b) at Grisson's Bridge, TN c) at La Fayette, TN d) near Moscow, TN
12	28	1863	Skirmish at Mount Pleasant, MS.
12	28	1863	Affair on John's Island, SC, with a Union naval gunboat shelling the Confederate batteries and positions.
12	28	1863	Action at Calhoun and skirmish at Charleston, TN, as Maj. Gen. Joseph Wheeler's, CSA, Confederate Cavalry attacks Maj. Gen. George H. Thomas, USA, commanding the Dept. of the Cumberland's supply train.
12	28	1863	Federal expedition from Nashville, TN, up the Cumberland River aboard 2 Union gunboats and 3 transports, to Creelsborough, KY, against Confederate guerrillas. 12/28-1/4/1864.
12	28	1863	Federal scouts from Vienna to Hopewell Gap, White Plains, etc, VA, and skirmish with some of Maj. John Singleton Mosby's Virginia Partisan Rangers, in addition to a company of the **Black Horse Cavalry.** 12/28-31/1863.

MONTH	DAY	YEAR	ACT
12	28	1863	Skirmish at Moorefield, WV.
12	29	1863	The Confederate attack on Waldron, AR, is repelled.
12	29	1863	Skirmish at Coldwater, MS.
12	29	1863	Federal scout to Bean's Station, TN, where it is reported only small bands of Confederates are in the immediate vicinity.
12	29	1863	Skirmish at Cleveland, TN.
12	29	1863	Skirmish at La Vergne, TN.
12	29	1863	Action at Mossy Creek, TN, where the Federals report incurring 109 casualties.
12	29	1863	Skirmish at Talbott's Station, TN.
12	29	1863	Skirmish on the Matagorda Peninsula, TX, including the US gunboats, **USS Monongahela, Granite City, Sciota, and** the destruction of the Confederate gunboat, **CSS Carr.**
12	29	1863	Maj. Gen. Winfield S. Hancock, USA, resumes the command of the 2nd US Army Corps, the Army of the Potomac, VA, etal.
12	30	1863	Skirmish at Waldron, AR.
12	30	1863	Skirmish near Saint Augustine, FL, as Confederate Cavalry attack a body of Union wood choppers, procuring fire-wood, capturing 24 Federals.
12	30	1863	Skirmish near Greenville, NC, as usual, with loss of life.
12	31	1863	Skirmish in Searcy County, AR.
12	31	1863	**The Bombardment of Charleston, SC.**
12	31	1863	Another deadly year comes to an end. 1864 will prove to be just as violent.

1864.

	Sunday.	Monday.	Tuesday.	Wednesday.	Thursday.	Friday.	Saturday.		Sunday.	Monday.	Tuesday.	Wednesday.	Thursday.	Friday.	Saturday.
Jan	....	....	....	....	....	1	2	**July**	....	....	....	....	....	1	2
	3	4	5	6	7	8	9		3	4	5	6	7	8	9
	10	11	12	13	14	15	16		10	11	12	13	14	15	16
	17	18	19	20	21	22	23		17	18	19	20	21	22	23
	24	25	26	27	28	29	30		24	25	26	27	28	29	30
	31	....	....	....	....	....	....		31	....	....	....	....	....	....
Feb	....	1	2	3	4	5	6	**Aug**	....	1	2	3	4	5	6
	7	8	9	10	11	12	13		7	8	9	10	11	12	13
	14	15	16	17	18	19	20		14	15	16	17	18	19	20
	21	22	23	24	25	26	27		21	22	23	24	25	26	27
	28	29	....	....	....	....	....		28	29	30	31	....	....	....
Mar	....	....	1	2	3	4	5	**Sept**	....	....	....	....	1	2	3
	6	7	8	9	10	11	12		4	5	6	7	8	9	10
	13	14	15	16	17	18	19		11	12	13	14	15	16	17
	20	21	22	23	24	25	26		18	19	20	21	22	23	24
	27	28	29	30	31	....	....		25	26	27	28	29	30	....
Apr	....	....	....	....	....	1	2	**Oct**	....	....	....	....	....	....	1
	3	4	5	6	7	8	9		2	3	4	5	6	7	8
	10	11	12	13	14	15	16		9	10	11	12	13	14	15
	17	18	19	20	21	22	23		16	17	18	19	20	21	22
	24	25	26	27	28	29	30		23	24	25	26	27	28	29
	....	....	....	....	....	....	....		30	31	....	....	....	....	....
May	1	2	3	4	5	6	7	**Nov**	....	....	1	2	3	4	5
	8	9	10	11	12	13	14		6	7	8	9	10	11	12
	15	16	17	18	19	20	21		13	14	15	16	17	18	19
	22	23	24	25	26	27	28		20	21	22	23	24	25	26
	29	30	31	....	....	....	....		27	28	29	30	....	....	....
June	....	....	....	1	2	3	4	**Dec**	....	....	....	....	1	2	3
	5	6	7	8	9	10	11		4	5	6	7	8	9	10
	12	13	14	15	16	17	18		11	12	13	14	15	16	17
	19	20	21	22	23	24	25		18	19	20	21	22	23	24
	26	27	28	29	30	....	....		25	26	27	28	29	30	31

xv

MONTH	DAY	YEAR	ACT
01	1	1864	Operations in Northeastern Arkansas, including skirmishes at Lunenburg, Sylamore, and on Sylamore Creek. 1/1-30/1864.
01	1	1864	Operations against Indians in the Humboldt Military District, CA, where a band of hostile Indians, mostly **Hoopas,** attacked a miners' camp on Pony Creek, a tributary of New River, taking their winter provisions, rifles, etc., then moving on to Plummer Creek, killing 2 white and 2 Chinamen, wounding 2 other Chinamen, and robbing a store of gold dust, supplies, etc. The next day they attack citizens gathered together, killing 3 whitemen, wounding 2 and another Chinamen, escaping into the wilds. 1/1-28/1864.
01	1	1864	The **Dept. of Kansas is re-established.** (it had been merged into merged into the Dept. of the Missouri, on Sept. 19, 1862).
01	1	1864	**Operations in Charleston Harbor and vicinity, SC.** 1/1-11/13/1864.
01	1	1864	Skirmish at Dandridge, TN.
01	1	1864	**Col. John M. Hugh's, CSA, Operations in Middle Tennessee.** 1/1-4/18/1864.
01	1	1864	Federal expedition from Bealeton through Chester Gap, to Front Royal, VA, braving the tremendous cold weather, picking up some Confederate prisoners, horses, etc. along the way, including the destruction of a tannery and a distillery. 1/1-4/1864.
01	1	1864	Skirmish at Rectortown, VA, where **Maj. John S. Mosby, CSA,** and the **43th VA Cavalry Battalion** continue to harass the Federals behind their lines, attacking them at will, seizing Union property whenever possible, repeatedly receiving the gratulations of his superior, Maj. Gen. JEB Stuart, CSA.
01	1	1864	Affair at Bunker Hill, WV, as Maj. Gen. Jubal Early's, CSA, boys attack and drive in the Union pickets.
01	2	1864	The Federal **occupation** of **Santa Catalina Island, off Los Angeles, CA.**
01	2	1864	Skirmish at La Grange, TN.
01	2	1864	Senator **George Davis** from North Carolina, succeeds **Wade Keyes** as **Attorney General** of the Confederate States of America.
01	3	1864	Federal scout from Memphis, TN, toward Hernando, MS, where it is determined the Confederates, under Maj. Gen. Nathan Bedford Forrest, CSA, are scattered over the countryside, from Coldwater to Senatobia, so as to obtain forage for the men and their horses.
01	3	1864	Maj. Gen. Francis J. Herron, USA, assumes the command of the Union forces on the Rio Grande, TX.
01	3	1864	Action at Jonesville, VA, where Brig. Gen. Orlando B. Wilcox, USA, is attacked and routed by Brig. Gen. William. E. "Grumble" Jones, CSA, and his cavalry; Jones capturing 383 Federals, 3 pieces of artillery and 27 6-mule wagons, etc.
01	3	1864	Federal reconnaissance from Charlestown, WV, to Winchester, VA, by way of Berryville, and skirmish, forcing Brig. Gen. John D. Imboden, CSA, to skedaddle.
01	3	1864	Confederate operations in Hampshire and Hardy Counties, WV, as Maj. Gen. Fitzhugh Lee, CSA, and his Cavalry captured a train of 40 wagons with 6 mules and horses to each wagon, loaded principally with artillery ammunition and hides, and 250 head of cattle, losing 120 during the night as they came over the mountains. The train belonged to Brig. Gen. Benjamin F. Kelley, USA, commanding the Dept. of West Virginia. The weather being extremely cold that it appears one Rebel's feet are so frozen the surgeon believes his feet will have to be amputated.
01	4	1864	Affair at Lockwood's Folly Inlet, NC.
01	4	1864	Federal operations about Sparta, TN, where the Union men kill, wound, and capture bushwackers, recapture supplies taken from sutlers, seize Confederate stragglers, horses, arms, clothing, etc. 1/4-14/1864.
01	4	1864	In an unpopular move, President Jefferson Davis authorizes Gen. Robert E. Lee, CSA, to requisition food supplies from the civilian population.
01	5	1864	The following are appointed Union Brigadier Generals: **Christopher Columbus Andrews,** USA **Cyrus Bussey,** USA **Philippe Regis Denis de geredern de Trobiand,** USA **John Wallace Fuller,** USA **John Franklin Miller,** USA
01	5	1864	Skirmish at Lawrence's Mill, TN, where the Union forage party attacked the Confederate pickets at Lawrence's Mill, 5 miles east of Mossy Creek, and captured 12 Rebels with their arms and 9 horses, without any loss.
01	5	1864	Skirmish on the Pecos River, near Fort Sumner, the New Mexico Territory, with hostile **Navajo Indians.**

The **Apaches** assist the Federals since their herd of horses were stolen. Many **Navajo** casualties. The weather is extremely cold.

| 01 | 6 | 1864 | The Dept. of Arkansas and the 7th US Army Corps are officially constituted. |

01 6 1864 The Dept. of Arkansas and the 7th US Army Corps are officially constituted.

01 6 1864 Skirmish at Dalton, GA.

01 6 1864 Maj. Gen. Joseph J. Reynolds, USA, assumes the command of the defenses of New Orleans, LA.

01 6 1864 The Confederate guerrilla attack on, and the disabling of, the Federal steamer transport, the **Delta**, on the Mississippi River.

01 6 1864 Federal expedition against the **Navajo Indians,** under Col. Christopher "Kit" Carson, USA, from Fort Canby to the Canon de Chelly area, the New Mexico Territory. The Navajo pay dearly in lifes for burning a Texan wagon train in Apache Canon on 3/28/1862. Brig. Gen. James H. Carleton, USA, commanding the Dept. of New Mexico is greatly concerned over the destitute condition of the captives, begging for authority to provide clothing for the women and children. He requests the Indian Dept. act immediately before it is too late. 1/6-21/1864.

01 6 1864 Affair at Flint Hill, VA, where charging dismounted Rebel Cavalry force the Union Cavalry pickets to fall back.

01 6 1864 President Jefferson Davis commutes the death penalty of a Confederate deserter, which will become more and more common.

01 7 1864 Skirmish at Martin's Creek, AR.

01 7 1864 Affair on Waccamaw Neck, near Charleston, SC, where the steamer, **Dan,** fails in her attempt to run the US naval blockade squadron off Wilmington, was run off, and beached herself, the men being captured, except for 3 who drowned.

01 7 1864 Skirmish at Warrenton, VA, where Maj. John S. Mosby, CSA, surprises a superior force of Yankees, capturing 30 men and 40 horses in addition to inflicting casualties. Maj. Gen. George G. Meade, USA, writes that it would seem that some one has been grossly derelict in duty.

01 7 1864 President Abraham Lincoln commutes the death penalty of a Union deserter, which also becomes more and more frequent for the Federals as well as the Confederates..

01 8 1864 The Federal gunboat bombardment of the Confederate works at the mouth of Caney Bayou, TX. 1/8-9/1864.

01 8 1864 Skirmish at Moorefield Junction, WV.

01 8 1864 Brig. Gen. John Hunt Morgan, CSA, who recently escaped from the Ohio State Penitentiary, Columbus, is honored at Richmond, VA.

01 9 1864 Skirmish at Terman's Ferry, KY, on the Sandy River between Louisa and Catlettsburg, KY, where the Confederates cross the river on the ice, and inflict death and casualties on the camped Federals. 20 Federals are sent to the hospital at Ashland, being badly frozen.

01 9 1864 Maj. Gen. Gouverneur K. Warren, USA, is temporarily in command of the 2nd US Army Corps, the Army of the Potomac, VA.

01 10 1864 Skirmish at King's River, AR.

01 10 1864 Federal expedition from Vicksburg, MS, aboard the steamers, **Era, Madison** and **Northerner,** up the Mississippi River, to Sunnyside Landing, AR, 200 miles, to disperse the Rebels that were obstructing navigation and reported to be attempting to move arms and ammunition from the east side to the west side of the Mississippi. Finding no Confederates, the Yankees retire. A cold day to be on transports on the river. Better yet, a good day not to have to exchange fire with the enemy. 1/10-16/1864.

01 10 1864 Federal scout from near Dandridge to Clark's Ferry, TN, and encounter with Col. George D. Dibrell's, CSA, Confederates, with casualties on both sides. 1/10-11/1864.

01 10 1864 Skirmish about 6 miles from Mossy Creek, TN, where a Union scouting party surprise attack the Rebels, inflicting casualties.

01 10 1864 Skirmish at Loudoun Heights, VA, where Maj. John S. Mosby, CSA, slips into the Federal camp and surprises a superior force of Yankees at 4:30 a.m.; however, the Yankees rally, and some of Mosby's men end up giving the ultimate in sacrifice for their cause.

01 10 1864 Federal scout to Sperryville, VA, by Brig. Gen. Wesley Merritt, USA, with Rebel prisoners.

01 10 1864 Skirmish at Petersburg, WV.

01 11 1864 Affair at Lockwood's Folly Inlet, NC, with the destruction of the Confederate Blockade-runner steamers, **Ranger,** and the **Vesta.**

01 11 1864 Federal scout to Lexington, TN, with report on Confederate movements.

01 11 1864 Federal expedition from Maryville up the Little Tennessee River, TN, to Chilhowee, where the Federals

			move against a nest of guerrillas comprised of absentees, deserters, paroled soldiers, and Rebel citizens who had been stealing goods from the loyal citizens of Blount and Monroe counties, and taking them to North Carolina to sell them. 1/11-12/1864.
01	11	1864	Sen. John B. Henderson of Missouri, proposed a joint resolution in the US Senate to abolish slavery, which will become the **13th amendment to the US Constitution, Washington, DC.**
01	12	1864	Skirmish at Marshall, KY, as minor skirmishing continues all over with no major troop movements lately.
01	12	1864	Affair at Matamoras, Mexico, where Union troops cross the Rio Grande, and move the US Consul to Mexico, Mr. L. Pierce, Jr., who is holding over $1,000,000, to Brownsville, TX and safety. 1/12-13/1864.
01	12	1864	Skirmish near Mossy Creek, TN, where a Union foraging party inflict 1 mortality and 15 prisoners on the Confederate outposts there.
01	12	1864	Affair near Accotink, VA, where some of Maj. Gen. Wade Hampton's, CSA, boys capture a couple citizens and horses.
01	12	1864	Affair near Ellis' Ford, VA.
01	12	1864	Federal raid on the Northern Neck, VA, arriving from Norfolk to Point Lookout, then moving through the county of Richmond, then into Lancaster and Northumberland, doing very little damage, other than taking some horses and a few negroes.
01	13	1864	Federal scout from Pine Bluff to Monticello, AR, where over 2,000 bushels of Confederate corn is destroyed. 1/13-14/1864.
01	13	1864	President Abraham Lincoln orders Maj. Gens. Quincy A. Gillmore in Florida, and Nathaniel P. Banks, in New Orleans, LA, to proceed at once in constructing free governments in the state of Florida and Louisiana.
01	13	1864	Skirmish at Ragland Mills, Bath County, KY, where Federals stationed at Mount Sterling attack and capture a third of the Confederates stationed at Ragland Mills (13 captured).
01	13	1864	Skirmish between Cavalry near Collierville, TN.
01	13	1864	Affair at Sevierville (13th), and skirmish at Schultz' Mill, Cosby Creek, TN. (**14th**), where Col. Robert B. Vance, CSA, captures a Federal train of 23 wagons, is pursued and the Federals recapture the wagons along with 1 ambulance loaded with medicines, 150 saddle horses and 100 stand of arms. 1/13-14/1864.
01	13	1864	Affair near Ely's Ford, VA, where the Rebels crossed the river on the ice and captured Brig. Gen. Judson Kilpatrick's Cavalry patrol.
01	14	1864	**Randall Lee Gibson,** CSA, is appointed Brig. Gen.
01	14	1864	Skirmish at Shoal Creek, AL.
01	14	1864	The **CSS Alabama** captures and burns the **Emma Jane** off the coast of Malabar, India, now having destroyed over 60 Union vessels.
01	14	1864	Federal scout to Baldwin's Ferry, Big Black River, MS, for the purpose of destroying any and all flatboats, ferries, or other means of crossing the river, which was carried out.
01	14	1864	Skirmish in Bollinger County, MO.
01	14	1864	Federal scout from Collierville, TN, to within 2 miles of Quinn's Mill, with no encounter with the Rebels.
01	14	1864	Skirmish at Dandridge, TN.
01	14	1864	Skirmish at Middleton, TN.
01	15	1864	Federal scouts near Round Prairie, Jackson County, MO, against guerrillas. 1/15-17/1864.
01	15	1864	Skirmish near Petersburg, WV.
01	16	1864	**Operations in Northwestern Arkansas.** 1/16-2/15/1864.
01	16	1864	Maj. Gen. Samuel R. Curtis, USA, assumes the command of the re-established Federal Dept. of Kansas.
01	16	1864	Skirmish at Oak Ridge, MS.
01	16	1864	Cavalry operations about Dandridge, TN, including skirmishes: a) at Kimbrough's Cross-Roads, (16th), and b) on the Bend of Chucky Road, (**17th**), and c) action near Dandridge (**17th**), with Lieut. Gen. James Longstreet, CSA, and Brig. Gen. Samuel D. Sturgis, USA, commanding Cavalry, Army of the Ohio, and Brig. Gen. Washington L. Elliott, USA, commanding Cavalry, Dept. of the Cumberland, 1/16-17/1864.
01	16	1864	Skirmish in White County, TN.
01	16	1864	Affair near Turkey Creek, VA.

01	17	1864	Federal scouts from Brownsville, AR, against guerrillas. 1/17-19/1864.
01	17	1864	Skirmish at Lewisburg, AR.
01	17	1864	Brig. Gen. Orlando B. Wilcox, USA, supersedes Brig. Gen. Robert B. Potter, USA, in the command of the 9th US Army Corps, Knoxville, TN.
01	17	1864	Affairs near Ellis' and Ely's Fords, VA, where the Rebels ambush, surround and capture a Yankee patrol at Ellis' Ford; also another party fires from dense pine trees on three sides into the Yankee patrol at Ely's Ford, killing and capturing these Yankees as well.
01	18	1864	Major opposition to the Confederate conscription law continues to develop in northwestern Georgia, western North Carolina and eastern Tennessee.
01	18	1864	Skirmish at Grand Gulf, MS, with Confederate guerrillas.
01	18	1864	Affair at Flint Hill, VA, where this time, the Union pickets stationed here are able to drive off the attacking Rebels.
01	19	1864	Skirmish at Branchville, AR, the site of a Confederate camp.
01	19	1864	Skirmish at Big Springs, near Tazewell, East TN, where a party of Confederates surprise and capture about 40 men. The Federal captain in charge escapes and is arrested by his Colonel for derelict of duty.
01	19	1864	Federal scouts from **Williamsburg, VA**, through Barhamsville, Twelve Mile Ordinary, New Kent Court-House, etc, and going as far as Bottom's Bridge before returning from their search for Confederates. In talking to an old man who just returned from Richmond, the Federals learned that Richmond was aware of their moves and had laid out an ambush for them. Lucky for them, they didn't go any further. 1/19-24/1864.
01	20	1864	**Nathaniel Harrison Harris,** CSA, is appointed Brig. Gen.
01	20	1864	**Clement Hoffman Stevens,** CSA, is appointed Brig. Gen.
01	20	1864	Federal naval reconnaissance of Forts Morgan and Gaines, at the mouth of Mobile Bay, AL.
01	20	1864	Skirmish at Island No. 76, Mississippi River.
01	20	1864	Operations in the District of North Carolina, as Federals under Brig. Gen. Innis Palmer, USA, commanding the Dept. of Virginia and North Carolina leave Plymouth, NC, to capture and destroy Rebel property; the expedition is highly successful, with over 150,000 pounds of pork, plus salt, sugar, etc. destroyed. 1/20-29/1864.
01	20	1864	Skirmish at Tracy City, TN, as Confederate cavalry arrive at Altamont, 2 dressed in Union uniform, call a Union captain out of the house he was in, and shoot and kill him when he comes out. They proceed to Tracy City where they overrun the Federals there and shoot another Union captain through the lung after he threw his weapon down, capturing and paroling other Union soldiers in the process.
01	21	1864	Federal scout from Waldron to Baker's Springs, AR, and skirmish with guerrillas. 1/21-25/1864.
01	21	1864	Federal scout from Rossville toward Dalton, GA, bivouacking for the night 3 miles from Summerville, and skirmish (**22nd**), with no casualties. 1/21-22/18/64.
01	21	1864	Maj. Gen. Carl Schurz, USA, is temporarily in command of the 11th US Army Corps, Knoxville, TN.
01	21	1864	Pro-Unionists meet in Nashville, TN, to propose a constitutional convention and to abolish slavery.
01	21	1864	Federal scout from Chattanooga to Harrison and Ooltewah, TN, and encounter with portions of Maj. Gen. Joseph Wheeler's, CSA, Cavalry.
01	21	1864	Skirmishes at Strawberry Plains (21st) and at Armstrong's Ferry, TN, as the Federals attempt to burn a bridge. (**22nd**). 1/21-22/18634.
01	21	1864	Federal reconnaissance on the Matagorda Peninsula, TX, including the accidentally killing of 2 Union soldiers from "friendly fire" from a US gunboat. The following Rebels vessels reported the impassable surf in Matagorda Bay: Cotton clads steamboats, **Carr** and **Cora,** steamers, **Lizzie Lake** and **Lucy Gwin,** and the schooners **Annie Dale** and **George Buckhart.** 1/21-25/1864.
01	22	1864	Skirmishes at Clear Creek and Tomahawk, in Northwestern AR.
01	22	1864	Affair at Subligna, GA, where a Federal surprise attack forces the Georgia State Guards to retire toward La Fayette, GA.
01	22	1864	Federal expedition from Union City to Trenton, TN, and due to the rising river and ice flow, are unable to cross the Obion River. 1/22-27/1864.
01	22	1864	The capture of 28 Confederate forage-wagons near Wilsonville, TN. Lieut. Gen. James Longstreet reports he has none to replace the ones lost, noting that the Federals have abandoned and burned 200 Federal wagons in their retreat to Knoxville. Maj. Gen. William Thompson Martin, CSA, captured 800 beef cattle.
01	22	1864	Affair at Ellis' Ford, VA, as the Federal Cavalry patrol is again attacked by the Confederates, the Yankees

			sustaining casualties, 1 mortal.
01	22	1864	Skirmish at Germantown, VA.
01	23	1864	**Operations in North Alabama.** 1/23-29/1864.
01	23	1864	Affair near Woodville, AL, as Confederate cavalry swoop down and capture 17 citizen teamsters and 90 corralled horses; the Rebels unknowingly capturing unserviceable horses.
01	23	1864	Affair at Bailey's, on Crooked Creek, in Northwestern AR.
01	23	1864	Skirmishes near Burrowsville, in Northwestern AR.
01	23	1864	Skirmish on Rolling Prairie, in Northwestern AR.
01	23	1864	Skirmish at Cowskin Bottom, the Indian Territory.
01	23	1864	Federal scout from La Grange, TN, to Riley, MS, with casualties.
01	23	1864	Affair at Cowskin Bottom, Newton County, MO, with bushwackers.
01	23	1864	Federal scout from Patterson, MO, to Cherokee Bay, AR, with fatalities to guerrilla forces. 1/23-27/1864.
01	23	1864	Skirmish near Newport, TN, where the Federals move to capture a reported Confederate forage train, finding only barren countryside that the Rebels had gleaned, transferring all valuable foodstuff across the river.
01	23	1864	Federal scout from Charlestown, WV, to Woodstock, VA, passing through Berryville, Millwood, White Post, Newtown, Middletown and Strasburg before attacking and driving the Rebels from Woodstock. The Federals withdraw to Winchester. 1/23-25/1864.
01	24	1864	**Brig. Gen. Stephen Gardner Champlin, USA,** dies at Grand Rapids, MI, from a painful and lingering hip wound he received May 31, 1862, at the Battle of Seven Pines, VA.
01	24	1864	Confederate operations near Natchez, MS, where Brig. Gen. Wirt Adams, CSA, reports the capture of 35 prisoners and 60 drays and teams.
01	24	1864	Union pickets are captured at Love's Hill, 5.5 miles northeast of Knoxville, TN. A couple lucky ones escape.
01	24	1864	Skirmish at Tazewell, TN, as the Confederates dash upon the town on the Big Springs and Bear Creek Roads, coming from the Clinch River, but are forced to withdraw after fighting.
01	24	1864	Federal expedition up the James River, VA, with the assistance of the gunboats, **General Jesup, Smith Briggs,** and the transport, **George Washington.** They leave Norfolk for Newport News, then to Brandon near Fort Powhatan, where a local doctor and his property is seized for dealing with the Rebels, while the **General Jesup** seizes two blockade runners, the sloop **Birdloe of Warwick,** and the schooner, **Thomas F. Dawson,** seizing gold, silver, US and Confederate Bank notes, etc. 1/24-25/1864.
01	25	1864	Skirmish at Bainbridge Ferry, North AL.
01	25	1864	Federal expedition from Scottsborough, AL, toward Rome, GA, as Brig. Gen. Morgan L. Smith, USA, of Maj. Gen. John A. Logan's command construct a pontoon bridge across the Coosa River, capturing prisoners, forage, etc, including $5,700 in Confederate money which proved to have been a State fund for the relief of soldiers' families. 1/25-2/5/1864.
01	25	1864	Skirmish near the Sweet Water, North AL.
01	25	1864	Skirmishes on the Little Missouri River and at Sulphur Springs, AR.
01	25	1864	Affair at Bayou Grand, FL, where the Federals prepare to move on Mobile, AL.
01	25	1864	**Corinth, MS, is evacuated** by the Union forces to consolidate their forces.
01	25	1864	Skirmish at Mount Pleasant, MS.
01	25	1864	Fort Sumter, SC, in again bombarded by Union batteries.
01	25	1864	Skirmish at La Grange, TN.
01	26	1864	Attack on Athens, North AL.
01	26	1864	Skirmish at Caddo Gap, AR.
01	26	1864	Affair in the San Andres Mountains, the New Mexico Territory, as Federal troops from Fort Craig overtake hostile Indians. The Federals are attacked during the night and forced to retreat with casualties on both sides.
01	26	1864	Operations about Dandridge, TN. 1/26-28/1864.
01	26	1864	Skirmishes at Flat Creek and Muddy Creek, near Dandridge, TN, with Maj. Gen. John G. Foster, USA, commanding the Army of the Ohio, pitted against Lieut. Gen. James Longstreet, CSA.
01	26	1864	Skirmish near Knoxville, TN.
01	26	1864	Skirmish at Sevierville, TN, as the Federals **evacuate Tazewell** and the Confederates of Lieut. Gen. James Longstreet's command **occupy Servierville.**
01	26	1864	Maj. Gen. John G. Parke, USA, resumes the command of the 9th US Army Corps, Knoxville, TN.

01	26	1864	The destruction of vast amounts of Confederate food in Hertford County, NC, by Brig. Gen. Innis N. Palmer, USA. The Federal list includes 200,000 pounds of pork, plus tobacco, cotton, wagons, etc.
01	27	1864	Affair on the Cumberland River, near Lebanon, KY, as Federal scouts attack and scatter the fleeing guerrillas.
01	27	1864	Skirmishes at Kelly's Ford (Fair Gardens), and McNutt's Bridge, near Dandridge, TN, with Maj. Gen. John G. Foster, USA, and Lieut. Gen. James Longstreet, CSA.
01	27	1864	Engagement near Fair Garden, near Dandridge, TN; Maj. Gen. John G. Foster, USA, versus Lieut. Gen. James Longstreet, CSA.
01	27	1864	Skirmish near Knoxville, TN, on the Strawberry Plains road with casualties before the attacking Confederates withdraw.
01	27	1864	Affair near Thoroughfare Mountain, VA, between enemy Cavalry scouting parties.
01	27	1864	Brig. Gen. John C. Caldwell, USA, is temporarily in command of the 2nd US Army Corps, Army of the Potomac, VA, etal.
01	27	1864	Operations in Hampshire and Hardy Counties, WV. 1/27-2/7/1864.
01	28	1864	Skirmish at Dallas, AR.
01	28	1864	Confederate expedition under Maj. Gen. George E. Pickett, CSA, against New Berne, NC. 1/28-2/10/1864.
01	28	1864	Lieut. Gen. Leonidas Polk's Confederate command is designated the **Confederate Dept. of Alabama, Mississippi and East Louisiana.**
01	28	1864	Federal expedition from Gallatin to the Cumberland Mountains, TN, as the Federals cross the Cumberland River at the mouth of the Caney Fork River, having numerous running skirmishes with the Rebels. The Union men find many citizens in this area actually starving, and discover that the Rebels in Jackson, Fentress and Overton counties are going to Glasgow and other towns in Kentucky to purchase goods. 1/28-2/8/1864.
01	28	1864	Skirmishes at Fain's Island, Indian Creek, Island Ford, Kelley's Ford, and Swann's Island, near Dandridge, TN, as Brig. Gen. Samuel D. Sturgis, under Maj. Gen. John G. Foster, USA, and his Union Cavalry, drive back Maj. Gen. William T. Martin's Confederate Cavalry, of Lieut. Gen. James Longstreet's command, inflicting approximately 200 killed, wounded and missing on the Rebels.
01	28	1864	Affair at Lee's House, on the Cornersville Pike, TN, where the Confederate cavalry wait in ambush and capture a Union forage train searching for corn and pork. Many of the Union men are shot but not mortally. They are taken 20 miles and given paroles signed by Maj. Gen. Nathan Bedford Forrest, CSA, and released. The Federals were kindly treated, although one was robbed of his watch.
01	28	1864	**Maj. Gen. John M. Schofield, USA, is assigned to the command of the Dept. of the Ohio,** and Maj. Gen. George Stoneman, USA, to the command of the 23rd US Army Corps, Army of the Cumberland, TN, etal.
01	28	1864	Cavalry skirmishes near Jonesville, VA. 1/28-29/1864.
01	28	1864	Maj. Gen. David B. Birney, USA, is temporarily in command of the 3rd US Army Corps, the Army of the Potomac, VA.
01	29	1864	Skirmish near Cobb's Mill, North AL.
01	29	1864	Skirmish near the Tennessee River, North AL.
01	29	1864	Federal expedition from Vicksburg, MS, to Waterproof, parish of Tensas, LA, and skirmishes, as the Federals raid numerous plantations, confiscating everything of value from gold and silver to farm animals and weapons. 1/29-2/23/1864.
01	29	1864	The Federal steamer, **Sir William Wallace,** is fired upon on the Mississippi River, near Vicksburg, MS, resulting in Union deaths to 3 men, and 4 severely wounded.
01	29	1864	Affair near Gloucester Court House, VA, as Brig. Gen. Isaac J. Wistar, USA, captures a couple of Rebs today.
01	29	1864	Federal expedition to Isle of Wight County, VA, with skirmishes near Benn's Church and at Smithfield, and the destruction of the US steamer, **Smith Briggs.** 1/29-2/1/1864.
01	30	1864	Federal expedition from Batesville to near Searcy Landing, AR. 1/30-2/3/1864.
01	30	1864	Skirmish at Chickamauga Creek, GA.
01	30	1864	**Maj. Gen. William S. Rosecrans, USA, supersedes Maj. Gen. John M. Schofield, USA,** in the command of the **Dept. of the Missouri** as Lincoln is unhappy with Schofield's performance in Missouri.
01	30	1864	Skirmish at Windsor, NC, where both sides claim victory. Isn't the first nor the last time this happens.
01	30	1864	Federal scout from Culpeper to Mount Zion Church, then to Madison Court-House, VA, returning to

			camp by way of Bethel Church and White's Shop.
01	30	1864	The capture of a wagon train at Medley, WV, by Maj. Gen. Jubal A. Early, CSA, with the assistance of local Partisan Rangers. The train consisted of 93 wagons loaded with commissary stores and forage, half had to be burned as their teams escaped.
01	31	1864	Federal expedition from Maryville, TN, to Quallatown, NC, where the Federals, aided by Pro-Northern Indians raid the town and inflict an estimated 265 casualties, before the Rebel gangs can flee into the mountains. 1/31-2/7/1864.
01	31	1864	Federal reconnaissance to Madison Court-House and Mount Carmel Church, VA, by Brig. Gen. Wesley Merritt, CSA.
02	1	1864	Skirmish at Waldron, AR.
02	1	1864	**Operations against Indians in the Humboldt Military District, CA.** 2/1-6/30/1864.
02	1	1864	**Operations in the Indian Territory,** as the Federal troops try to smoke the "peace pipe" with many of the hostile Indian tribes. 2/1-24/1864.
02	1	1864	Federal Cavalry expedition from Madisonville to Franklinton, LA, and vicinity. 2/1-3/1864.
02	1	1864	Federal scouts from Rolla, MO. 2/1-3/1/1864.
02	1	1864	**Operations in the New Mexico and Arizona Territories,** including a posse of Mexican citizens tracking **Navajoes** who stole their livestock. Over 2,500 Indians await transportation to reservations. Over 125 have died at Fort Canby within the last month alone. Now that the Federals are subduing the Indians, they begin to complain that they tire of feeding the Indians from their commissaries. 2/1-3/7/1864.
02	1	1864	Skirmish at Batchelder's Creek, NC, with Maj. Gen. George E. Pickett's, CSA, moving from Kinston, NC, aborts his attempt to recapture New Berne, NC, as Brig. Gen. Innis N. Palmer, USA, withdraws to the city's inner defenses. The Federals sustain 326 casualties.
02	1	1864	Federal expedition from Knoxville to Flat Creek, TN, with no engagements.
02	1	1864	Federal reconnaissance from Maryville toward Sevierville, TN, and 14 miles southwest of Dandridge, with no casualties. 2/1-2/1864.
02	1	1864	Federal scout in White and Putnam Counties, TN, including Cookville, up the Calfkiller River, near Yankeetown, and Lancaster, as the Federals killed and captured many notorious rebels under **Champ Ferguson** accused of engaging in murder, robbery, and rape. 2/1-7/1864.
02	1	1864	Skirmish at Bristoe Station, VA.
02	1	1864	President Abraham Lincoln orders a transport ship be sent to Ile a Vache, Santo Domingo, to bring back those Negro colonists wishing to return to the US, which retards Lincoln's plan to setup colonies for Negroes.
02	1	1864	President Abraham Lincoln, using the **Congressional Conscription Act,** orders that 500,000 men be drafted on March 10 to serve for 3 years or for the duration of the war, whichever comes first. Unlike in the past, Lincoln faces little opposition.
02	2	1864	Federal operations about Whitesburg, AL, where the Union men are busy constructing two boats that will carry 15 men each.
02	2	1864	The Federal steamer, **Mill Boy,** is wrecked 9 miles above Jacksonport, AR.
02	2	1864	Skirmish on Halcolm Island, MO, with the **Bolin gang.**
02	2	1864	Skirmish at Bogue Sound Block-house, NC, with Maj. Gen. George E. Pickett, CSA.
02	2	1864	Skirmish at Gales' Creek, NC, with Maj. Gen. George E. Pickett, CSA.
02	2	1864	The US Steamer, **Underwriter,** is captured near New Berne, NC, on the Neuse River, by Maj. Gen. George E. Pickett's CSA men.
02	2	1864	Skirmish at Newport Barracks, NC.
02	2	1864	The Confederate blockade-runner, **Preston,** is caught and destroyed at Charleston, SC.
02	2	1864	Skirmish near La Grange, TN, where the attacking Confederate Cavalry offered the Federals battle, which they declined, electing to remain safely in their fort.
02	2	1864	Skirmish near Strasburg, VA.
02	2	1864	Skirmish at Patterson's Creek, WV, as Union Cavalry unsuccessfully contest the Confederates who captured the Union wagon train on 1/30/1864. The Rebels burn the bridges.
02	3	1864	Federal expedition aboard the steamers, **J.M. Brown** and **Red Chief,** from Brashear City, LA, up Grand Lake into Lac Fausse Pointe, and into Grand River, etc. The Federals confiscate Rebel supplies and food, etc. 2/3-6/1864.
02	3	1864	**The Meridian, MS, Expedition,** and co-operating expeditions from Memphis, TN, and up the Yazoo

			River, to destroy Rebel railroads, and etc., in the vicinity. 2/3-3/6/1864.
02	3	1864	Gen. William T. Sherman's, USA, column advances from Vicksburg, MS, to be joined by Brig. Gen. William S. Smith's, USA Cavalry, the start of the **Meridian, MS, Expedition.**
02	3	1864	Action at Liverpool Heights, Yazoo River, MS.
02	3	1864	The Confederate capture and burning of the US steamer, **Levi,** on the Kanawha River, at Red House Landing, WV, at 5 a.m. in the morning as everybody aboard was asleep.
02	4	1864	**Allen Thomas,** CSA, is appointed Brig. Gen.
02	4	1864	Federal expedition from Helena up White River, AR, aboard the steamers, **Cheek, Emerald** and **Rike.** Among other events, the Negro Soldiers present seize some "secesh" chickens that had not "taken the oath of allegiance." The Yankee bellies will be full tonight. 2/4-8/1864.
02	4	1864	Skirmish at Mountain Fork, AR.
02	4	1864	Skirmish at Hot Springs, AR.
02	4	1864	Skirmish at Rolling Prairie, AR.
02	4	1864	Skirmish at Columbia, LA.
02	4	1864	Skirmish near Bolton Depot, MS, and following as Lieut. Gen. Leonidas Polk, CSA, falls back, the Meridian, MS, Expedition.
02	4	1864	Skirmish at Champion's Hill, MS, as Maj. Gen. James McPherson, USA, joins up with Maj. Gen. William T. Sherman, USA, the Meridian, MS, Expedition.
02	4	1864	Skirmish at Edwards' Ferry, MS, the Meridian, MS, Expedition.
02	4	1864	Skirmish opposite Liverpool Heights, the Meridian, MS, Expedition.
02	4	1864	Skirmish at Queen's Hill, MS, the Meridian, MS, Expedition.
02	4	1864	Skirmish at Moorefield, WV, as the Confederates under Maj. Gen. Jubal Early, CSA, commanding the Valley District, retreat over the mountains with their wagon train captured at Medley, in addition to 1,250 head of cattle, 550 sheep, 80 prisoners, etc.
02	5	1864	**The Florida Expedition,** begins as Brig. Gen. Truman Seymour, USA, moves from Hilton Head, SC, toward Jacksonville, FL. 2/5-22/1864 .
02	5	1864	Federal scout from Houston, MO, into Arkansas, with skirmishes. The Federal rout the large but poorly armed band of guerrillas. 2/5-17/1864.
02	5	1864	Skirmish on Crooked Creek, in Northwestern AR.
02	5	1864	Skirmish near Cape Girardeau, MO.
02	5	1864	Skirmish on Baker's Creek, MS, as Maj. Gen. William T. Sherman, USA, **occupies Jackson,** enroute to Meridian, MS.
02	5	1864	Skirmish at Clinton, MS, the Meridian, MS, Expedition.
02	5	1864	Skirmish at Jackson, MS, the Meridian, MS, Expedition.
02	5	1864	Skirmish near Aldie, VA, where the Federals capture some of Maj. John S. Mosby's Partisan Rangers who attacked their rear guard. Mosby's men were led by **William E. Ormsby** who deserted from the 2nd MA Cavalry on the night of 1/24/1864. Ormsby was tried by drumhead court-martial and **executed** on 2/7/1864.
02	5	1864	Affair at Winchester, VA.
02	6	1864	Col. Henry M. Black, 6th California Infantry, is assigned to the command the District of Humboldt, CA.
02	6	1864	Skirmish at Hillsborough, MS, the Meridian, MS, Expedition.
02	6	1864	Federal scout in the Sni Hills, MO, after bushwackers. 2/6-10/1864.
02	6	1864	Skirmish near Newport Barracks, NC, as this effectively ends Maj. Gen. George E. Pickett's, CSA, advance on New Berne, NC.
02	6	1864	Federal expedition to John's and James Islands and skirmishes (**9th-11th**) near Bugbee Bridge, Charleston Harbor, SC, and vicinity. 2/6-14/1864.
02	6	1864	Affair at Bolivar, TN, with Union foragers.
02	6	1864	**Expedition from Memphis, TN, to Wyatt, MS,** the Meridian, MS, Expedition. 2/6-18/1864.
02	6	1864	Maj. Gen. Gouverneur K. Warren, USA, is placed temporarily in command of the 2nd US Army Corps, Army of the Potomac, VA.
02	6	1864	Demonstration on the Rapidan, including engagement at Norton's Ford and skirmishes at Barnett's and Culpeper's Fords, VA, with the Federals forced to retreat back across the Rapidan. 2/6-7/1864 .
02	6	1864	Federal expedition from Yorktown against Richmond, VA, including skirmishes at Bottom's Bridge and near Baltimore Store, ordered by Maj. Gen. Benjamin F. Butler, USA, to release the Union prisoners held there. This moves meets with failure and the Confederates under Brig. Gen. Eppa Hunton, CSA, force a Union withdrawal. Hunton then sends his best wagon train teams to King and Queen county for pork.

The army must be fed. 2/6-8/1864.

02	7	1864	**Jacksonville, FL, is occupied** by Brig. Gen. Truman Seymour, USA, Maj. Gen. Quincy A. Gillmore, USA, in overall command, commanding the Dept. of the South.
02	7	1864	Skirmish at Vidalia, LA, where the **2nd MS Heavy Artillery of African descent** travel from Natchez, MS, aboard the steamer, **Diligent,** and rout the Rebels at Vidalia, LA.
02	7	1864	Skirmish at Brandon, MS, as Lieut. Gen. Leonidas Polk, CSA, offered little resistance to the advancing Maj. Gen. William T. Sherman, USA, the Meridian, MS, Expedition.
02	7	1864	Skirmish at Morton, MS, the Meridian, MS, Expedition.
02	7	1864	Skirmish at Satartia, MS, the Meridian, MS, Expedition.
02	7	1864	Affair at Waccomo Neck, NC.
02	7	1864	Affair at the mouth of Caney Bayou, TX, where the Federals fire 66 shots at the Confederate fort there "with great accuracy."

02	8	1864	Skirmish at Ten-Mile Run, near Camp Finegan, FL, as Brig. Gen. Truman Seymour, USA, marches inland from Jacksonville, FL.
02	8	1864	Skirmish at Ringgold, GA.
02	8	1864	Skirmish at Barboursville, KY.
02	8	1864	Skirmish at Donaldsonville, LA.
02	8	1864	Affair at Coldwater Ferry, MS, with Maj. Gen. W. Sherman, USA, the Meridian, MS, Expedition.
02	8	1864	Skirmish near Morton, MS, the Meridian, MS, Expedition.
02	8	1864	Skirmishes at and near Senatobia, MS, the Meridian, MS, Expedition. 2/8-9/1864.
02	8	1864	Federal scout near Maryville, TN, on the main Sevierville road, with no enemy encounters.

02	9	1864	Skirmish at Morgan's Mill, Spring River, AR, as the Federals, while hunting a large band of guerrillas, run into a full regiment of Confederate regulars. Big mistake by the Federals.
02	9	1864	Skirmish at Tomahawk Gap, AR.
02	9	1864	Skirmish in White County, AR.
02	9	1864	Federal expedition from Fernandina up Nassau River, FL. 2/9-10/1864.
02	9	1864	Skirmish near Point Washington, FL, with Brig. Gen. Seymour.
02	9	1864	Skirmish at New River, LA.
02	9	1864	**Yazoo City, MS, is occupied** by Maj. Gen. William T. Sherman, USA, on his way to Meridian, MS. 2/9-3/6/1864.
02	9	1864	Federal reconnaissance toward Swansborough, NC, and Young's Cross-Roads and the White River. The Rebels are reported to have retired to Jacksonville and Trenton.
02	9	1864	Skirmish in Hardin County, TN.
02	9	1864	Maj. Gen. John M. Schofield, USA, supersedes Maj. Gen. John G. Foster, USA, in the command of the Dept. of the Ohio, TN.
02	9	1864	109 Federal officers, led by Col. Thomas E. Rose, of PA, escape from Libby Prison, Richmond, VA, by digging a tunnel, with 2 drowning and 48 others being recaptured.
02	9	1864	**President Abraham Lincoln sits for several photographs,** including the one eventually to be used on the $5 bill at Washington, D.C.

02	10	1864	Skirmish at Lake Village, AR.
02	10	1864	Skirmish at Barber's Ford, FL, wit Brig. Gen. Truman Seymour, USA.
02	10	1864	The Federal capture of Camp Cooper, FL, by Brig. Gen. Truman Seymour, USA.
02	10	1864	Skirmish at Hillsborough, MS, with Maj. Gen. Sherman, USA, the Meridian, MS, Expedition.
02	10	1864	Skirmish at Morton, MS, the Meridian, MS, Expedition.
02	10	1864	Skirmish at Pocahontas, MO.
02	10	1864	The **USS Florida** captures and destroys two blockade runners off Masonbrough Inlet, NC.
02	10	1864	Maj. Gen. George Stoneman, USA, supersedes Brig. Gen. Jacob D. Cox, USA, in command of the 23rd US Army Corps, Army of the Cumberland, TN, etal.

02	11	1864	Skirmish at Lake City, FL, with Brig. Gen. Truman Seymour, USA.
02	11	1864	Skirmishes near Madisonville, LA, and, as usual, with loss of life.
02	11	1864	Affair at Raiford's Plantation, near Byhalia, MS, the Meridian, MS, Expedition.
02	11	1864	Brig. Gen. William Sooy Smith's, USA, Cavalry finally advances from Collierville, near Memphis, TN, on his way to join up with Maj. Gen. William T. Sherman, the Meridian, MS, Expedition.
02	11	1864	Federal descent upon Lamar, TX.

02	11	1864	Brig. Gen. H. W. Gilmor's raid of Confederate irregulars on the **Baltimore and the Ohio Railroad,** at Brown's Shop, between Kearneysville and Duffield's Depot, WV, succeed in derailing the express passenger train west and robbing the crew and passengers.
02	12	1864	**Charles William Field, C.S.A.,** is appointed Maj. Gen.
02	12	1864	Federal expedition from Batesville, AR, after Col. Freeman's command. Much activity including the jayhawkers who were captured were executed by rifle squad. Forage is becoming hard to come by. 2/12-20/1864.
02	12	1864	Skirmish at Caddo Gap, AR.
02	12	1864	Skirmish at Holly Springs, MS, the Meridian, MS, Expedition.
02	12	1864	Affair at Wall Hill, MS, the Meridian, MS, Expedition.
02	12	1864	Affair 4 miles west of the California House, MO, where bushwackers attack the stagecoach, but are repelled.
02	12	1864	Skirmish at Macon, MO.
02	12	1864	Skirmish at Rock House, WV.
02	13	1864	Federal expedition from Helena up the Saint Francis River, AR, with a large amount of Confederate prisoners taken. 2/13-14/1864.
02	13	1864	Skirmishes at Pease Creek, FL. 2/13-14/1864.
02	13	1864	Skirmishes between Chunky Creek and Meridian, MS, the Meridian, MS, Expedition. 2/13-14/1864.
02	13	1864	Skirmish at Wyatt, MS, the Meridian, MS, Expedition.
02	13	1864	Skirmish in Fentress County, TN.
02	13	1864	Federal scout near Knoxville, TN, to within sight of the Rebel camp, with no enemy encounters.
02	14	1864	Affair near Larkinsville, AL, with an attack by bushrangers.
02	14	1864	Skirmish at Ross' Landing, AR.
02	14	1864	Skirmish at Scott's Farm, Washita Cove, AR.
02	14	1864	Skirmish at Gainesville, FL, with Brig. Gen. Truman Seymour, USA.
02	14	1864	Union forces under Maj. Gen. Quincy A. Gillmore, USA, **occupy Gainesville, FL.**
02	14	1864	**Meridian, MS, is occupied** by Maj. Gen. William T. Sherman, USA, who promptly begins to destroy all Confederate contraband of importance; Brig. Gen. William S. Smith, USA, not having arrived as of yet, while Lieut. Gen. Leonidas Polk, CSA, watches the destruction taking place from outside the city, the Meridian, MS, Expedition. 2/14-20/1864.
02	14	1864	Affair near Brentsville, VA, where Confederates ambush a Union escort, killing 2, wounding 4 Federals.
02	15	1864	Skirmish at Saline River, AR.
02	15	1864	Federal expedition from Fernandina to Woodstock and King's Ferry Mills, FL, for the purpose of procuring lumber for military use. 2/15-23/1864.
02	15	1864	Skirmishes at Marion Station, MS, the Meridian, MS, Expedition. 2/15-17/1864.
02	15	1864	**Federal expedition from Vicksburg to Grand Gulf, MS,** as the **12th Louisiana Infantry of African descent** is sent on numerous excursions throughout the area, confiscating and transporting mainly Confederate cotton, with assistance by the Union steamers, **Shenango, Thomas E. Tutt, Autocrat, John Raines, Welcome,** the gunboat, **Pittsburg,** and the ram **Switzerland.** No encounter with the enemy, although seen. The Federals lose only one man who was captured and hung, and a couple accidently wounded by friendly fire. 2/15-3/6/1864.
02	15	1864	Affair near Charleston, MO, with guerrillas.
02	15	1865	Skirmish in Overton County, TN, with the Confederates defeating a party of buckwackers and tories, inflicting 19 casualties, including 17 dead, by Col. John M. Hughs', CSA, Confederate operations in Middle Tennessee.
02	15	1864	Skirmish at Laurel Creek, Wayne County, WV, 25 miles from Louisa, KY, with Rebel casualties and prisoners.
02	16	1864	**Robert Hall Chilton, C.S.A.,** is appointed Maj. Gen.
02	16	1864	**Operations about Mobile, AL,** as the Union naval fleet bombards the Confederate fortifications. 2/16-3/27/1864.
02	16	1864	Skirmish at Caddo Gap, AR.
02	16	1864	Skirmish at Indian Bay, AR.
02	16	1864	Skirmish at Lauderdale Springs, MS, between Maj. Gen. William T. Sherman, USA, and Lieut. Gen. Leonidas Polk, CSA, the Meridian, MS, Expedition.
02	16	1864	Affair at Fairfield, NC, where the US gunboat, **Foster,** transports Federals to the Alligator River where a

Confederate camp is surrounded and the entire Rebel company is captured; this all taking place during a severe snow storm.

02	16	1864	The Confederate vessels, **Pet** and **Spunky,** are captured off Wilmington, NC.
02	16	1864	Federal expedition against the Indians from Fort Walla Walla to the Snake River, Washington Territory. The **Palouse Indians** are unable to warn the particular Indian camp surrounded by the Yankees, who proceed to fire into the wigwams. The Federals employing the practice of "shoot first and ask questions later." The 31 bucks and 40 squaws and children not killed or mortally wounded were made prisoners. This action taking place 29 miles from a miners' camp, 80 miles from the post on the Snake River and 15 miles below the old **Nez Perces Reserve.** 2/16-23/1864.
02	17	1864	**James Patton Anderson, C.S.A.,** is appointed Maj. Gen.
02	17	1864	Skirmish at Black's Mill, AR.
02	17	1864	Skirmish at Horse Head Creek, AR.
02	17	1864	Skirmish in the Houlka Swamp, near Houston, MS, the Meridian, MS, Expedition.
02	17	1864	Skirmish near Pontotoc, MS, with Maj. Gen. W. T. Sherman, USA, the Meridian, MS, Expedition.
02	17	1864	The US steamer, **USS Housatonic,** is destroyed at the city of Charleston, SC, sunk by a torpedo from the **CSS H. L. Hunley,** the Confederate experimental submarine, which also sinks in the process.
02	17	1864	Federal expedition from Island No. 10 to Riley's Landing, TN, where the Federals capture a band of guerrillas caught asleep, lying with their pistols under the pillows.
02	17	1864	Federal expedition from Motley's Ford, TN, to Murphy and vicinity, NC, and the confiscation of large quantities of corn. 2/17-22/1864.
02	17	1864	Maj. Gen. William H. French, USA, resumes the command of the 3rd US Army Corps, the Army of the Potomac, VA.
02	17	1864	Federal scout from Warrenton, and skirmish near Piedmont, VA. It being very cold, the Federals marched rapidly, and happen to capture 13 of Maj. John S. Mosby's Partisan Rangers. 2/17-18/1864.
02	18	1864	**Alexander Travis Hawthorn,** CSA, is appointed Brig. Gen.
02	18	1864	Skirmish at Ringgold, GA.
02	18	1864	Skirmish at Aberdeen, MS, with Maj. Gen. William Sherman, USA, the Meridian, MS, Expedition.
02	18	1864	Affair near Okolona, MS, as Brig. Gen. William S. Smith's, USA, Cavalry forces attempt to join up with Maj. Gen. William T. Sherman, USA, at Meridian, MS.
02	18	1864	Affair near the headwaters of the Piney River, MO, with guerrillas and bushwackers sustaining casualties.
02	18	1864	Skirmish near Maryville, TN, with fatalities.
02	18	1864	Skirmish at Mifflin, TN.
02	18	1864	Federal scout from Ooltewah, TN, to Burke's and to Ellidge's Mills, GA, with a brief skirmish with Rebel pickets. 2/18-19/1864.
02	18	1864	Skirmish at Sevierville, TN.
02	19	1864	**Brig. Gen. William Edwin Baldwin, CSA,** dies near Dog River Factory, AL, after falling from his horse, when his saddle straps broke.
02	19	1864	Operations about Brown's Ferry, AL, as the Federals report that a considerable Confederate Cavalry force has got back into the Tuscumbia Valley, and the Federals attempt to repulse their crossing the river at three ferries.
02	19	1864	The Confederate capture of a Union forage train of 35 wagons at Waugh's farm, 12 miles from Batesville, AR.
02	19	1864	Skirmish at Grosstete, or Grosstete Bayou, LA.
02	19	1864	Skirmish at Egypt Station, MS, the Meridian, MS, Expedition.
02	19	1864	Skirmish near Houston, MS, the Meridian, MS, Expedition.
02	19	1864	Skirmish near Meridian, MS, the Meridian, MS, Expedition.
02	19	1864	Skirmish near Independence, MO.
02	20	1864	Federal expedition from Helena up White River, AR. 2/20-2 6/1864.
02	20	1864	**The Engagement at Olustee, or Ocean Pond, or Silver Lake, FL,** where Brig. Gen. Seymour Truman, USA, under Maj. Gen. Quincy A. Gillmore, USA, retreats toward Jacksonville, FL, with heavy casualties in its black Union regiments. after facing Brig. Gen. Joseph Finegan, CSA, commanding the District of East FL.
02	20	1864	Skirmish at Pease Creek, FL.
02	20	1864	Skirmish near West Point, MS, as Maj. Gen. William T. Sherman, USA, withdraws back towards Vicksburg, MS, after tiring of waiting for Brig. Gen. William Sooy Smith's Cavalry, tearing up

			Confederate railroad tracks all the way, the Meridian, MS, Expedition.
02	20	1864	Skirmish at Flat Creek, TN.
02	20	1864	Skirmish on the Sevierville Road, near Knoxville, TN.
02	20	1864	Skirmish at Strawberry Plains, TN.
02	20	1864	Skirmishes at Upperville and Front Royal, VA, where the Federals surprise **John S. Mosby's men who were celebrating John's promotion to Lieut. Colonel.** Mosby regroups and the superior fire power of the Federals using their carbines allows the Yankees to withdraw.
02	20	1864	Affair near Hurricane Bridge, WV, with a Union scouting party.
02	21	1864	Skirmish at Ellis' Bridge, MS, with Maj. Gen. Nathan Bedford Forrest, CSA, the Meridian, MS, Expedition.
02	21	1864	Skirmish near Okolona, MS, with Brig. Gen. W. S. Smith, USA, the Meridian, MS, Expedition.
02	21	1864	Skirmish at Prairie Station, MS, with Maj. Gen. Nathan Bedford Forrest, CSA, the Meridian, MS, Expedition.
02	21	1864	Skirmishes at Union, MS, the Meridian, MS, Expedition. 2/2 1-22/1864.
02	21	1864	Skirmish at West Point, MS, and with Brig. Gen. William Sooy Smith's, USA, Cavalry column retreating in the face of Maj. Gen. Nathan Bedford Forrest, CSA, the Meridian, MS, Expedition.
02	21	1864	Skirmishes near Circleville and Dranesville, VA, as Lieut. Col. John S. Mosby attacks and disperses a Union raiding party, killing 15 and capturing 70. Mosby has l killed and 4 slightly wounded. 2/21-22/1864.
02	21	1864	Federal scout from New Creek to Moorefield, WV. 2/21-22/1864.
02	22	1864	Skirmish at Luna Landing, AR.
02	22	1864	Demonstration on Dalton, GA, as Maj. Gen. George H. Thomas, USA, Army of the Cumberland makes reconnaissance on Lieut. Gen. Joseph E. Johnston's, CSA, Army of Tennessee, in winter quarters. 2/22-27/1864.
02	22	1864	Skirmish at Whitemarsh Island, GA, as the Confederates attempt to defend against the Federals landing a sizeable force here.
02	22	1864	Confederate raid on Mayfield, KY, robbing 3 stores, inflicting casualties, and burning everything else they didn't want.
02	22	1864	Skirmish at Ivey's Hill, or Farm, near Okolona, MS, and below:
02	22	1864	Engagement near Okolona, MS, with Maj. Gen. Nathan Bedford Forrest, CSA, Cavalry routing the Union forces under Brig. Gen. William S. Smith, USA, the Meridian, MS, Expedition.
02	22	1864	Skirmish on the Tallahatchie River, the Meridian, MS, Expedition.
02	22	1864	Skirmish at Lexington, MO.
02	22	1864	Federal operations about Warrensburg, MO, with guerrillas. 2/22-24/1864.
02	22	1864	Skirmish on Calfkiller Creek, TN, where the Confederates inflict severe casualties on the Federals, part of Col. John M. Hughs, CSA, Confederate operations in Middle Tennessee.
02	22	1864	Affair near Indianola, TX, where Confederate cavalry surround and capture 25 mounted Federal infantrymen.
02	22	1864	Skirmishes at Gibson's and Wyerman's Mills, on Indian Creek, VA, and Powell's Bridge, TN, as Brig. Gen. Theophilus T. Garrad, USA, commanding the District of the Clinch encounters Brig. Gen. William E. "Grumble" Jones', CSA, Cavalry.
02	22	1864	Secretary of the Treasury, Salmon P. Chase offers to resign in light of the **"Pomeroy Circular"** whereby Sen. Samuel C. Pomeroy of Kansas, advocates Chase running for the Presidency; Chase claims the notice is without Chase's approval.
02	23	1864	**William Brimage Bate, C.S.A.,** is appointed Maj. Gen.
02	23	1864	**Robert Charles Tyler,** CSA, is appointed Brig. Gen.
02	23	1864	Skirmishes near Dalton and at Catoosa Station and Tunnel Hill, GA, between Gen. Joseph E. Johnston, CSA, and Maj. Gen. John McCauley Palmer, USA, under Maj. Gen. George Henry Thomas, USA, the Army of the Cumberland.
02	23	1864	Maj. Gen. John A. McClernand, USA, resumes the command of the 13th US Army Corps, LA, etal.
02	23	1864	Federal scout from Springfield, MO, into Northern Arkansas, and skirmishes with guerrillas near Buffalo City (**March 1st**), and at Bennett's Bayou (**March 2nd**). One guerrilla killed was an ex-Baptist minister. 2/23-3/9/1864.
02	23	1864	Skirmish near New Albany, MS, the Meridian, MS, Expedition.
02	23	1864	In light of the **Pomeroy Circular,** President Lincoln meets with his Cabinet, without Secretary of

Treasury, Salmon P. Chase.

02	24	1864	Skirmishes at Tunnel Hill, Buzzard Roost, and Rocky Face Ridge (or Crow's Valley), GA, as Maj. Gen. John McCauley. Palmer's, USA, forces fail to force a retreat by Lieut. Gen. Joseph E. Johnston, CSA, effectively ending the Dalton, GA, excursion.
02	24	1864	Skirmish at Canton, MS, the Meridian, MS, Expedition.
02	24	1864	Skirmish at Tippah River, MS, the Meridian, MS, Expedition.
02	24	1864	Federal scout from Camp Mimbres, the New Mexico Territory, where the Federals kill 13 Indians including the chief of the **Mangas Indian** tribe; the Yankees capture from the Indians a Mexican woman who had been in captivity for 15 years. 2/24-29/1864.
02	24	1864	Gen. Braxton Bragg, CSA, is charged with the conduct of military operations in the Armies of the Confederacy, effectively becoming President Jefferson Davis' **Chief of Staff,** Richmond, VA.
02	25	1864	Affair near Hudsonville, MS, the Meridian, MS, Expedition.
02	25	1864	Maj. Gen. Oliver O. Howard, USA, resumes the command of the 11th US Army Corps, TN, etal.
02	25	1864	Federal scout from Whiteside's, TN, to Stevens' and Frick's Gaps, GA, where the Yankees gather all the meat and beef they could find. 2/25-26/1864.
02	25	1864	Maj. Gen. John C. Breckinridge, CSA, is assigned to the command of the **Trans-Alleghany** or the **Western Dept. of Virginia**, relieving from command, Maj. Gen. Samuel Jones, CSA.
02	26	1864	**Edward Porter Alexander,** CSA, is appointed Brig. Gen.
02	26	1864	**William Wirt Allen,** CSA, is appointed Brig. Gen.
02	26	1864	Skirmish near Canton, MS, as Maj. Gen. William T. Sherman, USA, continues to withdraw from Meridian, MS, the Meridian, MS, Expedition.
02	26	1864	Skirmish at Sulphur Springs, TN.
02	26	1864	The Confederate **capture of Washington, TN,** by , Col. John M. Hughs', CSA, Confederate operations in Middle Tennessee, inflicting 75 Union casualties.
02	27	1864	Skirmish at Pinos Altos, the Arizona Territory.
02	27	1864	The destruction of Confederate salt-works on Goose Creek near St. Mark's, FL.
02	27	1864	The Confederate **Prison Camp at Andersonville, GA,** (officially called **Camp Sumter**) is put in service near **Americus, GA,** to help relieve the overcrowding of prisoners at **Belle Isle, Richmond, VA.**
02	27	1864	Skirmish at Madisonville, MS, the Meridian, MS, Expedition.
02	27	1864	Skirmish at Sharon, MS, the Meridian, MS, Expedition.
02	27	1864	Skirmish at the Stone Church, near Catoosa Platform, MS, the final encounter during the Union demonstration on Dalton, GA.
02	27	1864	Affair near Poplar Bluff, MO, where the Yankee scouts burn a Rebel wagon train, killing some jayhawkers in the process.
02	27	1864	Skirmish in the Sequatchie Valley, TN, with many Union prisoners, Col. John M. Hughs, CSA, Confederate operations in Middle Tennessee.
02	28	1864	Skirmishes on the Pearl River, the Meridian, MS, Expedition.
02	28	1864	Skirmish near Yazoo City, MS, the Meridian, MS, Expedition.
02	28	1864	Skirmish at Dukedom, TN, with a Confederate party raiding the **Paducah Railroad.** The Federals attack and capture some men.
02	28	1864	Lieut. Gen. John Bell Hood, CSA, is assigned to the command of the 2nd Army Corps, the Confederate Army of Tennessee.
02	28	1864	Federal scout in Gloucester County, VA, with little action.
02	28	1864	Brig. Gen. George Armstrong Custer's, USA, Cavalry raid into Albemarle County, VA, as a diversionary tactic for Brig. Gen. Hugh Judson Kilpatrick's expedition against Richmond, VA. 2/28-3/1/1864.
02	28	1864	**Brig. Gen. Hugh Judson Kilpatrick's, USA, Cavalry Expedition against Richmond, VA,** in an attempt to rescue Federal Prisoners of War held at Belle Island Prison. 2/28-3/4/1864.
02	28	1864	Affair at Ely's Ford, VA, with Brig. Gen. Kilpatrick, USA.
02	29	1864	**Hiram Bronson Granbury,** CSA, is appointed Brig. Gen.
02	29	1864	Skirmish on Redwood Creek, CA, with the **Redwood Indians,** as Brig. Gen. George Wright, USA, commanding the Dept. of the Pacific, proclaims that the Indian war is being prosecuted vigorously and successfully.
02	29	1864	Skirmish near Canton, MS, the Meridian, MS, Expedition.
02	29	1864	Federal expedition from Rolla, MO, aboard the **Pacific Railroad,** to Batesville, AR, seizing corn and

fighting bushwackers. 2/29-3/13/1864.

02	29	1864	Skirmish at Stanardsville, VA, with Brig. Gen. George Armstrong Custer, USA.
02	29	1864	Skirmishes at Ballahock, on Bear Quarter road, and at Deep Creek, VA, with loss of life. 2/28-3/1/1864.
02	29	1864	Skirmish at Beaver Dam Station, VA, as Brig. Gen. H. Judson Kilpatrick USA, splits his command and sends part of it under Col. Ulric Dahlgren, USA, towards Goochland Court House, VA.
02	29	1864	Skirmish at Charlottesville, VA, as Brig. Gen. George A. Custer, USA, continues on his diversionary expedition.
02	29	1864	Skirmish near Taylorsville, VA, with Brig. Gen. Judson Kilpatrick's, USA, Cavalry raid on Richmond.
02	29	1864	The US expedition to Petersburg and the destruction of the saltpeter-works near Franklin, WV. 2/29-3/5/1864.

03	1	1864	The following are appointed Confederate Brigadier Generals: **Richard Lucian Page,** CSA **Claudius Wistar Sears,** CSA **William Feimester Tucker,** CSA
03	1	1864	Skirmish at Cedar Glade, AR.
03	1	1864	Skirmish in the Redwood Mountains, near Arcata, CA, with the **Redwood Indians.**
03	1	1864	Skirmishes at Cedar and McGirt's Creeks, FL, as the Federals advanced to ascertain the Confederates' position at Ten-Mile Station.
03	1	1864	Federal operations on the Ouachita River, LA, including actions at Trinity and Harrisonburg. The following US vessels were engaged: **Conestoga, Cricket, Fort Hindman, Lexington, Osage and the Ouachita.** 3/1-4/1864.
03	1	1864	Skirmish at Ashland, VA, as Brig. Gen. Judson Kilpatrick, USA, calls off his column's attack on Richmond and crosses the Chickahominy east of Richmond, VA.
03	1	1864	Skirmish near Atlee's, VA, with portions of the Union cavalry of the Kilpatrick raid on Richmond, VA.
03	1	1864	Skirmishes on the Brook turnpike, near Richmond, VA, as Col. Ulric Dahlgren, USA, abandons his attempt to enter Richmond, VA, from the north, at Short Pump, and hangs his guide, a young Negro lad for leading them astray.
03	1	1864	Skirmish at Burton's Ford, Rapidan River, VA, as Brig. Gen. George A. Custer's, USA, diversionary expedition ends today.
03	1	1864	Skirmish near Stanardsville, VA, with Brig. Gen. George A. Custer, USA.

03	2	1864	Federal expedition from Larkin's Landing to Gourd Neck and Guntersville, AL. 3/2-3/1864.
03	2	1864	Skirmish at Canton, MS, the Meridian, MS, Expedition.
03	2	1864	**Col. Ulric Dahlgren, USA, son of Rear Admiral John Dahlgren, USN,** is ambushed and killed at Mantapike Hill, near King and Queen Court House by Confederate forces led by Capt. E. Fox, with (supposedly) provoking orders on Dalgren's body to burn the Capitol of Richmond, and kill the Confederate government, including President Jefferson Davis. This orders will be vehemently denied as being authorized by the Union government. Gen. Robert E. Lee, USA, sends photostatic copies of the captured orders to Maj. Gen. George G. Meade, USA, commanding the Federal Army of the Potomac. Kilpatrick does not deny that his orders were indorsed in red ink "approved" over his official signature; just that he infers his original orders had been changed to include the above, subtly accusing the Confederates of tampering with his orders.
03	2	1864	Skirmish near Old Church, VA, with Brig. Gen. Hugh Judson Kilpatrick, USA.
03	2	1864	Skirmish near Walkerton, VA, as Brig. Gen. Judson Kilpatrick's Cavalry raid on Richmond, VA, ends in total failure.

03	3	1864	Skirmishes at Jackson and near Baton Rouge, LA.
03	3	1864	Skirmish at Brownsville, MS, the Meridian, MS, Expedition.
03	3	1864	Skirmish at Liverpool, MS, the Meridian, MS, Expedition.
03	3	1864	Skirmish near Petersburg, WV, with Union cavalry.

03	4	1864	**Operations in Florida,** as Maj. Gen. James Patton Anderson, CSA, assumes command of the District of Florida and reports the continuous landing of Federal troops while there is no let up in the number of Confederate troops in the district being drawn off for service in other parts of the Confederacy. 4/4-14/1864.
03	4	1864	Skirmish at Rodney, MS.
03	4	1864	Maj. Gen. William T. Sherman's, USA, Federal column arrives at Vicksburg, MS, from its Meridian, MS, Expedition.

03	4	1864	The US Senate confirms **Andrew Johnson as the Military Governor of Tennessee.**
03	4	1864	Skirmish near Murfreesborough, TN.
03	4	1864	Confederate demonstration on Portsmouth, VA, is repelled with the combined effort of Maj. Gen. David Birney, USA, Brig. Gen. Judson Kilpatrick's, USA, Cavalry, and Union gunboats. 3/4-5/1864 .
03	5	1864	**Alpheus Baker,** CSA, is appointed Brig. Gen.
03	5	1864	**Daniel Harris Reynolds,** CSA, is appointed Brig. Gen.
03	5	1864	Skirmish at Leet's Tan-yard, GA, where Maj. Gen. Joseph Wheeler's Confederate cavalry attacks Brig. Gen. Absalom Baird's Cavalry of the 3rd Division, 14th US Army Corps, capturing their camps, wagons, stores, prisoners, etc.
03	5	1864	Confederate attack on Yazoo City, MS, is repelled, the Meridian, MS, Expedition.
03	5	1864	Skirmish at Panther's Springs, TN, with Brig. Gen. Jacob D. Cox, USA.
03	5	1864	Maj. Gen. John C. Breckinridge, CSA, supersedes Maj. Gen. Samuel Jones, CSA, in the command of the Trans-Allegheny or Western Dept. of Virginia.
03	5	1864	Commander John Taylor Wood's Confederate raid on the Eastern Shore of Virginia, at Cherrystone Point, VA, where a telegraph station is seized. Wood also sinks a large schooner, bonds the steamer **Iolas,** escaping in the steam-tug, **Titan,** to Mathews County, in the neighborhood of Mobjack Bay.
03	6	1864	**John Bullock Clark, Jr.,** CSA, is appointed Brig. Gen.
03	6	1864	Skirmish at Flint Creek, AR.
03	6	1864	Confederate attack on the Union pickets at Columbus, KY.
03	6	1864	**Yazoo City, MS, is abandoned** by the Union forces, precipitated by the previous day's Confederate attack, effectively ending the Meridian, MS, Expedition.
03	6	1864	Confederates' unsuccessful torpedo boat attack on the **USS Memphis,** North Edisto River, near Charleston, SC.
03	6	1864	Affair near Island No. 10, TN, on the Mississippi River, as the Federals move to capture 3 men reported to have murdered a Negro the previous day, and also to capture a notorious horse thief.
03	6	1864	Skirmish at Snickersville, VA, where a Union detachment ordered to Purcellville, had by mistake marched to Snickersville. Big mistake. The entire party was either killed or captured.
03	7	1864	Skirmish at Decatur, AL.
03	7	1864	Skirmishes at Brownsville, MS. 3/7-8/1864.
03	7	1864	President Jefferson Davis prods Lieut. Gen. James Longstreet, CSA, at Greeneville, East TN, to take the offensive in Tennessee and Kentucky.
03	8	1864	Affairs at **Courtland and Moulton, AL,** where Brig. Gen. Grenville M. Dodge, USA, **captures** the two towns along with large quantities of stores, ammunition, salt, and other provisions.
03	8	1864	Skirmish near Baton Rouge, LA.
03	8	1864	Skirmish at Cypress Creek, LA.
03	8	1864	Maj. Gen. Simon B. Buckner, CSA, is temporarily in command of the Dept. of East Tennessee.
03	8	1864	**President Abraham Lincoln meets** his **new Lieut. General, Ulysses Simpson Grant for the first time,** at Washington, DC.
03	9	1864	Skirmish near Nickajack Gap, GA, with Brig. Gen. Absalom Baird, USA.
03	9	1864	Skirmish near Greenwich, VA, as Lieut. Col. John S. Mosby, with assistance from the 4th VA Cavalry and **Chincapin Rangers,** attack a Union Cavalry scouting party.
03	9	1864	Federal expedition into King and Queen County, VA, where Brig. Gen. Judson Kilpatrick, USA, and his cavalry drive the Rebels from their camp near Carlton's Store. The Federals burn a grain mill in addition to other property, as Kilpatrick proclaims the people in this area have been well punished for the murder of Colonel Dahlgren. 3/9-12/1864.
03	9	1864	Federal expedition to the Piankatank, and skirmish at Cricket Hill, VA, where the Union gunboats, **Brewster and Jesup,** sink a schooner under tow, capture a valuable steam saw-mill, etc. 3/9-22/1864.
03	9	1864	Skirmish near Suffolk, VA, where the Negro Cavalry behaved bravely in hand-to-hand combat with the Confederates, although Brig. Gen. Matthew W. Ransom, CSA, claims the Federals fled towards Portsmouth, VA. Who's telling the truth?
03	9	1864	After President Lincoln hands Grant his accommodation to Lieut. Gen., **Grant leaves Washington, DC,** for the Army of the Potomac, currently headquartered at Brandy Station, VA.
03	10	1864	Federal expedition from Batesville to Wild Haws, Strawberry Creek, etc, AR. 3/10-12/1864.
03	10	1864	Confederate guerrilla raid on Clinton, KY, taking government horses, and breaking into local stores.
03	10	1864	Confederate guerrilla raid on Mayfield, KY, breaking into stores of local Union men.

MONTH	DAY	YEAR	ACT
03	10	1864	**The Red River Campaign, LA,** begins as Maj. Gen. Nathaniel P. Banks, USA, begins to concentrate troops at New Orleans, LA, for a drive into the heartland of the Confederate Trans-Mississippi region. 3/10-5/22/1864.
03	10	1864	Detachment from the Army of the Tennessee, under the command of Brig. Gen. Andrew J. Smith, USA, embarks at Vicksburg, MS, to assist Maj. Gen. Nathaniel P. Banks, USA.
03	10	1864	Skirmish in White County, TN, with Union Cavalry; the Rebels are forced to retreat with casualties on both sides during **Col. John M. Hughs', CSA,** Confederate operations in Middle Tennessee.
03	10	1864	Skirmishes near Charlestown and at Kabletown, WV, where the superior Union force pursuing Lieut. Col. John S. Mosby, CSA gets the worst of this engagement.
03	10	1864	Maj. Gen. Franz Sigel, USA, supersedes Brig. Gen. Benjamin F. Kelley, USA, in the command of the Dept. of West Virginia.
03	11	1864	Federal Cavalry operations about Sparta, TN, including skirmishes on Calfkiller Creek and near Beersheba Springs, and confrontations with the Texas Rangers, etc. **The notorious Champ Ferguson is also killed.** 3/11-28/1864.
03	11	1864	After meeting with **Maj. Gen. George G. Meade,** USA, **Lieut. Gen. Ulysses S. Grant,** USA, returns to Washington, DC, and leaves for Nashville, TN, to meet with **Maj. Gen. William T. Sherman,** USA.
03	12	1864	Maj. Gen. Nathaniel P. Banks, USA, with the assistance of Union gunboats, under Admiral David Porter, USN, start up the Red River, LA.
03	12	1864	Federal scout to Nola Chucky Bend, near Morristown, TN.
03	12	1864	Skirmish near Union City, TN.
03	12	1864	The Union Army has the following changes in command: a) Lieut. Gen. Ulysses S. Grant, USA, is assigned to the **overall command of the Armies of the United States.** b) Maj. Gen. Henry W. Halleck, USA, is assigned as the **Chief of Staff of the US Armies.** c) Maj. Gen. William T. Sherman, USA, to the command of the **Military Division of the Mississippi,** which encompasses the Depts. of the Arkansas, the Cumberland, the Ohio, and the Tennessee, **(as Union departments were named after rivers).** d) Maj. Gen. James B. McPherson, USA, to the command of the **Dept. and Army of the Tennessee.**
03	13	1864	Skirmish at Carrollton, AR.
03	13	1864	Federal scouts from Yellville to Buffalo River, AR, including encounters with guerrillas and bushwackers. 3/13-26/1864.
03	13	1864	The Confederate steamer, **Sumter,** is captured in Lake George, FL, by the Federal armed tug, the **Columbine.**
03	13	1864	Skirmish at Cheek's Cross-Roads, TN.
03	13	1864	Skirmish at Spring Hill, TN.
03	13	1864	Skirmish at Los Patricios, TX, with Federal cavalry.
03	14	1864	Skirmish at Claysville, AL.
03	14	1864	Skirmish at Hopefield, AR.
03	14	1864	The advance of the Union forces from Franklin to Alexandria, LA, the Red River (LA) Campaign. 3/14-26/1864.
03	14	1864	The **capture of Fort De Russy,** near Simsport, LA, led by Brig. Gen. Andrew Jackson Smith, USA, under Maj. Gen. Banks, USA, the Red River (LA) Campaign.
03	14	1864	Federal operations in Jones County, MS, against guerrillas.
03	14	1864	Skirmish at Bent Creek, TN.
03	14	1864	The 9th US Army Corps, Maj. Gen. John G. Parke, USA, commanding, is ordered from East Tennessee to Annapolis, MD.
03	15	1864	Federal scout from Batesville to West Point, Grand Glaize, Searcy Landing, etc, AR. 3/15-21/1864.
03	15	1864	Skirmish at Clarendon, AR.
03	15	1864	The new Pro-Union governor Michael Hahn of Louisiana, is given powers previously held by the military governor as President Lincoln attempts to transfer authority back to civilian government in those southern areas controlled by the Union.
03	15	1864	The U.S. Naval forces arrives at Alexandria, LA, the Red River Campaign.
03	15	1864	Skirmish at Marksville Prairie, LA, with Maj. Gen. Banks, USA, the Red River (LA) Campaign.
03	15	1864	Skirmish at Bull's Gap, TN.

03	15	1864	Skirmish in Flat Creek Valley, TN.
03	16	1864	Maj. Gen. Sterling Price, CSA, supersedes Lieut. Gen. Theophilus H. Holmes, CSA, in the command of the District of Arkansas.
03	16	1864	Skirmish near Palatka, FL, with Brig. Gen. Truman Seymour, USA, commanding the District of Florida.
03	16	1864	Maj. Gen. Nathaniel P. Banks, USA, **occupies Alexandria, LA,** on the Red River, with the assistance of nine Union ironclads and gunboats, under Admiral David Porter, USN.
03	16	1864	Brig. Gen. Orlando B. Willcox, USA, resumes the command of the 9th US Army Corps, enroute to Annapolis, MD.
03	16	1864	Federal scout from Pilot Knob, MO, through Barnesville, to the Arkansas line, and skirmishes with guerrillas. 3/16-25/1864.
03	16	1864	**Maj. Gen. Nathan Bedford Forrest's, CSA, Confederate Expedition into West Tennessee and Kentucky.** 3/6-4/14/1864.
03	16	1864	Confederate raid on the **Nashville and Chattanooga Railroad,** near Tullahoma, TN, with the Rebel capture and destruction of a train of freight cars heavily laden with supplies for the Federal army at Chattanooga, with 60 Federal prisoners and about 20 Yankee Negroes killed, during Col. John M. Hughs', CSA, Confederate operations in Middle Tennessee.
03	16	1864	Skirmish at Santa Rosa, TX.
03	16	1864	Affair near Annandale, VA, where a Rebel party capture a couple of Union stragglers; the Federals escape by killing the Rebel guards.
03	16	1864	Skirmish at Bristoe Station, VA.
03	16	1864	Federal reconnaissance from Harper's Ferry, WV, toward Snicker's Gap, VA, meeting up with a couple of Lieut. Col. John S. Mosby's Partisan Rangers with little action. 3/16-18/1864.
03	16	1864	Federal scout in Cabell and Wayne Counties, WV, including to Barboursville and Wayne Court-House. 3/16-18/1864.
03	17	1864	Skirmish with Indians, on Red Mountain, 7 miles southwest of Blue Rock Station, CA, where the Federals rout an Indian party and pursuing them to the Eel River, fighting again 2 days later.
03	17	1864	Federal scout from Lebanon, MO, to Thomasville, Oregon County, MO, into Northern Arkansas, and skirmishes. 3/17-4/1/1864.
03	17	1864	Skirmish at Manchester, TN.
03	17	1864	Lieut. Gen. Ulysses S. Grant, USA, meets with Maj. Gen. William T. Sherman, USA, at Nashville, TN. They board a train and leave for Cincinnati, OH.
03	17	1864	Affair at Corpus Christi, TX, as the Confederates move to capture the Yankees reported to have landed at the Oso. The Federals withdraw after a fire fight.
03	17	1864	Federal reconnaissance to Sperryville, VA, where the Federals capture a Rebel major conscripting local boys for Confederate service. 3/17-18/1864.
03	17	1864	Federal expedition from the Yorktown wharf aboard the transport, **Convoy,** into Mathews and Middlesex Counties, VA, where to instill law and order in his men and to stop them from robbing the local citizens, the Federal officer in charge had one man shot in the shoulder as a lesson. 3/17-21/1864.
03	18	1864	Skirmish at Monticello, AR.
03	18	1864	Affair on Spring Creek, AR.
03	18	1864	**Maj. Gen. William T. Sherman, USA, officially assumes the command of the Military Division of the Mississippi,** as Sherman and Grant plot military strategy at Cincinnati, OH.
03	18	1864	Federal scout from Island No. 10, TN, aboard the steamer, **John Rowe,** to New Madrid, MO. The party included **Company C, 7th Louisiana Infantry of African descent,** with no encounters.
03	18	1864	**Lieut. Gen. James Longstreet, CSA, resumes the command of the Dept. of East Tennessee.**
03	19	1864	Federal expedition from Rolling Prairie to Batesville, AR, with skirmishes, where the Confederates suffer about 50 casualties, with loss of horses, etc. 3/19-4/4/1864.
03	19	1864	Skirmish with Indians on the Eel River, CA, where the Yankees kill 2 Indian men and capture 2 squaws.
03	19	1864	Skirmish on the Cumberland River, KY, with Brig. Gen. Edward H. Hobson, USA, with the loss of life on both sides.
03	19	1864	Skirmish at Black Bayou, LA, the Red River (LA) Campaign.
03	19	1864	Federal scout from Lexington, toward Jackson, MO, and encounters with guerrillas and bushwackers. 3/19-22/1864.
03	19	1864	Skirmish at Beersheba Springs, TN.

03	19	1864	Union attack on Laredo, TX. Even though the Federals have superior rifles, the Texans barricade the town and force a Union withdrawal.
03	19	1864	Federal scout to Salem and Orleans, VA, where Lieut. Col. John S. Mosby, CSA, is up to his old tricks and punishes the Yankees from coming into **Mosby's Confederacy.**
03	20	1864	Skirmish at Arkadelphia, AR.
03	20	1864	Skirmish at Roseville Creek, AR.
03	20	1864	Skirmish at Bayou Rapides, on the Red River, LA.
03	20	1864	Federal scouts in Jackson and La Fayette Counties, MO, with skirmishes, inflicting guerrilla casualties. 3/20-30/1864.
03	21	1864	Skirmish near Moulton, AL, with Brig. Gen. Grenville M. Dodge, USA, commanding the Left Wing, 16th US Army Corps, who reports sighting Maj. Gen. Nathan Bedford Forrest's Confederate Cavalry.
03	21	1864	Affair at Henderson's Hill, LA, with Brig. Gen. Joseph A. Mower, USA, defeating and capturing the better part of Maj. Gen. Richard Taylor, CSA, scouting arm of the CSA service, the Red River (LA) Campaign.
03	21	1864	Skirmish at Reynoldsburg, 65 miles from Union City, TN, where the Confederates capture the Federal garrison of 50 men there.
03	21	1864	Affair at Velasco, TX, as an armed blockade runner fires on the grounded Federal steamship, **Matagorda,** whose crew then abandoned her, opting to go to shore.
03	22	1864	**Brig. Gen. Nathan Kimball, USA, is assigned to the command of the Dept. of Arkansas,** north of the Arkansas River, during the absence in the field of Maj. Gen. Frederick Steele, USA.
03	22	1864	Skirmish with Indians at Bald Spring Canon, on the Eel River, CA, where 2 more Indian men are killed. The Yankees are relentless in their pursuit of hostile Indians.
03	22	1864	Affair at Fancy Farms, KY, 10 miles south of Mayfield, where the postmaster was shot, the Catholic chapel destroyed, and the Willet & Boswell's store was broken into by the Confederates.
03	22	1864	**Maj. Gen. Lewis Wallace, USA,** supersedes Brig. Gen. Henry H. Lockwood, USA, in the command of **the Middle Dept.,** currently headquartered at Baltimore, MD.
03	22	1864	Skirmish at Langley's Plantation, Issaquena County, MS, as the Federals travel aboard a tug to search for Confederates. The Union force included 1 company of the **66th US Colored Infantry.**
03	22	1864	Affair at Corpus Christi, TX.
03	22	1864	Affair at Winchester, VA.
03	23	1864	**The Camden (Arkansas) Expedition.** 3/23-5/3/1864.
03	23	1864	Maj. Gen. Frederick Steele's, USA, column advances from Little Rock, AR, toward the Red River and Maj. Gen. Nathaniel P. Banks, USA.
03	23	1864	Skirmishes on the Benton, AR, road, the Camden (AR) Campaign. 3/23-24/1864.
03	23	1864	The Army of the Potomac **discontinues the 1st US Army Corps** and assigns those troops to the 5th US Army Corps, VA.
03	23	1864	Maj. Gen. Gouverneur K. Warren, USA, supersedes Maj. Gen. George Sykes, USA, in the command of the 5th US Army Corps, the Army of the Potomac, VA.
03	24	1864	Federal expedition from Batesville to Coon Creek, Devil's Fork of the Red River, etal, and skirmish **(27th)** near Cross-Roads, AR. 3/24-31/1864.
03	24	1864	Skirmish (24th) at Oil Trough Bottom and skirmish **(27th)** near Cross-Roads, AR, with guerrillas. 3/24 & 3/27/1864.
03	24	1864	Skirmish near Goodrich's Landing, LA.
03	24	1864	Federal expedition from Camp Lincoln, under Brig. Gen. Benjamin Alvord, USA, commanding the District of Oregon, near Canyon City, to Harney Valley, Oregon, with skirmishes with Indians, as the Yankees move against Indians who are stealing horses and mules from various ranches in the area. 3/24-4/16/1864.
03	24	1864	The Confederate **capture of Union City, TN,** under Maj. Gen. Nathan Bedford Forrest, CSA.
03	24	1864	Maj. Gen. Winfield S. Hancock, USA, resumes the command of 2nd US Army Corps, the Army of the Potomac, VA.
03	24	1864	The **3rd US Army Corps is discontinued,** and the troops are distributed to the 2nd and the 6th US Army Corps, the Army of the Potomac, VA.
03	25	1864	Federal scout from Batesville to Fairview, AR, with little action. If more days were like this, a lot more men would still be alive. 3/25-26/1864.

03	25	1864	Skirmish at Dover, AR.
03	25	1864	Skirmish at Rockport, AR, the Camden (AR) Campaign.
03	25	1864	Skirmish in Van Buren County, AR.
03	25	1864	Skirmish near White River, AR, the Federals recapturing some of their men held as prisoners.
03	25	1864	The Confederate attack on, and **capture of, Paducah, KY,** on the Ohio River, by Maj. Gen. Nathan Bedford Forrest, CSA; however, Forrest failed to capture the Federal garrison at Fort Anderson, and withdraws toward Fort Pillow, Mississippi River.
03	25	1864	The Districts of Baton Rouge and La Fourche are attached to the Defenses of New Orleans, LA.
03	25	1864	Federal expedition from Beaufort aboard the US gunboat, **Britannia,** to Bogue and Bear Inlets, NC, with the burning of a blockade runner. The Federal landing party in their small landing boats had a dangerous time due to the rough seas, with several of the crafts capsizing, but no fatalities. 3/25-26/1864.
03	25	1864	Affair at McClellansville, SC, as the Federals unsuccessfully attempt to capture the Rebel steamer, **Little Ada.**
03	25	1864	Brig. Gen. David McM. Gregg, USA, supersedes Maj. Gen. Alfred Pleasonton, USA, in the command of the Cavalry Corps, the Army of the Potomac, VA.
03	26	1864	Skirmish near Quitman, AR.
03	26	1864	Skirmish at Campti, LA, the Red River (LA) Campaign.
03	26	1864	Skirmish at Clinton, MS.
03	26	1864	Skirmish near Black Jack Church, near Greenville, NC.
03	26	1864	Maj. Gen. James Birdseye McPherson, USA, assumes the command of the Army of the Tennessee, under Maj. Gen. William T. Sherman, USA.
03	26	1864	**Lieut. Gen. Ulysses S. Grant, USA, joins the Army of the Potomac,** currently headquarterd at Culpeper Court House, VA.
03	27	1864	Affair at Branchville, AR, the Camden (AR) Campaign.
03	27	1864	Skirmish at Brooks' Mill, AR, the Camden (AR) Campaign.
03	27	1864	Federal scout from Little Rock to Benton, AR, where the Yankees arrest 3 women who helped the Rebels hide some stolen bales of cotton. 3/27-31/1864.
03	27	1864	Federal expedition from Pine Bluff to Mount Elba and Long View, AR, the Camden (AR) Campaign. 3/27-31/1864.
03	27	1864	Skirmish with Indians on the Eel River, CA, where the pursuing Federals attack a large Indian camp, killing 5 Indian men, and capturing 3 women and 3 young children.
03	27	1864	Skirmish at Columbus, KY, with Maj. Gen. Nathan Bedford Forrest's, CSA, Cavalry.
03	27	1864	Skirmish at Livingston, MS.
03	27	1864	Affair in Deepwater Township, MO, where the Federals capture some notorious bushwackers. Given a trial, found guilt and ordered to be executed, the men were allowed to write letters, will their belongings and calmly walked over to their graves, knelt down and met death in a most courageous manner. If another convicted bushwacker wasn't so horribly mutilated by numerous buckshot, the Federals would have executed him too, but felt sorry for him. The doctor said he was going to die anyways.
03	27	1864	Affair at Louisville, TN, as a band of mounted Rebels dashed into town, captured a Union citizen, and fled towards Maryville.
03	28	1864	Federal scouts to Caperton's Ferry, AL, and encounters with bushwackers.
03	28	1864	Skirmish at Danville, AR.
03	28	1864	Skirmish at Mount Elba, AR, the Camden (AR) Campaign.
03	28	1864	Engagement with Indians on the Eel River, CA, where the Yankees attack a large party, killing 16 Indian men, and capturing 2 squaws. The Yankees note that there is still a large number of wild Indians known by the name, **Wileackee,** still living in this area. The Federals plan to move on them.
03	28	1864	Riot by a group of **Copperheads,** or members of the **Knights of the Golden Circle** at Charleston, Coles County, IL, sees the worst anti-war protesters since the **Draft Riot** protesters in New York City NY, in July, 1863, resulting in at least 6 deaths and 20 injuries.
03	28	1864	**Operations in Eastern Kentucky.** 3/28-4/16/1864.
03	28	1864	Affair at New Hope, KY, as the Confederates burn the passenger train there on the **Louisville and Nashville Railroad.**
03	28	1864	Maj. Gen. Nathaniel P. Banks', USA, column advances from Alexandria, LA, the Red River Campaign, while Maj. Gen. (soon to be Lieut. Gen) Richard Taylor, CSA, concentrates forces to contest Banks' advance into the Trans-Mississippi region.
03	28	1864	Skirmish on Obey's River, TN, with Brig. Gen. Edward H. Hobson, USA, commanding the District of

			South Central Kentucky.
03	28	1864	Federal scout to Aldie and Middleburg, VA, as the Federals traverse the Bull Run Battlefield searching for Lieut. Col. John S. Mosby, CSA and the 43rd Virginia Battalion Calvary 3/28-29/1864.
03	28	1864	Federal scout in Gloucester County, VA, to ascertain the truth of alleged rebel designs to capture oyster schooners.
03	28	1864	Affair at Bloomery Gap, WV.
03	29	1864	Affair at Caperton's Ferry, AL, as a party of Federals assisting a refugee in crossing the Tennessee River was attacked by a band of mounted Confederates. The Federals are shot and wounded as they refuse to surrender and attempt to flee in the skiff they were using.
03	29	1864	Skirmish at Arkadelphia, AR, the Camden (AR) Campaign.
03	29	1864	Federal scouts from Bellefonte, AR. 3/29-4/1/1864.
03	29	1864	Skirmish at Long View, AR, the Camden (AR) Campaign.
03	29	1864	Skirmish at Roseville, AR, 45 miles from Fort Smith, AR.
03	29	1864	Federal scout from Lookout Valley to Deer Head Cove, GA. 3/29-31/1864.
03	29	1864	Skirmishes about Monett's Ferry and Cloutierville, LA, on the Red River. 3/29-30/1864.
03	29	1864	Skirmish near Bolivar, TN, with Maj. Gen. Nathan Bedford Forrest's, CSA, Cavalry.
03	30	1864	Federal scout from Athens, AL, with the capture of the celebrated guerrilla, Capt. Moore, and 30 of his men.
03	30	1864	Federal scout from Woodville, AL, against guerrillas.
03	30	1864	Action at Mount Elba, AR, and the pursuit of the Confederates to Big Creek, AR, the Camden (AR) Campaign.
03	30	1864	Federal scout from Columbus to Clinton and Moscow, KY.
03	30	1864	Confederate attack on the outpost at Snyder's Bluff, MS, as Brig. Gen. Lawrence S. Ross, CSA, captures a Negro corral, 100 mules, some Negroes, burned all their quarters and killed 30.
03	30	1864	The capture of the Confederate outpost at Cherry Grove, NC, (by boats from the US Steamer, **Commodore Barney.)**
03	30	1864	Affair near Greenton, MO, with bushwackers.
03	30	1864	Federal reconnaissance from Lookout Valley, TN, to McLemore's Cove, GA. 3/30-4/1/1864.
03	31	1864	Federal scout from Bridgeport, AL, to Caperton's Ferry and vicinity, where a couple of men are found playing both sides of the allegiance game, with passes from both armies. Their mother is drawing rations from the government and has her house searched where the Federals find 80 bushels of corn, 20 of wheat, 3 barrels of flour, 10 bushels of rye, and some 200 pounds of bacon. Were the rations for the family? To be resold at a profit? Or maybe for the Confederate boys? 3/31-4/2/1864.
03	31	1864	Skirmish near Arkadelphia, AR, the Camden (AR) Campaign.
03	31	1864	Skirmish at Palatka, FL.
03	31	1864	Skirmish at Forks of Beaver, Eastern KY.
03	31	1864	Skirmish at Natchitoches, LA, with Maj. Gen. Nathaniel Prentiss Banks, USA.
03	31	1864	Affair at Spring Island, SC, where the Confederates report a Federal reconnoitering party landing from a Union gunboat and tug.
04	1	1864	Skirmish at Arkadelphia, AR, as Maj. Gen. Frederick Steele, USA, heads south to assist Maj. Gen. Nathaniel P. Banks, USA, in the Red River Campaign, LA.
04	1	1864	Action at Fitzhugh's Woods, 6 miles above Augusta, AR, on the White River, assisted by the US gunboat, **Covington.**
04	1	1864	Federal expedition aboard the **Harriet A. Weed,** from Palatka to Fort Gates, FL.
04	1	1864	The US transport, **Maple Leaf,** is destroyed in the Saint John's River, FL, after striking a Confederate mine.
04	1	1864	**The Pearl River (Louisiana), Expedition,** aboard the Federal steamer, **Lizzie Davis.** 4/1-10/1864.
04	1	1864	Affair near Bloomfield, MO, where 3 guerrillas are caught in the act of robbing a Union man's house.
04	1	1864	Skirmish near Plymouth, NC.
04	2	1864	Skirmishes at Antoine, or Terre Noir Creek, and on Wolf Creek, AR, the Camden (AR) Campaign.
04	2	1864	Skirmishes at Okolona, AR, the Camden (AR) Campaign. 4/2-3/1864.
04	2	1864	Skirmish on Cedar Creek, FL, with **Brig. Gen. John P. Hatch, USA, now commanding the District of Florida.**
04	2	1864	Skirmish at Cow Ford Creek near Pensacola, FL, with Rebel Cavalry.
04	2	1864	Skirmish at Crump's Hill, or Piney Woods, LA, the Red River (LA) Campaign.

04	2	1864	Skirmish at Grossetete Bayou, LA.
04	2	1864	The Confederate destruction of the two light-houses at Cape Lookout, NC.
04	2	1864	Skirmish at Cleveland, TN.
04	2	1864	Federal reconnaissance from Powder Springs Gap toward Rogersville and Bull's Gap, TN. 4/2-4/1864.
04	3	1864	Affair near Clarksville, AR, where the Federals surprise attack a guerrilla camp, capturing men and weapons.
04	3	1864	Engagement at Elkin's Ferry, Little Missouri River, AR, the Camden (AR) Campaign. 4/3-4/1864.
04	3	1864	Skirmish at Ducktown Road, GA.
04	3	1864	Skirmish near Fort Gibson, the Indian Territory.
04	3	1864	Skirmish at Grand Ecore, LA, on the Red River.
04	3	1864	Skirmish at Clinton, MS.
04	3	1864	Skirmish at Cypress Swamp, TN.
04	3	1864	Skirmish near Raleigh, TN, with Maj. Gen. Nathan Bedford Forrest's, CSA, Cavalry.
04	4	1864	Skirmish at Charlestown, AR.
04	4	1864	Skirmishes at Roseville, AR, 45 miles from Fort Smith, AR. 4/4-5/1864.
04	4	1864	Skirmish at Campti, LA, on the Red River.
04	4	1864	**The 11th and the 12th US Army Corps are consolidated as the 20th US Army Corps,** under the command of Maj. Gen. Joseph Hooker, USA, TN, etal, with the following assignments: Brig. Gen. Jacob D. Cox, USA, supersedes Maj. Gen. George Stoneman, USA, in the command of the 23rd US Army Corps. Maj. Gen. John M. Schofield, USA, is then assigned to the command of the 23rd US Army Corps, **Army of the Cumberland**, TN, superseding Brig. Gen Jacob D. Cox, USA.
04	4	1864	Maj. Gen. Philip H. Sheridan, USA, is assigned to the command of the Cavalry Corps, the Army of the Potomac, VA, superseding Brig. Gen. David McGregg, USA.
04	4	1864	Maj. Gen. Quincy A. Gillmore, USA, is ordered to proceed with all available forces to Fort Monroe, VA.
04	4	1864	The US House of Representatives passes a resolution denouncing any intentions by **Napoleon III** of France to install a monarchy in Mexico under **Maximilian.**
04	5	1864	Skirmish at Marks' Mills, AR, the Camden (AR) Campaign.
04	5	1864	Skirmish at Whiteley's Mills, AR, with guerrillas.
04	5	1864	Skirmish on Quicksand Creek, Eastern KY.
04	5	1864	Skirmish at Natchitoches, LA, with Maj. Gen. Richard Taylor, CSA, as the US transports are having difficulty with the low water level in the Red River, LA.
04	5	1864	Federal expedition from New Madrid, MO, and skirmishes in the swamps of Little River, near Osceola, and on Pemiscot Bayou. The commanding Union officer advises the men against making a fire, which they do anyways. The Federals are attacked as they slept. Men are killed and wounded. The Federals leave one man mortally wounded with the women of a nearby house who promise to bury him. Before leaving, the Yankees find the ground covered with the blood of wounded Rebels. A nasty affair war is. 4/5-9/1864.
04	5	1864	Affair near Blount's Creek, NC, where a Federal scouting party surprise and capture a Rebel command there.
04	6	1864	Skirmishes on the Arkansas River and near Prairie Grove, AR, with Brig. Gen. John B. Sanders, USA, commanding the District of Southwest Missouri. 4/6-7/1864.
04	6	1864	Skirmish on the Little Missouri, AR, the Camden (AR) Campaign.
04	6	1864	Skirmish at Piney Mountain, AR.
04	6	1864	Affair at Prairie Du Rocher, IL, where the Yankees pursue guerrillas and horse thiefs.
04	6	1864	**A Union constitutional convention meets in New Orleans, LA, and adopts a new state constitution which abolishes slavery.**
04	6	1864	**The Dept. of the Monongahela is merged into the Dept. of the Susquehanna, PA.**
04	6	1864	Brig. Gen. James B. Ricketts, USA, is temporarily commanding the 6th US Army Corps, the Army of the Potomac, VA.
04	7	1864	Skirmish at Woodall's Bridge, near Decatur, AL.
04	7	1864	Skirmish at Rhea's Mills, AR.
04	7	1864	Skirmish on Brushy Creek, Eastern KY.
04	7	1864	Skirmishes near Port Hudson, LA.
04	7	1864	Skirmish at Wilson's Plantation, near Pleasant Hill, LA, between Maj. Gen. Banks, USA, and Maj. Gen.

			R. Taylor, CSA, the Red River (LA) Campaign.
04	7	1864	Skirmish at the foot of the Sierra Bonita, the New Mexico Territory, where the pursuing Federals catch and kill **21 Apache Indians,** capturing 45 head of livestock.
04	7	1864	Lieut. Gen. James Longsteet's Confederate Army Corps is ordered from Greeneville, East Tennessee, where he has been since last September, to Virginia to rejoin the Army of Northern Virginia, and Gen. Robert E. Lee, CSA.
04	8	1864	<u>**Richard Taylor, C.S.A., is appointed Lieut. Gen.**</u>
04	8	1864	**Camille Armand Jules Marie Prince de Polignac, C.S.A.,** is appointed Maj. Gen.
04	8	1864	Skirmish at Paint Rock Bridge, near Larkinsville, AL.
04	8	1864	Federal expedition from Denver, the Colorado Territory, to the Republican River, KS, 200 miles east of Denver. The Federals pursue a band of **Cheyenne Indians** purported to have stolen some cattle, burning their village, including their stores of beef and buffalo meat, cooking utensils, etc. 4/8-23/1864.
04	8	1864	**The Engagement at Sabine Cross-Roads, or the Battle of Mansfield, or Pleasant Grove, LA,, the Red River (LA) Campaign.**
04	8	1864	**Brig. Gen. Jean Jaques Alfred Alexander Mouton, CSA,** is mortally wounded at the opening battle of the Red River Campaign, Sabine Crossroads, near Mansfield, LA, while leading his men in a charge against the Federal troops, as Lieut. Gen. Richard Taylor, CSA, contests Maj. Gen. Nathaniel P. Banks', USA, advance on Shreveport, LA; Banks withdrawing to Pleasant Hill, LA.
04	8	1864	Skirmish at Bayou De Paul (Carroll's Mill), near Pleasant Hill, LA.
04	8	1864	Confederate demonstration on James Island, Charleston Harbor, SC, and vicinity.
04	8	1864	Skirmish at Winchester, VA, with Federal cavalry.
04	9	1864	Skirmishes on Prairie D'Ane, AR, prevents Maj. Gen. Frederick Steele, USA, from assisting Maj. Gen. Nathaniel P. Banks, USA. The Camden (AR) Campaign. 4/9-12/1864.
04	9	1864	**The Engagement at Pleasant Hill, LA,** with Maj. Gen. Nathaniel P. Banks, USA, repulsing Lieut. Gen. Richard Taylor, CSA, but effectively halting Banks' Red River Campaign.
04	9	1864	Skirmish near Raleigh, TN, with Maj. Gen. Nathan Bedford Forrest's, CSA, Cavalry.
04	9	1864	Maj. Gen. George Stoneman, USA, is assigned to the command of the Cavalry Corps, the Dept. of the Ohio, TN, etal.
04	9	1864	Maj. Gen. John M. Schofield, USA, assumes the command of the 23rd US Army Corps, the Army of the Cumberland, TN, etal.
04	9	1864	**Federal offensive plans are laid for a general advance of the Armies of the United States as follows:** a) Maj. Gen. Nathaniel P. Banks, USA, **to advance on Mobile, AL.** b) Maj. Gen. William T. Sherman, USA, the Military Division of the Mississippi, **to advance on Georgia,** and the Confederate Army of Tennessee, under Gen. Joseph E. Johnston, CSA. c) Maj. Gen. Franz Sigel, USA, commanding the Dept. of West Virginia, **to advance down the Shenandoah Valley, VA.** d) Maj. Gen. Benjamin F. Butler, USA, commanding the Army of the James, **to advance upon Richmond,** VA, from the south side of the James River, VA. e) Maj. Gen. George G. Meade, USA, commanding the Army of the Potomac, **to advance upon the Confederate Army of Northern Virginia,** under Gen. Robert E. Lee, CSA.
04	10	1864	Skirmish at Prairie D'Ane, AR, as Maj. Gen. Frederick Steele, USA, retreats back to Little Rock, AR.
04	10	1864	Federal scout to Dedmon's Trace, GA.
04	10	1864	Lieut. Gen. E. Kirby Smith, CSA, orders Lieut. Gen. Richard Taylor, CSA, to **withdraw from Pleasant Hill** to Mansfield, LA.
04	10	1864	The Union forces, under Maj. Gen. Nathaniel P. Banks, USA, **retreat to Grand Ecore, LA,** effectively ending the Red River Campaign. 4/10-11/1864.
04	10	1864	Skirmish at Cypress Swamp, TN.
04	10	1864	Maj. Gen. Oliver O. Howard, USA, supersedes Maj. Gen. Gordon Granger, USA, in the command of the 4th US Army Corps, TN.
04	11	1864	Affair near Kelly's Plantation, Sulphur Springs Road, AL, where a band of robbers capture and burn the Federal wagon containing 10 days' rations, etc. The Federals track many fresh trails and believe they lead to a local resident's house who they will closely monitor.
04	11	1864	Federal scout from Stevenson to Caperton's Ferry, AL, and vicinity to arrest several prominent citizens residing on the south bank of the Tennessee River.

04	11	1864	A Pro-Union State Government is installed at Little Rock, AR, with **Dr. Isaac Murphy,** as governor, the next southern state after Louisiana, to reject the Confederacy, enticed by the controlling Union military forces occupying these states.
04	11	1864	Skirmish at Richland Creek, AR.
04	11	1864	Federal reconnaissance from Rossville to La Fayette, GA. 4/11-13/1864.
04	11	1864	Skirmish near Columbus, KY, with Maj. Gen. Nathan Bedford Forrest's, CSA, Cavalry.
04	11	1864	Affair in Chariton County, MO, with bushwackers.
04	11	1864	Affair at Catlett's Station, near Greenwich, VA, with Maj. Gen. JEB Stuart's Confederate cavalry, with fatalities.
04	12	1864	Federal reconnaissance from Bridgeport down the Tennessee River to the vicinity of Triana, AL, and various locations throughout this area. 4/12-16/1864.
04	12	1864	Skirmish near Florence, AL, where the Yankees surprise a Rebel camp, capturing and killing some of them.
04	12	1864	Skirmish at Van Buren, AR.
04	12	1864	Skirmish near Fremont's Orchard, on the north side of the Platte River, the Colorado Territory, where the Federals attack and kill many Indians purported to have been harassing the ranchers there. From the arrows sticking in some of the Yankees, it appears they are **Cheyennes.**
04	12	1864	The Engagement at Blair's (or Pleasant Hill) Landing, LA, including the participation of the Union gunboats, **Lexington,** and the **Osage,** the Red River (LA) Campaign. 4/12-13/1864.
04	12	1864	**Brig. Gen. Thomas Green, CSA,** is mortally wounded at the engagement at Blair's Landing, LA, by an exploding shell fired from the Federal Gunboats that accompanied Maj. Gen. Nathaniel P. Banks', USA, Red River Campaign Expedition.
04	12	1864	Skirmish at Fort Bisland, LA.
04	12	1864	Federal expedition from Point Lookout, MD, to Westmoreland County, VA, to search for Rebel contraband goods; 3 Union gunboats as well as the **36th US Colored Infantry** participating. 11/12-14/1864.
04	12	1864	**Maj. Gen. Simon B. Buckner, CSA, assumes the command of the Confederate Dept. of East Tennessee.**
04	12	1864	Skirmish at Pleasant Hill Landing, TN.
04	12	1864	**The Confederate capture of Fort Pillow, TN, by Maj. Gen. Nathan Bedford Forrest, CSA, and the reported massacre of defenseless Union troops, the majority of whom were black.**
04	12	1864	Federal expedition up Matagorda Bay, TX, where the gunboat, **Estrella,** exchanges shots with the Rebel gunboat, **Carr,** and the armed schooner, **Buckhart.** 4/12-13/1864.
04	13	1864	Skirmish near Decatur, AL, as usual, with loss of life.
04	13	1864	Skirmish at Indian Bay, AR.
04	13	1864	Action at Moscow, AR, the Camden (AR) Campaign.
04	13	1864	Skirmishes at and near Richland Creek, AR. 4/13-14/1864.
04	13	1864	Skirmish on Spring River, 8 miles west of Smithville, AR.
04	13	1864	Skirmish at Columbus, KY, with Maj. Gen. Nathan Bedford Forrest's, CSA, Cavalry.
04	13	1864	Skirmish at Paintsville, Eastern KY.
04	13	1864	Skirmish at Mink Springs, 6 miles from Cleveland, TN, where Rebel Cavalry surprise and capture the Union outpost on the Cleveland and Ducktown road.
04	13	1864	Federal expedition from Norfolk to Isle of Wight County, VA, and skirmishes near Cherry Grove Landing and at Smithfield. The Federal's superior naval power is shown again today as the following are just some of the Union vessels participating: transports, **Pentz, Thomas, Tracy, Tucker,** and **Woodis,** gunboats, **Brewster, Foster, Jesup, Nansemond,** and the **Reno,** along with the flag-ship, **Minnesota.** 11/13-15/1864.
04	13	1864	Affair near Nokesville, VA, with Confederate guerrillas getting the worse of it.
04	13	1864	Federal reconnaissance from Portsmouth to the Blackwater, VA, including the **2nd US Colored Cavalry.** 11/13-15/1864.
04	13	1864	Maj. Gen. John Sedgwick, USA, resumes the command of the 6th US Army Corps, the Army of the Potomac, VA.
04	13	1864	Maj. Gen. Ambrose E. Burnside, USA, resumes the command of the 9th US Army Corps, the Army of the Potomac, VA.
04	14	1864	Skirmish at Dutch Mills, AR, the Camden (AR) Campaign.

04	14	1864	Skirmish at White Oak Creek, AR, the Camden (AR) Campaign.
04	14	1864	Skirmish at Taylor's Ridge, GA.
04	14	1864	Federal expedition from Camp Sanborn, the Colorado Territory, to Beaver Creek, KS, in pursuit of Indians purported to have stolen livestock. Evidence point toward the **Cheyenne Indians.** 4/14-18/1864.
04	14	1864	Affair near Booneville, Eastern KY.
04	14	1864	Action at Half Mountain, on Licking River, Eastern KY.
04	14	1864	Skirmish at Paducah, KY, on the Ohio River, with Maj. Gen. Nathan Bedford Forrest's, CSA, Cavalry, which concludes his latest expedition into West Tennessee and Kentucky, which began 3/16/1864.
04	14	1864	Skirmish at Bayou Saline, LA, the Red River (LA) Campaign.
04	15	1864	Skirmish at Camden, AR, the Camden (AR) Campaign.
04	15	1864	Skirmish at Roseville, AR.
04	15	1864	Operations in the Indian Territory, with rebel forces that came in from the southeast from the **Choctaw Indian Nation.** 4/15-20/1864.
04	15	1864	Skirmish near Baton Rouge, LA.
04	15	1864	The Union ironclad, **USS Eastport,** is sunk by a Confederate torpedo, Red River (Campaign), LA, (later raised by the Union forces, only to be destroyed on April 26, 1864).
04	15	1864	Skirmish at Spencer's Ranch, near Presidio del Norte, the New Mexico Territory.
04	15	1864	Federal demonstration on Battery Island, Charleston Harbor, SC, and vicinity.
04	15	1864	Skirmish near Greeneville, TN, as Maj. Gen. John M. Schofield, USA, commanding the Dept. of the Ohio has his cavalry surprise the Rebel cavalry, killing and capturing 25 Confederates.
04	15	1864	Affair 1.5 miles from Bristoe Station and Milford, VA, where the Union commander accuses his vedettes of cowardice.
04	15	1864	Skirmish at Waterford, VA, where Lieut. Col. John S. Mosby, CSA, routs a marauding Federal cavalry party.
04	16	1864	Skirmishes about Camden, AR, the Camden (AR) Campaign. 4/16-18/1864.
04	16	1864	Skirmish at Liberty Post-Office, AR, the Camden (AR) Campaign.
04	16	1864	Affair on the Osage Branch of King's River, AR.
04	16	1864	The US transport, **Hunter,** is destroyed in the Saint John's River, FL, after striking a Confederate torpedo, near the wreck of the **Maple Leaf.**
04	16	1864	Skirmish at Salyersville, Eastern KY.
04	16	1864	Skirmish at Grand Ecore, LA, the Red River (LA) Campaign.
04	16	1864	Skirmish at Rheatown, TN.
04	16	1864	Affair near Catlett's Station, VA, with some of Maj. Gen. JEB Stuart's, CSA, men.
04	17	1864	Affair at Flint River, AL, as the Confederates attempt to cutoff a Federal scouting party with limited success, inflicting casualties.
04	17	1864	Skirmish in Limestone Valley, AR, where the Federals surprise attack and overrun a Confederate camp.
04	17	1864	Skirmish at Red Mound, AR, the Camden (AR) Campaign.
04	17	1864	The Confederate **capture of Plymouth, NC,** by Brig. Gen. Robert Frederick Hoke, CSA, assisted by the Confederate ram, the **CSS Albemarle.** 11/17-20/1864.
04	17	1864	Skirmish at Beaver Creek, NC, on the Kinston Road.
04	17	1864	Skirmish at Holly Springs, MS.
04	17	1864	Maj. Gen. Stephen A. Hurlbut, USA, is relieved from command of the 16th US Army Corps, and Maj. Gen. C. C. Washburn, USA, is assigned to the command of the District of West Tennessee.
04	17	1864	Affair near Ellis' Ford, VA.
04	17	1864	Lieut. Gen. Ulysses S. Grant, USA, issues a proclamation that from now on P.O.W.'s will only be exchanged or paroled for an equal amount of Union P.O.W.'s which has the effect of hurting the southern cause due to their limited resources of manpower.
04	18	1864	**Samuel Bell Maxey, C.S.A.,** is appointed Maj. Gen.
04	18	1864	Skirmish near Decatur, AL, where the Confederates repel a Union advance.
04	18	1864	Engagement at Poison Spring, about 8 miles from Camden, AR, with Maj. Gen. Sterling Price, CSA, forcing a Union retreat, the Camden (AR) Campaign.
04	18	1864	Federal expedition from Burkesville, KY, to Obey's River, TN, with prisoners including one Rebel accused of murdering a Union soldier. 4/18-20/1864.
04	18	1864	Affair at Hunnewell, MO, as local citizens attempt to fend off some plundering bushwackers with mortalities on both sides.

04	18	1864	**Gen. P. G. T. Beauregard, CSA, is assigned to the command of the Dept. of North Carolina and Southern Virginia.**
04	18	1864	Skirmish at Boykin's Mills, SC.
04	19	1864	Confederate operations against Unionists in Marion County, AL, as the Texas Cavalry captures a good many Union conscripts and Rebel deserters.
04	19	1864	Skirmish on King's River, AR. The Yankees lose a small wagon train and men. The Rebels lose a good many more men.
04	19	1864	Federal expedition up the Yazoo River, MS, with skirmishes at and near Mechanicsburg, with the capture of the US gun-boat, **Petrel (or Gunboat No. 5); Gunboat No. 11 (or Prairie Bird)** also participating in the expedition. 4/19-23/1864.
04	19	1864	Skirmishes near Charleston, MO, with guerrillas. 4/19-20/1864.
04	19	1864	The Union blockade ship, the **USS Southfield,** is rammed and sunk by the Confederate ram, the **CSS Albemarle,** off the coast of Plymouth, NC. The **USS Miami** is disabled.
04	19	1864	Skirmishes at Waterhouse's Mill and Boiling Springs, TN, with Union pickets repelling Confederate Cavalry strikes. 4/19-20/1864.
04	19	1864	Affair at Leesburg, VA, with Lieut. Col. John S. Mosby, CSA; as usual, some Union men depart from this earth as Mosby interrupts a Union wedding party celebration taking place, leaving greetings for the Federal troops with the Pro-Union citizens living in the area. A festivity turned tragic.
04	19	1864	Affair at Marling's Bottom, Pocahontas County, WV. The routed Federals flee toward Beverly, WV.
04	20	1864	**Robert Frederick Hoke, C.S.A.,** is appointed Maj. Gen.
04	20	1864	**James Blair Steedman, U.S.A.,** is appointed Maj. Gen.
04	20	1864	Skirmish near Camden, AR, the Camden (AR) Campaign.
04	20	1864	The Confederate attack on Jacksonport, AR, is repelled.
04	20	1864	Skirmishes about Natchitoches, LA, on the Red River, the Red River (LA) Campaign. 4/20-21/1864.
04	20	1864	Skirmish at Waterproof, LA.
04	20	1864	The Confederate forces under Brig. Gen. Robert F. Hoke, CSA, surround and capture the Union garrison at Plymouth, NC, with Hoke awarded by being promoted to Major General, effective this day, the 1st Southern victory in this military arena in quite some time.
04	20	1864	Federal expedition from Fort Dalles, Oregon, and from Fort Walla Walla, Washington Territory, to Southeastern Oregon, with skirmishes with Indians, including the **Snake Indians (June 18th)**, the Federals destroying all their lodges, capturing all their horses, etc., the **Cayuse Indians** assisting the Yankees. During this expedition, the Federals travel many hundreds of miles, encountering and killing hostile Indians, capturing squaws and children, destroying Indian villages, etc. Yankees and friendly Indians, including the **Pi-Utes,** and **Warm Springs Indians** also lose men, some horribly mutilated, having some scalped and disemboweled, etc. 4/20-10/26/1864.
04	20	1864	**Gen. P. G. T. Beauregard, CSA, is superseded by Maj. Gen. Samuel Jones, CSA, in the command of the Confederate Dept. of South Carolina, Georgia, and Florida.**
04	21	1864	Affair at Harrison's Gap, AL, where a party of Rebels led by an ex-Methodist preacher, are captured and paroled by orders of Maj. Gen. John Logan, USA, after having them take an oath of allegiance to the US.
04	21	1864	Affair at Cotton Plant, Cache River, AR, with little action as the Rebels flee before the advancing Yankees.
04	21	1864	Maj. Gen. Nathaniel P. Banks', USA, column retires from Grand Ecore to Alexandria, LA, the Red River (LA) Campaign. 4/21-25/1864.
04	21	1864	Affair at Tunica Bend, LA, the Red River (LA) Campaign.
04	21	1864	Skirmish at Red Bone, MS.
04	21	1864	The destruction of the Confederate salt-works at Masonborough Inlet, NC.
04	21	1864	Federal expedition from the Siletz River Block-House to Coos Bay, Oregon, as the Yankees pursue a party of Indians who fled the **Alsea Sub-Agency Reservation.** The Indians, in addition to others never living on the reservation, are captured and returned. The Union soldiers complain that the white settlers at Umpqua and Coos Bay always took the part of the Indians, assisting them to hide or escape to the hills. 4/21-5/12/1864.
04	22	1864	**Brig. Gen. Joseph Gilbert Totten, USA,** dies at Washington, DC, from pneumonia.
04	22	1864	**Richard Delafield,** USA, is appointed Brig. Gen.
04	22	1864	Federal expedition from Jacksonport to Augusta, AR, and skirmish near Jacksonport. 4/22-24/1864.
04	22	1864	Affair 18 miles above Cotton Plant, AR.

04	22	1864	Skirmishes at and near Cloutierville, LA, as Brig. Gen. Hamilton Bee, CSA, contests the Union withrawal under Maj. Gen. Nathaniel P. Banks, USA. 4/22-24/1864.
04	22	1864	Attack on the Union transports in the Red River, near Tunica Bend, LA, the Red River (LA) Campaign.
04	22	1864	Skirmish on the Duck River, TN.
04	22	1864	By an act of Congress, the first US coins are minted with the motto, **"In God We Trust."**

04	23	1864	**William Henry Fitzhugh Lee, C.S.A.,** is appointed Maj. Gen.
04	23	1864	**James Chesnut, Jr., C.S.A.** is appointed Brig. Gen.
04	23	1864	The Confederate demonstration on Camden, AR, the Camden (AR) Campaign.
04	23	1864	Affair at Swan Lake, AR, the Camden (AR) Campaign.
04	23	1864	Confederate surprise attack on the Union pickets at Nickajack Trace, GA, killing, wounding and capturing the Yankees.
04	23	1864	Engagement at Monett's Ferry, or Cane River Crossing, and Cloutierville, LA, the Red River (LA) Campaign.
04	23	1864	Skirmish at Independence, MO.
04	23	1864	Maj. Gen. Frank P. Blair, Jr, USA, is assigned to the command of the 17th US Army Corps, TN, etal.
04	23	1864	Affair near Hunter's Mills, Fairfax County, VA, which is only about 20 miles from Washington, DC, with none other than Lieut. Col. John S. Mosby, CSA, and his Partisan Rangers.

04	24	1864	Affair near Decatur, AL, with Gen. Joseph E. Johnston, CSA.
04	24	1864	Skirmish near Camden, AR, the Camden (AR) Campaign.
04	24	1864	Federal scout from Ringgold to La Fayette, GA. 4/24-25/1864.
04	24	1864	Skirmish at Pineville, LA.
04	24	1864	Skirmish near Middletown, VA; Rebels flee toward Winchester.

04	25	1864	**James Fleming Fagan, C.S.A.,** is appointed Maj. Gen.
04	25	1864	Action at Marks' Mills, AR, the Camden (AR) Campaign.
04	25	1864	Skirmishes in Moro Bottom, AR, the Camden (AR) Campaign. 4/25-26/1864.
04	25	1864	Skirmish at Cotile Landing, LA, Red River, as Maj. Gen. Nathaniel P. Banks, USA, arrives at Alexandria, LA.
04	25	1864	Skirmish near Natchez, MS.
04	25	1864	Federal expedition from Bull's Gap to Watauga River, TN, as the Yankees discover the Rebels have burned all the bridges from Bull's Gap to the Watauga and about 20 miles of railroad track. 4/25-27/1864.
04	25	1864	Confederate attack on the Union outpost near Hunter's Mills, in Fairfax County, VA, by Lieut. Col. John S. Mosby, CSA, who captures men and horses.
04	25	1864	Maj. Gen. Robert Ransom, Jr. CSA, is assigned to the command of the Dept. of Richmond, VA.

04	26	1864	**Hiram Burnham,** USA, is appointed Brig. Gen.
04	26	1864	Maj. Gen. Frederick Steele, USA, **retreats from Camden, AR,** unable to joinup with Maj. Gen. Nathaniel P. Banks, USA, the Camden (AR) Campaign.
04	26	1864	Skirmish near Little Rock, AR.
04	26	1864	Federal expedition from Jacksonville to Lake Monroe, FL, where Brig. Gen. William Birney, commanding the District of Florida reports the seizure of two blockade runners, **Fannie** and **Shell,** in addition to cotton, 400 head of cattle, etc. 4/26-5/6/1864.
04	26	1864	Skirmishes about Alexandria, LA, as Union troops from the Red River Campaign continue to return here. 4/26-5/13/1864.
04	26	1864	Skirmish at Bayou Rapides Bridge, near McNutt's Hill, LA, the Red River (LA) Campaign.
04	26	1864	Skirmish at Berwick, LA.
04	26	1864	Engagement at the junction of the Cane and Red Rivers, LA, the Red River (LA) Campaign. 4/26-27/1864.
04	26	1864	Engagement at Deloach's Bluff, LA, and the destruction of the Union ironclad, **Eastport,** the disabling of the ironclad, **Cricket,** and the explosion of the Union vessel, **Champion 3,** the Red River (LA) Campaign.
04	26	1864	Skirmish in Wayne County, MO.
04	26	1864	The Federals **evacuate Washington, NC,** due to the **capture of Plymouth, NC,** by the Confederate forces. ll/26-30/1864.
04	26	1864	Affair at Winchester, VA.

04	27	1864	The following are appointed Union Brigadier Generals: **Edward Hatch,** USA **Lewis Addison Grant,** USA **Edward Moody McCook,** USA
04	27	1864	Skirmish near Decatur, AL, as the Confederate dash on the Union picket-lines on the Courtland and Moulton road is repulsed.
04	27	1864	The Confederate commerce raider, the **CSS Alabama,** continues destroying merchant vessels, this time, the **Tycoon,** off Salvador, Brazil.
04	27	1864	The Confederate attack on the Union Pickets on Taylor's Ridge, near Ringgold, GA, belonging to Brig. Gen. Judson Kilpatrick's, USA, Cavalry.
04	27	1864	Skirmish on Troublesome Creek, Breathitt County, KY, where the Federal cavalry overtake, capture, and kill 35 Confederates.
04	27	1864	Skirmish at Dayton, MO.
04	27	1864	Affairs at Masonborough Inlet, NC. (between the US steamer, **Niphon,** and the Confederate batteries). 4/27-29/1864.
04	27	1864	Federal expedition from **Williamsburg, VA,** and skirmish at Twelve-Mile Ordinary, VA. A solid Confederate force is posted at Bottom's Bridge, VA, contesting any further Union advance in that direction. 4/27-29/1864.
04	28	1864	Skirmish near Princeton, AR, the Camden (AR) Campaign.
04	28	1864	Skirmish with Indians at the Big Bend of the Eel River, CA, where the Yankees kill 8 Indian men, wounding many more, and capturing 11 squaws and 1 young child.
04	28	1864	Skirmishes in Johnson County, MO, where Brig. Gen. Egbert B. Brown, USA, commanding the District of Missouri sends Union cavalry after the guerrillas, led by **William Clarke Quantrill,** who ambushed and killed some Federal soldiers. 4/28-30/1864.
04	28	1864	Federal scout from Springfield, MO, toward Fayetteville, AR, for the purpose of establishing telegraphic communications. 4/28-5/7/1864.
04	28	1864	Fort Sumter, SC, once again is bombarded by Union artillery for a week.
04	28	1864	Federal reconnaissance to Madison Court-House, VA, to ascertain if any Rebels are there or at Wolftown.
04	28	1864	Federal scout from Vienna toward Upperville, VA. With casualties, the Federals capture 2 blockade runners and some of Lieut. Col. John S. Mosby's Partisan Rangers. 4/28-5/1/1864.
04	29	1864	**James Dearing,** CSA, is appointed Brig. Gen.
04	29	1864	Skirmish at the Ouachita River, AR, with Maj. Gen. Frederick Steele, USA, the Camden (AR) Campaign.
04	29	1864	Skirmish near Saline Bottom, AR, with Maj. Gen. Frederick Steele, USA, the Camden (AR) Campaign.
04	29	1864	The Federal Districts of West Florida and of Key West and the Tortugas are attached to the Defenses of New Orleans.
04	29	1864	Federal reconnaissance from Ringgold toward Tunnel Hill, GA, with encounters between Brig. Gen. Judson Kilpatrick, USA and Brig. Gen. William Young Conn Humes, CSA.
04	29	1864	Skirmish at Grand Ecore, LA, the Red River (LA) Campaign.
04	29	1864	Skirmish in the Sni Hills, MO.
04	29	1864	Federal expedition from Newport Barracks to Swansborough, NC, where the Federals capture 3 fishing boats and 225 barrels of salted fish ready for shipment to Kinston, NC. 4/29-30/1864.
04	29	1864	Skirmish in Berry County, TN.
04	30	1864	**Mosby Monroe Parsons, C.S.A.,** is appointed Maj. Gen.
04	30	1864	Skirmish at Decatur, AL, with Maj. Gen. James B. McPherson, USA, Commanding the US Army of the Tennessee.
04	30	1864	**The Engagement (Rear-Guard) at Jenkins' Ferry, Saline River, AR, the Camden (AR) Campaign.**
04	30	1864	**Brig. Gen. William Read Scurry, CSA,** is mortally wounded at the engagement at Jenkins' Ferry, AR, where he bled to death, refusing to be taken from the battlefield to surgeons who probably could have saved his life.
04	30	1864	**Brig. Gen. Samuel Allen Rice, USA,** is severely wounded at the engagement at Jenkins' Ferry, AR, having his ankle bone shattered by a Confederate minieball, failing to recover, he died at his home at Oskaloosa, IA, on July 6, 1864.
04	30	1864	Skirmish at Whitmore's Mill, AR, the Camden (AR) Campaign.
04	30	1864	Federal expedition from Memphis, TN, to Ripley, MS, and skirmish (**May 2nd**) at Bolivar, TN, with Brig. Gen. Samuel D. Sturgis, USA. 4/30-5/9/1864.

MONTH	DAY	YEAR	ACT
04	30	1864	**President Jefferson Davis' son, Joseph, age 5,** falls out a second floor window at the Confederate White House, **and dies,** Richmond, VA.
05	1	1864	Skirmish at Lee's Creek, AR.
05	1	1864	Skirmish at Pine Bluff, AR.
05	1	1864	Affair with Indians at Booth's Run, CA, after which 15 bucks and 25 squaws and children burn their bows and arrows, and come into the Federal camp to surrender, having enough of the death and destruction from fighting the white man.
05	1	1864	**Brig. Gen. John P. Hatch, USA, assumes the command of the Dept. of the South,** FL, etal, replacing Brig. Gen. Quincy A. Gillmore, USA.
05	1	1864	Skirmish at Stone Church, GA, near Chattanooga, TN.
05	1	1864	Skirmish at Ashton, LA.
05	1	1864	Skirmish at Ashwood Landing, LA.
05	1	1864	Affair at Berwick, LA, with an attack by Confederate cavalry.
05	1	1864	Skirmish at Clinton, LA.
05	1	1864	The US transport, **Emma,** is captured at David's Ferry, Red River, LA, the Red River (LA) Campaign.
05	1	1864	Skirmishes at Governor Moore's Plantation, LA, the Red River (LA) Campaign. 5/1-4/1864.
05	1	1864	**Lieut. Col. John Mosby's Cavalry and Military Operations in Virginia,** begins with the capture of 8 of Maj. Gen. Franz Sigel's, USA, wagon train near Bunker Hill, Shenandoah Valley, VA. Mosby then proceeds to Martinsburg, capturing Federal men and horses. His men had a skirmish near Winchester, losing several good men. Mosby's men also attacked a heavily guarded wagon train near Strasburg, capturing about 30 men and same in horses. About **May 10th,** Mosby attacked the Union Cavalry outpost near Front Royal, capturing 16 men and 75 horses without any losses. About **May 20th,** Mosby failed to capture a heavily guarded Federal wagon train near Strasburg; however, this action prevented Maj. Gen. David Hunter, USA, from receiving this as well as future wagon trains. About **June 20th,** Mosby moved into Fairfax and routed a body of Union Cavalry near Centreville, VA, killing, wounding and capturing 39. About **June 22nd,** Mosby captured Duffield's Depot, on the **Baltimore & Ohio Railroad,** taking 50 prisoners, having another encounter near Harper's Ferry, capturing 19 Yankees and 27 horses. And on **July 4th,** Mosby moved to assist Lieut. Gen. Jubal Early, CSA, in his 2nd invasion of Maryland, fighting the Federals on **July 6th** near Mount Zion Church, assisting Early on the way, during and returning from his invasion of the North. The above activities described above were typical for John Mosby and would continue through the end of July. 5/1-8/3/1864.
05	2	1864	Skirmish with Indians on Kneeland's Prairie, CA, where the Federals surround a party of hostile savages, firing into the thick brush, killing squaws in the process; at least one Yankee was shot and had his throat cut.
05	2	1864	Skirmish at Lee's Cross-Roads, near Tunnel Hill, GA.
05	2	1864	Skirmish near Ringgold Gap, GA.
05	2	1864	Skirmishes at Bayou Pierre, LA, the Red River (LA) Campaign. 5/2-3/1864 .
05	2	1864	Skirmish at Wells' Plantation, LA, as Lieut. Gen. Richard Taylor, CSA, continues to harass Maj. Gen. Nathaniel P. Banks', USA, withdrawal to Alexandria, the Red River (LA) Campaign.
05	2	1864	Skirmish at Wilson's Landing, LA, the Red River (LA) Campaign.
05	2	1864	Brig. Gen. William H. Emory, USA, supersedes Maj. Gen. William B. Franklin, USA, in the command of the l9th US Army Corps, LA, the Red River (LA) Campaign.
05	2	1864	Affair on Bee Creek, MO, where the Yankees attack and destroy a small guerrilla camp.
05	2	1864	Skirmish at Bolivar, TN.
05	2	1864	Federal scout in Hickman and Maury Counties, TN. 5/2-12/1864.
05	2	1864	Federal expeditions against the **Virginia and Tennessee Railroad,** in southwestern VA. 5/2-19/1864.
05	2	1864	Federal expedition under the command of Brig. Gen. George Crook, USA, sets out from the Kanawha River, WV, for operations against the **Virginia and Tennessee Railroad.**
05	3	1864	Maj. Gen. Frederick Steele's, USA, column arrives at Little Rock, AR, ending the Camden expedition.
05	3	1864	Skirmish near the mouth of Richland Creek, AR, where guerrillas capture a Yankee wagon train. Although the Federals gave a good fight, the Yankees who came upon the battlefield believe many of the Yankees were slaughtered, it not being possible that they all fell dead (37 Yankees) with no survivors.
05	3	1864	Skirmish at Cedar Bluffs with the **Cheyenne Indians,** the Colorado Territory, killing 25 and wounding 40 more. One **Cheyenne** spy was about to be shot, when the Yankees spared him when it was learned he was only half **Cheyenne**; and half **Sioux,** if he would lead them to the **Cheyenne** camp.

MONTH	DAY	YEAR	ACT
05	3	1864	Skirmish at Catoosa Springs, GA.
05	3	1864	Skirmish at Chickamauga Creek, GA.
05	3	1864	Skirmish at Red Clay, GA.
05	3	1864	Skirmish between the Bayous Redwood and Olive Branch, at Comite bridge, near Baton Rouge, LA, with a Confederate attack.
05	3	1864	The US transport, **City Belle,** is captured, the Red River (LA) Campaign.
05	3	1864	Federal raid on Bulltown, WV, where they **burn the town.**
05	3	1864	President Abraham Lincoln and his Cabinet discuss the **alledged massacre** of surrendered, unarmed Federal troops, many black, by Maj. Gen. Nathan Bedford Forrest's, CSA, Cavalry command at Fort Pillow, TN.
05	4	1864	Skirmish on the Varnell's Station Road, GA, as Maj. Gen. William T. Sherman, USA, prepared to move on Atlanta, GA.
05	4	1864	Maj. Gen. Frank P. Blair, Jr, assumes the command of the 17th US Army Corps, GA, etal.
05	4	1864	Skirmish at Ashwood Landing, LA.
05	4	1864	Skirmish in Doubtful Canon, Steen's Peak, the New Mexico Territory, where the Yankees are attacked by **Apache Indians** while en route from Fort Cummings to Fort Bowie. The Federals report killing 10 and wounding another 20 more **Apaches.**
05	4	1864	Federal expedition from Vicksburg to Yazoo City, MS, with skirmishes at Benton **(7th and 9th),** at Luce's Plantation, **(13th),** and at other points, with Brig. Gen. John McArthur, USA, skirmishing with Brig. Gen. Wirt Adams, CSA.
05	4	1864	Engagement at David's Ferry, LA, with the destruction of the US steamer, **Covington,** and the capture of the US steamers, **Signal,** and **Warner,** the Red River (LA) Campaign. 5/4-5/1864.
05	4	1864	Operations about New Berne and in the Albemarle Sound, NC, with skirmishes on the Trent Road, (4th) on the south side of the Trent River, **(5th)** the engagement with the Confederate ironclad ram, the **Albemarle, (5th)** and the surrender of the Union outpost at Croatan, NC. **(5th).** 5/4-6/1864.
05	4	1864	**Campaign from the Rapidan to the James River, VA,** as Lieut. Gen. Ulysses S. Grant, USA, orders Maj. Gen. George G. Meade, USA, to move the Army of the Potomac across the Rapidan River, advancing on Gen. Robert E. Lee's, CSA, flank toward Richmond, VA, as Lee moved up from around Orange Court House, VA. 5/4-6/12/1864.
05	4	1864	Skirmish near Chancellorsville, VA, with Lee and Meade.
05	4	1864	**Operations on the South Side of the James River, VA,** as Maj. Gen. Benjamin F. Bulter, USA, and the Army of the James, started out in transports and prepared to attack Richmond, VA, from the south. 5/4-6/2/1864.
05	4	1864	Affair at Callaghan's Station, WV, as the Federals move against the **Virginia and Tennessee Railroad.**
05	5	1864	Federal scout in Craighead and Lawrence Counties, AR. 5/5-9/1864.
05	5	1864	Skirmish near the mouth of Richland Creek, AR.
05	5	1864	Skirmish near Tunnel Hill, GA.
05	5	1864	Federal scout in Meade and Breckinridge Counties, KY, with a skirmish on Beaver Creek with guerrillas.
05	5	1864	Engagement at Dunn's Bayou, Red River, LA, including the Union ironclad gunboat, **Signal,** the Union steamer, the **Covington,** and the Federal transport ship, the **Warner,** the Red River (LA) Campaign.
05	5	1864	Skirmish at Graham's Plantation, LA, on the Red River, the Red River (LA) Campaign.
05	5	1864	Skirmish at Natchitoches, LA, on the Red River, the Red River (LA) Campaign.
05	5	1864	The Confederate ironclad ram, **Albemarle,** disables the Federal blockade vessel, **Sassacus,** and encounters the following Union vessels: **Ceres, Commodore Hull, Mattabesett, Miami, Seymour, Wyalusing,** and the **Whitehead,** the Roanoke River, NC.
05	5	1864	Maj. Gen. Benjamin F. Butler, USA, lands at Bermuda Hundred and City Point (now Hopewell), VA, below Richmond, VA.
05	5	1864	Brig. Gen. August V. Kautz's, USA, raid against the **Petersburg and Weldon Railroad,** VA, including skirmishes: a) at the Birch Island Bridges, the Blackwater River **(6th),** b) Stony Creek Station **(7th),** and c) at Jarratt's Station and White's Bridge **(8th),** VA. 5/5-11/1864
05	5	1864	**The Battle of the Wilderness,** including combats with Maj. Gens. Gouverneur K. Warren, John Sedgwick, and William B. Franklin, USA, and Lieut. Gens. James Longstreet, Richard S. Ewell and A. P. Hill, CSA, at: a) **the Brock Road**

                  b) **Craig Meeting House**
                  c) **the Furnaces**
                  d) **Parker's Store**
                  e) **Todd's Tavern,** etc. Total casualties approximate 25,000. 5/5-7/1864.

05	5	1864	**Brig. Gen. Micah Jenkins, CSA,** is mortally wounded at the Battle of the Wilderness, dying the next day from a Federal Minieball that lodged in his brain.
05	5	1864	**Brig. Gen. John Marshall Jones, CSA,** is mortally wounded as his brigade opened the Battle of the Wilderness, VA, shot down from his horse while rallying his men from the initial Federal assault on the Confederate lines.
05	5	1864	**Brig. Gen. Leroy Augustus Stafford, CSA.,** is mortally wounded at the Battle of the Wilderness, VA, while leading his men against the Federals, dying three days later on May 8, 1864.
05	5	1864	**Maj. Gen. Alexander Hays, USA,** is mortally wounded at the Battle of the Wilderness, VA, while leading his men near the Brock and Orange Plank Road.
05	5	1864	Confederate raid on the **Baltimore and Ohio Railroad** between Bloomington and Piedmont, WV, under Capt. John H. McNeill, of the Virginia Partisan Rangers, as the Rebels **capture Piedmont** as well as freight trains, mail train, bridges, 104 prisoners, many railroad cars in depot, etc. Everything captured was **burned,** except the prisoners.
05	5	1864	US Cavalry expedition under Brig. Gen. William W. Averell, USA, sets out from Logan Court-House, WV, against the **Virginia and Tennessee Railroad.**
05	6	1864	The following are appointed Confederate Brigadier Generals:

                  John Bratton,   CSA
                  Samuel Jameson Gholson, CSA
                  Stand Watie,   CSA

05	6	1864	**James Samuel Wadsworth, U.S.A.,** is appointed Maj. Gen.
05	6	1864	**Brig. Gen. Micah Jenkins, CSA,** dies from the battle wound to his brain he received the day before at the Battle of the Wilderness, VA, receiving his wound near the same spot that Lieut. Gen. Thomas J. "Stonewall" Jackson, CSA, was killed a year earlier at the Battle of Chancellorsville, Va.
05	6	1864	**Maj. Gen. James Samuel Wadsworth, USA,** is mortally wounded at the Battle of the Wilderness, VA, receiving his deathwound with a Confederate minieball lodging in his brain, while he rode atop his horse and leading his men against a Confederate charge, dying two days later on May 8, 1864, being awarded the rank of Major General, this day of his mortal wound.
05	6	1864	Skirmish with Indians near Boynton's Prairie, CA, after which 15 Indians went to the Federals and surrendered, stating that they were the last of their tribe in this section of the country, the Yankees having done a good job of eliminating them.
05	6	1864	Affair at Tampa, FL, where a Federal expeditionary force from Key West temporarily **occupies Tampa.**
05	6	1864	Skirmishes at Tunnel Hill, GA. 5/6-7/1864.
05	6	1864	Skirmish near Morganfield, KY.
05	6	1864	Skirmishes at Bayou Lamourie, LA, Red River, the Red River (LA) Campaign. 5/6-7/1864.
05	6	1864	Skirmish at Boyce's Plantation, LA, the Red River (LA) Campaign.
05	6	1864	Confederate operations in the Calcasieu Pass, LA, where the Rebels capture the Union gunboats, **Granite City** and **Wave.** Federals report 174 killed, wounded and missing while the Rebels lose 21. The Confederates report that before boarding the Union ships, the Yankees had attached weights to many of their dead and thrown them overboard, at least 5 washing up on shore and believing an accurate count will never be known. 5/6-6/1864.
05	6	1864	Confederate raid on Napoleonville, LA, where the Rebels ransack the stores there.
05	6	1864	Skirmish at Well's Plantation, LA, the Red River (LA) Campaign.
05	6	1864	Federal scout from Bloomfield, MO, after guerrillas.
05	6	1864	Federal scout from Patterson, MO, and skirmish **(8th)** at Cherokee Bay, AR, where the Rebels attack but soon after skedaddle, leaving 12 dead behind. 5/6-11/1864.
05	6	1864	Encounter on the James River, near City Point, with the Union ironclad gunboat, the **Commodore Jones,** destroyed by a Confederate electronic torpedo, while Maj. Gen. Benjamin F. Butler's overwhelming Union army fails to take the city of Petersburg, VA, which is lightly defended by Maj. Gen. George Pickett, CSA.
05	6	1864	The Engagement at Port Walthall Junction and Chester Station, VA, with Maj. Gen. Benjamin F. Butler, USA, and the Army of the James. 5/6-7/1864.
05	6	1864	Skirmish at Princeton, WV, with Brig. Gen. William W. Averell, USA, and his movements on the

Virginia and Tennessee Railroad.

05	7	1864	**Edward Richard Sprigg Canby, U.S.A.,** is appointed Maj. Gen.
05	7	1864	**Oliver Edwards,** USA, is appointed Brig. Gen.
05	7	1864	**August Valentine Kautz,** USA, is appointed Brig. Gen.

05 7 1864 Skirmishes near Florence (7th), and at Decatur **(8th)**, AL, as Brig. Gen. John D. Stevenson's, USA, were attacked by the Rebels and forced to withdraw toward Lawrenceburg. 5/7-8/1864.

05 7 1864 Maj. Gen. William T. Sherman, USA, moves forward toward Dalton, GA, and Gen. Joseph E. Johnston, CSA, Sherman's army located as follows:
a) **Army of the Cumberland,** Maj. Gen. George H. Thomas, USA, near Ringgold, northwest of Dalton.
b) **Army of the Ohio,** Maj. Gen. John Schofield, north of Dalton
c) **Army of the Tennessee,** Maj. Gen. James McPherson northwest of Dalton, GA.

05 7 1864 Skirmish near Nickajack Gap, GA.

05 7 1864 Skirmish at Varnell's Station, GA.

05 7 1864 Skirmish at Bayou Boeuf, LA, the Red River (LA) Campaign.

05 7 1864 The **Military Division of West Mississippi is constituted,** under the command of Maj. Gen. Edward R. S. Canby, USA.

05 7 1864 The US gun-boat, **Shawsheen,** is captured at Turkey Island, the James River, VA, during Maj. Gen. Benjamin F. Butler's Union operations on the south side of the James River, VA.

05 7 1864 Lieut. Gen. Ulysses S. Grant, USA, breaks off the fighting around the Wilderness, and instead of retreating as some many Union commanders had done in the past, **moves toward Spotyslvania Court House,** Gen. Robert E. Lee, CSA, rushing troops to get there first.

05 7 1864 Maj. Gen. Richard H. Anderson, CSA, is assigned the command of the 1st Confederate Army Corps, the Army of Northern Virginia, as **Lieut. Gen. James Longstreet, CSA, is seriously wounded.**

05 8 1864 **Brig. Gen. Leroy Augustus Stafford, CSA,** dies at Richmond, VA, from wounds received during the first day of the Battle of the Wilderness, VA, on May 5, 1864.

05 8 1864 **Maj. Gen. James Samuel Wadsworth, USA,** dies in a Confederate field hospital from his battle wound received May 6, 1864, at the Battle of the Wilderness, Spotsylvania, VA.

05 8 1864 Skirmish 10 miles northeast of Maysville, AR.

05 8 1864 Federal demonstration against Resaca, with combats at Snake Creek Gap, Sugar Valley, and near Resaca, GA. 5/8-13/1864.

05 8 1864 Federal demonstration against Rocky Face Ridge, with combats at Buzzard Roost or Mill Creek Gap, and Dug Gap, GA.

05 8 1864 Skirmish at Bayou Robert, LA, the Red River (LA) Campaign.

05 8 1864 **The Operations about Spotsylvania Court-House, VA,** including combats at the following locations:
a) **Todd's Tavern** (8th)
b) **Corbin's Bridge** (8th)
c) **Alsop's Farm** (8th)
d) **Laurel Hill** (8th)
e) **Ny and the Po Rivers** (10th)
f) **The Angle or the Salient** (12th)
g) **Piney Branch Church** (15th)
h) **Harris' Farm** (19th)
i) **Stanard's Mill** (21st)
j) **Guiney's Station** (21st) 5/8-21/1864.

05 8 1864 Maj. Gen. Jubal A. Early, CSA, is assigned to the command of the 3rd Confederate Army Corps, the Army of Northern Virginia, replacing Lieut. Gen. A. P. Hill, CSA, who has taken ill.

05 8 1864 Affair at Halltown, WV, where the Union pickets are attacked.

05 8 1864 Skirmish at Jeffersonville, WV, during the Federal operations on the **Virginia and Tennessee Railroad.**

05 9 1864 **Maj. Gen. John Sedgwick, USA,** is mortally wounded at Spotsylvania, VA, foolishly exposing himself to a Confederate sniper, and right after bragging the sharpshooter couldn't hit an elephant, was instantly killed by a minie bullet to his left cheek.

05 9 1864 **Maj. Gen. Stephen D. Lee, CSA, assumes the command of the Dept. of Alabama, Mississippi, and East Louisiana.**

05 9 1864 **The Gila (Arizona Territory) Expedition,** against Indians, as the Yankees leave Fort Bowie to Tuscon, AZ, then forward burning Indian farms and property of the hostile Indians. The expedition ends with 51

dead Indians, 17 wounded and 16 women and children as prisoners. 5/9-6/3/1864 .

| 05 | 9 | 1864 | Skirmish at Eudora Church, AR. |

05 9 1864 Skirmish at Eudora Church, AR.

05 9 1864 Federal scout from the American Ranch to Cedar Bluffs, the Colorado Territory, where the Yankees run into peaceful **Sioux Indians** who stated that a war party of 25 **Cheyenne Indians** had gone to the Platte to steal horses to escape the pursuing Federals. 5/9-10/1864.

05 9 1864 The US transport, **Harriet A. Weed,** is destroyed in the Saint John's River, FL, by a torpedo, near the mouth of Cedar Creek and 12 miles below Jacksonville.

05 9 1864 **Demonstrations against Dalton,** with combats near Varnell's Station (9th and **12th**) and at Dalton **(13th)**, GA. 5/9-13/1864.

05 9 1864 **Brig. Gen. Samuel B. Maxey, CSA, resumes the command of the Indian Territory.**

05 9 1864 Federal expedition from Louisa, KY, to, and skirmish at, Rock-House Creek, WV. 5/9-13/1864.

05 9 1864 Skirmish near Pound Gap, KY, as the Federals beat up on some Rebels, and 125 veterans of the 14th KY Volunteers request furloughs. Appears they had enough of this war.

05 9 1864 The Federal ironclad gunboat, the **Lexington,** successfully passes through a man made dam above Lexington, LA.

05 9 1864 Federal expedition from Fort Crittenden, the Utah Territory, to Fort Mojave, the Arizona Territory, to determine whether a route from the Colorado River to Salt Lake City can be made superior to the present route from Carson City to Salt Lake. Along the difficult trails and many hardships the Yankees experience, they note how many of the Indian tribes have been relegated to disgusting beggars, never once mentioning who caused them to become like this. 5/9-6/22/1864.

05 9 1864 Skirmish at Brandon (or Brander's) Bridge, VA, with the Federal Army of the James.

05 9 1864 **Engagement at Cloyd's Mountain, or Cloyd's Farm, VA,** with Brig. Gen. William W. Averell, USA, Cavalry, moving on the **Virginia and Tennessee Railroad.**

05 9 1864 **Brig. Gen. Albert Gallatin Jenkins, CSA,** is mortally wounded at the Battle of Cloyd's Mountain, near Dublin, VA, Pulaski County, having his arm removed by Federal surgeons after being captured, and failing to recover, he died on May 21, 1864.

05 9 1864 Engagement at Fort Clifton, VA, as Maj. Gen. Benjamin F. Butler, USA, decides to withdraw back to City Point, VA.

05 9 1864 Engagement at Swift Creek, or Arrowfield Church, VA, with Maj. Gen. Benjamin F. Butler's, USA operations of the Army of the James south of the James River, VA.

05 9 1864 Skirmish at Ware Bottom Church, VA, with Maj. Gen. Benjamin F. Butler, USA.

05 9 1864 Maj. Gen. Philip Sheridan's, USA, Cavalry expedition from Todd's Tavern to the James River, including combats at:

a) **Davenport** (9th)
b) **Beaver Dam Station, North Anna and at the Davenport Ford,**(9th and **10th**)
c) **Ground Squirrel Bridge, or Church** **(11th)**
d) **Glen Allen Station** **(11th)**
e) **Ashland** **(11th)**
f) **Yellow Tavern** **(11th)**
g) **Meadow Bridge** **(12th)**
h) **Mechanicsville** **(12th)**
i) **Strawberry Hill** **(12th)**
j) **Brook Church or Richmond Fortifications** **(12th)**
k) **Jones Bridge, Mattapony Church, Haxall's, White House Landing, Hanover Court-House, etc.** 5/9-24/1864.

05 9 1864 Brig. Gen. Horatio G. Wright, USA, assumes the command of the 6th US Army Corps, the Army of the Potomac, VA, as Maj. Gen. John Sedgwick, USA, is killed by a Confederate sharpshooter.

05 10 1864 **Thomas Moore Scott,** CSA, is appointed Brig. Gen.

05 10 1864 **Francis Fessenden,** USA, is appointed Brig. Gen.

05 10 1864 **Brig. Gen. James Clay Rice, USA,** is mortally wounded at Spotsylvania, VA, having his thigh mangled by a Confederate minieball, and failing to rally from the operation which amputated that leg, dies that evening in a Union field hospital.

05 10 1864 **Brig. Gen. Thomas Greely Stevenson, USA,** is mortally wounded at Spotsylvania, VA, being instantly killed by a Confederate sharpshooter while at the head of his command.

05 10 1864 Skirmish at Dardanelle, AR.

05 10 1864 Federal scout from Pilot Knob, MO, to Gainesville, AR, that runs into an abundance of bushwackers, and

			destroys Rebel property everywhere. 5/10-25/1864.
05	10	1864	Skirmish on Pine Island, Charleston Harbor, SC, and vicinity.
05	10	1864	Affair with Confederate guerrillas at Winchester, TN, as the Federals drive them off.
05	10	1864	Action at Chester Station, VA, with Maj. Gen Benjamin F. Butler, USA, and the Army of the James.
05	10	1864	The Union destruction of the Confederate torpedo station, on the James River, VA, by the Federal Army of the James.
05	10	1864	Engagement at Cove Mountain, or Grassy Lick, near Wytheville, WV, during the Federal operations on the **Virginia and Tennessee Railroad.**
05	10	1864	Skirmish at Lost River Gap, WV, between Brig. Gen. Benjamin F. Kelley, USA, and Brig. Gen. John D. Imboden, CSA.
05	10	1864	Skirmish at New River Bridge, WV, during the **Virginia and Tennessee Railroad** operations.
05	11	1864	**Maj. Gen. James Ewell Brown "Jeb" Stuart,** CSA, is mortally wounded at the combat of **Yellow Tavern, VA,** while defending Richmond, VA, from Maj. Gen. Philip Henry Sheridan's, USA, cavalry raid, receiving a pistol wound in his stomach and dying painfully the next day in his nation's capital, Richmond, VA.
05	11	1864	Federal expedition from Point Lookout, MD, aboard the transport steamer, **Star,** and the gunboat, **Yankee,** to the Rappahannock River, VA, for the purpose of destroying Confederate torpedoes. 5/11-14/1864.
05	11	1864	Maj. Gen. Edward R. S. Canby, USA, assumes the command of the Military Division of West Mississippi.
05	11	1864	Federal reconnaissance from Hilton Head, aboard the US transports, **Croton, Plato** and **Thomas Foulks,** to Daufuskie Island, SC.
05	11	1864	Skirmish at Blacksburg, WV, during the Federal operations on the **Virginia and Tennessee Railroad.**
05	12	1864	**Horatio Gouverneur Wright, U.S.A.,** is appointed Maj. Gen.
05	12	1864	The following are appointed Union Brigadier Generals: **Joseph Bailey,** USA **John Rutter Brooke,** USA **Samuel Sprigg Carroll,** USA **Simon Goodell Griffin,** USA **John Frederick Hartranft,** USA **Joseph Hayes,** USA **Nelson Appleton Miles,** USA **Emory Upton,** USA
05	12	1864	**Maj. Gen. James Ewell Brown "Jeb" Stuart, CSA,** dies in Richmond, VA, from wounds received the day before at Yellow Tavern, VA.
05	12	1864	**Brig. Gen. Junius Daniel, CSA,** is mortally wounded at the Battle of the Wilderness, VA, at the "Bloody Angle," while leading his men in a valiant effort to regain the ground at the "mule shoe" which had been captured by the Federal troops. Total casualties approximate 12,000 today.
05	12	1864	**Brig. Gen. James Byron Gordon, CSA,** is mortally wounded at the combat near Meadow Bridge, VA, while defending Richmond, VA, from Maj. Gen. Philip Henry Sheridan's, USA, cavalry raid, a day after Maj. Gen. JEB Stuart, CSA, was mortally wounded, dying in his nation's capital on May 18, 1864.
05	12	1864	**Brig. Gen. Abner Monroe Perrin, CSA,** is mortally wounded at the Battle of the Wilderness, VA, while leading his men against the Federal lines, receiving several wounds while riding his horse.
05	12	1864	Skirmish at Jackson's Ferry (Hallowell's Landing), AL, with the Union gunboat, **Gunboat A.**
05	12	1864	Skirmish at Bayou Lamourie, LA, the Red River (LA) Campaign.
05	12	1864	Skirmish at Smith's Station, the Nebraska Territory.
05	12	1864	**The Engagement at Proctor's Creek and Drewry's Bluff (or Fort Darling), VA,** as Gen. Pierre G. T. Beauregard, CSA, now commanding at Petersburg, VA, deflects Maj. Gen. Benjamin F. Butler's, USA, advance. 5/12-16/1864.
05	12	1864	Maj. Gen. August V. Kautz's, USA, raid against the **Richmond and Danville Railroad,** including skirmish at Flat Creek Bridge, and Chula Depot **(14th),** VA, part of Maj. Gen. Benjamin F. Butler's operations south of the James River, below Richmond. 5/12-17/1864.
05	12	1864	Affair at Strasburg, VA, as Lieut. Col. John S. Mobsy, CSA, attacks yet another Union wagon train with casualties inflicted on the Federals.
05	12	1864	Skirmishes near Newport, at Brown's Ferry, Salt Ponds (or Salt Pond Mountain), and Gap Mountain, WV, during the Federal operations on the **Virginia and Tennessee Railroad.** 5/12-13/1864.

05	13	1864	Brig. Gen. Joseph O. Shelby's, CSA, operations north of the Arkansas River. 5/13-31/1864.
05	13	1864	Skirmish at Cypress Creek, Perry County, AR, with Brig. Gen. Joseph O. Shelby, CSA.
05	13	1864	Skirmish at Spavinaw, AR, where with the assistance of the **2nd Cherokee Regiment,** the Yankees rout the Rebels at their camp, destroying Rebel supplies; the Confederates skedaddle.
05	13	1864	Skirmish at Tilton, GA, as Gen. Joseph E. Johnston, CSA, **evacuated Dalton, GA,** and entrenches at Resaca, GA, awaiting the advance of Maj. Gen. William T. Sherman's, USA, Army.
05	13	1864	The Union fleet finally passes the falls at Alexandria, and Maj. Gen. Nathaniel P. Banks', USA, column is in full retreat to the Mississippi River, the Red River (LA) Campaign.
05	13	1864	Skirmish 6 miles northeast of Cuba, MO, with guerrillas.
05	13	1864	Affair on James Island, Charleston Harbor, SC, and vicinity.
05	13	1864	Skirmish at Pulaski, TN.
05	13	1864	Skirmish near New Market, VA, as Brig. Gen. John D. Imboden, CSA, routs the attacking Yankee Cavalry.
05	13	1864	With Gen. Robert E. Lee, CSA, repelling Lieut. Gen. Ulysses S. Grant, USA, at Spotsylvania Court House, VA, Grant slides his troops to the south and east of Lee's. The frightening list of casualties is taking its toll on both armies, but more so on Lee who is unable to replace his losses with new troops. Grant's plan of attrition continues. Grant is accused by some of being a butcher.
05	14	1864	**John Brown Gordon, C.S.A.,** is appointed Maj. Gen.
05	14	1864	**Andrew Jackson Smith, U.S.A.,** is appointed Maj. Gen.
05	14	1864	**The Battle of Resaca, GA.** 5/14-15/1864.
05	14	1864	Skirmish at Wilson's Landing, LA, the Red River (LA) Campaign.
05	14	1864	Skirmishes at Rude's Hill and New Market, VA, as Maj. Gen. Franz Sigel, USA, marches up the Shenandoah Valley, Brig. Gen. John D. Imboden's, CSA, Cavalry contesting Sigel's advance, and waiting to be joined by Maj. Gen. John Cabell Breckinridge's, CSA, infantry.
05	15	1864	Skirmish at Centre Star, AL, 14 miles from Florence, with the Federals whipping the Rebels, capturing 35, forcing the Confederates to withdraw across the Tennessee River.
05	15	1864	Skirmish near Dardanelle, AR, with Brig. Gen. Joseph O. Shelby, CSA.
05	15	1864	Skirmish at Armuchee Creek, at Tanner's Bridge, GA.
05	15	1864	Skirmish near Rome, GA, as Maj. Gen. William T. Sherman, USA, continues to confront Gen. Joseph E. Johnston, CSA.
05	15	1864	Skirmish at Avoyelles, or Marksville, Prairie, LA, the Red River (LA) Campaign.
05	15	1864	The Confederate attack on Mount Pleasant Landing, LA, where the Rebels capture the Union stockade there, burn the saw-mill and other buildings before being forced to skedaddle by the pursuing Federals.
05	15	1864	**The Engagement at New Market, VA,** as Maj. Gen. John C. Breckinridge, CSA, is assisted by the students from the **Virginia Military Institute (VMI),** at Lexington, VA, in defeating Maj. Gen. Franz Sigel, USA, sending him skedaddeling up the Shenandoah Valley.
05	15	1864	Skirmish near Strasburg, VA.
05	15	1864	Federal scout from Beverly through Pocahontas, Webster, and Braxton Counties, WV, captures 36 prisoners, 85 horses and 40 head of cattle. 5/15-30/1864.
05	15	1864	Brig. Gens. William W. Averell's and George Crook's, USA, Cavalry commands unite at Union, WV.
05	16	1864	Skirmish near Calhoun, GA.
05	16	1864	Skirmish at Floyd's Spring, GA.
05	16	1864	Action at Rome (or Parker's) Cross-Roads, GA.
05	16	1864	Action at Big Bushes, 3 miles from Smoky Hill, KS, where the **Cheyenne Indians** lose 3 chiefs including **Black Kettle,** and 25 warriors; the Yankees suffering 7 casualties.
05	16	1864	Skirmish at Pond Creek, Pike County, KY.
05	16	1864	Engagement at Mansura (Belle Prairie, or Smith's Plantation), LA, the Red River (LA) Campaign.
05	16	1864	Affair with Indians at Spirit Lake, Minnesota, where in one occasion a Yankee was found dead with 2 bullets and one arrow. He still had his scalp, though. Just one of many infractions.
05	16	1864	Skirmish near Drywood Creek, MO, 35 miles southeast of Fort Scott, with guerrillas.
05	16	1864	Federal expedition from Patterson to Bloomfield and Pilot Knob, MO, with among other incidents, the Yankees are attacked by bushwackers, but lose them in the swamp. 5/16-25/1864.
05	16	1864	Federal expedition against the **Apache Indians** from Fort Craig, the New Mexico Territory, and to establish Fort Goodwin, the Arizona Territory, on the Gila River, near the confluence of the Rio de Sauz. The Yankees proclaim that the **Apaches** have been run out of country in the Gila Valley, and will soon be

			forced to surrender. 5/16-8/2/1864.
05	16	1864	Skirmish on the Ashepoo River, SC.
05	16	1864	Gen. Pierre G. T. Beauregard, CSA, successfully attacks Maj. Gen. Benjamin F. Butler, USA, at Fort Darling, or Drewry's Bluff, VA, forcing Maj. Gens. William F. Smith and Quincy A. Gillmore, USA, to retreat to Bermuda Hundred, VA, where Butler is effectively "bottled in" with the James and Appomattox Rivers to the north and south and Gen. Beauregard, CSA, to the east. It is argued that if Butler had been successful (and probably should have) in taking Petersburg, and then marching on to Richmond, VA, the Civil War would have concluded much sooner than what actually occurred. Total casualties approximate 6,700.
05	16	1864	Skirmish at Port Walthall Junction, VA, part of the Army of the James' operations south of the James River.
05	17	1864	Affair at Madison Station, AL.
05	17	1864	Brig. Gen. Joseph O. Shelby's, Confederate scout in Northern Arkansas. 5/17-22/1864.
05	17	1864	The Confederate **capture of Dardanelle, AR,** by Brig. Gen. Joseph O. Shelby, CSA.
05	17	1864	Engagement at Adairsville, GA, as Gen. Joseph E. Johnston, CSA, is attacked by Maj. Gen. William T. Sherman, USA, as Johnston pulls back, heading toward Atlanta, GA.
05	17	1864	Action at Rome, GA, with Gen. Joseph E. Johnston, CSA.
05	17	1864	Action near Moreauville, LA, the Red River (LA) Campaign.
05	17	1864	Skirmish at Yellow Bayou, LA, the Red River (LA) Campaign.
05	17	1864	Operations on the Bermuda Hundred front, VA, with Maj. Gen. Benjamin F. Butler, USA, in charge. 5/17-6/2/1864.
05	17	1864	Skirmish near Waterford, Loudoun County, VA, as Lieut. Col. John S. Mosby, CSA, with his 43rd VA Cavalry battalion, attack the men who joined up with the Union and formed a company of independent cavalry; Mosby inflicting 9 casualties on these Virginian Federals.
05	18	1864	**Brig. Gen. Byron Gordon, CSA,** dies in Richmond, VA, from his death wounds received on May 12, 1864 at the combat at Meadow Bridge, the Battle of the Wilderness, VA.
05	18	1864	**Joseph Brevard Kershaw, C.S.A.,** is appointed Maj. Gen.
05	18	1864	**John McCausland,** CSA, is appointed Brig. Gen.
05	18	1864	Skirmish at Fletcher's Ferry, AL.
05	18	1864	Skirmish at Clarksville, AR.
05	18	1864	Affair near Searcy, AR, where the Yankees seize 80 good horses; cattle is almost non-existent in these parts by now.
05	18	1864	Combats near Cassville, GA, as Maj. Gen. William T. Sherman, USA, continues to pursue the retreating Gen. Joseph E. Johnston, CSA. 5/18-19/1864.
05	18	1864	Combats near Kingston, GA. 5/18-19/1864.
05	18	1864	Skirmish at Pine Log Creek, GA.
05	18	1864	Skirmish in Pike County, KY.
05	18	1864	Skirmish at Wolf River, KY, as the Yankees moving from Glasgow, kill a few Rebs, losing a couple men themselves.
05	18	1864	Engagement at Yellow Bayou (Bayou De Glaize, Calhoun Station, Norwood's Plantation, or Old Oaks), LA, the Red River (LA) Campaign.
05	18	1864	Federal scouts near Neosho and Carthage, MO, where no Rebels are found in force. The Yankees decide to scout into Arkansas where small bands of guerrillas are operating, stealing and robbing the citizens. The Federals will try to bring law and order to these parts. 5/18-23/1864.
05	18	1864	Skirmish at City Point, VA, with Maj. Gen. Benjamin F. Butler.
05	18	1864	Skirmish at Foster's Plantation, VA, with Maj. Gen. Benjamin F. Butler, USA.
05	19	1864	The following are appointed Confederate Brigadier Generals: **Clement Anselm Evans,** CSA **Martin Witherspoon Gary,** CSA **Bryan Grimes,** CSA **William Terry,** CSA
05	19	1864	Skirmish at Fayetteville, AR, with Brig. Gen. Joseph O. Shelby, CSA.
05	19	1864	Skirmish near Norristown, AR, with Brig. Gen. Joseph O. Shelby, CSA.
05	19	1864	Operations on the Saint John's River, FL, including affairs at Welaka and Saunders (19th), and the capture of the US steamer, **Columbine. (23rd).** 5/19-27/1864.

05	19	1864	The Union forces cross the Atchafalaya, LA, near Simsport, LA, ending the failed Red River Campaign under Maj. Gen. Nathaniel P. Banks, USA.
05	19	1864	Skirmish at Dandridge, TN.
05	19	1864	The Union forces of Brig. Gen. William W. Averell and George Crook, USA, reach Meadow Bluff, WV, concluding their operations against the **Virginia and Tennessee Railroad.**
05	20	1864	Skirmish at Stony Point, AR.
05	20	1864	Skirmish at Etowah River, near Cartersville, GA, as Gen. Joseph E. Johnston, CSA, is closely pursued by Maj. Gen. John Schofield, USA. Johnston decides to retreat after Lieut. Gen. John Bell Hood, CSA, retreats instead of attacking the Union army, incorrectly thinking he was being surrounded.
05	20	1864	Skirmish near Mayfield, KY.
05	20	1864	Skirmish near Lamar, MO, where **Brig. Gen. John B. Sanborn, USA, commanding the District of Southwest Missouri,** reports a Confederate attack on his troops at Lamar; the Rebs are repelled.
05	20	1864	Skirmish at Greenville, MS.
05	20	1864	Gen. Robert E. Lee, CSA, moves his troops to front the Army of the Potomac as Lieut. Gen. Ulysses S. Grant, USA, orders Maj. Gen. George G. Meade, USA, to cross the Mattaponi River, sliding to the south along Lee's lines towards Richmond, VA.
05	20	1864	Skirmish at Ware Bottom Church, VA, with Maj. Gen. Benjamin F. Butler, USA.
05	20	1864	Skirmish at Greenbrier River, WV.
05	21	1864	**Brig. Gen. Albert Gallatin Jenkins, CSA,** dies near Dublin, GA, from wounds received at the Battle of Cloyd's Mountain, GA, on May 9, 1864.
05	21	1864	**Bushrod Rust Johnson, C.S.A.,** is promoted to Maj. Gen.
05	21	1864	Skirmish at Pine Bluff, AR.
05	21	1864	Affair on the Blue River, MO, where bushwackers ambush the Federal escort team transporting a prisoner to Kansas City, dealing out death to some Yankee boys today.
05	21	1864	The detachment from the Army of the Tennessee, that had participated in the Red River Campaign, re-embarks for Vicksburg, MS. 5/21-22/1864.
05	21	1864	Federal demonstration on James Island, near Charleston, SC. 5/21-23/1864.
05	21	1864	Skirmish at Fort Powhatan, VA, with the Federal Army of the James under the command of Maj. Gen. Benjamin F. Butler, USA.
05	21	1864	Skirmish at Newtown, VA.
05	21	1864	**Maj. Gen. David Hunter, USA, supersedes Maj. Gen. Franz Sigel, USA, in the command of the Dept. of West Virginia,** due to Sigel's setbacks in the Shenandoah Valley dealt by Maj. Gen. John C. Breckinridge, CSA.
05	22	1864	Affair near Devall's Bluff, AR, where the Confederates surprise attack and capture some Yankees, escaping toward Des Arc.
05	22	1864	Skirmish near Mount Pleasant, MS, 14 miles from Tupelo, as the Confederates kill 12 Federals and capture 5.
05	22	1864	The Federal capture and the Confederate recapture of the schooner, **Stingaree,** off of Brazos, TX, as after a Federal steamer captures the ship, the Rebel commander and his crew served liquor to the Federals, got them drunk, overpowered them, and was able to beach the vessel, escaping from the Federal steamer that originally captured them.
05	22	1864	Skirmish at Front Royal, VA.
05	22	1864	**Operations on the line of the North Anna River, Pamunkey, and the Totopotomy Rivers, VA,** as Lieut. Gen. Ulysses S. Grant, USA, moving from Guiney's Station, VA, is confronted with Confederate entrenched lines at Hanover Junction, near Richmond, VA, with the following combats: a) **Dabney's Ferry** b) **Ford or Mills on the North Anna** c) **Hanover Junction** d) **Jericho Bridge** e) **Mount Carmel Church** f) **Ox Ford** g) **Quarles' Mills** h) **Sexton's Station** i) **Crump's Creek** (May 27th) j) **Hanovertown** (May 27th)

	k) **Hawe's Shop**	**(May 27th)**	
	l) **Jones' Farm**	**(May 27th)**	
	m) **Little Church**	**(May 27th)**	
	n) **Totopotomy River**	**(May 28th-31st)**	
	o) **Armstrong's Farm**	**(May 30th)**	
	p) **Matadequin Creek**	**(May 30th)**	
	q) **Old Church**	**(May 30th)**	
	r) **Shady Grove**	**(May 30th)**	
	s) **Bethesda Church**	**(May 31st)**	
	t) **Meschump's Creek**	**(May 31st)**	
	u) **Shallow Creek**	**(May 31st)**	
	v) **Turner's Farm**	**(May 31st)**	
	w) **Ashland**	**(June lst)** (during 5/22-6/1/1864)	

05   23   1864   Skirmish with Indians at Grouse Creek, CA.

05   23   1864   Action at Stilesborough, GA, as Maj. Gen. William T. Sherman, USA, attempts to turn Gen. Joseph E. Johnston's left flank, crosses the Etowah River, and heads towards Dallas, GA.

05   23   1864   Federal scout from Warrensburg, MO, which, among other things, searched for the guerrillas who attacked and killed some Yankee soldiers and citizens, including a local judge. 5/23-25/1864.

05   24   1864   **Stephen Elliott, Jr.,**   CSA, is appointed Brig. Gen.

05   24   1864   **Brickett Davenport Fry,** CSA, is appointed Brig. Gen.

05   24   1864   Skirmish near Little Rock, AR.

05   24   1864   Skirmish at Burnt Hickory (or Huntsville) GA, as Maj. Gen. Joseph Wheeler, CSA, Cavalry attacks Maj. Gen. William T. Sherman's supply lines.

05   24   1864   Skirmishes at Cass Station and Cassville, GA.

05   24   1864   Skirmish near Dallas, GA.

05   24   1864   Skirmish near Morganza, LA.

05   24   1864   Col. Colton Greene's Confederate operations on the west bank of the Mississippi River, capturing 2 Union vessels in the process. 5/24-6/4/1864.

05   24   1864   Skirmish at Holly Springs, MS.

05   24   1864   Skirmish near Nashville, TN.

05   24   1864   The 9th US Army Corps is assigned to the Army of the Potomac.

05   24   1864   Action at Wilson's Wharf, north side of the James River, below Fort Powhatan, VA, as Maj. Gen. Fitzhugh Lee's Confederate attack is repulsed by the two all Black Federal regiments garrisoned there.

05   24   1864   Skirmish near Charlestown, WV, as the Federals pursue some of Lieut. Col. John S. Mosby's, CSA, men towards Kabletown.

05   24   1864   Skirmish near Lewisburg, WV.

05   25   1864   Skirmish at Buck Horn, AR, with Brig. Gen. Joseph O. Shelby, CSA.

05   25   1864   Skirmish near Camp Finegan, FL, as Col. Robert Shaw, with 300 colored and 100 white soldiers is ordered to move toward Baldwin.

05   25   1864   Affair at Jackson's Bridge, near Pensacola, FL, with Rebel Cavalry.

05   25   1864   Operations on the line of Pumpkin Vine Creek, with combats at New Hope Church, Pickett's Mills, and other points, GA, as Lieut. Gen. John Bell Hood, CSA, repels multiple attacks by Maj. Gen. Joseph Hooker, USA, about 25 miles from Atlanta, GA. 5/25-6/5/1864.

05   25   1864   The capture of the Union steamers, **USS Lebanon** and the **USS Clara Eames,** Mississippi River, MS, by Col. Colton Greene, CSA.

05   25   1864   The engagement with the US steamer, **Curlew,** on the Mississippi River, MS, by Col. Colton Greene, CSA.

05   25   1864   Federal expedition from Fort Wingate, the New Mexico Territory, to the Gila and San Carlos Rivers, the Arizona Territory, with skirmishes with **Apache Indians (June 7th** and **8th)** on the San Carlos River. The Federals surround a large party of **Apaches** who proclaim they are peaceful, having recently signed a peace treaty with the white men with the assistance of the **Zuni Indians.** The Federals admit the **Zunis** are peaceful but have been assisting the hostile Indians, and refuse to accept their word of any treaty and demand they surrender and come with them to a reservation. The **Apaches** try to flee, whereupon the Yankees fire upon them, instantly killing 15 Indians; the Indians scatter into the mountains, the Federals pursuing, firing, reloading, firing, again, etc. 5/25-7/13/1864.

MONTH	DAY	YEAR	ACT
05	25	1864	Skirmish near Cripple Creek, on the Woodbury Pike, TN, as the Rebels flee into the cedar woods, in the vicinity of Shelbyville.
05	26	1864	Maj. Gen. John G. Foster, USA, assumes the command of the Dept. of the South, FL, etal.
05	26	1864	Combats at and about Dallas, GA, as both sides begin to entrench which changes the concept of this advance into a siege. 5/26-6/1/1864.
05	26	1864	**The Montana Territory is created, which previously was mostly a part of the Dakota Territory.**
05	26	1864	Affair on Lane's Prairie, Maries County, MO, with bushwackers.
05	26	1864	The destruction of the US transport, **Boston,** at Chapman's Fort, Ashepoo River, SC, by her crew, after running aground. Afterwards, the Confederates board her and find a large number of burnt horses.
05	26	1864	Lieut. Gen. Ulysses S. Grant, USA, continues to slide along the right of Gen. Robert E. Lee's, CSA, front toward Hanovertown.
05	26	1864	**The Lynchburg, VA, Campaign.** 5/26-6/29/1864.
05	26	1864	The Union forces, under Maj. Gen. David Hunter, USA, advance from Strasburg and Cedar Creek toward Lynchburg, VA, and vicinity, and will be opposed by Brig. Gen. William E. "Grumble" Jones.
05	27	1864	Skirmish at Pond Springs, AL.
05	27	1864	Brig. Gen. Joseph O. Shelby, CSA, assumes the command of all the Confederate troops north of the Arkansas River, AR.
05	27	1864	Skirmish at Thomas' House on the Trinity River, CA, as 66 bucks, 68 squaws and 24 children surrender near the junction of North Fork and the main Eel Rivers. The Federals move tomorrow to kill or capture what few hostiles are left in this section of the military district.
05	27	1864	Skirmish at Greenville, MS.
05	27	1864	The Dept. of the Missouri is embraced into the Military Division of West Mississippi.
05	27	1864	Skirmish near **Shanghai, MO**, where bushwackers **burn the town** over fighting with local citizens there.
05	27	1864	Maj. Gen. Philip H. Sheridan, USA, Cavalry crosses the Pamunkey River and **occupies Hanovertown, VA.**
05	28	1864	Skirmish near Little Rock, AR.
05	28	1864	Skirmish at Washington, AR.
05	28	1864	Skirmish with Indians at Big Flat, CA.
05	28	1864	Skirmish near Jacksonville, FL.
05	28	1864	Confederate reconnaissance under Lieut. Gen. William Hardee, CSA, sustain substantial casualties against Maj. Gen. James McPherson, USA, near Dallas, GA.
05	28	1864	The Confederate attack on the Pest House, opposite Port Hudson, LA, where the Rebels destroy medicines, capture the attending physician, destroy telegraph wires and poles toward Baton Rouge, etc.
05	28	1864	The destruction and **burning of Lamar, MO**, by bushwackers.
05	28	1864	Skirmish at Pleasant Hill, MO.
05	28	1864	Skirmish at Warrensburg, MO.
05	28	1864	The Army of Northern Virginia and Gen. Robert E. Lee, CSA, arrive from North Anna to the area north of the Chickahominy River and Mechaniscville, near Cold Harbor, in advance of Grant's crossing of the Pamunkey River near Hanovertown, VA.
05	29	1864	Action at Moulton, AL.
05	29	1864	The Confederate capture of a Union refugee wagon train at Salem, AR, that left from Jacksonport, AR. 80 men and some women are reported killed. The remaining civilians will starve if not aided by the Union army as the Confederates burned the entire train. Nasty business this war is out west.
05	29	1864	Skirmish on Bayou Fordoche Road, 5 miles from Morganza, LA.
05	29	1864	Skirmish at Yazoo River, MS.
05	29	1864	Confederate guerrilla depredations at Winchester, TN, as they move into town and rob the place and citizens of $10,000.
05	29	1864	Skirmish at Middleburg, VA.
05	29	1864	Skirmishes at Newtown, VA, as the Federals lose another wagon train to the Rebels, this time 16 wagons. 5/29-30/1864.
05	29	1864	Maj. Gen. Jubal A. Early, CSA, is assigned to the command of the Confederate 2nd Army Corps, the Army of Northern Virginia.
05	29	1864	Skirmish at Hamlin, WV.
05	30	1864	**Brig. Gen. James Barbour Terrill, CSA,** is mortally wounded during the Battle of Bethesda Church,

			VA, part of the overall Battles of the Wilderness and Spotsylvania Court-House, VA.
05	30	1864	**Brig. Gen. John Morgan's, CSA, Confederate Cavalry raid** into Kentucky, on Maj. Gen. William T. Sherman's, USA, supply lines. 5/30-6/20/1864.
05	30	1864	Federal expedition from Morganza to the Atchafalaya, LA, and skirmishes near Livonia and Morganza. 5/30-6/5/1864.
05	30	1864	Skirmishes on Mill and Honey Creeks, MO, where the Federals confront and kill two bushwackers who had just spent the day robbing some poor Union families along their way. The Yankees burn the Rebels' homes. These actions only caused further retaliations back and forth. 5/30-31/1864.
05	30	1864	Skirmish at Greeneville, TN.
05	30	1864	Skirmish at Ashland and Hanover, VA, as Lieut. Gen. Ulysses S. Grant, USA, arrives along the Totopotomoy River, almost within 10 miles of Richmond, VA, but blocking the way is the Army of Northern Virginia, north of the Chickahominy River.
05	30	1864	Skirmish at Old Church, VA.
05	30	1864	Brig. Gen. George Crook's, USA, Command sets out from Meadow Bluff, WV, for the Lynchburg, VA, vicinity, in cooperation with Maj. Gen. David Hunter's, USA, advance from Strasburg and Cedar Creek toward Lynchburg, VA.
05	31	1864	<u>**Richard Heron Anderson, C.S.A., is appointed Lieut. Gen.**</u>
05	31	1864	<u>**Jubal Anderson Early, C.S.A., is appointed Lieut. Gen.**</u>
05	31	1864	The following are appointed Confederate Brigadier Generals:

        William Ruffin Cox,   CSA
        William Gaston Lewis,   CSA
        Robert Doak Lilley,   CSA
        John Caldwell Calhoun Sanders,   CSA
        James Barbour Terrill,   CSA (killed the day before)
        William Richard Terry,   CSA
        Thomas Fentress Toon,   CSA
        Zebulon York,   CSA

05	31	1864	Federal expedition from Jacksonville and the capture on June 2nd of the Confederate Camp Milton, FL. 5/31-6/3/1864.
05	31	1864	**The Operations at and about Cold Harbor, VA.** (The battles of Cold Harbor and Bethesda Church were fought on June 1st-3rd). 5/31-6/12/1864.
05	31	1864	Dissatisfied over Lincoln's policies, a group of Radical Republicans meet in Cleveland, OH, and nominate **Maj. Gen. John Charles Fremont,** USA, and **Brig. Gen. John Cochrane,** USA as President and Vice-President in the upcoming elections.
06	1	1864	**Stephen Dodson Ramseur, C.S.A.,** is appointed Maj. Gen.
06	1	1864	The following are appointed Confederate Brigadier Generals:

        Rufus Barringer,   CSA
        James Conner,   CSA
        Adam Rankin Johnson,   CSA

06	1	1864	Skirmish near Pound Gap, KY, as Brig. Gen. John Hunt Morgan, CSA, continues to harass Maj. Gen. William T. Sherman's supply lines.
06	1	1864	Skirmish near Kingston, GA.
06	1	1864	Skirmish near Marietta, GA, as Maj. Gen. George Stoneman, USA, Cavalry **captures Allatoona Pass, GA,** an important rail link.
06	1	1864	The engagement with the US steamer, **Exchange,** on the Mississippi River, MS, during Col. Colton Greene's Confederate operations on the west bank of the Mississippi River.
06	1	1864	Skirmish near Arnoldsville and the raid on New Market, MO, where the Yankees capture a couple bushwackers accused of committing two murders.
06	1	1864	Maj. Gen. Philip H. Sheridan's, USA, Cavalry, using Spencer repeating rifles, repels both attacks led by Maj. Gen. Richard H. Anderson, CSA, near Old Cold Harbor, VA.
06	1	1864	Federal expedition from Memphis, TN, into Mississippi, toward Ripley, as Brig. Gen. Samuel Davis Sturgis, USA, is ordered against Maj. Gen. Nathan Bedford Forrest, CSA. 6/1-13/1864.
06	2	1864	**Brig. Gen. George Pierce Doles, CSA,** is mortally wounded near Bethesda Church, VA, killed instantly by a Union sharpshooter, while inspecting his troops' entrenchment lines.
06	2	1864	The engagement with the US steamers, **USS Adams** and the **USS Monarch,** Mississippi River, MS, with

			Col. Colton Green, CSA.
06	2	1864	Affair at Covington, VA, with Brig. Gen. William E. "Grumble" Jones, CSA, pitted against Maj. Gen. David Hunter, USA; Jones' is destined to die 3 days later.
06	3	1864	Skirmish at Searcy, AR.
06	3	1864	The US gun-boat, **Water Witch,** is captured by the Confederate forces in Ossabaw Sound, near Savannah, GA.
06	3	1864	Skirmish near Neosho, MO, where the Yankees pursue and kill some bushwackers, the bushwackers inflicting same on the Federals. A vicious, endless circle.
06	3	1864	Federal scout from Sedalia to the Blackwater River, MO, after some bushwackers shoot a Yankee and kill a civilian in front of the post office. These actions by lawless bands of barbarians are laying the groundwork for the wide open Wild Wild West after the end of the Civil War. 6/3-5/1864.
06	3	1864	**Lieut. Gen. Ulysses S. Grant, USA, loses about 7,000 men** in less than an hour in trying two frontal assaults on the entrenched Confederate lines at **Cold Harbor.** Grant, refusing defeat, does not negotiate a truce until June 7th to send rescue parties to help the wounded on the battlefield, resulting in further loss of life. Within the last month of the Army of the Potomac's advance, estimates of 50,000 Union and 32,000 Confederate casualties haunt the two armies; the Confederates, however, have no resources for new recruits to fill the dwindling ranks.
06	3	1864	Cavalry action at Haw's Shop, VA, part of the Cold Harbor attack.
06	3	1864	Skirmish near Via's House, VA, during the Campaign from the Rapidan to the James River, VA.
06	3	1864	Brig. Gen. William W. Averell's, USA, Cavalry command sets out from Bunger's Mills, Greenbrier County, WV, to join up with Maj. Gen. David Hunter, USA, on his way to Lynchburg.
06	4	1864	Federal scouts from Huntersville and Clinton, AR, in search of guerrilla bands. 6/4-17/1864.
06	4	1864	Action at Big Shanty and Acworth, GA, as Gen. Joseph E. Johnston, CSA, moves from New Hope Church area outside Atlanta to fortified positions fronting Maj. Gen. William T. Sherman, USA, at the Pine Mountain, GA.
06	4	1864	Affair at Hudson's Crossing, Neosho River, the Indian Territory, where the Federals followup and attack the bushwackers, who originally attacked the Federal Indian brigade moving to meet the refugee train at Hudson's Crossing and burn their camp. The Yankees rescue a colored woman and 4 children who are halfbreed **Cherokees.**
06	4	1864	Brig. Gen. John Hunt Morgan's, CSA, Cavalry forces enter Kentucky **(for the last time)** towards Lexington.
06	4	1864	Skirmish near Vicksburg, MS.
06	4	1864	Affair at Harrisonburg, VA, with Maj. Gen. David Hunter, USA, The Lynchburg, VA, Campaign.
06	4	1864	Affair at Port Republic, VA, with Maj. Gen. David Hunter, USA.
06	4	1864	Skirmish at Panther Gap, WV, with Maj. Gen. David Hunter, USA.
06	5	1864	Skirmish at Worthington's Landing, AR.
06	5	1864	The Federals maintain their sporadic bombardment of Fort Sumter, Charleston Harbor, SC.
06	5	1864	Federal scout from Forysth through Ozark and Douglas Counties, MO. 6/5-12/1864.
06	5	1864	Federal scout from Warrensburg to the North Blackwater River, MO, and encounters with bushwackers. 6/5-9/1864.
06	5	1864	**The skirmish and engagement near Piedmont, VA,** about 7 miles southwest of Port Republic, results in a Confederate defeat for the Confederate Dept. of Southwest Virginia, under Brig. Gen. W. E. Jones, CSA, by Maj. Gen. David Hunter, USA. An important loss for the Confederates, as the Federals begin taking control of the all important Shenandoah Valley, VA, the breadbasket of the Confederacy.
06	5	1864	**Brig. Gen. William Edmondson "Grumble" Jones, CSA,** is mortally wounded at the skirmish near Piedmont, VA, instantly killed while directing his men on the front lines.
06	6	1864	Skirmish at Bealer's Ferry, Little Red River, AR, with the loss of life.
06	6	1864	Engagement at Old River Lake, or Lake Chicot, AR. (Also known as the engagement at Ditch Bayou, Fish Bayou, Grand Lake and Lake Village). This fire fight proved to be very important to the 11 Yankees who sacrificed their lives today and the other 52 who withered in pain from their battle wounds, blood seeping from their bullet holes.
06	6	1864	The Federal **occupation of Stauton, VA,** by Maj. Gen. David Hunter, USA.
06	6	1864	Skirmish near Moorefield, Hardy County, WV, with Rebel Cavalry.
06	7	1864	**Grenville Mellen Dodge, U.S.A.,** is appointed Maj. Gen.
06	7	1864	**John Gibbon, U.S.A.,** is appointed Maj. Gen.

06	7	1864	**Byron Root Pierce,** USA, is appointed Brig. Gen.
06	7	1864	Skirmish at Sunnyside Landing, AR.
06	7	1864	Skirmish at Ripley, MS, with Brig. Gen. Samuel D. Sturgis, USA.
06	7	1864	Raid on New Frankfort, Saline County, MO, by bushwackers.
06	7	1864	Affair at Sikeston, MO, with guerrillas. The notorious Wright is killed. The Yankees also take 1 prisoner; he is too drunk to kill.

| 06 | 7 | 1864 | **The Trevilian Raid** (by Maj. Gen. Philip Henry Sheridan, USA) as Lieut. Gen. Ulysses S. Grant, USA, sends Sheridan's Cavalry to join up with Maj. Gen. David Hunter's Cavalry at **Charlottesville, VA,** so as to create a diversion while Maj. Gen. George G. Meade, USA, under Grant, moves the Army of the Potomac south across the James River to attack Richmond from the south by way of Petersburg, VA. Sheridan moved west between the North Anna and the Mattaponi Rivers against the Confederate rail line with combats at the following: |

a) **Trevilian Station** (11th and 12th)
b) **Newark or Mallory's Cross-Roads** (11th and 12th)
c) **King and Queen Court-House** (18th and 20th)
d) **White House or Saint Peter's Church** (21st)
e) **Black Creek or Tunstall's Station** (21st)
f) **Jones' Bridge** (23rd)
g) **Saint Mary's Church** (24th)

6/7-24/1864.

06	8	1864	Federal scout on the Osage and in its vicinity, AR, in search of bushwackers including traveling to Papinsville, Double Branches, Miami Mission, Balltown, the Little Osage, the main Marais des Cygnes timber, Butler, Hog Skin Prairie, Gilbreth's, on Panther Creek, Germantown and Harrisonville, etc. As the new ads of our age proclaim, "join the Marines (Army) and see the world (United States). 6/8-19/1864.
06	8	1864	The Confederate **capture** of the Federal garrison at **Mount Sterling, KY,** by Brig. Gen. John Hunt Morgan, CSA, who also loots a local bank of about $18,000.
06	8	1864	Naval engagement at Simsport, LA, with the US vessels, **Chillicothe, Fort Hindman,** and **Neosho,** and the Confederate batteries there.
06	8	1864	The Republican nominating Convention held at Baltimore, MD, selects Abraham Lincoln and surprisingly the military governor of Tennessee, Andrew Johnson, as Lincoln's running mate, slighting the incumbent vice-president Hannibal Hamlin.
06	8	1864	Affair at Indian Bayou, MS, near Greenville, MS.
06	8	1864	Federal expedition from Fort Churchill to the Humboldt River, Smoke Valley, and Surprise Valley, 200 miles east of Yreka, the Nevada Territory. 6/8-8/9/1864.
06	8	1864	The Cavalry commands of Brig. Gens. George Crook and William W. Averell, USA, join up with Maj. Gen. David Hunter's, USA.
06	9	1864	Skirmishes near Big Shanty and near Stilesborough, GA, as Maj. Gen. William T. Sherman, USA, prepares to attack Gen. Joseph E. Johnston, CSA, at Pine Mountain, GA.
06	9	1864	Action at Mount Sterling, KY, sees Brig. Gen. John Hunt Morgan, CSA, driven out of and away from Mount Sterling.
06	9	1864	Affair at Pleasureville, KY, as Brig. Gen. John Hunt Morgan, CSA, retreats toward Winchester, KY.
06	9	1864	Skirmish at Point of Rocks, MD.
06	9	1864	Affair near Breckinridge, MO.
06	9	1864	Federal scout from Cassville, MO, to Cross Hollow, AR, with bushwackers trying to break the telegraph lines, including two women caught red handed. 6/9-14/1864.
06	9	1864	Skirmish at La Fayette, TN.
06	9	1864	Affair in Loudoun County, VA.
06	9	1864	Engagement at Petersburg, VA, as Gen. Pierre Gustave Toutant Beauregard, CSA, throws back Maj. Gen. Benjamin F. Butler's, USA, feeble attempt to capture Petersburg, VA.
06	10	1864	**John Smith Preston,** CSA, is appointed Brig. Gen.
06	10	1864	Skirmish at Lewisburg, AR.
06	10	1864	Skirmish at Calhoun, GA.
06	10	1864	**Operations about Marietta, Georgia,** with combats between Gen. Joseph E. Johnston, CSA, and Maj. Gen. William T. Sherman, USA, at:

a) **Brush Mountain**

			b) **Cheney's Farm**

b) **Cheney's Farm**
c) **Gilgal Church**
d) **Kenesaw Mountain**
e) **Kolb's Farm**
f) **Lost Mountain**
g) **McAfee's Cross-Roads**
h) **Nickajack Creek**
i) **Noonday Creek**
j) **Noyes' Creek**
k) **Olley's Creek**
l) **Pine Hill**
m) **Powder Springs**
n) **other points** 6/10-7/3/1864.

06	10	1864	Affair near Benson's Bridge, KY, with Brig. Gen. John Hunt Morgan, CSA.
06	10	1864	Brig. Gen. John Hunt Morgan's Confederate demonstration on Frankfort, KY. 6/10-12/1864.
06	10	1864	The **capture of Lexington,** KY by Maj. Gen. John Hunt Morgan, CSA.
06	10	1864	Maj. Gen. John G. Walker, CSA, is assigned to the command of the District of West Louisiana, and vice Lieut. Gen. Richard Taylor, CSA, is relieved of command.
06	10	1864	**Operations in the District of Central Missouri,** against guerrillas, where Brig. Gen. Egbert B. Brown, USA, commanding the District of Central Missouri reports 23 Union casualties after logging 3,810 miles by the various Yankee expeditions against guerrillas. 6/10-23/1864.
06	10	1864	Affair near Saint James, MO, with guerrillas dressed in Union uniforms. The guerrillas burn two railroad box-cars.
06	10	1864	Federal scout from Sedalia to Renick's Farm, MO, and encounters with bushwackers, including 4 young ladies at a ranch where many bushwackers fled from. The young ladies admitted feeding them and would do so again. They were probably cooking a nice big pot of pork and beans when the Yanks dropped in uninvited. 6/10-15/1864.
06	10	1864	**The Engagement at Brice's Cross-Roads (or Tishomingo Creek), near Guntown, MS,** as Maj. Gen. Nathan Bedford Forrest, CSA, routs Brig. Gen. Samuel Davis Sturgis, USA, who had over twice as many men as Forrest. Sturgis flees toward Memphis, TN. Forrest reports capturing 1,618 prisoners and scores upon scores of Federal ammunition, weapons, etc, while he reports losing 492 men. Forrest is one of the few remaining Confederate commanders who has the upper hand in his dealings with the Federals.
06	10	1864	Skirmish at Brownsburg, VA, and below as Maj. Gen. John C. Breckinridge, CSA, attempts to intercept Maj. Gen. David Hunter's, USA, combined Union cavalry force on their way toward Lexington and Lynchburg.
06	10	1864	Skirmish at Middlebrook, VA, The Lynchburg, VA, Campaign.
06	10	1864	Affair near Newport, VA.
06	10	1864	Skirmish at Old Church, VA, part of the Campaign from the Rapidan to the James River, VA.
06	10	1864	Skirmish at Waynesborough, VA, The Lynchburg, VA, Campaign.
06	10	1864	Skirmish near Kabletown, WV, 5 miles above Snicker's Ferry.
06	11	1864	**Selden Connor,** USA, is appointed Brig. Gen.
06	11	1864	The **13th US Army Corps is discontinued,** the Dept. of Missouri, AR.
06	11	1864	The **CSS Alabama** arrives at Cherbourg, France, for repairs.
06	11	1864	The **capture of Cythiana,** KY, by Brig. Gen. John Hunt Morgan, CSA.
06	11	1864	Action at Keller's Bridge, near Cynthiana, KY, with Brig. Gen. John Hunt Morgan, CSA.
06	11	1864	Federal expedition from Point Lookout, MD, aboard the steam transports, **Charleston, Georgia, Favorite,** and the **Long Branch** to Pope's Creek, VA. At St. Mary's, the Union gunboat, **Resolute,** ran into the **Long Branch,** inflicting injuries, and sending the **Long Branch** back for repairs. The expedition proceeds and ends up capturing large amounts of much needed Confederate livestock, horses, mules, etc. 6/11-21/1864.
06	11	1864	Action at Ripley, MS, as Brig. Gen. Sturgis, USA, retreats while Maj. Gen. Nathan Bedford Forrest, CSA, advances.
06	11	1864	Skirmish at Salem, MS, with Maj. Gen. Nathan Bedford Forrest, CSA.
06	11	1864	Skirmish at Ridgely, MO, where the Federals battled Rebs. One Reb lieutenant, William Felland (Oldham), son of a local planter, was shot and taken prisoner. After taking down his confession, he was taken out and executed by the Yankees.

06	11	1864	The raid on Arrington's Depot, VA, by Maj. Gen. Hunter, USA, The Lynchburg, VA, Campaign.
06	11	1864	Skirmish at Lexington, VA, including the **burning of the Virginia Military Institute (VMI)** by Maj. Gen. D. Hunter, USA, The Lynchburg, VA, Campaign.
06	11	1864	Skirmish near Midway, VA.
06	11	1864	Gen. Robert E. Lee, CSA, dispatches Lieut. Gen. Jubal Early, CSA, to the Shenandoah Valley to assist Maj. Gen. John C. Breckinridge, CSA, in dealing with Maj. Gen. David Hunter, USA, there.
06	12	1864	Action at Cynthiana, KY, where Brig. Gen. Stephen G. Burdrige, USA, expels Brig. Gen. John Hunt Morgan, CSA, from Kentucky.
06	12	1864	Skirmish at Davis' Mills, MS, with Maj. Gen. Nathan Bedford Forrest, CSA, and Brig. Gen. Samuel D. Sturgis, USA.
06	12	1864	Guerrilla raid on Calhoun, MO, where they burnt 1 church, 1 tavern, 2 homes, and robbed 2 stores. Their leader, Dr. Beck, was killed.
06	12	1864	Skirmish near Kingsville, MO, with guerrillas.
06	12	1864	Affair at Montevallo, MO, 35 miles east of Fort Scott, where bushwackers attacked the town. A railroad train just arrived from Fort Smith with about 1,000 refugees.
06	12	1864	Brig. Gen. John Hunt Morgan's, CSA, Cavalry forces retreat to Abingdon, VA, effectively ending his last raid into Kentucky. Morgan has only a short time to live before the Federals catch up with him. 6/12-20/1864.
06	12	1864	Skirmish at Cedar Creek, VA.
06	12	1864	Action at Long Bridge, VA, as Lieut. Gen. Ulysses S. Grant, USA, begins to move the Army of the Potomac across the James River towards Petersburg, VA.
06	12	1864	Skirmish at Piney River, by Amherst Court-House, VA, The Lynchburg, VA, Campaign.
06	12	1864	Maj. Gen. Philip H. Sheridan, USA, is repelled by Maj. Gen. Wade Hampton, CSA, at Trevilian Station, VA. Sheridan retreats back to join Lieut. Gen. Ulysses S. Grant, USA, near Petersburg, VA, deciding against trying to meet up with Maj. Gen. David Hunter, USA, around Lynchburg, VA.
06	12	1864	Skirmish at White House Landing, VA, as the Campaign from the Rapidan to the James River, VA, is concluded.
06	13	1864	Federal scout from Fort Leavenworth, KS, to Weston, MO, after guerrillas. Among the many events, the Yankees capture an old man and accuse him of being a guerrilla, handling him very badly. His daughter comes out of their house with a pistol to defend her father. The old man is taken and ordered to show the Yanks where any guerrillas are. He refuses and is to be hung. He asked that his body be sent back to his wife. The Yanks then hang him (only slightly) and then release him, probably giving him one hell of a scare. One must conclude it did not make him hate the Yanks any less. Lasting memories by him, his wife, and his daughter to pass down to the next generation. 6/13-16/1864.
06	13	1864	Skirmish near Collierville, TN, as Brig. Gen. Samuel D. Sturgis', USA, Federal expedition against Maj. Gen. Nathan Bedford Forrest, CSA, is concluded.
06	13	1864	Federal raid from Morristown, TN, into North Carolina, and the capture **(June 28th)** of the Confederate Camp Vance, 6 miles from Morgantown, NC, by men under Maj. Gen. John M. Schofield, USA, commanding the Dept of the Ohio. As the war is beginning to move into the last phases, the Northern forces from the Ohio, are already moving into areas far from their original designated area. 6/13-7/15/1864.
06	13	1864	Skirmish near Buchanan, VA, The Lynchburg, VA, Campaign.
06	13	1864	Federal scout from Lexington to around Lynchburg, VA, by Maj. Gen. David Hunter, USA. 6/13-15/1864.
06	13	1864	**The Richmond (Virginia) Campaign,** begins with Gen. Robert E. Lee, CSA, beginning to move his troops to front Grant's Union move on Petersburg, VA. 6/13-7/31/1864.
06	13	1864	Skirmish at Riddell's Shop, VA, the Richmond, VA, Campaign.
06	13	1864	Skirmish at White Oak Swamp, VA, the Richmond, VA, Campaign.
06	13	1864	**Lieut. Gen. Richard S. Ewell, CSA, is assigned to the command of the Dept. of Richmond, VA, while vice Maj. Gen. Robert Ransom, Jr., CSA, is ordered to the Dept. of Western Virginia.**
06	14	1864	**Lieut. Gen. Leonidas Polk, CSA,** is mortally wounded at Pine Mountain, near Marietta, GA, during the opening of the Atlanta, GA, Campaign, killed instantly by a Federal Artillery shell through his chest, while he sat upon his horse examining the Federal position with Confederate Lieut. Gens. Joseph E. Johnston and William Joseph Hardee.
06	14	1864	**Hylan Benton Lyon,** CSA, is appointed Brig. Gen.

06	14	1864	The **USS Kearsarge** lies in wait for the **CSS Alabama,** off the port of Cherbourg, France.
06	14	1864	Skirmish near Lexington, MO, where the guerrillas attack the Yankees, and fight with valor, discipline and skill, the Federals commending their sworn enemy.
06	14	1864	Raid on **Melville, MO,** where bushwackers **burn the town.**
06	14	1864	Federal scouts from Pleasant Hill, MO, in search of guerrillas. 6/14-16/1864.
06	14	1864	Skirmish at Bean's Station, TN.
06	14	1864	Skirmish in Lincoln County, TN.
06	14	1864	Skirmish near Harrison's Landing, VA, the Richmond, VA, Campaign.
06	14	1864	Affair at New Glasgow, VA, Shenandoah Valley, The Lynchburg, VA, Campaign.
06	15	1864	The capture of the steamer, **J.R. Williams,** by Col. Stand Watie, CSA, in the Arkansas River, and skirmish at San Bois Creek, the Indian Territory. 6/15-16/1864.
06	15	1864	The attack on the Union gun-boats at: a) Ratliff's (15th) b) Como (15th and **16th**) c) Magnolia Landings (**16th**) d) and skirmish (**17th**) at Newport Cross-Roads, LA. 6/15-17/1864.
06	15	1864	Skirmish near White Hare, MO, where the Federals meet up with the guerrillas who burned Melville, MO, yesterday, routing the guerrillas. A large portion of the captured goods are turned over to the citizens from Melville.
06	15	1864	Skirmish near Moscow, TN.
06	15	1864	The Union forces **evacuate** Pass Cavallo, TX.
06	15	1864	Skirmish at Malvern Hill, VA, the Richmond, VA, Campaign.
06	15	1864	**Assaults on the Confederate Petersburg, VA, lines** fail as Gen. Pierre G.T. Beauregard resists Grant's attack; Lee still deceived into believing Grant's main army lies north of the James River, the Richmond, VA, Campaign. 6/15-18/1864.
06	15	1864	Skirmish near Smith's Store, VA, the Richmond, VA, Campaign.
06	15	1864	Brig. Gen. Alfred H. Terry, USA, is temporary in command of the 10th US Army Corps, over vice Maj. Gen. Quincy A. Gillmore, USA, , the Richmond, VA, Campaign.
06	16	1864	Skirmish at West Point, AR.
06	16	1864	Federal expedition from Kansas into Missouri, by order of Maj. Gen. Samuel R. Curtis, USA, commanding the Dept. of Kansas. 6/16-20/1864.
06	16	1864	Federal expedition from Fort Leavenworth, KS, to Farley, etal, MO. 6/16-17/1864.
06	16	1864	Maj. Gen. Joseph J. Reynolds, USA, is assigned to command of the forces being assembled at Morganza, LA, to operate against Mobile, AL.
06	16	1864	Affair on Big North Creek, near Preston, MO, with guerrillas.
06	16	1864	Action on the Bermuda Hundred, VA, front, as Gen. Pierre G.T. Beauregard, CSA, pulls most of his troops back to defend the Petersburg, VA, line, the Richmond, VA, Campaign.
06	16	1864	Actions at Fort Clifton, VA, the Richmond, VA, Campaign. 6/16-17/164.
06	16	1864	Skirmish at New London, VA, with Maj. Gen. Breckinridge, CSA, The Lynchburg, VA, Campaign.
06	16	1864	Skirmish on Otter Creek, near Liberty, VA, The Lynchburg, VA, Campaign.
06	16	1864	Skirmish at Spencer, WV.
06	17	1864	Skirmish on Monticello Road, near Pine Bluff, AR.
06	17	1864	Skirmish near Columbia, MO, with guerrillas.
06	17	1864	Skirmish on the Bermuda Hundred, VA, front, as Gen. Pierre G. T. Beauregard fends off the 2nd Corps under Maj. Gen. William Hancock, USA. Gen. Lee realizes Petersburg is Grant's target and sends the Army of Northern Virginia to Petersburg, the Richmond, VA, Campaign.
06	17	1864	**The Engagement at Lynchburg, VA,** where Lieut. Gen. Jubal A. Early, CSA, joins with Maj. Gen. John C. Breckinridge, CSA, and forces Maj. Gen. David Hunter, USA, to retreat toward Parkersburg and Martinsburg, VA, temporarily clearing the Shenandoah Valley of Federals. 6/17-18/1864.
06	17	1864	Skirmish at Diamond Hill, near Lynchburg, VA.
06	18	1864	**William Lindsay Brandon,** CSA, is appointed Brig. Gen.
06	18	1864	**Joshua Lawrence Chamberlain,** USA, is appointed Brig. Gen.
06	18	1864	Skirmish at Acworth, GA.
06	18	1864	Skirmish at Allatoona, GA.

06	18	1864	Federal scout from Kansas City, MO. 6/18-20/1864.
06	18	1864	Confederates from Chariton County descend on Laclede, MO, and are pursued by the Yankees, after raiding the town. 6/18-19/1864.
06	18	1864	Skirmish at King and Queen Court-House, VA, the Richmond, VA, Campaign.
06	18	1864	Maj. Gen. David B. Birney, USA, is temporary in command of the 2nd US Army Corps, VA, as Maj. Gen. Winfield S. Hancock, USA, is wounded, the Richmond, VA, Campaign.
06	18	1864	Brig. Gen. William T. H. Brooks, USA, assumes the command of the 10th US Army Corps, the Richmond, VA, Campaign.
06	19	1864	Skirmish at Hahn's Farm, near Waldron, AR, where the Yankees attack and rout the Texas Rangers.
06	19	1864	Skirmish at Iron Bridge, the Indian Territory.
06	19	1864	The Confederate Raider vessel, the **CSS Alabama,** is destroyed and sinks off the coast of Cherbourg, France, by the **USS Kearsarge,** after the **CSS Alabama** is credited with the capture of 65 Federal vessels.
06	19	1864	Affair at Bayou Grossetete, LA, where the Yankees drive in the Rebs and capture 100 head of cattle plus horses and mules.
06	19	1864	Federal scout from Mount Vernon, MO, with encounters with the Southerners; as usual, casualties occur. 6/19-25/1864.
06	19	1864	Affair at Eagle Pass, TX, where renegades attack the Confederate positions.
06	19	1864	**The Siege of Petersburg and Richmond, VA, by Lieut. Gen. Ulysses Simpson Grant, USA, and the Army of the Potomac.** 6/19-7/31/1864.
06	19	1864	The retreat of the Union forces under Maj. Gen. David Hunter, USA, from Lynchburg, VA, to Meadow Bluff, WV, with skirmishes: a) Liberty, VA (19th) b) Buford's Gap, VA **(20th)** c) Catawba Mountain, VA **(21st)** d) Salem, VA **(21st)** e) Cove Gap, WV **(23rd)** f) New Castle, VA **(23rd)** g) Sweet Sulphur Springs WV **(23rd),** effectively ending the Lynchburg, VA, Campaign. 6/19-29/1864.
06	19	1864	Affair near Petersburg, WV, as Capt. McNeill, and his Virginia Partisans initially meet with success but are driven off.
06	20	1864	**William Francis Bartlett,** USA, is appointed Brig. Gen.
06	20	1864	Federal scouts from Lewisburg, AR, to Norristown, Dover, Glass Village, etc, as the Federals deal death to some of the guerrillas operating in this area. 6/20-23/1864.
06	20	1864	**Operations on the White River, AR.** 6/20-29/1864.
06	20	1864	Federal scout from Cassville, MO, to Cross Hollow, AR, with yet another guerrilla death. The Yankees are continuing to exert their overwhelming power, reducing the ranks of the guerrillas, bushwackers and Confederates everyday. The Yankees receiving supplies and reinforcements, it appears, from an almost unlimited resources. 6/20-24/1864.
06	20	1864	Federal expedition from Batchelder's Creek to the vicinity of Kinston, NC, and skirmish **(22nd)** at Southwest Creek, where the Federals attack the strong Confederate position on Southwest Creek, 3.5 miles from Kinston, with limited success, and casualties on both sides, but with the Union capturing a good handful of Rebels. Were these men captured or were they just getting tired of fighting a losing war? 6/20-23/1864.
06	20	1864	Federal expedition against the **Wilmington and Weldon Railroad, NC,** and if possible, to burn the large covered bridge over the Northeast Cape Fear River, by men under Maj. Gen. David B. Birney, USA. The Federals get sidetracked a bit, but do end up seizing prisoners, weapons, horses, etc, as well as destroying 2 ferry boats and a schooner loaded with salt at Swansborough. 6/20-25/1864.
06	20	1864	Skirmish at White's Station, TN.
06	20	1864	Skirmish at King and Queen Court-House, VA, with Maj. Gen. Philip H. Sheridan, USA, Cavalry, the Richmond, VA, Campaign.
06	20	1864	Skirmish at White House, VA, the Richmond, VA, Campaign.
06	21	1864	Skirmish in Decatur County, TN.
06	21	1864	Action at Howlett's Bluff, VA, the Richmond, VA, Campaign.
06	21	1864	**President Abraham Lincoln tours the Petersburg, VA, siege lines on horseback** with Lieut. Gen.

06	21	1864	**President Abraham Lincoln tours the Petersburg, VA, siege lines on horseback** with Lieut. Gen. Ulysses S. Grant, USA, as both sides continue to entrench.
06	21	1864	Skirmishes at White House or Saint Peter's Church and Black Creek, or Tunstall's Station, VA, the Richmond, VA, Campaign.
06	21	1864	**Confederate Secretary of the Treasury, Christopher G. Memminger, resigns** due to severe criticism of his handling the Confederate Treasury, Richmond, VA.
06	22	1864	**Joseph Holt,** USA, is appointed Brig. Gen.
06	22	1864	**Elliott Warren Rice,** USA, is appointed Brig. Gen.
06	22	1864	Skirmish at White River Station, on the White River, AR.
06	22	1864	Federal scout from Piney Green to Snead's Ferry and Swansborough, NC, where the Union Cavalry is ambushed on the road through an impenetrable swamp, losing a few good men, but managing to burn a Rebel schooner laden with salt. 6/22-23/1864.
06	22	1864	Engagement near the Jerusalem Plank Road, Petersburg, VA, where Lieut. Gen. Ambrose Powell Hill, CSA, repels the forces under Maj. Gens. David B. Birney, USA, and Horatio G. Wright, USA, the Richmond, VA, Campaign.
06	22	1864	Federal expedition, with Brig. Gen. James H. Wilson, USA, Cavalry against the **South Side and Danville Railroad, VA,** with skirmishes at the following: a) Reams' Station (22nd) b) near Nottoway Court-House **(23rd)** c) at Stauton River Bridge, or Roanoke Station **(25th)** d) Sappony Church, or Stony Creek **(28th-29th)** e) Reams' Station **(29th),** the Richmond, VA, Campaign. 6/22-7/2/1864.
06	22	1864	Brig. Gen. John Hunt Morgan, CSA, assumes the command of the Dept. of Western VA, and East Tennessee.
06	23	1864	**Stephen Dill Lee,** **C.S.A., is appointed Lieut. Gen.**
06	23	1864	**Alexander Peter Stewart,** **C.S.A., is appointed Lieut. Gen.**
06	23	1864	Skirmish at Okolona, MS.
06	23	1864	Skirmish at Collierville, TN.
06	23	1864	Confederate attack on the train near La Fayette, TN.
06	23	1864	Skirmishes near Falls Church and Centreville, VA, with Lieut. Col. John S. Mosby, CSA. 6/23-24/1864.
06	23	1864	Skirmish at Jones' Bridge, VA, the Richmond, VA, Campaign.
06	23	1864	**Confederate operations in the Shenandoah Valley, VA, Maryland, and Pennsylvania.** 6/23-8/3/1864.
06	23	1864	Lieut. Gen. Jubal Early's, CSA, Confederate command advances from Lynchburg to Winchester, VA. 6/23-7/2/1864.
06	23	1864	President Lincoln returns to Washington, from Petersburg, VA.
06	24	1864	**Operations in the District of Northern Alabama.** 6/24-8/20/1864
06	24	1864	Skirmish at Curtis' Well, Northern AL.
06	24	1864	Affair near Fayetteville, AR, as Buck Brown, with over 200 men, steal the entire Yankee mule herd of 240, reportedly fleeing 40 miles with the mules to Maysville.
06	24	1864	The capture of the US steamer, **Queen City,** on the White River, AR, by Maj. Gen. Joseph O. Shelby, CSA.
06	24	1864	The engagement between the US steamers, **Fawn** and the **Naumkeag,** and Maj. Gen. Joseph O. Shelby and Brig. Gen. Robert C. Tyler, CSA, Confederate forces, AR. 6/24-25/1864.
06	24	1864	Action at La Fayette, GA.
06	24	1864	Indian attack on the wagon train on the John Day's Road, near Fort Klamath, Oregon. The Yankees blame the attack on the **Klamath, Lake, Modoc,** and **Goose Lake Indian tribes.** All Indians in the neighborhood are ordered to report to the Fort at once, and all absentees will be required to give an account of their whereabouts.
06	24	1864	Action at Hare's Hill, VA, the Richmond, VA, Campaign.
06	24	1864	Engagement at Saint Mary's Church, VA, where Maj. Gen. Philip H. Sheridan, USA, is driven off toward the James River with his wagon train of captured supplies, the Richmond, VA, Campaign.
06	25	1864	**Edward Stuyvesant Bragg,** USA, is appointed Brig. Gen.
06	25	1864	Confederate operations on the Yellow River, FL, where the Rebels capture two schooners, one being the **Osceola.**
06	25	1864	Skirmish at Allatoona, GA.
06	25	1864	Skirmish at Spring Place, GA.

06	25	1864	Affair at Point Pleasant, LA.
06	25	1864	Skirmish at Ashwood, MS.
06	25	1864	Skirmish at Rancho Las Rinas, TX, as the Texas Rangers attack and rout the Yankees, killing about 20 good men.
06	25	1864	**Federal sappers begin digging a tunnel** under the Confederate entrenched lines at Petersburg, VA.

06	26	1864	Skirmish near Claredon (26th) and the pursuit of the Rebels to Bayou De View, on the White River, AR. 6/26-28/1864.
06	26	1864	Affair 1.5 miles east of Sedalia, on the Sedalia and Marshall Road, MO, with bushwackers.
06	26	1864	Lieut. Gen. Jubal Early, CSA, **occupies Stauton, VA.**
06	26	1864	Skirmish at Smithfield, WV, with Capt. McNeill and his Virginia Partisans Rangers.
06	26	1864	Skirmishes at Wire Bridge and Springfield, WV, with Virginia Partisan Rangers.

06	27	1864	Skirmish in Big Cove Valley, , 6 miles northeast of Huntsville, AL, as the Federals chase the Rebels into the hills near Blevingston Gap.
06	27	1864	Federal scout from Brownsville, AR, to the vicinity of St. Charles, were bushwackers and Confederates are reported to be in large numbers. 6/27-29/1864.
06	27	1864	**The Battle of Kennesaw Mountain, GA,** where Gen. Joseph E. Johnston's, CSA, well entrenched army repels and slaughters the attacking columns of Maj. Gen. William T. Sherman, USA.
06	27	1864	**Brig. Gen. Charles Garrison Harker, USA,** is mortally wounded while leading his men in a charge atop his horse against the Confederate position at the Battle of Kennesaw Mountain, Marietta, GA, receiving his death wound from a Confederate sharpshooter.
06	27	1864	**Brig. Gen. Daniel McCook, Jr., USA,** is mortally wounded at the Battle of Kennesaw Mountain, Marietta, GA, while leading his men in a charge against the Confederate earthworks, dying three weeks later in **Steubenville, OH.**
06	27	1864	Affair at Crittenden, KY, as the town is attacked by Confederates assembling to capture a wagon train. The Federals rush foward men to protect the train.
06	27	1864	Affairs near Dunksburg, MO, against guerrillas. Upon entering the ranch house on the range of Mr. & Mrs. Spencer, who with 4 grown daughters were having breakfast, the Yankees were refused any food, as the Spencers needed what they had to feed their dogs. The Federals were reminded that the Confederates could enjoy dinner here anytime. 6/27-28/1864.
06	27	1864	Maj. Gen. Winfield S. Hancock, USA, resumes the command of the 2nd US Army Corps, the Army of the Potomac, the Richmond, VA, Campaign.

06	28	1864	**Bradley Tyler Johnson,** CSA, is appointed Brig. Gen.
06	28	1864	Skirmish at Tunnel Hill, GA.
06	28	1864	Action at Howlett's Bluff, VA, the Richmond, VA, Campaign.

06	29	1864	**Brig. Gen. Joseph Pannell Taylor, USA,** dies at Washington, DC, from natural causes.
06	29	1864	**Amos Beebe Eaton,** USA, is appointed Brig. Gen.
06	29	1864	Affair at Pond Springs, Northern AL.
06	29	1864	Skirmish at Meffleton Lodge, AR.
06	29	1864	Skirmish at Davis' Bend, LA.
06	29	1864	Skirmish at La Fayette, TN.
06	29	1864	Skirmishes at Charlestown and Duffield's Station, WV, as the Lieut. Col. John S. Mosby, CSA, captures 25, destroys a storehouse and telegraph wires, escaping across the Shenandoah Valley into Loundoun County by Berry's Ferry.

06	30	1864	Skirmish at Acworth, GA.
06	30	1864	Skirmish at Allatoona, GA.
06	30	1864	Skirmish at La Fayette, GA.
06	30	1864	Actions on Four-Mile Creek, at Deep Bottom, VA, the Richmond, VA, Campaign. 6/30-7/1/1864.
06	30	1864	Lieut. Gen. Jubal A. Early, CSA, **occupies New Market, VA,** on his way to invade the North.
06	30	1864	President Abraham Lincoln accepts **Salmon P. Chase, the US Secretary of the Treasury's, resignation.**

07	1	1864	**George Henry Chapman,** USA, is appointed Brig. Gen.
07	1	1864	**John Thomas Croxton,** USA, is appointed Brig. Gen.
07	1	1864	Operations in Arkansas. 7/1-31/1864.
07	1	1864	The **CSS Florida** captures the **Harriet Stevens** off Bermuda.

07	1	1864	The **CSS Florida** captures the **Harriet Stevens** off Bermuda.
07	1	1864	Brig. Gen. George Wright, USA, is assigned to the command of the District of California.
07	1	1864	Skirmish at Allatoona, GA.
07	1	1864	Skirmish at Howell's Ferry, GA.
07	1	1864	Skirmish at Lost Mountain, GA.
07	1	1864	**Operations on the West Coast of Florida,** where Federal troops, including the **2nd US Colored Infantry** perpetuate destruction to Rebel property, destroying railroad track, cotton, mills, livestock, store-houses, etc. 7/1-31/1864.
07	1	1864	**Federal operations against the Sioux Indians in the District of Minnesota,** including such events as 90 **Sioux** surrendering to the Federal authorities; other hostile Indians continuing to kill settlers, emigrants, including 3 citizen teamsters on 8/24/1864 on the Red River of the North; the **Sisseton Sioux** wishing to make peace with the white man; the defeat of the **Teton bands** of **Sioux Indians** with heavy losses, as well as the transfer of as many Indians as possible to various Indian reservations, etc, while continuing to subdue the remaining hostile independent Indian tribes, as the Yankees tirelessly continue to work toward changing the remaining Indians' way of life forever. 7/1-10/1/1864.
07	1	1864	Skirmish near Fayette, MO.
07	1	1864	**Maj. Gen. Irvin McDowell, USA, assumes the command of the Dept. of the Pacific.**
07	1	1864	President Lincoln appoints **William Pitt Fessenden** to replace Salmon P. Chase as the **new Secretary of the Treasury.**
07	2	1864	**Martin Davis Hardin,** USA, is appointed Brig. Gen.
07	2	1864	Gen. Joseph E. Johnston, CSA, withdraws from Kennesaw Mountain to below Marietta, GA, so as to not be flanked by Maj. Gen. William T. Sherman, USA.
07	2	1864	Skirmish on the Byhalia, MS, Road, 10 miles south of Collierville, TN, as the Confederates achieve an early victory, but the Federals regroup and drive the Rebels off.
07	2	1864	Federal expedition from Vicksburg to Pearl River, with skirmishes en route, and engagement **(July 7th)** near Jackson, MS, as Maj. Gen. Henry W. Slocum, USA, successfully moves to destroy the bridge over the Pearl River, but losing 220 men in the process. 7/2-10/1864.
07	2	1864	Skirmish at Fort Johnson, on James Island, Charleston Harbor, SC, where the Union troops establish a successful beachhead.
07	2	1864	Skirmish near Secessionville, Charleston Harbor, SC, and vicinity.
07	2	1864	Skirmish at Bolivar Heights, WV, as Lieut. Gen. Jubal Early, CSA, reaches Winchester, VA, and marches on Harper's Ferry, WV.
07	3	1864	Federal operations in the vicinity of Baton Rouge, LA, with skirmish near Benton's Ferry, 7 miles from the Amite River **(July 25th),** with the defeat of the Rebels at their own camp. 7/3-25/1864.
07	3	1864	Skirmish in Platte County, MO, as the Federals attack, kill and wound a band of guerrillas, bushwackers, and outright villains, in the general vicinity of St. Joseph, MO.
07	3	1864	Union assaults on Fort Johnson and Battery Simkins, Charleston Harbor, SC, are repulsed.
07	3	1864	Skirmish on John's Island, SC, where Union the assault is repulsed.
07	3	1864	Skirmish at King's Creek, Charleston Harbor, SC, and vicinity.
07	3	1864	Skirmish near White Point, SC.
07	3	1864	Skirmish near La Grange, TN.
07	3	1864	Skirmish at Buckton, VA, as Lieut. Gen. Jubal Early, CSA, drives Maj. Gen. Franz Sigel, USA, across the Potomac into Maryland.
07	3	1864	Skirmish at North River Mills, WV, with Lieut. Gen. Jubal A. Early, CSA.
07	3	1864	Skirmish at North Mountain, WV, with Lieut. Gen. Jubal A. Early, CSA.
07	3	1864	Skirmish at Martinsburg, WV, with Lieut. Gen. Jubal A. Early, CSA.
07	3	1864	Skirmish at Darkesville, WV, with Lieut. Gen. Jubal A. Early, CSA.
07	3	1864	Skirmish at Leetown, WV, with Lieut. Gen. Jubal A. Early, CSA.
07	3	1864	Brig. Gen. George Crook, USA, assumes the command of all US forces in the Dept. of West Virginia west of the Alleghanies and south of the **Baltimore and Ohio Railroad.**
07	4	1864	**Charles Jackson Paine,** USA, is appointed Brig. Gen.
07	4	1864	Skirmish in Searcy County, AR, as the Federals attack and rout Brig. Gen. Joseph O. Shelby, CSA.
07	4	1864	Skirmishes at Ruff's Mill, Neal Dow Station, and Rottenwood Creek, GA.
07	4	1864	Skirmish at Cross Bayou, LA.
07	4	1864	Skirmish in Clay County, MO.

| 07 | 4 | 1864 | The attack on Battery Pringle, James Island, SC. 7/4-9/1864. |

07 4 1864 Federal expedition from Memphis, TN, to Grand Gulf, MS, aboard the steamers, **Rose Hamilton, Madison, J. D. Perry, J. C. Snow, Silver Wave, Sunny South, Tycoon,** and the **Shenandoah,** including skirmishes at the following:
a) near Bolivar   **(July 6th)**
b) at Utica   **(July 13th)**
c) at Port Gibson   **(July 14th)**
d) at Grand Gulf   **(July 16th),** the Federals adding more pressure to the strained resources of the Southern armies in this district, as well as in most other military regions. 7/4-24/1864.

07 4 1864 Skirmish at Frankford, WV.

07 4 1864 The operations about Harper's Ferry, WV. 7/4-7/1864.

07 4 1864 Skirmish at Patterson's Creek Bridge, WV, as Lieut. Gen. Jubal Early, CSA, prepares to cross into Maryland.

07 4 1864 Skirmish at South Branch Bridge, WV.

07 5 1864 Operations on the line of the Chattahoochee River, with skirmishes at Howell's, Turner's, and Pace's Ferries, Isham's Ford, and other points, GA, as Maj. Gen. William T. Sherman, USA, presses Gen. Joseph E. Johnston's CSA line. 7/5-17/1864.

07 5 1864 Federal expedition from Morganza to Simsport, LA, on the Atchafalaya, to ascertain the Confederate position under Brig. Gen. Gabriel C. Wharton, CSA. 7/5-7/1864.

07 5 1864 Affair at Keedysville, MD, as Lieut. Gen. Jubal Early, CSA, crosses the Potomac into Maryland.

07 5 1864 Affair at Noland's Ferry, MD.

07 5 1864 Skirmish at Point of Rocks, MD.

07 5 1864 Affair at Solomon's Gap, MD.

07 5 1864 Federal scouts from Big Piney, MO, including the killing of a guerrilla who attempted to flee from his Federal captors, shot in the back as he ran away. 7/5-6/1864.

07 5 1864 Federal expedition from New Madrid to Caruthersville, MO, with skirmishes with bushwackers. 7/5-10/1864.

07 5 1864 The call is made upon New York and Pennsylvania for 24,000 militia, to help defend Washington, DC, from the advance of Lieut. Gen. Jubal A. Early, CSA.

07 5 1864 **Maj. Gen. Andrew J. Smith's, USA, Federal expedition from La Grange, TN, to Tupelo, MS.** 7/5-21/1864.

07 5 1864 Maj. Gen. Andrew J. Smith's, USA, command moves from La Grange, TN, in search of Maj. Gen. Nathan Bedford Forrest, CSA.

07 6 1864 **Brig. Gen. Samuel Allen Rice, USA,** dies at his home at Oskaloosa, IA, from a shattered ankle received at the engagement at Jenkins' Ferry, AR, on April 30, 1864.

07 6 1864 **Edward Cary Walthall, C.S.A.,** is appointed Maj. Gen.

07 6 1864 Federal scout from Fort Goodwin, in Southeastern Arizona, against hostile Indians. 7/6-24/1864.

07 6 1864 Skirmish near Benton, AR, as the Federals return from a scout to Norristown, capturing some Confederate deserters.

07 6 1864 Affair at the Antietam, MD.

07 6 1864 The Confederate **capture of Hagerstown, MD,** by Lieut. Gen. Jubal A. Early, CSA, as Cavalry Brig. Gen. John McClausland, CSA, levies $20,000 on the residents of Hagerstown in retribution for the destruction dealt the Shenandoah Valley by Maj. Gen. David Hunter, USA.

07 6 1864 Federal operations in **Western Missouri,** under Maj. Gen. Samuel R. Curtis, USA, commanding the Dept. of Kansas. 7/6-30/1864.

07 6 1864 Skirmish near the Little Blue, Jackson County, Western MO.

07 6 1864 Action at Mount Zion Church, near Aldie, VA, with Lieut. Col. John S. Mosby, CSA.

07 6 1864 Skirmish at Big Cacapon Bridge, WV.

07 6 1864 Skirmish at Sir John's Run, WV.

07 7 1864 **Henry Delmar Clayton,   C.S.A.,** is appointed Maj. Gen.

07 7 1864 **John Carpenter Carter,   CSA,** is appointed Brig. Gen.

07 7 1864 **James Thadeus Holtzclaw,   CSA,** is appointed Brig. Gen.

07 7 1864 Skirmish at Van Buren, AR, with Maj. Gen. Frederick Steele, USA, commanding the Dept. of Arkansas.

07 7 1864 Affair at Brownsville, MD.

07 7 1864 Skirmish at Frederick, MD.

07	7	1864	Skirmish at Middletown, MD.
07	7	1864	Affair at Solomon's Gap, MD.
07	7	1864	The 3rd Division, 6th US Army Corps, Army of the Potomac, arrives at Baltimore, MD, from its position in front of Petersburg, VA, to aid Washington DC from Lieut. Gen Jubal Early, CSA. 7/7-8/1864.
07	7	1864	Skirmish near Ripley, MS, with Brig. Gen. Andrew J. Smith, USA, and his Federal expedition to Tupelo, MS.
07	7	1864	Guerrilla attack on Parkville, Western MO.
07	7	1864	Skirmish on John's Island, SC, as the Yankees fail to maintain the beachhead they are attempting to establish.
07	7	1864	Federal scouts (7th-**9th** and **12th-18th**) from Kingston to England Cove, TN, including actions against guerrillas under **Champ Ferguson's Command.** 7/7-18/1864.
07	8	1864	Skirmish 3 miles from Vienna, AL, as the Federals are ambushed by guerrillas or (more aptly called) bushwackers.
07	8	1864	Skirmish near Huntersville, AR.
07	8	1864	Skirmish at Antietam Bridge, MD, with Lieut. Gen. Jubal A. Early, CSA.
07	8	1864	Skirmish at Frederick, MD.
07	8	1864	Skirmish at Sandy Hook, MD.
07	8	1864	Federal scout from Patterson to Buffalo Creek, in Ripley County, MO, where the Yankees come across 3 jayhawkers at different locations and kill them. The Yankees are serious in putting down the guerrilla warfare in the area. 7/8-12/1864.
07	8	1864	Skirmish near Richmond, MO, with guerrillas belonging to Maj. Gen. Sterling Price's Confederate Army.
07	8	1864	Skirmish near Kelly's Mill, MS, as Maj. Gen. Andrew J. Smith, USA, moves on Tupelo, MS.
07	8	1864	Brig. Gen. Albrion P. Howe, USA, supersedes Maj. Gen. Franz Sigel, USA, in the command at Harper's Ferry, WV.
07	9	1864	Maj. Gen. William T. Sherman, USA, pushes Gen. Joseph E. Johnston, CSA, and the Army of Tennessee back to the defenses of Atlanta, GA.
07	9	1864	The Confederate forces under Lieut. Gen. Jubal Early, CSA, levy the city of Frederick, MD for $200,000 in retribution for the suffering extracted on the Shenandoah Valley by Maj. Gen. David Hunter, USA.
07	9	1864	The **CSS Florida** continues to harass Union shipping, this time off the coast of Eastern shore of Maryland.
07	9	1864	**The Battle of Monocacy, MD,** where Lieut. Gen. Jubal A. Early, CSA, routs the Federals under Maj. Gen. Lewis Wallace, USA, and heads toward Washington, DC.
07	9	1864	Skirmish at Urbana, MD.
07	9	1864	Federal operations against guerrillas in the vicinity of Wellington, MO, with skirmishes at Warder's Church **(10th)**, and at Columbus, Johnson County, with the notorious guerrilla **Wilhite** ending up with 28 balls through him or in him, another of his companions receiving 18 rifle balls. **(12th)**. 7/9-13/1864.
07	9	1864	Action at Burden's Causeway, John's Island, SC.
07	9	1864	2 additional divisions of the 6th Army Corps, Army of the Potomac, embark at City Point, VA, the Petersburg, VA, lines for the defense of Washington, DC, against Jubal Early, CSA. Maj. Gen. George Meade, USA, orders additional pressure to be exerted on Gen. Robert E. Lee's Petersburg, VA, lines.
07	10	1864	Maj. Gen. Lovell H. Rousseau's, USA, raid from Decatur, AL, to the **West Point and Montgomery Railroad,** with skirmishes:
			a) near Coosa River, at Stone's Ferry, AL. **(13th)**
			b) near Greenpoint and at Ten Island Ford, AL. **(14th)**
			c) near Auburn, GA. **(18th)**
			d) near Checaw (Station), GA **(18th)** 7/10-22/1864.
07	10	1864	Skirmish 20 miles north of Little Rock, AR, with the scouting Federals capturing some Confederates and inflicting casualties.
07	10	1864	Skirmish near Petit Jean, AR.
07	10	1864	Skirmish at Clinton, KY, with mounted Rebels under **Outlaw and Kesterson.**
07	10	1864	Affair with guerrillas at Platte City, Western MO.
07	10	1864	The burning of the Gunpowder Bridge, MD.
07	10	1864	Skirmish near Monocacy, MD.
07	10	1864	Skirmish at Rockville, MD.
07	10	1864	Skirmishes at Cherry Creek and Plentytude, MS, with Maj. Gen. Andrew J. Smith, USA.

MONTH	DAY	YEAR	ACT
07	10	1864	Skirmish in Issaquena County, MS.
07	10	1864	Federal expedition from Vicksburg to Grand Gulf, MS, with skirmishes at Port Gibson **(14th)** and at Grand Gulf **(16th),** as the Confederate attacks on them are repulsed; the Federals returning to Vicksburg aboard the steamer, **Madison.** 7/10-17/1864.
07	10	1864	Affair at Platte City, MO.
07	10	1864	The unsuccessful Federal attack on Fort Johnson and Battery Simkins, Charleston Harbor, SC.
07	11	1864	Federal scout from Gunter's Landing to Warrenton, AL, and skirmish with die hard Confederates refusing to yield, but are driven back, while others are no quite so patriotic, as the Yankees capture men who are deserters.
07	11	1864	The US Naval destruction of Confederate saltworks near Tampa, FL.
07	11	1864	The Confederate capture of railroad trains at Magnolia, MD.
07	11	1864	Skirmish at Frederick, MD.
07	11	1864	The District of Columbia militia is called into service of the United States.
07	11	1864	Skirmishes at and near Pontotoc, MS, with Maj. Gen. Andrew J. Smith, USA, and Confederates under Lieut. Gen. Stephen D. Lee, CSA, commanding the Dept. of Alabama, Mississippi and East Louisiana. 7/11-12/1864.
07	11	1864	Maj. Gen. Edward O. C. Ord, USA, is assigned to the command of the 8th US Army Corps and of the troops in the Middle Dept., VA.
07	11	1864	**The Skirmish near Fort Stevens, Washington, DC,** between Lieut. Gen. Jubal A. Early, CSA, and the hastily assembled Union troops, where after skirmishing, Early decides to terminate any attempt to carry Washington, D.C. President Abraham Lincoln observes the fighting from the trenches.
07	11	1864	The 1st and 2nd Divisions, 6th US Army Corps, and an advanced detachment of the 19th US Army Corps, arrive at Washington, DC. 7/11-12/1864.
07	11	1864	Maj. Gen. Quincy A. Gillmore, USA, is assigned to the command of the detachment of the 19th US Army Corps in the Dept. of Washington, DC.
07	12	1864	Federal scout in Lincoln County, TN, where 9 miles southwest of Tullahoma, on Hurricane Creek, the Federals put 2 brothers up to watch the house of Mr. Blade, and kill Mr. McNight, which they do when he shows up. The Yankees move out on the Huntsville road, where they kill Garland Miller. These encounters are not isolated, as the Federals work to eliminate guerrillas operating independently, although there are many cases when the innocent are blamed for crimes they never committed. 7/12-15/1864.
07	12	1864	The Governor of New Jersey calls out volunteers for the defense of Washington, D.C.
07	12	1864	Skirmish at Turkey Creek, Lee's Mills, near Ream's Station, VA, the Richmond, VA, Campaign.
07	12	1864	Skirmish at Warwick Swamp, VA, the Richmond, VA, Campaign.
07	12	1864	Action near Fort Stevens and skirmishes along the northern defenses of Washington, DC, before Lieut. Gen. Jubal A. Early, CSA, retreats.
07	13	1864	Skirmish near Brownsville, AR, where the attacking Confederates almost overwhelm the Yankees there.
07	13	1864	Federal expedition from Helena, AR, to Buck Island, in the Mississippi River, as Brig. Gen. Napoleon B. Buford, USA, commanding the District of Eastern Arkansas, pursues Brig. Gen. Joseph O. Shelby, CSA. 7/13-16/1864.
07	13	1864	Federal reconnaissance from Pine Bluff, AR, down the river in search of Confederates, who they don't meet. A wary but peaceful, hot and sunny day with no loss of life.
07	13	1864	Skirmish at Bell Mines, KY.
07	13	1864	Federal scout from Munfordville to Big Spring, KY, against guerrillas. 7/13-15/1864.
07	13	1864	Affair at Rockville, MD.
07	13	1864	Action near Camargo Cross-Roads, near Tupelo, MS, as Maj. Gen. Nathan Bedford Forrest, CSA, contests the advance of Maj. Gen. Andrew J. Smith, USA.
07	13	1864	Action with guerrillas at Camden Point, Western MO.
07	13	1864	Affair with guerrillas at Versailles, Western MO.
07	13	1864	Maj. Gen. Horatio G. Wright, USA, is assigned to the command of all the forces moving against the Confederate forces in retreat from Washington, DC.
07	13	1864	Brig. Gen. William H. Emory, USA, is assigned to the command of the detachment of the 19th US Army Corps, Washington, DC.
07	14	1864	Action at Bayou des Arc, or Farr's Mills, AR, with Rebels after the Federals return from scouting in Saline, Hot Springs and Montgomery Counties.

			Saline, Hot Springs and Montgomery Counties.
07	14	1864	Operations in Webster and Union Counties, KY, including skirmishes (14th) at Morganfield and **(15th)** at Geiger's Lake, with guerrillas. 7/14-18/1864.
07	14	1864	Affair at Poolesville, MD, as Lieut. Gen. Jubal A. Early's, CSA, Confederate troops cross the Potomac River at White's Ford, Leesburg, VA.
07	14	1864	Skirmish near Bloomfield, MO, with bushwackers.
07	14	1864	Skirmish with guerrillas near Fredericksburg, Western MO.
07	14	1864	**The Engagement at Harrisburg, near Tupelo, MS,** where Maj. Gen. Nathan Bedford Forrest, CSA, is defeated (only twice in his career) by Maj. Gen. Andrew Jackson Smith, USA. Total casualties approximate 2,200, and prevents Forrest from attacking Maj. Gen. William T. Sherman's supply lines. As Maj. Gen. Nathan Bedford Forrest goes on to write, **"The Battle of Harrisburg will furnish the historian a bloody record, but it will also stamp with immortality the gallant dead and the living heroes it has made...etal. Future generations will never weary in hanging garlands upon their graves.** How right he was. 7/14-15/1864.
07	14	1864	Action at Malvern Hill, VA, the Richmond, VA, Campaign.
07	14	1864	Maj. Gen. Lewis Wallace, USA, resumes the command of the 8th US Army Corps, VA.
07	15	1864	Federal expedition from Jacksonville and skirmish (15th) at Trout Creek, FL, with the destruction of Rebel property including the huge rotary circular saw machinery valued at $50,000. 7/15-20/1864.
07	15	1864	Action at Old Town Creek, MS, with Nathan Bedford Forrest, CSA, and Maj. Gen. Andrew J. Smith, USA.
07	15	1864	Guerrilla attack on Huntsville, Western MO.
07	15	1864	Affair at Lindley, Grundy County, MO, as a band of guerrillas ride into town and rob the citizens of money, horses, and guns.
07	15	1864	Affair at Accotink, VA.
07	15	1864	Skirmishes near Hillsborough, VA. 7/15-16/1864.
07	16	1864	**Brig. Gen. John Randolph Chambliss, CSA,** is mortally wounded on the Charles City Road, outside Richmond, VA, during an encounter with the Federal Cavalry under Brig. Gen. David M. McMutrie Gregg, USA.
07	16	1864	**Brig. Gen. Victor Jean Baptiste Girardey, CSA,** is mortally wounded near Fussell's Mill, on the Darbytown Road, VA, while resisting a Federal attack on the east end of Richmond, VA.
07	16	1864	**Daniel McCook, Jr,** USA, is appointed Brig. Gen., one day before he dies from battle wounds.
07	16	1864	Cavalry skirmish at Ellistown, MS, with Maj. Gen. Forrest, CSA, and Maj. Gen. Andrew J. Smith, USA.
07	16	1864	Skirmish on the Clear Fork, near Warrensburg, Western MO.
07	16	1864	Skirmish on the Fayette road, near Huntsville, Western MO.
07	16	1864	Skirmish on James Island, Charleston Harbor, SC, and vicinity.
07	16	1864	Action at Four-Mile Creek, VA, the Richmond, VA, Campaign.
07	16	1864	Action at Malvern Hill, VA, the Richmond, VA, Campaign.
07	16	1864	The capture of the Confederate wagon train near Purcellville, VA, as Lieut. Gen. Jubal Early, CSA, heads back to the Shenandoah Valley, VA.
07	16	1864	Skirmish at Wood Grove, VA.
07	17	1864	**Brig. Gen. Daniel McCook, Jr., USA, dies at Steubenville, OH,** from his battlewounds received at the Battle of Kennesaw Mountain, GA, on June 27, 1864.
07	17	1864	Federal scout from Lewisburg, AR, to Norristown, Dover, etc, with the killing of 3 bushwackers below Norristown on the Arkansas River.
07	17	1864	Federal scout on the South Platte River, the Colorado Territory, against Indians who on many occasions, are stealing horses, etc. from settlers and ranchers. 7/17-28/1864.
07	17	1864	Federal scout from Columbus aboard the steamer, **Convoy,** to Hickman, KY, who search houses for guerrillas. As each day passes, it is becoming riskier to be a southern bushwacker or guerrilla. 7/17-18/1864.
07	17	1864	Federal expedition from Baton Rouge to Davidson's Ford, near Clinton, LA, against Rebel property and men. 7/17-18/1864.
07	17	1864	Action with guerrillas near Fredericksburg, Ray County, in Western MO.
07	17	1864	Skirmish at Herring Creek, near Harrison's Landing, VA, the Richmond, VA, Campaign, which is near the vicinity that Maj. Gen. George McClellan, USA, retreated to after his defeat at the gates of Richmond, VA, during his Peninsula Campaign in 1862.

Gen. Jubal Early's, CSA, path into the Shenandoah Valley. 7/17-18/1864.

| 07 | 18 | 1864 | **John Bell Hood, C.S.A., is appointed Full General, the last to be promoted in the Confederacy.** |

07 18 1864 Federal expedition against **Apache Indians** to the Pinal Mountains, the Arizona Territory, including the surrender of Indians, who come into the Federal camp to give up. A squaw is shot and killed as she tries to run away refusing to be tied up. The 5th CA Infantry is ordered over the mountains west of Pinal Creek to kill all buck Indians big enough to carry arms and capture all squaws and children they come across. The Yankees kill an Indian who ends up being a squaw. **(August lst).** The Yankees hang 2 buck hostages at sundown **(August 3rd).** The Federals report that on **August 6th,** they fired upon 15 Indians who approached the Yankees, killing 5 instantly. 7/18-8/7/1864.

07 18 1864 Skirmish at Buck Head, GA.

07 18 1864 **Gen. John Bell Hood, CSA, supersedes Gen. Joseph E. Johnston, CSA, in command of the Confederate Army of the Tennessee.** President Jefferson Davis, never getting along with Johnston and disappointed in his handling of the Army of the Tennessee in the face of Maj. Gen. William T. Sherman, USA, replaces Johnston with Hood, a known fighter, but questionable leader.

07 18 1864 Federal scout against guerrillas who were herding their stolen horses on Rock Creek, 65 miles from Salem, at Hay Hollow in the southeast corner of Shannon County, MO. 7/18-21/1864.

07 18 1864 Federal operations in Southeast Missouri and Northeastern Arkansas, with skirmishes with guerrillas at:
a) Scatterville, AR   **(July 28th),** at
b) Osceola, AR   **(Aug. 2nd)** and at
c) Elk Chute, MO   **(Aug. 4th)** 7/18-8/6/1864.

07 18 1864 Federal operations in Southwest Missouri, Brig. Gen. John B. Sanborn, USA, commanding the District of Southwest Missouri, with skirmishes against guerrillas at:
a) near Maysville, AR **(20th),** and
b) near Carthage, MO **(21st).**

07 18 1864 Federal scout from Falls Church, VA, is ambushed by the Rebels, losing men and horses. 7/18-21/1864.

07 18 1864 Brig. Gen. Alfred H. Terry, USA, is temporary in command of the 10th US Army Corps, VA, , the Richmond, VA, Campaign.

07 18 1864 Affair at Kabletown, WV.

07 18 1864 President Abraham Lincoln calls for 500,000 volunteers.

07 19 1864 Skirmish on the Benton road, near Little Rock, AR, with guerrillas, who ambush and inflict casualties on the Yankees.

07 19 1864 Operations on the White River, AR, and the Confederate attack **(July 24th)** on, and the burning of, the Federal steamer, **Clara Bell.** 7/19-25/1864.

07 19 1864 Skirmishes on Peach Tree Creek, GA, as Gen. John Bell Hood, CSA, plans to attack Maj. Gen. William T. Sherman's, Union army currently stationed as follows:
a) **Army of the Cumberland** - Maj. Gen. George H. Thomas, USA, stationed along Peachtree Creek, north of Atlanta.
b) **Army of the Ohio**   - Maj. Gen. John M. Schofield, USA, positioned east of Atlanta.
c) **Army of the Tennessee**   - Maj. Gen. James B. McPherson, USA, located near Decatur, GA.

07 19 1864 Federal scout to Taos, Western MO, against guerrillas.

07 19 1864 The guerrilla attack on Webster, Washington County, MO, 15 miles southwest of Potosi, where they rob the town of goods, kill 1 man, and take 2 others, including horses, etc. This type of lawless will prevail after the Civil War and become known as part of the Wild Wild West.

07 19 1864 Skirmish at Ashby's Gap, VA, as Lieut. Gen. Jubal Early, USA, moves his command toward Winchester.

07 19 1864 The Engagement at Berry's Ford, VA.

07 19 1864 Brig. Gen. John H. Martindale, USA, is in temporary command of the 18th US Army Corps, vice Maj. Gen. William F. Smith, USA, is relieved of command, VA, , the Richmond, VA, Campaign.

07 19 1864 Skirmish at Bunker Hill, WV.

07 19 1864 Skirmish at Charlestown, WV.

07 19 1864 Skirmish at Darkesville, WV.

07 19 1864 Skirmish at Kabletown, WV.

07 20 1864 Federal expedition from Fort Boise to Boonville, the Idaho Territory, against Indians. Upon returning to Boonville, the Federal troops learn that local citizens took the law into their own hands, attacking a large party of (mostly women and .children) Indians, scalping 35, of which only about 5 were men. Infants were thrown against rocks and killed. Not every engagement of the Civil War was fought by gentlemen, or of a civilized nature. 7/20-8/17/1864.

07	20	1864	**The Battle of Peach Tree Creek, GA,** as Gen. John Bell Hood, CSA, fails disastrously in his attack, under Lieut. Gen. William Hardee, CSA, on the Union lines under Maj. Gen. George H. Thomas, losing almost 3 men to every 1 Union loss; a loss Hood could not afford. Total casualties approximate 6,600.
07	20	1864	**Brig. Gen. Clement Hoffman Stevens, CSA,** is mortally wounded at the Battle of Peach Tree Creek, GA, while leading his men, dying 5 days later on July 25, 1864.
07	20	1864	Guerrilla attack on Arrow Rock, Western MO.
07	20	1864	Federal operations in La Fayette and Johnson Counties, MO, with skirmishes with guerrillas in the vicinity of Arrow Rock and Mount Prairie. 7/20-31/1864.
07	20	1864	The Federals continue to bombard Fort Sumter, Charleston Harbor, SC.
07	20	1864	Skirmish in Blount County, TN.
07	20	1864	Skirmish at Philomont, VA.
07	20	1864	Engagement at Stephenson's Depot, VA, as Union cavalry under Brig. Gen. William W. Averell, USA, capture over 250 Confederates, as Lieut. Gen. Jubal Early, CSA, withdraws up the Shenandoah Valley towards Strasburg, VA.
07	21	1864	Federal expedition from Barrancas, FL, toward Pollard, AL, and skirmishes: a) at Camp Gonzales, FL **(22nd)** b) near Pollard, AL **(23rd)** 7/21-25/1864.
07	21	1864	Engagement at Bald (or Leggett's) Hill, GA, as Maj. Gen. James B. McPherson's Army of the Tennessee attacks and carry the hill which overlooks the city of Atlanta, GA, and defended by Maj. Gen. Patrick Cleburne, CSA.
07	21	1864	Skirmish at Atchafalaya, LA.
07	21	1864	Guerrilla attack on Plattsburg, Western MO.
07	22	1864	Skirmish near Pine Bluff, AR, with the Yankees surprising the Rebels, destroying a large amount of provisions and medical supplies the Confederates can't afford to lose.
07	22	1864	**The Battle of Atlanta, GA,** as Gen. John B. Hood, CSA, is unsuccessful in defeating Maj. Gen. William T. Sherman, USA, with a flank attack by Lieut. Gen. William Hardee, CSA, on the Army of the Tennessee, led by Maj. Gen. James B. McPherson, USA, again losing 3 to 4 men for every Union loss. Total casualties approximate 12,000.
07	22	1864	**Maj. Gen. William Henry Talbot Walker, CSA,** is mortally wounded during the Battle of Atlanta, GA, instantly shot dead by a Federal picket of the 16th US Army Corps, during Lieut. Gen. William J. Hardee, CSA, attack on the Federal left wing.
07	22	1864	**Brig. Gen. Samuel Benton, CSA,** is mortally wounded at the Battle of Atlanta, GA, struck near the heart with an artillery shell fragment and also having his foot amputated, dying six days later on July 28, 1864.
07	22	1864	**Maj. Gen. James Birdseye McPherson, USA,** is mortally wounded at the Battle of Atlanta, GA, while riding upon his horse, he tried to reach his command whose position had been overrun by the Confederates. Maj. Gen. William T. Sherman, USA, weeps profusely for the loss of his dear friend and colleague.
07	22	1864	**Maj. Gen. John A. Logan, USA, succeeds Maj. Gen. James B. McPherson, USA, in the command of the Army of the Tennessee.**
07	22	1864	Garrard's raid to Covington, GA. 7/22-24/1864.
07	22	1864	Skirmish at Concordia, LA.
07	22	1864	Skirmish near Vidalia, LA.
07	22	1864	Skirmish at Coldwater River, MS.
07	22	1864	Skirmishes with guerrillas near Camden Point and Union Mills, Western MO.
07	22	1864	Skirmish in Wright County, MO.
07	22	1864	President Jefferson Davis' orders the Confederate armies of the **Trans-Mississippi** to aid the Army of Tennessee, Gen. John B. Hood, CSA. The Confederates, under Lieut. Gen. E. Kirby Smith, CSA, attempt to transfer their troops to the east bank of the Mississippi River, although Kirby and Lieut. Gen. Richard Taylor, CSA, believe it to be a foolish attempt. Ultimately, it can't be done due to the Federal gunboats patrolling the Mississippi. Instead, Kirby Smith decides to move with Maj. Gen. Sterling Price in his operations against Maj. Gen. Frederick Steele, USA. 7/22-8/22/1864.
07	22	1864	Skirmishes at Clifton, TN. 7/22-23/1864.
07	22	1864	Skirmish near Berryville, VA.
07	22	1864	Skirmish at Newtown, VA.

| 07 | 22 | 1864 | Skirmish at Newtown, VA. |
| 07 | 22 | 1864 | Maj. Gen. Edward O. C. Ord, USA, assumes the command of the 18th US Army Corps, the Richmond, VA, Campaign. |

| 07 | 23 | 1864 | The successful Federal raid from Jacksonville on Baldwin, FL, and skirmishes. 7/23-28/1864. |
| 07 | 23 | 1864 | Operations about Atlanta, GA, including the: |

a) battle of Ezra Church **(July 28th)**

b) assault at Utoy Creek **(August 6th),** and other combats, GA. 7/23-8/25/1864.

07	23	1864	Brig. Gen. Morgan L. Smith, USA, is temporary in command of the 15th US Army Corps, GA.
07	23	1864	Skirmish with guerrillas near Liberty, Western MO.
07	23	1864	Federal operations in Randolph County, MO, with skirmishes at:

a) Allen   (23rd) and

b) Huntsville **(24th),** with guerrillas. 7/23-24/1864.

07	23	1864	Federal expedition against **Apache Indians** in Southwestern New Mexico Territory. 7/23-10/10/1864.
07	23	1864	Skirmish near Kernstown, VA, as Lieut. Gen. Jubal Early, CSA, moves down the Shenandoah Valley against Maj. Gen. David Hunter, USA.
07	23	1864	Maj. Gen. David B. Birney, USA, assumes the command of the 10th US Army Corps, VA, the Richmond, VA, Campaign.

07	24	1864	Federal scout from Lewisburg, AR, to 8 miles beyond Camp Myrick, killing 10 of Brig. Gen. Joseph O. Shelby's Confederates.
07	24	1864	Skirmish at Whitesville, FL.
07	24	1864	Skirmish near Cartersville, GA.
07	24	1864	Skirmish near Collierville, TN, 20 miles east of Memphis, on the **Memphis and Charleston Railroad,** with guerrillas.
07	24	1864	The engagement at Kernstown, or the **Battle of Winchester, VA,** where Lieut. Gen. Jubal A. Early, CSA, routs Maj. Gen. George Crook, USA, who retreats towards Harper's Ferry, WV.
07	24	1864	Skirmish at Falling Waters, WV.

07	25	1864	**Brig. Gen. Clement Hoffman Stevens, CSA,** dies at Atlanta, GA, from battle wounds received at the **Battle of Peach Tree Creek,** GA, on July 20, 1864.
07	25	1864	Federal Cavalry expedition from Decatur to Courtland, AL, and skirmish. 7/25-28/1864.
07	25	1864	Affair at Courtland, Northern AL.
07	25	1864	Affair at Benton, AR, where the Yankees kill **Brig. Gen. George M. Holt, of the Arkansas militia.**
07	25	1864	Federal scout in Yell County, AR, with skirmishes, where the Yankees kill the 2 Newsom brothers. 7/25-8/11/1864.
07	25	1864	**Federal expedition against the Sioux Indians in the Dakota Territory,** Maj. Gen. John Pope, USA, of the Eastern Campaign fame, is now commanding the **Dept. of the Northwest.** The 2 great Indian nations which occupy this military department are the **Chippewas** who inhabit the region between Lake Superior and Rainy Lake River on the east and the Red River of the North on the west, and the powerful **Sioux** or **Dakota Nation,** which, divided, into several strong and warlike tribes, claims and roams over the vast region from the western frontier of Minnesota on the east to the Rocky Mountains on the west, and from the frontier of Iowa and the line of the Platte River on the south to the British possessions on the north. Other tribes include the **Yanktonais, Unkpapas,** the **Rees,** etc. The Federals will work on making the Indians know who's in charge in these parts. 7/25-10/8/1864.
07	25	1864	Skirmish at Williamsport, MD.
07	25	1864	Federal scout from Fulton, MO, against bushwackers. 7/25-26/1864.
07	25	1864	Skirmish at Pleasant Hill, MO.
07	25	1864	Skirmish at Martinsburg, WV.
07	25	1864	Skirmish at Bunker Hill, WV, as Lieut. Gen. Jubal Early, CSA, pursues the retreating Federals.

| 07 | 26 | 1864 | The following are appointed Confederate Brigadier Generals: |

Robert Houstoun Anderson,	CSA
Samuel Benton,	CSA (mortally wounded July 22, 1864)
William Felix Brantley,	CSA
George Gibbs Dibrell,	CSA
George Doherty Johnston,	CSA
Felix Huston Robertson,	CSA
Jacob Hunter Sharp,	CSA

Alabama, Mississippi, and East Louisiana.

| 07 | 26 | 1864 | Federal scout to Searcy and West Point, AR, with encounter with Rebel forces and loss of life. 7/26-28/1864. |

07 26 1864 — Action at Wallace's Ferry, Big Creek, AR.

07 26 1864 — Federal expedition from Paducah aboard the steamer, **Olive,** to Haddix's Ferry, KY, and skirmish with guerrillas. 7/26-27/1864.

07 26 1864 — Skirmish at Falling Waters, MD.

07 26 1864 — Skirmish at Muddy Branch, MD.

07 26 1864 — Federal scout in Johnson County, MO, against guerrillas. 7/26-31/1864.

07 26 1864 — Confederate attack on Shelbina, MO, where they proceed to tear up railroad track, burn 2 trains of railroad cars, etc.

07 26 1864 — Skirmish at White's Station, TN.

07 26 1864 — Federal scout toward Rapidan Station, VA, noting that Lieut. Gen. Richard S. Ewell, CSA, is in force near Culpeper, VA.

07 27 1864 — Action at Massard Prairie, 7 miles from Fort Smith, AR, where the Confederates overpower the Yankees, capturing 82, both sides inflicting mortal wounds on each other.

07 27 1864 — Skirmish at Whiteside, Black Creek, FL.

07 27 1864 — Maj. Gen. Alexander McDowell McCooks's, USA, raid on the **Atlanta, West Point, Macon and Western Railroads,** with skirmishes:

a) near Campbellton	**(July 28th)**
b) near Lovejoy's Station	**(July 29th)**
c) at Clear Creek	**(July 30th)** and
d) action near Newman	7/27-31/1864.

07 27 1864 — Maj. Gen. George Stoneman's Cavalry raid to Macon, GA, to destroy Confederate railroad lines, with combats at:

a) Macon and Clinton	**(July 30th)**
b) Hillsborough	**(July 30th-31st)**
c) Mulberry Creek and Jug Tavern	(August 3), GA.

07 27 1864 — Brig. Gen. Kenner Garrard's, USA, raid to South River, with skirmishes at:

| a) Snapfinger Creek | (July 27th) |
| b) Flat Rock Bridge, and Lithonia | **(July 28th),** GA. |

07 27 1864 — **Maj. Gen. Oliver O. Howard, USA, assumes the command of the Army of the Tennessee, GA.**

07 27 1864 — Maj. Gen. David S. Stanley, USA, succeeds Maj. Gen. Oliver O. Howard, USA, in the command of the 4th US Army Corps, GA.

07 27 1864 — Maj. Gen. John A. Logan, USA, resumes the command of the 15th US Army Corps, GA.

07 27 1864 — Brig. Gen. Alpheus S. Williams, USA, **succeeds Maj. Gen. Joseph Hooker,** USA, in the temporary command of the 20th US Army Corps, GA, as **Hooker resigns,** feeling slighted with the promotion of Maj. Gen. Oliver O. Howard, to the command of the Army of the Tennessee.

07 27 1864 — Skirmishes with guerrillas on the Blackwater River (27th), and on Big Creek, MO. **(28th).** 7/27-28/1864.

07 27 1864 — Federal scout in Chariton County, MO, under Brig. Gen. Clinton B. Fish, USA, commanding the District of North Missouri, with skirmishes with guerrillas **(30th)** on the Chariton Road, near Keytesville, and at Union Church. 7/27-30/1864.

07 27 1864 — Demonstration on the north bank of the James River and engagement at Deep Bottom (or Darbytown, Strawberry Plains, and New Market Road), VA, by Lieut. Gen. Ulysses S. Grant, USA, the Richmond, VA, Campaign. 7/27-29/1864.

07 27 1864 — Skirmish near Lee's Mill, VA, the Richmond, VA, Campaign.

07 27 1864 — Federal expedition from Norfolk, VA, into North Carolina, having successfully accomplished their objects of capturing horses, cotton, and other contraband property, visiting such places as Gatesville, Winton, Wintonville, and Elizabeth City. The Federals note that three fifths of the people of the counties of Perquimans and Chowan Counties have a deep feeling for the Union and wish they could be rid of the guerrillas that still infest the country through which the Federals keep moving through. 7/27-8/4/1864.

07 27 1864 — Skirmish at Back Creek Bridge, WV.

07 27 1864 — **Maj. Gen. Henry W. Halleck, Chief of Staff, USA, is assigned to the command over the Middle Dept. and the Depts. of Washington, West Virginia, and the Susquehanna, Pennsylvania.**

07 28 1864 — **Brig. Gen. Samuel Benton, CSA,** dies at Griffin, GA, from battle wounds received July 22, 1864, at the Battle of Atlanta, GA.

07	28	1864	Affair on the Danville road, near Decatur, Northern AL.

07 28 1864 Action against the **Sioux Indians** at the Tahkahokuty Mountain, the Dakota Territory, on the Knife River.

07 28 1864 **The Battle of Ezra Church, GA,** where Gen. John B. Hood, CSA, attacks, and is repelled by, Maj. Gen. Oliver Otis Howard, USA, with tremendous loss of Southern life. Total casualties approximate 600 Union and 5,000 Confederate. Hood is losing too many valiant men he will never be able to replace.

07 28 1864 Skirmish on the Morgan's Ferry road, near Morganza, LA, with Brig. Gen. Michael K. Lawler's, USA, men scattering the Rebels.

07 28 1864 Federal expedition from New Berne to Manning's Neck, NC, as Brig. Gen. Innis N. Palmer, USA, commanding the District of North Carolina, sent men aboard the gunboat, **Whitehead,** up the Chowan River to Manning's Neck to communicate with the cavalry at work on the **Weldon and Petersburg Railroad.** They succeed in capturing cotton, tobacco, etc. and all the Rebel commissary supplies at Winton, in addition to capturing the Rebel steamer, **Arrow.** 7/28-31/1864.

07 28 1864 Skirmish at Long's Mills, near Mulberry Gap, TN, as the Yankees whip the Rebels.

07 28 1864 Action at Four-Mile Creek, VA, the Richmond, VA, Campaign.

07 28 1864 Maj. Gen. Lewis Wallace, USA, is reassigned to the command of the Middle Dept. and the 8th US Army Corps, VA.

07 28 1864 Maj. Gen. Edward O. C. Ord, USA, is assigned to the command of the 18th US Army Corps, VA.

07 29 1864 **Thomas Benton Smith,** CSA, is appointed Brig. Gen.

07 29 1864 Skirmishes near Napoleonville, LA, between Paincourtville and Lake Natchez, where the attacking Rebels are repulsed, with loss of life.

07 29 1864 Affair at Highland Stockade, near Baton Rouge, LA, where some Union pickets were shot and severely wounded by the Rebels.

07 29 1864 Federal expedition from Warrensburg to Chapel Hill, MO, with skirmish near Chapel Hill. **(July 30th),** again, as usual, with loss of human life. 7/29-8/2/1864.

07 29 1864 Skirmish at Hagerstown, MD, as Lieut. Gen. Jubal Early, CSA, orders Confederate cavalry under Brig. Gen. John McCausland to move back into Maryland and Pennsylvania.

07 29 1864 Skirmish at Clear Spring, MD.

07 29 1864 Skirmish at Mercersburg, PA, with Brig. Gen. John McCausland, CSA.

07 30 1864 **William Mahone,**   **C.S.A.,** is appointed Maj. Gen.

07 30 1864 **Victor Jean Baptiste Girardey,** CSA, is appointed Brig. Gen.

07 30 1864 **David Addison Weisiger,**   CSA, is appointed Brig. Gen.

07 30 1864 The following are appointed Union Brigadier Generals:

William Worth Belknap,	USA
Luther Prentice Bradley,	USA
Joseph Alexander Cooper,	USA
William Grose,	USA
James William Reilly,	USA
John Wilson Sprague,	USA
Charles Carroll Walcutt,	USA

07 30 1864 Skirmish at Paint Rock Station, AL.

07 30 1864 Skirmish at Hay Station, No. 3, near Brownsville, AR, as the Rebel attack is repulsed, but they manage to take some civilians hostage.

07 30 1864 Skirmish near Pine Bluff, AR, as the Federal party sent to repair the cut telegraph wires are attacked and return to camp, mourning some of their comrades, whose lifeless bodies they bring with them.

07 30 1864 Maj. Gen. Henry W. Slocum, USA, is assigned to the command of the 20th US Army Corps, GA.

07 30 1864 Skirmish at Bayou Tensas, LA.

07 30 1864 Affair at Emmitsburg, MD.

07 30 1864 Skirmish at Monocacy Junction, MD.

07 30 1864 **The Confederate Burning of Chambersburg, PA,** is ordered by Brig. Gen. John McCausland, CSA, Cavalry, after the town could not or would not raise the $500,000 (or $100,000 in gold) assessment for the destruction of property in the Shenandoah Valley by Maj. Gen. David Hunter, USA.

07 30 1864 Skirmish at McConnellsburg, PA, with Early's Cavalry and the Union cavalry under Brig. Gen. William W. Averell, USA.

07 30 1864 Federal scout against guerrillas in Phelps and Maries Counties, MO. 7/30-8/1/1864.

07 30 1864 Skirmish at Clifton, TN.

07 30 1864 **Brownsville, TX, is reoccupied** by the Confederate forces.

07	30	1864	Skirmish at Lee's Mill, VA.
07	30	1864	**The Explosion of the mine and the Assault on the Crater, the Petersburg Line, VA,** that results in a Union disaster due in part to **Brig. Gen. James H. Ledlie's** failure to take command of the advancing troops, opting to remain in a bombproof. The mine had taken a month to dig, was almost 6 football fields in length and packed with explosives, killing almost 300 Confederates when it was detonated who are blown to bits. Maj. Gen. William Mahone, CSA, responds and inflicts 4,000 Union casualties, while the Rebels sustain 1,500, the Richmond, VA, Campaign.
07	30	1864	Skirmish near Shepherdstown, WV.
07	31	1864	Affair near Watkins' Plantation, Northern AL.
07	31	1864	Action near Fort Smith, AR, with Federals under the command of Maj. Gen. Frederick Steele, USA, commanding the Dept. of Arkansas.
07	31	1864	Affair at Orange Grove, near Donaldsonville, LA, where the Confederate attack on the Union pickets results in no casualties on either side.
07	31	1864	Skirmish at Hancock, MD, as Brig. Gen. William W. Averell, USA, Cavalry is ordered against the Confederate Cavalry under Brig. Gen. John McCausland, CSA, which burned Chambersburg, PA.
08	1	1864	**Powell Clayton,** USA, is appointed Brig. Gen.
08	1	1864	Federal operations in Eastern Arkansas, with skirmish (August 1st) at Lamb's Plantation, near Helena, with guerrillas. 8/1-5/1864.
08	1	1864	Federal scout against Indians on the Smoky Hill Fork, KS. From present indications, the Yankees believe the Indians are upon the Saline, Solomon, and Republican Rivers, as the **buffalo** are plenty upon these streams, and they depend entirely upon them for a living. 8/1-5/1864.
08	1	1864	Federal scout to Baxter Springs, KS, with skirmish, where after a few shots, the Confederates are routed.
08	1	1864	Operations in Eastern Kentucky pits Brig. Gen. Napoleon B. Buford, USA, against Brig. Gen. Joseph O. Shelby, CSA, with skirmishes near: a) Bardstown (Aug. 1st) and b) **near New Haven, KY. (Aug. 2nd)** 8/1-31/1864.
08	1	1864	The Confederates attack Cumberland, MD, as the Union Cavalry under Brig. Gen. William W. Averell, USA, closes in on Brig. Gen. John McCausland, CSA.
08	1	1864	Affair at Flintstone Creek, MD.
08	1	1864	**Federal operations in Southwest Missouri,** under Brig. Gen. John Sanborn, USA, commanding the District of Southwest Missouri, with skirmishes: a) at Diamond Grove Prairie (Aug. 1st) b) at Rutledge **(Aug. 4th)** c) near Enterprise and on Buffalo Creek **(Aug. 7th).** 8/1-28/1864.
08	1	1864	Federal scout on the Independence road to Gunter's Mills, MO, near Pleasant Hill, MO. 8/1-3/1864.
08	1	1864	Skirmishes near Independence, MO, as Maj. Gen. Alfred Pleasonton, USA, commanding the District of Western Missouri reports his men overrunning 2 Rebel camps.
08	1	1864	Skirmish at Rolla, MO.
08	1	1864	The pursuit of the Confederates forces who attacked Athens, TN, into North Carolina, and skirmishes: a) at Athens, TN, (Aug. 1st), and b) near Murphy, NC, **(Aug. 2nd)** 8/1-3/1864.
08	1	1864	**Federal expedition from La Grange, TN, to Oxford, MS.** 8/1-30/1864.
08	1	1864	Federal scout from Strawberry Plains to Greeneville, TN, with instructions to destroy the railroad bridges over the Hoston and Wataugo River, and skirmish at Morristown, TN. **(Aug. 2nd)** 8/1-5/1864.
08	1	1864	**The Richmond (Virginia) Campaign.** 8/1-12/31/1864.
08	1	1864	Skirmish at Deep Bottom, VA, the Richmond, VA, Campaign.
08	2	1864	**William Miller,** CSA, is appointed Brig. Gen.
08	2	1864	Federal operations in Mobile Bay, AL, as the Federals attempt to close one of the last two Confederate open ports; the other being Wilmington, NC; Maj. Gen. Edward R.S. Canby, USA, commanding the Military Division of the West Mississippi, with Maj. Gen. Gordon Granger, USA, commanding the landing forces. 8/2-23/1864.
08	2	1864	Federal naval expedition to McIntosh County, GA, as the Yankees continue to exert pressure on the dwindling Confederate forces in this area of the Confederacy. 8/2-4/1864.
08	2	1864	Federal reconnaissance from Berwick to Pattersonville, LA, as Brig. Gen. Robert A. Cameron, USA, commanding the District of La Fource sends the **93rd US Colored Infantry** along.

08	2	1864	Skirmish at Hancock, MD, with Brig. Gen. John McCausland, CSA.
08	2	1864	Skirmish at Old Town, MD.
08	2	1864	Federal operations near Holden, MO, with skirmish on Norris Creek, as the Yankees chase the Rebels away from a Union crew working to repair the telegraph lines that were torn down. **(8th).** 8/2-8/1864.
08	2	1864	Skirmish at Green Springs Run, WV.

08	3	1864	**John Decatur Barry,** CSA, is appointed Brig. Gen.
08	3	1864	US forces, under Maj. Gen. Gordon Granger, USA, land on Dauphin Island and invest Fort Gaines, AL, at the entrance to Mobile Bay, AL.
08	3	1864	Confederate operations about Woodville, MS, against the advancing Federals, including on the Bayou Sara, Laurel Hill, Saint Francisville, etc. 8/3-6/1864.
08	3	1864	Skirmish near Fayette, MO, as the Yankees pursue the small band of Confederates over 15 miles before giving up.
08	3	1864	Federal scouts from Fort Sumner, the New Mexico Territory, with many many stories to be told, which include the skirmish at the Sacramento Mountains with the **Apache Indians,** who are aided by their brethren, the **Coyoteros;** the Yankees aided by the **Navajoes,** who act as guides, scouts, and spies. **(Aug. 26th).** The Federals note that east of the Sacramento Mountains, the country is aflush of red roses and wild flowers blossoming in every direction; cherries, plums and raspberries abound; elk and black-tailed deer are numerous in the mountains and herds of antelope are seen east of Sacramento. Wild turkeys are seen by the hundreds at every camp, and many are killed by the men when they are allowed to shoot. In some instances, panthers are seen, and one specimen of the American lion is seen, but could not be killed. 8/3-11/4/1864.
08	3	1864	Federal scout from Cumberland Gap, TN, into Lee County, VA, and to Tazewell, TN, and skirmish near Jonesville, VA. **(4th).** The Federals estimate Lee County to produce 200,000 bushels of corn this year and are on the lookout for Brig. Gen. John Hunt Morgan's Confederates to occupy the county. 8/3-6/1864.
08	3	1864	Skirmishes at Triune, TN. 8/3-4/1864.
08	3	1864	Action near Wilcox's Landing, VA, the Richmond, VA, Campaign.

08	4	1864	**John Calvin Brown, C.S.A.,** is appointed Maj. Gen.
08	4	1864	**Bryan Morel Thomas,** CSA, is appointed Brig. Gen.
08	4	1864	Skirmish at Antietam Ford, MD, with Brig. Gen. John McCausland's, Confederate Cavalry.
08	4	1864	Federal expedition from Natchez, MS, to Gillespie's Plantation, LA, about 5 miles below Vidalia and 5 miles east of Trinity, with skirmish. 8/4-6/1864.
08	4	1864	Federal scout from Fort Union Nation, the New Mexico Territory, where they begin to move against the hostile **Kiowas** and **Comanches Indian tribes.** There are also Mexican bandits operating in the area, with the Indians being blamed for their deprivations. 8/4-9/15/1864.
08	4	1864	Federal operations in the vicinity of Brazos Santiago, TX, with skirmish at Point Isabel **(August 9th).** 8/4-15/1864.
08	4	1864	Skirmish at Tracy City, TN.
08	4	1864	Action near Harrison's Landing, VA, the Richmond, VA, Campaign.
08	4	1864	Action at New Creek, WV, with Brig. Gen. William W. Averell's, USA, Cavalry command defeating the Rebels, capturing men, property, etc., and reporting back to Maj. Gen. Philip H. Sheridan, USA, in the Shenandoah Valley, near Harper's Ferry.

08	5	1864	**Philip Cook,** CSA, is appointed Brig. Gen.
08	5	1864	**Archibald Campbell Godwin,** CSA, is appointed Brig. Gen.
08	5	1864	**Joseph Abel Haskin,** USA, is appointed Brig. Gen.
08	5	1864	The passage of Fort Morgan, Mobile, AL, by the US fleet, including the monitors, **Chickasaw, Manhattan, Tecumseh,** and **Winnebago,** and engagement in Mobile Bay, AL, by Admiral Daniel Farragut, USN.
08	5	1864	The US monitor, **Tecumseh,** is sunk by a torpedo near Fort Morgan, AL, when Farragut is reported to have said, **"Damn the torpedos, full speed ahead!"**
08	5	1864	The capture of the Confederate ram, **Tennessee,** and the gun-boat, **Selma,** AL, by Admiral Farragut during the Battle of Mobile Bay, AL.
08	5	1864	**Fort Powell, AL, is evacuated** by the Confederates, after being bombarded from the rear by the ironclad **USS Chickasaw** that passed Fort Morgan.
08	5	1864	Skirmish near Remount Camp, AR, as the Yankees lose men when the Confederates, dressed in Union

			garb, surprise attack them.
08	5	1864	Skirmish at Concordia Bayou, LA.
08	5	1864	Affair at Doyal's Plantation, LA, where the Federals are surrounded by the Confederates, but refuse to surrender, and escape by cutting a path through the Rebels.
08	5	1864	Skirmish at Olive Branch, LA.
08	5	1864	Skirmish at Keedysville, MD.
08	5	1864	Skirmishes at Williamsport and Hagerstown, MD.
08	5	1864	Skirmish at Cabin Point, VA, the Richmond, VA, Campaign.
08	5	1864	**The explosion of a Confederate mine** in front of the 18th US Army Corps, the Richmond, VA, Campaign.
08	5	1864	Skirmish at Huttonsville, WV.
08	6	1864	The affair on the Somerville road, near Decatur, Northern AL.
08	6	1864	Federal expedition with men under Maj. Gen. Frederick Steele, USA, from Little Rock to Little Red River, AR, and with skirmishes with Brig. Gen. Joseph O. Shelby, CSA, at the following locations:

a) Hickory Plains **(August 7th)**
b) Bull Bayou **(August 7th)**
c) Hatch's Ferry **(August 9th)**
d) near Augusta **(August 10th)**
e) near Searcy **(August 13th)** 8/6-16/1864.

08	6	1864	Federal scout in Saline County, MO, with skirmishes at Arrow Rock. **(August 7th)**. 8/6-9/1864.
08	6	1864	Skirmish at Indian Village, LA.
08	6	1864	Skirmish at Plaquemine, LA.
08	7	1864	Affair with the **Commanches** and **Kiowas** Indians near Fort Lyon, the Colorado Territory.
08	7	1864	Affair at Bayou Grand, FL, where the Union gunboats shell the Confederate Cavalry there, setting fire to numerous (Rebel) buildings.
08	7	1864	Brig. Gen. Richard W. Johnson, USA, succeeds Maj. Gen. John M. Palmer, USA, in the temporary command of the 14th US Army Corps, GA.
08	7	1864	Skirmish at Enterprise, MO.
08	7	1864	Skirmish 5 miles south of Huntsville, MO, with guerrillas.
08	7	1864	Federal scout from Independence into La Fayette County, MO, against guerrillas. 8/7-8/1864.
08	7	1864	Skirmishes at the Tallahatchie River, MS, with Brig. Gen. Joseph A. Mower, USA. 8/7-9/1864.
08	7	1864	The Confederate raid in Union County, TN, by the notorious Bill Gibbs, at the head of the most villainous gang of cutthroats, robbers, and assassins which the country is cursed with. Arriving from Thorn Hill, Grainger County, they murdered 3 men, taking many others as prisoners, robbing houses at will, killing those who tried to escape. For today at least, lawlessness prevailed in Union City, TN, and men paid for it with their lives.
08	7	1864	**The (FINAL) Shenandoah Valley, Virginia, Campaign,** as Maj. Gen. Philip Henry Sheridan, USA, moves against the Confederates under Lieut. Gen. Jubal Anderson Early, CSA, and his cavalry commander, **Maj. Gen. Lunsford Lindsay Lomax, CSA.** 8/7-11/28/1864.
08	7	1864	**The Middle Military Division (Middle Dept. and the Dept. of Washington, of the Susquehanna, and of West Virginia) is constituted, (to be known as the Army of the Shenandoah)** and Maj. Gen. Philip H. Sheridan, USA, is assigned to its temporary command, VA, as Lieut. Gen. Ulysses S. Grant, USA, orders Maj. Gen. Sheridan to clear the Shenandoah Valley of Rebels once and for all.
08	7	1864	Engagement at Oldfields, near Moorefield, WV, as Brig. Gen. William W. Averel'sl, USA, cavalry overwhelms Lieut. Gen. Jubal A. Early's, CSA, cavalry under Brig. Gen. John McClausand.
08	8	1864	**James Deering Fessenden,** USA, is appointed Brig. Gen.
08	8	1864	**Fort Gaines, AL,** Dauphin Island, in Mobile Bay, **is surrendered** by Col. Charles D. Anderson, CSA, without the approval of his superiors.
08	8	1864	Federal scout against Indians from Camp Anderson to Bald Mountain, CA, where the Indians flee into the thick timber in the direction of the Hoopa Valley. 8/8-12/1864.
08	8	1864	Action with the **Sioux Indians** on the Little Missouri River, the Dakota Territory.
08	8	1864	Federal scout against Indians armed only with bows and arrows, from Salina to Mulberry Creek, KS. 8/8-11/1864.
08	8	1864	Skirmish at Salem, KY.
08	8	1864	Skirmish at La Fayette, TN.

MONTH	DAY	YEAR	ACT
08	8	1864	Skirmish at Fairfax Station, VA.
08	9	1864	**The Federal siege of Fort Morgan, Mobile Bay, AL,** begins as the Federals surround the fort, now that Forts Gaines and Powell had surrendered. 8/9-22/1864.
08	9	1864	Skirmish near Pond Springs, Northern AL.
08	9	1864	Federal operations in Central Arkansas, with skirmishes with Confederates, guerrillas and bushwackers. 8/9-15/1864.
08	9	1864	Bvt. Maj. Gen. Jefferson C. Davis, USA, is assigned to the command of the 14th US Corps, GA.
08	9	1864	Skirmish at Hurricane Creek, MS, as Brig. Gen. Joseph A. Mower, USA, moves from La Grange, TN, on Oxford, MS.
08	9	1864	Skirmish at Oxford, MS, with Brig. Gen. Jospeh A. Mower, USA.
08	9	1864	The explosion of Federal ammunition at City Point, VA, takes places as two Confederate agents smuggle a bomb aboard an ordnance supply ship unloading at the docks, causing a chain reaction of explosions, the Richmond, VA, Campaign.
08	9	1864	Affair near Sycamore Church, Richmond, VA.
08	9	1864	**Lieut. Col. John S. Mosby's, 43rd Virginia Cavalry Confederate operations in Virginia,** including his routing of Federal Cavalry at Fairfax Station (August 9th), capturing men and horses; an attack **(August 13th)** on Berryville and the Union supply train, capturing and destroying 75 loaded wagons, and 200 head of beef cattle, 500 horses, etc., under Brig. Gen. John Reese Kenly, USA; attacking and capturing Yankees at Kernstown and Charlestown **(circa August 15th),** crossing back through Snicker's Gap, and capturing men and horses at Charlestown **(August 20th);** attacking and capturing a Federal outpost in Fairfax **(Sept. 3rd);** attacking the Yankees around Berryville and near Charlestown, **(Sept. 5th),** and attacking the Federal rear near Charlestown, **(Sept. 8th).** Although Mosby was effective and doing all he possibly do, he was becoming more and more a nuisance in the side of Federals, and less of a military threat to strategic positions. 8/9-10/14/1864.
08	10	1864	**Lundsford Lindsay Lomax, C.S.A.,** is appointed Maj. Gen.
08	10	1864	Skirmishes at Baldwin, FL, where the Rebels attack and capture a small Federal force who were preoccupied with ripping up railroad track.
08	10	1864	**Maj. Gen. John Wheeler's, CSA, Confederate raid** to disrupt the Union supply and communication lines of Maj. Gen. William T. Sherman, USA, in North Georgia and East Tennessee, with combats at Dalton **(August 14th-15th)** and other points, GA. 8/10-9/9/1864.
08	10	1864	Federal scouts from Morganza, LA, with skirmishes 3 miles south of Williamsport with the Confederates. 8/10-12/1864.
08	10	1864	Skirmish at the Tallahatchie River, MS, with Brig. Gen. Joseph A. Mower's, USA, expedition from La Grange, TN, on Oxford, MS.
08	10	1864	Skirmish near Stone Chapel, VA, the Shenandoah Valley, VA, Campaign.
08	11	1864	**Daniel Davidson Bidwell,** USA, is appointed Brig. Gen.
08	11	1864	Skirmish in Crawford County, AR.
08	11	1864	Federal expedition mostly of Negro forces, from Helena, aboard the steamer, **H.A. Homeyer,** to Kent's Landing, AR. 8/11-13/1864.
08	11	1864	Skirmish on White Oak Creek, AR.
08	11	1864	Skirmish with the **Kiowas Indians** near Sand Creek, the Colorado Territory, as the Federals plan to kill every Indian they come in contact with.
08	11	1864	Skirmish at Hartville, MO.
08	11	1864	Federal operations in Johnson County, MO, with skirmish near Holden **(12th),** with bushwackers. 8/11-19/1864.
08	11	1864	Operations against the **Brule Sioux Indians** in the Nebraska Territory, with skirmish near Fort Cottonwood **(Sept. 20th);** the **Pawnees** and **Ogalalla Sioux Indians** are encountered along the way but are friendly with the white man. 8/11-10/28/1864.
08	11	1864	The **CSS Tallahassee** captures seven Federal vessels off the coast of Sandy Hook, NJ, burning all except one for the Federal crews to escape on.
08	11	1864	Lieut. Gen. Jubal Early, CSA, moves his forces from Winchester, VA, up the Shenandoah Valley toward Cedar Creek as Maj. Gen. Philip Sheridan, USA, who recently replaced Maj. Gen. David Hunter, USA, marches with the newly formed US **Army of the Shenandoah** against Early.
08	11	1864	Action at Newtown, VA, with Lieut. Gen. Jubal Early, CSA.

08	11	1864	Action at Newtown, VA, with Lieut. Gen. Jubal Early, CSA.
08	11	1864	Action at Toll-Gate, near White Post, VA, the Shenandoah Valley, VA, Campaign.
08	11	1864	Skirmish near Winchester, VA, the Shenandoah Valley, VA, Campaign.
08	12	1864	**Joseph Anthony Mower, U.S.A.,** is appointed Maj. Gen.
08	12	1864	Federal operations in Madison County, AL, near Fayetteville, and New Market. 8/12-14/1864.
08	12	1864	Skirmish at Van Buren, AR.
08	12	1864	Federal scout from Camp Anderson to Bald Mountain, CA. 8/8-12/1864.
08	12	1864	Federal scout against guerrillas on the Fort Union road, near Fort Garland, the Colorado Territory. 8/12-16/1864.
08	12	1864	Skirmishes at Baldwin, FL.
08	12	1864	Affair with Indians in the San Andres Mountains, the New Mexico Territory, as the Federals overtake the fleeing Indians.
08	12	1864	The Confederate raider, **CSS Tallahassee,** captures six more Federal vessels off the coast of New Jersey and New York, causing alarm up and down the eastern seaboard.
08	12	1864	Federal operations in Ray and Carroll Counties, MO, and skirmish with guerrillas who attack the Yankees but are repulsed (12th) at Fredericksburg, MO. 8/12-16/1864.
08	12	1864	Skirmish at Cedar Creek, VA, as Lieut. Gen. Jubal A. Early, CSA, against Maj. Gen. Philip H. Sheridan, USA, begin to meet up with each other.
08	13	1864	Federal expedition from Fort Barrancas, FL, to capture the nearby Rebel camp, which the Yankees find deserted. 8/13-14/1864.
08	13	1864	Skirmish at Palatka, FL.
08	13	1864	Federal operations about Shawneetown, IL, against Pro-Southerns, as Maj. Gen. Samuel P. Heintzelman, USA, commanding the Northern Dept., order troops to move against Col. Johnson who captured 3 steamers loaded with Government cattle and crossed the Ohio River near Shawneetown into Illinois.
08	13	1864	Skirmishes at Hurricane Creek, MS, with Maj. Gen. Nathan Bedford Forrest, CSA, contesting the advance of Maj. Gen. Joseph A. Mower, USA. 8/13-14/1864.
08	13	1864	Federal operations under Maj. Gen. Alfred Pleasonton, USA, commanding the District of Central Missouri, against guerrillas, including **William Clarke Quantrill,** in La Fayette, Saline, and Howard Counties, MO, with skirmishes. 8/13-22/1864.
08	13	1864	The **CSS Tallahassee** captures and burns two more Federal vessels off the coast of New York.
08	13	1864	Affair at Berryville, VA, the Shenandoah Valley, VA, Campaign.
08	13	1864	Actions at Four-Mile Creek and Dutch Gap, VA.
08	13	1864	Federal demonstration on the north bank of the James River, at Deep Bottom, as Maj. Gen. Ulysses S. Grant, USA, attempts to divert Gen. Robert E. Lee's, CSA, attention away from Petersburg, VA, with little success, including combats at: a) **White's Tavern** b) **Charles City Road** c) **New Market Road** d) **Fussell's Mill** e) **Gravel Hill** f) **Bailey's Creek** g) **Deep Run (or Creek)**, etc, the Richmond, VA, Campaign. 8/13-20/1864.
08	13	1864	Skirmish near Strasburg, VA, as the action begins to pickup between Lieut. Gen. Jubal Early, CSA, and Maj. Gen. Philip Sheridan, USA.
08	14	1864	Federal scout from Mayfield, KY, and skirmish 2.5 miles from town at Bethel Church where scoundrels were playing a card game with an old Union man. After taking $250 from him, they were planning on killing him when the game was over, but the Federals arrived to break up their scheme. They are now spending time in jail. 8/14-15/1864.
08	14	1864	Skirmish at Lamar, MS, with Maj. Gen. Nathan Bedford Forrest, CSA, and Maj. Gen. Joseph A. Mower, USA.
08	14	1864	Skirmish near Strasburg, VA, as Lieut. Gen. Jubal Early, CSA, and Maj. Gen. Philip Sheridan, USA, continue to spar.
08	14	1864	Maj. Gen. John G. Parke, USA, is placed in the command of the 9th US Army Corps, the Richmond, VA Campaign.
08	15	1864	**Brig. Gen. Daniel Phineas Woodbury, USA,** dies from camp fever (yellow fever) at his post at Key

08	15	1864	**George Washington Gordon,** CSA, is appointed Brig. Gen.
08	15	1864	**William Hugh Young,** CSA, is appointed Brig. Gen.
08	15	1864	**Lieut. Gen. Richard Taylor, CSA, is assigned to the command the Dept. of Alabama, Mississippi, and East Louisiana.**
08	15	1864	Federal scout from Triana to Valhermoso Springs, AL, with the capture of some mules, horses, and oxen and the destruction of 2 salt-peter works.
08	15	1864	The Union raid on the **Florida Railroad,** including action at Gainesville, FL, **(August 17th),** Brig. Gen. John P. Hatch, USA, commanding the District of Florida. 8/15-19/1864.
08	15	1864	Skirmishes at Sandtown and Fairburn, GA.
08	15	1864	Federal expedition from Paincourtville to Lake Natchez, LA, with skirmish on Grand River. 8/15-21/1864.
08	15	1864	Skirmish at Dripping Spring, Boone County, MO, with guerrillas led by the notorious Bill Anderson, and with Federal casualties.
08	15	1864	Federal operations in Southwest Missouri and Northwestern Arkansas, Brig. Gen. John B. Sanborn, USA, commanding the District of Southwest Missouri, with skirmishes: a) at Carrollton, AR (15th) b) on Richland Creek, AR **(16th),** and c) at Mud Town, AR **(24th).** 8/15-24/1864.
08	15	1864	The **CSS Tallahassee** continues to wreak havoc on the Federal shipping, this time capturing six more, burning five, releasing one with all the Federal crew to safety off the New England coast.
08	15	1864	Confederate raid on the **Nashville and Northwestern Railroad,** TN, as 600 cords of wood is destroyed, with employees carried off, and feared murdered by the Rebels.
08	15	1864	Skirmish at Cedar Creek, VA, the Shenandoah Valley, VA, Campaign.
08	15	1864	Skirmish at Fisher's Hill, near Strasburg, VA, the Shenandoah Valley, VA, Campaign.
08	15	1864	Skirmish near Charlestown, WV.
08	16	1864	Federal expedition from Mount Vernon, IN, aboard the steamers, **Cottage, Dunleath, General Halleck, Jennette Hopkins,** and the **Jeannette Rogers,** into Kentucky, to deflect the Confederate advance under Cols. Johnson and Sypert into Indiana, including skirmishes: a) at White Oak Springs **(17th)** b) Geiger's Lake **(18th)** and c) Smith's Mills **(19th).** 8/16-22/1864.
08	16	1864	Skirmish with Indians near Smoky Hill Crossing Run, KS.
08	16	1864	Skirmish 10 miles northwest of Columbia, MO, as the Yankees rout Brig. Gen. James Thadeus Holtzclaw, CSA.
08	16	1864	The **CSS Tallahassee** captures and burns five more Union ships off the coast of New England.
08	16	1864	Engagement at Cedarville (Guard Hill or Front Royal or Crooked Creek), VA, the Shenandoah Valley, VA, Campaign.
08	17	1864	Federal expedition from Decatur to Moulton, and skirmish **(18th-19th)** near Antioch Church, Northern AL. 8/17-20/1864.
08	17	1864	The Confederate capture and burning of the Federal steamer, **Miller,** on the Arkansas River, 10 miles below Pine Bluff, AR, as the steamer, **Annie Jacobs,** lies stuck on a sand bar.
08	17	1864	Skirmish at South Newport, GA, where the Federals land and surprise the Rebels, capturing 38, in addition to 5 citizens and 51 Negroes, and burning the bridge over the South Newport River as they left.
08	17	1864	Skirmish in Issaquena County, MS.
08	17	1864	Action at Winchester, VA, as Lieut. Gen. Jubal Early, CSA, attacks the rear guard of Maj. Gen. Philip Sheridan, USA, who is withdrawing toward Berryville, VA.
08	18	1864	**Eli Long,** USA, is appointed Brig. Gen.
08	18	1864	Skirmish at Benton, AR, as the Confederate Cavalry which temporarily **occupied Benton,** is driven off in a hurry.
08	18	1864	Skirmishes near Pine Bluff, AR.
08	18	1864	Maj. Gen. Judson H. Kilpatrick's, USA, Cavalry raid from Sandtown to Lovejoy's Station, in an unsuccessful attempt to destroy the **Macon and Western Railroad,** as Maj. Gen. William T. Sherman, USA, attempts to force the Confederates out of Atlanta, GA, with combats at: a) Camp Creek (18th) b) Red Oak **(19th)** c) Flint River **(19th)**

			c) Flint River **(19th)**
			d) Jonesborough **(19th)**
			e) Lovejoy's Station **(20th),** GA. 8/18-22/1864.
08	18	1864	Skirmish at Charleston, TN.
08	18	1864	Skirmish at Opequon Creek, VA, as Lieut. Gen. Jubal Early, CSA, attempts to head off Maj. Gen. Philip Sheridan's, USA, march to Harper's Ferry, WV.
08	18	1864	**The Battle of the Weldon Railroad** (including combats at Globe Tavern, Yellow House, and Blick's Station), VA, as Lieut. Gen. Ulysses S. Grant, USA, sends the 5th US Army Corps, under Maj. Gen. Gouverneur K. Warren, westward outside Petersburg, in an attempt to surround Gen. Robert E. Lee, CSA, in Petersburg, the Richmond, VA, Campaign. 8/18-21/1864.
08	19	1864	Federal scout for Indians on the Republican River, KS. 8/19-24/1864.
08	19	1864	Skirmish at Hurricane Creek, MS, with Maj. Gen. Joseph A. Mower, USA.
08	19	1864	Lieut. Gen. A. P. Hill, CSA, attacks the Union forces on the **Weldon Railroad,** capturing 2,500 and pushing the Federals back, but not away from the railroad, a vital Confederate link.
08	19	1864	Skirmish at Berryville, VA, with Lieut. Gen. Jubal Early, CSA, the Shenandoah Valley, VA, Campaign.
08	19	1864	Skirmish near Opequon Creek, on the Berryville and Winchester Pike, VA, with Maj. Gen. Philip H. Sheridan, USA, the Shenandoah Valley, VA, Campaign.
08	19	1864	Skirmish at Franklin, WV.
08	20	1864	Skirmish near Rocheport, MO.
08	20	1864	**The burning of Legareville, SC,** by the Federal forces, near Charleston Harbor, SC, and vicinity.
08	20	1864	Skirmish at Pine Bluff, TN, as the Confederates defeat the Federals confronting them, and are reported to have terribly mutilated some 8 Yankees by beating their heads and faces to a pulp, pumping a couple bullets in each body.
08	20	1864	Skirmish at Berryville, VA, the Shenandoah Valley, VA, Campaign.
08	20	1864	Skirmish at Opequon Creek, VA, the Shenandoah Valley, VA, Campaign.
08	20	1864	Skirmish at Bulltown, WV.
08	21	1864	**Brig. Gen. John Caldwell Calhoun Sanders, CSA,** is mortally wounded during the siege of Petersburg, VA, on the **Weldon Railroad,** bleeding to death after having both of his femoral arteries in his thighs severed by a Federal Minie ball, unable to stem to massive flow of his life blood from his body.
08	21	1864	Federal expedition in Washington and Benton Counties, AR, with skirmishes with hostile Indians and bushwackers in the vicinity of Cane Hill. 8/21-27/1864.
08	21	1864	The Skirmish at Grubb's Cross-Roads, KY.
08	21	1864	Skirmish at Diamond Grove, MO.
08	21	1864	**The Confederate attack on, and occupation of Memphis, TN,** by Maj. Gen. Nathan Bedford Forrest, CSA, as he captures about 250-100 days men.
08	21	1864	Skirmishes at Rogersville (Aug. 21st) and at Blue Springs **(Aug. 23rd),** and pursuit of the Confederates to Greeneville, TN. 8/21-23/1864.
08	21	1864	In an important move, Gen. Robert E. Lee, CSA, concedes the Weldon Railroad, a vital railroad link of Richmond and Petersburg, after Lieut. Gen. A. P. Hill's latest attack on the Federal lines fails to force the Yankees to retreat.
08	21	1864	Skirmish near Berryville, VA, the Shenandoah Valley, VA, Campaign.
08	21	1864	Skirmish in Loudoun County, near Leesville, VA, with the Federals capturing a small band of Lieut. Col. John S. Mosby's men.
08	21	1864	Skirmish at Middleway, WV, the Shenandoah Valley, VA, Campaign.
08	21	1864	Skirmish near Summit Point, WV, the Shenandoah Valley, VA, Campaign.
08	21	1864	Skirmish at Welch's (or Flowing) Spring, near Charlestown, WV, the Shenandoah Valley, VA, Campaign.
08	22	1864	**John Dunovant,** CSA, is appointed Brig. Gen.
08	22	1864	**Lucius Jeremiah Gartrell,** CSA, is appointed Brig. Gen.
08	22	1864	**Joseph Barnes,** USA, is appointed Brig. Gen.
08	22	1864	Federal scout from Helena aboard the steamers, **Dove** and **Homeyer,** up the Saint Francis River to Mount Vernon, AR. 8/22-25/1864.
08	22	1864	Skirmish in Yell County, AR.
08	22	1864	Bvt. Maj. Gen. Jefferson C. Davis, USA, assumes the command of the 14th US Army Corps, GA.
08	22	1864	Skirmishes at Canton and Roaring Spring, KY, as the Yankees rout the Rebels down the north bank of the Cumberland River.

08	22	1864	Federal operations in La Fayette County, MO, against bushwackers. 8/22-30/1864.
08	22	1864	Skirmish on the Vaughan Road, VA, the Richmond, VA, Campaign.
08	22	1864	Skirmish at Charlestown, WV, as Lieut. Gen. Jubal Early, CSA, continues to move against Maj. Gen. Philip Sheridan, USA, who has moved to the vicinity of Harpers Ferry, WV.
08	23	1864	**The Confederate surrender of Fort Morgan, Mobile Bay, AL,** leaves Wilmington, NC, as the last port open for Confederate blockade runners.
08	23	1864	Federal expedition to Clinton, LA, with skirmishes at Olive Branch and the Comite River **(August 25th),** 17 miles from Baton Rouge, LA. 8/23-29/1864.
08	23	1864	Federal expedition from Cassville, MO, to Fayetteville, AR, with skirmish at Gerald Mountain, AR. 8/23-28/1864.
08	23	1864	Federal scout from Ozark, MO, to Dubuque Crossing and Sugar Loaf Prairie. 8/23-26/1864.
08	23	1864	Affair at Webster, MO, as 50 guerrillas enter the town and plunder and rob it, before moving on.
08	23	1864	Skirmish at Abbeville, MS, as Brig. Gen. Joseph A. Mower's, USA, expedition from La Grange, TN, to Oxford, MS, draws to an end.
08	23	1864	Action on the Dinwiddie Road, near Reams' Station, VA, as the Union 5th Army Corps begins to dismantle the **Weldon Railroad,** the Richmond, VA, Campaign.
08	23	1864	Skirmish at Kearneysville, WV, the Shenandoah Valley, VA, Campaign.
08	24	1864	Action at Ashley's and Jones' (Hay) Stations, near Devall's Bluff, AR, as Brig. Gen. Joseph O. Shelby, CSA, attacks Maj. Gen. Frederick Steele's Federals, destroying telegraph lines, tearing up railroad tracks, torching hay and machinery. Steele had enough of this Rebel monkey business, and requests a Union gunboat.
08	24	1864	Skirmish on Gunter's Prairie, the Indian Territory, where the Federals kill 20 Rebels and capture 14, as well as 150 mules and horses, and burn a large quantity of hay.
08	24	1864	Skirmish at Annandale, VA, with Lieut. Col. John S. Mosby, 43rd Virginia Battalion and his Virginia Partisan Irregulars.
08	24	1864	Skirmish near Reams' Station, VA, on the **Weldon Railroad,** the Richmond, VA, Campaign.
08	24	1864	Action on the Vaughan Road, near Reams' Station, VA, the Richmond, VA, Campaign.
08	24	1864	Skirmish at Halltown, WV, the Shenandoah Valley, VA, Campaign.
08	24	1864	Affair at Huttonsville, WV.
08	24	1864	Skirmish at Sutton, WV.
08	25	1864	Skirmishes at Morgan's Ferry and on the Atchafalaya River, LA.
08	25	1864	Federal scout to Crisp's Mill, on Big Creek, MO, with skirmishes near Rose Hill. 8/25-30/1864.
08	25	1864	Federal scout in Platte County, MO. 8/25-30/1864.
08	25	1864	Federal operations on the Texas Prairie, in Jackson County, MO, against guerrillas. 8/25-30/1864
08	25	1864	Federal scouts in Jackson and Cass Counties, MO, with skirmish near Pleasant Hill **(26th)** with bushwackers. 8/25-29/1864.
08	25	1864	The **CSS Tallahassee,** refueling in Nova Scotia, and after three weeks at sea and capturing 31 Union vessels, slips through the blockade at Wilmington, NC, ending her short lived but illustrious career.
08	25	1864	**The Battle of Reams' Station, on the Weldon Railroad, VA,** as Lieut. Gen. Ambrose P. Hill, CSA, attacks the 2nd US Army Corps under Maj. Gen. Winfield Scott Hancock, USA, who are in the process of destroying the **Weldon Railroad.** Hill retreats back to Petersburg, VA. Total casualties approximate 3,100, the Richmond, VA, Campaign.
08	25	1864	Skirmish at Halltown, WV, as Lieut. Gen. Jubal Early, CSA, threatens to invade the north again.
08	25	1864	Action near Kearneysville, WV, the Shenandoah Valley, VA, Campaign.
08	25	1864	Action near Shepherdstown, WV, the Shenandoah Valley, VA, Campaign.
08	26	1864	Federal operations at the **Chattahoochee railroad bridge** and at Pace's and Turner's Ferries, GA, with skirmishes, as Maj. Gen. James Schofield, USA, part of Maj. Gen. William T. Sherman's, USA, command attempt to surround Lieut. Gen. John Bell Hood, CSA, around Atlanta, GA. 8/26-9/1/1864.
08	26	1864	Skirmish near Bayou Tensas (26th), and expedition from Goodrich's Landing to Bayou Macon, LA. **(28th-31st).** 8/26-31/1864.
08	26	1864	Affair at Williamsport, MD, as Lieut. Gen. Jubal Early, CSA, crosses back into Maryland.
08	26	1864	Skirmish near Charlestown, WV, the Shenandoah Valley, VA, Campaign.
08	26	1864	Action at Halltown, WV, the Shenandoah Valley, VA, Campaign.
08	27	1864	Federal scout 30 miles down the Arkansas River, near Pine Bluff, AR, with skirmishes. 8/27-28/1864.

08	27	1864	Federal scout 30 miles down the Arkansas River, near Pine Bluff, AR, with skirmishes. 8/27-28/1864.
08	27	1864	Skirmish at Fayetteville, AR.
08	27	1864	Federal expeditions from Little Rock and Devall's Bluff to Searcy, Fairview, and Augusta, AR. 8/27-9/6/1864.
08	27	1864	Maj. Gen. Henry W. Slocum, USA, assumes the command of the 20th US Army Corps, GA.
08	27	1864	Federal expedition against the **Oywhee Indians** from Fort Boise to Salmon Falls, the Idaho Territory, with skirmishes. These Indians normally moved to the Upper Owyhee River this time of year to hunt and fish, but have sought the Snake River instead to avoid Federal cavalry movements, but to no avail as the Federals track them down. 8/27-10/5/1864.
08	27	1864	Skirmish at Owensborough, KY.
08	27	1864	Maj. Gen. Edward O. C. Ord, USA, is temporarily in command of the Army of the James, the Richmond, VA, Campaign.
08	27	1864	Skirmish at Duffield's Station, WV, the Shenandoah Valley, VA, Campaign.
08	27	1864	Skirmish at Nutter's Hill, WV, the Shenandoah Valley, VA, Campaign.
08	28	1864	**Walter Husted Stevens,** CSA, is appointed Brig. Gen.
08	28	1864	Skirmish at Fayetteville, AR.
08	28	1864	Affair near Holly Springs, MS.
08	28	1864	Skirmish in Polk County, MO, in the vicinity of Jacksonport.
08	28	1864	Skirmish near Rocheport, MO, with Maj. Gen. Alfred Pleasonton, USA.
08	28	1864	Skirmishes at Leetown and Smithfield, WV, as Maj. Gen. Philip H. Sheridan, USA, marches towards Charles Town, WV.
08	29	1864	**Maj. Gen. Sterling Price's, CSA, Missouri Expedition,** in a futile attempt to retake Missouri for the Confederacy. 8/29-12/2/1864.
08	29	1864	Maj. Gen. Sterling Price, CSA, assumes the command of the expeditionary forces at Princeton, AR.
08	29	1864	Federal expedition up White River from Helena, AR, with affair **(Sept. 3rd)** at Kendal's Grist-Mill, AR. 8/29-9/3/1864.
08	29	1864	Skirmish at Milton, FL, as the Federals travel from Barrancas aboard the steamers, **Clinton** and **Planter,** to confront the Confederate Cavalry at Milton.
08	29	1864	Skirmish near Red Oak, GA, as Maj. Gen. William T. Sherman, USA, prepares to tighten the noose on Atlanta, GA, and Lieut. Gen. John Bell Hood, CSA.
08	29	1864	Skirmish near Ghent, KY.
08	29	1864	The attack on the Federal steamer, **White Cloud,** on the Mississippi River, near Port Hudson, LA, partly disabling her, while the **Henry Choteau** escapes major damage further up the river.
08	29	1864	Operations in East Tennessee, including skirmishes at Park's Gap and at Greeneville, **(Sept. 4th),** and the **death of Brig. Gen. John H. Morgan,** CSA. 8/29-9/4/1864.
08	29	1864	Skirmish at Charlestown, WV, the Shenandoah Valley, VA, Campaign.
08	29	1864	Engagement at Smithfield Crossing of the Opequon, WV, with Maj. Gen. Philip Sheridan, USA, defeating Lieut. Gen. Jubal A. Early, CSA.
08	30	1864	Skirmish near Dardanelle, AR, where the Yankees rout the Rebels, the Rebs making good their escape by swimming Betty's Mill Creek.
08	30	1864	Skirmish near East Point, GA, as the Federals **capture the West Point-Atlanta Railroad,** leaving only the **Macon Railroad** line open into Atlanta, GA.
08	30	1864	Action at Flint River Bridge, GA.
08	30	1864	The **Democratic National Convention** meeting in Chicago, IL, **nominates Maj. Gen. George B. McClellan** as their candidate for the Presidency in the upcoming election, who is running on a peace platform.
08	30	1864	Federal expedition to Natchez Bayou, LA, with skirmish near Gentilly's Plantation, near Bay Natchez, which is below Lake Natchez. **(Sept. 1st),** as the Confederates surprise and capture some of the Yankee Cavalry. 8/30-9/2/1864.
08	30	1864	**Brig. Gen. George Crook, USA, is assigned to the command of the the Dept. of West Virginia,** vice Maj. Gen. David Hunter, USA, is relieved.
08	30	1864	Skirmish near Smithfield, WV, the Shenandoah Valley, Campaign.
08	31	1864	**The Battle of Jonesborough, GA,** where Lieut. Gen. William Hardee, CSA, under Lieut. Gen. John Bell Hood, CSA, is repulsed by Maj. Gen. Oliver O. Howard, USA. 8/31-9/1/1864.
08	31	1864	Skirmish near **Rough and Ready Station, GA,** as Maj. Gen. James Schofield's, USA, Army of the Ohio,

			capture the final railroad line, the **Macon Railroad,** into Atlanta, leaving Hood with the inevitable of evacuating Atlanta.
08	31	1864	Affair at **Steelville, MO,** as a gang of bushwackers **capture** and plunder the town, killing militia men and citizens who tried to obstruct them.
08	31	1864	Skirmish at Clifton, TN.
08	31	1864	Skirmish near the Davis House, the Richmond, VA, Campaign.
08	31	1864	Skirmish at Martinsburg, WV, the Shenandoah Valley, Campaign.
09	1	1864	**Giles Alexander Smith, U.S.A.,** is appointed Maj. Gen.
09	1	1864	Skirmish near Beatty's Mill, AR, with a large force of bushwackers. Interestingly, the Federals capture a lot of Spanish brown, which the bushwackers were using to disguise themselves as Indians.
09	1	1864	Skirmish at Fort Smith, AR.
09	1	1864	Federal scout against Indians from Camp Grant to the North Fork of the Eel River, CA. 9/1-29/1864.
09	1	1864	Federal operations in the Trinity River Valley, CA, against Indians committing deprivations on ranchers and settlers in this vicinity. 9/1-12/3/1864.
09	1	1864	**The Confederate Army of Tennessee evacuates Atlanta, GA,** as Lieut. Gen. John Bell Hood, CSA, burns the huge munitions and supply depots, creating fires that burn out of control, burning much of the railroad yards, as he leaves the city. A "Gone with the Wind" scene.
09	1	1864	Federal operations in Johnson County, MO, with skirmish (1st) near Lone Jack, as once again the Yankee attacks exert a deadly toll on guerrillas. 9/1-9/1864.
09	1	1864	The Confederate attack on, and **capture of, Tipton, MO,** then fleeing toward Boonville.
09	1	1864	Skirmish at Opequon Creek, WV, the Shenandoah Valley, Campaign.
09	2	1864	**Brig. Gen. John Herbert Kelly, CSA,** is mortally wounded at the Battle of Franklin, TN, dying 2 days later on 9/41864.
09	2	1864	Skirmish at the Tannery, near Little Rock, AR, where the Confederate attack on the tannery is repulsed with losses.
09	2	1864	Skirmish 8 miles from Quitman, AR.
09	2	1864	**The Union forces under Maj. Gen. William Tecumseh Sherman, USA, occupy Atlanta, GA.**
09	2	1864	Actions at Lovejoy's Station, southeast of Atlanta, GA, as Lieut. Gen. John Bell Hood, regroups his remaining forces which have been decimated and weakened by all the losses sustained in the recent fighting and attacks on Union positions in front of Atlanta. 9/2-5/1864
09	2	1864	Guerrilla raid on Owensborough, KY, who are reported to have murdered 3 Union soldiers and 1 civilian after they surrendered.
09	2	1864	Federal scouts on the Little Blue River, in Jackson County, MO, where bushwackers try to surprise the Federals by stringing wire across the road between two trees which the Yankee horses ran into. 9/2-10/1864.
09	2	1864	Skirmish near Mount Vernon, MO, with Union cavalry.
09	2	1864	Federal expedition from Sedalia, MO, to Scott's Ford, on the Blackwater, patrolling for Confederates. 9/2-4/1864.
09	2	1864	Skirmishes at and near Union City, TN.
09	2	1864	Federal scout from Whiteside's, TN, to Sulphur Springs, GA. 9/2-5/1864 .
09	2	1864	Federal reconnaissance beyond Yellow Tavern, on the **Weldon Railroad,** south of Petersburg, VA, the Richmond, VA, Campaign.
09	2	1864	Action at Bunker Hill, WV, the Shenandoah Valley, Campaign.
09	2	1864	Skirmish at Darkesville, WV, the Shenandoah Valley, Campaign.
09	3	1864	**Thomas Wilberforce Egan,** USA, is appointed Brig. Gen.
09	3	1864	Skirmish in Sibley County, KY.
09	3	1864	Skirmishes near Rocheport, MO, as the Federals are constantly fighting with guerrillas, the Yankees reporting that Boone and Howard are swarming with guerrillas.
09	3	1864	**The Engagement near Berryville, VA,** where Maj. Gen. Philip H. Sheridan, USA, compels the Confederates under Lieut. Gen. Richard H. Anderson, CSA, to retreat toward Winchester, VA, as his army corps was enroute under order to join the Confederate lines at Petersburg, VA, under Gen. Robert E. Lee.
09	3	1864	Affair near Sycamore Church, near Richmond, VA, the Richmond, VA, Campaign.
09	3	1864	Action at Bunker Hill, WV, the Shenandoah Valley, Campaign.

MONTH	DAY	YEAR	ACT
09	4	1864	**Brig. Gen. John Hunt Morgan, CSA,** is mortally wounded near Knoxville, TN, killed by a Federal detachment and shot by Private Andrew Campbell, of Company C, 13th TN Cavalry, in the garden of the house he had slept at the night before. John was best known for his calvary jaunts into the north, as another legend's part in the Civil War comes to an end. Many had already come to an end. More were yet to come.
09	4	1864	Skirmish at Brownsville, AR.
09	4	1864	The Confederate attack on the Federal steamers, **Celeste** and **Commercial,** at Gregory's Landing, on the White River, AR, is unable to capture or damage the vessels, but inflicting human casualties just the same.
09	4	1864	Affair 9 miles above Donaldsonville, LA, as the Rebels attack Federal couriers coming from Plaquemine to Donaldsonville.
09	4	1864	After two straight months, the Yankees end their **3rd massive bombardment of Fort Sumter, Charleston Harbor, SC,** without the fort succumbing, after almost 15,000 shells fired into the fort.
09	4	1864	Skirmish at Berryville, VA, as Lieut. Gen. Jubal Early, CSA, pulls his forces back up the Shenandoah Valley, with Maj. Gen. Philip Sheridan, USA, in hot pursuit.
09	4	1864	Maj. Gen. John Gibbon, USA, is in temporary command of the 18th US Army Corps, the Petersburg, VA, siege lines, the Richmond, VA, Campaign.
09	5	1864	Skirmish near Stephenson's Depot, north of Winchester, VA, on the Opequon river, with Early and Sheridan exchanging punches.
09	5	1864	Federal reconnaissance to Sycamore Church, outside Richmond, the Richmond, VA, Campaign.
09	5	1864	Maj. Gen. David B. Birney, USA, is in temporary command of the Army of the James, the Richmond, VA, Campaign.
09	6	1864	**Lieut. Gen. Richard Taylor, CSA, assumes the command of the Dept. of Alabama, Mississippi, and East Louisiana.**
09	6	1864	Operations in the vicinity of Lewisburg, AR, with skirmishes a) at Norristown (Sept. 6th) and b) near Glass Village **(Sept. 8th)**. 9/6-8/1864.
09	6	1864	Federal scout from Little Rock to Benton, AR, as the Yankees chase the Rebels out of Benton, fleeing across the Saline River. The Yankees report that the main body of Confederates under Maj. Gen. Sterling Price, CSA, has retired to Arkadelphia. 9/6-7/1864.
09	6	1864	Skirmish at Richland, AR.
09	6	1864	Skirmish at Searcy, AR.
09	6	1864	Federal expedition from Morganza to Bayou Sara, LA, with no engagements. 9/6-7/1864.
09	6	1864	Skirmish near the Eight-Mile Post, on the Natchez and Liberty Road, MS.
09	6	1864	Federal scouts in Boone and Howard Counties, MO, with skirmishes in Boone County, **(Sept. 7th and 8th)**. 9/6-12/1864.
09	6	1864	Affair near Brunswick, MO, where a band of Yankees are captured by guerrillas, stripped and robbed, but fortunately not of their lives.
09	6	1864	Federal forces begin another bombardment of Fort Sumter, Charleston Harbor, SC. 9/6-14/1864.
09	6	1864	Skirmish at Readyville, Stone's River, TN, as the defeated Confederates are pursued to Woodbury, 5 miles away, losing 130 men captured and over 200 horses.
09	6	1864	Skirmish at the Palmetto Ranch, near Brazos Santiago, TX, with the 1st Texas Cavalry.
09	7	1864	Under protest from Lieut. Gen. John B. Hood, CSA, Maj. Gen. William T. Sherman, USA, orders the **civilian evacuation of Atlanta, GA,** citing his lack of supplies to feed the population. This will create much hardship on the civilian population who is forced to leave behind most of their worldly possessions.
09	7	1864	Federal expeditions to Grand Lake, Grand River, Lake Fausse Pointe, Bayou Pigeon, and Lake Natchez, LA, under Brig. Gen. Robert A. Cameron, USA, commanding the District of La Fourche, with affair at Labadieville, **(Sept. 8th)**. 9/7-11/1864.
09	7	1864	Affair at Centralia, MO, where guerrillas stopped a freight train on the **North Missouri Railroad,** stealing 4 car-loads of horses therefrom.
09	7	1864	Skirmishes near Brucetown and near Winchester, VA, the Shenandoah Valley, Campaign.
09	7	1864	**Maj. Gen. Benjamin F. Butler, USA, resumes the command of the Army of the James,** the Richmond, VA, Campaign.
09	8	1864	The destruction of over 50 Confederate boats at Salt House Point, Mobile Bay, AL, by the Federals.

			Richmond, VA, Campaign.
09	8	1864	The destruction of over 50 Confederate boats at Salt House Point, Mobile Bay, AL, by the Federals.
09	8	1864	Skirmishes 4 miles below Hornersville and Gayoso, MO, as the Federals continue to deal out death to guerrillas they happen across.
09	8	1864	**Maj. Gen. George B. McClellan, USA, accepts the Democratic nomination for President** of the U.S.A., at Orange, NJ.
09	9	1864	Federal expeditions from Mobile Bay to Bonsecours and Fish Rivers, AL, and the destruction of the immense salt-works at Bonsecours, and the barracks at Camp Anderson. 9/9-11/1864.
09	9	1864	The Confederate rifle attack on the Federal steamer, **J.D. Perry,** just below Clarendon, AR, with little damage done.
09	9	1864	Federal scout of the **60th US Colored Infantry,** from Helena to Alligator Bayou, AR. 9/9-14/1864.
09	9	1864	Federal scout from Lewisburg to Norristown and Russellville, AR, with skirmishes with guerrillas. 9/9-12/1864.
09	9	1864	Federal expedition from Pine Bluff toward Monticello, AR, with skirmishes near: a) Monticello **(Sept. 10th)** and b) at Brewer's Lane **(Sept. 11th)**. 9/9-11/1864.
09	9	1864	Federal expedition from Fort Pike, LA, aboard the steamer, **J.D. Swain,** up the Pearl River, to Deer Island Landing. 9/9-12/1864.
09	9	1864	Affair on the Warrensburg road, near Warrensburg, MO, as the Federals happen upon 4 guerrillas robbing the Warrensburg mail. The guerrillas escape, although one may be wounded.
09	9	1864	The Confederate capture and burning of the mail steamer, **Fawn,** and skirmish at Currituck Bridge, VA. The Federals find the body of a man belonging to the 23rd MA Volunteers, another seriously wounded, and the burned out shell of the vessel; the rest of the command missing, captured by the Rebels. The Federals quickly move to reopen this route.
09	10	1864	Affair at Campbellton, GA, as the attacking Confederates capture the 60 man strong Union foraging party, along with their wagons.
09	10	1864	Operations in East Louisiana, including skirmishes: a) at Leesburg **(Sept. 28th)** and b) at Duvall's Ford, **(Sept. 30th)**. 9/10-10/13/1864.
09	10	1864	Skirmish near Dover, MO.
09	10	1864	Skirmish 5 miles northeast of Pisgah, Cooper County, MO.
09	10	1864	Skirmish just east of Roanoke, in Howard County, MO, as the Federals rout Brig. Gen. James T. Holtzclaw's, CSA, men.
09	10	1864	Skirmish at Woodbury, TN.
09	10	1864	The assault on the Confederate works at the Chimneys, the Richmond, VA, Campaign.
09	10	1864	Skirmish at Darkesville, WV, the Shenandoah Valley, Campaign.
09	11	1864	Skirmish near Fort Smith, AR.
09	11	1864	Federal expedition from Fort Rice, the Dakota Territory, to relieve Capt. Fisk's emigrant train. Upon arriving at their assistance, the Yankees find the emigrants in a fortified position, refusing to go any further into the **Bad Lands** without proper protection; Capt. Fisk urging them on; the Federals ready to censure Fish for his stupidity in trying to make the emigrants move out into danger without proper protection. On the way back to Fort Rice, the Federals have some 30 horses stolen by Indians. Even the soldiers aren't safe, let along unprotected emigrants. 9/11-30/1864.
09	11	1864	Operations in the **Cherokee Nation,** the Indian Territory, with actions at Hay Station, near Fort Gibson **(Sept. 16th),** and at Cabin Creek and Pryor's Creek, **(Sept. 19th),** as Maj. Gen. George Sykes, USA, commanding the District of South Kansas reports the Union debacle at Cabin Creek where the Confederates capture over 300 wagons as well as the same in men. 9/11-25/1864.
09	11	1864	Skirmish at Hodge's Plantation, LA, where yet another Rebel attack is repelled.
09	11	1864	Federal scouts in Moniteau and Morgan Counties, MO. 9/11-18/1864.
09	11	1864	Federal operations against guerrillas in Monroe and Ralls Counties, MO. 9/11-16/1864.
09	12	1864	**Brig. Gen. Joshua Blackwood Howell, USA,** is critically wounded near Petersburg, VA, where he suffers a fall from his horse, dying two days later on Sept. 14, 1864.
09	12	1864	**Alexander Brydie Dyer,** USA, is appointed Brig. Gen.
09	12	1864	**Joshua Blackwood Howell,** USA, is appointed Brig. Gen.

			at Iron Mountain, as well as destroying the telegraph office, etc.
09	12	1864	Skirmish near Memphis, TN.
09	12	1864	President Abraham Lincoln notifies Lieut. Gen. Ulysses S. Grant of his dismay over Maj. Gen. Philip H. Sheridan's lack of progress in the Shenandoah Valley.
09	13	1864	**Joseph Roswell Hawley,** USA, is appointed Brig. Gen.
09	13	1864	**William Henry Seward, Jr.,** USA, is appointed Brig. Gen.
09	13	1864	Skirmish near Searcy, AR, as the Rebels attack and wound every Yankee sent out with dispatches. (4)
09	13	1864	Federal expedition from Morganza to Fausse River, LA, with skirmishes:

09 13 1864   Federal expedition from Morganza to Fausse River, LA, with skirmishes:
a) near Bayou Maringouin   (13th)
b) near Rosedale   **(15th)** and
c) near Bayou Maringouin   **(16th)**. 9/13-17/1864.

09	13	1864	Skirmish at Longwood, MO, with guerrillas.
09	13	1864	Skirmish at Abraham's Creek, near Winchester, VA, as Early and Sheridan continue to spar here as well as at the following:
09	13	1864	Affair near Berryville, VA.
09	13	1864	Skirmish at Gilbert's Ford, Opequon Creek, VA.
09	13	1864	Affair at Locke's Ford, Opequon Creek, VA.
09	13	1864	Federal scout to Poplar Spring Church, VA, the Richmond, VA, Campaign.
09	13	1864	Skirmish at Bunker Hill, WV.
09	14	1864	**Brig. Gen. Joshua Blackwood Howell, USA,** dies near Petersburg, VA, from injuries suffered on September 12, 1864, when he fell off his horse, being promoted to Brig. Gen. the day of his injury.
09	14	1864	Affair near Weston, KY, as the Confederate guerrillas shoot and kill the Federals protecting the steamer, **Colossus,** as they make off with the vessel.
09	14	1864	Skirmish at Bullitt's Bayou, LA, where the Rebels attack the Union pickets along the river-bank by sneaking up through the brush.
09	14	1864	Federal scout in Texas County, MO, with skirmish at Thomasville, MO. **(Sept. 18th)**. 9/14-21/1864.
09	14	1864	Skirmish near Berryville, VA, as Lieut. Gen. Richard H. Anderson, CSA, and his army corps again leaves for the Petersburg, VA, siege lines, depleting Lieut. Gen. Jubal Early, CSA, of much needed men. Gen. Robert E. Lee, CSA, is facing the same situation as Lieut. Gen. Ulysses S. Grant, USA, is extending his Union siege lines around Petersburg, VA.
09	14	1864	Skirmish near Centerville, WV, where the Federals overtake and kill some of the party of 30 horse thieves.
09	15	1864	**Basil Wilson Duke,** CSA, is appointed Brig. Gen.
09	15	1864	Skirmish in Lumpkin County, GA.
09	15	1864	Skirmish at Snake Creek Gap, GA.
09	15	1864	Federal operations in Randolph, Howard, and Boone Counties, MO, with skirmishes at Columbia **(Sept. 16th)**. 9/15-19/1864.
09	15	1864	Federal reconnaissance toward Dinwiddie Court-House, and skirmish, Richmond, VA, Campaign.
09	15	1864	Skirmish at Seivers' Ford, Opequon Creek, VA, the Shenandoah Valley, Campaign.
09	16	1864	Federal operations under Brig. Gen. Michael K. Lawler, USA, in the vicinity of Morganza, LA, with skirmishes:

09 16 1864   Federal operations under Brig. Gen. Michael K. Lawler, USA, in the vicinity of Morganza, LA, with skirmishes:
a) at Williamsport   (Sept. 16th)
b) at the Atchafalaya River   **(Sept. 17th)** and
c) at Bayou Alabama and Morgan's Ferry   **(Sept. 20th)**. 9/16-25/1864.

09	16	1864	**Maj. Gen. Nathan Bedford Forrest's, CSA, Cavalry Raid into Northern Alabama and Middle Tennessee,** to cut the supply and communication lines of Maj. Gen. William T. Sheman, USA. 9/16-10/10/1864.
09	16	1864	Maj. Gen. Nathan Bedford Forrest, CSA, sets out from Verona, MS.
09	16	1864	The affair at Coggins' Point (16th) and the pursuit of the Confederates, the Richmond, VA, Campaign. 9/16-17/1864.
09	16	1864	Skirmishes at Snicker's Gap, VA, the Shenandoah Valley, Campaign. 9/16-17/1864.
09	16	1864	Lieut. Gen. Ulysses S. Grant, USA, travels to Charles Town, WV, to meet with Maj. Gen. William T. Sherman, USA, to discuss a Union offensive against Lieut. Gen. Jubal Early, CSA, whose army has been depleted with the reinforcement of Gen. Robert E. Lee, CSA, at Petersburg, VA.
09	17	1864	**Charles Miller Shelley,** CSA, is appointed Brig. Gen.

09	17	1864	Affair at Limestone Ridge, VA, the Shenandoah Valley, Campaign.
09	17	1864	Lieut. Col. Vincent A. Witcher's, CSA, Confederate expedition into West Virginia, including skirmishes at Buckhannon, as he visits Bulltown, Jacksonville, Westover, Buckhannon, Walkersville and Weston, destroying $1,000,000 worth of stores, capturing 300 prisoners, and much needed 500 horses and 200 beef-cattle for the ragged Army of Northern Virginia. **(Sept. 27th-28th).** 8/17-28/1864.
09	18	1864	Federal expedition from Barrancas to Marianna, FL, including affair: a) at Euchee Anna Court-House **(Sept. 23rd)** and b) action at Marianna. **(Sept. 27th).** 9/18-10/4/1864.
09	18	1864	Skirmish 7 miles from Lexington, MO, in Ray County, as the Confederate guerrillas attack the state militia camp there.
09	18	1864	Federal scout against Indians on the Cimarron River, in Northeastern New Mexico Territory. The Federals believe the deprivations committed in this area is the work of the **Kiowas** and **Commanches.** 9/18-10/5/1864.
09	18	1864	The affair near Martinsburg, WV, as Lieut. Gen. Jubal Early, CSA, moves from the vicinity of Winchester, VA, against the **Baltimore and Ohio Railroad,** near Martinsburg, WV, with a force of 12,000 against Maj. Gen. Philip H. Sheridan's force, USA, of 40,000.
09	19	1864	**Matthew Calbraith Butler, C.S.A.,** is appointed Maj. Gen.
09	19	1864	**James Lawson Kemper, C.S.A.,** is appointed Maj. Gen.
09	19	1864	Federal expeditions from Natchez to Buck's Ferry (19th-**21st**) and Farrar's Plantation, MS, and skirmishes en route. 9/19-22/1864.
09	19	1864	Maj. Gen. Sterling Price's, CSA, Confederate Cavalry column of 12,000 **enters Missouri from Arkansas,** the **last major Confederate** thrust to take control of Missouri.
09	19	1864	Affair at Doniphan, MO, with Maj. Gen. Sterling Price, CSA.
09	19	1864	Two Confederates, Capt. John Yates Beall, CSN, and Capt. John H. Cole, CSA, plan to capture Union vessels, sail to Johnson's Island, and release the Confederate prisoners there, near Sandusky, OH. Beall captures the Federal steamer, **Philo Parons** on Lake Erie, then captures and burns the **Island Queen.** Cole fails to capture the **Michigan,** forcing Beall to burn the **Philo Parsons** at Sandwich, Canada, and abandon their plans.
09	19	1864	Skirmish at Culpeper, VA.
09	19	1864	Federal scout to Lee's Mill and Proctor's House, Richmond, VA. Campaign. 9/16-17/1864.
09	19	1864	**The Battle of Winchester (or the Opeguon), VA,** as Maj. Gen. Philip H. Sheridan, USA, makes good on his plan to attack Lieut. Gen. Jubal Early, CSA, and his depleted force of 12,000, with fighting taking place along the Opequon River, Martinsburg Pike, Stevensburg Depot, Berryville Pike, etc. Total casualties approximate 7,950. Early is shaken.
09	19	1864	**Brig. Gen. Archibald Campbell Godwin, CSA,** is mortally wounded at the Battle of Winchester, VA, instantly killed by a Federal artillery shell fragment.
09	19	1864	**Brig. Gen. Robert Emmett Rodes, CSA,** is mortally wounded at the Battle of Winchester, VA, while leading his men in a counterattack against the Federal lines.
09	19	1864	**Brig. Gen. David Allen Russell, USA,** is mortally wounded at the Battle of Winchester, VA, instantly killed by a Confederate artillery shell fragment through his heart, while at the head of his command.
09	20	1864	<u>**Simon Bolivar Buckner, C.S.A., is appointed Lieut. Gen.**</u>
09	20	1864	The following are appointed Confederate Brigadier Generals: **Edwin Gray Lee,** CSA **Patrick Theodore Moore,** CSA **William Henry Wallace,** CSA
09	20	1864	Skirmish at Cartersville, GA.
09	20	1864	Federal raids from Kentucky and East Tennessee into Southwestern Virginia, by Bvt. Maj. Gen. Stephen G. Burbridge, USA, against Maj. Gen. John C. Breckinridge, CSA, commanding the Dept. of Western Virginia and East Tennessee. 9/20-10/17/1864.
09	20	1864	Skirmish at McCormick's Gap, KY.
09	20	1864	The Union **surrender of Keytesville, MO,** as Maj. Gen. Sterling Price, CSA, presses on to relieve pressure from Union advances in the south.
09	20	1864	Federal scout in La Fayette County, MO, with skirmish on the Arrow Rock Road with guerrillas **(Sept. 23rd).** 9/20-25/1864.
09	20	1864	Skirmish at Ponder's Mill, Little Black River, MO, with Maj. Gen. Sterling Price, CSA.

pressure from Union advances in the south.

09	20	1864	Federal scout in La Fayette County, MO, with skirmish on the Arrow Rock Road with guerrillas **(Sept. 23rd)**. 9/20-25/1864.
09	20	1864	Skirmish at Ponder's Mill, Little Black River, MO, with Maj. Gen. Sterling Price, CSA.
09	20	1864	Skirmish near Cedarville, VA, as Union cavalry pursue the fleeing Confederates under Lieut. Gen. Jubal Early, CSA.
09	20	1864	Skirmish at Middletown, VA, the Shenandoah Valley, Campaign.
09	20	1864	Skirmish at Strasburg, VA, the Shenandoah Valley, Campaign.
09	21	1864	Affair near Council Grove, KS, as two normally peaceful, but drunk, Indians pull knives on some Union men, swearing they will kill them unless they give them some whiskey. One of the Union men picks up a rifle and bayonets one of the Indians. Men in those days had a different way of settling disputes or threats. Also, it was Indians pulling the knifes, which justified the whiteman's actions.
09	21	1864	Federal expeditions from Vicksburg to Deer Creek, MS, and skirmishes near Rolling Fork. **(22nd-23rd)**. 9/21-26/1864.
09	21	1864	Maj. Gen. Nathan Bedford Forrest, CSA, crosses the Tennessee River, TN, and moves on Athens.
09	21	1864	Maj. Gen. Philip H. Sheridan, USA, is assigned to the permanent command of the Middle Military Division, VA.
09	21	1864	Skirmish at Fisher's Hill, VA, as both Lieut. Gen. Jubal A. Early, CSA, and Maj. Gen. Philip H. Sheridan, USA, dig in.
09	21	1864	Skirmish at Front Royal, VA, the Shenandoah Valley, Campaign.
09	21	1864	Skirmish at Strasburg, VA, the Shenandoah Valley, Campaign.
09	22	1864	Federal scout from Helena to Alligator Bayou, AR. 9/22-28/1864.
09	22	1864	Skirmish at **Carthage, MO,** as guerrillas **capture** the town, then **burn** it to the ground.
09	22	1864	Skirmish 6 miles north of Longwood, MO, with guerrillas.
09	22	1864	Affair at Patterson, MO, with Maj. Gen. Sterling Price, CSA.
09	22	1864	Skirmish near Sikeston, MO, with Maj. Gen. Sterling Price.
09	22	1864	**The Battle of Fisher's Hill, VA,** as Maj. Gen. Philip H. Sheridan, USA, inflicts serious damage to Lieut. Gen. Jubal Early's, CSA, forces of the Shenandoah, as Maj. Gen. George Crook, USA, flanks Early and causes a panic and rout as Early's men flee up the Shenandoah. Total casualties approximate 1,750.
09	22	1864	Skirmish at Milford, VA, the Shenandoah Valley, Campaign.
09	22	1864	Maj. Gen. Edward O.C. Ord, USA, resumes command of the 18th Army Corps, the Richmond, VA Campaign.
09	23	1864	Skirmish at Athens, AL, with Maj. Gen. Nathan Bedford Forrest, CSA.
09	23	1864	Affair near Fort Smith, AR.
09	23	1864	Skirmishes near Rocheport, MO, with Maj. Gen. Sterling Price, CSA.
09	23	1864	Maj. Gen. Stephen A. Hurlbut, USA, assumes the command of the Dept. of the Gulf, MO, etal.
09	23	1864	Skirmish at Edenburg, VA, as small parcels of the armies under Early and Sheridan toss bullets back and forth here and the following during the Shenandoah Valley, Campaign
09	23	1864	Skirmish at Front Royal, VA.
09	23	1864	Skirmish at Mount Jackson, VA.
09	23	1864	Skirmish at Woodstock, VA.
09	23	1864	Maj. James H. Nounnan's Federal expedition into the Kanawha Valley, WV, including skirmish at Coalsmouth, **(Sept. 30th)**. 9/23-10/1/1864.
09	24	1864	**Isaac Hardin Duval,** USA, is appointed Brig. Gen.
09	24	1864	**John Edwards,** USA, is appointed Brig. Gen.
09	24	1864	The action at and **surrender of Athens, AL,** to Maj. Gen. Nathan Bedford Forrest, CSA, and his cavalry.
09	24	1864	Skirmish at Magnolia, FL.
09	24	1864	Skirmish at Farmington, MO, with Maj. Gen. Sterling Price.
09	24	1864	Confederate attack on Fayette, MO, by Maj. Gen. Sterling Price, CSA.
09	24	1864	Skirmish at Jackson, MO, with Maj. Gen. Sterling Price, CSA.
09	24	1864	Skirmish at Forest Hill (or Timberville), VA, as the Shenandoah Valley, Campaign continues to be fought here and at the following locations today:
09	24	1864	Skirmish at Luray, VA.
09	24	1864	Skirmish at Mount Jackson, VA.

Confederate Army will come from the Shenandoah Valley.

09	25	1864	Federal expedition from Little Rock to Fort Smith, AR, with skirmishes: a) at Clarksville, **(Sept. 28th)** b) White Oak Creek **(Sept. 29th)** c) at Clarksville **(Oct. 9th)**. 9/25-10/13/1864.
09	25	1864	The action at and the **surrender of Sulphur Branch Trestle, AL,** to Maj. Gen. Nathan Bedford Forrest, CSA.
09	25	1864	Skirmish near Henderson, KY.
09	25	1864	Skirmish at Walnut Creek, KS, where Maj. Gen. James G. Blunt, USA commanding the District of Upper Kansas, reports a large group of hostile Indians not less than 4,000, 1,500 of whom at least are warriors of the **Cheyenne** and **Arapahoe Indian Nations,** are moving upon the Sante Fe road, possibly on the warpath against frontier settlements.
09	25	1864	Skirmish at Farmington, MO, with Maj. Gen. Sterling Price, CSA.
09	25	1864	Affair at Huntsville, MO, with Maj. Gen. Sterling Price, CSA.
09	25	1864	Skirmish near Johnsonville, TN.
09	26	1864	Skirmish at Vache Grass, AR.
09	26	1864	Skirmish near Roswell, GA.
09	26	1864	Skirmish at Osage Mission, KS.
09	26	1864	Federal expedition from Napoleonville to Grand River and Bayou Pigeon, LA. 9/26-30/1864.
09	26	1864	Federal expedition from Natchez, MS, to Waterproof and Sicily Island, LA. 9/26-10/30/1864.
09	26	1864	Skirmishes in Arcadia Valley, Shut-in Gap, and Ironton, MO, as Maj. Gen. Sterling Price, CSA, heads towards St. Louis, MO.
09	26	1864	Skirmish at Richland Creek, near Pulaski, TN, with Maj. Gen. Nathan Bedford Forrest, CSA.
09	26	1864	Skirmish at Brown's Gap, VA, as the Shenandoah Valley's skies are darkened with the black smoke of burning barns, fields, and houses, by the torches of Maj. Gen. Philip Henry Sheridan, including the following:
09	26	1864	Skirmish at Port Republic, VA.
09	26	1864	Skirmish at Weyer's Cave, VA.
09	27	1864	Skirmishes at Arcadia and Ironton, MO, with Maj. Gen. Sterling Price, CSA.
09	27	1864	Affair at **Centralia, MO,** where a band of Confederate guerrillas, under **Bloody Bill Anderson,** which included **Frank** and **Jesse James,** sack and **burn the town**, massacring over 20 unarmed Union soldiers as they are arriving aboard a train. Later, the Federals are ambushed and 116 more Yankees are killed in a tragic loss of life.
09	27	1864	The Confederate attack on Fort Davidson, Pilot Knob, MO, by Maj. Gen. Sterling Price, CSA.
09	27	1864	Skirmish at Mineral Point, MO, with Maj. Gen. Sterling Price, CSA.
09	27	1864	Skirmishes at Lobelville and Beardstown, TN.
09	27	1864	Skirmish at Pulaski, TN, with Maj. Gen. Nathan Forrest, CSA.
09	27	1864	Skirmish at Port Republic, VA, the Shenandoah Valley, Campaign.
09	27	1864	Skirmish at Weyer's Cave, VA, the Shenandoah Valley, Campaign.
09	28	1864	Skirmish near Decatur, GA, 5 miles out on the Decatur Road.
09	28	1864	Skirmish at Brownsville, MS.
09	28	1864	Skirmish at Caledonia, MO, with Maj. Gen. Sterling Price, CSA.
09	28	1864	Skirmish near Centralia, MO, with Maj. Gen. Sterling Price, CSA.
09	28	1864	Skirmish in Polk County, MO.
09	28	1864	Skirmish near Rheatown, TN, with Bvt. Maj. Gen. Stephen G. Burbridge, CSA.
09	28	1864	Skirmish at Wells' Hill, TN.
09	28	1864	Skirmish at Port Republic, VA, the Shenandoah Valley, Campaign.
09	28	1864	Skirmish at Rockfish Gap, VA, the Shenandoah Valley, Campaign.
09	28	1864	The Yankees and Rebels around Petersburg, VA, continue to incur losses as snipers (needlessly) pick off men on both sides of the siege lines.
09	29	1864	Skirmish at Moore's Bluff, MS.
09	29	1864	Federal expedition from Vicksburg to Rodney and Fayette, MS, and skirmish at Port Gibson, **(Sept. 30th)**. 9/29-10/3/1864.
09	29	1864	Affair at Cuba, MO, with Maj. Gen. Sterling Price, CSA.

09	29	1864	Skirmishes at Leasburg or Harrison, MO, with Maj. Gen. Sterling Price, CSA. 9/29-10/1/1864.
09	29	1864	**Operations against Indians in the Nebraska and Colorado Territories.** 9/29-11/30/1864.
09	29	1864	Affair with Indians near Plum Creek, the Nebraska Territory.
09	29	1864	Action in Scuppernong River, NC.
09	29	1864	**Operations in North Georgia and North Alabama, as Maj. Gen. William Tecumseh Sherman, USA, assisted by Maj. Gen. George Henry Thomas, USA, etc.,** spar with the Confederates all over the area in AL, and GA. 9/29-11/13/1864.
09	29	1864	Skirmish at Centreville, TN.
09	29	1864	Skirmish at Jonesborough, TN, with Bvt. Maj. Gen. Stephen G. Burbridge, CSA.
09	29	1864	Skirmish near Lynchburg, TN, with Maj. Gen. Nathan Bedford Forrest, CSA.
09	29	1864	Skirmish at the Watauga River, TN, with Bvt. Maj. Gen. Stephen G. Burbridge, CSA.
09	29	1864	**The Battle of Chaffin's Farm,** as Lieut. Gen. Ulysses S. Grant, USA, sends the 10th and 18th US Army Corps north of the James River to attack the outer defenses of Richmond directly, including combats at: a) Fort Harrison (**captured** by Brig. Gen. George Stannard, USA) b) Fort Gilmer (where the Confederates halt the Union advance) c) New Market Heights d) Laurel Hill, the Richmond, VA campaign. 9/29-30/1864. The Confederate lines, already pressured, are further stretched to the breaking point.
09	29	1864	**Brig. Gen. Hiram Burnham, USA,** is mortally wounded as he led him men against the Confederate's outer defense works of Richmond, VA, at Fort Harrison.
09	29	1864	**The Battle of Poplar Spring Church,** including combats at Wyatt's, Peebles', and Pegram's Farms, Chappell House, and the Vaughan Road, Richmond, VA, Campaign, as Lieut. Gen. A. P. Hill, CSA, beats back the Union offensive. However, the Union lines are extended which further stretches the already thin Rebel lines. 9/29-10/2/1864.
09	29	1864	Skirmish at Waynesborough, VA, as Lieut. Gen. Jubal A. Early, CSA, and Maj. Gen. Philip H. Sheridan, USA, continue to clash.
09	30	1864	Skirmish at Camp Creek, GA.
09	30	1864	The Confederate capture of the steamer, **Ike Davis,** between the mouth of the Rio Grande and New Orleans, LA, as the Rebels disguise themselves as passengers and board her.
09	30	1864	Skirmish at Waynesville, MO, with guerrillas under the notorious Bill Anderson.
09	30	1864	Skirmishes at Carter's Station, TN, with Bvt. Maj. Gen. Stephen A. Burbridge, USA. 9/30-10/1/1864.
10	1	1864	**Brig. Gen. John Dunovant,** CSA, is mortally wounded during the fighting on the Vaughn Road, south of the James River, VA, following the Federal capture of Fort Harrison, VA.
10	1	1864	**John Henry Ketcham,** USA, is appointed Brig. Gen.
10	1	1864	**Thomas Alfred Smyth,** USA, is appointed Brig. Gen.
10	1	1864	Skirmishes at Athens, AL, as Maj. Gen. Nathan Bedford Forrest, CSA, and his Confederate cavalry is on the prowl. 10/1-2/1864.
10	1	1864	Skirmish near Huntsville, AL, as Maj. Gen. Nathan Bedford Forrest, CSA, continues on his expedition.
10	1	1864	Operations in Arkansas, under Maj. Gen. Frederick Steele, USA, commanding the Dept. of Arkansas. 10/1-31/1864.
10	1	1864	Federal scout from Helena aboard the mail-boat, **Diligence,** to Alligator Bayou, AR, with the capture of some Rebels. 10/1-4/1864.
10	1	1864	Skirmish at Salt Spring, GA, as Lieut. Gen. John Bell Hood, CSA, moves the remnants of his Army of Tennessee south around Atlanta to assault Maj. Gen. William T. Sherman's, USA, railroad lines.
10	1	1864	Skirmish at Franklin, MO, with Maj. Gen. Sterling Price, CSA.
10	1	1864	Skirmish near Lake Springs, MO, with Maj. Gen. Sterling Price, CSA.
10	1	1864	Skirmish at Union, MO, with Maj. Gen. Sterling Price, CSA.
10	1	1864	Federal expedition against hostile **Apache Indians** from Fort Craig, the New Mexico Territory, to Fort Goodwin, the Arizona Territory. 10/1-11/27/1864.
10	1	1864	The British blockade runner, **Condor,** runs aground near Cape Fear at Fort Fisher, NC, while pursued by the **USS Niphon.**
10	1	1864	Skirmishes at Clinch Mountain and at Laurel Creek Gap, TN, with Bvt. Maj. Gen. Stephen A. Burbridge, USA.
10	1	1864	The surrender of the block-houses at Carter's Creek Station, TN, by Maj. Gen. Nathan Bedford Forrest's, CSA, men.

MONTH	DAY	YEAR	ACT
10	1	1864	Skirmishes at Clinch Mountain and at Laurel Creek Gap, TN, with Bvt. Maj. Gen. Stephen A. Burbridge, USA.
10	1	1864	The surrender of the block-houses at Carter's Creek Station, TN, by Maj. Gen. Nathan Bedford Forrest's, CSA, men.
10	1	1864	Bvt. Maj. Gen. Godfrey Weitzel, USA, is in temporary command of the 18th US Army Corps, the Richmond, VA, campaign.
10	2	1864	Skirmish at Big Shanty and the Kennesaw Water Tank, GA, as Lieut. Gen. John B. Hood's, CSA, men start tearing up the track of the **Western and Atlantic Railroad,** which is Maj. Gen. William T. Sherman's, USA, supply line.
10	2	1864	Skirmish at the crossing of Flat Rock and McDonough roads, GA.
10	2	1864	Skirmish near Sand Mountain, GA.
10	2	1864	Skirmishes at Shadna Church and Westbrook's, near Fairburn, GA.
10	2	1864	Skirmishes at the Sweet Water and Noyes' Creeks, near Powder Springs, GA. 10/2-3/1864.
10	2	1864	Federal expeditions to the Amite River, New River, and Bayou Manchac, LA. 10/2-8/1864.
10	2	1864	The Confederate **occupation of Washington, MO,** which is 50 miles west of St. Louis, MO, by Maj. Gen. Sterling Price, CSA.
10	2	1864	Operations in Southwest Mississippi and East Louisiana, including skirmish at Marianna, FL. 10/2-11/1864.
10	2	1864	Descent on Fayette, MS.
10	2	1864	Skirmish near Columbia, TN, with Maj. Gen. Nathan Bedford Forrest, CSA.
10	2	1864	Skirmish at Bridgewater, Shenandoah Valley, VA.
10	2	1864	Skirmish at Mount Crawford, Shenandoah Valley, VA.
10	2	1864	Federal action by Bvt. Maj. Gen. Stephen A. Burbridge, USA, near the Confederate salt-works at Saltville, VA, is repulsed.
10	3	1864	Skirmish near Mount Elba, AR.
10	3	1864	Skirmish at Big Shanty, GA, as Maj. Gen. William T. Sherman, USA, is becoming annoyed at Hood's destruction and Forrest's raids.
10	3	1864	Skirmish at Kennesaw Water-Tank, GA, as Lieut. Gen. John B. Hood, CSA, continues tearing up the **Atlanta to Chattanooga railway line.**
10	3	1864	Federal expedition from Morganza to Bayou Sara, LA, and skirmishes. 10/3-6/1864.
10	3	1864	Skirmish at Hermann, MO, with Maj. Gen. Sterling Price, CSA.
10	3	1864	Affair at Miller's Station, west of St. Louis, MO, with Maj. Gen. Sterling Price, CSA.
10	3	1864	On his way back to Richmond, VA, President Jefferson Davis delivers a speech of encouragement to the citizens of Columbia, SC, as he predicts a total defeat for Maj. Gen. William T. Sherman, USA, currently at Atlanta, GA.
10	3	1864	Skirmish at Mount Jackson, VA, Shenandoah Valley, Campaign.
10	3	1864	Skirmish at North River, VA, Shenandoah Valley, Campaign.
10	4	1864	**Ferdinand Van Derveer,** USA, is appointed Brig. Gen.
10	4	1864	Federal reconnaissance from Little Rock toward Monticello and to Mount Elba, AR. 10/4-11/1864.
10	4	1864	Skirmish at Acworth, GA, as Lieut. Gen. John B. Hood, CSA, continues destroying railroad track with his Army of Tennessee.
10	4	1864	Skirmishes near Lost Mountain, GA. 10/4-7/1864.
10	4	1864	Skirmish at Moon's Station, GA.
10	4	1864	Skirmishes at and near Bayou Sara, LA.
10	4	1864	Federal expedition from Natchez to Woodville, MS, and skirmishes. (Oct. **5th** and **6th**). 10/4-12/1864.
10	4	1864	Skirmish near Richwoods, MO, as Maj. Gen. Sterling Price, CSA, and his Confederate raiders move away from St. Louis, MO.
10	4	1864	Skirmish near Memphis, TN.
10	4	1864	Skirmish at Salem, VA.
10	4	1864	President Lincoln's Cabinet welcomes the recently appointed **Postmaster General** of the US, **William Dennison.**
10	5	1864	**The Engagement at Allatoona, GA,** as Brig. Gen. John M. Corse, USA, repels Lieut. Gen. John B. Hood's forces led by Maj. Gen. Samuel G. French, CSA, in their attempt to capture the garrison there. Total casualties approximate 1,500, or almost a 40% loss ratio for the forces involved.

10	5	1864	Skirmish at Atchafalaya, LA.
10	5	1864	Federal expedition from Baton Rouge, LA, to Clinton, Greensburg, Osyka, and Camp Moore, LA, where the Federals capture 4,000 pounds of bacon, 12 barrels of whiskey, 100 dozen pairs of boots and shoes, 2,000 pounds of salt, etc. 10/5-9/1864.
10	5	1864	Skirmish at Saint Charles, LA.
10	5	1864	Skirmish at Thompson's Creek, near Jackson, LA.
10	5	1864	Federal expedition from Natchez to the Homochitto River, MS. 10/5-8/1864.
10	5	1864	Federal expedition from Tunica Landing to Fort Adams, MS. 10/5-8/1864.
10	5	1864	Skirmishes on the Osage River, MO, with Maj. Gen. Sterling Price, CSA. 10/5-6/1864.
10	5	1864	**Lieut. Gen. William J. Hardee, CSA, assumes the command of the Confederate Dept. of South Carolina, Georgia, and Florida,** as he and Lieut. Gen. John Bell Hood, CSA, who could not get along, are separated by President Jefferson Davis.
10	6	1864	Skirmishes at Florence, AL, with Maj. Gen. Nathan Bedford Forrest, CSA, and Maj. Gen. William T. Sherman's, USA, rear guard. 10/6-7/1864.
10	6	1864	Skirmish in Cole County, MO, as Maj. Gen. Sterling Price, CSA, continues moving away from St. Louis.
10	6	1864	Skirmish at Kingsport, TN, with Bvt. Maj. Gen. Stephen A. Burbridge, USA.
10	6	1864	Skirmish near Brock's Gap, VA, where Brig. Gen. George Armstrong Custer, USA, repels Brig. Gen. Thomas L. Rosser, CSA, and also at the following skirmish.
10	6	1864	Skirmish near Fisher's Hill, VA, as the Confederate Army in the Shenandoah under Lieut. Gen. Jubal Early, CSA, refuse to quit.
10	7	1864	The Confederate commerce raider, **CSS Florida,** is captured at Bahia, Brazil, by the **USS Wachusett.**
10	7	1864	Skirmish at Dallas, GA, with Lieut. Gen. John B. Hood's, CSA, Confederates against Maj. Gen. William T. Sherman, USA, as Hood begins to move his army toward Alabama.
10	7	1864	Federal operations in Montgomery County, MD, in the vicinity of Sandy Springs, Barnesville, Middlebrook and Mechanicsville against a small roving band of Confederate guerrillas in the area. 10/7-11/1864.
10	7	1864	Skirmish at Jefferson City, the state capital of Missouri, as Maj. Gen. Sterling Price, CSA, continues to march on.
10	7	1864	Skirmish at Moreau Creek, MO, with Maj. Gen. Sterling Price, CSA.
10	7	1864	Skirmish at Tyler's Mills, Big River, MO, with Maj. Gen. Sterling Price, CSA.
10	7	1864	Skirmish with Indians on the Elk Creek, the Nebraska Territory.
10	7	1864	Skirmish at Kingston, TN.
10	7	1864	Skirmish on the Black road, near Strasburg, VA, the Shenandoah Valley, Campaign.
10	7	1864	Skirmish near Columbia Furnace, VA, the Shenandoah Valley, Campaign.
10	7	1864	The engagement on the Darbytown and New Market Roads, including combats at Johnson's Farm and Four-Mile Creek, as Confederate forces attack and try to push back the Union siege forces around Petersburg, VA, but to no avail, the Richmond, VA, Campaign.
10	7	1864	**Brig. Gen. John Gregg, CSA,** is mortally wounded in the action while attempting to push back the Federal troops on the Darbytown Road, below Richmond, VA.
10	8	1864	The new **(and last)** Confederate commerce raider, the **CSS Shenandoah,** (aka **Sea King**), embarks from London, England.
10	8	1864	The capture of the Confederate mail and the recapture of Union flags, near Saint Joseph, on the west side of the Mississippi River, LA.
10	8	1864	Skirmish in Barry County, MO, with Maj. Gen. Sterling Price, CSA.
10	8	1864	Skirmish near Jefferson City, MO, with Maj. Gen. Sterling Price, CSA, and his Confederate expeditionary force.
10	8	1864	Skirmish at Rogersville, TN, with Bvt. Maj. Gen. Stephen A. Burbridge, USA.
10	8	1864	Skirmish in Luray Valley, VA, between Cavalry forces, the Shenandoah Valley, Campaign.
10	8	1864	Skirmish at Tom's Brook, near Strasburg, VA, the Shenandoah Valley, Campaign.
10	8	1864	Federal reconnaissance on the Vaughan and Squirrel Level Roads, near Petersburg, the Richmond, VA, Campaign.
10	9	1864	The attack on the US Steamer, **Sebago, in** Mobile Bay, AL.
10	9	1864	Skirmishes near Van Wert, GA. 10/9-10/1864.
10	9	1864	Skirmishes near Bayou Sara, LA. 10/9-10/1864.
10	9	1864	Skirmish at, and the **capture of, Boonville, MO,** by Maj. Gen. Sterling Price, CSA.

10	9	1864	Skirmish at, and the **capture of, California, MO,** by Maj. Gen. Sterling Price, CSA.
10	9	1864	Skirmish at, and the **capture of, Russellville, MO,** by Maj. Gen. Sterling Price, CSA.
10	9	1864	Federal scout in Saint Francois County, MO, with skirmishes with guerrillas.
10	9	1864	Skirmish near Piedmont, VA.
10	9	1864	Engagement at Tom's Brook, near Strasburg, VA, as the Union cavalry under Brig. Gens. Alfred T. Torbert, George Armstrong Custer, and Welsey Merritt, USA, rout the Confederates led by Maj. Gen. Lunsford Lindsay Lomax, and Brig. Gen. Thomas L. Rosser, CSA, who lose over 300 men captured.
10	10	1864	Skirmish with the **Cheyenne Indians** near Valley Station, the Colorado Territory, where the Yankees kill 10, and write that they will clean them out of the country between the Platte and Arkansas directly.
10	10	1864	Skirmishes near Rome, GA, as Lieut. Gen. John B. Hood, CSA, and Maj. Gen. William T. Sherman, USA, continue to butt heads. 10/10-11/1864.
10	10	1864	Action at Eastport, MS, where Maj. Gen. Nathan B. Forrest, CSA, repels a Federal attack aboard the Union transports, **Aurora, City of Pekin, Key West, Krenton,** and the **Undine,** disabling a few of the transports before they could even land troops. The Yankees retreat "with honor."
10	10	1864	Federal scout in Pemiscot County, MO, including a skirmish with guerrillas 4 miles below Caruthersville. 10/10-12/1864.
10	10	1864	**Operations in East Tennessee.** 10/10-28/1864.
10	10	1864	The affair at South Tunnel, near Gallatin, TN.
10	10	1864	Skirmish at Thorn Hill, near Bean's Station, TN.
10	10	1864	Skirmish near Rectortown, VA, as Maj. Gen. Philip H. Sheridan, USA, moves into a strong position near Cedar Creek, along the Valley Pike, the Shenandoah Valley, and awaits the oncoming forces under Lieut. Gen. Jubal Early, CSA.
10	11	1864	The Confederate attack on the steamer, **Resolute,** on the White River, 12 miles above Clarendon, AR, by bushwackers who fire into the vessel, inflicting 4 casualties, including one fatality. The attack appears senseless.
10	11	1864	Federal expedition from Atlanta to Flat Creek, GA, and skirmishes, as Maj. Gen. William T. Sherman, USA, concentrates his forces around Rome, GA; Lieut. Gen. John B. Hood, CSA, is just south of the city. 10/11-14/1864.
10	11	1864	Skirmishes near Boonville, MO, as Maj. Gen. Sterling Price, CSA, continues with the last Confederate thrust into Missouri. 10/11-12/1864.
10	11	1864	Skirmish at Brunswick, MO, with Maj. Gen. Sterling Price, CSA.
10	11	1864	Federal scout from Camp Palmer to Gum Swamp, NC, as the Yankees capture some Rebels as well as some black men hired by the Confederate Government to work on the railroad there. 10/11-13/1864.
10	11	1864	Skirmish near Fort Donelson, TN, as Confederate Cavalry fails to raid the Union black recruiting post there.
10	11	1864	Federal scout toward Stony Creek Station, the Richmond, VA, Campaign.
10	11	1864	Skirmish near White Plains, VA.
10	11	1864	Bvt. Maj. Gen. Alfred H. Terry, USA, is in temporary command of the 10th US Army Corps, the Richmond, VA, Campaign.
10	11	1864	Skirmish 2 miles south of Petersburg, WV, with some of Brig. Gen. John D. Imboden's Confederate cavalry.
10	12	1864	Skirmishes on the Coosaville road, near Rome, GA, as Maj. Gen. William T. Sherman, USA, edges closer to Lieut. Gen. John Bell Hood, CSA. 10/12-13/1864.
10	12	1864	Skirmish at La Fayette, GA.
10	12	1864	Skirmishes at Resaca, GA.
10	12	1864	The Indian attack on the Overland Stage Coach at Freeman's Ranch, near Plum Creek, the Nebraska Territory.
10	12	1864	Rear Admiral David D. Porter, USN, relieves Rear Admiral Samuel P. Lee, USN, as commander of the **North Atlantic Blockading Squadron,** off Wilmington, NC.
10	12	1864	Skirmish at Greeneville, TN, as the Federal raids from Kentucky and East Tennessee into southwestern Virginia, under Bvt. Maj. Gen. Stephen A. Burbridge, USA, are concluded.
10	12	1864	**Chief Justice of the United States, Roger Brooke Taney,** dies at the age of 89, in Washington, DC.
10	13	1864	Federal expedition from Pine Bluff to Arkansas Post, AR. 10/13-18/1864.
10	13	1864	Combat at Buzzard Roost Gap, GA. 10/13-14/1864.

MONTH	DAY	YEAR	ACT
10	13	1864	The Union **surrender of Dalton, GA.**
10	13	1864	The Union **surrender of Tilton, GA,** as Lieut. Gen. John B. Hood's, CSA, men seize the important railroad line in the vicinity.
10	13	1864	Federal reconnaissance from Rome on the Cave Springs Road, GA, and skirmishes.
10	13	1864	Skirmish with Indians near Mullahla's Station, the Nebraska Territory.
10	13	1864	Federal scout against **Apache Indians** from near Tularosa, into the Sacramento Mountains, the New Mexico Territory. With frost and heavy snow, their travels are dangerous enough without having to deal with the possibility of confronting hostile Indians. 10/13-21/1864.
10	13	1864	Federal operations against Indians near Fort Belknap, TX, with skirmish (Oct. 13th) 16 miles above Fort Belknap on Elm Creek, TX. The Yankees are tracking down the Indians responsible for the latest murders of white settlers. 10/13-20/1864.
10	13	1864	Action at Cedar Creek, VA, as Lieut. Gen. Jubal Early, CSA, moves into position at his old entrenched lines at Fisher's Hill.
10	13	1864	Engagement on the Darbytown Road, the Richmond, VA, Campaign.
10	13	1864	**John Mosby's Irregular Confederate Partisans** capture and **burn** the railroad train on the **Baltimore and Ohio Railroad** near Kearneysville and west of Harper's Ferry, WV, seizing over $170,000 from the Union paymaster.
10	14	1864	Skirmish near Fort Smith, AR.
10	14	1864	Skirmish at Adamstown, MD.
10	14	1864	Maj. Gen. Sterling Price's, CSA, attack on Danville, MO, where the Rebels burn the post office. Destruction of this nature will do little damage to the Yankee military machine.
10	14	1864	Skirmish near Glasgow, MO, as Maj. Gen. Sterling Price, CSA, forces continue to wear down, both man power and horses.
10	14	1864	Skirmish at the Boca Chica Pass, TX.
10	14	1864	Skirmish at Strasburg (or Hupp's Hill), VA, as Lieut. Gen. Jubal Early, CSA, and Maj. Gen. Philip H. Sheridan, USA, forces are only a couple miles apart from each other.
10	14	1864	Affair at Duffield's Station, WV, Shenandoah Valley Campaign.
10	15	1864	Skirmish at Snake Creek Gap, GA.
10	15	1864	Skirmish at Bayou Liddell, LA.
10	15	1864	Skirmish at Hernando, MS.
10	15	1864	The action at, and **capture of Glasgow, MO,** by Maj. Gen. Sterling Price, CSA.
10	15	1864	The **surrender of Paris, MO,** to Maj. Gen. Sterling Price, CSA.
10	15	1864	The affair at, and **occupation of Sedalia, MO,** by Brig. Gen. Joseph O. Shelby, CSA, under Maj. Gen. Sterling Price.
10	15	1864	Skirmish at Mossy Creek, TN.
10	15	1864	Federal expedition from Bernard's Mills to Murfree's Station, VA, and skirmish **(16th)** at the **Blackwater,** as the Yankees continue to destroy precious and limited Confederate supplies, including bacon and 4 barrels of apple brandy. I wonder if the brandy was really destroyed? 10/15-17/1864.
10	16	1864	Federal expedition from Devall's Bluff aboard the steamer, **Celeste,** on the Cache River, toward Clarendon, AR, in search of Confederates. 10/16-17/1864.
10	16	1864	Skirmish at Ship's Gap, GA, as Lieut. Gen. John B. Hood, CSA, and Maj. Gen. William T. Sherman, USA, continue to spar.
10	16	1864	Skirmish near Morganza, LA.
10	16	1864	The Confederate **capture of Ridgely, MO,** by Maj. Gen. Sterling Price, CSA.
10	16	1864	**Maj. Gen. Nathan Bedford Forrest's, CSA, Cavalry raid into West Tennessee.** 10/16-11/10/1864.
10	16	1864	Skirmish near Bull's Gap, TN.
10	16	1864	Federal expedition from City Point into Surry County, VA, as the Federals traveled every main and by road between the Blackwater and James Rivers, below Bacon Castle and City Point, (now called Hopewell) visiting every residence, capturing all the citizens, negroes and stock available. Even though there is corn in the fields and potatoes in the ground, this area is becoming barren of any livestock. 10/16-18/1864.
10	17	1864	Skirmish at Eddyville, Lyon County, KY, as the Federals move from Louisville.
10	17	1864	**Gen. Pierre Gustave Toutant Beauregard, CSA, assumes the command of the Confederate Military Division of the West,** east of the Mississippi River.
10	17	1864	The surrender of, and Confederate **occupation of, Carrollton, MO,** by Maj. Gen. Sterling Price, CSA.

10/16-18/1864.

| 10 | 17 | 1864 | Skirmish at Eddyville, Lyon County, KY, as the Federals move from Louisville. |

10 17 1864 **Gen. Pierre Gustave Toutant Beauregard, CSA, assumes the command of the Confederate Military Division of the West,** east of the Mississippi River.

10 17 1864 The surrender of, and Confederate **occupation of, Carrollton, MO,** by Maj. Gen. Sterling Price, CSA.

10 17 1864 Skirmish near Lexington, MO, as the Union forces begin to close in on the invading Confederates under Maj. Gen. Sterling Price, CSA.

10 17 1864 The **burning of Smithville, MO,** by Maj. Gen. Sterling Price, CSA.

10 17 1864 Affair at Cedar Run Church, VA, the Shenandoah Valley Campaign.

10 17 1864 **Lieut. Gen. James Longstreet, CSA, is ordered to resume command** of his army corps, the Richmond, VA, Campaign, after recovering from battle wounds received at the Wilderness in May, 1864.

10 18 1864 **Maj. Gen. David Bell Birney, USA,** dies at his home in Philadelphia, PA, from camp fever (malaria) contracted in the summer of 1864 during Gen. Ulysses S. Grant's Overland Campaign through Virginia.

10 18 1864 Skirmish near Huntsville, AL, as Lieut. Gen. John B. Hood, CSA, moves his Army of Tennessee towards Gadsden, AL, away from Maj. Gen. William T. Sherman's, USA, railroad line on the **Chattanooga to Atlanta Railroad.**

10 18 1864 Skirmish near Summerville, GA.

10 18 1864 Skirmish near Milton, FL, as the Confederates attack the US steamer, **Planter,** which is busy gathering logs in Blackwater Bay, at Battledonge. Later the **Planter** enters Escambia Bay and carries away 15,000 new brick and a lot of doors and window sashes.

10 18 1864 Skirmish in Barry County, MO.

10 18 1864 Skirmish at Clinch Mountain, TN.

10 18 1864 Confederate raids on the **Nashville and Northwestern Railroad, TN,** as the Rebels burn nearly all the Negro and other dwellings along the railroad for two miles.

10 19 1864 The following are appointed Union Brigadier Generals:
Alfred Gibbs,   USA
Rutherford Birchard Hayes, USA
Charles Russell Lowell,   USA
William Henry Powell,   USA

10 19 1864 Skirmish in Crawford County, AR, with guerrillas attacking local militia men, with casualties.

10 19 1864 Federal reconnaissance from Little Rock to Princeton, AR, with skirmish **(Oct. 23rd)** at Hurricane Creek. 10/19-23/1864.

10 19 1864 Skirmish at Ruff's Station, GA.

10 19 1864 Skirmishes near Turner's and Howell's Ferries, GA.

10 19 1864 Action at Lexington, MO, with Maj. Gen. Sterling Price, CSA.

10 19 1864 Skirmish near Montevallo, MO.

10 19 1864 Lieut. Bennett H. Young, CSA, and his band of about 25 Confederates cross the Canadian border about 15 miles and move on St. Albans, Vermont, where they rob 3 banks of over $200,000 before a dozen of the raiders flee back across the border and are captured but later released by the Canadian officials. Similar to the English authorities, many foreign officials, though not officially acknowledging the Confederate States of America, will go out of their way to assist them, unofficially.

10 19 1864 **The Battle of Cedar Creek, (or Bell Grove), VA,** where Lieut. Gen. Jubal Early and his subordinates, Maj. Gens. John Brown Gordon and Joseph Brevard Keshaw, CSA, attack and overwhelm the Union forces and where Maj. Gen. Philip Sheridan, USA, regroups the disorganized, beaten back and retreating Union army of the 6th, 8th, and 19th US Army Corps, and repels the Confederate onslaught and effectively terminates the last major Confederate threat in the Shenandoah Valley, VA. Total casualties approximate 8,575. The Confederates will continue to annoy the Federals but will **never be able to effectively stage another major offensive in the Shenandoah Valley.**

10 19 1864 **Maj. Gen. Stephen Dodson Ramseur, CSA,** is mortally wounded at the Battle of Cedar Creek, VA, shot through both of his lungs, he was captured and died the next morning.

10 19 1864 **Brig. Gen. Daniel Davidson Bidwell, USA,** is mortally wounded at the Battle of Cedar Creek, VA, while leading his men against the Confederates.

10 19 1864 **Brig. Gen. Charles Russell Lowell, USA,** is mortally wounded at the Battle of Cedar Breek, VA, while at the head of his brigade, receiving his deathwound during the Union counter attack against Lieut. Gen. Jubal Anderson Early's, CSA.

10	20	1864	Skirmish at Blue Pond, AL.
10	20	1864	Skirmish at Little River, AL.
10	20	1864	Skirmish in Benton County, AR, with Maj. Gen. Sterling Price, CSA.
10	20	1864	Skirmish near Waterloo, LA.
10	20	1864	Skirmish at Dover, MO, as Maj. Gen. Sterling Price, CSA, is becoming alarmed at the Union Calvary forces under Maj. Gen. Alfred Pleasonton, the **Army of the Border** under Maj. Gen. Samuel Ryan Curtis, as well as Brig. Gen. Andrew Jackson Smith, USA, are surrounding and hemming him in.
10	20	1864	The Indian attack on the settlements in the Platte Valley, near Alkali Station, the Nebraska Territory.
10	20	1864	Skirmish near Memphis, TN.
10	20	1864	Skirmish at Fisher's Hill, VA, as Lieut. Gen. Jubal Early, licks his wounds, and retreats southward with the last remnants of Confederate opposition in the Shenandoah Valley.
10	20	1864	President Abraham Lincoln officially sets the last Thursday in November to be forever celebrated as **"Thanksgiving."**
10	21	1864	**George Crook,** U.S.A., is appointed Maj. Gen.
10	21	1864	**William Badger Tibbits,** USA, is appointed Brig. Gen.
10	21	1864	Skirmish at Leesburg, AL.
10	21	1864	Skirmish at Bryant's Plantation, FL.
10	21	1864	Skirmish at Harrodsburg, KY.
10	21	1864	Action at the Little Blue, MO, where Brig. Gen. Joseph O. Shelby, CSA, forces Maj. Gen. Samuel R. Curtis, USA, to retreat to Bush Creek, near Westport, MO. Maj. Gen. Sterling Price, CSA, continues to exert muscle.
10	21	1864	Skirmish with Indians, at Alkali Station, the Nebraska Territory.
10	21	1864	Skirmish in Clinch Valley, near Sneedville, TN.
10	21	1864	The Confederate raids on the **Nashville and Northwestern Railroad, TN,** by forces under Lieut. Gen. John B. Hood, CSA.
10	22	1864	The Confederate guerrilla attack on the Union transport, on the White River, near Saint Charles, AR, where the Rebel rifle shots kill 3 and wound 14 men of the **53rd US Colored Infantry.**
10	22	1864	Federal expedition from Brashear City to Belle River, LA. 10/22-24/1864.
10	22	1864	Action at the Big Blue (Byram's Ford, etc.), MO, where Brig. Gen. Joseph O. Shelby, CSA, forces Maj. Gen. Samuel R. Curtis, USA, to retreat to Bush Creek, near Westport, MO.
10	22	1864	Action at, and Federal **evacuation of, Independence, MO,** because of Maj. Gen. Sterling Price, CSA.
10	22	1864	Action at State Line, MO, with Maj. Gen. Sterling Price, CSA.
10	22	1864	Skirmish with Indians near Midway Station, the Nebraska Territory.
10	23	1864	Skirmish at King's Hill, AL.
10	23	1864	The engagement at the Big Blue, MO, with Maj. Gen. Sterling Price, CSA.
10	23	1864	**The Engagement at Westport, MO,** near present day Kansas City, MO, as Brig. Gen. Joseph O. Shelby, CSA, attacks; Maj. Gen. Alfred Pleasonton, USA, and his cavalry counterattack; Brig. Gen. John S. Marmaduke, CSA, and the rest of Maj. Gen. Sterling Price's Confederate force see the Union troops reverse yesterday's defeat; Sterling withdraws southward which effectively ends the last Confederate threat in Missouri.
10	23	1864	The destruction of the blockade-runner, **Flamingo,** at Charleston, SC.
10	23	1864	Skirmish at Dry Run, VA, the Shenandoah Valley Campaign.
10	24	1864	**Brig. Gen. James Jay Archer, CSA,** dies from deteriorating health developed as a Federal prisoner of war after being captured July 3, 1863 with most of his brigade of Heth's division at the Battle of Gettysburg, Pa. Exchanged, he died in his nation's capital, of Richmond, VA.
10	24	1864	Federal scout from Pine Bluff toward Mount Elba, AR. 10/24-27/1864.
10	24	1864	Skirmish near Magnolia, FL, where Union Cavalry battle the Confederate forces stationed near Waldo, with casualties.
10	24	1864	Skirmish near South River, GA.
10	24	1864	Federal operations in Issaquena and Washington Counties, MS, and skirmish **(25th)** at Steele's Bayou, as the Yankees capture cotton, horses, mules, sheep, beef-cattle, in addition to prominent rebels throughout this here country. 10/24-31/1864.
10	24	1864	Maj. Gen. Sterling Price, CSA, concludes his Missouri expedition, moving his long train of captured Federal supplies along the Kansas state line.

10	25	1864	Skirmish on the Gadsden road, AL, as Lieut. Gen. John B. Hood, CSA, and Maj. Gen. William T. Sherman, USA, continue to spar.
10	25	1864	Skirmish near Round Mountain, AL.
10	25	1864	Skirmish at Turkeytown, AL.
10	25	1864	Federal operations about Fayetteville, AR, during the invasion by Maj. Gen. Sterling Price, CSA. 10/25-11/4/1864.
10	25	1864	Skirmish near the Half-way House, between Little Rock and Pine Bluff, AR.
10	25	1864	Federal expedition up the Blackwater Bay and skirmish (Oct. 26th) at Milton, FL, as the Federals, including Negro soldiers, drive off the Rebels, and seize over 100,000 feet of seasoned Rebel lumber. 10/25-28/1864.
10	25	1864	The engagement on Little Osage River or Mine Creek KS, as Brig. Gen. Joseph O. Shelby, CSA, and his cavalry attempt to protect the Rebel wagon train from the Yankee advance. Price loses about a third of his wagon train.
10	25	1864	Engagement at the Marais des Cygnes, KS, as Maj. Gen. Sterling Price, CSA, continues to retreat.
10	25	1864	Skirmishes at Mound City and Fort Lincoln, KS, with Maj. Gen. Sterling Price, CSA.
10	25	1864	Confederate attack on Clinton, MO, by Maj. Gen. Sterling Price, CSA.
10	25	1864	Engagement at the Marmiton, or battle of Charlot, MO, with Maj. Gen. Sterling Price, CSA.
10	25	1864	Skirmish near Memphis, TN.
10	25	1864	Skirmishes at Milford, VA, the Shenandoah Valley Campaign. 10/25-26/1864.
10	26	1864	Confederate demonstration against Decatur, AL. 10/26-29/1864.
10	26	1864	Federal expedition from Brownsville to Cotton Plant, AR. 10/26-11/2/1864.
10	26	1864	Federal expedition from Little Rock to Irving's Plantation, AR. 10/26-28/1864.
10	26	1864	Federal expedition from Atlanta to Trickum's Cross-Roads, GA, and skirmishes **(Oct. 27th)** near Trickum's Cross-Roads and Lawrenceville. 10/26-29/1864.
10	26	1864	Federal scout from Vidalia to the York Plantation, LA. 10/26-27/1864.
10	26	1864	Skirmish at Albany, MO, with Maj. Gen. Sterling Price, CSA.
10	26	1864	Skirmish near Glasgow, MO, with Maj. Gen. Sterling Price, CSA.
10	26	1864	The outlaw Confederate guerrilla, **"Bloody" Bill Anderson,** is killed in a Federal ambush near Richmond, MO.
10	26	1864	Affair in Scott County, VA, as the Federals kill the notorious guerrilla leader, Capt. Burleson.
10	26	1864	Skirmish at Winfield, WV, with Confederate Cavalry.
10	27	1864	**Gilbert Moxley Sorrel,** CSA, is appointed Brig. Gen.
10	27	1864	The destruction of the Confederate ram, the **Albemarle,** by Lieut. William B. Cushing, USA, using a torpedo, at Plymouth, NC. 10/27-28/1864.
10	27	1864	The unsuccessful Confederate guerrilla attack on the steamer, **Belle Saint Louis,** at Fort Randolph, TN.
10	27	1864	Skirmishes at Mossy Creek and Panther Springs, TN.
10	27	1864	The engagement at Boydton Plank Road or Hatcher's Run, the Richmond, VA, Campaign. 10/27-28/1864.
10	27	1864	The engagement at Fair Oaks and Darbytown Road, the Richmond, VA, Campaign, as Lieut. Gen. Ulysses S. Grant, USA, attempts to move on Petersburg, VA, before winter, but to no avail as Maj. Gens. Henry Heth and William Mahone, CSA, repel Maj. Gens. Winfield Scott Hancock and Gouverneur K. Warren, USA. (The final) Winter is fast approaching. 10/27-28/1864.
10	27	1864	Skirmish in front of Fort Morton and Fort Sedgwick, the Richmond, VA, Campaign.
10	28	1864	Skirmish at Goshen, AL, as Lieut. Gen. John B. Hood, CSA, moves his Army of Tennessee westward.
10	28	1864	Skirmish at Ladiga, AL, as Hood moves westward and contrary to previous army theory, Maj. Gen. William T. Sherman, USA, moves eastward back towards Atlanta, GA.
10	28	1864	Engagement at Newtonia, southwest MO, where Maj. Gen. Samueul R. Curtis, USA, forces Maj. Gen. Sterling Price, CSA, to continue his retreat.
10	28	1864	Skirmish with Indians near Midway Station, the Nebraska Territory.
10	28	1864	Action at Morristown, TN, with Maj. Gen. Nathan Bedford Forrest, CSA.
10	28	1864	Skirmish at Russellville, TN.
10	28	1864	Skirmish near Newtown, VA, the Shenandoah Valley Campaign.
10	28	1864	Operations about Snicker's Gap (Oct. 28th) and skirmish **(Oct. 29th)** at Upperville, VA, where the 8th IL Cavalry proclaims to have whipped Lieut. Col. John S. Mosby's men badly, killing 7 or 8, and capturing 9. 10/28-29/1864.

10	28	1864	Action at Morristown, TN, with Maj. Gen. Nathan Bedford Forrest, CSA.
10	28	1864	Skirmish at Russellville, TN.
10	28	1864	Skirmish near Newtown, VA, the Shenandoah Valley Campaign.
10	28	1864	Operations about Snicker's Gap (Oct. 28th) and skirmish **(Oct. 29th)** at Upperville, VA, where the 8th IL Cavalry proclaims to have whipped Lieut. Col. John S. Mosby's men badly, killing 7 or 8, and capturing 9. 10/28-29/1864.
10	29	1864	**Brig. Gen. Thomas Edward Greenfield Ransom, USA,** dies from complications developed from battlewounds received during his career, near Rome, GA.
10	29	1864	The capture of the Union steamer, **Mazeppa,** by Maj. Gen. Nathan B. Forrest, CSA, near Forts Henry and Heiman, Tennessee River, KY.
10	29	1864	The Confederate attack on Vanceburg, KY, is repulsed by the loyal citizens of the town, the rebels fleeing toward Fox Creek, Fleming County.
10	29	1864	The Federal expedition to Quincy, MO, with skirmishes **(Nov. 1st and 2nd)** near Quincy. 10/29-11/8/1864.
10	29	1864	Skirmish at Upshaw's Farm, Barry County, MO, with Maj. Gen. Sterling Price, CSA.
10	29	1864	Skirmish near Warrenton, MO.
10	29	1864	Skirmish at Nonconnah Creek, TN, along the Pigeon Roost Road.
10	29	1864	Skirmish at Johnson's Farm, the Richmond, VA, Campaign. 10/27-28/1864.
10	29	1864	Action at Beverly, WV, as after two hours' hard fighting the Confederates are routed and fail in their attack on the town.
10	30	1864	Skirmish at Muscle Shoals (or Raccoon Ford), near Florence, AL.
10	30	1864	The capture of the gun-boat, **Undine (No. 55)** and transports near Fort Heiman, KY, by Maj. Gen. Nathan Bedford Forrest, CSA.
10	30	1864	The **CSS Olustee, formerly the CSS Tallahassee,** eludes the Federal blockade off Wilmington, NC, and begins looking for Federal commerce vessels to raid.
10	30	1864	Skirmish at Bainbridge, TN.
10	31	1864	Skirmish near Shoal Creek, AL, as Lieut. Gen. John Bell Hood, CSA, prepares to move his Confederate army into Tennessee, assuming Maj. Gen. William T. Sherman, USA, will pursue him. Instead, Sherman will move in the opposite direction toward the sea.
10	31	1864	**Nevada is admitted as the 36th State of the Union.**
10	31	1864	The Union naval **occupation of Plymouth, NC.**
11	1	1864	**Thomas Lafayette Rosser,** C.S.A. is appointed Maj. Gen.
11	1	1864	**William Henry Fitzhugh Payne,** CSA, is appointed Brig. Gen.
11	1	1864	**Federal Operations against guerrillas in Central Arkansas.** 11/1-30/1864.
11	1	1864	Skirmish on the Big Piney, near Waynesville, MO, with bushwackers.
11	1	1864	Affair at Greenton, MO, as 3 Union officers stop and wait at a lady's house for the woman to cook them dinner, their command continuing to march on. The officers tell the men they'll catch up with them. After dinner, 3 guerrillas capture the Yankees, quickly taking them into the bush and where the Federals find their officers the next morning, all 3 shot through the head. Nasty busy, this guerrillas warfare.
11	1	1864	Skirmish near Lebanon, MO, where the Confederates attack a Union forage train.
11	1	1864	Skirmish at Rolla, MO.
11	1	1864	The 1st and 3rd Division, 16th US Army Corps are transferred from Missouri to Nashville, Tennessee, and the command of Maj. Gen. George H. Thomas, USA, as the Confederate expedition into Missouri by Maj. Gen. Sterling Price, CSA, had concluded. The Federals moving manpower where needed. 11/1-30/1864.
11	1	1864	Skirmishes at Union Station, TN.
11	1	1864	Federal scout from Bermuda Hundred into Charles City County, VA, the Richmond, VA, Campaign. 11/1-5/1864.
11	1	1864	Affair at Green Springs Run, WV, with Bvt. Maj. Gen. Benjamin F. Kelley's, USA, Yankees repelling the Confederates.
11	2	1864	Affair at Hazen's Farm, near Devall's Bluff, AR, as a party of Yankees sent to collect bricks at the Hazen's Farm, were captured, robbed, then paroled by the Confederates. Upon hearing of this, the furious Federal officer in charge orders the arrest of the paroled Yankees.
11	2	1864	Federal expedition from Little Rock to Benton, AR. 11/2-3/1864.

MONTH	DAY	YEAR	ACT
11	3	1864	The 4th US Army Corps arrives at Pulaski, TN, to block any move in that direction by Lieut. Gen. John B. Hood, CSA.
11	4	1864	**William MacRae,** CSA, is appointed Brig. Gen.
11	4	1864	**Peter Burwell Starke,** CSA, is appointed Brig. Gen.
11	4	1864	**Maj. Gen. John C. Breckinridge's, CSA, Confederate advance into** East Tennessee. 11/4-17/1864.
11	4	1864	The destruction of the gun-boats, the **Tawah (No. 29), Key West (No. 32),** and the **Elfin (No.52),** Tennessee River, TN, near Johnsonville, TN, by Maj. Gen. Nathan Bedford Forrest, CSA, and his captured vessels with the assistance of Confederate shore batteries. Forrest loses the captured **Undine,** but accomplishes his goal of disrupting Federal supply line and water traffic to the estimated damage of $6,700,000, after bombarding Johnsonville. Forrest moves south to meet up with Lieut. Gen. John B. Hood, CSA, via Corinth, MS.
11	4	1864	Action at Johnsonville, TN, as this encounter as well as the above effectively concludes Maj. Gen. Nathan Bedford Forrest's latest expedition. 11/4-5/1864.
11	5	1864	Skirmishes at Shoal Creek, AL. 11/5-6/1864.
11	5	1864	Federal expedition from Lewisburg to Fort Smith, AR, with skirmishes. 11/5-23/1864.
11	5	1864	Federal operations against Indians in the Colorado Territory, this time of year experiencing deep snows. 11/5-14/1864.
11	5	1864	Skirmishes at Big Pigeon River, KY. 11/5-6/1864.
11	5	1864	Skirmish at Bloomfield, KY.
11	5	1864	Operations in Mississippi County, MO, with skirmishes at Charleston (Nov. 5th) and near Sikeston **(Nov. 6th),** as a band of guerrillas make a quick dash into town. 11/5-6/1864.
11	5	1864	Federal expedition from Rolla to Licking, Texas County, MO, with skirmish **(Nov. 9th)** near Licking. 11/5-9/1864.
11	5	1864	Federal expedition from Springfield, MO, to Fort Smith, AR, with skirmishes **(Nov. 6th)** near Cincinnati, AR. 11/5-16/1864.
11	5	1864	Skirmishes in front of Forts Haskell and Morton, the Richmond VA, Campaign.
11	5	1864	Lieut. Col. Vincent A. Witcher's, CSA, Confederate operations in the Kanawha Valley, WV, including the capture and burning of the US steamers, **Barnum** and **Fawn** on the Big Sandy River, WV. 11/5-12/1864.
11	6	1864	Skirmish at Cane Hill, AR, with Maj. Gen. Sterling Price, CSA, after retreating from Missouri.
11	6	1864	Affairs at Fort Lyon, the Colorado Territory, where the new commander orders the arrest of all the peaceful **Arappahoe Indians** who have been camped 2 miles from the Fort and come everyday to the Fort for provisions, demanding all their weapons and horses belonging to the US Government. The Indians immediately agree to any demands made by the Yankees. The Commander proclaims they are all his prisoners. 9 **Cheyenne Indians** come to the Fort telling the Commander that 600 more are on their way, plus an additional 2,000 once the weather breaks. The officer writes he will not allow this as he does not have the provisions to feed all these Indians. He also writes of no love lost for the hostile **Arapahoes, Sioux, Cheyenne, Kiowas** and **Commanches,** as well as the **Apaches.** The Federals fought to disarm the hostile Indians, and when they finally achieve peace, they turn their backs on the Indians. A no win situation for the Indian Nations. 11/6-16/1864.
11	6	1864	Skirmish on the McDonough road, near Atlanta, GA.
11	6	1864	Federal expedition from Vicksburg, MS, to Gaines' Landing and Bayou Macon, LA. 11/6-8/1864.
11	6	1864	Federal scout in Callaway County, MO. 11/6-7/1864.
11	6	1864	Skirmish with Indians at the Sand Hills Stage Station, the Nebraska Territory.
11	6	1864	Federal expedition from New Creek to Moorefield, WV, and skirmish with the Yankees bringing off 460 head of sheep, and provisions the Confederates desperately need. 11/6-8/1864.
11	7	1864	**Samuel Read Anderson,** CSA, is appointed Brig. Gen.
11	7	1864	The **6th US Army Corps,** TN, etal. **is abolished.**
11	7	1864	Skirmish near Edenburg, VA, the Shenandoah Valley Campaign.
11	7	1864	Federal reconnaissance toward Stony Creek, the Richmond, VA, Campaign.
11	7	1864	The 2nd Session of the 2nd Congress of the Confederate States of America opens in Richmond, VA, destined to be the final session of the Confederate states government.
11	8	1864	**Abraham Lincoln's** political worries over his past commanding general cease as Lincoln receives 55% of the general vote to defeat McClellan and be **reelected President of the United States of America;** the Union troops overwhelming voting to keep Lincoln and his campaign against the Confederacy going.

11	9	1864	Skirmish at Florence, AL.
11	9	1864	Skirmish at Shoal Creek, AL.
11	9	1864	Federal scout from Devall's Bluff to Searcy and Clinton, AR. 11/9-15/1864.
11	9	1864	Skirmish near Atlanta, GA.

11   9   1864   In preparation of his march to the sea, Maj. Gen. William T. Sherman, USA, who believes Maj. Gen. George H. Thomas, USA, at Nashville, TN, can handle Lieut. Gen. John Bell Hood, CSA, reorganizes his army as follows:

a) **Right Wing - Maj. Gen. Oliver O. Howard, USA.**
        1. 15th US Army Corps
        2. 17th US Army Corps

b) **Left Wing - Maj. Gen. Henry W. Slocum, USA.**
        1. 14th US Army Corps
        2. 20th US Army Corps

11   9   1864   Federal expedition from Memphis to Moscow, TN. 11/9-13/1864.

11   10   1864   **Josiah Gorgas,** CSA, is appointed Brig. Gen.

11   10   1864   The following are appointed Union Brigadier Generals:
Edmund Jackson Davis,   USA
Thomas John Lucas,   USA
James Richard Slack,   USA

11   10   1864   Federal scout from Kingston, GA, as Maj. Gen. William T. Sherman, USA, moves back to Atlanta, GA, burning all railroad lines and supplies that could assist the Rebels. 11/10-11/1864.

11   10   1864   Skirmish at Neosho, MO.

11   10   1864   Federal scout near Memphis, TN, with the capture of a few Rebels.

11   10   1864   Skirmish near Kernstown, VA, as Lieut. Gen. Jubal Early, CSA, with his feeble force of Confederates, move north from New Market towards Maj. Gen. Philip H. Sheridan, USA, and the Army of the Shenandoah.

11   11   1864   **William Montague Browne,** CSA, is appointed Brig. Gen.

11   11   1864   Skirmish at Shoal Creek, AL.

11   11   1864   The destruction of all military facilities at Rome, GA, by the retreating Union army heading for Atlanta.

11   11   1864   Federal scout from Springfield, MO, to Huntsville and Yellville, AR, with skirmishes. 11/11-21/1864.

11   11   1864   Action at Bull's Gap, TN, with Maj. Gen. John C. Breckinridge, CSA. 11/11-13/1864.

11   11   1864   Skirmish at Russellville, TN, with Maj. Gen. John Cabell Breckinridge, CSA, commanding the Dept. of Western Virginia and East Tennessee and Maj. Gen. George Henry Thomas, USA, commanding the Dept. of the Cumberland.

11   11   1864   Skirmish near Kernstown, VA, the Shenandoah Valley Campaign.

11   11   1864   Skirmish at Manassas Junction, VA.

11   12   1864   The **Federal destruction of Atlanta, GA,** continues as Maj. Gen. William T. Sherman, USA, prepares to launch his **"march to the sea"** campaign.

11   12   1864   Skirmish with bushwackers 12 miles northwest of Centreville, MO.

11   12   1864   Action at Cedar Creek, VA, the Shenandoah Valley Campaign.

11   12   1864   The **USS Wachusett** arrives off Hampton Roads, VA, with its prize in tow, the **CSS Florida,** in tow since October 7th, when it was captured at the Brazilian port of Bazhia.

11   12   1864   Action at Newtown (or Middletown), VA, as Lieut. Gen. Jubal Early, CSA, and Maj. Gen. Philip H. Sheridan, USA, meet again.

11   12   1864   Action at Nineveh, VA, the Shenandoah Valley Campaign.

11   13   1864   Skirmish with Indians at Ash Creek, 12 miles from Fort Larned, KS, as the hostile Indians attack and capture 5 wagons loaded with corn, and kill one Yankee, while injuring 4.

11   13   1864   Federal scout for Confederate guerrillas in Pemiscot County, MO, with skirmish. 11/13-16/1864.

11   13   1864   Lieut. Gen. Jubal Early, CSA, breaks off contact with Maj. Gen. Philip H. Sheridan, USA, and withdraws south back to New Market, VA, as his beleaguered force is further weakened when a large portion of his force is sent to assist Gen. Robert E. Lee's, CSA, dwindling siege lines around Petersburg, VA. Early having fought over 70 plus engagements in his Valley Campaign, and taking the war north to Washington, DC, is not normally remembered in the same vain as Stonewall Jackson's Valley Campaign, ultimately because of Jackson's success and Early's defeat.

11   14   1864   **The Campaign in North Alabama and Middle Tennessee.** 11/14/1864-1/23/1865.

11	14	1864	Skirmish on Cow Creek, KS.
11	14	1864	Federal expedition from Baton Rouge, LA, to Brookhaven, MS, and skirmishes. 11/14-21/1864.
11	14	1864	Maj. Gen. John M. Schofield, USA, assumes the command of the US forces at Pulaski, TN, consisting of two US Army Corps, the first line of defense against Lieut. Gen. John Bell Hood, CSA.
11	14	1864	Action near Russellville, TN, with Maj. Gen. John C. Breckinridge, CSA.
11	14	1864	President Abraham Lincoln **officially ends Maj. Gen. George Brinton McClellan's military career** by accepting George's resignation. **Another major player in the American Civil War bows out of the arena for good.**
11	15	1864	**Joseph Benjamin Palmer,** CSA, is appointed Brig. Gen.
11	15	1864	**The Savannah (Georgia) Campaign.** 11/15-12/21/1864.
11	15	1864	Maj. Gen. William T. Sherman's, USA, starts from Atlanta, GA, on his famous **"March to the Sea,"** destroying everything of military value in sight.
11	15	1864	Skirmish near East Point, GA, the "March to the Sea," Campaign by Maj. Gen. Wm Sherman.
11	15	1864	Skirmish at Jonesborough, GA, the "March to the Sea," Campaign by Maj. Gen. Wm Sherman.
11	15	1864	Skirmishes near Rough and Ready and Stockbridge, GA, the "March to the Sea," Campaign by Maj. Gen. Wm Sherman.
11	15	1864	Skirmish at Clinton, LA.
11	15	1864	Skirmish near Collierville, TN.
11	16	1864	**Dudley McIver DuBose,** CSA, is appointed Brig. Gen.
11	16	1864	Skirmishes on the line of Shoal Creek, AL. 11/16-20/1864.
11	16	1864	Federal scout from Devall's Bluff to West Point, AR, with skirmishes. 11/16-18/1864.
11	16	1864	Federal expedition from Barrancas to Pine Barren Bridge, FL, in the vicinity of Pensacola and Montgomery, where the Yankees capture the Rebel picket, move on and capture the next inner picket guards, wait and capture the Rebs coming to relieve these men, cross the rickety bridge and virtually capture the entire Confederate camp without a Union man injured. Well done. 11/16-17/1864.
11	16	1864	Skirmish at Bear Creek Station, GA, the "March to the Sea," Campaign by Maj. Gen. Wm Sherman.
11	16	1864	Skirmish at Cotton River Bridge, GA, the "March to the Sea," Campaign by Maj. Gen. Wm Sherman.
11	16	1864	Action at Lovejoy's Station, GA, the "March to the Sea," Campaign by Maj. Gen. Wm Sherman.
11	16	1864	Federal expedition from Brookfield to Brunswick, Keytesville, and Salisbury, MO. 11/16-23/1864.
11	16	1864	Federal expedition against guerrillas from Cape Girardeau to Patterson, Wayne County, MO, with skirmishes at: a) Reeves' Mill (Nov. 19th), and at b) Buckskull, Randolph County, AR. **(Nov. 20th).** 11/16-25/1864.
11	16	1864	Skirmishes at Strawberry Plains, TN, with the Confederates under Maj. Gen. John C. Breckinridge, CSA. 11/16-17/1864.
11	16	1864	Skirmish near Lee's Mill, the Richmond, VA, Campaign.
11	17	1864	**Godfrey Weitzel, U.S.A.,** is appointed Maj. Gen.
11	17	1864	Skirmish near Maysville, AL.
11	17	1864	Skirmish near New Market, AL.
11	17	1864	Federal expedition from Little Rock to Fagan's Ford, Saline River, AR. 11/17-18/1864.
11	17	1864	Affair at Towaliga Bridge, GA, as Maj. Gen. William T. Sherman, USA, takes four different routes to the sea in an attempt to confuse the Confederates.
11	17	1864	Federal expedition from Brashear City to Bayou Portage, LA, with skirmish **(Nov. 18th)** at Lake Fausse Pointe, LA. 11/17-19/1864.
11	17	1864	Skirmish at Flat Creek, TN, as Maj. Gen. John C. Breckinridge's, CSA, latest expedition is concluded.
11	17	1864	President Jefferson Davis, CSA, strongly objects to any notion by several Georgia State Senators wishing to discuss a separate peace treaty with the Federal government, Richmond, VA.
11	18	1864	Skirmish at Fayette, MO, with Confederate guerrillas who continue to harass the Federal troops.
11	18	1864	Skirmish at Kabletown, WV, the Shenandoah Valley Campaign.
11	18	1864	President Jefferson Davis orders Maj. Gen. Howell Cobb, CSA, commanding the Georgia reserves, to contest Maj. Gen. William T. Sherman's, USA, march to the sea with every available man including Negroes to dig obstructions, fell trees, etc.
11	19	1864	Skirmish at Duckett's Plantation, near Paint Rock River, AL.
11	19	1864	Skirmish at Buck Head Station, GA, the "March to the Sea," Campaign by Maj. Gen. Wm Sherman.

11	19	1864	Federal expedition from Terre Bonne to Bayou Grand Caillou, LA, with affair **(Nov. 23rd)** at Bayou Grand Caillou. 11/19-27/1864.
11	19	1864	Skirmish with Indians, near Plum Creek Station, the Nebraska Territory.
11	19	1864	With little threat of Confederate intervention, President Abraham Lincoln lifts the Federal blockade of the southern ports at Norfolk, VA, and at Fernandina and Pensacola, FL.

11	20	1864	Skirmish near Clinton, GA, with Maj. Gen. William T. Sherman, USA, as he continues to skirmish on his march to the sea, including the following skirmishes in Georgia:
11	20	1864	Skirmish at East Macon, GA.
11	20	1864	Skirmish at Griswoldville, GA.
11	20	1864	Skirmish at Walnut Creek, GA.
11	20	1864	Skirmish with Indians near Fort Zarah, KS, as two Yankees are severely injured with arrow wounds.
11	20	1864	Skirmish at Kabletown, WV, the Shenandoah Valley Campaign.

11	21	1864	The **Confederate Army of Tennessee,** under Lieut. Gen. John Bell Hood, CSA, sets out from Florence, AL, for Tennessee under the following commands: a) Maj. Gen. Benjamin Franklin Cheatham's Army Corps b) Lieut. Gen. Stephen Dill Lee's Army Corps c) Lieut. Gen. Alexander Peter Stewart's Army Corps d) Maj. Gen. Nathan Bedford Forrest Cavalry Corps
11	21	1864	Skirmish at Clinton, GA, the "March to the Sea," Campaign by Maj. Gen. Wm Sherman, and the following skirmishes in Georgia: 11/21-23/1864.
11	21	1864	Skirmish near Eatonton, GA.
11	21	1864	Skirmish at Gordon, GA.
11	21	1864	Skirmish at Griswoldville, GA, as Maj. Gen. William T. Sherman, USA, roughs up the Georgia state militia force.
11	21	1864	Skirmish near Macon, GA.
11	21	1864	Operations in the vicinity of Fulton, MO, with skirmish **(Nov. 28th)** near Fulton, against guerrillas who have been busy robbing and terrorizing the local citizens. 11/21-30/1864.

11	22	1864	Federal scout from Devall's Bluff to Augusta, AR, with the Rebel pickets fleeing as soon as the Yankees approached the town. 11/22-24/1864.
11	22	1864	Engagement at Griswoldville, GA, the "March to the Sea," Campaign by Maj. Gen. William T. Sherman.
11	22	1864	Action at Lawrenceburg, TN.
11	22	1864	Skirmish at Front Royal, VA, the Shenandoah Valley Campaign.
11	22	1864	Action at Rude's Hill, near Mount Jackson, VA, the Shenandoah Valley Campaign.

11	23	1864	Skirmishes at Balls' Ferry and the **Georgia Central Railroad Bridge,** Oconee River, GA, the "March to the Sea," Campaign by Maj. Gen. Wm. Sherman. 11/23-25/1864.
11	23	1864	Skirmish near, and Federal **occupation of Milledgeville,** the state capital of Georgia, by Maj. Gen. William T. Sherman, USA.
11	23	1864	Skirmishes at Morganza, LA, with fatalities.
11	23	1864	Federal expedition from Vicksburg under Maj. Gen. Edward R.S. Canby, USA, commanding the Military Division of West Mississippi and Maj. Gen. Napoleon J.T. Dana, USA, commanding the Districts of West Tennessee and Vicksburg, to Yazoo City, MS, and skirmish at Big Black Bridge on the **Mississippi Central Railroad (Nov. 27th)** and action at Concord Church **(Dec. lst).** This expedition successfully cuts Lieut. Gen. John B. Hoods', CSA, communications with Mobile, AL, and cuts the Confederate Army from the large quantities of supplies and stores accumulated at Jackson. The **3rd US Colored Cavalry** participates in the destruction of 30 miles of railroad track, wagon bridges, railroad depots and buildings, 2,600 bales of cotton, 2 locomotives, 4 cars, 4 stage coaches, 20 barrels of salt, and $166,000 of stores at Vaughn Station. The destruction of Confederate stores is typical of these expeditions. MS. 11/23-12/4/1864.
11	23	1864	Federal expedition from Fort Wingate against Indians in New Mexico Territory, with skirmish **(Dec. lst)** on the Red River, as the Federals pursue a small band of Indians trying escape with some stolen sheep into the mountains and maintain their freedom and own way of living. The party is comprised of 8 **Apaches** with their families, 3 **Navajoes** with their families, and 5 **Navajoes** who left their families behind. The Yankees catch up, take a couple of squaws and children prisoners, kill one buck, retake all the sheep and burn everything else the fleeing Indians left behind. 11/23-12/10/1864.

11	23	1864	Skirmish at Fouche Springs, TN, as Lieut. Gen. John B. Hood, CSA, continues his advance on Columbia.
11	23	1864	Skirmish at Henryville, TN.
11	23	1864	Action at Mount Pleasant, TN.
11	24	1864	Skirmish at Saint Charles, AR.
11	24	1864	Action at Campbellsville, TN.
11	24	1864	Skirmishes in front of Columbia, TN, as Maj. Gen. Nathan Bedford Forrest, CSA, and his cavalry attack the Federals there and are repulsed. 11/24-27/1864.
11	24	1864	Skirmish at Lynnville, TN.
11	24	1864	Skirmish at Parkins' Mill, VA, the Shenandoah Valley Campaign.
11	24	1864	Skirmish near Prince George Court-House, VA, the Richmond, VA, Campaign.
11	24	1864	The Federal **Attorney General, Edward Bates,** not of much value or heard from in the Lincoln Cabinet, **resigns his post.**
11	25	1864	Skirmish near Sandersville, GA, with Maj. Gen. Joseph Wheeler's, CSA, Cavalry and Maj. Gen. John Schofield, USA, the "March to the Sea," Campaign by Maj. Gen. Wm. Sherman.
11	25	1864	Affair at Raccourci, near Williamsport, LA, where Lieut. Thatcher, USN, commanding the **Gazelle Gunboat, No. 50,** while on shore, was murdered by guerrillas and horribly mutilated.
11	25	1864	Affair with Indians near Plum Creek Station, the Nebraska Territory.
11	25	1864	The engagement with **Kiowa, Comanche, Arapahoe** and **Apache** Indians at Adobe Fort, on the Canadian River, the New Mexico Territory, where, among other things, the Yankees destroy their village, including 150 lodges, large amounts of dried meats, berries, buffalo robes, powder, etc. The Federals continue with their war of attrition against the hostile Indian tribes.
11	25	1864	Southern agents, arriving from Canada, set fire to 10 hotels in New York City, NY, will little damage, as most fires are extinguished. One of the southern agents, R. C. Kennedy is captured and will be hanged for setting fire to Barnum's Museum, again, with little damage.
11	25	1864	Maj. Gen. Andrew A. Humphreys, USA, is assigned to the temporary command of the 2nd US Army Corps, the Richmond, VA, Campaign.
11	26	1864	**Lucius Bellinger Northrop,** CSA, appointed Brig. Gen.
11	26	1864	Federal expedition from Lewisburg to Strahan's Landing, AR. 11/16-12/2/1864.
11	26	1864	Skirmish at Sandersville, GA, as Maj. Gen. William T. Sherman, USA, continues to press on through the state of Georgia, causing destruction on his way.
11	26	1864	Skirmish at Osage, MO.
11	26	1864	Affair with Indians near Plum Creek Station, the Nebraska Territory.
11	26	1864	Skirmish with Indians at Spring Creek, the Nebraska Territory.
11	26	1864	Skirmish at Fairfax Station, VA.
11	27	1864	Federal scout from Little Rock to Benton, AR, where the Yankees are ambushed by a party of bushwackers. 11/27-30/1864.
11	27	1864	Skirmish at Sylvan Grove, GA, the "March to the Sea," Campaign by Maj. Gen. Wm. Sherman.
11	27	1864	Action at Waynesborough, GA, with Maj. Gen. William T. Sherman, USA, and opposing Confederate Cavalry. 11/27-28/1864.
11	27	1864	Federal expedition from Baton Rouge, LA, against the **Mobile and Ohio Railroad,** and skirmish at the Chickasawha Bridge, MS. **(Dec. 10th),** as Maj. Gen. Dabney H. Maury, CSA, commanding the District of the Gulf confronts Brig. Gen. John W. Davidson, USA's expedition. As an indication of the destruction in this district, the Federals have a difficult time moving through the region due to destroyed bridges, and roads. The Federals manage to cross the Amite, Pearl and Black Rivers, as well as Red Creek, traveling through Greensburg, Franklinton, Fordville, Columbia, Augusta, and over the Leaf and Chickasawha Rivers, cutting a path of destruction along the way. 11/27-12/13/1864.
11	27	1864	The explosion of the federal vessel, **Greyhound,** Maj. Gen. Benjamin F. Butler's, USA, floating headquarters, on the James River, VA, possibly by Confederate agents.
11	27	1864	Skirmishes at: a) Moorefield (27th and **28th**), where Brig. Gen. Thomas L. Rosser, CSA, surrounds and captures a small party of Union soldiers. b) affair at New Creek **(28th),** where Rosser surprises and captures Fort Kelley, along with 200 wagons, large amount of quartermaster, ordnance and commissary stores and c) skirmish **(28th)** at Piedmont, WV. Maj. Gen. Philip H. Sheridan, USA, is upset and calls the capture of

| 11 | 27 | 1864 | The explosion of the federal vessel, **Greyhound,** Maj. Gen. Benjamin F. Butler's, USA, floating headquarters, on the James River, VA, possibly by Confederate agents. |

11 27 1864 Skirmishes at:

a) Moorefield (27th and **28th**), where Brig. Gen. Thomas L. Rosser, CSA, surrounds and captures a small party of Union soldiers.

b) affair at New Creek **(28th),** where Rosser surprises and captures Fort Kelley, along with 200 wagons, large amount of quartermaster, ordnance and commissary stores and

c) skirmish **(28th)** at Piedmont, WV. Maj. Gen. Philip H. Sheridan, USA, is upset and calls the capture of Fort Kelley, a Federal disgrace. Sheridan's nature is not of one to accept such actions. 11/27-28/1864.

11 28 1864 Federal expedition from Brownsville to Fairview, AR. 11/28-12/8/1864.

11 28 1864 Skirmish at Buck Head Church, GA, as Maj. Gen. William T. Sherman, USA, presses on towards Savannah, GA.

11 28 1864 Engagement at Buck Head Creek, or Reynolds' Plantation, GA, the "March to the Sea," Campaign by Maj. Gen. Wm. Sherman.

11 28 1864 Skirmish near Davisborough, GA, the "March to the Sea," Campaign by Maj. Gen. Wm. Sherman.

11 28 1864 Skirmish near Waynesborough, GA, the "March to the Sea," Campaign by Maj. Gen. Wm. Sherman.

11 28 1864 Skirmish on Cow Creek, KS.

11 28 1864 The Federal Dept. of Mississippi is created, and Maj. Gen. Napoleon J. T. Dana, USA, is assigned to its command, MS.

11 28 1864 Skirmishes at crossings of Duck River, TN, as Maj. Gen. Nathan Bedford Forrest, CSA, and his cavalry attempt to ford above Columbia, TN, in cooperation with Lieut. Gen. John B. Hood's, infantry assault from the south on Maj. Gen. George Thomas, USA.

11 28 1864 Skirmish at Shelbyville, TN.

11 28 1864 Skirmish at Goresville, VA, where the Independent Battalion of Virginia Cavalry **(Loudoun Rangers)** fight with Lieut. Col. John S. Mosby's Partisan Rangers, driving the Rebels off. Mosby does not have a monopoly on recruiting irregulars as Virginia men are doing the same for the Union cause.

11 28 1864 Federal scout toward Stony Creek Station, the Richmond, VA, Campaign.

11 28 1864 Federal expedition from Winchester into Faquier and Loudoun Counties, VA, by Bvt. Maj. Gen. Wesley Merritt, destroying over $410,000 of property including: 87 horses, 474 Beef-cattle, 100 sheep, 230 barns, 8 mills, 1 distillery, 10,000 tons of hay and 25,000 bushels of grain. 11/28-12/3/1864.

11 28 1864 Maj. Gen. Winfield S. Hancock, USA, is assigned to the command of a new veteran volunteer army corps (to be organized), the Richmond, VA, Campaign.

11 28 1864 Federal expedition from Kernstown to Moorefield, & etc, WV. 11/28-12/2/1864.

11 29 1864 **Robert Bullock,** CSA, is appointed Brig. Gen.

11 29 1864 The Confederate Cavalry attack on the steamer, **Alamo,** on the Arkansas River, near Dardanelle, AR, the Rebels inflicting little damage to the vessel and men aboard except for riddling the vessel with 87 bullet holes.

11 29 1864 The engagement with friendly, **peaceful Cheyenne Indians on Sand Creek,** the Colorado Territory, with the **Union massacre of Cheyenne women and children,** 40 miles south of Fort Lyon, Denver, by **Col. John M. Chivington,** 1st Colorado Cavalry; Chivington boasts he just about annihilated the entire tribe, and belittles **Capt. Silas S. Soule** for thanking God that he had killed no Indians. This action will later be condemned by the US Government. The Major ordered to investigate Col. Chivington's actions acquire sworn testimony of fellow officers and soldiers at the massacre, and if, true, **the atrocities** the Federals committed against these human beings go beyond the scope of reporting in this book, as their actions go beyond **barbarism and savagery.**

11 29 1864 Skirmish near Louisville, GA, as Maj. Gen. William T. Sherman, USA, continues on his march to the sea.

11 29 1864 Skirmish at Doyal's Plantation, LA, with a small party of jayhawkers, near Donaldsonville.

11 29 1864 Federal scout from Warrensburg to the Greenton Valley, MO, against guerrillas, with no encounters. 11/29-12/3/1864.

11 29 1864 Skirmish near Boyd's Landing, SC.

11 29 1864 Action at the Columbia Ford, TN.

11 29 1864 Skirmish at Mount Carmel, TN.

11 29 1864 Skirmish near Rally Hill, TN.

11 29 1864 **The Engagement at Spring Hill (or Thompson's Creek), TN,** as Maj. Gen. John M. Schofield, USA, retreats to Franklin, TN, after the Confederates crossed the Duck River and attempted to flank the

11	30	1864	The engagement at Honey Hill, near Grahamville, SC, as the Union expeditionary force from Hilton Head, under Maj. Gen. John G. Foster, USA, commanding the Dept. of the South, and his subordinate, Brig. Gen. John P. Hatch, USA, are repulsed by an inferior Southern force, but with a strong defensive position; the Yankees report 746 casualties.
11	30	1864	**The Battle of Franklin, TN,** where Maj. Gen. John M. Schofield, USA, repulses repeated Confederate attacks under Lieut. Gen. John Bell Hood, CSA, with very severe fighting near the Gin House, the Carter House, and along the Columbia and Lewisburg Pikes. Schofield withdrawing across the Tennessee River, toward Nashville, TN. Hood continues to pursue Schofield. Hood's continuous brash and repeated assaults since his promotion to command the Confederate Army of Tennessee is taking a severe toll on the strength of his army, losing men he cannot replace. Total casualties approximate 8,575.
11	30	1864	**Brig. Gen. John Adams, CSA,** is mortally at the Battle of Franklin, TN, as he charged the Federal breastworks on his horse.
11	30	1864	**Maj. Gen. Patrick Ronayne Cleburne, CSA,** is mortally wounded at the Battle of Franklin, TN, as he was leading his troops against the Federals.
11	30	1864	**Brig. Gen. States Rights Gist, CSA,** is mortally wounded at the Battle of Franklin, TN, killed instantly as he led his troops in a frontal assault on the Federal breastworks.
11	30	1864	**Brig. Gen. Hiram Bronson Granbury, CSA,** is mortally wounded at the Battle of Franklin, TN, as he led his troops in a frontal assault on the Federal breastworks.
11	30	1864	**Brig. Gen. Otho French Strahl, CSA,** is mortally wounded at the Battle of Franklin, TN, as he handed rifles up to his men so they could fire down in the Federal works.
11	30	1864	**Brig. Gen. John Carpenter Carter, CSA,** is mortally wounded at the Battle of Franklin, TN, as he led his men in a frontal assault on the Federal breastworks, dying ten days later on December 10, 1864.
11	30	1864	Skirmish at Thompson's Station, TN.
11	30	1864	Skirmish at Snicker's Gap, VA.
11	30	1864	Skirmish at Kabletown, WV.
12	1	1864	**Operations in Central Arkansas.** 12/1-31/1864.
12	1	1864	Federal expedition down the Arkansas River to Pine Bluff, AR.
12	1	1864	Skirmish near Cypress Creek, Perry County, AR, with guerrillas.
12	1	1864	Federal expedition against guerrillas from Helena, AR, to Friar's Point, MS. 12/1-5/1864.
12	1	1864	Skirmish at Millen's (or Shady) Grove, GA, as Maj. Gen. William T. Sherman, USA, has completed more than half of his march to the sea at Savannah, GA, facing little Confederate resistance along the way.
12	1	1864	Operations in the vicinity of Waynesville, MO, with skirmish **(Dec. 2nd)** on the Big Piney, with bushwackers. 12/1-3/1864.
12	1	1864	Operations against hostile **Cheyenne Indians** in the Nebraska Territory, with skirmish **(Dec. 8th)** 6 miles east of Plum Creek, with the Indians who attacked a wagon train. 12/1-31/1864.
12	1	1864	The designation of the Federal Dept. of the Susquehanna is changed to the Dept. of Pennsylvania.
12	1	1864	**Operations about Nashville, TN,** where Maj. Gen. John M. Schofield, USA, combines forces with the well entrenched Maj. Gen. George Thomas, USA, against the pursuing Lieut. Gen. John B. Hood, CSA, and the Confederate Army of Tennessee, who is not far behind. 12/1-14/1864.
12	1	1864	Action of Owen's Cross-Roads, TN.
12	1	1864	Federal expedition to Stony Creek Station, and skirmish, the Richmond, VA, Campaign.
12	1	1864	President Abraham Lincoln appoints **James Speed** from Kentucky to replace Edward Bates, who recently resigned, as **US Attorney General.**
12	2	1864	**Brig. Gen. Archibald Gracie, Jr., CSA,** is mortally wounded during the siege of Petersburg, VA, instantly killed by a Federal artillery shell, the day after his 32nd birthday, as he observed the enemy through his telescope.
12	2	1864	Maj. Gen. Sterling Price's, CSA, command reaches Laynesport, AR, effectively ending his latest and last expedition into Missouri. Yet another last hurrah for the Confederacy.
12	2	1864	Skirmish at Buck Head Creek, GA, the "March to the Sea," Campaign by Maj. Gen. Wm. Sherman.
12	2	1864	Skirmish at Rocky Creek Church, GA, the "March to the Sea," Campaign by Maj. Gen. Wm. Sherman.
12	2	1864	Maj. Gen. Greenville M. Dodge, USA, is appointed to the command of the Dept. of the Missouri, and vice Maj. Gen. William S. Rosecrans, USA, is relieved, mainly due to Rosecrans' inability to effectively command this Department due, in part, to the various divided political groups in this department.
12	2	1864	Confederate operations against the stockades and block-houses on the **Nashville and Chattanooga**

Railroad, as Lieut. Gen. John Bell Hood, CSA, approaches the Union defensive lines of Nashville, TN. 12/2-4/1864.

| 12 | 2 | 1864 | Brig. Gen. Thomas J. Wood, USA, assumes the command of the 4th US Army Corps, because vice Maj. Gen. David S. Stanley, USA, is wounded at the battle of Franklin, TN. |

12 3 1864 Skirmish in Perry County, AR, and as usual, with casualties and loss of life.

12 3 1864 Skirmish at Thomas' Station, GA, along Maj. Gen. William T. Sherman's, USA, march to the sea, with Sherman cutting a path of destruction along the way, his men living off the land.

12 3 1864 Skirmish near New Madrid, MO, with a small band of guerrillas.

12 3 1864 The **10th and the 18th US Army Corps are discontinued** and the following are organized, and commanded by:

a) 24th US Army Corps - Maj. Gen. Edward O. C. Ord, USA

b) 25th US Army Corps - Maj. Gen. Godfrey Weitzel, USA

12 3 1864 President Abraham Lincoln and Lieut. Gen. Ulysses S. Grant, USA, urge Maj. Gen. George H. Thomas, USA, to attack the Confederate Army of Tennessee, outside Nashville, TN. Thomas defers, instead waiting to build his army's strength with incoming reinforcements and the solidifying of his entrenched defensive works.

12 4 1864 **James Monroe Goggin,** CSA, is appointed Brig. Gen.

12 4 1864 Skirmish at the Little Ogeechee River, GA, the "March to the Sea," Campaign by Maj. Gen. Wm. T. Sherman, including the following skirmishes in Georgia:

12 4 1864 Skirmish near Lumpkin's Station, GA.

12 4 1864 Skirmish near Statesborough, GA.

12 4 1864 Skirmish at Station No. 5, on the **Georgia Central Railroad,** GA.

12 4 1864 The engagement at Waynesborough, GA, as Maj. Gen. Joseph O. Wheeler's, CSA, Confederate cavalry attacks Maj. Gen. William T. Sherman's Cavalry, under Brig. Gen. Judson Kilpatrick who was guarding the Union men who were occupied destroying railroad tracks. Wheeler is eventually driven off.

12 4 1864 Skirmish with Indians on Cow Creek, 15 miles east of Fort Zarah, KS, as the Indians attack and capture a 6-mule team and wagon loaded with ammunition for the Fort. The Federals worry about this much ammunition getting into the Indians hands, arguing the wagon was not properly guarded.

12 4 1864 Skirmish on the New Texas road, near Morganza, LA, as Rebels dressed in Federal uniforms fire on the Union pickets there.

12 4 1864 Action at Bell's Mills, TN.

12 4 1864 Skirmish at White's Station, near Memphis, TN, where the anxious Union advance guards and flankers charge after the withdrawing Rebels, only to find themselves surrounded and made prisoners.

12 4 1864 Skirmish near Davenport Church, the Richmond, VA, Campaign.

12 5 1864 Skirmish near Lewisburg, AR.

12 5 1864 Skirmish 1.5 miles from Dalton, GA, the "March to the Sea," Campaign by Maj. Gen. William T. Sherman, as the Confederates unsuccessfully and ineffectively continue to contest Sherman's march, but to little avail against the overwhelming Union army. The Rebels manage to capture 30 Federals and cut the telegraph lines before retreating. These minor incidences are nothing more than a nuisance for Sherman; the Rebels lack the manpower and firepower to do serious damage to the Union army.

12 5 1864 Skirmish at the Little Ogeechee River, GA, as Maj. Gen. William T. Sherman, USA, presses on towards Savannah, GA.

12 5 1864 Confederate demonstrations against Murfreesborough, TN, by Maj. Gen. Nathan B. Forrest, CSA, against Maj. Gen. Lovell H. Rousseau, USA. Forrest retreats back towards Nashville, TN. 12/5-7/1864.

12 5 1864 The Confederate capture of the tug-boat, **Lizzie Freeman,** while towing the barge, **Zimmerman,** near Smithfield, VA, as they went to Aiken's Island to procure paving stones. The crew was captured as they slept and are paroled by the Rebels. Brig. Gen. George Foster, USA, commanding, is outraged that the captain took the ship without authorization, and told him to forget about sitting out the rest of the war as he would not recognize his capture and parole, so get back to work.

12 6 1864 **Patrick Henry Jones,** USA, is appointed Brig. Gen.

12 6 1864 Federal expedition from Brownsville to Des Arc, with skirmish near Des Arc, AR.

12 6 1864 Skirmish at Lewisburg, AR.

12 6 1864 Federal demonstrations against the **Charleston and Savannah Railroad,** SC, with little success, Maj. Gen. Samuel Jones, CSA, commanding the District of South Carolina, defending. However, Maj. Gen.

William Tecumseh Sherman, USA, will soon be on his way to change all of this. The Rebs lose 52 men. 12/6-9/1864.

| 12 | 6 | 1864 | Action at Bell's Mills, TN, between the Union naval flotilla comprised of the Union gunboat, **USS Neosho,** and Federal steamers, **USS Fairplay, USS Moose** and the **USS Silver Lake,** and Confederate shore batteries, with little damage to the Union vessels. |

12 6 1864 **Brig. Gen. Hylan Benton Lyon's, CSA, Confederate Raid** from Paris, TN, to Hopkinsville, KY, etc., and skirmishes. Lyon has under his command 800 poorly equipped, undisciplined new recruits, many without shoes and proper clothing. Upon learning of Lieut. Gen. John B. Hoods' defeat and of his army leaving Tennessee, 500 of Lyon's men deserted and returned to their homes. Before they deserted, Lyon was able to capture 3 Federal steamers, burn 8 court-houses, railroad bridges, depots, etc., and caused Maj. Gen. McCook's entire division of cavalry to be withdrawn from Nashville, which aided in Hood's retreat from the Nashville area. 12/6/1864-1/15/1865.

12 6 1864 Federal expedition from Portsmouth, VA, to Hertford, NC, and the successful capture of guerrillas, horses, cattle, etc. The Yankees continue to grind and wear down the dwindling remaining Confederate resources. 12/6-10/1864.

12 6 1864 President Abraham Lincoln appoints former Secretary of the Treasury, **Salmon P. Chase, as Chief Justice of the US Supreme Court,** replacing the deceased Roger B. Taney. It is suggested Lincoln did so to eliminate Chase's political aspirations.

12 7 1864 Skirmish near Paint Rock Bridge, AL.

12 7 1864 Federal expedition from Brownsville to Arkansas Post, AR. 12/7-13/1864.

12 7 1864 Federal expedition from Devall's Bluff to Augusta, AR. 12/7-8/1864.

12 7 1864 Skirmish at Buck Creek, GA, as Maj. Gen. William T. Sherman, USA, creeps closer to Savannah, GA, with skirmishes at the following Georgia sites:

12 7 1864 Skirmish at Cypress Swamp, near Sister's Ferry, GA.

12 7 1864 Skirmish at Jenks' Bridge, Ogeechee River, GA.

12 7 1864 Affair at Moselle Bridge, on the **Southwest Branch Pacific Railroad,** near Franklin, MO, as a lone Confederate is instantly killed, shot dead with 6 rifle balls passing through him, as he tried to burn the bridge.

12 7 1864 **Federal operations to and operations against Fort Fisher, NC.** 12/7-27/1864.

12 7 1864 Federal expedition to Hicksford, and skirmishes, the Richmond, VA, Campaign. 12/7-12/1864.

12 7 1864 Lieut. Gen. Ulysses S. Grant, USA, commander of the Union Armies, contemplates removing Maj. Gen. George H. Thomas, USA, if Thomas does not immediately obey orders and attack Lieut. Gen. John Bell Hood, CSA.

12 8 1864 Skirmish near Bryan Court-House, GA, the "March to the Sea, Campaign by Maj. Gen. Wm Sherman.

12 8 1864 Skirmish at Ebenezer Creek, GA, the "March to the Sea," Campaign by Maj. Gen. Wm Sherman.

12 8 1864 Affair at **Tuscumbia, MO,** where Confederate Cavalry **captures** the town and disarmed and paroled 25 Yankees stationed there.

12 8 1864 Maj. Gen. Napoleon J. T. Dana, USA, assumes the command of the Dept. of Mississippi.

12 8 1864 Maj. Gen. Benjamin F. Butler, USA, and 6,500 Union men are transported down the James River to Fortress Monroe, VA, to join the naval expeditionary force assembling there for the planned assault on Fort Fisher, to close the last remaining open Confederate port at Wilmington, NC.

12 8 1864 Skirmish at Hatcher's Run, south of Petersburg, VA, the Richmond, VA, campaign.

12 9 1864 Skirmish at Cuyler's Plantation, GA, as Maj. Gen. William T. Sherman, USA, reaches the outskirts of Savannah, GA, with skirmishes at the following Georgia locations:

12 9 1864 Skirmish between Eden and Pooler Stations, GA.

12 9 1864 Skirmish at Monteith Swamp, GA.

12 9 1864 Skirmish at Ogeechee Canal, GA.

12 9 1864 Maj. Gen. Greenville M. Dodge, USA, assumes the command of the Dept. of the Missouri, MO, etal.

12 9 1864 The **USS Otesgo** and the tugboat, **Bazely,** are sunk by Confederate torpedoes on the Roanoke River, near Jamesville, NC.

12 9 1864 Federal reconnaissance to Hatcher's Run, and skirmishes, the Richmond, VA, Campaign, as military activity along the siege lines of Petersburg, VA, begin to pick up. 12/9-10/1864.

12 10 1864 **Brig. Gen. John Carpenter Carter, CSA,** dies from wounds he received at the Battle of Franklin, TN, on November 30, 1864.

| 12 | 10 | 1864 | Federal expedition against **Tonto Apache Indians** in Central Arizona, with skirmish **(Dec. 15th)** on Hassayampa Creek, where the Yankees kill 11 of 15 Apache warriors, the other 4 fleeing, leaving large blood trails to follow. The Federals then burn their camp. 12/10-23/1864. |

| 12 | 10 | 1864 | Skirmish near Savannah, GA, as Maj. Gen. William T. Sherman, USA, opts not to attack the fortified Confederate positions under Lieut. Gen. William Hardee, CSA, but instead, to lay siege to the city. |

| 12 | 10 | 1864 | The capture and burning of the Confederate steamer, **Ida,** on the Savannah, River, GA, the "March to the Sea," Campaign by Maj. Gen. Wm Sherman. |

| 12 | 10 | 1864 | Skirmish near Springfield, GA, the "March to the Sea," Campaign by Maj. Gen. Wm Sherman. |

| 12 | 10 | 1864 | Federal scout from Core Creek to Southwest Creek, NC, and skirmishes, with the dismounted Confederates with little consequence to either side, except a few men depart this earth, while others will carry battle scars for life, their own testimony to having met today in this obscure field of battle of the American Civil War. 12/10-15/1864. |

| 12 | 10 | 1864 | Federal expedition from East Tennessee into Southwestern Virginia, to destroy Confederate salt works and supplies, by Maj. Gen. George Stoneman, USA. 12/10-29/1864. |

| 12 | 10 | 1864 | Brig. Gen. Alvan C. Gillem's, USA, command starts from Knoxville, TN, part of Maj. Gen. George Stoneman's forces. |

| 12 | 10 | 1864 | Skirmish in front of Fort Holly, near Petersburg, VA, as Lieut. Gen. Ulysses S. Grant, USA, keeps mounting pressure on the Confederate defensive lines. 12/9-10/1864. |

| 12 | 11 | 1864 | **The Federal Investment of Savannah, GA,** as Maj. Gen. William T. Sherman, USA, begins to rebuild the 1,000 foot bridge over the Ogeechee River to Fort McAllister, which was destroyed by the Confederates. 12/11-21/1864. |

| 12 | 11 | 1864 | Operations about Broadwater Ferry and Chowan River, VA, against the Confederates as Brig. Gen. Israel Vogdes, USA, commanding the US forces at Portsmouth, VA, grabs and detains a squadron of the 20th NY Cavalry heading for the front, to be used for this work instead. The general is improvising. The Cavalry probably doesn't mind staying here instead of the going to the front. Unfortunately, Rebel bullets are just as deadly in this work as anywhere else. Just maybe not as many in this region. 10/11-19/1864. |

| 12 | 12 | 1864 | The capture of the Confederate steamer, **Resolute,** on the Savannah, River, GA, the "March to the Sea," Campaign by Maj. Gen. Wm Sherman. |

| 12 | 12 | 1864 | Communications are established between Gen. William T. Sherman's USA, and the **South Atlantic Blockading Squadron,** under the command of Rear-Admiral Dahlgren, Savannah, GA. Maj. Gen. William T. Sherman has now truly reached the sea. |

| 12 | 12 | 1864 | Skirmish on the Amite River, LA. |

| 12 | 12 | 1864 | Maj. Gen. George H. Thomas, USA, prepares to attack Lieut. Gen. John B. Hood, CSA, outside Nashville, TN, as soon as the ice and sleet melts. |

| 12 | 12 | 1864 | Maj. Gen. George Stoneman's, USA, command (that of Brig. Gen. Stephan G. Burbridge's and Brig. Gen. Alvan C. Gillem's forces) advances from Bean's Station, TN, with the following skirmish: |

| 12 | 12 | 1864 | Skirmish at Big Creek, near Rogersville, TN. |

| 12 | 13 | 1864 | **Cyrus Hamlin,** USA, is appointed Brig. Gen. |

| 12 | 13 | 1864 | Federal expedition up the White River aboard the steamers, **Sir William** and **Kate Hart,** from Devall's Bluff, AR, with the Federal seizure of large quantities of Confederate property. 12/13-15/1864. |

| 12 | 13 | 1864 | Affair 3 miles east of Devall's Bluff, AR, with Union pickets. |

| 12 | 13 | 1864 | Federal expedition from Barrancas, FL, by the **97th US Colored Infantry**, to, and the **capture of, Pollard, AL,** with destruction to public buildings, property, clothing, military equipment, etc, and skirmishes at all the streams from the Little Escambiato Pine Barren Creek. Gen. Pierre G.T. Beauregard, CSA, is unable to muster a strong force from Mobile to contest the Yankees.12/13-19/1864. |

| 12 | 13 | 1864 | The engagement at and **Federal capture of Fort McAllister,** outside Savannah, GA, by the 15th US Army Corps, which effectively dooms the city to the Union invaders, the "March to the Sea," Campaign by Maj. Gen. William T. Sherman. |

| 12 | 13 | 1864 | Federal expedition from Morganza to and beyond Morgan's Ferry, LA. 12/13-14/1864. |

| 12 | 13 | 1864 | Action at Kingsport, TN, where Brig. Gen. Basil W. Duke, CSA, commanding the remnants of the late Brig. Gen. John Hunt Morgan's Confederate forces, is defeated by Maj. Gen. George Stoneman's, USA, latest expedition. |

| 12 | 13 | 1864 | The Confederate attack on the railroad train near Murfreesborough, TN. |

| 12 | 13 | 1864 | Lieut. Gen. Ulysses S. Grant, USA, orders Maj. Gen. John Logan, USA, to Nashville, TN, and relieve Maj. Gen. George H. Thomas, USA, of command, if Thomas fails to attack Lieut. Gen. John B. Hood, CSA, once the weather breaks. |

William Tecumseh Sherman, USA, will soon be on his way to change all of this. The Rebs lose 52 men. 12/6-9/1864.

12	6	1864	Action at Bell's Mills, TN, between the Union naval flotilla comprised of the Union gunboat, **USS Neosho,** and Federal steamers, **USS Fairplay, USS Moose** and the **USS Silver Lake,** and Confederate shore batteries, with little damage to the Union vessels.
12	6	1864	**Brig. Gen. Hylan Benton Lyon's, CSA, Confederate Raid** from Paris, TN, to Hopkinsville, KY, etc., and skirmishes. Lyon has under his command 800 poorly equipped, undisciplined new recruits, many without shoes and proper clothing. Upon learning of Lieut. Gen. John B. Hoods' defeat and of his army leaving Tennessee, 500 of Lyon's men deserted and returned to their homes. Before they deserted, Lyon was able to capture 3 Federal steamers, burn 8 court-houses, railroad bridges, depots, etc., and caused Maj. Gen. McCook's entire division of cavalry to be withdrawn from Nashville, which aided in Hood's retreat from the Nashville area. 12/6/1864-1/15/1865.
12	6	1864	Federal expedition from Portsmouth, VA, to Hertford, NC, and the successful capture of guerrillas, horses, cattle, etc. The Yankees continue to grind and wear down the dwindling remaining Confederate resources. 12/6-10/1864.
12	6	1864	President Abraham Lincoln appoints former Secretary of the Treasury, **Salmon P. Chase, as Chief Justice of the US Supreme Court,** replacing the deceased Roger B. Taney. It is suggested Lincoln did so to eliminate Chase's political aspirations.
12	7	1864	Skirmish near Paint Rock Bridge, AL.
12	7	1864	Federal expedition from Brownsville to Arkansas Post, AR. 12/7-13/1864.
12	7	1864	Federal expedition from Devall's Bluff to Augusta, AR. 12/7-8/1864.
12	7	1864	Skirmish at Buck Creek, GA, as Maj. Gen. William T. Sherman, USA, creeps closer to Savannah, GA, with skirmishes at the following Georgia sites:
12	7	1864	Skirmish at Cypress Swamp, near Sister's Ferry, GA.
12	7	1864	Skirmish at Jenks' Bridge, Ogeechee River, GA.
12	7	1864	Affair at Moselle Bridge, on the **Southwest Branch Pacific Railroad,** near Franklin, MO, as a lone Confederate is instantly killed, shot dead with 6 rifle balls passing through him, as he tried to burn the bridge.
12	7	1864	**Federal operations to and operations against Fort Fisher, NC.** 12/7-27/1864.
12	7	1864	Federal expedition to Hicksford, and skirmishes, the Richmond, VA, Campaign. 12/7-12/1864.
12	7	1864	Lieut. Gen. Ulysses S. Grant, USA, commander of the Union Armies, contemplates removing Maj. Gen. George H. Thomas, USA, if Thomas does not immediately obey orders and attack Lieut. Gen. John Bell Hood, CSA.
12	8	1864	Skirmish near Bryan Court-House, GA, the "March to the Sea, Campaign by Maj. Gen. Wm Sherman.
12	8	1864	Skirmish at Ebenezer Creek, GA, the "March to the Sea," Campaign by Maj. Gen. Wm Sherman.
12	8	1864	Affair at **Tuscumbia, MO,** where Confederate Cavalry **captures** the town and disarmed and paroled 25 Yankees stationed there.
12	8	1864	Maj. Gen. Napoleon J. T. Dana, USA, assumes the command of the Dept. of Mississippi.
12	8	1864	Maj. Gen. Benjamin F. Butler, USA, and 6,500 Union men are transported down the James River to Fortress Monroe, VA, to join the naval expeditionary force assembling there for the planned assault on Fort Fisher, to close the last remaining open Confederate port at Wilmington, NC.
12	8	1864	Skirmish at Hatcher's Run, south of Petersburg, VA, the Richmond, VA, campaign.
12	9	1864	Skirmish at Cuyler's Plantation, GA, as Maj. Gen. William T. Sherman, USA, reaches the outskirts of Savannah, GA, with skirmishes at the following Georgia locations:
12	9	1864	Skirmish between Eden and Pooler Stations, GA.
12	9	1864	Skirmish at Monteith Swamp, GA.
12	9	1864	Skirmish at Ogeechee Canal, GA.
12	9	1864	Maj. Gen. Greenville M. Dodge, USA, assumes the command of the Dept. of the Missouri, MO, etal.
12	9	1864	The **USS Otesgo** and the tugboat, **Bazely,** are sunk by Confederate torpedoes on the Roanoke River, near Jamesville, NC.
12	9	1864	Federal reconnaissance to Hatcher's Run, and skirmishes, the Richmond, VA, Campaign, as military activity along the siege lines of Petersburg, VA, begin to pick up. 12/9-10/1864.
12	10	1864	**Brig. Gen. John Carpenter Carter, CSA,** dies from wounds he received at the Battle of Franklin, TN, on November 30, 1864.

12	10	1864	Federal expedition against **Tonto Apache Indians** in Central Arizona, with skirmish **(Dec. 15th)** on Hassayampa Creek, where the Yankees kill 11 of 15 Apache warriors, the other 4 fleeing, leaving large blood trails to follow. The Federals then burn their camp. 12/10-23/1864.
12	10	1864	Skirmish near Savannah, GA, as Maj. Gen. William T. Sherman, USA, opts not to attack the fortified Confederate positions under Lieut. Gen. William Hardee, CSA, but instead, to lay siege to the city.
12	10	1864	The capture and burning of the Confederate steamer, **Ida,** on the Savannah, River, GA, the "March to the Sea," Campaign by Maj. Gen. Wm Sherman.
12	10	1864	Skirmish near Springfield, GA, the "March to the Sea," Campaign by Maj. Gen. Wm Sherman.
12	10	1864	Federal scout from Core Creek to Southwest Creek, NC, and skirmishes, with the dismounted Confederates with little consequence to either side, except a few men depart this earth, while others will carry battle scars for life, their own testimony to having met today in this obscure field of battle of the American Civil War. 12/10-15/1864.
12	10	1864	Federal expedition from East Tennessee into Southwestern Virginia, to destroy Confederate salt works and supplies, by Maj. Gen. George Stoneman, USA. 12/10-29/1864.
12	10	1864	Brig. Gen. Alvan C. Gillem's, USA, command starts from Knoxville, TN, part of Maj. Gen. George Stoneman's forces.
12	10	1864	Skirmish in front of Fort Holly, near Petersburg, VA, as Lieut. Gen. Ulysses S. Grant, USA, keeps mounting pressure on the Confederate defensive lines. 12/9-10/1864.
12	11	1864	**The Federal Investment of Savannah, GA,** as Maj. Gen. William T. Sherman, USA, begins to rebuild the 1,000 foot bridge over the Ogeechee River to Fort McAllister, which was destroyed by the Confederates. 12/11-21/1864.
12	11	1864	Operations about Broadwater Ferry and Chowan River, VA, against the Confederates as Brig. Gen. Israel Vogdes, USA, commanding the US forces at Portsmouth, VA, grabs and detains a squadron of the 20th NY Cavalry heading for the front, to be used for this work instead. The general is improvising. The Cavalry probably doesn't mind staying here instead of the going to the front. Unfortunately, Rebel bullets are just as deadly in this work as anywhere else. Just maybe not as many in this region. 10/11-19/1864.
12	12	1864	The capture of the Confederate steamer, **Resolute,** on the Savannah, River, GA, the "March to the Sea," Campaign by Maj. Gen. Wm Sherman.
12	12	1864	Communications are established between Gen. William T. Sherman's USA, and the **South Atlantic Blockading Squadron,** under the command of Rear-Admiral Dahlgren, Savannah, GA. Maj. Gen. William T. Sherman has now truly reached the sea.
12	12	1864	Skirmish on the Amite River, LA.
12	12	1864	Maj. Gen. George H. Thomas, USA, prepares to attack Lieut. Gen. John B. Hood, CSA, outside Nashville, TN, as soon as the ice and sleet melts.
12	12	1864	Maj. Gen. George Stoneman's, USA, command (that of Brig. Gen. Stephan G. Burbridge's and Brig. Gen. Alvan C. Gillem's forces) advances from Bean's Station, TN, with the following skirmish:
12	12	1864	Skirmish at Big Creek, near Rogersville, TN.
12	13	1864	**Cyrus Hamlin,** USA, is appointed Brig. Gen.
12	13	1864	Federal expedition up the White River aboard the steamers, **Sir William** and **Kate Hart,** from Devall's Bluff, AR, with the Federal seizure of large quantities of Confederate property. 12/13-15/1864.
12	13	1864	Affair 3 miles east of Devall's Bluff, AR, with Union pickets.
12	13	1864	Federal expedition from Barrancas, FL, by the **97th US Colored Infantry**, to, and the **capture of, Pollard, AL,** with destruction to public buildings, property, clothing, military equipment, etc, and skirmishes at all the streams from the Little Escambiato Pine Barren Creek. Gen. Pierre G.T. Beauregard, CSA, is unable to muster a strong force from Mobile to contest the Yankees.12/13-19/1864.
12	13	1864	The engagement at and **Federal capture of Fort McAllister,** outside Savannah, GA, by the 15th US Army Corps, which effectively dooms the city to the Union invaders, the "March to the Sea," Campaign by Maj. Gen. William T. Sherman.
12	13	1864	Federal expedition from Morganza to and beyond Morgan's Ferry, LA. 12/13-14/1864.
12	13	1864	Action at Kingsport, TN, where Brig. Gen. Basil W. Duke, CSA, commanding the remnants of the late Brig. Gen. John Hunt Morgan's Confederate forces, is defeated by Maj. Gen. George Stoneman's, USA, latest expedition.
12	13	1864	The Confederate attack on the railroad train near Murfreesborough, TN.
12	13	1864	Lieut. Gen. Ulysses S. Grant, USA, orders Maj. Gen. John Logan, USA, to Nashville, TN, and relieve Maj. Gen. George H. Thomas, USA, of command, if Thomas fails to attack Lieut. Gen. John B. Hood, CSA, once the weather breaks.

12	14	1864	The US Naval attack on Forts Rosedew and Beaulieu, the Vernon River, GA, until the Confederates surrendered on the 21st, the "March to the Sea," Campaign by Maj. Gen. William T. Sherman. 12/14-21/1864.
12	14	1864	Federal operations in the vicinity of the Hermitage Plantation, near Morganza, LA. 12/14/1864-1/5/1865.
12	14	1864	Skirmish in the Cypress Swamp, near Cape Girardeau, MO, where the Federals kill 3 guerrillas.
12	14	1864	Affair at Bristol, TN, as Maj. Gen. George Stoneman's, USA, Cavalry raid captures over 300 Confederates.
12	14	1864	Skirmish on the Germantown road, near Memphis, TN, as Maj. Gen. George H. Thomas, USA, prepares to attack the Confederate Army of Tennessee the following day.
12	14	1864	**Maj. Gen. Edward O.C. Ord, USA, is in temporary command of the Army of the James,** the Richmond, VA, Campaign.
12	15	1864	The Confederate capture of the railroad train near Murfreesborough, TN.
12	15	1864	**The Battle of Nashville, TN, as the last major battle in the West** is fought around the capital of Tennessee. In two days fighting, Maj. Gen. George H. Thomas, USA, overwhelms the Confederate Army of Tennessee, forcing Lieut. Gen. John B. Hood, CSA, to withdraw toward Columbia. Fighting occurs at Montgomery Hill, Brentwood Hills, astride the Franklin and Granny White pikes, etc. Total casualties approximate 4,560. With no means of restocking the army, Lieut. Gen. John B. Hood's, Confederate Army of the Tennessee remains a force but diminished. 12/15-16/1864.
12	15	1864	Federal expedition from Fortress Monroe to Pagan Creek, VA, aboard the steamer, **John Tracy,** to capture Rebels reported by a spy who will be celebrating a wedding at a local residence there. The steamer runs aground unfamiliar shoals and oyster beds, not arriving until after 11 p.m. The alerted Rebs move the wedding up 3 hours, enjoy the festivities and are long gone before the Yankees surround the place.
12	15	1864	Skirmish near Abingdon, VA, with Maj. Gen. George Stoneman, USA.
12	15	1864	Skirmish near Glade Springs, VA, with Maj. Gen. George Stoneman, USA.
12	16	1864	Skirmish at Hinesville, GA, as Maj. Gen. William T. Sherman, USA, resupplies his army with supplies from the Union vessels off the Atlantic coast.
12	16	1864	Federal expedition from Morganza to the Atchafalaya River, LA. 8/16-19/1864.
12	16	1864	Action at Marion and the Federal **capture of Wytheville, VA,** by Maj. Gen. George Stoneman, USA, as Maj. Gen. John C. Breckinridge, CSA, commanding the Dept. of Western Virginia and East Tennessee musters as many Confederates in the region to block Stoneman's latest raid.
12	17	1864	The **USS Louisiana,** loaded with 350 tons of gunpowder is towed off Fort Fisher, near Wilmington, NC, to be exploded, as the huge naval flotilla with Maj. Gen. Benjamin F. Butler's 6,500 men sail from Fortress Monroe, Hampton Roads, VA.
12	17	1864	Action at Franklin, TN, as Union cavalry under Brig. Gen. James H. Wilson, USA, pursue the retreating Confederate Army of Tennessee.
12	17	1864	Action at Hollow Tree Gap, TN.
12	17	1864	Action at West Harpeth River, TN.
12	17	1864	The capture and the destruction of the Lead Mines in southwest Virginia by Maj. Gen. George Stoneman, USA, as another Federal expeditionary force continues to destroy valuable Rebel supplies. The wheels continue to come off the Confederate military machine.
12	17	1864	The engagement near Marion, VA, with Maj. Gen. George Stoneman, USA. 12/17-18/1864.
12	17	1864	Skirmish near Mount Airy, VA, with Maj. Gen. George Stoneman, USA .
12	18	1864	Skirmish near Dudley Lake, AR.
12	18	1864	Lieut. Gen. William Hardee, CSA, refuses Maj. Gen. William T. Sherman's, USA, demand of the surrender of **Savannah, GA,** opting to **evacuate** the city instead.
12	18	1864	Skirmish on Little River, in New Madrid County, MO, with guerrillas.
12	18	1864	Skirmish at Spring Hill, TN, with the Confederate Army of Tennessee.
12	19	1864	**William Lowther Jackson,** CSA, is appointed Brig. Gen.
12	19	1864	Skirmish at Rector's Farm, AR.
12	19	1864	Skirmish at Curtis's Creek, TN.
12	19	1864	Skirmish at Rutherford's Creek, TN.
12	19	1864	Federal expedition from Kernstown to Lacey's Springs, VA, and action at Lacey's Springs **(21st),** as Bvt. Maj. Gen. George Armstrong Custer, USA, and his Federal cavalry drive against the Rebels, destroying

surrender of **Savannah, GA,** opting to **evacuate** the city instead.

12	18	1864	Skirmish on Little River, in New Madrid County, MO, with guerrillas.
12	18	1864	Skirmish at Spring Hill, TN, with the Confederate Army of Tennessee.

12	19	1864	**William Lowther Jackson,** CSA, is appointed Brig. Gen.
12	19	1864	Skirmish at Rector's Farm, AR.
12	19	1864	Skirmish at Curtis's Creek, TN.
12	19	1864	Skirmish at Rutherford's Creek, TN.
12	19	1864	Federal expedition from Kernstown to Lacey's Springs, VA, and action at Lacey's Springs **(21st),** as Bvt. Maj. Gen. George Armstrong Custer, USA, and his Federal cavalry drive against the Rebels, destroying property, inflicting casualties, and disrupting communications. The sanctity of the South's beautiful Shenandoah Valley has just about been totally destroyed by the Federals. 12/19-22/1864.
12	19	1864	Federal Cavalry expedition led by Brig. Gen. Alfred T. A. Torbert, USA, from Winchester to near Gordonsville, VA, including skirmishes at:

a) Madison Court-House **(Dec. 21st)**
b) Liberty Mills **(Dec. 22nd)**
c) near Gordonsville, **(Dec. 23rd).** Military activity in the Shenandoah Valley is greatly diminished as the majority of Lieut. Gen. Jubal Early, CSA, and Maj. Gen. Philip H. Sheridan, USA, armies are sent to the battle front at Petersburg, VA. 12/19-28/1864.

12	20	1864	**John McArthur, U.S.A.,** is appointed Maj. Gen.
12	20	1864	The Confederate **evacuation of Savannah, GA,** by Lieut. Gen. William Hardee, CSA.
12	20	1864	Federal expeditions from Cape Girardeau and Dallas, MO, to Cherokee Bay, AR, and the Saint Francis River, with skirmishes, with guerrillas. 12/20/1864-1/4/1865.
12	20	1864	The **USS Hartford,** arrives in New York City Harbor for repairs. The ship and its commander, Admiral Daniel G. Farragut's part in the American Civil War has come to an end.
12	20	1864	Engagement at Poplar Point, NC. 12/20-22/1864.
12	20	1864	Skirmish near the Pocotaligo Road, SC, as the **33rd US Colored Infantry** drives off the 300+ plus Rebels contesting their advance near the Tullifinny Creek, capturing men and supplies.
12	20	1864	Skirmish at Columbia, TN.
12	20	1864	The capture and the destruction of the salt-works at Saltville, VA, by Maj. Gen. George Stoneman, USA. 12/20-21/1864.

12	21	1864	The 20th US Army Corps **occupies Savannah, GA.**
12	21	1864	Skirmish at Franklin Creek, MS. 12/21-22/1864.
12	21	1864	Federal expedition, under Brig. Gen. Benjamin H. Grierson, USA, from Memphis, TN, to destroy the **Mobile and Ohio Railroad,** about 100 miles of railroad track, and capturing 800 Confederates with nearly enough horses to mount them all. 12/21/1864-1/5/1865.

12	22	1864	**James Edward Harrison,** CSA, is appointed Brig. Gen.
12	22	1864	**John Doby Kennedy,** CSA, is appointed Brig. Gen.
12	22	1864	Maj. Gen. Joseph J. Reynolds, USA, supersedes Maj. Gen. Frederick Steele in the command of the Dept. of Arkansas.
12	22	1864	Skirmish on Franklin Creek, MS.
12	22	1864	Skirmish at Duck River, TN, as Maj. Gen. George H. Thomas, USA, pursues the retreating Lieut. Gen. John B. Hood, CSA.
12	22	1864	The Union forces under Maj. Gen. George Stoneman, USA, retire from Saltville, VA.

12	23	1864	Federal expedition from Baton Rouge to Clinton, LA. 12/23-24/1864.
12	23	1864	The **USS Louisiana,** loaded with 350 tons of explosives, is blown up near Fort Fisher, Wilmington, NC, with no damage to the fort. So much for that idea.
12	23	1864	Skirmish at Warfield's, near Columbia, TN.
12	23	1864	The US Government honors **Daniel G. Farragut**'s naval role by promoting him to the newly created rank of **Vice Admiral-the Army equivalent of Lieut. Gen.**

12	24	1864	Skirmish near Fort Smith, AR.
12	24	1864	Federal scout from Pine Bluff to Richland, AR, with skirmish (Dec. 24th) near Richland. 12/24-25/1864.
12	24	1864	Skirmish at Lynnville, TN.
12	24	1864	Action at Richland Creek, TN.

| 12 | 24 | 1864 | Skirmish at Taylorstown, VA. |

Maj. Gen. Benjamin F. Butler, USA, resumes the command of the Army of the James, the Richmond, VA, Campaign.

(12 24 1864)

12	25	1864	Engagement at Verona, MS, with Brig. Gen. Benjamin H. Grierson's Union expedition.
12	25	1864	Actions at King's (or Anthony's) Hill, or Devil's Gap, TN, with the Confederate Army of Tennessee.
12	25	1864	Skirmish at Richland Creek, TN, with Lieut. Gen. John B. Hood, CSA.

12 25 1864 Skirmish near White's Station, TN, with Maj. Gen. George H. Thomas, USA, as about 100 men of his advance guard are surrounded and captured by the Confederates; the Federals not suspecting that large of a Rebel force in the area. In many instances of these captures, the Rebels, unable to provide for their prisoners, parole them; the Union commanders refuse to recognize these paroles and send these men back into the action, in lieu of releasing them from their military assignment.

12 26 1864 Federal expedition against Indians in Central Arizona, with skirmish **(Jan. lst)** at Sycamore Springs, the Arizona Territory. 12/26/1864-1/1/1865.

12 26 1864 Action at Sugar Creek, TN, as Lieut. Gen. John B. Hood, CSA, and the remnants of the Confederate Army of Tennessee cross the Tennessee River towards Tupelo, MS, signifying the end to Hood's campaign north. Hood's a total failure while Sherman's a complete success after the fall of Atlanta, GA.

12 26 1864 Federal scout from Fairfax Court-House to Hopewell Gap, VA, with the Federals capturing two soldiers belonging to the 4th VA Cavalry at Thoroughfare Gap, at Mrs. Lewis' house. 12/26-27/1864.

| 12 | 27 | 1864 | Skirmish at Decatur, AL. |
| 12 | 27 | 1864 | Federal scout from Pine Bluff to Simpson's Plantation, AR. |

12 27 1864 After extensive naval bombardment of Fort Fisher and the landing of an expeditionary force, Maj. Gen. Benjamin F. Butler's, USA, infantry, under Brig. Gen. Adelbert Ames, USA, are transported back to Fortress Monroe, VA, aboard the ocean transports, **C. W. Thomas** and **Wedbosset,** and the steamers, **Baltic, Haze, Idaho, S. Moore, Perit,** and the **Starlight.** Butler's plan to take Fort Fisher and close the sole remaining Confederate port of Wilmington, NC, is a total failure, not uncommon for this Union general.

12 27 1864 Skirmish at Okolona, MS, with Brig. Gen. Benjamin H. Grierson, USA.

12 27 1864 Maj. Gen. Stephen G. Burbridge's, USA, command reaches Pound Gap, VA, after taking part in Maj. Gen. George Stoneman's expedition into Southwestern Virginia.

| 12 | 28 | 1864 | The Engagement at Egypt, MS, with Brig. Gen. Benjamin H. Grierson, USA. |
| 12 | 28 | 1864 | Skirmish near Decatur, AL. |

12 29 1864 Skirmish at Hillsborough, AL, as the few remaining fire fights with the Confederate Army of Tennessee take place.

12 29 1864 Skirmish at Pond Springs, AL.

12 29 1864 Brig. Gen. Alvan C. Gillem's, USA, command reaches Knoxville, TN, after taking part in Maj. Gen. George Stoneman's expedition into Southwestern Virginia.

12	30	1864	**Pierce Manning Butler Young, C.S.A.,** is appointed Maj. Gen.
12	30	1864	**James Phillip Simms,** CSA, is appointed Brig. Gen.
12	30	1864	Skirmish near Leighton, AL.

12 30 1864 Skirmish 15 miles below Caruthersville, MO, where the Yankees pursue the fleeing guerrillas. The Federals believe more guerrillas would have been killed or captured if it weren't for the noise made by the horses on frozen ground, giving them advance notice who then fled.

12 30 1864 **Maj. Gen. John G. Parke, USA, is in temporary command of the Army of the Potomac,** and Bvt. Maj. Gen. Orlando B. Wilcox, USA, is in command of the 9th US Army Corps, the Richmond, VA, Campaign.

12 31 1864 **President Abraham Lincoln contemplates removing Maj. Gen. Benjamin F. Butler,** USA, from command for the botched assault on Fort Fisher, Wilmington, NC.

| 12 | 31 | 1864 | Affair at Paint Rock Bridge, AL. |
| 12 | 31 | 1864 | Skirmish at Russellville, AL. |

12 31 1864 Skirmish at Sharpsburg, KY, with Confederates arriving from the direction of Owingsville, as 1864 comes to a close with the last of American boys to lose their life during this bloody year.

1865.

	Sunday.	Monday.	Tuesday.	Wednesday.	Thursday.	Friday.	Saturday.
Jan	1	2	3	4	5	6	7
	8	9	10	11	12	13	14
	15	16	17	18	19	20	21
	22	23	24	25	26	27	28
	29	30	31	....	....	....	....
Feb....	....	....	....	1	2	3	4
	5	6	7	8	9	10	11
	12	13	14	15	16	17	18
	19	20	21	22	23	24	25
	26	27	28	....	....	....	....
Mar ...	....	....	....	1	2	3	4
	5	6	7	8	9	10	11
	12	13	14	15	16	17	18
	19	20	21	22	23	24	25
	26	27	28	29	30	31	....
Apr ...	....	....	....	....	....	....	1
	2	3	4	5	6	7	8
	9	10	11	12	13	14	15
	16	17	18	19	20	21	22
	23	24	25	26	27	28	29
	30	....	....	....	....	....	....
May...	....	1	2	3	4	5	6
	7	8	9	10	11	12	13
	14	15	16	17	18	19	20
	21	22	23	24	25	26	27
	28	29	30	31	....	....	....
June...	....	....	....	....	1	2	3
	4	5	6	7	8	9	10
	11	12	13	14	15	16	17
	18	19	20	21	22	23	24
	25	26	27	28	29	30	....
	....	....	....	....	....	....	....

	Sunday.	Monday.	Tuesday.	Wednesday.	Thursday.	Friday.	Saturday.
July...	....	....	....	....	....	....	1
	2	3	4	5	6	7	8
	9	10	11	12	13	14	15
	16	17	18	19	20	21	22
	23	24	25	26	27	28	29
	30	31	....	....	....	....	....
Aug ...	....	....	1	2	3	4	5
	6	7	8	9	10	11	12
	13	14	15	16	17	18	19
	20	21	22	23	24	25	26
	27	28	29	30	31	....	....
Sept ..	....	....	....	....	....	1	2
	3	4	5	6	7	8	9
	10	11	12	13	14	15	16
	17	18	19	20	21	22	23
	24	25	26	27	28	29	30
Oct....	1	2	3	4	5	6	7
	8	9	10	11	12	13	14
	15	16	17	18	19	20	21
	22	23	24	25	26	27	28
	29	30	31	....	....	....	....
Nov ...	....	....	....	1	2	3	4
	5	6	7	8	9	10	11
	12	13	14	15	16	17	18
	19	20	21	22	23	24	25
	26	27	28	29	30	....	....
Dec ...	....	....	....	....	....	1	2
	3	4	5	6	7	8	9
	10	11	12	13	14	15	16
	17	18	19	20	21	22	23
	24	25	26	27	28	29	30
	31	....	....	....	....	....	....

| 01 | 1 | 1865 | Federal operations against guerrillas in Arkansas, including the **11th US Colored Infantry,** and the use of the steamers, **Alamo, Annie Jacobs,** and the **Chippewa,** with actions at: |

a) Dardanelle,   **(Jan. 14th)**

b) Ivey's Ford,   **(Jan. 17th)** and skirmish at

c) Boggs' Mills,   **(Jan. 14th),** where the Yankees destroy Rebel supplies including 1,200 bushels of wheat near Chickalah. 1/1-27/1865.

01	1	1865	Skirmish at Bentonville, AR, with Confederate guerrillas.
01	1	1865	**The Campaign of the Carolinas, by Maj. Gen. William Tecumseh Sherman, USA.** 1/1-4/26/1865.
01	1	1865	Federal operations on the Canyon City Road, Oregon, with skirmishes with the **Snake Indians,** including the killing of bucks and squaws who attempted to flee local citizens who demanded they surrender and move to a reservation. 1/1-11/30/1865.
01	1	1865	**The Richmond, Virginia, Campaign Continues,** as the last large Confederate army remains on the siege lines at Petersburg, VA. 1/1-4/3/1865.
01	1	1865	Maj. Gen. Benjamin F. Butler, USA, abandons his latest project to blow a hole at Dutch Gap, on the James River, VA, after the large explosion of gunpowder fails.
01	2	1865	Engagement at Franklin, MS, with Confederates along the **Mobile and Ohio Railroad,** as Brig. Gen. Benjamin H. Grierson's latest Federal expedition moves on.
01	2	1865	Skirmish at Lexington, MS, with Brig. Gen. Benjamin H. Grierson, USA.
01	2	1865	Federal scout for bushwackers in Shannon County, MO, with excursions to Jack's Ford, Birch Prairie and within 8 miles of Thomasville. The Yankees report the whole county is full of bushwackers as the notorious guerrilla, **Freeman,** disbanded his whole army until spring. While the Federals were down in Shannon County, the guerrillas were active in Texas County in the neighborhood of Rolla, MO, robbing several families of everything they had. 1/2-7/1865.
01	2	1865	Federal scout from Fort Wingate to Sierra del Datil, the New Mexico Territory, as they followed the trail of Indians who stole a number of sheep from people residing near the post. After forced marches in severe snow-storms, the Yankees give up trying to catch the thieves. The Union men suffered greatly, living on boiled wheat for 3 days. 1/2-10/1865.
01	2	1865	Federal scout from Benvard's Mills to South Quay, VA, on the Blackwater.
01	2	1865	Bvt. Maj. Gen. Samuel W. Crawford, USA, is placed in temporary command of the 5th US Army Corps, the Richmond, VA, Campaign.
01	2	1865	Brig. Gen. Charles Devens, USA, is placed in temporary command of the 24th US Army Corps, the Richmond, VA, Campaign.
01	3	1865	Skirmish near Mechanicsburg, MS, with Union forces under Brig. Gen. Benjamin H. Grierson, on the **Mobile and Ohio Railroad** line.
01	3	1865	The Federal expedition to and the capture of Fort Fisher, NC, and its dependencies. 1/3-17/1865.
01	3	1865	Skirmish near Hardeeville, SC.
01	3	1865	The larger portion of the Army of the Tennessee, under Maj. Gen. Oliver O. Howard, USA, is transferred from Savannah, GA, to Beaufort, SC, as Maj. Gen. William T. Sherman, USA, prepares to move north and invade South Carolina. 1/3-17/1865.
01	4	1865	Skirmish near Thorn Hill, AL, with remnants of the Confederate Army of Tennessee.
01	4	1865	Federal expedition from Brownsville, across the White River aboard the steamers, **Belle Peoria** and **Ella,** to Augusta, AR. The Yankees seize 407 head of cattle, sending 330 head back by boat to Devall's Bluff; the rest, well, let's just say the men got their stomach's full at the expense of the Rebels. 1/4-27/1865.
01	4	1865	Skirmish at the Ponds, MS, along the **Mobile and Ohio Railroad,** as Brig. Gen. Benjamin H. Grierson's expedition which began back on 12/21/1864, effectively comes to an end, with a partial list of destruction: 200,000 feet of bridges and trestle-work; 10 miles of track (rails bent and ties burned); 20 miles of telegraph (poles cut down and wire destroyed), 14 locomotives and tenders, 95 railroad cars, over 300 army wagons, 30 warehouses full of Confederate commissaries, machine shops, 5,000 new arms, 700 head of fat hogs, immense amount of grain, etc., as the list goes on.
01	4	1865	Federal expedition from Bloomfield to Poplar Bluff, MO, and vicinity, as the Yankees brave ice and snow, crossing swamps, and swimming across the St. Francis River. The men suffer greatly from exposure to the elements, but manage to kill 19 Rebels, wounding and capturing more, in addition to seizing depleted Confederate stock. 1/4-16/1865.
01	4	1865	The 2nd expedition to Fort Fisher, near Wilmington, NC, embarks at Bermuda Landing, VA, Brig. Gen.

Alfred H. Terry, USA, commanding the armed forces and Admiral David D. Porter, USN, commanding the large naval fleet. Maj. Gen. Benjamin F. Butler, USA, remaining behind this time. 1/4-5/1865.

| 01 | 6 | 1865 | **Richard Lee Turberville Beale,** CSA, is appointed Brig. Gen. |
| 01 | 6 | 1865 | Skirmish at Huntsville, AR. |

01	7	1865	Skirmish in Johnson County, AR.
01	7	1865	Federal expedition from Pine Bluff, AR, and skirmish **(9th),** with guerrillas, and casualties. 1/7-9/1865.
01	7	1865	Skirmishes with Indians at Valley Station and Julesburg, the Colorado Territory, as the hostile savages attacked and burned the wagon train at Valley Station, killing 12 men. They were unable to capture the wagon train at Julesburg, being driven off, but killing 2 white men. The stations are now closed, as the operators have left. The Yankees fear that unless troops are rapidly sent, many emigrants will starve.
01	7	1865	Federal scout against Indians from Fort Ellsworth, KS, traveling to Smoky Hill, Buffalo Creek, up the Saline River to Walnut Creek, then to Pawnee Rock which is 15 miles northeast of Fort Larned, to the mouth of Big Creek, about 50 miles due north of Fort Larned. The Federals find no signs of Indians, and report that **buffalo is tolerably plenty and very tame,** showing that they have not been hunted by the Indians. 1/7-11/1865.
01	7	1865	The 2nd Division, 19th US Army Corps, leaves the Shenandoah Valley, VA, en route to Savannah, GA, as more troops are moved from the Shenandoah Valley for other strategic points.
01	7	1865	Urged on by Lieut. Gen. Ulysses S. Grant, USA, President Abraham Lincoln **removes Maj. Gen. Benjamin F. Butler, USA, from active service in the US Army,** after his last failure on the assault on Fort Fisher, Wilmington, NC; one of many in his career. **This effectively removes yet another Civil War figure from any future part in the war.**

01	8	1865	Skirmish near Ivey's Ford, AR.
01	8	1865	The naval fleet under Rear-Admiral David D. Porter, USN, and the transport fleet containing the expeditionary forces against Fort Fisher, arrive at redenzvous off Beaufort, NC.
01	8	1865	Maj. Gen. John A. Logan, USA, resumes the command of the 15th US Army Corps, relieving Maj. Gen. Peter J. Osterhaus, USA, TN, etal.
01	8	1865	Action with Indians, mainly **Kickapoos** and **Pottawatomies,** at Dove Creek, Concho River, TX. It is here where another injustice was done to a tribe of Indians. The friendly Indians sent a woman with child under a flag of truce to the Yankees who refused to recognize any friendly Indians on the Texas frontier and then declined to accept her offer of being their prisoner, as the officer in charge stated, "he takes no prisoners," whereupon they killed her, the young lad escaping into the bushes. Attacking the tribe in their wigwams, many Indians were massacred before they finally returned fire, killing and wounding about 15 before the Yankees called off the attack during a heavy snow-storm. The Indians flee towards Mexico, leaving behind most of their provisions they can't afford to lose, in their haste to get away from the white devils.
01	8	1865	Maj. Gen. Edward O. C. Ord, USA, assumes command of the Dept. of Virginia and North Carolina, as well as the Army of the James, vice Maj. Gen. Benjamin F. Butler, USA, relieved from command.

01	9	1865	Federal scouts about Mount Sterling, KY, capturing 4 men dressed in rebel uniform, mounted and armed. It is very cold this time of year, as the men are piling the earth around the bottom of the tents to keep out the cold. The earth is frozen. 1/9-2/15/1865.
01	9	1865	President Abraham Lincoln sends US Secretary of War, Edwin Stanton, to Savannah, GA, for discussions with Maj. Gen. William T. Shermin, USA, on military strategy and his alledged mistreatment of black freedmen.
01	9	1865	Federal reconnaissance from Eastport to Iuka, MS, as Lieut. Gen. John B. Hood, USA, arrives in Tupelo, MS, with the remnants of the Confederate Army of Tennessee.
01	9	1865	Skirmishes with guerrillas in Texas County, MO. 1/9-11/1865.
01	9	1865	Skirmish near Disputanta Station, VA, the Richmond, VA, Campaign.

| 01 | 10 | 1865 | Skirmish with guerrillas near Glasgow, MO, as the Yankees divy up the spoils from one dead guerrilla which included a belt and 6 revolvers, 4 purses containing $ 72.25, pocketknives, 1 pocket compass, 1 gold pen and silver holder, and the likenesses of 2 young ladies, in addition to his hat and boots. This episode was not an isolated incident. |

| 01 | 11 | 1865 | Federal expeditions from Helena, AR, aboard the steamer, **Dove,** up the Mississippi River to Harbert's Plantation, MS, where the **60th US Colored Infantry** surround Mr. Harbert and find him asleep out in his corncrib. Mr. Harbert, you see, is in a bit of trouble, as he is a Negro enlisted Union soldier who |

decided he had enough of the war and deserted back to his plantation-farm. 1/11-13/1865.

| 01 | 11 | 1865 | Skirmish with guerrillas near Lexington, MO, as the beaten bushwackers flee towards Greenton. |

01 11 1865 Skirmish with guerrillas near Lexington, MO, as the beaten bushwackers flee towards Greenton.

01 11 1865 Federal scout against **Navajo Indians** from Fort Wingate to Sierra Del Datil and vicinity, the New Mexico Territory. The Yankees find no Indians in the area. 1/11-21/1865.

01 11 1865 The Federal forces numbering over 580, at Beverly, Randolph County, WV, are captured, by Maj. Gen. Thomas L. Rosser, CSA, in a surprise cavalry raid.

01 11 1865 **Maj. Gen. George G. Meade, USA, resumed command of the Army of the Potomac,** the Richmond, VA, Campaign.

01 11 1865 Federal scout from New Creek through Greenland Gap, and through Petersburg to Franklin, WV, for the purpose of surprising any Confederates in the area, which meets with little success. 1/11-15/1865.

01 12 1865 The following are appointed Union Brigadier Generals:

John Grant Mitchell, USA
John Morrison Oliver, USA
Benjamin Franklin Potts, USA
James Sidney Robinson, USA
Robert Kingston Scott, USA

01 12 1865 Affair near Sugar Loaf Prairie, AR, where the notorious guerrilla, **Cook,** is smoked out of his hole up in a cave by the Yankees. Bad move on Cook's part to be caught in this cave as he won't live to see tomorrow. Some of his band join him, while the remainder are captured.

01 12 1865 Federal expedition from Morganza, LA, with skirmishes with a few Confederates who the Yankees happen upon. Bad move on the Rebels' part. The Yankees also seize Rebel supplies. The Confederacy is an empty shell by now in this area. 1/12-15/1865.

01 12 1865 Federal scout against guerrillas from Camp Grover to Texas Prairie, MO, with limited success. 1/12-15/1865.

01 12 1865 Federal scout from Warrensburg to Miami, MO, as the Yankees search for reported bushwackers proves futile. 1/12-17/1865.

01 12 1865 The Federal expedition convoyed by the fleet of Rear-Admiral David D. Porter, USN, sails from the rendezvous off Beaufort, NC, for Fort Fisher.

01 12 1865 The above expedition arrives at Federal Point, NC, for Fort Fisher, Wilmington, NC. 1/12-13/1865.

01 12 1865 The State of North Carolina is merged into the Dept. of the South.

01 12 1865 Maj. Gen. John G. Parke, USA, resumes command of the 9th US Army Corps, the Richmond, VA, Campaign.

01 13 1865 **James Alexander Williams,** USA, is appointed Brig. Gen.

01 13 1865 At Tupelo, MS, **Lieut. Gen. John Bell Hood, CSA, resigns as commander of the Confederate Army of Tennessee.** Too late, as the damage has already been done.

01 13 1865 The combined military and naval operations against Fort Fisher, NC. 1/13-15/1865.

01 13 1865 The bombardment of Fort Fisher, NC, by the naval fleet, including the **USS Brooklyn, USS Canonicus, USS Monadnock, USS New Ironsides,** and the **USS Saugus.**

01 13 1865 The landing of the Union expeditionary forces against Fort Fisher, NC.

01 13 1865 Skirmish near Fort Fisher, NC.

01 14 1865 **Thomas Harrison,** CSA, is appointed Brig. Gen.

01 14 1865 Operations on the **Overland Stage Coach Road** between Julesburg and Denver, the Colorado Territory, and skirmishes with Indians:

a) Beaver Creek Stage Coach Station, 82 miles west of Denver, found burned **(Jan. 14th).**

b) Godfrey's Ranch, 70 miles west of Denver, where 4 whitemen succeed in driving the Indians off. **(Jan. 14th)**

c) Lillian Springs Ranch, 33 miles west of Denver, where 3 whitemen fought off 500 Indians and escape. The ranch is burned. **(Jan. 17th)**

d) near Moore's Ranch, or Washington Ranch, 50 miles west of Denver, several whitemen were able to drive the Indians off. **(Jan. 26th)**

e) Morrison's or the American Ranch, 68 miles west of Denver, where Indians attacked, captured, and burned the ranch. A passing train found 3 Indians and 7 white bodies in the ruins partly burned. Mr. Morrison, his wife, and child are missing. **(Jan. 26th)**

f) Wisconsin Ranch, 56 miles west of Denver, where a few ranchmen hold off and kill 3 Indians, managing to escape; the ranch is burned by the Indians. **(Jan. 26th)**

g) near Valley Station, 53 miles west of Denver, where the Federal troops were present and killed 13 Indians after they were able to burn 100 tons of hay. **(Jan. 28th).**

h) Antelope Stage Coach Station, 15 miles, Buffalo Ranch Springs, 18 miles, Harlow's Ranch, 22 miles, and Spring Hill Stage Coach Station, 27 miles west of Denver, were burned **(Jan. 28th).**

i) additional incidents, with all cattle between Julesburg and the Wisconsin Ranch, about 1,500 head, were driven off and taken by the Indians. 1/14-29/1865.

01	14	1865	**Gen. Pierre G. T. Beauregard, CSA, assumes temporary command of the Confederate Army of Tennessee,** at Tupelo, MS.
01	14	1865	The advance of the Union forces from Beaufort to Pocotaligo, SC, and skirmishes, under Maj. Gen. William T. Sherman, USA.
01	15	1865	Skirmish in Madison County, AR.
01	15	1865	Federal expeditions against guerrillas from Pine Bluff, AR. One local doctor fled from his house with about 25 other guerrillas as the Yankees gave pursuit. His wife screamed at the top of her lungs from her porch to the Federals, pleading with them not to kill her husband. Back then, life was lived day by day. 1/15-18/1865.
01	15	1865	Federal scout against the **Sioux Indians** from Fort Larned to Pawnee Fork, Walnut Creek, and Smoky Hill River, KS. The Yankees fail to find any **Sioux,** but report the buffalo which were plentiful along their trip suddenly disappeared, indicating that the Indian tribes were in the vicinity and on the hunt. 1/15-21/1865.
01	15	1865	Federal expedition from New Orleans aboard the schooner, **Cazador,** to Mandeville, LA, and capture of some prisoners, and provisions. 1/15-17/1865.
01	15	1865	**The assault on and the capture of Fort Fisher, near Wilmington, NC,** by the expeditionary forces under Brig. Gen. Alfred H. Terry, USA, which effectively closes the last major Confederate port for blockade runners. Total casualties approximate 1,840.
01	15	1865	**Maj. Gen. William Henry Chase Whiting, CSA,** is mortally wounded at the Federal assault on Fort Fisher, NC, captured by the Federals and dying as a prisoner of war, on March 10, 1865.
01	15	1865	The US monitor, **USS Patapsco,** is destroyed in the Charleston Harbor, SC, after striking a Confederate torpedo.
01	15	1865	The 23rd US Army Corps, under Maj. Gen. James Schofield, USA, embarks at Clifton, TN, by water transports for the East, by way of Cincinnati, OH, then by rail to Washington, DC, and finally by ocean transport to later capture Wilmington, NC. 1/15-18/1865.
01	15	1865	Maj. Gen. John Gibbon, USA, assumes the command of the 24th US Army Corps, the Richmond, VA, Campaign.
01	16	1865	**Alfred Howe Terry, U.S.A.,** is appointed Maj. Gen.
01	16	1865	Federal expedition from Brashear City aboard the Union gunboat, **No. 41,** and the steamer, **Carrie,** to Whiskey Bayou, LA. The Yankees visit numerous plantations on their excursion, taking everything of value, destroying what they can't take with them. As these excursions continue, each day the locals pray the Federals won't be marching in their direction. 1/16-18/1865.
01	16	1865	Federal operations about Waynesville, MO, including skirmish with guerrillas near McCourtney's Mills, on Big Piney. 1/16-22/1865.
01	16	1865	Fort Caswell is blown up and the defensive works at Smithville and Reeves' Point, NC, are abandoned by the Confederate forces under Gen. Braxton Bragg, CSA. 1/16-17/1865.
01	16	1865	The powder magazines at the captured Fort Fisher, NC, accidentally explode, causing over 100 Union casualties. Rumor has it a some drunken Union soldiers and/or sailors may have unknowingly set off the explosion.
01	16	1865	The State of North Carolina is designated as the District of North Carolina in the Dept. of the South.
01	16	1865	Federal scouts about Franklin, TN, against bushwackers, where some are surrounded and killed at the house of a Mrs. Cherry. The anguish and terror felt by Mrs. Cherry who was an eyewitness to the killings can only be imagined today by the contemporary reader. 1/16-2/20/1865.
01	17	1865	The 2nd Division, 19th US Army Corps, commanded by Bvt. Maj. Gen. Cavier Grover, USA, arrives at Savannah, GA. 1/17-20/1865.
01	17	1865	Bvt. Maj. Gen. George W. Getty, USA, is placed in temporary command of the 6th US Army Corps, the Richmond, VA, Campaign.
01	18	1865	Skirmish at Clarksville, AR.
01	18	1865	Federal expedition from Napoleonville by men under Brig. Gen. Robert A. Cameron, USA, commanding

the District of La Fourche, to Grand River, LA. The main incidence of this night occurs when the surround a residence suspected of housing rebels. The Union Lieut. enters the house and comes running out when he hears shots being fired outside (at a dog). It being very dark, a Yankee private takes aim at the person fleeing out of the house (the Union Lieut.) and proceeds to fire a bullet into his forehead. A night of deadly friendly fire. 1/18-19/1865.

01	18	1865	Federal scout against guerrillas from Warrensburg to the Snibar Hills, MO. Due to the horrendous weather and current provisions in the area, the Yankees decide not to bring in any livestock, etc., from the local area, as the women and children living on farms in the area would greatly suffer, irregardless if their husbands and fathers are bushwackers. 1/18-22/1865. This bunch of Federals are decent men.
01	18	1865	Affair near Lovettsville, VA, where Maj. Gen. Thomas L. Rosser, CSA, and his Confederate Cavalry surprise attacks the Union vedettes and reserve force near Harper's Ferry; the Yankees pursue Rosser to Purcellville, but could not overtake him.
01	19	1865	Federal scout from Donaldsonville, LA. 1/19-20/1865.
01	19	1865	Skirmish at Corinth, MS.
01	19	1865	Federal reconnaissance to Myrtle Sound and skirmish at the Half Moon Battery, NC, with assistance from the gunboat, **USS Buckingham.**
01	19	1865	Federal expedition from Memphis, TN, to Marion, AR, with skirmishes with bushwackers **(Jan. 20th and 21st)** at and near Marion. 1/19-22/1865.
01	19	1865	Bowing to political pressure from the Confederate Congress, President Jefferson Davis will appoint and **Gen. Robert E. Lee, CSA, will grudgingly accept, the position of Commander of all the Confederate forces in the field.**
01	20	1865	**William McComb,** CSA, is appointed Brig. Gen.
01	20	1865	The Territory of Arizona is re-annexed to the Dept. of the Pacific.
01	20	1865	Skirmish near Fort Larned, KS, as the **Cheyenne** and **Arapahoe Indians** attack the sutler wagon train destined for Fort Lyon. The Yankee escort repels the Indian attacks, but the train returns back to Fort Larned, with casualties on both sides.
01	20	1865	Skirmish at the Point of Rocks or the Nine-Mile Ridge, KS.
01	20	1865	Federal reconnaissance from Pocotaligo to the Salkehatchie River, SC, and skirmish, as the Confederates have few men to assemble against the advancing Maj. Gen. William T. Sherman, USA.
01	20	1865	Secretary of War Stanton briefs President Lincoln on his recent meetings with Maj. Gen. William T. Sherman, USA.
01	21	1865	Federal expedition from Brashear City aboard the Union gunboat, **No. 43,** to Bayou Sorrel, LA, against Rebels and torpedoes. 1/21/-22/1865.
01	22	1865	Skirmish on the Benton Road, near Little Rock, AR, with guerrillas.
01	22	1865	Federal expedition from Little Rock to Mount Elba, AR, with skirmishes at Saline River. 1/22-2/4/1865.
01	23	1865	Skirmish with guerrillas at Thompson's Plantation, in the vicinity of Donaldsonville, LA.
01	23	1865	Federal scout from Cumberland Gap, TN, and the death of 12 Rebel guerrillas. The Yankees have orders to shoot a guerrilla whenever and wherever he is found, and not to take any prisoners on any account, and that's exactly what they do. 1/23-27/1865.
01	23	1865	**Lieut. Gen. Robert Taylor, CSA, assumes command of the Army of Tennessee,** vice Lieut. Gen. John Bell Hood, CSA, resigning January 13, 1865.
01	23	1865	A Confederate fleet sails from Richmond, VA, down the James River to attack the Federal supply depot at City Point, only to have the **Drewry, CSS Richmond, Scorpion,** and **Virginia No. 2** run aground.
01	23	1865	Action at Fort Brady on the James River, the Richmond, VA, Campaign.
01	24	1865	Skirmish at Fayetteville, AR.
01	24	1865	Skirmish near Bayou Goula, LA, with guerrillas.
01	24	1865	The expedition from Cape Girardeau, MO, to Eleven Points River, AR, as the Yankees find many families starving. The Federals use their own funds to buy food for the destitute, taking money from the wealthier Rebel families they come across. Many families profess their men have been taken off by the Confederates, conscripted. Whether they went voluntarily or not, the families are fed tonight out of the goodness of these Federal soldiers who passed their way this evening. 1/24-2/22/1865.
01	24	1865	Maj. Gen. Nathan Bedford Forrest, CSA, assumes the command of the District of Mississippi, East Louisiana, and West Tennessee.
01	24	1865	Bvt. Maj. Gen. Orlando B. Wilcox, USA, is placed in temporary command of the 9th US Army Corps,

the Richmond, VA, Campaign.

01	25	1865	The Confederate commerce raider, **CSS Shenandoah,** arrives at Melbourne, Australia, for repairs and provisions.
01	25	1865	Skirmish near Simpsonville, Shelby County, KY, where the Union cattle guard composed of negro soldiers are attacked with a number killed and wounded.
01	25	1865	Federal reconnaissance from Pocotaligo to the Salkehatchie River, SC. by Maj. Gen. William T. Sherman, USA.
01	25	1865	Federal expedition from Irish Bottom to Evans' Island, TN, to secure beef cattle; the river being so full of ice, the Yankees could not get them off the island.
01	25	1865	Skirmish near Powhatan, VA, the Richmond, VA, Campaign.
01	26	1865	Skirmish at Paint Rock, AL.
01	26	1865	Federal scout from Pine Bluff toward Camden and Monticello, AR, with skirmishes, as both sides leave men lying on the ground in final peaceful serenity. 1/26-31/1865.
01	26	1865	Federal expedition from Plaquemine to The Park, LA, with skirmish **(Feb. 4th)** at The Park. 1/26-2/4/1865.
01	26	1865	Skirmish near Pocotaligo, SC, with Maj. Gen. William T. Sherman, USA.
01	26	1865	Federal expedition from Memphis, TN, into Southeastern Arkansas and Northeastern Louisiana, as the Yankees lay waste to vast amounts of Confederate provisions, food, etc., including the capture of the Rebel transport, **Jim Barkman,** that was loading corn for the Rebels at Camden. 1/26-2/11/1865.
01	27	1865	**Thomas John Wood,** U.S.A., is appointed Maj. Gen.
01	27	1865	**Charles Camp Doolittle,** USA, is appointed Brig. Gen.
01	27	1865	Skirmish at Elrod's Tan-yard, De Kalb County, AL, with bushwackers, as the **18th US Colored Infantry** lose men as they traveled from Bridgeport, AL, aboard the US transport, **Bridgeport,** and encounter guerrillas.
01	27	1865	Federal expedition from Fort Pinney aboard the Union gunboat, **No. 28,** to Kimball' s Plantation, AR, where because Mrs. Kimball lied about her husband's whereabouts (he was hiding under the floorboards), the Yankees burn their plantation to the ground.
01	27	1865	Maj. Gen. Nathan Bedford Forrest, CSA, is assigned to the command of the District of Mississippi and East Louisiana.
01	27	1865	Skirmish at Ennis' Cross-Roads, SC.
01	27	1865	The Federals capture and refloat the Confederate torpedo boat, **Scorpion,** on the James River, below Richmond, VA.
01	27	1865	Maj. Gen. Gouverneur K. Warren, USA, resumes the command of the 5th US Army Corps, the Richmond, VA, Campaign.
01	28	1865	The unsuccessful Confederate attack on the US Steamer, **Octorara,** while in Mobile Bay, AL, by the torpedo boat **St. Patrick.** The torpedo failing to explode on contact. Amid a rain of Union shelling, the **St. Patrick** safely withdraws, to attempt this courageous endeavor another day.
01	28	1865	Federal operations against Indians on the Upper Arkansas, with skirmish **(Feb. lst)** at Fort Zarah, KS, as the hostile Indians attack a Yankee party cutting wood. 1/28-2/9/1865.
01	28	1865	Skirmish at Combahee River, SC, with Maj. Gen. Sherman, USA.
01	28	1865	Action at Athens, TN, as the Yankees prevent the attacking Confederates from capturing the town; the Federals lose at least 20 men as prisoners to the Rebels though.
01	28	1865	Federal expedition from Strawberry Plains to Clinch Mountain, TN, with skirmish with bushwackers. 1/28-31/1865.
01	28	1865	After various meetings with Francis Preston Blair, Jr, regarding peace discussions, **President Jefferson Davis appoints Vice President Alexander Stephens, John A. Campbell, former US Supreme Court Justice and R. M. T. Hunter,** as commissioners to meet with Federal authorities to further discuss potential peace overtures.
01	29	1865	Affair at Danville, KY, where guerrillas, dressed in Union garb, enter the town, rob the citizens and 1 boot store, and leave on the Perryville pike at 11:15 a.m.
01	29	1865	Skirmish 5 miles west of Harrodsburg, KY, where the Yankees overtake 40 guerrillas, killing and capturing 12.
01	29	1865	Federal scouts from Bayou Goula to Grand River, LA, with skirmish **(Jan. 30th)** at Richland Plantation. 1/29-2/7/1865.
01	29	1865	Skirmish at Robertsville, SC.

01	30	1865	Skirmish 3 miles east of Chaplintown, KY, with guerrillas.
01	30	1865	Federal expedition from Thibodeaux to Lake Verret and Bayou Planton, LA, with skirmish (Jan. 30th) near Lake Verret. 1/30-31/1865.
01	30	1865	Skirmish in La Fayette County, MO.
01	30	1865	**The Military Division of the Missouri is created,** which includes the Depts. of the Missouri and the Northwest.
01	30	1865	The Dept. of Kansas is merged into the Dept. of the Missouri.
01	30	1865	**Maj. Gen. John Pope, USA, is assigned to the command of the Military Division of the Missouri.**
01	30	1865	**Maj. Gen. Samuel R. Curtis, USA, is transferred to the command of the Dept. of the Northwest.**
01	30	1865	Skirmish near Lawtonville, SC.
01	30	1865	Federal scout to Long Bridge and Bottom's Bridge, VA, the Richmond, VA, Campaign.
01	31	1865	**Operations in North Alabama and East Tennessee.** 1/31-4/24/1865.
01	31	1865	Skirmish 2 miles south of Oxford, KS, with a gang of treacherous guerrillas.
01	31	1865	Federal expedition from Fort Pike to Bayou Bonfouca, LA, with skirmish (Jan. 31st). 1/31-2/1/1865.
01	31	1865	Federal expedition from Morganza aboard the sloop, **Rosetta,** to New Roads, LA, where a band of Confederates fire into the sloop; the Yankees suffer no casualties and are able to stop the Rebels from capturing and burning the schooner, **Perserverance,** which is loaded with lumber.
01	31	1865	**The Dept. of North Carolina is constituted,** to consist of the State of North Carolina, and **Maj. Gen. John M. Schofield, USA, is assigned to its command.**
01	31	1865	Maj. Gen. David S. Stanley, USA, assumes the command of the 4th US Army Corps, during the operations in North Alabama and East Tennessee.
01	31	1865	**Gen. Robert E. Lee, CSA, is appointed General-in-Chief of all the Confederate Armies;** a promotion too late in coming to have any effect.
01	31	1865	The US House of Representatives votes 119 to 56 in favor of a Constitutional amendment to abolish slavery, Washington, DC.
01	31	1865	President Abraham Lincoln instructs Secretary of State, William Seward, to travel to Fortress Monroe, VA, and hold peace discussions with the recently appointed Confederate Commission.
02	1	1865	**Stephen Thomas,** USA, is appointed Brig. Gen.
02	1	1865	**Maj. Gen. John Bankhead Magruder, CSA, assumes the command of the District of Arkansas.**
02	1	1865	Union naval operations against Confederate salt-works at St. Andrews Bay, FL.
02	1	1865	Federal operations against Indians about Fort Boise, the Idaho Territory, with skirmish **(Feb. 15th)** near the Bruneau Valley. Many Indians, including emigrants are destitute in this region. 2/1-20/1865.
02	1	1865	Illinois becomes the 1st state to ratify the 13th Amendment which abolishes slavery.
02	1	1865	Federal scout against guerrillas from Warrensburg to Tabo Creek, Dover, Oaklin Church, and Davis' Creek, MO. 2/1-5/1865.
02	1	1865	Federal scout from Warrensburg to Wagon Knob, Big Grove, Greenton, and Texas Prairie, MO, against guerrillas. The Federals are getting the upper hand in these parts, as they visit various guerrilla homes, finding women with their flock of children at each place; the men with their older sons having fled to the thick bushes. 2/1-5/1865.
02	1	1865	Skirmish at Hickory Hill, SC, as Maj. Gen. William T. Sherman, USA, proceeds into South Carolina with minor obstruction by Lieut. Gen. William J. Hardee, CSA, as he awaits reinforcements from the Army of Tennessee, on its way from Tupelo, MS.
02	1	1865	Skirmish at Whippy Swamp Creek, SC, with Maj. Gen. William T. Sherman, USA.
02	1	1865	Skirmish in McLemore's Cove, TN, in the vicinity of Ringgold, as the Federals attack and smash a Confederate camp.
02	1	1865	Bvt. Brig. Gen. William W. Morris, USA, is in temporary command of the Middle Dept., VA.
02	1	1865	Bowing to political pressure, President Jefferson Davis accepts the **resignation** of the Confederate **Secretary of War, James A. Seddon.**
02	1	1865	The troops in the trenches around Petersburg, VA, continue to suffer from the harsh winter weather as the James River threatens to freeze over.
02	2	1865	**Federal operations against Indians on the North Platte River in the Colorado and Nebraska Territories.** 2/2-18/1865.
02	2	1865	The hostile Indians attack the **Overland Stage Station at Julesburg, the Colorado Territory,** and burn it to the ground.
02	2	1865	Skirmish on Saint John's River, FL, with the US Naval operations against the Confederate salt-works there.

MONTH	DAY	YEAR	ACT
02	2	1865	Rhode Island becomes the 2nd and Michigan becomes the 3rd US state to ratify the 13th amendment abolishing slavery.
02	2	1865	Skirmish at Barker's Mill, Whippy Swamp, SC, as Lieut. Gen. William J. Hardee, CSA, uses all available Confederate cavalry to hinder Maj. Gen. William T. Sherman's, USA, advance into South Carolina.
02	2	1865	Skirmish at Duck Branch, near Loper's Cross-Roads, SC.
02	2	1865	Skirmish at Lawtonville, SC.
02	2	1865	Skirmishes at Rivers' and Broxton's Bridges, Salkehatchie River, SC.
02	2	1865	Maj. Gen. John G. Parke, USA, resumes the command of the 9th US Army Corps, the Richmond, VA, Campaign.
02	2	1865	President Abraham Lincoln travels from Washington, DC, to Fortress Monroe, VA, and joins his Secretary of State, William H. Seward, aboard the **River Queen,** where they plan to meet with the Confederate peace delegation the next day.
02	3	1865	Skirmish at Ladd's House, Hog Jaw Valley, AL, with guerrillas, who skedaddle into the mountains. 2/3-4/1865.
02	3	1865	Federal scout against the party of hostile Indians suspected of being **Kiowas** and **Comanches,** from Fort Larned to South Fork of Pawnee Creek and Buckner's Branch, KS. The Yankees traveled long distances across the open ranges in pursuit of this party of Indians but are unable to catch up with them. 2/3-8/1865.
02	3	1865	Maryland, New York, and West Virginia become the 4th, 5th, and 6th states to ratify the 13th amendment which abolishes slavery.
02	3	1865	**The Confederate District of North Mississippi and West Tennessee is formed, and Brig. Gen. Marcus J. Wright, CSA, is assigned to its command.**
02	3	1865	**The Confederate District of South Mississippi and East Tennessee is formed, and Brig. Gen. Wirt Adams, CSA, is assigned to its command.**
02	3	1865	The detachment Army of the Tennessee, commanded by Maj. Gen. Andrew J. Smith, USA, is ordered from the Dept. of the Cumberland to the Military Division of West Mississippi.
02	3	1865	The 7th Division, Cavalry Corps, Military Division of the Mississippi, is ordered from the Dept. of the Cumberland to the Military Division of West Mississippi.
02	3	1865	Federal scouts in La Fayette County, MO, killing bushwackers and guerrillas. 2/3-8/1865.
02	3	1865	Skirmish at Dillingham's Cross-Roads or Duck Branch, SC.
02	3	1865	Action at Rivers' Bridge, Salkehatchie River, SC, as Maj. Gen. William T. Sherman's, USA, 17th US Army Corps press on northward towards the state capital of Columbia.
02	3	1865	**President Abraham Lincoln and Secretary of State William Seward meet with Confederate Vice President Alexander Stephens, John A. Campbell, and R.M.T. Hunter to discuss peace proposals.** Lincoln reiterates there will be no peace until the southern states recognize the Federal government as the only national government, which the southern states are a part of it.
02	3	1865	Affair near Harper's Ferry, WV, where a Confederate force derail a train on the **Baltimore and Ohio Railroad.** In a fit of rage, the commanding Union officer accuses the Lieut. in charge, of derelict of duty, if not drunk then full of opium all the time, feels it would be a waste of time to court martial him, and suggests a quick solution - hang him. Undoubtedly, his wish was not carried out.
02	4	1865	**Robert Lowry,** CSA, is appointed Brig. Gen.
02	4	1865	Action with Indians at Mud Springs, a telegraph station 105 miles east of Fort Laramie, in the Nebraska Territory, where the Indians attack this desolate outpost. 2/4-6/1865.
02	4	1865	Skirmish at Angley's Post-Office, SC, as Maj. Gen. William T. Sherman, USA, and his 4 US Army Corps press on northward.
02	4	1865	Skirmish at Buford's Bridge, SC.
02	4	1865	**Maj. Gen. John Pope, USA, assumes the command of the Military Division of the Missouri.**
02	4	1865	Federal expedition from Winchester, VA, to Moorefield, WV, where the Cavalry forces continue to spar with each other. 2/4-6/1865 .
02	4	1865	President Abraham Lincoln returns to Washington, DC, believing nothing was accomplished the previous day.
02	5	1865	Action at Braddock's Farm, near Welaka, FL.
02	5	1865	Skirmish at Combahee Ferry, SC.
02	5	1865	Skirmish at Duncanville, SC.

MONTH	DAY	YEAR	ACT
02	5	1865	The latest Confederate ironclad, the **CSS Stonewall,** arrives at Ferrol, Spain, for refueling.
02	5	1865	Skirmish near McMinnville, TN, as the Yankees attack the Rebel desperadoes, or as the Federals put it, with some of the Southern Chivalry. As usual, men on both sides die here.
02	5	1865	**The Battle of Hatcher's Run, or Dabney's Mill, VA,** as Lieut. Gen. Ulysses S. Grant, USA, extends Gen. Robert E. Lee's CSA, defensive lines around Petersburg, VA, by sending the 2nd and 5th US Army Corps south and westward toward the Boydton Plank Road and Hatcher's Run, the Richmond, VA, Campaign. 2/5-7/1865 .
02	5	1865	Skirmish at Charlestown, WV.
02	6	1865	**Brig. Gen. John Pegram, CSA,** is mortally wounded at Hatcher's Run, or Dabney's Mill, VA, instantly killed by a Federal minie ball through his heart as he led his troops against the Federal positions of Maj. Gen. Gouverneur K. Warren's, USA, 5th US Army Corps, with the Confederates being repulsed.
02	6	1865	Federal operations in Ozark County, MO, as the Yankees move to remove yet another guerrilla from this area. 2/6-8/1865.
02	6	1865	Skirmish near Barnwell, SC.
02	6	1865	Skirmish at Cowpen Ford, Little Salkehatchie River, SC, as Maj. Gen. William T. Sherman, USA, presses onward.
02	6	1865	Action at Fishburn's Plantation, near Lane's Bridge, Little Salkehatchie River, SC.
02	6	1865	Affair at Corn's Farm, Franklin County, 12 miles from Hillsborough, TN as a Confederate is shot as he tried to flee from the Corn's barn where he had been sleeping for the night.
02	6	1865	Federal scout from Fairfax Court-House to Brentsville, VA, where the Yankees had a hard time crossing Bull Run as it was frozen over. 2/6-7/1865.
02	6	1865	President Jefferson Davis appoints Maj. Gen. John Cabell Breckinridge, CSA, as the new Confederate Secretary of War.
02	6	1865	Maj. Gen. Edward O.C. Ord, USA, is assigned to the command of the Dept. of Virginia, the Richmond, VA, Campaign.
02	6	1865	**Gen. Robert E. Lee, CSA, assumes the position of General-in- Chief of all the Confederate armies, a move too late to be of any significance.**
02	7	1865	**Brig. Gen. John Henry Winder, CSA,** dies of mental fatigue of his military position that eventually had overwhelmed him, at Florence, SC.
02	7	1865	Federal scouts from Morganza to Fausse River and Grossetete Bayou, LA, under Brig. Gen. Daniel Ullmann, USA. 2/7-10/1865.
02	7	1865	Maine and Kansas become the 7th and 8th states to ratify the 13th amendment to the US Constitution, which abolishes slavery.
02	7	1865	Skirmish at Blackville, SC, as Maj. Gen. William T. Sherman, USA, marches on basically unopposed.
02	7	1865	Federal reconnaissance to Cannon's Bridge, South Edisto River, SC .
02	7	1865	Skirmish at the Edisto Railroad Bridge, SC.
02	7	1865	Federal scout on the Hernando Road, TN, where the Yankees are unable to catchup with several squads of Rebels belonging to Lieut. Gen. Nathan Bedford Forrest's Cavalry. These men were making their headquarters at the home of Mrs. Heldinbrand, about 14 miles from Memphis, between the Hernando and Hollow Ford Roads.
02	8	1865	**George Baird Hodge,** CSA, is appointed Brig. Gen.
02	8	1865	Federal expedition down the Arkansas River, aboard the steamer, **Davenport,** near Little Rock, AR, against guerrillas. 2/8-9/1865 .
02	8	1865	Federal scout from Helena to Madison, AR, with skirmish **(Feb. 12th),** with guerrillas near Madison, also destroying about 2,500 bushels of corn and large amounts of bacon. 2/8-13/1865.
02	8	1865	**Maj. Gen. Grenville M. Dodge, USA, assumes the command of the territory formerly comprised in the Dept. of Kansas.** Later, he will be merciless on the hostile Indians.
02	8	1865	Affair at **(1)** New Market (8th), where guerrillas captured and burned a train of 9 wagons; **(2)** skirmish at Bradfordsville (8th), where the guerrillas murder 3 train guards they took as hostages, and **(3)** skirmish at Hustonville, KY, where the pursuing Yankees make the guerrillas pay for what they've done. **(Feb. 9th).** 2/8-9/1865.
02	8	1865	Massachusetts and Pennsylvania become the 9th and 10th states to ratify the 13th amendment, which will abolish slavery.
02	8	1865	Action with Indians on the North Platte River, near Rush Creek, the Nebraska Territory. 2/8-9/1865.
02	8	1865	Skirmish at Cannon's Bridge, South Edisto River, SC.
02	8	1865	Skirmish at Walker's or Valley Bridge, Edisto River, SC.

02	8	1865	Skirmish near White Pond, SC.
02	8	1865	Skirmish at Williston, SC, with Maj. Gen. William T. Sherman, USA.
02	9	1865	**James Isham Gilbert,** USA, is appointed Brig. Gen.
02	9	1865	Brig. Gen. Elias S. Dennis, USA, assumes the command of the District of South Alabama.
02	9	1865	Federal scout from Pine Bluff to Devall's Bluff, AR, with skirmish with guerrillas. 2/9-19/1865.
02	9	1865	**The Northern Division of Louisiana is formed,** to consist of the Districts of Baton Rouge and of Port Hudson, and the Post of Morganza, while **Maj. Gen. Francis J. Herron, USA, is assigned to its command.**
02	9	1865	The Defenses of New Orleans, LA, is changed to the Southern Division of Louisiana, with Brig. Gen. Thomas W. Sherman, USA, in command.
02	9	1865	**Maj. Gen. John M. Schofield, USA, assumes the command of the Dept. of North Carolina.**
02	9	1865	The advance of the 23rd US Army Corps from Tennessee, arrives at Fort Fisher, NC, under command of Maj. Gen. John M. Schofield, USA, and prepares for an assault on Wilmington, NC.
02	9	1865	**Maj. Gen. Quincy A. Gillmore, USA, assumes the command of the Dept. of the South,** over vice Maj. Gen. John G. Foster, SC, etal.
02	9	1865	Skirmish at Binnaker's Bridge, South Edisto River, SC.
02	9	1865	Skirmish at Holman's Bridge, South Edisto River, SC.
02	9	1865	Skirmish near Memphis, TN, where the Confederates attack and capture a Union wood train and its escort. A Negro moving his family to Memphis told the pursuing Yankees he passed a Rebel force with a large number of mules about 12 miles from Hernando. The Yankees moved out in that direction.
02	9	1865	Gen. Robert E. Lee, CSA, who assumed the command of all the Confederate Armies, and proposes granting a pardon to all deserters who return to their commands within 30 days; President Jefferson Davis concurs.
02	10	1865	Skirmish in Johnson's Crook, GA, as Maj. Gen. James B. Steedman, USA, commanding the District of the Etowah, has his men surprise the Confederates here, inflicting casualties.
02	10	1865	The Dept. of the Cumberland is declared to consist of the State of Tennessee and such parts of Northern Georgia, Alabama, and Mississippi as may be occupied by the troops under the command of Maj. Gen. George H. Thomas, USA.
02	10	1865	**The Dept. of Kentucky (that consists of the State of Kentucky), is created, and assigned is Maj. Gen. John M. Palmer, USA, to its command.**
02	10	1865	All troops in the Depts. of Kentucky and the Cumberland are declared subject to orders of Maj. Gen. George H. Thomas, USA, except those posts on the east bank of the Mississippi River, which were subject to the order of Maj. Gen. Edward Sprigg Canby, USA.
02	10	1865	Federal expedition from Brashear City to Lake Verret, LA. 2/10-11/1865.
02	10	1865	Skirmish at Kittredge's Sugar House, near Napoleonville, LA, with a small band of Confederates.
02	10	1865	The Dept. of the Gulf is declared to embrace the States of Louisiana and Texas.
02	10	1865	Federal expedition from Thibodeaux to Lake Verret, LA, as the Yankees continue to try to ferret out guerrillas; this time coming up empty handed as they traversed the plantations in the area. 2/10-13/1865.
02	10	1865	The Dept. of Mississippi is declared to embrace as much of the State of Mississippi as was occupied by the troops of the Military Division of West Mississippi on the river.
02	10	1865	Federal scout from Friar's Point, MS, and skirmish, with yet another lone guerrilla who is surrounded by the Yankees at his ranch, only to face the same treatment as many other guerrillas faced before him; staring down the wrong end of a gun barrel, where in most cases, surrender was not an option.
02	10	1865	Ohio and Missouri become the 11th and 12th states to ratify the 13th amendment which will abolish slavery.
02	10	1865	Skirmish at James Island, SC.
02	10	1865	Skirmish at Johnson's Station, SC.
02	10	1865	Affair 9 miles from Triune, TN, at the house of the widow Patterson, where the Yankees surround Confederates, belonging to Lieut. Gen. John B. Hood's Army of the Tennessee, who were enjoying a ball held there. The Yankees estimate they killed 4 when they fired into the house, as the citizens removed the bodies to hide the fact there were guerrillas partaking in the festivities. One must wonder if that was the case, or if they were removing their own to bury.
02	10	1865	**Capt. Raphael Semmes is promoted to Confederate Rear Admiral, CSN,** and placed in command of the James River Squadron, VA, replacing Commodore J. K. Mitchell, CSN.
02	11	1865	Skirmish at Clear Creek, AR.
02	11	1865	Skirmish near Pine Bluff, AR.

02	11	1865	Action near Sugar Loaf, NC.
02	11	1865	Action at Aiken, SC, as Maj. Gen. William T. Sherman, USA, reaches the **Augusta and Charleston Railroad,** now in a position to attack the Confederates at Augusta, GA, and/or the Charleston, SC, vicinity.
02	11	1865	Attack on Battery Simkins, SC.
02	11	1865	Action at Johnson's Station, SC.
02	11	1865	Skirmishes about Orangeburg, SC. 2/11-12/1865.
02	11	1865	Federal expedition from Bermuda Hundred to Fearnsville and to Smithfield, VA, finds no Confederate resistance of any kind in this area. 12/11-15/1865.
02	11	1865	Affair at Williamsburg, VA, as the Rebel Cavalry forces, dressed in Union garb, attack the Union picket-post and charge upon the reserves, inflicting casualties, receiving some in return.
02	12	1865	Skirmish at Waterloo, AL.
02	12	1865	Skirmish 20 miles north of Lewisburg, AR, as a Yankee column of 100 men attacked the guerrilla **Capt. Jeff Williams** at his home, terminating his existence on this earth.
02	12	1865	Federal operations about Forts Riley and Larned, KS, with little excitement. 2/12-20/1865.
02	12	1865	Skirmish near Columbia, MO, as the Yankees attacked Jim Carter's camp, killing 3 and wounding the rest of the guerrilla outlaws.
02	12	1865	Skirmish at Macon, MO.
02	12	1865	Skirmishes at the North Edisto River, SC, as Maj. Gen. William T. Sherman, USA, continues on his march northward toward Columbia, SC, causing vast destruction along the way. 2/12-13/1865.
02	13	1865	**Maj. Gen. Samuel R. Curtis, USA, assumes the command of the Dept. of the Northwest, consisting of the Colorado Territory, etal.**
02	13	1865	Action at Station Four, FL, as the **2nd US Colored Infantry** contribute their quota of dead privates today, as the Yankees' path of destruction in this area is contested today by the Confederates, Maj. Gen. Samuel Jones, CSA, commanding the District of Florida, fighting a losing battle.
02	13	1865	Skirmish with bushwackers in Mississippi County, MO.
02	13	1865	Federal expedition from Camp Russell (near Winchester) to Strasburg, Edenburg and Little Fort Valley, VA, and skirmishes with Brig. Gen. John McCausland's, CSA, Cavalry, with fatalities on both sides. 2/13-17/1865.
02	14	1865	<u>**Wade Hampton, C.S.A., is appointed Lieut. Gen.**</u>
02	14	1865	**Maj. Gen. Francis J. Herron, USA, assumes the command of the Northern Division of Louisiana.**
02	14	1865	Federal expeditions from Donaldsonville to Grand Bayou and Bayou Goula, LA, with skirmish **(Feb. 15th)** at Martin's Lane, with guerrillas, most from the 2nd LA Cavalry. 2/14-18/1865.
02	14	1865	Skirmish at Gunter's Bridge, North Edisto River, SC, as Maj. Gen. William T. Sherman, USA, crosses the Congaree River and pushes on for Columbia, SC. The Confederacy is in dire straits with little hope of reversal.
02	14	1865	Skirmish at Wolf's Plantation, SC, as Lieut. Gen. William J. Hardee, CSA, contemplates the evacuation of Charleston, SC.
02	14	1865	**Maj. Gen. George Stoneman, USA, is assigned to the command of the District of East Tennessee.**
02	14	1865	Maj. Gen. Horatio G. Wright, USA, resumes the command of the 6th US Army Corps, the Richmond, VA, Campaign.
02	15	1865	**Bryan Grimes,** **C.S.A.,** is appointed Maj. Gen.
02	15	1865	**John Horace Forney,** CSA, is appointed Brig. Gen.
02	15	1865	**Thomas Muldrup Logan,** CSA, is appointed Brig. Gen.
02	15	1865	**Green Berry Raum,** USA, is appointed Brig. Gen.
02	15	1865	**Charles John Stolbrand,** USA, is appointed Brig. Gen.
02	15	1865	**Brig. Gen. Mosby M. Parsons, CSA, is assigned to the temporary command of the District of Arkansas.**
02	15	1865	**Brig. Gen. Alexander Asboth, USA, assumes the command of the District of West Florida, vice Brig. Gen. Thomas J. McKean, USA, is relieved.**
02	15	1865	Skirmish at Bates' Ferry, Congaree River, SC, as the Confederates desperately attempt to slow Maj. Gen. William T. Sherman's, USA, and his 4 US Army Corps advance with the aid of the Union Cavalry under Brig. Gen. Judson Kilpartick, USA.
02	15	1865	Skirmish at Congaree Creek, SC.
02	15	1865	Skirmish at Red Bank Creek, SC.

02	15	1865	Skirmish at Savannah Creek, SC.
02	15	1865	Skirmish at Two League Cross-Roads, near Lexington, SC.
02	15	1865	Federal scout from Nashville, on the Nolensville Pike, TN. 2/15-16/1865.
02	15	1865	Federal scout from Fairfax Court-House to Aldie and Middleburg, VA, with the capture of 8 Confederate Cavalrymen. Indeed, a good night for the Yankees. 2/15-16/1865.

02	16	1865	**Milledge Luke Bonham, C.S.A.,** is appointed Maj. Gen.
02	16	1865	**Isaac Munroe St. John,** CSA, is appointed Brig. Gen.
02	16	1865	Skirmish 3.5 miles from Gurley's Tank, AL, as the Confederates attack a Federal foraging party.
02	16	1865	Federal operations about Bennett's Bayou and Tolbert's Mill, AR, where the Yankees burn the mill, considered to be a meeting place for guerrillas. 2/16-18/1865.
02	16	1865	Skirmish near Cedar Keys, FL.
02	16	1865	Indiana, Louisiana and Nevada become the 13th, 14th, and 15th US states to ratify the 13th Amendment which abolishes slavery.
02	16	1865	Federal scout from Fort Larned, KS, to the North fork of the Pawnee, northwest to Walnut Creek, up the South Fork of Walnut Creek, to a large body of timber about 120 miles from Fort Zarah, with no signs of Indians. 2/16-21/1865.
02	16	1865	Federal scout in Ozark County, MO, and Marion County, AR, against bushwackers. 2/16-20/1865.
02	16	1865	Skirmishes about **Columbia, SC,** between Maj. Gen. William T. Sherman, USA, and Gen. G. T. Beauregard, CSA, as the Union forces arrive on the south bank of the Congaree River, as Beauregard **evacuates** the city. 2/16-17.1865.
02	16	1865	The Confederate Cavalry attacks by Brig. Gen. John Crawford Vaughn, CSA, upon the garrisons of Athens and Sweet Water, TN, 45 miles below Knoxville, TN, with the Rebels capturing both garrisons.

02	17	1865	Skirmish at Fort Buchanan, the Arizona Territory, as the **Apaches Indians,** on the warpath, attack the Fort, capturing rations, weapons, killing and horribly mutilating some Federal soldiers, before fleeing.
02	17	1865	Federal scout from Pine Bluff, AR, to the Arkansas River, with skirmish (Feb. 17th) near Bayou Meto, AR. 2/17-18/1865.
02	17	1865	Skirmish in Washington County, AR.
02	17	1865	Federal expedition from Plaquemine to The Park, LA. 2/17-22/1865.
02	17	1865	Federal expedition from Eastport to Iuka, MS, to capture the Rebels who were making a habit of going into Iuka every night, and remaining there until morning. Upon moving on Iuka, the Yankees find that Lieut. Gen. Nathan Bedford Forrest, CSA, had moved all his men about a week ago to West Point, MS, about 100 miles below Verona. 2/17-18/1865.
02	17	1865	Skirmish near Smithville, NC.
02	17	1865	The Confederate forces, under Lieut. Gen. William J. Hardee, CSA, **evacuate Charleston, SC,** and heads to Cheraw, SC.
02	17	1865	The Union forces, under Maj. Gen. William T. Sherman, USA, **occupy Columbia,** SC. Lieut. Gen. Wade Hampton's Confederate cavalry set fire to cotton bales before fleeing. Union soldiers uncover barrels of whiskey, and that night the majority of Columbia catches fire and burns. Yankees blame the Rebels, but to most Southerners, this is a gross humiliation of the North's deprivations exerted by the victorious Union armies that will have lasting effects.
02	17	1865	Federal expedition from Whitesburg aboard the gunboats, **Sherman** and **Stone River,** to Fearn's Ferry, TN, and skirmish with guerrillas 3 miles from Warrenton. 2/17-18/1865.
02	17	1865	The Territory of Utah and that part of the Nebraska Territory, lying west of the 22d degree longitude, is added to the Dept. of the Missouri.

02	18	1865	The following are appointed Confederate Brigadier Generals: **Collett Leventhorpe,** CSA **William Raine Peck,** CSA **Reuben Lindsay Walker,** CSA
02	18	1865	**Galusha Pennypacker,** USA, is appointed Brig. Gen.
02	18	1865	The Confederate commerce raider, **CSS Shenandoah,** leaves the port of Melbourne, Australia.
02	18	1865	The Confederate guerrilla attack on Fort Jones, near Colesburg, KY, the **12th US Colored Heavy Artillery** sustaining fatalities.
02	18	1865	**Maj. Gen. John M. Palmer, USA, assumes the command of the Dept. of Kentucky.**
02	18	1865	**The 13th and the 16th US Army Corps are constituted;** the former from the Reserve Corps, the Military Division of West Mississippi, the latter from the troops arriving from the Army of the

Cumberland, MO.

| 02 | 18 | 1865 | Maj. Gen. Gordon Granger, USA, is assigned to the command of the 13th US Army Corps, MO. |

02 18 1865 Maj. Gen. Andrew J. Smith, USA, is assigned to the command of the 16th US Army Corps, MO, etal.

02 18 1865 Action at Fort Anderson, near Wilmington, NC, as Maj. Gen. Jacob Dolson Cox, USA, lands his troops, and advances on the fort while the US Navy bombards the fort.

02 18 1865 Skirmish at Orton Pond, NC.

02 18 1865 The Union forces, led by Brig. Gen. Alexander Schimmelfennig, USA, of Maj. Gen. Sherman's army, **occupies Charleston, SC.**

02 18 1865 Maj. Gen. William T. Sherman, USA, orders the burning of all important buildings, railroad tracks, and military stores that were not already burned by the fire that swept through Columbia, SC, adding additional insult to injury.

02 18 1865 Federal expedition from Camp Averell (near Winchester) into Loudoun County, VA, and skirmish **(Feb. 19th)** at Ashby's Gap, as the Federals take 2 deserters from Lieut. Col. John S. Mosby's, CSA, command along to point out the houses that belonged to Mosby's men. The Yankees find themselves attacked by a superior Cavalry force, with the majority of the expeditionary force killed, captured, or wounded. (78 men). 2/18-19/1865.

02 18 1865 Federal scout in Prince William County, VA, with the destruction of Rebel property. 2/18-19/1865.

02 19 1865 Federal expedition with the **56th US Colored Infantry,** from Helena, AR, aboard the steamer, **Curlew,** to Friar's Point, MS. 2/19-22/1865.

02 19 1865 Federal expedition from Barrancas to Milton, FL, to obtain an interview with the Rebel Captain Keyser, and make arrangements for the surrender of his command. Upon arriving here, the Yankees find that Keyser had been ordered to Pollard, AL.

02 19 1865 Federal expedition from Eastport, MS, to Russellville, AL, with skirmishes **(20th)** near Tuscumbia, AL, in the Federal advance on Selma. 2/19-23/1865.

02 19 1865 Skirmish at Town Creek, near Wilmington, and the Cape Fear River, NC, as Maj. Gen. Jacob D. Cox, USA, attempts to flank the Confederates and capture Wilmington. 2/19-20/1865.

02 19 1865 The Union **capture of Fort Anderson,** near Wilmington, NC.

02 20 1865 **Brig. Gen. John S. Morgan, USA, is assigned to the command of the District of Arizona.**

02 20 1865 The Confederate attack on Fort Myers, FL, is repulsed.

02 20 1865 Skirmish at Center Creek, MO.

02 20 1865 Federal expedition to Greeneville and Warrensburg, TN, in the pouring rain, with skirmishes **(Feb. 21st and 22nd)** near Greeneville as elections were held in the town.

02 20 1865 Federal expedition from Nashville to Pine Wood, Hickman County, TN, and encounter with guerrillas. 2/20-24/1865.

02 21 1865 **William Flank Perry,** CSA, is appointed Brig. Gen.

02 21 1865 **William Paul Roberts,** CSA, is appointed Brig. Gen.

02 21 1865 Brig. Gen. Elias S. Dennis, USA, assumes the command of the US forces on Dauphin Island, AL.

02 21 1865 Brig. Gen. William P. Benton, USA, assumes the temporary command of the US forces at Mobile, AL.

02 21 1865 Federal scout from Pine Bluff to Douglas' Plantation, AR, and skirmish with the Confederates as the rain fell in torrents. **(22nd).** 2/21-22/1865.

02 21 1865 Federal operations, under Maj. Gen. John Newton, USA, commanding the District of Key West and Tortugas, in the vicinity of Saint Mark's, FL, with the assistance of the Federal steamers, **Fort Henry, Hibiscus, Honduras, Iuka, Magnolia, Mahaska, Proteus,** and the **Stars and Stripes,** with the schooners **O.H. Lee, Matthew Vasar** and the **Two Sisters,** move against the remaining Confederate resistance in the vicinity. The Yankees' military might is overpowering. 2/21-3/7/1865 .

02 21 1865 **Brig. Gen. Douglas H. Cooper, CSA, is assigned to the command of the District of the Indian Territory.**

02 21 1865 The Confederate Raid on Cumberland, MD, where Lieut. Gen. Jubal A. Early's, CSA, Cavalry of Partisan Rangers under Capt. Jesse McNeill, sweeps into the well fortified town, **capturing Maj. Gen. George Crook, USA,** and **Bvt. Maj. Gen. Benjamin F. Kelley, USA,** a most embarrassing event for the Yankees, especially the 2 Union Major Generals. They were taken to Richmond, and eventually paroled.

02 21 1865 Skirmish at Eagle Island, NC, as Maj. Gen. John Schofield's, USA, army rapidly advanced on Wilmington, NC.

02 21 1865 Skirmish at Fort Strong, NC, as Gen. Braxton Bragg **evacuates Wilmington** at nightfall, burning vast precious Confederate supplies.

02	22	1865	Federal scout from Pine Bluff to Bayou Meto, AR, and skirmishes at Mrs. Voche's **(Feb. 23rd)** and Bayou Meto **(Feb. 24th).** 2/22-24/1865 .
02	22	1865	Federal expedition under Brig. Gen. Alexander Asboth, USA, commanding the District of West Florida, from Barrancas, aboard the steamer, **Matamoras,** to Milton, FL, and skirmishes. The Yankees capture prisoners and supplies. 2/2-25/1865.
02	22	1865	**Brig. Gen. John McNeil, USA, is assigned to the command of the District of Central Missouri.**
02	22	1865	Maj. Gen. Andrew J. Smith, USA, assumes the command of the 16th US Army Corps, MO, etal.
02	22	1865	Skirmish at Northeast Ferry, NC.
02	22	1865	Skirmish at Smith's Creek, NC.
02	22	1865	The Union forces **occupy Wilmington, NC,** the **last major Confederate seaport** as Gen. Braxton Bragg, CSA, evacuated the city the night before.
02	22	1865	Skirmish near Camden, SC, as Maj. Gen. William T. Sherman, USA, continues marching northward.
02	22	1865	Skirmish near Wateree River, SC.
02	22	1865	**Gen. Joseph E. Johnston, CSA, is assigned by Gen. Robert E. Lee, CSA, to the command of the Army of Tennessee, and all the troops in the Confederate Dept. of South Carolina, Georgia, and Florida.**
02	22	1865	Circumstances and fast moving events are beginning to explode out of control for the Confederacy.
02	22	1865	Gen. Robert E. Lee, CSA, laid optional plans to retreat to Burkeville, VA, and unite with the Confederate forces in North Carolina if he was forced to leave his defensive position around Petersburg and Richmond, VA.
02	23	1865	**Thomas Ewing, Jr., U.S.A.,** is appointed Maj. Gen.
02	23	1865	Federal expedition from Barrancas to Milton, FL, and skirmishes. 2/22-25/1865.
02	23	1865	Bvt. Maj. Gen. Stephen G. Burbridge, USA, is relieved from the command of the District of Kentucky.
02	23	1865	Federal scouts from Salem and Licking, MO, to Spring River Mills, AR, with skirmishes, as the Yankees continue to do a number on the guerrillas, who can't be feeling so confident anymore. 2/23-3/2/1865.
02	23	1865	Skirmish near Camden, SC, as Maj. Gen. William T. Sherman, USA, crosses the Catawba River and heads for North Carolina. Heavy rains will slow his progress over the next several days.
02	23	1865	Federal expedition from Yorktown aboard the gunboat, **USS Mystic,** to West Point, VA, where the Yankees are unsuccessful in their attempt to capture Col. Richardson of Gen. Robert E. Lee's staff who was home on 60 days leave; he was warned by a spy. The Yankees also missed breaking up a wedding where a band of Rebels were supposed to attend; they got the wrong date, as it is scheduled for March 2nd. The Yankees proceed to burn Richardson's home, and other barns, with thousands of pounds of bacon and about 25,000 bushels of corn and grain, before returning to Yorktown, VA. 2/23-24/1865.
02	24	1865	Federal scout with the **60th US Colored Infantry,** from Helena, aboard the steamer, **Curlew,** to Clarke's Store, AR.
02	24	1865	Affair at Switzler's Mill, MO, where the guerrilla Poe kills a man and hangs two negroes, besides robbing another citizen. Lawlessness still prevails in some sections of this part of the United States.
02	24	1865	Skirmish at Camden, SC, as Maj. Gen. William T. Sherman, USA, and Lieut. Gen. Wade Hampton, CSA, argue in writing over the murders of certain Union soldiers who were foraging. Hampton informs Sherman that he has ordered the death of all Federal soldiers caught burning the homes and properties of citizens of the Confederacy.
02	25	1865	Brig. Gen. James Veatch, USA, assumes the command of the US forces on Dauphin Island, AL.
02	25	1865	Maj. Gen. Frederick Steele, USA, is assigned to the command of the troops operating from Pensacola Bay, FL.
02	25	1865	Skirmish at Piketon, KY.
02	25	1865	The Union forces **occupy Camden, SC,** on the Wateree River.
02	25	1865	Skirmish at West's Cross-Roads, SC.
02	25	1865	**Gen. Joseph E. Johnston, CSA, assumes the command of the Army of Tennessee** and all troops in the Confederate Dept. of South Carolina, Georgia, and Florida. Johnston notifies Gen. Robert E. Lee, CSA, that he believes a combination of his troops with Gen. Braxton Bragg, CSA, in North Carolina is necessary to mount any kind of obstruction to the forces under Maj. Gen. William T. Sherman, USA.
02	25	1865	Maj. Gen. Gordon Granger, USA, assumes the command of the 13th US Army Corps, TN, etal.
02	26	1865	Federal expedition from Pine Bluff to McMilley's Farm, AR, with skirmish **(Feb. 27th)** with guerrillas at McMilley's Farm. 2/26-28/1865.

02	26	1865	Skirmish at Lynch's Creek, SC, as Maj. Gen. William T. Sherman, USA, marches on.
02	26	1865	Skirmish near Stroud's Mill, SC, as Maj. Gen. William T. Sherman's, USA, 20th US Army Corps reaches Hanging Rock, NC.
02	26	1865	**Maj. Gen. Winfield S. Hancock, USA, is assigned to the command of the Dept. of West Virginia,** and temporarily of all the troops of the Middle Military Division not under the immediate command of Maj. Gen. Philip Henry Sheridan, USA.
02	27	1865	Brig. Gen. John M. Thayer, USA, is assigned to the command of the Post of Saint Charles, AR.
02	27	1865	Skirmish at Spring Place, GA.
02	27	1865	Brig. Gen. Edmund J. Davis, USA, assumes the temporary command of the US forces at Morganza, LA.
02	27	1865	**Brig. Gen. Morgan L. Smith, USA, assumes the command of the District of Vicksburg, MS.**
02	27	1865	**Brig. Gen. John McNeil, USA, assumes the command of the District of Central Missouri.**
02	27	1865	Skirmish near Sturgeon, MO, with guerrillas in the dark.
02	27	1865	Skirmish at Cloud's House, SC.
02	27	1865	Skirmish near Mount Elon, SC.
02	27	1865	**Operations (Final) in the Shenandoah Valley, VA.** 2/27-4/23/1865.
02	27	1865	**Federal expedition from Winchester, VA, to the front of Petersburg, VA.** 2/27-3/28/1865.
02	27	1865	Maj. Gen. Philip Henry Sheridan's US command starts from Winchester, VA, to Petersburg, VA, as Brig. Gen. Wesley Merritt, USA, moves with 10,000 Union Cavalry to operate against the **Virginia Central Railroad** and the **James River Canal.** Merrit is also ordered to capture Lynchburg, VA. Lieut. Gen. Jubal Early, CSA, attempts to gather as many Confederates as possible to deflect this latest Union advance.
02	27	1865	Gen. Robert E. Lee, CSA, is and has been concerned over the large number of desertions his army has been facing. The Confederate Army of Northern Virginia's strength is rapidly dwindling.
02	28	1865	**<u>Nathan Bedford Forrest, CSA, is appointed Lieut. Gen.</u>**
02	28	1865	**Tyree Harris Bell,** CSA, is appointed Brig. Gen.
02	28	1865	Skirmish near Cheraw, SC, with the advancing Union forces under Maj. Gen. William Tecumseh Sherman, USA.
02	28	1865	Skirmish near Rocky Mount, SC.
02	28	1865	The following commands are reorganized as follows: a) **District of Middle Tennessee** - Maj. Gen. Lovell H. Rousseau b) **District of West Tennessee** - Maj. Gen. Cadwallder Washburn c) **District of East Tennessee** - Maj. Gen. George Stoneman d) **District of Etowah, Tennessee** - Maj. Gen. James B. Steedman,
03	1	1865	**Alexander William Campbell,** CSA, is appointed Brig. Gen.
03	1	1865	**Ellison Capers,** CSA, is appointed Brig. Gen.
03	1	1865	Federal expedition from Gravelly Springs to Florence, AL. 3/1-6/1865.
03	1	1865	Skirmish at Holly Creek, GA.
03	1	1865	**Brig. Gen. Douglas H. Cooper, CSA, assumes the command of the District of the Indian Territory** and the superintendency of Indian Affairs.
03	1	1865	Federal expedition from Baton Rouge to Jackson and Clinton, LA, as the Yankees experience terrible weather, having to rebuild bridges across White's Bayou, Redwood and the Comite. The Rebels leave the impression they are about to abandon this area very soon; the local citizens are beginning to show a strong disposition to get on good terms with the Federal authorities. 3/1-12/1865.
03	1	1865	Brig. Gen. Benjamin H. Grierson, USA, is assigned to the command of the Military Division of West Mississippi.
03	1	1865	Maj. Gen. Jacob D. Cox, USA, assumes the command of the District of Beaufort, SC.
03	1	1865	With Admiral John Dahlgren aboard, his flagship, the **Harvest Moon,** strikes a Confederate torpedo near Charleston Harbor, SC, and sinks. The after effects of a military campaign will continue even after the last shots have been fired.
03	1	1865	Skirmish at Wilson's Store, SC, as Maj. Gen. William T. Sherman, USA, continues his march through the Carolinas.
03	1	1865	Skirmish near Philadelphia, TN, as Brig. Gen. Davis Tillson, USA, commends the Federal officer in charge for his resolve of taking no guerrillas as prisoners, all the enemy being killed today.
03	1	1865	Skirmish at Mount Crawford, VA, as Maj. Gen. Philip H. Sheridan, USA, and Brig. Gen. Wesley Merritt, USA, Union Cavalry meet up with Lieut. Gen. Jubal Early, CSA.

MONTH	DAY	YEAR	ACT
03	1	1865	Wisconsin becomes the 16th state to ratify the 13th amendment which will abolish slavery, if passed.
03	2	1865	Brig. Gen. Benjamin H. Grierson, USA, assumes the command of the cavalry forces in the Military Division of West Mississippi.
03	2	1865	Skirmish at Chesterfield, SC.
03	2	1865	Maj. Gen. William T. Sherman's, USA 20th US Army Corps **occupies Chesterfield, SC.**
03	2	1865	Skirmish at Thompson's Creek, near Chesterfield, SC.
03	2	1865	Federal operations about Athens, TN, and within 14 miles of Murphy, as the Federals extract a heavy levy on guerrillas' lives today. 3/2-4/1865.
03	2	1865	The Federal **occupation of Stauton,** VA, by Maj. Gen. Philip H. Sheridan, USA.
03	2	1865	Affair at Swoope's Depot, VA, with Maj. Gen. Philip H. Sheridan, USA.
03	2	1865	**The Engagement at Waynesborough, VA,** where Brig. Gen. George Armstrong Custer, USA, completely routs the Confederates under Lieut. Gen. Jubal A. Early, CSA, capturing over 1,000 and over 200 wagon of supplies. The Confederates easily gave way which indicates the current morale of the Southern man fighting in the Shenandoah Valley, as compared to the "invincibility" felt by the Rebel "foot cavalry" under Lieut. Gen. Thomas Jonathan "Stonewall" Jackson, in earlier days of glory, which now seemed so far away. The Confederate remnants under Lieut. Gen. Jubal Early march toward Richmond, VA. **This engagement is effectively the last in the Shenandoah Valley, VA.**
03	3	1865	Skirmish at Decatur, AL.
03	3	1865	Skirmish near Tunnel Hill, GA, as Maj. Gen. Joseph Wheeler's Confederates capture a small squad of Yankees out and about repairing downed telegraph wires.
03	3	1865	The Idaho Territory is attached to the District of Oregon.
03	3	1865	Brig. Gen. Thomas J. McKean, USA, assumes the command of the District of Morganza, LA.
03	3	1865	Federal expeditions from Bloomfield, 25 miles into Dunklin County, MO, with skirmishes (Mar. 3rd and **7th)** near Bloomfield and **(Mar. 4th)** in Dunklin County, where the Yankees kill 6 Rebels, in fierce fighting. The Confederates are not yet ready to throw in the towel. 3/3-7/1865.
03	3	1865	Affair near Big Black Creek, SC.
03	3	1865	Skirmish near Blakeny's, SC.
03	3	1865	The Union forces, under Maj. Gen. William T. Sherman, USA, **occupy Cheraw, SC,** as the Confederates retreat across the Pee Dee River, and yield large depots of precious military supplies.
03	3	1865	Skirmish at Juniper Creek, near Cheraw, SC.
03	3	1865	Skirmish at Thompson's Creek, near Cheraw, SC.
03	3	1865	Skirmish near Hornsborough, SC.
03	3	1865	Federal reconnaissance from Cumberland Gap, TN, toward Jonesville, VA, with skirmishes **(Mar. 4th)** at Ball's Bridge, VA, and **(Mar. 5th)** at Tazewell, TN. 3/3-5/1865.
03	3	1865	Federal expedition from Memphis, TN, into Northern Mississippi. 3/3-11/1865.
03	3	1865	The **occupation of Charlottesville, VA,** by the Federal troops under Maj. Gen. Philip Henry Sheridan, USA, who continue to ride toward Petersburg, VA.
03	3	1865	Federal operations about Warrenton, Bealeton Station, Sulphur Springs, Salem, and Centreville, VA, and encounters with guerrillas dressed in Union garb. The Union officer in charge commenting how the Federal cavalry is misbehaving badly as they pillage and plunder farms and houses along their ride. 3/3-8/1865.
03	3	1865	The Federals begin moving their convoy of Confederate prisoners up the Shenandoah Valley from Waynesborough to Winchester, VA, with skirmishes along the way at: a) Harrisonburg **(Mar. 5th)** b) Mount Jackson **(Mar. 7th)** c) Rude's Hill **(Mar. 7th)**
03	3	1865	Before adjourning, the 38th Congress of the U.S.A. establishes the **Bureau for the Relief of Freedmen and Refugees,** designed to manage and supervise all abandoned lands controlled by the US and to provide assistance to the refugees and freed slaves.
03	4	1865	**William Wirt Allen,** C.S.A., is appointed Maj. Gen.
03	4	1865	**Young Marshall Moody,** CSA, is appointed Brig. Gen.
03	4	1865	Affair near Pine Bluff, AR, where the Yankees sneak up on the camp of a small band of Rebels in the dark and scatter the Confederates in all directions, as they are taken by surprise.
03	4	1865	The US transport, **Thorn,** strikes a torpedo on the Cape Fear River and sinks near Fort Anderson, NC.
03	4	1865	Skirmish at Phillips' Cross-Roads, NC.

MONTH	DAY	YEAR	ACT
03	4	1865	Federal expedition from near Cheraw to Florence, SC, and skirmishes. 3/4-6/1865.
03	4	1865	Maj. Gen. Cadwallader C. Washburn, USA, assumes the command of the District of West Tennessee.
03	4	1865	US Chief Justice, Salmon P. Chase swears in **Abraham Lincoln** for his 2nd term as President, Washington, DC.
03	5	1865	Federal scouts from Waynesville to Hutton Valley, Rolla, and Lebanon, MO, in search of the guerrillas who captured and murdered a citizen of Waynesville, MO. One can only imagine what he had done to deserve such a fate. 3/5-12/1865.
03	5	1865	Skirmish near Cheraw, SC, as Maj. Gen. William T. Sherman, USA, prepares to invade North Carolina, crossing the Pee Dee River, and striking for Fayetteville.
03	5	1865	Federal expedition from Fortress Monroe to Fredericksburg, VA, with the destruction of all Confederate property of value along the way. 3/5-8/1865.
03	5	1865	President Abraham Lincoln appoints **Hugh McCulloch, Comptroller of the Currency,** to the position of **Secretary of the Treasury** to replace **William Fessenden** who resigned after being reelected to the Senate from his home state of Maine.
03	6	1865	**Maj. Gen. Alexander McD. McCook, USA, is assigned to the command of the District of Eastern Arkansas.**
03	6	1865	Skirmish at Natural Bridge, FL.
03	6	1865	**Gen. Joseph E. Johnston, CSA, assumes the command of all the troops in the Confederate Dept. of North Carolina.**
03	7	1865	Skirmish at Elyton, AL.
03	7	1865	Federal expedition from Jacksonville into Marion County, FL, and skirmish. 3/7-12/1865.
03	7	1865	Skirmish with Indians 80 miles west of Fort Larned, KS, as the Indians attack a wagon train but are driven off.
03	7	1865	Federal scout from Glasgow to the Perche Hills, MO, in Howard and Boone Counties, in search of guerrillas. The Federals use a local to point out the homes of suspected bushwackers, killing any they run into; burning their homes along the way. The Federals complain that too many locals house and feed these marauders, which makes it more difficult to suppress their actions. The Yankees report chasing a guerrilla band for 2 days in their sight, but unable to overtake them. 3/7-15/1865.
03	7	1865	Federal operations about Licking, MO, where the Yankees report that just about everyday, they kill and wound guerrillas, capturing horses, guns, food, etc. It has become very dangerous to have chosen the life of a guerrilla/bushwacker. 3/7-25/1865.
03	7	1865	Maj. Gen. Sterling Price, CSA, is assigned to the command of the Missouri Division of Infantry, and Brig. Gen. Mosby M. Parsons, CSA, is assigned to the command of Parson's Missouri Brigade.
03	7	1865	Maj. Gen. Jacob D. Cox, USA, is removed to New Berne, NC, to setup a base to supply the army of Maj. Gen. William T. Sherman, USA, after it was learned that Wilmington, NC, is not as advantageous to use for the same.
03	7	1865	Skirmish at Rockingham, NC, as Maj. Gen. William T. Sherman, USA, marches into North Carolina.
03	7	1865	Skirmish at Southwest Creek, NC, with Maj. Gen. William T. Sherman, USA.
03	7	1865	Brig. Gen. Benjamin Alvord, USA, is relieved from the command of the District of Oregon.
03	7	1865	Skirmish near Flint Hill, VA, with guerrillas dressed in Union garb, and again, as usual, with loss of life.
03	8	1865	Skirmish with Indians at Poison Creek, the Idaho Territory.
03	8	1865	Maj. Gen. Sterling Price, CSA, assumes the command of the Missouri Division of Infantry.
03	8	1865	**Col. Edwin C. Catherwood, 13th US Missouri Cavalry, assumes the command of the District of Rolla, MO.**
03	8	1865	**The Battle of Kinston, or Wise's Forks, NC,** as Maj. Gen. Jacob D. Cox, USA, repels Gen. Braxton Bragg, CSA, who contested Cox's latest move, with fresh troops received from the Confederate Army of Tennessee, but to no avail. 3/8-10/1865.
03	8	1865	Skirmish at Love's or Blue's Bridge, SC.
03	8	1865	Skirmish in Jackson County, TN.
03	8	1865	The Headquarters of the Dept. of Mississippi is transferred from Vicksburg, MS, to Memphis, TN.
03	8	1865	Skirmish at Duguidsville, VA, with Maj. Gen. Philip H. Sheridan, USA, who is moving toward Petersburg, VA, from the Shenandoah Valley.
03	9	1865	**Christopher Columbus Andrews, U.S.A., is appointed Maj. Gen.**

03	9	1865	**Maj. Gen. Alexander McD. McCook, USA, assumes the command of the District of Eastern Arkansas.**
03	9	1865	Federal scout from Fort Larned to Coon Creek, Mulberry Creek, then on to Crooked Creek, KS, where the Yankees find a friendly village of **Arapahoes** of **Little Raven's** band, with many bucks, squaws and papooses. The Federals learn there are a few thousand of **Comanches, Apaches** and **Kiowas** in the vicinity and deem it advisable not to burn any of the deserted Indian villages they discovered in the area, opting to return back to Fort Larned as fast as possible. Good idea. 3/9-15/1865.
03	9	1865	Skirmish at Howard's Mills, KY.
03	9	1865	Federal scout against guerrillas from Cape Girardeau into Bollinger, Wayne, and Stoddard Counties, MO. The Yankees report there are a few less agitators in this region after this scout. 3/9-15/1865.
03	9	1865	**Maj. Gen. George Stoneman, USA, assumes the command of the District of East Tennessee.**
03	9	1865	Vermont becomes the 17th state to ratify the 13th amendment abolishing slavery.
03	9	1865	The Federal **occupation of Columbia, VA,** by Maj. Gen. Philip H. Sheridan, USA.
03	9	1865	President Abraham Lincoln accepts the **resignation of his Secretary of the Interior, John P. Usher,** effective May 15.
03	10	1865	**Maj. Gen. William Henry Chase Whiting, CSA,** dies as a prisoner of war at Fort Columbus, NY, from his wounds received at the Federal assault on Fort Fisher, NC, on January 15, 1865.
03	10	1865	Skirmish between Boyd's and the Woodville Station, AL.
03	10	1865	Federal scout from Little Rock to Clear Lake, AR, with skirmish **(Mar. 11th)** at Clear Lake. 3/10-13/1865.
03	10	1865	Engagement at Monroe's Cross-Roads, SC, where Brig. Gen. Hugh Judson Kilpatrick, USA, defeats Lieut. Gen. Wade Hampton, CSA.
03	10	1865	Federal expedition from Suffolk, VA, to Murfree's Depot, NC, with skirmish (10th) at South Quay, VA. 3/10-11/1865.
03	11	1865	Skirmish at Washington, AR.
03	11	1865	Brig. Gen. Edmund J. Davis, USA, is assigned to the command of the District of Baton Rouge, LA.
03	11	1865	Affair near the Little Blue River, MO.
03	11	1865	Skirmish at Fayetteville, NC, as the Union vessels, **USS Eolus, Lenapee, USS Maratanza** and **Nyack** sail up the Cape Fear River towards Fayetteville.
03	11	1865	The Union forces, under Maj. Gen. William T. Sherman, USA, **occupy Fayetteville, NC,** as Sherman now prepares to do battle with the Confederate forces under Gen. Joseph E. Johnston, CSA, who awaits his further march.
03	11	1865	Federal expedition from Fortress Monroe aboard steamers, into Westmoreland County, VA, with skirmish **(Mar. 12th)** near Warsaw, VA, and with the destruction of all Confederate property of any value. 3/11-13/1865.
03	11	1865	Skirmish at Goochland Court-House, VA, as Maj. Gen. Philip Henry Sheridan, USA, threatens Richmond, VA.
03	12	1865	Federal scout from Lewisburg into Yell and Searcy Counties, AR, where the Yankees deal death to guerrillas near Danville, and in Searcy County. The Federals also seize some wheat. 3/12-23/1865.
03	12	1865	Skirmish at Morganza Bend, LA.
03	12	1865	Federal expedition from Vicksburg, MS, by the **53rd US Colored Troops,** aboard the steamer, **Diana,** and accompanied by the Union gunboat, **Mound City,** to Grand Gulf and vicinity. 3/12-14/1865.
03	12	1865	Brig. Gen. Mosby M. Parsons, CSA, is assigned to the command of the Missouri District of Infantry, vice Maj. Gen. Sterling Price, CSA, is relieved.
03	12	1865	Affair near Lone Jack, MO.
03	12	1865	Federal expeditions from Fort Churchill to Pyramid and Walker's Lakes, Nevada, with skirmish with **Smoke Creek Indians:** a) at Mud Lake and **(Mar. 14th)** b) affair near Walker's Lake, Nevada. **(Mar. 16th).** 3/12-19/1865.
03	12	1865	Federal scout in Loudoun County, VA, in pursuit of Maj. John S. Mosby's Partisan Rangers. Mosby is wary, and evades the Yankees. As usual, he normally puts himself in a position of confronting the Yankees at his own choosing. 3/12-14/1865.
03	12	1865	Skirmish near Peach Grove, 2 miles from Vienna, VA, with guerrillas, resulting in loss of Union life and casualties.

03	13	1865	**George Washington Getty,** U.S.A., is appointed Maj. Gen.
03	13	1865	**James Brewerton Ricketts,** U.S.A., is appointed Maj. Gen.
03	13	1865	**Wager Swayne,** USA, is appointed Brig. Gen.
03	13	1865	Affair 1 mile from Dalton, GA, as the attacking Confederates capture 5 railroad hands on the Cleveland road. The Yankees pursue and kill 2 of the cusses, and capture 1.
03	13	1865	**Col. John Morrill, 64th Illinois Infantry, is assigned to the command of the District of Rolla, MO.**
03	13	1865	Skirmish near Fayetteville, NC.
03	13	1865	Skirmish near Beaver Dam Station, VA, with Maj. Gen. Philip H. Sheridan's, USA, Cavalry force on their way to joinup with the Union forces under Lieut. Gen. Ulysses S. Grant, USA, on the siege lines of Petersburg, VA.
03	13	1865	After delays and debate which has been going on for quite some time, the Confederate Congress approves putting Negroes in the Confederate Army to shore up the weak numbers. President Jefferson Davis signs the bill immediately.
03	13	1865	Skirmish near Charlestown, WV.
03	14	1865	Skirmish near Dalton, GA, where the Yankees are surprised to capture a Rebel belonging to Gen. Robert E. Lee's Virginian Army. Wonder how he got down there? Maybe he was one of those who had enough of the war and was working his way back home, taking up the cause along the way.
03	14	1865	Federal reconnaissance from Fayetteville on the Goldsborough road to Black River, NC, and skirmish.
03	14	1865	Federal reconnaissance from Fayetteville on the Raleigh road to Silver Run Creek, NC, and skirmish.
03	14	1865	The Union forces, under Maj. Gen. Jacob D. Cox, USA, **occupy Kinston, NC.**
03	14	1865	The limits of the District of Oregon is extended to include the entire State of Oregon.
03	14	1865	Skirmish at the South Anna Bridge, VA, as Maj. Gen. Philip H. Sheridan, USA, and his cavalry move towards Petersburg, VA.
03	14	1865	Skirmish at Woodstock, VA.
03	14	1865	Federal scout from New Creek to Moorefield, WV, in search of any Confederates still in the area; a mopping up campaign. 3/14-17/1865.
03	14	1865	Federal scout from Philippi to Carricks's Ford, WV, in search of any Confederate forces still in the area. 3/14-16/1865.
03	15	1865	**Thomas Casimer Devin,** USA, is appointed Brig. Gen.
03	15	1865	Skirmishes at Boyd's Station and Stevenson's Gap, AL, as the vanquished Confederates do everything they can in their losing battle. Today, they attack and capture men of the **101st US Colored Infantry.** 3/15-18/1865.
03	15	1865	Federal scout from Fort Sumner, the New Mexico Territory, to the Rio Conchas, Rio Turpentino, Anton Chico, the Pecos, the town of Anton Chico, etc., to ascertain the truth of whether **Navajo** and **Apache Indians** from the local reservation were stealing sheep and cattle. The Yankees are convinced this is not the case but more of unscrupulous whitemen who sell inferior stock and to save themselves blame the Indians when they disappear. In addition, there are even reports a group of **Navajoes** returned a large flock of sheep they found that were lost in the blinding snowstorms. And finally, it appears that anytime livestock is missing, the Indians are blamed for it. An easy scapegoat. 3/15-21/1865.
03	15	1865	Skirmish near Smith's Mills, Black River, NC, as Maj. Gen. William T. Sherman, USA, marches on, and while Gen. Joseph E. Johnston, CSA, attempts to assemble a respectable Confederate force to contest his advance.
03	15	1865	Skirmish at South River, NC.
03	15	1865	Skirmish near Ashland, VA, with Maj. Gen. Philip H. Sheridan, USA.
03	15	1865	Skirmish at Hanover Court-House, VA, with Maj. Gen. Philip H. Sheridan, USA.
03	16	1865	**The Battle of Averasborough (or Taylor's Hole Creek), NC,** between Maj. Gen. Henry W. Slocum's column of Sherman's Army, and Lieut. Gen. William J. Hardee, CSA; Hardee withdrawing toward Bentonville, NC, to join up with the main body of Gen. Joseph E. Johnston's Confederate Army. Total casualties approximate 1,550.
03	16	1865	Skirmish at Little Cohera Creek, NC.
03	16	1865	Gen. Pierre Gustave Toutant Beauregard, CSA, is announced as 2nd in command of Gen. Joseph E. Johnston's Confederate Army, NC, etal.
03	16	1865	Lieut. Gen. Alexander P. Stewart, CSA, is assigned to the command of the infantry and artillery of the Army of Tennessee.

MONTH	DAY	YEAR	ACT
03	16	1865	Federal scout from near Winchester to Front Royal, VA.
03	16	1865	Federal scout from Summit Point, through Kabletown and Myerstown, to the Shenandoah Ferry, WV. 3/16-17/1865.

| 03 | 17 | 1865 | The following are appointed Confederate Brigadier Generals: |

Richard Montgomery Gano,   CSA
Henry Gray,   CSA
William Polk Hardeman,   CSA
Walter Paye Lane,   CSA

03	17	1865	**The Mobile, Alabama, Campaign.** 3/17-5/4/1865.
03	17	1865	The advance of the Union forces (Maj. Gen. Edward R. Canby's, USA, column, Dept. of West Mississippi) moves forward from Mobile Point, AL, toward Mobile, AL. Canby's forces outnumber the Confederates under Brig. Gen. Randall Lee Gibson, CSA, 30,000 to 3,000.
03	17	1865	Federal expedition against guerrillas from Pine Bluff to Bass' Plantation, AR, crossing the river aboard the steamer, **Argosy,** with no encounters with the enemy. 3/17-20/1865.
03	17	1865	**Col. John Morrill, 64th Illinois Infantry, assumes the command of the District of Rolla, MO.**
03	17	1865	Skirmish at Averasborough, NC, with Maj. Gen. William T. Sherman, USA.
03	17	1865	Skirmish at Falling Creek, NC.
03	17	1865	Federal scout from Winchester to Edenburg, VA. 3/17-19/1865.

03	18	1865	**Thomas James Churchill,** C.S.A., is appointed Maj. Gen.
03	18	1865	**John Sappington Marmaduke,** C.S.A., is appointed Maj. Gen.
03	18	1865	**Richard Waterhouse,** CSA, is appointed Brig. Gen.
03	18	1865	**Charles Ewing,** USA, is appointed Brig. Gen.
03	18	1865	Federal expedition from Dauphin Island to Fowl River Narrows, AL, and skirmishes, the Mobile, AL, Campaign. 3/18-22/1865.
03	18	1865	Federal expedition from Fort Gibson to the following in the Indian Territory:

a) Deep Fork, 50 miles from Fort Gibson
b) We-wo-ka, 85 miles southwest of Fort Gibson
c) Little River Town, 25 miles southwest of We-wo-ka
d) Hillabee, 20 miles east of We-wo-ka
e) Canadian River, 20 miles southeast of We-wo-ka, with no encounters with the enemy. The Yankees report there are no longer any citizens living in this part of the Territory. 3/18-30/1865.

03	18	1865	Skirmish at the Amite River, LA.
03	18	1865	**Col. John G. Fonda, 118th Illinois Infantry, is assigned to the temporary command of the District of Baton Rouge, LA.**
03	18	1865	Brig. Gen. Joseph L. Brent, CSA, assumes the command of the Cavalry Forces, of the Front Lines, of the District of West Louisiana.
03	18	1865	Skirmish near Benton's Cross-Roads, NC, as Gen. Joseph E. Johnston's Confederate Army of 20,000 faces the total combined army of Maj. Gen. William T. Sherman, USA, of 100,000. Johnston decides to attack the Union column of 30,000 under Maj. Gen. Henry W. Slocum, USA, with Lieut. Gen. Wade Hampton's, CSA, Cavalry attacking Brig. Gen. Judson Kilpatrick and his Union Cavalry. Such valiant men.
03	18	1865	Skirmish at Bushy Swamp, NC.
03	18	1865	Skirmish at Mingo Creek, NC.
03	18	1865	Maj. Gen. Jacob D. Cox, USA, is relieved from the command of the District of Beaufort, SC, and is assigned to command the Provisional Corps, SC.
03	18	1865	Skirmish at Livingston, TN.
03	18	1865	Skirmish near Dranesville, VA, as the Federal Cavalry patrol confronts and routs a party of Rebel Cavalry, inflicting casualties.

03	19	1865	**Brig. Gen. Thomas Kilby Smith, USA, assumes the command of the District of South Alabama, the Mobile, AL, Campaign.**
03	19	1865	Skirmishes at Welaka and Saunders, FL.
03	19	1865	Federal scout from Warrensburg to Columbus, MO, with skirmish with guerrillas near Greenton. 3/19-23/1865.
03	19	1865	**The Battle of Bentonville, NC,** as Gen. Joseph E. Johnston, CSA, squares off in front of Maj. Gen. Henry W. Slocum's Union column. 3/19-21/1865.

| 03 | 19 | 1865 | Skirmish at the Neuse River Bridge, near Goldsborough, NC. |

03 19 1865 Skirmishes at and near Cox's Bridge, Neuse River, near Goldsborough, NC, with Maj Gen. John M Schofield's, USA, column of Maj. Gen. William T. Sherman's, USA, Army, which is marching towards Goldsborough, NC. 3/19-20/1865.

03 19 1865 Skirmish at Celina, TN.

03 20 1865 The advance of the Union forces (Maj. Gen. Frederick Steele's column, of Maj. Gen. Edward R. S. Canby's Army) starts from Pensacola, FL, for Mobile AL.

03 20 1865 Skirmish at Talbot's Ferry, AR.

03 20 1865 Skirmish at Ringgold, GA, with Union pickets and guerrillas.

03 20 1865 Federal expedition with the **93rd US Colored Infantry** from Brashear City aboard the gunboat, **No. 49,** to Bayou Pigeon, LA, to bring within the Union lines the family of a government employee, with skirmish **(Mar. 21st)** at Bayou Teche, LA. 3/20-22/1865.

03 20 1865 Federal scout against guerrillas from Lexington, MO, to Tabo Church, 12 miles east, Wellington, the Snibar Hills, etc. The Yankees recommend the banishment of certain widows (including the widow of the late **Wilhite,** killed a year ago) who are continuing to aid and abet the bushwackers in the vicinity.

03 20 1865 Skirmish near Falling Creek, NC.

03 20 1865 Maj. Gen. George Stoneman's US Raid in East Tennessee, Southwestern Virginia, and Western North Carolina, to aid in part, Maj. Gen. William T. Sherman's advance on the Confederate Army under Gen. Joseph E. Johnston, CSA, at Bentonville, NC. 3/20-4/27/1865.

03 20 1865 Federal scout from Winchester to Edenburg, VA, with skirmish **(Mar. 21st)** near Fisher's Hill, VA, the Shenandoah Valley.

03 20 1865 Federal scout from Harper's Ferry into Loudoun County, VA, with skirmishes **(Mar. 21st)** near Hamilton and **(Mar. 23rd)** at Goose Creek.

03 20 1865 Federal scout to Kabletown, Myerstown, and Myers' Ford, WV.

03 21 1865 The Dept. of Arkansas and the Indian Territory is transferred from the Military Division of West Mississippi to the Military Division of Missouri.

03 21 1865 Federal scout from Pine Bluff to Monticello, AR, for the purpose of breaking up some conscripting and bushwacking parties that were in this section of the country. As usual for this time of the war, the Yankees did not come home empty handed. 3/21-23/1865.

03 21 1865 The Union forces **occupy Goldsborough, NC.**

03 21 1865 **Brig. Gen. Innis N. Palmer, USA, assumes the command of the District of Beaufort, SC.**

03 21 1865 Federal expedition from East Tennessee into Southwestern Virginia and Western North Carolina, by Maj. Gen. George Stoneman, USA, commanding the District of East Tennessee. 3/21-4/25/1865.

03 22 1865 **Theodore Washington Brevard,** CSA, is appointed Brig. Gen.

03 22 1865 Brig. Gen. James Harrison Wilson's US Cavalry Raid, 13,500 strong, from Chickasaw to Selma, AL, and Macon, GA, in an attempt to **destroy one of the last remaining munitions manufacturing** facilities of the **Confederacy.** The Confederacy might be standing on one leg. 3/22-4/24/1865.

03 22 1865 Brig. Gen. Edward Hatch, USA, assumes the command of all the troops of the Cavalry Corps, the Military Division of the Mississippi, remaining at Eastport, MS.

03 22 1865 Guerrillas operations about Stephenson's Mill, 16 miles southwest of Salem, MO, on the Current River, as bushwackers set fire to, and burn the fort there, in part, for retaliation for the local miller failing to have the quantity of meal ground for 250 rebels they had demanded yesterday. The Yankees plan on killing these boys for committing such a deed. Only one way to deal with guerrillas. 3/22-23/1865.

03 22 1865 Skirmish at Black Creek, NC.

03 22 1865 Skirmish at Hannah's Creek, NC.

03 22 1865 Skirmish at Mill Creek, NC.

03 22 1865 Skirmish at Celina, TN.

03 22 1865 Skirmish 9.5 miles from Patterson Creek Station, WV, as the Federal Cavalry attacks McNeill's Partisan Rangers.

03 23 1865 Skirmishes near Dannelly's Mills, AL, as Brig. Gen. James H. Wilson, and his Union Cavalry move toward Lieut. Gen. Nathan Bedford Forrest, CSA, and his Cavalry, the Mobile, AL, Campaign. 3/23-24/1865.

03 23 1865 **Brig. Gen. Michael K. Lawler, USA, is assigned to the command of the District of Baton Rouge, LA.**

03 23 1865 Federal scout from Donaldsonville to Bayou Goula, LA, where the Yankees capture a few Confederates

			hiding out in local plantation homes. 3/23-24/1865.
03	23	1865	Skirmish at Cox's Bridge, Neuse River, NC, as Maj. Gen. William T. Sherman, USA, concentrates his forces around Bentonville, NC, to square off against the last remaining Confederate forces in North Carolina under Gen. Joseph E. Johnston, CSA.
03	23	1865	**Col. Reuben F. Maury, 1st Oregon Cavalry, assumes the command of the District of Oregon.**
03	23	1865	Brig. Gen. Benjamin Alvord, USA, relinquishes the command of the District of Oregon.
03	23	1865	President Abraham Lincoln departs from Washington, DC, with his wife and son, to confer with Lieut. Gen. Ulysses S. Grant and Maj. Gen. William T. Sherman, USA, at City Point, VA, outside Petersburg, VA.
03	24	1865	Affair near Dannelly's Mills, AL, the Mobile, AL, Campaign.
03	24	1865	Affair near Evergreen, AL, the Mobile, AL, Campaign.
03	24	1865	Federal scout in search of Confederates, through the swamps, from Bayou Boeuf to Bayou Chemise, LA.
03	24	1865	Affair about 7 miles west of Rolla, MO, on the Springfield Road, where guerrillas dressed in Union garb surprise and capture a band of Yankees taking a breather along the road. The Union officers are attacked in the nearby house they went into to get a drink of water, firing through the window and killing a mounted guerrilla; the rest take off with their Yankee prisoners; the Union prisoners not heard from since.
03	24	1865	Skirmish near Moccasin Creek, NC.
03	24	1865	The **CSS Stonewall** embarks from the port of Ferrol, Spain, as the two wooden US frigates, **USS Niagara** and **USS Sacramento** fail to challenge her. The commanding Union Naval officer, Commodore T. T. Craven will later be court martialed for his (un)(warranted) lack of action.
03	25	1865	Skirmishes on the Deer Park Road, AL, the Mobile, AL, Campaign, and at the following Florida locations:
03	25	1865	Action at Canoe Creek, or Bluff Spring, FL.
03	25	1865	Skirmish at Cotton Creek, FL.
03	25	1865	Skirmish at Escambia River, FL.
03	25	1865	Skirmish at Mitchell's Creek, FL.
03	25	1865	Skirmish near Glasgow, KY.
03	25	1865	Federal expedition with the **93rd US Colored Infantry,** from Brashear City, aboard the gunboat, **No. 43,** to Indian Bend, LA, for the purpose of destroying or capturing a barge said to have been used by the Rebels for transporting a number of horses over Grand Lake and into their lines. 3/25-27/1865.
03	25	1865	Federal expedition from Brashear City, aboard the steamer, **Cornie,** down the Atchafalaya River, to near Oyster Bayou, LA, for the purpose of taking possession of a large oyster boat which lay stranded on the beach at a point 6 miles west of Oyster Bayou. 3/25-28/1865.
03	25	1865	Skirmish at Brawley Forks, TN.
03	25	1865	**The Confederate assault upon and capture of Fort Stedman,** led by Maj. Gen. John Brown Gordon, CSA, as Gen. Robert E. Lee, CSA, orders a surprise attack at 4:00 a.m. to force Lieut. Ulysses S. Grant, USA, to contract his siege line and protect his supply depot at City Point, VA. As the Confederates lack the (initiative) or manpower to press forward, the Federals regroup and counter attack, forcing the Confederates back to their original defensive lines. Total casualties approximate 5,500, the Richmond, VA, Campaign.
03	25	1865	Action at Fort Fisher, VA, the Richmond, VA, Campaign.
03	25	1865	Action at the Watkins House, VA, the Richmond, VA, Campaign.
03	26	1865	Skirmish at Muddy Creek, AL, the Mobile, AL, Campaign.
03	26	1865	Union forces **enter Pollard, AL,** the Mobile, AL, Campaign.
03	26	1865	Skirmish near Spanish Fort, AL, with Maj. Gen. E.R.S. Canby.
03	26	1865	Skirmish in Bath County, beyond Owingsville, KY.
03	26	1865	Federal expedition from Bonnet Carre to the Amite River, LA, in search of the Confederate guerrillas who captured the local provost-marshal of this parish, meeting with no success, as they searched everywhere. 3/26-29/1865.
03	26	1865	Maj. Gen. Philip Henry Sheridan's US Cavalry command crosses the James River, VA, to combine forces with Lieut. Gen. Ulysses S. Grant, USA. As Grant laid low and continued to apply pressure on the Army of Northern Virginia, he allowed the other Union armies to one by one dissect the bowels of the Confederacy. Now, with only Lee's army remaining as an obstacle, Grant will plunge into the heart of the Confederacy.

03	27	1865	**The Federal siege and the Capture of the Spanish Fort, AL,** the Mobile, AL, Campaign. 3/27-4/8/1865.
03	27	1865	Maj. Gen. Frederick Steele's US column reaches Canoe Station, AL, the Mobile, AL, Campaign.
03	27	1865	The 10th US Army Corps is reorganized and Maj. Gen. Alfred H. Terry, USA, is assigned to its command, NC, etal.
03	27	1865	Brig. Gen. Elkanah Greer, CSA, is assigned to the command of the Reserve Corps in the State of Texas, vice Brig. Gen. Jerome B. Robertson, CSA, is relieved, and assigned to the command of a brigade.
03	27	1865	**President Abraham Lincoln meets with Lieut. Gen. Ulysses S. Grant, Maj. Gen. William T. Sherman, and Admiral David Porter, USN, at City Point, VA, aboard the River Queen, to discuss his policy on Confederate surrender and reconstruction.**
03	27	1865	Federal scout from Winchester to Woodstock, VA. 3/27-29/1865.
03	28	1865	Skirmish near Elyton, AL, with Brig. Gen. James H. Wilson.
03	28	1865	Federal expedition from Fort Pike, LA, aboard the sloop, **Rosetta,** to Bay Saint Louis, MS, in an unsuccessful attempt to capture some of Lieut. Gen. Nathan Bedford Forrest's Confederate Cavalry troops. 3/28-30/1865.
03	28	1865	Skirmish at Bull Creek, Christian County, MO.
03	28	1865	Brig. Gen. Robert E. Mitchell, USA, is relieved from the command of the District of Nebraska, and is assigned to the command of the District of North Kansas.
03	28	1865	Skirmish at Boone, NC, with Maj. Gen. George Stoneman, USA.
03	28	1865	Skirmish near Snow Hill, NC, with Maj. Gen. George Stoneman's USA, Cavalry approaching from the west.
03	28	1865	Skirmish at Germantown, TN, with the Union pickets there.
03	28	1865	**The District of the Plains is formed,** to consist of the Districts of Utah, Colorado, and Nebraska. **Brig. Gen. Patrick E. Connor, USA, is assigned to its command.**
03	28	1865	Federal expedition from Deep Bottom, VA, with the assistance of transports, ferries, and gunboats, to near Weldon, NC, where the Yankees meet little resistance, and with minor skirmishes, capturing some prisoners and Confederate supplies, cotton, etc. 3/28-4/11/1865.
03	29	1865	**Thomas Maley Harris,** USA, is appointed Brig. Gen.
03	29	1865	Maj. Gen. Frederick Steele's US column reaches Weatherford, AL, the Mobile, AL, Campaign.
03	29	1865	Skirmish as Blackwater River, KY.
03	29	1865	Col. William H. Dickey, **84th US Colored Troops,** assumes the command of the US Forces at Morganza, LA.
03	29	1865	Skirmish in Southwest Missouri.
03	29	1865	Federal scout from Waynesville, MO, to Rolla, camping at Jackson's Mills, and Coppage's Mill, on Spring Creek, to the Big Piney, with one reported bushwacker shot to death today. 3/29-4/2/1865 .
03	29	1865	Skirmish near Moseley Hall, NC, with Maj. Gen. Stoneman, USA.
03	29	1865	Skirmish at Wilkesborough, NC, with Maj. Gen. George Stoneman's, USA, Cavalry.
03	29	1865	**The Appomattox (Virginia) Campaign,** as Lieut. Gen. Ulysses S. Grant, after conferring with the President, begins the final assault on the Confederate lines at Petersburg, VA. 3/29- 4/9/1865 .
03	29	1865	Engagement at Lewis Farm near Gravelly Run, VA, as Gen. Robert E. Lee, CSA, sends Maj. Gens. Fitzhugh Lee and George Pickett, CSA, to repel the Federal attack, the Richmond, VA, Campaign.
03	29	1865	Skirmish at the junction of the Quaker and Boydton Roads, VA, as Maj. Gens. George Pickett and Fitzhugh Lee, CSA, fend off Lieut. Gen. Ulysses S. Grant's, USA, steady advance, the Richmond, VA, Campaign.
03	29	1865	Skirmish on the Vaughan Road, near Hatcher's Run, VA, the Richmond, VA, Campaign.
03	29	1865	Federal scout from Stephenson's Depot, VA, the Shenandoah Valley, to Smithfield, WV.
03	30	1865	Skirmish at Montevallo, AL, with Lieut. Gen. Nathan Bedford Forrest, CSA, contesting the advance of Brig. Gen. James H. Wilson, USA.
03	30	1865	Federal expeditions from Baton Rouge to Clinton and the Comite River, LA, including the capture of 2 Confederate soldiers who had slept in the woods and were enjoying a hot breakfast at the home of a Mrs. Simms. One of the Rebels' grey horse indicates these are Confederate Cavalrymen. 3/30-4/2/1865.
03	30	1865	**Brig. Gen. Patrick E. Connor, USA, assumes the command of the District of the Plains,** the Nebraska Territory, etal.
03	30	1865	Skirmish near Five Forks, VA, the Richmond, VA, Campaign.
03	30	1865	Skirmishes on the line of Hatcher's Run and Gravelly Run, VA, the Richmond, VA, Campaign.

03	30	1865	Affair near Patterson's Creek, WV, about 10 miles east of Cumberland, MD, where a band of guerrillas attacked, captured and robbed a passenger train on the **Baltimore & Ohio Railroad.** The railroad refuses to accept Federal soldiers aboard for protection without receiving any compensation from the Union government. That's gratitude for you.
03	31	1865	Union troops **occupy Asbyville, AL,** with Brig. Gen. James H. Wilson, USA.
03	31	1865	Action near Montevallo, AL, where Brig. Gen. James Harrison Wilson, USA, and his Cavalry force destroys iron furnaces, etc, while combating Lieut. Gen. Nathan Bedford Forrest, CSA.
03	31	1865	Action at Six-Mile Creek, AL, with Brig. Gen. James H. Wilson.
03	31	1865	Maj. Gen. Frederick Steele's, USA, column reaches Stockton, AL, the Mobile, AL, Campaign.
03	31	1865	Federal operations about Aquia Eria, the New Mexico Territory, as the Yankees respond to a scared rancher that hostile Indians had crossed his ranch last night. Upon further scouting, the Yankees determine the horse tracks had been made by either peaceful **Navajo** or **Pueblo Indians.** The tracks close to his house that the nervous rancher referred to where his own. 3/31-4/1/1865.
03	31	1865	Skirmish at Gulley's, NC.
03	31	1865	Skirmish at Hookerton, NC.
03	31	1865	Maj. Gen. Jacob D. Cox, USA, resumes the command of the 23rd US Army Corps, NC, etal.
03	31	1865	Skirmish at Magnolia, TN.
03	31	1865	Maj. Gen. John Bankhead Magruder, CSA, is assigned to the command of the District of Texas, New Mexico, and Arizona, and vice Maj. Gen. John G. Walker, CSA, is relieved of command.
03	31	1865	Action at Crow's House, VA, the Richmond, VA, Campaign.
03	31	1865	Action at Hatcher's Run, or Boydton Road, VA, the Richmond, VA, Campaign.
03	31	1865	**The Engagement at Dinwiddie Court-House, VA,** where Maj. Gen. George Pickett, CSA, repels the attacks by Maj. Gens. Philip H. Sheridan and Gouvenour Warren, USA, however retreating to Five Forks, which weakens the Petersburg, VA, line, which will ultimately help cause the final break in Lee's defensive position.
03	31	1865	The engagement at the White Oak Road, or White Oak Ride, VA, the Richmond, VA, Campaign.
04	1	1865	**William Babcock Hazen, U.S.A.,** is appointed Maj. Gen.
04	1	1865	**Wesley Merritt,** **U.S.A.,** is appointed Maj. Gen.
04	1	1865	Skirmish near Blakely, AL, as Maj. Gen. Edward R. S. Canby, USA, moves on Mobile AL, and where the Union ironclad, **USS Rudolph,** is sunk by a Confederate torpedo.
04	1	1865	Skirmish at Centerville, AL, with Brig. Gen. James H. Wilson, USA, and at the following Alabama locations:
04	1	1865	Action at Ebenezer Church, near Maplesville, AL.
04	1	1865	Skirmish at Maplesville, AL.
04	1	1865	Skirmish at Plantersville, AL.
04	1	1865	Skirmish near Randolph, AL.
04	1	1865	Skirmish at Trion, AL.
04	1	1865	Federal scout from Pine Bluff to Bayou Bartholomew, AR. 4/1-4/1865.
04	1	1865	The affair 15 miles northwest of Fort Garland, the Colorado Territory, as 5 hostile **Ute Indians** attack a Mexican ranch and kill 1 Mexican and some beeves. As most **Utes** are friendly, the local Federal officer will await further instructions before declaring a regular war against the entire **Ute Indian Nation tribe.**
04	1	1865	Federal operations against Indians west of Fort Laramie, the Dakota Territory, with skirmish **(May 20th)** at Deer Creek Station, as a white man, supposed to be **Bill Comstock,** formerly of Fort Laramie, seems to have command of the Indians, who have attacked the station. 4/1-5/27/1865.
04	1	1865	Federal expedition from Dalton to Spring Place and the Coosawattee River, GA, with skirmishes. 4/1-4/1865.
04	1	1865	Federal scouts against guerrillas from Licking, MO, to places such as Piney Fork of the Gasconade River, Hog Creek, etc, where the Yankees are successful in killing more guerrillas, seizing provisions, and destroying anything of value. 4/1-30/1865.
04	1	1865	Gen. William T. Sherman's US army is reorganized, NC, etal.
04	1	1865	Skirmish near Snow Hill, NC, with Maj. Gen. William T. Sherman, USA.
04	1	1865	Skirmish at White Oak Creek, TN.
04	1	1865	**The Battle of Five Forks, VA,** as Maj. Gen. Philip H. Sheridan's Cavalry and Maj. Gen. Gouverneur K. Warren's, 5th US Army Corps attack and overwhelm and separate Maj. Gen. George E. Pickett, CSA from the rest of the Army of Northern Virginia, almost completely surrounding Petersburg, VA, in the process. **Lee realizes that both Petersburg and Richmond are now lost to the Confederacy.**

04	1	1865	Bvt. Maj. Gen. Charles Griffin, USA, relieves Maj. Gen. Gouverneur K. Warren, USA, of the command of the 5th US Army Corps, VA, as Maj. Gen. Philip H. Sheridan, USA, removes Warren from command during the height of the Battle of Five Forks for being slow is reacting to Sheridan's orders. Warren will later be acquitted but the damage to his military had already been done.
04	1	1865	Skirmish at the White Oak Road, near Petersburg, VA, with Maj. Gen. Andrew A. Humphreys, USA, and his 2nd US Army Corps under Lieut. Gen. Ulysses S. Grant, USA, the Richmond, VA, Campaign.
04	2	1865	**Charles Griffin, U.S.A.,** is appointed Maj. Gen.
04	2	1865	The Federal siege and **capture of Fort Blakely, AL,** an important fortification of Mobile, AL, by Maj. Gen. Edward R. S. Canby, USA, the Mobile, AL, Campaign. 4/2-9/1865.
04	2	1865	Skirmish near Centerville, AL, with Brig. Gen. James H. Wilson, USA, and at the following Alabama locations:
04	2	1865	Skirmish near Scottsville, AL.
04	2	1865	**The Engagement at Selma, AL,** where Lieut. Gens. Nathan Bedford Forrest and Richard Taylor, CSA, retreat from the Union onslaught under Maj. Gen. James H. Wilson, USA, with Wilson capturing over 2,700 prisoners. Forrest is finally found to be not invincible but his troop's strength has been greatly diminished during his last campaigns.
04	2	1865	The Union troops **occupy Selma, AL,** as Lieut. Gens. Nathan Bedford Forrest and Richard Taylor, CSA, barely escape capture themselves.
04	2	1865	Skirmish at Summerfield, AL.
04	2	1865	Skirmish 4 miles form Hickory Station, AR, on the **Little Rock and Devall's Railroad,** where the Confederates derail part of the train but are driven off by the Federal troops aboard. While the attack was progressing, most of the passengers fled into the prairie, only returning when the coast was clear. Included was a Yankee from the 12th MI Infantry who threw his saber away in the brush, retrieving it after danger had passed. The men got the train back on the rails and proceed forward. Do you suppose the brave saber yielding Yankee told his family of this adventure when he returned home?
04	2	1865	Skirmish 2 miles from Van Buren, AR, as the Yankees kill 2 Confederates who just recently robbed several local citizens. Papers found on the bodies indicate they were from Fulton, TX, enroute to Missouri. I wonder if they were just passing through, trying to seize enough provisions to last them, or were they really vile men, stealing and murdering along the way? We'll never know.
04	2	1865	Federal expedition from the Hermitage, across the Amite, to the French Settlement, LA, in pursuit of guerrillas. 4/2-5/1865 .
04	2	1865	Federal expeditions from Thibodeaux, Bayou Boeuf, and Brashear City, to Lake Verret, Grand Bayou, and The Park, LA, with skirmish **(Apr. 4th)** at Grand Bayou, LA. 4/2-10/1865.
04	2	1865	Skirmish near Goldsborough, NC, as Maj. Gen. William T. Sherman, USA, presses forward towards the war's end.
04	2	1865	Maj. Gen. Joseph A. Mower, USA, assumes the command of the 20th US Army Corps, NC., etal.
04	2	1865	Skirmish at Gravelly Ford, on Hatcher's Run, VA, the Richmond, VA, Campaign.
04	2	1865	The Federal **assault upon and the capture** of the fortified Confederate lines in front of Petersburg, VA, as Maj. Gen. Horatio Wright's 6th US Army Corps breaks through. The Confederate defenders at Fort Baldwin and Fort Gregg **buy Lee time to evacuate the rest of his army,** as he moves toward and orders the troops at Richmond, VA, to concentrate at Amelia Court-House, 40 miles west, the Richmond, VA, Campaign.
04	2	1865	**Lieut. Gen. Ambrose Powell Hill, CSA,** is mortally wounded by a Federal straggler, while attempting to reach his own lines, soon after Lieut. Gen. Ulysses S. Grant's final Federal assault on the Confederate lines at Petersburg, VA.
04	2	1865	**A large portion of Richmond, VA, including factories, gun-boats on the James River, are set afire as the Confederates evacuate their capital; Jefferson Davis leaves for Danville, VA, aboard a special train.**
04	2	1865	Action at Scott's Cross-Roads, VA, the Richmond, VA, Campaign.
04	2	1865	The engagement at Sutherland's Station, on the South Side Railroad, the Richmond, VA, Campaign.
04	3	1865	Federal scout from Huntsville to near Vienna, AL. 4/3-4/1865.
04	3	1865	Action at Northport, near Tuscaloosa, AL, between Lieut. Gen. Nathan Bedford Forrest, CSA, and Maj. Gen. James H. Wilson, USA.
04	3	1865	The unsuccessful Federal pursuit of bushwackers near Farmington, MO, as they kill men in their way, and stealing their teams of horses to escape the pursuing Yankees, etc.

04	3	1865	Federal expedition to Asheville, NC, by Maj. Gen. David S. Stanley, USA, commanding the 4th US Army Corps. 4/3-11/1865.
04	3	1865	Skirmish at Mount Pleasant, TN.
04	3	1865	Skirmish near Hillsville, VA, with Maj. Gen. George Stoneman, USA.
04	3	1865	Action at Namozine Church, the Appomattox Campaign, VA, as Maj. Gen. Philip H. Sheridan and his Union cavalry press the retreating Confederate Army of Northern Virginia.
04	3	1865	**The occupation of Petersburg and Richmond, VA,** by the Union forces, as Brig. Gen. Godfrey Weitzel, USA, and the Army of the James formally accepts the city's surrender, the Richmond, VA, Campaign.
04	3	1865	**President Abraham Lincoln visits Petersburg, VA,** as the majority of the city was spared from being burned by the fleeing Confederates.
04	4	1865	The Union Cavalry troops, under Brig. Gen. James Harrison Wilson, USA, **occupy Tuscaloosa, AL.**
04	4	1865	Skirmishes at East River Bridge, FL. 3/4-5/1865.
04	4	1865	The capture of the steamer, **Harriet De Ford,** near Fair Haven, Chesapeake Bay, MD, as Gen. Robert E. Lee, CSA, sends the courageous Capt. Fitzhugh, 5th VA Cavalry and some of his men, in hopes of capturing one of Lieut. Gen. Ulysses S. Grant's supply vessels, using Maj. John S. Mosby's men to transport the badly needed supplies to Lee's men in the trenches around Petersburg and Richmond. Unable to capture the **Eolus, Titan,** or the **Highland Light,** Fitzhugh captures the **Harriet De Ford,** boarding the vessel disguised as wood choppers. Upon moving up the Chesapeake Bay, he hears the guns blasting around Petersburg, which are celebrating the Union victory there. Fitzhugh desperately attempts to get the supplies to Lee, but is pursued by Union gunboats, he runs the vessel aground, taking what supplies he could.
04	4	1865	**Maj. Gen. J. Bankhead Magruder, CSA, assumes the command of the Confederate District of Texas, New Mexico and Arizona.**
04	4	1865	Skirmish at Amelia Court-House, VA, as Gen. Robert E. Lee, CSA, does not receive the much needed supplies at Richmond and Lynchburg to feed his army. Meanwhile, Lee's route toward North Carolina is blocked as Maj. Gen. Philip H. Sheridan, arrives at Jetersville, which is southwest of Amelia Court-House and his men block the **Danville Railroad** line that way. Maj. Gen. George G. Meade, USA, is closing in from the east, the Appomattox, VA, Campaign.4/4-5/1865.
04	4	1865	Skirmish at Tabernacle Church, or Beaver Pond Creek, VA, the Appomattox, VA, Campaign.
04	4	1865	President Abraham Lincoln visits Richmond, VA, after arriving aboard the **USS Malvern,** taking time to sit in Jefferson Davis' chair in the Confederate White House.
04	5	1865	**Frederick Tracy Dent,** USA, is appointed Brig. Gen.
04	5	1865	Federal scout from Huntsville to New Market, Maysville, etc, AL. 4/5-7/1865.
04	5	1865	Federal expedition from Camp Bidwell to Antelope Creek, CA. 4/5-18/1865.
04	5	1865	Skirmishes at Newport Bridge, FL. 3/5-6/1865.
04	5	1865	The destruction of US transports on Neuse River, NC. 4/5-7/1865.
04	5	1865	Federal expedition from Charleston to the Santee River, SC. 4/5-15/1865.
04	5	1865	Federal expedition from Georgetown to Camden, SC, and skirmishes at: a) Dingle's Mill, near Sumterville **(Apr. 9th)** b) near Statesburg **(Apr. 15th)** c) Boykins' Mill **(Apr. 18th)** d) Bradford Springs **(Apr. 18th)** e) Beech Creek, near Statesburg **(Apr. 19th)** f) Denkins' Mill **(Apr. 19th).** 4/5-25/1865.
04	5	1865	The engagement at Amelia Springs, VA, as Gen. Robert E. Lee, CSA, unable to feed his hungry army, orders food be sent by rail from Lynchburg, and turns his army toward Farmville. Maj. Gen. George G. Meade, USA, refrains Maj. Gen. Philip H. Sheridan, USA, from an all out attack until more Federal reinforcements arrive, the Appomattox, VA, Campaign.
04	5	1865	Skirmish at Paine's Cross-Roads, VA, the Appomattox, VA, Campaign.
04	6	1865	**Maj. Gen. John Austin Wharton, CSA,** is mortally wounded, shot to death by Col. George W. Baylor, of the 2nd Confederate Texas Cavalry, after arguing over general military affairs in General Wharton's Houston, TX, hotel room.
04	6	1865	Skirmish at King's Store, AL, as Brig. Gen. James H. Wilson, USA, continues to spar with Lieut. Gen. Nathan Bedford Forrest, CSA.

04	6	1865	Skirmish near Lanier's Mill, Sipsey Creek, AL, with Brig. Gen. James H. Wilson, USA, and Lieut. Gen. Nathan Bedford Forrest, CSA.
04	6	1865	Action at Natural Bridge, FL.
04	6	1865	Skirmish at Flat Creek, near Amelia Springs, VA, the Appomattox, VA, Campaign.
04	6	1865	Action near High Bridge, VA, the Appomattox, VA, Campaign.
04	6	1865	**Brig. Gen. James Dearing, CSA,** is mortally wounded at the action at High Bridge, VA, from a pistol duel with **Bvt. Brig. Gen. Theodore Read, USA,** who also died from this duel on April 6, 1865, **Bvt. Brig. Gen. Dearing** dying on April 23, 1865.
04	6	1865	**The Engagement at Sayler's Creek, VA,** where the Confederate Army separates into two columns heading in different directions, and Lieut. Gen. Richard S. Ewell's entire Confederate Army Corps is overwhelmed by Maj. Gens. Philip H. Sheridan and Horatio Wright's 6th US Army Corps, and forced over 8,000 Confederates to surrender. This will be the <u>**last fight between the Army of Northern Virginia and the Federal Army of the Potomac.**</u>
04	6	1865	The engagement at Rice's Station, VA, as the other Confederate column under Lieut. Gen. James Longstreet, CSA, encounters the Federals under Maj. Gen. Edward O.C. Ord, USA, the Appomattox, VA, Campaign.
04	6	1865	Action at Wytheville, VA, with Maj. Gen. George Stoneman, USA.
04	6	1865	Affair near Charlestown, WV, where Lieut. Col. John S. Mosby, CSA, and his Virginia Partisan Irregular Rangers surprise the camp of the Loudoun County Rangers, capturing a number of men and nearly all their horses. This will prove to be **Mosby's final escapade** against the Federal military forces, not surprisingly, ending his Confederate career with a victory.
04	7	1865	Federal scout from near Blakely toward Stockton, AL, the Mobile, AL, Campaign.
04	7	1865	Skirmish at Fike's Ferry, Catawba River, AL, as Lieut. Gen. Nathan Bedford Forrest, CSA, and Brig. Gen. James H. Wilson, USA, continue to spar with their cavalry commands.
04	7	1865	**Brig. Gen. George D. Wagner, USA, is assigned to the command of the Saint Louis, MO, District.**
04	7	1865	Tennessee becomes the 18th state to ratify the 13th amendment which will abolish slavery.
04	7	1865	Lieut. Gen. Ulysses S. Grant, USA, confers with Gen. Robert E. Lee, CSA, through messages about the surrender of the Confederate Army under Lee, near Appomattox Court-House, VA, as the starving and worn remnants of Gen. Robert E. Lee's Confederate Army cross the Appomattox River and receive much needed rations at Farmville, as the Union forces continue to surround them.
04	7	1865	The Engagement at Farmville, VA, as the Union forces continue to press Gen. Robert E. Lee, CSA, the Appomattox, VA, Campaign.
04	7	1865	**Brig. Gen. Thomas Alfred Smyth, USA,** is mortally wounded at the engagement at Farmville, VA, while riding his horse and encouraging him men on the firing line, receiving his death wound from the rifle of a Confederate sharpshooter, shot in the mouth, and dying two days later.
04	7	1865	The engagement at High Bridge, VA, the Appomattox, VA, Campaign.
04	7	1865	Skirmish at Prince Edward Court-House, VA, the Appomattox, VA, Campaign.
04	8	1865	**Brig. Gen. George D. Wagner, USA, assumes the command of the Saint Louis, MO, District.**
04	8	1865	Federal pursuit of guerrillas in Northeast Missouri, where 3 notorious guerrillas were captured and brought back to Macon City to face trial for their crimes. 4/8-10/1865.
04	8	1865	Action at Martinsville, NC.
04	8	1865	**The Engagement at Appomattox Station, VA,** as Maj. Gen. George G. Meade, USA, continued to press Gen. Robert E. Lee, CSA, while Maj. Gen. Philip H. Sheridan, USA, and his cavalry capture the Confederate supply trains at Appomattox Station. Lee now faced the following: a) Behind Lee: Maj. Gen. George G. Meade and the 2nd US Army Corps - Maj. Gen. Andrew A. Humphreys, USA, Commanding and the 6th US Army Corps - Maj. Gen. Horatio G. Wright, USA, Commanding b) To Lee's Left: Maj. Gen. Philip H. Sheridan's Cavalry 5th US Army Corps - Maj. Gen. Charles Griffin, USA, Commanding. c) In Lee's front towards Lynchburg - Maj. Gen. E.O.C. Ord, USA, and the US Army of the James.
04	8	1865	Federal scout from Fairfax Court-House into Loudoun County, VA, in search of Lieut. Col. Gen. John S. Mosby, CSA and his Virginia Battalion. 4/8-10/1865.
04	8	1865	Federal scout from Vienna into Loudoun County, VA, in search of Lieut. Col. John S. Mosby's Virginia Partisan Rangers, with no luck. However, the Yankees are closing in. 4/8-10/1865.

04	9	1865	Federal expedition from Blakely to Claiborne, AL, and skirmish (**11th**) near Mount Pleasant, the Mobile, AL, Campaign. 4/9-17/1865.
04	9	1865	The Federal bombardment and the **capture of Batteries Huger and Tracy, near Mobile, AL,** as Mobile is on the verge of surrender by Maj. Gen. Dabney H. Maury, CSA. 4/9-11/1865.
04	9	1865	**Engagement at Appomattox Court-House, VA,** as Gen. Robert E. Lee, CSA, orders one last assault to break through the Union lines. Initially, Maj. Gens. John Brown Gordon and Fitzhugh Lee, CSA, break through the Union cavalry only to find solid lines of Federal infantry blocking the way. Lee realizes there is nothing more he can do without the useless loss of life.
04	9	1865	**THE SURRENDER OF THE ARMY OF NORTHERN VIRGINIA AT APPOMATTOX COURTHOUSE, VA. by General Robert Edward Lee, CSA, to Lieut. General Ulysses Simpson Grant, USA, at the Wilbur McLean Residence.**
04	9	1865	**Brig. Gen. Thomas Alfred Smyth, USA,** dies near Burkeville, VA, from his deathwound received two days before at Farmville, VA, the <u>last Federal General</u> to die from combat wounds in the American Civil War.
04	9	1865	President Jefferson Davis, representing the remnants of the Confederate Government, vows to carry on the fight for Southern independence at the new capital of Danville, VA.
04	10	1865	Skirmish at Benton, AL, as Lieut. Gen. Nathan Bedford Forrest, CSA, and Brig. Gen. James H. Wilson, USA, and their cavalry continue to fight the war between the states.
04	10	1865	Skirmish at Lowndesborough, AL, with Lieut. Gen. Nathan Bedford Forrest, CSA, and Brig. Gen. James H. Wilson, USA.
04	10	1865	Maj. Gen. William T. Sherman's US army moves from Goldsborough toward Raleigh, NC, and Gen. Joseph E. Johnston's Confederate Army.
04	10	1865	Skirmish at Boonville, NC, with Maj. Gen. William T. Sherman, USA.
04	10	1865	Skirmish at Moccasin Swamp, NC, with Maj. Gen. William T. Sherman, USA.
04	10	1865	Skirmish near Nahunta Station, NC, with Maj. Gen. William T. Sherman, USA.
04	10	1865	Skirmishes near Burke's Station and at Arundel's Farm, VA, as the Union Cavalry inflicts casualties on the Rebels operating in this area.
04	10	1865	Jefferson Davis and some of his cabinet leaves Danville, VA, for Greensborough, NC, hoping to evade Maj. Gen. George Stoneman's USA Cavalry.
04	10	1865	**Gen. Robert E. Lee, CSA, issues Order No. 9, which is Lee's formal farewell to the troops and officially disbands the Confederate Army of Northern Virginia. From this point in time, there will only be memories for the soldiers.**
04	11	1865	The Confederate forces under Maj. Gen. Dabney Herndon Maury, CSA, **evacuate Mobile, AL,** including Forts Huger and Tracy, withdrawing to Meridian, MS, the Mobile, AL, Campaign.
04	11	1865	Skirmish at Saint Charles, AR.
04	11	1865	**Brig. Gen. Robert B. Mitchell, USA, assumes the command of the District of North Kansas.**
04	11	1865	Skirmish near Beulah, NC, with Maj. Gen. William T. Sherman.
04	11	1865	Affair near Pikeville, NC.
04	11	1865	Skirmish near Mocksville, NC, with Maj. Gen. George Stoneman, USA, and his Union cavalry.
04	11	1865	Skirmish at Shallow Ford, NC, with Maj. Gen. George Stoneman, USA, in a mopping up campaign.
04	11	1865	Skirmish near Smithfield, NC, with Maj. Gen. George Stoneman.
04	11	1865	The Union forces, under Maj. Gen. William T. Sherman, USA, **occupy Smithfield, NC.**
04	11	1865	Federal scout from Winchester, VA, to Timber Ridge, WV. 4/11-12/1865.
04	11	1865	President Abraham Lincoln, along with the citizens of Washington, DC, continue to rejoice to the news coming from Lieut. Gen. Ulysses S. Grant, USA, informing of the surrender by Gen. Robert E. Lee.
04	12	1865	The Union forces, under Maj. Gen. Eward R. S. Canby, USA, **occupy Mobile, AL,** the Mobile, AL, Campaign.
04	12	1865	Skirmish on the Columbus Road, near Montgomery, AL, with Brig. Gen. James H. Wilson, USA.
04	12	1865	The Union forces, under Brig. Gen. James H. Wilson, USA, **occupy Montgomery, AL.**
04	12	1865	Federal scout from Tallahassa Mission, the Indian Territory, in the direction of Concharty, with a long range skirmish with outlaws. 4/12-13/1865.
04	12	1865	Federal expedition from Port Hudson to Jackson, LA, with the Union capture of various Confederate officers and men. 4/12-13/1865.
04	12	1865	Federal scout against Indians, from Dakota City, the Nebraska Territory, to Elk Creek, the West Fork of Badger Creek, westerly toward the South Fork of the Elk Creek, thence up to the Chalk Branch, finding

			and capturing some **Omaha Indians,** probably from the Omaha Indian Reserve. Whether they did anything, who knows.. and back then.. who cares.. 4/12-16/l865 .
04	12	1865	Federal scout from Fort Stanton, the New Mexico Territory, in pursuit of 4 Indians who stole a few head of cattle from a ranch on the Carrizo and Ruidoso Creeks. The Yankees pursue; the Indians split up; the Federals track one lone Indian for days on end, through canons, brush, mountains, etc. Fortunately for the Indian, he was able to evade them until the Yankees give up and return to their Fort. 4/12-25/1865.
04	12	1865	**President Jefferson Davis meets with Gen. Joseph E. Johnston, CSA, at Greensborough, NC, and permits Johnston to meet with Maj. Gen. William T. Sherman, USA, to discuss the issue of surrender.**
04	12	1865	Action near Raleigh, NC, with Maj. Gen. William T. Sherman, USA, and Gen. Joseph E. Johnston, CSA.
04	12	1865	Skirmish near Raleigh, NC, with Sherman and Johnston.
04	12	1865	The Union forces under Maj. Gen. William T. Sherman, USA, **occupy Raleigh, NC,** the capital of North Carolina.
04	12	1865	Skirmish at Grant's Creek, near Salisbury, NC, with Maj. Gen. George Stoneman, USA.
04	12	1865	Engagement at Salisbury, NC, with Maj. Gen. George Stoneman.
04	12	1865	The Union forces, under Maj. Gen. George Stoneman, USA, **occupy Salisbury, NC,** capturing over 1,300 Confederate prisoners.
04	12	1865	Action at Swift Creek, NC, with Gen. Joseph E. Johnston and Maj. Gen. William T. Sherman.
04	12	1865	**Maj. Gen. Joshua Chamberlain, USA, receives the official surrender of the Army of Northern Virginia by Maj. Gen. John Brown Gordon, CSA, at Appomattox Court-House (or Clover Hill).**
04	13	1865	The **USS Ida** sinks in Mobile Bay, AL, after hitting a Confederate torpedo.
04	13	1865	Maj. Gen. Frederick Steele, USA, is assigned to the command of all the troops and posts on the east side of Mobile Bay, AL, with the exception of the troops belonging to the 16th US Army Corps.
04	13	1865	Skirmish at Wetumpka, AL, with Brig. Gen. James H. Wilson.
04	13	1865	Skirmish at Whistler or Eight Mile Creek Bridge, AL, the Mobile, AL, Campaign.
04	13	1865	Federal scouts about Lexington, KY. 4/13-16/1865.
04	13	1865	Skirmish at Morrisville, NC, as Gen. Joseph E. Johnston's, CSA, men continue to contest the advance of Maj. Gen. William T. Sherman, USA, towards the new temporary capital of the Confederacy at Greensborough, NC.
04	14	1865	Skirmish on the Columbus Road, near Tuskegee, AL, with Brig. Gen. James H. Wilson's, USA, Cavalry.
04	14	1865	Still on the prowl, the Confederate commerce raider, **CSS Shenandoah,** embarks from the Eastern Caroline Islands in the Pacific Ocean and heads for the Kurile Islands.
04	14	1865	Skirmish near Morrisville, NC, between Johnston and Sherman.
04	14	1865	Affair near Saunders' Farm, NC, between Johnston and Sherman; Johnston proposing a suspension of hostility to allow peace talks.
04	14	1865	Maj. Gen. Robert Anderson, USA, who surrendered Fort Sumter, SC, raises the same Union flag he lowered 4 years ago to the day over the Federal controlled Fort Sumter, Charleston Harbor, SC..
04	14	1865	Skirmish at Mount Pleasant, TN.
04	14	1865	<u>**PRESIDENT ABRAHAM LINCOLN IS MURDEROUSLY ASSAULTED AND ASSASSINATED BY JOHN WILKES BOOTH AT FORD'S THEATER, WASHINGTON, DC, as he watches the comedy, our American Cousin.**</u>
04	15	1865	**George Armstrong Custer, U.S.A.,** is appointed Maj. Gen.
04	15	1865	Skirmish at McKenzie's Creek, near Patterson, MO, where the Yankees surprise a Rebel camp, killing and wounding the occupants there.
04	15	1865	Skirmish near Chapel Hill, NC.
04	15	1865	President Jefferson Davis flees Greensborough, NC.
04	15	1865	Federal scout through the counties of Randolph and Pocahontas, WV, and of Bath and Highland, VA, with a hodge podge of events, including capturing weapons, prisoners, stragglers, deserters; running into paroled men of Gen. Robert E. Lee's Army of Northern Virginia on their way home, etc. 4/15-23/1865.
04	15	1865	<u>**THE DEATH OF PRESIDENT ABRAHAM LINCOLN,**</u> **at 7:22 a.m.** from injuries received at the hands of John Wilkes Booth the night before, Washington, DC. The pistol shot had entered the back of the President's head and lodged near his right eye. Secretary of War, Edwin Stanton, proclaims, **"Now he belongs to the ages." Lincoln is granted enough time on this earth to see his part through to the end — the end of the American Civil War which he guided the United States successfully through.**
04	16	1865	Skirmish at Crawford, AL, with Brig. Gen. James H. Wilson, USA.

04	16	1865	Skirmish at Girard, AL, with Brig. Gen. James H. Wilson, USA.
04	16	1865	Skirmish near Opelika, AL, with Brig. Gen. James H. Wilson, USA.
04	16	1865	Action at Columbus, GA, with Brig. Gen. James H. Wilson, USA.
04	16	1865	The Union troops under Brig. Gen. James H. Wilson, USA, **occupy Columbus, GA.**
04	16	1865	The Federal attack on Fort Tyler, near West Point, GA.
04	16	1865	The Union troops under Brig. Gen. James H. Wilson, USA, Cavalry, **occupy West Point, GA.**
04	16	1865	**Brig. Gen. Robert Charles Tyler, CSA,** is mortally wounded by a Federal sharpshooter, while defending a Confederate earth work on the west side of the town of West Point, GA, called Fort Tyler, against the advancing Federal cavalry under Brig. Gen. James H. Wilson, USA.
04	16	1865	President Jefferson Davis with the remnants of the Confederate government arrive at Lexington, NC.
04	17	1865	Federal expedition from Blakely, AL, to Georgetown, GA, and Union Springs, AL, the Mobile, AL, Campaign.
04	17	1865	The destruction of the Confederate ironclad gun-boat, the **CSS Jackson** or the **Muscogee,** at Columbus, GA, by Maj. Gen. George H. Thomas, USA.
04	17	1865	Action at the Catawba River, near Morgantown, NC, with Maj. Gen. George Stoneman, USA.
04	17	1865	Meeting at the Bennett House, near Durham Station, NC, to discuss surrender of the Confederate Army, between Gen. Joseph E. Johnston, CSA, and Maj. Gen. William T. Sherman, USA.
04	17	1865	President Jefferson Davis and his entourage arrive at Salisbury, NC.
04	17	1865	Brig. Gen. Thomas A. Davies, USA, is assigned to the command of the District of Wisconsin.
04	17	1865	President Abraham Lincoln's remains lie in state in the East Room of the White House, Washington, DC, until his funeral on 4/19/1865.
04	18	1865	Skirmish at the Double Bridges, over the Flint River, GA, as Brig. Gen. James H. Wilson, USA, and his Union Cavalry presses on.
04	18	1865	Skirmish at Pleasant Hill, GA, with Brig. Gen. James H. Wilson, USA.
04	18	1865	Skirmish near Taylorsville, KY.
04	18	1865	**Hostilities** between the armies of Generals William T. Sherman, USA, and of Joseph E. Johnston, CSA, **are suspended,** NC, as a broad agreement is reached that attempts to cross military boundaries and borders on a political plan that will have to be approved by the US Government. 4/18-26/1865.
04	18	1865	Skirmish 6 miles from Germantown, TN.
04	19	1865	The **Confederate Districts of Arkansas and West Louisiana are consolidated to form the District of Arkansas and West Louisiana, and Lieut. Gen. Simon B. Buckner, CSA, is assigned to its command.**
04	19	1865	Skirmish near Barnesville, GA, with Brig. Gen. James H. Wilson, USA, and his Union Cavalry.
04	19	1865	Federal expedition from Terre Bonne to Pelton's Plantation and Grand Cailou, LA, in search of Confederates. 4/19-25/1865.
04	19	1865	The negotiations for the surrender of the Confederate forces in the Trans-Mississippi Dept., that are commanded by Gen. Edmund Kirby Smith, CSA, are presented by Maj. Gen. John Pope, USA, commanding the Military Division of the Missouri. 4/19-5/27/1865.
04	19	1865	Federal expedition with the 3rd US Colored Infantry, from Memphis, TN, aboard the steamers, **Sallie List, Dove,** and **Pocahontas,** to Brownsville, MS. The area is infested with insects as 8 horses die from buffalo gnats. 04/19-23/1865.
04	19	1865	President Jefferson Davis and his fleeing entourage arrive at Charlotte, NC.
04	19	1865	Maj. Gen. Lewis Wallace, USA, resumes the command of the Middle Dept. VA.
04	19	1865	The **Military Division of the James is organized,** to consist of the Dept. of Virginia and such parts of North Carolina not occupied by the command of Maj. Gen. William T. Sherman, and **Maj. Henry W. Halleck, USA, is assigned to its command.**
04	19	1865	A funeral procession removes President Abraham Lincoln's remains to be shown at the Rotunda of the Capitol.
04	20	1865	The Union troops under Brig. Gen. James H. Wilson, USA, **occupy Macon, GA,** as well as skirmishing at the following places: a) at Montpelier Springs, AL b) at Rocky Creek Bridge, AL c) at Mimm's Mills, on the Tobesofkee Creek, GA d) near Spring Hill, GA
04	20	1865	Arkansas becomes the 19th state to ratify the 13th amendment, abolishing slavery.

04	20	1865	Bvt. Brig. Gen. Guy V. Henry, 40th Massachusetts Infantry, assumes the command of the **South Sub-District of the Plains.**
04	20	1865	Gen. Robert E. Lee, CSA, writes to President Jefferson Davis of his opposition to Davis' idea of transforming the struggle for Southern independence into guerrilla warfare.
04	21	1865	Federal expedition against guerrillas from Donaldsonville to Bayou Goula, LA. 4/21-22/1865.
04	21	1865	Federal scout from Rolla toward Thomasville, MO, and skirmish with guerrillas at Spring Valley, 30 miles south of Licking, MO. **(23rd).** 4/21-27/1865.
04	21	1865	<u>**Maj. John Singleton Mosby, CSA, refusing to surrender to the Yankees, disbands the 43rd Virginia Cavalry Battalion and his Virginia Partisan Rangers at Millwood, VA.**</u> "Mosby's Confederacy" forever reserving his place in the halls of Civil War history. However, the majority of Mosby's command, now under Lieut. Col. Chapman, CSA, rode to Winchester, VA, where they surrendered and were paroled.
04	21	1865	President Abraham Lincoln's funeral railroad train leaves Washington, DC, for Springfield, IL, to stop at many locations along the long circuitous route, including Philadelphia, then Harrisburg, etc.
04	22	1865	Union troops, under Brig. Gen. James H. Wilson, USA, **occupy Talladega, AL.**
04	22	1865	Federal scout from Deer Creek to Sage Creek, the Dakota Territory, and skirmish with Indians **(Apr. 22nd)** on the Sage Creek with encounter with hostile **Cheyenne** and **Sioux Indians.** The Indians, attacking at night, are driven off; losses can't be determined as the Indians carry off all (if any) dead and wounded. 4/22-23/1865.
04	22	1865	Skirmish at Buzzard Roost, GA, with Brig. Gen. James H. Wilson, USA, and his Union cavalry, as his mopping up operations will soon be coming to an end.
04	22	1865	Maj. Gen. Nathaniel P. Banks, USA, resumes the command of the Dept. of the Gulf, LA, etal.
04	22	1865	Skirmish with guerrillas near the mouth of the Big Gravois, MO, near the Osage.
04	22	1865	Skirmish near Linn Creek, MO, where the Yankees kill several guerrillas.
04	22	1865	Federal scout against Indians from Dakota City, the Nebraska Territory, to Middle Bow River. 4/22-27/1865.
04	22	1865	Skirmish at Howard's Gap, Blue Ridge Mountains, NC, with Maj. Gen. George Stoneman, USA.
04	22	1865	**Maj. Gen. Henry W. Halleck, USA, assumes the command of the Military Division of the James, VA.**
04	23	1865	**Brig. Gen. James Dearing, CSA, is the last of the Confederate General to die** from wounds received in action, from a pistol duel with a Federal Bvt. Brig. Gen. Theodore Read, USA, on April 6, 1865, dying in a hospital at Lynchburg, VA.
04	23	1865	Action at Munford's Station, AL, with Maj. Gen. James H. Wilson, USA.
04	23	1865	Skirmish with guerrillas on the Snake Creek, the Arizona Territory.
04	23	1865	Affair near Fort Zarah, KS, as the Yankees come across 5 Mexicans murdered by hostile Indians, with 4 having been scalped.
04	23	1865	Action at Hendersonville, NC, with Maj. Gen. George Stoneman, USA, and his Union Cavalry.
04	23	1865	Federal scout from Pulaski, TN, to Rogersville, AL. 4/23-26/1865.
04	23	1865	Federal expedition from Burkeville and Petersburg to Danville and South Boston, VA, as Maj. Gen. Horatio G. Wright, USA, commanding the 6th US Army Corps and his cavalry under Bvt. Maj. Gen. Wesley Merritt, USA, capture 500 prisoners, the few remaining Confederate railroad locomotives, cannons, and other military stoers. 4/23-29/1865.
04	23	1865	The Headquarters of the Middle Military Division is transferred from Winchester, VA, to Washington, DC, thus closing the history books on the events taking place in the Shenandoah Valley, VA.
04	24	1865	Skirmish near Boggy Depot, the Indian Territory, with retreating Confederates.
04	24	1865	The destruction of the Confederate steamer, **CSS Webb,** 25 miles below New Orleans, on the Mississippi River, LA, after being pursued by the Union gunboats **Hollyhock and the Richmond.**
04	24	1865	**Bvt. Brig. Gen. Chester Harding, Jr, 43rd Missouri Infantry, assumes the command of the District of Central Missouri.**
04	24	1865	Skirmish near Miami, MO, with bushwackers; the Yankees report killing 7 of the 13 they encountered.
04	24	1865	President Abraham Lincoln's body lies in state in New York City, NY.
04	24	1865	President Andrew Johnson rejects the agreement between Maj. Gen. William T. Sherman, USA, and Gen. Joseph E. Johnston, CSA, believing Sherman went beyond his authority to negotiate such terms. **Sherman is furious.** Lieut. Gen. Ulysses S. Grant is ordered to assume all remaining military movements.
04	25	1865	Federal scout from Pine Bluff to Rodgers' Plantation, AR, with skirmish at Rodgers' Plantation.

04	25	1865	Skirmish at Linn Creek, MO.
04	25	1865	President Abraham Lincoln's funeral train leaves for Albany, NY.
04	26	1865	**La Fayette Curry Baker,** USA, is appointed Brig. Gen.
04	26	1865	Federal scout from Little Rock to the Saline River, AR. 4/26-29/1865 .
04	26	1865	Affair near Fort Rice, the Dakota Territory, with either **Cheyenne** or **Platte Indians,** as the Indians attack and kill some of the Yankees herding horses toward Fort Rice.
04	26	1865	**THE SURRENDER OF THE CONFEDERATE ARMY IN NORTH CAROLINA AT BENNETT'S HOUSE, NEAR DURHAM'S STATION, NC, by Gen. Joseph Eggleston Johnston, CSA, to Lieut. Gen. Ulysses Simpson Grant, accompanied by Maj. Gen. William Tecumseh Sherman, USA, this time the terms are the same as those given Gen. Robert E. Lee, CSA.**
04	26	1865	President Jefferson Davis and his entourage sets out from Charlotee, NC, headed for the territory west of the Mississippi to carry on the struggle for Southern independence. **Secretary of the Treasury, G.A. Trenholm,** resigns due to poor health and will be replaced by **Postmaster General Reagan.**
04	26	1865	Federal operations in the Shenandoah Valley, VA, including shots fired by a small band of guerrillas at the Federals (April 26th), and the refusal of Col. Thompson, CSA, and his Jackson's Confederate Cavalry command of about 100 to accept terms of surrender. This patriotic group of diehards disbands into the hills around the Shenandoah Valley. 4/26-5/5/1865
04	26	1865	**John Wilkes Booth and David E. Herold are captured** at Richard H. Garrett's Farm, near Port Royal, and north of Bowling Green, VA, where **Booth is mortally wounded.**
04	27	1865	Brig. Gen. James C. Veatch, USA, is assigned to command the Post and the District of Mobile, AL.
04	27	1865	Col. William H. Dickey, **84th US Colored Troops, assumes the command of the District of Morganza, LA.**
04	27	1865	Affair near James Creek, in the vicinity of Mount Vernon, MO, as 2 bushwackers are confronted and laid to rest.
04	27	1865	The loss of the steamer, **Sultana,** in the Mississippi River, near Memphis, TN, as its boiler explodes, causing massive loss (1,200 to 1,900?) of returning Federal Prisoners of War. The actual loss will never be determined.
04	27	1865	President Abraham Lincoln's funeral train passes through Rochester and Buffalo, NY.
04	28	1865	Federal scout against Indians, from Fort Cummings, the New Mexico Territory. 4/28-5/13/1865.
04	28	1865	President Abraham Lincoln's funeral train arrives in Cleveland, OH, where over 50,000 mourners view his coffin.
04	29	1865	Skirmish on the Cumberland River, near Eddyville, in Lyon County, KY, where the **USS Moose** captures a Confederate raiding party numbering about 200 Confederates of Brig. Gen. Abram Burford's command.
04	29	1865	Federal expedition from Saint Louis, MO, to receive the surrender of Bvt. Brig. Gen. M. Jeff. Thompson, CSA. 4/29-6/11/1865.
04	29	1865	President Jefferson Davis and his entourage arrives at Yorkville, SC.
04	29	1865	President Abraham Lincoln's funeral train arrives at Columbus, OH, where the mourning masses pay their last respects.
04	30	1865	Federal operations in the vicinity of Brashear City, LA, with skirmishes at: a) Chacahoula **(Apr. 3rd)** b) Bayou Black **(Apr. 4th)** c) Bayou Goula **(Apr. 9th)** · d) Brown's Plantation **(Apr. 11th)**. 4/30-5/12/1865.
04	30	1865	Maj. Gen. Edward R. S. Canby, USA, meets with Lieut. Gen. Richard Taylor, CSA, near Mobile, AL, to agree upon an end to hostilities and the surrender of the remaining Confederate forces in Alabama and Mississippi.
04	30	1865	President Abraham Lincoln's funeral train arrives at Indianapolis, IN.
05	1	1865	The following are appointed Union Brigadier Generals: **James Sanks Brisbin,** USA **Thomas Odgen Osborn,** USA **Joseph Haydn Potter,** USA
05	1	1865	**Maj. Gen. Governeur K. Warren, USA, is ordered to relieve Maj. Gen. Napoleon J. T. Dana, USA, in the command of the Dept. of Mississippi.**

MONTH	DAY	YEAR	ACT
05	1	1865	Federal scout against Indians from Ojo de Anaya, the New Mexico Territory. 5/1-9/1865.
05	1	1865	**The pursuit and the capture of Confederate President Jefferson Davis,** currently at Cokesburg, SC, and heading for the Florida coast. 5/1-10/1865.
05	1	1865	President Abraham Lincoln's funeral train arrives in Chicago, IL, where his body lies in state at the courthouse.
05	2	1865	Affair on the Blue Earth River, Minnesota, where a party of hostile **Sioux Indians** massacred a family of whites, consisting of 4 or 5 grown persons, and wounded a child.
05	2	1865	**Bvt. Brig. Gen. John E. Smith, USA, is assigned to the command the District of West Tennessee,** vice Maj. Gen. Stephen Gano Burbridge, USA, is relieved of command.
05	2	1865	President Jefferson Davis and his entourage arrive at Abbeville, SC, headed for Washington, GA. President Andrew Johnson puts a $100,000 reward out for the capture of Davis. The Confederate navy turns over their cargo of bullion and archives to Davis' escort commander, Brig. Gen. Basil Duke, and disbands. Confederate **Secretary of the Navy, Stephen R. Mallory,** officially resigns and leaves for La Grange, GA.
05	3	1865	Federal expedition against **Cheyenne Indians** from Fort Laramie to Wind River, the Dakota Territory. 5/3-21/1865.
05	3	1865	Federal operations about Fort Adams, MS, with the assistance of the steamer, **Magnet,** and the gunboat, **Chillicothe.** Rumor has it Davis, with a small escort, crossed the river at Quitman. News is arriving of the surrender of Lieut. Gen. Richard Taylor's Confederate forces. 5/3-6/1865.
05	3	1865	Federal expedition from Rodney to Port Gibson, MS, with skirmishes. 5/3-6/1865.
05	3	1865	Skirmishes on the Missouri River about 15 miles south of Boonville, MO, as the Federals surprise and kill numerous guerrillas attempting to ford the Missouri River.
05	3	1865	Affair with attacking guerrillas near Pleasant Hill, MO, the outlaws escaping towards the Snibar Hills.
05	3	1865	Federal expeditions from Fort Churchill to Carson Lake and the Truckee and Humboldt Rivers, Nevada, against a threatened Indian uprising. The Federals find that the $25,000 appropriated for the purpose of cultivating the **Truckee** and **Walker River Indian** reservations had disappeared and nothing was being raised on either reservation for the Indians. The agents are determined to continue in their ways, even being so bold as to graze herds of stock on the reserves, depleting all the grass and seed. The Federals are surprised the Indians haven't revolted by now, and promise that the Great Father in Washington will see to their needs. 5/3-6/15/1863.
05	3	1865	President Jefferson Davis' entourage continues to dwindle as **Confederate Secretary of State, Judah P. Benjamin,** resigns and flees, eventually reaching England.
05	3	1865	**President Abraham Lincoln's funeral train reaches its final destination of Springfield, IL.**
05	4	1865	Skirmish at Wetumpka, AL, the Mobile, AL, Campaign.
05	4	1865	Federal scout from Pine Bluff to Noble's Farm, AR, against a lawless band of robbers. 5/4-6/1865.
05	4	1865	Skirmish with guerrillas at the Star House, 2 miles from Lexington, MO. The attacking guerrillas are repulsed.
05	4	1865	**THE SURRENDER OF THE CONFEDERATE FORCES IN THE DEPT. OF ALABAMA, MISSISSIPPI, AND EAST LOUISIANA, AT CITRONELLE, AL, 40 miles north of Mobile, by Lieut. Gen. Richard Taylor, CSA, to Maj. Gen. Edward Richard Sprigg Canby, USA., the Mobile, AL, Campaign.**
05	4	1865	President Abraham Lincoln, the 16th President of the United States of America is laid to rest, returning to his hometown of Springfield, IL. So very much has happened since his departure just a short 4 years ago.
05	5	1865	Connecticut becomes the 20th state to ratify the 13th amendment which will abolish slavery.
05	5	1865	Skirmish at Summerville, GA.
05	5	1865	Col. Charles Everett, 2nd Louisiana Infantry, is assigned to the command of the District of Bonnet Carre, LA.
05	5	1865	Skirmish with guerrillas in the Perche Hills, MO.
05	5	1865	The Indian attack on the wagon train near Mullahla's Station, the Nebraska Territory.
05	5	1865	President Jefferson Davis and the few remnants of Confederate political authority arrive at Sandersville, GA, with Jefferson fearing for his life.
05	5	1865	Federal expedition from Pulaski, TN, to New Market, AL. 5/5-13/1865.
05	6	1865	**James Harrison Wilson, U.S.A.,** is appointed Maj. Gen.
05	6	1865	Federal scout with the **79th US Colored Infantry,** from Little Rock, aboard the steamer, **Rose Hamilton,** to Bayou Meto and Little Bayou, AR. 5/6-11/1865.

05	6	1865	Federal expedition from Richmond to Stauton and Charlottesville, VA, including the **surrender of Maj. Gen. Thomas L. Rosser, CSA, Cavalry** at Lexington. Rosser states that the remainder of his command would only come in and surrender in small groups, which would require weeks to accomplish. Rosser also admits he has stashed artillery pieces, and munitions at various places. The Yankees believe there is a large stash of Rebel property concealed around Charlottesville, which has yet to be found. 5/6-14/1865.
05	6	1865	Maj. Gen. David Hunter, USA, is appointed to head the commission which will try those accused of assassinating President Abraham Lincoln, Washington, DC.
05	7	1865	**Col. Simon Jones, USA, 93rd US Colored Troops, assumes the command of the Carrollton District, LA.**
05	7	1865	Maj. Gen. William T. Sherman's, USA, army continues marching northward to Washington, DC, for the final Grand Review of his army.
05	8	1865	**James Meech Warner,** USA, is appointed Brig. Gen.
05	8	1865	Federal expedition from Spring Hill, AL, to Baton Rouge, LA. 5/8-22/1865 .
05	8	1865	Skirmish near Readsville, Callaway County, MO, as bushwackers dressed in Union uniform, try to fool an advancing Yankee command; when that fails, the bushwackers fire and disperse the Union cavalry, leaving behind gallant men with blood oozing from their wounds.
05	8	1865	Federal scout against guerrillas in Saline, La Fayette, and Cooper Counties, MO. 5/8-10/1865.
05	8	1865	Federal scout from Plum Creek to Midway Station, the Nebraska Territory, against the hostile Indians who attacked the wagon train near Mullahla's Station on May 5th. 5/8-20/1865.
05	9	1865	President Jefferson Davis and his wife Varina, are reunited on the Oconee River, near Dublin, GA.
05	9	1865	**Lieut. Gen. Nathan Bedford Forrest, CSA, officially disbands his Cavalry command, ending a very illustrious military career. So long General.**
05	10	1865	**Maj. Gen. Samuel Jones, CSA, surrenders his Confederate command at Tallahassee, FL.**
05	10	1865	**President Jefferson Davis is captured** near Irwinville, GA, by the 4th Michigan Cavalry. **The Confederate Government ceases to exist.** Davis will be taken to Macon, GA, on to Richmond, VA, and finally to imprisonment at Fortress Monroe, Hampton Roads, VA.
05	10	1865	Federal irregulars mortally wound **William Clarke Quantrill,** the notorious guerrilla leader, near Taylorsville, Spencer County, KY. Quantrill will be transferred to Louisville for medical treatment where he dies on June 6, 1865, in his 27th year of age. Other members of his group will go on to earn more notoriety, including **Frank and Jessee James and Cole Younger.**
05	10	1865	Federal scout from Fort Sumner, the New Mexico Territory, in the direction of Fort Bascom to Rioi de las Conchas and Chaperita, to the Pecos and back, as the Yankees meet up with friendly **Navajoes** who report hostile **Comanches** are in the area, although a whiteman reports the killing of a hostile **Navajo** who tried to steal 3 of his horses. It makes it difficult to determine what Indian tribe is guilty and who are innocent and only guilty of having red skin. 5/10-19/1865.
05	11	1865	**Lewis Baldwin Parsons,** USA, is appointed Brig. Gen.
05	11	1865	**Brig. Gen. M. Jeff Thompson, CSA, surrenders his Confederate command at Chalk Bluff, AR.**
05	11	1865	The Confederate Commerce Raider, CSS Stonewall, arrives at Havana, Cuba.
05	11	1865	Federal expedition with the **62nd US Colored Infantry,** from Brazos Santiago, TX, with skirmishes **(May 12th and 13th)** at Palmetto Ranch and (May 13th) at White's Ranch. 5/11-14/1865.
05	12	1865	Maj. Gen. Oliver O. Howard, USA, is assigned to duty as the Commissioner of the Bureau of Refugees, Freedman, and Abandoned Lands, FL, etal.
05	12	1865	Bvt. Maj. Gen. Adelbert Ames, USA, assumes the command of the 10th US Army Corps, FL, etal.
05	12	1865	Federal scout against hostile Indians, from Cottonwood, the Nebraska Territory, to Gilman's Station, 15 miles east of Post Cottonwood. Other encounters are also described. 5/12-14/1865.
05	12	1865	**The Last Engagement of any significance of the American Civil War takes place with the skirmish at Brownsville, or the Union capture, under Col. Theodore H. Barrett, USA, of the Confederate position at Palmetto Ranch, TX, led by Col. John S. Ford, CSA. The fighting will rage on until the following day. 5/12-13/1865.**
05	13	1865	**Brig. Gen. John M. Thayer, USA, is assigned to the command of the District of Eastern Arkansas.**
05	13	1865	Skirmish with Indians at Dan Smith's Ranch, 5 miles below Gilman's, near Julesburg, the Colorado Territory, as 25 Indians attempt to run off the livestock there.

MONTH	DAY	YEAR	ACT
05	13	1865	Lieut. Gen. Edmund Kirby Smith, CSA, meets with the Confederate governors of Arkansas, Louisiana and Missouri at Marshall, TX, where Smith is advised to surrender his army. Brig. Gen. Joseph Orville Shelby, CSA, threatens to arrest Smith if he does.
05	14	1865	Federal expedition from Brashear City, aboard the steamer, **Cornie,** to Ratliff's Plantation, LA, where the Yankees send out word that continued resistance is futile. 5/14-16/1865.
05	14	1865	**Maj. Gen. Gouverneur K. Warren, USA, assumes the command of the Dept. of Mississippi.**
05	14	1865	Skirmish with guerrillas on the Little Piney, MO, with a detachment of Texas and Pulaski County militia.
05	15	1865	Federal scout against guerrillas from Pine Bluff to Johnson's Farm, AR, with skirmish **(May 16th)** on the Monticello Road. 5/15-17/1865.
05	17	1865	**THE CONFEDERATE TROOPS IN FLORIDA SURRENDER TO BVT. BRIG. GEN. ISRAEL VOGDES, USA.** 5/17-20/1865.
05	17	1865	**Maj. Gen. Edward R. S. Canby, USA, is assigned to the command,** and Maj. Gen. Nathaniel P. Banks, USA, is relieved from command of the **Dept. of The Gulf.**
05	17	1865	The State of Mississippi is added to the Dept. of the Gulf, LA, etal.
05	17	1865	**The Military Division of West Mississippi is abolished, and the Dept. of the Gulf is constituted** from the states of Louisiana, Mississippi, Alabama, Florida, and the District of Key West and the Tortugas.
05	17	1865	Maj. Gen. Philip H. Sheridan, USA, is assigned to the general command west of the Mississippi River and South of the Arkansas River.
05	18	1865	Federal expedition against the **Sioux Indians** in the Dakota Territory, where the Yankees rescue a white woman prisoner and her little daughter, who had been purchased from the **Cheyenne Indians** when they killed her husband. The Federals capture 2 Sioux Indians chief, **Two Face and Black Foot,** who they tie up by the neck with a trace chain, suspended from a beam of wood, and leave them without any foothold. **Is this tortue of what?** 5/18-27/1865.
05	18	1865	Skirmish with Indians on the Coteau, Minnesota, as a party of Union Indian Scouts with the assistance of some half-breeds attack a war party of **Sioux Indians;** the Federals using the employ of their own kind to track and fight their brethren who are still refusing to give in to the ways of the whiteman, holding on to their way of life. The "civilized" redman, under the auspices of the whiteman, help to eliminate their own way of life that others (Indians) are dying for.
05	18	1865	Federal scout against guerrillas from Lebanon to Warsaw, MO. 5/18-20/185.
05	18	1865	Skirmish with Indians near Fort Kearny, the Nebraska Territory, as many Union soldiers receive arrow wounds. In the final outcome, will arrows or lead bullets win out?
05	18	1865	The 25th US Army Corps is ordered to be held in readiness for transportation to Texas.
05	19	1865	The following are appointed Union Brigadier Generals: **James William Forsyth,** USA **Joseph Eldridge Hamblin,** USA **Richard Henry Jackson,** USA **William Wells,** USA
05	19	1865	The Confederate Commerce Raider, **CSS Stonewall,** surrenders to the Union officials at Havanna, Cuba.
05	19	1865	Federal scout against Indians from Sweetwater Bridge to Whisky Gap of the Medicine Bow Mountains, the Dakota Territory. 5/19-20/1865.
05	19	1865	Maj. Gen. William B. Hazen, USA, is assigned to the command of the 15th US Army Corps, FL.
05	19	1865	Federal scout from Kingsville, MO. 5/19-22/1865.
05	19	1865	Federal scout against Indians from Fort Kearny to the Little River, the Nebraska Territory. 5/19-6/2/1865.
05	19	1865	Federal scout against Indians from Fort Kearny, the Nebraska Territory. 5/19-26/1865.
05	19	1865	**Maj. Gen. John A. Logan, USA, is assigned to the command of the Army of the Tennessee.**
05	20	1865	Federal scout against Indians from Camp Plumb, the Dakota Territory, to the Red Buttes, on Deer Creek, then east to Box Elder Canon, then north to the North Platte River when the Yankees observe a party of 100 Indians across the river; the river being too hide to ford, all they can do is watch them. 5/20-22/1865.
05	20	1865	Skirmishes with Indians on Deer Creek, the Dakota Territory, as the Yankees repel an Indian attack of about 50, killing and wounding a few.
05	20	1865	Federal operations against Indians about Three Crossings Station, the Dakota Territory, as the Yankees pursue the Indians who attacked the station, tore down telegraph lines and stole one horse; they cross the Sweetwater River, and head toward their families at Wind River. 5/20-22/1865.

05	20	1865	Former **Confederate Secretary of War, Stephen R. Mallory, is captured** at LaGrange, GA, and transferred to Fort Lafayette, New York, where he will remain until paroled in March, 1866.
05	20	1865	Affair near Pawnee Rock, KS, as Indians attacked 2 men coming from Fort Larned, killing one while the other escaped.
05	20	1865	Skirmish on the Blackwater, near Longwood, MO, with roving Confederate bushwackers, as the Federal officer in charge believes troops should be stationed at Dresden, MO, to be near the **Pacific Railroad,** and close to forage and provisions.
05	21	1865	**Charles Hale Morgan,** USA, is appointed Brig. Gen.
05	22	1865	Skirmish at Valley Mines, MO, as the Federals attack 5 men caught robbing a store there, killing one, wounding another.
05	22	1865	**President Jefferson Davis, the last symbol of the Confederacy is imprisoned at Fortress Monroe, off Hampton, VA.**
05	23	1865	Federal scout from Pine Bluff to Monticello, AR, with skirmish **(May 24th)** at Monticello, as the Yankees pursue a party of Confederates under Captain Kidd who have not yet surrendered. The Yankees inform the Rebels they were going to remain in the area until they surrender or until every corndodger and pound of meat was eaten and every ear of corn was properly disposed of to the US Cavalry horses. 5/23-27/1865.
05	23	1865	Maj. Gen. William B. Hazen, USA, assumes the command of the 15th US Army Corps, FL, etal.
05	23	1865	Federal scout from Thibodeaux by way of Brule Texas, passing through Labadierville, to Lake Verret, LA.
05	23	1865	Federal scout from Warrensburg, MO, to the mouth of Coal Camp Creek, near the Osage, as the Yankees track bushwackers accused of killing 12 discharged soldiers and citizens in Hickory and Benton Counties. 5/23-26/1865.
05	23	1865	Skirmish 10 miles northwest of Waynesville, MO, as the Yankees attack a band of bushwackers, inflicting casualties.
05	23	1865	**The Army of the Potomac, under Maj. Gen. George Gordon Meade, USA,** is reviewed in the city of Washington, DC.
05	24	1865	Federal scout from Napoleonville to Bayou Saint Vincent, LA.
05	24	1865	Skirmish 6 miles from Rocheport, MO, as the Yankees surround the house where 11 Confederate guerrillas were holed up, killing 5, wounding and capturing the rest, who may end up swinging from the end of a rope.
05	24	1865	**Bvt. Brig. Gen. George Spalding, USA, 12th Tennessee Cavalry, is assigned to the command of the District of North Missouri, vice Fisk.**
05	24	1865	**Maj. Gen. William Tecumseh Sherman's, USA, Union Army** is reviewed in the city of Washington, DC, a part of the **G.A.R. Grand Armies of the Republic. This celebrated event will soon become only a memory as the last line of Union soldiers march by the reviewing stand.**
05	25	1865	**Francis Channing Barlow, U.S.A.,** is appointed Maj. Gen.
05	25	1865	The unintentional explosion of the Confederate ordnance depot at Mobile, AL, which cause $ 5,000,000 in damages to buildings, boats, etc. 20 tons of gunpowder causes approximately 300 casualties.
05	25	1865	Federal expedition from Bayou Boeuf to Bayou De Large, LA, with affair **(May 27th)** at Bayou De Large, as the Yankees surprise the camp of 11 Confederates behind J. Terrion's plantation, capturing all of their weapons and provisions, as the Rebels fled into the woods. 5/25-27/1865.
05	25	1865	Federal expedition from Fort Ruby to the Humboldt Valley, Nevada, with skirmish **(May 29th)** near Austin, Nevada, with the **Pi-Ute** and **Bannock Indians** who were committing deprivations against ranchers' livestock, about Austin, Grass Valley and in the Reese River Valley. As was usually the case, many Indians were laid to rest, along with a few white men and friendly Indians. 5/25-6/15/1865.
05	26	1865	**Gershom Mott, U.S.A.,** is appointed Maj. Gen.
05	26	1865	Federal scout after a band of roving Confederates and skirmishes in Carroll and Ray Counties, MO, including in the Crook River timber, as the Yankees continue to inflict serious damage to the remaining Rebels, bushwackers and guerrillas. 5/26-27/1865.
05	26	1865	Federal scout against Indians from Plum Creek, the Nebraska Territory to the vicinity of Mullahla's Station, where a few head of cattle were stolen. 5/26-27/1865.
05	26	1865	Federal operations against Indians on the **Overland Stage Road** on the Platte and Sweetwater Rivers, with skirmishes at:

			a) Saint Mary's Station **(May 27th)**
			b) Sweetwater Station **(May 26th, 28th, and June lst)**
			c) Platte Bridge, Dakota Territory **(June 3rd)**
			d) Sage Creek, Colorado Territory **(June 8th).** The attacking Indians burn some of the above stations, tear down telegraph lines, kill quite a few whitemen and soldiers, sometimes horribly mutilating and scalping their victims, in addition to wounding many others, etc. 5/26-6/9/1865.

05 26 1865 **LIEUT. GEN. EDMUND KIRBY SMITH, CSA, SURRENDERS ALL THE CONFEDERATE TROOPS IN THE TRANS-MISSISSIPPI DEPT., TO MAJ. GEN. EDWARD RICHARD SPRIGG CANBY, USA. Lieut. Gen. Simon Bolivar Buckner, CSA, represents Smith while Maj. Gen. Peter Joseph Osterhaus, USA, represents Canby as the agreement takes place at New Orleans, LA. Brig. Gen. Joseph Orville Shelby, CSA, refuses to surrender, opting to go to Mexico, dispersing the remainder who refused to go along with him.**

05 27 1865 **Benjamin Henry Grierson, U.S.A.,** is appointed Maj. Gen.

05 27 1865 **Maj. Gen. Peter J. Osterhaus, USA, is assigned to the command the Dept. of Mississippi,** relieving Maj. Gen. Gouverneur K. Warren, USA.

05 27 1865 Skirmish in Chariton County, MO, with guerrillas.

05 27 1865 Skirmish at Switzler's Mill, Chariton County, MO, with guerrillas.

05 28 1865 **Bvt. Brig. Gen. George Spalding, USA, 12th Tennessee Cavalry, assumes the command of the District of North Missouri.**

05 29 1865 **The Territory in the Trans-Mississippi, south of the Arkansas River, is designated the Military Division of the Southwest, by Maj. Gen. Philip H. Sheridan, USA.**

05 29 1865 The Army of the Tennessee and the Army of Georgia (except the troops belonging to the East) are ordered to Louisville, KY.

05 29 1865 **The District of East Louisiana is formed,** to consist of the Districts of Baton Rouge and Port Hudson and the Post of Clinton, and Brig. Gen. Michael K. Lawler, USA, is assigned to its command.

05 29 1865 Federal operations against guerrillas in Johnson County, MO.

05 29 1865 **Maj. Gen. Philip H. Sheridan, USA, assumes the command of the Military Division of the Southwest.**

05 29 1865 **Bvt. Maj. Gen. John E. Smith, USA, assumes the command of the District of West Tennessee.**

05 29 1865 **Federal operations under Maj. Gen. Philip Henry Sheridan, USA, in Texas and on the Rio Grande River, TX,** as Sheridan begins a mopping up campaign after the surrender of Lieut. Gen. E. Kirby Smith, CSA, overseeing the renamed Military Division of the Southwest, relocating troops, chasing Indians, and overall acting like a big cheese. 5/29/1865-11/14/1866.

05 29 1865 In an act of reconciliation, President Andrew Johnson grants amnesty and pardons to all those who participated in the rebellion.

05 30 1865 The 4th US Army Corps is ordered from the Dept. of the Cumberland to the Military Division of the Southwest, TN.

05 31 1865 The following are appointed Union Brigadier Generals:
Henry Alanson Barnum, USA
Robert Francis Catterson, USA
William Thomas Clark, USA
Americus Vespucius Rice, USA
William Burnham Woods, USA

05 31 1865 Federal expedition from Barrancas aboard the transports, **Peabody, N.P Banks, Clyde, Hussar,** and **Tampico,** and with the steamer, **Itasca,** to Apalachicola, FL. 5/31-6/6/1865.

06 1 1865 Federal expedition through Pocahontas and Pendleton Counties, WV, and Highland County, VA, in search of horse thieves. The Yankees traveled to Huttonsville, Gatewood's, Back Creek Valley, Galltown, Monterey, New Hampton, etc., without finding any horse thieves. **The final chapter on the American Civil War in this region has now been written. 6/1-13/1865.**

06 2 1865 Federal operations against Indians in the vicinity of Crystal Palace Bluff, about Fort Rice, the Dakota Territory, as one man is reported dying from the efforts of his arrow wounds.

06 3 1865 Skirmish with Indians at Dry Creek, the Dakota Territory, as the Indians attack the Platte Bridge Station,

killing quite a few Union soldiers, scalping a few when time permitted, and wounding others, before being driven off.

| 06 | 3 | 1865 | **Maj. Gen. Edward R. S. Canby, USA, assumes the command of the Dept. of the Gulf,** LA, etal. |
| 06 | 3 | 1865 | <u>**The 6th US Army Corps is reviewed in Washington, DC.**</u> |

06 4 1865 Federal operations against Indians near Fort Collins, the Colorado Territory, as the Yankees travel to Virginia Dale and towards Laramie in search of horse stealing Indians, Frenchmen and half-breeds. 6/4-10/1865.

06 5 1865 Bvt. Maj. Gen. Benjamin H. Grierson, USA, is assigned to the command of the Cavalry Forces, the Dept. of the Gulf, LA.

06 5 1865 The veteran portion of the 4th Army Corps is ordered to proceed from the Dept. of the Cumberland to New Orleans, LA.

06 6 1865 The notorious guerrilla, **William Clarke Quantrill** dies in Louisville, KY, at age 27, from wounds received on May 10, 1865, **as another player in the Civil War departs the living.**

06 8 1865 Attack by Indians on the **Overland Stage Road** in Kansas and Colorado, with skirmishes at:
a) Fort Dodge, Kansas   **(June 8th and 12th)**
b) Chavis Creek, near Cow Creek Station   **(June 9th)**
c) near Cow Creek Station, Plum Butte and Pawnee Rock, KS, **(June 12th).** 6/8-14/1865.

06 9 1865 Maj. Gen. Peter J. Osterhaus, USA, assumes the command of the Dept. of Mississippi.

06 9 1865 The unintentional explosion of the ordnance building at Chattanooga, TN, causing approximately 10 casualties. The commanding officer orders the arrest of the ordnance officer for dereliction of duty.

06 10 1865 Col. John D. Allen, 15th US Missouri Cavalry, assumes the command of the District of Southwest Missouri.

06 12 1865 Federal expedition from the **Pawnee Indian Village** to the Platte and Niobrara Rivers, the Dakota Territory, in search of hostile Indians, with many experiences to write about. 6/12-7/5/1865.

06 13 1865 Federal expedition against hostile Indians from Dun Glen to Fairbanks Station, Nevada, with no encounters. 6/13-26/1865.

06 13 1865 Federal scout against Indians from Camp Nichols, the New Mexico Territory, with action **(June 14th)** with attacking Indians on the Sante Fe Road, as the Indians lance one man to death, with other casualties, etc. 6/13-17/1865.

06 14 1865 Action with Indians at Horse Creek, the Dakota Territory, where approximately 2,000 **Sioux** attack and kill 4 Yankees, wounding 4 others. The Federals "circle" the wagons but the Indians withdraw in lieu of attacking the well defended Yankees.

06 14 1865 Col. Carroll H. Potter, 6th US Volunteer Infantry, assumes the command of the South Sub-District of the Plains, Dakota, etal.

06 15 1865 Federal scout from Fort Sumner to the Oscura Mountains, the New Mexico Territory, where the Yankees destroy the camp of **Delgaditos Largo's Navajo Indian** tribe. The area is totally void of water, the Yankees finding holes dug in every ravine where the Indians were trying to find the life saving water. 6/15-22/1865.

06 17 1865 Federal expedition from Denver, the Colorado Territory, to Fort Halleck, the Dakota Territory. 6/17-19/1865.

06 17 1865 Skirmish with Indians on Dead Man's Fork, the Dakota Territory.

06 17 1865 Maj. Gen. Gordon Granger, USA, assumes the command of all troops within the State of Texas.

06 19 1865 Brig. Gen. Thomas J. McKean, USA, is assigned to the command of the District of Southwest Missouri.

06 20 1865 **The Powder River Indian Expedition, the Dakota Territory,** with Maj. Gen. Grenville M. Dodge, USA, commanding the Dept. of the Missouri, and US Forces in Kansas and the Territories report the construction of the **Union Pacific Railroad** is progressing; law and order has mostly be restored with the guerrillas and bushwackers lying down their weapons; Maj. Gen. Dodge has been quite busy cleaning out the overcrowded jails and prisons of many outlaws, captured Rebel prisoners of war, etc., many of whom were immediately released when it was learned they were lodged in jail with no charges against them; certain friendly Indians are rebelling on their reservations; there are continued reports of the Indian agents absconding the Federal funds appropriated for the welfare of the peaceful Indians; fighting

continued between the hostile Indians, many tribes of which have been dealt with very harshly by the Federals, with the principal hostile Indian tribes being the **Northern Cheyennes** and **Sioux,** occupying the country north of the North Platte River; the **Arapahoes,** occupying the country between the North Platte and South Platte and east of the Rocky Mountains; the **Southern Cheyennes,** the country immediately south of the Arkansas River, but who claim the country between the Arkansas and South Platte; and the **Comanches, Kiowas** and **Apaches,** occupying the country south of the Arkansas River, and bordering on New Mexico. 6/20-10/7/1865.

06	20	1865	Brig. Gen. James A. Williamson, USA, is assigned to the command of the District of Saint Louis, MO.
06	20	1865	Maj. Gen. Jacob D. Cox, USA, is temporary in command of the Dept. of North Carolina.
06	20	1865	Bvt. Maj. Gen. Thomas H. Ruger, USA, is in temporary command of the 23rd US Army Corps, NC, etal.
06	20	1865	Maj. Gen. George H. Thomas, USA, assumes the command of the Military Division of the Tennessee.
06	21	1865	Brig. Gen. James C. Veatch, USA, is assigned to the command of the Union forces in West Louisiana.
06	22	1865	Brig. Gen. Morgan L. Smith, US Army, is relieved from the command of the District of Vicksburg, MS.
06	22	1865	Unaware that the war is over, the **CSS Shenandoah** continues to prey on Union whaling ships in the Bering Sea.
06	23	1865	**Brig. Gen. Stand Watie, CSA, the Cherokee Indian Nation, surrenders his Confederate Forces, comprised of Cherokee, Creek, Osage, and Creek Indians. at Doaksville, near Fort Townson, Indian Territory, later Oklahoma. This surrender will comprise of the last organized Confederate force to officially surrender.**
06	23	1865	Brig. Gen. Thomas J. McKean, US Army, assumes the command of the District of Southwest Missouri.
06	23	1865	**Rear admiral Samuel F. DuPont dies unexpectedly at Philadelphia, PA.**
06	24	1865	Federal operations about Rock Creek Station and Seven Mile Creek, the Dakota Territory, in search of Indians rumored to have run off livestock in this area. The Yankees fail to catch up with any Indians as they repeatedly write how their horses are inferior to the Red Man's. The Federals do meet small groups of whitemen reporting attacks upon their wagon trains. In addition, the Yankees find upon reaching the town of **Virginia Dale,** a man by the name of James Enos, who, whilst out hunting, was fired upon by a party of Indians, supposed to be **Arapahoes.** He was severely wounded in the back by an arrow. It is of the opinion of the surgeon that he cannot live. Such was the life of the early pioneers trying to settle or cross the plains. 6/24-30/1865.
06	24	1865	**The Dept. of Mississippi is created,** embracing the State of Mississippi, and Maj. Gen. Henry W. Slocum, USA, is assigned to its command.
06	24	1865	By now, all military blockades of all southern ports, including restrictions on the Mississippi River, have been raised by President Andrew Johnson, Washington, DC.
06	25	1865	Bvt. Brig. Gen. Chester Harding, Jr, 43rd Missouri Infantry, relinquishes his command of the District of Central Missouri.
06	26	1865	**George Peabody Estey,** USA, is appointed Brig. Gen.
06	26	1865	Federal expedition against **Apache Indians,** from Fort Bowie to the Gila River, the Arizona Territory, with skirmishes **(July 3rd)** at Cottonwood Creek and **(July 4th)** at Cavalry Canon, Arizona Territory, the Yankees destroying Apache rancheros, crops, retaking cattle, etc. 6/26-7/6/1865.
06	26	1865	The Confederate commerce raider, **CSS Shenandoah,** captures 6 Union whaling vessels in the Bering Sea.
06	26	1865	Brig. Gen. John Newton, USA, is assigned to the command the District of Florida.
06	26	1865	The 2nd Division, 15th US Army Corps, is ordered from Louisville, KY, to Little Rock, AR.
06	26	1865	The 4th US Army Corps arrives at New Orleans, LA, en route to Texas. 6/26-29/1865.
06	26	1865	Bvt. Brig. Gen. John L. Beveridge, 17th llinois Cavalry, assumes the command of the District of Central Missouri.
06	27	1865	**William Henry Penrose,** USA, is appointed Brig. Gen.
06	27	1865	The US Army announced the following assignments:

         A) **Military Division of the Atlantic** - Maj. Gen. George Meade
              1) Dept. of Alabama   - Maj. Gen. Charles R. Woods
              2) Dept. of Florida   - Maj. Gen. John G. Foster
              3) 23rd US Army Corps, FL   - Brig. Gen. Samuel P. Carter
              4) Dept. of Georgia   - Maj. Gen. James B. Steedman

        5) Dept. of North Carolina   - Maj. Gen. John M. Schofield
    B) **Military Division of the Gulf**   - Maj. Gen. Philip Sheridan
        1) Dept of Louisiana & Texas   - Maj. Gen. Edward R.S. Canby
        2) Union Post of Galveston TX   - Col. Frederick W. Moore, 83rd Ohio Infantry, in addition to the
            3rd Brigade, 2nd Division, the 13th US Army Corps.
    C) **Military Division of the Mississippi** - Maj. Gen. William T. Sherman (reorganized)
        1) Dept. of Mississippi   - Maj. Gen. Henry W. Slocum
        2) Dept. of the Missouri   - Maj. Gen. John Pope
        3) Dept. of Arkansas   - Maj. Gen. Joseph J. Reynolds
        4) Dept. of Kentucky   - Maj. Gen. John M. Palmer
        5) Middle Dept.   - Maj. Gen. Winfield S. Hancock
        6) Dept. of the East   - Maj. Gen. Joseph Hooker
        7) Dept. of Virginia   - Maj. Gen. Alfred H. Terry
        8) 1st Sub-District of St. Louis, MO, Col David Moore, 51st MO Infantry - Col. David Moore, 41st
            Missouri Infantry, vice Col. Joseph Weydemeyer, Missouri Infantry, is relieved of command.
        9) Dept. of the Ohio   - Maj. Gen. Edward O. C. Ord
    D) **Military Division of the Pacific** is created, to consist of the Dept. of California and the Columbia.
        1) Military Division of the Pacific - Maj. Gen. Henry W. Halleck
        2) Dept. of California is created, to consist of the States of California and Nevada and the Territories
            of New Mexico and Arizona.
        3) Dept. of California   - Maj. Gen. Irvin McDowell
        4) Dept. of the Columbia is created, to consist of the State of Oregon and the Territories of Idaho and
            Washington.
        5) Dept. of the Columbia, Oregon, etal - Brig. Gen. George Wright
        6) Dept. of Washington   - Maj. Gen. Christopher C. Augur
    E) **Military Division of Tennessee**   - Maj. Gen. George H. Thomas
        1) Dept. of Tennessee   - Maj. Gen. George Stoneman

06	28	1865	**The District of Kansas is formed,** from the Districts of North and South Kansas, and Brig. Gen. Robert B. Mitchell, is assigned to its command.
06	28	1865	On its final days of operation against Federal shipping, the Confederate commerce raider, the **CSS Shenandoah** captures 11 Union whalers in the Bering Sea. At least the whales were happy.
06	29	1865	Skirmish with Indians near Fort Dodge, Kansas, as a party of about 40 hostile Indians charged upon one of the cattle herds belonging to a Mexican train, killing 2 Mexican herdsmen and scalping another; the Indians fail to capture any livestock as the Yankees are fast on their trail in chasing them away. Due to the poor shape of their horses, the Yankees cannot catch the skillful Indian horsemen on their well cared for horses.
06	30	1865	Skirmish with Indians at Rock Creek, the Dakota Territory, where the Indians are reported to have ran off 60 head of cattle from Rock Creek and killing one soldier. Also at Willow Springs Station they have stolen all the stock belonging to the stage coach company.
06	30	1865	Maj. Gen. Henry W. Halleck, US, relinquishes his command of the Military Division of the James, VA.
06	30	1865	The US Military Commission finds all of the following guilty of conspiring to murder President Abraham Lincoln with the following sentences doled out:

        1) **Samuel Arnold**   - life imprisonment
        2) **George Atzerodt**   - death by hanging
        3) **David Herold**   - death by hanging
        4) **Dr. Samuel Mudd**   - life imprisonment
        5) **Michael O'Laughlin** - life imprisonment
        6) **Lewis Payne**   - death by hanging
        7) **Edward Spangler**   - 6 yrs. imprisonment
        8) **Mrs. Mary Surratt**   - death by hanging

| 07 | 1 | 1865 | New Hampshire becomes the 21st state to ratify the 13th amendment which will abolish slavery. |
| 07 | 2 | 1865 | Federal expedition against Indians from Camp Lyon, the Idaho Territory, to the headwaters of the Malheur River, Oregon, with skirmish with **Snake Indians** and possibly some **Boise Indians. (July 9th).** The Indians are no match for the Federals, who fight valiantly, but with only one possible outcome. 7/2-13/1865. |

07	7	1865	**The sentence of hanging** the 4 condemned to death for conspiring to assassinate President Abraham Lincoln was carried out at the Old Penitentiary Building, Washington DC. The other 4 are transferred to Fort Jefferson on Dry Tortugas, off the Florida Keys near Key West with the final results: 1) Michael O'Laughlin will die in prison of yellow fever in 1867. 2) Dr. Samuel Mudd will be pardoned and released from prison in 1868. 3) Samuel Arnold will be pardoned and released in 1869. 4) Edward Spangler will be pardoned and released in 1869.
07	10	1865	Federal expedition against **Apache Indians,** from Fort Bowie to Maricopa Wells, the Arizona Territory, with many events but no encounters with hostile Indians. 7/10-21/1865.
07	17	1865	Skirmish with Indians on the Owyhee River, the Idaho Territory, as the Federals pursue and hunt down the Indians with their stock of horses, as they try to evade the Yankees in the steep canons of the area, but to no avail, as the Union soldiers send some Indians to meet their maker.
07	21	1865	**Francis Trowbridge Sherman,** USA, is appointed Brig. Gen.
07	22	1865	**James Hughes Stokes,** USA, is appointed Brig. Gen.
07	26	1865	**Emerson Opdycke,** USA, is appointed Brig. Gen.
07	26	1865	Skirmish with Indians at Platte Bridge, the Dakota Territory.
07	30	1865	**Brig. Gen. George Wright, USA,** drowns at sea off the coast of Northern California in the wreck of the steamship, **Brother Jonathan.**
08	1	1865	**George Leonard Andrews, U.S.A.,** is appointed Maj. Gen.
08	1	1865	Affairs with Indians at Big Laramie and Little Laramie, the Dakota Territory.
08	13	1865	Skirmish with Indians near Powder River, the Dakota Territory.
08	15	1865	A peace treaty is signed at the mouth of the Little Arkansas River, with the following Indian Nation Tribes: a) **Apache** b) **Arapahoe** c) **Comanche** d) **Kiowa**
08	16	1865	Skirmish with Indians near Powder River, the Dakota Territory.
08	26	1865	**Brig. Gen. Marcellus Monroe Crocker, USA,** dies at Washington, DC, from camp fever (tuberculosis) that afflicted him for a very long time.
08	28	1865	Action with Indians at Tongue River, the Dakota Territory.
09	1	1865	Skirmish with Indians on the east side of the Powder River, the Montana Territory, with little fighting as the Indians flee from the advancing Federals.
09	2	1865	Skirmish with Indians at Powder River, the Montana Territory.
09	4	1865	Skirmish with Indians at Powder River, the Montana Territory, as about 150 Indians of a total group estimated to be from 500 to 2,000 attack a party of Federal Cavalry, killing 2 and wounding another; the Indians have about 5 killed. The Indians regroup and attack again, this time leaving another 7 or 8 dead on the field.
09	5	1865	**Brig. Gen. Alexander Schimmelfennig, USA,** dies near Wernersville, PA, while trying to recuperate from camp fever (tuberculosis) which afflicted him for a very long time.
09	5	1865	Engagement with Indians at Powder River, the Montana Territory.
09	7	1865	Skirmish with Indians at Powder River, the Montana Territory, as a Federal tracking party engage a party of about 40 Indians, killing two or three and losing one Yankee boy.
09	8	1865	Engagement with Indians at Powder River, the Montana Territory, as a large considerable force of Indians attack the rear of the Federal's wagon train.
09	14	1865	A peace treaty is signed at Fort Smith, AR, with the following Indian Nation Tribes: 1) **Cherokee** 2) **Creek** 3) **Choctaw** 4) **Chickasaw**

5) **Osage**
6) **Seminole**
7) **Seneca**
8) **Shawnee**
9) **Quapaw**

| 09 | 23 | 1865 | <u>**Skirmish with Indians in the Harney Lake Valley, Oregon, which action commenced at 12 a.m. and ended at 7 p.m. that night, the last reported hostilities occurring during the era of the American Civil War per the Official Records of the War of the Rebellion. It is finally over. Ironically, the last encounter reported has the Federals being routed, luckily escaping with only one injury.**</u> |

09 25 1865 **William Gamble,**   USA, is appointed Brig. Gen.

09 25 1865 **Louis Douglass Watkins,**   USA, is appointed Brig. Gen.

09 27 1865 **Charles Henry Van Wyck,** USA, is appointed Brig. Gen.

09 29 1865 **Robert Brown Potter,**   U.S.A., is appointed Maj. Gen.

11 6 1865 The Confederate Commerce Raider, the **CSS Shenandoah,** after an illustrious career, surrenders to British authorities at Liverpool, England.

11 9 1865 **Francis Fessenden, U.S.A.,** is appointed Maj. Gen.

11 10 1865 **Capt. Henry Wirz, CSA,** the commander of the notorious **Confederate prison camp at Andersonville, GA,** and who proclaims his innocence to the end, and after being found guilty of atrocities to Union prisoners, **is hanged today.**

11 11 1865 **Morgan Henry Chrysler,** USA, is appointed Brig. Gen.

11 13 1865 South Carolina, where it all began 4 years ago, is the 23rd state of the Union to ratify the 13th amendment, which abolishes slavery.

11 20 1865 **Joel Allen Dewey,** USA, is appointed Brig. Gen.

12 2 1865 Alabama becomes the 24th state to ratify the 13th amendment, abolishing slavery.

12 4 1865 North Carolina becomes the 25th state to ratify the 13th amendment, abolishing slavery.

12 5 1865 Georgia becomes the 26th state to ratify the 13th amendment which abolishes slavery.

12 11 1865 Oregon becomes the 27th state to ratify the 13th amendment to the Constitution of the United States, which officially abolishes slavery, one of the main causes of the American Civil War.

12 21 1865 **Brig. Gen. James Heyward Trapier, CSA,** dies from camp fever sickness developed during the Civil War, near Georgetown, SC.

Many more generals and soldiers will die from related battle wounds and sicknesses, but our coverage stops here, as 1865 is the cutoff of the differences between Northern and Southern States. No further conflicts and only the remaining agony and suffering from the damage caused. Many of those afflicted will slip off into obscurity. Those fortunate to have escaped the war unscathed will become statistics, notwithstanding, of the toll that time takes upon us all. We would love to report the rest of those fallen generals who pass on after 1865, as well as events of interest, but must limit ourself to the bracket of years that the ultimate war of American history was fought, and where the Official Records of the War of the Rebellion concludes.

With this we say....

Take a breather, relax, and Now, go back to 1860, like the author has so many, many, times and start over again..

Only this time, put on your stereo headset, pop in a CD such as the soundtrack from Ken Burns' "The Civil War" and enjoy.

Good luck, and may we see each other with the fallen in the next life.

MAPS

from

The Official Military Atlas of the
CIVIL WAR

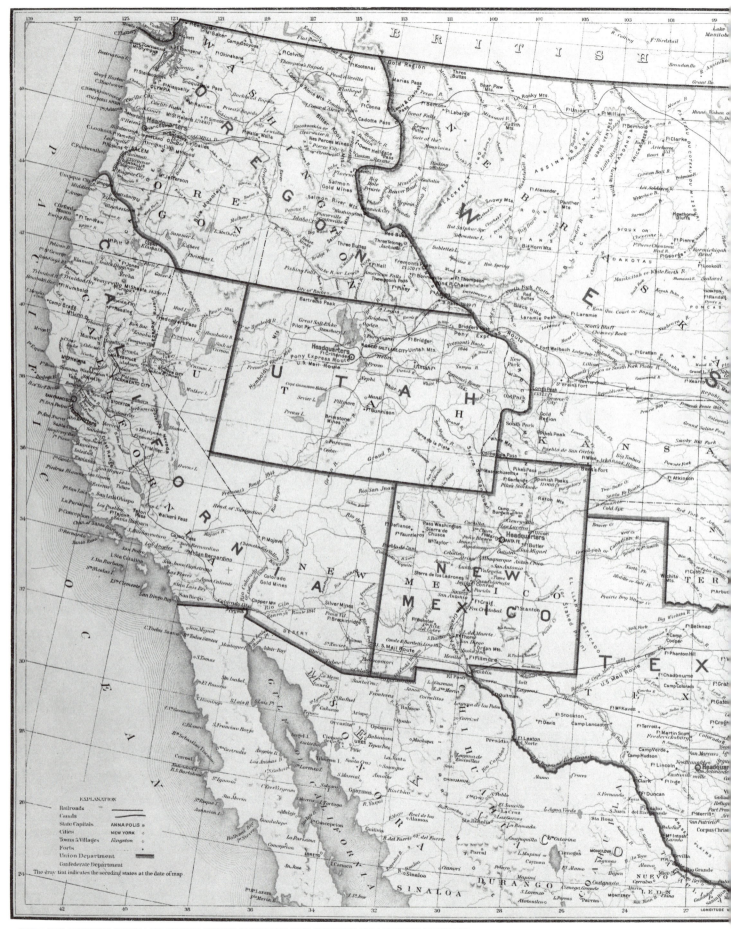

MAP
OF THE
UNITED STATES
OF AMERICA,
SHOWING THE
BOUNDARIES
OF THE
UNION AND CONFEDERATE
GEOGRAPHICAL DIVISIONS
AND
DEPARTMENTS,
DEC. 31, 1860.

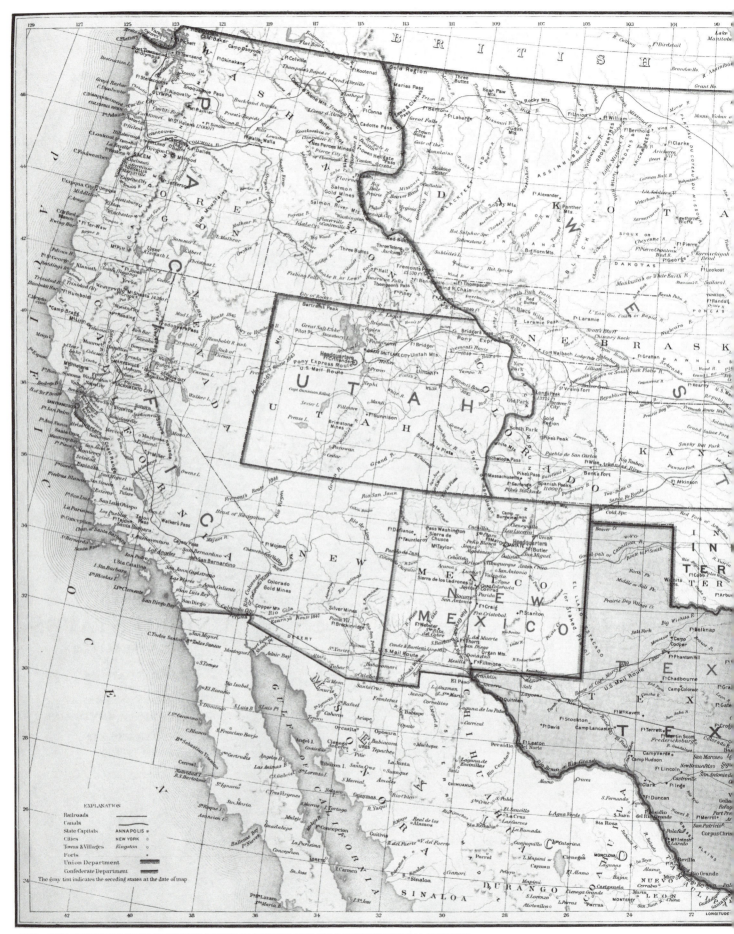

MAP
OF THE
UNITED STATES
OF AMERICA,
SHOWING THE
BOUNDARIES
OF THE
UNION AND CONFEDERATE
GEOGRAPHICAL DIVISIONS
AND
DEPARTMENTS,
JUNE 30, 1861.

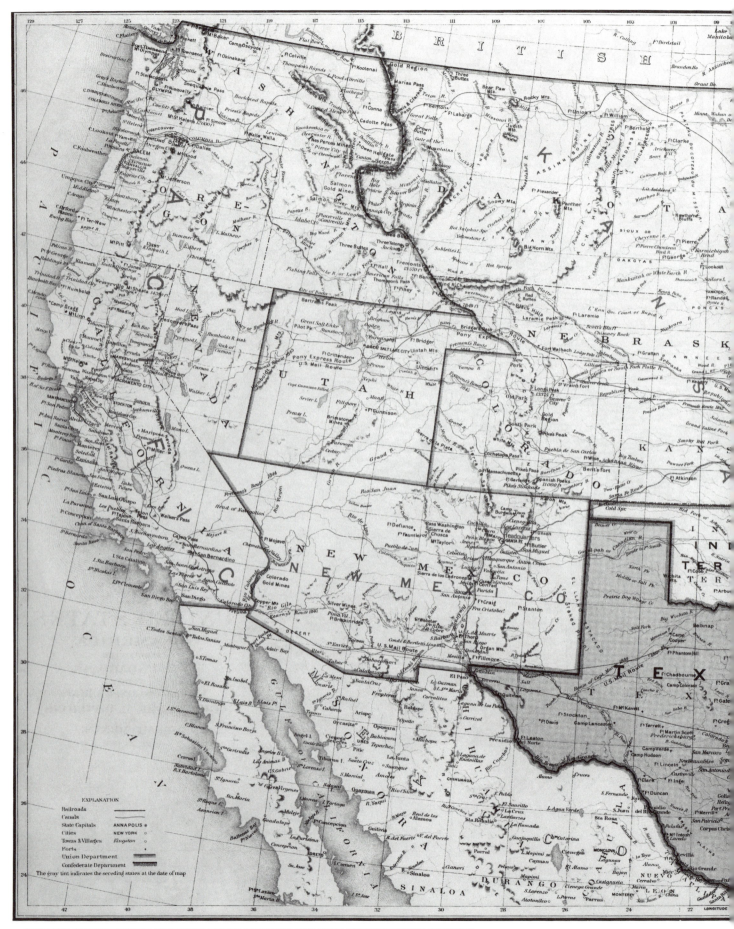

MAP
OF THE
UNITED STATES
OF AMERICA,
SHOWING THE
BOUNDARIES
OF THE
UNION and CONFEDERATE
GEOGRAPHICAL DIVISIONS
AND
DEPARTMENTS,
DEC. 31, 1861.

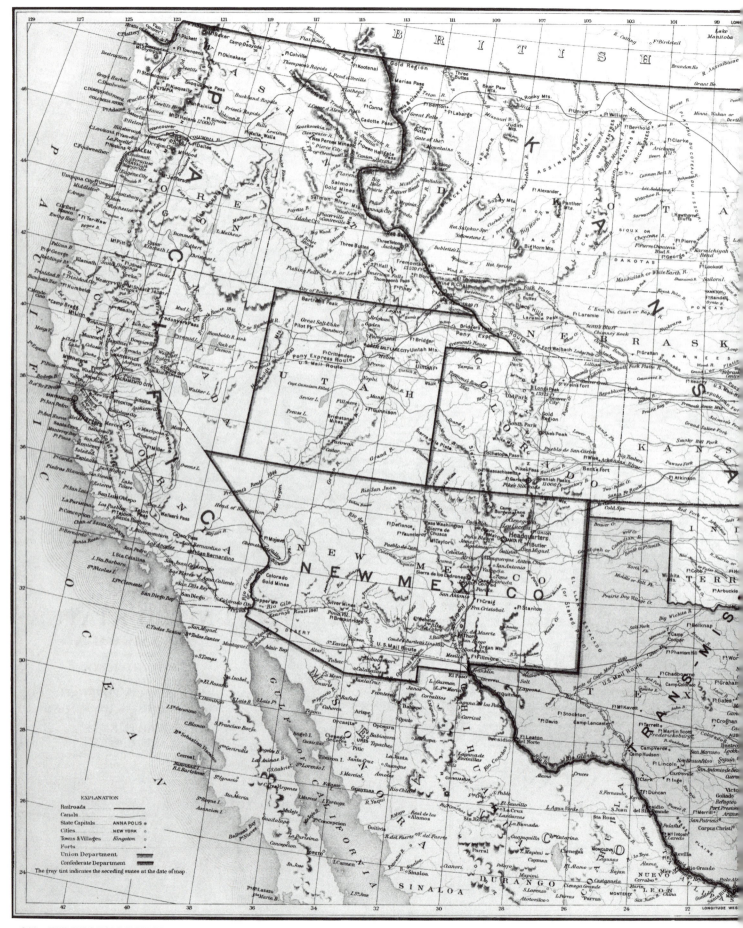

MAP
OF THE
UNITED STATES
OF AMERICA,
SHOWING THE
BOUNDARIES
OF THE
UNION AND CONFEDERATE
GEOGRAPHICAL DIVISIONS
AND
DEPARTMENTS,
JUNE 30, 1862.

*U.S. Forces belonging to the Rappahannock, Shenandoah
and Mountain Departments consolidated June 26,1862,
into the Army of Virginia under POPE.
On June 30, 1862, the Army of the Potomac (McCLELLAN)
and the Army of Northern Virginia (LEE) were operating in
the Vicinity of Richmond, Virginia.

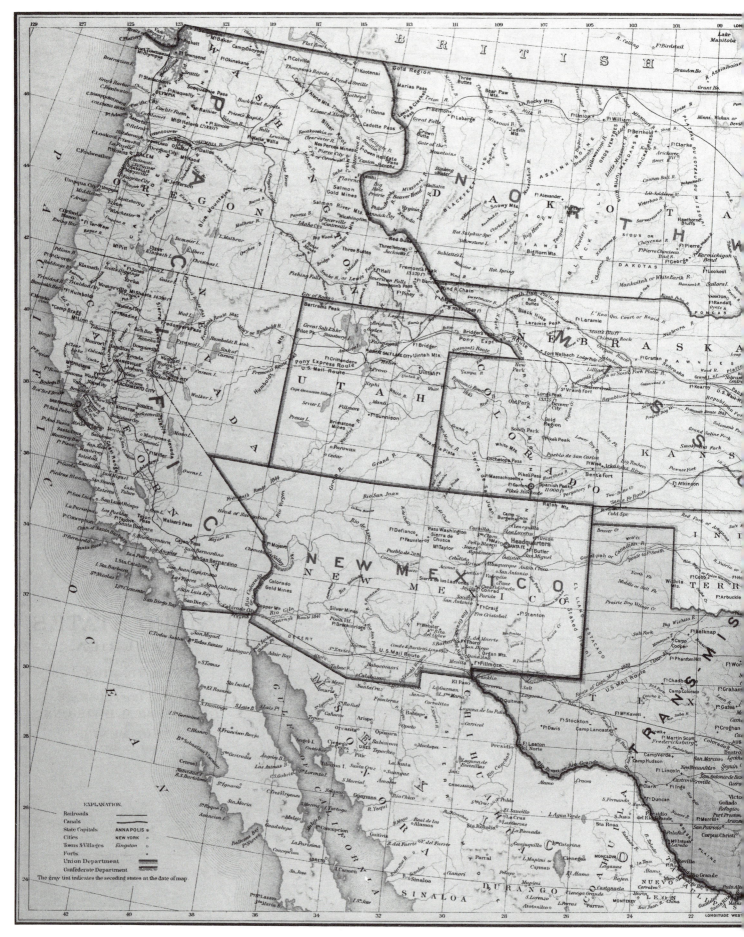

MAP
OF THE
UNITED STATES
OF AMERICA,
SHOWING THE
BOUNDARIES
OF THE
UNION AND CONFEDERATE
GEOGRAPHICAL DIVISIONS
AND
DEPARTMENTS,
DEC. 31, 1862.

✳ On Dec. 31, 1862, the Army of the Potomac (BURNSIDE) and the Army of Northern Virginia (LEE) were operating in the Vicinity of Fredericksburg Vᵃ.

✳ Department of the West ———————

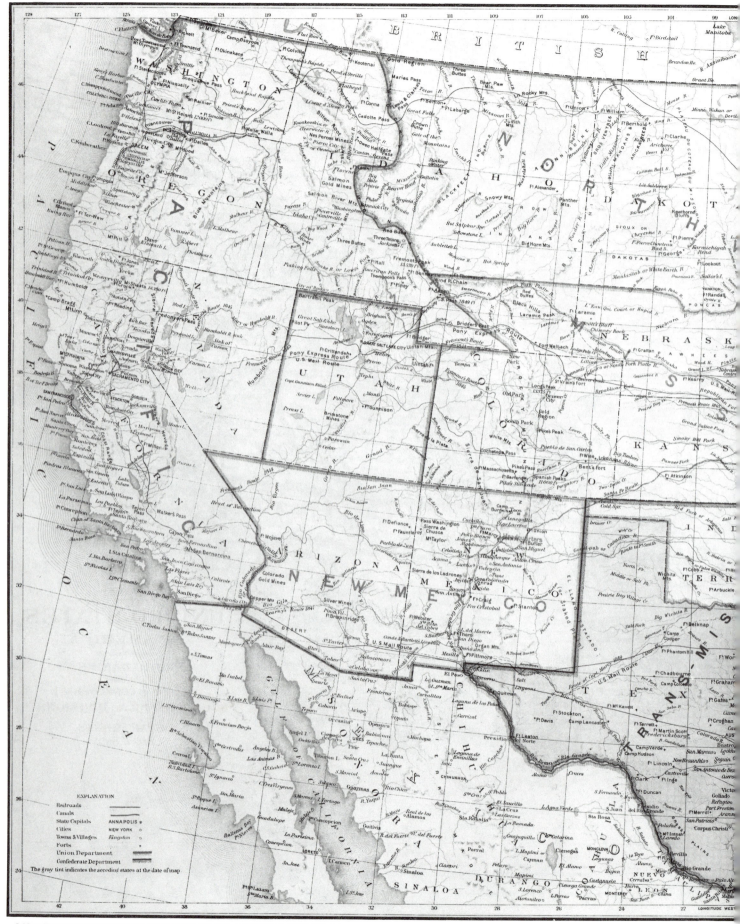

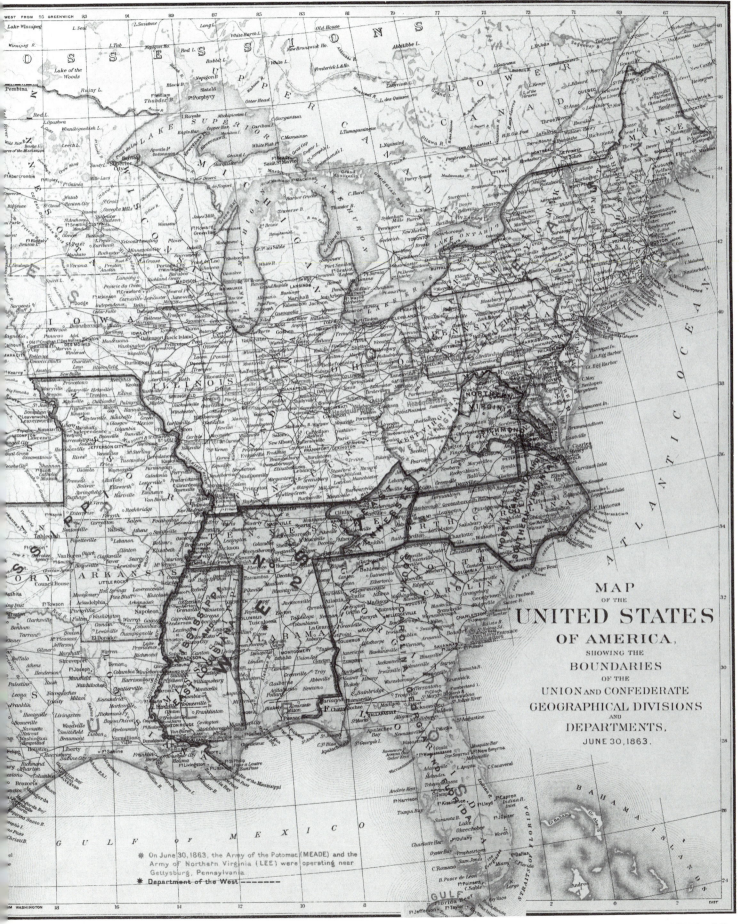

MAP
OF THE
UNITED STATES
OF AMERICA,
SHOWING THE
BOUNDARIES
OF THE
UNION AND CONFEDERATE
GEOGRAPHICAL DIVISIONS
AND
DEPARTMENTS,
JUNE 30, 1863.

＊ On June 30, 1863, the Army of the Potomac (MEADE) and the Army of Northern Virginia (LEE) were operating near Gettysburg, Pennsylvania.
＊ Department of the West ――――――

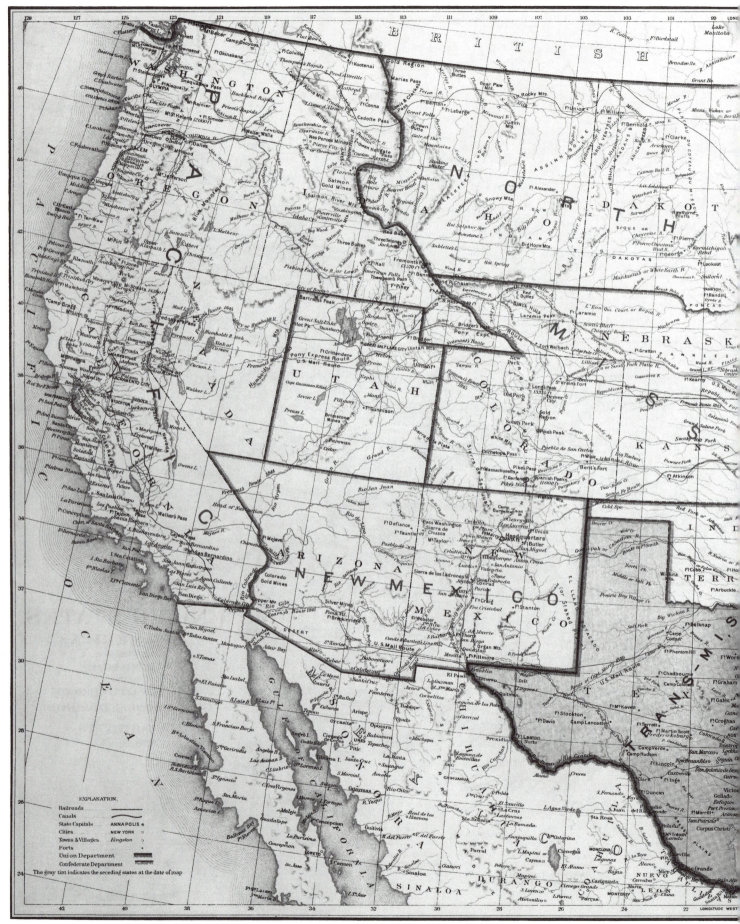

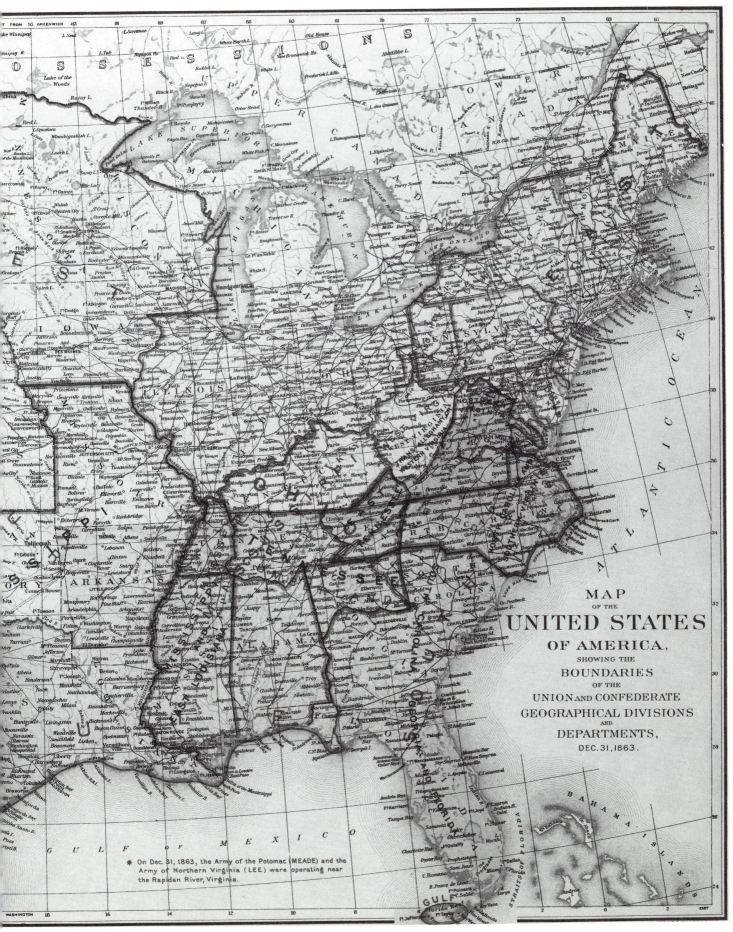

MAP
OF THE
UNITED STATES
OF AMERICA,
SHOWING THE
BOUNDARIES
OF THE
UNION AND CONFEDERATE
GEOGRAPHICAL DIVISIONS
AND
DEPARTMENTS,
DEC. 31, 1863.

✳ On Dec. 31, 1863, the Army of the Potomac (MEADE) and the
Army of Northern Virginia (LEE) were operating near
the Rapidan River, Virginia.

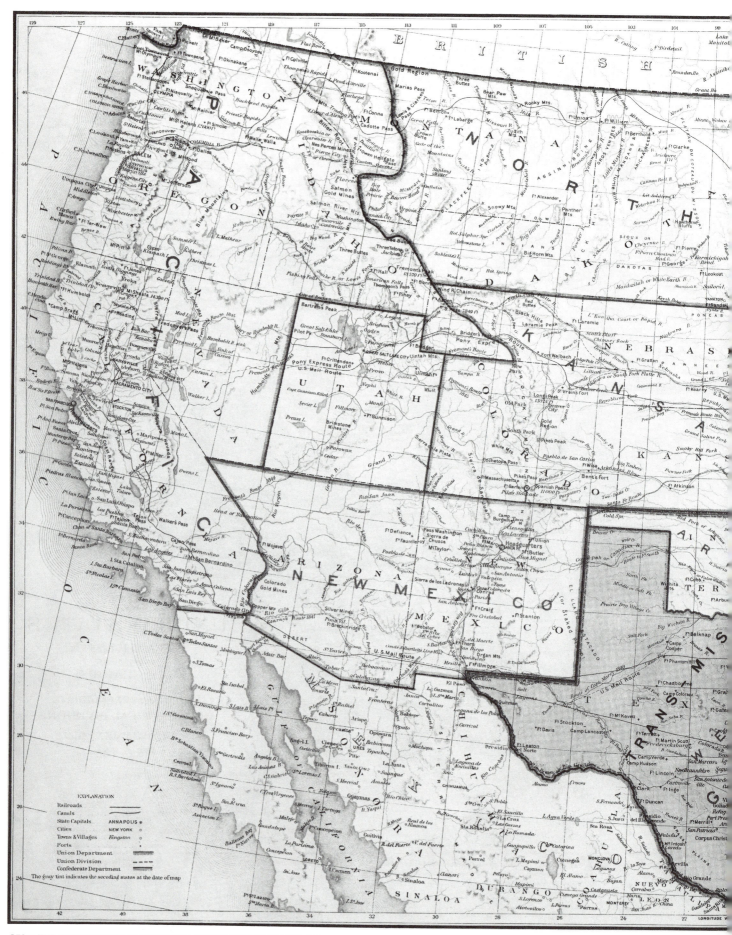

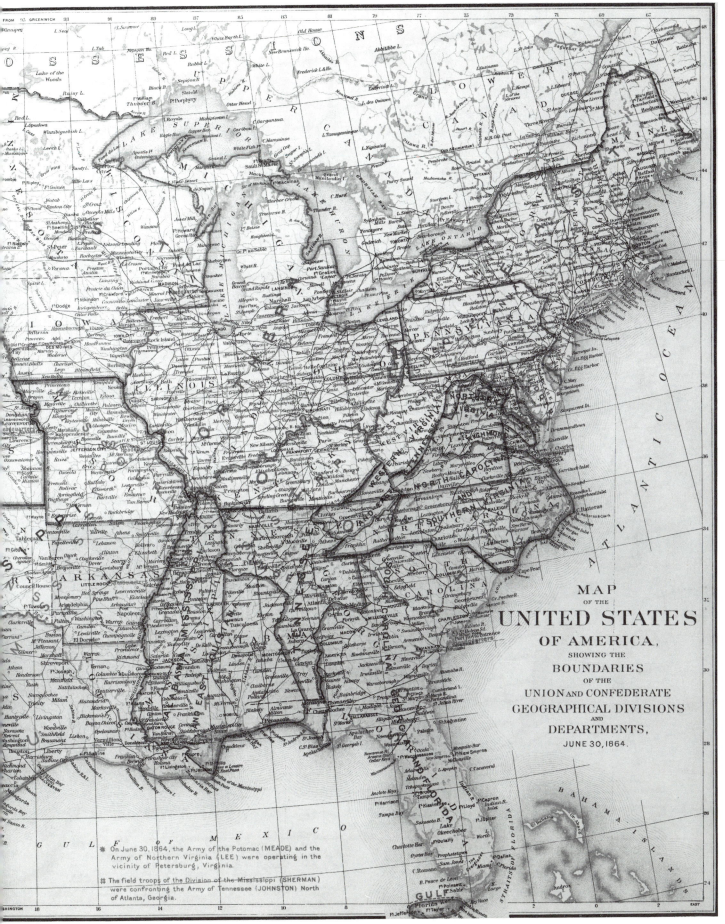

MAP
OF THE
UNITED STATES
OF AMERICA,
SHOWING THE
BOUNDARIES
OF THE
UNION and CONFEDERATE
GEOGRAPHICAL DIVISIONS
AND
DEPARTMENTS,
JUNE 30, 1864.

✻ On June 30, 1864, the Army of the Potomac (MEADE) and the
Army of Northern Virginia (LEE) were operating in the
vicinity of Petersburg, Virginia.

The field troops of the Division of the Mississippi (SHERMAN)
were confronting the Army of Tennessee (JOHNSTON) North
of Atlanta, Georgia.

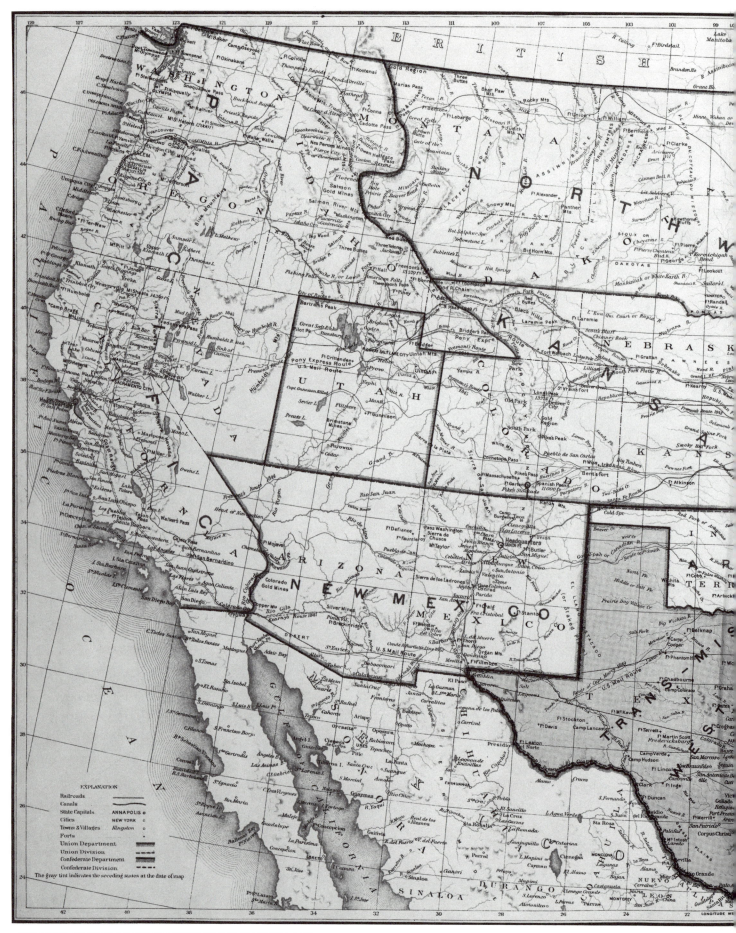

MAP
OF THE
UNITED STATES
OF AMERICA,
SHOWING THE
BOUNDARIES
OF THE
UNION AND CONFEDERATE
GEOGRAPHICAL DIVISIONS
AND
DEPARTMENTS,
DEC. 31, 1864.

✳ On Dec. 31, 1864, the Army of the Potomac (MEADE) and the
Army of Northern Virginia (LEE) were operating in the
vicinity of Petersburg, Virginia.

The Union forces under SHERMAN were located at and
about Savannah, Georgia.

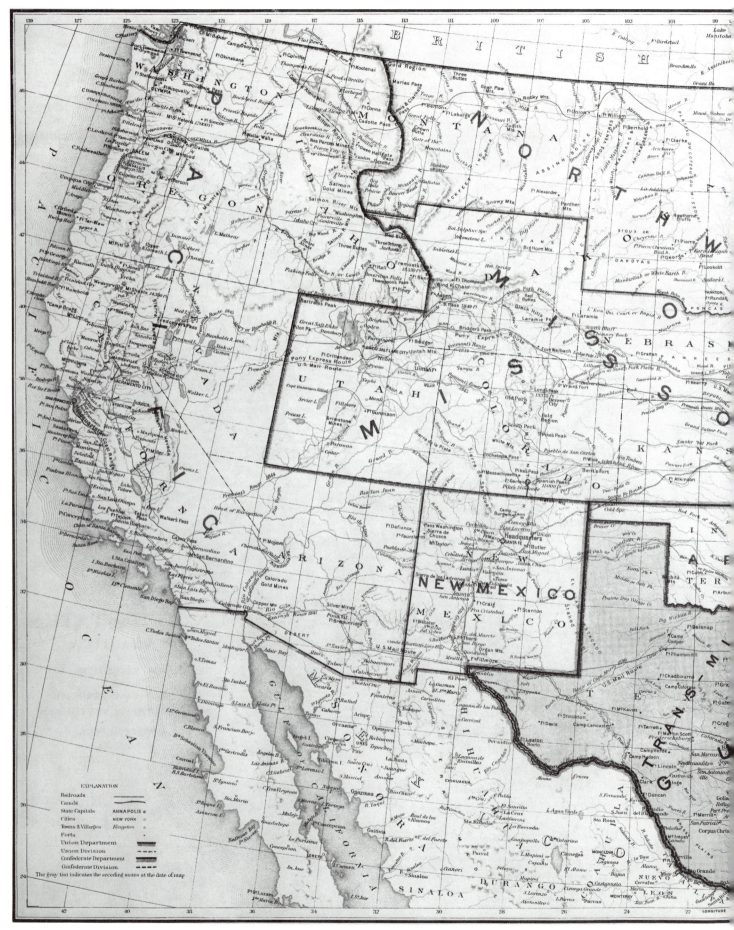

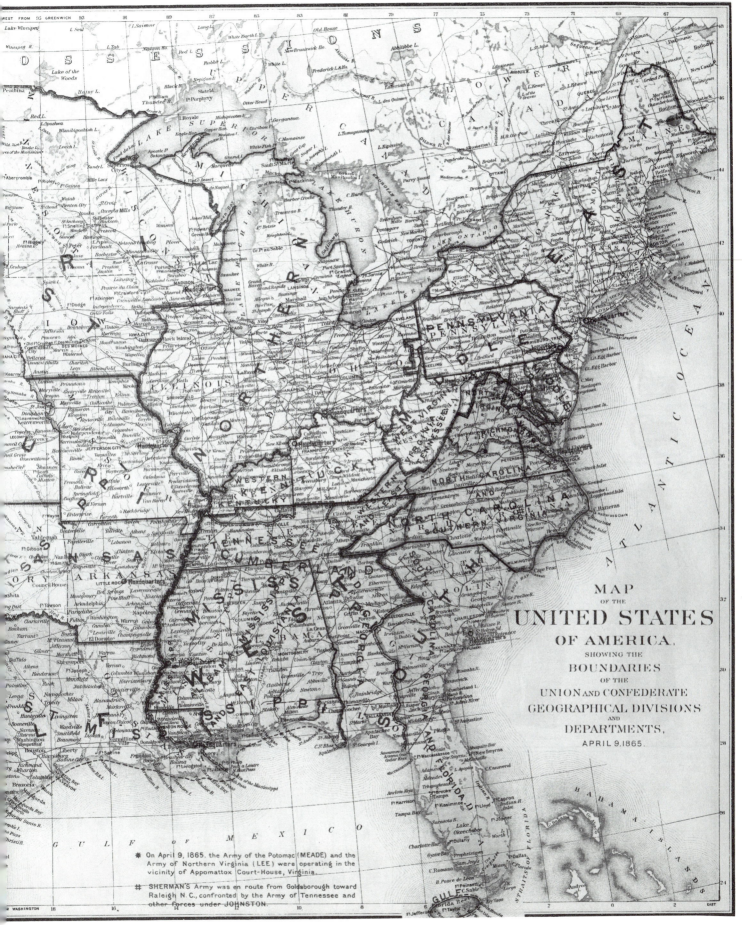

MAP
OF THE
UNITED STATES
OF AMERICA,
SHOWING THE
BOUNDARIES
OF THE
UNION AND CONFEDERATE
GEOGRAPHICAL DIVISIONS
AND
DEPARTMENTS,
APRIL 9, 1865.

✳ On April 9, 1865, the Army of the Potomac (MEADE) and the Army of Northern Virginia (LEE) were operating in the vicinity of Appomattox Court-House, Virginia.

SHERMAN'S Army was en route from Goldsborough toward Raleigh N.C., confronted by the Army of Tennessee and other forces under JOHNSTON.

Schedule to track the various Army Commands

Army Corps	Date	Commanding General	District Field of Service, etc	Under, campaign, Notes of importance
		example		
13		MG John McClernand	Vicksburg	MG Ulysses S Grant
13	July 1863	MG Edward O C Ord	Dept of Missouri	Siege of Vicksburg, MS
13		MG John Schofield		

Organization of the Army commanded by Brig. Gen. Irvin McDowell at the Battle of Bull Run, or Manassas, VA, July 21, 1861.

1st Division BG Daniel Tyler	2nd Division Col David Hunter Col Andrew Porter	3rd Division Col Samuel P Heintzelman	4th Division (Reserve) BG Theodore Runyon	5th Division Col Dixon Miles
1st Brigade Col Erasmus D Keyes 2 ME 1 CT 2 CT 3 CT	1st Brigade Col Andrew Porter 14 NY 27 NY Battalion, US Inf Battln, US Marines Battln, US Cavalry 8 NY Militia 5 US Art-Battery D	1st Brigade Col William B Franklin 5 MA 11 MA 1 MN 1 US Art-Battery I	(3 Months Volunteers) 1 NJ 2 NJ 3 NJ 4 NJ	1st Brigade Col Louis Blenker 8 NY (Vol) 29 NY 39 NY 27 PA 2 US Art-Battery A Bookwood's NY Batln
2nd Brigade BG Robert C Schenck 2 NY 1 OH 2 OH 2 US Art-Battery E	2nd Brigade Col Ambrose E Burnside 2 NH 1 RI 2 RI 79 NY	2nd Brigade Col Orlando B Wilcox 4 MI 11 NY (Fire Zouave) 2 US Art-Battery D	(3 Years Volunteers) 1 NJ 2 NJ 3 NJ 41 NY	2nd Brigade Col Thomas A Davies 16 NY 18 NY 31 NY 32 NY 2 US Art-Battery G
3rd Brigade Col William T Sherman 13 NY 69 NY 79 NY 2 WI 3 US Art-Battery E		3rd Brigade Col Oliver O Howard 3 ME 4 ME 5 ME 2 VT		
4th Brigade Col Israel B Richardson 1 MA 12 NY 2 MI 3 MI 1 US Art-Battery G 2 US Art-Battery M				

Organization of the Confederate forces combined at the Battle of Bull Run, or Manassas, VA July 21, 1861, under the command of Brig. Gen. Joseph E. Johnston, CSA.

Army of the Potomac (Afterwards the 1st Corps) BG Pierre Gustave Toutant Beauregard			Army of the Shenandoah (Johnston's Division) BG Joseph Eggleston Johnston	
1st Brigade BG Milledge L Bonham 11 NC 2 SC 3 SC 7 SC 8 SC	4th Brigade BG James Longstreet 5 NC 1 VA 11 VA 17 VA	Troops Not Brigaded 7 LA 8 LA Hampton (SC) Legion 30 VA Cavalry Harrison's Battln Cav (10) Independt Cav Cos Washington (LA) Art	1st Brigade Col Thomas J Jackson 2 VA 4 VA 5 VA 27 VA Pendleton's Battery	4th Brigade Col Arnold Elzey 1 MD Battln 3 TN 10 VA 13 VA Grove's Battery
2nd Brigade BG Richards S Ewell 5 AL 6 AL 6 LA	5th Brigade Col P St George Cooke 1 LA Battln 8 VA-7 Co 18 VA 19 VA 28 VA 49 VA-3 Co	Artillery Kemper's Battery Latham's Battery Loudoun Battery Shield's Battery Camp Pickens Battery	2nd Brigade Col F S Bartow 7 GA 8 GA 9 GA Duncan's (KY) Battln Pope's (KY) Battln Alburtis' Battery	Troops Not Brigaded 1 VA Cav 33 VA
3rd Brigade BG David R Jones 17 MS 18 MS 5 SC	6th Brigade Col Jubal A Early 13 MS 4 SC 7 VA 24 VA		3rd Brigade BG Barnard E Bee 4 AL 2 MS 11 MS 1 TN Imboden's Battery	

Organization of the Army of the Tennessee, Brig. Gen. Ulysses S. Grant, USA Commanding at the Battle of Pittsburg Landing, or Shiloh, TN. April 6-7, 1862.					
1st Division	2nd Division	3rd Division	4th Division	5th Division	6th Division
MG John A McClernand	BG Wm H Wallace	MG L Wallace	BG S A Hurlbut	BG W T Sherman	BG B M Prentiss
1st Brigade	1st Brigade	1st Brigade	1st Brigade	1st Brigade	1st Brigade
8 IL 18 IL	2 IA 7 IA	8 MO	3 IA 28 IL	6 IA 46 OH	21 MO 25 MO
11 IA 13 IA	12 IA	11 IN	32 IL	40 IL	16 WI
2 IL LT-Bat A	14 IA	24 IN	41 IL	6 IN Battery	12 MI
2nd Brigade	2nd Brigade	2nd Brigade	2nd Brigade	2nd Brigade	2nd Brigade
11 IL 20 IL	9 IL 12 IL	1 NE 23 IN	25 IN 14 IL	55 IL	18 MO
45 IL	81 OH 13 MO	58 OH	15 IL	54 OH	61 IL
48 IL	14 MO Birge Sharp	68 OH	46 IL	71 OH	16 IA
3rd Brigade	3rd Brigade	3rd Brigade	3rd Brigade	3rd Brigade	Not Brigaded
17 IL 29 IL	8 IA 7 IL	20 OH 56 OH	31 IN 44 IN	53 OH	11 IL Cav-8 Co's
43 IL 49 IL	50 IL 51 IL	76 OH	17 KY	75 OH	5 OH Bat 1 MN Bat
Carmichael's IL Cav	57 IL 58 IL	78 OH	25 KY	77 OH	18 WI 23 MO
Not Brigaded	Not Brigaded	Not Brigaded	Not Brigaded	4th Brigade	15 IA
Stewart's IL Cav	2 US Cav-Co C	1 MO Lt-Bat I	5 OH Cav-1,2 Batt	48 OH 70 OH	Unassigned Troops
1 IL Lt-Bat D	4 US Cav-Co I	9 IN Batt	13 OH Bat	72 OH	15 WI 14 WI
14 OH Bat	2 II Cav-Co A,B	5 OH Cav-3rd Batt	MO Lt-Mann's Bat	Not Brigaded	8 OH
	1 IL Lt-Bat A	11 IL Cav-3rd Batt	2 MI Bat	4 IL Cav-1,2, Batt	1 IL Lt-Bat H,I
	1 MO Lt-Bat D,H,K			1 IL Lt-Bat B,E	2 IL Lt-Bat B,F

Army of the Ohio, Maj. Gen. Don Carlos Buell, USA, Commanding at the Battle of Pittsburg Landing/Shiloh, TN.			
2nd Division	4th Division	5th Division	6th Division
BG A McD McCook	BG William Nelson	BG Thomas Crittenden	BG T J Wood
4th Brigade	10th Brigade	11th Brigade	20th Brigade
15 US Inf-1 Bat	6 OH	19 OH	64 OH
16 US Inf-1 Bat	24 OH	59 OH	65 OH
19 US Inf-1 Bat	36 IN	9 KY	13 MI
1 OH 6 IN		13 KY	51 IN
5 KY			
5th Brigade	19th Brigade	14th Brigade	21st Brigade
77 PA 29 IN	6 KY 9 IN	13 OH 11 KY	15 IN 40 IN
30 IN 34 IL	41 OH	26 KY	5 IN 24 KY
6th Brigade	22nd Brigade	Not Brigaded	
15 OH 49 OH	1 KY 2 KY	3 KY Cav	
32 IN 39 IN	20th KY	1 OH Lt-Bat G	
5 US Art-Bat H	2 IN Cav	4 US-Bat H,M	

Organization of the Confederate Army of the Mississippi Commanding at the Battle of Pittsburg Landing, or Shiloh, TN. April 6-7, 1862.					
1 Army Corps Maj Gen Leonidas Polk		2nd Army Corps Maj Gen Braxton Bragg		3rd Corps Maj Gen Wm J Hardee	Reserve Corps BG John Breckinridge
1st Division	2nd Division	1st Division	2nd Division		
BG Charles Clark	BG B F Cheatham	BG Daniel Ruggles	BG Jones M. Withers		
1st Brigade	1st Brigade	1st Brigade	1st Brigade	1st Brigade	1st Brigade
Col. R. M. Russell	BG B. R. Johnson	Col. R. L. Gibson	BG A. H. Gladden	Col. T C Hindman	Col R P Trabue
11 LA	2 TN	1 AR	21 AL	2 AR	4 AL 31 AL
12 TN	15 TN	4 LA	22 AL	5 LA	15 AR 3 KY
13 TN	154 TN	13 LA	25 AL	6 AR AR	4 KY 5 KY
22 TN	Polk's Bat.	19 LA	26 AL	3rd Confederate	Chew's TN Battln
Bankhead's Battery	Blythe's MS Battery	Bains' Battery	1 LA	Miller's Battery	Byrne's Battery
			Robertson's Bat	Swett's Battery	Lyon's Battery
2nd Brigade	2nd Brigade	2nd Brigade	2nd Brigade	2nd Brigade	2nd Brigade
BG A. P. Stewart	Col W H Stephens	BG Patton Anderson	Col J R Chalmers	BG P R Cleburne	BG J S Bowen
13 AR	7 KY	1 FL (Battln)	5 MS 7 MS	15 AR 6 MS	9 AR
4 TN	1 TN	17 LA	9 MS 10 MS	5 (35th) MS	10 AR
5 TN	6 TN	20 LA	51 TN	23 TN 24 Tn	2nd Confederate
33 TN	9 TN	9 TX	52 TN	Shoup's Art Bat	1 MO
Stanford's Battery	Smith's Bat	Hodgsons' Bat	Gage's Bat	Watson's Bat	Hudson's Bat
		3rd Brigade	3rd Brigade	3rd Brigade	3rd Brigade
		Col. Preston Pond	BG J K Jackson	BG S A M Wood	Col W S Statham
		16 LA	17 AL 18 AL	7 AL 16 AL	15 MS 22 MS
		18 LA	19 AL 2 TX	8 AR 9 AR Bat	19 TN 20 TN
		38 TN	AL Bat	3 MS Bat 27 TN	28 TN
		Cresent (LA) Reg	AR Bat	44 TN 55 TN	45 TN
		Ketchum's Bat	Giradey's Bat	Harper's Bat	Rutledge's Bat

Organization of the Federal Forces during the Valley Campaign, June 25-July 2, 1862.

Forces at Kernstown — March 23, 1862
- BG James Shields
- Col Nathan Kimball
- 1st Brigade
- Col Nathan Kimball
- 14 IN 8 OH
- 67 OH 84 PA
- 2nd Brigade
- Col Jeremiah Sullivan
- 39 IL 13 IN
- 5 OH 62 OH
- 3rd Brigade
- Col Erastus B Tyler
- 7 IN 7 OH
- 29 OH 110 PA
- Cavalry
- Col Thorton Brodhead
- 1 PA Squadron
- MD Independent Co's
- 1 WV Battalion
- 1 OH-Co A,C
- Artillery
- Col Philip Daum
- WV Art-Bat A,B
- 1 OH Art-Bat E,L

Forces at Kernstown — May 8, 1862
- BG Robert C Schenck
- Milroy's Brigade
- BG Robert H Milroy
- 25 OH 32 OH
- 73 OH 75 OH
- 2 WV 3 WV
- 1 OH-Bat I
- 12 OH Battery
- 1 WV Cavalry-3 Co's
- Schneck's Brigade
- BG Robert C Schenck
- 55 OH 82 OH
- 5 WV
- 1 CN Cavalry Battln
- 1 OH Artillery

Bank's Command — May 23-25, 1862
- MG Nathaniel Banks
- 1st Division
- 1st Brigade
- Col Dudley Donnell
- 5 CT 28 NY
- 46 PA 1 MD
- 3rd Brigade
- Col George H Gordon
- 2 MA 29 PA
- 27 IN 3 WI
- Cavalry
- 1 MI-5 Co's
- Artillery
- Capt Robert Hampton
- 1 NY-Bat F
- 4 US Art-Bat F
- Cavalry
- BG John P Hatch
- 1 ME-5 Co's
- 1 VT 5 NY
- 1 MD-5 Co's
- Unattached
- 10 ME 8 NY Cav
- PA Zouaves d'Afrique
- PA Art-Bat E

Forces at Harper's Ferry — May 26-30, 1862
- BG Rufus Saxton
- BG James Cooper
- BG John P Slough
- Col Dixon S Miles
- Cole's MD Cav
- 1 MD Cav-6 Co's
- 5 NY Cav-4 Co's
- 8 NY Cav-4 Co's
- 1 NY Art-Bat L
- 60 NY 78 NY
- 102 NY 109 PA
- 111 PA 3 DE
- 1 MD 3 MD
- MD Punrell Legion
- 1 DC
- 8 US Battalion
- 12 US Battalion
- Naval Battery

Fremont's Command — June 1-9, 1862
- MG John C Fremont
- Blenker's Division
- BG Louis Blenker
- 1st Brigade
- BG Julius Stahel
- 8 NY 39 NY
- 41 NY 45 NY
- 27 PA
- 2 NY Battery
- WV Art-Bat C
- 2nd Brigade
- Col John A Koltes
- 29 NY 68 NY
- 73 PA 13 NY Bat
- 3rd Brigade
- BG Henry Bohlen
- 54 NY 58 NY
- 74 PA 75 PA
- 1 NY Art-Bat I
- Cavalry
- 4 NY
- Unattached Cavalry
- 6 OH 3 WV-detchmnt
- Advance Brigade
- Col Gustave Cluseret
- 60 OH 8 WV
- Milroy's Brigade
- BG Robert H Milroy
- 2 WV 3 WV
- 5 WV 25 OH
- 1 WV Cav-detchment
- WV Art-Bat G
- 1 OH Art-Bat I
- 12 OH Battery
- Schenck's Brigade
- BG Robert C Schenck
- 32 OH 55 OH
- 73 OH 75 OH 82 OH
- 1 CT Cav Bttln
- 1 OH Art-Bat K
- IN Battery
- Bayard's Brigade
- BG George D Bayard
- 1 NJ Cav 1 PA Cav
- 13 PA Reserves or
- 1st Rifles Bttln

Shield's Division — June 8-9, 1862
- BG James Shields
- 1st Brigade
- Col Nathan Kimball
- 14 IN 4 OH
- 8 OH 7 WV
- 2nd Brigade
- BG Orris Ferry
- 39 IL 13 IN
- 62 OH 67 IN
- 3rd Brigade
- BG Erastus B Tyler
- 5 OH 7 OH
- 29 OH 66 OH
- 4th Brigade
- Col Samuel Carroll
- 7 IN 84 PA
- 110 PA 1 WV
- Artillery
- Col Philip Daum
- 1 VA Art-Bat A,B
- 1 OH Art-Bat H,L
- 4 US Art-Bat E
- Cavalry
- 1 OH-detachment
- 1 RI Battalion
- 1 WV detachment

Organization of the Confederate Forces, Maj. Gen. Thomas J. Jackson, CSA, Commanding during the Valley Campaign, March 23-June 10, 1852.

Forces at Kernstown — March 23, 1862
- Garnett's Brigade
- BG Richard B Garnett
- 2 VA 4 VA
- 5 VA 27 VA
- 33 VA
- Rockbridge Bat
- West Augusta Bat
- Burks' Brigade
- Col Jesse S Burks
- 21 VA 42 VA
- 1 VA (Irish) Battln
- VA Battery
- Fulkerson's Brigade
- Col Samuel V Fulkerson
- 23 VA 37 VA
- Danville Art
- Cavalry
- Col Turner Ashby
- 7 VA
- Chew's VA Battery

Forces at McDowell — May 8, 1862
- 2nd Brigade
- Col John A Campbell
- 21 VA 42 VA
- 48 VA
- 1 VA (Irish) Battln
- Third Brigade
- BG Wm Taliaferro
- 10 VA 23 VA
- 37 VA
- ARMY OF THE NORTHWEST
- BG Edward Johnson
- 1st Brigade
- Col Z T Conner
- 12 GA 25 VA
- 31 VA
- 2nd Brigade
- Col W C Scott
- 44 VA 52 VA
- 58 VA

Forces in the Operations — May 20-June 10, 1862
- 1st Brigade
- BG Charles S Winder
- 2 VA 4 VA
- 5 VA 27 VA
- 33 VA
- 2nd Brigade
- Col John A Campbell
- Col John M Patton
- 21 VA 42 VA
- 48 VA
- 1 VA (Irish) Battln
- 3rd Brigade
- Col Samuel Fulkerson
- BG Wm Taliaferro
- 10 VA 23 VA
- 37 VA
- Artillery
- Col S Crutchfield
- 6 VA Batteries

Ewell's Division
- MG Richard S Ewell
- 2nd Brigade
- Col W C Scott
- BG George H Steuart
- 44 VA 52 VA
- 58 VA 1 MD
- 4th Brigade
- BG Arnold Elzey
- Col J A Walker
- 25 VA 31 VA
- 12 GA
- 2nd Brigade
- BG Isaac R Trimble
- 21 NC 21 GA
- 15 AL 16 MS
- 8th Brigade
- BG Richard Taylor
- 6 LA 7 LA
- 8 LA 9 LA
- LA Battalion
- Cavalry
- Col Thomas Flournoy
- BG George Steuart
- BG Turner Ashby
- Col Thomas Munford
- 6 VA 7 VA
- Chew's VA Battery

Organization of the Army of the Potomac, Maj. Gen. George Brinton McClellan, USA, Commanding at the Seven Days' Battle outside Richmond, VA.

during the Peninsula Campaign, June 25-July 2, 1862.

General Headquarters
Capt James B McIntyre
Indep Co-Onedida (NY)
4 US Cav-Co A,E

Vol Engineer Brigade
BG Daniel P Woodbury
15 NY   50 NY

Reg Engineer Brigade
Capt James C Duane

Provost Guard
BG Andrew Porter
2 US Cav-7 Co's
McClellan (IL) Drgoons
93 NY
8 US-2 Co's

Headquarters Guard
Maj Granville Haller
Sturges (IL) Rifles

Men at White House
BG Silas Casey
11 PA Cav-Co BDFIK
1 NY Lt-Bat F
93 NY-Co BCDEGI

2nd Army Corps
BG Edwin V Sumner

1st Division
BG Israel Richardson

1st Brigade
Col John C Caldwell
5 NH   7 NY
61 NY   81 PA

2nd Brigade
BG Thomas F Meagher
Col Robert Nugent
Col John Burke
29 MA   63 NY
69 NY   88 NY

3rd Brigade
BG William H French
52 NY   57 NY
64 NY   66 NY
53 PA   2 DE

Artillery
Capt George Hazzard
1 NY Lt-Bat B
4 US-Bat A
4 US-Bat C

Cavalry
6 NY Cav-Co D
6 NY Cav-Co F
6 NY Cav-Co H
6 NY Cav-Co K

2nd Division
BG John Sedgwick
1st Brigade
Col Alfred Scully
15 MA   1 MN
34 NY   82 NY
MA Sharpshooter-1 Co
MN Sharpshooter-2 Co

2nd Brigade
BG William W Burns
69 PA
71 PA
72 PA
106 PA

3rd Brigade
BG Napoleon JT Dana
19 MA   20 MA
7 MI
42 NY

Artillery
Col Charles Tompkins
1 RI Lt-Bat A
1 US-Bat I

Corps Art Reserve
1 NY Lt-Bat G
1 RI Lt-Bat B,G

Cavalry
6 NY-Co D,F,H,K

3rd Army Corps
BG S P Heintzelman

2nd Division
BG Joseph Hooker

1st Brigade
BG Cuvier Grover
1 MA   11 MA
16 MA   2 NH
26 PA

2nd Brigade
BG Daniel E Sickles
70 NY   71 NY
72 NY
73 NY
74 NY

3rd Brigade
Col Joseph B Carr
5 NJ   6 NJ
7 NJ   8 NJ
9 NY

Artillery
1 NY Lt-Bat D
NY Lt Art-4th Bat
1 US Art-Bat H

3rd Division
BG Philip Kearny
1st Brigade
BG John C Robinson
20 IN   87 NY
57 PA
63 PA
105 PA

2nd Brigade
BG David B Birney
3 ME   4 ME
38 NY
40 NY
101 NY

3rd Brigade
BG Hiram G Berry
2 MI   3 MI
5 MI   1 NY
37 NY

Artillery
1 RI Lt-Bat E
2 US-Bat G

Corps Art Reserve
Capt G A De Russy
NY Lt-6 Bat
NJ Lt-2 Bat
4 US-Bat K

Cavalry
Col Wm W Averell
3 PA

4th Army Corps
BG Erasmus K Keyes

1st Division
BG Darius Couch

1st Brigade
BG Albion P Howe
55 NY   62 NY
93 PA   98 PA
102 PA

2nd Brigade
BG John Abercrombie
65 NY   67 NY
23 PA
31 PA
61 PA

3rd Brigade
BG Innis Palmer
7 MA   10 MA
36 NY
2 RI

Artillery
1 PA Lt-Bat C
1 PA Lt-Bat D

2nd Division
BG John J Peck
1st Brigade
BG Henry M Naglee
11 ME   56 NY
100 NY
52 PA
104 PA

2nd Brigade
BG Henry W Wessels
81 NY   85 NY
92 NY   96 NY
98 NY   85 NY
101 PA   103 PA

Artillery
1 NY Lt-Bat H
NY Lt-7 Bat

Corps Art Reserve
Maj Robert M West
NY Lt-8 Bat
1 PA Lt-Bat E
1 PA Lt-Bat H
5 US-Bat M

Cavalry
Col D McM Gregg
8 PA

5th Army Corps
BG Fitz John Porter

1st Division
BG George W Morrell

1st Brigade
BG John Martindale
2 ME   18 MA
22 MA   1 MI
13 NY   25 NY
MA Sharp-2nd Co

2nd Brigade
BG Charles Griffin
9 MA   4 MI
4 MI
14 NY
62 PA

3rd Brigade
BG Dan Butterfield
12 NY   17 NY
44 NY   83 PA
MI Sharp-Brady's CO

Artillery
Capt William Weeden
MA Lt-Bat C,E
1 RI Lt- Bat C
5 US-Bat D

Sharpshooters
1 US Sharpshooters
Col Hiram Berdan

2nd Division
BG George Sykes
1st Brigade
Col Robert Buchanan
3 US
4 US
12 US
14 US

2nd Brigade
MG Charles S Lovell
2 US   6 US
10 US
11 US
17 US

3rd Brigade
Col Gouveneur Warren
5 NY
10 NY

Artillery
Capt Stephen Weed
3 US-Bat L
3 US-Bat M
5 US-Bat I

3rd Division
BG John A McCall

1st Brigade
BG Truman Seymour
BG John F Reynolds
Col Seneca Simmons
Col Biddle Roberts
PA Reserves-1,2,5,8
13 PA Res-Co ABDEFK

2nd Brigade
BG George Meade
Col Albert Magilton
3 PA Res   4 PA Res
7 PA Res
11 PA Res

3rd Brigade
BG Truman Seymour
Col Feger Jackson
6 PA Res   9 PA Res
10 PA Res   12 PA Res

Artillery
1 PA Lt-Bat A
1 PA Lt-Bat B
1 PA Lt-Bat G
5 US Art-Bat C

Cavalry
Col James Childs
4 PA
Col John Farnsworth
8 IL

Artillery Reserve
Col Henry Hunt
1st Brigade (Horse)
LCol William Hays
2 US Art-Bat A,B
2 US Art-Bat M
3 US Art-Bat C
3 US Art-Bat G

2nd Brigade
LCol George Getty
1 US Art-Bat E,G,K
4 US Bat G
5 US-Bat A
5 US-Bat K

3rd Brigade
Maj Albert Arndt
NY Lt Btln-Bat A,B
NY Lt Btln-Bat C
NY Lt Btln-Bat D

4th Brigade
Maj ER Petherdridge
MD Lt-Bat A
MD Lt-Bat B

5th Brigade
Capt Howard Carlisle
2 US Art-Bat E
3 US-Bat F,K

Unattached
1 NY Lt-Bat G
NY Lt-5 Bat

Siege Train
Col Robert O Tyler
1 CT Heavy Art

6th Army Corps
BG Wm B Franklin

1st Division
BG Henry W Slocum

1st Brigade
BG George W Taylor
1 NJ
2 NJ
3 NJ
4 NJ

2nd Brigade
Col Joseph Bartlett
5 ME
16 NY
27 NY
96 PA

3rd Brigade
BG John Newton
18 NY   31 NY
32 NY
95 NY

Artillery
Capt Edward Platt
MA Lt-Bat A
NJ Lt-1 Bat
2 US-Bat D

2nd Division
BJ William F Smith
1st Brigade
BG Winfield Hancock
6 ME   43 NY
49 PA
137 PA
5 WI

2nd Brigade
BG W T H Brooks
2 VT   3VT
4 VT
5 VT
6 VT

3rd Brigade
BG John Davidson
7 ME   20 NY
33 NY   49 NY
77 NY

Artillery
Capt Romeyn B Ayres
1 NY Lt Art-Bat E
NY Lt Art-Bat 1,2
5 US Art-Bat F

Cavalry
5 PA-Co I,K

Unattached Cavalry
1 NY

Cavalry Reserve
BG St George Cooke
6 PA   6 US
1 US-Co A,C,F,H
5 US-Co A,D,F,H,I
Vol Engineer Brigade
BG Daniel Woodbury
15 NY   50 NY

Organization of the Army of Northern Virginia, Gen. Robert E. Lee, CSA, Commanding during the Seven Days' Battle outside Richmond, VA, during the Peninsula Campaign, June 25-July 2, 1862.

Jackson's Corps — MG Thomas J Jackson		Magruder's Corps — MG John B Magruder			Dept of N Carolina — MG Theophilus Holmes

Jackson's Corps
MG Thomas J Jackson

Whiting's Division
BG Wm H C Whiting

1st Texas Brigade
BG John Bell Hood
18 GA 1 TX
4 TX 5 TX
Hampton (SC) Legion

3rd Brigade
Col E McIver Law
4 AL 2 MS
11 MS 6 NC

Artillery
Balthis' Bat-
Stauton (VA) Art
Reilly's Bat-
Rowan (NC) Art

Jackson's Division
1st Brigade
BG Charles S Winder
2 VA 4 VA
5 VA 27 VA
33 VA
Carpenter's (VA) Bat
Poague's Bat-
Rockbridge (VA) Art
2nd Brigade
LCol RH Cunningham
BG John R Jones
21 VA 42 VA
48 VA 1 VA Battln
Caskie's Bat-
Hampden (VA) Art
3rd Brigade
Col S V Fulkerson
Col E T H Warren
BG Wade Hampton
10 VA 23 VA
37 VA
Wooding's Bat-
Danville (VA) Art
4th Brigade
BG Alexander R Lawton
13 GA 26 GA
31 GA 38 GA
60 GA 61 GA

Hill's Division
MG Daniel H Hill

1st Brigade
BG Robert E Rodes
3 AL 5 AL
6 AL 12 AL
26 AL

2nd Brigade
BG George Anderson
2 NC 4 NC
14 NC 30 NC

3rd Brigade
BG Samuel Garland
5 NC 12 NC
13 NC 20 NC
23 NC

4th Brigade
Col Alfred Colquitt
13 AL 6 GA
23 GA 27 GA
28 GA

5th Brigade
BG Roswell S Ripley
44 GA 48 GA
1 NC 3 NC

Artillery
Bondurant's Bat-
Jeff Davis (AL) Bat
Carter's (VA) Bat
King Willam (VA) Bat
Clark's (VA) Bat
Hardaway's (AL) Bat
Nelson's Bat-
Hanover (VA) Art
Peyton's Bat-
Orange (VA) Bat
Rhett's (SC) Art

Ewell's Divison

MG Richard S Ewell
4th Brigade
BG Arnold Elzey
Col James A Walker
BG Jubal Early
13 VA 25 VA
31 VA 44 VA
52 VA 58 VA
12 GA
7th Brigade
BG Isaac R Trimble
15 AL 21 GA
16 MS 21 NC
1 NC Battalion
Courtney's (VA) Bat
8th Brigade
BG Richard Taylor
Col I G Seymour
Col L A Stafford
6 LA 7 LA
8 LA 9 LA
1 LA Special Battln
Charlottesville (VA)
(Carrington's Bat)
Maj A R Courtney
Maryland Line
Col Bradley Johnson
1st MD
Brockenbrough's Bat-
Baltimore (MD) Art

Magruder's Corps
MG John B Magruder

1st Division
BG David R Jones

1st Brigade
BG Robert Toombs
2 GA 15 GA
17 GA

3rd Brigade
Col George Anderson
1 GA (Reg) 7 GA
8 GA 9 GA
11 GA

Artillery
Brown's Bat-
Wise (VA) Art
Hart's Bat -
Washington (SC) Art
Lane's (GA) Bat
Moody's (LA) Bat
Woolfolk's Bat-
Ashland (VA) Bat

2nd Brigade
BG Howell Cobb
16 GA 24 GA
2 LA 15 NC
Cobb's (GA) Legion
Troup (GA) Art

3rd Brigade
BG Richard Griffin
Col William Barksdale
13 MS 17 MS
18 MS 21 MS
McCarthy's (VA) Bat

Artillery
Col Stephen D Lee
Kirkpatrick's Bat-
Amherst (VA) Art
Page's Bat -
Magruder (VA) Art
Read's Bat -
Pulaski (GA) Art
Richardson's Bat

McClaw's Division
MG Lafayette McClaws

1st Brigade
BG Paul J Semmes
10 GA 53 GA
15 VA 32 VA
5 LA 10 LA
Manly's (NC) Bat

4th Brigade
BG Joseph B Kershaw
2 SC 3 SC
7 SC 8 SC
Kemper's Bat-
Alexandria (VA) Bat

Cavalry
BG James E B Stuart
1 NC 1 VA
3 VA 4 VA
5 VA 9 VA
10 VA
Cobb's (GA) Legion
Critcher's (VA) Bttln
Hampton (SC) Legion
Jeff Davis Legion
Stuart Horse Art

Longstreet Division
MG James Longstreet

1st Brigade
BG James L Kemper
1 VA 7 VA
11 VA 17 VA
24 VA
Roger's (VA) Bat

2nd Brigade
BG RH Anderson
Col M Jenkins
2 SC 4 SC
5 SC 6 SC
Palmetto (SC) Sharp

3rd Brigade
BG George E Pickett
Col Eppa Hunton
Col JB Strange
8 VA 18 VA
19 VA 28 VA
56 VA

4th Brigade
BG Cadmus M Wilcox
8 AL 9 AL
10 AL 11 AL
Anderson's (VA) Art

5th Brigade
BG Roger A Pryor
14 AL 2 FL
14 LA 1 LA Battln
3 VA
Donaldsonville(LA)Bat

6th Brigade
BG Winfld Featherston
12 MS 19 MS
2 MS Battalion
3rd Richmond Hwtzr

Artillery
Washington (LA) Bttln

Huger's Division
MG Benjamin Huger

2nd Brigade
BG William Mahone
6 VA 12 VA
16 VA 41 VA
49 VA
Grimes' (VA) Bat
Moorman's (VA) Bat

3rd Brigade
BG Ambrose R Wright
44 AL 3 GA
4 GA 22 GA
1 LA
Huger's (VA) Bat
Ross' (GA) Bat

4th Brigade
BG Lewis A Armistead
9 VA 14 VA
38 VA 53 VA
57 VA 5 VA Battln
Fauquier (VA) Bat
Turner's Bat

Hill's Light Dvsion
MG Ambrose P Hill

1st Brigade
BG Charles W Field
40 VA 47 VA
55 VA 60 VA

2nd Brigade
BG Maxcy Gregg
1 SC (Prov) 12 SC
1 SC Rifles 13 SC
14 NC

3rd Brigade
BG Joseph Anderson
Col Edward Thomas
14 GA 35 GA
45 GA 49 GA
3 LA Battln

4th Brigade
BG Lawrence O Branch
7 NC 18 NC
28 NC 33 NC
37 NC

5th Brigade
BG James J Archer
5 AL Bat 19 GA
1 TN 7 TN
14 TN

6th Brigade
BG William D Pender
16 NC 22 NC
34 NC 38 NC
2 AR Bttln
22 VA Bttln

Artillery
LCol Lewis Coleman
Andrews' (MD) Bat
Crenshaw's (VA) Bat
Bachman (SC) Bat
Fredericksburg (VA)
(Braxton's Bat)
Letcher (VA) Art
(Davidson's Bat)
Johnson's (VA) Bat
Masters' (VA) Bat
McIntosh's Bat-
Pee Dee (SC)
Pegram's (VA) Bat

Dept of N Carolina
MG Theophilus Holmes

2nd Brigade
BG Robert Ransom, Jr
24 NC 25 NC
26 NC 35 NC
48 NC 49 NC

3rd Brigade
BG Julius Daniel
43 NC 45 NC
50 NC
Burrough's Cavalry

4th Brigade
BG J G Walker
Col Van H Manning
3 AR GA Battln
27 NC 46 NC
30 VA 57 VA
Goodwyn's Cav

Artillery
Col James Deshler
Branch's (VA) Bat
Brem's (NC) Bat
French's (VA) Bat
Graham's (VA) Bat
Grandy's (VA) Bat
Lloyd's (NC) Bat

Wise's Command
BG Henry A Wise
26 VA 46 VA
4 VA Heavy Art
10 VA Cav
Andrew's (VA) Bat
Armistead's (VA) Bat
French's (VA) Bat
Rive's (VA) Bat

Reserve Artillery
BG W N Pendleton
1st VA Artillery
Col J T Brown
Coke' Bat
Macon's Bat
Richardson's Bat
Smith's Bat
Watson's Bat
Jone's Battalion
Maj H P Jones
Clark's (VA) Bat
Peyton's (VA) Bat
Rhett's (SC) Bat
Nelson's Battalion
Maj William Nelson
Huckstep's (VA) Bat
Kirkpatrick's (VA)
R C M Page's Bat
Richardson's Battln
Maj Chas Richardson
Ancell's (VA) Bat
Milledge's (GA) Bat
Woolfolk's Bat-
Ashland (VA) Art
Sumter (GA) Battln
LCol A S Cutts
Blackshear's Bat
Lane's Bat
Price's Bat
Ross' Bat
Miscellaneous
Dixie (VA) Chapman
Dabney's (VA) Bat
Dearing's Bat
Grimes' (VA) Bat
Hamilton's Bat

General Headquarters
Capt James B McIntyre
Indep Co-Oneida (NY)
4 US Cav-Co A,E

Vol Engineer Brigade
BG Daniel P Woodbury
15 NY 50 NY

Reg Engineer Brigade
Capt James C Duane

Provost Guard
Maj William H Wood
2 US Cav-Co E,F,H,K
8 US Inf-Co A,D,F,G
19 US Inf-Co G,H

Headquarters Guard
Maj Granville Haller
Sturges (IL) Rifles

Quartermaster's Guard
1 US Cav-Co B,C,H,I

Cavalry Division
BG Alfred Pleasonton
1st Brigade
Maj Charles Whiting
5 US 6 US
2nd Brigade
Col John Farnsworth
8 IL 3 IN
1 MA 8 PA
3rd Brigade
Col Richard Rush
4 PA 6 PA
4th Brigade
Col A McReynolds
1 NY 12 PA
5th Brigade
Col Benjamin Davis
8 NY 3 PA
Artillery
2 US-Bat A,B,L,M
3 US-Bat C,G
Unattached
1 ME Cav
15 PA Cav-detachment

1st Army Corps
MG Joseph Hooker
BG George G Meade

Escort
2 NY Cav-Co A,B,I,K

1st Division
BG Rufus King
BG John P Hatch
BG Abner Doubleday

1st Brigade
Col Walter Phelps
22 NY 24 NY
30 NY
84 NY (14 Militia)
2 US Sharpshooters

2nd Brigade
BG Abner Doubleday
Col Wm P Wainsworth
7 IN 76 NY
95 NY 56 PA

3rd Brigade
BG Marsena R Patrick
21 NY 23 NY
35 NY 80 NY

4th Brigade
BG John Gibbon
19 IN 2 WI
6 WI 7 WI

Artillery
Capt J Albert Monroe
NH Lt-1 Bat
1 RI Lt Bat-D
1 NY Lt Bat-L
4 US Bat-B

2nd Division
BG James B Ricketts
1st Brigade
BG Abram Duryea
97 NY 104 NY
105 NY 107 NY

2nd Brigade
Col Wm A Christian
Col Peter Lyle
26 NY 94 NY
88 NY 90 PA

3rd Brigade
BG George Hartsuff
Col Richard Coulter
16 ME 12 MA
13 MA 11 PA
83 NY-(9 Militia)

Artillery
1 PA Lt-Bat F
PA Lt-Bat C

3rd Division
BG George G. Meade
BG Truman Seymour
1st Brigade
BG Truman Seymour
Col Biddle Roberts
1 PA Res 2 PA Res
5 PA Res 6 PA Res
13 PA Res

2nd Brigade
Col Albert Magilton
3 PA Res 4 PA Res
7 PA Res 8 PA Res
3rd Brigade
Col Thomas Gallagher
LCol Robert Anderson
9 PA Res 10 PA Res
11 PA Res 12 PA Res
Artillery
1 PA Lt-Bat A,B,G
5 US-Bat C

2nd Army Corps
MG Edwin V Sumner

Escort
6 NY Cav-Co D,K

1st Division
MG Israel Richardson
BG John C Caldwell
BG Winfield S Hacock

1st Brigade
Col John C Caldwell
5 NH 7 NY
61 NY 64 NY
81 PA

2nd Brigade
BG Thomas F Meagher
Col John Burke
LCol J Wm Hofmann
29 MA 63 NY
69 NY 88 NY

3rd Brigade
Col John R Brooke
2 DE 52 NY
57 NY 66 NY
53 PA

Artillery
1 NY Lt-Bat B
4 US Bat-A,C

2nd Division
MG John Sedgwick
BG Oliver O Howard
1st Brigade
BG Willis A Gorman
15 MA 1 MN
34 NY 82 NY
MA Sharpshooter-1 Co
MN Sharpshooter-2 Co

2nd Brigade
BG Oliver O Howard
Col Joshua T Owen
Col De Witt C Baxter
69 PA 71 PA
72 PA 106 PA

3rd Brigade
BG Napoleon JT Dana
Col Norman J Hall
19 MA 20 MA
7 MI 42 NY
59 NY

Artillery
1 RI Lt-Bat A
1 US-Bat I

3rd Division
BG William H French
1st Brigade
BG Nathan Kimball
14 IN 8 OH
132 PA 7 WV

2nd Brigade
Col Dwight Morris
14 CT 108 NY
130 PA

3rd Brigade
BG Max Weber
Col John W Andrews
1 DE 5 MD
4 NY

Unattached Artillery
1 NY Lt-Bat G
1 RI Lt-Bat B,G

4th Army Corps
(attached to 6 US Corps)

1st Division
MG Darius Couch
[Assigned as 3d Div]
[6th US Arm Corps]

1st Brigade
BG Charles Devens
7 MA 10 MA
36 NY 2 RI

2nd Brigade
BG Albion P Howe
62 NY 93 PA
98 PA 102 PA
139 PA

3rd Brigade
BG John Cochrane
65 NY 67 NY
122 NY 23 PA
61 PA 82 PA

Artillery
NY Lt-3rd Bat
1 PA Lt-Bat C,D
2 US-Bat G

5th Army Corps
MG Fitz John Porter

Escort
1 ME Cav-detachment

1st Division
MG George W Morrell

1st Brigade
Col James Barnes
2 ME 18 MA
22 MA 1 MI
13 NY 25 NY
118 PA
MA Sharp-2nd Co

2nd Brigade
BG Charles Griffin
2 DC 9 MA
32 MA 4 MI
14 NY 62 PA

3rd Brigade
Col T B W Stockton
20 ME 16 MI
12 NY 17 NY
44 NY 83 PA
MI Sharp-Brady's CO

Artillery
MA Lt-Bat C
1 RI Lt- Bat C
5 US-Bat D

Sharpshooters
1 US Sharpshooters

2nd Division
BG George Sykes

1st Brigade
LC Robert Buchanan
3 US 4 US
12 US-1,2 Battalion
14 US-1,2 Battalion

2nd Brigade
MG Charles S Lovell
1 US 6 US
2 US 10 US
11 US 17 US

3rd Brigade
Col Gouverneur Warren
5 NY 10 NY

Artillery
1 US-Bat E,G
5 US-Bat I,K

3rd Division
BG Andrew Humphreys
1st Brigade
BG Erastus B Tyler
91 PA 126 PA
129 PA 134 PA

2nd Brigade
Col Peter Allabach
123 PA 131 PA
133 PA 155 PA
Artillery
1 NY Lt-Bat C
1 OH Lt-Bat L

Artillery Reserve
1 Battalion NY Lt-
Batteries A,B,C,D
NY Lt-5 Bat
1 US-Bat K
4 US-Bat G

6th Army Corps
MG Wm B Franklin

Escort
6 PA Cav-Co B,G

1st Division
MG Henry W Slocum

1st Brigade
Col Alfred Torbert
1 NJ 2 NJ
3 NJ 4 NJ

2nd Brigade
Col Joseph Bartlett
5 ME 16 NY
27 NY 96 PA

3rd Brigade
BG John Newton
18 NY 31 NY
32 NY 95 NY

Artillery
Capt Emory Upton
MD Lt-Bat A
MA Lt-Bat A
NJ Lt-Bat A
2 US-Bat D

2nd Division
MJ William F Smith

1st Brigade
BG Winfield Hancock
Col Amasa Cobb
6 ME 43 NY
49 PA 137 PA
5 WI

2nd Brigade
BG W T H Brooks
2 VT 3VT
4 VT 5VT
6 VT

3rd Brigade
Col William Irwin
7 ME 20 NY
33 NY 49 NY
77 NY

Artillery
Capt Romeyn B Ayres
MD Lt-Bat B
NY Lt-1 Bat
5 US-Bat F

9th Army Corps
MG Ambrose Burnside
MG Jesse Reno
BG Jacob D Cox

Escort
1 ME Cav-Co G

1st Division
BG Orlando Willcox

1st Brigade
Col Benjamin Christ
28 MA 17 MI
79 NY 50 PA

2nd Brigade
Col Thomas Welsh
8 MI 46 NY
45 PA 100 PA

Artillery
MA Lt-8 Bat
2 US-Bat E

2nd Division
BG Samuel D Sturgis
1st Brigade
BG James Nagle
2 MD 6 NH
9 NH 48 PA

2nd Brigade
BG Edward Ferrero
21 MA 35 MA
51 NY 51 PA

Artillery
PA Lt-Bat D
4 US-Bat E

3rd Division
BG Isaac P Rodman
1st Brigade
Col H S Fairchild
9 NY 89 NY
103 NY

2nd Brigade
Col Edward Harland
8 CT 11 CT
16 CT 4 RI

Artillery
5 US-Bat A

Kanawha Division
BG Jacob D Cox
Col Eliakim Scammon
1st Brigade
Col Eliakim Scammon
Col Hugh Ewing
12 OH 23 OH
30 OH
WV Cav-Gilmore's
WV Cav-Harrison's

2nd Brigade
Col George Crook
11 OH 28 OH
36 OH
Chicago Dragoons
KY Lt-Simmond's

Unattached
6 NY Cav-(8 Co's)
OH Cav-3rd Indep
3 US-Bat L,M

12th Army Corps
MG Joseph Mansfield
BG Alpheus Williams

Escort
1 MI Cav-Co L

1st Division
BG Alpheus Williams
BG Samuel Crawford
BG George Gordon

1st Brigade
BG Samuel Crawford
Col Joseph Knipe
5 CT 10 ME
28 NY 46 PA
124 PA 125 PA
128 PA

3rd Brigade
BG George Gordon
Col Thomas Ruger
27 IN 2 MA
Zouaves d'Afrique-PA
3 WI

2nd Division
BG George S Greene
1st Brigade
LCol Hector Tyndale
Maj Orrin J Crane
5 OH 7 OH
29 OH 66 OH
28 PA

2nd Brigade
Col Henry Stainrook
3 MD 102 NY
109 PA 111 PA

3rd Brigade
Col Wm B Goodrich
LCol Jonathan Austin
3 DE 60 NY
Purnell Legion-MD
78 NY

Artillery
Capt Clermont Best
ME Lt-4,6 Bat
1 NY-Bat M
NY Lt-10 Bat
PA Lt-Bat E,F
4 US-Bat F

Organization of the Confederate Army of Northern Virginia, Gen. Robert E. Lee, CSA, Commanding during the Battle of Antietam, Sharpsburg, MD, or the Maryland Campaign, September, 1862.

Longstreet's Corps MG James Longstreet			Jackson's Corps MG Thomas J Jackson			
McLaws Division MG Lafayette McLaws	**Jones' Division** BG David R Jones	**Hood's Division** BG John Bell Hood	**Ewell's Division** BG Alex R Lawton		**Hill's Division** MG Daniel H Hill	**Nelson's Battalion** Maj William Nelson
Kershaw's Brigade BG Joseph B Kershaw 2 SC 3 SC 7 SC 8 SC	Toombs' Brigade BG Robert Toombs Col Henry L Benning 2 GA 15 GA 17 GA 20 GA	Hood's Brigade Col W T Wofford 18 GA 1 TX 4 TX 5 TX Hampton (SC) Legion	BG Jubal A Early Lawton' Brigade Col M Douglass Maj J H Lowe Col John H Lamar 13 GA 26 GA 31 GA 38 GA 60 GA 61 GA	Thomas' Brigade Col Edward L Thomas 14 GA 35 GA 45 GA 49 GA	Ripley's Brigade BG Roswell S Ripley Col George Doles 4 GA 44 GA 1 NC 3 NC	Amherst (VA) Art - (Kirkpatrick's Bat) Fluvanna (VA) Art - (Ancell's Bat) Huckstep's (VA) Bat Johnson's (VA) Bat Milledge (GA) Art- (Milledge's Bat)
Cobb's Brigade BG Howell Cobb LCol C C Sanders LCol William MacRae 16 GA 24 GA Cobb's (GA) Legion 15 NC	Drayton's Brigade BG Thomas F Drayton 50 GA 51 GA 15 SC	Law's Brigade Col E McIver Law 4 AL 2 MS 11 MS 6 NC	Early's Brigade BG Jubal A Early Col William Smith 13 VA 25 VA 31 VA 44 VA 49 VA 52 VA 58 VA	Artillery Maj R L Walker Branch (NC) Art (A C Latham's Bat) Crenshaw's (VA) Bat Fredericksburg (VA) (Braxton's Bat)	Rodes' Brigade BG Robert E Rodes 3 AL 5 AL 6 AL 12 AL 26 AL	Miscellaneous Cutshaw's (VA) Bat Dixie (VA) Art - (Chapman's Bat) Magruder (VA) Art - (T J Page, Jr's Bat) Rice's (VA) Art
Semmes' Brigade BG Paul J Semmes 10 GA 53 GA 15 VA 32 VA	Pickett's Brigade Col Eppa Hunton BG Richard B Garnett 8 VA 18 VA 19 VA 28 VA 56 VA	Artillery Maj B W Frobel German Art (SC) Palmetto Art (SC) Rowan Art (NC)	Trimble's Brigade Col James A Walker 15 AL 12 GA 21 GA 21 NC 1 NC Battalion	Letcher (VA) Art (Davidson's Bat) Middlesex (VA) Art (Fleet's Bat) Pee Dee (SC) Art (McIntosh's Bat)	Garland's Brigade BG Samuel Garland Col D K McRae 5 NC 12 NC 13 NC 20 NC 23 NC	Thomas (VA) Art - (E J Anderson's Bat)
Barksdale Brigade BG William Barksdale 13 MS 17 MS 18 MS 21 MS	Kemper's Brigade BG James L Kemper 1 VA 7 VA 11 VA 17 VA 24 VA	Evan's Brigade BG Nathan G Evans Col P F Stevens 17 SC 18 SC 22 SC 23 SC Holcombe (SC) Legion Macbeth (SC) Art	Hay's Brigade BG Harry T Hays 5 LA 6 LA 7 LA 8 LA 14 LA	Purcell (VA) Art (Pegram's Bat) Jackson's Division BG John R Jones	Anderson's Brigade BG George Anderson Col R T Bennett 2 NC 4 NC 14 NC 30 NC	Cavalry MJ James E B Stuart Hampton's Brigade BG Wade Hampton 1 NC 2 SC Cobb's (GA) Legion Jeff Davis Legion 10 VA
Artillery Maj S P Hamilton Col Henry C Cabell Manly's (NC) Bat Pulaski (GA) Bat Richmond (Fayette) Bat Richmond Howitzrs-1 Co Troup (GA) Art	Jenkin's Brigade Col Joseph Walker 1 SC 2 SC 5 SC 6 SC 4 SC Battalion Palmetto (SC) Sharp	Artillery Washington (LA) Art Col J B Walton Co 1,2,3,4 Lee's Battalion Col Stephen D Lee Ashland (VA) Art Bedford (VA) Art Brooks (SC) Art Eubank's (VA) Bat Madison (LA) Lt Art Parker's (VA) Bat	Artillery Maj A R Courtney Charlottesville (VA) (Carrington's Bat) Chesapeake (MD) Art (Brown's Bat) Courtney (VA) Art (Latimer's Bat) Johnson's (VA) Bat Louisiana Guard Art (D'Aquin's Bat) 1 MD Bat-(Dement's) Stauton (VA) Art (Balthis Bat)	BG William E Starke Col A J Grigsby Winder's Brigade Col A J Grigsby LCol R D Gardner Maj H J Williams 2 VA 4 VA 5 VA 27 VA 33 VA	Colquitt's Brigade Col Alfred Colquitt 13 AL 6 GA 23 GA 27 GA 28 GA	Lee's Brigade BG Fitzhugh Lee 1 VA 3 VA 4 VA 5 VA 9 VA
Anderson's Division MG Richard Anderson Wilcox's Brigade Col Alfred Cumming 8 AL 9 AL 10 AL 11 AL	Anderson's Brigade Col George Anderson 1 GA (Reg) 7 GA 8 GA 9 GA 11 GA			Taliaferro's Brigade Col E T H Warren Col James W Jackson Col James Sheffield 47 AL 48 AL 10 VA 23 VA 37 VA	Artillery Maj S F Pierson Hardaway's (AL) Bat Jeff Davis (AL) Bat Jones' (VA) Bat King Willam (VA) Bat	Robertson's Brigade BG Beverly Robertson Col Thomas T Munford 2 VA 6 VA 7 VA 12 VA 17 VA Battln
Mahone's Brigade Col William A Parham 6 VA 12 VA 16 VA 41 VA 61 VA	Artillery Fauquier (VA) Art - (Stribling's Bat) Loudoun (VA) Art - (Roger's Bat) Turner (VA) Art - (Leake's Bat) Wise (VA) Art - (J S Brown's Bat)		Hill's Light Division MG Ambrose P Hill Branch's Brigade BG Lawrence O Branch Col James H Lane 7 NC 18 NC 28 NC 33 NC 37 NC	Jones' Brigade Col Bradley Johnson BG John R Jones Capt John E Penn Capt A C Page Capt R W Withers 21 VA 42 VA 48 VA 1 VA Battln	Reserve Artillery BG William Pendleton Brown's Battalion Col J Thompson Brown Powhatan-(Dance's) Rchmnd Hwtzr-2 Co (Watson's Bat) Rchmnd Hwtzr-3 Co (Smith's Bat) Salem - (Hupp's Bat) Williamsburg Art (Coke's Bat)	Horse Artillery Capt John Pegram Chew's (VA) Bat Hart's (SC) Bat Pelham's (VA) Bat
Featherston's Brigade BG Winfld Featherston Col Carnot Posey 12 MS 16 MS 19 MS 2 MS Battalion			Gregg's Brigade BG Maxcy Gregg 1 SC (Prov) 12 SC 1 SC Rifles 13 SC 14 NC	Starke's Brigade BG William E Starke Col Leroy A Stafford Col Edmund Pendleton 1 LA 2 LA 9 LA 10 LA Coppens' (LA) Battln 15 LA	Cutts' Battalion LCol A S Cutts Blackshears (GA) Bat Irwin (GA) Art - (Lane's Bat) Lloyd's (NC) Bat Patterson's (GA) Bat Ross' (GA) Bat	
Armistead's Brigade BG Lewis A Armistead Col J G Hodges 9 VA 14 VA 38 VA 53 VA 57 VA	Walker's Division BG John Walker Walker's Brigade Col Van H Manning Col E D Hall 3 AR 27 NC 46 NC 48 NC 30 VA French's (VA) Bat		Field's Brigade Col J M Brockenbrough 40 VA 47 VA 55 VA 22 VA	Artillery Maj L M Shumaker Alleghany (VA) Art (Carpenter's Bat) Brockenbrough (MD) Danville (VA) Art (Wooding's Bat)	Jones' Battalion Maj H P Jones Morris (VA) Art - (R C M Page's Bat) Orange (VA) Art - (Peyton's Bat) Turner's (VA) Bat Wimbish's (VA) Bat	
Pryor's Brigade BG Roger A Pryor 14 AL 2 FL 8 FL 3 VA	Ransom's Brigade BG Robert Ransom, Jr 24 NC 25 NC 35 NC 49 NC Branch's (VA) Art		Archer's Brigade BG James J Archer Col Peter Turney 5 AL Bat 19 GA 1 TN 7 TN 14 TN	Hampden (VA) Art (Caskie's Bat) Lee (VA) Bat (Raine's Bat) Rockbridge (VA) Art (Poague's Bat)		
Wright's Brigade BG Ambrose R Wright 44 AL 3 GA 22 GA 48 GA			Pender's Brigade BG William D Pender Col R H Brewer 16 NC 22 NC 34 NC 38 NC			
Artillery Maj John S Saunders Donaldsonville (LA) - Art-(Maurin's Bat) Huger's (VA) Bat Moorman's (VA) Bat Thompson's (Grimes) - VA Bat						

Organization of the Army of the Potomac at the Battle of Fredericksburg, VA, Dec. 11-15, 1862, Maj. Gen. Ambrose E Burnside, USA, Commanding.

Escort, etc.	Right Grand Division MG Edwin V Sumner	9th Army Corps BG Orlando B. Wilcox	Center Grand Division MG Joseph Hooker		Left Grand Division MG William B Franklin Escort - 6 PA Cav	
Onedida (NY) Cav 1 US Cav-(detach) 4 US Cav-Co A,E	2nd Army Corps MG Darius Couch	Escort 6 NY Cav-Co B,C	3rd Army Corps BG George Stoneman	5th Army Corps BG Daniel Butterfield	1st Army Corps MJ John F Reynolds	6th Army Corps MJ Wm F Smith
	1st Division BG Winfield Hancock	1st Division BG William W Burns	1st Division BG David Birney	1st Division BG Charles Griffin	1st Division BG Abner Doubleday	1st Division BG Wm T H Brooks
Provost Guard BG Marsena Patrick McClellan Dragns-Co A McClellan Dragns-Co B 2 US Cav 8 US Inf 9 NY Inf 23 NY Inf	1st Brigade BG John Caldwell Col George Schauk 5 NH 7 NY 61 NY 64 NY 81 PA 145 PA	1st Brigade Col Orlando M Poe 2 MI 17 MI 20 MI 79 NY	1st Brigade BG John C Robinson 20 IN 63 PA 68 PA 105 PA 114 PA 141 PA	1st Brigade Col James Barnes 2 ME 18 MA 22 MA 1 MI 13 NY 25 NY 118 PA-MA Sharp/Co 2	1st Brigade Col Walter Phelps 22 NY 24 NY 30 NY 84 NY 2 US Sharp	1st Brigade Col Alfred Tolbert 1 NJ 2 NJ 3 NJ 4 NJ 15 NJ 23 NJ
Vol Engineer Brig BG Daniel Woodbury 15 NY 50 NY	2nd Brigade BG Thomas F Meagher 28 MA 63 NY 69 NY 88 NY 116 PA	2nd Brigade Col Benjamin Christ 29 MA 8 MI 27 NJ 46 NY 50 PA	2nd Brigade BG J H Hobard Ward 3 ME 4 ME 38 NY 40 NY 55 NY 57 PA 99 PA	2nd Brigade Col Jacob B Sweitzer 9 MA 32 MA 4 MI 14 NY 62 PA	2nd Brigade Col James Gavin 7 IN 76 NY 95 NY 56 PA	2nd Brigade Col Henry L Cake 5 ME 16 NY 27 NY 121 NY 96 PA
Battalion US Eng Lieut Charles Cross	3rd Brigade Col Samuel K Zook 27 CT 2 DE 52 NY 57 NY 66 NY 53 PA	3rd Brigade Col Daniel Leasure 36 MA 45 PA 100 PA	3rd Brigade BG Hiram G Berry 17 ME 3 MI 5 MI 1 NY 37 NY 101 NY	3rd Brigade Col T B W Stockton 20 ME 16 MI 12 NY 17 NY 44 NY MI Sharp-Brady	3rd Brigade Col Wm F Rogers 21 NY 23 NY 35 NY 80 NY	3rd Brigade BG David A Russell 18 NY 31 NY 32 NY 95 NY
					4th Brigade BG Solomon Meredith Col Lysander Cutler 19 IN 24 MI 2 WI 6 WI 7 WI	
Artillery BG Henry J Hunt	Artillery 1 NY Lt-Bat B 4 US Art-Bat C	Artillery 1 NY Lt-Bat D 3 US Bat-L,M	Artillery Capt George Randolph 1 RI Lt-Bat E 3rd US Art-Bat F,K	Artillery MA Lt-3rd,5th Bat 1 RI Lt-Bat C 5 US Art-Bat D 1 US Sharp	Artillery Capt George Gerrish Capt John Reynolds NH Lt-1st Bat 4 US Art-Bat B	Artillery MD Lt-Bat A MA Lt-1st Bat (A) NJ Lt-1st Bat 2 US Art-Bat D
Artillery Reserve NY Lt-5 Bat 1 Battln NY-Bat A,B,C,D 1 US Art-Bat K 2 US Art-Bat A 4 US Art-Bat G 5 US Art-Bat K 32 MA Inf	2nd Division BG Oliver O Howard 1st Brigade BG Alfred Scully 19 ME 15 MA 34 NY 82 NY 1 MN MA Sharp MN Sharp-2nd Co	2nd Division BG Samuel D Sturgis 1st Brigade BG James Nagle 2 MD 6 NH 9 NH 48 PA 7 RI 12 RI	2nd Division BG Daniel E Sickles 1st Brigade BG Joseph B Carr 1 MA 11 MA 16 MA 2 NH 11 NJ 26 PA	2nd Division BG George Sykes 1st Brigade LC Robert C Buchanan 3 US 4 US 12 US-1st,2nd Battln 14 US-1st,2nd Battln	2nd Division BG John Gibbon BG Nelson Taylor 1st Brigade Col Adrian R Root 16 ME 94 NY 104 NY 105 NY 107 PA	2nd Division BG Albion P Howe 1st Brigade BG Calvin E Pratt 6 ME 43 NY 49 PA 119 PA 5 WI
Unattached Artillery Maj Thomas Trumbull 1 CT Heavy Art-Bat B,M	2nd Brigade Col Joshua T Owen 69 PA 71 PA 72 PA 106 PA	2nd Brigade BG Edward Ferrero 21 MA 35 MA 11 NH 51 NY 51 PA	2nd Brigade Col George B Hall 70 NY 71 NY 72 NY 73 NY 74 NY 120 NY	2nd Brigade Maj George L Andrews Maj Charles S Lovell 6 US 7 US 10 US 11 US 1,2,17,19 US Battln	2nd Brigade Col Peter Lyle 12 MA 26 NY 90 PA 136 PA	2nd Brigade Col Henry Whiting 26 NJ 2 VT 3 VT 4 VT 5 VT 6 VT
	3rd Brigade Col Norman J Hall Col William R Lee 19 MA 20 MA 7 MI 42 NY 59 NY 127 PA		3rd Brigade BG Joseph W Revere 5 NJ 6 NJ 7 NJ 8 NJ 2 NY 115 PA	3rd Brigade BG Gouverneur Warren 5 NY 140 NY 146 NY	3rd Brigade BG Nelson Taylor Col Samuel Leonard 13 MA 83 NY 97 NY 11 PA 88 PA	3rd Brigade BG Francis L Vinton Col Robert F Taylor BG Thomas H Neill 21 NY 20 NY 33 NY 49 NY 77 NY
	Artillery 1 RI Lt-Bat A 1 RI Lt-Bat B	Artillery 2 NY Lt-Bat L PA Lt-Bat D 1 RI Lt-Bat D 4 US Art-Bat E	Artillery Capt James E Smith NJ Lt-2nd Bat NY Lt-4th Bat 1 US Art-Bat H 4 US-Bat K	Artillery 1 OH Lt-Bat L 5 US-Bat L	Artillery Capt George Leppien ME Lt-2nd Bat ME Lt-5th Bat PA Lt-Bat C 1 PA Lt-Bat F	Artillery MD Lt-Bat B NY Lt-1st Bat NY Lt-3rd Bat 5th US Art-Bat F
	3rd Division BG William H French 1st Brigade BG Nathan Kimball Col John S Mason 14 IN 24 NJ 28 NJ 4 OH 8 OH 7 WV	3rd Division BG George W Getty 1st Brigade Col Rush C Hawkins 10 NH 13 NH 25 NY 9 NY 89 NY 103 NY	3rd Division BG Amiel W Whipple 1st Brigade BG A Sanders Platt Col Emlen Franklin 86 NY 124 NY 122 PA	3rd Division BG Andrew A Humphreys 1st Brigade BG Erastus B Tyler 91 PA 126 PA 129 PA 134 PA	3rd Division BG George G Meade 1st Brigade Col Wm Sinclair Col Wm McCandless 1st,2nd PA Reserves 6th,13th PA Reserves 121 PA	3rd Division BG John Newton 1st Brigade BG John Cochrane 65 NY 67 NY 122 NY 23 PA 61 PA 82 PA
	2nd Brigade Col Oliver H Palmer 14 CT 108 NY 130 PA	2nd Brigade Col Edward Harland 8 CT 11 CT 15 CT 16 CT 21 CT 4 RI	2nd Brigade Col Samuel S Carroll 12 NH 163 NY 84 NY 110 PA	2nd Brigade Col Peter H Allabach 123 PA 131 PA 133 PA 155 PA	2nd Brigade Col Albert Magilton 3rd,4th PA Reserves 7th,8th PA Reserves 142 PA	2nd Brigade BG Charles Devens 7 MA 10 MA 37 MA 36 MA 2 RI
	3rd Brigade Col John W Andrews LC William Jameson LC John W Marshall 1 DE 4 NY 10 NY 132 PA	Artillery 2 US Art-Bat E 5 US Art-Bat A Cavalry Division BG Alfred Pleasonton 1st Brigade BG John F Farnsworth 8 IL 3 IN 8 NY	3rd Brigade NY Lt-10th Bat NY Lt-11th Bat 1 OH Lt-Bat H	Artillery 1 NY Lt-Bat C 1 US Art-Bat E,G Cavalry Brigade BG William W Averell 1 MA 3 PA 4 PA 5 US	3rd Brigade BG C Geder Jackson Col Joseph Fisher LC Robert Anderson 5,9 PA Reserves 10,11 PA Reserves 12th PA Reserves	3rd Brigade Col Thomas Rowley BG Frank Wheaton 62 NY 93 PA 98 PA 102 PA 139 PA
	Artillery 1 NY Lt-Bat G 1 RI Lt-Bat G				Artillery 1 PA Lt-Bat A 1 PA Lt-Bat B 1 PA Lt-Bat G 5 US Art-Bat C	Artillery 1 PA Lt-Bat C 1 PA Lt-Bat D 1 PA Lt-Bat D 2 US Art-Bat G
	Artillery Reserve Capt Charles Morgan 1 US Art-Bat I 4 US Art-Bat A	2nd Brigade Col David McM Gregg Col Thomas C Devin 6 NY 8 PA 6 US		Artillery 2 US Art-Bat B,L		Cavalry Division BG George D Bayard Col David McM Gregg 1 ME 1 NJ 2 NY 10 NY 1 PA DC Indep Co
		Artillery 2 US Art-Bat M				

Organization of the Confederate Army of Northern Virginia, Gen. Robert Edward Lee, CSA, Commanding during the Battle of Fredericksburg, VA, December 11-15, 1862.

1st Corps — LG James Longstreet

McLaws Division — MG Lafayette McLaws

Kershaw's Brigade — BG Joseph B Kershaw
2 SC 3 SC
7 SC 8 SC
15 SC 3 SC

Barksdale Brigade — BG William Barksdale
13 MS 17 MS
18 MS 21 MS

Cobb's Brigade — BG T R R Cobb / Col Robert McMillan
16 GA 18 GA
24 GA
Cobb's (GA) Legion

Semmes' Brigade — BG Paul J Semmes
10 GA 50 GA
51 GA 53 GA

Artillery — Col Henry C Cabell
Manly's (NC) Bat
Reads' (GA) Bat
Richmond Howitzrs-1 Co
Troup (GA) Art

Anderson's Division — MG Richard Anderson

Wilcox's Brigade — BG Cadmus M Wilcox
8 AL 9 AL
10 AL 11 AL
14 AL

Mahone's Brigade — BG William Mahone
6 VA 12 VA
16 VA 41 VA
61 VA

Featherston's Brigade — BG Winfld Featherston
12 MS 16 MS
19 MS 48 MS

Wright's Brigade — BG Ambrose R Wright
3 GA 22 GA
48 GA 2 GA Battln

Perry's Brigade — BG Edward A Perry
2 FL 5 FL
8 FL

Artillery
Donaldsonville (LA) - Art-(Maurin's Bat)
Huger's (VA) Bat
Lewis' (VA) Bat
Norfolk (VA) Lt Blues

Pickett's Division — MG George E Pickett

Garnett's Brigade — BG Richard B Garnett
8 VA 18 VA
19 VA 28 VA
56 VA

Armistead's Brigade — BG Lewis A Armistead
9 VA 14 VA
38 VA 53 VA
57 VA

Kemper's Brigade — BG James L Kemper
1 VA 3 VA
7 VA 11 VA
24 VA

Jenkin's Brigade — BG Micah Jenkins
1 SC 2 SC
5 SC 6 SC
Hampton Legion
Palmetto Sharp

Corse's Brigade — BG Montgomery Corse
15 VA 17 VA
30 VA 32 VA

Artillery
Dearing's (VA) Bat
Faquier (VA) Art-(Stribling's Bat)
Richmond (Fayette)-(Macon's) Bat

Hood's Division — MG John Bell Hood

Law's Brigade — BG E McIver Law
4 AL 44 AL
6 NC 54 NC
57 NC

Robertson's Brigade — BG Jerome B Robertson
3 AR 1 TX
4 TX 5 TX

Anderson's Brigade — BG George T Anderson
1 GA 7 GA
8 GA 9 GA
11 GA

Toomb's Brigade — Col Henry L Benning
2 GA 15 GA
17 GA 20 GA

Artillery
German Art (SC)
Palmetto Art (SC)
Rowan Art (NC)

Ransom's Division — BG Robert Ransom, Jr

Ransom's Brigade — BG Robert Ransom, Jr
24 NC 25 NC
35 NC 49 NC
Branch's (VA) Bat

Cooke's Brigade — BG John R Cooke / Col E D Hall
15 NC 27 NC
46 NC 48 NC
Cooper's (VA) Bat

1st Corps Artillery
Washington (LA) Art
Col J B Walton
1,2,3,4, Company

Alexander's Battln — LC E Porter Alexander
Bedford (VA) Art
Eubanks's (VA) Art
Madison's Lt Art (LA)
Parker's (VA) Bat
Rhett's (SC) Bat
Woolfolk's (VA) Bat

2nd Corps — LG Thomas J Jackson

D H Hill's Division — MG Daniel H Hill

1st Brigade — BG Robert E Rodes
3 AL 5 AL
6 AL 12 AL
26 AL

2nd-Ripley's Brigade — BG George Doles
4 GA 44 GA
1 NC 3 NC

3rd Brigade — BG Alfred H Colquitt
13 AL 6 GA
23 GA 27 GA
28 GA

4th Brigade — BG Alfred Iverson
5 NC 12 NC
20 NC 23 NC

5th Brigade — Col Bryan Grimes
2 NC 4 NC
14 NC 30 NC

Artillery — Maj H P Jones
Hardaway's (AL) Bat
Jeff Davis (AL) Bat
King Willam (VA) Bat
Morris (VA) Art - Page's Bat
Orange (VA) Art - Fry's Bat

A P Hill's Division — MG Ambrose P Hill

1st (Field's) Brigade — Col J M Brockenbrough
40 VA 47 VA
55 VA 22 VA

2nd Brigade — BG Maxcy Gregg / Col D H Hamilton
1 SC (Prov) 12 SC
1 SC Rifles 13 SC
14 NC

3rd Brigade — Col Edward L Thomas
14 GA 35 GA
45 GA 49 GA

4th Brigade — BG James H Lane
7 NC 18 NC
28 NC 33 NC
37 NC

5th Brigade — BG James J Archer
5 AL Battln 19 GA
1 TN 7 TN
14 TN

6th Brigade — BG William D Pender / Col A M Scales
13 NC 16 NC
22 NC 34 NC
38 NC

Artillery — LC R L Walker
Branch (NC) Art
Crenshaw's (VA) Bat
Johnson's (VA) Bat
Letcher (VA) Art
Pee Dee (SC) Art
Purcell (VA) Art

Ewell's Division — BG Jubal A Early

Lawton' Brigade — Col C A Evans
13 GA 26 GA
31 GA 38 GA
60 GA 61 GA

2nd Brigade — Col R F Hoke
15 AL 12 GA
21 GA 21 NC
1 NC Battalion

Early's Brigade — Col J A Walker
13 VA 25 VA
31 VA 44 VA
49 VA 52 VA
58 VA

Hay's (1 LA) Brigade — BG Harry T Hays
5 LA 6 LA
7 LA 8 LA
9 LA

Artillery — Capt J W Latimer
Charlottesville (VA)
Chesapeake (MD) Art
Courtney (VA) Art
1st MD Bat
Louisiana Guard Art
Stauton (VA) Art

Jackson's Division — BG Wm B Talliaferro

1st Brigade — BG Elisha F Paxton
2 VA 4 VA
5 VA 27 VA
33 VA

2nd Brigade — BG John R Jones
21 VA 42 VA
48 VA 1 VA Battln

3rd (Taliaferro's) — Col E T H Warren
47 AL 48 AL
10 VA 23 VA
37 VA

4th (Starke's) Brigade — Col Edmund Pendleton
1 LA 2 LA
10 LA 14 LA
Coppens' (LA) Battln
15 LA

Artillery — Capt J B Brockenbrough
Carpenter's (VA) Bat
Danville (VA) Bat
Hampden (VA) Art
Lee (VA) Bat
Lusk's (VA) Bat

Reserve Artillery — BG William Pendleton

Brown's Battalion — Col J Thompson Brown
Brook's (VA) Bat
Dance's Bat (Powhatan)
Hupp's Bat-Salem Art
Poague's (VA) Bat - Rockbridge Art
Smith's Bat
Watson's Bat-2nd Hwtzr

Cutts' (GA) Battalion
Lane's Bat
Patterson's (GA) Bat
Ross' (GA) Bat

Nelson's Battalion — Maj Wm Nelson
Kirkpatrick's (VA) Bat
Massie's (VA) Bat
Milledge's (GA) Bat

Misc Batteries
Ells' (GA) Bat
Nelson's (VA) Bat

Cavalry — MJ James E B Stuart

1st Brigade — BG Wade Hampton
1 NC 1 SC
Cobb's (GA) Legion
Phillips' (GA) Legn
2 SC

2nd Brigade — BG Fitzhugh Lee
1 VA 2 VA
3 VA 4 VA
5 VA

3rd Brigade — BG W H F Lee
2 NC 9 VA
10 VA 13 VA
15 VA

4th Brigade — BG W E Jones
6 VA 7 VA
12 VA 17 VA
White's (VA) Battln

Artillery — Maj John Pelham
Breathed's (VA) Bat
Chew's (VA) Bat
Hart's (SC) Bat
Henry's (VA) Bat
Moorman's (VA) Bat

Organization of the 14 US Army Corps or the Army of the Cumberland, Maj. Gen. William S Rosecrans, USA, commanding during the Stone's River or Murfreesboro, TN, Campaign, December 26, 1862-January 5, 1863.

Artillery
Col James Barnett
Provost Guard
10 OH Infantry
General Escort
Anderson Troop, PA Cav

RIGHT WING
MG Alexander McD McCook

1st (late 9th) Division	3rd (Late 11th) Division
BG Jefferson C Davis	BG Philip H Sheridan
Escort	Escort
36 IL Cav-Co B	2 KY Cav-Co L
2 KY Cav-Co G	
1st (late 30th) Brigade	1st (late 37th) Brigade
Col P Sidney Post	BG Joshua W Sill
59 IL 74 IL	Col Nicholas Greusel
75 IL 22 IN	36 IL 88 IL
	21 MI 24 WI
2nd (late 31st) Brigade	2nd (late 35th) Brigade
Col William P Carlin	Col Frederick Schaefer
21 IL 38 IL	LCol Bernard Laiboldt
101 OH 15 WI	44 IL 73 IL
	2 MO 15 MO
3rd (late 32nd) Brigade	3rd Brigade
Col William E Woodruff	Col George W Roberts
25 IL 35 IL	Col Luther P Bradley
81 IN	22 IL 27 IL
	42 IL 51 IL
Artillery	Artillery
2 MN Battery	Capt Henry Hescock
5 WI Battery	1 IL Art-Battery C
8 WI Battery	4 IN Battery
	1 MO Art-Bat G

2nd Division
BG Richard W Johnson
1st (late 6th) Brigade
BG August Willich
Col William Wallace
Col William H Gibson
89 IL 32 IN
39 IN 15 OH 49 OH
2nd (late 5th) Brigade
BG Edward N Kirk
Col Joseph B Dodge
34 IL 79 IL
29 IN 30 IN
77 PA
3rd (late 4th) Brigade
Col Philemon P Baldwin
6 IN 5 KY
1 OH 93 OH
Artillery
5 IN Battery
1 OH Art-Battery A
1 OH Art-Battery E
Cavalry
3 IN-Co's G,H,I,K

CENTER
MG George H Thomas

Provost Guard
9 MI
1st (late 3rd) Division
MG Lovell H Rousseau

1st (late 9th) Brigade	3rd (Late 1st) Division
Col Benjamin Scribner	BG Speed S Fry
38 IN 2 OH	Escort
33 OH 94 OH	2 KY Cav-Co B
10 WI	1st Brigade
	Col Moses B Walker
	82 IN 12 KY
	17 OH 31 OH
	38 OH
2nd (late 17th) Brigade	2nd Brigade
Col John Beatty	Col John M Harlan
42 IN 88 IN	10 IN 74 IN
15 KY 3 OH	4 KY 10 KY
	14 OH
3rd (late 28th) Brigade	3rd Brigade
Col John C Starkweather	BG James B Steedman
24 IL 79 PA	87 IN 2 MN
1 WI 21 WI	9 OH 35 OH
4th Brigade	42 IL 51 IL
LCol Oliver L Shepherd	Artillery
15 US-1 Battln	1 MI Art-Bat D
16 US-1 Battln	1 OH Art-Bat C
18 US-1,2 Battln	4 US Art-Bat I
19 US-1 Battln	4th (late 7th) Division
Artillery	BG Robert B Mitchell
Capt Cyrus O Loomis	1st Brigade
KY Art-Bat A	BG James D Morgan
1 MI-Bat A	10 IL 16 IL
5 US Art-Bat H	60 IL 10 MI 14 MI
Cavalry	2nd (late 36th) Brigade
2 KY-6 Co's	Col Daniel McCook
2nd (late 8th) Division	85 IL 86 IL
BG James S Negley	125 IL 52 OH
1st (late 25th) Brigade	Cavalry
BG James G Spears	2 IN-Co A
1 TN 2 TN	5 KY 3 TN
3 TN 5 TN	Artillery
6 TN	2 IL Art-Bat I
2nd (late 29th) Brigade	10 WI Battery
Col Timothy R Stanley	Unattached Infantry
19 IL 11 MI	8 KS-5 Co's
18 OH 69 OH	1 Middle (10th) TN
3rd (late 7th) Brigade	Artillery Reserves
Col John F Miller	11,12 IN Bat
37 IN 21 OH	1 MI-Bat E
74 OH 78 PA	5th (late 12th) Division
Artillery	BG Joseph J Reynolds
KY Art-Bat B	1st (late 33rd) Brigade
1 OH Art-Bat G	Col Albert S Hall
1 OH Art-Bat M	80 IL 123 IL
	101 IN 105 OH
	2nd (late 40th) Brigade
	Col Abram O Miller
	98 IL 17 IN
	72 IN 75 IN
	Artillery
	18,19 IN Battery
	19 IN Battery

LEFT WING
MG Thomas L Crittenden

1st (late 6th) Division	3rd (late 5th) Division
BG Thomas J Wood	BG Horatio Van Cleve
BG Milo S Hascall	Col Samuel Beatty
1st (late 15th) Brigade	1st (late 11th) Brigade
BG Milo S Hascall	Col Samuel Beatty
Col George P Buell	Col Benjamin C Grider
100 IL 58 IN	79 IN 9 KY
3 KY 26 OH	11 KY 19 OH
2nd (late 21st) Brigade	2nd (late 14th) Brigade
Col George D Wagner	Col James P Fyffe
15 IN 40 IN	44 IN 86 IN
57 IN 97 OH	13 OH 59 OH
3rd (late 20th) Brigade	3rd (late 23rd) Brigade
Col Charles G Harker	Col Samuel W Price
51 IN 73 IN	35 IN 8 KY
13 MI 64 OH	21 KY 51 OH
65 OH	99 OH
Artillery	Artillery
Maj Seymour Race	Capt George R Swallow
8,10 IN Battery	7 IN Battery
6 OH Battery	PA Art-Bat B
2nd (late 4th) Division	3 WI Battery
BG John M Palmer	
1st (late 22nd) Brigade	
BG Charles Cruft	
31 IN 1 KY	
2 KY 90 OH	
2nd (late 19th) Brigade	
Col William B Hazen	
110 IL 9 IN	
6 KY 41 OH	
3rd (late 10th) Brigade	
Col William Grose	
84 IL 36 IN	
23 KY 6 OH	
24 OH	
Artillery	
Capt William Standart	
1 OH Lt-Bat B,F	
4 US-Bat H,M	

Cavalry Corps
BG David S Stanley
Cavalry Division
Col John Kennett

1st Brigade
Col Robert H G Minty
2 IN 3 KY
4 MI 7 PA
2nd Brigade
Col Lewis Zahm
1 OH 3 OH
4 OH
Artillery
1 OH Art-Bat D
Reserve Cavalry
15 PA 2 TN
1 Middle (5th) TN
Unattached
4 US Cavalry
MISCELLANEOUS
Pioneer Brigade
Capt James St Morton
1,2,3 Battalion
IL Lt Art-Stokes' Bat

Engineers & Mechanics
1 MI

POST OF GALLATIN, TN
BG Eleazer A Paine
Ward's (late 8th) Brig
BG William T Ward
102 IL 105 IL
70 IN 79 OH
IN Lt Art-13 Bat

Cavalry
1 KY 7 KY
11 KY

Organization of the Confederate Army of Tennessee, commanded by Gen. Braxton Bragg, CSA, during the Stone's River, or Murfreesboro, TN, Campaign, December 26, 1862-January 6, 1863.

POLK'S CORPS		HARDEE'S CORPS			CAVALRY
LG Leonidas Polk		LG William J Hardee			BG Joseph Wheeler
1st Division	2nd Division	1st Division	2nd Division	McCown's Division	Wheeler's Brigade
MG Benjamin F Cheatham	MG Jones M Withers	MG John C Breckenridge	MG Patrick Cleburne	MG John Porter McCown	BG Joseph Wheeler
1st Brigade	1st (Deas') Brigade	1st Brigade	1st Brigade	1st Brigade	1 AL 3 AL
BG Daniel S Donelson	Col J Q Loomis	BG Daniel W Adams	BG Leonidas E Polk	BG Matthew D Ector	51 AL 1 TN
8 TN 16 TN	19 AL 22 AL	Col Randall L Gibson	1 AR 13 AR	10 TX Cav 11 TX Cav	8 Confederate
38 TN 51 TN	25 AL 26 AL	32 AL 13 LA	15 AR 5 Confederate	14 TX Cav 15 TX Cav	TN Battln
84 TN	39 AL 1 LA (Reg)	20 LA 16 LA	2 TN 5 TN	TX Battery	AR Battery
Carnes (TN) Bat	17 AL Battln Sharp	25 LA 14 LA Battln	Helena (AR) Art		Buford's Brigade
	Robertson's Bat	Washington Art (5th Bat)			BG Abraham Buford
					3 KY 5 KY
2nd Brigade	2nd Brigade	2nd Brigade	2nd Brigade	2nd Brigade	6 KY
BG Alexander P Stewart	BG James R Chalmers	Col J B Palmer	BG St John R Liddell	BG James E Rains	Pegram's Brigade
4 TN 5 TN	Col T W White	BG Gideon J Pillow	2 AR 5 AR	Col R B Vance	BG John Pegram
19 TN 24 TN	7 MS 9 MS	18 TN 26 TN	6 AR 7 AR	3 GA Battln 9 GA Battln	1 GA 1 LA
31 TN 33 TN	10 MS 41 MS	28 TN 32 TN	8 AR	29 NC 11 TN	
MS Battery	9 MS Battln Sharp	45 TN	Swett's (MS) Bat	Eufaula (AL) Lt Art	
	Blythe's (MS) Reg	Moses' (GA) Bat			Wharton's Brigade
	Garrity's (AL) Bat				BG John A Wharton
3rd Brigade	3rd Brigade	3rd Brigade	3rd Brigade	3rd Brigade	14 AL Battalion
BG George Maney	BG J Patton Anderson	BG William Preston	BG Bushrod R Johnson	BG Evander McNair	1,3 Confederate
1 TN 27 TN	45 AL 24 MS	1 FL 3 FL	17 TN 23 TN	Col R W Harper	2 GA 3 GA (detchmnt)
4 TN 6 TN	27 MS 29 MS	4 FL 60 NC	44 TN	1,2 AR Mounted Rifles	2 TN 4 TN
9 TN TN Sharp	30 MS 39 NC	20 TN	Jefferson (MS) Art	4 AR 30 AR	8 TX
Smith's (MS) Bat	MO Battery	TN Battery		4 AR Battln	Murray's (TN) Reg
4th Brigade	4th Brigade	4th Brigade	4th Brigade	AR Battery	Escort Company
BG Preston Smith	Col A M Manigault	BG Roger W Hanson	BG Sterling A M Wood		McCown's Escort Co
Col Alfred Vaughan, Jr	24 AL 28 AL	Col R P Trabue	16 AL 33 AL		White's (TN) Bat
12 TN 13 TN	34 AL 10 SC	41 AL 2 KY	3 Confederate 45 MS		
29 TN 47 TN	19 SC	4 KY 6 KY	15 MS Battln Sharp		ARTILLERY
154 TN 9 TX	AL Battery	9 KY	AL Battery		Baxter's (TN) Bat
Allin's (TN) Sharp		KY Battery			Byrne's (KY) Bat
TN Battery		Jackson's Brigade			Gibson's (GA) Bat
		BG John K Jackson			
		5 GA 5 MS			
		8 MS 2 GA Battln Sharp			
		Pritchard's (GA) Bat			
		Lumsden's (AL) Bat			

General Headquarters

Provost-Marshal
BG Marsena R. Patrick
93 NY   6 PA
8 US, Co A,B,C,D,F,G

Patrick's Brigade
Col William F. Rogers
21 NY   23 NY
35 NY   80 NY
OH Lt Art-12th Bat
MD Lt Art-Bat D

Engineer Brig
BG Henry W. Benham
15 NY   50 NY
Battln US Eng

Signal Corps
Capt Samuel T Cushing

Ordnance Dept
Lieut. John R. Edie

Guards and Orderlies
Oneida (NY) Cav

Artillery
BG Henry J Hunt

Artillery Reserve
Capt William Graham
BG Robert O. Tyler
1 CT-Bat B, M
NY Lt-5,15,29,30,32 Bat
1 US Art-Bat K
3 US Art-Bat C
4 US Art-Bat G
5 US Art-Bat K
32 MA Inf

Train Guard
Col William Birney
Capt Robert S. Johnston

1st US Army Corps — MG John F. Reynolds

Escort
1 ME Cav-Co L

1st Division — BG James Wadsworth
- 1st Brigade — Col Walter Phelps / 22 NY 24 NY / 30 NY 84 NY
- 2nd Brigade — BG Lysander Cutter / 7 IN 76 NY / 95 NY 56 PA / 147 NY
- 3rd Brigade — BG Gabriel R. Paul / 22 NJ 29 NJ / 30 NJ 31 NJ / 137 PA
- 4th Brigade — BG Solomon Meredith / 19 IN 24 MI / 2 WI 6 WI / 7 WI
- Artillery — Capt John Reynolds / NH Lt-1st Bat / 4 US Art-Bat B / 1 NY Lt-Bat L

2nd Division — BG John C. Robinson
- 1st Brigade — Col Adrian R Root / 16 ME 94 NY / 104 NY 107 NY
- 2nd Brigade — BG Henry Baxter / 12 MA 26 NY / 90 PA 136 PA
- 3rd Brigade — Col Samuel Leonard / 13 MA 83 NY / 97 NY 11 PA / 88 PA
- Artillery — Capt Dunbar R Ransom / ME Lt-2nd Bat (B) / ME Lt-5th Bat (E) / PA Lt-Bat C / 5 US-Bat C

3rd Division — BG Abner Doubleday
- 1st Brigade — 121 PA 135 PA / 142 PA 151 PA
- 2nd Brigade — Col Roy Stone / 143 PA 149 PA / 150 PA
- Artillery — Maj Ezra W Matthews / 1 PA Lt-Bat B / 1 PA Lt-Bat F / 1 PA Lt-Bat G

2nd US Army Corps — MG Darius N Couch

Escort
6 NY Cav-Co D,K

1st Division — MG Winfield S Hancock
- 1st Brigade — BG John C Caldwell / 5 NH 61 NY / 81 PA 148 PA
- 2nd Brigade — BG Thomas F Meagher / 28 MA 63 NY / 69 NY 88 NY / 116 PA
- 3rd Brigade — BG Samuel K Zook / 52 NY 57 NY / 66 NY 140 PA
- 4th Brigade — Col John R Brooke / 27 CT 2 DE / 64 NY 53 PA / 145 PA
- Artillery — 1 NY Lt-Bat B / 4 US Art-Bat C

2nd Division — BG John Gibbon
- 1st Brigade — BG Alfred Scully / Col Henry W Hudson / Col Byron Laflin / 19 ME 15 MA / 1 MN 34 NY / 82 NY (2nd Militia) / MN Sharp-2nd Co
- 2nd Brigade — Col Joshua T Owen / 69 PA 71 PA / 72 PA 106 PA
- 3rd Brigade — Col Norman J Hall / 19 MA 20 MA / 7 MI 42 NY / 59 NY 127 PA
- Artillery — 1 RI Lt-Bat A,B / Sharpshooters / 1 Co MA

3rd Division — BG William H French
- 1st Brigade — Col Samuel S Carroll / 14 IN 24 NJ / 28 NJ 4 OH / 8 OH 7 WV
- 2nd Brigade — BG William Hays / Col Charles J. Powers / 14 CT 12 NJ / 108 NY 130 PA
- 3rd Brigade — Col John D MacGregor / Col Charles Albright / 1 DE 4 NY / 132 PA
- Artillery — 1 NY Lt-Bat G / 1 RI Lt-Bat G
- Artillery Reserve — 1 US Art-Bat I / 4 US Art-Bat A

3rd US Army Corps — MG Daniel Sickles

1st Division — BG David B Birney
- 1st Brigade — BG Charles K Graham / Col Thomas C Egan / 57 PA 63 PA / 68 PA 105 PA / 114 PA 141 PA
- 2nd Brigade — BG J H Hobard Ward / 3 ME 4 ME / 38 NY 40 NY / 20 IN 99 PA
- 3rd Brigade — Col Samuel B Hayman / 17 ME 3 MI / 5 MI 1 NY / 37 NY
- Artillery — Capt A Judson Clark / 1 RI Lt-Bat E / 3rd US Art-Bat F,K / NJ Lt-Bat B

2nd Division — MG Hiram Berry / BG Joseph B Carr
- 1st Brigade — BG Joseph B Carr / 1 MA 11 MA / 16 MA 11 NJ / 26 PA
- 2nd Brigade — BG Joseph W Revere / Col J Egbert Farnum / 70 NY 71 NY / 72 NY 73 NY / 74 NY 120 NY
- 3rd Brigade — BG Gershom Mott / Col William J Sewell / 5 NJ 6 NJ / 7 NJ 8 NJ / 2 NY 115 PA
- Artillery — Capt Thomas W Osborn / 1 NY Lt-Bat D / NY Lt-4th Bat / 1 US Art-Bat H / 4 US-Bat K

3rd Division — BG Amiel W Whipple / BG Charles K Graham
- 1st Brigade — Col Emlen Franklin / 86 NY 124 NY / 122 PA
- 2nd Brigade — Col Samuel M Bowman / 12 NH 84 PA / 110 PA
- 3rd Brigade — Col Hiram Berdan / 1 US Sharpshooters / 2 US Sharpshooters
- Artillery — Capt A Puttkammer / Capt James Huntington / NY Lt-10th Bat / NY Lt-11th Bat / 1 OH Lt-Bat H

5th US Army Corps — MG George G Meade

1st Division — BG Charles Griffin
- 1st Brigade — BG James Barnes / 2 ME 18 MA / 22 MA 1 MI / 13 NY 25 NY / 118 PA-MA Sharp/Co 2
- 2nd Brigade — Col James McQuade / Col Jacob B Sweitzer / 9 MA 32 MA / 4 MI 14 NY / 62 PA
- 3rd Brigade — Col T B W Stockton / 20 ME 16 MI / 12 NY 17 NY / 44 NY 83 PA / MI Sharp-Brady
- Artillery — Capt Augustus Martin / MA Lt-3rd,5th Bat / 1 RI Lt-Bat C / 5 US Art-Bat D

2nd Division — MG George Sykes
- 1st Brigade — BG Romeyn B Ayres / 3 US 4 US / 12 US-1st,2nd Bat / 14 US-1st,2nd Battln
- 2nd Brigade — Col Sidney Burbank / 6 US 7 US / 10 US 11 US / 17 US-1st Bat / 17 US-2nd Bat / 2 US-Co B,C,F,I,K
- 3rd Brigade — Col Patrick H O'Rorke / 5 NY 140 NY / 146 NY
- Artillery — Capt Stephen Ward / 1 OH Lt-Bat L / 5 US-Bat I

3rd Division — BG Andrew A Humphreys
- 1st Brigade — BG Erastus B Tyler / 91 PA 126 PA / 129 PA 134 PA
- 2nd Brigade — Col Peter H Allabach / 123 PA 131 PA / 133 PA 155 PA
- Artillery — 1 NY Lt-Bat C / 1 US Art-Bat E,G

6th US Army Corps — MG John Sedgwick

Escort
Hugh H Janeway
1 NJ Cav-Col L
1 PA Cav-Co H

1st Division — BG W T H Brooks / Provost-4 NJ-Co A,C,H
- 1st Brigade — Col Henry W Brown / Col William H Penrose / Col Samuel L Buck / Col William H Penrose / 1 NJ 2 NJ / 3 NJ 4 NJ / 15 NJ 23 NJ
- 2nd Brigade — BG Joseph J Bartlett / 5 ME 16 NY / 27 NY 121 NY / 96 PA
- 3rd Brigade — BG David A Russell / 18 NY 32 NY / 49 PA 95 PA / 119 PA
- Artillery — Maj John A Tompkins / MA Lt-1st Bat (A) / NJ Lt-Bat A / MD Lt-Bat A / 2 US-Bat D

2nd Division — BG Albion P Howe
- 2nd Brigade — Col Henry Whiting / 26 NJ 2 VT / 2 VT 4 VT / 5 VT 6 VT
- 3rd Brigade — BG Thomas H Neill / 21 NY 20 NY / 33 NY 49 NY / 7 ME 77 NY
- Artillery — NY Lt-1st Bat / 5th US Art-Bat F

3rd Division — BG John Newton
- 1st Brigade — Col Alexander Shaler / 65 NY 67 NY / 122 NY 23 PA / 82 PA
- 2nd Brigade — Col William H Browne / Col Henry L Eustis / 7 MA 10 MA / 37 MA 36 NY / 2 RI
- 3rd Brigade — BG Frank Wheaton / 62 NY 93 PA / 98 PA 102 PA / 139 PA
- Artillery — 1 PA Lt-Bat C,D / 2 US Art-Bat G

Light Division — Col Hiram Burnham
6 ME 31 NY
43 NY 61 PA
5 WI
NY Lt Art-3 Bat

11th US Army Corps — MG Oliver O Howard

Escort
1 IN Cav-Co I,K

1st Division — BG Charles Devens / BG Nathaniel McLean
- 1st Brigade — Col Leopold von Gilsa / 41 NY 45 NY / 54 NY 153 PA
- 2nd Brigade — BG Nathaniel McLean / Col John C Lee / 17 CT 25 OH / 55 OH 75 OH / 107 OH
- Unattached — 8 NY-1 Co
- Artillery — NY Lt-13 Bat

2nd Division — BG Adolph Von Steinwehr
- 1st Brigade — Col Adolphus Buschbeck / 29 NY 154 NY / 27 PA 73 PA
- 2nd Brigade — BG Francis C Barlow / 33 MA 134 NY / 136 NY 73 OH
- Artillery — 1st NY Lt-Bat I

3rd Division — MG Carl Schurz
- 1st Brigade — BG A Schimmelfennig / 82 IL 68 NY / 157 NY 61 OH / 74 PA
- 2nd Brigade — Col W Krzyzanowski / 58 NY 119 NY / 75 PA 26 WI
- Unattached — 82 OH
- Artillery — 1st OH Lt-Bat I
- Reserve Artillery — LCol Louis Schirmer / NY Lt-2nd Bat / 1st OH Lt-Bat K / 1st WV Lt-Bat C

12th US Army Corps — MG Henry W Slocum

Provost Guard
10 ME (Battln)

1st Division — BG Alpheus Williams
- 1st Brigade — BG Joseph F Knipe / 5 CT 28 NY / 46 PA 128 PA
- 2nd Brigade — Col Samuel Ross / 20 CT 3 MD / 123 NY 145 NY
- 3rd Brigade — BG Thomas H Ruger / 27 IN 2 MA / 13 NJ 107 PA / 3 WI
- Artillery — NY Lt-6th Bat

2nd Division — BG John W Geary
- 1st Brigade — Col Charles Candy / 5 OH 7 OH / 29 OH 66 OH / 28 PA 147 PA
- 2nd Brigade — Col Thomas L Kane / 29 PA 109 PA / 111 PA 124 PA / 125 PA
- 3rd Brigade — BG George S Greene / 60 NY 78 NY / 102 NY 137 NY / 149 NY
- Artillery — 2 US-Bat A

Cavalry Division — BG George Stoneman

First Division — BG Alfred Pleasonton
- 1st Brigade — Col Benjamin F Davis / 8 IL 3 IN / 8 NY 9 NY
- 2nd Brigade — Col Thomas C Devin / 6 NY 8 PA / 1 MI 17 PA

2nd Division — BG William W Averell
- 1st Brigade — Col Horace B Sargent / 1 MA 4 NY / 6 OH 1 RI
- 2nd Brigade — Col John B McIntosh / 3 PA 4 PA / 16 PA

3rd Division — BG David McM Gregg
- 1st Brigade — Col Judson Kilpatrick / 1 ME 2 NY / 10 NY
- 2nd Brigade — Col Percy Wyndham / 12 IL 1 MD / 1 NJ 1 PA

Reg Reserve Cavalry — BG John Buford
6 PA 1 US
2 US 5 US
6 US

Artillery — Capt James Robertson
2nd US-Bat B,L,M
4th US-Bat E

1st Corps / McLaws Division	Anderson's Division	2nd Corps	D H Hill's Division	Early's Division	Artillery	Cavalry
MG Lafayette McLaws Wofford's Brigade BG Wm T Wofford 16 GA 18 GA 24 GA Cobb's GA Legion Phillips' GA Legion	MG Richard Anderson Wilcox's Brigade BG Cadmus M Wilcox 8 AL 9 AL 10 AL 11 AL 14 AL	LG Thomas J Jackson MG Ambrose P Hill BG Robert E Rodes MG JEB Stuart A P Hill's Division MG Ambrose P Hill BG Henry Heth BG WD Pender BG James Jay Archer	BG Robert E Rodes BG Samuel D Ramseur 3 AL 5 AL 6 AL 12 AL 26 AL	MG Jubal A Early Gordon's Brigade BG John B Gordon 13 GA 26 GA 31 GA 38 GA 60 GA 61 GA	Carrington's (VA) Bat- Charlottesville Art Garber's (VA) Bat- Stauton Art Latimer's (VA) Bat- Courtney Art Thompson's Bat- LA Guard Art	MJ James E B Stuart 1st Brigade BG Wade Hampton 1 NC 1 SC Cobb's (GA) Legion Phillips' (GA) Legn 2 SC
Semmes' Brigade BG Paul J Semmes 10 GA 50 GA 51 GA 53 GA	Wright's Brigade BG Ambrose R Wright 3 GA 22 GA 48 GA 2 GA Battln	Heth's Brigade BG Henry Heth Col J M Brockenbrough 40 VA 47 VA 55 VA 22 VA	Colquitt's Brigade BG Alfred H Colquitt 6 GA 19 GA 23 GA 27 GA 28 GA	Hoke's Brigade BG Robert F Hoke 6 NC 21 NC 54 NC 57 NC 1 NC Battln		
Kershaw's Brigade BG Joseph B Kershaw 2 SC 3 SC 7 SC 8 SC 15 SC 3 SC	Mahone's Brigade BG William Mahone 6 VA 12 VA 16 VA 41 VA 61 VA	Thomas' Brigade BG Edward L Thomas 14 GA 35 GA 45 GA 49 GA	Ramseur's Brigade BG Samuel D Ramseur Col F M Parker 2 NC 4 NC 14 NC 30 NC	Smith's Brigade BG William Smith 13 VA 49 VA 52 VA 58 VA	Artillery Reserve Dance's Bat (Powhatan) Hupp's Bat-Salem Art Watson's Bat-2nd Hwtzr Smith's Bat-3rd Hwtzr Brooke's (VA) Bat	2nd Brigade BG Fitzhugh Lee 1 VA 2 VA 3 VA 4 VA
Barksdale Brigade BG William Barksdale 13 MS 17 MS 18 MS 21 MS	Posey's Brigade BG Carnot Posey 12 MS 16 MS 19 MS 48 MS	Lane's (4th Brigade) BG James H Lane 7 NC 18 NC 28 NC 33 NC 37 NC	Doles' Brigade BG George Doles 4 GA 12 GA 21 GA 44 GA	Hay's Brigade BG Harry T Hays 5 LA 6 LA 7 LA 8 LA 9 LA	McIntosh's Battalion Hurt's (AL) Bat Johnson's (VA) Bat Lusk's (VA) Bat	3rd Brigade BG W H F Lee 2 NC 5 VA 9 VA 10 VA 13 VA 15 VA
	Perry's Brigade BG Edward A Perry 2 FL 5 FL 8 FL	McGowan's Brigade BG S McGowan Col O E Edwards Col A Perrin Col D H Hamilton 1 SC (Prov) 12 SC 1 SC Rifles 13 SC 14 NC	Iverson's Brigade BG Alfred Iverson 5 NC 12 NC 20 NC 23 NC		Reserve Artillery BG William Pendleton Patterson's (GA) Bat Ross' (GA) Bat Wingfield's Bat	4th Brigade BG W E Jones 6 VA 7 VA 11 VA 12 VA 1 MD Battin 34 VA Battin 35 VA Battin
Artillery Col Henry C Cabell Manly's (NC) Bat McCarthy's (VA) Bat Carlton's (GA) Bat Fraser's (GA) Bat	Artillery LCol J J Garnett Lewis' (VA) Bat Grandy's (VA) Bat Maurin's (LA) Bat Moore's-ex Huger (VA)	Archer's (5th Brigade) BG James J Archer Col B D Fry 13 AL 5 AL 1 TN 7 TN 14 TN	Artillery LCol T H Carter Reese's (AL) Bat- Jeff Davis Art Carter's (VA) Bat- King William Art Fry's (VA) Bat- Orange Art Page's (VA) Bat- Morris' Art	Artillery Brown's (MD) Bat- Chesapeake Art Carpenter's (VA) Bat Dement's (MD) Bat Raine's (VA) Bat- Lee's Art	Nelson's Battalion LC W Nelson Kilpatrick's (VA) Bat Massie's (VA) Bat Milledge's (GA) Bat	Horse Artillery Maj R F Beckman Lynchburg Beauregards Stuart Horse Art VA Bat Washington (SC) Art
	Artillery Reserve Alexander's Battln LC E Porter Alexander Jordon's (VA) Bat Woolfolk's (VA) Bat Moody's (LA) Bat Parker's (VA) Bat Rhett's (SC) Bat Washington (LA) Art Eshleman's 4th Co Miller's 3rd Co Richardson's 2nd Co Squire's 1st Co	Pender's Brigade BG William D Pender 13 NC 16 NC 22 NC 34 NC 38 NC Artillery Brunson's (SC) Bat Crenshaw's (VA) Bat Davidson's (VA) Bat- Letcher Art McGraw's (VA) Bat Mayre's (VA) Bat		Trimble's Division BG Richard E Colston Paxton's (1st) Brigade BG E F Paxton Col J H S Funk 2 VA 4 VA 5 VA 27 VA 33 VA Jones' (2nd) Brigade BG John R Jones Col T S Garrett Col A S Vandeventer 21 VA 42 VA 44 VA 48 VA 50 VA Colston's (3rd) Brigade Col E T H Warren Col T V Williams LCol S T Walker LCol S D Thurston LCol H A Brown 1 NC 3 NC 10 VA 23 VA 37 VA Nicholl's (4th) Brigade BG F T Nicholls Col J M Williams 1 LA 2 LA 10 LA 14 LA 15 LA		

Organization of the Army of the Potomac, Maj. Gen. George Gordon Meade, USA, Commanding General at the Battle of Gettysburg, PA, July 1-3, 1863.

General Headquarters
Provost Marshall-Gen
BG Marsena R Patrick
93 NY 8 US-8 Co's
2 PA Cav 6 PA Cav
1,2,5,6 US Cav detch

Signal Corps
Capt Lemuel B Norton

Guards and Orderlies
Oneida (NY) Cav

Artillery
BG Henry J Hunt

Engineer Brigade
BG Henry W Benham
15 NY-3 Co's
50 NY US Battln

1st Army Corps
MG Abner Doubleday
MG John Newton

General Headquarters
1 ME Cav-Co L

1st Division
BG James S Wadsworth
1st Brigade
BG Solomon Meredith
Col William Robinson
19 IN 24 MI
2 WI 6 WI
7 WI

2nd Brigade
BG Lysander Cutler
7 IN 76 NY
84 NY 95 NY
147 NY 56 PA

2nd Division
BG John C Robinson
1st Brigade
BG Gabriel R Paul
Col Samuel H Leonard
Col Adrian R Root
Col Richard Coulter
Col Peter Lyle
Col Richard Coulter
16 ME 13 MA
94 NY 104 NY
107 NY

2nd Brigade
BG Henry Baxter
12 MA 83 NY
97 NY 11 PA
88 PA 90 PA

3rd Division
BG Thomas A Rowley
MG Abner Doubleday
1st Brigade
Col Chapman Biddle
BG Thomas A Rowley
Col Chapman Biddle
80 NY 121 NY
142 PA 151 PA

2nd Brigade
Col Roy Stone
Col Langhorne Wister
Col Edmund L Dana
143 PA 149 PA
150 PA

3rd Brigade
BG George J Stannard
Col Francis Randall
12 VT 13 VT
14 VT 15 VT
16 VT

Artillery
Col Chas Wainwright
ME Lt-2,5 Bat
1 NY Lt-L
1 PA Lt-B
4 US Bat B

2nd Army Corps
MG Winfield S Hancock
BG John Gibbon

General Headquarters
6 NY Cav-Co D,K

1st Division
BG John C Caldwell
1st Brigade
Col Edward E Cross
Col H Boyd McKeen
5 NH 61 NY
81 PA 148 PA

2nd Brigade
Col Patrick Kelly
28 MA 63 NY
69 NY 88 NY
116 PA

3rd Brigade
BG Samuel K Zook
LCol John Fraser
52 NY 57 NY
66 NY 140 NY

4th Brigade
Col John R Brooke
27 CT 2 DE
64 NY 53 PA
145 PA

2nd Division
BG John Gibbon
BG William Harrow
1st Brigade
BG William Harrow
Col Francis E Heath
19 ME 15 MA
1 MN 82 NY

2nd Brigade
BG Alexander S Webb
69 PA 71 PA
72 PA 106 PA

3rd Brigade
Col Norman J Hall
19 MA 20 MA
7 MI 42 NY
59 NY

Unattached
MA Sharpshooters-Co 1

3rd Division
BG Alexander Hays
1st Brigade
Col Samuel S Carroll
14 IN 4 OH
8 OH 7 WV

2nd Brigade
Col Thomas A Smyth
LCol Francis E Pierce
14 CT 1 DE
12 NJ 10 NJ
108 NY

3rd Brigade
Col George L Williard
Col Eliakim Sherrill
LCol James M Bull
39 NY 111 NY
125 NY 126 NY

Artillery
Capt John G Hazard
1 NY Lt-Bat B
1 RI Lt-Bat A,B
1 US-Bat I
4 US-Bat A

3rd Army Corps
MG Daniel E Sickles
MG David B Birney

1st Division
MG David B Birney
BG J H Hobard Ward
1st Brigade
BG Charles K Graham
Col Andrew H Tippin
57 PA 63 PA
68 PA 105 PA
114 PA 141 PA

2nd Brigade
BG J H Hobard Ward
Col Hiram Berdan
20 IN 3 ME
4 ME 86 NY
124 NY 99 PA
1,2 US Sharp

3rd Brigade
Col P R de Trobriand
17 ME 3 MI
5 MI 40 NY
110 PA

2nd Division
BG Andrew A Humphreys
1st Brigade
BG Joseph B Carr
1 MA 11 MA
16 MA 12 NH
11 NJ 26 PA
84 PA

2nd Brigade
Col William Brewster
70 NY 71 NY
72 NY 73 NY
74 NY 120 NY

3rd Brigade
Col George C Burling
2 NH 5 NJ
6 NJ 7 NJ
8 NJ 115 PA

Artillery
Capt George Randolph
Capt A Judson Clark
NJ Lt-2 Bat
1 NY Lt-Bat D
1 RI Lt-Bat E
4 US-Bat K

5th Army Corps
MG George Sykes

General Headquarters
12 NY-Co D,E
17 PA Cav-Co D,H

1st Division
BG James Barnes
1st Brigade
Col William S Tilton
18 MA 22 MA
1 MI 118 PA

2nd Brigade
Col Jacob B Sweitzer
9 MA 32 MA
4 MI 62 PA

3rd Brigade
Col Strong Vincent
Col James C Rice
20 ME 16 MI
44 NY 83 PA

2nd Division
BG Romeyn B Ayres
1st Brigade
Col Hannibal Day
3 US 4 US
6 US 12 US
14 US

2nd Brigade
Col Sidney Burbank
2 US 7 US
10 US 11 US
17 US

3rd Brigade
BG Stephen H Weed
Col Kenner Garrard
140 NY 146 NY
91 PA 166 PA

3rd Division
BG Samuel W Crawford
1st Brigade
Col Wm McCandless
1,2 PA Reserves
6,13 PA Reserves

3rd Brigade
Col Joseph W Fisher
5,9 PA Reserves
10,11 PA Reserves
12 PA Reserves

Artillery
Capt Augustus Martin
MA Lt-3 Bat
1 NY Lt-Bat C
1 OH Lt-Bat L
5 US-Bat D,I

6th Army Corps
MG John Sedgwick

General Headquarters
1 NJ Cav-Co L
1 PA Cav-Co H

1st Division
BG Horatio G Wright

Provost Guard
4 NJ-3 Co's

1st Brigade
BG A T A Tolbert
1 NJ 2 NJ
3 NJ 15 NJ

2nd Brigade
BG Joseph Bartlett
5 ME 121 NY
95 PA 96 PA

3rd Brigade
BG David A Russell
6 ME 49 PA
119 PA 5 WI

2nd Division
BG Albion P Howe
2nd Brigade
Col Lewis A Grant
2 VT 3 VT
4 VT 5 VT
6 VT

3rd Brigade
BG THomas H Neill
7 ME 33 NY
43 NY 49 NY
77 NY 61 PA

3rd Division
MG John Newton
BG Frank Wheaton
1st Brigade
BG Alexander Shaler
65 NY 67 NY
122 NY 23 PA
82 PA

2nd Brigade
Col Henry L Eustis
7 MA 10 MA
37 MA 2 RI

3rd Brigade
BG Frank Wheaton
Col David J Nevin
62 NY 93 PA
98 PA 102 PA
139 PA

Artillery
Col Charles Tompkins
MA Lt-1 Bat
NY Lt-1,3 Bat
1 RI Lt-Bat C,G
2 US-Bat D,G
5 US-Bat E

11th Army Corps
MG Oliver O Howard

General Headquarters
1 IN Cav-Co I,K
8 NY-1 Co

1st Division
BG Francis Barlow
BG Adelbert Ames
1st Brigade
Col Leopold von Gilsa
41 NY 54 NY
68 NY 153 PA

2nd Brigade
BG Adelbert Ames
Col Andrew L Harris
17 CT 25 NY
75 OH 107 OH
2nd Division
BG A von Steinwehr

1st Brigade
Col Charles R Coster
134 NY 154 NY
27 PA 73 PA

2nd Brigade
Col Orlando Smith
33 MA 136 NY
55 OH 73 OH

3rd Division
MG Carl Schurz
1st Brigade
BG A Schimmelfennig
Col G von Amsberg
82 IL 45 NY
157 NY 61 OH
74 PA

2nd Brigade
Col W Krzyzanowski
58 NY 119 NY
82 OH 75 PA
26 WI

Artillery
Maj Thomas W Osborn
1 NY Lt-Bat I
1 OH Lt-Bat I,K
4 US-Bat G

12th Army Corps
MG Henry W. Slocum
BG Alpheus S Williams

Provost Guard
10 ME-4 Co's

1st Division
BG Alpheus S Williams
BG Thomas H Ruger
1st Brigade
Col Archbld McDougall
5 CT 20 CT
3 MD 123 NY
145 NY 46 PA

2nd Brigade
BG Henry H Lockwood
1 MD-Potomac
1 MD-East Sh
150 NY

3rd Brigade
BG Thomas H Ruger
Col Silas Colgrove
27 IN 2 MA
13 NJ 107 NY
3 WI

2nd Division
BG John W Geary
1st Brigade
Col Charles Candy
5 OH 7 OH
29 OH 66 OH
28 PA 147 PA

2nd Brigade
Col George Cobham, Jr
BG Thomas L Kane
Col George Cobham, Jr
29 PA 109 PA
111 PA

3rd Brigade
BG George S Greene
60 NY 78 NY
102 NY 137 NY
149 NY

Artillery
Lieut Ed Muhlenberg
1 NY Lt-Bat M
PA Lt-Bat E
4 US-Bat F
5 US-Bat K

Artillery Reserve
BG Robert O Tyler
Capt James Robertson

Headquarters Guard
32 MA-Co C

1 Reg Brig
Capt Dunbar R Ransom
1 US-Bat H
3 US-Bat F,K
4 US-Bat C
5 US-Bat C

1 Vol Brig
LCol F McGilvery
MA Lt-5,9 Bat
NY Lt-15 Bat
PA Lt-Bat C,F

2nd Vol Brig
Capt Elijah D Taft
1 CT Hvy-Bat B,M
CT Lt-2 Bat
NY Lt-5 Bat

3rd Vol Brig
Capt Jm Huntington
NH Lt-1 Bat
1 OH Lt-Bat H
1 PA Lt-Bat F,G
WV Lt-Bat C

4th Vol Brigade
Capt Robert Fitzhugh
ME Lt-6 Bat
MD Lt-Bat A
NJ Lt-1 Bat
1 NY Lt-Bat G,K

Cavalry Corps
MG Alfred Pleasonton
1st Division
BG John Buford

1st Brigade
Col William Gamble
8 IL 12 IL
3 IN 8 NY

2nd Brigade
Col Thomas C Devin
6 NY 9 NY
17 PA 3 WV

Res Brigade
BG Wesley Merritt
6 PA 1 US
2 US 5 US
6 US

2nd Division
BG David McM Gregg

Headquarters Guard
1 OH-Co A

1st Brigade
Col John B McIntosh
1 MD
Purnell-Co A
1 MA 1 NJ
1 PA 3 PA
3 PA Hvy Art-H

2nd Brigade
Col Pennock Huey
2 NY 4 NY
6 OH 8 PA

3rd Brigade
Col J Irvin Gregg
1 ME 10 NY
4 PA 16 PA

3rd Division
BG Judson Kilpatrick

Headquarters Guard
1 OH-Co C

1st Brigade
BG Elon Farnsworth
Col Nathan Richmond
5 NY 18 PA
1 VT 1 WV

2nd Brigade
BG George A Custer
1 MI 5 MI
6 MI 7 MI
Horse Art

1st Brigade
Capt James Robertson
9 MI Bat
2 US-Bat B,L
2 US-Bat M
4 US-Bat E

2nd Brigade
Capt John C Tidball
1 US-Bat E,G
1 US-Bat K
2 US-Bat A
3 US-Bat C

Organization of the Army of Northern Virginia, Gen. Robert E. Lee, CSA, Commanding at the Battle of Gettysburg, PA, July 1-3, 1863.

1st Army Corps
LG James Longstreet

McLaws Division
MG Lafayette McLaws

Kershaw's Brigade
BG Joseph B Kershaw
2 SC   3 SC
7 SC   8 SC
15 SC   3 SC

Barksdale Brigade
BG William Barksdale
Col B G Humphreys
13 MS   17 MS
18 MS   21 MS

Semmes' Brigade
BG Paul J Semmes
Col Goode Bryan
10 GA   50 GA
51 GA   53 GA

Wofford's Brigade
BG Wm T Wofford
16 GA   18 GA
24 GA
Cobb's GA Legion
Phillips' GA Legion

Artillery
Col Henry C Cabell
1 NC Artillery-Bat A
Pulaski (GA) Artillery
1 Richmond Hwtzrs
Troup (GA) Artillery

Pickett's Division
MG George E Pickett

Garnett's Brigade
BG Richard B Garnett
Maj C S Peyton
8 VA   18 VA
19 VA   28 VA
56 VA

Kemper's Brigade
BG James Lawson Kemper
Col Joseph Mayo, Jr
1 VA   3 VA
7 VA   11 VA
24 VA

Armistead's Brigade
BG Louis A Armistead
Col W R Aylett
9 VA   14 VA
38 VA   53 VA
57 VA

Artillery
Maj James Dearing
Faquier (VA) Art
Hampden (VA) Art
Richmond Fayette Art
Virginia Battery

Hood's Division
MG John Bell Hood

Law's Brigade
BG Evander M Law
Col James Sheffield
4 AL   15 AL
44 AL   47 AL
48 AL

Robertson's Brigade
BG Jerome B Robertson
3 AR   1 TX
4 TX   5 TX

Anderson's Brigade
BG George T Anderson
LCol William Luffman
7 GA   8 GA
9 GA   11 GA
59 GA

Benning's Brigade
BG Henry L Benning
2 GA   15 GA
17 GA   20 GA

Artillery
Maj M W Henry
Branch (NC) Art
German (SC) Art
Palmetto (SC) Lt Art
Rowan (NC) Art

Artillery Reserve
Col J B Walton
Alexander's Battalion
Col E P Alexander
Ashland (VA) Art
Bedford (VA) Art
Brooks (SC) Art
Madison (LA) Lt Art
Virginia Battery #1
Virginia Battery #2
Washington's (LA) Art
Maj B F Eshleman
1,2,3,4, Co's

2nd Army Corps
LG Richard S Ewell

Escort
Randolph's VA Cav

Early's Division
MG Jubal A Early

Hay's Brigade
BG Harry T Hays
5 LA   6 LA
7 LA   8 LA
9 LA

Smith's Brigade
BG William Smith
31 VA   49 VA
52 VA

Hoke's Brigade
Col Isaac E Avery
Col A C Godwin
6 NC   21 NC
57 NC

Gordon's Brigade
BG John B Gordon
13 GA   26 GA
31 GA   38 GA
60 GA   61 GA

Artillery
Charlottesville (VA) Art
Courtney (VA) Art
LA Guard Artillery
Stauton (VA) Art

Johnson's Division
MG Edward Johnson

Steuart's Brigade
BG George H Steuart
1 NC   3 NC
10 VA   23 VA
37 VA
1 MD Battalion

Stonewall Brigade
BG James A Walker
2 VA   4 VA
5 VA   27 VA
33 VA

Nicholl's Brigade
Col J M Williams
1 LA   2 LA
10 LA   14 LA
15 LA

Jone's (2nd) Brigade
BG John M Jones
LC R H Dungan
21 VA   25 VA
42 VA   44 VA
48 VA   50 VA

Artillery
1st MD Battery
Alleghany (VA) Art
Chesapeake (MD) Art
Lee's (VA) Art

Rode's Division
MG Robert E Rodes

Daniel's Brigade
BG Junius Daniel
32 NC   43 NC
15 NC   53 NC
2 NC Battalion

Dole's Brigade
BG George Doles
4 GA   12 GA
21 GA   44 GA

Iverson's Brigade
BG Alfred Iverson
5 NC   12 NC
20 NC   23 NC

Ramseur's Brigade
BG Samuel D Ramseur
2 NC   4 NC
14 NC   30 NC

O'Neal's Brigade
Col E A O'Neal
3 AL   5 AL
6 AL   12 AL
26 AL

Artillery
LCol Thomas Carter
Reese's (AL) Bat-
Jeff Davis (AL) Art
King William (VA) Art
Morris' (VA) Art
Orange (VA) Art

Artillery Reserve
Col J Thompson Brown
1st VA Artillery
Capt Willis J Dance
2 Richmond (VA) Hwtzr
3 Richmond (VA) Hwtzr
Powhatan (VA) Art
Rockbridge (VA) Art
Salem (VA) Art

Nelson's Battalion
LCol William Nelson
Amherst (VA) Art
Fluvanna (VA) Art
Georgia Battery

3rd Army Corps
LG Ambrose P Hill

Anderson's Division
MG Richard Anderson

Wilcox's Brigade
BG Cadmus M Wilcox
8 AL   9 AL
10 AL   11 AL
14 AL

Mahone's Brigade
BG William Mahone
6 VA   12 VA
16 VA   41 VA
61 VA

Wright's Brigade
BG Ambrose R Wright
Col William Gibson
BG Ambrose R Wright
3 GA   22 GA
48 GA   2 GA Battln

Perry's Brigade
Col David Lang
2 FL   5 FL
8 FL

Posey's Brigade
BG Carnot Posey
12 MS   16 MS
19 MS   48 MS

Artillery -
(Sumter Battalion)
Co's A,B,C

Heth's Division
MG Henry Heth
BG James J Pettigrew

1st Brigade
BG James J Pettigrew
Col J K Marshall
11 NC   26 NC
47 NC   52 NC

2nd Brigade
Col J M Brockenbrough
40 VA   47 VA
55 VA
22 VA Battalion

3rd Brigade
BG James J Archer
Col B D Fry
LCol S G Shepard
13 AL   5 AL
1 TN   7 TN
14 TN

4th Brigade
BG Joseph R Davis
2 MS   11 MS
42 MS   55 NC

Artillery
Donaldsonville (LA)
Huger (VA) Art
Lewis (VA) Art
Norfolk Lt Art Blues

Pender's Division
MG William D Pender

1st Brigade
BG James H Lane

2nd Brigade
BG Isaac R Trimble

1st Brigade
BG James H Lane
Col Amber Perrin
Col O E Edwards
1 SC (Prov)
1 SC Rifles   12 SC
13 SC   14 SC

2nd Brigade
BG James H Lane
Col C M Avery
7 NC   18 NC
28 NC   33 NC
37 NC

3rd Brigade
BG Edward L Thomas
14 GA   35 GA
45 GA   49 GA

4th Brigade
BG Alfred M Scales
LCol G T Gordon
Col W Lee Lowrance
13 NC   16 NC
22 NC   34 NC
38 NC

Artillery
Albemarle (VA) Art
Charlotte (SC) Art
Madison (MS) Lt Art
VA Battery

Artillery Reserve
Col R Lindsay Walker
McIntosh's Battalion
Maj D G McIntosh
Danville (VA) Art
Hardaway (AL) Art
2nd Rockbridge (VA) Art
VA Battery

Pegram's Battalion
Maj W J Pegram
Capt E B Brunson
Crenshaw (VA) Bat
Fredericksburg (VA) Art
Letcher (VA) Art
Pee Dee (SC) Art
Purcell (VA) Art

Cavalry
Stuart's Division
MJ James E B Stuart

Hampton's Brigade
BG Wade Hampton
Col L S Baker
1 NC   1 SC
Cobb's (GA) Legion
Jeff Davis' Legion
Phillips (GA) Legion
2 SC

Robertson's Brigade
4 NC   5 NC

Fitz Lee's Brigade
BG Fitzhugh Lee
1 VA   2 VA
3 VA   4 VA
5 VA
1 MD Battalion

Jenkin's Brigade
BG Albert G Jenkins
Col M J Ferguson
14 VA   16 VA
17 VA
34 VA Battalion
36 VA Battalion
Jackson's (VA) Bat

Jones' Brigade
BG William Jones
6 VA   7 VA
11 VA

W H F Lee's Brigade
Col J R Chambliss, Jr
2 NC   9 VA
10 VA   13 VA

Stuart Horse Artillery
Maj R F Beckman
Breathed's (VA) Bat
Chew's (VA) Bat
Griffin's (MD) Bat
Hart's (SC) Bat
McGregor's (VA) Bat
Moorman's (VA) Bat

Imboden's Command
BG John D Imboden
18 VA Cav
62 VA Inf (Mounted)
VA Partisan Rangers
VA Battery

Organization of the Union Forces operating against Vicksburg, MS, Maj. Gen. Ulysses S. Grant, USA, Commanding,
the Army of the Tennessee, May 18-July 4, 1863.

Escort
4 IL Cav-Co A

Engineers
1 Battln Eng of West

9th Army Corps
MG John G Parke
1st Division
BG Thomas Welsh
1st Brigade
Col Henry Bowman
36 MA 17 MI
27 MI 45 PA

3rd Brigade
Col Daniel Leisure
2 MI 8 MI
20 MI 79 NY
100 PA
Artillery
PA Lt-Bat D

2nd Division
BG Robert B Potter
1st Brigade
Col Simon G Griffin
6 NH 9 NH
7 RI

2nd Brigade
BG Edward Ferrero
35 MA 11 NH
51 NY 51 PA

3rd Brigade
Col Benjamin Christ
29 MA 46 NY
50 PA

Artillery
2 NY Lt-Bat L
Artillery Reserve
2 US-Bat E

Escort
3 IL Cav-Co L

Pioneers
KY Inf-Indepndnt

13 Army Corps
MJ John A McClernand
MJ Edward O C Ord
9th Division
BG Peter Osterhaus
1st Brigade
BG Albert L Lee
Col James Keigwin
118 IL 49 IN
69 IN 7 KY
120 OH

2nd Brigade
Col Daniel W Lindsey
54 IN 22 KY
16 OH 42 OH
114 OH

Cavalry
2 IL-5 Co's
3 IL-3 Co's
6 Mo-7 Co's

Artillery
Capt Jacob T Foster
MI Lt-7 Bat
WI Lt-1 Bat

10th Division
BG Andrew J Smith
Escort
4 IN Cav-Co C
1st Brigade
BG Stephen Burbridge
16 IN 60 IN
67 IN 83 OH
96 OH 23 WI

2nd Brigade
Col William Landram
77 IL 97 IL
130 IL 19 KY
48 OH

Artillery
IL Lt-Chicago
OH Lt-17 Bat

Escort
1 IN Cav-Co C

12th Division
BG Alvin P Hovey
1st Brigade
BG George C McGinnis
11 IN 24 IN
34 IN 46 IN
29 WI

2nd Brigade
Col James R Slack
87 IL 47 IN
24 IA 2 IA
56 OH

Artillery
1 MO Lt-Bat A
OH Lt-2 Bat
WI Lt-1,16 Bat

14th Division
BG Eugene A Carr
Escort
34 IL Cav-Co G
1st Brigade
BG William P Benton
Col Henry Washburn
Col David Shunk
33 IL 99 IL
8 IN 18 IN
1 US (Siege Guns)

2nd Brigade
BG Michael Lawler
21 IA 22 IA
23 IA 11 WI

Artillery
2 IL Lt-Bat A
IN Lt-1 Bat

15th Army Corps
MG William T Sherman
1st Division
MG Frederick Steele
1st Brigade
Col Francis Manter
Col Bernard Farrar
13 IL 27 MO
29 MO 30 MO
31 MO 32 MO

2nd Brigade
Col Charles R Woods
25 IA 31 IA
3 MO 12 MO
17 MO 76 OH

3rd Brigade
BG John M Thayer
4 IA 9 IA
26 IA 30 IA

Artillery
IA Lt-1 Bat
2 MO Lt-Bat F
OH Lt-4 Bat

Cavalry
Kane Cty IL-Indpt Co
3 IL, Co D

2nd Division
MG Frank P Blair
1st Brigade
Col Giles A Smith
113 IL 116 IL
6 MO 8 MO
13 US-1 Battln

2nd Brigade
Col Thomas K Smith
BG Joseph Lightburn
55 IL 127 IL
83 IN 54 OH
57 OH

3rd Brigade
BG Hugh Ewing
30 OH 37 OH
47 OH 4 WV

Artillery
1 IL Lt-Bat A,B,H
OH-8 Bat

Cavalry
Theilemann's IL
10 MO

3rd Division
BG James M Tuttle
1st Brigade
BG Ralph Buckland
Col Wm L McMillen
114 IL 93 IN
72 OH 95 oH

2nd Brigade
BG Joseph A Mower
47 IL 5 MN
11 MO 8 WI

3rd Brigade
BG Charles Matthies
Col Joseph Woods
8 IA 12 IA
35 IA

Artillery
Capt Nelson Spoor
1 IL Lt-Bat E
IA Lt-2 Bat

Unattached Cavalry
4 IA

Escort
7 IL Cav-Co B

16th Army Corps
MG Cadwlldr Washburn
1st Division
BG William S Smith
1st Brigade
Col John M Loomis
26 IL 90 IL
12 IL 100 IL

2nd Brigade
Col Stephen G Hicks
40 IL 103 IL
15 MI 46 OH

3rd Brigade
Col Joseph Cockehill
97 IL 99 IN
53 OH 70 OH

4th Brigade
Col Wm W Sanford
48 IL 6 IA

Artillery
Capt Wm Cogswell
1 IL Lt-Bat F,I
IL Lt-Cogswell's Bat
IN Lt-6 Bat

4th Division
BG Jacob G Lauman
1st Brigade
Col Isaac C Pugh
41 IL 53 IL
3 IA 33 WI

2nd Brigade
Col Cyrus Hall
14 IL 15 IL
46 IL 76 IL
53 IN

3rd Brigade
Col George Bryant
Col Amory Johnson
28 IL 32 IL
12 WI

Cavalry
15 IL-Co's F,I

Artillery
Capt George Gumbart
2 IL Lt-Bat E,K
OH Lt-5,7,15 Bat

Provisional Division
BG Nathan Kimball
Englemann's Brigade
Col Adolph Englemann
43 IL 61 IL
106 IL 12 MI

Richmond's Brigade
Col Jonathan Richmond
18 IL 54 IL
126 IL 22 OH

Montgomery's Brigade
Col Milton Montgomery
40 IA 3 MN
25 WI 27 WI

Escort
4 Co-OH Cav

17th Army Corps
MG James B McPherson
3rd Division
MG John A Logan
1st Brigade
BG John E Smith
BG Mortimer Leggett
20 IL 31 IL
45 IL 124 IL
23 IN

2nd Brigade
BG Mortimer Leggett
Col Manning Force
30 IL 20 OH
68 OH 78 OH

3rd Brigade
BG John Stevenson
8 IL 17 IL
81 IL 7 MO
32 OH

Artillery
Maj Chas Stolbrand
1 IL Lt-Bat D
2 IL Lt-Bat G,L
MI Lt-8 Bat
OH Lt-3 Bat

6th Division
BG John McArthur
Escort
11 IL Cav-Co G
1st Brigade
BG Hugh T Reid
1 KS 16 WI

2nd Brigade
BG Thomas E Ransom
11 IL 72 IL
95 IL 14 WI
17 WI

3rd Brigade
Col William Hall
Col Alex Chambers
11 IA 13 IA
15 IA 16 IA

Artillery
Maj Thomas Maurice
2 IL Lt-Bat F
MN Lt-1 Bat
1 MO Lt-Bat C
OH Lt-10 Bat

Escort
4 MO Cav-Co F

7th Division
BG Isaac F Quinby
BG John E Smith
1st Brigade
Col John Sanborn
48 IN 39 IN
4 MN 18 WI

2nd Brigade
Col Samuel Holmes
Col Green Raum
56 IL 17 IA
10 MO 24 MO
80 OH

3rd Brigade
Col George Boomer
Col Holden Putnam
BG Charles Matthies
93 IL 5 IA
10 IA 26 MO

Artillery
Capt Frank Sands
Capt Henry Dillon
1 MO Lt-Bat M
OH Lt-11 Bat
WI Lt-6,12 Bat

Herron's Division
MG Francis Herron
1st Brigade
BG William Vandever
37 IL 26 IN
20 IA 34 IA
1 MO Lt-Bat E,F

2nd Brigade
BG William W Orme
94 IL 19 IA
29 WI
1 MO Lt Art-Bat B

Unattached Cavalry
Col Cyrus Bussey
5 IL 3 IA
2 WI

District of
N.E. Louisiana

BG Elias S Dennis
Detached Brigade
Col George W Neely
63 IL 108 IL
120 IL 131 IL
10 IL Cavalry

African Brigade
Col Isaac F Shepard

Post at
Miliken's Bend, LA

Col Hiram Schofield
8 LA 9 LA
11 LA 13 LA
1 MS 3 MS

Post at
Goodrich's Landing

Col William F Wood
1 AR 10 LA

Stevenson's Division	Forney's Division	Smith's Division	Bowen's Division	River Batteries
MG Carter L Stevenson	MG John H Forney	MG Martin Luther Smith	MG John S Bowen	1 LA Heavy Artillery
1st Brigade	Hebert's Brigade	Baldwin's Brigade	1st MO Brigade	22 LA
BG Seth M Barton	BG Louis Hebert	BG William E Baldwin	Col Francis M Cockrell	1 TN Heavy Artillery
40 GA 41 GA	3 LA 21 LA	17 LA 31 LA	1 MO 2 MO	TN Batteries (3)
42 GA 43 GA	36 MS 37 MS	4 MS 46 MS	3 MO 5 MO	Vaiden (MS) Battery
52 GA	38 MS 43 MS	TN Battery	6 MO	
Hudson's (MS) Battery	7 MS Battalion		Guibor's (MO) Battery	Miscellaneous
Pointe Coupee (LA)-	2 AL Art Battalion-		Landis' (MO) Battery	54 AL-detachment
Art, Co. A,C	Company C		Wade's (MO) Battery	City Guards
	Appeal (AR) Bat			Signal Corps

2nd Brigade	Moore's Brigade	Vaughn's Brigade	2nd Brigade
BG Alfred Cumming	BG John C Moore	BG John C Vaughn	Col T P Dockery
34 GA 36 GA	37 AL 40 AL	60 TN 61 TN	15 AR 19 AR
39 GA 56 GA	42 AL 35 MS	62 TN	20 AR 21 AR
57 GA	40 MS 2 TX	20 LA	1 AR Cavalry Battalion
Cherokee (GA) Art	1 MS Lt Artillery		12 AR Battalion-
	AL Battery		Sharpshooters
	Pointe Coupee (LA)-		1 MO Cavalry
	Art, Co. B		3 MO Cavalry
			3 MO Battery
			Lowe's (MO) Battery

3rd Brigade		Shoup's Brigade
BG Stephen D Lee		BG Francis A Shoup
20 AL 23 AL		26 LA 27 LA
30 AL 31 AL		28 [29] LA
46 AL		McNally's (AR) Battery
AL Battery		

4th Brigade		MS State Troops
Col A W Reynolds		BG John V Harris
39 TN 43 TN		5 Regiment
59 TN		3 Battalion
3 TN (Provisional)		
3 MD Battery		

Waul's Texas Legion		Attached
Col T N Waul		14 MS Lt Art Battalion
1 Battalion Infantry		MS Partisan Rangers
2 Battalion Infantry		Signal Corps
Cavalry Battalion		
Artillery Company		

Attached
1 TN Cavalry-
Carter's Regiment-Co C
Botetourt (VA) Art
Signal Corps

Organization of the Army of the Cumberland, commanded by Maj. Gen. William S Rosecrans, USA, at the battle of Chickamauga, GA, September 19 and 20, 1863.

General Headquarters 1 Battln OH Sharp 10 OH Inf-15 PA Cav				
14th Army Corps MG George H Thomas General Headquarters Provost Guard 9 MI Infantry Escort 1 OH Cavalry-Co L	**20th Army Corps** MG Alexander McD McCook General Headquarters Provost Guard 81 IN Infantry Escort 2 KY Cavalry-Co I	**21st Army Corps** MG Thomas L Crittenden General Headquarters Escort 15 IL Cavalry-Co K	**Reserve Army Corps** MG Gordon Granger	**Cavalry Corps** BG Robert B Mitchell
1st Division BG Absalom Baird 1st Brigade Col Benjamin Scribner 38 IN 2 OH 33 OH 94 OH 10 WI	**1st Division** BG Jefferson C Davis 1st Brigade Col P Sidney Post 59 IL 74 IL 75 IL 22 IN WI Lt Art-5 Bat	**1st Division** BG Thomas J Wood 1st Brigade Col George P Buell 100 IL 58 IN 13 MI 26 OH	**1st Division** BG James B Steedman 1st Brigade BG Walter C Whitaker 96 IL 115 IL 84 IN 22 MI 40 OH 89 OH OH Lt Art-18 Bat	**1st Division** Col Edward M McCook 1st Brigade Col Archibald Campbell 2 MI 9 PA 1 TN
2nd Brigade BG John Starkweather 24 IL 79 PA 1 WI 21 WI	**2nd Brigade** BG William P Carlin 21 IL 38 IL 8 IN 101 OH MN Lt Art-2 Bat	**2nd Brigade** BG George D Wagner 15 IN 40 IN 57 IN 97 OH	**2nd Brigade** Col John G Mitchell 78 IL 98 OH 113 OH 121 OH 1 IL Lt Art-Bat M	**2nd Brigade** Col Daniel M Ray 2 IN 4 IN 2 TN 1 WI 1 OH Lt Art-Bat D
3rd Brigade BG John H King 15 US-1 Battln 16 US-1 Battln 18 US-1,2 Battln 19 US-1 Battln Artillery IN Lt-4 Bat 1 MI Lt-Bat A 5 US-Bat H	**3rd Brigade** Col Hans C Heg Col John A Martin 25 IL 35 IL 8 KS 15 WI WI Lt Art-8 Bat	**3rd Brigade** Col Charles G Harker 3 KY 64 OH 65 OH 125 OH Artillery IN Lt-8 Bat IN Lt-10 Bat OH Lt-6 Bat		**3rd Brigade** Col Louis D Watkins 4 KY 5 KY 6 KY
2nd Division MG James S Negley 1st Brigade BG John Beatty 104 IL 42 IN 88 IN 15 KY	**2nd Division** BG Richard W Johnson 1st Brigade BG August Willich 89 IL 32 IN 39 IN 15 OH 49 OH 1 OH Lt Art-Bat A	**2nd Division** MG John M Palmer 1st Brigade BG Charles Cruft 31 IN 1 KY 2 KY 90 OH	**2nd Division** 2nd Brigade Col Daniel McCook 85 IL 86 IL 125 IL 52 OH 69 OH 2 IL Lt Art-Bat I	**2nd Division** BG George Crook 1st Brigade Col Robert H G Minty 3 IN Battalion 4 MI 7 PA 4 US
2nd Brigade Col Timothy Stanley 19 IL 11 MI 18 OH				
3rd Brigade Col William Sirwell 37 IN 21 OH 74 OH 78 PA	**2nd Brigade** Col Joseph B Ddoge 79 IL 29 IN 30 IN 77 PA OH Lt Art-20 Bat	**2nd Brigade** BG William B Hazen 9 IN 6 KY 41 OH 124 OH		**2nd Brigade** Col Eli Long 2 KY 1 OH 3 OH 4 OH
Artillery IL Lt-Bridges' Bat 1 OH Lt-Bat G,M	**3rd Brigade** Col Philemon P Baldwin Col William W Berry 6 IN 5 KY 1 OH 93 OH IN Lt Art-5 Bat	**3rd Brigade** Col William Grose 84 IL 36 IN 23 KY 6 OH 24 OH		**Artillery** Chicago (IL) - - [Board of Trade Art]
3rd Division BG John M Brannan 1st Brigade Col John M Connell 82 IN 17 OH 31 OH 38 OH		**Artillery** Capt William Standart 1 OH Lt-Bat B,F 4 US-Bat H,M		
2nd Brigade Col John T Croxton 10 IN 74 IN k 4 KY 10 KY 14 OH		**Unattached** 110 IL Battalion		
3rd Brigade Col F Van Derveer 87 IN 2 MN 9 OH 35 OH	**3rd Division** MG Philip H Sheridan 1st Brigade BG William H Lytle Col Silas Miller 36 IL 88 IL 21 MI 24 WI IN Lt Art-11 Bat	**3rd Division** BG Horatio Van Cleve 1st Brigade BG Samuel Beatty 79 IN 9 KY 17 KY 19 OH		
Artillery 1 MI Lt-Bat D 1 OH Lt-Bat C 4 US-Bat I				
4th Division MG Joseph J Reynolds 1st Brigade Col John T Wilder 92 IL 98 IL 123 IL 17 IN 72 IN	**2nd Brigade** Col Bernard Laiboldt 44 IL 73 IL 2 MO 15 MO 1 MO Lt Art-Bat G	**2nd Brigade** Col George F Dick 44 IN 86 IN 13 OH 59 OH		
2nd Brigade Col Edward A King 68 IN 75 IN 101 IN 105 OH 14 OH	**3rd Brigade** Col Luther P Bradley Col Nathan H Walworth 22 IL 27 IL 42 IL 51 IL 1 IL Lt Art-Bat C	**3rd Brigade** Col Sidney M Barnes 35 IN 8 KY 21 KY 51 OH 99 OH		
3rd Brigade BG John B Turchin 18 KY 11 OH 36 OH 92 OH		**Artillery** IN Lt-7 Bat PA Lt-16 Bat WI Lt-3 Bat		
Artillery IN Lt-18,19,21 Bat				

Organization of the Confederate Army of Tennessee, commanded by Gen. Braxton Bragg, CSA, at the battle of Chickamauga, GA, September 19 and 20, 1863.

Army Headquarters
Escort
Capt Guy Dreux
Guy Dreux's Co LA Cav
Holloway's Co AL Cav

RIGHT WING
LG Leonidas Polk
Escort
Greenleaf's Co-LA Cav

Cheatham's Division
MG Benjamin F Cheatham
Escort
2 GA Cav-Co G
Jackson's Brigade
BG John K Jackson
1 GA   5 GA
5 MS   8 MS
2 GA Battln Sharp

Smith's Brigade
BG Preston Smith
Col Alfred Vaughan, Jr
11 TN   12 TN
47 TN   13 TN
154 TN 29 TN
Dawson's Battln Sharp

Maney's Brigade
BG George Maney
1 TN   27 TN
4 TN   6 TN
9 TN   24 TN

Wright's Brigade
BG Marcus J Wright
8 TN   16 TN
28 TN   38 TN
51 TN   52 TN

Strahl's Brigade
BG Otho F Strahl
4 TN   5 TN
19 TN   24 TN
31 TN   33 TN

Artillery
Maj Melancthon Smith
Carne's (TN) Bat
Scogin's (GA) Bat
Scott's (TN) Bat
Smith's (MS) Bat
Stanford's (MS) Bat

HILL'S CORPS
LG Daniel Henry Hill

Cleburne's Division
MG Patrick Cleburne
Escort
Sander's Co TN Cavalry
Wood's Brigade
BG Sterling A M Wood
16 AL   33 AL
45 AL   32 MS
45 MS   18 AL Battln
15 MS Battln Sharp

Polk's Brigade
BG Lucius E Polk
1 AR   2 TN
35 TN   48 TN
3 Confederate
5 Confederate

Deshler's Brigade
BG James Deshler
Col Roger Q Mills
9 AR   24 AR
6 TX   10 TX
[15,17,18,24,25]
[TX Cavalry]

Artillery
Maj T R Hotchkiss
Capt Henry C Semple
Calvert's (AR) Bat
Douglas' (TX) Bat
Semple's (AL) Bat

Breckenridge's Division
MG John C Breckenridge
Escort
Foules' Co-MS Cavalry
Helms' Brigade
BG Benjamin H Helm
Col Joseph H Lewis
41 AL   2 KY
4 KY   6 KY
9 KY

Adam's Brigade
BG Daniel W Adams
Col Randall L Gibson
32 AL   13 LA
20 LA   16 LA
25 LA   19 LA
14 LA Battln

Stovall's Brigade
BG Marcellus A Stovall
1 FL   3 FL
4 FL   47 GA
60 NC

Artillery
Cobb's (KY) Bat
Graves' (KY) Bat
Mebane's (TN) Bat
Slocomb's (LA) Bat

Reserve Corps
MG William H Walker

Walker's Division
BG States R Gist
Gist's Brigade
BG States Rights Gist
Col Peyton H Colquitt
LCol Leroy Napier
8 GA Battalion
46 GA   16 SC
24 SC

Ector's Brigade
BG Matthew D Ector
Stone's (AL) -
(Sharpshooters)
Pound's (MS) -
(Sharpshooters)
29 NC   9 TX
10 TX Cav   14 TX Cav
32 TX Cav

Wilson's Brigade
Col Claudius C Wilson
25 GA   29 GA
30 GA   4 LA Battln
1 GA Battln Sharp

Artillery
Ferguson's (SC) Bat
Howell's (GA) Bat
Lindell's (GA) Bat
BG St. John R Liddell

Liddell's Division
Liddell's Brigade
Col Daniel C Govan
2 AR   15 AR
5 AR   13 AR
6 AR   7 AR
8 AR   1 LA (Regs)

Walthall's Brigade
BG Edward C Walthall
Col Samuel Benton
24 MS   27 MS
29 MS   30 MS
34 MS

Artillery
Capt Charles Swett
Fowler's (AL) Bat
Warren Lt Art (MS) Bat

LEFT WING
LG James Longstreet
Hindman's Division
MG Thomas C Hindman
BG Patton Anderson
Escort
Lenoir's Co-AL Cav
Anderson's Brigade
BG Patton Anderson
Col J H Sharp
7 MS   9 MS
10 MS   41 MS
44 MS
9 MS Battln Sharp
Garrity's (AL) Bat

Deas' Brigade
BG Zachariah C Deas
19 AL   22 AL
25 AL   39 AL
50 AL
17 AL Battln Sharp
Dent's (AL) Bat

Manigault's Brigade
BG Arthur M Manigault
24 AL   28 AL
34 AL   10 SC
19 SC
Water's (AL) Bat

BUCKNER'S CORPS
MG Simon B Buckner
Escort
Clark's Co-TN Cav
Stewart's Division
MG Alexander Stewart
Johnson's Brigade
BG Bushrod R Johnson
Col John S Fulton
17 TN   23 TN
25 TN   44 TN

Bate's Brigade
BG William B Bate
58 AL   37 GA
15 TN   37 TN
20 TN
4 GA Battln Sharp

Brown's Brigade
BG John C Brown
Col Edmund Cook
18 TN   26 TN
32 TN   45 TN
23 TN Battalion

Clayton's Brigade
BG Henry D Clayton
18 AL   36 AL
38 AL

Artillery
Maj J Wes Eldridge
1 AR Battery
Dawson's (GA) Bat
Eufaula (AL) Art
9 GA Art Battln-Co E

Preston's Division
BG William Preston
Gracie's Brigade
BG Archibald Gracie
43 AL   63 TN
1,2,3,4, AL Battalion

Trigg's Brigade
Col Robert C Trigg
6 FL   7 FL
54 VA
1 FL Cavalry

Third Brigade
Col John H Kelly
65 GA   5 KY
58 NC   63 VA

Artillery Battalion
Maj A Leyden
Jeffress' (VA) Bat
Peeples' (GA) Bat
Wolihin's (GA) Bat

RESERVE CORPS
ARTILLERY
Maj Samuel C Williams
Baxter's (TN) Bat
Darden's (MS) Bat
Kolb's (AL) Bat
McCant's (FL) Bat

Johnson's Division
BG Bushrod R Johnson
Gregg's Brigade
BG John Gregg
Col Cyrus A Sugg
3 TN   10 TN
30 TN   41 TN
50 TN   7 TX
1 TN Battalion
Bledsoe's (MO) Bat

McNair's Brigade
BG Evander McNair
Col David Coleman
1,2 AR Mounted Rifles
25 AR   39 NC
4 AR   31 AR
Culpeper's (SC) Bat

LONGSTREET'S CORPS
MG John Bell Hood
M'Laws' Division
BG Joseph B Kershaw
2 SC   3 SC
7 SC   8 SC
15 SC   3 SC Battln
Humphrey's Brigade
BG Benjamin Humphreys
13 MS   17 MS
18 MS   21 MS

Wofford's Brigade
BG William T Wofford
16 GA   18 GA
24 GA
3 GA Battln Sharp
Cobbs (GA) Legion
Phillips (GA) Legion

Bryan's Brigade
BG Goode Bryan
10 GA   50 GA
51 GA   53 GA

Hood's Division
MG John Bell Hood
BG E McIver Law
Jenkins' Brigade
BG Micah Jenkins
1 SC   2 SC Rifles
5 SC   6 SC
Hampton Legion
Palmetto Sharp

Robertson's Brigade
BG Jerome Robertson
Col Van H Manning
3 AR   1 TX
4 TX   5 TX

Law's Brigade
BG E McIver Law
Col James L Sheffield
4 AL   15 AL
44 AL   47 AL
48 AL

Anderson's Brigade
BG George T Anderson
7 GA   8 GA
9 GA   11 GA
59 GA

Benning's Brigade
BG Henry L Benning
2 GA   15 GA
17 GA   20 GA

Corps Artillery
Col E Porter Alexander
Fickling's (SC) Bat
Jordan's (VA) Bat
Moody's (LA) Bat
Parker's (VA) Bat
Taylor's (VA) Bat
Woolfolk's (VA) Bat

RESERVE ARTILLERY
Maj Felix Robertson
Barret's (MO) Bat
Le Gardeur's (LA) Bat
Havis' (GA) Bat
Lumsden's (AL) Bat
Massenburg's (GA) Bat

CAVALRY
MG Joseph Wheeler
Wharton's Division
BG John A Wharton
1st Brigade
Col C C Crews
Malone's (AL) Reg
2 GA   3 GA   4 GA
2nd Brigade
Col Thomas Harrison
3 Confederate 3 KY
4 TN   8 TX   11 TX
White's (TN) Bat

Martin's Division
1st Brigade
Col John T Morgan
1 AL   3 AL
51 AL   8 Confederate
2nd Brigade
Col A A Russell
4 AL (Russell's Reg)
1 Confederate
JH Wiggins' (AR) Bat

FORREST'S CORPS
BG Nathan B Forrest
Escort
Jackson's Co-TN Cav
Armstrong's Division
BG Frank C Armstrong
Armstrong's Brigade
Col James T Wheeler
3 AR   2 KY
6 TN   18 TN

Forrest's Brigade
Col George G Dibrell
4 TN   8 TN
9 TN   10 TN   11 TN
Shaw's Battalion
O P Hamilton's Battln
RD Allison's Squadron
Huggins' (TN) Bat
Morton's (TN) Bat

Pegram's Division
BG John Pegram
Davidson's Brigade
BG Henry B Davidson
1 GA   6 GA   6 NC
Rucker's (1 TN) Legion
12,16 TN Battalion
Huwald's (TN) Bat

Scott's Brigade
Col John S Scott
10 Confederate
1 LA   2 TN   5 TN
NTN Robinson's (LA) Bat

Detachment of John-
Hunt Morgan's Command

Organization of the Union Army, with Lieut. Gen. Ulysses S. Grant, USA, Commanding General at the Campaign for Petersburg and Richmond, VA, at December 31, 1864.

Escort
5 US Cav-Co's B,F,K

ARMY OF THE POTOMAC
MG George G Meade
(on leave)
MG John G Parke

Provost Guard
BG Marsena R Patrick
8 DE-3 Co's 1 MA Cav
1 IN Cav 68 PA
1 MA Cav 114 PA
80 NY (20 Militia)

Engineer Brigades and
Defense of City Point
BG Henry W Benham
1 ME Sharp 61 MA
MI Sharp 18 NH
15 NY 50 NY

Battalion US Engineers
Maj Franklin Harwood

Guards and Orderlies
Oneida (NY) Cav

Artillery
BG Henry J Hunt

Engineer Brigade
BG Henry W Benham

SIEGE ARTILLERY
Col Henry L Abbot
1 CT Heavy 3 CT Bat

Artillery Reserve
Capt Ezekiel R Mayo
14 MA 2 ME
3 ME 15 NY Heavy
1 RI 3 VT

2nd Army Corps
MG Andrew A Humphreys

1st Division
BG Nelson A Miles

1st Brigade
Col George N Macy
26 MI 5 NH
2 NY Heavy Art 61 PA
81 PA 140 PA
183 PA

2nd Brigade
Col Robert Nugent
28 MA 63 NY
69 NY 88 NY
7 NY Heavy

3rd Brigade
Col Clinton MacDougall
7 NY 39 NY
52 NY 111 NY
125 NY 126 NY

4th Brigade
Col William Glenny
4 NY Heavy Art 64 NY
66 NY 53 PA
116 PA 145 PA
148 PA

2nd Division
BG John Gibbon
(on leave)
BG Thomas A Smyth

Provost Guard
1st Brigade
Col James M Willett
19 ME 19 MA
20 MA 7 MI
1 MN 59 NY
152 NY 184 NY
36 WI

2nd Brigade
Col Mathew Murphy
8 NY Heavy Art
155 NY 164 NY
170 NY 182 NY

3rd Brigade
LCol Francis E Pierce
14 CT 1 DE
12 NJ 10 NY Battln
108 NY 4 OH Battln
69 PA 106 PA Battln
7 WV

3rd Division
BG Gershom Mott

1st Brigade
BG P R de Trobriand
20 IN 1 ME Heavy Art
17 ME 40 NY
73 NY 86 NY
124 NY 99 PA
110 PA 2 US Sharp

2nd Brigade
BG Bryron R Pierce
1 MA Heavy Art
5 MI 93 NY
57 PA 84 PA
105 PA 141 PA
1 US Sharp

3rd Brigade
Col John Ramsey
11 MA Battln 11 NJ
7 NJ Battalion
8 NJ Battalion
120 NY

ARTILLERY BRIGADE
Maj John G Hazard
6 ME 10 MA
1 NH 2 NJ
3 NJ 1 NY Art-Bat G
4 NY Heavy Art-Bat C,L
11 NY 12 NY
1 PA Art-Bat F
1 RI Art-Bat B
4 US Art-Bat K
5 US Art-Bat C,I

5th Army Corps
MG Gouverneur K Warren

Escort
4 PA Cav-detachment

Provost Guard
5 NY-Co E,F, 104 NY

1st Division
BG Charles Griffin
(on leave)
BG Joseph J Bartlett

1st Brigade
BG Joshua Chamberlain
185 NY 198 PA

2nd Brigade
Col Edgar M Gregory
187 NY 188 NY
189 PA

3rd Brigade
Col Alfred L Pearson
20 ME 32 MA
1 MI 16 MI
83 PA 91 PA
118 PA 155 PA

2nd Division
BG Romeyn B Ayres
(on leave)
Col James Gwyn

1st Brigade
Col Frederick Winthrop
5 NY 15 NY Heavy Art
140 NY 146 NY

2nd Brigade
Col Andrew W Denison
1 MD 4 MD
7 MD 8 MD

3rd Brigade
Col William Sergeant
3 DE 4 DE
157 PA 190 PA
191 PA 210 PA

3rd Division
BG Samuel W Crawford

Sharpshooters
1 NY Battalion

1st Brigade
BG Edward S Bragg
(on leave)
Col Henry A Morrow
24 MI 143 PA
149 PA 150 PA
6 WI 7 WI

2nd Brigade
BG Henry Baxter
16 ME 39 MA
97 NY 11 PA
88 PA 107 PA

3rd Brigade
Col J William Hoffman
76 NY 94 NY
95 NY 147 NY
56 PA 121 PA
142 PA

ARTILLERY BRIGADE
Col Charles Wainwright
(on leave)
Maj Robert H Fitzhugh
5 MA 9 MA
1 NY-Art-Bat C,D,E,H,L
1 PA Art-Bat B
4 US Art-Bat B
5 US Art-Bat D,G

6th Army Corps
MG Horatio G Wright

Escort
21 PA Cav-Co E

1st Division
BG Frank Wheaton

1st Brigade
Capt Baldwin Hufty
1 NJ 2 NJ
4 NJ 10 NJ
15 NJ 40 NJ

2nd Brigade
BG Ranald Mackenzie
2 CT Heavy Art
65 NY 121 NY
95 PA

3rd Brigade
Col Thomas S Allen
37 MA 49 PA
82 PA 119 PA
2 RI 5 WI

2nd Division
BG George W Getty
(on leave)
BG Lewis A Grant

1st Brigade
Col James M Warner
(on leave)
Col George P Foster
62 NY 93 PA
98 PA 102 PA
139 PA

Second Brigade
LCol Charles Hunsdon
1 VT Heavy Art
2 VT 3 VT
4 VT 5 VT
6 VT

3rd Brigade
Col Thomas W Hyde
1 ME 43 NY
49 NY 77 NY
122 NY 61 PA

3rd Division
BG Truman Seymour

1st Brigade
Col William S Truex
14 NJ 106 NY
151 NY 87 PA
10 VT

2nd Brigade
Col Benjamin F Smith
6 MD 9 NY Heavy Art
110 OH 122 OH
126 OH 67 PA
138 PA

ARTILLERY BRIGADE
Col Charles Tompkins
4 ME 1 NJ
3 NY 1 OH
56 PA 1 RI Lt-Bat E
5 US-Bat E

CAVALRY
2nd Division
BG David McM Gregg
(on leave)
BG Henry E Davies

1st Brigade
Col Hugh H Janeway
1 MA 1 NJ
10 NY 24 NY
1 PA
2 US Art-Bat A

2nd Brigade
Col J Irvin Gregg
2 PA 4 PA
8 PA 13 PA
16 PA
1 US Art-Bat H,I

3rd Brigade
Col Charles H Smith
1 ME 6 OH
2 NY Mounted Rifles
21 PA

Unattached
13 OH

9th Army Corps
BG Orlando B Willcox

Escort
2 PA Cav-detachment

Provost Guard
79 NY

1st Division
Col N McLaughlin

1st Brigade
Col Samuel Harriman
8 MI 27 MI
109 NY 51 PA
37 WI 38 WI

2nd Brigade
Col Byron M Cutcheon
1 MI Sharpshooters
46 NY 60 OH
50 PA

3rd Brigade
LCol Gilbert Robinson
3 MD 29 MA
57 MA 59 MA
14 NY Heavy Artillery
100 PA

Acting Engineers
17 MI

2nd Division
BG Robert B Potter

1st Brigade
BG Simon G Griffin

1st Brigade
Col John I Curtin
35 MA 36 MA
58 MA 39 NJ
51 NY 45 PA
48 PA 4 RI
7 RI

2nd Brigade
Col Herbert B Titus
31 ME 2 MD
56 MA 6 NH
9 NH 11 NH
179 NY 186 NY
17 VT

3rd Division
BG John F Hartranft

1st Brigade
Col Charles W Diven
200 PA 208 PA
209 PA

2nd Brigade
Col Joseph A Mathews
205 PA 207 PA
211 PA

ARTILLERY BRIGADE
Col John C Tidball
7 ME 11 MA
19 NY 27 NY
34 NY
PA Art-Bat D

ARMY OF THE JAMES
MG Benjamin F Butler

Engineer
1 NY

Naval Brigade
BG Charles K Graham

24 Army Corps
MG Edward O C Ord
(on leave)
BG Alfred H Terry

Headquarters Guard
8 CT

Provst Grd/Orderlies
4 MA Cav-Co's F,K

1st Division
BG Robert S Foster

1st Brigade
Col Thomas O Osborn
39 IL 62 OH
67 OH 199 PA

2nd Brigade
BG Joseph R Hawley
6 CT 7 CT
3 NH 7 NH
16 NY Heavy Art

3rd Brigade
Col Harris Plaisted
10 CT 11 ME
24 MA 100 NY
206 PA

4th Brigade
Col James Jordan
8 ME 89 NY
148 NY 158 NY
55 PA

2nd Division
BG Adelbert Ames

1st Brigade
Col N Martin Curtis
3 NY 112 NY
117 NY 142 NY

2nd Brigade
Col G Pennypacker
47 NY 48 NY
76 PA 97 PA
203 PA

3rd Brigade
Col Louis Bell
13 IN 9 ME
4 NH 115 PA
169 NY

3rd Division
BG Chas Devens, Jr

1st Brigade
LCol John B Raulston
11 CT 13 NH
81 NY 98 NY
139 NY 19 WI

2nd Brigade
Col Joseph H Potter
5 MD 10 NH
12 NH 96 NY
118 NY 9 VT

3rd Brigade
Col Guy V Henry
21 CT 40 MA
2 NH 58 PA
188 PA

1ST INFANTRY DIVISION
ARMY OF WEST VIRGINIA
Col Thomas M Harris

1st Brigade
LCol Thomas F Wiles
34 MA 116 OH
123 OH

2nd Brigade
Col William B Curtis
23 IL 54 PA
12 WC

3rd Brigade
Col Milton Wells
10 WV 11 WV
15 WV

ARTILLERY BRIGADE
Maj Charles C Abell
3 NY Art-Bat E,H,K,M
7 NY 16 NY
17 NY
1 PA Art-Bat A
1 RI Art-Bat F
4 US Art-Bat L
5 US Art-Bat A,F

25th Army Corps
MG Godfrey Wetzel
4 MA Cav-Co E,H
BG Charles J Paine

1st Brigade
Col Delevan Bates
1 US 27 US
30 US

2nd Brigade
Col John W Ames
4 US 6 US
39 US

3rd Brigade
Col Elias Wright
5 US 10 US
37 US 107 US

2nd Division
BG William Birney

1st Brigade
Col Charles Russell
7 US 109 US
116 US 117 US

2nd Brigade
Col Ulysses Doubleday
8 US 45 US
127 US

3rd Brigade
Col Henry C Ward
28 US 29 US
31 US

3rd Division
BG Edward A Wild

1st Brigade
Col Alonzo G Draper
22 US 36 US
38 US 118 US

2nd Brigade
Col Edwrd Martindale
29 CT 9 US
41 US

3rd Brigade
BG Henry G Thomas
19 US 23 US
43 US

Unassigned
2 US Colored Cav
(dismounted)

ARTILLERY BRIGADE
LCol Richard Jackson
1 CT 4 NJ
5 NJ 16 NY Heavy
1 PA Art-Bat E
3 RI Art-Bat C
1 US Art-Bat D,M
3 US Art-Bat E
4 US Art-Bat D

CAVALRY DIVISION
BG August V Kautz

1st Brigade
Col Robert M West
20 NY 5 PA

2nd Brigade
Col Samuel P Spear
1 DC 11 PA

3rd Brigade
Col Andrew W Evans
1 MD 1 NY Mounted

ARTILLERY
4 WI
1 US Art-Bat B

DEFENSES OF
BERMUDA HUNDRED
BG Edward Ferrero

1st Brigade
Col William Heine
41 NY 104 PA

2nd Brigade
LCol G De P Arden
6 NY Heavy Art
10 NY Heavy Art

Provisional Brigade
Col William McClure
13 NH-detachment
2 PA Heavy Art-bttln

SIEGE ARTILLERY
13 NY Heavy-Bat A,H
3 PA Heavy-Bat E,G,M

Pontoniers
3 MA Heavy-Bat I

SEPARATE BRIGADE
Col Wardell Robinson

FORT POCHANTAS
Maj William Tantum
38 NJ 16 NY Heavy
33 NY Bat
1 US Colored Cavalry

HARRISON LANDING
LCol Wm McKinley
4 MA Cav 184 NY
3 PA Heavy Art

FORT POWHATAN
Col William J Sewell
38 NJ 3 PA Heavy
1 US Colored Cav-Co E

Organization of the Army of Northern Virginia, Gen. Robert E. Lee, CSA, Commanding at the Campaign for Petersburg and Richmond, VA, December 31, 1864.

		3RD ARMY CORPS	Mahone's Division	ANDERSON'S CORPS	CAVALRY
Provost Guard	**Wofford's Brigade**	**2ND ARMY CORPS**	LG Ambrose P Hill	MG William Mahone	LG Richard H Anderson	MJ Wade Hampton

Provost Guard
1 VA Battalion
39 VA Battalion
Engineer Troops
1st Regiment

1ST ARMY CORPS
LG James Longstreet
Pickett's Division
MG George E Pickett
Steaurt's Brigade
BG George H Steaurt
9 VA   14 VA
38 VA   53 VA
57 VA

Corse's Brigade
BG Montgomery D Corse
15 VA   17 VA
29 VA   30 VA
32 VA

Hunton's Brigade
BG Eppa Hunton
8 VA   18 VA
19 VA   28 VA
56 VA

Terry's Brigade
BG William R Terry
1 VA   3 VA
7 VA   11 VA
24 VA

Field's Division
MG Charles W Field
Anderson's Brigade
BG George T Anderson
7 GA   8 GA
9 GA 11 GA 59 GA

Law's Brigade
Col W F Perry
4 AL   15 AL
44 AL 47 AL 48 AL

Gregg's Brigade
Col F S Bass
3 AR   1 TX
4 TX   5 TX

Benning's Brigade
BG Henry L Benning
2 GA   15 GA
17 GA   20 GA

Bratton's Brigade
BG John Bratton
1 SC   5 SC
6 SC 2 SC Rifles
Palmetto (SC) Sharp

Wofford's Brigade
BG Dudley M DuBose
16 GA 18 GA 24 GA
3 GA Battln Sharp
Cobb's GA Legion
Phillips' GA Legion

Humphrey's Brigade
BG Benjamin G Humphreys
13 MS   17 MS
18 MS   21 MS

Bryan's Brigade
BG Goode Bryan
10 GA   50 GA
51 GA   53 GA

Conner's Brigade
BG James Conners
2 SC   3 SC
7 SC   8 SC
15 SC   20 SC
3 SC Battalion

Artillery
BG Edward P Alexander
Cabell's Battalion
VA Battalion
GA (2) Batteries
NC Battery
Huger's Battalion
LCol F Huger
SC Battery
LA Battery
VA (2) Batteries

Hardaway's Battalion
LC R A Hardaway
VA (3) Batteries

Haskell's Battalion
Maj John C Haskell
NC (2) Batteries
SC Battery
VA (2) Batteries

Starke's Battalion
LCol A W Starke
LA Battery
VA (2) Batteries

2ND ARMY CORPS
MG John B Gordon
Battle's Brigade
3 AL   5 AL
6 AL   12 AL
61 AL

Grime's Brigade
32 NC   43 NC
45 NC   53 NC
2 NC Battalion

Cox's Brigade
1 NC   2 NC
3 NC   4 NC
14 NC   30 NC

Cook's Brigade
4 GA   12 GA
21 GA   44 GA

Early's Division
BG John Pegram
5 NC   12 NC
20 NC   23 NC
1 NC Battalion

Lewis' Brigade
6 NC   21 NC
54 NC   57 NC

Pegram's Brigade
13 VA   31 VA
49 VA   52 VA
58 VA

Gordon's Division
BG Clement A Evans
13 GA   26 GA
31 GA   38 GA
60 GA   61 GA
12 GA Battalion

Terry's Brigade
2 VA   4 VA
5 VA   10 VA
21 VA   23 VA
25 VA   27 VA
33 VA   37 VA
42 VA   44 VA
48 VA

York's Brigade
1 LA   2 LA
5 LA   6 LA
7 LA   8 LA
9 LA   10 LA
14 LA   15 LA

3RD ARMY CORPS
LG Ambrose P Hill
Heth's Division
MG Henry Heth
Davis's Brigade
BG Joseph R Davis
1 Confederate Battalion
2 MS   11 MS
26 MS   42 MS

Cooke's Brigade
BG John Rogers Cooke
15 NC   27 NC
46 NC   48 NC
55 NC

MacRae's Brigade
11 NC   26 NC
44 NC   47 NC
52 NC

Archer's Brigade
Col R M Mayo
13 AL 1 TN (Prov Army)
7 TN   14 TN

Walker's Brigade
2 MD Battalion
22 VA Battalion
40 VA   47 VA
55 VA

Johnson's Brigade
12 TN   23 TN
25 TN   44 TN
63 TN

Wilcox's Division
MG Cadmus M Wilcox
14 GA   35 GA
45 GA   49 GA

Lane's Brigade
BG James H Lane
7 NC   18 NC
28 NC   33 NC
37 NC

McGowan's Brigade
BG Samuel McGowan
12 SC   13 SC
14 SC
1 SC (Prov Army)
Orr's SC Rifles

Seales's Brigade
BG Alfred M Scales
13 NC   16 NC
22 NC   34 NC
38 NC

Mahone's Division
MG William Mahone
Sander's Brigade
MG John C Sanders
BG James H Lane
8 AL   9 AL
10 AL   11 AL
13 AL   14 AL

Weisiger's Brigade
BG David A Weisiger
6 VA   12 VA
16 VA   41 VA
61 VA

Harris' Brigade
BG Nathaniel H Harris
12 MS   16 MS
19 MS   48 MS

Sorrel's Brigade
BG Gilbert M Sorrel
3 GA   22 GA
48 GA   64 GA
2, 10 GA Battalion

Finegan's Brigade
BG Joseph Finegan
2 FL   5 FL
8 FL   9 FL
10 FL   11 FL

Artillery
Col R L Walker
AL Battery
MD (2) Batteries
VA (3) Batteries

Pegram's Battalion
Col W J Pegram
MS Battery
SC Battery
VA (4) Batteries

Poague's Battalion
Col W T Poague
NC Battery
VA (2) Batteries

Eshleman's Battalion
LCol B F Eshleman
LA (4) Batteries

Richardson's Battalion
LCol Charles Richardson
LA Battery
VA (3) Batteries

Lane's Battalion
Maj John Lane
GA (3) Batteries

Owen's Battalion
Maj William M Owen
VA (3) Batteries

ANDERSON'S CORPS
LG Richard H Anderson
Hoke's Division
[started for Wilmington]
[NC, Dec 20, 1864]
MG Robert F Hoke
Hagood's Brigade
BG Johnson Hagood
11 SC   21 SC
25 SC   27 SC
7 SC Battalion

Colquitt's Brigade
BG Alfred H Colquitt
6 GA   19 GA
23 GA   27 GA
28 GA

Clingman's Brigade
8 NC   31 NC
51 NC   61 NC

Kirkland's Brigade
BG William W Kirkland
17 NC   42 NC
66 NC

Johnson's Division
MG Bushrod R Johnson
Wise's Brigade
BG Henry A Wise
26 VA   34 VA
46 VA   59 VA

Elliott's Brigade
BG Stephen Elliott, Jr
17 SC   18 SC
22 SC   23 SC
26 SC
Holcombe SC Legion

Gracie's Brigade
BG Archibald Gracie, Jr
41 AL   43 AL
59 AL   60 AL
23 AL Battalion

Ransom's Brigade
BG Matt Whitaker Ransom
24 NC   25 NC
35 NC   49 NC
56 NC

Artillery
Col H P Jones
Moseley's Battalion
GA Battery
NC Battery
VA (2) Batteries

Blount's Battalion
VA (4) Batteries

Coil's Battalion
LA Battery
MS Battery
VA Battery

Martin's Battalion
VA (2) Batteries

CAVALRY
MJ Wade Hampton
Butler's Brigade
Col H K Aiken
4 SC   5 SC
6 SC

Young's Brigade
Col J F Waring
10 GA
Cobb's GA Legion
Phillips' GA Legion
Jeff Davis' MS Legion

Lee's Division
MG Wm Henry F Lee
Barringer's Brigade
BG Rufus Barringer
1 NC   2 NC
3 NC   5 NC

Beale's Brigade
BG Richard Lee T Beale
9 VA   10 VA
13 VA

Dearing's Brigade
BG James Dearing
8 GA   4 NC
16 NC Battalion

Horse Artillery
Maj R Preston Chew
SC (Hart's) Battery
VA (2) Batteries

ARMY OF THE CUMBERLAND
MG George H Thomas
Escort
1 OH Cav-Co I
Artillery
BG John M Brannan

4th Army Corps
MG Oliver Howard
MG David Stanley

1st Division
MG David Stanley
BG William Grose
BG Nathan Kimball

1st Brigade
BG Charles Cruft
Col Isaac Kirby
21 IL 38 IL 31 IN
81 IN 1 KY 2 KY
90 OH 101 OH

2nd Brigade
BG Walter Whitaker
Col Jacob Taylor
59 IL 96 IL 115 IL
35 IN 84 IN 21 KY
23 KY 40 OH
45 OH 51 OH 99 OH

3rd Brigade
Col William Grose
Col P Sidney Post
BG William Grose
Col John Bennett
59 IL 75 IL
80 IL 84 IL
9 IN 30 IN
36 IN 84 IN 77 PA
Artillery
Capt Peter Simonson
Capt Samuel McDowell
Capt Theo Thomasson
IN Lt-5 Bat
PA Lt-B Bat

2nd Division
BG John Newton

1st Brigade
Col Francis Sherman
BG Nathan Kimball
Col Emerson Opdycke
36 IL 44 IL
73 IL 74 IL
88 IL 28 KY
2 MO 15 MO 24 WI

2nd Brigade
BG George Wagner
Col John W Blake
100 IL 40 IL
57 IN 28 KY
26 OH 97 OH

3rd Brigade
BG Charles Harker
BG Luther Bradley
22 IL 27 IL
42 IL 51 IL
79 IL 3 KY
64 OH 65 OH 125 OH
Artillery
Capt Chas Aleshire
Capt Wilbur Goodspeed
1 IL Lt-Bat M
1 OH Lt-Bat A

3rd Division
BG Thomas J Wood
Col P Sidney Post

1st Brigade
BG August Willich
Col William Grose
Col Chas T Hotchkiss
25 IL 35 IL 89 IL
32 IL 8 KS 15 OH
49 OH 15 WI

2nd Brigade
BG William B Hazen
Col Oliver H Payne
Col P Sidney Post
59 IL 6 IN 5 KY
6 KY 23 KY 1 OH
6 OH 41 OH
71 OH 93 OH 124 OH

3rd Brigade
BG Samuel Beatty
Col Frederick Knefler
79 IN 86 IN
9 KY 17 KY
13 OH 19 OH 52 OH
Artillery
Capt Cullen Bradley
IL Lt-Bridge's
OH Lt-6 Bat
Artillery Brigade
Maj Thomas Osborn
Capt Lyman Bridges
1 IL Lt-Bat M
IL Lt-Bridge's
IN Lt-5 Bat
1 OH Lt-Bat A,M
OH Lt-6 Bat
PA Lt-Bat B

HQ Guard
7 Co OH Sharpshtr
Artillery
BG William F Barry

14th Army Corps
MG John Palmer
BG Richard Johnson
BG Jeff Davis

1st Division
BG Richard Johnson
BG John H King
BG William Carlin
Provost Guard
16 US-Co D,1st Battn

1st Brigade
BG William Carlin
Col Anson G McCook
Col Marion Taylor
104 IL 42 IN
88 IN 15 KY
2 OH 33 OH
94 OH 10 WI
21 WI

2nd Brigade
BG John H King
Col Wm Stoughton
Col Marshall Moore
95 NY
Maj John R Edie
11 MI 69 OH
15 US 16 US
18 US 19 US

3rd Brigade
Col Benjmn Scribner
Col Josiah Given
Col Marshall Moore
37 IN 38 IN
21 OH 74 OH
78 PA 79 PA
1 WI
Artillery
Capt Lucius Drury
1 IL Lt-Bat C
1 OH Lt-Bat I

2nd Division
BG Jefferson C Davis
BG James D Morgan

1st Brigade
BG James D Morgan
Col Robert Smith
Col Charles M Lum
10 IL 16 IL
60 IL 10 MI
14 MI 17 NY

2nd Brigade
Col John G Mitchell
34 IL 78 IL
98 OH 108 OH
113 OH 121 OH

3rd Brigade
Col Daniel McCook
Col Oscar Harmon
Col Caleb Dilworth
LCol James Langley
85 IL 86 IL
110 IL 125 IL
22 IN 52 OH
Artillery
Capt Charles Barnett
2 IL Lt-Bat I
WI Lt-5 Bat

3rd Division
BG Absalom Baird

1st Brigade
BG John Turchin
Col Moses Walker
19 IL 24 IL
82 IN 23 MO
11 OH 17 OH
31 OH 89 OH
92 OH

2nd Brigade
Col F Van Derveer
Col Newell Gleason
75 IN 87 IN
101 IN 2 MN
9 OH 35 OH
105 OH

3rd Brigade
Col George P Este
10 IN 74 IN
10 KY 18 KY
14 OH 38 OH
Artillery
Capt George Estep
IN Lt-7,19 Bat
Artillery Brigade
Maj Chas Houghtaling
1 IL Lt-Bat C
2 IL Lt-Bat I
IN Lt-Bat 7,19,20
1 OH Lt-Bat I
WI Lt-5 Bat

20th Army Corps
MG Joseph Hooker
BG Alpheus Williams
MG Henry W Slocum

1st Division
BG Alpheus Williams
Escort
15 IL Cav-Co K

1st Division
BG Alpheus Williams
BG Joseph Knipe

1st Brigade
BG Joseph Knipe
5 CT 3 MD-detch
123 NY 141 NY
46 PA

2nd Brigade
BG Thomas H Ruger
Col Wm Stoughton
27 IN 2 MD
13 NJ 107 NY
150 NY 3 WI

3rd Brigade
Col Thomas Robinson
Col Horace Boughton
82 IL 101 IL
45 NY 143 NY
61 OH 82 OH
31 WI
Artillery
Capt John Woodbury
1 NY Lt-Bat I,M

2nd Division
BG John W Geary

1st Brigade
BG James D Morgan
Col Charles Candy
Col Ario Pardee, Jr
5 OH 7 OH
29 OH 66 OH
28 PA 147 PA

2nd Brigade
Col Adolphus Buschbeck
Col John T Lockman
Col Patrick Jones
Col George W Mindil
33 NJ 119 NY
134 NY 154 NY
27 PA 73 PA
109 PA

3rd Brigade
Col David Ireland
Col William Rickards
Col George Cobham, Jr
60 NY 78 NY
102 NY 137 NY
149 NY 29 PA 111 PA
Artillery
Capt William Wheeler
Capt Charles Aleshire
NY Lt-13 Bat
PA Lt-Bat E

3rd Division
MG Daniel Butterfield
BG William T Ward

1st Brigade
BG William T Ward
Col Benjamin Harrison
102 IL 105 IL
129 IL 70 IN 79 OH

2nd Brigade
Col Samuel Ross
Col John Coburn
20 CT 33 IN
85 IN 19 MI 22 WI

3rd Brigade
Col James Wood, Jr
20 CT 33 MA
136 NY 55 OH
73 OH 26 WI
Artillery
Capt Marco B Gary
1 MI Lt-Bat I
1 OH Lt-Bat C
Artillery Brigade
Maj John A Reynolds
1 MI Lt-Bat I
1 NY Lt-Bat I,M
NY Lt-13 Bat
1 OH Lt-Bat C
PA Lt-Bat C
5 US-Bat K

UNATTACHED TROOPS
Reserve Brigade
Col Joseph W Burke
Col Heber Le Favour
10 OH 9 MI
22 MI
Pontoniers
Col George P Buell
58 IN
Pontoon Battalion
Siege Artillery
11 IN Battery
Ammunition Train Guard
1 Battln OH Sharp

Cavalry Corps
BG Washington Elliott
Escort
4 OH-Co D

1st Division
BG Edward M McCook

1st Brigade
Col Joseph B Dorr
Col John T Croxton
LCol James Brownlow
BG John T Croxton
8 IA 4 KY
2 MI 1 TN

2nd Brigade
Col Oscar La Grange
LCol James W Stewart
LCol Horace P Lamson
LCol William H Torrey
2 IN 4 IN
150 NY 3 WI

3rd Brigade
Col Louis D Watkins
Col John K Faulkner
4 KY 6 KY
7 KY
Artillery
18 IN Bat

2nd Division
BG Kenner Garrard

1st Brigade
Col Robert H G Minty
4 MI 7 PA
4 US

2nd Brigade
Col Eli Long
Col Beroth Eggleston
1 OH 3 OH
4 OH
(Mounted Infantry)
Col John T Wilder
Col Abram O Miller
98 IL 123 IL
17 IN 72 IN
Artillery
Chicago (IL) Board
of Trade Battery

3rd Division
BG Judson Kilpatrick
Col Eli H Murray
Col William W Lowe

1st Brigade
LCol Robert Klein
LCol Matt Patrick
Maj J Morris Young
3 IN-4 Co's
5 IA

2nd Brigade
Col Charles C Smith
Maj Thomas Sanderson
LCol Fielder A Jones
8 IN 2 KY
10 OH

3rd Brigade
Col Eli H Murray
Col Smith D Atkins
92 IL (Mounted Inf)
3 KY 5 KY
Artillery
10 WI Battery

ARMY OF THE TENNESSEE
MG James B McPherson
MG John A Logan
MG Oliver O Howard
Escort
4th Co-OH Cav
1 OH Cav

15th Army Corps
MG John A Logan
BG Morgan L Smith

1st Division
BG Peter J Osterhaus
BG Charles R Woods
MG Peter J Osterhaus

1st Brigade
BG Charles R Woods
Col Milo Smith
26 IA 30 IA
27 MO 76 OH

2nd Brigade
Col James Williamson
4 IA 9 IA
25 IA 31 IA

3rd Brigade
Col Hugo Wangelin
3 MO 12 MO
17 MO 29 MO
31 MO 32 MO
Artillery
Maj C Landgraeber
2 MO Lt-Bat F
OH LT-4 Bat

2nd Division
BG Morgan L Smith
BG Joseph Lightburn
BG William B Hazen

1st Brigade
BG Giles A Smith
Col James S Martin
Col Theodore Jones
55 IL 111 IL
116 IL 127 IL
6 MO 8 MO
30 OH 57 OH

2nd Brigade
BG Joseph Lightburn
Col Wells S Jones
111 IL 83 IN
30 OH 37 OH
47 OH 53 OH
54 OH
Artillery
Capt Francis De Gress
1 IL Lt-Bat A,B,H

3rd Division
BG John E Smith
Escort
4 MO Cav-Co F

1st Brigade
Col Jesse Alexander
Col Joseph B McCown
63 IL 48 IN
59 IN 4 MN
18 WI

2nd Brigade
Col Green B Raum
13 IL 56 IL
17 IA 10 MO
24 MO 80 OH

3rd Brigade
BG Charles Matthies
Col Benjamin Dean
Col Jabez Banbury
93 IL 5 IN
10 IA 26 MO
Artillery
Capt Henry Dillon
WI Lt-6,12 Bat
Cavalry
5 OH

4th Division
BG William Harrow

1st Brigade
Col Reuben Williams
Col John M Oliver
26 IL 48 IL
90 IL 12 IN
99 IN 100 IN
75 MI 70 OH

2nd Brigade
BG Charles Walcutt
40 IL 103 IL
97 IN 6 IA
46 OH

Third Brigade
Col John M Oliver
48 IL 99 IN
15 MI 53 OH
70 OH
Artillery
Capt Henry Griffiths
Maj John T Cheney
Capt Josiah Burton
1 IL Lt-Bat F
IA Lt-1 Bat

16th Army Corps
MG Greeneville Dodge
BG Thomas E Ransom
General Headquarters
1 AL Cav
52 IL-Co A

2nd Division
BG Thomas W Sweeny
BG Elliott W Rice
BG John M Corse

1st Brigade
BG Elliott W Rice
52 IL 66 IN
2 IA 7 IA

2nd Brigade
Col Patrick E Burke
LCol Robert N Adams
Col August Mersy
9 IL (Mounted)
12 IL 66 IL
81 OH

3rd Brigade
Col Moses M Bane
BG William Vandever
Col Henry Cummings
Col Richard Rowett
7 IL 50 IL
57 IL 39 IA
Artillery
Capt Fredrck Welker
1 MI Lt-Bat B
1 MO Lt-Bat H,I
OH Lt-3 Bat

4th Division
BG James C Veatch
BG John W Fuller
BG Thomas E Ransom

1st Brigade
BG John W Fuller
Col John Morrill
64 IL 18 MO
27 OH 39 OH

2nd Brigade
BG John W Sprague
35 NJ 43 OH
63 OH 25 WI

3rd Brigade
Col James H Howe
Col William Grower
Col John Tillson
10 IL 25 IN
17 NY 32 WI
Artillery
Capt Jerome Burrows
Capt George Robinson
1 MI Lt-Bat C
OH Lt-14 Bat
2nd US-Bat F

17th Army Corps
MG Frank P Blair, Jr
Escort
1 OH Cav-Co M
9 IL (Mounted Inf)
11 IL Cav-Co G

3rd Division
BG Mortimer Leggett
BG Charles R Woods
Escort
1 OH Cav-Co D

1st Brigade
BG Manning Force
Col George E Bryant
20 IL 30 IL
31 IL 45 IL
12 WI 16 WI

2nd Brigade
Col Robert K Scott
LCol Greenberry Wiles
20 OH 32 OH
68 OH 78 OH

3rd Brigade
Col Adam G Malloy
17 WI
Worden's Battalion
Artillery
Capt Wm S Williams
1 IL Lt-Bat D
1 MI Lt-Bat H
OH Lt-3 Bat

4th Division
BG Walter Gresham
Col William Hall
BG Giles A Smith
Escort
11 IL Cav-Co G

1st Brigade
Col Wm L Sanderson
Col Benjamin F Potts
32 IL 53 IL
23 IN 53 IN
3 IA 32 OH
12 WI

2nd Brigade
Col George C Rogers
Col Isaac C Pugh
14 IL 15 IL
32 IL 41 IL
53 IL

3rd Brigade
Col William Hall
Col John Shane
BG William W Belknap
11 IA 13 IA
15 IA 16 IA
Artillery
Capt Edward Spear
Capt William Clayton
2 IL Lt-Bat F
MN Lt-1 Bat
1 MO Lt-Bat C
OH Lt-19,15 Bat

ARMY OF THE OHIO
(23rd Army Corps)
MG John M Schofield
BG Jacob D Cox
Escort
7 OH Cav-Co G
Engineer Battalion
Capt Chas McAlester
Capt Oliver McClure

1st Division
BG Alvin P Hover
1st Brigade
Col Richard Barter
120 IN 124 IN
128 IN

2nd Brigade
Col John McQuiston
Col Peter Swaine
123 IN 129 IN
130 IN 99 OH
Artillery
IN Lt-23,24 Bat

2nd Division
BG Henry M Judah
BG Milo S Hascall

1st Brigade
BG Nathaniel McLean
BG Joseph A Cooper
80 IN 91 IN
13 KY 25 MI
45 OH 3 TN
6 TN

2nd Brigade
BG Milo S Hascall
Col John R Bond
Col William Hobson
107 IL 80 IN
13 KY 23 MI
45 OH 111 OH
118 O H

3rd Brigade
Col Silas Strickland
14 KY 20 KY
27 KY 50 OH
Artillery
Capt Joseph Shields
IN Lt-22 Bat
1 MI Lt-Bat F
OH Lt-19 Bat

3rd Division
BG Jacob D Cox
Col James Reilly

1st Brigade
Col James W Reilly
Col James W Gault
BG James W Reilly
112 IN 16 KY
100 OH 104 OH
8 TN

2nd Brigade
BG Mahlon D Manson
Col John S Hurt
Col John Casement
Col Daniel Cameron
65 IL 63 IN
65 IN 24 KY
103 OH 5 TN

3rd Brigade
BG Nathaniel McLean
Col Robert Byrd
Col Israel N Stiles
11 KY 12 KY
1 TN 5 TN
Dismounted Cavalry
Col Eugene Crittenden
16 IL 12 KY
Artillery
Maj Henry W Wells
IN Lt-15 Bat
1 OH Lt-Bat D

CAVALRY
MG George Stoneman
Col Horace Capron
Escort
7 OH-Co D

1st Brigade
Col Israel Garrard
9 MI 7 OH

2nd Brigade
Col James Biddle
Col Thomas Butler
16 IL 5 IN
6 IN 12 KY

Third Brigade
Col Horace Capron
14 IL 8 MI
McLaughlin's OH Squad
Independent Brigade
Col Alexander Holeman
LCol Silas Adams
1 KY 11 KY
Artillery
24 IN Bat

Organization of the Confederate Army during the Atlanta, GA, Campaign, Gen. Joseph E. Johnston, CSA,
then Gen John Bell Commanding, May 3-September 8, 1864, with redeployment of forces

ARMY OF TENNESSEE
Gen Joseph E Johnston
Escorts
Army Headquarters
Guy Dreux's Co LA Cav
Holloway's Co AL Cav
Hardee's Corps
LG William J Hardee
MG Patrick Cleburne
Escort
Raum's Co MS Cav
Cheatham's Division
MG Benjamin F Cheatham
BG George Maney
BG John C Carter
Escort
Co G, 2 GA Cav
Maney's Brigade
BG George Maney
Col George C Porter
1 TN   27 TN
4 TN   6 TN
9 TN   41 TN
50 TN   24 TN
Strahl's Brigade
BG Otho F Strahl
4 TN   5 TN
19 TN   24 TN
31 TN   33 TN
Wright's Brigade
BG John C Carter
8 TN   16 TN
28 TN   38 TN
51 TN   52 TN
Vaughan's Brigade
BG Alfred Vaughan, Jr
Col M Magevney, Jr
BG George W Gordon
11 TN   12 TN
47 TN   29 TN
13 TN   154 TN
Cleburne's Division
MG Patrick Cleburne
BG Mark P Lowrey
Escort
Sander's Co TN Cav
Polk's Brigade
BG Lucius E Polk
1 AR   15 AR
2 TN   35 TN
48 TN   5 Confederate
Govan's Brigade
BG Daniel C Govan
Col Peter V Green
2 AR   24 AR
5 AR   13 AR
6 AR   7 AR
8 AR   19 AR
3 Confederate
Lowrey's Brigade
BG Mark P Lowrey
Col John Weir
16 AL   33 AL
45 AL   32 MS
45 MS   3 MS Battln
Granbury's Brigade
BG Hiram B Granbury
BG James A Smith
LCol R B Young
6 TX   15 Cav
7 TX   10 TX
10,15,17,18,24,25
TX Cavalry-(Dismounted)

Walker's Division
MG William H T Walker
BG Hugh Weedon Mercer
Escort Co G, 53 AL Vol
[Partisan Rangers]
Jackson's Brigade
BG John R Jackson
1 GA   5 GA
47 GA   65 GA
5 MS   8 MS
2 GA Battln Sharp
Gist's Brigade
BG States Rights Gist
Col James McCullough
8 GA Battalion
46 GA 16 SC 24 SC
Steven's Brigade
BG Clement H Stevens
BG Henry Rootes Jackson
Col W D Mitchell
25 GA   29 GA
30 GA   66 GA
1 GA Battln Sharp
26 GA Battalion
Bate's Division
MG William B Bate
MG John C Brown
Escort-Foules'Co MS Cav
Lewis' Brigade
BG Joseph H Lewis
2 KY   4 KY
5 KY 6 KY 9 KY
Smith's [Tyler's]
Brigade
BG Thomas Benton Smith
37 GA   10 TN
15 TN   37 TN
4 GA Battln Sharp
Finley's Brigade
BG Jesse J Finley
Col R Bullock
1 FL Cav-dismounted
3 FL   1 FL
4 FL 6 FL 7 FL
Mercer's Brigade
BG Hugh Weedon Mercer
Col W Barkuloo
LCol C S Guyton
Col C H Olsmtead
1 GA   54 GA
57 GA   63 GA
ARTILLERY
BG Francis A Shoup
Hardee's Corps
Col Melancthon Smith
Hoxton's Battalion
AL Bat   MS Bat
Marion (FL) Lt Art
Martin's Battalion
Bledsoe's (MO) Bat
Ferguson's (SC) Bat
Howell's (GA) Bat
Hotchkiss' Battalion
AR Battery
Semple's (AL) Bat
Warren (MS) Lt Art
Cobb's Battalion
Cobb's (KY) Bat
Johnston (TN) Art
Washington (LA) -
Lt Art-(5 Co)
Artillery Reserve
LC James Hallonquist
Palmer's Battalion
AL Bat   GA Bat (2)

HOOD'S [or LEE'S] CORPS
LG John B Hood
MG Carter L Stevenson
MG Benjamin Cheatham
LG Stephen D Lee
Hindman's Division
MG Thomas C Hindman
MG John C Brown
MG Patton Anderson
MG Edward Johnson
Escort
Co B-3 AL
Deas' Brigade
BG Zachariah C Deas
Col J G Coltart
LCol H T Toulmin
19 AL   22 AL
25 AL   39 AL
50 AL
17 AL Battln Sharp
Tucker's or [Sharp's]
Brigade
BG William F Tucker
BG Jacob H Sharp
7 MS   9 MS
10 MS   41 MS
44 MS
9 MS Battln Sharp
Manigault's Brigade
BG Arthur M Manigault
24 AL   28 AL
34 AL   10 SC
19 SC
Walthall's or
[Brantly's] Brigade
BG Edward C Walthall
Col Samuel Benton
BG William F Brantly
24 MS   27 MS
29 MS   30 MS
34 MS
Stevenson's Division
MG Carter L Stevenson
Brown's Brigade
BG John C Brown
Col Edward C Cook
Col Joseph B Palmer
3 TN Vol 18 TN
26 TN   32 TN
45 TN   23 TN Battln
Reynold's Brigade
BG Alexander Reynolds
Col R C Trigg
Col John B Palmer
58 NC   60 NC
54 VA   63 VA
Cumming's Brigade
BG Alfred Cumming
Col C M Shelley
34 GA   36 GA
39 GA   56 GA
2 GA State Troops
Pettus' Brigade
BG Edmund W Pettus
20 AL   23 AL
30 AL   31 AL
46 AL

Stewart's Division
MG Alexander Stewart
MG Henry D Clayton
Escort
Co A, 10 Confed Cav
Stovall's Brigade
BG Marcellus Stovall
Col Abda Johnson
40 GA   41 GA
42 GA   43 GA
52 GA
Gibson's Brigade
BG Randall Gibson
1 LA   13 LA
16 LA   25 LA
19 LA 20 LA 30 LA
4 LA Battalion
14 LA Battln Sharp
Clayton's Brigade
BG Henry D Clayton
Col Bushrod Jones
18 AL   32 AL
58 AL   36 AL
38 AL
Baker's Brigade
BG Alpheus Baker
37 AL   40 AL
42 AL   54 AL
Artillery
Hood's Corps
Col Robert F Beckham
Courtney's Battalion
AL Battery (2)
Douglas' (TX) Bat
Eldridge's Battalion
Eufaula (AL) Art
LA Bat
MS Bat
Johnston's Battalion
Cherokee (GA) Bat
Stephens (GA) Lt Art
TN Bat
Cavalry Corps
LC Felix Robertson
Ferrell's (GA) Bat
Huwald's (TN) Bat
TN Bat
Wiggins' (AR) Bat
Artillery Reserve
LC James Hallonquist
Waddell's Battalion
AL Battery
Bellamy's (AL) Bat
MO Battery
Williams' Battalion
Barbour (AL) Art
Jefferson (MS) Art
Nottoway (VA) Art
Detachments
Cantey's Brigade
BG James Cantey
17 AL   29 AL
37 MS
Battln AL Sharp
Engineer Troops
(3rd Regiment)
Maj Stephen Presstman
Co's A,B,C,D,F,G

CAVALRY CORPS
MG Joseph Wheeler
Martin's Division
MG William T Martin
Morton's Brigade
BG John T Morgan
1 AL   3 AL
4 AL   7 AL
51 AL   12 AL Battln
Iverson's Brigade
BG Alfred Iverson
1 GA   2 GA
3 GA   4 GA
6 GA
Kelly's Division
BG John H Kelly
Allen's Brigade
BG William W Allen
3,8,10,12 Confederate
5 GA
Dibrell's Brigade
BG George G Dibrell
4 TN   8 TN
9 TN   10 TN
11 TN
Humes' Division
BG William Y C Humes
Humes' Brigade
Col James T Wheeler
1 [6] TN 2 TN
4 TN   5 TN
9 TN Battalion
Harrison's Brigade
Col Thomas Harrison
3 AR   8 TX
11 TX   4 TN
Grigsby's [Williams']
Brigade
Col J Warren Grigsby
1 [3] KY 2 KY
9 KY
Allison's (TN) Squad
Dortchs (KY) Battln
Hamilton's (TN) Battln
Hannon's Brigade
Col Moses W Hannon
53 AL   24 AL Battln

ARMY OF MISSISSIPPI
LG Leonidas Polk
MG William W Loring
LG Alexander Stewart
MG Benjamin Cheatham
Escort
Orleans Light Horse
Loring's Division
MG William W Loring
BG Winfld Featherston
1st Brigade
BG Winfld Featherston
Col Robert Lowry
3 MS   22 MS
31 MS   33 MS
40 MS   1 MS
1 MS Battln Sharp
2nd Brigade
BG John Adams
6 MS   14 MS
15 MS   20 MS
23 MS   43 MS
1 MS Battln Sharp
3rd Brigade
Col Thomas M Scott
27 AL   35 AL
49 AL   55 AL
57 AL   12 LA
Artillery Battalion
Maj John D Myrick
Barry's (TN) Bat
Bouanchaud's (LA) Bat
Cowan's (MS) Bat
French's Division
MG Samuel G French
1st Brigade
BG Matthew D Ector
BG William H Young
29 NC   39 NC
9 TX
10,14,32 TX Cav-
(dismounted)
2nd Brigade
BG Francis Cockrell
Col Elijah Gates
1 MO   2 MO
3 MO   4 MO
5 MO   6 MO
1,3 MO Cav-dismounted
3rd Brigade
BG Cladius W Sears
Col W S Barry
4 MS   35 MS
36 MS   39 MS
46 MS   7 MS Battln
Artillery Battalion
Maj George S Storrs
Guibor's (MO) Bat
Hoskin's (MS) Bat
Ward's (AL) Bat

Cantey's Division
BG James Cantey
MG Edward C Walthall
1st Brigade
BG Daniel Reynolds
1 AR   2 AR
4 AR   9 AR
25 AR
2nd Brigade
Col Virgil Murphey
1 AL   17 AL
26 AL   29 AL
37 AL
Cantey's Brigade
Col V S Murphey
Col E A O'Neal
17 AL   26 AL
29 AL   37 MS
Quarles' Brigade
BG William A Quarles
1 AL   42 TN
46 TN   55 TN
48 TN   49 TN
52 TN
Artillery Battalion
Maj William Preston
Selden's (AL) Bat
Tarrant's (AL) Bat
Yates' (MS) Bat
Cavalry Division
BG William H Jackson
1st Brigade
BG Frank C Armstrong
6 AL   1 MS
2 MS   28 MS
Ballentine's MS Reg
2nd Brigade
BG Lawrence S Ross
3 TX   6 TX
9 TX   27 TX
3rd Brigade
BG Samuel W Ferguson
2 AL   12 MS
56 AL   11 MS
Miller's (MS) Reg
Perrin's (MS) Reg
Artillery Battalion
Croft's (GA) Bat
King's (MO) Bat
Waties' (SC) Bat

Organization of the Union Army, Lieut. Gen. Ulysses S. Grant, USA, Commanding General at Appomattox Courthouse, April 15, 1865.

Escort
5 US Cav-Co's B,F,K
Headquarters Guard
4 US

ARMY OF THE POTOMAC
MG George G Meade

Provost Guard
Col George N Macy
1 IN Cav   3 PA Cav
1 MA Cav-Co C,D
11 US-1 Battalion
14 US-2 Battalion

Headquarters Guard
3 US

Quartermaster's Guard
Oneida (NY) Cav

Engineer Brigade
Defense of City Point
BG Henry W Benham
15 NY-9 Co's 50 NY
Battalion US Engineers
Capt Franklin Harwood

Artillery
BG Henry J Hunt

SIEGE TRAIN
Col Henry L Abbot
1 CT Heavy 3 CT Bat

Artillery Reserve
BG William Hays
2 ME 3 ME 4 ME
6 ME 5 MA 9 MA
3 NJ 1 NY-Co C,E,G,L
12 NY 1 OH-Co H
1 PA-Co B,F 1 RI-Co E
3 VT 5 US-Co C,I

2nd Army Corps
MG Andrew A Humphreys

1st Division
BG Nelson A Miles

1st Brigade
Col George W Scott
26 MI 5 NH Battln
2 NY Heavy Art 61 PA
81 PA 140 PA

2nd Brigade
Col Robert Nugent
28 MA 63 NY 69 NY
88 NY 4 NY Heavy

3rd Brigade
Col Henry J Madill
Col Clinton MacDougall
7 NY 39 NY 52 NY
111 NY 125 NY 126 NY

4th Brigade
Col John Ramsey
64 NY 66 NY
53 PA 116 PA
145 PA 148 PA 183 PA

2nd Division
BG William Hays
(assigned to Art Res)
(on April 6, 1865)
BG Francis C Barlow

1st Brigade
Col William A Olmsted
19 ME 19 MA 20 MA
7 MI 1 MN 59 NY
152 NY 184 PA 36 WI

2nd Brigade
Col James P McIvor
8 NY Heavy 155 NY
164 NY 170 NY 182 NY

3rd Brigade
BG Thomas A Smyth
Col Daniel Woodall
14 CT 1 DE
12 NJ 10 NY Battln
108 NY 4 OH
69 PA 106 PA 7 WV

Unattached
MN Sharp-2 Co's

3rd Division
BG Gershom Mott
BG P R De Trobriand

1st Brigade
BG P R de Trobriand
Col Russell Shepherd
20 IN 1 ME Heavy Art
40 NY 73 NY 86 NY
124 NY 99 PA 110 PA

2nd Brigade
BG Bryron R Pierce
1 MA Heavy Art
5 MI 93 NY 57 PA
17 ME 105 PA 141 PA

3rd Brigade
Col Robert McAllister
11 MA 7 NJ
8 NJ 11 NJ 120 NY

ARTILLERY BRIGADE
Maj John G Hazard
10 MA 1 NH 2 NJ
11 NY 1 RI Art
4 NY Heavy Art-Bat C,L
11 NY 12 NY
4 US Art-Bat K

5th Army Corps
MG Gouverneur K Warren
BG Charles Griffin

Escort
4 PA Cav-Co C

Provost Guard
104 NY

1st Division
BG Charles Griffin
BG Joseph J Bartlett

1st Brigade
BG Joshua Chamberlain
185 NY 198 PA

2nd Brigade
Col Edgar M Gregory
187 NY 188 NY
189 NY

3rd Brigade
BG Joseph J Bartlett
Col Alfred L Pearson
20 ME 32 MA
1 MI 16 MI
83 PA 91 PA
118 PA 155 PA
1 ME Sharpshooters

2nd Division
BG Romeyn B Ayres

1st Brigade
Col Frederick Winthrop
BG Joseph Hayes
5 NY 15 NY Heavy Art
140 NY 146 NY

2nd Brigade
Col Andrew W Denison
Col Richard Bowerman
Col David L Stanton
1 MD 4 MD
7 MD 8 MD

3rd Brigade
Col James Gwyn
3 DE 4 DE
8 DE 157 PA
190 PA 191 PA
210 PA

3rd Division
BG Samuel W Crawford

1st Brigade
Col John A Kellogg
91 NY 6 WI
7 WI

2nd Brigade
BG Henry Baxter
16 ME 39 MA
97 NY 11 PA
107 PA

3rd Brigade
Col Richard Coulter
94 NY 95 NY
147 NY 56 PA
88 PA 121 PA
142 PA

Unattached
NY Sharp-1 Battln

ARTILLERY BRIGADE
Col Charles Wainwright
1 NY Art-Bat B,D,H
15 NY Heavy Art-Bat M
4 US Art-Bat B
5 US Art-Bat D,G

6th Army Corps
MG Horatio G Wright

Escort
21 PA Cav-Co E

1st Division
BG Frank Wheaton

1st Brigade
Col William H Penrose
1 NJ Battln 2 NJ
4 NJ Battln 3 NJ
10 NJ 15 NJ
40 NJ

2nd Brigade
Col Joseph E Hamblin
2 CT Heavy Art
65 NY 121 NY
95 PA

3rd Brigade
Col Oliver Edwards
37 MA 49 PA
82 PA 119 PA
2 RI 5 WI

2nd Division
BG George W Getty

1st Brigade
Col James M Warner
62 NY 93 PA
98 PA 102 PA
139 PA

2nd Brigade
BG Lewis A Grant
LCol Amasa S Tracy
Maj Charles Mundee
1 VT Heavy Art
2 VT 3 VT
4 VT 5 VT
6 VT

3rd Brigade
Col Thomas W Hyde
1 ME 43 NY
49 NY 77 NY
122 NY 61 PA

3rd Division
BG Truman Seymour

1st Brigade
Col William S Truex
14 NJ 106 NY
151 NY 87 PA
10 VT

2nd Brigade
Col J Warren Keifer
6 MD 9 NY Heavy Art
110 OH 122 OH
126 OH 67 PA
138 PA

ARTILLERY BRIGADE
Capt Andrew Cowan
1 NJ 1 NY
3 NY 9 NY Heavy Art
1 RI Lt Art-Bat G,H
5 US-Bat E
1 VT Heavy Art

9th Army Corps
MG John G Parke

Provost Guard
79 NY

1st Division
BG Orlando B Wilcox

1st Brigade
Col Samuel Harriman
8 MI 27 MI
109 NY 51 PA
37 WI 38 WI

2nd Brigade
LCol Ralph Ely
1 MI Sharpshooters
2 MI 20 MI
46 NY 60 OH
50 PA

3rd Brigade
LCol Gilbert Robinson
Col James Bintliff
3 MD Battln 29 MA
57 MA 59 MA
18 NH 100 PA
14 NY Heavy Artillery
Acting Engineers
17 MI

2nd Division
BG Robert B Potter
BG Simon G Griffin

1st Brigade
Col John I Curtin
35 MA 36 MA
58 MA 39 NJ
51 NY 45 PA
48 PA 7 RI

2nd Brigade
BG Simon G Griffin
Col Walter Harriman
31 ME 2 MD
56 MA 6 NH
9 NH 11 NH
179 NY 186 NY
17 VT

3rd Division
BG John F Hartranft

1st Brigade
LCol W H H McCall
Col Alfred McCalmont
200 PA 208 PA
209 PA

2nd Brigade
Col Joseph A Mathews
205 PA 207 PA
211 PA

ARTILLERY BRIGADE
Col John C Tidball
7 ME 11 MA
19 NY 27 NY
34 NY
PA Art-Bat D

CAVALRY
2 PA

Independent Brigade
Col Charles Collis
1 MA Cav 61 MA
80 NY (20 Militia)
68 PA 114 PA

CAVALRY DIVISION
MG Philip H Sheridan

ARMY OF THE SHENANDOAH
BG Wesley Merritt

1st Division
BG Thomas C Devin

1st Brigade
Col Peter Stagg
1 MI 5 MI
6 MI 7 MI

2nd Brigade
Col Charles Fitzhugh
6 NY 9 NY
19 NY 17 PA
20 PA

3rd (Reserve) Brigade
BG Alfred Gibbs
2 MA 6 PA
1 US 5 US
6 US

ARTILLERY
4 US Art-Bat C,E

3rd Division
BG George A Custer

1st Brigade
Col William Heine
41 NY 104 PA

2nd Brigade
Col Alex Pennington
1 CT 3 NJ
2 NY 2 OH

2nd Brigade
Col William Wells
8 NY 15 NY
1 VT

3rd Brigade
Col Henry Capehart
1 NY 1 WV
2 WV 3 WV

**SECOND DIVISION
ARMY OF THE POTOMAC**
MG George Crook

1st Brigade
BG Henry E Davies
1 NJ 10 NY
24 NY 1 PA
2 US Art-Bat A

2nd Brigade
Col J Irvin Gregg
Capt Samuel Young
4 PA 8 PA
16 PA 21 PA
1 US Art-Bat H,I

3rd Brigade
Col Charles H Smith
1 ME 6 OH
13 OH
2 NY Mounted Rifles

ARMY OF THE JAMES
MG Edward O C Ord

Headquarters Guard
3 PA Art-Bat D,I

Engineer
1 NY

Pontoniers
3 MA Art-Bat I

Unattached Cavalry
4 MA-Co's I,L,M
7 NY (1 Mount Rifles)

**DEFENSES OF
BERMUDA HUNDRED**
MG George L Hartsuff

Infantry Division
BG Edward Ferrero

1st Brigade
Bvt BG Gil McKibbin
41 NY 103 NY
2 PA Heavy Art
104 PA

2nd Brigade
Col George C Kibbe
6 NY Heavy Art
10 NY Heavy Art

Artillery
33 NY

ARTILLERY
13 NY Heavy-Bat A,H
3 PA Heavy-Bat E,M
7 NY

Separate Brigade
BG Joseph B Carr

FORT POCAHONTAS
LCol Ashbel W Angel
38 NJ 20 NY Cav-Co D
16 NY Heavy-Bat E,H
184 NY-Co I

HARRISON'S LANDING
Col Wardell Robinson
188 PA
1 US Colored Cav-Co I

FORT POWHATAN
Col William Sewell
38 NJ 3 PA Heavy Art
20 NY Cav-Co F
1 US Colored Cav-Co E

24th Army Corps
MG John Gibbon

Headquarters Guard
Capt Charles Thomas
4 MA Cav-Co F,K

1st Division
BG Robert S Foster

1st Brigade
Col Thomas Osborn
39 IL 62 OH
67 OH 85 PA
199 PA

3rd Brigade
Col George B Dandy
10 CT 11 ME
24 MA 100 NY
206 PA

4th Brigade
Col H Fairchild
8 ME 89 NY
148 NY 158 NY
55 PA

3rd Division
BG Charles Devens Jr

1st Brigade
Col Edward Ripley
11 CT 13 NH
81 NY 98 NY
139 NY 19 WI

2nd Brigade
Col Michael Donohoe
8 CT 5 MD
10 NH 12 NH
96 NY 118 NY
9 VT

3rd Brigade
Col Samuel H Roberts
21 CT 40 MA
2 NH 58 PA
188 PA

Independent Division
BG John W Turner

1st Brigade
LCol Andrew Potter
34 MA 116 OH
123 OH

2nd Brigade
Col William B Curtis
23 IL 54 PA
12 WV

3rd Brigade
Col Thomas M Harris
10 WV 11 WV
15 WV

ARTILLERY
Maj Charles C Abell
3 NY Art-Bat E,H,K,M
17 NY 1 PA-Bat A
1 RI Art-Bat
1 US Art-Bat B
4 US Art-Bat L
5 US Art-Bat A,F

25th Army Corps
MG Godfrey Wetzel

Provost Guard
4 MA Cav-Co E,H

1st Division
BG August V Kautz

1st Brigade
Col Alonzo Draper
22 US 36 US
38 US 118 US

2nd Brigade
BG Edward A Wild
29 CT 9 US
115 US 117 US

3rd Brigade
BG Henry G Thomas
19 US 23 US
43 US 114 US

Attached Brigade
Col Charles S Russell
10 US 28 US

Cavalry
2 US Colored

2nd Division
BG William Birney

1st Brigade
Col James Shaw, Jr
7 US 109 US
116 US

2nd Brigade
Col Ulysses Doubleday
8 US 41 US
45 US 127 US

3rd Brigade
Col William Woodward
29 US 31 US

ARTILLERY BRIGADE
Capt Loomis Langdon
1 CT 4 NJ
5 NJ
1 PA Art-Bat E
3 RI Art-Bat C
1 US Art-Bat D
4 US Art-Bat D

Cavalry Division
BG Ranald Mackenzie

1st Brigade
Col Robert M West
20 NY-Co G
5 PA

2nd Brigade
Col Samuel P Spear
1 DC Battalion
1 MD 11 PA

Artillery
4 WI

Organization of the Army of Northern Virginia, Gen. Robert E. Lee, CSA, Commanding at Appomattox Courthouse, April 15, 1865

	2ND ARMY CORPS	Gordon's Division	3RD ARMY CORPS	Mahone's Division	ANDERSON'S CORPS	CAVALRY
Provost Guard	LG John B Gordon	BG Clement A Evans	LG Ambrose P Hill	MG William Mahone	LG Richard H Anderson	MJ Fitzhugh Lee
1 VA Battalion	Grime's [late Rhode's]	Evan's Brigade	(killed)	Forney's Brigade	Johnson's Division	Fitzhugh Lee's Division
44 VA Battalion	Division	Col J H Lowe	Provost Guard	BG William H Forney	MG Bushrod R Johnson	BG Thomas T Munford
Escort	MG Bryan Grimes	13 GA 26 GA	5 AL Battalion	8 AL 9 AL	Wise's Brigade	Munford's Brigade
39 VA Battalion	Battles' Brigade	31 GA 38 GA	Heth's Division	10 AL 11 AL	BG Henry A Wise	1 VA 2 VA
Engineer Troops	Col Edwin L Hobson	60 GA 61 GA	MG Henry Heth	13 AL 14 AL	26 VA 34 VA	3 VA 4 VA
Col T M R Talcott	3 AL 5 AL	9 GA Battln Art	Davis's Brigade	Weisiger's Brigade	46 VA 59 VA	Payne's Brigade
1st, 2nd Regiment	6 AL 12 AL	12 GA Battln Art	BG Joseph R Davis	BG David A Weisiger	Wallace's Brigade	BG William H Payne
1ST ARMY CORPS	61 AL	18 GA Battln Art	1 Confederate Battalion	6 VA 12 VA	BG William H Wallace	Col R B Boston
LG James Longstreet	Grimes' Brigade	Terry's Brigade	2 MS 11 MS	16 VA 41 VA	17 SC 18 SC	5 VA 6 VA
Pickett's Division	Col D G Cowand	Col T V Williams	26 MS 42 MS	61 VA	22 SC 23 SC	8 VA 36 VA Battln
MG George E Pickett	32 NC 43 NC	2 VA 4 VA	Cooke's Brigade	Harris' Brigade	26 SC	Gary's Brigade
Steuart's Brigade	45 NC 53 NC	5 VA 10 VA	BG John Rogers Cooke	BG Nathaniel H Harris	Holcombe SC Legion	BG Martin W Gary
BG George H Steuart	2 NC Battalion	21 VA 23 VA	15 NC 27 NC	12 MS 16 MS	Moody's Brigade	7 GA 7 SC
9 VA 14 VA	Cox's Brigade	25 VA 27 VA	46 NC 48 NC	19 MS 48 MS	BG Young M Moody	24 VA
38 VA 53 VA	BG William R Cox	33 VA 37 VA	55 NC	Sorrel's Brigade	41 AL 43 AL	Hampton's SC Legion
57 VA	1 NC 2 NC	42 VA 44 VA	MacRae's Brigade	Col George E Tayloe	59 AL 60 AL	W H F Lee's Division
Corse's Brigade	3 NC 4 NC	48 VA	BG William MacRae	3 GA 22 GA	23 AL Battalion	MG Wm Henry F Lee
BG Montgomery D Corse	14 NC 30 NC	York's Brigade	11 NC 26 NC	48 GA 64 GA	Ransom's Brigade	Barringer's Brigade
Col Arthur Herbert	Cook's Brigade	Col Eugene Waggaman	44 NC 47 NC	2, 10 GA Battalion	BG Matt Whitaker Ransom	BG Rufus Barringer
15 VA 17 VA	Col Edwin A Nash	1 LA 2 LA	52 NC	Finegan's Brigade	24 NC 25 NC	1 NC 2 NC
29 VA 30 VA	4 GA 12 GA	6 LA 7 LA	McComb's Brigade	Col David Lang	35 NC 49 NC	3 NC 5 NC
32 VA	21 GA 44 GA	8 LA 9 LA	BG William McComb	2 FL 5 FL	56 NC	Beale's Brigade
Hunton's Brigade	GA (Patterson's) Bat	10 LA 14 LA	2 MD Battalion	8 FL 9 FL		Capt S H Burt
BG Eppa Hunton	Archer's Battalion	15 LA	1 TN (Prov Army)	10 FL 11 FL	**ARTILLERY**	9 VA 10 VA
Maj Michael P Spessard	LCol F H Archer	**ARTILLERY**	7 TN 14 TN	**ARTILLERY**	Blount's Battalion	13 VA 14 VA
8 VA 18 VA	3 VA Battln Reserves	BG Armistead L Long	17 TN 23 TN	BG Reuben L Walker	GA Battery	Robert's Brigade
19 VA 28 VA	44 VA Battln Reserves	Braxton's Battalion	25 TN 44 TN	McIntosh's Battalion	NC (Cumming's) Bat	BG William P Roberts
56 VA	Early's Division	LCol Carter M Braxton	63 TN	LCol William M Owen	VA (Miller's) Bat	4 NC
Terry's Brigade	BG James A Walker	VA (Carpenter's) Bat	Wilcox's Division	AL (Hurt's) Bat	VA (Young's) Bat	16 NC Battalion
BG William R Terry	Johnston's Brigade	VA (Cooper's) Bat	MG Cadmus M Wilcox	LA (Owen's) Bat	Coil's Battalion	Rosser's Division
Maj William B Bentley	Col John W Lea	VA (Hardwicke's) Bat	Thomas's Brigade	MD (Chew's) Bat	MS (Bradford's) Bat	MG Thomas L Rosser
1 VA 3 VA	5 NC 12 NC	Cutshaw's Battalion	BG Edward L Thomas	VA (Chamberlayne's) Bat	VA (Pegram's) Bat	Dearing's Brigade
7 VA 11 VA	20 NC 23 NC	Capt C W Fry	14 GA 35 GA	VA Battery	VA (Wright's) Bat	BG James Dearing
24 VA	1 NC Battalion	AL (Reese's) Bat	45 GA 49 GA	VA (Donald's) Bat	Stribling's Battalion	Col A W Harman
Field's Division	Lewis' Brigade	VA (Carter's) Bat	Lane's Brigade	Poague's Battalion	VA (Dickerson's) Bat	7 VA 11 VA
MG Charles W Field	Capt John Beard	VA (Montgomery's) Bat	BG James H Lane	LCol W T Poague	VA (Marshall's) Bat	12 VA 35 VA Battln
Perry's Brigade	6 NC 21 NC	VA (Fry's) Bat	18 NC 28 NC	MS (Richard's) Bat	VA (Macon's) Bat	McCausland's Brigade
(late Law's)	54 NC 57 NC	VA (Garber's) Bat	33 NC 37 NC	NC Bat	VA (Sullivan's) Bat	16 VA 17 VA
BG William F Perry	Walker's Brigade -	VA (Jones') Bat	McGowan's Brigade	VA (3) Batteries	Smith's Battalion	21 VA 22 VA
4 AL 15 AL	(late Pegram's)	Hardaway's Battalion	BG Samuel McGowan	Richardson's Battalion	Capt William F Dement	**ARTILLERY**
44 AL 47 AL	Maj Henry Kyd Douglas	LCol Robert Hardaway	12 SC 13 SC	LCol Charles Richardson	1 MD Battery	LCol R B Chew
48 AL	13 VA 31 VA	VA (Dance's) Bat	14 SC	LA Battery	VA (Johnson's) Bat	Chew's Battalion
Anderson's Brigade	49 VA 52 VA	VA (Graham's) Bat	1 SC (Prov Army)	VA (Moore's) Bat	VA (Neblet's) Bat	VA (Graham's) Bat
BG George T Anderson	58 VA	VA (Griffin's) Bat	Orr's SC Rifles	VA (Grandy's) Bat	VA (2) Batteries	VA (McGregor's) Bat
7 GA 8 GA		VA (Smith's) Bat	Seales's Brigade	Pegram's Battalion		Breathed's Battalion
9 GA 11 GA		Johnson's Battalion	Col Joseph H Hyman	Col William J Pegram		Maj James Breathed
59 GA		LCol Marmaduke Johnson	13 NC 16 NC	SC Battery		VA (P P Johnston's) Bat
Benning's Brigade		VA (Clutter's) Bat	22 NC 34 NC	VA (2) Batteries		VA (Shoemaker's) Bat
BG Henry L Benning		VA (Clutter's) Bat	38 NC	VA (Brander's) Bat		G W Custis Lee's Div
2 GA 15 GA		VA (Pollock's) Bat				MG George W Custis Lee
17 GA 20 GA		Lightfoot's Battalion				BG Seth Barton's Brigade
Gregg's Brigade		VA (Caroline) Art				Crutchfield's Brigade
Col R M Powell		VA (Nelson) Art				
3 AR 1 TX		VA (Surry) Art				
4 TX 5 TX		Stark's Battalion				
Bratton's Brigade		LCol Alexander W Stark				
BG John Bratton		LA (Green's) Bat				
1 SC 5 SC		VA (French's) Bat				
6 SC 2 SC Rifles		VA (Armistead's) Bat				
Palmetto (SC) Sharp						
Kershaw's Brigade						
MG Joseph B Kershaw						
Du Bose's Brigade						
BG Dudley M DuBose						
Capt J F Espy						
16 GA 18 GA						
24 GA						
3 GA Battln Sharp						
Cobb's GA Legion						
Phillips' GA Legion						
Humphrey's Brigade						
Col W H Fitzgerald						
Capt G R Cherry						
13 MS 17 MS						
18 MS 21 MS						
Simm's Brigade						
BG James P Simms						
Capt G W Waldron						
10 GA 50 GA						
51 GA 53 GA						
ARTILLLERY						
BG Edward P Alexander						
Haskell's Battalion						
LCol John C Haskell						
NC Battery						
Ramsey's (NC) Bat						
SC Battery						
VA (Lamkin's) Bat						
Huger's Battalion						
Maj Tyler C Jordan						
LA (Moody's) Bat						
SC (Fickling's) Bat						
VA (Parker's) Bat						
VA (Taylor's) Bat						
VA (3) Batteries						

RECOMMENDED READING

"The Official Records of the War of the Rebellion," 128 volumes, reprinted 1985 by the National Historical Society.

"The American Heritage Picture History of the Civil War," 1960. ISBN # 0-517-385562, published 1982 by Bonanza Books, and distributed by Crown Publishers, Inc.

"Antietam," by William A. Frassanito, 1978. ISBN # 0-684-17645-9, published by Macmillan Publishing Company.

"Battles and Leaders of the Civil War," Volumes I, II, III, and IV. ISBN # 0-89009-569-8, originally 1887. 1982, by Castle, a division of Book Sales, Inc.

"Bloody Roads South, the Wilderness to Cold Harbor," by Noah Andre Trudeau, 1989. ISBN # 0-316-85326-7, published 1989 by Little, Brown and Company.

"The Blue and the Gray," by Henry Steele Commager, 1950. ISBN # 0-517-383799, published 1982 by the Fairfax Press, Inc., distributed by Crown Publishers, Inc.

"The Blue and the Gray," 1992 by the National Geographic Society. ISBN # 0-87044-876-3.

"Matthew Brady's Illustrated History of the Civil War," ISBN # 0-517-225190, published by the Fairfax Press, and distributed by Crown Publishers, Inc.

"Campfire and Battlefield, The Classic Illustrated History of the Civil War," by Rossiter Johnson, 1978. ISBN # 0-517-26925-2, published 1978 by the Fairfax Press, Inc., distributed by Crown Publishers, Inc.

"Campfire and Battlefield, A Pictorial Narrative of the Civil War," by Rossiter Johnson, 1958, published by the Blue and Grey Press, Inc.

"The Civil War Almanac," 1983 by Bison Books. ISBN # 0-911818-36-7, distributed by Ballantine Books, a division of Random House Company, Inc.

"The Civil War, Day by Day. An Almanac 1861-1865," by E.B. Long. ISBN # 0-306-80255-4, 1971, published by Da Capo Press, Inc.

"The Civil War Years, A Day-by-Day Chronicle of the Life of a Nation," by Robert E. Denney, 1992. ISBN # 0-8065-8519-4, Sterling Publishing Co., Inc., New York.

Bruce Catton's, **"The Civil Year,"** 1984. ISBN # 0-517-447711, published 1984 by Fairfax Press, Inc., distributed by Crown Publishers, Inc.

"The Civil War, a Narrative," by Shelby Foote. A 3 boxed set:
a) Fort Sumter to Perryville, 1958
b) Fredericksburg to Meridian, 1963
c) Red River to Appomattox, 1974
ISBN # 0-394-74913-8, published 1986 by Random House Company, Inc.

"Harper's Pictorial History of the Civil War," originally published 1866. ISBN # 0-517-224224, published by the Fairfax Press, Inc., and distributed by Crown Publishers, Inc.

"The Photographic History of the Civil War, Forts and Artillery, the Navies," ISBN # 1-55521-200-X, published 1987 by the Blue and Grey Press, Inc., a division of Book Sales, Inc.

"The Civil War, an Illustrated History," by Geoffrey C. Ward, with Rick Burns and Ken Burns, 1990. ISBN # 0-394-56285-2, published 1991 by Alfred A. Knopf, Inc.

"A Civil War Treasury of Tales, Legends and Folklore," by B. A. Botkin, 1960. ISBN # 0-88394-049-3, published 1981 by Promontory Press.

"A Pictorial History of the Confederacy," by Lamont Buchanan. LCN # 51-12017, distributed by Bonanza Books, a division of Crown Publishers, Inc.

"Jefferson Davis, the Rise and Fall of the Confederate Government," 1961 by Peter Smith, reprinted 1971 by the Crowell-Colbin Publishing Company.

"Decision in the West, the Atlanta Campaign of 1864," by Albert Castel, 1992, published by the University Press of Kansas. ISBN # 0-7006-0562-2.

"Decisive Battles of the Civil War," by William Swinton, 1992. ISBN # 0-88394-064-7, published 1992 by Promontory Press, a division of LDAP, Inc.

"Grant and Lee, the Virginia Campaigns, 1864-1865," by William A. Frassanito, 1983. ISBN # 0-684-17873-7, published by Charles Scribner's Sons.

"Generals in Gray," by Ezra J. Warner, 1959. ISBN # 0-8071-0823, published 1992 by Louisiana State University Press.

"Generals in Blue," by Ezra J. Warner, 1964. ISBN # 0-8071-0882-7, published 1991 by Louisiana State University Press.

"They Met at Gettysburg," by Edward Stackpole, originally 1956. ISBN # 0-517-112000, 1984 published by Bonanza Books, and distributed by Crown Publishers, Inc.

"Great Battles of the Civil War," by the Editors of Civil War Times Illustrated, 1984 by Historical Times, Inc., published by Gallery Books.

"This Hallowed Ground, the Story of the Union Side of the Civil War," by Bruce Catton, 1956, published by Doubleday & Company.

"Illustrated History of the Civil War," edited by Henry Steele Commager, 1976, by Grolier Enterprise, Inc. ISBN # 0-671-06806-7, 1984 by Exter Books, distributed by Bookthrift.

"History of the Confederate States Navy, from its Organization to the Surrender of its last vessel," by J Thomas Scharf. Fairfax Press, Inc. ISBN # 0-517-239132, distributed by Crown Publishers, Inc.

"The Killer Angels," by Michael Shaara, 1974. ISBN # 0-345-34810-9, published 1993 by Ballantine Books, a division of Random House Company, Inc.

"Memoirs of Robert E. Lee," A. L. Long. ISBN # 0-89009-694-5, 1983 published by the Blue and Grey Press, Inc., a division of Book Sales, Inc.

"Lifeline of the Confederacy, Blockade Running during the Civil War," by Stephen R. Wise, 1988. ISBN # 0-87249-554-X, published by the University of South Carolina Press, Columbia, SC.

"Mr. Lincoln's Camera Man, Matthew B. Brady," by Roy Meredith, 1946. ISBN # 0-486-23021-X, published 1974 by Dover Publications, Inc.

"Mosby's Rangers, a Record of the Operations," by James S. Williamson, published 1896, by the Polhemus Press. ISBN # 8094-4225-6.

"Rebels and Yankees, the Commanders of the Civil War," by William C. Davis, 1990. ISBN # 0-86101-510-X, published by Salamander Books Limited, distributed by Hodder and Stoughton Services.

"Richmond Redeemed, the Siege of Petersburg," by Richard J. Sommers, 1981, published by Leslie's. ISBN # 0-385-15626-X, distributed by Doubleday and Company, Inc.

"They Called Him Stonewall," by Burke Davis, 1954. ISBN # 0-517-66204-3, published 1988 by the Fairfax Press, Inc., distributed by Crown Publishers, Inc.

"Jeb Stuart, the Last Cavalier," by Burke Davis, 1957. ISBN # 0-517-18597-0, published 1992 by Wing Books, distributed by Outlet Book Company, Inc., a Random House Company.

"Tragic Years, 1860-1865, a Documentary History of the American Civil War, 1860-1865," by Paul M. Angle and Earl Schenck Miers, 1960. LC # 60-8012, by Kingsport Press, Inc., Kingsport, TN.

"Uniform and Dress of the Army and Navy of the Confederate States," by Ray Riling, 1960, Philadelphia, PA. LC # 60-16421.

NOTES

NOTES

Antioch Church	259
Asbyville	318
Athens	61,62,201,216,268, 270
Bainbridge Ferry	201
Barton Station	134,178,179,180
Battery Huger	322
Battery Tracy	322
Bear Creek	57
Benton	322
Big Cove Valley	243
Black Creek	137
Blakely	318,321,322,324
Blount's Plantation	137
Blountsville	137
Blue Pond	276
Bolivar	60
Boyd's Station	312,313
Bridgeport	59,60,61,85,158, 159,173,178,179, 184,216,219,300
Broomtown Valley	166
Brown's Ferry	207
Buckhorn Tavern	175
Burnsville	146
Camp Anderson	265
Cane Creek	178,179
Canoe Station	317
Caperton's Ferry	165,215,216,218
Cedar Bluff	138
Centerville	318,319
Centre	137
Centre Star	230
Cherokee Station	109,134,178,180
Chickasaw	46,55,315
Citronelle	327
Claiborne	322
Claysville	212
Cobb's Mill	202
Columbus Road	322,323
Courtland	78,133,211,251
Courtland Bridge	78
Crawford	323
Crooked Creek	137
Curtis' Well	242
Dannelly's Mills	315,316
Danville Road	253
Dauphin Island	255,256,307,308,314
Davis Gap	165
Decatur	57,75,81,84,183, 211,217,219,220, 222,223,227,246, 251,253,256,259, 277,291,310
Deer Park Road	316
De Kalb County	300
Devil's Backbone	165
Dickson Station	134,135,178
Duckett's Plantation	281
Ebenezer Church	318
Eight Mile Creek Bdg	323
Elkton Station	62

Elrod's Tan-yard	300
Elyton	311,317
Evergreen	316
Fayetteville	258
Fletcher's Ferry	231
Florence	45,129,135,143,190, 219,227,230,272, 278,280,282,309
Gadsden	137,275
Gadsden Road	277
Girard	324
Goshen	277
Gourd Neck	210
Gravelly Springs	309
Great Bear Creek	134
Greenpoint	246
Gunter's Landing	164,247
Guntersville	78,80,83,210
Gurley's Tank	306
Hallowell's Landing	229
Hillsborough	291
Hog Jaw Valley	302
Hog Mountain	137
Hunt's Mill	172
Huntsville	57,68,74,81,86,155, 243,270,275,319, 320
Jackson's Ferry	229
Jonesborough	78
Kelly's Plantation	218
King's Store	320
Ladd's House	302
Ladiga	277
Lamb's Ferry	63
Lanier's Mill	321
Larkin's Landing	210
Larkinsville	85,172,206,218
Lawrenceburg	227
Law's Landing	78
Lebanon	166
Leesburg	276
Leighton	135,291
Limestone Bridge	61
Little Bear Creek	109,179
Lowndesborough	322
Lundy's Lane	134
Madison County	258
Madison Station	231
Marion County	221
Maplesville	318
Maysville	163,176,181,183, 281,320
Mobile	5,6,9,15,77,119, 201,206,218,240, 282,288,307,314, 315,316,317,318, 319,321,322,323, 324,326,327,330
Mobile Bay	87,200,254,255,256, 257,261,264,265, 272,300,323
Montevallo	317,318

Montgomery	5,7,8,11,14,77,322
Montpelier Springs	324
Mooresville	61
Moseley's Plantation	81
Moulton	211,214,223,234, 259
Mount Pleasant	322
Mount Vernon	5
Muddy Creek	316
Munford's Station	325
Muscle Shoals	174,278
New Market	80,175,258,281,320, 327
Northport	319
Old Deposit Ferry	78
Opelika	324
Paint Rock	300
Paint Rock Bridge	60,218,253,287,291
Plantersville	318
Pollard	250,288,307,316
Pond Springs	234,243,257,291
Port Deposit	164
Raccoon Ford	278
Randolph	318
Rawlingsville	166
Rock Cut	135
Rocky Creek Bridge	324
Rogersville	63,325
Round Mountain	277
Russellville	74,291,307
Salt House Point	264
Sand Mountain	137,193
Scottsborough	201
Scottsville	319
Selma	307,315,319
Shoal Creek	199,278,279,280, 281
Sipsey Creek	321
Six-Mile Creek	318
Somerville Road	256
Spangler's Mill	78
Stevenson	78,86,165,167,218
Stockton	318,321
Sulphur Branch Trestle	269
Sulphur Springs Road	218
Summerfield	319
Sweet Water	201
Talladega	325
Ten Island Ford	246
Town Creek	131,136
Trenton	178
Triana	259
Trinity	78,84
Trion	318
Turkeytown	277
Tuscaloosa	319,320
Tuscumbia	58,59,60,109,125, 135,136,178,307
Tuscumbia Valley	207
Tuskegee	323
Union Springs	324
Valhermoso Springs	259

ARKANSAS	(continued)
Talbot's Ferry	59,315
Tannery	263
Taylor's Creek	140
Terre Noir Creek	216
Threlkeld's Ferry	122
Tolbert's Mill	306
Tomahawk	200
Trenton	78,97
Tulip	175,179
Vache Grass	269
Van Buren	104,111,113,120, 122,219,245,258,319
Van Buren County	215
Vance's Store	173
Village Creek	65,70,72
Vine Prairie	122
Waddell's Farm	70
Waldron	168,188,189,190,194, 200,203,241
Wallace's Ferry	252
Washington	234,312
Washington County	260,306
Washita Cove	206
Waugh's Farm	207
West Point	66,162,212,240,252, 281
Whiteley's Mills	217
White County	66,205
White Oak Creek	220,257,269
White Springs	117
Whitmore's Mill	223
Wild Haws	211
Wittsburg	159
Wolf Creek	216
Worthington Landing	236
Yell County	251,260,312
Yellville	59,72,97,105,212, 280

ARIZONA	TERRITORY
Arizona Territory	125,233
Cavalry Canon	333
Central Arizona	291
Chiricahua Mountains	167
Cottonwood Creek	333
Gila	227
Gila Valley	230
Hassayampa Creek	288
Maricopa Wells	335
Mesilla	9
Picacho	58
Pinal Creek	249
Pinal Mountains	181,249
Pinos Altos	209
Rio de Sauz	230
San Pedro Crossing	92,163
Snake Creek	325
Sycamore Springs	291
Tuscon	58,62,65,227

CALIFORNIA	
Albee's Ranch	79
Angel's Ranch	63
Antelope Creek	320
Arcata	56,68,83,210
Bald Mountain	256,258
Bald Spring Canon	214
Bannock City Mines	139
Bell Spring	14
Big Bend	223
Big Flat	234
Bishop's Creek	52
Blue Rock Station	213
Booth's Run	224
Boyton's Prairie	226
Buena Vista County	28
Camp Anderson	256,258
Camp Babbitt	133
Camp Bidwell	320
Camp Grant	263
Camp Latham	52,70
Croghan's Ranch	62
Cutterback's House	74
Daley's Ferry	68
Del Norte County	38
Elk Ranch	79
Fawn Prairie	69,145
Fernandina	101
Franklinton	203,283
Grouse Creek	233
Honey Lake Valley	101
Hoopa Valley	166,256
Humboldt	6
Humboldt County	38
Hydesville	98
Keatuck Creek	14
Kellog's Lake	22
Kettenshaw	14
Keysville	133
Klamath County	38
Kneeland's Prairie	224
Larrabee's	14
Light Prairie	83
Los Angeles	36,37,197
Los Angeles County	28
Mattole Valley	69
Mendocino County	38
Mendocino Reservation	139
Miller's Ranch	79
Napa County	38
Oak Camp	137,145
Oak Grove	28,30
Owen's Lake	70
Owen's River Valley	52
Pitt River Valley	21
Plummer Creek	197
Pony Creek	197
Red Mountain	213
Redwood Creek	88,154,209
Redwood Mountains	210
Round Valley	21,157
Saint Simon's Island	101
San Diego County	28

CALIFORNIA	
San Bernardino	28
San Bernardino County	28
San Francisco	12
San Francisco Harbor	128
San Jose Valley	36
San Louis Obispo County	28
Santa Ana Canyon	26
Santa Barbara County	28
Santa Catalina Island	197
Shelter Cove	139
Simmons' Ranch	98
Sonoma County	38
Spaulding's	102
Table Bluff	55
Temecula Ranch	28,30
Thomas' House	234
Trinity County	38
Tulare County	28
Van Dusen's Creek	10,67,74
Warner's Ranch	36,37
Weaverville Crossing	75
Whitney's Ranch	78
Williams' Valley	132
Willow Creek	184
Yreka Road	92

COLORADO	TERRITORY
American Ranch	228,297
Antelope Stage Coach Station	298
Beaver Creek Stage Coach Station	297
Boonville	249
Buffalo Ranch Springs	298
Camp Sanborn	220
Cedar Bluffs	224,228
Colorado City	132
Colorado Territory	248,279,305
Denver	218,297,298,332
Denver City	54
Fremont's Orchard	219
Gilman's	328
Godfrey's Ranch	297
Harlow's Ranch	298
Julesburg	296,297,298,301, 328
Laramie	332
Lillian Springs Ranch	297
Moore's Ranch	297
Morrison's Ranch	297
Overland Stage Coach Rd	297,330,332
Overland Stage Station	301
Sage Creek	331
Sand Creek	257,284
Smith's, Dan Ranch	328
Squirrel Creek Crossing	132
Valley Station	273,296,298
Washington Road	297
Wisconsin Ranch	297,298
Virginia Dale	332,333

DAKOTA TERRITORY		FLORIDA		GEORGIA	
Bad Lands	265	Jacksonville	51,56,95,129,130,163,	Alexander's Bridge	170
Big Laramie	335		204,205,207,222,228,	Alexander's Creek	271
Box Elder Canon	329		234,235,248,251,311	Allatoona	240,242,243,244,271
Camp Plumb	329	Key West	6,22,118,226,258,335	Allatoona Pass	235
Crystal Palace Bluff	331	King's Ferry Mills	206	Alpine	166,167,168,169
Dakota Territory	329	Lake Beresford	95	Americus	209
Dead Man's Fork	332	Lake City	205	Andersonville	209,336
Deer Creek	325,329	Lake George	212	Armuchee Creek	230
Deer Creek Station	318	Lake Monroe	222	Atlanta	167,180,225,231,233,
Dry Creek	331	Little Escambia	288		236,239,246,249,250,
Horse Creek	332	McGirt's Creek	210		251,252,259,261,262,
Little Laramie	335	Magnolia	268,276		270,271,273,277,279,
Medicine Bow Mtns.	329	Marianna	267,271		280,281,291
Overland Stage Road	330	Marion County	311	Auburn	246,263
Platte Bridge	331,335	Mayport Mills	94	Augusta	6,271,283,305
Platte Bridge Stn.	331	Milton	70,81,262,275,277,307,	Ball's Ferry	282
Red Buttes	329		308	Barnesville	324
Rock Creek	334	Mitchell's Creek	316	Bear Creek Station	281
Rock Creek Station	333	Montgomery	281	Big Shanty	236,237,271
Sage Creek	325	Mosquito Inlet	53	Brunswick	145
Saint Mary's Stn.	331	Natural Bridge	311,321	Brush Mountain	237
Seven Mile Creek	333	Newport Bridge	320	Bryan Court-House	287
Sweetwater Bridge	329	Ocean Pond	207	Buck Creek	287
Sweetwater Station	331	Ocklockonnee Bay	129	Buck Head	249
Tahkahokuty Mtns	253	Olustee	207	Buck Head Church	284
Three Crossings Stn.	329	Palatka	130,213,216,258	Buck Head Creek	284,285
Willow Springs Stn.	334	Pease Creek	206,207	Buck Head Station	281
		Pensacola	5,6,7,9,10,25,26,30,	Burke's Mill	207
			36,50,63,70,72,81,216,	Burnt Hickory	233
			233,281,282,315	Buzzard Roost	209,227,325
FLORIDA		Pensacola Bay	308	Calhoun	230,237
Amelia Island	49	Pine Barren Bridge	281	Campbellton	252,265
Apalachicola	5,55	Pine Barren Creek	288	Camp Creek	259,270
Bagdad	81	Point Washington	205	Camp Sumter	209
Baldwin	233,251,257,258	St. Andrew's Bay	56,128,301	Cartersville	232,251,267
Barber's Ford	205	St. Augustine	5,23,127,194	Cass Station	233
Barrancas	250,262,267,281,	St. John's Bluff	89,91,94	Cassville	231,233
	288,307,308	St. John's Mill	163	Catoosa Springs	225
Barrancas Barracks	5	St. Joseph's	118	Catoosa Station	208
Battledonge	275	St. Mark's	70,209,307	Cave Springs Road	274
Bayou Grand	201,256	Santa Rosa Island	5,10,30,54	Chattahoochee	261
Black Creek	252	Saunders	231,314	Cheney's Farm	238
Blackwater Bay	275,277	Silver Lake	207	Checaw (Station)	246
Bluff Spring	316	Smyrna	53	Chickamauga	162,163,164,165,166,
Braddock's Farm	302	Station Flour	305		167,168,169,170,171,
Bryant's Plantation	276	Tallahassee	5,32,328		172,189,190
Camp Cooper	205	Tampa	73,226,247	Chickamauga Creek	169,202,225
Camp Finegan	205,233	Tampa Bay	177	Clear Creek	252
Camp Gonzales	250	Ten Mile Run	205	Clinton	252,282
Camp Milton	235	Ten Mile Station	210	Cloutierville	216
Canoe Creek	316	Township	121	Cloyd's Mountain	232
Cedar Creek	210,216,228	Trout Creek	248	Cockspur Island	57
Cedar Keys	44,306	Waldo	276	Coosaville Road	273
Choctawhatchie Bay	190	Welaka	231,302,314	Covington	250
Cotton Creek	316	Whiteside	252	Crawfish Springs	190
Cow Ford Creek	216	Whitesville	251	Crow's Valley	209
Dry Tortugas	6,22,335	Woodstock	206	Cuyler's Plantation	287
Escambia Bay	275			Cypress Swamp	287
Euchee Anna C-H	267			Dallas	233,234,272
Fernandina	57,205,206,282	GEORGIA		Dalton	188,193,198,200,208,
Gainesville	206,259	Acworth	236,240,243,271		209,227,228,230,257,
Goose Creek	209	Adairsville	231		274,284,286,313,318
Jackson's Bridge	233				

GEORGIA	(continued)
Varnell's Station Road	225
Venus Point	47
Walnut Creek	282
Warsaw Sound	48,147
Washington	327
Watkins' Ferry	61
Waynesborough	283,284,286
Westbrook's	271
W. Chickamauga Creek	170
West Point	324
Whitemarsh Island	54,58,208
Wilmington Island	54,58
Wilmington Narrows	45

IDAHO	TERRITORY
Bruneau Valley	301
Camp Lyon	334
Grand Pass	154
Idaho Territory	159,335
Meadows, the	163
Poison Creek	311
Salmon Falls	262
Snake Indian Country	138
Soda Springs	163

ILLINOIS	
Bird's Point	29
Cairo	11,22,23,26,29, 30,43,45,47
Charleston	215
Chicago	144,262,327
Chicago Times	144
Coles	6
Coles County	215
Evansville	75
Prairie Du Rocher	217
Shawneetown	258
Springfield	6,7,15,325,327
Sterling	159

INDIANA	
Corydon	154
Evansville	77
Geiger's Lake	259
Indiana State	259
Indianapolis	326
Mount Vernon	259
Newburg	77
Paoli	147
Pekin	155
Rome	147
Salem	154
Smith's Mills	259
Vernon	155
White Oak Springs	259

INDIAN	TERRITORY
AKA Oklahoma	
Barren Fork	191,192
Bayou Bernard	78
Beattie's Prairie	98
Bird Creek	38
Boggy Depot	325
Brazil Creek	175
Cabin Creek	151,157,265
Cherokee Country	119
Chustenahlah	39
Chusto-Talasah	38
Concharty	322
Cowskin Bottom	201
Creek Agency	139
Deep Fork	314
Doaksville	333
Elk Creek	156
Fourteen Mile Creek	180
Greenleaf Prairie	145,183
Gunter's Prairie	261
Hay Station	265
High Shoal	38
Hillabee	314
Honey Springs	156
Hudson's Crossing	236
Iron Bridge	241
Locust Grove	74
Old Fort Wayne	98
Perryville	164
Pryor's Creek	265
Round Grove	68
Round Mountain	36
San Bois Creek	240
Sheldon's Place	191
Tahlequah	75,130
Tallahassa Mission	322
Tulsa	38
Webber's Falls	132,135,167,175
We-wo-ka	314

IOWA	
Oskaloosa	223,245

KANSAS	
Ash Creek	280
Aubrey	51
Bass County	164
Baxter Springs	174,254
Beaver Creek	220
Big Bushes	230
Big Creek	296
Booth's Ranch	168
Brooklyn	163
Buckner's Branch	302
Buffalo Creek	296
Cass County	164
Cato	102
Chavis Creek	332

KANSAS	
Coon Creek	312
Cottonwood	132
Council Grove	268
Cow Creek	281,284,286
Cow Creek Station	332
Crooked Creek	312
Crossing Run	259
Hickory Grove	82
Humboldt	132
Jackson County	164
Kansas City	164
Lawrence	163,164
Marais des Cygnes	165,277
Mine Creek	277
Mound City	277
Mulberry Creek	256,312
Nine Mile Ridge	299
Osage Mission	269
Overland Stage Road	332
Oxford	301
Paola	163
Pawnee Creek	302,306
Pawnee Rock	296,298,330,332
Plum Butte	332
Point of Rocks	299
Salina	256
Sante Fe Road	269
Shawneetown	145
Walnut Creek	269,296,298,306

KENTUCKY	
Albany	28,29,163
Alcorn's Distillery	139
Ashbysburg	93
Athens	125
Augusta	93
Bacon Creek	112
Bacon Creek Bridge	37
Barboursville	27,88,136,205
Bardstown	95,98,128,153,254
Bardstown Pike	94,95,96
Barren Mound	97
Bath County	97,147,199,316
Bear Wallow	91
Beach Fork	95
Bear Wallow	112
Beaver Creek	152,225
Beech Grove	44
Bell Mines	247
Benson's Bridge	238
Bethel Church	258
Big Rockcastle Creek	97
Big Spring	247
Bloomfield	98,279
Booneville	220
Boston	113,149
Bourbon County	97
Bowling Green	27,33,45,46,47,88, 137,139
Bowling Green Road	91
Bradenburg	89,154

Bradfordsville	303	Estill County	97	Laurel Bridge	33
Breathitt County	223	Fair Grounds	95	Laurel County	28,33
Breckinridge County	225	Falmouth	91	Lawrenceburg	96,97,99
Brimstone	168	Fancy Farms	214	Lawrence County	165
Brooksville	93	Fern Creek	94	Lebanon	45,75,153,202
Brownsville	36	Fishing Creek	38,43,44	Lebanon Junction	93
Brushy Creek	217	Flat Lick	82	Lexington	21,75,87,98,128,162,236,
Burkesville	102,145,220	Fleming County	278		238,323
Burkesville Road	112	Florence	91	Lick Ford	47
Burnt Cross-Roads	95	Floyd County	108	Little Sandy	45
Calhoun	105	Forks of Beaver	216	Lockridge Mills	62
Camp Beauregard	40	Fox Creek	278	Logan County	178
Camp Dick Robinson	21,26	Fox Springs	147	Logan's Cross-Roads	44
Camp Goggin	37	Frankfort	75,87,238	Log Church	89
Camp Joe Underwood	32	Frankfort Road	94	London	82,96,98,158
Camp Nelson	162	Franklin	89,96,97,153,270,	Louisa	39,127,129,198,206,228
Camp Wildcat	32,98		287	Louisville	27,30,75,86,93,94,154,
Canton	260	Fry Mountain	34		274,328,331,332,333
Carter County	165	Gallatin County	97	Louisville Pike	94
Caseyville	36	Garrettsburg	101	Lucas Bend	28
Catlettsburg	198	Gault House	93	Lusby's Mill	71
Cave City	63,91	Geiger's Lake	87,248	Lyon County	274,326
Cedar Church	94	Ghent	262	McClean County	35
Celina	134,136	Glasgow	89,91,94,112,	Mackville	75
Chaplin Hills	96		145,174,231,316	Mackville Pike	96
Chaplintown	301	Goose Creek Salt-wks	99	Madison Road	98
Chesser's Store	96	Gradyville	38	Madisonville	84,88,130
Christianburg	151	Grassy Mound	95	Mammoth Cave	82
Clark County	97	Green Chapel	112	Manchester	97,99
Clark's Neck	165	Greensburg	45,91	Marrowbone	152
Clay County	28	Greenville	168,188	Marrowbone Creek	171
Clay Village	95	Grider's Ferry	39	Marshall	199
Clinton	157,211,216,246	Grubb's Cross-Roads	260	Martin Creek	154
Clinton County	189	Haddix's Ferry	252	Mayfield	27,208,211,214,232,258
Coal Run	152	Half Mountain	220	Maysville	89,147
Colesburg	306	Hamilton's Ford	113	Meade County	225
Columbia	127,150,153,186,189	Harrodsburg	95,96,97,276,300	Merry Oaks	91
Columbus	25,27,34,36,44,45,	Hazle Green	127,128	Middle Creek	43
	49,93,159,211,215,	Henderson	73,77,90,269	Mill Springs	37,39,44,142,143
	216,219,248	Henderson County	100	Monterey	70
Coombs' Ferry	124	Henry County	97	Montgomery County	97
Covington	89,161,163	Hickman	25,156,159,248	Monticello	136,139,146,187
Crab Orchard	97,98,163	Hickman's Bridge	130	Morgan County	174
Crab Orchard Road	97	Hillsborough	30	Morganfield	79,86,226,242,248
Creek Head	135	Hodgensville	32	Morgantown	33
Creelsborough	134,150,193	Hopkinsville	29,287	Moscow	216
Crittenden	243	Horse Cave	91	Mountain Side	98
Cross-Roads	98	Horseshoe Bend	140	Mount Carmel	147
Cumberland Ford	28	Horseshoe Bottom	140	Mount Sterling	124,128,129,188,197,237
Cummings' Ferry	154	Howard's Mills	146,312		296
Cynthiana	76,238,239	Hustonville	303	Mount Vernon	97,147
Cypress Bridge	35	Irvine	159	Mount Washington	94
Danville	96,129,130,300	Ivy Mountain	34	Mount Zion Church	86
Danville Cross-Roads	96	Jackson	188	Mud Creek	147
Dick's Ford	97	Jamestown	144	Mud Lick Springs	147
Dog Walk	96	Jennie's Creek	43	Munfordville	37,39,90,91,92,112,247
Dresden	62	Johnson's Ferry	113	Negro Head Cut	136
Dry Ridge	96	Keller's Bridge	238	Nelson's Cross-Roads	98
Eddyville	33,36,274,326	Kettle Creek	145	New Albany	147
Edmonton	145	La Fayette	187	New Haven	93,113,254
Elizabethtown	113	Lancaster	97,159	New Hope	215
Elizabethtown Road	93	Lancaster Road	97	New Hope Station	158

KENTUCKY	(continued)	KENTUCKY		LOUISIANA	
New Market	114,303	Tompkinsville	68,75,104,105	Bayou De Large	330
Nolin	112	Triplett's Bridge	147	Bayou De Paul	218
Oakland Station	90	Troublesome Creek	223	Bayou des Allemands	71,87
Olympian Springs	174	Union County	248	Bayou Dunn's	225
Owensborough	91,262,263	Uniontown	86	Bayou Fordoche Road	234
Owen County	70,71,97	Valley Wood	98	Bayou Goula	148,299,300,305,315,
Owensville	77	Vanceburg	278		325,326
Owingsville	291,316	Viola	40	Bayou Grand	305,319
Paducah	23,25,34,44,45,50,	Volney	178	Bayou Grand Caillou	282
	165,170,215,220,252	Waitsborough	145	Bayou Grossetete	207,217,241,303
Paint Lick Bridge	159	Webster County	248	Bayou Indian	182
Paintsville	43,219	West Liberty	32,93,175	Bayou Lafourche	99
Paris	77,79,127,134,159	Weston	266	Bayou Lamourie	226,229
Perryville	95,96,98,300	Whippoorwill Creek	37	Bayou Liddell	274
Phillips Fork	140	White's Farm	86	Bayou Macon	140,163,172,261,279
Pike County	133,152,230,231	Wild Cat	98	Bayou Manchac	271
Piketon	34,45,101,133,308	Wild Cat Mountain	97	Bayou Maringouin	266
Pitman's Cross-Roads	98	Williamsburg	158	Bayou Montesano	128
Pleasureville	237	Winchester	159,237	Bayou Natchez	262
Pond Creek	153,230	Woodburn	89,136,140,153	Bayou Olive Branch	225
Powell County	97,113	Woodbury	33	Bayou Oyster	316
Prestonburg	34,43,108	Woodsonville	39,90	Bayou Phelp's	135,136
Quicksand Creek	217	Yates' Ford	86	Bayou Pierre	224
Ragland Mills	199			Bayou Pigeon	264,269,315
Red Bird Creek	84,140			Bayou Planton	301
Richmond	85,86,98,159			Bayou Plaquemine	123
Roaring Spring	260	**LOUISIANA**		Bayou Portage	186,281
Rockcastle Hills	31,32	Alexandria	139,140,212,213,215,	Bayou Rapides	214
Rogersville	158		221,222,224,230	Bayou Rapides Bridge	222
Rolling Fork	113	Algiers	71	Bayou Redwood	225
Rowan County	147	Amite	319	Bayou Robert	227
Rowlett's Station	39	Ashton	224	Bayou Saint Vincent	330
Rumsey	35	Ashwood Landing	224,225	Bayou Saline	220
Russellville	36,38,79,94,150	Atchafalaya	144,167,170,232,235,	Bayou Sara	81,84,182,264,271,
Sacramento	40		245,250,272		272
Salem	256	Avoyelles Prairie	230	Bayou Sara Road	141
Salyersville	175,180,187,188,220	Barre's Landing	135,142,178	Bayou Sorrel	299
Saratoga	33	Baton Rouge	5,6,62,64,69,71,80,	Bayou Teche	119,133,142,158,315
Scottsville	146,189		83,111,126,134,137,	Bayou Teche Country	173,183
Scottsville Road	89		140,142,170,171,210,	Bayou Tensas	139,161,253,261
Sharpsburg	291		211,220,225,234,244,	Bayou Tunica	182
Shelby County	300		248,253,261,272,281,	Bayou Vermillion	134,174,183,185,186,
Shelbyville	87		283,290,309,317,328		187
Shepherdsville	88,94,154	Bayles Cross Roads	30	Bayou Whiskey	298
Shepherdsville Road	94	Bay Natchez	262	Bayou White's	309
Sibley County	263	Bayou Alabama	266	Bayou Yellow	231
Simpsonville	300	Bayou Black	213,326	Bayou Vidal	132,133
Slate Creek	124	Bayou Boeuf	136,227,316,319,330	Belle Prairie	230
Slaughterville	87	Bayou Boeuf Crossing	149	Benton's Ferry	78,244
Smith's	89	Bayou Boeuf Road	135	Berwick	142,144,222,224,254,
Snow's Pond	93	Bayou Bonfouca	104,301	Berwick Bay	100,132,173
Somerset	37,38,39,43,130	Bayou Bourbeau	181	Bethel Place	133
Southerland's Farm	91	Bayou Bullitt's	266	Blair's Landing	219
South Union	140	Bayou Carrion Crow	176,177,181,183,185	Bonnet Carre	98,129,316
Spencer County	328	Bayou Chemise	316	Boutte Station	87
Springfield	95,113	Bayou Choctaw	135,136	Boyce's Bridge	140
Stanford	97,159	Bayou Clark's	135,136	Boyce's Plantation	226
Stoner Bridge	124	Bayou Concordia	256	Brashear City	148,149,158,203,276,
Tait's Ferry	86	Bayou Cotile	140		281,298,299,304,315,
Taylorsville	324,328	Bayou Courtableau	142		316,319,326,329
Tebb's Bend	153	Bayou Cross	244	Breaux Bridge	134
Terman's Ferry	198	Bayou De Glaize	231	Brown's Plantation	326

Dripping Spring	259	High Grove	159	Lindley	248
Dry Fork	186	Hog Creek	318	Linn Creek	31,81,325,326
Dry Fork Creek	17	Hog Island	141	Little Blue	35,37,64,68,245,276
Dry Wood	102,154	Holden	255,257	Little Compton	81
Dry Wood Creek	230	Honey Creek	177,235	Little Niangua	56
Dubuque Crossing	261	Hopewell	99,160,164,178,	Little Piney	329
Dug Fort	175	Hornersville	64,127,170,265,	Little Sante Fe	34,36,53
Dug Springs	20,21	Horse Creek	62,169	Little Sni	55
Dunksburg	37,243	Hoyle's Run	56	Lone Jack	82,263,312
Dutch Hollow	31	Houston	39,168,181,184,185,	Longwood	266,268,330
Edina	21		186,190,204	Lookout Station	23
Eleven Points	67,99	Hudson	39	Lost Creek	58
Eliott's Mills	27	Humansville	53,54,56,82,174,177	Lotspeich Farm	75
Elk Chute	249	Hunnewell	23,43,220	Lucas Bend	26,30
Eminence	71	Huntsville	102,248,251,256,269	McCourtney's Mills	298
Enterprise	167,169,254,256	Hutton Valley	167,311	McCulla's Store	20,21
Etna	20	Iberia	25,85	McKay's Farm	53
Eureka	92	Independence	37,47,53,64,70,81,	McKenzie's Creek	323
Farley	240		82,99,123,129,135,	Macon (City)	206,305,321
Farmington	17,186,268,269,319		136,164,207,222,254,	Madrid Bend	48
Fayette	244,248,255,268,281		256,276	Man's Creek	176
Fishlake	23	Indian Creek Valley	56	Marias-des-Cygnes	61
Flat Creek	47	Inman Hollow	75	Marmiton	277
Florence	155	Iron Mountain	266	Marshall	51,159,174,176,243
Florida	18,65,67,77,	Ironton	21,26,31,33,269	Marshfield	46,98
Forsyth	19,20,80,81,82,193,236	Island Mound	100	Martinsburg	19
Four Mile	83,84	Island No. 10	48,51,54,55,56,98	Martin's House	139
Fox Creek	49,50	Jack's Fork	162,181,295	Medde	23
Frankfort	68	Jackson	17,55,57,136,213,268	Medicine Creek	56
Fredericksburg	248,258	Jackson's Mill	317	Melville	240
Fredericktown	23,31,32,135	James Creek	326	Merrill's Crossing	175
French Point	140	Jefferson City	16,272	Mexico	19
Fulton	19,33,78,79,251,282	Johnstown	37,177	Miami	66,68,297,325
Gadfly	56	Jollification	94	Middle Creek Bridge	135
Garden Hollow	161	Jonesborough	23,175	Milford	39
Gasconade	148	Kansas City	12,82,84,142,232,241,	Mill Creek	235
Gayoso	80,265		276	Mill Creek Bridge	135
Gladden Valley	186	Keetsville	48,104	Miller's Station	271
Glasgow	274,277,296,311	Kennett	127	Millsville	19
Golden Grove	160	Keytesville	48,252,267,281	Mineral Point	269
Gouge's Mill	54	King's House	179	Mingo Creek	48
Granby	56,92,95,126	Kingsville	239,329	Mingo Swamp	122
Greenfield	105,160,169,173	Kirksville	23,80	Monagan Springs	60,67
Greenton	99,216,278,297,301,314	Klapsford	23	Monday's Hollow	31
Greenton Valley	178,284	Knobnoster	44	Monroe Station	18
Greenville	35,48,77	Lake Springs	270	Montevallo	56,58,80,81,239,275
Gum Slough	127	Lamar	84,101,232	Monticello Bridge	25
Gunter's Mills	254	La Mine Bridge	175	Moore's Mill	78,79
Halcolm Island	203	Lamine Crossing	175	Moreau Creek	272
Hallsville	40	Lancaster	37,88	Morristown	27,43
Hambright Station	71	Lane's Prairie	234	Morse's Mills	24
Hamburg	21,22	Lebanon	44,51,213,278,311,329	Moselle Bridge	287
Harrison	270	Leasburg	270	Mountain Grove	49,50
Harrisonville	19,20,70,101,	Leesville	52	Mountain Store	78,143
	179,	Lexington	24,26,27,28,31,39,51,	Mount Ida	188
Hartville	118,142,257		98,138,159,160,165,	Mount Prairie	250
Hay Hollow	249		181,192,208,213,240,	Mount Vernon	47,92,241,263,326
Hazel Bottom	97		267,275,297,315,327	Mount Zion Church	40
Henrytown	31	Liberty	10,95,251	Muscle Fork	82
Hermann	271	Licking	62,66,279,308,311,	Neosho	17,56,60,67,83,86,87,
Hernando	274		318,325		88,110,125,134,173,
Hickory Grove	84,92	Linden	131		181,231,236,280

MONTANA	TERRITORY	
Powder River	335	

NEBRASKA	TERRITORY	
Alkali Station	276	
Badger Creek	322	
Chalk Branch	322	
Cottonwood	328	
Dakota City	322,325	
Elk Creek	272,322	
Freeman's Ranch	273	
Gilman's Station	328	
Midway Station	276,277,328	
Mud Springs	302	
Mullahla's Station	274,327,328,330	
Nebraska Territory	257,317	
Niobrara	188,189	
Omaha	70	
Platte Valley	276	
Plum Creek	270,273,285,328,330	
Plum Creek Station	282,283	
Post Cottonwood	328	
Rush Creek	303	
Sand Hills Stage St.	279	
Sierra Nevada Mtns	105	
Spring Creek	283	

NEVADA	TERRITORY	
Austin	330	
Big Mound	158	
Camp Ruby	163	
Carson City	228	
Carson Lake	327	
Dead Buffalo Lake	158	
Dakota Territory	159	
Dun Glen	332	
Fairbanks Station	332	
Grass Valley	330	
Humboldt Valley	330	
Mud Lake	312	
Pyramid Lake	312	
Smith's Station	229	
Smoke Valley	237	
Stony Lake	159	
Surprise Valley	237	
Walker's Lake	312	
Yreka	237	

NEW HAMPSHIRE		
Portsmouth	155	

NEW JERSEY		
Orange	265	
Sandy Hook	257	

NEW MEXICO	TERRITORY	
Alamoosa	30	
Albuquerque	49,56	
Anton Chico	313	
Apache Canon	54,198	
Apache Pass	76,136	
Aquia Eria	318	
Cajoude Arivaypo	139	
Camp Mimbres	209	
Camp Nichols	332	
Camp Robledo	29	
Canada Alamosa	28	
Canon de Chelly	198	
Carrizo Creek	323	
Chaperita	328	
Conchas Springs	159	
Cook's Canon	155,158	
Cubero	49	
Doubtful Canon	225	
Glorieta	54	
Jacob's Well	169	
Johnson's Ranch	54	
Jornada del Muerto		
Desert	147	
La Glorieta Pass	54	
Mesilla	20,21	
New Mexico Terr.	125,163,333	
Ojo de Anaya	327	
Ojo Redondo	169	
Oscura Mountains	332	
Paraje	65	
Pecos	313,328	
Peralta	57,58	
Pigeon's Ranch	54	
Pinos Altos Mines	121	
Presidio del Norte	220	
Pueblo Colorado	163	
Rio Bonito	130	
Rio de las Animas	157	
Rio de las Conchas	313,328	
Rio Hondo	157	
Rio Turpentino	313	
Ruidoso Creek	323	
Sacramento Mountains	274	
San Andres Mountains	139,201,258	
San Augustine Spring	20	
Santa Fe	49,54	
Sante Fe Road	332	
Sierra Bonita	218	
Sierra del Datil	295,297	
Socorro	60	
Spencer's Ranch	220	
Steen's Peak	225	
Tularosa	274	
Utah Creek	96	
Valerde	47	

NEW YORK		
Albany	7,326	
Barnum's Museum	283	
Buffalo	7,326	
Greenpoint	33,45	
Lindenwald	78	
Long Island	45	
New York City	5,8,9,10,23,47,72, 150,155,157,159,215, 283,290,325	
New York Harbor	49	
Rochester	326	
Rockland County	180	
Syracuse	129	
Troy	155	
West Point	35,72	

NORTH CAROLINA		
Albemarle Sound	46,225	
Asheville	320	
Averasborough	313,314	
Batchelder's Creek	61,79,123,142,203,241	
Bear Inlet	193,215	
Beaufort	53,215,296,297,298	
Beaver Creek	220	
Bennett's House	324,326	
Benton's Cross-Roads	314	
Bentonville	313,314,315,316	
Beulah	322	
Big Swift Creek	134	
Black Creek	315	
Black Jack Church	215	
Blount's Creek	132,217	
Blue Ridge Mountains	68,325	
Bogue Inlet	215	
Bogue Sound Block-Hs	203	
Boone	317	
Boonville	322	
Bushy Swamp	314	
Camden	59,300	
Camden County	59,160	
Camden Court-House	177,189	
Camp Palmer	273	
Camp Vance	239	
Cape Fear	39,270	
Cape Hatteras	18,24,33,75,114,	
Cape Lookout	217	
Cedar Point Road	56	
Cedar Point	126,155,188	
Charlotte	324,326	
Cherokee County	179	
Cherry Grove	216	
Chesapeake/Albemarle	Canal 59	
Chicamacomico	29,30	
Chicoa Creek	191	
Chowan County	252	
Clinton	65	
Cobb's Point	46	
Core Creek	104,126,134,148, 288	
Cox's Bridge	315	
Croatan	225	

OHIO			PENNSYLVANIA			SOUTH CAROLINA	

OHIO	
Athens	158
Berlin	156
Buffington	157
Camp Chase	130
Camp Dennison	156
Cheshire	157
Cincinnati	7,75,89,139,155,156, 160,162,213,298
Cleveland	7,235,326
Columbus	7,130,158,187,198, 326
Covington	155
Eagleport	158
Hamden	156
Hamilton	155
Hockingport	157
Holmes County	147
Johnson's Island	267
New Lisbon	158
Newport	155
Ohio St Penitentiary	158,187,198
Pomeroy	157
Rockville	158
Salineville	158
Sandusky	267
Springfield	158
Steubenville	158,243,248
Washington	158
Wooster	155

OREGON	
Alsea Sub-Agency Reservation	221
Butter Creek	7
Camp Lincoln	214
Canyon City	214
Canyon City Road	295
Coos Bay	221
Harney Lake Valley	336
Harney Valley	214
John Day's Road	242
Portland	70
Umpqua	221
Willow Creek	7

PENNSYLVANIA	
Big Round Top	151,152
Caledonia Iron-Works	153
Carbon County	98
Carlisle	151
Cashtown	150
Cemetery Ridge	151
Chambersburg	96,147,150,152,253, 254
Chambersburg Pike	151
Devil's Den	151
Easton	23
Emmitsburg Road	151
Fairfield	151,153
Fountain Dale	150

PENNSYLVANIA	
Gettysburg	73,97,144,149,150,151, 152,154,156,161,185, 191,276
Greencastle	149,153
Green Oak	153
Hanover	151
Harrisburg	8,12,64,151,325
Herr Ridge	151
Hunterstown	152
Little Round Top	151,152
Luzerne County	98
McConnellsburg	149,150,253
McPherson's Ridge	151
McPherson's Woods	151
Mercersburg	153,253
Oak Ridge	151
Oyster Point	150
Peach Orchard	151
Philadelphia	8,11,12,275,325,333
Pittsburgh	7
Railroad Cut	151
Schuylkill County	98
Seminary Ridge	151
Spangler's Spring	151
Steven's Furnace	153
Wernersville	335
West Chester	23
Wheatfield	151
Willoughby Run	151
Wrightsville	150
York	150

RHODE ISLAND	
Newport	12

SOUTH CAROLINA	
Abbeville	327
Aiken	305
Angley's Post-Office	302
Barker's Mill	302
Barnwell	303
Barnwell's Island	46,159
Battery Cheves	169
Battery Gregg	166,167
Battery Island	65,167,220
Battery Pringle	244
Battery Simkins	244,247,305
Battery Wagner	155,156,157,161,162, 164,167
Bay Point	34
Beaufort	34,38,100,120,132,295
Beech Creek	320
Big Black Creek	310
Binnaker's Bridge	304
Blackville	303
Blakeny's	310
Blue's Bridge	311
Bluffton	52,144
Boyd's Landing	284

SOUTH CAROLINA	
Boykins' Mills	221,320
Braddock's Point	35
Bradford Springs	320
Broxton's Bridge	302
Buckingham	52
Buford's Bridge	302
Bugbee Bridge	204
Bull Island	121
Bulls Bay	99
Burden's Causeway	246
Camden	308,320
Cannon's Bridge	303
Castle Pickney	1
Caston Plantation	99
Chapman's Fort	234
Charleston	1,5,6,8,9,10,12,22, 31,34,35,38,39,44, 63,68,69,73,95,117, 121,123,129,132,141, 146,155,156,161,162, 163,165,167,169,174, 176,180,181,189,190, 194,197,198,203,204, 207,211,218,220,229, 230,232,236,244,247, 248,250,264,276,298, 305->309,320,323
Cheraw	306,309,310,311
Chesterfield	310
Chisolm's Island	39
Cloud's House	309
Cole's Island	65
Columbia	271,305,306,307
Combahee Ferry	302
Congaree Creek	305
Coosawhatchie	99
Cowpen Ford	303
Cummings' Point	160
Cunningham's Bluff	186
Daufuskie Island	121,229
Denkins' Mill	320
Dillingham's C-R	302
Dingle's Mill	320
Dixon's Island	66,149
Duck Branch	302
Duncanville	302
Edisto Island	44,54,55,59,148
Edisto RR Bridge	303
Ennis' Cross-Roads	300
Fenwick's Island	75
Field's Point	144
Fishburn Plantation	303
Florence	303,311
Folly Island	132
Frampton Plantation	99
Georgetown	82,320,336
Grahamville	285
Grimball's Landing	156
Hardeeville	295
Heyward Plantation	186
Hilton Head	34,35,39,51,70,94, 100,143,204,229,285

Chambers Creek	119	Davidson's Ferry	278	Grisson's Bridge	193
Charleston	172,186,188,193,260	Davis' Bridge	93,94	Hamburg	119
Charlotte	127	Davis Mill	129,128,131,132	Hamburg Landing	143
Chattanooga	35,50,56,57,69,77,85,	Decatur	76	Hardin Pike	108
	87,103,151,154,155,	Decherd	80,150	Harpeth Shoals	105,118
	162,163,165,166,167,	Denmark	79,86,160	Harrison	200
	169,170,171,172,173,	Dixon Springs	148	Harrison's Landing	164
	174,175,177,179,180,	Dobbin's Ferry	109	Hartsville (Road)	83,106,109,134,135,175
	181,184,186,200,213,	Double Bridge	104	Hatchie Bottom	79
	224,332	Dover		Hay's Ferry	192
Cheek's Cross-Roads	190,212	Drakes' Creek	83	Henderson	168
Cherry Valley	131	Dresden	61	Henderson's Mill	175
Chewalla	95	Duck River Island	136	Henderson's Station	105
Chickamauga Creek	186	Ducktown Road	219	Henryville	283
Chickamauga Station	187	Dukedom	209	Hermitage Ford	98
Chilhowee	198	Dunlap	173	Hernando (Road)	153,154,157,303,304
Christiana	126,149,174	Durhamville	91,93	Hickory	98
Chucky Road	199	Dyersburg	81,83,121	Hillsborough	150
Clarksburg	114	Eagleville (Pike)	125,130,134,138,146,	Hollow Fork Road	303
Clark's Creek Church	168		189	Horn Lake Creek	141
Clark's Ferry	198	Eastport	180	Horn Lake Road	153
Clarksville	47,83,88,103,105,	Edgefield	105	Hornet's Nest	56
	142,180	Edgefield Junction	83,103	Huff's Ferry	183
Cleveland	170,174,186,192,194,	Edmondson Pike	112	Humboldt	79,88,96,111
	217,219,313	Elk Fort	112	Huntingdon	113,114,193
Clifton	110,117,118,124,250,	England Cove	246	Huntsville	82,247
	253,263,298	Estenaula	192	Hurricane Creek	247
Clinch Mountain	179,189,270,275,300	Estill Springs	152	Indian Creek	202
Clinch Valley	276	Evans' Island	300	Insane Asylum	117
Clinton Ferry	78	Fain's Island	202	Irish Bottom	300
College Grove	128,136	Fairfield	150	Island Ford	202
Collierville	98,121,127,142,156,	Fair Garden	202	Island No. 10	48,177,185,207,211,213
	175,181,193,199,205,	Farmington	174	Jacksborough	50,51,165
	239,242,244,251,281	Fayetteville	64,176,180,189	Jack's Creek	193
Columbia	283	Fearn's Ferry	306	Jackson	49,69,78,82,111,128,
Columbia Ford	284	Flat Creek (Valley)	201,203,208,213,281		131,145,155,156,170
Columbia (Pike)	76,89,125,126,127,	Florence	188	Jasper	68,71,173
	131,156,179,271,283,	Fosterville	150,174	Jefferson (Pike)	113,114
	284,285,289,290	Fouche Springs	283	Johnsonville	269,278,279
Colwell's Ford	185	Franklin	108,109,110,113,121,	Jonesborough	171,172,270
Como	170		122,125,126,127,129,	Jordan's Store	144
Concord Church	126		130,132,144,263,284,	Kelly's Ford	202
Concordia	156		285,286,287,289,298	Kimbrough's C-R	199
Conyersville	165	Friar's Island	167	Kimbrough's Mill	108
Cookville	203	Friendship Church	172	Kinderhook	81
Cornersville	202	Gainesville	131	Kingsport	170,272,288
Corn's Farm	303	Gallatin (Pike)	51,82,83,88,98,102,	Kingston	184,186,189,246,272
Cosby Creek	199		175,202,273	Knob Creek	118
Cotton Port Ford	172	Galloway Switch	98	Knoxville	12,14,38,74,111,148,166
Covington	93,127	Garrison's Creek	174		181,183,184,185,186,187
Cowan	155,174	Gatlinburg	190		188,189,190,191,192,200
Craven's Farm	186	Germantown (Road)	72,121,154,156,157,		201,202,203,206,208,264
Cripple Creek	234	Gin House	285		288,291,306
Crossville	190	Glasgow	202	La Fayette	127,140,181,189,193,
Crump's Landing	50,55	Goodlettsville	94		237,242,256
Cumberland Iron Works	84,122	Grand Junction	92,100,101,104,129,	La Fayette Landing	94
Cumberland Mountains	61,82,177,190,202		131,159	La Fayette Station	72
Curtis's Creek	289	Granger's Mill	191	La Grange	92,101,102,111,121,124,
Cypress Swamp	217,218	Granny White's Pike	50,289		126,127,129,130,131,132
Dandridge	192,193,197,198,199	Greeneville	17,55,173,190,191,		134,136,140,141,142,147
	201,202,203,223		211,218,220,235,254,		161,168,190,197,201,203
Dandridge's Mill	190		260,262,273,307		244,245,254,257,261

Lancaster	203	Mifflin	207	Perkins' Mill	112
La Vergne	96,104,105,109,113,	Mill Creek	105,108,118,120	Perryville	127
	114,117,140,194	Milton	128	Petersburg	112,126
Lawrenceburg	55,181,282	Mink Springs	219	Philadelphia	172,176,178,179,188,309
Lawrence's Mill	197	Missionary Ridge	186	Pillowville	184
Lebanon (Road)	62,97,102,131,140,147	Monterey	55,58,61,63,117	Pilot Knob	83
Leesburg	172	Montevale Springs	134	Pine Bluff	260
Lee's House	202	Montezuma	168	Pine Mountain	82
Leiper's Ferry	180	Montgomery	148	Pine Wood	307
Lenoir's Station	148,184	Morning Sun	73	Piney Factory	181
Lewisburg Pike	125,131	Morristown	190,191,212,239,254,	Pittsburg Landing	48,49,51,53,55,56,61
Lexington	111,124,130,150,198		277	Pitt's Cross-Roads	173
Liberty	120,122,124,128,131,	Moscow	123,124,127,130,172,	Pocahontas	93,145,146,148
	132,140		181,188,193,240,280	Powell's Bridge	208
Lick Creek	59	Mossy Creek	193,194,197,198,199,	Powell Valley	149
Limestone Station	167		274,277	Prim's Blacksmith	112
Linden	140	Mossy Creek Station	193	Pulaski	62,63,85,156,179,188,
Little Ford	85	Motley's Ford	207		190,191,230,269,279,
Little Rock Landing	136	Mount Carmel	284		281,325
Livingston	77,79,191,314	Mount Pleasant	76,82,283,320	Purdy (Road)	50,54,57,61,62
Lizzard	113,137	Muddy Creek	201	Quinn's Mill	199
Lobelville	269	Mulberry Village	192	Railroad Bridge	174
Locke's Mill	172	Murfreesboro(ugh)	47,52,53,75,85,88,103,	Railroad Crossing	111
Lockridge's Mill	61		113,114,117,118,119,	Railroad Tunnel	174
Log Mountain	188		120,121,122,123,124,	Raleigh	158,217,218
Long Ford	190		126,127,129,131,135,	Randolph	93
Long's Mill	253		137,140,142,143,144,	Rankin's Ferry	71
Lookout Mountain	171,186		159,174,211,286,288,	Rawhide	188
Lookout Valley	167,180,216		289	Readyville	69,131,174,264
Loudoun	176,183,184,189	Murphy	207,310	Red Mound	114
Louisville	215	Narrows	165	Reynoldsburg	214
Lower Post Ferry	78	Nashville	47,48,50,77,87,94,95,	Reynolds' Station	85
Lowry's Ferry	119		97,98,101,102,103,108,	Rheatown	168,175,220,269
Lynchburg	270		109,110,112,113,119,	Richland Creek	85,99,269,290
Lynnville	283,290		121,132,138,173,193,	Richland Station	128
Lytle's Creek	117		200,212,213,233,278,	Riley's Landing	207
McLemore's Cove	301		280,284,285,286,287,	Ripley	118,235
McLemoresville	170		288,289,306,307	Rising Sun	73
McMinnville	53,85,135,173,192,303	Neely's Bend	95,97	Rock Creek Ford	152
McNutt's Bridge	202	New Castle	193	Rockford	183
Macon	130	New Madrid Bend	178,188	Rock Island Ferry	160
Magnolia	318	New Market	193	Rock Spring	114
Manchester	53,117,120,150,213	Newport	201	Rogersville	182,217,260,272,288
Manchester Pike	117,125,137,143,147	New Providence	88	Rome	106
Manscoe Creek	83	Nola Chucky Bend	212	Round Mountain	85
Maryville	183,198,203,205,207	Nolensville	108,113,114,119,124,	Rover	122,124,126,127,128,
Maynardville	188		306		139,149,150
Medon (Station)	82,86,96	Nonconah Creek	79,131,141,278	Rural Hills	104
Memphis	47,58,68,77,87,92,111,	Obion Plank Road	139	Russellville	188,190,192,277,280,281
	119,124,131,134,142,	Ooltewah	200,207	Rutherford Creek	126,127,289
	143,147,148,153,157,	Orchard Knob	186	Rutherford Station	111
	158,161,162,174,175,	Overall's Creek	114	Rutledge	189,191,192
	185,190,197,204,205,	Owen's Cross-Roads	285	Salem (Pike)	127,129,142,146
	223,235,238,245,251,	Palmyra	183	Saulsbury	81,122,126,129,131,132,
	260,266,271,276,277,	Panther's Springs	211,277		134,188
	280,286,289,290,299,	Paris	50,54,61,169,287	Savannah	51,57,58,59
	300,303,304,310,311,	Parker's Cross-Roads	114	Schultz' Mill	199
	324,326	Peach Orchard	56	Sequatchie Valley	158,173,209
Meriwether's Ferry	82,185	Pea Ridge	58,60	Sevierville (Road)	199,201,203,205,207,208
Middleburg	112	Pea Vine Valley	187	Shelby Depot	98
Middleton	95,121,126,142,146,	Peck's House	193	Shelbyville (Pike)	53,59,118,120,124,135,
	149,199	Pelham	152		144,145,150,174,234,284

Catlett's Station	84,93,98,111,118,177, 176,178,180,181,187, 191,219,220	Crump's Creek	232	Fairfax Station	257,283
		Crump's Cross-Roads	152	Fair Oaks (Station)	67,69,71,72,73,277
Cedar Creek	234,235,239,257,258, 259,273,274,275,280	Cub Run	19,118	Falls Church	35,36,87,162,242,249
		Culpeper (C-H)	62,75,79,81,101,145, 146,147,158,160,169, 173,175,182,192,202, 215,252,267	Falmouth	58,104,114,123,125, 132,136,181,182
Cedar Creek Valley	133			Fant's Ford	84
Cedar Mountain	81			Farmville	320,321,322
Cedar Run	51,81	Culpeper Ford	204	Fayetteville	178
Cedar Run Church	275	Cunningham's Ford	83	Fearnsville	305
Cedarville	146,259,268	Currioman Bay	123	Fitzhugh's Crossing	137
Centreville	19,29,50,85,86,93, 125,162,171,176,224, 242,310	Currituck Bridge	265	Five Forks	317,318,319
		Curtis Farm	17	Flat Creek Bridge	229,321
		Dabney's Ferry	232	Fleetwood	176
Chaffin's Farm	270	Dabney's Mill	303	Flemming Cross-Roads	138
Chancellor House	137	Dam # 1	58	Fog Island	171
Chancellorsville	136,137,138,139,143, 225,226	Dam # 4	38	Forge Bridge	83
		Dam # 5	38,39	Foster's Plantation	231
Chantilly	86,106,113,123,125, 129,146,177	Danville	319,322,325	Four Mile Creek	243,248,253,258,272
		Darbytown (Road)	248,252,272,274,277	Fox's Ford	176
Chapmansville	29	Darnestown	26	Franklin	86,94,100,104,108, 128
Chappel House	270	Davenport Church	286		
Charles City (C-H)	71,73,74,75,190,	Davenport (Ford)	228	Franklin's Crossing	137,145
Charles City Road	248,258	Davis House	263	Frazier's Farm	73
Charleston	48	Deep Bottom	243,252,254,258,317	Fredericksburg	144
Charlottesville	183,210,237,310,328	Deep Creek (Run)	137,145,210,258	Fredericksburg	59,63,64,65,69,77, 78,80,82,86,88,103, 104,105,108,109,110, 112,120,124,131,132, 136,137,138,145,311
Cherry Grove Lndng	219	Deserted House	121		
Cherrystone Point	211	Devereux Station	186		
Chesapeake Bay	170	Diascund Bridge	111,146,148		
Chesapeake/OH Canal	38	Dinwiddie C-H	266,318		
Chesnessex Creek	175	Dinwiddie Road	261	Fredericks' Hall St	80
Chester Station	226,229	Dispatch Station	73	Freeman's Ford	83,84
Chimneys	265	Disputanta Station	296	Freestone Point	28
Chincoteague Inlet	33	Doolan's Farm	35	French's Field	72
Chincoteague Lt Hse	175	Dover	149	Front Royal	65,66,67,73,140,145, 197,208,224,232,259, 268,282,314
Chuckatuck	126,135,138,	Dowdall's Tavern	137		
Chula Depot	229	Dranesville	37,38,39,123,124, 145,208,314		
Circleville	208			Frying Pan	113,145,175,177
City Point	65,225,226,228,231, 246,257,274,316,317	Drewry's Bluff	64,156,229,231	Frying Pan Church	177
		Dry Run	276	Furnaces	226
Clark's Mountain	83	Dublin	228	Fussell's Mill	248,258
Cloyd's Farm	228	Duffield's Depot	224	Gaines' Cross-Roads	64,103,158,176
Cloyd's Mountain	228	Duguidsville	311	Gaines' Mill	65,72
Cockletown	55,	Dumfries	50,52,108,109,113, 126,128,130,141	Gainesville	52,85,145,149,176,178
Coggin's Point	79,80,266			Garlick's Landing	70
Cold Harbor	65,72,234,235,236	Eastville	170	Garnett's Farm	72,73
Columbia	312	Edenburg	55,184,268,279,305, 314,315	Garrett's Farm	326
Columbia Bridge	62,77			Germanna Ford	137,175,185
Columbia Furnace	56,58,272	Edenton (Road)	133,134,135	Germantown	86,125,184,190,193, 201
Conrad's Ferry	96	Edward's Ferry	32		
Conrad's Store	62	Elk Run	61,118,133	Gibson's Mill	208
Corbin's Bridge	227	Ellis' Ford	114,189,199,200,220	Gilbert's Ford	266
Corbin's C-R	103,166	Ellison's Mill	66,72	Gill's Bluff	71
Covington	65,164,182,192,236	Eltham's Landing	62	Glade Springs	289
Coyle's Tavern	164	Elvington Heights	74	Gladesville	153
Craig Meeting House	226	Ely's Ford	138,188,199,200,209	Glendale	73
Crater, Petersburg	255	Evansport	50	Glen Allen Station	228
Crew's Farm	73	Fairfax Court-House	15,19,36,37,39,46, 87,96,105,113,118, 121,127,131,143,145, 150,159-61,164,176, 178,185,192,193,224, 257,291,303,306,321	Glove Tavern	260
Crook's Run	137			Gloucester(Point)C-H	12,104,132,133,141, 158,202,209,216
Crooked Creek	259				
Crooked Run	170			Goochland C-H	210,312
Cross Keys	69			Golding's Farm	73
Crow's House	318			Goose Creek	158,315

VIRGINIA	(continued)	VIRGINIA		VIRGINIA	
Muddy Run	160,169,182	Parkin's Mill	283	Richmond	11,14,18,19,21,23,34,36,
Mulberry Point	62	Payne's Farm	187		37,44,48,49,52,58,64,66,
Murfree's Stn (Depot)	274,312	Peach Grove	312		69,70,71,72,73,86,87,97,
Namozine Church	320	Peach Orchard	73		104,109,111,119,124,127,
Neersville	95,172	Peebles' Farm	270		131,133,138,153,154,158,
Nelson's Farm	73	Pegram's Farm	270		173,182,188,189,200,204,
Newark	237	Peninsula	53,65,71,80,82,148,248		205,209,210,218,224,225,
New Baltimore	166,178,179	Petersburg	54,80,112,143,226,229,		227,228,229,231,232,235,
New Bridge	66,68,71		231,237,239,240,241,		236,239,240,241,242,243,
Newby's Cross-Roads	103,158		242,243,246,254,258,		247,248,249,251,252,253,
New Castle	65,241		260,261,263,264,265,		254,255,256,257,258,260,
New Glasgow	240		266,269,272,277,280,		261,262,263,264,265,266,
New Hope Church	187		285,287,288,290,295,		267,268,270,271,272,273,
New Kent Court-House	63,72,73,74,182,200		301,303,308,309,310,		274,275,276,277,278,279,
New London	240		311,313,316,317,318,		281,283,284,285,286,287,
New Market (Road)	19,35,39,59,69,70,		319,320,325		289,290,291,295,296,297,
	70,184,230,243,252,	Philomont	101,103,104,250,		298,299,300,301,302,303,
	258,268,272,280	Piedmont	59,207,236,273		305,307,308,310,312,316,
New Market C-R	73	Piedmont Station	141		317,318,319,320,328
New Market Heights	270	Piney Branch Church	227	Richmond Road	76
Newport	238	Pocomoke Sound	175	Riddell's Shop	239
Newport News	15,16,17,18,32,39,	Pohick Church (Run)	23,29,35,39,43,48,49,	Rixeyville	182
	83,123,127,128,201		177	Rixeyville's Ford	160,166
Newtown	66,145,146,160,201,	Poindexter's Farm	73	Roanoke Station	242
	232,234,250,257,	Point Lookout	199	Robertson's Ford	169,171
	277,280	Point of Rocks	72	Robertson's Tavern	187
Nine Mile	147	Pollock's Mill Creek	137	Robinson House	19
Nine Mile Road	71	Pony Mountain	169	Robinson Plantation	141
Nineveh	280	Pope's Creek	238	Saint Mary's Church	79,237,238,242
Nokesville	219	Poplar Spring Church	266,270	St. Peter's Church	237,242
Nomini Bay	123	Port Conway	135,164,166	St. Stephen's Church	176
Norfleet House	133,134,	Port Republic	68,69,236,269	Salem (Church)	55,85,101,138,139,164,
Norfolk	5,10,11,14,15,63,	Port Royal	82,108,109,135,326		191,214,241,271,310
	129,189,199,172,	Port Walthall Jctn	226,231	Salem Heights	138
	201,219,252,282	Portsmouth	63,158,161,211,219,	Salient (The)	227
Northern Neck	199		287,288	Saltville	271,290
North Mount Station	156	Potomac Creek	23,111,114	Sangster's Station	50,186,191
Norton's Ford	204	Powell's Fort Valley	73,74	Sappony Church	242
Nottoway Court-House	242	Powhatan	300	Savage Station	73
Oak Grove	72,136,166,	Pratt's Landing	123	Sayler's Creek	321
Occoquan	35,48,49,50,111,	Prince Edward C-H	321	Scott's	192
	113,129,	Prince George C-H	283	Scott's Cross-Roads	319
Occoquan Bridge	45	Princess Anne C-H	171	Seiver's Ford	266
Occoquan Village	45	Pritchard's Mill	26	Seleeman's Ford	129
Old Cold Harbor	235	Proctor's Creek	229	Seven Pines	66,67,68,70,101,201
Old Church	65,70,210,233,235,	Proctor's House	267	Sewell Mountain	26
	238	Providence Church	103,113,118,133,138,	Sewell's Point	14,63
Olive Branch Church	122,123		141,	Sexton's Station	232
Opequon Creek	147,260,266	Purcellville	211,248,299	Shady Grove	233
Orange Court-House	75,76,78,79,82,169,	Quaker Road	317	Shallow Creek	233
	171,177,225	Quarles' Mills	232	Shannon's Cross-Road	138
Orange Plank Road	137,226	Raccoon Ford	79,83,137,169,170,171,	Shenandoah Valley	17,19,20,48,52,53,55,61,
Orchard	72		175,187,188,189		64,65,66,68,69,99,101,105,
Orleans	214	Rapidan Station	75,83,137,169,252		135,140,146,156,189,219,
Otter Creek	240	Rappahannock Bridge	122,133,178		224,230,232,239,240,242,
Ox Ford	232	Rappahannock-(Statn)	54,84,102,103,118,122,		243,245,246,248,249,250,
Pagan Creek	289		178,180,182,191		251,253,255,256,257,258,
Paine's Cross-Roads	320	Reams' Station	242,247,261		259,260,261,262,263,264,
Paris	97	Reed's Ferry	138		265,266,267,268,269,271,
Parker's Ford	248	Rectortown	197,273		272,273,274,275,276,277,
Parker's Store	187,226	Rice's Station	321		279,280,281,282,283,290,
Parkersburg	240	Richard's Ford	114,172		296,309,310,311,315,317,
					325,326

VERMONT

Rutland	155
St. Albans	275

DISTRICT OF COLUMBIA

Washington, DC	5,6,7,8,10,11,12,15,
	16,20,24,29,30,32,37,
	44,45,52,53,55,59,72,
	79,80,84,86,87,95,117,
	132,143,147,163,174,
	188,189,191,199,205,
	211,212,221,222,242,
	243,245,246,247,273,
	280,298,301,302,311,
	316,322,323,324,325,
	328,330,332,333,335

WASHINGTON TERRITORY

Grande Ronde	
Prairie	81
Nez Perces	
Reserve	207

WEST VIRGINIA

WEST VIRGINIA	COUNTIES
Boone	127,178
Braxton	40,230
Cabell	131,213
Calhoun	141,167
Clay	40
Frederick	189
Gilmer	135
Greenbrier	103,236
Hampshire	139,184,189,197,202
Hardy	102,189,197,202,236
Harrison	134
Jefferson	103
Logan	127,131
Marion	57
Mercer	46
Pendleton	101,331
Pocahontas	101,120,221,230,323,331
Randolph	297,323
Roane	38,168
Shenandoah	189
Tucker	102
Webster	40,176,230
Wayne	206,213
Wyoming	78,123,127

WEST VIRGINIA	TOWNS, CITIES, ETC.
Addison	59,176
Allegheny Mtns	244
Alpine Depot	43
Armstrong Creek	89
Arnoldsburg	62
Back Creek Bridge	176,252
Back Creek Valley	331
Ball's Mill	165

WEST VIRGINIA

Barboursville	18,19,213
Barke's Ridge	78
Bath	43,167
Bath Springs	117
Beckley	40
Beech Creek	81
Beech Fork	167
Belington	18
Beller's Mill	25
Berkeley Springs	43
Beverly	18,133,135,151,
	152,165,181,193,
	221,230,278,297
Big Bend	68,69
Big Birch	95
Big Cacapon Bdge	245
Big Run	24
Big Sewell	190
Blacksburg	229
Blake's Farm	35
Bloomington	226
Blue's House	24
Blue Stone	46,82
Blue Sulphur	191
Bolivar Heights	31,89,95,103,
	105,108,244
Boone Court-House	25,123,178
Boothsville	57
Bowman's Place	19
Braxton Court-Hse	40
Bridgeport	137
Brown's Ferry	229
Brown's Shop	206
Buckhannon	18,86,170,267
Buffalo	93
Buffalo Mountain	38
Bulltown	176,225,260,267
Bunger's Mills	236
Burlington	25,132,136,160,
	176,184
Cacapon	59
Cacapon Mountain	160
Cackleytown	181
Cairo Station	139
Callaghan Station	225
Camp Allegheny	38
Camp Chase	48
Camp Creek	61
Camp McDonald	62
Camp Piatt	122,127,131,148
Cannelton	89
Carnifex Ferry	26
Carrick's Ford	18,21,313
Cassville	28
Cedar Creek	183
Centerville	266
Chapmanville	28,59
Charleston	20,90,177,178,
	181,183
Charlestown	67,87,93,95,98,
	103,105,108,112,
	123,141,174,184,

WEST VIRGINIA

Charlestown	197,201,212,233,243,249,
	257,259,260,261,262,266,
	284,303,313,321
Cheat Mountain	26,38
Cheat Mountain Pass	169
Cheat River Valley	18
Cherry Run	39
Chesapeake/OH Canal	43
Clark's Hollow	61
Coalsmouth	268
Cockrall's Mill	105
Cold Knob Mountain	105
Columbian Iron Works	189
Cove Mountain	229
Cross-Lanes	24
Darkesville	88,109,244,249,263,265
Droop Mountain	182
Dry Fork	43
Duffield's Station	206,243,262,274
Elizabeth	180
Elizabeth Court-Hse	141
Elk Mountain	52,183
Elk Run	164
Elk Water	26
Fairmont	57,137
Falling Waters	17,251
Fayetteville	35,89,141,144,153,156,
	159,168
Flat Top	78
Flat Top Mountain	78
Flowing Creek	260
Frankfort	17,245
Franklin	62,63,66,133,163,210,260,
	297
Galltown	331
Gap Mountain	229
Gatewood's	190,331
Gauley (Bridge)	20,32,33,35
Gauley Ferry	89
Giles Court-House	63
Glenville	18,86,94,163,164
Goings' Ford	132
Grafton	15,22
Grass Lick	59
Grassy Lick	229
Great Cacapon Bridge	43
Greenbrier	29,33
Greenbrier Bridge	171
Green Springs Run	126,255,278
Guyandotte	35,104
Guyandotte Valley	44
Halltown	105,111,156,227,261
Hamlin	234
Hanging Rock	94
Hanging Rock Pass	28,43
Harper's Ferry	10,11,12,13,16,17,19,25,
	30,31,48,53,66,67,84,87,
	89,90,91,92,93,94,97,109,
	128,147,154,156,161,168,
	171,173,190,213,224,245,
	246,251,255,260,261,274,
	299,302,315

CONFEDERATE ARMIES	AND C.S.A. ARMY CORPS	FEDERAL ARMIES	AND UNION ARMY CORPS
Army of Mobile, AL	45	Army of the Potomac-(cont)	139,142,151,154,162,165,169,171,174,
Army of Pensacola, FL	36,45		182,186,187,188,191,194,198,202,204,
Army of Kentucky	82,95		207,210,211,214,215,217,218,219,225,
Army of Central Kentucky	33,37,48,54		228,232,233,236,237,239,241,243,246,
Army of the Mississippi	54,62,74,77,82,85,102,103,178,		291,297,320,330
	191	Right Grand Division	103,121,122
Army of Mississippi	49,54	Center Grand Division	103,104,120,121,122
1st (Polk's) Army Corps	102,105	Left Grand Division	103,104,120,122
2nd (Hardee's) Army Corps	102,103	Reserve Grand Division	118,122
Army of Mississippi/East LA	109	Cavalry Corps	217
1st (Van Dorn's) Army Corps	109	1st US Army Corps	55,72,73,89,91,93,117,122,125,151,
2nd (Price's) Army Corps	109		160,214
Northwestern Army	19	1st Cavalry Division	160
Army of Tennessee	98,103,104,105,128,154,157,162,	2nd US Army Corps	72,85,87,89,96,113,117,121,122,142,
	166,167,169,178,181,182,188,		162,191,194,198,202,204,214,240,243,
	191,208,209,218,249,263,275,		261,263,283,303,319,321
	277,282,285,286,289,290,291,	3rd US Army Corps	72,82,83,88,89,100,122,151,158,202,
	295,296,297,298,299,301,304,		207,214
	308,311,313	4th US Army Corps	65,151,159,175,187,218,252,279,286,
2nd Army Corps	157,182,191,209,246,270,271		300,302,305,320,331,332,333
Cavalry Corps	128	2nd Division	187
Army of Middle Tennessee	100,120	3rd Division	187
Army of Northern Virginia	85,87,91,94,99,102,105,108,	5th US Army Corps	52,55,65,82,83,103,104,112,121,122,
	124,133,138,139,144,145,146,		124,125,214,260,261,295,300,303,318,
	148,149,152,154,167,169,170,		319,321
	173,177,218,227,234,235,240,	6th US Army Corps	65,84,104,122,145,214,217,219,228,
	309,316,318,320,321,322,323		246,279,298,305,319,321,325,332
1st (Longstreet's) Army Corps	102,124,133,144,145,150,167,	1st Division	247
	169,218,227	2nd Division	247
2d (Jackson-Ewell) Army Corps	28,85,101,102,138,139,144,145,	3rd Division	246
	321	2nd Brigade	70
3d (AP Hill-Early) Army Corps	144,145,227,234	7th US Army Corps	77,151,157,159,174,198
Cavalry Corps-JEB Stuart	144,145,149	2nd Division	151,174
Army of the Peninsula, VA	54	8th US Army Corps	161,165,189,247,248,253
Army of Southwest Virginia	63	9th US Army Corps	77,87,90,96,119,122,123,127,128,131,
Army of the Southwest	119,123		144,145,160,161,163,200,201,212,213,
Army of the West	71,74,93		219,233,258,291,297,299,302
1st Army Corps	93	1st Division	128,161
		2nd Division	128,160,163
		3rd Division	127,128
		Cavalry Corps	122,142
FEDERAL ARMIES	AND UNION ARMY CORPS	10th US Army Corps	87,240,241,249,251,270,273,286,317,
Army of the Border	276		328
Army of the Cumberland	102,118,162,166,170,171,172,	11th US Army Corps	89,109,120,122,125,130,131,151,162,
	174,178,186,187,202,205,208,		171,173,174,187,200,209,217
	217,218,227,249,306,307	2nd Division	187
Cavalry Corps	187	12th US Army Corps	89,90,91,98,122,165,169,171,173,
2nd Division	187		174,217
Army of the Frontier	99,102,131	13th US Army Corps	99,111,122,148,161,169,178,179,208,
Army of Georgia	331		238,306,307,308,334
Army of the James	218,225,226,228,229,231,232,	2nd Division	334
	262,264,289,290,296,320,321	3rd Division	334
Army of the Mississippi	76,99,117,119	14th US Army Corps	99,118,180,187,211,256,257,260,280
Army of Mississippi	48,61	Cavalry Division	211
Army of the Ohio	54,61,199,201,218,227,249,262	3rd Division	211
Cavalry Corps	218	15th US Army Corps	111,119,171,174,180,187,190,251,252,
7th US Division	54		251,280,288,296,329,330,333
Army of the Potomac	20,22,23,50,51,52,55,62,64,65,	1st Division	171
	66,70,71,73,75,77,79,82,83,87,	2d Division	171,333
	88,89,90,91,93,94,96,97,98,99,	4th Division	171
	100,102,103,104,105,108,109,	16th US Army Corps	111,124,147,214,220,250,278,306,
	110,112,113,117,118,119,120,		307,308,323
	121,122,123,125,129,136,137,		

FEDERAL ARMIES AND UNION ARMY CORPS

FEDERAL ARMIES AND UNION ARMY CORPS	
16th US Army Corps	
1st Division	278
3rd Division	278
17th US Army Corps	111,119,188,222,225,280,302
18th US Army Corps	112,159,163,249,251,253,256,
	264,268,270,271,286
19th US Army Corps	110,224,247,296,298
2nd Division	296,298
20th US Army Corps	118,175,217,252,253,262,280,
	290,309,310,319
21th US Army Corps	118,124,175
22th US Army Corps	122,176
23th US Army Corps	143,172,192,202,205,217,218,
	298,304,318,333
24th US Army Corps	286,295,298
25th US Army Corps	286,329
29th US Army Corps	163
Reserve Army Corps	71,306,317
Army of the Shenandoah	256,257,280
Army of the Southwest	74,85,95
Army of the Tennessee	75,76,111,118,168,171,179,
	212,215,223,227,232,249,250,
	252,295,302,329,331
5th Division	75
Army of Virginia	72,73,82,83,87,88,89

CONFEDERATE

CONFEDERATE	REGIMENTS
2d Cherokee Mntd Rifles	40,230
GA State Guard	200
3 GA Cav	93
4 GA	65
1 Reg LA	6
1 LA Cav	50
2 LA Cav	305
27 MS	50
MS Cav	33
MS Cav-1 Battalion	46
MO State Guard	14,22,33,75
2 NC Volunteers	57
1 TN Cav	45
14 TN	32
1 TX Cav	264
2 TX Cav	320
1 TX Rifles	25,28
9 TX	36
Texas Legion	136
Texas Rangers	48,87,91,105,110,112,212,221
Terrel's Texas Cav	168
VA Militia	12,13
VA Volunteers	11
1 VA Cav	36
4 VA Cav	211,291
5 VA Cav	320
6 VA Cav	164
30 VA	23
45 VA	46
Mosby's Partisan Cav	128,274
43 VA Cav Battalion	197,216,231,257,261,325
VA Black Horse Cav	193
VA Chatham Grays, Cav	15
VA Chincapin Cav Rangers	211
VA McNeill Partisan Cav	315

UNION REGIMENTS

UNION	REGIMENTS
1 US Dragoons	24,26
1 US Art	6
2 US Art	10
5 US Art	26
2 US	12
3 US	9
6 US	332
7 US	20,30,32,62
8 US	11
9 US	26,28,29,31,33
19 US	15,56
1 US Cav	11,12,32
2 US Cav	6,8,11
2 US Colored	244,305
2 US Colored Cav	219
3 US Colored	324
3 US Colored Cav	282
11 US Colored	295
12 US Colored Heavy Art	306
18 US Colored	300
33 US Colored	290
36 US Colored	219
53 US Colored	276,312
56 US Colored	307
60 US Colored	265,298,308
62 US Colored	328
66 US Colored	214
79 US Colored	327
84 US Colored	317,326
93 US Colored	254,315,316,328
97 US Colored	288
101 US Colored	313
1 CA	31,35,45,64,84,88
1 Bttln Mntaineer	155
2 CA	38,43,155
3 CA	80
4 CA	57,123,130,132,148
5 CA	64,88,249
6 CA	204
1 CO Cav	284
2 IL Cav	185
3 IL Cav	192
7 IL Cav	53
8 IL	28,277
11 IL	25
13 IL	37,38
16 IL	18
17 IL	333
23 IL	27
29 IL	31
37 IL	44
38 IL	31
64 IL	313,314
118 IL	314
1 IN	26
11 IN	16,17
20 IN	71
22 iN	26
24 IN	26
1 IA Cav	54
2 IA Cav	142
3 IA Cav	47

UNION REGIMENTS

UNION	REGIMENTS
5 IA Cav	53,54
18 IA	166
1 KS Cav	43
2 KS Cav	53
5 KS Cav	52
8 KS	d
KY Volunteers	33
1 KY Cav	47
12 KY	29
14 KY	228
2 LA	327
7 LA African	213
8 LA	144
12 LA African	207
2 MA Cav	204
4 MA	10
6 MA	10,13
8 MA	13
17 MA	64
23 MA	61,265
24 MA	68
40 MA	325
54 MA	143,144,
	146,157
12 MA Cav	79
9 MD	177
1 ME Cav	58
2 ME	22
12 ME	68
2 MI	24
3 MI	24,45
1 MI Cav	72
4 MI Cav	192,328
2 MS Afr H Art	205
MO Militia	37,56
MO Cav-1 Batt	50
MO Reserve-1	12
MO Reserve-2	12
MO Reserve-3	12
MO Reserve-4	12
MO Reserve-5	12
1 MO Cav	44,54
2 MO Cav	37
4 MO Cav	49
6 MO Cav	141,178
13 MO Cav	311
15 MO Cav	332
1 MO	142
4 MO	21
7 MO	45
8 MO	21,22
10 MO	39
11 MO	31
41 MO	334
43 MO	325,333
51 MO	334
6 NH	56
2 NJ	31
3 NJ	24
9 NJ	82
3 NY Cav	67,72
20 NY Cav	288

UNION	REGIMENTS
7 NY	11
11 NY	14
16 NY	19
26 NY	29
31 NY	29
34 NY	27
79 NY	22,26
103 NY	60
OH Militia	12
1 OH Cav	45
5 OH	142
27 OH	24
36 OH	59
71 OH	83
83 OH	334
1 OR Cav	316
PA Militia	10,11
3 PA Cav	37,66
5 PA Cav	46,47,89,123
6 PA Cav (Lancers)	62,65,66
9 PA Cav	68
11 PA Cav	72
26 PA	10
28 PA	26,54
63 PA	49
69 PA	29
71 PA	29
103 PA	126
1 RI Cav	58
1 RI Lt Art	61
12 TN Cav	330,331
13 TN Cav	264
Loudoun VA Rangers	284,321
1 WV Cav	138
1 WA Territory	59,62
2 WI Cav	142
5 WI	26

CONFEDERATE MILITARY	DEPARTMENTS AND DISTRICTS
Dept No. 1	31,72
Dept No. 2 or Western Dept	18,25,28,66,71,72,73,74,77,99,101
1st or Western Div/Dept # 2	27
TransMississippi Dist/Dept	43,45,66,67,76,79,83,123,125,168, 250,324,331
Dept/Dist of Arkansas	83,128,213,301,303,305,324
District of Arkansas/West LA	324
Dept of Alabama & West FL	31,38,48,49,61,73
District of Florida	210,305
District of East Florida	95
District of West Florida	95
Middle & East Florida	23,30,32,51,52,56,59,207
Dept of AL, MS & East LA	202,227,247,251,252,259,264,327
District of the Gulf	74,110,112,136,283
Dept of Georgia	33
District of Henrico, VA	54
Dept/Dist-Indian Territory	36,228,307,309
Central Div of Kentucky	27
District of Louisiana	83
District of West Louisiana	67,83,238,314,324
District of the Mississippi	74,88,192
Dept of Miss/East LA/West TN	71,94,97,109,192,299,300
[aka Dept of the Southwest]	

CONFEDERATE MILITARY	DEPARTMENTS AND DISTRICTS
Dist of North Miss/West TN	302
Dist of South Miss/East TN	302
Dist of Missouri Infantry	311,312
Dept of the Navy	8
Dept of Norfolk, VA	57
Dept of North Carolina	52,53,71,76,125,131,143,156,171,311
District of Cape Fear, NC	172
Defense of Wilmington, NC	172
Dept of South Carolina	23
Dept of S Carolina/Georgia	85,92
SC GA & E. FL	34,49,51,221,272,286,308
Dept/District of Tennessee	77,158,191,192,193
Dept/Division of East TN	68,77,84,86,100,112,119,136,140, 158,211,213,219
District of the Clinch, TN/VA	208
District of Texas	25,27,71
District of TX, NMex & AZ	108,318,320
Dept of N Carolina & S VA	92,124,221
Dept of VA & N Carolina	92,125,175
Dept of Southern Virginia	131
Dept/Dist-SW VA/East TN	182,236,242,267,280,289
Dept of Western Virginia	97,103,105,109,209,211,239
[aka the Trans-Allegheny]	
Dept (Army) of Northern VA	32
a) Aquia District	32
b) Potomac District	32
c) [Shenandoah] Valley Dist	32,34,70,157,177,191,204
Dept of the Peninsula, VA	57
Dept of Richmond, VA	131
Dept/Military Div of the West	155,274

FEDERAL MILITARY	DEPARTMENTS AND DISTRICTS
Annapolis, MD	11,13,18
Dist of Northern Alabama	242
Dist of South Alabama	304,314
Dept of Alabama	333
Dist of Mobile, AL	326
District of Arizona	85,307
District of Western AZ	88
Dept of Arkansas	198,212,214,245,254,270,290
Dist of Eastern Arkansas	247,311,312
Military Div-the Atlantic	333
Dept/Dist of California	6,244,334
Dist of Southern CA	28,29,31,35,45,57,64,123,130,132,148
Dist of Humboldt, CA	38,43,53,127,155,166,197,203,204
Dept of the Columbia	334
Dist of Colorado	317
Dept of the Cumberland	22,27,99,100,177,193,199,212,280, 302,304,331,332
Cumberland, KY & TN	30,34
Dept of the East	117,119,157,334
Dept/Dist of Florida	10,47,51,213,216,222,259,333
Dept/Dist of Key West, FL	43,223,307,329
Dist of the Tortugas, FL	223,307,329
District of West Florida	223,305,308
District of the Frontier	181
Dept of Georgia	333
Dept of GA, SC & FL	65
Dept of the Gulf	48,52,81,102,110,161,169,268,304, 325,329,332
Military Div of the Gulf	334

FEDERAL MILITARY	DEPARTMENTS AND DISTRICTS	FEDERAL MILITARY	DEPARTMENTS AND DISTRICTS
Dept Harper's Ferry, WV and Cumberland, MD	32	Dept of Pennsylvania	11,20,23,285
District of Cairo, IL	47,76	Dist of the Plains	317,325
Dept/Dist of Kansas	34,36,50,55,57,61,62,92,197,199, 240,245,269,301,334	Dept of the Potomac	23
		Dept of the South	51,54,59,81,86,88,91,99,120,144, 146,205,224,239,285,297,298,304
Dist of North Kansas	317,322,334	Military Div of the Southwest	331,332
Dist of South Kansas	265,334	Dept of the Susquehanna, PA	146,217,252,256,285
Dept/Dist of Kentucky	306,308,334	Military Div of the Tennessee	333,334
Dist of Southcentral KY	215,216	Dept of the Tennessee	92,97,99,161,177,212,334
Dist of Baton Rouge, LA	215,304,312,314,315,331	Dept/Dist of Middle Tennessee	93,309
Dist of Bonnet Carre, LA	327	Dept/Dist of East Tennessee	93,305,309,312,315
Dist of Clinton, LA	331	Dist of West Tennessee	47,76,92,220,282,309,311,327,331
Dist of East Louisiana	331	Dist of the Etowah, TN	304,309
District-La Fourche, LA	215,254,264,299	Dept of Texas, then (LA & TX)	7,8,11,334
Dist of Morganza, LA	304,310,326	Dist of Galveston, TX	334
Defenses-New Orleans, LA	118,215,223,241,304	District of Utah	80,163,317
Dist of Port Hudson, LA	304,331	Dept of the Rappahannock, VA	55,72,
Northern Division of LA	304,305	Dept of the Shenandoah, VA	20,23,55,57,69,72
Southern Division of LA	304	Dist of Beaufort, SC	309,314,315
Dept of Maryland	20	Dept of Virginia/N Carolina	23,68,77,122,132,149,156,157,159, 183,200,298,303,324,334
District of Minnesota	244		
Middle Military Dept	53,68,69,112,127,161,165,189,214, 247,252,253,256,301,309,324,334	Military Div-James River, VA	324,325,334
		Dept of Western Virginia	27,30,51
Middle Military Division	256,268,325	Defense of Harper's Ferry, WV	97
Military Div-Mississippi	177,179,212,213,218,302,315,334	Dept/Dist of West Virginia	97,149,150,212,218,232,244,252, 252,256,262,309
Military Div-West Miss	227,229,254,282,302,304,306,309, 310,314,315,329		
		Dist of Wisconsin	324
Dept of the Mississippi	50,51,69,76	The Western Dept	12,17,20,32,33,169
Dept of Mississippi	284,287,304,311,326,329,331,332, 333,334	Dept/Dist of Washington, DC	11,23,55,57,88,89,99,104,122,123, 176,247,252,256
Dist of Vicksburg, MS	282,309,333	Dept of Washington (State)	334
Dept of the Missouri	34,36,44,50,92,97,129,142,197, 202,234,238,285,287,301,306,332, 334		
		FORTS	
Dist of Central Missouri	258,308,309,325,333	Fort Abercrombie, Dak Terr	87,88,92,93
Dist of Southeast Missouri	39	Fort Adams, MS	176,272,327
Dist of Southwest Missouri	39,217,232,249,254,259,332,333	Fort Adobe, New Mexico Terr	283
Dist of Western Missouri	254	Fort Anderson, CA	55,78
Dist of Ironton, MO	21	Fort Anderson, KY	215
Dist of Rolla, Missouri	311,313,314	Fort Anderson, NC	127,307,310
Dist of St. Louis, Missouri	43,47,321,333,334	Fort Arbuckle, Indian Terr	12
Military Div of the Missouri	301,302,315,324	Fort Baker, CA	60
Dept of the Monongahela, PA	146,217	Fort Baldwin, VA	319
Mountain Department	51,54,69,72	Fort Barrancas, FL	5,36,43,258
Dist of Nebraska	317	Fort Bascom, New Mexico Terr	328
Dept of New England	29	Fort Beaulieu, GA	289
Dept/District of New Mexico	37,84,91	Fort Beauregard, LA	140,167
Dept of Northeastern Va	15,23	Fort Beauregard, SC	34
Northern Department	258	Fort Belnap, TX	274
Dept of the Northwest	88,251,301,305	Fort Bisland, LA	133,219
Dept of New Mexico Territory	9,16,17,34,56,119,198,	Fort Blakely, AL	319
Dept/Dist of North Carolina	43,44,75,112,156,200,253,301, 304,298,333,334	Fort Bliss, TX	9,24
		Fort Boise, Idaho Terr	159,249,262,301
District of Albemarle, NC	153	Fort Bowie, Arizona Terr	135,165,225,227,333,335
Dept of the Ohio	12,13,15,20,27,34,35,50,83,84, 92,128,129,131,133,139,144,162, 168,177,178,189,190,202,205,212, 218,220,239,,334	Fort Brady, VA	299
		Fort Breckinridge, New Mex T	18
		Fort Brooke, FL	177,193
		Fort Brown, TX	9,180
Dept/District of Oregon	6,24,26,30,32,59,62,72,75,214, 310,311,313,316	Fort Buchanan, New Mexico T	20,306
		Fort Canby, New Mexico Terr	198,203
Dept of the Pacific	6,9,11,31,33,36,209,244,299	Fort Caswell, NC	5,10,125,298
Military Div. of the Pacific	334	Fort Cedar, Utah Territory	130

FORTS	(continued) T=territory	FORTS	T = territory	FORTS	T = territory
Fort Chadbourne, TX	9	Fort Johnston, NC	5,10	Fort Randolph, TN	93,277
Fort Chapman, SC	234	Fort Jones, KY	306	Fort Ridgely, MN	83,84
Fort Churchill, NM T	101,153,237,312,327	Fort Keanry, Neb T	329	Fort Rice, Dakota T	265,326,331
Fort Clark, NC	24	Fort Kelley, VA	283,284	Fort Riley, KS	305
Fort Clark, TX	9,81	Fort Klamath, Oregon	242	Fort Riley, TN	95
Fort Clifton, VA	228,240	Fort Knox, KY	113	Fort Rosedew, GA	289
Fort Cobb, Ind. T	12	Fort Lafayette, MD	21,29	Fort Ruby, Nevada T	94,105,330
Fort Collins, Colorado T	332	Fort Lafayette, NY	27,330	Fort Saint Philip, LA	5,58,59,61
Fort Columbus, NY	312	Fort Lancaster, TX	9	Fort Sanders, TN	187
Fort Cottonwood, Neb T	rr 257	Fort Lapwai, Idaho T	163	Fort Scott, KS	24,101,139,
Fort Craig, NM T	23,30,47,65,201,230,270	Fort Laramie, Dakota T	318,327		145,167
Fort Crittenden, Utah T	228	Fort Laramie, Neb T	302	Fort Scott, MO	25,230,239
Fort Crook, CA	21,22,92,101	Fort Larned, KS	166,168,280,296,	Fort Sedgwick, VA	277
Fort Cummings, NM T	225,326		298,299,302,305,	Fort Smith, AR	11,104,126,
Fort Dalles, Oregon T	7,221		306,311,312,330		141,165,216,
Fort Darling, VA	64,160,229,231	Fort Lawrence, MO	305,306		217,239,252,
Fort Davidson, MO	269	Fort Leavonworth, KS	11,12,15,82,88,239,		254,263,265,
Fort Davis, TX	10,22		240		268,269,274,
Fort Defiance, TN	47	Fort Lincoln, KS	277		279,290,335
Fort Delaware, VA	146	Fort Livingston, LA	60	Spanish Fort, AL	316,317
Fort De Russy, LA	138,212	Fort Loudon, TN	187	Fort Stanton, NM T	21,24,323
Fort Dodge, KS	334	Fort Lyon, Colorado T	166,256,279,284,299	Fort Stedman, VA	316
Fort Donelson, TN	36,45,46,47,50,84,88,91,	Fort Lyon, Denver		Fort Stevens, DC	247
	99,117,122,150,159,170,	Fort Lyon, VA	154	Fort Stockton, TX	11
	273	Fort McAllister, GA	121,122,125,126,127	Fort Strong, NC	307
Fort Duncan, TX	9	Fort McCook, TN	85	Fort Sumner, NM T	163,197,255,
Fort Ellsworth, KS	296	Fort McIntosh, TX	9		313,328,332
Fort Esperanza, TX	187,188	Fort McLane, NM T	17	Fort Sumter, SC	1,5,6,8,9,
Fort Fillmore, NM T	20,21,81	Fort McRee, FL	5,36,43		22,30,161,
Fort Fisher, NC	270,287,289,290,291,295,	Fort Macomb, LA	6		162,163,165,
	296,297,298,304,312	Fort Macon, NC	10,53,60		167,179,180,
Fort Fisher, VA	316	Fort Magruder, VA	130,133		181,184,185,
Fort Foote, TN	46	Fort Marion, FL	5		189,201,223,
Fort Furnance, VA	673	Fort Mason, TX	9		236,250,264,
Fort Gaines, AL	5,200,255,256,257	F Massachusetts, LA	6		323
Fort Garland, Colo T	175,258,318	Fort Mitchel, KY	89	Fort Taylor, FL	6
Fort Gaston, CA	80,137,145,154,193	Fort Morgan, AL	5,73,175,200,255,	Fort Thorn, NM T	28,85
Fort Gates, FL	216		257,261	Townson, Indian T	333
Fort Gibson, Indian T	75,78,97,125,137,140,	Fort Mojave, AZ T	228	Fort Tracy, AL	322
	141,142,143,145,191,	Fort Monroe, VA	6,10,13,14,15,16,35,	Fort Tyler, GA	324
	193,217,265,314		43,52,55,62,68,73,	Fort Union, Colo T	258
Fort Gibson, MS	193		85,217,287,288,289,	Fort Union, NM T	96,255
Fort Gilmer, VA	240		291,301,302,311,	Fort Wagner, SC	157,159
Fort Goodwin, Ariz T	230,245,270		312,328,330	Fort Walker, SC	34
Fort Gregg, VA	319	Fort Morgan, AL	5,73,175,200,255,	Walla Walla, Wash T	7,81,207,221
Fort Halleck, Dak T	124,154,332		257,261	Fort Warren, MA	35,37,40
Fort Harrison, VA	270	Fort Morton, VA	277,279	Washita, Indian T	10,11,12
Fort Haskell, VA	279	Fort Moultrie	1	Fort Wingate, NM T	169,233,282,
Fort Hatteras, NC	24	Fort Myers, FL	307		295,297
Fort Heiman, KY	143,278	Fort Pemberton, MS	125,127	Fort Wood, LA	60
Fort Heiman, TN	45,46	Fort Peyton, FL	127	Fort Wright, CA	132
Fort Henry, KY	278	Fort Pickens, FL	5,6,7,9,10,17,30	Fort Zarah, KS	282,286,300,
Fort Henry, TN	36,44,45,46,91,117,119	Fort Pike, LA	6,60,265,301,317		306,325
Fort Hindman, AR	117,118	Fort Pillow, TN	5,8,63,65,68,123,		
Fort Hindman, LA	237		125,160,170,185,		
Fort Holly, VA	288		219,225		
Fort Holt, KY	37,39	Fort Pinney, AR	300		
Fort Huger, AL	322	Fort Powell, AL	255,257		
Fort Inge, TX	9,30	Fort Powhatan, VA	156,201,232,233		
Fort Jackson, LA	5,6,58,59,61,190	Fort Pulaski, GA	5,36,57,81,144		
Fort Jefferson, FL	6,335,	Fort Quitman, LA	60		
Fort Johnson, SC	5,244,247	Fort Quitman, TX	9,85		

MOUNTAIN	GAPS	MOUNTAIN	GAPS	HILLS	
Anderson's Gap, TN	173	Mulberry Gap, TN	185,253	Culp's Hill, PA	151
Ashby's Gap, VA	92,101,147,155,157, 249,307	Neal's Gap, AL	165,169	Diamond Hill, VA	240
		Nickajack Gap, GA	211,227	Dutton's Hill, KY	130
Berry's Ford Gap, VA	100	Panther Gap, WV	236	Fisher's Hill, VA	135,171,259,268,272, 274,276,315
Big Creek Gap, KY	70	Park's Gap, TN	262		
Big Creek Gap, TN	50,51,70,89	Petersburg Gap, WV	166	Fleetwood Hill, VA	146
Blevingston Gap, AL	243	Pine Mountain Gap, TN	88	Flint Hill, VA	46,47,87,198,200,311
Bloomering Gap, WV	47,217	Pound Gap, KY	51,228,235,291	Forrest Hill, VA	268
Blooming Gap, VA	47	Powder Spring Gap, TN	149,192,217	Gravel Hill, VA	258
Blue Bird Gap, GA	168	Ringgold Gap, GA	157,224	Green Hill, TN	132,147
Blue's Gap, WV	43,94	Rockfish Gap, VA	269	Guard Hill, VA	259
Boonsborough Gap, MD	90	Rocky Gap, KY	146	Hare's Hill, VA	242
Brock's Gap, VA	272	Rocky Gap, WV	164	Henderson's Hill, LA	214
Brown's Gap, VA	269	Roger's Gap, TN	69,86,89,148	Hickory Hill, SC	301
Buford's Gap, VA	241	Shallow Ford Gap, TN	171	Hill's Plantation, AR	75
Bull's Gap, TN	212,217,222,274,280	Ship's Gap, GA	274	Hill's Point, NC	131,134
Buzzard Roost Gap, GA	273	Shut In Gap, MO	269	Hill's Point, VA	134,138
Caddo Gap, AR	182,188,201,206	Snake Creek Gap, GA	227,266,274	Honey Hill, SC	285
Catlett's Gap, GA	169	Snicker's Gap, VA	99,101,144,147, 156,158,213,257, 266,277,285	Hupp's Hill, VA	274
Chester Gap, VA	104,157,158,197			Independent Hill, VA	126
Clinch Gap, TN	191			Indian Hill, TN	186
Clinch Mountain Gap,	TN 191	Solomon's Gap, MD	245,246	Ivey's Hill, MS	208
Cold Spring Gap, WV	160	Stevens Gap, AL	313	Jone's Hill, TN	
Cove Gap, WV	241	Stevens Gap, GA	167,170,209	King's Hill, AL	276
Crab Gap, TN	189	Swift Run Gap, VA	61	King's Hill, TN	290
Cumberland Gap, TN	47,53,54,61,71,75, 79,82,84,85,91,98, 167,171,183,188, 255,299,310	Tap's Gap, AL	165	Laurel Hill, MS	255
		Thoroughfare Gap, VA	85,90,98,148, 149,185,291	Laurel Hill, VA	227,270
				Laurel Hill, WV	18
		Tomahawk Gap, AR	205	Leggett's Hill, GA	250
Davis' Gap, AL	75	Whisky Gap, Dak Terr	329	Liscombe's Hill, CA	69
Day's Gap, AL	137	Wilson's Gap, KY	71	Love's Hill, TN	201
Devil's Gap, TN	290	Wilson's Gap, TN	71	Malvern Hill, VA	73,74,79,80,240,248
Dogwood Gap, WV	26	Winston's Gap, AL	166,167	Mantapike Hill, VA	210
Dutch Gap, GA	168	Winter's Gap, TN	165	Mathews Hill, VA	19
Dutch Gap, VA	160,258,295	Woodson's Gap, TN	59,69	McNugh's Hill, LA	222
Fairfield Gap, PA	153			Muldraugh's Hill, KY	113,114
Frick's Gap, GA	209			Montgomery Hill, TN	289
Fox's Gap, VA	90		HILLS	Munson's Hill, VA	24,29
Greenland Gap, WV	136,297	Anthony's Hill, TN	290	Nutter's Hill, WV	262
Guy's Gap, TN	150,227	Ash Hills, KY	161	Oak Hill, VA	176
Harrison's Gap, AL	221	Bald Hill, GA	250	Ox Hill, VA	86
Henderson's Gap, AL	168	Big Hill, KY	84,85,98	Park Hill, Ind Terr	75
Hill's Gap, TN	173	Big Hill, TN	95	Perche Hills, MO	311,327
Hollow Tree Gap, TN	289	Black Fork Hills, MO	153	Pigeon Hills, TN	187
Holly Tree Gap, TN	108	Brown Hill, KY	98,98	Pine Hill, GA	238
Hoover's Gap, TN	149	Buffalo Hill, KY	29	Pink Hill, MO	54,68,70,71
Hopewell Gap, VA	162,193,291	Bunker Hill, VA	19,49,156,224	Pleasant Hill, GA	324
Howard's Gap, NC	325	Bunker Hill, WV	19,87,109,147,197, 249,251,263,266	Pleasant Hill, LA	217,218,219
Kanawha Gap, WV	28			Pleasant Hill, MO	75,141,163,166,234, 240,251,254,261,327
Knob Gap, TN	113	Cane Hill, AR	102,105,108,111, 260,279	Pott's Hill, AR	47
Laurel Creek Gap, TN	270			Queen's Hill, MS	154,204
Liberty Gap, TN	149	Cemetery Hill, PA	151	Rally Hill, TN	284
Lost River Gap, WV	229	Champion's Hill, MS	141,204	Riggin's Hill, TN	88
Luray Gap, VA	65	Chapel Hill, MO	74,99,253	Rocky Hill, KY	98
McCormick's Gap, KY	267	Chapel Hill, NC	323	Rose Hill, MO	43,261
Manassas Gap, VA	101,157,158	Chapel Hill, TN	126,133,136	Round Hill, AR	75
Mechanicsburg Gap, WV	28	Clover Hill, VA	323	Rude's Hill, VA	59,230,282,310
Millcreek Gap, GA	227	Coal Hill, OH	157	Smoky Hill, KS	230,254,259,298
Moccasin Gap, TN	113	Cotton Hill, WV	31,33,35,89	Sni Hills, MO	204,223,315
Monterey Gap, PA	153	Cox Hill, TN	117	Snibar Hills, MO	299,327
Mountain Gap, KY	97	Cricket Hill, VA	211	Snodgrass Hill, TN	170
Mountain Gap, TN	173	Crump's Hill, LA	216		

HILLS (continued)

Hill	Page
Snow Hill, NC	317,318
Snow Hill, TN	131
Sporting Hill, PA	151
Spring Hill, AL	328
Spring Hill, CO	298
Spring Hill, GA	324
Spring Hill, MO	33,59,66
Spring Hill, TN	126,128,139,145, 212,284,289
Strawberry Hill, VA	228
Thompson's Hill, MS	137
Thorn Hill, AL	295
Thorn Hill, TN	256,273
Tunnel Hill, GA	208,209,223,224, 225,226,243,310
Tunnel Hill, KY	104
Tunnel Hill, TN	186
Upton's Hill, KY	30
Upton's Hill, VA	90
Vaught's Hill, TN	128
Vinegar Hill, KY	92
Wall Hill, MS	206
Walnut Hill, MS	140
Well's Hill, TN	269
White Stone Hill, Dak T	166

RAILROADS

Railroad	Page
Atlanta Railroad	252,262,271,275
Baltimore and Ohio RR	13,15,43,135,206, 225,226,244,267, 274,302,318
Central Pacific Railroad	74
Charleston & Augusta RR	305
Charleston-Savannah RR	286
Chattanooga to Atlanta RR	271,275
Danville, VA Railroad	229,242,320
East Tennessee-Georgia RR	186
Eastern Texas Railroad	93
Florida Railroad	259
Fredericksburg, VA RR	153
Georgia Central Railroad	282,286
Hannibal-St. Joseph, MO	23,27
Iron Mountain Railroad	135
Jackson, LA Railroad	129,139,140
Little Rock & Devall's	319
Louisville & Lexington, KY	151
Louisville & Nashville RR	63,83,132,215
Macon, GA RR	252,259,262
McMinnville-Manchester	135
Memphis to Charleston	57,61,63,64,178, 180,181,183,187, 188,189,251
Mississippi Central RR	86,100,161,282
Southside Richmond RR	319
Mobile, TN & Ohio RR	51,61,62,64,94, 105,110,283,290, 295
Nashville & Chattanooga	132,213,225
Nashville & Decatur	85
Nashville & Northwestern	259,275,277
New Orleans & Jackson	140
Norfolk & Petersburg RR	141
North Missouri	264
Northwestern RR	135
Orange & Alexandria RR	54,103
Pacific RR	209,287,331
Paducah RR	209
Petersburg and Weldon	225,253,260, 261,263
Richmond RR	153,229
Richmond & Danville RR	229
Richmond-Fredericksburg	67,153
Richmond and York River	73
Seaboard & Roanoke RR	140
Southside & Danville RR	242
Union Pacific RR	74,332
Virginia Central RR	65,67,72,309
Virginia and Tennessee	189,193,224, 225,226,227, 228,229,232
Western RR	252,271
West Point & Montgomery	246,252,262
Wilmington and Weldon	153,154,241

RIVERS

River	Page
Aestham River, VA	167
Alligator River, NC	206
Amite River, LA	72,78,129,132, 133,134,137, 171,244,271, 283,288,315, 316
Appomattox River, VA	72,143,231,321
Arkansas River	118,119,122, 168,214,217, 230,234,240, 248,259,261, 273,284,285, 300,303,306, 329,331,333, 335
Ashepoo River, SC	231,234
Atchafalaya River, LA	123,261,266, 289,316
Back River, VA	19,20
Bear River, Idaho Terr	139
Bear River, Utah Terr	121
Belle River, LA	276
Big Black River, MS	138,141,146, 148,149,150, 153,166,168, 172,176,199
Big Coal River, WV	122,148
Big Hatchie MS	95
Big Pigeon River, KY	279
Big River, MO	31,272
Big Sunflower River, MS	142
Big Warrior River, AL	137
Black River, LA	123,283
Black River, MO	26,75,90,236, 252
Black River, NC/SC	82,313
Big Sandy River, WV	279
Blackwater River, KY	317
Blackwater, VA	94,95,100,108,109, 112,118,133,146, 169,181,219,225, 274,295
Blue Earth River, Minn	327
Blue River, MO	232
Bonsecours River, AL	265
Brier River, MO	54
Buffalo River, AR Terr	118,191,212
Bull River, SC	48
Cache River, AR	66,75,221,274
Calfkiller River, TN	203
Canadian River, NM Terr	96,283,314
Cane River, LA	222
Caney Fork River, TN	202
Cape Fear River, NC	10,102,183,241, 307,310,312
Castor River, MO	136,159
Catawba River, AL	321
Catawba River, NC/SC	308,324
Chariton River, MO	81,82
Chattahoochie River, GA	143,245
Chattooga River, GA	168
Cheat River, WV	18,19,43,172,189
Chickahominy River, VA	65,67,69,72,79, 105,164,210,234, 235
Chickasawha River, MS	66,283
Choctawhatchee Rvr, SC	101
Chowan River, NC/VA	145,181,253,288
Cimarron, New Mex Terr	267
Clinch River, TN	188,189,192,201
Coal River, WV	168,178
Coan River, VA	123,126
Coldwater River, MS	77,88,106,124,125, 128,134,140,147, 148,161,163,174, 181,194,197,250
Colorado River	228
Columbia River Wash Terr	9
Columbus River, Oregon	7
Comite River, LA	127,137,261,377
Combahee River, SC	144,169,300
Concho River, TX	296
Congaree River, SC	305,306
Coosa River, AL	201,246
Coosaw River, SC	43
Coosawatte River, GA	318
Cotton River, GA	281
Crook River, MO	330
Crooked River, FL	65
Cumberland River, KY/TN	25,27,34,36,39,44, 45,46,47,95,97, 108,112,117,119, 140,153,159,186, 187,193,202,213, 260,326
Current River, MO	84,134,315
Doboy River, GA	103,104
Doe River, TN	36

BLOCKADE RUNNER/CLIPPER FRIGATE/IRON CLAD/MAIL SHIP/MORTAR
BOAT/PRIVATEER/RAM/ SCHOONER/ SLOOP/STEAMER/
TRANSPORT/TUGBOAT/ WHALER/ WOODEN VESSEL

Shell, br/sch	222
CSS Shenandoah, raider	272,300,306,323, 333,334,326
Spunky, br	207
Stingaree, schooner	232
CSS Stonewall, ic	303,316,328,329
CSS Sumter, st/tr/prvtr	7,17,18,33,38, 165,212
Tacony, privateer	147,149,150
CSS Tallahassee, raider	258,259,260, 261,262,278
CSS Teazer, gb	74
CSS Tennessee, ram	255
CSS Theodora, br	31
Vesta, br/st	198
City of Vicksburg, st	122
Victory, br/st	38
W.B. Terry, st	23
Joseph H. Toone, br/sch	30
CSS Venus, tr/st	278
CSS Virginia No. 2, gb	299
CSS Webb, st	325
Key West, st	113
Sallie Wood, st	46

UNION	VESSELS
John Adams, st	120,155
Albert Adams, wv	18
Adams, st	235
USS Adele, i/c	177
William Aiken, cutter	1
USS Albatross, gb	26,129,130,138
Alamo, st	284,295
Alert, wv/sch	89
Alexandria, sch	170
USS Ethan Allen, gb	118
Alliance, sch	170
USS Allison, st/gb	126
Altahama, whaler	91
Harder Andrew, gb	53
USS Anglo-American, gb	85
Ann, st	73
Annie, st	191
Annie Jacobs, st	295
Argosy, st	314
Ariel, st	75
USS Arizona, gb	166
USS Aroostook, ic	64
Arrow, st	141
USS Arthur, bark/gb	59,82
Augusto, bark/wv	36
Aurora, st/tr	273
USS Autocrat, st	206
Baltic, st	9,12, 179,291
N.P. Banks, st/tr	331
USS Barataria, st	132
USS Barney, gb	46,160
USS Barnum, st	279
USS Bazely, tb	287
Clara Bell, st	249
USS Jacob Bell, cl	123
USS City Belle, tr	225
Hamilton Belle, st	183
Louisana Belle, st	142
USS Benton, gb/ic	68,80,136
USS Black Hawk, gb	118
USS Boston, tr	234
Bragg, ram	80
Brewster, gb	211,219
USS Bridgeport, tr	300
USS Smith Briggs, st/gb	145,173,201,202
Brinker, gb	46
USS Britannia, gb	215
USS Brooklyn, st/fr/tr	5,7,14,17,144,297
Brother Jonathan st	335
G. Brown, st	104
USS Buckingham, gb	299
USS Cairo, ic	21,68,109
USS Calhoun, gb	119
USS Carondolet, ic	21,45,46,55,56, 68,76,134,136,185
Carrie, st	298
USS Lewis Cass, rev cttr	6
Catahoula, st	77
USS Catskill, ic	132
USS Cayuga, gb	80
Cazador, schooner	298
Celeste, st	264,274
USS Ceres, st,gb	56,46,75,225
USS Champion 3, st/tr	
Charleston, st/tr	238
Chassett, tb	160
Chasseur, st/gb	46
Check, st	204
Chesapeake, wv/sch	189,191
Chesterfield, st	66
USS Chickasaw, ic	255
USS Chillicothe gb	237,327
USS Chippewa, st/gb	60,295
USS Choctaw, gb	145,185
USS Chocura, st	62
USS Choteau, Henry, st	262
USS Cincinnati, ic	21,45,63,118,143
City of Alton, st	40
Henry Clay, st	134
USS Clifton, gb	117,166
Clinton, st	262
Clyde, st/tr	331
USS Cohassett, ic	160
USS Coleman, gb	189
Allen Collier, st	179
USS Colorado, gb	26
USS Colossus, st	266
USS Columbia, gb	119
USS Columbine, tb	212,231
Commercial, st	264
Commodore, st/gb	46,55
Commodore Barney, st/ic	160,216
Commodore Hull, gb	225
Commodore Jones, gb	145,173,223
Commodore Morris, gb	131,145
Commodore Perry, gb	46
Commonwealth, wv	134
USS Conestoga, st/gb	22,26,27,33,45, 46,70,123,210
USS Canonicus, gb	297
USS Congress, frigate	50
Constitution, st	12,37
Convoy, st/tr	213,248
Parker Cook, st	108
Cornie, st	316,329
Corris, wv	120
Corypheus, yacht/gb	117
Cottage, st	259
USS Courser, whaler	91
USS Covington, st/gb	216,225
Crescent City, st/gb	141
Creole, st	71
USS Cricket, gb/ic	162,210,222
Croton, st/tr	229
Cuba, st/wv	18
USS Cumberland, sloop	24,50
USS Curlew, st	233,307,308
USS Currituck, gb	49
USS Caleb Cushing, ctr	150
USS Cyane, sloop/gb	128
Darlington, st	101
Davenport, st	303
USS Ike Davis, st	270
USS Lizzie Davis, st	216
USS Dawn, gb	122,125
USS Daylight, gb	19,60,193
Enoch Dean, st	155
Ben DeFord, st	120
Harriet de Ford, st	320
USS Baron de Kalb, gb	118,119,155
USS Delaware, gb	46,181
USS De Soto, gb	124
USS Diana, st/gb	119,312
Diligence, st/mailboat	270
Eben Dodge, whaler	38
USS Henry Dodge, ctr	8
Dove, st	260,296,324
USS Dragon, gb	125
Elisha Dunbar, whaler	91
Dunleath, st	259
Ben Dunning, wv	18
Eagle, st	56
Clara Eames, st	233
USS Eastport, ic	220,222
USS Elfin, gb	279
Ella, st	191,295
USS Ellis, st	105
Emerald, st	204
Emma, st/tr	224
Emma Jane, wv/sch	199
Enchantress, wv/sch	18
USS Eolus, st	312,320
USS Essex, ic	45,76,77,80, 81,83,84,88,
USS Estrella, gb	119,219

BLOCKADE RUNNER/CLIPPER BOAT/PRIVATEER/RAM/ TRANSPORT/TUGBOAT/		FRIGATE/IRON SCHOONER/ WHALER/	CLAD/MAIL SHIP/MORTAR SLOOP/STEAMER/ WOODEN VESSEL		
Eugene, st	175	J.J. Houseman, sch	170	Manhattan, tr/gb	142,255
USS Exchange, st	235	USS Howquah, gb	193	USS Marmora, ic	147
Fair Play, st	287	USS Hunchback, gb	46	USS Maratanza, ic	64,312
USS Fanny, tr	21,24,29	USS General Hunter, tr	220	USS Marblehead, gb	193
Favorite, st/tr	238	Hussar, gb/tr	46,331	Mariner, st/tr	162
USS Fawn, st	177,242,265,279	Iatan, st	80,85	USS Massachusetts, st	17,27
Fernandia, wv	39	USS Ida, gb	323	Matagorda, st	214
Flo, wv	36	Idaho, st	291	Matamoras, st	308
USS Florida, gb	205	USS Indianola, ic	124,125	USS Mattabesett, gb	225
USS Fort Hindman, gb	210	Iolas, st	211	Mazeppa, st	278
USS Foster, gb	206,219	USS New Ironsides, st/ic	132,163,167,	Memphis, st	211
Thomas Foulks, st/tr	229		174,297	Mercedita, st	121
W.W. Fraizer, st	129	USS Iroquois, st	62,63	USS Miami, gb	181,221,225
USS Franklin, gb	185	Island Queen, st	267	USS Michigan, st	267
USS Freeborn, gb	17,125	Isabella, st	9	Miller, st/tr	259
Lizzie Freeman, tug	286	USS Itasca, st/gb	59,69,331	Governor Milton, tb/tr	155
USS Galena, ic	64	USS Iuka, st	307	USS Minnesota, wv/flagsh	24,50,219
USS Gazelle, gb	283	Annie Jacobs, st	259	USS Mississippi, gb	56,127
USS Gemsbok, bark/gb	60	Henry James, mortar	104	Mist, st	178
General Halleck, st	259	Jamestown, st/gb	25	Monadnock, gb	297
USS General Jesup, gb	173,201,211,219	USS Kanawha, gb	175	USS Monarch, ram	68,80,179,235
Georgia, bark/gb	60	USS Kearsarge, st/ic	240,241	USS Monitor, ic	33,45,49,50,
Georgia, st/tr	238	USS Kenwood, gb	155		64,114
Golden Rule, wv	121	USS Keokuk, ic	132	USS Monongahela, gb	128,181,194
Gramphus No. 2, st/gb	119	USS Keystone State, st	121	USS Montauk, gb/ic	125,132
USS Granite City, gb	46,166,194,226	Lewis Killiam, st	18	Monticello, st	14,24
Greyhound, st	283	USS Key West, tr/gb	273,278	S. Moore, st	291
USS Gunboat A, gb	229	USS Kineo, gb	80	USS Moose, st/gb	287,326
USS Gunboat No. 5, gb	221	USS Kinsman, gb	119	USS Morse, gb	46,141
USS Gunboat No. 11, gb	221	Krenton, tr	273	USS Mound City, st/ic	21,63,69,70,
USS Gunboat No. 28, gb	300	Lafayette, whaler	99		80,134,136,312
USS Gunboat No. 29, gb	278,279	USS La Fayette, tr	134	USS Mystic, gb	308
USS Gunboat No. 41, gb	298	USS Lancaster, gb	129	USS Nahant, gb/ic	126,132,147
USS Gunboat No. 43, gb	299,316	Lancer, ic	92	USS Nansemond, gb	219
USS Gunboat No. 49, gb	315	Maple Leaf, st/tr	146,173,216,220	USS Nantucket, ic	132
USS Gunboat No. 50, gb	283	Lebanon, st	233	USS Naumkeag, st	242
USS Gunboat No. 52, gb	279	USS O. H. Lee, st/sch	307	USS Neosho, gb	237,287
USS Gunboat No. 55, gb	273,278	USS Lenapee, st	312	New Moon, st	108
USS Hale E.B., ic	132,163	Levi, st	204	New National, st/gb	155
USS Fort Henry, st	307	USS Lexington, st/gb	22,23,25,26,30,	New River, st	105
Rose Hamilton, st	245,327		33,45,46,48,49,	Niad, wv	18
Hannibal, st	22		56,70,118,145,	USS Niagara, st/wv/fr	12,15,36,316
USS Harriet Lane, st/gb	9,15,24,117		162,210,219,228	USS Niphon, st	223,270
Harriet Stevens, st	243	Little Blue, st	71	No. 7, ic	83
Kate Hart, st	288	Lockwood R.J., st	46	Northerner, st	122,126,198
USS Hartford, gb	128,129,130,290	London, st	71	North State, tr/gb	125,126
USS Harvest Moon, st	309	Long Branch, st/tr	238	USS Norwich, ic	163
USS Hatteras, wv	44,119	USS Louisiana, gb	46,289,290	Nyack, st	312
Haze, st	291	USS Louisville, st/ic	21,47,68,80,	O'Brien, st	185
USS Hercules, rev cutter	124		118,134,136	Ocean Rover, wv	89
USS Hetzel, gb	46	Seth Lowe, st/tb	49,64	Ocmulgee, wv	88
USS Hibiscus, st	307	Luella, st	21	USS Octorara, st	300
Highland Light, st	320	McClelland Robert-Rev/Cttr	6	Olive, st	252
Highlander, wv/sch	193	Machia, wv	18	USS Oneida, st	63,87
USS Hollyhock, gb	325	Madison, st	245,247	USS Osage, gb	210,219
Homeyer H.A., st	257,260	Magnet, st	327	USS Osceola, sch	242
Honduras, st	307	USS Magnolia, st	307	Otesgo, gb	287
Jennie Hopkins, st	259	USS Mahaska, st	307	USS Ottawa, wv	51
USS Housatonic, st	207	USS Malvern	320	USS Ouachita, gb	210
		Manchester, wv	97	USS Owasco, gb	117,181
				Philo Parons, st	267
				USS Passaic, gb/ic	126,132
				USS Patapsco, gb/ic	126,132,298

CONFEDERATE GENERALS	
* Brigadier General	
** Major General	
*** Lieutenant General	
**** Full General	
xxxxx Died (1861-1865)	

Adams, Daniel Weisiger CSA *	56,65
Adams, John CSA * xxxxx	113,285
Adams, William Wirt CSA **	38,171,188,201,225,302
Alexander, Edward Porter CSA *	209
Allen, Henry Watkins CSA *	163
Allen, William Wirt CSA **	209,310
Anderson, George Burgwyn CSA * xxxxx	69,90,97
Anderson, George Thomas CSA *	100
Anderson, James Patton CSA **	46,207,210
Anderson, Joseph Reid CSA *	25,52,53
Anderson, Richard Heron CSA ***	19,30,75,227,235,263,266
Anderson, Robert Houstoun CSA *	251
Anderson, Samuel Read CSA *	279
Archer, James Jay CSA * xxxxx	68,90,276
Armistead, Lewis Addison CSA * xxxxx	55,152
Armstrong, Frank Crawford CSA *	120
Ashby, Turner CSA * xxxxx	31,50,55,65,68
Baker, Alpheus CSA *	211
Baker, Laurence Simmons CSA *	158
Baldwin, William Edwin CSA * xxxxx	91,207
Barksdale, William CSA * xxxxx	82,109,151,152
Barringer, Rufus CSA *	235
Barry, John Decatur CSA *	255
Barton, Seth Maxwell CSA *	50
Bate, William Brimage CSA **	94,208
Battle, Cullen Andrews CSA *	163
Beale, Richard Lee Turberville CSA *	296
Beall, William Nelson Rector CSA *	57
Beauregard, Pierre G Toutant CSA****	8,10,15,16,17,19,29,32, 45,49,54,56,61,63,64,65, 67,71,85,92,95,101,167, 221,229,231,237,240,274, 288,298,306,313
Bee, Barnard Elliott CSA * xxxxx	16,19,20
Bee, Hamilton Prioleau CSA *	49,222
Bell, Tyree Harris CSA *	309
Benning, Henry Lewis CSA *	119
Benton, Samuel CSA * xxxxx	250,251,252
Blanchard, Albert Gallatin CSA *	27
Boggs, William Robertson CSA *	101
Bonham, Milledge Luke CSA **	11,14,15,306
Bowen, John Stevens CSA ** xxxxx	51,137,143,155
Bragg, Braxton CSA ****	5,9,26,30,31,36,43,48, 49,54,55,62,71,72,77,78, 82,85,87,88,89,90,91,92, 93,95,96,97,98,99,100, 101,102,103,105,110,113, 114,117,120,125,145,149, 151,152,154,155,157,158, 162,188,209,298,307,308, 311
Branch, Lawrence O'Bryan CSA * xxxxx	35,51,90
Brandon, William Lindsay CSA *	240
Brantley, William Felix CSA *	251
Bratton, John CSA *	226
Breckenridge, John Cabell CSA **	33,57,80,100,103,117, 183,191,209,211,230,232, 238,239,240,267,279,280, 281,289,303
Brevard, Theodore Washington CSA *	315
Brown, John Calvin CSA **	85,255
Browne, William Montague CSA *	280
Bryan, Goode CSA *	165
Buckner, Simon Bolivar CSA ***	26,27,28,29,33,47,110, 112,136,140,211,219,267, 324,331
Buford, Abraham *	87,326
Bullock, Robert CSA *	284
Butler, Matthew Culbraith CSA **	165,267
Cabell, William Lewis CSA *	120,165
Campbell, Alexander William CSA *	309
Cantey, James CSA *	118
Capers, Ellison CSA *	309
Carroll, William Henry CSA *	33
Carter, John Carpenter CSA * xxxxx	245,285,287
Chalmers, James Ronald CSA *	46,55,173,174,175,176,181
Chambliss, John R. Jr CSA * xxxxx	192,248
Cheatham, Benjamin Franklin CSA **	18,50,282
Chestnut, James Jr CSA *	10,222
Chilton, Robert Hall CSA **	98,206
Churchill, Thomas James CSA **	49,118,314
Clanton, James Holt CSA *	184
Clark, Charles CSA *	14
Clark, John Bullock Jr CSA *	211
Clayton, Henry DeLamar CSA **	135,245
Cleburne, Patrick Ronayne CSA** xxxxx	49,109,186,187,250,285
Clingman, Thomas Lanier CSA *	64
Cobb, Howell CSA **	46,70,167,281
Cobb, Thomas Reade Rootes CSA * xxxxx	100,110
Cocke, Philip St. George CSA * xxxxx	31,39
Cockrell, Francis Marion CSA *	156
Colquitt, Alfred Holt CSA *	86
Colston, Raleigh Edward CSA *	39
Conner, James CSA *	235
Cook, Philip CSA *	255
Cooke, John Rogers CSA *	100
Cooper, Douglas Hancock CSA *	93,94,137,307,309
Cooper, Samuel CSA ****	8,13
Corse, Montgomery Dent CSA *	100
Cosby, George Blake CSA *	120
Cox, William Ruffin CSA *	235
Crittenden, George Bibb CSA **	22,34,35,44,54
Cumming, Alfred CSA *	100
Daniel, Junius CSA * xxxxx	86,229
Davidson, Henry Brevard CSA *	163
Davis, Joseph Robert CSA *	90
Davis, William George Mackey CSA *	101
Dearing, James CSA * xxxxx	223,321,325
Deas, Zachariah Cantey CSA *	110
de Lagnel, Julius Adolph CSA *	58
Deshler, James CSA * xxxxx	158,170
Dibrell, George Gibbs CSA *	178,198,251
Dockery, Thomas Pleasant CSA *	161
Doles, George Pierce CSA * xxxxx	100,235
Donelson, Daniel Smith CSA ** xxxxx	18,119,134
Drayton, Thomas Fenwick CSA *	28
DuBose, Dudley McIver CSA *	281
Duke, Basil Wilson CSA *	266,288,327

CONFEDERATE GENERALS	
* Brigadier General	
** Major General	
*** Lieutenant General	
**** Full General	
xxxxx Died (1861-1865)	

Duncan, Johnson Kelly CSA * xxxxx	43,111
Dunovant, John CSA * xxxxx	260,270
Early, Jubal Anderson CSA ***	19,119,150,151,191,197,
	203,204,224,227,234,235,
	239,240,242,243,244,245,
	246,247,248,249,250,251,
	253,256,257,258,259,260,
	261,262,264,266,267,268,
	270,272,273,274,276,276,
	280,290,307,309,310
Echols, John CSA *	58,97,182
Ector, Matthew Duncan CSA *	84
Elliott, Stephen Jr CSA *	233
Elzey, Arnold Jones CSA **	21,108,109,131
Evans, Clement Anselm CSA *	231
Evans, Nathan George CSA *	32,70
Ewell, Richard Stoddert CSA ***	16,44,65,69,142,144,145,
	146,147,151,158,225,239,
	252,321
Fagan, James Fleming CSA **	89,222
Featherston, Winfield Scott CSA *	49
Ferguson, Samuel Wragg CSA *	158,189
Field, Charles William CSA **	50,206
Finegan, Joseph CSA *	55,56,59,95,207
Finley, Jesse Johnson CSA *	184
Floyd, John Buchanan CSA * xxxxx	5,14,22,24,26,31,33,36,
	46,47,50,164
Forney, James Horace CSA **	50,61,74,95,99,110
Forney, William Henry CSA *	305
Forrest, Nathan Bedford CSA ***	36,40,47,48,75,77,85,98,
	101,109,110,111,113,114,
	117,122,124,125,129,138,
	140,146,155,157,170,183,
	187,188,189,192,193,197,
	202,208,213,214,215,216,
	217,218,219,220,225,235,
	238,239,245,247,248,258,
	260,266
Frazer, John Wesley CSA *	141
French, Samuel Gibbs CSA **	32,38,86,124,131,271
Frost, Daniel Marsh CSA *	12,49
Fry, Brickett Davenport CSA *	233
Gano, Richard Montgomery CSA *	314
Gardner, Franklin CSA **	57,110,113,154
Gardner, William Montgomery CSA *	35
Garland, Samuel Jr CSA * xxxxx	65,90
Garnett, Richard Brooke CSA * xxxxx	35,152
Garnett, Robert Selden CSA * xxxxx	11,16,18,19
Garrott, Isham Warren CSA * xxxxx	143,147
Gartrell, Lucius Jeremiah CSA *	260
Gary, Martin Witherspoon CSA *	231
Gatlin, Richard Caswell CSA *	18,23,52
Gholson, Samuel Jameson CSA *	226
Gibson, Randall Lee CSA *	199
Gilmer, Jeremy Francis CSA **	164
Girardey, Victor Jean B. CSA * xxxxx	248,253
Gist, States Rights CSA * xxxxx	52,285

Gladden, Adely Hogan CSA * xxxxx	29,56,57
Godwin, Archibald C. CSA * xxxxx	255,267
Goggin, James Monroe CSA *	286
Gordon, George Washington CSA *	259
Gordon, James Byron CSA * xxxxx	172,229,231,275,316,322,
	323
Gordon, John Brown CSA **	100,230
Gorgas, Josiah CSA *	280
Govan, Daniel Chevilette CSA *	125
Gracie, Archibald Jr CSA * xxxxx	101,285
Granbury, Hiram Bronson CSA * xxxxx	209,285
Gray, Henry CSA *	314
Grayson, John Breckinridge CSA* xxxxx	22,23,32
Green, Martin Edwin CSA * xxxxx	77,150
Green, Thomas CSA * xxxxx	141,219
Greer, Elkanah Brackin CSA *	96,317
Gregg, John CSA * xxxxx	85,140,272
Gregg, Maxcy CSA * xxxxx	16,38,90,109,110
Griffith, Richard CSA * xxxxx	35,73
Grimes, Bryan CSA **	231,305
Hagood, Johnson CSA *	77
Hampton, Wade CSA ***	65,160,185,199,239,305,
	306,308,312,314
Hanson, Roger Weightman CSA * xxxxx	110,117
Hardee, William Joseph CSA ***	16,20,30,37,54,74,96,102,
	103,104,114,157,178,186,
	188,191,234,239,250,262,
	272,288,289,290,301,305,
	302,306,313
Hardeman, William Polk CSA *	314
Harris, Nathaniel Harrison CSA *	200
Harrison, James Edward CSA *	290
Harrison, Thomas CSA *	297
Hatton, Robert Hopkins CSA * xxxxx	65,67
Hawes, James Morrison CSA *	49
Hawthorn, Alexander Travis CSA *	207
Hays, Harry Thompson CSA *	78
Hebert, Louis CSA *	66,92
Hebert, Paul Octave CSA *	22,23,27,67,71
Helm, Benjamin Hardin CSA * xxxxx	51,170,191
Heth, Henry CSA **	43,63,64,66,119,142,152,
	276,277
Higgins, Edward CSA *	180
Hill, Ambrose Powell CSA *** xxxxx	48,66,72,81,90,91,138,
	139,142,144,145,150,151,
	176,191,225,227,242,260,
	261,270,319
Hill, Benjamin Jefferson CSA *	284
Hill, Daniel Henry CSA ***	18,29,53,62,76,125,127,
	130,131,132,133,134,135,
	146,151,152,153,155,157,
	187
Hindman, Thomas Carmichael CSA *	28,36,39,57,67,75,93,105,
	108,113,191
Hodge, George Baird CSA *	303
Hogg, Joseph Lewis CSA * xxxxx	47,64
Hoke, Robert Frederick CSA **	119,220,221
Holmes, Theophilus Hunter CSA ***	15,30,32,53,76,79,96,128,
	153,213
Holtzclaw, James Thadeus CSA *	245,259,265
Hood, John Bell CSA ****	49,72,96,170,151,209,232,
	233,249,250,253,261,262,
	263,264,270,271,272,273,

Benton, William Plummer USA * — 60,307

Berry, Hiram Gregory USA ** xxxxx — 106,138

Bidwell, Daniel Davidson USA * xxxxx — 257,275

Birge, Henry Wagner, USA * — 170

Birney, David Bell USA ** xxxxx — 47,141,203,211,222,

Birney, William USA * — 142

Blair, Francis Preston Jr USA ** — 81,106,143,180,190,222, 225,300

Blenker, Louis Ludwig USA * xxxxx — 22,37,54,180

Blunt, James Gillpatrick USA ** — 56,61,62,105,106,108, 113,156,164,165,174,269

Bohlen, Henry USA * xxxxx — 60,83

Bowen, James USA * — 96

Boyle, Jeremiah Tilford USA * — 34

Bradley, Luther Prentice USA * — 253

Bragg, Edward Stuyvesant USA * — 242

Brannan, John Milton USA * — 28,43,88,99

Brayman, Mason USA * — 92

Briggs, Henry Shaw USA * — 76

Brisbin, James Sanks USA * — 326

Brooke, John Rutter USA * — 229

Brooks, William T. Harbaugh USA ** — 28,120,146,241

Brown, Edbert Benson USA * — 106,223,238

Buchanan, Robert Christie USA * — 106

Buckingham, Catharinus Putnam USA * — 76

Buckland, Ralph Pomeroy USA * — 106

Buell, Don Carlos USA ** — 13,34,35,37,48,53,56,61, 69,78,90,92,95,93,96,99, 100

Buford, John USA ** xxxxx — 78,151,153,160,171,191

Buford, Napoleon Bonaparte USA * — 58,247,254

Burbridge, Stephen Gano USA * — 69,239,267,269,270,271, 272,273,288,291,308,327

Burnham, Hiram USA * xxxxx — 222,270

Burns, William Wallace USA * — 28

Burnside, Ambrose Everett USA ** — 21,43,44,46,51,52,53,59, 75,77,80,97,102,103,104, 105,109,110,112,120,121, 128,129,133,139,143,144, 145,162,166,167,168,170, 171,174,178,179,181,183, 184,187,188,189,190,219

Bussey, Cyrus USA * — 197

Busteed, Richard USA * — 81

Butler, Benjamin Franklin USA ** — 10,11,13,14,15,16,17,18, 21,23,24,29,37,48,52,58, 61,64,69,87,99,102,110, 112,183,204,218,225,226, 227,228,229,231,232,237, 264,283,287,289,290,291 295,296

Butterfield, Daniel USA ** — 25,104,106

Cadwalader, George USA * — 13,15,18,60

Caldwell, John Curtis USA * — 60,191,202

Cameron, Robert Alexander USA * — 161,254,264,298

Campbell, Charles Thomas USA * — 106

Campbell, William Bowen USA * — 73

Canby, Edward Richard Sprigg USA ** — 16,34,47,56,57,67,91,227, 254,282,304,314,315,316, 318,319,

Carleton, James Henry USA * — 31,35,45,57,60,64,84,91, 198

Carlin, William Passmore USA * — 31,100

Carr, Eugene Asa USA * — (appointed 3/7/62),95

Carr Joseph Bradford USA * — 88

Carrington, Henry Beebee USA * — 52

Carroll, Samuel Sprigg USA * — 229

Carter, Samuel Powhatan USA * — 61,111,113,114,333

Casey, Silas USA ** — 24,67

Catterson, Robert Francis USA * — 331

Chamberlain, Joshua Lawrence USA * — 152,235,323

Chambers, Alexander USA * — 161

Champlin, Stephen G. USA * xxxxx — 45,106,201

Chapin, Edward Payson, USA * xxxxx — 143

Chapman, George Henry USA * — 243

Chetlain, Augustus Louis USA * — 191

Chrylser, Morgan Henry USA * — 336

Clark, William Thomas USA * — 331

Clay, Cassius Marcellus USA * — 57

Clayton, Powell USA * — 52,254

Cluseret, Gustave Paul USA * — 97

Cochrane, John USA * — 76,235

Connor, Patrick Edward USA * — 80,130,317

Connor, Selden USA * — 238

Cook, John USA * — 52

Cooke, Philip St. George USA * — 36

Cooper, James USA * xxxxx — 13,130

Cooper, Joseph Alexander USA * — 253

Copeland, Joseph Tarr USA * — 106

Corcoran, Michael USA * xxxxx — 79,121,185

Corse, John Murray USA * — 161,271

Couch, Darius Nash USA ** — 13,74,96,113,121,122,146

Cowdin, Robert USA * — (appointed 9/26/62)

Cox, Jacob Dolson USA ** — 13,18,19,20,35,61,66,81, 90,95,96,97,192,205,211, 217,307,309,311,313,314, 318,333

Craig, James USA * — 53

Crawford, Samuel Wylie USA * — 60,78,295

Crittenden, Thomas Leonidas USA ** — 24,40,75,76,118,170,172

Crittenden, Thomas Turpin USA * — 60

Crocker, Marcellus M. USA * xxxxx — 106,335

Crook, George USA ** — 79,127,225,230,232,235, 237,244,251,262,268,276, 307

Croxton, John Thomas USA * — 243

Cruft, Charles USA * — 76

Cullum, George Washington USA * — 33,48,49

Curtis, Newton Martin USA * — (appointed 1/12/65)

Curtis, Samuel Ryan USA ** — 13,30,39,46,47,48,49,52, 61,77,84,92,99,142,199, 240,245,276,277,300,305

Custer, George Armstrong, USA ** — 150,185,209,210,272,273, 289,310,323

Cutler, Lysander USA * — 106

Dana, Napoleon Jackson USA ** — 106,179,282,284,287,326

Davidson, John Wynn USA * — 45,159,283

Davies, Henry Eugene ** — (appointed BG 9/10/63) (appointed MG 4/2/65)

Davies, Thomas Alfred USA * — 19,49,324

UNION GENERALS	
* Brigadier General	
** Major General	
*** Lieutenant General	
xxxxx Died (1861-1865)	

Davis, Edmund Jackson USA *	280,309,312
Davis Jefferson Columbus USA *	26,38,93,257,260
Deitzler, George Washington USA *	106
Delafield, Richard USA *	221
Dennis, Elias Smith USA *	106,144,304,307
Dent, Frederick Tracy USA *	320
Denver, James William USA *	22,37,55
De Russy, Gustavus Adolphus USA *	142
de Trobiand, Philippe Regis Denis *	197
Devens, Charles Jr USA *	58,295
Devin, Thomas Casimer USA *	313
Dewey, Joel Allen USA *	336
Dix, John Adams USA *	13,20,33,34,53,68,77,89, 94,99,105,149,157
Dodge, Charles Cleveland USA *	106,126
Dodge, Grenville Mellen USA **	54,133,135,211,214,236, 285,287,303,332
Doolittle, Charles Camp USA *	300
Doubleday, Abner *	(appointed 4/23/61),151
Dow, Neal USA *	60
Duffie, Alfred Napoleon Alexander *	149,181,182,183
Dumont, Ebenezer USA *	25,62
Duryee, Abram USA *	24
Duval, Isaac Hardin USA *	268
Dwight, William USA *	106
Dyer, Alexander Brydie USA *	265
Eaton, Amos Beebe USA *	243
Edwards, John USA *	268
Edwards, Oliver USA *	227
Egan, Thomas Wilberforce USA *	263
Ellet, Alfred Washington USA *	100
Elliott, Washington Lafayette USA *	70,186,199
Emory, William Hemsley USA **	11,12,51,224,247,
(appointed MG 9/25/65)	
Estey, George Peabody USA *	333
Eustis, Henry Lawrence USA *	168
Ewing, Charles USA *	314
Ewing, Hugh Boyle USA *	106
Ewing, Thomas Jr USA **	127,164,308
Fairchild, Lucius USA *	177
Farnsworth, John Elon USA * xxxxx	150,152
Farnsworth, John Franklin USA *	37
Ferraro, Edward USA *	89
Ferry, Orris Sanford USA *	51
Fessenden, Francis USA **	228,336
Fessenden, James Deering USA *	256
Fisk, Clinton Bowen USA *	105,252
Force, Manning Ferguson USA *	161
Forsyth, James William USA *	329
Foster, John Gray USA **	29,75,76,78,110,111,112, 142,157,163,183,185,189, 190,201,202,205,234,285, 304,333
Foster, Robert Sanford USA *	146
Franklin, William Buel USA *	13,23,29,59,62,65,90, 103,104,109,110,120,121, 163,167,173,174,176,177,
Franklin, William Buel USA * (cont)	178,179,180,181,182,183, 185,186,187,224,225
Fremont, John Charles USA **	13,20,22,24,25,26,27,28, 30,31,32,33,34,54,62,64, 66,69,70,71,235
French, William Henry USA **	28,106,158,207
Fry, James Barnet *	
Fry, Speed Smith USA *	53
Fuller, John Wallace USA *	197
Gamble, William USA *	336
Garfield, James Abraham USA **	43,51,173
Garrard, Kenner USA *	158,252
Garrard, Theophilus Toulmin USA *	106,208
Geary, John White USA *	26,28,54,60,64,73,180
Getty, George Washington USA **	93,151,157,298,313
Gibbon, John USA **	61,78,80,236,264,298
Gibbs, Alfred USA *	275
Gilbert, Charles Champion *	87
Gilbert, James Isham USA *	304
Gillem, Alvan Cullem USA *	162,288,291
Gillmore, Quincy Adams USA **	57,58,60,144,146,154,155, 163,167,199,205,206,207, 217,224,231,240,247,304
Gordon, George Henry USA *	69
Gorman, Willis Arnold USA *	25,117
Graham, Charles Kinnaird USA *	106
Graham, Lawrence Pike USA *	21
Granger, Gordon USA **	54,90,95,132,175,187,218, 254,255,307,308,332
Granger, Robert Seaman USA *	94
Grant, Lewis Addison USA *	223
Grant, Ulysses Simpson ***	13,21,22,24,25,26,27,30, 34,39,43,44,45,46,47,50, 51,53,55,56,57,60,61,69, 73,76,78,97,98,99,101,102, 106,108,109,110,111,119, 120,121,122,124,126,127, 133,135,138,140,141,142, 148,153,168,171,174,177, 179,180,181,184,186,211, 212,213,232,234,235,236, 237,239,240,241,242,252, 256,258,260,266,268,270, 275,277,286,287,288,296, 303,313,316,317,319,320, 321,322,325,326
Greene, George Sears USA *	60
Gregg, David McMurtie USA *	106,160,167,215,217,248
Gregg, James Irvin USA *	79
Gresham, Walter Quintin USA *	161
Grierson, Benjamin Henry USA **	88,127,129,130,134,135,136 137,140,144,192,193,290, 291,295,309,310,331,332
Griffin, Charles USA **	69,121,319,321
Griffin, Simon Goodell USA *	229
Grose, William USA *	253
Grover, Cuvier USA *	58,298
Hackleman, Pleasant A. USA * xxxxx	60,94
Halleck, Henry Wager USA **	23,34,36,39,40,44,50,51,61 62,63,64,65,67,75,76,77,80 111,134,139,147,212,252, 324,325,334
Hamblin, Joseph Eldridge USA *	329

UNION GENERALS	
* Brigadier General	
** Major General	
*** Lieutenant General	
xxxxx Died (1861-1865)	

Name	Pages
McCook, Daniel Jr USA * xxxxx	243,248
McCook, Edward Moody USA *	223
McCook, Robert Latimer USA * xxxxx	53,80
McDowell, Irvin USA **	13,15,19,20,48,51,53,55, 59,64,65,66,68,69,72,85, 88
McGinnis, George Francis USA *	107
McIntosh, John Baillie USA *	130
McKean, Thomas Jefferson USA *	36,305,310,332,333
McKinstry, James USA *	25
McLean, Nathaniel Collins USA *	107
McMillan, James Winning USA *	107
McNeil, John USA *	107,181,308,309
McPherson, James B. USA ** xxxxx	83,96,111,119,136,140, 141,188,204,212,215,223, 227,234,249,250
Mackenzie, Ranald Slidell USA *	275
Maltby, Jasper Adalmorn USA *	160
Mansfield, Joseph King USA ** xxxxx	11,13,30,31,76,90,91
Manson, Mahlon Dickerson USA *	53,172,192
Marcy, Randolph Barnes USA *	28
Marston, Gilman USA *	107
Martindale, John Henry USA *	22,104,249
Mason, John Sanford USA *	107
Matthies, Charles Leopold USA *	107
Meade, George Gordon USA **	24,38,91,106,112,121,122 150,152,154,157,169,174, 175,176,182,187,188,198, 210,212,218,225,232,237, 246,297,320,321,330,333
Meagher, Thomas Francis *	45
Meigs, Montgomery Cunningham USA *	13
Meredith, Solomon USA *	95
Meredith, Sullivan Amory USA *	107
Merritt, Wesley USA **	150,186,198,203,273,284, 309,318,325
Miles, Nelson Appleton USA *	229
Miller, John Franklin USA *	197
Miller, Stephen USA *	179
Milroy, Robert Huston USA **	25,38,57,101,106,141,147
Mitchel, Ormsby M. USA ** xxxxx	26,27,30,47,57,61,63,68, 69,86,87,91,99,100
Mitchell, John Grant USA *	297
Mitchell, Robert Byington USA *	53,56,317,322,334
Montgomery, William Reading USA *	13
Morgan, Charles Hale USA *	330
Morgan, Edward Dennison USA **	28
Morgan, George Washington USA *	35,54,71,86,91
Morgan, James Dada USA *	50,76
Morrell, George Webb USA **	22,74
Morris, William Hopkins USA *	107,127,161
Morton, James St. Clair, USA * xxxxx	107;(KIA) 6/17/1864 near Petersburg VA
Mott, Gershom USA **	88,330
Mower, Joseph Anthony USA **	128,214,256,257,258,260, 261,319
Nagle, James USA *	89

Name	Pages
Naglee, Henry Morris USA *	46
Negley, James Scott USA *	29,101
Neill, Thomas Hewson USA *	107
Nelson, William USA ** xxxxx	27,32,34,76,93
Newton, John USA **	28,120,130,307,333
Nickerson, Franklin Stillman USA *	107
Oglesby, Richard James USA **	28,53,106
Oliver, John Morrison USA *	297
Opdycke, Emerson USA *	335
Ord, Edward Otho Cresap USA **	26,61,92,95,148,161,169,247 251,253,262,268,289,296,303 321,334
Orme, William Ward USA *	107
Osborn, Thomas Ogden USA *	326
Osterhaus, Peter Joseph USA *	(appointed 6/9/62), 296,331,332
Owen, Joshua Thomas USA *	107
Paine, Charles Jackson USA *	244
Paine, Elezear Arthur USA *	25
Paine, Halbert Eleazer USA *	132
Palmer, Innis Newton USA *	28,159,200,202,203,253,315
Palmer, John McCauley USA **	39,106,180,208,209,256,304,
Parke, John Grubb USA **	36,53,60,76,128,145,201,212 258,291,297,302
Parsons, Lewis Baldwin USA *	328
Patrick, Marsena Rudolph USA *	52
Patterson, Francis Engle USA* xxxxx	57,105
Paul, Gabriel Rene USA *	87
Peck, John James USA **	23,74,162,175
Pennypacker, Galusha USA *	306
Penrose, William Henry USA *	333
Phelps, John Smith USA *	77
Phelps, John Walcott USA *	13
Piatt, Abram Sanders USA *	61
Pierce, Byron Root USA *	237
Pile, William Anderson USA *	193
Pitcher, Thomas Gamble USA *	107
Pleasonton, Alfred USA **	76,101,142,146,149
Plummer, Joseph Bennett USA * xxxxx	31,32,81
Poe, Orlando Metcalfe USA *	107
Pope, John USA **	13,20,26,37,39,48,51,53,56, 61,68,69,71,72,75,76,79,80, 81,82,83,84,85,86,87,88,251 301,302,324,334
Porter, Andrew USA *	13
Porter, Fitz John USA **	14,65,72,74,85,103,118,120
Potter, Edward Elmer USA *	107,157,158
Potter, Joseph Haydn USA *	326
Potter, Robert Brown USA **	127,163,200,336
Potts, Benjamin Franklin USA *	297
Powell, William Henry USA *	275
Pratt, Calvin Edward USA *	89
Prentiss, Benjamin Mayberry USA **	14,27,37,40,56,106,153
Prince, Henry USA *	59
Quinby, Isaac Ferdinand USA *	52,65,92
Ramsay, George Douglas USA *	169
Ransom, Thomas E. G. USA * xxxxx	101,107,278
Raum, Green Berry USA *	305
Rawlins, John Aaron USA *	161
Reid, Hugh Thompson USA *	127
Reilly, James William USA *	253
Reno, Jesse Lee USA ** xxxxx	5,35,59,76,87,90
Revere, Joseph Warren USA *	99

Steele, Frederick USA ** (cont)	261,270,290,304,308,315, 317,318,323,333
Stevens, Isaac Ingalls USA ** xxxxx	29,39,76
Stevenson, John Dunlap USA *	107,227
Stevenson, Thomas G. USA * xxxxx	127,228
Stokes, James Hughes USA *	11,335
Stolbrand, Charles John USA *	305
Stone, Charles Pomeroy USA *	5,16,24,30,31,32
Stoneman, George USA **	29,51,62,72,100,106,122, 137,138,139,202,205,217, 218,235,252,288,289,290, 252,288,289,290,291,305, 309,312,315,317,320,321, 322,323,324,334
Stoughton, Edwin Henry USA *	101,127
Strong, George Crockett USA ** xxxxx	107,156,157,159
Strong, William Kerley USA *	22
Stuart, David USA *	107
Stumbaugh, Frederick Shearer USA *	107
Sturgis, Samuel Davis USA *	22,57,71,190,199,202, 223,235,237,238,239
Sully, Alfred USA *	93
Sumner, Edwin Vose USA ** xxxxx	9,11,23,31,51,67,96,103, 109,110,121,129
Swayne, Wager USA *	313
Sweeny, Thomas William USA *	20,107
Sykes, George, USA **	21,34,106,122,124,214, 265
Taylor, George William USA * xxxxx	24,63,86
Taylor, Joseph Pannel USA * xxxxx	123,243
Taylor, Nelson USA *	88
Taylor, William USA * xxxxx	63,86
Terrill William Rufus USA * xxxxx	88,96
Terry, Alfred Howe USA **	60,240,249,273,296,298, 317,334
Terry, Henry Dwight USA *	76
Thayer, John Milton, USA *	95,309,328
Thomas, George Henry USA **	25,26,29,35,44,60,61,92, 118,170,177,178,180,186, 187,193,208,227,249,250, 270,278,280,284,285,286, 287,288,289,290,304,324, 333,334
Thomas, Henry Goddard USA *	284
Thomas, Lorenzo USA *	27
Thomas, Stephen USA *	145,301
Thruston, Charles Mynn USA *	36
Tibbits, William Badger USA *	276
Tillson, David USA *	107
Todd, John Blair Smith *	1
Torbert, Alfred Thomas A. USA *	107,276,290
Totten, Joseph Gilbert USA * xxxxx	7,52,53,54,55,57,151,221
Tower, Zealous Bates USA *	51
Turchin, John Basil USA *	76
Turner, John Wesley USA *	167
Tuttle, James Madison USA *	73
Tyler, Daniel USA *	19,53
Tyler, Erastus Barnard USA *	28,69
Tyler, Robert Ogden USA *	107
Tyndale, Hector USA *	132
Ullman, Daniel USA *	119,303
Underwood, Adin Ballou USA *	182
Upton, Emory USA *	229
Van Alen, James Henry USA *	58
Van Cleve, Horatio Phillips USA *	55
Van Derveer, Ferdinand USA *	271
Vandever, William USA *	107
Van Vliet, Stewart *	29
Van Wyck, Charles Henry USA *	336
Veatch, James Clifford USA *	60,308,326,333
Viele, Egbert Ludovicus USA *	(appointed 8/17/61)
Vincent, Strong USA * xxxxx	152,154
Vinton, Francis Laurens USA *	91
Vogdes, Israel USA *	107,288,329
von Willich, August, USA *	76
von Seinwehr, Adolph Wilhelm USA *	22,125
Wade, Nelancthon Smith USA **	53,56,57
Wadsworth, James Samuel USA **xxxxx	25,52,117,125,226,227
Wagner, George Day USA *	107,321
Wallace, William Harvey USA * xxxxx	27,57
Wallace, Lewis USA **	16,17,25,40,52,54,214, 246,248,253,324
Walcutt, Charles Carroll USA *	253
Ward, John Henry Hobart USA *	95
Ward, William Thomas USA *	14
Warner, James Meech USA *	328
Warren, Fitz Henry USA *	76
Warren, Gouverneur Kemble USA **	93,138,151,162,198,204, 214,225,260,277,300,303, 318,319,326,329,331
Washburn, Cadwallader Colden USA **	76,106,161,178,220,309, 311
Watkins, Louis Douglass USA *	336
Webb, Alexander Stewart USA *	149
Weber, Max USA *	60
Webster, Joseph Dana USA *	107
Weed, Stephen Hinsdale, USA * xxxxx	145,152
Weitzel, Godfrey USA **	85,99,119,140,271,281, 286,320
Wells, William USA *	190,329
Welsh, Thomas USA * xxxxx	107,162
Wessels, Henry Walton USA *	60,153
West, Joseph Rodman USA *	88,99
Wheaton, Frank USA *	107
Whipple, Amiel Weeks USA * xxxxx	58,138,139
Whipple, William Denison USA *	156
Whitaker, Walter Chiles USA *	149
White, Julius USA *	69,87
Wild, Edward Augustus USA *	135,189
Willcox, Orlando Bolivar USA *	83,96,119,131,197,200, 213,291,299
Williams, Alpheus Starkey USA *	29,49,50,87,91,165,252
Williams, David Henry USA *	107
Williams, James Alexander USA *	297,333
Williams, Nelson Grosvenor USA *	107
Williams, Seth USA *	30
Williams, Thomas USA * xxxxx	31,52,71,80
Wilson, James Harrison USA **	56,180,242,289,315,317, 318,319,320,321,322,323, 324,325,327

UNION GENERALS	
* Brigadier General	
** Major General	
*** Lieutenant General	
xxxxx Died (1861-1865)	

Wistar, Isaac Jones USA *	108,202
Wood, Thomas John USA **	30,124,286,300
Woods, Charles Robert USA *	160,333
Woods, William Burnham USA *	331
Woodbury, Daniel Phineas USA * xxxxx	29,228
Wool, John Ellis USA **	23,27,30,63,64,68,69, 112,119
Wright, George USA * xxxxx	26,28,29,31,33,36,209, 244,334,335
Wright, Horatio Gouverneur USA **	27,83,84,129,228,229, 242,247,305,319,321,325
Zook, Samuel Kosciuszko USA * xxxxx	108,152

NATIVE AMERICAN	INDIAN NATION TRIBES
Indians - (tribe not identified)	7,10,22,26,29,74,78,81, 88,117,121,127,130,131, 154,156,157,157,162,163, 166,179,180,189,192,197, 203,213,214,221,223,224, 226,227,228,233,234,254, 254,256,258,259,260,270, 272,273,274,276,277,279, 280,282,283,291,296,297, 298,300,301,309,311,322, 325,327,328,329,330,331, 332,333,334,335,336
Apache	22,24,76,130,135,136,139 198,218,225,230,233,249, 251,255,270,274,279,282, 283,306,312,313,333,335
Apache - Mescalero	163
Apache - Tonto	288
Arapahoe	269,279,283,299,312,333, 335
Boise	334
Bannock	330
Cayuse	221
Cherokee	11,29,36,38,39,40,60,67, 75,98,108,125,135,230, 236,265,333,335
Cheyenne	218,219,220,224,228,230, 269,273,279,284,285,299, 325,327,329,333,336
Chickasaw	10,11,12,18,38,40,60,335
Chippewa	251
Choctaw	7,11,18,38,40,60,174, 175,182,220,335
Comanche	255,256,267,279,283,302, 312,328,333,335
Coyoteros	255
Creek	11,18,36,38,39,40,98, 333,335
Dakota	251
Delgaditos Largo's Navajo	332
Goose Lake	242
Goshutes	129

NATIVE AMERICAN	INDIAN NATION TRIBES
Great Osage	29
Hoopas	197
Kickapoo	296
Kiowa	255,256,257,267,279,283, 302,312,333,335
Klamath	242
Lake	242
Lipan	30
Mangas	209,
Modoc	242
Navajo	154,155,163,169,197,198, 255,282,297,313,318,328, 332
Nez Perce	163
Omaha	323
Osage	333,336
Owen's River	133
Oywhee	262
Palouse	207
Pawnee	257,332
Pin	108
Pi-Ute	221,330
Platte	326
Ponca	188
Pottawatomie	296
Pueblo	318
Quapaw	336
Redwood	209,210,
Rees	251
Sagwich	139
Seminole	11,40,336
Seneca	29,336
Shawnee	29,336
Shoshone	159
Sioux	83,84,87,88,89,92,93, 113,147,158,159,224,228, 244,251,253,256,279,298, 325,327,329,332,333
Sioux - Brule	257
Sioux - Ogalalla	257
Sioux - Sisseton	244
Smoke Creek	312,
Snake	83,138,163,221,295,334
Tehachapie	133
Teton - Sioux	244
Truckee	327
Ukie	157
Unkpapas	251
Ute	124,148,154,163,318
Walker River	327
Warm Springs	221
Wileackee	215
Yanktonais	251
Zuni	154,163,169,233

NOTES

NOTES